EXPANSION 1775-1867

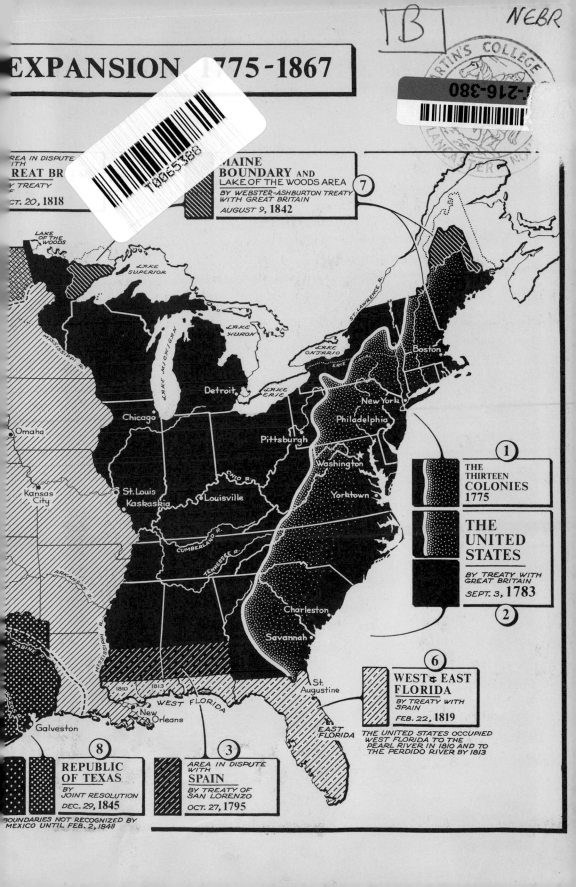

B

AREA IN DISPUTE
WITH
GREAT BRITAIN
BY TREATY
OF
OCT. 20, 1818

MAINE
BOUNDARY AND
LAKE OF THE WOODS AREA ⑦
*BY WEBSTER–ASHBURTON TREATY
WITH GREAT BRITAIN*
AUGUST 9, 1842

LAKE OF THE WOODS

LAKE SUPERIOR

LAKE MICHIGAN

LAKE HURON

LAKE ONTARIO

LAKE ERIE

ST. LAWRENCE R.

MISSISSIPPI R.

Boston

Detroit

Chicago

New York

Philadelphia

Omaha

Pittsburgh

Washington

OHIO R.

Kansas City

St. Louis
Kaskaskia

Louisville

Yorktown

CUMBERLAND R.

TENNESSEE R.

ARKANSAS R.

Charleston

Savannah

MISSISSIPPI R.

SABINE R.

1810   1813

WEST FLORIDA

New Orleans

St. Augustine

EAST FLORIDA

Galveston

BRAZOS R.

① THE
**THIRTEEN
COLONIES**
1775

② **THE
UNITED
STATES**
*BY TREATY WITH
GREAT BRITAIN*
SEPT. 3, 1783

⑥ **WEST & EAST
FLORIDA**
*BY TREATY WITH
SPAIN*
FEB. 22, 1819

THE UNITED STATES OCCUPIED
WEST FLORIDA TO THE
PEARL RIVER IN 1810 AND TO
THE PERDIDO RIVER BY 1813

⑧ **REPUBLIC
OF TEXAS**
BY JOINT RESOLUTION
DEC. 29, 1845

BOUNDARIES NOT RECOGNIZED BY
MEXICO UNTIL FEB. 2, 1848

③ AREA IN DISPUTE
WITH
SPAIN
*BY TREATY OF
SAN LORENZO*
OCT. 27, 1795

THE GROWTH OF
AMERICAN
FOREIGN POLICY

A HISTORY

THE GROWTH OF
AMERICAN
FOREIGN POLICY

A HISTORY

BY

Richard · W · Leopold

PROFESSOR OF HISTORY,
NORTHWESTERN UNIVERSITY

New York : Alfred · A · Knopf

L. C. catalog card number: 62–13894

THIS IS A BORZOI BOOK,
PUBLISHED BY ALFRED A. KNOPF, INC.

PUBLISHED 1962
REPRINTED 1964, 1965, 1966, 1967

TO

Frederick Merk

Raymond J. Sontag

Frederick R. Whitman
(1876–1957)

Preface

IN OFFERING a new history of American foreign policy to the public, the author owes some explanation of what he has tried to do and how his work differs from several excellent surveys already in print. An outgrowth of over twenty years of teaching and research, this volume seeks to provide an organization and emphasis suited to the needs of the general reader and college student of the 1960's. It reflects a conviction that the drastic changes in America's international position in the last two decades and the complex problems facing its citizens today have rendered obsolete the traditional treatment which devotes as much space to the intricacies of the Maine boundary and Newfoundland fisheries disputes as to the controversies over arms control and divided Berlin. It recognizes that practical considerations also dictate a fresh approach. No longer can a scholar encompass in a single usable book or a teacher complete in a single year's course the entire sweep of United States foreign policy from 1775 to 1961 without subordinating some periods to others.

I have chosen to subordinate the early period and have therefore been relatively brief on developments prior to 1889, so as to deal at length with events since that date. Yet to compress is not to slight, and by giving up a chronological coverage of the republic's formative years, I feel I have been able to set forth more fully than other writers the principles and practices of that era which continued to shape American foreign policy in the twentieth century. Omitted are the details of treaties long since superseded, of border clashes long since resolved, and of expansionist projects long since consummated or abandoned. What I have sought to do is to depict in broad strokes the course of

American foreign policy from 1775 to 1889; to trace the growth in that period of the basic guidelines—isolationism, neutrality, and the Monroe Doctrine; to note the interplay of ideals and self-interest in external affairs; and to analyze the constitutional conflict between the executive and legislative branches for control of foreign policy. By concentrating on those topics, I have found it possible to move quickly through the first century of independence and still extract the lessons it has to teach.

The detailed narrative opens with the inauguration of Benjamin Harrison on March 4, 1889, and closes with that of John F. Kennedy on January 20, 1961. The first date is not a decisive one; it simply ushered in a decade of conflicting impulses, which saw the United States acquire an overseas empire and begin to play a larger role in world affairs. The government grew increasingly concerned about events beyond its borders, and some of the problems which disturbed American leaders in the fifteen years before the First World War broke out in 1914 persisted in various forms until Dwight D. Eisenhower surrendered his responsibility as a chief spokesman for the free world. To those who may complain that I have allotted too much space to recent times and argue that current events are not the province of the historian, I reply that most of the period from 1889 to 1945 is hardly recent and that the experience derived from those years is much more significant than that gained between 1775 and 1889. As to the years from 1945 to 1961, the historian can supply a better perspective than any other scholar. Thanks to the prompt publication of vital documents —even archival materials and personal papers—he is able to describe fully what happened only yesterday. He cannot always tell so quickly why things occurred, but he can go as far as his evidence warrants and then frankly concede what he does not know.

The major concern of this book is foreign policy, not diplomacy or foreign relations. By foreign policy I mean those objectives and aims set by the government for promoting the nation's interest and welfare in the world at large. Diplomacy I take to be the art or profession of transacting business among governments. Foreign relations I define as the sum total of all connections—official, private, commercial, and cultural—among different countries and different peoples. I shall not ignore the relations between the United States and other powers, but they will be described only when they shed light on American foreign policy as a whole. Nor shall I neglect diplomacy, but the labors of the diplomats will be subordinated to the decisions of the policy makers. In short, the core of this volume is the formulation of foreign policy in the United States and the steady growth of that policy from the beginnings of independence to the present day.

What novelties does this survey contain? Besides the unusual organization of the material before 1889, it offers after that date character sketches of every president and secretary of state, as well as of congressional leaders who shaped foreign policy. Within an integrated narrative, it traces the evolution of basic policies, such as isolationism and neutrality, and the operation of constitutional provisions, such as the handling of treaties and the armed forces. Three of the first eight chapters deal with the struggle between the executive and the legislature for the control of foreign policy, and that theme reappears in the introductory chapters to the remaining five time periods into which the work is divided. I have also emphasized the problem of meshing foreign policy with military capability. For the years from 1889 to 1921, the book embodies the research of the author as well as that of other scholars. For the years from 1921 to 1939, it presents an interpretation and coverage in depth which may help retrieve that period from the clichés and oversimplification to which it has been subjected. The momentous changes that took place in foreign policy between 1939 and 1953 I have discussed in the light of the nation's earlier experiences and the lessons that most Americans drew from the past. The treatment of the Eisenhower era, I believe, is fuller and more up to date than in any comparable volume, especially for those areas—South and Southeast Asia, Africa, and the Middle East—in which the United States had been previously little concerned.

Much, of course, had to be omitted in a one-volume work. I would have liked to develop more systematically the influence of public opinion and interest groups, but I chose instead to stress decision making in the White House and on Capitol Hill. I had hoped to trace in greater detail the conflict between ideals and self-interest in American foreign policy, but I had to be content with a single introductory chapter and some illustrations within the general narrative. I would have preferred to sketch more fully the international setting, and I am aware that the American scene is depicted more adequately than the foreign. Too often in these pages other governments seem monolithic, when actually they too had to cope with internal divisions. Finally, I had wished to elaborate upon the views of historians where they differed from my own, but I decided reluctantly that such historiographical forays were of more interest to specialists than to the general reader and undergraduate for whom this book has been written. At a few places in the bibliographical essay I have indicated books and articles whose conclusions run counter to those I have reached.

It is impossible in a work of this type to cite all the sources drawn upon. The bibliographical essay suggests the richness of the literature without exhausting the printed and manuscript materials I have used. Nor does it make sense to give references for the short extracts quoted in the text. I have taken presidential statements from the *Messages and*

Papers compiled by James D. Richardson in 1897 and from the published works of the individuals concerned. The diplomatic notes quoted can be found in the *Foreign Relations* series, in other collections issued by the State Department, and in the digests of international law edited by John Bassett Moore and Green H. Hackworth. To facilitate the task of those wishing to consult the entire document, I have always appended the complete date. I have also supplied the full name and title of every person when he is first mentioned and, in the case of members of Congress, the state he represents and the party to which he belongs. I have kept footnotes to a minimum, upon the assumption that something worth saying is worth saying in the text. I have indulged in the practice, perhaps a bit old-fashioned these days, of providing the reader with a sufficient array of facts, so that he can judge for himself the difficult decisions American statesmen often faced. The last impression I would wish to leave is that the course of foreign policy was predetermined and that reasonable men cannot honestly disagree over choices made in the past.

Nor is it possible to express adequately my obligations to others. Over the years I have absorbed facts and interpretations so long in the public domain that I am not always sure which ideas are my own. I have probably borrowed without proper acknowledgment from my good friends Samuel F. Bemis, Julius W. Pratt, Thomas A. Bailey, and Richard W. Van Alstyne who, in addition to their notable contributions to scholarship, have written textbooks from which beginners and specialists alike profit.

From the inception of this work Mr. Alfred A. Knopf, that great benefactor of historians, has demonstrated his continuing interest. Two heads of his College Department—Mr. John T. Hawes and Mr. Joseph G. Sutton—have come to my aid on many occasions. Mrs. Wayland W. Schmitt has edited the manuscript with skill and discrimination. Mr. Theodore R. Miller, an outstanding cartographer, has enriched the volume with his maps. Miss Bridget Gellert was most helpful and patient in preparing the manuscript for publication. And Professor Walter Johnson of the University of Chicago must bear some responsibility, as an emissary of the house of Knopf, for persuading me to undertake this sort of a book.

I wish to thank, too, Dr. Robert Oppenheimer, the Director, and Mr. George F. Kennan, a permanent Member, for their good offices in providing a year of uninterrupted writing under ideal conditions at The Institute for Advanced Study in Princeton. With typical generosity, Dean Simeon E. Leland of the College of Liberal Arts, Northwestern University, made it possible for me to accept an annual membership at The Institute after having granted me a few years earlier a Spring Quarter leave of absence. Acting Dean Robert H. Baker of the

Graduate School, Northwestern University, kindly provided a small grant to defray last-minute expenses. Of the many helpful people in Deering Library, I can single out for thanks only the late Aleene Baker, head of the Documents Division. Mrs. Marion G. Hartz, Mrs. Elizabeth S. Gorman, Miss Elizabeth I. Horton, Mrs. Grace Armour, and Mrs. Lorna P. Gallagher did yeoman service in typing various parts of the manuscript.

No author could have asked for more sympathetic yet critical readers. Words cannot express my gratitude to those friends who saved me from factual errors, questionable statements, and stylistic crudities. Professor Richard N. Current of the University of Wisconsin read the entire manuscript; Professor John M. Blum of Yale University read all but the last thirteen chapters; Professor Roger F. Hackett of the University of Michigan read every chapter or section dealing with East Asia; and Dr. John C. Campbell of the Council on Foreign Relations read those chapters covering the period from 1939 to 1961. My greatest debt is to my loyal friend and former colleague, Professor Arthur S. Link of Princeton University, who struggled with the first overly long version and showed me how to shorten and improve the work. His frequent encouragement, his generous sharing of an unmatched knowledge of the Wilson era, and his constant readiness to assist helped enormously at every stage of my labors.

I have dedicated this volume to three former teachers: to the late Frederick R. Whitman, who awakened my interest in history when I was a schoolboy at the Phillips Exeter Academy; to Professor Raymond J. Sontag of the University of California, who did much to settle my choice of a profession when I was an undergraduate at Princeton University; and to Professor Frederick Merk of Harvard University, who revealed to me the delights of scholarship when I was a graduate student at Harvard University.

R. W. L.

Evanston, Illinois,
September 1961

Contents

Contents

BOOK III: THE FIRST TEST: THE GREAT CRUSADE, 1905–21

BOOK IV: INTERLUDE: THE INTERWAR COMPROMISE, 1921–39

BOOK VI: THE CONTINUING TEST: NEITHER PEACE NOR WAR, 1953–61

Maps

DRAWN BY THEODORE R. MILLER

BOOK·I

THE FORMATIVE YEARS

1775–1889

In which the American people embrace fundamental principles, develop procedural practices, and achieve security through an independent foreign policy.

I

The Course of American Foreign Policy to 1889

THE UNITED STATES benefited from a wise foreign policy during its formative years. Mistakes and miscalculations did occur, and at times external dangers threatened the national security or forced a temporary abandonment of national ideals. But the problems and perils which then beset the republic seem minor when compared with to-day's, while certain favorable conditions—geographic, economic, and strategic—permitted the country after 1825 to cease worrying about shifts in the European balance of power and to concentrate upon developments in the Americas. By 1889 these advantageous circumstances had begun to change, yet the attitudes they had produced and the hopes they had encouraged persisted into the twentieth century. In commencing a history of American foreign policy, therefore, it is desirable to survey briefly this early period, to describe the world in which the United States grew to maturity, and to analyze the diplomatic principles which almost all citizens endorsed and the procedural practices which their unique Constitution imposed.

THE QUEST FOR INDEPENDENCE

The first goal in the foreign policy of the recalcitrant colonies in 1775 was to obtain assistance in the rebellion against England. Recognition by the states of Europe would help somewhat; armed support would do still more. On February 6, 1778, after months of strenuous efforts, Benjamin Franklin and his colleagues persuaded France, Britain's ancient foe, to conclude an alliance. This treaty conferred recognition upon the United States, brought France into the war, and bound the allies to act together in conducting the fighting and negotiating the peace. No other power went that far. The Netherlands and Sweden granted recognition in treaties of amity and commerce on October 8, 1782, and April 3, 1783, respectively, while Spain entered the fray as a result of an understanding with the French. But Spain did not recognize the United States until it knew Britain would acknowledge the thirteen colonies to be free and sovereign. This the British did in the definitive peace treaty of September 3, 1783.

Victory on the battlefield meant political but not diplomatic independence. The statesmen in London, Paris, and Madrid continued to regard the new nation as they had the former colonies, as a pawn in their own territorial and commercial rivalries in the Western Hemisphere. They believed the democratic experiment across the Atlantic would fail, and another forty years passed—including a second war with England, a quasi-war with France, and frequent skirmishes with Spain—before they conceded the young republic the right to stand on its own feet and make its own decisions in foreign affairs. Other states delayed recognition: Prussia until 1785, Portugal until 1791, Russia until 1809. The exchange of envoys was slow and begrudging. As late as September, 1817, only nine European monarchies maintained diplomatic missions in Washington, while American diplomatic posts abroad numbered seven.

For a decade after 1783 the major goals in American foreign policy were to gain the respect which an independent status warranted and to eliminate the controversies which the peace settlement had bequeathed. The United States found its boundaries questioned, its representatives snubbed, and the ships of its citizens barred from certain foreign ports. With England there were disputes over the execution of the treaty of 1783, over the intrigues among the Indians carried on by Canadian officials, and over the exclusion of American vessels from the West Indian trade. With Spain there was disagreement over the location of the southern frontier and the right of American citizens to use the Mississippi River as it flowed through Spanish territory to the Gulf of Mexico. With France, an ally, there was the danger of being reduced to a satellite.

Then, in 1793, the wars of the French Revolution ushered in a twenty-year period that entangled the new nation increasingly in Europe's quarrels. The administration of George Washington attempted to stay aloof. It proclaimed American neutrality and tried to demonstrate to the cynical eighteenth-century world that such a policy meant impartiality, or at least as much impartiality as the weak could muster when menaced by the strong. To avoid being drawn into the struggle, the United States did sign the Jay Treaty with England on November 19, 1794; and while yielding to the Mistress of the Seas on maritime matters, it secured the final withdrawal of British troops from American soil. Taking advantage of suspicions among the belligerents, the United States did negotiate the Treaty of San Lorenzo with Spain on October 27, 1795, and obtained thereby its claim to the southern boundary and the right of its citizens to use the Mississippi freely and to deposit their cargoes in Spanish territory preparatory to reloading into ocean-going vessels.

Impartial neutrality angered the French, who had expected non-military aid. The irate government in Paris turned upon its ally, tried through agents in America to sway the voters into electing a president from the party opposed to Washington, recalled its minister, twice refused—once under insulting circumstances—to receive American envoys, and seized American ships without a semblance of legality. Congress responded with measures to bolster the nation's defenses, to insure loyalty at home, and to retaliate against indignities abroad. On July 7–9, 1798, the legislature adopted bills to end the treaty of 1778 and to employ force against armed French vessels. Two years of desultory fighting in the Caribbean ensued, until a convention of September 30, 1800, regularized the unilateral abrogation of the alliance and terminated the undeclared war. With the breaking of the French bond, the United States had taken another step along the road to diplomatic independence.

Thomas Jefferson's inauguration on March 4, 1801, provided no respite from external dangers and no change in basic policies. The Republican President and his successor, James Madison, did not differ from their Federalist predecessors, Washington and John Adams, in their desire to be free of European ties and tutelage. Yet as the struggle between Napoleon and the British-led coalition continued, the republic found itself deeply affected by events abroad. The belligerents preyed upon its burgeoning seaborne trade. Their economic reprisals cut profits in maritime commerce and lowered prices of agricultural produce. England's need for seamen compelled it to engage in the humiliating practice of impressing American citizens into the Royal Navy from the decks of American merchantmen and, in exceptional cases, of American warships. Try as he might, Jefferson could not gain permanent relief by playing one side off against the other; his sole diplomatic success in eight years, the purchase of the huge Louisiana tract from France on April 30, 1803, did not check his mounting troubles. In desperation, he persuaded Congress to pass the Embargo Act of December 22, 1807. This experiment in peaceable coercion closed American ports to all foreign ships, belligerent and neutral, and restricted Ameri-

convincing. Economic benefits and strategic considerations did not disappear; indeed James K. Polk's zeal to acquire California stemmed from a desire for ports on the Pacific and a fear of Anglo-French intrusion. Yet as the republic matured, expansionists talked more in terms of geographic determinism, institutional superiority, and enlarging the area of freedom. By the first, contemporaries meant that certain nearby lands were destined by their very location to become part of the Union. Texas, Oregon, California, and Cuba fitted that elastic formula. By the second, they meant that the governmental system developed by the Anglo-Saxons enabled them to rule more wisely and utilize more expertly the areas under their control. In the Western Hemisphere the untutored aborigines and weaker Latins must eventually yield to the hardier Nordics. By the third, they meant that America had a mission to extend the blessings of liberty. This could be done by serving as a beacon of hope for those living under tyranny and by demonstrating the advantages of democracy. It could be accomplished, too, by providing a wider setting for the republican experiment, by making the American continent, as the Democratic platform said in 1844, "the asylum of the oppressed of every nation." It was this last point, stressed by Ralph Waldo Emerson and Walt Whitman, that kept the concept of manifest destiny, often regarded as a rationale for American cupidity, also an expression of American idealism.

Not everyone accepted this brief for adding territory, and some feared democracy would break down in a nation stretching from ocean to ocean. To suspicious antislavery advocates such as James Russell Lowell, the manifest destiny of the antebellum period was one half ignorance and one half rum. But most Americans shared the conviction that they had been chosen by providence to exemplify the virtues of free government on a bountiful continent, separated from the tribulations of the Old World.

Linked to the question of why the young nation wished to expand is that of how expansion was effected. Was the record discreditable? Were the tactics used ones that the United States would condemn today? Did the government in Washington resort to treachery, bullying, subversion, or naked aggression? The answer varies with each annexation. In purchasing Louisiana on April 30, 1803, the United States merely accepted a beneficial offer, one resulting from Napoleon's military setback in Haiti, his diplomatic frustrations in Italy, and his willingness to renew the war with England.

In the Floridas, on the other hand, there is much to criticize. Jefferson's claim under the Louisiana treaty to part of West Florida was tortured; his attempt to substantiate it by bribery and bluff, unworthy. Madison probably did not instigate the uprising against Spain in the Baton Rouge district in 1810, though some experts think he did; but he took advantage of the development to occupy—gradually, in the following three years—Spanish territory west of Mobile. He also sent a former Revolutionary general, George Mathews, to East Florida to stir up sentiment for annexation, allowed the army and navy to cooperate in the venture, and disavowed his agent on April 4, 1812, only when failure was evident. Even then, the President kept American troops on neutral soil until May, 1813, hoping the inhabitants might rebel. In the final disposition of the Floridas by the treaty of February 22, 1819, force played a potential rather than an actual part. Spain had to bow to the inevitable and obtain the best possible terms. Spain's impotence and European indifference would have allowed the United States to seize the colony whenever it wished.

The addition of Texas in December, 1845, is often deplored because of the methods employed. Critics accuse American citizens of accepting cheap land from Mexico in bad faith and of settling on foreign soil with every intention of joining it to the country of their birth. The critics also charge that American aid insured the success of the insurrection which began in 1835 and that the manner of incorporation in 1845 was unconstitutional. These allegations are largely wide of the mark. The settlers were free men, not government agents. Their grievances against Mexican misrule were genuine. Their rebellion would have triumphed without assistance from the American Southwest, although admittedly the Jackson administration enforced the neutrality laws laxly. The Lone Star Republic remained independent for nine years and twice had overtures for annexation ignored in Washington. Mexico was unable to reconquer the lost province. It had no legal basis for complaint if the Texans chose to merge with another people. The United States was unrealistic in insisting upon the Rio Grande as a boundary. The acquisition of territory by a joint resolution rather than by a treaty was unprecedented. But neither a weak border claim nor an unusual constitutional procedure nor Mexico's warning that annexation meant war alters the conclusion that the annexation of Texas was a legitimate act of two sovereign states.

Oregon presents a simpler case. The flow of population to the Pacific Northwest did bring about a partition favorable to the United States. But those pioneers did not move to alien soil. By a treaty of August 6, 1827, extending the convention of 1818, the land west of the Rockies between the forty-second parallel and 54°40′ was open to citizens of both countries. The pioneers did not rebel; they simply outnumbered the British residents. Their presence was an important factor, but only one, paving the way for a treaty on June 15, 1846, which gave the United States the bulk of the area actually in dispute. Time, geography, and a foreign policy that was often blustering and sometimes reckless were also responsible.

Perhaps the most controversial episode in the diplomacy of continental expansion was the acquisition of California. In June, 1846, American-born settlers in the Sacramento Valley rose against Mexico and established the Bear Flag Republic. In view of President Polk's known desire for California and the recent outbreak of the Mexican War, this insurrection seemed a calculated aggression by the United States. The actions of Captain John C. Frémont, an army officer and son-in-law of an expansionist Senator, appeared to implicate the government in Washington. Frémont led an armed exploring expedition into California during the spring, gave Mexican authorities constant trouble, professed to receive secret orders from Polk, and rendered immediate aid to the rebels. Yet his sealed instructions are still an impenetrable mystery, and Frémont's course actually upset Polk's strategy. The President wanted annexation, but by peaceful means. He welcomed an uprising against Mexico, but he insisted that it be led by native Californians, not foreign settlers. He hoped the residents of the West Coast would ask to be incorporated into the Union, as had the Texans. But Frémont's rashness antagonized the Californians and obliged the United States to gain the province as a spoil of war, not as a freewill offering. It took a military conquest and the peace treaty of February 2, 1848, to complete the annexation.

Mexico's crushing defeat led some Americans to talk of absorbing the entire country. Other enthusiasts advocated placing all of the Western Hemisphere under the jurisdiction of the United States. The years from 1848 to 1854 witnessed not only the most ambitious schemes of continental expansion but also the first faltering projects for overseas territory. The initial offer to purchase Cuba was made on June 17, 1848. Six years later came an attempt to buy or lease Samaná Bay in the Dominican Republic. Concern for an interoceanic canal prompted agents on the spot to urge seizing strategic sites along the Central American coast. An annexation treaty with Hawaii was signed on September 15, 1854. But no overseas possession materialized, and only one small strip of contiguous land was added. On December 30, 1853, a bankrupt Mexican government sold 30,000 square miles in the Gila River Valley for the construction of a railroad to the Pacific by the southern route. Soon thereafter the Kansas-Nebraska Act aroused such sectional antagonisms that the free states resolutely opposed the acquisition of any territory in which slavery could exist.

INTERNAL CRISIS AND EXTERNAL ADJUSTMENT

The outbreak of the Civil War compelled the United States to devote its foreign policy to preserving the Union. Expansionist dreams were put aside for the moment, as the Lincoln administration concentrated on the task of insulating the domestic conflict from the rest of the world, of denying the Confederacy allies and aid, and of gaining European acquiescence in certain measures for suppressing the rebellion. It sought to prevent recognition of Southern independence, forestall European intervention, and win approval abroad of the Northern blockade.

To prevent recognition of Southern independence would isolate the Confederate States and sap their morale. Conversely, acceptance into the family of nations would flatter their pride and bolster their hope for outside support. On this, as on all diplomatic matters in the Civil War, England held the key; the rest of Europe took its cue from her. Hence, when the Palmerston cabinet acknowledged the belligerent status of Jefferson Davis' government on May 13, 1861, the reaction in Washington was sharp. Fearing that the move foreshadowed full recognition, Secretary of State William H. Seward called it unfriendly and premature. Actually, the British were legally correct, and Lincoln had strengthened their case by imposing the blockade. Before proceeding further, however, the men in London waited to see how the fighting progressed. Since the Federals produced few victories and suffered many defeats, recognition remained a possibility until mid-1863. The turning point really came in October, 1862, when Palmerston decided, on hearing of Lee's retreat after Antietam, not to go ahead with the recognition tentatively agreed upon a month earlier. Never again did Britain come so close to taking that step.

Forestalling European intervention was necessary if the Union was to survive. Much depended, of course, on the form such intervention would take. A military alliance between the Confederacy and one or more European states was not likely unless Lincoln and Seward blundered badly. Unneutral aid would be serious but not disastrous. The greatest danger was forcible mediation, in which England and France would demand the prompt cessation of hostilities on the basis of a divided republic and on pain of armed reprisals if the ultimatum were ignored. Early in the war the South believed and the North feared that Anglo-French dependence on raw cotton might bring about that kind of intervention; but Seward quickly made it clear that he would reject mediation, even if it meant adding to the list of foes on the battlefield. Thus the question of intervention was decided when the Confederate military tide crested at Antietam and then ebbed.

Winning approval of the blockade proved to be the easiest of Seward's tasks. In this matter, as with recognition and intervention, England declined to take any action which might needlessly lead to involvement. Only intolerable assaults upon its national honor or material well-being could make it act otherwise, and the blockade was not such an assault. Although at first Lincoln's navy drew a very loose cordon around the South—the kind of cordon Jefferson and Madison had protested against—the British accepted it as valid on February 15, 1862. Nor did they seriously object to later questionable practices respecting broken voyages. In both instances the government was motivated by a desire to have the North set maritime precedents which could be appealed to in the future when Great Britain was at war and the United States at peace. Loopholes in England's neutrality laws and an initial tardiness in plugging them, however, indirectly jeopardized the blockade. During 1862 the Confederates were able to build in British yards two merchant hulls which, after putting to sea, took on sufficient armament to imperil unprotected Northern cargo ships. Heavy damage by the *Florida* and *Alabama* compelled the United States to release vessels from patrol duty along the Eastern and Gulf coasts. A more immediate danger lay in the construction for the South near Liverpool of two ironclads, more powerful than any of the Union's wooden cruisers or armored monitors. Only a belated purchase of the two rams for the Royal Navy on September 5, 1863, averted a serious diplomatic and naval crisis. Thus, when Lee surrendered, the blockade was still intact, the Davis regime still unrecognized, and the European monarchies still neutral. Skillful diplomacy by the North, bitter rivalries on the Continent, and Palmerston's determination to stay aloof contributed to the outcome.

From 1865 to 1872 the most pressing item in foreign affairs was a quarrel with England over an alleged lack of neutrality during the Civil War. The United States demanded that its citizens be compensated for the destruction of their property by Confederate cruisers built in British ports. It estimated the damage done directly at $15,000,000. Some Americans also wanted reparation for indirect damages, such as the rise in insurance rates, the loss of trade to foreign vessels, and the cost of running down the raiders. Extremists argued that Britain was responsible for prolonging the war by eighteen months; they computed the indirect claims at $2,250,000,000. That sum could be paid only by ceding Canada to the United States. Since the British government did not believe it had been negligent and since the Canadian people did not wish to change rulers, some compromise was necessary. It took six years, many fiery speeches, new leaders, a war scare abroad, and a political quarrel at home to bring about the Treaty of Washington of May 8, 1871. Among other matters, that agreement referred to arbitration the claims against England, and by the Geneva Award of September 14, 1872, the United States received $15,500,000.

Other external adjustments accompanied the return to peace. During the war Spain had reannexed the Dominican Republic, and France had placed an Austrian archduke on the Mexican throne against the wishes of most Mexicans. By April, 1865, the Spanish venture had collapsed, but French bayonets still protected Maximilian of Habsburg from the republican forces under Benito Juarez. Seward could do little until the war ended; then he exerted strong pressure on Napoleon III to withdraw his troops. Faced with the victorious Union army along the border, with stubborn resistance by Juarez in the field, and with mounting troubles in Europe, the Emperor yielded. By March, 1867, the last French soldiers had sailed for home; three months later the deserted Maximilian fell before a firing squad. Simultaneously, a brief revival of expansionist activity subsided in the face of domestic problems. The settlement of the *Alabama* claims thwarted the United States demand for Canada, while premature attempts to acquire all or part of the Danish West Indies and the Dominican Republic failed. A similar fate befell treaties granting special privileges to the United States in the Hawaiian and Samoan Islands. The sole territorial additions at this time were Alaska, purchased from Russia on March 30, 1867, and the unoccupied atoll of Midway, claimed on August 28, 1867.

The remaining years before 1889 marked the nadir of American diplomatic activity. Never before or since have external affairs seemed less important; never again would the United States appear so immune from developments beyond its borders. Possessed of an independent foreign policy, surfeited with a continental expanse for the democratic experiment, and absorbed in internal rebuilding, the nation grew steadily in strength until during the last decade of the century new factors at home and abroad forced it once more to look outward.

THE WORLD OF THE YOUNG REPUBLIC

The world in which the republic was born and reached maturity helped shape the course of its foreign policy. The configuration of power on the European continent, the existence of European colonies in the Western Hemisphere, the slow means of communication, and the rudimentary weapons of war, all played a part and distinguished that early period from today. And to the United States before 1889—again in contrast to today—the outside world meant Europe. Save for occasional trade contacts and missionary endeavors, the Middle East, Africa, and almost all of Asia were of trifling significance.

No nation or alliance dominated the continent of Europe for long between 1775 and 1889. At first there was a superficial equilibrium which barely concealed the might of Great Britain. Then came a slight shift as many of England's foes gave aid, secret or open, to the rebellious colonies, but the peace of 1783 still left the British with a vast empire in North America, insular outposts in the Caribbean, and continued superiority at sea. A decade later revolutionary France made a bid for hegemony, and by 1812 Napoleon Bonaparte controlled a greater area than any man until 1941. The United States soon discovered how events overseas could menace its security; it also learned to reap advantages from the strife of Europe. Several early diplomatic triumphs—indeed, independence itself—resulted from rivalries and unrest in the Old World.

After Napoleon's downfall in 1815 Europe entered upon a century of relative peace. Rebellions and wars erupted every so often, but none of the former had the unsettling effect of the French Revolution and none of the latter matched the global consequences of the struggle just ended. The new period saw no one state supreme. It opened with an attempt to keep the peace by a concert of the big powers; it closed with the formation of an alliance system that lasted until 1914. To most Americans, the Continental developments—the creation of national states in Germany and Italy, the democratic trend in England, the frequent governmental changes in France, and the persistence of absolutism in Russia—seemed less significant than the diplomatic activity of the European nations in the Western Hemisphere and the future of their empires there.

Spain's possessions in the Americas were reduced by 1825 to Cuba and Puerto Rico. Except during such abnormal times as the Civil War, Spain could not hurt the United States save through weakness. England's colonies far outnumbered France's, but each was eager to uphold some balance of power in the New World. For that reason they tried to check the expansion of the republic by encouraging Texas to remain independent and by advising Mexico to avoid war. Both wanted to keep California out of Yankee hands but succeeded only in convincing Washington of their own ambitions there. Both wished to see Spain retain Cuba; twice they vainly proposed an Anglo-American-French guarantee of the *status quo* for that island. France took advantage of the Civil War to resurrect a monarchy in Mexico, but with the death of Maximilian in 1867 and the rout by Prussia in 1871, the French ceased to threaten the security of the United States. Indeed, by 1889 only Great Britain and the new German Empire seemed capable of causing trouble across the Atlantic, and the latter could not do so effectively until it had acquired some naval bases.

In the world of the young republic, men and messages traveled slowly. It took Benjamin Franklin thirty-eight days in 1776, amidst the perils of November gales and British cruisers, to sail from the United States to France. Sixty years later a new ambassador consumed three weeks getting to the English capital. Even in 1861 the Boston-London journey lasted thirteen days. In the 1780's over two months had to elapse before a reply could be received to a message sent to a minister in Europe; not until 1867 did the Atlantic cable make for instantaneous communication. Other regions were more remote. Critical dispatches from the State Department to the consul at Monterey, California, in 1845 were six months in transit; a treaty signed with China on July 3, 1844, reached Washington 192 days later. A telegraph to the Pacific was operating by 1861, but in 1889 agents in Hawaii and Samoa still had to use ships.

Under these conditions representatives abroad enjoyed a wide area of discretion and initiative. Their instructions had to be couched in general terms, to be ignored as unforeseen circumstances dictated. Neither the president nor the secretary of state could control every important transaction. Such a system had disadvantages. Developments at home and abroad might render obsolete the original objectives of a negotiation or nullify a carefully drafted treaty. But it also had benefits. It permitted time for reflection. The glare of publicity and the sense of urgency which so hamper modern statesmen were absent.

Before 1889 the nature of warfare, like the slowness of communications, posed diplomatic problems very different from today's. In the United States a repugnance against standing armies kept the land forces woefully undermanned and unprepared to engage in large-scale operations. Except for the periods 1812–15, 1846–8, and 1861–5, their main experience was Indian fighting and garrison duty in the West. Until the ideas of Alfred T. Mahan gained currency in the 1890's, the navy was regarded as something to be improvised after hostilities had begun and then to be employed primarily for commerce raiding. In peace its few ships were widely dispersed to show the flag, not trained for fleet action. Ordnance of all types was changing very slowly. As late as 1883, when Congress authorized the nucleus of a modern navy, it stipulated that the ships carry auxiliary sails, even though the first steam frigate had been launched forty years earlier.

There was little coordination before 1889 in the work of the diplomat and the soldier. No liaison existed between the State, War, and Navy Departments. No officer in either service was assigned to drafting war plans, much less meshing them with foreign policy. The Naval War College was not founded at Newport until 1884; its army counterpart was not established at Washington until 1901. The president and his cabinet made the vital decisions, sometimes quite oblivious of their military implications. A single example will suffice. During the crisis over Oregon in January, 1846, Polk insisted that the United States must look John Bull "straight in the eye," while extremists in the Senate demanded England's expulsion from North America. Yet at that moment the United States could muster seven steam warships, built or building, mounting 39 guns to oppose the Royal Navy's 141 steam vessels with 698 guns. And most of the fighting, if war came.

would be on the seas. Such irresponsibility seemed to justify Alexis de Tocqueville's observation in 1835 that "almost all the defects inherent in democratic institutions are brought to light in the conduct of foreign affairs." Such bumptious and uninformed diplomacy would be suicidal once the world of the young republic changed and the United States had to deal, as it did after 1889, with events far beyond its shores.

2

❯❯❯-❯❯❯-❯❯❯-❯❯❯❮❮❮-❮❮❮-❮❮❮-❮❮❮

The Persistence of

Isolationism

THE CARDINAL PRINCIPLE undergirding the foreign policy of the young republic was isolationism. Precisely defined, this set of ideas was, in itself, largely negative—a limitation upon the action of the United States government. It required the avoidance of permanent alliances and of involvement in the diplomatic affairs of other continents. But taken together with such other major concepts as neutrality and the Monroe Doctrine and such lesser ones as nonintervention, recognition of *de facto* governments, and equality of trade opportunity, it provided a positive and realistic course for a young and weak nation.

For convenience in analysis, isolationism will be treated apart from those other concepts, but it should always be thought of as simply one element of a larger whole and one means by which the American people strove to establish their independence on the international stage. Isolationism as a policy must not be confused with the geographic isolation of the United States, which steadily diminished as the republic matured, or with the sentiment of escapism, which the settlers brought from Europe in the seventeenth and eighteenth centuries, although both physical aloofness and a desire to be free of the tribulations of the Old World made the policy seem wise and inevitable. Nor should isolationism be regarded as a hermitlike policy which barred official relations with other countries or forbade commercial intercourse. In 1783, the United States could not live alone, and the founding fathers knew it.

THE FIRST ALLIANCE

Paradoxically, one of the first acts of the United States flew in the face of that colonial experience and contravened the cardinal principle of its subsequent foreign policy. As an inescapable step to independence, the young republic concluded a permanent alliance with France on February 6, 1778. Intended to supplement a treaty of amity and commerce signed the same day and to anticipate a declaration of war upon France by England, the pact obligated the two parties to fight together and not to negotiate a separate peace. Some of the articles divided between the allies the British territory that might be conquered during the war, but the most significant one for the future was a promise by the United States to guarantee "from the present time and forever" the French possessions in America, both those then held and those to be acquired in the peace settlement. No mention was made as to how long the alliance would last or how it might be terminated.

Enthusiasm for this wartime expedient did not long survive the end of the conflict. Although many Americans remained grateful for the indispensable French assistance and some became, after 1789, ardent admirers of all things Gallic, most citizens saw no advantage in replacing the imperial tie by a permanent bond with one of England's traditional foes. To be sure, the obligations assumed in 1778 were not unduly burdensome or dangerous; but since European chancelleries continued to think of the New World as part of the balance of power of the Old, it seemed desirable to reduce diplomatic commitments to a minimum. The suspicions engendered by the peacemaking, when France was prepared to sacrifice America's needs to Spain's, were not quickly forgotten; and it is hardly surprising that on June 12, 1783 the Congress resolved that "the true interest of these states requires that they should be as little as possible entangled in the politics and controversies of European nations."

One other factor made the alliance less desirable in peace than in war. Although it did not require the United States to defend French soil in the Old World or come to her aid on European battlefields, it did encourage representatives of His Most Christian Majesty to meddle in American domestic affairs. During the struggle for independence the French envoy secured the support of several members of the Continental Congress by judicious loans and subsidies, and it was only natural for the court at Versailles to look upon the new state as a ward. Such a relationship would be objectionable at any time; it became fraught with peril in the 1790's when the wars of the French Revolution aroused diverse sympathies in the United States for the major belligerents.

For a decade after 1783, however, there was no real demand to abrogate the first alliance. Occasionally American diplomats considered appealing to France to help solve boundary and navigation disputes with Spain and England. But no new bonds were forged, though in its zeal for vital commercial privileges and the free use of the Mississippi River, the United States came perilously close to guaranteeing forever Spanish sovereignty over vast tracts in the interior of North America. Such a pledge would not have constituted an alliance, but it might have made impossible the diplomatic goal of limiting European power in the Western Hemisphere and freeing American foreign policy of all European influences.

With the beheading of Louis XVI on January 21, 1793, and the outbreak eleven days later of a war that soon became global in scope, the Washington administration had to re-examine the implications of the alliance of 1778. Had it been nullified by a change of rulers in France? Was it incompatible with a policy of neutrality? Did it imperil the national security? To all those questions Secretary of State Jefferson answered in the negative; and the President accepted his views over those of Secretary of the Treasury Hamilton, who wished to grasp the opportunity to end once and for all a contract the benefits of which had been exhausted but the obligations of which remained. Thus the eventual termination of the treaty of 1778 resulted, not from an embarrassing call upon the United States for armed assistance, but from the intolerable French assaults upon American neutral shipping and the infuriating attempts of their agents to sway the American voters prior to the presidential election of 1796. But before the first alliance passed out of existence, those events drew from the retiring chief executive on September 19, 1796, a final admonition which, although intended mainly to guide his countrymen during the current crisis and immediate future, helped to shape the policy of isolationism for many generations to come.

WASHINGTON'S "GREAT RULE OF CONDUCT"

Washington's Farewell Address constituted a foreign policy of independence, not of isolationism. The first President did speak of alliances —their dangers and their advantages—but his primary concern was to keep the operation of his government immune from foreign intrigue and the decisions of his people free from alien domination. He did advocate a great rule of conduct for the nation's adolescence, but he was farsighted enough to suggest that a different course might be adopted when the United States reached maturity.

Only a sixth of this influential document dealt with foreign policy, and that portion was carefully integrated with solemn warnings on the dangers of sectional hostilities and of violent partisan feelings in domestic affairs. After deploring the tendency of these emotions to divide the American people and after excoriating the machinations of French agents in this country, Washington declared:

Observe good faith and justice toward all nations. Cultivate peace and harmony with all. . . . Nothing is more essential than that permanent, inveterate antipathies against particular nations and passionate attachments for others should be excluded. . . . The great rule of conduct for us in regard to foreign nations is, in extending our commercial relations to have with them as little *political* connection as possible. So far as we have already formed engagements let them be fulfilled with perfect good faith. Here let us stop. Europe has a set of primary interests which to us have none or a very remote relation. Hence she must be engaged in frequent controversies, the causes of which are essentially foreign to our concerns. Hence, therefore, it must be unwise in us to implicate ourselves by artificial ties in the ordinary vicissitudes of her politics or the ordinary combinations and collisions of her friendships or enmities. Our detached and distant situation invites and enables us to pursue a different course. If we remain one people, under an efficient government, the period is not far off when . . . we may take such an attitude as will cause the neutrality we may at any time resolve upon to be scrupulously respected . . . when we may choose peace or war, as our interest, guided by justice, shall counsel. Why forego the advantages of so peculiar a situation? Why quit our own to stand upon foreign ground? Why, by interweaving our destiny with that of any part of Europe, entangle our peace and prosperity in the toils of European ambition, rivalship, interest, humor, or caprice? It is our true policy to steer clear of permanent alliances. . . . Taking care always to keep ourselves by suitable establishments on a respectable defensive posture, we may safely trust to temporary alliances for extraordinary emergencies.

In short, Washington's great rule was to have as little political, as distinct from commercial, relationship with Europe as possible. The French tie must be respected, but in the near future permanent alliances must be avoided. In the ordinary vicissitudes of European diplomacy the United States should play no part, but in dire emergencies, such as that of 1778, it could form temporary alliances. For the more distant future, when it had grown in strength, the nation would be free to remain neutral, select allies, and choose war or peace as its interests, guided by its ideals, dictated. Nowhere did Washington use the word "isolationism"; to him, it was a means, not an end. The end was an independent foreign policy.

Less than two years after Washington's testament, Congress decided that the first alliance need no longer be respected, and on September 30, 1800, it was ended by a treaty with France. Six months later, just to make clear that the principles of the Farewell Address were shared by both political parties, Jefferson's inaugural message of March 4, 1801, called for "peace, commerce, and honest friendship with all nations, entangling alliances with none." The Virginian also omitted the term "isolationism," but his inclusion of the phrase "no entangling alliances" was the form in which that policy has come ringing down the years.

Like Washington, Jefferson avoided a doctrinaire approach to foreign affairs, and his definition of isolationism left room for temporary alliances during extraordinary emergencies. Such a case he recognized in 1802. For a few years before, as Franco-American relations deteriorated, there had been a *rapprochement* between the United States and England. But even the most ardent Anglophile dared not think of an alliance, and to overtures from the British foreign secretary, Hamilton remarked pithily early in 1798, " 'Twill be best not to entangle." In these sentiments the incoming Republicans concurred. When, however, it seemed likely that a vigorous France, spurred by dreams of a revived empire in North America, would replace a feeble Spain at the mouth of the Mississippi River, Jefferson thought of countering with a defensive alliance. "The day that France takes possession of N. Orleans," he wrote on April 18, 1802, "we must marry ourselves to the British fleet and nation." Although there was an element of calculated bluff in these words and although they were contingent upon the failure of negotiations at Paris, Jefferson's threat did not stand alone; and he returned to it on several occasions, even with hints in public, until the purchase of Louisiana eliminated any necessity of forging a second alliance.

As the War of 1812 approached and as American neutral rights suffered grievously from Anglo-French belligerent practices, there was no disposition to align the United States with either side. Indeed, when national pride combined with sectional and territorial ambition to bring about hostilities, a margin of only two votes prevented a declaration against France as well as Great Britain. Far from allying itself with England's foe, the young republic almost fought both. The ensuing conflict did not jeopardize the policy of isolationism. It was essentially an Anglo-American contest, divorced as far as possible from the European struggle. No troops were sent abroad; the fighting was confined to the New World and the high seas. The Madison administration did not care about the balance of power and gave no thought to joining the concert of peace that emerged in 1815.

THE PANAMA DEBATE AND THE REVOLUTIONS OF 1848

By 1825 Washington's warning had hardened into a hallowed tradition, and isolationism was a revered principle of American foreign policy. Men in public life could disagree with neither; the only matter open to question was their exact application to a specific situation. Such a discussion occurred in the winter of 1825–6, when President John Quincy Adams proposed to send delegates to a Congress of American States at Panama. That meeting had been planned originally by Simon Bolívar as a purely Latin American affair for the primary purpose of promoting unity among the newly created republics. A series of treaties looking to that end had already been negotiated by Colombia, Mexico, and Peru. Only later was it decided to place on the agenda such items as the defense of the hemisphere, the liberation of Cuba and Puerto Rico, the definition of neutral rights, and an inter-American agreement that would convert the noncolonization principle contained in Monroe's message of December 2, 1823, into a multi-lateral obligation. The invitation to the United States was also an afterthought and tentative in nature. Great Britain and the Netherlands, who held possessions in the Caribbean, were asked to be present as observers.

When, during a legislative recess, Adams indicated he would be receptive to a bid and when, later, he announced the nomination of two delegates subject to confirmation by the Senate and an appropriation by the House, he stirred up a veritable hornets' nest. Did the Farewell Address and the policy it embodied prohibit attendance at this international conference? The motives of the legislators who opposed participation were a mixture of sectional antipathies, constitutional scruples, racial prejudice, political partisanship, personal animosities, and sincere conviction. It would, therefore, be foolish to accept an appeal to the principle of avoiding entangling alliances as conclusive proof that the speaker was genuinely concerned with isolationism. But the very fact that so many Congressmen deemed it expedient to invoke the shades of George Washington on the issue is in itself most significant.

Adams told the Senate on December 26, 1825, that the American delegates would not "contract alliances" or engage in undertakings hostile to any nation. He envisaged no departure from the pattern of past diplomacy. When this assurance failed to convince the House, the President on March 15, 1826, addressed himself to the question of whether attendance at Panama would "change the policy, hitherto invariably pursued by the United States, of avoiding all entangling alliances." Far from conflicting with the Farewell Address, such a course was "directly deducible from and conformable to it." Washington's counsel, he observed, dealt with a contemporary problem, and its author had predicted that changed conditions in the future might require a different policy. That time had come. In 1796 there had been no independent Spanish-American republics; in 1826 there were eight. In 1796 it was Europe that had a set of primary interests which had only a remote relation to the United States. In 1826 all of the Americas had a set of primary interests that were of no concern to Europe. Adams, too, had reversed himself. In 1821 he had opposed Clay's call for an "American equipoise" against the Holy Alliance; now he agreed with Jefferson's remark of 1823 that "America, North and South, has a set of interests distinct from those of Europe, and peculiarly her own." That difference, he believed, consisted of an allegiance to democracy.

To John Quincy Adams, the most experienced diplomat the young republic had yet produced, a policy of isolationism in 1826 did not preclude participation in an inter-American conference called to stimulate trade, clarify maritime rights, and promote peace. But for good reasons or bad, an articulate majority on Capitol Hill maintained that freedom from despotism or monarchy in the New World was of no direct concern to the United States. Three future presidents argued further that the aims of the Panama Congress lay outside the proper diplomatic activity of the nation and that United States attendance would violate the precepts of the Father of his Country. James Buchanan asserted that the American people regarded the Farewell Address as the palladium of their liberty and accused Adams of trying to explain away its principles. Martin Van Buren denied that the states of the New World had common interests and raised the specter of an alliance that would infringe upon the prerogative of the legislature to declare war. In campaigning for re-election to Congress, James K. Polk took pride in having opposed Adams' recommendation.

This important debate ended in an anticlimax. The Senate finally confirmed the delegates on March 14, 1826, and the House voted the necessary appropriations on April 22. But one of the envoys died en route, and the other stopped short of his destination because the conference had adjourned. The gathering accomplished very little. The episode is not to be remembered, therefore, as a precursor of the inter-American movement—that would not come until 1889—or as a discussion of the wisdom of isolationism. The latter was taken for granted. Rather, it was significant as an attempt to define the limits of an accepted policy.

Not for another twenty years was there a similar debate on the meaning of isolationism. During that interval the principle of avoiding both permanent alliances and involvement in the diplomatic affairs of other continents retained the unquestioning allegiance of leaders in both major parties. When at mid-century a somewhat unrealistic discussion arose, the issue was not one of forging a second alliance but of whether the cause of democracy elsewhere in the world was of direct concern to the United States. Should the American people promote republican institutions solely by the example they set at home, or should they intervene abroad in behalf of those struggling for liberty? By the 1850's the geographic area at stake had extended from the New World to the Old.

Let it be said at once that there was not the remotest possibility of armed intervention by the United States in Europe. To be sure, the liberal revolutions that swept the continent in 1848, like many earlier uprisings, aroused intense popular interest as democrats on this side of the Atlantic looked forward to the downfall of monarchy on the other. To be sure, the heroic bid for independence in Hungary captured the people's imagination as few such distant events had done before, and the highly publicized visit to this country in 1851–2 of the dynamic Louis Kossuth encouraged normally discreet statesmen to say things that sounded faintly ridiculous a few years later. To be sure, a tiny but noisy faction of the Democratic party took the name of Young America in 1852 and dedicated itself, in addition to nominating Stephen A. Douglas for the presidency, to a bold and vigorous foreign policy, one that contemplated the possibility of alliances and crusades to make Europe safe for democracy. Yet interesting as are these faint stirrings of concern for freedom abroad and significant as may seem the first competent critique of the Farewell Address, the real importance of the debates following the uprisings of 1848 is the evidence they reveal of the firm popular attachment to the policy implicit in Washington's counsel of 1796. Certainly contemporaries set greater store by the continuing defense of isolationism than by the transitory and scattered attacks upon it.

At no time did Congress vote directly upon the naked question of intervening in Europe. The issue presented was always tangential. In 1849 it was a move to suspend diplomatic relations with Austria in order to show displeasure at the crushing of a revolt within its empire. In 1850 there was an expression of sympathy for the Hungarians and a disclaimer of meddling in the domestic affairs of other nations. In 1851 the President was requested to place a warship at Kossuth's disposal for travel to the United States, and the nature of the reception to be accorded was argued at length. In 1852 a resolution was introduced to reaffirm the doctrine of noninvolvement. In short, words of encouragement were freely uttered, public transportation for the Magyar leaders was provided, and a warm welcome was arranged; but assistance in the form of men, money, arms, and even diplomatic support was not forthcoming.

A disconcerting vagueness characterized most critics of isolationism during the intermittent Congressional debates of 1849–52. The United States, they contended, had come of age and must assume an active role in world affairs. It must protest against the Russian intervention in Hungary. But few reasonable lawmakers told how they would translate words into deeds. There was no disposition to ally with England against the Continental autocracies. There was no demand for naval reprisals, much less for an expeditionary force. Even the Farewell Address was, for the most part, treated with respect. Senators such as Lewis Cass and William H. Seward took pains to point out that Washington had not prohibited resolutions of displeasure or, indeed, temporary alliances. Yet they did not themselves advocate such alliances.

The most intelligent and reasoned appraisal of isolationism in these years is to be found in a little pamphlet by William H. Trescot, a conservative Democrat from South Carolina. Entitled *A Few Thoughts on the Foreign Policy of the United States* and published in 1849, before the Kossuth craze reached its height, it deplored the tendency to stereotype the Farewell Address into what Trescot called a "political proverb." The changed diplomatic status of the United States, which Washington foresaw, had arrived. The growth of its settlements on the Pacific coast gave the country a vital concern for Asia where, the author believed, the future of Europe would be decided. Similarly, the importance of the Caribbean, where Anglo-American interests ran parallel, suggested the desirability of an alliance with Great Britain. As to the question of the hour, Trescot concluded: "There is but one principle upon which American intervention in the international relations of Europe can be justified . . . and it is this, that wherever the changes among European powers are such as to modify the respective weight of its colonial empires, we are directly interested in the resulting balance of power."

None of the defenders of isolationism peered so far into the future as Trescot, and most looked back to the age of Washington and Jefferson. But they were not vague and they did reflect the sentiments of the vast majority of Americans. The dying Clay, when visited by Kossuth in January, 1852, touched a responsive chord when he said bluntly that it was best for free men everywhere that the United States stay out of "the distant wars of Europe" and "keep our lamp burning brightly on this Western shore, as a light to all nations." Others appealed to the precepts of the first President, and one influential Senator went still further. On April 6, 1852, James M. Mason, Democrat of Virginia and chairman of the Foreign Relations Committee from 1851 to 1861, declared that peace and amity could best be promoted "by avoiding all alliances, whether transient or permanent." And at the political level the Whig platform of 1852 proclaimed: "We still adhere to the doctrine of the Father of His Country, as announced in the Farewell Address, of keeping ourselves free from all entangling alliances with foreign countries."

Pleas for intervention in order to promote the cause of democracy in Europe led several Presidents to tell Congress that the traditional policy should not be modified. In his inaugural address of March 4, 1849, Zachary Taylor observed that "we are warned by the admonitions of history and the voice of our own beloved Washington to abstain from entangling alliances." On December 2, 1851, Millard Fillmore stated: " 'Friendly relations with all, but entangling alliances with none' has long been a maxim with us. Our true mission is not to . . . impose upon other countries our form of government by artifice or force, but to teach by example and show by our success . . . the advantages of free institutions." A year later Fillmore devoted a large portion of his last annual message to that theme and flatly denied that the growth in material power by the United States or changed conditions in transportation and communication warranted any departure from isolationism. And just to demonstrate that the conservative Whigs were not alone in their thinking, James Buchanan, an expansionist-minded Democrat, asserted on March 4, 1857: "To avoid entangling alliances has been a maxim of our policy since the days of Washington, and its wisdom no one will attempt to dispute."

THE PROBLEM OF INTERNATIONAL CONFERENCES

Nor did many disputants emerge before 1889. Even as the United States grew in strength and the world shrank in size, men continued to believe, or said they believed, that the national interest required barring permanent ties with other countries and avoiding diplomatic involvement in other continents. In 1884 the Republican platform endorsed "a policy which shall keep us from entangling alliances with foreign nations," and the Democrats replied by recommending close commercial relations with neighbors of the hemisphere "but entangling alliances with none."

One problem dating back to the days of John Quincy Adams recurred with increasing frequency after the Civil War. Did isolationism mean that the United States should not attend international conferences whose primary purpose was to discuss social and economic matters that cut across national boundaries? Were diplomats quitting their own to stand upon foreign ground when they signed agreements protecting the use of submarine cables, establishing a Bureau of Weights and Measures, or providing for an exchange of official documents? Was it impolitic or dangerous to adhere to multilateral treaties designed to promote peace through arbitration or a world court?

Prior to 1861 the United States was not represented at a single international conference. Then, in May, 1863, John A. Kasson attended a gathering in Paris to consider postal regulations, but no formal treaty was concluded. The following year the minister to Switzerland acted as observer at a meeting in Geneva which drafted a convention to ameliorate the condition of the wounded in time of war. Several times in the next few years the United States was invited to adhere to this innocuous and humanitarian endeavor, but Seward declined. This country, he wrote on March 31, 1868, already followed the rules agreed upon at Geneva; moreover it has always been deemed "at least a questionable policy, if not unwise, for the United States to become a party to any instrument to which there are many other parties. Nothing but the most urgent necessity should lead to a departure from this rule."

Fourteen years later, without fanfare or protest, President Chester A. Arthur declared the adherence of the United States to the Geneva Convention as amended in 1868. On March 16, 1882, the Senate gave its unanimous consent. In fact, such had been the change since Seward's day that Arthur referred on December 4, 1882, to four different meetings with which the United States was concerned. He requested, "in view of the frequent occurrences of conferences for the consideration of important matters of common interest to civilized nations," that he be invested "with discretionary powers to send delegates to such conventions."

Yet none of the conferences mentioned threatened to involve the United States in the diplomatic toils of other continents, much less to entangle it in an alliance. To many, however, such a danger appeared in the General Act of Berlin of February 26, 1885, to which the American government was a party. Dealing with Africa, the treaty provided for, among other things, suppression of the slave traffic, free trade in the Congo basin, and the neutrality of the area should war among the powers break out elsewhere. A commission composed of one delegate from each nation was to execute the terms of the Act, and it possessed considerable authority, including the right, under certain conditions, to call upon the warships of the signatories.

Fearing legislative sensibilities, the Arthur administration had cautioned the American delegates at Berlin not to commit the country to any course "contrary to its well-known policy." Congress, nevertheless, quickly protested. A report by the Republican minority of the House Committee on Foreign Affairs called participation in the Congo Conference "unfortunate" and asserted "that no prospect of commercial advantage warrants a departure from the traditional policy . . . which forbids entangling alliances." The Democratic majority, "heedful of the admonitions of Washington," dissented from the President's original decision to attend the conference. Given these adverse reports, it was unlikely that the incoming Grover Cleveland, who had little taste for novelty in foreign affairs, would look with favor upon the Berlin treaty. He gave some inkling of what was to follow when, in his inaugural address on March 4, 1885, he rejected "any share in foreign broils and ambitions upon other continents" and pledged himself to a Jeffersonian policy of friendship with all nations, entangling alliances with none. He refused to submit the Congo agreement to the Senate on the ground that the country could never join in any pact for "the conservation of the territorial integrity of distant regions where we have no established interests or control." He told the Congress on December 8, 1885, that "to share in the obligation of enforcing neutrality in the remote valley of the Kongo [sic] would be an alliance." Actually, the treaty bound the United States only to respect the neutrality of the Congo basin, not to defend it, but Cleveland's distortion passed almost unnoticed.

From 1796 until 1889—and well beyond—the American people endorsed Washington's "great rule of conduct" in foreign affairs with a reverence befitting the Father of his Country and with a unanimity facilitating the task of the diplomats. Once the French alliance had been abrogated, no new bonds, permanent or temporary, were forged. In 1826 some citizens contended that peace and stability in the Western Hemisphere was a legitimate concern of the nation. At mid-century a tiny minority argued that the suppression of free institutions in Europe could not be regarded with indifference. Only an occasional Trescot, however, called attention to the way in which a shift in the continental balance of power, especially in colonial areas, could affect the United States. As the period drew to a close, international conferences that confined themselves to social and economic problems proved to be acceptable; those which suggested diplomatic involvement in other continents did not. In short, for the world in which the young republic was born and spent its adolescence, the policy of isolationism was both possible and desirable. Indeed, it was beneficial and indispensable.

The Quest for Neutrality

SECOND ONLY to isolationism as a polestar of American diplomacy in the formative years was the principle of neutrality. As a legal concept, dealing with technical problems no longer common today, neutrality also requires precise definition. It is the policy of a nation in remaining aloof from a war between other states, while expecting from them certain rights and observing for them certain duties. As a policy, it can be adhered to, modified, or abandoned as the national interest dictates. By staying aloof, the neutral does not favor one belligerent at the expense of the other or feel obliged to decide which cause is just. A war between other states embraces civil as well as foreign conflicts. The rights of a neutral are normally secured by treaties, while his duties are defined by international agreements and domestic laws.

Historically, neutrality evolved as a compromise between the divergent interests of neutrals and belligerents. It attempted to adjust the latter's desire to bar his foe from all commerce with the outside world and the former's wish to trade uninterruptedly with all nations, those at war as well as those at peace. In both cases self-interest plays a major role. The belligerent usually tolerates some neutral trade, lest he add another enemy to those he is already fighting; the neutral often endures galling interferences as a lesser evil than war. But at any moment, when the lives of nations are at stake, the delicate balance can be upset. The belligerent may decide he has more to gain by starving his opponent into submission, even though he enlarges the conflict in the process. Or the neutral may conclude he has less to lose by joining the fray than by having his economy destroyed. In short, neutrality is no automatic safeguard for peace. It presupposes the neutral's in-difference to the outcome of the fighting, or at least a conviction that his participation would be worse than the triumph of one side or the other. To the young republic, eager to avoid diplomatic involvement in the Old World, intent on reducing European influence in the New, and dependent upon the sinews of commerce for its very existence, the quest for neutrality was logical and desirable, though not always suc-cessful.

THE BENEFITS OF NEUTRAL RIGHTS

Since nations, like individuals, are more concerned with their preroga-tives than with their obligations, the concept of neutral rights devel-oped before that of neutral duties. These rights were mainly of two kinds. The first pertained to the right of a nonparticipant to be free from invasion and other wartime operations. Its territory must not be occupied or used as a base from which one belligerent attacks the other. The second embraced the right of a neutral's seaborne commerce to be exempt from undue interference by the warring powers. Neutrals claimed the right to trade with either belligerent except in contraband articles and through blockaded ports.[1] They expected to be left alone in their intercourse with other neutrals unless it could be demonstrated that their acts were a subterfuge to conceal traffic with the enemy. They hoped their flag would protect all cargo other than contraband, even that owned by another state. For their part, neutrals understood that there was no general agreement as to what constituted undue interference by the warring powers and that each nation could enjoy these rights only if it possessed treaty guarantees or a navy strong enough to defend its shipping.

In the United States, where overseas commerce was indispensable to the economy and where hopes for insulation from Europe's wars were high, the statesmen had an added incentive to think first of the advantages accruing to a nonbelligerent. Less than eleven weeks after declaring independence, the Continental Congress drafted a model plan for securing neutral rights through treaties. Reflecting both the nation's lack of sea power and its abundance of exportable grain, the plan set

---

[1] Contraband is that which cannot be supplied to a belligerent except at the risk of seizure and confiscation. Before 1889 it was divided into absolute contra-band—goods intended solely for war use—and conditional contraband—goods normally employed in peaceful pursuits but adaptable for warlike purposes. A blockade is a naval cordon drawn around the ports and coasts of a foe to prevent all ships, enemy and neutral, from entering or departing. Even noncontraband articles can be confiscated if found on a vessel attempting to pierce the blockade. A legitimate blockade is one in which there is actual danger of interception by the patrolling squadron; an illegal, or paper, blockade is one in which there are too few warships to cover the blockaded area adequately.

forth three objectives. The first was that neutral ships could carry without fear of capture all goods other than contraband, no matter who held the title. This theory that the neutral flag of the vessel protected its cargo was known as "free ships make free goods." The second goal was to give a narrow definition to contraband of war. Specifically, the United States wished to confine those articles that could be confiscated to arms and munitions and to exempt foodstuffs and naval stores. A final aim was to establish the right of neutrals to transport goods other than contraband from one unblockaded port to another, even to those which under normal conditions were closed to foreign nations.

This plan of September 17, 1776, did not correspond to eighteenth-century maritime practices. It was objectionable to England, Spain, and other countries who in time of peace monopolized the trade of their empires and who in time of war counted on their fleets to deprive the enemy of all seaborne commerce. The doctrine that free ships make free goods was not widely accepted, and a British Rule of 1756 forbade neutrals to enter during war those harbors from which they were barred in peace. The big-navy powers tended to expand, not contract, the contraband list and to declare a coast under blockade even when it was insufficiently patrolled. In the face of such opposition, the Plan of 1776 remained largely an ideal. Agreements incorporating its provisions were signed with France on February 6, 1778, with Holland on October 8, 1782, and with Sweden on April 3, 1783. No agreements could be obtained from England, Spain, or Russia. These omissions left American shipping unprotected during any war involving the Mistress of the Seas. Yet on May 7, 1784, Congress adopted a second and more ambitious plan. It proposed to abolish contraband entirely and to define blockades precisely. Only one treaty, that with Prussia on September 10, 1785, was concluded under the Plan of 1784.

Undoubtedly the founding fathers expected the young republic to reap, not relinquish, the benefits of neutral rights in a global conflict. On July 11, 1787, Madison insisted that wartime trade was a source of wealth the United States ought not to deny its citizens. Jefferson expressed the hope on July 4, 1790, that "the new world will fatten on the follies of the old." After hostilities had commenced, President Washington urged Congress on December 7, 1796, to create a navy so as to prevent those violations of rights which might leave the neutral no option but to declare war. On May 16, 1797, President John Adams argued that it was imperative to consult other neutrals to safeguard those rights and that such consultation would not violate the policy of isolationism. In short, there was little disposition to withdraw into a continental economy whenever the world was at war. On the other hand, these early statesmen were neither foolhardy nor doctrinaire. Although not prepared to abandon neutral rights at the first sign of danger, they were unwilling to insist upon them at the cost of war. Between 1794 and 1812 they made many concessions to escape involvement in the European struggle, but they did not lose sight of their long-range goal, and they renewed their attempts after 1815 to vindicate those rights.

Four months before he helped formulate the Monroe Doctrine, Secretary of State John Quincy Adams drafted another document; if it had gone into force, it would have rivaled the President's message as a paramount contribution to American foreign policy. His project of July 28, 1823, was to be the basis for both an Anglo-American convention on neutral practices and a multilateral pact among all the maritime powers of the world. In it Adams returned to the principle embodied in the Plan of 1784, but on two points he broke new ground. First, his project would push the idea that free ships make free goods to its logical conclusion and confer complete immunity on all private property at sea. Second, it would outlaw privateers. The commissioning of privately owned vessels to serve as armed auxiliaries against enemy merchant craft was an old custom to which all small-navy powers clung in order to augment their fleets in time of crisis, but the abuses revealed in the decade after 1815 by Spain's rebellious colonies persuaded Adams that the practice should be renounced, provided the belligerent right to capture private property at sea be abolished simultaneously. That proviso doomed the plan to failure. Although privateering was declining in Europe, few Continental monarchies were yet ready to eliminate private warfare on the oceans. The Adams project did not lead to any treaties, but it remained the ideal for which the United States strove in the long stretch of comparative peace after the wars of the French Revolution.

Only one episode in that period need be mentioned. The Crimean War revived interest in neutral rights on both sides of the Atlantic, and Secretary of State William L. Marcy tried in vain to commit the belligerents to a long-term treaty embodying the principle that free ships make free goods. At the close of the conflict, however, England, France, Russia, Prussia, Austria, Turkey, and Sardinia signed the Declaration of Paris on April 16, 1856. It abolished privateering; exempted from seizure, except as contraband of war, neutral goods on belligerent ships as well as belligerent property on neutral vessels; and stipulated that blockades, to be binding, must be maintained by a force sufficient to prevent access to the enemy coast. Although these were articles for which the United States had long contended, Marcy declined to adhere to the Declaration. He reasoned much as Adams had thirty years earlier. If privateering was abolished without simultaneously granting complete immunity to all seaborne property, the small-navy powers would be at the mercy of the large. The American government had not com-

missioned a single privateer since 1815, but it felt that such ships remained a useful threat until the Adams project was universally accepted and thus insured for all nonbelligerents, strong and weak alike,
the full benefits of their neutral rights.

NEUTRAL RIGHTS IN TWO WARS

Two widely separated wars revealed inherent limitations in the practical workings of neutral rights, but they did not shake the faith of the
American people in that policy. During the titanic struggle which
lasted from 1793 to 1815 a quest for neutrality brought the young republic to a state of quasi-hostilities with France and was partly responsible in 1812 for the second conflict with England. During the ordeal of
the Union from 1861 to 1865 the Federal navy engaged in practices
which contravened the traditional American position on belligerent
rights and set valuable precedents for the British for the war of 1914
to 1918.

The first lesson learned in the 1790's was the futility and the
danger of negotiating treaties under the Plan of 1776 unless England
was included. By the agreement of 1778, France was bound to respect
British goods, not contraband, on United States vessels, but England
was not obliged to exempt from seizure French cargoes carried in
American bottoms. The situation was made worse in 1794, when John
Jay negotiated a comprehensive settlement, part of which dealt with
neutral rights. In this pact, designed primarily to check a perilous drift
toward an Anglo-American war, the United States acknowledged that,
so far as England was concerned, free ships did not make free goods,
that naval stores were contraband, and that the Rule of 1756 must be
obeyed. Although Jay had no choice but to make these concessions, the
French regarded them as calculated violations of the treaty of 1778
and started down the path that led to the undeclared war of 1798–1800.

During this first decade of world conflict the United States did not
choose to fight for all its neutral rights. Unable to gain Great Britain's
acceptance of the Plan of 1776, the Washington administration settled
for considerably less, and so did its successors. On July 15, 1797, Secretary of State Timothy Pickering asserted that until all maritime
powers shared America's views, it was folly to incorporate them in
treaties with a few. On September 9, 1801, President Jefferson wrote
that, laudable as was his country's concept of neutral rights, "in the
present state of things they are not worth a war."

A second lesson was driven home in the next decade. It taught that
in a life-and-death struggle fewer and fewer neutral rights are respected. As England moved after 1805 to strangle the Continental em-

pire and Napoleon countered with attempts to isolate the island of shopkeepers, American shipping was trapped between the French decrees and the British orders-in-council. Sweeping blockades were proclaimed and important ports closed. Vessels were diverted and delayed, their cargoes sometimes confiscated and their crews occasionally imprisoned. Belligerent cruisers hovered off the American coast and frequently violated territorial waters. And in the background lurked a well-grounded suspicion that some of the British depredations were undertaken to cripple the American merchant marine in the postwar era.

Even in the face of these and other outrages, the American people tried to steer a middle course. They were unwilling to renounce completely the benefits of neutral rights and yet reluctant to fight for them. To be sure, the government did impose a variety of commercial restrictions, ranging from nonimportation to total embargo; but those experiments in peaceable coercion were designed to bring pressure upon the belligerents, not yield to their indignities. To be sure, the United States did on June 18, 1812, declare war upon one of its oppressors, and British infractions of neutral rights comprised four of the six grievances listed in Madison's message to Congress on June 1. But the vote was close, and today historians still disagree whether the war came mainly because of violations of neutrality, the allied issue of impressments, a feeling of national frustration, English incitement of Indians along the frontier, American lust for Canada and the Floridas, or inept diplomacy that lured the country into a position from which it dared not retreat.[2]

The final lesson to be comprehended before 1889 was that the rights of a neutral look very different when viewed through belligerent eyes. During the Civil War traditional roles were reversed. England was at peace and the United States, with its very existence at stake, resorted to practices it had long denounced. It instituted loosely patrolled blockades, questioned the validity of broken voyages, and removed Confederate diplomats from a British vessel. This turnabout should have shown the unstable nature of neutrality; but if it did, Americans manifested no desire to modify or abandon that basic element of their diplomacy.

[2] The galling practice of impressing British deserters into the Royal Navy from the deck of an American merchantman, together with the all-too-frequent cases of mistaken identity by which citizens of the United States were condemned to serve under the Union Jack, transcended the simple question of a belligerent's right to visit and search private neutral vessels. It involved arbitrary acts by English officers and a complete Anglo-American disagreement on the right of individuals to change their allegiance. The United States was never able to secure protection from that practice by treaty, but after 1815 Great Britain had little need to resort to it. In a convention of May 13, 1870, the British finally accepted the American position on naturalization.

THE WISDOM OF NEUTRAL DUTIES

If the American policy of neutral duties emerged slightly later than that of neutral rights, it made a more novel and satisfying contribution to international law. It was more novel because the United States demonstrated to the cynical eighteenth century that neutrality could be true impartiality, not a thinly disguised device to give covert aid to one of the belligerents. It was more satisfying because the American government could fulfill its duties by its own efforts, whereas the enjoyment of rights depended on the willingness of other countries to sign treaties.

The wisdom of assuming the duties of a neutral was quickly seen when the European war erupted in 1793. The major belligerents held territory in the Western Hemisphere, and each would have gladly used American soil as a base from which to attack its enemies' colonies. Each owned warships that wished to replenish and refurbish along the Atlantic coast. Each was eager to augment its navy by commissioning privateers in neutral ports and having those vessels return to those ports when disposing of their prizes. Such practices would have brought hostilities to the door of the United States and were clearly dangerous to its security. Then, too, the American people were sharply divided in their sympathies, yet their government was bound by the alliance of 1778 to defend, if called upon, the French possessions in the New World and to deny France's foes the right to outfit private armed vessels in American harbors. In short, strict neutrality held out the best prospect of peace, and even Jefferson and Hamilton could agree that peace was indispensable.

It was one thing to grasp the wisdom of accepting the duties of a neutral; it was another to discover trustworthy precedents to follow. Pioneering on new ground, the Washington administration recognized two types of obligations. The first was negative and obliged the neutral to abstain from certain acts; for example, the government must not aid the belligerents or join the fighting in any way. The second was positive and required the neutral to prevent certain acts; its government must see that neither its citizens nor those of the belligerents used neutral soil for the benefit of one side or the other. Once a government had determined to be neutral, the acts of prevention posed the greater task.

In adjusting these generalities to the specific problems of the hour, Washington and his cabinet decided, first, that the United States must remain at peace and that it could be neutral without abrogating the alliance of 1778. They knew France did not seek armed assistance and preferred to exploit its ally as a carrier of foodstuffs. Second, the

President and his associates decided that neutral citizens must not, within the United States, join any expedition to be launched against a friendly neighbor. Third, the administration concluded that England could not complain of being barred from outfitting privateers in American ports if France was likewise forbidden. This last point outraged the impetuous French minister, who argued that the treaty prohibition on France's foes implied a grant to France.

Washington instituted his policy of neutral duties while Congress was not in session. On April 22, 1793, after a full cabinet discussion, he issued a proclamation that was general in nature and did not use the word "neutrality." It declared that "the duty and interest of the United States require that they should . . . pursue a conduct friendly and impartial toward the belligerent powers." It admonished American citizens to avoid all acts which belied that impartiality and warned that they would not be protected if they engaged in contraband trade or otherwise violated international law. This initial proclamation, however, lacked legal authority, and on December 3, 1793, Washington told the reassembled Congress that it ought "to correct, improve, or enforce" what the executive had done. He spoke of "our duties to the rest of the world" and urged prompt legislation. The lawmakers were still deliberating when an armed expedition was raised in Kentucky with the avowed purpose of marching southward under the French flag to invade the territory of Spain, with whom America was at peace. Once again the President acted, and in a proclamation of March 24, 1794, he cautioned the participants that their actions were "contrary to the laws of nations and to the duties incumbent on every citizen of the United States." He ordered them to desist, but he had no legal sanction to back up this command.

On June 5, 1794, the first neutrality law was finally enacted. It enjoined American citizens within the United States in four different ways: from accepting commissions to serve a foreign power, from securing the enlistment of others into the armed forces of a belligerent, from launching attacks against a nation with whom their country was at peace, and from arming or equipping private ships for operations against a nation with whom the United States was at peace. There was nothing to prevent individual citizens from selling munitions or granting loans to the warring powers, though that omission was not surprising, given the state of American finances and manufactures in the 1790's. The vote of 13 to 12 in the Senate and of 48 to 38 in the House indicated divided counsels and presaged difficulties in enforcement, but the administration was determined to set a high standard of neutrality. Under the Jay Treaty of November 19, 1794, it agreed to pay England $143,000 for damages inflicted by privateers which France had illegally commissioned in American ports. On June 14, 1797, Congress passed a new statute extending the prohibition against outfitting privateers to American citizens outside the country. By those means the United States solved the problem of neutral duties at a time when failure to do so might have spelled disaster.

The foundations laid by Washington and his colleagues were completed a generation later when the Latin American Wars of Independence raised anew the question of what constituted the obligations of a neutral. Once again the sympathies of United States citizens were enlisted in a belligerent cause; once again privateers were commissioned in American ports and operated in territorial waters. Another statute was passed on March 3, 1817, by a margin of 23 to 10 in the Senate and of 83 to 62 in the House. It applied the prohibitions contained in the laws of 1794 and 1797 to civil wars or rebellions and then attempted to prevent unneutral deeds before they occurred as well as to punish them after they had happened. Specifically, it required owners of armed private vessels leaving American ports to post bond that they themselves would not violate the law or sell their ships to anyone who might. Customs officials were authorized to seize any privateer they suspected of illegal activity.

Finally, on April 20, 1818, the acts of 1794 and 1817 were combined into a single statute which remained, save for a period of two years, the law of the land until 1889.[3] By all this legislation the United States set an unprecedented standard of neutral conduct. It prompted George Canning, certainly no lover of things American, to tell the House of Commons on April 16, 1823: "If I wished for a guide in the system of neutrality, I would take that laid down in America in the days of the presidency of Washington." Even more significant than that unexpected tribute is the incontrovertible fact that a policy of neutral duties served the nation well at a time when it had no real stake in the outcome of European wars or in the world balance of power.

NEUTRAL DUTIES IN WAR AND PEACE

It is not to be supposed that the restless American people universally approved or easily maintained a strict fulfillment of neutral obligations. Even in 1794, when involvement in the Anglo-French conflict would have been suicidal, the first neutrality act passed the Senate only by the casting vote of the Vice President and passed the House by the narrow margin of ten. Even in those perilous days the law was frequently violated, and local juries were reluctant to indict the guilty. Right down to 1889 the concept of neutral duties has been assailed, in

[3] An act of March 10, 1838, gave the government two years' additional authority to detain vehicles and arms as they crossed the border into an adjacent state or colony if it was believed they were intended for use in a military expedition against a country with whom the United States was at peace.

war and in peace, whenever enough citizens believed the national interest would be advanced by the triumph of one side or the other. Such convictions often nullified attempts to strengthen existing laws and led to repeated demands to repeal or modify what was already on the statute books.

Although the legislation of the Washington administration was enacted begrudgingly and enforced with difficulty, the Latin American Wars of Independence revealed more fully the popular ambivalence toward duty. When President Madison recommended on December 26, 1816, that Congress put additional teeth into the neutrality laws, Henry Clay countered with an appeal not to take any action that might impede the spread of democracy in the Western Hemisphere. On January 24, 1817, the Speaker of the House argued that, in contrast to 1793, the United States had a stake in the outcome of this conflict, that it would benefit from the overthrow of the Spanish Empire in the Americas, and that it should be guided by the dictates of national interest, not the obligations of international law.

Clay's battle against the Neutrality Acts of 1817 and 1818 ended in failure, as did his related struggles to speed recognition of Spain's rebellious colonies. But Clay's arguments reappeared with countless variations throughout the century. In 1836 popular sympathy for the Texan rebels led to a shockingly lax discharge of neutral duties, and President Jackson did nothing to remedy the defects of the existing law. A year later an uprising in both Canadas aroused similar emotions and created comparable problems. Moving with a determination that contrasted sharply with the dilatoriness of his predecessor, President Martin Van Buren issued proclamations on January 5 and November 21, 1838, exhorting all citizens to refrain from supporting the insurrection and warning them of punishment. He also managed to persuade Congress to pass a temporary statute on March 10, 1838, which contained preventive clauses for unneutral deeds on land as well as on sea. President Tyler published a similar proclamation on September 25, 1841, but his recommendation of July 10 to revive the act of 1838 fell on deaf legislative ears.

By 1849 the golden age of filibustering had dawned as American citizens launched armed expeditions from the United States to subvert, for good reasons and bad, governments in nearby regions. Spanish Cuba, independent Hawaii, strife-torn Nicaragua, and Mexico's remote peninsula of Lower California were the main targets. These raids challenged the integrity of both President and Congress. The response of the executive branch was moderately good. All the incumbents from 1849 to 1861 took action to check these infractions, and a few were effective. Zachary Taylor issued one proclamation with respect to Cuba on August 11, 1849, and his rigid enforcement measures incurred resentment in the expanionist-minded South. Millard Fillmore was an even stauncher supporter of neutral duties. On April 25, 1851, he enjoined all citizens from invading Cuba, and on October 22, 1851, he took similar action on Mexico. In his message of December 2, 1851, he reminded Congress of the inadequacies in the act of 1818. Franklin Pierce, a champion of territorial extension, felt obliged to proclaim neutrality on three occasions—for Mexico on January 18, 1854, for Cuba on May 31, 1854, and for Nicaragua on December 8, 1855. Some of Pierce's other actions, notably his hasty recognition of the regime in Nicaragua set up by William Walker, a notorious American filibuster, blunted the effect of these utterances. James Buchanan also dealt with Nicaragua. He issued one proclamation on October 30, 1858, and told Congress earlier that he was determined to execute the law. Like Fillmore, however, he left it to that body to decide in what ways the statutes might be strengthened.

The record of the legislative branch, on the other hand, was bad. Far from bolstering a toothless enforcement machinery, Congress seriously considered suspending or repealing the existing law. During the 1850's several concerted efforts, led by Southerners, were made in that direction. Senator John Slidell of Louisana sponsored such a move on May 1, 1854, when rumors had it that Spain was about to free the slaves in Cuba. Three Mississippians, all with an eye on the Walker expeditions, followed suit: Albert G. Brown in the Senate on March 3, 1855, John A. Quitman in the House on January 18, 1858, and William Barksdale in the House on February 16, 1860. Quitman, who had been indicted but not convicted for his part in an abortive invasion of Cuba, introduced his resolution during the excitement caused by the illegal arrest of Walker on Nicaraguan soil by Commodore Hiram Paulding of the United States Navy. Paulding's excessive zeal in apprehending the man who had made a mockery of the neutrality law led to his removal from command and his denunciation in some quarters as a traitor. There were, however, those who remembered that Walker, not Paulding, was the real culprit, and despite a flood of oratory, the Quitman resolution did not pass.

After the Civil War, Northern hotheads replaced Southern fire-eaters as the chief foes of neutral duties. At the very moment the American government was straining every nerve to bring England to book for the shabby performance of its neutral obligations during 1862 and 1863, Nathaniel P. Banks, Republican of Massachusetts and chairman of the House Committee on Foreign Affairs, urged a relaxation of the existing statute. Ostensibly, his motion was in retaliation for Canada's failure to prevent a handful of Confederate raiders from crossing the frontier and destroying Northern property. Actually, Banks hoped to facilitate the task of the Fenian Brotherhood, an organization dedicated to the emancipation of Ireland but not averse to hitting John Bull wherever he was vulnerable. On June 6, 1866, President

Andrew Johnson issued a proclamation admonishing American citizens not to join with "certain ill-disposed persons" who were about to invade Canada, and he followed this with steps to enforce the law. Nevertheless, the House unanimously agreed on July 28, 1866, to suspend certain provisions in the act of 1818. With more courage and disinterestedness than he is usually credited with, Charles Sumner, Republican of Massachusetts and chairman of the Senate Foreign Relations Committee, kept the Banks bill off the floor. The Fenian nuisance persisted, however, and on May 24, 1870, President Ulysses S. Grant had to reiterate Johnson's warning of four years earlier.

Simultaneously, American neutrality was threatened in another quarter. The ten-year insurrection that began in Cuba in 1868 aroused the sympathy of many persons in the United States and led to demands that the belligerent status of the rebels be recognized. Others were intent on giving assistance in men, arms, and money. Grant was confronted, as Presidents Grover Cleveland and William McKinley would be at a later date, with the difficult and uncongenial task of enforcing the neutrality law, and he was not entirely successful. The old Clay theme could be heard again—it was to America's interest to see Spain ejected from the New World. Grant did issue a proclamation on October 12, 1870, but his heart was not in it. If it had not been for Secretary of State Hamilton Fish, who wanted no additional complications while settling the *Alabama* claims with Great Britain, the performance would have been still poorer.

In 1889 the quest for neutrality by the United States remained as strong as it had been a century earlier. Seventy-five years of relative peace in Europe had caused most Americans to forget how difficult it was to enjoy unhampered their neutral rights in an all-out war. Few could foresee that the revolution in naval weapons and tactics then going on would further complicate the problems of maritime commerce for nonbelligerents in the future. Moreover, the Geneva Award of September 14, 1872, by which the United States received $15,500,-000 for the direct damage done by Confederate raiders built in England during the Civil War, together with the three rules of conduct incorporated in the Treaty of Washington of May 8, 1871, seemed to place the duties of a neutral in a clearer light than ever before. Actually, the conditions which had made neutrality a possible and desirable policy were already changing. Once the young republic became a world power, as it was to do within a decade, it would no longer be distant and aloof from the rest of mankind. Shifts in the global balance of power might endanger its vital interests, and its people might lose their indifference to the outcome of wars in Europe and Asia. Yet such was the appeal of neutrality that it continued to shape the foreign policy of the United States until the fifth decade of the twentieth century.

4

>>>->>>->>>->>><<<-<<<-<<<-<<<

The Growth of
the Monroe Doctrine

THE MONROE DOCTRINE was the third major concept underlying American foreign policy before 1889. Although this principle was not precisely defined until December, 1823, or fully accepted until the Civil War, it too reflected the colonial desire to be spared the turmoil and wars of Europe. Like isolationism and neutrality, its aim was to promote the safety and interests of the United States, but the method differed. Isolationism was a self-imposed ban upon permanent alliances and involvement in the diplomatic affairs of other continents; its realization depended solely on America's own efforts. Neutrality was also a voluntary curb on the activities of American citizens in war and peace, as well as a limitation on foreign belligerents; its enjoyment was contingent upon the tolerance of the large maritime nations and the strength of the young democratic government. The Monroe Doctrine sought to restrict in a specific geographic area the operations of the European monarchies; it could be upheld only insofar as the republic had the will and the power to do so. To drive Europe from the Western Hemisphere was, before 1889, an impossible task, but to confine and eventually nullify her influence was a legitimate and continuing goal. To limit, not eliminate, the activity of the Old World in the New was the cardinal objective of the Monroe Doctrine.

ANTECEDENTS

Those passages in the message of December 2, 1823, that contain
the Monroe Doctrine in its pristine form were a blend of past experience and current exigencies. From the colonial era came the theory of
the two spheres, a belief—a fervent hope—that the diplomatic concerns of the two hemispheres could be kept apart. This idea can be
traced to the Anglo-French Treaty of Whitehall in 1686, which provided
that a war between colonies in the New World would not automatically
lead to hostilities in the Old and, conversely, that a conflict in Europe
should not, in itself, precipitate fighting in the Americas. This concept
also paralleled isolationism; in his Farewell Address Washington
wrote that "Europe has a set of primary interests which to us have none
or a very remote relation." A quarter of a century later Secretary of
State John Quincy Adams restated the theory when he told his minister
in Russia on July 5, 1820, that "for the repose of Europe as well as of
America, the European and American political systems should as separate and distinct from each other as possible." In advising Monroe how
to handle Britain's proposal for an Anglo-American warning to the
Continental monarchies to let alone the rebellious Spanish colonies,
Jefferson declared on October 24, 1823: "America, North and South,
has a set of interests distinct from those of Europe, and peculiarly her
own."

A more immediate antecedent of the Monroe Doctrine was contemporary opposition to further European colonization in the New
World. Although this hostility was implicit in the expansionist dreams
of the young republic, it remained for John Quincy Adams to state it
explicitly. While discussing a disputed boundary with the British minister on January 26, 1821, he exclaimed: "Keep what is yours, but leave
the rest of the Continent to us." On July 17, 1823, he announced to the
Russian envoy "that the American continents are no longer subjects for
any new European colonial establishments." Five days later he instructed Richard Rush in London to emphasize the noncolonization
principle in his forthcoming negotiations with Great Britain and
Russia.

One way of reducing European influence in the Americas was to
prevent the staking out of new claims. Another, though more indirect,
was to bar the transfer of existing colonies from one nation to another.
Strategically situated territory might be less dangerous to the republic
if it belonged to a weak Spain rather than a powerful England. As early
as January 25, 1786, Jefferson observed that the Gulf coast, which
encompassed the mouths of many rivers that drained the interior,
could not be in better hands for the time being; but he feared lest it be
wrested from Spain before the United States was strong enough to do

the acquiring itself. This apprehension, voiced privately, was repeated with variations in official dispatches at the turn of the century, when it seemed likely that Louisiana and both the Floridas would become part of a new French empire in North America. The United States resolutely opposed such a transfer, and alarm over its prospect prompted Jefferson to talk in 1802 of marrying the British fleet the day Napoleon took over New Orleans.

In 1811 this no-transfer policy finally received the sanction of both the executive and legislative branches. Worried lest England seize the Floridas, President Madison secretly asked Congress on January 3 to declare in executive session that such a move would jeopardize the nation's security. Twelve days later he signed a joint resolution which affirmed that the United States could not "without serious inquietude" see any part of the Floridas pass to a foreign power and that, under certain conditions, it might have to control the territory temporarily. The conditions were two: a request for protection by local Spanish officials and a threat of prior occupation by a European monarchy. In short, the United States was not content simply to express opposition to the transfer of colonies; it might even use force to prevent that transfer.

Florida was not the only Spanish dependency whose cession to a European nation was objected to in Washington. Writing to his minister in Madrid on April 28, 1823, Adams conceded that "the transfer of Cuba to Great Britain would be an event unpropitious to the interests of this Union." That understatement, however, was not followed by an appeal to Congress to authorize, even provisionally, an anticipatory occupation of the Pearl of the Antilles. Nor did the no-transfer principle find its way into the President's message of December 2, 1823. It continued, nonetheless, to be applied to other sites—such as Puerto Rico on October 25, 1825—and by 1870 it had come to be regarded as an essential part of the Monroe Doctrine.

Such were some of the precedents upon which James Monroe and his advisers could draw when they were confronted by a potential crisis in the summer and autumn of 1823. To a vague threat that Russia and Great Britain were about to enlarge their North American holdings was added the fear that the Quadruple Alliance, or a segment thereof, was planning to reconquer the recently recognized Latin American republics. In April, acting under a mandate from the Congress of Verona, French troops crossed the Pyrenees to restore the monarchy in Spain, and rumors were rife that those energies would soon be turned to establishing Bourbon princes on thrones in the New World. To the apprehensive, Cuba seemed menaced by both England and France. To devout republicans, the apparent crushing of the Greek bid for independence was another blow to the cause of liberty. Should not the United States grasp Canning's bid of August 16, 1823, and with England stem this surging tide of reaction?

THE MESSAGE OF 1823

In dealing with the events of 1823, historians have questioned whether the threatened reconquest of the former Spanish colonies by a European concert was genuine, whether George Canning's overture for an Anglo-American warning to those powers was sincere, and whether Monroe was the actual author of the doctrine that bears his name. Today, the answers to those questions are less significant than an exact knowledge of what the message said, how it was interpreted in the United States, why it took the form it did, and whether the executive and legislature cooperated in shaping this cardinal principle of foreign policy.

The last point can be disposed of easily. The Monroe Doctrine was a presidential statement, drafted after a long debate in the cabinet and with the advice of the retired Jefferson and Madison. There was no consultation, formal or informal, with Congress; that body was not requested to take any steps to implement the declaration. The cabinet debate determined the form the pronouncement took. Joint action with England was ruled out—partly because its sincerity was suspect; partly because Canning lost interest after obtaining pledges from Count Polignac, the French ambassador; but mainly because, as Adams put it on November 7, "it would be more candid, as well as more dignified, to avow our principles explicitly to Russia and France, than to come in as a cock-boat in the wake of the British man-of-war." The President, however, overruled the Secretary's plan to confine this affirmation to a diplomatic note, which might not be published for months or years. It was Monroe who was responsible for including it in his state of the Union message of December 2, 1823, for all the world to read.

At the very outset the President turned to foreign affairs. After alluding to impending negotiations with Russia and England over rival claims to the Pacific Northwest, he reiterated the noncolonization principle adumbrated by Adams in the preceding months. "The American continents," Monroe said, "by the free and independent condition which they have assumed and maintain, are henceforth not to be considered as subjects for future colonization by any European powers." Then, some forty paragraphs later, he expressed a fervent hope that Greece might again be free. This wish, however, did not mean the United States would quit its own to challenge the Quadruple Alliance on foreign ground, for Monroe went on to assert:

In the wars of the European powers in matters relating to themselves we have never taken any part, nor does it comport with our policy to do so. It is only when our rights are invaded or seriously menaced that we resent injuries or make preparations for our defense. With the movements in this hemisphere we are of necessity more immediately connected. . . . The political system of the allied powers is essentially different . . . from that of America. . . . We owe it, therefore, to candor and to the amicable relations existing between the United States and those powers to declare that we should consider any attempt on their part to extend their system to any portion of this hemisphere as dangerous to our peace and safety. With the existing colonies or dependencies of any European power we have not interfered and will not interfere. But with the Governments who have declared their independence and maintained it, and whose independence we have . . . acknowledged, we could not view any interposition for the purpose of oppressing them, or controlling in any other manner their destiny, by any European power in any other light than as the manifestation of an unfriendly disposition toward the United States.

As stated in 1823, the Monroe Doctrine left untouched existing European dependencies in the New World but forbade future colonization. The transfer of monarchical institutions across the Atlantic was said to be dangerous to the safety of the United States, while any European interference in the domestic concerns of the Latin republics was branded as an unfriendly act. So long as Spain alone attempted reconquest, the United States would remain neutral; but that attitude might change if Madrid secured assistance from others. Finally, this country would abstain from participating in any war outside of the Western Hemisphere until its interests were directly affected or its rights menaced.

There were certain topics on which the Doctrine, as originally set forth, was silent. It did not define European interposition or interference in the New World. It said nothing about the adjustment of boundary disputes, the forcible collection of debts, the transfer of colonies from one European state to another, or the voluntary cession of territory by an American republic to a European monarchy. Monroe did not indicate that the United States might be more concerned with developments in the Caribbean than in Patagonia; in no place did he pledge the nation to use force to uphold the principles he enunciated. Nor did he give an unqualified promise never to take part in Europe's wars.

Almost at once men at home and abroad asked what Monroe meant and what he would do if the potential peril from the allied autocracies became actual. Since Congress alone could authorize military and naval measures, the views of the legislature were most significant. The failure of the President to seek them in advance and to make any recommendation for strengthening the armed forces suggests that he did not anticipate having to back up his words with deeds. Although most lawmakers appeared to endorse the warning to Europe, they were not eager to record that opinion officially. In fact, if it had not been for a pro-Hellenic bloc which resented Monroe's seeming indifference to the Greek cause and which sponsored demands to send an agent to Athens, Congress might never have discussed the Monroe Doctrine in the winter of 1823. But with the Hellenists forcing his hand, on January 20, 1824, Clay introduced a joint resolution avowing that the American people "would not see, without serious inquietude, any forcible interposition by the Allied Powers of Europe in behalf of Spain to reduce to their former subjection those parts of the continent" which had won their independence. The only real opposition in the House came from John Randolph of Virginia, a chronic dissenter and a bitter foe of Clay. Either because of the link to the Greek question or because it was learned that French intervention in the Western Hemisphere was unlikely, Clay's resolution was never brought to a vote in the House or even discussed in the Senate. Legislative inaction, however, did not signify disagreement. During the Panama debate two years later several speakers strongly supported Monroe's position.

How did the Monroe administration and its successor, headed by Adams and Clay, interpret the Doctrine? Was it a maxim to be applied universally, or was it to be restricted to specific situations? Since the posture of the United States on the world scene hardly justified needless invocations, caution was the order of the day. Thus, by recognizing Brazil's independence on May 26, 1824, the government at Washington revealed that it would tolerate monarchies in the Americas if they represented the wishes of the people. To Colombia on August 6, 1824, Secretary Adams disclosed that he did not object to the employment of Spanish troops in the New World while France controlled the Iberian homeland. That same note evaded Colombia's bid for a defensive alliance against European interlopers and said that Congress must decide, after England had been consulted, how the United States would resist armed intervention from abroad. On December 7, 1824, Monroe told the legislature that the Latin American countries were free to adopt any institutions they desired. On April 13, 1825, Secretary of State Clay assured Brazil that its request for an alliance against Portugal was premature and that the United States would remain neutral in wars between a former colony and the mother country. Lastly, on November 9, 1825, Clay ignored Mexico's plea for aid against an alleged French menace. In short, during the supposed crisis of 1823 President Monroe did not seek the cooperation, military or diplomatic, of the other American republics; in the calmer days of 1825 President Adams evinced no desire for a hemispheric system of reciprocal assistance.

THE POLK REVIVAL

Where the policy of isolationism limited the diplomatic activity of the United States, the Monroe Doctrine sought to reduce European influence in the New World. Since it is always easier for a nation to control itself than to restrict others, the tenets of the Farewell Address were more faithfully observed in the years after their promulgation than the words of James Monroe. At no time before 1889 did the transatlantic powers regard the message of 1823 as binding upon them. It could be viewed, as a British foreign secretary wrote on May 2, 1854, "only as the dictum of the distinguished person who announced it, and not as an international axiom which ought to regulate the conduct of European states." Indeed, for more than two decades after its birth the Monroe Doctrine was virtually forgotten, even by the United States.

One reason for this neglect is that in 1823 Monroe's message had done little to protect the Western Hemisphere. Whatever plans of reconquest the reactionary allies may have envisaged, they were effectively checkmated on October 9, 1823, when France assured England that it would not use armed force against Spain's rebellious colonies. This Polignac Memorandum, not the Monroe Doctrine, proved to be the shield—if one was needed—for the Latin republics; and Canning, never overly modest about his own accomplishments, was quick to impress upon their leaders this debt to Great Britain. Somewhat inaccurately he boasted, "I called the New World into existence to redress the balance of the Old." But there was enough truth in that exaggeration to persuade the new nations to look for guidance and support to London, not to Washington.

From 1826 to 1845 the Monroe Doctrine was not only virtually forgotten; it was also frequently violated. The noncolonization feature was the chief victim, and England was the main culprit. In one way or another Britain extended its sovereignty over the Falkland Islands in 1833, over Roatán in the Gulf of Honduras in 1838, and over San Juan del Norte in Nicaragua in 1841. England pushed the frontier of Belize steadily southward between 1833 and 1836, at the expense of the Central American Federation. But these transgressions were in remote regions, not vital to the security of the United States, and thus passed unchallenged even by President Jackson. The noninterference aspect of the Doctrine was not so badly breached. In 1838 France did institute a naval blockade of both Mexico and Argentina. In the first case, Mexican citizens were fired upon; in the second, French forces occupied an island in the River Plate and French officers meddled in Argentina's domestic affairs. But these reprisals, like others undertaken by England, were designed to secure unpaid claims, not subvert existing regimes. They did elicit from Congress a request for information, but that body did not yet consider that collecting debts by force fell under Monroe's interdict.

When European activity occurred closer to home, the United States manifested more concern. By the early 1840's the expansionist impulse to annex Texas and California and to settle the Oregon dispute was growing rapidly, yet in each of those areas England or France or both seemed to be trying to thwart American ambitions. In Oregon, open on terms of equality to citizens of both nations under the treaty of 1827, the Hudson's Bay Company was attempting to divert the influx of pioneers. In Texas, Anglo-French representatives were striving to patch up a peace between that republic and Mexico; and they were prepared to guarantee Texan independence by a diplomatic act, in which the United States could join or not as it saw fit. In California, loosely governed from Mexico City, there was talk of a European protectorate and even of outright cession. These schemes, which never got far beyond the blueprint stage, were based on the assumption, blatantly expressed in June, 1845, by Prime Minister François Guizot, that Europe must maintain a balance of power in North America to curb the westward march of the young republic. Although this idea of a balance of power did negate the theory of the two spheres, there was nothing in the original Doctrine to prohibit independent Mexico from ceding California to France. Nor could the Doctrine be invoked to require the Oregon boundary to be drawn at a particular place.

Nevertheless, if an appeal to Monroe's memory bolstered his diplomacy as trouble loomed over Texas, Oregon, and California, Polk was not one to hold back. With virtually no foreshadowing, with very little discussion in the cabinet, and with only an occasional talk with a congressional leader, the President revived and reoriented the principles which had lain dormant for two decades. In his message of December 2, 1845, he began, as Monroe had begun twenty-two years before, with foreign affairs. He branded Anglo-French action in Texas as "interference" and prophesied that similar "intrigues" elsewhere would also fail. He did not, however, speak directly of California. After a long review of the Mexican and Oregon problems, Polk turned to the balance-of-power theory and denied that it could apply to the Western Hemisphere. Europe must keep its hands off the New World, just as the United States abstained from involvement in the Old. The American people would resist any attempt by foreign powers, in the name of the balance of power, to restrict their expansion. As to the noncolonization principle, he said:

> The present is deemed a proper occasion to reiterate and reaffirm the principle avowed by Mr. Monroe and to state my cordial concurrence. . . . The reassertion of this principle, especially in reference to North America, is at this day but the promulgation of a policy which no European power should cherish any disposition to resist. Existing rights of every European nation should be respected, but it is due alike to our safety and our interests . . . that it should be distinctly announced to the world as our settled policy that no future European colony or dominion shall with our consent be planted or established on any part of the North American continent.

Polk's revival seemed both to narrow and to enlarge the original Doctrine. By repeated references to North America, as distinct from the Western Hemisphere, the President suggested that the principles of 1823 might apply with greater force to nearby areas than to distant regions. On the other hand, by indicting Anglo-French negotiations with Texas, he appeared to place diplomatic interposition under the same ban as armed intervention. Some historians argue that the words "planted or established" barred the transfer of existing colonies as well as the creation of new ones.

In 1846, as in 1824, the legislature debated this executive pronouncement without conferring explicit approval. On January 26 a bellicose endorsement by Senator William Allen, Democrat of Ohio, was referred to the Foreign Relations Committee, of which he was chairman. No report was ever made, but the mere introduction of the resolution provoked a brief exchange. John C. Calhoun, Democrat of South Carolina, who had been in Monroe's cabinet in 1823, deplored indiscriminate appeals to the Doctrine and warned that abstract declarations of policy did more harm than good. Lewis Cass, Democrat of Michigan and later Secretary of State under James Buchanan, disagreed and cited the fact of British aggression. John M. Clayton, Whig of Delaware, another future head of the State Department, contended that both President Polk and Secretary Buchanan had reversed the stand they had taken in the Panama debate of 1825–6.

Two years later Polk had another opportunity to define the Monroe Doctrine. An unusual situation in Yucatan raised the question of whether a free people in the New World could voluntarily transfer its land to a European state.[1] After consulting many congressional leaders, the President declared in a message of April 29, 1848, that the United States sympathized with Yucatan but did not seek to annex it. "Yet, according to our established policy," he continued, "we could not consent to a transfer of this 'dominion and sovereignty' either to Spain, Great Britain, or any other European power." Quoting Monroe's words of 1823 and his own of 1845, Polk concluded that because of Yucatan's proximity to the United States, it would in foreign hands be "dangerous to our peace and security." Yet eager as he was, for humanitarian and strategic reasons, to aid the Yucatecos, Polk saw no easy solution and therefore asked Congress for advice and, if necessary, authority to take positive action. To his disgust, that body debated rather than decided. On May 4, the Senate Foreign Relations Committee reported a bill for the temporary occupation of the peninsula, but it encountered indifference and opposition. Calhoun again rose to deprecate the tendency to read into the message of 1823 more than Monroe had intended. He denied the Doctrine had become an "established policy" or that it could be applied to the present case. Polk's supporters were few and none too enthusiastic. With the danger from England and Spain not materializing and the Democratic national convention diverting legislative minds to more immediate problems, the Yucatan episode faded into history, though not until some Americans had been reminded once more of Monroe's message of 1823.

Until the Civil War the Monroe Doctrine received no additional gloss, but it was kept in the public eye by the controversy with Great Britain over the Clayton-Bulwer Treaty of April 19, 1850. By that pact, the two nations agreed to share equally in the construction and operation of any future isthmian canal and, also, not to "occupy, or fortify, or colonize . . . or exercise any dominion over Nicaragua, Costa Rica, the Mosquito Coast, or any part of Central America." Unfortunately, the negotiators failed to make clear whether this prohibition applied only to new colonies or whether it required England to relinquish those recently annexed. Moreover, since the treaty, no matter how interpreted, tied the hands of American expansionists in a region of growing importance, it ran into severe criticism on other grounds. These strictures could hardly be justified by the Monroe Doctrine, for that document was intended to curtail European activity in the New World, not rationalize America's. But when Britain insisted that it was not obligated by the agreement to give up territory added since 1823, a

---

[1] A province of Mexico, Yucatan remained aloof from the war that began in 1846. Early in 1848 an aboriginal uprising threatened to exterminate the white ruling class. The latter appealed for aid to the United States, England, and Spain, offering, if necessary, to transfer their "dominion and sovereignty" to whomever succored them.

cry could be raised—and was—that the treaty of 1850 tacitly recognized violations of the noncolonization dictum. What the critics conveniently ignored was that this same treaty, by forbidding further enlargement of territory by England in Central America, actually gave substance and support to the Monroe Doctrine.

Thus the 1850's saw added publicity given to the message of 1823. During a debate in January, 1853, Monroe's pronouncement was for the first time consistently referred to in Congress and in the press as a "doctrine." Theretofore such words as "principle" and "declaration" had been employed. On January 6, 1854, the Doctrine was appealed to for the first time in a diplomatic note to another country. In June, 1856, the Democratic platform began the now familiar practice of lauding the Doctrine. Yet this evidence should not obscure the fact that prior to 1861 the Monroe Doctrine was still not accepted by all citizens as a sound and incontrovertible policy, to be invoked whenever their interests in the Western Hemisphere seemed menaced. It had never been formally endorsed by Congress. To many it looked like the property of expansionist-minded Democrats, and those of cautious temperament preferred not to act in its name until the need was clearly apparent and unless the people were prepared to back words with deeds.

CHALLENGE AND RESPONSE

What transformed the Monroe Doctrine from a diplomatic principle of limited utility with distinct partisan overtones into a dogma of universal application, concurred in by all Americans irrespective of political ties, was the challenge it encountered between 1861 and 1867. Before that period it had been challenged and even violated, but rarely in areas so vital to the national security and never with so flagrant a disregard of public opinion. Earlier infringements—such as the seizure of the distant Falklands, the extension of the Belize frontier through the Central American jungle, the occupation of tiny Roatán in the Gulf of Honduras—and previous threats in Texas and California pale into insignificance before the reannexation of the Dominican Republic by Spain in 1861 and the re-establishment of a monarchy in Mexico by France in 1864.

For present purposes, the details of those challenges are less important than the reaction they aroused in the United States. At the diplomatic level the response had to be restrained. Not until April, 1865, when the Union was restored and its huge armed forces were free to be turned against foreign interlopers, could Seward back words with deeds. By then the restoration of Spanish rule in Haiti had collapsed; by then trouble in Europe and resistance in Mexico prompted Napoleon III to think of liquidating the ill-starred venture; by then, after early mistakes, Seward was moving with consummate skill. Never invoking the words of the fifth President but always speaking his language, the Secretary made it clear that sooner or later the twin principles of noncolonization and noninterference in the New World would be vindicated, by might if need be. At the popular level there was less restraint. Inveighing against France or Spain and cheering for the Monroe Doctrine were useful ways of releasing frustrated emotions during the dreary months before the tide turned in favor of the North. Beginning in 1862, giant rallies pledged allegiance to the principles of 1823. Famous men of the day spoke out in their behalf; writings more hortatory than historical poured from the press. Even an organization named the Defenders of the Monroe Doctrine was formed.

Public agitation precipitated congressional action. Against the known wishes of Lincoln and Seward, resolutions were introduced condemning France and requesting the administration to compel withdrawal from Mexico. Thanks to Sumner, all such moves in the Senate were buried in the Foreign Relations Committee, but by 1864 delay was no longer possible in the House. Without a dissenting vote that chamber on April 4 resolved that "it does not accord with the policy of the United States to acknowledge any monarchical government erected on the ruins of any republican government in America under the auspices of any European Power." Although it mentioned no names, the House had in mind French interference in Mexico's internal strife and the transfer of monarchical institutions from the Old World to the New. At the cost of an unpleasant controversy with the chairman of the Foreign Affairs Committee involving recognition rather than the Monroe Doctrine, the executive managed to retain control of Mexican affairs and by steady but dignified pressure contributed to the evacuation of Napoleon's troops in 1867.

From 1867 to 1889 the Monroe Doctrine continued to grow quietly. Two trends may be noted. One was the final consolidation of the no-transfer principle with the Doctrine itself. This was effected in President Ulysses Grant's message to Congress on May 31, 1870, and in Secretary Hamilton Fish's memorandum to the Senate on July 14, 1870, although as late as August, 1877, there was no protest from Washington when the government of Norway and Sweden sold the Caribbean island of St. Bartholomew to France. The second was a contention that the construction of an interoceanic canal in the Western Hemisphere by a European state violated the Monroe Doctrine. On June 25, 1879, Ambrose E. Burnside, Republican of Rhode Island and better remembered for his military than his senatorial career, offered a resolution terming a foreign-built canal dangerous to the nation's peace and safety; and he rested his case on the message of 1823. On May 8, 1882, Secretary of State Frederick T. Frelinghuysen invoked the Doctrine in an attempt to persuade Great Britain to abrogate the Clayton-Bulwer Treaty. Although the Burnside resolution failed to pass and the English refused to heed Frelinghuysen's plea, these new pretensions foreshadowed a further growth that occurred at the turn of the century

By the time the French withdrew from Mexico, the Monroe Doctrine had come of age. Promulgated but qualified in the 1820's, forgotten and violated in the 1830's, revived but disputed in the 1840's, publicized but monopolized by one party in the 1850's, it had emerged from the ordeal of the 1860's strengthened and acclaimed, enshrined as never before in the hearts of the American people. With new pretensions advanced in its name after 1867, no responsible statesmen on either side of the Atlantic dared—though a few might try—to ignore the powerful prejudice in the United States against any type of intervention by the Old World in the affairs of the New.

Ideals and Self-Interest

SUPPLEMENTING the basic concepts of isolationism, neutrality, and the Monroe Doctrine as guidelines in American foreign policy before 1889 was a group of lesser principles, no one of which merits detailed analysis but all of which taken together shed light on the diplomacy of the young republic. Nonintervention in the domestic affairs of other countries, prompt recognition of established governments, a respect for treaty obligations, the peaceful settlement of international disputes, and a reluctance to wage war indicate, too, some of the ideals which the United States tried to live up to in dealing with other nations. Yet from the outset these ideals clashed with self-interest, and America's leaders learned very early that they must try to avoid the intoxication of moral abstractions on the one hand and the cynicism of unscrupulous practices on the other. How far they succeeded in promoting the national interest without tarnishing a standard of conduct they held dear may be seen as these minor principles are examined.

NONINTERVENTION AND RECOGNITION

Nonintervention was a standard of conduct deeply cherished by the American people. The idea that one state should keep its hands off another and not subvert the regime in power was perfectly in line with the people's own needs and fully consonant with its policies of isolationism, neutrality, and the Monroe Doctrine.

Yet intervention is difficult to define. It can take many forms, some of which are permissible under international law. Thus, one country may send troops into another so as to protect its citizens and their property from disorder. A consistent refusal to pay debts was long considered a just cause for armed reprisals. Efforts to promote peace may be regarded as intervention by that belligerent which is winning at the moment. Sometimes a failure to act is called intervention; a lax discharge of neutral duties or a delay in recognizing a government which, according to precedents, is entitled to recognition are cases in point.

Despite its devotion to the principle of nonintervention, the United States before 1889 occasionally departed from it. Overly zealous military men and apprehensive consular officials were mostly to blame. To Spain, Brigadier General Jackson's punitive expedition into the Floridas in April, 1818, appeared provocative. The Mexicans could not view with amusement the comic-opera capture of Monterey in October, 1842, by Commodore Thomas ap Catesby Jones, who mistakenly thought war had broken out, or the inflammatory acts of Captain Frémont in the spring of 1846. Commodore Paulding's arrest of William Walker near San Juan del Norte in December, 1857, violated Nicaraguan sovereignty. Several diplomatic agents, desiring to thwart real or imaginary Anglo-French designs, were guilty of meddling in the affairs of Central America, the Dominican Republic, and the Hawaiian Kingdom. But in none of these cases was there specific authorization from Washington, and only the first helped the United States gain an important objective of foreign policy.

Much more censurable was direct governmental interference. The Madison administration was clearly implicated in the machinations of George Mathews and others in East Florida in March, 1812, and the nation gained nothing at all. Another flagrant departure from nonintervention occurred in Mexico between 1853 and 1861. Faced with chaos below the Rio Grande, Presidents Pierce and Buchanan were willing to buy territory from whatever faction could and would sell, even if the gold enabled a dictator to retain power. More than that, they baldly sought the right to intervene. The first of the McLane-Ocampo projects of December 14, 1859, granted the United States—in exchange for $4,000,000, half of which was to go to American creditors—three rights of transit across Mexico, with special privileges affecting mail, troops, and supplies. In cases of exceptional danger, American armed forces could be used for protection without prior permission from Mexico. The second project gave the United States virtually a free hand to intervene whenever its treaty rights were violated or Mexico found itself unable to cope with threats to lives and property. Fortunately for the good name of the former and the unimpaired sovereignty of the latter, the Senate on May 31, 1860, defeated the first agreement by a margin of 27 to 18 and then refused to vote on the

second. It would be difficult to show that the national interest suffered
thereby.

A desire to alleviate hardship and misery has also threatened the
policy of nonintervention. The ten-year rebellion that devastated Cuba
from 1868 to 1878 provides the best example, although in that case
selfish motives were mingled with humanitarianism. Enthusiasm for
the cause of liberty in the New World and a traditional dislike of Spain
made some citizens wish to intervene, but there were practical reasons
as well. The destruction of American property and the peril to American investments, while less serious than after 1895, produced the
same demand for action to which McKinley reluctantly yielded in
April, 1898. The government faced the same burdensome task of patrolling coastal waters and the same unpopular duty of stopping armed
expeditions. With unspeakable atrocities occurring on the island and
with neither side seemingly able to win, intervention in the name
of peace and humanity might have been a blessing for all concerned,
but the Grant administration held back. It did suggest in July, 1869, a
settlement which embraced Cuban independence, emancipation for
the slaves, and an indemnity to Spain guaranteed by the United States;
but this was not made an ultimatum. It did wait six years before, on
November 5, 1875, sounding out England and others regarding joint
mediation; but it declined to go ahead alone when the replies turned
out to be discouraging. Hence, when the fighting finally ceased on
February 10, 1878, nonintervention had survived its most grueling
test, and no one could say that abstention had hurt the national interest.

Prompt recognition of established governments was another ideal
which normally promoted the welfare of the United States. Given their
own revolutionary experience, the founding fathers believed in the
right of self-determination. As Secretary of State Jefferson wrote on
November 7, 1792: "It accords with our principles to acknowledge any
Government to be rightful which is formed by the will of the people
substantially declared." Nor did it make any difference what form that
government took. "We surely cannot deny," he said on March 12, 1793,
"to any nation the right whereon our own Government is founded—
that every one may govern itself according to whatever form it pleases,
and change those forms at its own will." Thus the United States quickly
indicated that the facts of the situation, not sympathy or hostility,
would decide the question of diplomatic intercourse. If a government
had popular support, then it made no difference whether it was a democracy, monarchy, or oligarchy, for recognition did not confer or imply moral approval. Yet it was not easy to put this criterion into practice. How did one determine "the will of the people substantially declared"? What should a new regime do to demonstrate its stability, a

sense of responsibility, and a willingness to discharge its international obligations?

During its formative years the young republic was tempted to extend recognition promptly rather than to deliberate unduly. Belief in the right of self-determination, eagerness to see democracy replace monarchy, and memories of its own struggle for acceptance motivated American thinking. Yet the record to 1889 shows relatively few instances of premature recognition. Caution characterized the Monroe administration's handling of Spain's rebellious colonies from 1817 to 1822, while President Jackson moved warily before recognizing Texan independence on March 3, 1837. In both cases the United States stood to benefit from the emergence of new nations; in both, however, the executive wished to avoid trouble with the mother country. After the triumph over Mexico, the government in Washington and its representatives abroad manifested less discretion. On February 28, 1848, Minister Richard Rush acted without authority in being the first to recognize the Second French Republic. On June 18, 1849, Secretary John Middleton Clayton sent A. Dudley Mann to Central Europe to report on the Hungarian uprising with instructions that stopped just short of empowering him to recognize a nonexistent state. President Franklin Pierce extended a premature recognition to a shaky Walker-supported regime in Nicaragua on May 14, 1856, in order to advance his own political ambitions and to retard England's diplomatic aspirations. On April 7, 1859, President Buchanan accepted the Juarez faction as the legitimate rulers of Mexico in a move calculated to gain territorial concessions and transit privileges from a grateful recipient. A congressional demand in April, 1869, for according a belligerent status to the Cuban rebels had freedom of the island as its ultimate goal, but the Grant administration managed to persuade the House that such recognition was not then in the national interest.

RESPECT FOR TREATY OBLIGATIONS

Just as democratic America regarded nonintervention and a prompt recognition of stable governments as the proper standard of conduct among nations, so did it believe that treaty obligations should be respected. The cynical eighteenth-century attitude never took root in the young republic, not because of the superior virtue of its citizens, but because they understood that it was to the interest of the weak to scrupulously observe written agreements. Similarly, its realistic leaders did not seek pledges that other countries might be tempted to break at the first convenient opportunity. Yet they did not condone breaches of contracts. When Algiers failed to live up to its commitments of 1795, the United States dispatched a naval squadron to teach the

Mediterranean corsairs a lesson in international honesty. When Spain was unwilling or unable to abide by the promises made at San Lorenzo in 1795, the American government sought redress through negotiation. On December 1, 1834, President Jackson asked Congress for provisional authority to sequester the property of French citizens in the United States in retaliation for the procrastination of the Chamber of Deputies in honoring the obligations assumed in a treaty of July 4, 1831. By May, 1846, Polk's cabinet was ready to go to war because Mexico had, among other things, defaulted on debts it had twice agreed in formal treaties to pay.

Turning to the reverse of the coin, there were few cases before 1889 in which the United States failed to abide by its treaty obligations. In negotiating with England the provisional peace of November 30, 1782, the American envoys may have violated their instructions from home, but they did not transgress the letter of the French alliance. Nor was Washington guilty of deserting a beleaguered ally when he proclaimed neutrality on April 22, 1793. The Anglo-American treaty of November 19, 1794, was interpreted in Paris as a flagrant violation of the commercial pact of 1778, but Jay was both realistic and correct in recognizing that he could not compel the British to adhere to the Plan of 1776. The unilateral abrogation of the first alliance by Congress on July 7, 1798, was improper, but legal niceties were set aright by the treaty of September 30, 1800. Careless drafting of the peace with Mexico on February 2, 1848, made some breach of the obligations it contained unavoidable, but the subsequent Gadsden Treaty of December 30, 1853, remedied the situation.

The most serious threats to past pledges grew out of the unpopular Clayton-Bulwer Treaty of 1850 and the delicate problem of Chinese immigration. The former, negotiated when the United States was too weak to build an interoceanic canal alone, had become obsolete by 1880; and from that time until November, 1901, several administrations tried vainly to terminate it by mutual consent. These diplomatic efforts were stimulated by the possibility of another unilateral abrogation by the legislature. The trouble over the admission of coolie laborers also stemmed from an outdated treaty. By the Seward-Burlingame accord of July 28, 1868, signed when Oriental workers were welcome in California, the United States assured to China the most-favored nation treatment with respect to travel and residence. Bloody riots on the Pacific coast in the next decade led Congress to virtually annul the pact, but President Rutherford B. Hayes protected the nation's honor by his veto of March 1, 1880. A new treaty of November 17, 1880, permitted the United States to limit and suspend but not exclude immigrant labor; yet in implementing that agreement, Congress frequently violated its spirit and perhaps its letter. On April 4,

1882, President Chester A. Arthur vetoed a twenty-year ban as an unreasonable interpretation of its terms and "a breach of our national faith"; but both he and Cleveland reluctantly approved in 1884 and 1888—two election years—statutes one of which the Supreme Court later ruled contravened existing treaties. Despite these infractions, where domestic needs took precedence over foreign commitments, one of the most important legacies of this early period was a respect for treaty obligations and, perhaps, even an undue faith in the pledged word of nations.

PEACEFUL SETTLEMENT OF DISPUTES

If Americans believed they were a divinely chosen people, manifestly destined to spread the blessings of free institutions across the continent, they were also convinced of their unique dedication to the pacific settlement of international disputes. Peace, friendship, and a hands-off policy, they liked to assert, was the way of life in the New World; whereas war, intervention, and broken promises characterized the Old. How valid were these boasts? What procedures were utilized in order to avoid a resort to force?

Prior to 1889 four devices were commonly employed to settle controversies amicably. The most frequent was direct negotiation. But when diplomatic relations had been suspended or a rupture was imminent, a third party could be useful in promoting communication between the disputants. This attempt to bring together the nations at odds is called good offices; it does not embrace any proposition to resolve the quarrel. A third method is mediation. A mediator suggests to the disputants a specific plan for composing their differences, although neither side is obliged to accept it. The fourth and most far-reaching method is arbitration. Arbitration involves the voluntary submission of a dispute to an impartial body for a final decision which both parties agree in advance to obey. That body can be chosen in various ways, and it may consist of a single individual, a specially selected commission, or a permanent tribunal. What distinguishes arbitration from direct negotiation, good offices, and mediation is the binding character of the verdict. Except where the arbitrators exceed their authority or become deadlocked, a solution is always forthcoming.

Historically, arbitration has proved to be most useful in determining conflicting interpretations of treaties or the validity and amount of claims held by one state or its citizens against another. It has been least successful when it attempted to deal with some point of vital interest or national honor. Thus, up to 1889 the United States concluded twenty claims conventions with eight republics of the New World and four Continental monarchies of Europe. Its record with Great Britain was even more impressive. The two countries reintroduced arbitration into modern diplomacy when the Jay Treaty of November 19, 1794, referred to separate commissions such questions as the identity of a river described in an earlier treaty, the amount of compensation due British creditors for pre-Revolutionary debts they had been unable to collect, and the validity of claims raised by English shippers for losses incurred because of a lax discharge of neutral duties by the United States. Twenty years later the Treaty of Ghent created four arbitral boards to handle boundary differences. In 1818 the Tsar of Russia was asked to clarify a clause in that treaty; in 1827 the disputed frontier between Maine and New Brunswick was submitted to the King of the Netherlands for settlement. In 1853 and 1863 the two countries signed conventions to dispose of outstanding claims. The most spectacular accomplishment came in the Treaty of Washington of May 8, 1871, which sent four controversies to arbitration: the damages due the United States for the depradations of the *Alabama* and her sisters, the claims of Englishmen for loss of property in the United States, the ownership of several small islands near Vancouver which had remained unclear since the Oregon partition of 1846, and the amount to be paid by the American government for the right of its citizens to fish in certain territorial waters of Newfoundland and Canada.

Not all of the arbitral commissions thus established were able to reach an agreement, and the findings of some were unpopular. Thus, the United States was so infuriated by the Halifax Award of November 23, 1877, which set a price of $5,500,000 on the inshore fishing privileges, that it paid the bill with reluctance and terminated the agreement at the first moment it was legally entitled to do so. Yet in no case did the nation fail to abide by the decision of the arbitrators, and in no case did the national interest suffer by upholding the ideal of arbitration. A knotty problem arose on January 10, 1831, when the King of the Netherlands departed from his prescribed powers and handed down a diplomatic recommendation rather than an arbitral verdict. Although both England and Jackson thought this solution of the Northeastern boundary an equitable one, the President questioned his authority to accept it and turned to the Senate for advice. On June 16, 1832, that body defeated by a vote of 35 to 8 a favorable report of the Foreign Relations Committee and a week later, by a margin of 23 to 22, it counseled the executive to renew negotiations with the British. In thus rejecting the irregular Dutch proposition, the United States may have been unwise; for a final settlement of the boundary did not come until August 9, 1842. Yet it had a perfectly legal right to do what it did.

In one dangerous quarrel the United States purposely avoided arbitration. Between January 21, 1845, and February 4, 1846, Presidents

Tyler and Polk rejected three British offers to settle the Oregon boundary dispute by that method. The former based his refusal on the ground that arbitration would retard rather than expedite a solution. Polk used two arguments. One was that the terms proposed by England were a virtual invitation to the arbitrator to reach a diplomatic compromise rather than a judicial decision. The second was that the national interest of the United States could not permit entrusting so important a matter to an outside party. In these three contentions—delay, vital interest, and the tendency of arbitrators to ignore valid claims and split the difference—are found limitations of the arbitral process. Sometimes, of course, such pleas were simply a pretext for avoiding a peaceful settlement; but since the Oregon crisis was resolved by direct negotiation within four months of Polk's second refusal, the United States should not be censured for turning down the British suggestions of 1845–6.

Up to 1889 there occurred only four significant occasions on which American diplomats had to decide whether to compose their difficulties through the good offices or mediation of a third party. Twice they chose to do so; twice they did not. On March 11, 1813, President Madison accepted with alacrity a Russian offer to mediate in the War of 1812. In fact, he did not even wait to hear whether England would follow suit—something it did not do. On January 27, 1836, the British chargé in Washington expressed his country's willingness to mediate the controversy involving France's tardiness in making payments under the treaty of 1831. Although the disputants agreed with varying qualifications to utilize those services, the imbroglio was liquidated before they could be exploited. On the other hand, Polk rejected British mediation during the Mexican War. After ignoring several hints, he informed England on September 11, 1846, that its offer would not be needed because direct negotiations looking to a peace had already begun. Similarly, the North would not consider European offers to help stop the Civil War. As early as June 19, 1861, Seward instructed Charles Francis Adams in London to inform the Foreign Office that "we cannot solicit or accept mediation from any, even the most friendly quarter." From that resolute stand he never deviated.

A concern for peaceful settlements did not lead the United States before 1889 to offer freely its own good offices and mediation. Only after the Civil War, when it began to think about closer hemispheric ties, did the government try to act as peacemaker. The record was not very impressive. The outstanding success occurred between 1866 and 1871, when Secretaries Seward and Fish helped arrange for a conference in Washington beginning on October 29, 1869, which eventually effected an armistice between Spain on the one hand and Chile, Peru, Ecuador, and Bolivia on the other. The most notable failure took place from 1879 to 1884 when three successive secretaries of state were unable to end the War of the Pacific. Certainly, if peace in the world, or even in the Americas, had been more vital to the interests of the United States, the attempts to compose differences between nations would have been more numerous.

THE WAR RECORD

On five occasions before 1889 the United States resorted to armed force rather than settle a dispute by peaceful means. There has been little disposition to condemn the two undeclared wars with the Barbary pirates from 1801 to 1805 and in 1815 or the quasi-war with France from 1798 to 1800. All three seemed called for by every dictate of honor and self-respect; none jeopardized needlessly the nation's security. But both Madison and Polk have been accused of yielding to popular passion or territorial cupidity and of failing to exhaust all possibilities of a peaceful settlement with England in 1812 and with Mexico in 1846. Each has been charged with double-dealing and aggressive designs. Both are said to have betrayed America's ideals when neither the realities of the situation nor the national interest required the course they chose.

Madison actually left the decision for war to Congress, but in his message of June 1, 1812, he marshaled a telling case against England. He blamed the British for impressing American citizens into the Royal Navy from the decks of American vessels, for committing warlike acts within American territorial waters, for resorting to unjustifiable paper blockades, for hampering legitimate neutral trade by illegal orders-in-council, for crippling future American commerce under the false guise of belligerent rights, and for inciting the Indians of the Northwest to attack American frontiersmen. Some historians, however, regard that brief as fallacious and deceptive. The problem of impressments, they argue, was less acute in 1812 than in 1807, and the President revived it simply to stir up popular indignation. Although British cruisers did hover off the American coast, they usually kept beyond the three-mile limit. American neutral rights were abridged, as they are in every major war, but despite that fact, most shippers preferred to remain at peace and make what money they could. The repeal of the orders-in-council could have been predicted, so these critics contend, if the administration had kept a competent minister in London.[1] As for the Indian trouble, British incitement was less important,

[1] News of their repeal on June 23, 1812, did not reach Washington until early August, by which time Congress had adjourned. If a transatlantic cable had existed then, the Senate might not have passed the war resolution on June 17; but a failure to declare war at that time would not necessarily have avoided hostilities in the future.

it has been argued, than the steady pressure from American fur traders and settlers or the refusal of the United States to abide by its treaties with the aborigines.

Some of the charges against the Madison administration are valid. It had blundered badly in the past, notably in accepting as genuine the alleged revocation of the French decrees, so that the diplomatic dead end of 1812 was partly its own fault. Its decisions during that fateful year were taken in almost complete ignorance of the portentous military and political changes occurring abroad. It did come to accept, though not pusillanimously bow to, the demands of a reckless and bellicose West, which talked of national honor but made little provision for national defense. It did share the hopes of the War Hawks that the Floridas and Canada would be conquered and annexed. Some of its deeds were censurable. In buying, sight unseen, in February, 1812, the worthless Henry letters at the cost of a badly needed frigate in order to expose the supposed intrigues of the New England Federalists, Madison and Secretary of State Monroe looked like fools as well as knaves.

Although the United States was to blame for some of the events leading to the second war with Great Britain, its decision to take up arms did not outrage the accepted canons of international morality. The grievances that it nursed and the affronts that it suffered were no less real because they had been long endured, because they might soon be ended, or because France was equally culpable. It is not enough to argue that hostilities could have been avoided, for except in cases of invasion, all wars can be escaped by passive submission. The real question is whether a resort to force promoted the national interest.

At first glance the answer would appear to be in the negative. No invader had yet set foot on American soil. At sea the American navy was hopelessly outnumbered. The army was unprepared to execute the grandiose plans of conquest. The country was not united behind the President, and disaffection spread as time passed. The administration shrank from joining hands with England's enemies, yet a French defeat in Europe would free veteran British troops for operations in the New World. The futility of the war seems to be symbolized by the burning of the Capitol, the flight of the President, the subversive talk at the Hartford Convention, and the Treaty of Ghent which neither eliminated the causes of the conflict nor reaped the territorial spoils the War Hawks had promised.

Yet on closer examination, the fighting had brought something more than a peace without victory. By accident as much as by design, the national interest was served. Merely by surviving a clash with the Mistress of the Seas, the American people secured a release from the feeling of frustration and impotence which had accumulated during the Jeffersonian experiment in economic coercion and the studied insolence of British statesmen. A few isolated naval victories and Jackson's belated triumph at New Orleans offset the more numerous disasters on land and sea and enabled the republic to emerge from the fray with a deeper sense of nationalism. That spirit was strengthened by the subsequent peopling of the West, one result of the war. Canada had eluded the grasp of the expansionists, but the decline of England's prestige after 1815 among the Indians of the Lakes region was instrumental in the rapid growth of that area. Similarly, Jackson's defeat of the Creeks at Horseshoe Bend on March 27, 1814, destroyed the barrier to the rich cotton lands of southern Georgia and central Alabama. Last but not least, in the postwar years England treated the United States with unprecedented civility, while Spain regarded the republic with such fear, especially after Jackson's raid in April, 1818, that it capitulated and made the best possible sale of the Floridas in the Transcontinental Treaty of February 22, 1819.

Unlike the War of 1812, which involved a powerful foe who had been guilty of repeated insults and injuries, the quarrel with Mexico in 1846 has seemed to many historians contrived and provocative, designed to win by force what diplomacy could not obtain. The fact that the former brought no additional territory and the latter ended with a cession of about 530,000 square miles has helped to foster the conclusion that Polk, in seeking to promote the national interest, grossly violated those standards of international conduct which most Americans hold dear.

On May 11, 1846, Polk asked Congress to recognize that a state of war existed by act of Mexico itself. He cited numerous instances of Mexican bad faith, culminating in a sneak attack on American troops on allegedly American soil. He blamed Mexico for defaulting on debts it had repeatedly promised to pay, for destroying American trade by systematic extortion, for threatening the safety of the American Southwest, for breaking off diplomatic relations unreasonably, and for refusing to restore them through the mission of John Slidell.

These contentions have often been dismissed as misleading or untrue. The title to the spot where American lives were lost, it has been argued, was in dispute. By ordering Zachary Taylor's forces to the Rio Grande on January 13, 1846, the President had needlessly courted trouble, and the general's actions upon his arrival had made a clash inevitable. The unredressed monetary claims, so the argument runs, did not justify using force against a weaker neighbor, especially since Mexico was unable rather than unwilling to meet the obligations. The rejection of Slidell was technically defensible, for Mexico had agreed only to receive a commissioner to discuss the Texan boundary, not a minister to liquidate all outstanding issues. Finally, the alleged menace to Texas was sheer fabrication; no Mexican soldiers entered the uninhabited strip between the Nueces and the Rio Grande until Taylor's advance.

Most of these accusations against the Polk administration are unanswerable. Even if we acquit the President, as we must, of the more extreme charges, the conclusion is inescapable that he made fewer concessions to the preservation of peace than any occupant of the White House, before or since. He was prepared to recommend war over unpaid debts, yet less than a decade earlier two American states had repudiated their obligations to European bondholders. He was willing to take up arms over Mexico's refusal to resume normal diplomatic relations, yet he had given Slidell higher rank and broader instructions than the Mexicans had stipulated when they agreed to receive him. The threat to Texas was illusory, yet Polk ordered Taylor into a contested area, where there was no American citizen to protect. He did not incite rebellion in California, but he let it be known that a revolutionary government would be welcomed into the Union. Technically correct on almost every point, Polk manifested little patience and no sympathy for a blustering but weaker neighbor.

The truth is that Polk was determined to acquire California and to settle once and for all the disputed Texas boundary. He wanted to reach those goals by peaceful methods, and he sincerely believed he could. When, however, his hopes were dashed, he did not shrink from resorting to force. Only Mexican rashness saved him from the unhappy predicament of recommending war on grounds which few Americans today would support and which many Americans then would have denounced. Whether the President could have gotten what he wanted by watchful waiting, whether Congress would have given him the authority he was on the verge of requesting, we shall never know; but certainly the national interest did require a showdown with Mexico in May 1846. The best that can be said for Polk is that he did not deliberately seek war in order to despoil a helpless foe, that he tried to end the fighting as quickly as possible, and that the peace terms of 1848 were not so harsh as some of his followers demanded or as the defeat of Mexico would have permitted.

6

❯❯❯-❯❯❯-❯❯❯-❯❯❯❮-❮❮❮-❮❮❮-❮❮❮

The Conduct of Foreign
Policy: The Problem

IF THE FOREIGN POLICY of the United States before 1889 rested on a few basic principles which most Americans accepted, it also adhered to certain procedural practices which derived from their unique constitutional system. That system had three distinctive features. First, the young republic operated under a written charter. Its jurisdiction was limited to explicit grants of authority and to those which could reasonably be implied from specific clauses. Second, the Constitution set up a federal union in which the individual states had a definite role to play. Under the Tenth Amendment, all powers not expressly delegated to the central government and not prohibited to the states were reserved for the latter. Third, the national government consisted of three coordinate branches—the executive, the legislative, and the judicial. This separation and balance were designed to prevent either the president or the Congress or the judiciary from becoming predominant.

So far as the conduct of foreign policy is concerned, the first two features have been less important than the third. To be sure, the silence or ambiguity of the Constitution on matters of external affairs has often been disturbing. There have also been instances when a state in exercising its prerogatives has embarrassed the federal government and even jeopardized the national interest. But the division of authority between the executive and the legislature has been a more constant influence. "The Constitution," Edward S. Corwin once observed, "is an invitation to struggle for the privilege of directing American foreign policy." What that instrument does, and all it does, is to confer upon the president certain powers respecting external relations, upon the Senate other powers, and upon the House of Representatives still others. Which body has the final say is left for time, men, and events to determine. That struggle for control was always present before 1889, but its intensity and outcome varied greatly according to the character and convictions of the men in the White House and on Capitol Hill.[1]

THE CONSTITUTIONAL FRAMEWORK

The president's powers in diplomacy fall into four categories. It is his duty to communicate with foreign nations, to plan and initiate policies, to negotiate and ratify treaties, and to serve as commander-in-chief of the armed forces. All but the second are clearly granted in the Constitution; the authority to plan and initiate must be implied from his other prerogatives. The Senate and the House acting together have the power to declare war, to provide for the common defense, to raise and equip the armed forces, to levy and collect taxes, to regulate foreign commerce, to determine qualifications for naturalization, to legislate for the federal territories, to admit new states into the Union, to impeach and remove the president, to propose amendments to the Constitution, and to call a convention to frame such amendments. Their acts are subject to a presidential veto but can become law if they are repassed by a two-thirds majority. Both houses can also offer advice through resolutions, conduct investigations, and call for papers in executive hands. The Senate alone is empowered to approve certain nominations and to consent, by a vote of two thirds of the members present, to all treaties. The House alone is entitled to originate money bills. When these prerogatives impinge upon or are shared with those of the president, they often precipitate the struggle to which Corwin referred.

Without doubt the framers of the Constitution intended the president and his appointees to transact business with other countries. They authorized him to receive ambassadors and, with the advice and consent of the Senate, to appoint those who represent the United States

[1] Prior to the installation of the Constitution on March 4, 1789, the direction of foreign policy was in the hands of a unicameral legislature which functioned through a Committee of Secret Correspondence (1775–7), a Committee for Foreign Affairs (1777–81), and a Department of Foreign Affairs (1781–9). The last was under a secretary who was responsible to the Congress. A Department of Foreign Relations was created on July 27, 1789, and renamed the Department of State on September 15, 1789. Its secretary reported to the new president. The Constitution forbade the states to make treaties or alliances, commission privateers, levy tonnage duties without congressional consent, maintain troops in peacetime, or engage in war unless actually invaded or immediately threatened. It declared treaties with foreign nations to be the supreme law of the land.

abroad. Thus Jefferson said on November 22, 1793, that the executive branch "is the only channel of communication between this country and foreign nations," while John Marshall asserted on March 7, 1800, that "the President is the sole organ of the nation in its external relations." But does the right to act as the medium through which diplomacy is conducted include the right to decide with whom the republic will have official intercourse? To this vital question the Constitution supplies no clear answer. Although Congress has conceded that the president may recognize other states, it has consistently denied that his authority is exclusive and has frequently contested the manner in which he has, or has not, used it. Recognition, then, is one of the main points of friction in the struggle to direct American foreign policy.

The treaty-making process is another. The framers of the Constitution purposely compelled the president to share his authority with the Senate. He alone determines whether a treaty will be drafted, but the upper house can suggest or prod. He alone negotiates with other nations and decides whether the finished product should be submitted to the Senate, but that body can refuse to give its consent. The president alone has the power to ratify or withhold ratification; but once a treaty has gone into force, he has no more right than Congress to interpret controversial clauses or terminate unpopular provisions. The president can create friction by concluding executive agreements that evade the treaty-making process, but before 1889 the number of these was very small.

A third source of friction stems from an overlapping of authority with respect to the armed forces. The Constitution explicitly states that the president will be commander-in-chief, but with equal clarity it empowers the Congress to declare war. In theory these provisions do not conflict; in practice they do. Generals and admirals have traditionally looked to the White House rather than to the Capitol, not only because the president is their titular superior but also because the civilian heads of the War and Navy Departments belong to the executive branch. Then, too, the president has insisted upon his right to station men and ships wherever, in his judgment, the security of the republic demands. He has decided when it is necessary to protect American merchant vessels with armed escorts. He has determined where detachments must be landed to safeguard American citizens and their property. He has even given assurances that he would, within the limits of his constitutional power, defend a friendly state while a treaty of annexation was being drafted and approved. Yet the execution of these orders might be construed by a potential enemy as a provocative act and thus precipitate hostilities, at which point a declaration of war by the legislature would be a mere formality. Small wonder, then, that Congress has sought to retain its war-making prerogative against encroachments by the president.

Friction has also resulted from an intrusion upon the president's power to plan and initiate foreign policy. Here again, Congress does not deny his authority; it simply argues that it too can operate in that area. Sometimes the two branches work at cross purposes. By enacting statutes dealing with neutrality, immigration, and tariffs, the legislature can narrow the executive's opportunity to bargain with foreign nations. While negotiations are in progress, it can call for secret papers which, if published, could imperil the very goals the president might be seeking. Congress can launch investigations and hold hearings at which cabinet members, ambassadors, and military officers may be required to testify. At any moment it can go on record as opposing this policy or that and thus weaken the hand of "the sole organ of the nation in its external relations."

In this struggle with Congress to direct foreign affairs, the president has enjoyed certain advantages that go beyond his constitutional prerogatives. The legislature lacks unity and centralized responsibility, while unlimited debate in the Senate may cause long delays. The executive can more easily move with dispatch, impose secrecy, undertake long-range planning, and focus public attention on its program. It possesses fuller information on events abroad, operates continuously without recess, and maintains the only official contacts with foreign representatives. Yet even the strongest presidents have discovered that they propose only to have the Congress dispose. Although the initiative in foreign policy does rest with the executive and although he has more often than not determined its substance, this paramountcy has not been constant and can be upset at any time by a resolute legislature. Hence, before analyzing in detail this struggle with respect to treaty making and the armed forces, we shall consider a few examples that have to do with appointments, appropriations, investigations, the call for papers, and recognition.

APPOINTMENTS AND APPROPRIATIONS

While the Senate rejected relatively few diplomatic appointments before 1889, it tried to employ its constitutional prerogative so as to shape foreign policy. The upper house refused to confirm some presidential selections because of personal or partisan dislikes and because of legal qualms, but it also balked when it felt that a legation in a particular country was not desirable. On December 30, 1791, the Senate questioned the expediency of sending permanent ministers to England, France, and Spain but finally bowed to Washington's request. It challenged the President again in April, 1794, when he nominated John Jay to be envoy extraordinary to Great Britain. Ostensibly, it objected because Jay was then Chief Justice and because a regular minister was already in London. Actually, most of the opposition feared the kind of settlement Jay sought, and some preferred war to any treaty at all. After a bitter debate, Jay was approved by a vote of 18 to 8. In another attempt to dictate policy, the Senate opposed John Adams' nomination on February 18, 1799, of William Vans Murray as minister to France. In this instance the President's own party fought the appointment because intransigence toward the French had proved to be a winning issue at the polls. Adams refused to heed the advice and, if the British envoy is to be believed, actually threatened to resign if Murray was not confirmed. This drastic solution was avoided by a compromise in which two prominent Federalists joined Murray in a commission which the Senate quickly approved.

This use by the Senate of its prerogative over appointments to determine with whom the United States will have diplomatic relations continued for another quarter of a century. President Jefferson's wish to exchange ministers with Russia ran afoul of senatorial opposition; his nomination of William Short failed on February 27, 1809, to obtain a single vote. Since the lawmakers could see no need of a permanent representative at St. Petersburg, they rejected John Quincy Adams for the same position on March 6. Three months later, however, the swiftly changing situation on the Continent suggested the wisdom of having a listening post in Eastern Europe, and on June 27, 1809, Adams was confirmed by a margin of 19 to 7. A final example has already been discussed. Early in 1826 the Senate held up for eleven weeks the nomination of two delegates to the Congress at Panama, not because the men were unqualified, but because many members of the upper house thought the United States had no business participating in an inter-American conference.

More familiar and less related to the constitutional issue was the Senate's rejection of appointments on personal, partisan, or legal grounds. On July 19, 1813, Albert Gallatin failed by one vote of confirmation as commissioner to negotiate peace with England because he was still Secretary of the Treasury; but seven months later, after resigning from the cabinet, he was approved. On January 25, 1832, former Secretary of State Martin Van Buren was rejected, also by a single vote, as minister to Great Britain; then the Senate's motive was so patently political that it helped to make Van Buren Jackson's chosen successor in the White House. Equally partisan in character was the defeat of Andrew Stevenson as minister to Great Britain in June, 1834; of Henry A. Wise as minister to France in March, 1843; and of George H. Proffit as minister to Brazil in January, 1844. The first lost to a coalition of Jackson's foes; the others, because they stood by President Tyler in his battle with the Whigs. It should be noted, however, that no nominee to head the State Department was turned down. Henry Clay came the closest in March, 1825, after accepting that position from John Quincy Adams, to whom he had just thrown his support in the House of Representatives in the balloting for president. The vote on Clay was 27 to 14. The very existence of the senatorial veto has probably prevented some controversial names from being submitted as secretary of state. Certainly party leaders talked Madison out of nominating Gallatin in March, 1809.

A final source of conflict over appointments has been the use of executive agents. Washington himself established the practice of assigning some diplomatic tasks to men whose subordinate status eliminated the need for confirmation by the Senate. He did so not to evade the constitutional requirement but because such agents were more appropriate than ministers resident or chargés d'affaires to conduct negotiations prior to inaugurating formal relations, to explore the possibility of resuming ties that had been ruptured, and to visit new nations not yet recognized. Thus he sent Gouverneur Morris to England on October 13, 1790, to discuss unofficially the restoration of relations that had been suspended for eighteen months. On August 11, 1790, he dispatched David Humphreys to investigate appointing a chargé d'affaires to Portugal.

It was the potential abuse, not the proper use, of executive agents that caused trouble for later presidents. More particularly, the Senate feared such agents might be empowered to sign treaties. Jackson was the first to grant that power to an agent, and it led to a bitter debate in the upper house in February, 1831. Twelve years later Tyler was criticized for giving a recess appointment to the man who negotiated the initial treaty with China. On January 9, 1883, the Senate appended a reservation to a treaty with Korea which, in effect, denied the right of the president to conclude such agreements through naval officers whose appointment for diplomatic missions had not been consented to. In May, 1888, a Republican assault upon a Democratic fisheries accord with England employed the argument that the preliminary discussion had been conducted by commissioners who had never been confirmed by the upper house. Partisan maneuvering for the coming election, however, did more to defeat that treaty than constitutional scruples over appointments.

At no time before 1889 did legislative intransigence over appropriations cripple the executive's conduct of foreign policy. That is not to say that American representatives abroad were maintained on an ample basis, that funds for foreign intercourse were cheerfully voted, or that presidential requests to strengthen the diplomatic corps were quickly granted. On the contrary, for more than a century the State Department and Foreign Service suffered from congressional parsimony, indifference, suspicion, and outright hostility. Nor is it to deny that a few contests over the power of the purse set precedents for the future.

One such precedent had to do with the contingent fund. Washington had quickly learned that no annual provision for foreign affairs could take care of every emergency and that the executive might be compelled to make some unexpected disbursement when the legislature was not in session and could not be convened quickly. Hence, starting in 1806, Congress appropriated each year an item for contingent expenses separate from the regular diplomatic budget. Although some lawmakers later argued that the fund enabled the president to employ executive agents illegally, the main objection was to the secrecy. "I am fully aware of the strong and correct public feeling which exists," Polk told Congress on April 20, 1846, "against secrecy of any kind in the administration of the Government, and especially in reference to public expenditures." Yet the experience of every nation had demonstrated, he continued, the necessity of making expenditures "the very object of which would be defeated by publicity." On July 1, 1790, Congress had anticipated Polk's reasoning by permitting the president, when he deemed it essential to the national interest, to make payments without specifying publicly the recipient or the purpose. This provision for secrecy was continued in later statutes, and Polk himself was to make the most vigorous defense of its wisdom.

In 1846 Charles J. Ingersoll, Democrat of Pennsylvania and chairman of the House Foreign Affairs Committee, charged that Daniel Webster had misused the contingent fund while Secretary of State in the previous Whig administration. On April 9 the House asked Polk to furnish, among other things, a statement of all confidential payments made under Webster and not publicly accounted for, the names of the recipients, and the purposes for which the money had been used. Although Webster was a political foe of Polk and a caustic critic of his Oregon policy, the President refused to comply. To do so, he asserted on April 20, 1846, would nullify the very purpose for which the secret-service feature had been created. The president alone must decide whether a disbursement should be kept confidential, and it would be improper for any incumbent to reverse a decision of his predecessor. Polk then told the House how much Webster had spent, but he did not reveal to whom the money had been given or for what end. The House accepted his judgment.

Two other kinds of conflict over appropriations appeared before 1889. One was the reluctance of Congress to make extraordinary appropriations for negotiations the nature of which the president cannot or will not divulge. Twice during Jefferson's tenure, but only after a bitter struggle, did the legislature vote sums for an undisclosed purpose. On February 26, 1803, it placed at his disposal $2,000,000 to defray expenses incurred in resolving the crisis precipitated by Spain's retrocession of Louisiana to France. On February 13, 1806, it gave him a similar amount with which to clear up the dispute with Spain over West Florida. Polk was less successful in August, 1846, when he asked for $2,000,000 with which to initiate peace talks with Mexico, the terms of which he did not reveal, while in 1858 and 1860 Buchanan got nowhere when he sought a larger sum with which to institute negotiations for acquiring Cuba. The second type of conflict arose when a treaty required some expenditure if it was to be carried out. The purchase of Louisiana is a case in point. On this and on several other occasions to be discussed later, the House showed its resentment at being excluded from the treaty-making process by insisting upon a long debate before voting the money.

DOCUMENTS AND INVESTIGATIONS

Another matter on which president and Congress clashed in the conduct of foreign policy was a legislative request to see documents in executive hands. The Senate and House often needed such papers to pass intelligent laws or vote wisely on treaties. Although some calls stemmed from idle curiosity or attempts to embarrass the administration, the vast majority had a very worthy purpose and no ulterior motive. In almost every case, moreover, the resolution containing the request explicitly urged the president to withhold information the publication of which would harm the national interest. The number of conflicts on this point before 1889 were relatively few, but they did establish practices which would carry over into the modern era.

Washington was the first president who refused to submit documents. On March 24, 1796, the House of Representatives requested by a vote of 62 to 37 to see all correspondence bearing on the Jay Treaty, excepting any which might affect adversely current negotiations. The President declined to comply. Although the record contained little that could embarrass him, although the resolution allowed him to keep secret any item he wished, and although the treaty had already been ratified, Washington chose to challenge the House at every point. Not content with saying its perusal of the papers was unnecessary and dangerous, he recalled that the framers of the Constitution had intentionally excluded the House from the treaty-making process. Foreign negotiations, he said on March 30, depended "on secrecy; and even when brought to a conclusion a full disclosure of all the measures, demands, or eventual concessions which may have been proposed or contemplated would be extremely impolitic." That is why the drafting and approval of treaties had been confined to a single executive and a small Senate. To submit to the larger House the details of such negotiations would "establish a dangerous precedent." In the present instance that body had in the text of Jay's agreement all the data needed in order to pass the supplementary legislation. Obviously the majority in the House did not relish this rebuff, but its control was too tenuous to force a showdown. It was content, therefore, to adopt a new resolution on April 6, 1796, which simply asserted the right of the members to see all pertinent documents. Then on April 30, the House voted by a margin of 51 to 48 to take the steps necessary to carry out the terms of the Jay Treaty.

Fifty years later Tyler and Polk reaffirmed the stand taken by Washington. The former, a president without a party, denied at least seven requests for papers in four years, but the most important episode came on February 2, 1843, when the House inquired into the seizure of Monterey in Mexican California the previous October by Commodore Thomas ap Catesby Jones. It asked to see all relevant correspondence and omitted the customary proviso that documents should be submitted only when it was "compatible with the public interest." Since Jones had acted without authority and since the papers would not endanger the nation's security, Tyler complied, but in so doing he redefined the prerogatives of the president. After noting that the House had not allowed him to use his judgment, he declared that crises might arise, even in peacetime, in which the publication of instructions to military officers "would be highly injudicious." In such cases, Tyler concluded in his message of February 18, 1843, "the discretion of the Executive can not be controlled by the request of either House of Congress for the communication of papers."

Polk was equally firm. As part of the unrelenting Whig attack upon his administration for its role in bringing on the Mexican War, the House on January 4, 1848, adopted a resolution by a vote of 145 to 15 calling for all correspondence relating to the mission of John Slidell. Slidell had gone to Mexico City in November, 1845, in an effort to restore diplomatic relations and to secure, if possible, both a settlement of the disputed Texas boundary and the acquisition of the much coveted California. Mexico's refusal to receive Slidell had been an important link in the chain of events that led to the outbreak of hostilities in May, 1846. In making the request at this time, the Whigs hoped to embarrass the President and gain political advantage in an election year. Polk did not give them that satisfaction. His reply of January 12 deplored the omission of the customary clause permitting him to withhold materials whose publication was not in the national interest. He cited Washington's refusal of 1796, even though the House resolution then had included that proviso. In the present instance, he said, the call affected negotiations still in progress and documents which, if known to the enemy, might prevent a reasonable peace. Under these circumstances Polk believed it to be his constitutional right and duty to hold back the papers. This message touched off a heated debate that continued intermittently for the next few months, but the irate legislators could do little but talk. On July 6, 1848, after the peace treaty of Guadalupe Hidalgo had been ratified, Polk sent to the House all of the Slidell correspondence.

Legislative investigations played little part in the conduct of foreign policy before 1889. This practice, inherited from the British Parliament, was designed to insure honesty and efficiency in governmental operations and to promote informed lawmaking. During the nineteenth century the hearings differed markedly from the highly publicized and often televised spectacles of today. A few that bore on external affairs were an inquiry into the defeat of Major General Arthur St. Clair on the Wabash in 1792, a probe into Madison's foolish purchase of the worthless Henry letters in 1812, and an examination of Jackson's punitive raid into the Floridas in 1818. None provoked a clash between president and Congress. The custom of holding hearings on all important treaties did not begin until the 1920's, and it was only then that these investigations assumed a major role in influencing American diplomacy

RECOGNITION

Recognition, on the other hand, created more tensions between the executive and the legislature before 1889 than after that date. The silence of the Constitution meant that procedures had to be worked out by trial and error. Since there are few functions in foreign affairs that surpass in importance the recognition of a new nation, the recognition of a new government within an existing state, or the recognition of the belligerent status of a people struggling for independence, it is not surprising that in these formative years president and Congress repeatedly tried to stake out their rival claims in this area.

No real conflict arose on September 21, 1792, when France deposed its king and became a republic. Washington consulted only his cabinet and upon its advice promptly received the envoy of the new regime on May 19, 1793. Congress acquiesced silently on that occasion, but not twenty-five years later when the question of acknowledging the independence of Spain's rebellious American colonies had to be decided. Although the insurrection had begun in 1808 and although a committee of the House as early as December 10, 1811, had expressed a willingness to "unite with the executive" in establishing relations with the belligerent governments to the south, it was not until 1818 that Speaker Clay challenged the hands-off policy of President Monroe and

Secretary Adams. The motives of the executive were clear. It was negotiating with Spain over the Floridas, monetary damages, and a transcontinental boundary. Premature recognition would jeopardize those efforts; it might even provoke war with the mother country. Clay's motives were mixed. An ardent nationalist and republican, he wished to eliminate all European influence and royal trappings from the New World. A staunch expansionist, he feared that the treaty with Spain might sacrifice American rights to Texas. A skillful politician, he was eager to embarrass Monroe, who had failed to name him secretary of state, and to champion ideas that might lead to the White House.

Three times between 1818 and 1821 Clay tried to secure recognition of the Latin American nations. On March 24–5, 1818, he proposed to amend an appropriation bill by adding $10,000 for the salary of a minister to Buenos Aires, to be spent whenever the executive deemed it expedient to despatch an envoy there. His motion was beaten twice. On May 10, 1820, he pushed through the House an expression of opinion that it was wise to provide for such ministers as the president, with the consent of the Senate, might send to South American governments then maintaining their independence. Monroe ignored the hint. On February 9, 1821, another resolution to allot money for ministers not yet appointed was lost. In short, Clay failed to vindicate his doctrine that the legislature, acting alone, could recognize new states; he was also unsuccessful in trying to force the hand of the executive. Yet when Monroe deemed the time propitious, he asked Congress to join him in extending recognition. On March 8, 1822, after telling why the independence of the former Spanish colonies should be acknowledged, he invited the Senate and the House, if they concurred in his views, to vote the appropriations needed to make that step effective. The President hoped "there might be such cooperation between the two departments of the Government as their respective rights and duties may require." Obviously, Monroe considered it the right of the executive to decide when recognition should be granted and the duty of the legislature to provide stipends for the envoys.

Andrew Jackson also believed that the president and Congress should act together in recognizing new states. On March 2, 1836, the province of Texas declared its independence of Mexico and subsequently won it on the battlefield of San Jacinto on April 21. On June 18 Senator Clay, the chairman of the Foreign Relations Committee, presented a report which argued, among other things, that although the executive normally takes the initiative in extending recognition, the legislature could ask him to act and could itself recognize a new state by enacting a statute regulating foreign commerce. Clay did not say that Jackson was being dilatory, but he did think Texas should be recognized whenever it was clear that it had a government competent to fulfill the obligations of a sovereign nation. Five days later Jackson told the Senate that the evidence was insufficient and that for this reason he had sent an agent to investigate.

On December 21, 1836, Jackson submitted extracts from the findings of that agent. He also recommended further delay until Mexico had acknowledged Texan independence, until a major European state had done so, or until the lapse of time and the course of events had proved beyond cavil that Texas could stand on its own feet. He reminded the legislature that recognition "is at all times an act of great delicacy and responsibility." Authorities, he said, did not agree "as to whom belonged the power of originally recognizing a new State—a power the exercise of which is equivalent under some circumstances to a declaration of war." Because of that risk, he believed the executive should not act without "a previous understanding with that body by whom war can alone be declared." Thus spoke one of the young republic's strong presidents on a vital constitutional issue. And he suited the deed to the words. Not until Congress had appropriated a salary for a diplomatic agent, to be appointed whenever the president deemed it expedient, and the Senate had resolved by a vote of 23 to 19 that the independence of Texas should be acknowledged did Jackson nominate on March 3, 1837, his last day in office, a chargé d'affaires to the Republic of Texas.

The next major battle did not occur until 1864, when the House sought to restrain the president from granting recognition to a new government in Mexico he had no intention of recognizing. This tempest in a teapot ranged far beyond the original point and eventually embraced the entire conduct of foreign policy. The debate must be read in the context of a simultaneous domestic controversy over Reconstruction. Indeed, some of the principals were the same—Lincoln, Seward, and Henry Winter Davis, Republican of Maryland, chairman of the House Foreign Affairs Committee and coauthor of the Wade-Davis bill of July 2, 1864, which Lincoln killed with a pocket veto. The diplomatic background was France's restoration of a monarchy under Archduke Ferdinand Maximilian of Habsburg.

Six days before Maximilian accepted the throne, Davis offered and the House unanimously endorsed a declaration that the United States should not recognize any monarchical government erected by a European power upon the ruins of a republic in the Americas. In explaining the meaning of this resolution of April 4, 1864, to the French, Seward warned that the sentiments were truly those of the American people; but he went on to say that granting recognition was a "purely executive function." The Davis resolution, he said, would require the Senate's concurrence and the President's approval to become law, and in any case, the United States did not contemplate a change in its course toward Mexico.

When a summary of these ill-chosen words appeared in the Paris press, the irate Davis pushed through a call for documents. Lincoln complied on May 25, 1864, and the fat was in the fire. The Representatives were angered not only by Seward's impugning their role in recognition but also by his disclosing the disagreement between the two branches. On June 27 Davis submitted a blistering report from his committee. It repudiated the idea that the power to recognize belonged solely to the executive. It recalled the desire of both Monroe and Jackson for legislative cooperation. It accused the administration of blunting the force of the House's action on April 4. It recommended the adoption of a resolution asserting "that Congress has a constitutional right to an authoritative voice in declaring and prescribing the foreign policy of the United States, as well as in the recognition of new powers as in other matters." It further stipulated that the president must respect that legislative authority and refrain from negotiating on any subject under discussion in Congress. The House adjourned before voting on this resolution which a later Senate memorandum described as "the first attempt in our history to establish the doctrine that Congress has a paramount authority in foreign affairs." Nor did it ever pass, although on December 19, 1864, the House expressed the opinion, in a form which did not require either senatorial or presidential approval, that Congress did have the right to formulate foreign policy, the according of recognition included, and that the executive ought not to offer any explanations to a foreign state on a proposition pending on Capitol Hill.

A final episode in this continuing struggle involved recognition of Cuba's belligerency in 1869. To acknowledge the status of belligerency means that an outside nation recognizes that a revolt within another state has attained the magnitude of a full-scale war. The status of a belligerent entitles the rebels to certain benefits and imposes upon them certain obligations. The former include the right to borrow money, to impose a blockade, to visit and search on the high seas, and to gain entrance into neutral ports. The major obligation is to observe the accepted rules of warfare. Granting belligerency is a lesser boon than according independence, but it is a delicate and dangerous step. Premature recognition of belligerency may be regarded by the mother country as intervention and encouragement of those in rebellion. The United States nursed a deep grievance against England for accepting the Confederacy as a belligerent on May 13, 1861.

The outbreak in 1868 of a ten-year insurrection in Cuba provided a test of strength between president and Congress on this issue. With public opinion strongly favoring the rebels, legislators argued that the least the United States could do was accord the gallant freedom fighters the status of belligerents. Such pleading rested, however, on sentiment —sympathy for the Cubans or hatred of Spain; under international law the facts did not justify recognition of any sort. Secretary Fish, moreover, was especially opposed to such a move, for he was then striving to bring England to account for its alleged culpability in 1861.

Nathaniel P. Banks, who had succeeded Davis as chairman of the Foreign Affairs Committee, spearheaded the drive in the House. On April 10, 1869, he won an overwhelming vote of sympathy for the Cuban cause and a promise to support the President if he granted belligerent status to those in rebellion. The Senate did not join this demonstration because Sumner agreed with Fish and would not report the resolution out of the Foreign Relations Committee. In no way discouraged and believing Grant to be on their side, Banks and his associates renewed the fight at the next session. Although the annual message of December 6, 1869, ruled out any recognition of belligerency, the President was known to be unpredictable. Indeed, on August 14 he had instructed Fish to prepare to recognize Cuban belligerency; this order the Secretary pigeonholed temporarily. With rumors rife that the executive branch was split on the issue, Fish threatened to resign unless Grant came out unequivocally for a hands-off policy. With much reluctance the hero of Appomattox capitulated; and on June 13, 1870, in a strongly worded message written by Fish, he flatly opposed belligerent status for the Cubans. It caught Banks and his followers by surprise. In vain did the angry legislators turn their fire on the President, terming his message the most impudent one ever sent to Congress and an unwarranted interference in the deliberations of a coordinate branch of government. Banks called it a veto in advance. But harsh words did not change votes, and on June 16, 1870, a resolution to acknowledge the belligerent status of the Cuban rebels was defeated by a count of 100 to 70. Once again the executive had prevailed.

The Conduct of Foreign Policy: Treaty Making

THE MOST DISTINCTIVE, publicized, and controversial feature of the American constitutional system influencing the conduct of foreign policy is the treaty-making process. It has also been, over the years, the most prolific source of conflict between the executive and the legislature. The conclusion of treaties with other nations was indispensable for the young republic if it was to establish trade relations, define neutral rights, safeguard fishing privileges, protect naturalized citizens, expedite extradition cases, collect monetary claims, settle boundary disputes, and acquire new territory. Yet in this vital area of diplomacy the framers of the Constitution knowingly forced the president and the Senate to share the responsibility and purposely excluded the House from the process. This division of authority inevitably contributed to the struggle between president and Congress and before 1889 created many precedents for the modern era.

INITIATION AND NEGOTIATION

In the beginning the division of authority was regarded as an asset rather than a liability. In all the preliminaries to treaties, the delegates at Philadelphia anticipated close cooperation between the newly created president and the small, indirectly elected Senate. The latter might suggest—formally by a resolution or informally by private conversations—the expediency of concluding an agreement with a foreign country. Or the former might ask the Senate's advice on the wisdom of entering into such an accord. In either case it was expected that the president would go in person to the Senate chamber and discuss the exact terms of the proposed treaty. He could even request the legislature to vote on specific clauses in draft form to see if a two-thirds majority approved. The Senate had still another opportunity to express its views if the negotiation was entrusted to an envoy extraordinary or a commission whose nomination it must confirm. Such was the case with Jay in 1794 and with Murray and his associates in 1799.

Washington's administration established different and unforeseen practices. Only once, on December 6, 1791, with regard to redeeming captive seamen from Algiers, did the Senate formally resolve that the executive should negotiate a treaty. When the President went to the upper house on August 22, 1789, to consult on an agreement with the Creek Indians, he felt the reception to be so frigid and the benefits so minimal that he never again resorted to the personal approach. For a time he continued to seek the Senate's advice in writing, but the emergence of partisan alignments in his second term caused him to abandon that procedure. The preliminaries to the Jay Treaty set the precedent which his successors, with few exceptions, followed. In nominating the Chief Justice for a special mission to England, he conferred with only the leading Federalists; and when on April 17, 1794, the Republican opposition requested him to make known "the whole business with which the proposed Envoy is to be charged," his supporters defeated the motion.

After Washington's retirement the Senate exercised sparingly its right to initiate treaties. On February 14, 1806, it requested the president to demand indemnity for British seizures of American neutral shipping and to reach some solution to the impressment problem. Although a few Republicans decried the move as infringing upon an executive prerogative, Jefferson seemed glad to have this backing and promptly named a two-man commission to reopen negotiations in London. A decade later the Senate was more reluctant to advise. When a leading Federalist proposed that Madison be urged to seek additional commercial privileges from England, a committee reported adversely on February 15, 1816. It declared that the President was the one "most competent to determine when, how, and upon what subject" treaties should be undertaken and reminded the members that differences among themselves or with the executive "could not fail to give the nation with whom we might be disposed to treat the most decided advantage." It was on that ground that Polk objected to secret senatorial advice during the tense negotiations over Oregon. When Calhoun told him on February 25, 1846, that the upper house might in executive session enact a resolution suggesting he renew discussions looking toward a settlement along the forty-ninth parallel, a line the British had recently rejected, the President demurred. He spoke of the impropriety of taking the matter out of executive hands and warned that a failure of the Calhoun scheme to obtain a two-thirds majority or a disclosure of differences between the executive and legislature would seriously weaken the bargaining position of the United States.

A few other examples of legislative initiative will suffice. On March 3, 1835, the Senate requested Jackson to consider acquiring treaty rights in the isthmian region for those citizens wishing to construct an interoceanic canal; but after investigating the subject, the President replied on January 9, 1837, that it was not feasible to act. On February 14, 1859, the House joined the Senate in resolving that instructions be given all ministers and consuls to promote the tobacco trade. A joint resolution of March 2, 1867, directed the secretary of state to negotiate with Colombia about canal rights; one of March 2, 1883, asked the president to renew a commercial convention with Venezuela. Several attempts by the House to initiate treaties were denounced by its own members as irregular, but by 1880 the step had been taken twice. On March 8, 1888, however, Cleveland reaffirmed the primacy of the president. A week earlier the Senate had called for a new treaty with China to exclude coolie labor. Since negotiations had been in progress for some time, this motion by a Republican Senate under a Democratic President in an election year had partisan overtones. Cleveland's rejoinder stated that the executive had not overlooked the matter and that it was the branch of government charged by the Constitution with formulating treaties. Indeed, information about the current discussions had been available to those Senators desiring it. Four days later the revised agreement was signed.

Still more sparingly did Washington's successors seek senatorial approval of treaties before they were concluded. Not until 1846 did Polk return to the procedure envisaged by the framers, and then he did so in order to escape from a political trap of his own making. On July 12, 1845, he had offered to divide the Oregon country roughly along the forty-ninth parallel. He had taken that step despite earlier speeches and out of deference to his predecessors, several of whom had made comparable proposals. When the British minister in Washington rejected the plan without even referring it to London, Polk publicly reasserted the American claim to all of Oregon. Many of his followers professed to believe that he would fight rather than accept less. The President never committed himself that far, but he was convinced that he must look John Bull straight in the eye to gain reasonable terms. In this view he was correct. Once Congress had, on April 27, 1846, adopted a joint resolution terminating the treaty of 1827, the British quickly indicated a willingness to settle on the forty-ninth parallel. Given the exaggerated expectations on Capitol Hill, Polk felt obliged to make sure the Senate would endorse such a solution. On June 10 he submitted a draft convention embracing England's terms and warned that he would not proceed unless two thirds of the members signified their approval in advance. Two days later the Senate advised him, by a vote of 38 to 12, to complete the transaction. On June 18, 1846, the treaty itself, signed three days earlier, was consented to by a margin of 41 to 14.

Polk's insistence on senatorial approval before the President concluded a treaty was repeated several times before 1889. Buchanan on February 21, 1861, and Lincoln on March 16 vainly sought advice on the wisdom of arbitrating with England a dispute over San Juan Island. On December 17, 1861, and on January 24, 1862, Lincoln sounded out the upper house on two treaties his minister to Mexico wished to sign; on February 25, 1862, that body voted 28 to 8 that it was inexpedient to do so. On February 10, 1868, Johnson asked the Senate to approve in advance a plan to acquire Samaná Bay from the Dominican Republic, and on January 15, 1869, he made a similar request for a projected naturalization treaty with England. The first proposition drew no response, but on April 15, 1869, Grant was advised to go ahead with the second. Grant himself twice resorted to the practice—on May 13, 1872, for a supplementary article to the Treaty of Washington and on June 18, 1874, for a reciprocity pact with Canada. The Senate was lukewarm on the former and opposed to the latter. On June 9, 1884, Arthur tried in vain to commit the Senate in advance to a renewal of the Hawaiian treaty of January 30, 1875, but in the end he had to make the move on his own responsibility.

CONSENT AND DEFEAT

When the Senate receives a signed treaty, it may take one of five steps. First, it may give its unqualified consent, provided two thirds of the members present concur. Second, it may give its consent with amendments, again by a two-thirds vote, although an amendment itself can be incorporated by a simple majority in the resolution conferring consent. Amendments that alter the text by additions or excisions require formal approval by the other signatory or signatories. Third, it may give its consent with reservations, again by a two-thirds majority. A reservation is a statement inserted in the resolution of consent by which the Senate interprets or defines the obligations assumed by the United States; it does not normally require explicit acceptance by the other party or parties. The distinction between amendments and reservations is tenuous, and the words are often used interchangeably. They differ not in the objective sought but in the form by which a qualified consent is given. Fourth, the Senate may block a treaty by refusing to consider it or by tabling it after debate. Fifth, the Senate may defeat a treaty whenever one third plus one of the members vote against the resolution of consent.

Up to 1889 the Senate approved without qualification a very large percentage of all treaties with foreign nations. Since many of those consented to were routine or noncontroversial in content, it should be added that a bare majority of the truly important ones also passed without change. Out of sixty-five treaties in that period which today seem noteworthy either because of conditions at the time or because of what has happened since, thirty-three were consented to without modification. Fifteen were subjected to amendments or reservations; eight of those were accepted by the other signatories and ratified. Seventeen were defeated, nine after a formal vote and eight for want of definitive action. In short, forty-one of the sixty-five major treaties submitted to the Senate before 1889 went into effect in their original or revised form. The details are summarized in a note at the end of this chapter.

Two other points deserve brief mention. In a sense the Senate can defeat treaties without even considering them. Fear of rejection by the upper house may induce a president not to negotiate or to withhold the pact after it is signed. It is impossible to estimate the number of treaties that were never negotiated, but before 1889 there were hardly a dozen which the executive decided not to submit for approval. In some instances, the president himself was dissatisfied; such was the case with Jefferson and the Monroe-Pinkney Treaty of December 31, 1806, dealing with impressments. In others, a change in the international situation or reports of hostility by the other signatory made submission unwise or unnecessary. Occasionally, American representatives abroad have acted without authorization or, upon second thought, have deemed it inexpedient to send home what they had drafted. Lastly, the president may withdraw a pact already under consideration out of fear that it will be defeated. Yet in the sole important case of that sort before 1889, the Senate had already acted adversely before the newly inaugurated Cleveland asked for the return. And Cleveland's reason was a dislike of the provisions, not an alarm over a possible rejection.

Finally, there is the two-thirds rule which, after the defeat of the Versailles Treaty in 1920, was widely blamed as an obstacle to the efficient conduct of foreign policy. Undoubtedly on some occasions a president might have been more ready to negotiate if he had needed to muster merely a simple majority, yet before 1889 this constitutional requirement accounted for the loss of only two of the sixty-five treaties, and these might well have failed anyway. The Hawaiian reciprocity agreement of May 21, 1867, passed a thin Senate by a single vote, 20 to 19, and it is doubtful whether the legislation needed to put it into effect could have overcome the formidable opposition in the House. The Frelinghuysen-Zavala canal convention of December 1, 1884, with Nicaragua cleared the Senate on January 29, 1885, by a wider but still insufficient margin of 32 to 23 before Cleveland withdrew it from further consideration.

RATIFICATION AND IMPLEMENTATION

Common usage notwithstanding, ratification is the action taken by the president to bring a treaty into force. After the Senate has given its consent, the executive decides whether to exchange ratifications with the other party and to issue the proclamation making the agreement effective. Until these final steps are taken, all preliminaries may be in vain. Actually, at no time before 1889 did a president refuse to ratify an important treaty which the Senate had approved. There were some which did not go into effect, however, because the other parties were unwilling to complete ratification. Their refusal stemmed mainly from changes made by the Senate, although chaotic conditions or new developments abroad were also responsible.

Almost every treaty requires some implementation. Very few can be carried out unless additional legislation is enacted, and the laws that are needed usually involve money. This fact has enabled the House of Representatives, which is technically excluded from the treaty-making process, to make its influence felt by exercising its prerogative to originate all appropriation bills. As early as 1796 a bitter fight arose over a relatively small grant needed to put into operation the mixed commissions established by the Jay Treaty. Having been rebuffed by Washington in their call for pertinent documents bearing upon that controversial settlement with England, many Congressmen wished to impress upon the executive the power of the purse. Only after a long debate had brought forth all sides of the knotty constitutional issue did the House finally vote on April 30, by the narrow margin of 51 to 48, to carry out the terms of the Jay Treaty, and subsequently it agreed to appropriate funds.

Not every request for money to implement a treaty has provoked a similar struggle. In 1802 Congress took less than a week to authorize the $2,664,000 required to execute a claims convention with Great Britain. A year later Jefferson went to extraordinary lengths to avoid difficulties over the Louisiana Purchase. At first he contemplated submitting all three treaties with France to both houses simultaneously for their approval. Although dissuaded from establishing that precedent, he did inform the Representatives on October 17, 1803, the very day the agreements went to the Senate, that they would soon be called upon to exercise those functions entrusted to them by the Constitution. Eight days later, even before the Senate gave its consent, the House voted 90 to 25 that the French treaties should be put into effect. And for sixty-five years thereafter the lower chamber fulfilled with a minimum of protest the obligations incurred whenever the president and the Senate concluded treaties involving money. In 1824, $5,000,000 was allocated to implement the treaty of 1819 with Spain. Between 1849 and 1852 three grants totaling $13,800,000 were made in support of the peace of Guadalupe Hidalgo with Mexico. Another $10,000,000 was voted in 1854 to pay that country for the territory acquired by James Gadsden the previous year.

Seward's purchase of Alaska on March 30, 1867, for $7,200,000 touched off the next major fracas. The reasons were partly a postwar reaction against executive leadership, partly a Republican hostility to the Johnson administration, partly a mounting opposition to Seward's grandiose schemes for expansion, and partly a justifiable suspicion over the secrecy surrounding the treaty with Russia. Although the Senate gave its consent on April 9 by a vote of 37 to 2, the House delayed for more than a year before taking final action. During that interval, when Seward agreed to pay Denmark $7,200,000 for two of its West Indian islands, the representatives formally resolved on November 25, 1867, that they had no obligation to appropriate funds for any new possessions until it could be shown that a need greater than the present one existed. On July 14, 1868, the House passed an enabling statute for Alaska, with a preamble which asserted its right to be consulted in advance in any future purchase of territory. The Senate struck out the preamble, not caring for this infringement of its power to act alone with the president in the treaty-making process. The House, in turn, would not admit that it must automatically carry out the wishes of the president and Senate. In the act of July 27, 1868, which appropriated funds to pay for Alaska, it inserted a compromise declaration to the effect that the approval of both houses was required to implement that particular treaty.

Although the House has relied most frequently upon the power of the purse, it has not ignored other means of establishing its right to be consulted in implementing certain types of treaties. It has argued, not always successfully, that no territory can be ceded by the United States without its consent and that no reciprocity agreement can take effect without its sanction. The most sweeping assertion of the first claim was made by Clay in 1820 against that part of the Transcontinental Treaty with Spain which drew the western boundary along the Sabine River instead of the Rio Grande. On March 28 he presented a resolution asserting that Congress alone had the authority to alienate territory and that no cession was valid without the concurrence of both houses. Spain, however, exchanged ratifications before the motion came to a vote. A variation on this theme occurred on June 16, 1846, the day after Secretary Buchanan signed the Oregon treaty with England but before the Senate gave its consent. An advocate of 54°40′ tried to place before the House a series of resolutions attacking the compromise settlement and insisting that Polk and the Senate defer further action until the people had expressed their views. Just how the popular will might be ascertained was not divulged; in any case the resolutions were not allowed to be introduced.

Only after the Civil War did the power of the House to implement commercial treaties become a source of friction. Even the controversial Marcy-Elgin agreement of June 5, 1854, caused no difficulty, since England had explicitly acknowledged that Congress must pass certain laws before its terms would go into force. Subsequent reciprocity conventions were not so fortunate. The enabling law to the Hawaiian pact of January 30, 1875, required eighteen months to clear the legislative hurdle. A similar battle occurred when the treaty was renewed on December 6, 1884. The Senate did not give its approval until January 20, 1887; then the House had its turn. A report on March 3 by the Judiciary Committee called the entire negotiation illegal and accused the President and the Senate of using the treaty-making process to destroy the House's jurisdiction over tariffs. Cleveland paid no heed to the committee's demand that he withhold ratification until the House had passed an enabling law.

TERMINATION AND EVASION

From a diplomatic point of view, the termination of a treaty may be a routine affair or it may provoke a major crisis. Much depends on whether an agreement provides for its own demise and, if not, whether the other signatory feels the ending deprives it of existing benefits.[1] From a constitutional point of view, the termination of a treaty may create friction between the executive and the legislature, for the framers did not specify which branch had the sole or paramount authority. In the century before 1889 practices varied considerably, but they did not lead to any major clash between president and Congress.

Among the treaties providing for their own termination, three merit attention. By December 2, 1845, President Polk was convinced

[1] Where the duration of a treaty was not clearly stated, international law traditionally justified terminating it on the following grounds: the fulfillment of all obligations assumed therein; the violation of its terms by the other signatory; the effect of changed conditions; and the consequences of war.

that the only way to settle the Oregon boundary dispute was to invoke the clause in the British treaty of August 6, 1827, which permitted either party to abrogate the pact twelve months after notifying the other of its wishes. He eagerly sought legislative cooperation and recommended that Congress empower him to give such a notice. The authority contained in the joint resolution of April 27, 1846, proved to be the key to a prompt and equitable compromise.

On the other hand, when President Pierce made a similar request on December 4, 1854, in order to get rid of a treaty of April 26, 1826, under which the United States paid tolls for vessels traversing Danish waters between the North and Baltic Seas, only the Senate complied. On March 3, 1855, it secretly authorized the President, at his discretion, to notify Denmark that in one year the treaty would lapse, and the government in Copenhagen was so notified. Eleven months later Senator Sumner challenged the legality of what had been done and argued that the concurrence of the House was needed, but his colleagues decided otherwise. After hearing a report from the Foreign Relations Committee on April 7, 1856, it held the previous action to be valid.

A third case concerned the Rush-Bagot agreement of April 1817, limiting Anglo-American armaments on the Great Lakes. Piqued by wartime incidents, the House on June 18, 1864, adopted a joint resolution directing the President to give the six-month notice required for abrogation. Although the Senate failed to respond before the session ended, Lincoln notified England on November 23 and so informed Congress when it reassembled. Since some lawmakers questioned his power to make such a move alone, both houses on February 9, 1865, passed a second resolution approving the President's act "as if the same had been authorized by Congress." But early in 1865 the diplomatic skies were clearing, and on March 8 Seward instructed Adams to tell the British that the United States was willing to let the agreement stand. In effect, the executive withdrew the notice after the legislature had directed that it be given.

Those treaties which did not provide for their own termination presented other problems. Two deserve notice. On July 6, 1798, the House joined the Senate in a resolution annulling the French alliance of February 6, 1778. France's illegal seizure of American shipping and its contemptuous refusal to negotiate on terms of equality produced a vote of 14 to 5 in one chamber and 47 to 37 in the second. Although President Adams had not recommended this move, he signed the measure the next day. Eighty years later President Rutherford B. Hayes reacted differently to a case of legislative initiative. To a House bill curbing Chinese immigration the Senate on February 15, 1879, added an amendment requiring the abrogation of two articles in the Seward-

Burlingame Treaty of July 28, 1868. In a veto on March 1, Hayes
conceded the authority of Congress to express the nation's will not to
adhere to a treaty, but he denied its right to modify by deletion existing
agreements. The amended bill, he insisted, was beyond the competence of the legislature. Although Hayes prevailed momentarily
when a motion to repass failed to muster the necessary two-thirds
majority, it was only a matter of time before the Burlingame Treaty
and its supplement of November 17, 1880, were effectively violated,
not terminated, by subsequent laws.

Evasion of the constitutional requirement is a final source of
conflict between president and Congress in the treaty-making process.
The most publicized evasion is the executive agreement upon which
the Senate does not vote. Actually, there are three types of executive
agreements: those authorized by Congress, those concluded under the
president's diplomatic prerogatives, and those entered into under his
powers as commander-in-chief. Only the second was common before
1889; that type was used to adjust claims of individual citizens and
to provide temporary arrangements pending the negotiation of a
treaty. Thus Secretary of State John Forsyth agreed with the British
minister on February 27, 1839, to recommend to the state of Maine
and the province of New Brunswick certain regulations to be observed
in a disputed zone until a permanent settlement could be reached. On
June 22, 1885, the successors of those two men agreed to allow
American citizens to enjoy until the end of the year those fishing
privileges they had possessed under a treaty the United States had
recently abrogated.

Less frequent were the other two kinds of executive agreements.
An example of the first was a law of June 19, 1886, which led to an
agreement with Spain on October 27 for suspending discriminatory
duties on trade with Cuba and Puerto Rico; but it was the McKinley
Tariff four years later that provided a legal basis for reciprocity conventions that were not submitted to the Senate. The most significant
example of the third type was the exchange of notes by Acting Secretary Richard Rush and British Minister Charles Bagot on April 28–9,
1817, restricting armaments on the Great Lakes, but Monroe sent
that accord to the Senate for its approval. Similar in nature was a
memorandum signed on July 29, 1882, by Secretary Frelinghuysen
and Mexican Minister Matias Romero which permitted the troops of
each nation to cross the border into the territory of the other when in
pursuit of Indian marauders. But neither of these agreements based
on the president's military powers created the amount of friction that
arose after 1941 or led to demands that their use be curbed.

Actually, the most flagrant evasion of the treaty-making process
before 1889 was a joint executive-legislative undertaking. On June

8, 1844, a coalition of Whigs and Van Buren Democrats decisively rejected a treaty to annex Texas which President Tyler and Secretary Calhoun had negotiated. Personal and partisan sentiments combined with sincere convictions in causing more than two thirds of the Senate to vote against the pact. Undaunted by this setback, Tyler turned to the House two days later and appealed for aid. Although he regarded the annexation of Texas by treaty as "the most suitable form in which it could be effected," he stood ready to cooperate fully "should Congress deem it proper to resort to any other expedient compatible with the Constitution." The question, he said, "is not as to the manner in which it shall be done, but whether it shall be accomplished or not." With only a week left before adjournment and with the presidential campaign already under way, Congress was in no mood to decide anything; but when it reconvened in December, the picture had changed. Polk, the expansionist, had been elected over Clay, who had straddled the Texas issue. Although the margin of victory was narrow and although other factors had played a decisive role, Tyler chose to interpret the result as a popular mandate for immediate action. On December 3, 1844, he spelled out the alternative to which he had alluded the previous June. Mindful that the Whigs still controlled the Senate, he recommended that annexation be accomplished by "a joint resolution or act to be perfected and made binding by the two countries when adopted in a like manner by the Government of Texas."

The constitutionality of this procedure was challenged at once and debated at length. On January 25, 1845, the House passed by a margin of 120 to 98 the kind of joint resolution Tyler envisaged, but the Senate Foreign Relations Committee reported it adversely. Legal doubts, a concern for prerogatives, partisan politics, and antislavery fears all created an apparently insurmountable roadblock. At that point Robert J. Walker, Democrat of Mississippi, proposed an amendment that would allow the President the option of dealing with Texas under the joint resolution or of negotiating a new treaty. It was intimated that Polk, if not Tyler, would follow the second course. On February 27, by identical tallies of 27 to 25, the Senate accepted the Walker proposal and adopted the amended resolution. The House concurred in the change by a count of 132 to 76, and on March 1, 1845, Tyler signed the measure.

By this vaguely worded document, explained by even vaguer assurances, the President and Congress circumvented the treaty-making process. To the consternation of five Senators who had supported the Walker amendment only because they believed a new treaty would be drafted, Tyler on his last day in office chose to approach Texas under the first option. On March 10, 1845, Polk decided to do the same. On June 23 the Texan Congress unanimously accepted the requirements of the resolution, and on July 4 a special convention at Austin voted 55 to 1 for incorporation by the United States. On December 29, 1845, Polk signed a second joint resolution admitting Texas into the Union. There was no new treaty.

Both the propriety and the constitutionality of annexing Texas by joint resolution have been subjects of continuing discussion. Whatever might be the merits of that method—and it can be argued that approval by a simple majority in both houses is more democratic than consent by a two-thirds vote in only one—there was no similar evasion of the constitutional requirement until the acquisition of Hawaii in July 1898. Indeed, only once again before 1889 did a president suggest that territory be added by a joint resolution. On December 5, 1870, Grant raised the question when his treaty to annex the Dominican Republic seemed certain to fail; but the legislature ignored his hints. In the future the conflict between president and Congress over evading the treaty-making process would lie in other areas.

Note on the Senate's Handling of Treaties, 1789–1889

AMONG the thirty-three treaties mentioned above to which the Senate gave its unqualified consent were the Treaty of San Lorenzo with Spain determining boundaries and granting free navigation of the Mississippi (October 27, 1795); the three constituting the Louisiana Purchase from France (April 30, 1803); the peace of Ghent with England (December 24, 1814); a commercial convention with Great Britain (July 3, 1815); a convention with England dealing with the fisheries and the northern frontier (October 20, 1818); a treaty with Spain ceding the Floridas and drawing a transcontinental boundary (February 22, 1819); an agreement with Russia partitioning the northwest Pacific coast (April 17, 1824); a treaty with England providing free and equal access to the Oregon country (August 6, 1827); a treaty with England referring to arbitration disputed territory in the Northeast (September 29, 1827); a claims convention with France disposing of damages to American shipping (July 4, 1831); the Webster-Ashburton Treaty with Great Britain settling the Maine boundary and other questions (August 9, 1842); a treaty with England partitioning the Oregon country at the forty-ninth parallel (June 15, 1846); the Clayton-Bulwer Treaty with Great Britain dealing with an interoceanic canal and the noncolonization of Central America (April 19, 1850); the Marcy-Elgin Treaty, also with England, providing for commercial reciprocity and fishing privileges (June 5, 1854); a convention with Great Britain regulating the African slave trade (April 7, 1862); a treaty with Russia purchasing Alaska (March 30, 1867); and the Treaty of Washington with England sending to arbitration the *Alabama* claims and three other disputes (May 8, 1871).

Of the fifteen treaties which the Senate subjected to amendments or reservations, the following were accepted by the other signatories and ratified: the Jay Treaty with Great Britain dealing with the Northwest posts, neutral rights, and commerce (November 19, 1794); a convention with

France settling several differences (September 30, 1800); the Treaty of Guadalupe Hidalgo restoring peace with Mexico (February 2, 1848); the Gadsden purchase adjusting the boundary with Mexico (December 30, 1853); the Seward-Burlingame Treaty with China concerning trade and immigration (July 28, 1868); a treaty of friendship with Samoa (January 17, 1878); a treaty of friendship with Korea (May 22, 1882); and a reciprocity agreement with Hawaii permitting the United States to develop a naval station on the Pearl River (December 6, 1884).

Nine of the seventeen treaties defeated by the Senate were rejected by a formal vote. They were a convention with Colombia regulating the African slave trade (December 10, 1824); a treaty to annex Texas (April 12, 1844); the McLane-Ocampo Treaty with Mexico granting transit privileges (December 14, 1859); a reciprocity treaty with Hawaii (May 21, 1867); the Johnson-Clarendon attempt to dispose of the *Alabama* and other claims with England (January 14, 1869); a treaty to annex the Dominican Republic (November 29, 1869); the Frelinghuysen-Zavala Treaty with Nicaragua concerning canal rights and a guarantee of territory (December 1, 1884); an extradition pact with England (June 25, 1886); and the Bayard-Chamberlain Treaty with Great Britain dealing with the fisheries (February 15, 1888). Eight others were lost when the Senate failed to act. These were the reciprocity agreement with Hawaii (July 20, 1855); the second McLane-Ocampo Treaty with Mexico conferring rights of intervention (December 14, 1859); two treaties with Mexico relating to a loan and the repayment thereof, signed without authority on April 6, 1862; a treaty with Denmark for the purchase of St. Thomas and St. John (October 24, 1867); a treaty with England to settle the San Juan Island dispute (January 14, 1869); a treaty with the Dominican Republic for the lease of Samaná Bay (November 29, 1869); and a treaty with Colombia concerning rights to construct a canal (January 26, 1870).

8

⟫⟫⟫-⟫⟫-⟫⟫⟪⟪⟪-⟪⟪-⟪⟪-⟪⟪

The Conduct of Foreign
Policy: The Armed Forces

A FINAL FEATURE of the constitutional system shaping the conduct of foreign policy before 1889 was the divided control of the armed forces. The potential conflict between the president's authority as commander-in-chief and Congress' power to declare war affected the diplomacy of the young republic in its formative years, although not so frequently as the clash over treaties. Until the 1920's the treaty-making process continued to pose more difficulties; but with the advent of weapons capable of instantaneous and mass destruction, the question of who orders the military into action has assumed greater importance.

DECLARED WARS

Entering a declared war with a foreign nation before 1889 was a rather leisurely procedure, in which there was time for deliberation and debate. In the two wars in which the United States engaged the constitutional machinery functioned exactly as the framers had intended. On June 1, 1812, President Madison laid before Congress a list of long-standing grievances covering England's practices on the high seas and its intrigues along the western frontier. He did not, however, make any specific recommendation. Although he believed the evidence disclosed "on the side of Great Britain a state of war against the United States and on the side of the United States a state of peace toward

Great Britain," he concluded that whether the country should remain passive under these accumulated wrongs was "a solemn question which the Constitution wisely confides to the legislative department." Madison likewise made no recommendation regarding France, whose assaults upon American property and self-respect he alluded to at the end of the special message.

Congress cast the die for war with England. But the debate was longer and the vote closer than on all subsequent occasions—1846, 1898, 1917, 1941—when a formal declaration was made. In the Senate the margin was 19 to 13 and in the House 79 to 49. A motion to include France as an enemy failed in the Senate by only two votes; another to restrict the fighting to defensive reprisals on the high seas ended in a tie. These narrow majorities led the disgruntled delegates at the Hartford Convention on January 4, 1815, to suggest an amendment to the Constitution which would forbid Congress to declare war except in cases of invasion, unless two thirds of the members of both houses concurred. Congress ignored the proposal, and no such amendment ever materialized.

On May 11, 1846, President Polk presented to the legislature a full account of "the existing state of relations" with Mexico. After reviewing Mexico's persistent unwillingness or inability to live up to past treaties and a recent refusal to receive, as it had allegedly promised to receive, a special envoy to discuss all outstanding differences, he described an attack of April 25 upon American troops in a disputed zone between the Nueces and Rio Grande Rivers. He noted that just before the skirmish the Mexican general had notified the American commander that "he considered hostilities commenced" and would pursue them to the fullest. "The cup of forbearance has been exhausted," Polk asserted. "After reiterated menaces, Mexico has passed the boundary line of the United States, has invaded our territory and shed American blood upon the American soil." In the name of national security Polk invoked "the prompt action of Congress to recognize the existence of the war, and to place at the disposition of the Executive the means of prosecuting the war with vigor, and thus hastening the restoration of peace."

Confronted with a *fait accompli*, with fighting already in progress and the country presumably invaded, Congress responded immediately. The House passed in one day, by a count of 113 to 14, and the Senate in two days, by a tally of 40 to 2, the legislation the President requested. This dispatch was in contrast to the seventeen days consumed in 1812. The real contest was over the adoption of the preamble which attributed the war to Mexican aggression. On that, the vote in the House was 123 to 67 and in the Senate 28 to 18. Senator Calhoun argued vainly for delay. He reminded his listeners that war could exist only by an act of Congress and that they had no documentary evidence of a Mexican invasion. For the time being, he said, the legislature should do no more than authorize defensive operations. But Calhoun was not heeded in this first instance of a President's provoking a war through his powers as commander-in-chief.

UNDECLARED WARS

Between 1789 and 1889 the United States fought three undeclared wars. The first and most severe was the so-called quasi-war with France from 1798 to 1800. Aroused by insults of the French Directory and by depredations of French cruisers, Congress passed without executive urging a series of laws designed to place the nation on a war footing, to protect its citizens and their property at sea, and to prevent subversion at home. Three of these statutes bore directly upon the undeclared war. The first, of May 28, 1798, permitted American naval craft to capture French privateers hovering off the coastline. A second, of June 25, allowed American armed merchantmen to make prizes of any armed French vessel that might attack them. A third, of July 9, 1798, authorized United States warships and privateers to seize all armed French vessels, public or private, anywhere on the high seas. That last act passed two days after Congress had voted to abrogate the alliance of 1778.

These measures led to two years of intermittent maritime reprisals, mostly in the West Indies. War was not declared; unarmed French commercial shipping was not molested. France was too occupied with events in Europe to spare major warships for duty in American waters and had to rely upon privateers, supported by a few frigates and sloops. There was no fleet action and only desultory minor engagements. Yet in two years the United States navy sank about eighty-five enemy craft, with but one important casualty of its own. No attempt was made to capture French possessions in the New World; American soil was not invaded. A treaty of September 30, 1800, brought the fighting to a welcome close.

An undeclared war of another sort and in a different area began the following year. Ever since gaining independence, the United States had tried by treaties and tribute to protect its seaborne commerce from the Barbary corsairs whose vessels scoured the Mediterranean and the Eastern Atlantic, destroying ships and selling their crews into slavery. The money expended in tribute and ransom could have built a sizable navy, which might have taught the greedy potentates to honor their treaty obligations. Then, in the spring of 1801, without consulting Congress, Jefferson decided to station a permanent squadron near Gibraltar. The ships sailed during a legislative recess, just as Tripoli, the weakest of the Barbary states, resumed its piratical operations. By the time the lawmakers reassembled, the President learned that his vessels had in self-defense captured an enemy cruiser. On December 8 he suggested that Congress empower the squadron to shoot first if it had to. The result was a law of February 6, 1802, "for the protection of commerce and seamen," and it was under such statutes that the United States fought Tripoli until the peace of June 4, 1805. Jefferson did not ask for nor did he receive a formal declaration of war.

The third conflict barely deserves the title of war, undeclared or otherwise. It involved a brief accounting with Algiers, whose avarice and treachery had by 1815 brought armed reprisals by some half-dozen maritime nations of Europe. Perhaps its chief significance is that it provided the sole example of a legislative refusal to comply with an executive recommendation to declare war. On February 23, 1815, five days after the peace treaty with England had been proclaimed, Madison asked Congress to declare the existence of a state of war and to insure its vigorous prosecution. The bright prospects for Mediterranean trade, now that Napoleon was overthrown, made prompt action desirable. The legislature, however, did not think it expedient to go that far, and in a statute of March 3, 1815, it simply authorized the commander-in-chief to equip and employ such naval vessels as might be needed to wage effective hostilities. Two squadrons were formed, and by July 3, 1815, after only a couple of engagements, a satisfactory settlement was reached.

THE USE OF FORCE SHORT OF WAR

Throughout its formative years the young republic used armed force short of war. These police actions normally sought to safeguard American citizens and their property in foreign lands and on international waters. By far the largest number were embarked upon by the executive under his prerogatives as commander-in-chief and without authorization by the legislature. Sometimes the president might ask Congress to empower him to act; occasionally that body might refuse to do so. None of these measures provoked widespread public protest or precipitated clashes between the two branches of government, such as were to come during the Boxer uprising in 1900, the Mexican revolution in 1916, or the Korean conflict in 1950. Usually the units involved were small in size, the fighting brief in duration, and the diplomatic consequences slight in nature.

Typical of the resort to force by the president alone was Jackson's dispatch of a warship in 1831 to the Falkland Islands to release an American merchant vessel illegally seized by men claiming to represent the government at Buenos Aires. Acting first and informing Congress afterward, Jackson suggested on December 6 that the legislature might "clothe the Executive with such authority and means" as it deemed necessary for the protection of American citizens. On July 13, 1854, Captain George N. Hollins of the USS *Cyane* bombarded and burned part of San Juan del Norte in Nicaragua as retaliation for unredressed outrages against American nationals and their property. The secretary of the navy authorized that mission, and Congress was notified upon its completion.

In the same category were various warlike acts in Far Eastern waters during the 1850's and 1860's. On November 20–2, 1856, Commander Andrew H. Foot destroyed four forts below Canton, China. On June 25, 1859, Commodore Josiah Tattnall rendered armed assistance to the British fighting the Chinese at Taku, near Tientsin. On July 16, 1863, the USS *Wyoming* sank two Japanese ships off Shimonoseki. None of these demonstrations was authorized by Congress; none elicited much criticism or protest.

One exception to the rule was Jackson's pursuit of the Seminole Indians into the Floridas in April, 1818. Crossing the border to abate a nuisance Spain could not or would not control, the brigadier general temporarily occupied key towns, deposed local governors, and executed two British citizens on Spanish soil. Whether he acted under instructions from the president is still a matter of historical controversy. Monroe insisted he had not authorized the seizure of East Florida or the subversion of Spanish rule; Jackson maintained that he had been secretly told, in a letter since burned, to undertake those very acts. On Capitol Hill this punitive raid did not pass unnoticed, although the ensuing criticism stemmed as much from partisan as from constitutional considerations. In the Senate, a committee report condemning Jackson's conduct was tabled. In the House, Clay denounced his political rival, likened his course to the most treacherous misdeeds of the Napoleonic era, and warned against the defiance of civilian authority by the military. But on February 8, 1819, a resolution to disapprove of the execution of the two Britons was lost by a count of 90 to 50. Even more important was the defeat the same day, by a vote of 112 to 42, of a bill designed to prohibit any future movement of American troops into foreign territory without an express order by Congress.

Sometimes the executive resorted to force short of war under powers granted by the legislature. The authority to undertake naval reprisals against the Barbary pirates in 1802 and 1815 has already been noted. On January 3, 1811, President Madison recommended that Congress permit him, under certain conditions, to occupy temporarily all or part of the Spanish Floridas in order to forestall their seizure by another nation. Behind closed doors the Senate voted 23 to 7 and the House 76 to 44 to incorporate that request in a joint resolution of January 15, 1811. A statute of March 3, 1819, asking the President to employ armed force against slavers and pirates provided the basis for operations off the African coast between 1820 and 1823. On March 3, 1839, Congress authorized President Van Buren to resist any attempt by England to bolster with force its claim to exclusive jurisdiction over a disputed area between Maine and New Brunswick. On June 2, 1858, the legislature empowered President Buchanan to resort to force short of war in order to obtain redress from Paraguay for various injuries, including the firing upon an American naval vessel three years earlier.

Occasionally Congress has denied a presidential request to use force short of war. On February 6, 1837, Jackson declared that the United States was justified under international law in going to war over Mexico's persistent refusal to pay long-standing claims for damages incurred on its soil. He preferred to await one more demand, but he would make it from an American warship off the Mexican coast. A failure to comply would then lead to reprisals—presumably a bombardment and blockade such as the French would soon undertake. Since the legislature was about to adjourn, he requested authority to adopt that policy during the recess. Neither house met this appeal directly, but the replies of both were negative in effect. Both agreed that one more attempt at peaceful settlement should be tried; and although the executive was allowed some discretion as to the method, he was not granted permission to employ the fleet against the hapless and helpless Mexicans.

On December 19, 1859, Buchanan returned to the problem. After vainly attempting to persuade Congress to assume a temporary protectorate over northern Chihuahua and Sonora and to establish a line of military posts there, he asked for authority to send a punitive expedition across the border. Its objective would be "indemnity for the past and security for the future." The President would obtain, if possible, the consent of the friendly Juarez government, which had been recognized in April but which had not yet asserted its control over the interior where the hostile Miramon regime was permitting the destruction of American lives and property. Should Congress withhold its assent, Buchanan warned, some European nation would eventually step in and perhaps set up a new colony in violation of the Monroe Doctrine. With the antislavery controversy nearing its climax, Congress was unable and unwilling to follow the President's advice, even though the subsequent Maximilian venture proved Buchanan to have been a good prophet.

DEPLOYMENT

As commander-in-chief, the president can order the armed forces to any place he believes will promote the nation's safety. In the early years of the republic this deployment did not normally raise serious constitutional problems or generate friction between the executive and the legislature. Indeed, before 1889 there was only one instance where this prerogative of the president encroached upon the power of Congress to declare war. For the most part, the man in the White House moved military units at will and without protest; in doing so, he rarely exposed himself to the charge of provoking another nation to fire the first shot. Through his secretary of the navy he assigned permanent cruising squadrons to the Mediterranean in 1815, the Pacific in 1821, the Caribbean in 1822, the South Atlantic in 1826, the Far East in 1835, and the African coast in 1842. The purpose of these squadrons was to show the flag, protect shipping, and encourage commerce. No contingents were regularly stationed on foreign soil, either to garrison an overseas base or to honor a diplomatic commitment. Not until the nature of war changed and the international obligations of the United States broadened did the deployment of men, ships, and planes become a source of discord between president and Congress.

Only in the case of Texas and the Mexican War did the executive encroach upon the legislature's constitutional prerogative. During the negotiation of an annexation treaty in January, 1844, the Texan chargé in Washington requested protection by the United States against a possible Mexican invasion between the time the pact was signed and the Texan Senate gave its consent. Secretary of State Abel P. Upshur, who was unjustifiably confident that the treaty would be quickly approved by both parties, promised that orders would be issued to the armed forces as soon as the signatures were affixed. On February 14 William S. Murphy, the American chargé in Texas, made a similar pledge, although he lacked instructions to do so. Two weeks later Upshur was killed, and on March 11 the acting Secretary told Murphy he had exceeded his authority and must withdraw the assurances he had given.

John C. Calhoun, who succeeded Upshur, managed to satisfy the Texans and still keep within the proper sphere of executive jurisdiction. On April 11, 1844, he stipulated that "during the pendency of the treaty" the President would deem it his duty "to use all the means placed within his power by the Constitution to protect Texas from all foreign invasion." Naval units would be concentrated in the Gulf of Mexico to cope with any contingency, and troops would man the southern border. Since the Senate defeated the treaty of April 12 two months later, this action by the Tyler administration did not arouse much criticism; but John Quincy Adams argued in the House that the very negotiation of a treaty which threatened to involve the nation in hostilities was a flagrant usurpation of the war-making power of the legislature.

By April, 1845, the newly installed Polk faced a comparable problem. The Texan Congress had been summoned to meet in two months' time to consider the American offer. Since Mexico had repeatedly proclaimed that annexation meant war and had broken off diplomatic relations as soon as Tyler had signed the joint resolution of March 1, the President understandably moved to meet a crisis. With the slow means of communication then prevailing, he had to anticipate all contingencies and give commanders in the field instructions they might never have to use. On June 15 Polk ordered Brigadier General Zachary Taylor to move his main units in the Southwest from Fort Jesup in west-central Louisiana to a point south of the Nueces River and as close to the Rio Grande as prudence dictated. By July 25, 1845, Taylor had established his Army of Observation at Corpus Christi on the south bank of the Nueces and on the northern edge of the uninhabited and disputed zone between the Republics of Texas and Mexico. On June 24 Commodore John S. Sloat was instructed to keep his small Pacific Squadron on the alert, to stay near Mexican ports, and in case of war to capture San Francisco. These dispatches did not reach Sloat until February, 1846. On July 11, 1845, Commodore David Conner, in charge of the Gulf Squadron based on Pensacola, was directed to defend Texas from any attack. As part of this mission he convoyed Taylor's troops to Corpus Christi and maintained a watch of the Veracruz area. All commanders were cautioned not to antagonize the Mexicans in any way.

Polk believed he had the authority to order these dispositions during a recess of Congress; but when the legislature reconvened, he informed it fully of what he had done. On December 2, 1845, he said that Mexico had broken off relations with the avowed intention of making war. He told of the Texan request for aid. He declared that "the moment the terms of annexation offered by the United States were accepted by Texas the latter became so far part of our own country as to make it our duty to afford such protection and defense." After describing the location of the American forces, he concluded: "But though our Army and Navy were placed in a position to defend our own and the rights of Texas, they were ordered to commit no act of hostility against Mexico unless she declared war or was herself the aggressor by striking the first blow."

Thus far Polk could not be accused of encroaching upon the right of Congress to declare war. He had not withheld any essential information from the legislature. He still hoped for a peaceful solution through the Slidell mission. Then on January 12, 1846, the President learned that his envoy would not be received. The very next day he ordered Taylor to advance to the Rio Grande. Whether this move had been long contemplated, whether the cabinet backed it unanimously, whether congressional leaders had been consulted, we do not know; for the President's extraordinarily full diary is strangely silent at that point. What is certain is that this directive made possible the attack upon American troops on the north bank on April 25; this action in turn led to full-scale war with Mexico. What is also clear is that this decision of January 13, 1846, was unnecessary, short-sighted, and provocative. It was unnecessary because the disputed zone was uninhabited and free of Mexican forces. It was short-sighted because the question of peace or war was thereby thrust into the hands of the field commanders. It was provocative because the proud Mexicans, who until then had only blustered, now felt compelled to counter with a military display. Most important of all, it cast doubt upon the validity of Polk's subsequent allegation to Congress that American blood had been shed upon American soil, and it became the chief staple in the argument that his administration had caused the war by maneuvering Mexico into firing the first shot.

If it seems remarkable that the executive took so vital a step without seeking legislative collaboration, it is even more incredible, in view of the later harsh criticism of Polk's diplomacy, that so little protest was voiced on Capitol Hill in the subsequent three months. To be sure, Polk made no official announcement and sent no official message; but Taylor's movements could not be kept secret. On March 14, 1846, the widely-read *Niles' Register* reported the beginning, six days previous, of the trek southward. Yet the only real objection raised in Congress came on March 26, during a debate on an appropriation bill in the House. Then a Whig from Pennsylvania opposed voting further funds for Taylor's army on the ground that the President had exceeded his constitutional authority by sending the troops beyond the Nueces into Mexican territory. Whatever may have been the wisdom or folly of the order of January 13, 1846, the silent acquiescence by the legislature destroys some of the complaint that the executive had usurped its war-making powers.

That is not to say that Polk was blameless. On the contrary, he remains the sole president in history who, by needlessly deploying the armed forces, provoked an attack by a potential enemy. War with Mexico may have been justified; it may even have been inevitable. On those matters historians still disagree. But there can be no dissent from the judgment that its commencement is on constitutional grounds to be deplored. Protection of a territory about to be annexed is one matter; needless occupation of an uninhabited and disputed boundary strip is something else again.

There was only one other faintly comparable case before 1889. On November 29, 1869, the Grant administration signed two treaties with the Dominican Republic, the first providing for annexation and the second for a lease of Samaná Bay. Simultaneously it promised to protect that country from adjacent Haiti while a plebiscite was held on the island and while the United States Senate deliberated. The President maintained a naval cordon well into 1871, even though the upper house defeated the first treaty on June 30, 1870, and never voted on the other. At that point Charles Sumner, who had broken with Grant and had been deposed as chairman of the Foreign Relations Committee, introduced a series of resolutions assailing the President's blockade as an unlawful assumption of the legislature's power to make war. The Senate tabled these resolutions on March 29, 1871, by a margin of 39 to 16, but soon thereafter the American gunboats were withdrawn from Dominican waters.

BOOK·II

EMERGENCE
AS A
WORLD POWER

1889–1905

*In which the American people respond
to internal and external forces, acquire
an overseas empire, and hasten thereby
their emergence as a world power.*

9

The Shaping of Foreign
Policy, 1889–1905

IN ONE SENSE, the United States was a world power long before 1889. Its ideas on self-determination and democracy knew no political boundaries. Its moral influence reached distant shores through missionaries and educators. Its commercial thrust broke down the self-imposed seclusion of Japan and helped do the same in Korea. Its latent strength to dominate the Western Hemisphere and affect the balance of power in Europe was recognized. American vessels carried the flag to every sea; American farmers produced staples upon which other countries came to depend. Yet none of these factors made the republic a world power by the criteria men began to apply after 1900. By then, colonies in the Western Pacific and the South China Sea gave the United States more than an economic stake in the equilibrium of East Asia. By then, the alliance system abroad caused the chancelleries of the Old World to seek support in the New as they had not done even in the days of Vergennes and Canning. By then, a novel concern for international affairs developed at home and was evident in the press, the consular reports, and the congressional debates. By then, the presidents commenced—tentatively, to be sure—to draw upon the diplomatic, economic, and military potential of the nation in order to preserve and promote peace in critical areas of the globe.

The gradual emergence of the United States as that type of world power between 1889 and 1905 did not lead to the abandonment of any basic principle of foreign policy. Isolationism, neutrality, and the Monroe Doctrine continued to be guidelines for the diplomats and cherished ideals for the people. All three were deemed desirable; all three were considered possible. Even the acquisition of an overseas empire could, men believed, be fitted into the traditional pattern. Nor did these years bring a marked change in the conduct of foreign affairs. The constitutional framework remained unaltered. The conflict between the executive and the legislature persisted. Yet forces were at work which tended to erode the landmarks of the past and set the stage for the first test that confronted the United States during the period 1905–21.

THE PRESIDENTS

As "the sole organ of the nation in its external relations," the presidency merits primary attention in an analysis of the shaping of foreign policy. Of the four men who sat in the White House from 1889 to 1905, none had prior experience in diplomacy and none was elected because of his ideas on world affairs. Such was the rule, not the exception, in those years. James Buchanan had been the last incumbent to serve an apprenticeship as secretary of state or as minister to a first-rank nation.

Benjamin Harrison, Republican of Indiana, could claim in 1889 as qualifications for the presidency a distinguished Civil War record, a successful legal career, and a single term in the Senate. In the upper house from 1881 to 1887, he devoted himself mainly to domestic matters, yet he also steered through a bill granting civil government to Alaska, demanded respect for treaty obligations in the case of Chinese immigrants, and served for one year on the Foreign Relations Committee. Elected on a platform which arraigned his Democratic predecessor for timidity in the conduct of foreign affairs, Harrison was forthright and aggressive, a robust but sometimes indiscreet champion of American rights. An old soldier, the bearded Hoosier was quick to resent any slight to the flag or to members of the armed forces; a wily partisan, he was not oblivious to the political value of making the eagle scream. The boldness and vigor which characterized the diplomacy of his administration stimulated a rising interest among the American people in developments overseas and was one factor in the eventual triumph of imperialism in 1898.

Grover Cleveland, a Democrat from New York, replaced Harrison when the voters in 1892 reversed the close decision of 1888. Once again domestic issues dominated the campaign. Yet the two candidates differed in their personalities and their approach to diplomacy. The iron-willed Cleveland, who had held no federal or military office before becoming president in 1885, had shown during his first term that he was a hard worker, an honest administrator, an unimaginative thinker, and a thorough traditionalist in foreign policy. He had refused to submit to the Senate the Act of Berlin of February 26, 1885, lest it entangle the United States in colonial rivalries in Africa. He had withdrawn from the Senate the Frelinghuysen-Zavala Treaty of December 1, 1884, lest it expose the republic to the charge of repudiating an existing agreement with England. During his second term Cleveland would continue to avoid, for the most part, new departures in foreign affairs, and he would try on several occasions to reverse innovations which Harrison had launched. Yet if his traditionalism and moralism caused him to cling to the policies of nonintervention and anti-imperialism, his sympathy for the underdog led him into the most extreme interpretation to date of the Monroe Doctrine.

William McKinley, Republican of Ohio, succeeded Cleveland in 1897. Initially he had little relish for foreign adventures. Although he took office absorbed in plans for domestic legislation, he was compelled after a time to devote most of his attention to external affairs and to make decisions which profoundly affected the place of the United States on the international stage. For such a task he was ill-prepared. Although he looked like Napoleon, he demonstrated no qualities of dynamic leadership. Possessed of a pedestrian mind, a parochial outlook, and a platitudinous oratory, he knew little of Europe or Asia and accepted unquestioningly the religious and moral standards of rural America at the end of the nineteenth century. During the Civil War he had risen from a private to a major. In 1877, after an interlude of law, he entered the House of Representatives, where he sat, save for nine months, until 1891 and where his chief concern was the tariff. Two terms as governor and the support of prominent businessmen led to the presidential nomination in 1896. Protectionism and the currency were the main issues in his first campaign against William Jennings Bryan, but the Republican platform also spoke out on such objectives as construction of a Nicaraguan canal, purchase of the Danish West Indies, control of the Hawaiian Islands, and restoration of peace in Cuba. Avoiding the unwarranted haste of Harrison and the unyielding opposition of Cleveland, McKinley moved slowly toward many of those goals, occasionally in the van of congressional and public opinion, more frequently in the wake. Yet by the time an anarchist shot him to death in September, 1901, early in his second term, the nation's foreign policy had changed in several respects. The McKinley administration opened a new era in American diplomacy; and although some of the developments would have occurred no matter who occupied the White House, the colorless but considerate Ohioan did much, however uneasily and reluctantly, to shape the emergence of the United States as a world power.

Theodore Roosevelt, on the other hand, faced the challenges of the new era resolutely and eagerly. Prior to his election as Vice President in 1900, the New York Republican had held no federal office higher than Assistant Secretary of the Navy, but he was better fitted by training and temperament to deal with foreign affairs than any incumbent of this period. A keen student of history and an avid follower of current events, he had a wide circle of talented friends, at home and abroad, with whom he talked and corresponded incessantly. An incurable romantic in some fields, Roosevelt was a realist in diplomacy. He sought to preserve peace by a reasonable balance of power rather than by paper agreements, and he stressed in season and out the importance of the armed forces in international relations. Impulsive by nature, given to exaggeration, never modest about himself, and a captive of late-Victorian concepts of morality, he sometimes seemed ridiculous and occasionally erred badly.

On two matters Roosevelt stood well ahead of most contemporaries. First, he sensed intuitively the leadership the president must provide in twentieth-century diplomacy. Power and responsibility, he asserted, must go hand in hand; the chief executive must employ not only those prerogatives which the Constitution explicitly granted to him but also those which it did not specifically assign to the legislature. Second, he understood clearly the enlarged role the nation must play in world affairs. The people of the United States, he insisted, had no alternative; all they could do was to approach the task manfully with confidence or ignobly with misgivings. Yet, until he was elected in his own right in 1904, Roosevelt did not give free rein to his views on America's obligation to promote world peace. His good offices in terminating the Russo-Japanese War, his aid in liquidating the Moroccan crisis, and his correspondence with heads of state in Europe belong to his second term and will be covered in Book Three.

THE SECRETARIES OF STATE

One continuing question is whether a president or his secretary of state is primarily responsible for shaping foreign policy. As head of the executive branch, the former is entitled to claim credit for successes, just as he must shoulder the blame for failures. In spite of generalizations to the contrary, very few presidents have been consistently their own secretary of state. They may make many of the vital decisions and occasionally negotiate in person, but their other duties prevent them from devoting full attention to external affairs.

James G. Blaine of Maine, who served under Harrison until June 4, 1892, was a secretary of state who made a definable contribution to

American foreign policy. Known as "the Plumed Knight" by his friends and as "Jingo Jim" by his foes, he was a perennial seeker of the presidency and had lost to Cleveland in 1884. As a member of the House from 1863 to 1876 and of the Senate from 1876 to 1881, he had won enormous acclaim as a Republican chieftain. He had first headed the State Department in 1881 but resigned after nine months when Garfield died of an assassin's bullet. Some observers predicted that the less experienced Harrison would be overshadowed by Blaine's prodigious energy and eloquent oratory, but such was not the case. The Secretary turned out to be more cautious on most issues and never infringed upon the President's prerogatives. He was, however, mainly responsible for the International Conference of American States which met in Washington on October 2, 1889, and inaugurated the modern inter-American movement.

John W. Foster, originally of Indiana, finished out Harrison's term when bad health forced Blaine to resign his post. Bewhiskered and erudite, Foster had better previous training than any incumbent of this period, but his tenure was too brief to permit him to make policy.

Walter Q. Gresham, also of Indiana, was Cleveland's choice as secretary of state in March, 1893. A modest and likable man, he had been a life-long Republican until he split with his party over the McKinley Tariff. A gallant soldier and a competent lawyer, he had no special qualifications to preside over the nation's foreign affairs except that he shared Cleveland's impulse to resist innovation and to uphold tradition. He frowned upon overseas expansion and denied that war in Korea affected the vital interests of the United States. He died in office on May 28, 1895, without having contributed anything substantial of his own.

Richard Olney of Massachusetts, Cleveland's second secretary of state, differed from Gresham in training and temperament. Square-hewn and forbidding of figure, with a drooping mustache and stern eyes, Olney had been an able corporation lawyer with no love for publicity until Cleveland made him Attorney General in 1893. In that office he urged federal firmness and the use of national troops during the Pullman Strike in Chicago in 1894. In the State Department he was less bound to the past than Gresham, but the contrast was chiefly in manner and personality. Where Gresham was conciliatory and mild, Olney was strong-willed and outspoken. Where Gresham handled an Anglo-Nicaraguan controversy in the spring of 1895 with a minimum of pressure, Olney a few months later magnified the Anglo-Venezuelan boundary dispute out of all proportion and encouraged Cleveland to present the British with a virtual ultimatum. Olney was also a vigorous defender of executive prerogatives, notably in the area of recognition.

After leaving office, he had some perceptive things to say about the policy of isolationism in the twentieth century.

Under McKinley, the State Department had three heads within a space of five months. First the President appointed seventy-four-year-old John Sherman of Ohio, mainly to vacate a Senate seat for his friend Mark Hanna. Sherman had held office continuously since 1855—six years in the House, thirty-two in the Senate, and four as Secretary of the Treasury. He had also been chairman of the Foreign Relations Committee from 1886 to 1893 and again from 1895 to 1897. But failing faculties and embarrassing lapses of memory made him a poor selection and placed the burden of work on his competent Assistant Secretary, William R. Day, also of Ohio. With Sherman's retirement on April 27, 1898, Day became secretary in name as well as in fact. A shy, imperturbable individual, Day was probably McKinley's most intimate associate; and since the two agreed essentially on all public matters, it is not easy to tell where one man's contribution ends and the other's begins. Day's tenure was brief. On September 16, 1898, McKinley named him chairman of the commission to negotiate the peace treaty with Spain and soon thereafter appointed him to the federal judiciary.

John Hay, the third Ohioan to be McKinley's secretary of state, served from September 30, 1898, until his death on July 1, 1905. His was the longest incumbency between Hamilton Fish's retirement in 1877 and Cordell Hull's accession in 1933. Born in Illinois but mostly a resident of Cleveland and Washington, a protégé of Lincoln and a poet of repute, Hay had filled minor positions in three European legations before becoming Assistant Secretary in 1879. A man of wealth and culture, fastidious in manners and sensitive to criticism, he welcomed a nomination by McKinley in March 1897 to be ambassador to Great Britain. During the next year and a half he was instrumental in forging a firm Anglo-American diplomatic friendship, and a determination to preserve and strengthen that bond colored his work as secretary of state. His part in popularizing the open door policy for China is generally regarded as his most important contribution to American diplomacy, and his name customarily appears near the top of any list of outstanding secretaries. Actually, a chronic hypochondria kept him from his desk for long stretches of time, and his conspicuous inability to get along with the Senate spelled defeat for many of his treaties. In retrospect, it is clear that occasionally Hay should have encouraged McKinley to adopt a bolder course or Roosevelt a more cautious one, but he was always careful not to encroach upon the prerogatives of the president. To his credit, he gave loyal and devoted service to two chief executives of completely opposite personalities and retained the love and esteem of both.

THE CONGRESSIONAL LEADERS

It is not to be supposed that the legislature allowed the executive a free hand in shaping foreign policy between 1889 and 1905. On the contrary, a few members of Congress exerted considerable influence of a positive or negative sort. Those who presided over key committees had the best opportunity for constructive work, yet the names of most chairmen of the Senate Committee on Foreign Relations and the House Committee on Foreign Affairs are deservedly forgotten. An exception was Cushman K. Davis, Republican of Minnesota, a member of the Senate since 1887 and chairman from May, 1897, until his death in November, 1900. Learned but partisan, an expert parliamentarian rather than a compelling speaker, he won fame as a champion of imperialism. As one of the peace commissioners in Paris, he demanded that Spain cede the entire Philippine archipelago, and he then skillfully steered the treaty to victory in the Senate. Davis was also largely responsible for the amendments to the first Hay-Pauncefote agreement of February 5, 1900; by insisting upon changes that were extremely distasteful to the Secretary, he paved the way for a second pact which was much more favorable to the United States.

To his intense disappointment, Henry Cabot Lodge, Republican of Massachusetts, did not succeed Davis as chairman of the Foreign Relations Committee. First the rule of seniority and then control of the chamber by the Democrats kept the coveted prize from him until May, 1919. Nonetheless, this thin, wiry man with a haughty and aristocratic mien, whose light-brown hair and close-cropped beard were beginning to be streaked with gray, was in these years the most articulate and best informed spokesman on external affairs on Capitol Hill. An ardent expansionist, a resolute defender of the Monroe Doctrine, a vigorous exponent of an American-controlled canal, a constant advocate of a big navy, and a leading architect of the new colonial system, Lodge reflected the changing character of American foreign policy. An eloquent orator and an effective floor leader, he was a lifelong intimate of Roosevelt. But Lodge wore no man's collar. A supreme egotist, he regarded himself as the successor to Webster and Sumner in the Senate. Such was his fierce pride in the prerogatives of that body that he did not hesitate to defy Roosevelt or wreck a cherished friendship with Hay.

No other legislator matched Lodge's intense concern with foreign affairs during the years from 1889 to 1905. A few Republican senators made a contribution, but their main interests lay elsewhere. Those deserving mention are Joseph B. Foraker of Ohio, for his insistence on armed intervention in Cuba and authorship of Puerto Rico's first organic law; Nelson B. Aldrich of Rhode Island, for his part in passing the peace treaty with Spain; Mark Hanna of Ohio, for a comparable role in gaining legislation which made Panama the route of the future canal; Redfield Proctor of Vermont, for a single speech on Cuban atrocities which convinced the noninterventionists in his party that a showdown with Spain could not be avoided; and Albert J. Beveridge of Indiana, for his passionate advocacy of overseas expansion and the white man's burden.

Being in a minority for most of this period, the Democrats had less opportunity to shape foreign policy in a positive way. They controlled the White House for only four of the sixteen years and the Congress for but two. Compelled to criticize and oppose, their main contributions were negative in character. When their attacks coincided with divisions in the ranks of their rivals, they could, for example, force the McKinley administration to accept armed intervention in Cuba or important amendments to the Hay-Pauncefote Treaty. The severity of the Democratic indictment of imperialism made a continuation of the colonial adventure less likely, and the political implications of their appeal to Anglophobia obliged Hay to limit his collaboration with Great Britain. The Democrats' outstanding spokesman on Capitol Hill in these years was Senator John T. Morgan of Alabama, who deplored Cleveland's refusal to annex Hawaii, urged freeing Cuba from Spanish tyranny, championed Nicaragua as the canal route, and denounced Roosevelt's role in the Panama uprising.

THE CONSTITUTIONAL CONFLICT

However intense or subdued were America's interests in foreign policy, the historic conflict for control did not flag. In the years 1889–1905 president and Congress continued to stake out their claims. Some new practices were imposed upon those developed in the preceding period; certain established customs remained unchanged. More and more treaties ran afoul of the Senate; on one occasion the legislature talked of impeaching the executive for defying its wishes in recognition.

In the realm of appointments, the Senate did not challenge the presidents' selections of secretaries of state, and every nomination to that post was quickly confirmed. Lesser diplomats fared almost as well. In 1889 the upper house did reject Murat Halstead as minister to Germany because of his newspaper attacks on the Senate, and in 1897 its leaders persuaded McKinley to appoint the inexperienced Charles P. Bryan as minister to Brazil rather than to China. The use of executive agents provoked the customary grumbling, but more because of the policies they pursued than because of the status they held. Two new irritants arose, however, in this area. One was the growing tendency of presidents to send delegates to international conferences without seeking senatorial approval. The second was McKinley's choice of senators to help negotiate the peace with Spain. In July, 1813, the Senate had declined to confirm Gallatin as envoy to Ghent until he had resigned as Secretary of the Treasury. In September, 1898, with Congress not in session, McKinley named Davis, William P. Frye, and George Gray to a five-man commission which completed its labors before the lawmakers reassembled. Several irate senators argued that their colleagues were ineligible to serve, and they condemned the President for violating the principle of the separation of powers. McKinley is alleged to have promised, under pressure, not to indulge in the practice again.

Tension over appropriations was conspicuously absent between 1889 and 1905. There were no stormy debates over the contingent fund or demands that a president make a public accounting, no important attempts to abolish legations in order to register displeasure toward the country involved, and no major battles over treaties requiring the House to defray the costs. With appropriations, as with appointments, the legislature did little to impede the executive's direction of foreign policy.

Congressional requests for information about the conduct of diplomacy likewise failed to embitter relations with the president. The call for documents was constant. The entanglements in Hawaii and Samoa, the crises with Chile and England, the prolonged negotiations with Spain, the polemical debates over the Philippines, the siege of the legations at Peking, the battle over the canal route, and the charges of executive usurpation in Panama and the Dominican Republic, all whetted legislative curiosity. But the request for papers invariably contained a proviso that nothing harmful to the public interest should be divulged. The president was thus free to decide which documents might be withheld. Similarly, the growing use of committee investigations barely affected the handling of external affairs. Inquests probed into the uprising in Hawaii in 1893 and the insurrection in the Philippines in 1899, but they did not result in a censure of executive policies. The resort to public hearings on controversial treaties still lay in the future.

Recognition, on the other hand, generated considerable friction between president and Congress. As in the past, there was more trouble when the issue involved newly created states or groups seeking belligerent status than when it concerned the change of regime in an existing nation. In a period that saw frequent revolutions in the turbulent countries of the New World, the State Department adhered to Jefferson's principle of acknowledging any stable government which represented the will of the people and discharged its international obligations. Only in the case of Hawaii did disagreement arise. The

Democrats and the anti-imperialists deplored as precipitate and premature Harrison's recognition of the new republic on January 28, 1893; the Republicans and the annexationists attacked as belated and begrudging Cleveland's acceptance of the same regime, after he failed to restore the monarchy, on August 17, 1894. But these differences were over policy, not prerogative.

More substantial divergences arose over the recognition of new states. Cuba was one storm center. On December 9, 1896, Senator J. Donald Cameron, Republican of Pennsylvania, introduced a joint resolution directing the President to acknowledge the independence of the Cuban rebels. Since such a step was not justified by the facts and might have led to an immediate war with Spain, the Cleveland administration held back. Fearful, however, lest the Republican-controlled Foreign Relations Committee submit a favorable report, Secretary Olney issued a release on December 19 in which he insisted that the power to recognize independent states rested "exclusively with the Executive." Arguing that a joint resolution on that subject was "important only as advice of great weight voluntarily tendered," he left the impression that Cleveland would ignore any congressional instructions to recognize the so-called Cuban Republic.

Olney's claim to exclusive jurisdiction went beyond traditional practices and goaded the Senate into an angry reply. Davis conceded that customarily the president did extend recognition alone but denied that the prerogative was solely his. Congress, too, could decide to act; and if the executive failed to carry out its wishes, he could be impeached and removed from office. The legislature refrained, however, from forcing a showdown on conflicting claims. Although the Cameron resolution was favorably reported on December 21, 1896, it never came to a vote. Instead, Olney encouraged the influential Eugene Hale, Republican of Maine, to read into the record on January 11, 1897, a memorandum prepared by the Assistant Attorney-General which cited numerous precedents to show that the executive had always been the one to recognize new states.

The case of Panama might have provoked a similar controversy if Congress had been in session. On November 13, 1903, Secretary Hay accorded recognition to that new and unstable republic one week after its independence had been proclaimed. Unlike Monroe in 1822 and Jackson in 1837, Roosevelt did not seek legislative collaboration in this vital decision. Many lawmakers subsequently blamed the President for moving too hastily and for seeming to substantiate the charge that the United States had conspired to destroy Colombian sovereignty on the isthmus. But because of the timing, the criticism involved the propriety of the action, not its constitutionality.

Only during the Cuban insurrection did the question of granting belligerent status threaten to embroil the President and Congress. Premature recognition could be dangerous, as the British learned after 1861, and during 1893 and 1894 Secretary Gresham had proceeded most circumspectly toward a revolution in Brazil. Such restraint was more difficult in the case of nearby Cuba. By large majorities the Senate on February 28, 1896, and the House on April 6 passed a concurrent resolution declaring that the belligerency of the rebels ought to be recognized. Since that resolution did not require him to act, Cleveland did nothing. A second attempt to force the hand of the executive came under McKinley when the Senate, by concurrent resolution, recommended that Cuba's belligerency be acknowledged. Administration leaders in the House buried that proposal and thus avoided aligning a Republican Congress against a Republican president.

The treaty-making process, like recognition, kept alive the struggle for control of foreign policy. By 1889 the Senate no longer exercised a compelling voice in the initiation and negotiation of treaties, while Congress as a whole raised fewer objections to implementing international agreements. In the next sixteen years the Clayton-Bulwer pact was the only one to raise the question of who terminates treaties, and there the issue was one of diplomatic method, not of constitutional power. On the other hand, the battle to gain senatorial consent grew more intense, and the evasion of the two-thirds rule by executive agreements became more frequent.

Statistically, the Senate approved without change most of the major treaties from 1889 to 1905. These included the agreement with England and Germany establishing a condominium in Samoa (June 14, 1889); a convention with Great Britain referring to arbitration the Bering Sea fur seals controversy (February 29, 1892); the Treaty of Paris with Spain concluding peace and ceding territory (December 10, 1898); a convention to settle disputes by pacific means, signed at the First Hague Conference (July 29, 1899); the agreement with England and Germany partitioning the Samoan group (December 2, 1899); the second Hay-Pauncefote Treaty with Great Britain dealing with an interoceanic canal (November 18, 1901); an abortive pact with Denmark purchasing its West Indian islands (January 24, 1902); the Hay-Herrán Treaty with Colombia conferring rights to build a canal (January 22, 1903); an accord with England submitting the Alaskan boundary controversy to a tribunal of jurists (January 24, 1903); a pact with Cuba defining the future relations of the two countries (May 22, 1903); and an agreement with Panama permitting the construction of a canal through a ten-mile strip in which the United States could act as if it were sovereign (November 18, 1903).

Several important treaties won senatorial consent only after they had been amended. Not all of them went into effect. The Cuban reciprocity agreement of December 11, 1902, did, but others fell by the wayside. The British rejected changes made in the first Hay-Pauncefote Treaty of February 5, 1900, while Roosevelt refused to accept the modifications made by the Senate in a general arbitration pact with England of December 12, 1904. The upper house approved a treaty signed at Brussels on July 2, 1890, only after appending reservations, and it probably would have done the same to the Hague Convention for the Pacific Settlement of International Disputes of July 29, 1899, if the American delegates had not already inserted a disclaimer to safeguard the policies of isolationism and the Monroe Doctrine. The presidents did not challenge the right of the Senate to interpret through such reservations the treaty obligations assumed by the United States.

Actually, the Senate defeated directly only one significant treaty in this period. On May 5, 1897, the vote on the amended Olney-Pauncefote arbitration agreement stood at 43 to 26, three short of the necessary majority. That pact was also the sole important victim of the two-thirds rule. The Senate did kill three treaties by failing to act. Lack of sufficient support for the Hawaiian annexation convention of June 16, 1897, caused its sponsors to delay and then resort to a joint resolution. A reciprocity agreement with Newfoundland of November 8, 1902, was not reported until February 11, 1905, at which time it was tabled. A treaty of February 7, 1905, setting up a customs control in the Dominican Republic was not brought to a vote because the antecedents had angered many senators. Cleveland's withdrawal, not the Senate's procrastination, was responsible for the demise of the Hawaiian annexation treaty of February 18, 1893, but the President's motive was dislike of the terms, not fear of rejection. On the other hand, it is impossible to say how many treaties were never concluded because of the senatorial veto.

Only once did an attempt to evade the treaty-making process create friction between the two branches of government. That was when Roosevelt sought initially to set up the Dominican customs control by an executive agreement of January 20, 1905. Such was the protest on Capitol Hill that he quickly recast the arrangements in treaty form. On the other hand, McKinley did not provoke criticism with the armistice protocol of August 12, 1898, which was a logical extension of his authority as commander-in-chief, or with Hay's modus vivendi of October 20, 1899, which paved the way for ending the Clayton-Bulwer Treaty and settling the Alaskan boundary. Indeed, the most flagrant evasion of these years came in the joint resolution of July 7, 1898, to annex Hawaii, when President and Congress agreed to act without a treaty.

Divided control of the armed forces did not, between 1889 and

1905, paralyze the conduct of foreign policy or place undue strains on the relations of president and Congress. In the one declared war of the period, the constitutional machinery functioned exactly as the framers had intended. When McKinley had exhausted the resources of diplomacy in dealing with Spain, he felt unable to intervene militarily in Cuba without legislative authority. "The issue," he concluded in a special message of April 11, 1898, "is now with Congress." That body responded by empowering him to employ the army and the navy to eject the Spaniards from the island. These years witnessed no undeclared wars but many police actions. At least thirty such operations occurred in the Caribbean, while American sailors and marines landed in Argentina, Chile, Hawaii, Samoa, Korea, Ethiopia, Turkey, and Morocco. The most formidable expedition was the one to rescue the legations at Peking in 1900. About 3,000 men were in the relief column that left Tientsin on August 4, a number exceeded only by Russia and Japan. On that occasion a few Democrats charged the Republican president with usurping the prerogatives of Congress; but since the legislature had adjourned before the crisis broke and since neither party desired a special session in an election year, these complaints produced no results.

There were a few episodes in this period which revealed how profoundly the president's powers as commander-in-chief could influence foreign policy, but in none did they actually encroach upon Congress' prerogative to declare war. Harrison's dispatch of a cruiser in May, 1891, to capture a Chilean merchantmen that had violated American neutrality laws might have provoked hostilities. McKinley's sending the *Maine* on a goodwill mission to Havana in January, 1898, helped bring on the conflict with Spain. Roosevelt exploited a previously planned naval concentration in the Caribbean during the winter of 1902–3 to support his suggestion—later his ultimatum—that Germany end its reprisals against Venezuela. He also insured the success of the uprising in Panama in November, 1903, by interposing American warships between Colombian reinforcements and the isthmus. Yet the subsequent criticism of Roosevelt was based upon his alleged collusion with the rebels and his questionable reading of the Colombian treaty, not upon a breach of his military authority or an infringement upon the rights of Congress.

As in the past, the executive made most of the important decisions in foreign policy. The plans for retaining the Philippines were perfected after the Senate and House had adjourned. The two corollaries to the Monroe Doctrine—Olney's in July, 1895, and Roosevelt's in December, 1904—never received legislative sanction. The two open door notes were dispatched in September, 1899, and July, 1900, when Congress was not in session. The President was primarily responsible for American attendance at the First Hague Conference in May, 1899, for the ultimatum to Germany to end the Venezuelan blockade in December, 1902, and for the choice of the Panama route even after Colombia had rejected the Hay-Herrán Treaty in August, 1903. Occasionally a frustrated president, such as Cleveland, might dump a puzzling problem into the lap of Congress for a solution; more frequently the men on Capitol Hill consciously sought to shape foreign policy. Thus it was pressure from the legislature that brought about armed intervention in Cuba in April, 1898. The Senate was chiefly instrumental in securing more favorable terms when the Clayton-Bulwer Treaty was abrogated in November, 1901. It also blocked all Anglo-American agreements for compulsory arbitration. Congress as a whole can claim credit for giving impetus to the calling of the First International Conference of American States in 1888, to the stiffening of the Cleveland administration's attitude toward the Venezuelan boundary controversy in 1895, and to the new opposition of the State Department, in 1903, to the forcible collection of debts by European powers in the Americas. In short, the conflict which the framers of the Constitution bequeathed did not prevent each branch from playing a distinct role in the shaping of foreign policy.

IO

❯❯❯-❯❯❯-❯❯❯-❯❯❮❮❮-❮❮❮-❮❮❮-❮❮❮

The Roots of Imperialism

THE CENTRAL PROBLEM in diplomacy for the period 1889–1905 is why the United States broke with tradition and annexed an overseas empire. The consequences of that momentous step in reorienting American foreign policy now elicit little disagreement, but the reasons for it are still a matter of dispute. Imperialism in the 1890's was, of course, the product of many forces and of a world very different from today's.[1] To understand it fully we must analyze its roots, examine the main events that insured its triumph, and discuss the decisions of men whose ideas are no longer popular or germane. We must also keep in mind that the acquisition of colonies was partly fortuitous and irrational, a development that cannot be explained solely as the work of a few dedicated expansionists with a definite goal.

THE STRATEGIC ROOT

Of all the roots of American imperialism, the strategic is the easiest to isolate. National security had always been a consideration in earlier additions of territory. During the era of continental expansion, there was a plea to obtain defensible frontiers, to eliminate bellicose neighbors, and to forestall European monarchies. The first stirrings of overseas expansion in the 1850's reflected the need for improved communi-

---

[1] "Imperialism" is used here in the narrowest sense: the rule or dominion of one state or people over another. More specifically, it denotes the establishment of colonies. Where states or people are controlled for economic or other purposes without complete loss of independence or sovereignty, the word "protectorate" is employed.

cation between the Atlantic and Pacific coasts and for coaling stations to service the new steam warships. These dreams of noncontinental possessions, both before the Civil War and immediately after, were premature; they did not face up to the difficult question of whether distant and different peoples would be admitted into the Union promptly and on a footing of complete equality. That was one reason why, for almost a quarter-century after Appomattox, the general public remained largely indifferent to any outward thrust.

In dispelling that apathy the navy played an important part. Since the professional sailor has a duty to plan for the future and to prepare for all contingencies, he has tended to be a staunch expansionist, eager to acquire insular outposts from which his vessels could operate against the enemy. During the 1880's, however, his primary concern was with the technical problems connected with the building of the so-called "new navy"—the size of ships, the caliber of guns, the capacity of bunkers, the width of armor plate. Hence the case for imperialism on strategic grounds was stated best initially, not by a board of experts after surveying existing facilities for the fleet, but by a single officer after inquiring into the history of the British Empire.

Alfred T. Mahan's *The Influence of Sea Power upon History, 1660–1783*, published in May, 1890, was the first of several scholarly treatises designed to explain the source of England's current greatness. That explanation Captain Mahan found in maritime supremacy. The British had wisely brought together a flourishing foreign commerce which enriched their citizens, a healthy merchant marine which transported their trade, an incalulably strong navy which protected their shipping throughout the globe, a convenient chain of overseas bases at which their naval craft could refuel and repair, and a far-flung empire which supplied raw materials for their industry and a ready market for their manufactures. These five elements were mutually self-supporting; taken together, they spelled power and prosperity. Without them nations would fall behind in the march of civilization. The lesson for Americans was clear.

Mahan realized that the United States could not rival England at once. The planting of colonies was the last step, not the first. Initially the government must perservere in its construction of modern warships that could control the waters around the North American continent. Next it must deny to potential enemies certain strategic sites within its defensive perimeter. Finally it must occupy key positions along the main water routes of the world. Since both political parties were already committed to building up the navy, Mahan, in his nonhistorical writings, concentrated on the last two steps. Beginning in December, 1890, with "The United States Looking Outward," he printed in leading magazines a series of articles which called attention to the strategic features of the Caribbean, the need to secure an insular foothold there, and the changes in commerce and warfare that the future interoceanic canal would bring about. Cuba, the Isthmus of Panama, and Hawaii he linked together in a single system vital to American security. With an uncanny sense of timing Mahan completed these essays as the newspaper headlines spoke of German ambitions in Hawaii, British intransigence toward Venezuela, and Spanish impotence in Cuba. Collected in book form in 1897 under the title *The Interest of America in Sea Power, Present and Future*, these pieces familiarized many intelligent citizens with the outlying areas the United States would some day control.

Just as important was the acceptance of Mahan's theories by men well placed to shape foreign policy. The gist of his thinking can be read in the reports of Navy Department officials and in the speeches of Congressmen eager to strengthen the fleet. Three of his most effective exponents were Theodore Roosevelt, Henry Cabot Lodge, and Benjamin F. Tracy, all of whom Mahan knew personally by 1890. As Secretary of Navy under Harrison, Tracy was partly responsible for giving Mahan the leisure in which to develop his ideas on sea power and for readying the ships which vindicated his doctrines during the War with Spain. Lodge served on the House Naval Affairs Committee from 1889 to 1893 and on the Senate Foreign Relations Committee beginning in 1895. Roosevelt became Assistant Secretary of the Navy in March, 1897. It was Lodge, for example, who told the Senate on March 2, 1895, that "without sea power no nation has been really great" and that without possession of the Hawaiian Islands, "the key of the Pacific," it would be folly to build an interoceanic canal. Mahan had argued that until it established Caribbean bases, the United States would suffer, not gain, from a piercing of the isthmus; to illustrate that point, Lodge exhibited on Capitol Hill a large map showing every British naval facility prominently marked with a red maltese cross.

Pre-eminence as a spokesman for expansion did not mean that Mahan advocated indiscriminately the annexation of territory. Prior to April, 1898, he did not recommend the acquisition of Guam, the Philippines, or any island west of Hawaii. In the Caribbean, he was not interested in densely populated Cuba, Haiti, or Puerto Rico. Before that date he was content to own the Hawaiian group and one of the Danish West Indies, to control the interoceanic canal, and to lease a harbor in Central or South America. Nor did Lodge or Roosevelt ask for much more until the War with Spain began. In 1897 Roosevelt did allude frequently to the Philippines, but not with the thought of annexing them; he simply wished to hit the Spanish navy wherever it could be found. Dewey's victory in Manila Bay opened new vistas to these expansionists, and by September, 1898, the more extreme had gone far beyond the program which Mahan had previously developed in an attempt to sell imperialism on strategic grounds.

THE ECONOMIC ROOT

Care must be taken in examining the economic root of American imperialism. As far as Europe is concerned, recent scholarship has tended to play down the familiar motivations for overseas expansion: the need of new markets for disposing of surplus manufactures, the need of new investment opportunities for accumulated capital, the need of additional living space for an expanding population, and the need of an uninterrupted source of raw materials for the factory system. It has assigned more and more weight to psychological and political forces. Yet there is no denying that the rapid development of the American economy in the last quarter of the nineteenth century did prompt many thoughtful observers to assert that the need for new markets was becoming critical. Steel production, for example, jumped from 389,799 tons in 1875 to 8,932,857 in 1898, and the number of bales of cotton being consumed by industry rose from 796,616 in 1870 to 3,873,165 in 1900. Even more pertinent are the statistics on foreign trade. In 1897 the value of manufactured articles exported by the United States for the first time exceeded the value of those imported. The same year the margin by which the value of total exports exceeded that of total imports stood at $286,263,144, the largest in history. By 1898 the amount had soared to $615,432,676. These and other figures convinced the American industrialist that, under truly competitive conditions, he could outsell his foreign rivals anywhere in the world. Yet it is significant that when he first began to express concern over a restriction of potential markets, he did not talk about colonies.

This ability to distinguish between the need for markets and the need for colonies can be illustrated in several ways. The First International Conference of American States met in 1889 primarily to stimulate trade among the nations of the New World. A customs union for the Western Hemisphere and experiments in reciprocity not overseas dependencies, were felt to be the solution for new commercial outlets. Even more revealing was the initial reaction to the disintegration of China after the Sino-Japanese War of 1894–5, a process which some feared might eliminate 400 million customers in Asia. No one seriously urged the United States to annex part of the Asiatic mainland or islands in the Western Pacific. The main goal was to prevent the European powers from partitioning the Celestial Kingdom into spheres of influence where special privileges would destroy equality-of-trade opportunity. How this might be achieved was not clear at the end of

1897, but all Americans agreed that diplomacy, not force or land grabbing, must be relied upon.

Which territories, if any, did the expansionists actually seek for their economic benefits prior to the War with Spain? The discussion on that point was distressingly vague. Men talked of new acquisitions in the name of duty and destiny or on such grounds as national security, international advantage, racial superiority, and the white man's burden. With the business community indifferent and even hostile to colonialism before 1898, the material rewards had to be stressed by Mahan and those political leaders who demanded a vigorous foreign policy. Mahan never doubted that overseas possessions were a source of wealth which would promote commerce, strengthen the merchant marine, bolster the navy, and enrich both industry and agriculture. Yet even his territorial program was limited, and he was more interested in Hawaii and a Caribbean foothold for their strategic advantages than for their economic benefits.

Not until the very eve of the War with Spain was the economic case for imperialism fully articulated, and its subsequent elaboration must be attributed to the broadening horizons that a military victory revealed. Albert J. Beveridge, still an unknown Republican from Indiana, was among the first to insist that the United States could win new markets only by establishing "trading-posts throughout the world as distributing points for American products." Speaking at Boston on April 27, 1898, four days before Dewey overwhelmed the Spaniards at Manila Bay, Beveridge prophesied that great self-governing colonies would grow about those trading posts and carry American civilization to "shores hitherto bloody and benighted." At Indianapolis on September 16, the day McKinley instructed his commissioners on the peace terms, Beveridge referred to the existing glut in capital and labor. He predicted that over 10,000 Americans would emigrate to Puerto Rico, Hawaii, and the Philippines to develop their forests, fields, and mines. That same month Charles A. Conant, an authority on banking and finance, argued in *The North American Review* that new markets and opportunities must be found if the nation's surplus capital was to be profitably employed. If the United States were to sit idly by and allow others to monopolize the trade of Africa and Asia, Conant warned, a social revolution would ensue at home.

These belated economic arguments for imperialism were not responsible for American intervention in Cuba in April, 1898. The War with Spain was humanitarian in its origin, not materialistic. Although some individuals in the United States—holders of devastated property on the island, shipowners engaged in Cuban trade, publishers of the yellow press, and those who might obtain governmental contracts—stood to gain from the conflict, the vast majority of citizens simply yielded to an outraged conscience and a traditional hatred of Spain. The business community tried for three years to withstand those emotions. Editorials in trade journals, petitions sent to Washington, and the proceedings of chambers of commerce suggest that the articulate banking, mercantile, and industrial groups were loath to embark upon any crusade for humanity that might jeopardize the return of prosperity. Recovery from the depression which began in 1893 had been delayed twice, once by the war scare over Venezuela in 1895 and again by the free silver campaign in 1896. The upturn of 1897, it was felt, must not suffer a similar fate.

Under the warming rays of easy military victories, opposition by business leaders to foreign adventures quickly evaporated. Two factors account for this abrupt change during 1898. One was the realization that the war would not last very long or harm the process of recovery. The second was the opportunity that Dewey's triumph at Manila offered in the impending contest for the threatened markets of Asia. It was widely assumed that a foothold in the Philippines would nullify the advantages that Russia, Germany, England, and France had recently gained by extracting long-term leaseholds from China. The hard-headed businessman yielded as readily as the expansionist politician to the dream that colonies in the Western Pacific would be economically profitable; he was no more perceptive than the zealous naval officer in sensing that such possessions might be a strategic liability, not a military asset.

THE RELIGIOUS ROOT

More difficult to define is the religious root of imperialism. It is easy enough to show that foreign missions provided the first contacts with certain islands in the Pacific and with several kingdoms in the Orient. It is well known that the United States government often saw conditions in those remote regions through missionary eyes. It is true that an occasional closing of areas to missionary activity aroused protest in religious circles. It has also been demonstrated that American churches, particularly the Protestant denominations, were deeply stirred by the bloodshed in Cuba and that increasingly in 1898 they urged armed intervention on moral grounds. Nor can it be denied that during the same summer many clergymen were dazzled by the boundless opportunities to labor for the Lord in East Asia, just as many businessmen were swept away by visions of an inexhaustible market in China. But the question recurs: did working in the vineyard require the acquisition of colonies? Actually, the men of the cloth failed to explore the problem fully, just as the men of the counting house too easily assumed that trade followed the flag and just as the men in uniform too readily argued that unfortified footholds in the Western Pacific would be a strategic asset.

Only after the War with Spain had begun did American religious bodies and periodicals launch a systematic campaign for overseas territory. For some years before, however, they had helped develop a climate of opinion which made that campaign successful. By asserting that injustice and suffering everywhere is the concern of all and by stressing the responsibility of the powerful to lift up the weak, they contributed toward destroying the provincialism of American citizens and toward reminding them of their obligations before God and man. In 1885 the American Home Missionary Society forged an important link between religious duty and manifest destiny by publishing *Our Country: Its Possible Future and Its Present Crisis* by Josiah Strong, a Congregational minister.

Like many of his nonclerical contemporaries, Strong was imbued with racist notions. He saw the Anglo-Saxon as the ultimate victor in the struggle for existence which the pressure of population upon the means of subsistence caused. Strong viewed that triumph with equanimity because he believed that the Anglo-Saxon possessed a "genius for colonizing" and exemplified the merits of civil liberty and spiritual Christianity. It is manifest, he wrote, that "the Anglo-Saxon holds in his hands the destinies of mankind" and that the United States will become "the principal seat of his power." Strong expected that virile nation to "move down upon Mexico, down upon Central and South America, out upon the islands of the sea, over upon Africa and beyond." In his pages there is more than a single religious motivation for overseas expansion, but the impulse of a militant, self-confident Christianity is clearly evident.

THE EMOTIONAL ROOT

The most difficult root of American imperialism to isolate and identify is the emotional . The simplest element in the mixture was a desire for adventure. To some Americans in the 1890's the long years of peace since Appomattox had become oppressive. They contended that the routine business of making a living, with its emphasis on material accomplishments and divisive competition, was sapping the moral fiber of the people, destroying their sense of national unity, and unfitting them to cope with future crises. Many of these men looked with envy upon the stirring deeds of empire building in which their European contemporaries were engaged. Roosevelt was only the most prominent of those who preached the gospel of the strenuous life and stressed the need for a revival of patriotism and valor. His views were shared by

Beveridge, who had hoped for a military rather than a political career; by Oliver Wendell Holmes, Jr., who never forgot in his judicial chambers his own ordeal by fire in the Civil War; by Brooks Adams, who idolized the warrior in his gloomy survey of Western civilization; and by Albert Shaw, who reflected the rising tide of jingoism in his informative *Review of Reviews*.

To this desire for adventure were added conscious and subconscious sentiments of force, combativeness, and even brutality. These stemmed not from the example of other nations but from the tensions and frustrations within American society. The last decade of the century, especially the years of depression beginning in 1893, witnessed widespread anxiety and restlessness. The increasing disparity between rich and poor, the growing bitterness of the farmer, the rising violence in labor disputes, the futile march of Coxey's army, and the dire forebodings over the apparent end of free land and the ostensible overproduction in industry caused many to look to the future with misgiving. This pessimism found an outlet in frequent displays of pugnacity and jingoism.

From a desire for adventure and conflict it was but a short step to rationalizing their inevitability. Here the biological theories of Charles Darwin proved useful. In his *Origin of Species* in 1859 the British scientist suggested that all plant and animal life had evolved through a struggle for existence among competing species. Nature selected for survival those species which best adapted themselves to a changing environment. In 1871 Darwin linked the human race to this evolutionary process in his *Descent of Man*. Subsequently Herbert Spencer and his American disciples transferred the concept to the realm of economics and sociology to justify the capitalistic system and a laissez-faire ideology of government. By the middle of the 1880's racists and political scientists were also drawing upon the Darwinian hypothesis when they described international relations as a jungle in which the weak were crushed and the virile spread themselves over the globe. It was impossible, they declared, for any nation to remain aloof. To stand still was to fall behind in the march of civilization. In the steaming tropics, in the vast expanse of Africa, and in the broad Pacific the struggle for survival among states went on. For their own safety the American people must look outward. They must meet the challenge of their generation.

Annexing distant possessions, then, promoted the national interest and insured the nation's survival. But it did more. It benefited backward peoples by raising their standard of living and by teaching them the art of self-government. Here was an ennobling purpose, a civilizing mission that it was the duty—indeed, the destiny—of certain races to undertake. It was a task for those who had demonstrated their superior fitness to utilize fully nature's resources, to develop wisely a national state, and to reproduce their political organization in new areas. It was a job, so these racists and publicists contended, for the Anglo-Saxons. The British and the Germans had already taken the field. When would the Yankee stock vindicate its blood and its heritage?

This challenge to Americans appeared in various writings which combined pseudo-scientific theories and unalloyed prophecy. In *Harper's Magazine* in March, 1885, John Fiske, a leading popularizer of Darwin in the United States, predicted that "every land on the earth's surface that is not already the seat of an old civilization shall become English in its language, in its religion, in its political habits." The title of his essay was "Manifest Destiny." That same year Josiah Strong expounded similar ideas in a chapter of *Our Country* headed "The Anglo-Saxon and the World's Future." In 1890 James K. Hosmer's *Short History of Anglo-Saxon Freedom* conveyed the impression that democracy was the contribution of a single race. Also in 1890 John W. Burgess, a leading political scientist at Columbia University, argued that "there is no human right to the status of barbarism." In an otherwise scholarly book on constitutional law he justified imperialism on the ground that the politically unfit must be ruled, in the interest of all mankind, by the able and the strong. These champions of order and stability would be Anglo-Saxons.

Precedent existed for this appeal to racial pride and institutional superiority. During the Mexican War some expansionists had warned that in the New World the weaker Latins must yield to the hardier Anglo-Saxons. One thing that distinguished the manifest destiny of the 1890's from that of fifty years before was the intrusion of racist jargon and the evolutionary hypothesis. In both periods the United States seemingly had no choice but to expand, yet in the 1840's the emphasis had been on enlarging the area of freedom so that the democratic experiment could be conducted on a continental scale. Before the Civil War the contiguous lands annexed were to be erected into new states and admitted into the Union on a basis of complete equality. At the end of the century sovereignty was to be established over distant areas for economic, strategic, and humanitarian purposes. Since the inhabitants were regarded as backward and in need of both spiritual uplift and political apprenticeship, they were to be kept in the status of a dependency.

There was still another difference between the old manifest destiny and the new. International relations, argued the exponents of the latter, had entered a new phase. In a world in which all nations had to struggle for survival, it was no longer possible for the United States to play a passive role, to serve simply as a beacon of republicanism for others to observe and copy. Clay could tell Kossuth in January, 1852, that it was best for free men everywhere that the lamp of liberty be kept "burning brightly on this Western Shore, as a light to all nations." Half a century later men wished to carry the torch into darkest Africa and distant Asia. The appeal to power, while not wholly absent in the days of Polk, was much more prominent in the era of Harrison. In 1851, for example, Fillmore declared that the mission of America was not to "impose upon other countries our form of government by artifice or force, but to teach by example and show by our success." In 1890 Burgess asserted that the institutionally superior nations were obliged "not only to answer the call of the unpolitical populations for aid and direction, but also to force organization upon them by any means necessary."

Before the War with Spain very few writers subjected this new manifest destiny to critical analysis. The pseudo-scientific theories on which it rested were not widely challenged. Mahan was left unanswered, while his followers in Congress were dismissed as jingoes and opportunists. The typical anti-imperialist was preoccupied with domestic issues, and he grossly underestimated the lure of tropical adventures. He could not believe that the nation might abandon its traditional policy, grounded as it was in the principles of democracy, equality, and government with the consent of the governed. Before 1898 the venerable Carl Schurz and the scholarly Theodore S. Woolsey did expatiate on the evils of overseas expansion, but even they did not realize until too late how fully the virus of imperialism had entered the American body politic.

One other factor weakened resistance to the virus. That was a series of diplomatic crises which played upon popular emotions between 1889 and 1898. First came a seemingly unavoidable clash with Germany and England over the Samoan Islands, a conflict which a hurricane helped avort in March, 1889, by virtually wiping out the rival squadrons in Apia harbor. Later that year Americans in the North Pacific became embroiled with the British over fur seals. The *Baltimore* fracas occurred in October, 1891, and war with Chile appeared likely in January, 1892. A year later began the long debate on the wisdom of annexing Hawaii, during which men raised the specter of a prior seizure by England or Germany. Perfidious Albion reappeared as a threat to the New World in March, 1895, in a dispute with Nicaragua, and in December, 1895, in a quarrel with Venezuela. Finally, in February, 1895, a bloody rebellion erupted in Cuba which inflamed American passions for three years and eventually drove the nation into a crusade to free the island from Spanish tyranny.

Although colonies brought little benefit to the United States, the strategic, economic, and religious roots of imperialism were not unimportant. Arguments based upon them may have been misleading and unsound and may seem as out of date in today's world as the concept of manifest destiny and the white man's burden; but millions of citizens accepted them at the time. In retrospect, the emotional root appears the most significant. Indeed, it may be argued that the American people quickly turned away from overseas dependencies because once their emotional needs were satisfied, the other pressures were too weak to uphold a policy that did not accord with their traditional ideals or the principles upon which their institutions rested.

II

The Lure of the Pacific

OF ALL the diplomatic developments from 1889 to 1898 which nurtured the roots of imperialism in the United States, those in the Pacific were the most revealing. Although events in the Caribbean provoked the War with Spain, Hawaii and Samoa provided the first full debate on the annexation of distant lands. For that reason a narrative of the steps leading to the acquisition of a colonial empire should begin with them.

THE GEOGRAPHIC SETTING

Distances are great in the vast Pacific, and few Americans in 1889 knew much about the islands that would soon become a factor in American diplomacy. Most familiar was the independent Hawaiian Kingdom with its capital at Honolulu on Oahu. This large group was strategically situated 2,100 miles from San Francisco and was the only one whose control by a hostile nation could endanger American security. Some alarmists thought England and Germany had designs on Hawaii. No such fears existed for the bleak and desolate Aleutians, an appendage of Alaska, or for the atoll of Wake, unoccupied and unclaimed, or for Midway, where the American flag had been raised on August 28, 1867. Although Congress soon thereafter appropriated $50,-000 to dredge a channel into the central lagoon, the funds were quickly exhausted. By December 9, 1887 Midway was so completely forgotten that Secretary Bayard recommended a symbolic act to demonstrate that the United States had not abandoned its title.

In the more remote reaches of the Pacific, Spain, Germany, and England were the paramount powers. Spain owned the Marianas, the Carolines, and the Philippines. The first contained Guam. The last was part of East Asia but sprawled across an area 1,152 miles long and 688 miles wide. Its capital was Manila on Luzon, an island the size of Ohio. Germany was a latecomer on the colonial scene, but within a few years it had acquired the Marshalls, the Bismarck Archipelago, and part of New Guinea and the Solomons. England shared New Guinea and the Solomons; it either had or would soon annex several groups in the South Pacific. Like Germany and the United States, Britain was interested in Samoa, whose fourteen islands—the largest of which were Savaii, Upolu, and Tutuila—were ruled by native chieftains. Located 4,100 miles from the California coast, the Samoan group was not vital to America's safety, but it did offer opportunities to spread the gospel, exploit the copra trade, and establish coaling stations for steamship lines and naval vessels.

HAWAII: THE ANNEXATION TREATY

American interests in Hawaii date back to the 1820's. Whalers, missionaries, and merchants preceded the diplomats in realizing the importance of the islands, and Honolulu was a thriving port when San Francisco was an unknown harbor. The first formal agreement between the Sandwich Islands, as they were then called, and the United States was signed on December 23, 1826. By December 19, 1842, Secretary Webster could assert that his country was "more interested in the fate of the islands and of their Government than any other nation." That same year brought a presidential statement opposing all attempts by European powers to annex Hawaii. Since the group lay outside of the Americas, it was not protected by the Monroe Doctrine; but, in terms reminiscent of 1823, John Tyler told Congress on December 20 that if any nation sought "to take possession of the islands, colonize them, and subvert the native Government," it could not but "create dissatisfaction on the part of the United States." This Tyler Doctrine, as it came to be known, was reiterated at least seven times in the next decade and was supplemented by two related declarations. One was that the United States might feel justified in using force to prevent Hawaii from falling prey to European aggression; the other that the United States would not enter into a joint arrangement with England and France to guarantee the *status quo.*

It was one thing to claim paramount interest in Hawaii and to warn other nations not to violate its sovereignty. It was something else again to seek annexation, a course which few responsible leaders advocated before 1893. The government in Washington repeatedly pro-

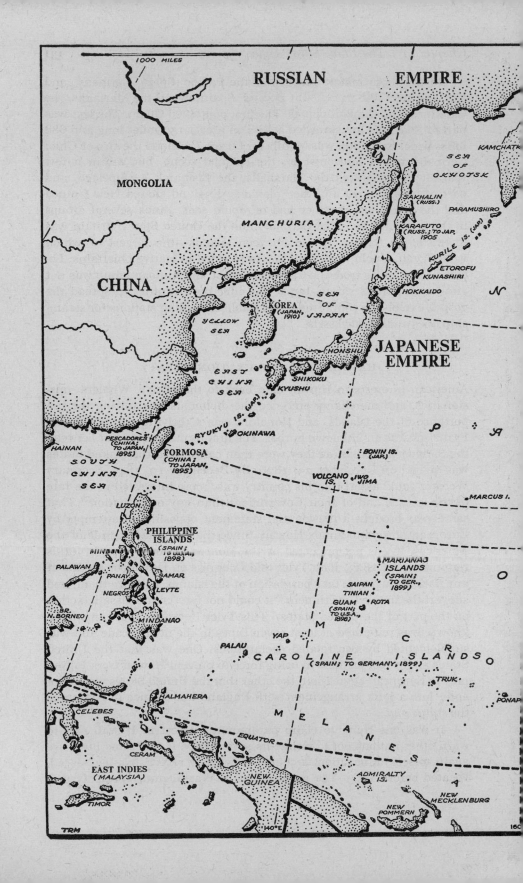

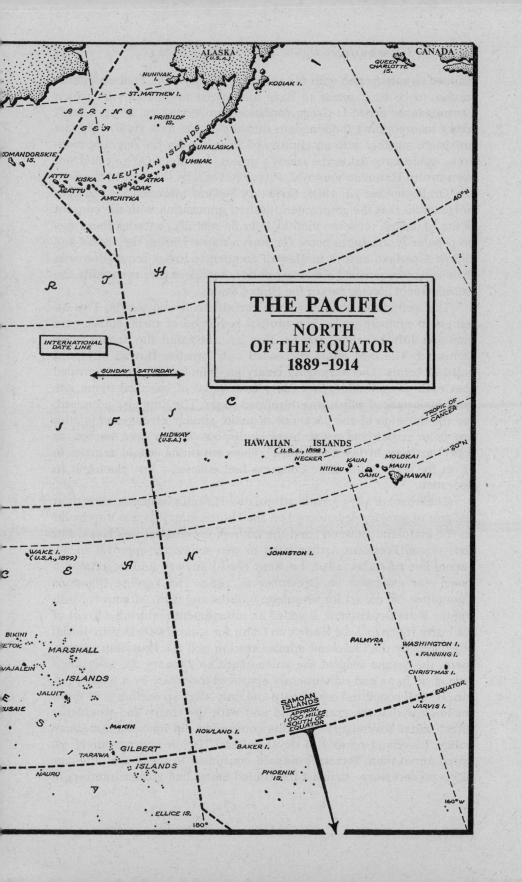

THE PACIFIC

NORTH
OF THE EQUATOR
1889-1914

INTERNATIONAL
DATE LINE

SUNDAY ← → SATURDAY

claimed its satisfaction with the existing situation. The Pierce administration, to be sure, seems to have authorized negotiations by which Commissioner David L. Gregg concluded on August 19, 1854, a draft treaty incorporating the kingdom into the Union as a state. This last provision, together with an annuity of $300,000 for the reigning monarch, would have led to the treaty's defeat; but since Gregg could not even insure Hawaiian approval, Pierce never sent the pact to the Senate. On September 12, 1867, Secretary Seward informed his minister in Honolulu that the government desired annexation with the consent of the islanders; yet seven months later he ruefully conceded there was no popular sentiment at home for such a move. During the 1870's and 1880's American envoys in Hawaii frequently urged acquisition, but their superiors pursued a waiting policy, confident that eventually the islands would become part of the United States.

This confidence stemmed from certain economic trends. Two attempts to promote trade by a mutual reduction of tariff duties were made on July 20, 1855, and on May 21, 1867, but the Senate twice demurred. The next effort succeeded only because Hawaii offered a political bonus. The reciprocity treaty on January 30, 1875, provided that each party would admit, duty free, a list of specified items, the most important of which was unrefined sugar. The King also promised, for the duration of the pact, not to make similar arrangements with any other nation and not to lease or dispose of "any port, harbor, or other territory in his dominions." The convention would remain in effect for seven years after Congress had enacted a law placing it in operation.

The treaty of 1875 greatly stimulated Hawaii's economy, though at the cost of growing dependence on the United States. It was unpopular on the mainland, however, and the outlook for renewal was bleak. For that reason President Arthur tried to win senatorial approval in advance; but when he failed, he went ahead anyway and negotiated a seven-year extension on December 6, 1884. The Foreign Relations Committee did not act for seventeen months and then, without consulting the State Department, it added an amendment requiring a grant of exclusive rights to Pearl Harbor on Oahu for a naval site. Despite initial objections by the Cleveland administration and the Hawaiian government, the Senate adopted the amendment on January 20, 1887, by a vote of 28 to 21 and subsequently approved the treaty by a wider margin. Hawaii concurred reluctantly and only after an exchange of notes made clear that the grant would end with the treaty and would not affect native sovereignty. Yet this concession did not alter American policy. Cleveland refused to develop Pearl Harbor and resolutely opposed annexation. Secretary Bayard continued to speak the language of his predecessors—to insist the United States had greater interests in the islands than any other power and to reject all suggestions for preserving the *status quo* by multilateral guarantees.

Soon thereafter conditions in Hawaii thrust annexation to the fore. A white minority, largely but not exclusively of American descent, dominated the production of sugar as well as the supporting commercial and transportation enterprises. These men had prospered economically under a burgeoning trade with the mainland and politically under a constitution they had imposed upon a weak king in 1887. This bright picture darkened suddenly as a result of the McKinley Tariff of October 1, 1890, and the accession of Queen Liliuokalani on January 29, 1891. The first virtually nullified the benefits of the treaty of 1884, by placing imported sugar on the free list and giving a bounty of two cents a pound to American producers. The second brought to the throne a talented but tactless woman who was determined to restore the power of the monarchy. By January, 1893, the depressed state of the economy and the obvious intention of Liliuokalani to overthrow the constitution of 1887 led to a revolution whose immediate aim was the formation of a republican government and whose ultimate goal was annexation to the United States.

Harrison and Blaine did nothing to foment the uprising. Although both were advocates of a bold foreign policy and overseas expansion, they were absorbed until January, 1892, in the Samoan crisis and a war scare with Chile. In his messages to Congress before 1893 the President never went beyond recommending completion of a cable from the mainland and improvement of the site at Pearl Harbor. Blaine was equally circumspect; he gave Minister John L. Stevens no instructions regarding annexation and passed over in silence all questions that sought to discover what the United States might do if a rebellion occurred. By the end of 1892, to be sure, administration papers were predicting imminent trouble in the islands; Stevens was insisting that the hour to strike had come; and the secretary of the navy was telling the commander of the Pacific Squadron that the government wished to acquire Hawaii. Still, it is unlikely that a lame-duck president would have made a decisive move before March 4, 1893, if the impetus to act had not come from the islands.

If the overthrow of the monarchy on January 16–17, 1893, compelled the American people to face prematurely the question of annexing Hawaii, the irresponsible and unauthorized actions of Stevens injected an additional moral issue. The minister did not instigate the revolution, but his relations with the insurgents were incompatible with his diplomatic status. He recognized the provisional government much too quickly and, having asked for sailors and marines from the cruiser *Boston* then in port, stationed them so that they served more to intimidate the Queen than to protect his legation. Since the insurrec-

tion could not have dethroned Liliuokalani without his support, the
question of Hawaii involved something more than the benefits or disadvantages of imperialism.

Stevens' derelictions were compounded by the precipitate action
of the Harrison administration. Without waiting for all the facts, Secretary Foster extended recognition on January 28, 1893, and signed an
annexation treaty on February 14. Such haste was unjustified and unwise. Despite later allegations, there was no danger of foreign intervention or counterrevolution. The treaty was concluded before spokesmen for the deposed Queen reached Washington, and it left unresolved
the status of Hawaii within the Union. Nor did Harrison hesitate when,
on the day of the signing, he learned that Stevens had raised the
American flag and proclaimed a protectorate, a step Foster had to disavow. Although the President would have preferred a plebiscite in the
islands, he sent the treaty to the Senate on February 15 with a request
for immediate approval. He asserted that "the overthrow of the monarchy was not in any way promoted by this Government," and he argued that the choice lay between permanent acquisition and temporary
control. The Senate chose neither. Although a Republican-dominated
Foreign Relations Committee rushed through a favorable report in two
days, no vote was taken before adjournment on March 4. President-
elect Cleveland made it known that he wished to deal with the treaty,
and opposition on the part of the Democrats ruled out any possibility
of mustering a two-thirds majority.

HAWAII: THE ANNEXATION DEBATE

Once in office, Cleveland handled the Hawaiian problem in a way that
insured a full and partisan debate for the next five years. On March 9,
1893, he withdrew the treaty from the Senate. On March 11 he appointed James H. Blount, Democrat of Georgia and late chairman of
the House Committee on Foreign Affairs, to investigate the causes of
the revolution and the sentiment in the islands for annexation. Commissioned as an executive agent, Blount reached Honolulu on March 29
and at once terminated the protectorate established by Stevens. Three
days later he returned the military contingent to the *Boston*. He then
held extended hearings, from which he concluded that Stevens had
played a grossly improper role and that the islanders did not wish to
join the Union. His findings were undoubtedly correct, but his report of
July 17, 1893, misled Cleveland into thinking that the provisional regime was about to disintegrate. As a result, the President hoped he
could undo the wrong and restore Liliuokalani to her throne. But since
the republican leaders held a firm grip on the reins of government and

since the absolutist Queen threatened to behead her opponents, Cleveland's policy seemed to require the use of force and to repair one injustice by creating another.

Faced with this unhappy prospect, the President forsook his venture in gallantry and dumped the problem into the lap of Congress. On December 18, 1893, he reported Blount's findings, called Stevens' use of troops "an act of war," and summarized his own failure to regain the situation of 1892. He hoped "the extended powers and wide discretion" of the legislature would find a solution "consistent with American honor, integrity, and morality" which he could endorse. Upon receiving this hot potato from a frustrated executive, the lawmakers began a five-month debate which heaped praise and blame on all the principals and contained some prophetic views on overseas expansion. Two resolutions eventually passed. The House version, adopted on February 7, 1894, by a vote of 177 to 78, termed annexation "inexpedient," criticized Stevens, and reaffirmed the principles of the Tyler Doctrine. The Senate resolution, carried unanimously on May 31, 1894, declared that the islanders had a right to choose their own form of government, that the American people must not interfere, and that intervention by a foreign nation in Hawaii would be regarded as an act unfriendly to the United States.

With the President opposed to annexation and Congress maintaining a hands-off attitude, the leaders of the provisional regime took steps to establish a more permanent government, one that would last at least until Cleveland left the White House. During the summer of 1894 they organized a rather undemocratic republic which empowered the executive, under certain conditions, to enter into a political and commercial union with the United States. The American minister promptly extended recognition, a move which Cleveland confirmed on August 17, 1894. The passage of the Wilson-Gorman Tariff that month restored to insular sugar producers the favored position they had enjoyed before 1890; but before its effects could be felt, an unsuccessful royalist coup early in 1895 precipitated another bitter debate on Capitol Hill.

This time Cleveland was on the defensive. His opponents accused him of encouraging Liliuokalani's followers and of facilitating their task by withdrawing all naval forces from Hawaiian waters. They called him blind to American interests because he had allowed Great Britain to lease for cable purposes an island only 500 miles from Honolulu. They introduced into both houses resolutions urging the dispatch of warships to the scene and the start of new negotiations for annexation. The Democrats in Congress again upheld the President. The House refused to concur in a $500,000 appropriation for building a cable to

Hawaii, while the Senate reaffirmed its earlier stand on noninterference. But where the vote on May 31, 1894, was 55 to 0, that on January 26, 1895, was 24 to 22. Expansionist sentiment was rising.

The second Hawaiian debate did more than reflect a growing demand for annexation. It presented a dress rehearsal for the arguments that would be voiced four years later when the nation pondered the wisdom of acquiring colonies after the War with Spain. A division between the two parties was taking shape, with most Republicans advocating a limited program of noncontinental possessions and most Democrats opposing. Two Senators prominent in that later debate summarized the difference. "I do not believe," said George Gray, Democrat of Delaware and future member of the peace commission, that "the traditions, the true interests of this country are consistent with annexation. I believe our policy is a continental one." To which Lodge, a later champion of the treaty of 1898, replied: "I do not mean that we should enter on a widely extended system of colonization. That is not our line." But he did think "we should take all outlying territory necessary to our own defense, to the protection of the Isthmian Canal, to the upbuilding of our trade and commerce, and to the maintenance of our military safety everywhere."

The outbreak of the insurrection in Cuba in February, 1895, and the threat of war with England over Venezuela in December pushed Hawaiian affairs into the background, where they remained during the McKinley-Bryan campaign of 1896. The acquisition of Pacific islands was of minor significance compared with the free-silver issue, but the party platforms that year revealed a persistent division over territorial expansion. Where the Democrats were content with a word of sympathy for the Cuban rebels and a pledge of allegiance to the Monroe Doctrine, the Republicans pushed beyond generalities. They demanded the United States bring peace and independence to Cuba, control Hawaii, purchase the Danish West Indies, and own the Nicaraguan canal.

McKinley's inauguration on March 4, 1897, was the signal for fresh efforts by annexationists in Hawaii and on the mainland. The new President had not shown any interest in expansion, but several factors made him look favorably on Hawaii. Foremost was the need to fulfill his campaign promise for a higher tariff without destroying the reciprocity treaty of 1884. When American sugar interests urged him to end that accord, he decided that annexation offered the safest escape. Tension between Japan and Hawaii also helped. By 1896 Japanese laborers had come to constitute a quarter of the entire population. The government in Tokyo, flushed with a recent victory over China, was in no mood to see that immigration curtailed; and when barriers were raised in March, 1897, it dispatched a cruiser to Honolulu. This move alarmed expansionists in the United States and prompted Assistant Secretary Roosevelt, who wished to establish a protectorate at once, to draft a plan for immediate use if Japan pushed the Hawaiian Republic too far.

In view of these developments, McKinley agreed in May, 1897, to accept Hawaii's pending offer of annexation. Former Secretary Foster drafted the treaty in terms almost identical to those of 1893. Secretary Sherman did the actual signing on June 16, 1897, even though he had just told the Japanese minister, in his absent-minded way, that no negotiations for acquiring the islands were contemplated. This blunder may have encouraged the government in Tokyo to protest, temperately but firmly, on June 19. While disavowing ambitions of its own, it declared that "the maintenance of the status quo in Hawaii is essential to the good understanding of the Powers which have interests in the Pacific." Japan withdrew this protest on December 22, after being assured the rights of its citizens would be safeguarded; but the episode was a portent of the future.[1]

Despite this help from alleged foreign meddling, the annexation treaty encountered rough sailing. It went to the Senate on June 17, 1897, along with a message in which McKinley called the incorporation of Hawaii a "necessary and fitting sequel" to all that had gone before and "a consummation," not a change in policy. The Foreign Relations Committee reported favorably on July 14, but no action could be taken in the ten days of the session that remained. When Congress reassembled in December, the prospect for approval was not bright. Domestic sugar producers, the American Federation of Labor, and anti-imperialist Democrats all voiced hostility. The mounting crisis with Spain over Cuba added another complication, and by March, 1898, the friends of the treaty had to confess they could not muster a two-thirds vote. They turned, therefore, to the device used for annexing Texas. This was a joint resolution, which required only a simple majority in each house. The Foreign Relations Committee introduced such a resolution on March 16, but another delay ensued. As the nation lurched toward war with Spain, most legislators felt that Hawaii could wait, and the executive was inclined to agree. The islands did not become part of the United States until August 12, 1898.

[1] The protest stemmed mainly from Hawaiian delays in meeting Japanese claims, American discrimination against Japanese laborers on the West Coast, and domestic criticism of the cabinet. Although Japan planned no hostile move, the Navy Department prepared for an emergency. On July 12, 1897, it instructed the commander of the Pacific Squadron to proclaim a provisional protectorate in Hawaii if Japan resorted to force. On July 13 it warned the captain of the only battleship in the Pacific to be ready to proceed to the islands at a moment's notice. On July 14 it told the attaché at Yokohama to inform the Department of any significant movements of the Japanese fleet.

SAMOA: EXPERIMENT IN JOINT RULE

Samoa posed a different problem for American expansionists. Its great distance from the California coast—twice that of Hawaii—meant that it attracted little American investment and almost no American residents. Lying beyond the defensive perimeter of the United States, it did not tempt a Marcy or a Seward into thoughts of annexation or even reciprocity. Its proximity to New Zealand and Australia would have made a Tyler Doctrine sound ridiculous. Actually, the situation was reversed; it was England who announced in 1844 that it could not see with indifference any other power assume control of the islands. And while American missionaries and steamship promoters showed some interest in the group, it was Germany who gained economic predominance after the Civil War.

In spite of that predominance, the United States became badly entangled in Samoa beginning in 1878. The entering wedge was a treaty of friendship and commerce of January 17.[2] Aside from the customary clauses relating to trade, it granted the United States the right, but not an exclusive one, to develop for its navy and merchant marine a coaling station at Pago Pago, an excellent landlocked harbor on Tutuila. It also obligated the American government to employ its good offices in disputes between the Samoans and other friendly governments. Although the Senate unanimously approved the pact with only minor amendments, the next decade was one of constant bickering with Germany and England, as the consul of each country, free from telegraphic control, sought by force and intrigue to outstrip his rivals in special concessions. An experiment in joint rule for the municipality of Apia on Upolu did not help, and on June 1, 1886, Secretary Bayard suggested that a conference be held in Washington for the purpose of establishing order under one chief who would be chosen by the natives and supported by the three powers. Bayard also hoped for a tripartite declaration which would bar the signatories from annexing the islands or imposing a protectorate over them.

The Washington Conference met from June 25 to July 26, 1887, and adjourned without reaching a settlement. A prior understanding between Great Britain and Germany, whereby the former promised the latter a free hand in Samoa in return for compensation elsewhere, killed any hope for agreement. Since the United States claimed a paramount interest in Hawaii on strategic and economic grounds, the Eu-

[2] On February 17, 1872, Commander Richard W. Meade negotiated on his own responsibility an agreement with the leading chief on Tutuila. In return for conceding to the United States the exclusive right to establish a naval station on the island, the chief and his people were to enjoy the friendship and protection of the American government. Grant suggested that the Senate modify the protective clause, but the Foreign Relations Committee did not even report the treaty.

ropean countries felt that the government in Washington should recognize the predominant position of Germany in Samoa. But Bayard refused to regard the two problems as related and insisted that the islands remain independent.

Yet a free and peaceful Samoa seemed impossible to attain. For another twenty months fighting continued, and to impartial observers the Germans appeared determined to gain by force what they could not secure by diplomacy. They deposed one king in August, 1887, and made war upon another in December, 1888. Stories of brutality, often exaggerated, finally aroused opinion in the United States; and since 1888 was an election year, the Republicans attacked Cleveland for not upholding American property rights and other interests. On January 15, 1889, the President virtually dared Congress to do more than he had done. Except for two appropriations—one of $500,000 to defend American interests and another of $100,000 to survey, improve, and occupy Pago Pago—the legislature was content to await the advent of Harrison. But as Cleveland and Bayard left office, they had the satisfaction, on February 4, 1889, of receiving a German bid for a new conference at Berlin.

Before the delegates assembled, a dramatic incident publicized as nothing else could the distant Samoan Islands. On March 15–16, 1889, a violent hurricane struck Apia Harbor, destroying or disabling six of the seven warships gathered there in anticipation of trouble. Fifty American sailors lost their lives as two of the three wooden vessels foundered in the boiling surf. All three German craft sank, and only superior engines enabled the sole British cruiser to escape. This act of nature did not prevent a war, for the diplomats had already paved the way for a peaceful solution. But it did ease the task of the conference at Berlin, it did bolster sentiment for a modern American navy, and it did turn attention in the United States outward.

During the deliberations at Berlin from April 29 to June 14, 1889, Secretary Blaine refused to sanction a partition of the islands. Like Bayard, he insisted upon an independent Samoa. To attain that ideal, he reluctantly accepted a treaty which entangled the nation further and looked superficially like a quasi-alliance. This act for the "Neutrality and Autonomous Government of the Samoan Islands" provided for the restoration of the king who had been deposed in 1887 and for the selection of his successor by the native tribes. Although it proclaimed the monarch to be sovereign, it gave the real authority to a chief justice, who was picked by the signatories, and to a revived municipal council of Apia, the president of which was chosen in the same way. Each of the three powers promised to respect the territorial integrity of the islands and the equality of commercial opportunity for all citizens. The arrangement would last three years or longer, unless one party decided otherwise. Called by Harrison "an honorable, just, and equal settlement," the Berlin agreement won the consent of the Senate on February 4, 1890, by a vote of 38 to 12. Properly interpreted, it marked not a new departure into world affairs but the last attempt to preserve an old policy.

Although it helped reduce bloodshed, the condominium of 1889 was neither successful in Samoa nor popular in the United States. On December 1, 1890, Harrison spoke of the arrangement with pride and hope; for the rest of his incumbency he virtually ignored it. Cleveland was not so complacent. During his first term he had endorsed the Bayard formula of preserving Samoan independence; by 1893 he professed to believe that the Republicans had paid too high a price. In his message of December 9 he referred to the "triple protectorate" and pointed to the consequences as illustrating "the impolicy of entangling alliance with foreign powers." Gresham also used the word "alliance" loosely in a report of May 9, 1894, but he was quite accurate when he described the condominium as "a tripartite foreign government imposed upon the natives." With this appeal to isolationism and anti-imperialism in mind, Cleveland told Congress on December 3, 1894, that the Berlin Treaty clearly defied the teachings of the founding fathers, and he invited that body to express its judgment on the propriety of withdrawing from the pact.

To this invitation, renewed on December 2, 1895, the legislature did not respond. The cure of terminating the experiment in joint rule seemed worse than the disease of continuing it. Congressional leaders were not yet ready to divide the islands and thus acquire territory below the equator, but they were also unwilling to renounce the prospect of a coaling station at Pago Pago. The President, on the other hand, having been castigated for hauling down the flag in Hawaii in 1894, did not wish to provoke further criticism by giving up a right held since 1878. Hence he handed the problem on to his successor. But McKinley was not eager to act, and even a successful war, which brought other distant lands beneath the Stars and Stripes, did not affect Samoa. Yet the islands had compelled the American people to think of overseas possessions long before they considered the Philippines; and the eventual partition of the group on December 2, 1899, with Tutuila going to the United States, created no protest or surprise.

12

The Changing Far East

IF THE PACIFIC provided an arena for incidents which nurtured the roots of imperialism in the United States, the Far East between 1889 and 1898 offered little more than a gauge for measuring the profound changes in American foreign policy at the close of the century. Where the debates over Hawaii in the 1890's revealed an increasing popular interest in strategic lands beyond the continental shores and where the negotiations over Samoa disclosed a growing governmental concern for remote islands of negligible economic value, events in East Asia attracted a minimum of attention at the start of the decade and a disproportionate amount at the end. Yet developments in the Orient played a major role in McKinley's decision, after the War with Spain, to retain the Philippines and thereby transform the United States into not only a colonial empire but also a Far Eastern power.

GEOGRAPHY AND TRADE

Like the Pacific, the Far East or East Asia in 1889 was a vast area about which the American people knew very little.[1] The densely populated, sprawling empire of China was the most familiar, thanks to missionary endeavors and a lucrative pre-Civil War commerce. Greater China was

---

[1] The "Far East" and "East Asia" are used interchangeably in this work to denote the area consisting of China, Manchuria, Korea, Japan, eastern Siberia, Mongolia, Sinkiang, and Tibet. The areas known today as "Southeast Asia" and "South Asia" are defined on page 691. In the 1890's the former was regarded as part of the Far East.

larger than all Europe, but by the 1890's the Manchu dynasty exercised only nominal control over Manchuria, while its suzerainty over the once-tributary kingdom of Korea was fast slipping away. The central government had long since agreed to abridgments of its sovereignty and violations of its territorial integrity. Treaties with various European countries had curtailed its authority to levy tariff duties, to collect customs receipts, and to try foreigners in Chinese courts. It had also ceded Hong Kong to England in 1842 and Macao to Portugal in 1887.

China's strongest neighbors were Japan and Russia. Until 1854 the former had remained secluded in the four islands of Hokkaido, Honshu, Shikoku, and Kyushu, which parallel the coast of Siberia and Korea for over a thousand miles. In that year an American expedition under Commodore Matthew C. Perry opened Nippon to the outside world, and by 1868 a period of westernization and stupendous material advancement had begun. Using Britain and the United States as models, the ambitious Japanese founded steamship lines, built railroads, developed manufactures, and created modern military forces. They also extended their authority to the Kuriles in 1875, the Bonins in 1876, and the Ryukyus in 1879. Russia's prominence in East Asia dates from 1858, when it seized from China a vast domain north of the Amur River. Two years later it obtained peacefully the Maritime Province of eastern Siberia. In 1875 Russia renounced its claims to the Kuriles in exchange for Sakhalin, a long narrow island that came within thirty miles of Hokkaido. Russia's chief military base was the port of Vladivostok, close to the boundary of Manchuria and Korea, roughly 700 miles from Tokyo and Peking.

Korea was the weakest of China's neighbors and, by 1889, a likely target for future Russo-Japanese expansion. Known as the Land of the Morning Calm, it had long been under Chinese suzerainty and closed to the outside world. In 1876 the Japanese began to pry open the door with a trade agreement, and six years later, in obvious imitation of Perry, Commodore Robert W. Shufeldt negotiated at the cannon's mouth a treaty of commerce and friendship. Korea, however, did not follow Japan along the road to modernization but became the focal point of a three-cornered rivalry. The Chinese undertook belatedly to regain their former dominant position. The Japanese, eager for a foothold on the mainland, considered the peninsula a logical jumping off place, for it was only a hundred miles from Honshu. The Russians also eyed the kingdom covetously. Since Vladivostok's contact with the European portion of the Romanov empire was by sea and since that harbor froze over in winter, the government at St. Petersburg adopted two significant policies. One was to construct the Trans-Siberian Railroad connecting Vladivostok with the Urals region; the other was to seek a warm-water outlet in Korea or southern Manchuria.

EAST ASIA, 1889-1914

American interests in East Asia had been confined to trade and missionary work, with territorial ambitions conspicuously absent. It would be an exaggeration to say the United States had formulated a Far Eastern policy by 1889, but it had pursued a course designed to promote the economic welfare of its citizens. The objective was to preserve equality of commercial opportunity for all comers, and the means was a general treaty containing the most-favored-nation clause. Such a clause insured that each concession granted to another country, even as a result of force, would automatically extend to the United States. And though in its initial agreements the government at Washington insisted upon extraterritorial rights for its citizens and some control over the tariffs levied by China and Japan, American interests during the nineteenth century seemed best served by maintaining the political independence and territorial integrity of the Manchu empire and by opposing European leaseholds and spheres of influence where discriminatory practices might flourish. Annexations were not seriously contemplated.

Before 1898 America's economic stake in the Far East hardly justified a more positive policy. In the preceding three decades the value of its Asiatic commerce never exceeded 7 per cent of the entire foreign trade, and the average figure was under 6. As late as 1897 the value of exports to all Asia had risen to only 3.7 per cent of the total exports of the United Sates and the value of its imports to but 11.4 per cent of the whole. In that year American investments in Asia amounted to 3.3 per cent of all investments abroad; in round numbers, its $23 million looked small when contrasted with $200 million for Mexico alone. In contrast to the British, few American citizens obtained advisory positions in the Chinese Customs Service, and one result was that concessions for building railroads and telegraph lines, laying submarine cables, and developing mines went almost wholly to Europeans. Of course, so long as American businessmen were occupied with exploiting the home market, they did not regret these lost opportunities abroad; but when they felt a pressing need at the end of the century to dispose of surplus manufactures and to invest accumulated capital, their attitude changed abruptly.

THE SINO-JAPANESE WAR

Before that shift occurred, the State Department revealed its aloofness from diplomatic developments in East Asia. In the spring of 1894 the long smoldering rivalry between China and Japan for control of Korea was about to erupt into armed conflict. On June 22 instructions went to the American minister at Seoul to use his best efforts to preserve peace; three days later he associated himself with his British, French, and Russian colleagues in urging both sides to withdraw their troops from Korean soil. On July 7 Secretary Gresham told his envoy in Tokyo that the President would be grievously disappointed if hostilities ensued. But that was as far as the Cleveland administration went. It had fulfilled the promise in the treaty of 1882 to employ America's good offices in any quarrel threatening Korea; thereafter it declined to join with England alone or with any group of states in bringing pressure upon Japan to desist from war. This caution also reflected domestic politics. The Republicans, already aroused over Cleveland's Hawaiian policy, had begun criticizing his extension of good offices as unfriendly to Japan. When the fighting finally broke out in August, 1894, American opinion overwhelmingly favored the sons of Nippon.

To the amazement of the world, Japan's modern forces quickly crushed their ill-equipped adversaries. They routed the Chinese from Pyongyang on September 15, 1894, and two days later scored an important victory off the mouth of the Yalu. On October 25 they drove beyond that river boundary into southern Manchuria, and by November 21 they had captured the fortress at Port Arthur on the tip of the Liaotung Peninsula. During the winter one column moved north toward Mukden, while an amphibious expedition crossed the Gulf of Chihli to land in northeastern Shantung. The destruction of the remnants of the Chinese fleet and the surrender of the fortified harbor of Weihaiwei on February 12, 1895, compelled the Peking government to sue for an armistice.

As the fighting progressed, the United States maintained its aloofness. On October 6, 1894, England suggested that the two countries combine with Russia, France, and Germany to bring about a peace which would give Japan a huge indemnity and place Korea under international supervision. Neither the President nor the Secretary of State would consider joint intervention, diplomatic or military, much less a multilateral guarantee to keep Korea independent. On November 6 Gresham told his minister in Tokyo: "The deplorable war between Japan and China endangers no policy of the United States in Asia." Although his attitude was that of "an impartial and friendly neutral," he did warn Japan that a crushing defeat of China might prompt other powers with interests in the Orient to "demand a settlement not favorable to Japan's future security." In his message of December 3, 1894, Cleveland simply described the failure of his good offices and reiterated that the conflict imperiled no basic policy of the United States. But he was prepared, he said, "to heed any intimation that our friendly aid for the honorable termination of hostilities would be acceptable to both belligerents."

Peace came, however, through direct negotiations. By the Treaty of Shimonoseki of April 17, 1895, China recognized Korea as an independent state and ceded to Japan the island of Formosa, the nearby Pescadores group, and the Liaotung Peninsula of southern Manchuria. It also agreed to pay a large indemnity and to permit temporary occupation of Weihaiwei. Europe's reaction showed Gresham to have been a good prophet. The transfer of Formosa caused no strenuous objection, for it merely brought Japan closer to the Spanish Philippines. But a foothold on the mainland was another matter. The Liaotung Peninsula, with excellent harbors at Port Arthur and Dairen, dominated the sea approaches to North China. Once established there, Japan could control Korea and spill over into the rest of Manchuria. Although Great Britain twice refused to collaborate, Russia persuaded Germany and France to join in offering friendly counsel to Tokyo. Liaotung in Japanese hands, the three powers argued on April 23, would menace Peking, render Korea's independence illusory, and jeopardize the peace of the Orient. They strongly advised returning the peninsula to China. Significantly, they did not invite the United States to participate in this move.

Japan's civil leaders had foreseen that sort of intervention. They had been driven by the triumphant military to demand some acquisition on the mainland; and since they could not have Korea, they settled for the Liaotung Peninsula. They were prepared, however, to beat a strategic retreat. They did sound out the United States and England to see whether they could muster support for resisting the tripartite advice, but there was no disposition in either capital to intervene against the intervenors. After making one final effort to retain only Port Arthur, the Japanese signed a revised treaty on May 5, 1895, in which they handed back the Liaotung Penisula and secured a larger indemnity.

The war of 1894–5 marked a turning point in the history of the Far East. It revealed the growing power of Japan and the appalling weakness of China. It turned Europe's attention to East Asia and ushered in a period of diplomatic maneuvers and imperialistic tensions. It eventually led England to seek allies in Washington and Tokyo. But the United States—beset with depression, racked by labor strife, frightened over a shrinking gold reserve, and facing an ugly Venezuelan controversy—did not seem at first to grasp the significance of what was happening. In his message of December 2, 1895, Cleveland devoted four long paragraphs to recent antimissionary riots in China but only a brief one to the war itself. There he underlined his hands-off policy and boasted that, in attempting to promote direct negotiations between the belligerents, the republic had "sought no advantages and interposed no counsels."

THE SCRAMBLE FOR CONCESSIONS

Such aloofness could not survive the scramble for concessions in the next three years. This development, which threatened China's territorial integrity and administrative entity and ultimately alarmed American businessmen looking for new markets, began on June 20, 1895, when France obtained a rectification of its Indochinese boundary and several economic advantages. Then on September 8, 1896, Russia gained the right to complete the Trans-Siberian line by building straight across northern Manchuria to Vladivostok and thus avoid the circuitous route along the Amur and Ussuri Rivers.[2] Later known as the Chinese Eastern, this railway was finished in 1903. Germany, the third of China's protectors in 1895, did not receive its compensation until March 6, 1898. It had long desired a foothold on the southern coast of the Shantung Peninsula, and the murder of two missionaries in 1897 enabled it to drive a hard bargain. The resulting convention leased for ninety-nine years spacious Kiaochow Bay and granted extensive railroad and mining privileges.

This sign of Manchu generosity—or weakness—touched off a second round of concessions. On March 27, 1898, Russia leased for twenty-five years the tip of the Liaotung Peninsula, including the sites at Port Arthur and Dairen which the Tsar's government had recently advised the victorious Japanese to retrocede. From this Kwantung leasehold a neutral area extended north to the base of the peninsula, while the Russian-controlled Chinese Eastern Railway was permitted to construct a branch from its main tracks at Harbin south to Dairen. Not to be outdone, the French won on April 10, 1898, a ninety-nine year lease on Kwangchow Bay in the extreme south. Suitable for development as a naval station, Kwangchow also guarded the sea lanes to northern Indochina.

England was the last to join in this scramble for concessions. As the chief beneficiary of the old order, it viewed with dismay the breakup of China into foreign leaseholds. Unwilling to stand idly by, Britain first sounded out the United States regarding some joint action or declaration which would give Anglo-American support to the principle of equal commercial opportunity for all. This confidential and unofficial overture of March 8, 1898, was badly timed and coldly received. Occupied with the Cuban crisis, President McKinley had no desire to complicate his task by arousing anti-British sentiments at home, especially since he judged London's aim to be selfish and its alarm exaggerated.

[2] The price of the grant was a fifteen-year secret alliance of June 3, 1896. Among other things, it promised mutual aid against a Japanese attack and the use of China's ports in wartime by the Russian navy.

On March 17 Sir Julian Pauncefote, England's ambassador, was told that while the United States wished to see preserved "open trade in China," there was no evidence at the moment of interference that would justify departing from the traditional policy of avoiding foreign alliances or involvement in Europe's affairs. Rebuffed by this obeisance to isolationism, England moved within a week to counter the latest Russo-German gains. On March 25, 1898, it decided to seek a naval site at Weihaiwei on the northern tip of the Shantung Peninsula, about halfway between Port Arthur and Tsingtao on Kiaochow Bay. On July 1 Britain signed an agreement with the Peking government to lease that harbor for so long a period as Russia occupied Port Arthur.

AMERICAN INTERESTS ON THE EVE

By the eve of the War with Spain in April, 1898, these onrushing developments in East Asia had assumed a new significance in American eyes. With prosperity returning, some exporters and entrepreneurs began to fear they might be excluded from the vast market and lucrative investments in China. Since six months later McKinley would demand in the peace treaty all of the Philippines, it is necessary to ask whether a desire for that archipelago played any part in the policy of the United States toward the changing Far East.

The answer is clearly no. The remoteness of the islands from North China and Korea disassociated them from the dramatic events of the 1890's. The Asiatic Squadron, based on Japan, did not operate that far south; and when George Dewey assumed command late in 1897, the most recent information he found in the files of the Bureau of Navigation dated from 1876. To be sure, a rebellion against Spanish misrule broke out in August, 1896, but unlike the insurrection in Cuba, the Filipino revolt attracted very little attention in the United States. Even the expansionist-minded Albert Shaw said in the *Review of Reviews* that he knew all too little about the islands and was prepared to see them go to Japan eventually. In any case, peace was restored on December 14, 1897, when Spain agreed to institute reforms and pay an indemnity of over $700,000 to Emilio Aguinaldo and the other insurgent leaders. By the beginning of 1898 Aguinaldo had gone into exile on the mainland, and with a few exceptions most Americans forgot about the Philippines.

One exception was Theodore Roosevelt. Yet before May 1, 1898, this disciple of Mahan evinced no desire to annex the Philippines or even to acquire a coaling station there. His concern with them during the summer of 1897, when he served as Acting Secretary of the Navy, was purely military. He wanted to hit the prospective foe wherever he

could, and there was a Spanish detachment, albeit a decrepit one, at
Manila. For that reason Roosevelt embarked upon a one-man crusade
to familiarize the President and the cabinet with the need for offensive
operations in the Western Pacific. For that reason he strained every
nerve to keep the vacant command of the Asiatic Squadron out of the
hands of a conventional officer and to entrust it to Dewey, who could
be relied upon to move aggressively against the enemy with a minimum of instructions from Washington. For that reason Roosevelt aided
Dewey, after his appointment, by adding to the squadron and delivering
more ammunition before hostilities began. Most important of all, Roosevelt charted the course Dewey was to follow if the impending conflict
materialized. On February 25, 1898, after Secretary John D. Long had
left for the day, Roosevelt sent a secret cable instructing the Commodore to concentrate every effective unit at Hong Kong and to keep fully
coaled at all times. If war came, he should prevent the Spanish flotilla
from leaving Asiatic waters and undertake an offensive against the
Philippine Islands.

Roosevelt's dispatch of February 25, 1898, was not the irresponsible and insubordinate act it has often been alleged to be. Dewey's orders
took effect only after hostilities had commenced. Nor was it a surreptitious and irrevocable deed that forced the hand of the peacefully inclined McKinley administration. The Assistant Secretary composed the
message with the help of Rear Admiral Arent S. Crowninshield, Chief
of the Bureau of Navigation and the officer charged with deploying
the fleet. Although there is no evidence that Roosevelt was told to transmit the cable and every reason to suppose that he was not, Long refrained from countermanding the instructions either that evening,
when he first heard of them, or at any time in the next two months.
Actually, Roosevelt's dispatch was anticipatory in nature. The decisive
orders did not go out until April 24, 1898, following a long conference
at the White House in which the Assistant Secretary did not participate.
The second message informed Dewey that war was inevitable and
directed him to proceed immediately against the Spanish detachment in
Manila Bay.

Neither Roosevelt's preliminary alert of February 25, 1898, nor
McKinley's final order of April 24 indicated a yearning for colonies in
the Western Pacific. There was not a word in the two dispatches, or any
other before May 1, about conquering the Philippines during the war
and annexing them after the peace. Incredible as it may seem, Dewey
received no instructions beyond destroying the Spanish flotilla. Only
upon learning of his victory did the administration take steps to provide
him with additional ships and a landing force. Only then did indifference to the future of the archipelago disappear in Washington. A sim-

ple act of naval strategy released emotional, economic, and diplomatic pressures long building. These, combined with the dramatic events in Manila Bay during the summer of 1898 and the apparent breakup of China into foreign leaseholds, played a part in McKinley's fateful decision to embark upon the path of imperialism.

13

⇥⇥⇥⇥⇥⇥⇥⇥⇥⇥⇤⇤⇤⇤⇤⇤⇤⇤

New Pretensions
in the New World

EXCEPT for the insurrection in Cuba, events in the New World did little between 1889 and 1898 to impel the United States along the road to empire. Although the countries of the Western Hemisphere were better known than those of the Pacific and the Far East, diplomatic inter-course with them remained largely routine. Although the volume of commerce with the neighbors to the south exceeded that with Asia, it did not compare with that with Europe. And although the new manifest destiny underlined the need for overseas expansion, its champions seemed content to seek close to home only a foothold or two in the Caribbean. Hence the most publicized and significant developments of those years—again excluding the rebellion against Spanish rule—were the new pretensions of a maturing republic as it strove for improved economic contacts within the hemisphere, magnified a minor incident with Chile into a major war scare, demanded an American-controlled interoceanic canal, and stretched the original meaning of the Monroe Doctrine beyond all recognition.

LEADERSHIP IN THE AMERICAS

Even before 1889 leaders in many walks of life had urged upon the government in Washington measures to foster better economic ties with the neighbors below the Rio Grande. Among the suggestions were a customs union, a railroad to link the two continents, direct subsidies to steamship lines, a roving commission to report on business opportunities, and a conference of all the American states. This last idea found a champion in James G. Blaine. On November 29, 1881, during his first brief tenure as secretary of state, he invited all the nations of the New World to meet in Washington the next year. Never before had the United States participated in a hemispheric gathering, much less served as the host. For various reasons—personal, political, and diplomatic—this project for assuming leadership in the Americas ran into difficulties when Blaine resigned on December 19. On April 18, 1882, Arthur asked Congress for advice on whether he should proceed; and when the indifferent lawmakers failed to respond, the President withdrew the invitations.

Six years later sentiment had changed. With the controversial Blaine no longer involved, the legislature on its own initiative passed a bill providing for a conference to study the economic problems of the hemisphere and to draft a plan for the compulsory arbitration of disputes between countries of the New World. Fresh invitations were issued on July 13, 1888, but by a curious turn of the political wheel, Blaine again headed the State Department when the delegates from every nation except the Dominican Republic assembled in Washington on October 2, 1889. Sitting until April 19, 1890, they spent most of their time talking about trade and even undertook a six-week tour of various industrial centers. Harrison underscored this commercial emphasis by choosing as representatives one lawyer, one veteran diplomat, one retired politician, and seven prominent businessmen, including Andrew Carnegie the steel magnate.

The results of this First International Conference of American States were disappointing. The only tangible economic gain was the establishment in Washington of a Commercial Union of the American Republics—renamed the Pan American Union in 1910—whose function was to disseminate information on trade. The plan for the hemispheric customs union was shelved; as a substitute, bilateral reciprocity agreements were suggested. Other schemes for strengthening business ties never got beyond the recommendation stage. Three of the resolutions dealing with noneconomic matters deserve mention. One embodied the principle that foreigners residing in an American republic were not entitled to special diplomatic protection by their country; the United States alone dissented. A second called upon the signatories not to recognize any territory obtained by conquest; it foreshadowed the Hoover-Stimson Doctrine of 1932. The third resolution contained the outline of a treaty which would make obligatory the submission to an impartial tribunal for final settlement all disputes involving boundaries, navigation rights, indemnities, diplomatic privileges, and the interpretation of treaties.

This pioneer experiment in multilateral arbitration never went into effect. A treaty embodying a report to the conference was signed on April 28, 1890, by the United States and ten other participants, but Harrison did not send it to the Senate. On September 3, 1890, he spoke of the proposal as "one of the happiest and most helpful incidents in the history of the Western Hemisphere"; and on December 9, 1891, after the deadline for ratification had passed, he urged that the time be extended. Only by so acting and by consenting to its terms, said the President, could the United States "conserve the influential initiative it has taken." But the legislature was unable to negotiate a treaty; and since the executive never submitted an instrument for senatorial approval, a general inter-American arbitration pact had to wait until January, 1929.

Despite its meager accomplishments, the First International Conference of American States was important. It brought together for an exchange of views all but one of the nations of the New World. It set a precedent for subsequent gatherings, the next of which met in Mexico City on October 22, 1901. It marked the initial attempt by the United States to assume leadership in hemispheric affairs. Lastly, Blaine's tact and charm persuaded many Latins, temporarily at least, that their northern neighbor was willing to deal with them as equals. Unfortunately, this promise of 1889 was not immediately fulfilled. The ensuing reciprocity agreements led to mutual recriminations. The Chilean crisis, the quest for footholds in the Caribbean, and the new pretensions regarding an interoceanic canal and the Monroe Doctrine blocked for many years hope of an inter-American solidarity based upon equality, nonintervention, and joint responsibility for the defense of the Western Hemisphere.

WAR WITH CHILE?

Ironically, the same Harrison administration displayed a needlessly bellicose attitude in handling a minor controversy with Chile. During 1891 a civil war in that distant land, already alienated by events of a decade before, brought into power men who nursed several grievances against the United States. One was the refuge given their political foes by the American minister at Santiago. A second was the attempt by an overly zealous customs official at San Diego to prevent legitimate purchases of arms and munitions. A third was the dramatic pursuit on the high seas by the cruiser *Charleston* of the *Itata*, a merchant ship which had departed illegally from an American port. Just as that incident came to a peaceful close, a street brawl occurred on October 18, 1891, at Valparaiso in which two sailors from the cruiser *Baltimore* were killed, sixteen injured, and others beaten or imprisoned. Since the police did nothing to restrain the mob, and may even have assisted it, the affair was interpreted in Washington as a deliberate insult to the United States.

To make matters worse, the Chilean government adopted a dilatory and provocative policy. It offered no expression of regret in the six weeks before Congress met. It dismissed as unwarranted and threatening a demand by the United States for satisfaction. It eventually requested the recall of the American minister. In his annual message of December 9, 1891, Harrison managed to restrain himself. He simply recited the facts of the case, regretted the "offensive tone" assumed by Chile, and promised, should the reply from Santiago be disappointing or unduly delayed, to submit a special message to the legislature "for such action as may be necessary." At this juncture the temporary Chilean minister of foreign affairs precipitated a major crisis by publicly questioning the truthfulness of Harrison and Secretary of the Navy Tracy.

Harrison then exhibited a jingoism and impatience that would reappear under others during the Venezuelan controversy in 1895 and the Cuban crisis in 1898. He seemed unwilling to wait for the inauguration of the permanent regime. He directed the arsenals and navy yards to prepare for hostilities. He declined to accept anything less than a full apology and reparation for the *Baltimore* fracas. He required amends for the letter impugning his veracity. Chile's failure to comply, he said on January 19, 1892, would oblige him to sever diplomatic relations. Two days later Harrison rewrote a dispatch prepared by Blaine and transformed it into a virtual ultimatum. When the Chilean president's absence from his capital caused further delay, Harrison sent Congress on January 25 a vast array of documents and a detailed narrative of the imbroglio. While he privately thought a clash was inevitable and publicly insisted that the demands made of Chile "be adhered to and enforced," he did not ask for authority to wage war. In concluding, he simply stated his belief that he "ought not to delay longer in bringing these matters to the attention of Congress for such action as may be deemed appropriate."

If the executive was inviting the legislature to empower him to use armed force, the latter showed no disposition to do so. Indeed, there was hardly time. Only a few hours after the President's message was read on Capitol Hill, the State Department began to decipher a dispatch of January 23 from Santiago. When this document was examined at the White House the next day, it was seen to meet every American demand. Chile expressed regret over the *Baltimore* affair,

SOUTH AMERICA
1889-1961

CUBA
(INDEP. 1902)

JAMAICA

HAITI
(HISPANIOLA)

DOMINICAN
REP.

VIRGIN IS.
(USA)
(1916)

PUERTO
RICO
(USA)
(1899)

GUADELOUPE

MARTINIQUE

BARBADOS

CARIBBEAN SEA

ARUBA   CURAÇAO

TRINIDAD

PANAMA
(INDEP. 1903)

Barranquilla

Caracas

VENEZUELA

ORINOCO

Georgetown
Paramaribo
Cayenne

GUIANA
(BR.) (NETH.) (FR.)

Bogotá

ORINOCO

COLOMBIA

Quito

EQUATOR

ECUADOR

Guayaquil

NEGRO

Manaus   AMAZON

Belém

Leticia

Fortaleza
(Ceará)

JURUÁ

MADEIRA

TAPAJÓZ

UCAYALI

Natal
Recife
(Pernambuco)

CHIMBOTE
HARBOR

ANDES

B R A Z I L

SÃO FRANCISCO

São
Salvador
(Bahia)

Callao   Lima

Cuzco

LAKE
TITICACA

La Paz

Brasília

BRAZILIAN
HIGHLANDS

PERU

PERU

BOLIVIA

Sucre

Belo
Horizonte

Tacna
Arica

CHACO

PARAGUAY

PARANÁ

ANDES

Antofagasta

GRAN CHACO

PARAGUAY

São Paulo

Rio de Janeiro
Santos

TROPIC OF
CAPRICORN

Tucumán

Asunción

CHILE

PARANÁ

Porto Alegre

Valparaíso   Mendoza

Santiago

Buenos
Aires

URUGUAY

Montevideo
RIO DE LA PLATA

ARGENTINA

Valdivia

PATAGONIA

ANDES

P A C I F I C   O C E A N

A T L A N T I C   O C E A N

A T L A N T I C   O C E A N

STR. OF
MAGELLAN

FALKLAND
ISLANDS

1000 MILES   CAPE HORN

70°W   50°W

TRM

consented to pay whatever reparation was fixed by the United States Supreme Court or some arbitral body, and officially withdrew the letter criticizing Harrison and Tracy. This complete capitulation brought the crisis to an end, and Harrison so informed Congress on January 28, 1892.

Why did the United States take so strong a stand on so minor an incident? Why were the President and the Secretary of the Navy more intransigent than the Congress and the Secretary of State? It has been suggested that Harrison wanted a popular issue on which to seek re-election and that Tracy wished a telling case with which to request larger appropriations. It has been pointed out that Chile's stubbornness and procrastination were also to blame. Undoubtedly those factors played a part. Certainly the need for modern armored ships, overseas bases, and the interoceanic canal was dramatized. Yet in the last analysis the episode is most comprehensible, not in terms of political ambitions, naval propaganda, or foreign bungling, but against the temperament of the ex-soldier in the White House whose extreme patriotism and aggressive inclinations not only embodied the new pretensions in the New World but also foreshadowed the triumph of imperialism in American foreign policy.

NAVAL BASES AND THE FUTURE CANAL

Even before the war scare with Chile revealed several handicaps in operating the fleet, Harrison and Blaine had taken steps to remove one of them. For coaling stations in the New World they turned their attention to Môle St. Nicholas in northwestern Haiti, Samaná Bay in the northeastern sector of the Dominican Republic, and Chimbote in northern Peru. Blaine knew about the last, for in 1881 he had had to reject a concession there which had been negotiated without his consent. But with the final triumph of steam over sail, the navy became more insistent about its needs along the west coast of South America. On May 27, 1889, the Secretary instructed his minister at Lima to lease Chimbote for the exclusive use of the United States; but when the Peruvians started to talk of territorial guarantees, Blaine's interest waned. On December 31, 1891, as trouble with Chile mounted, Harrison urged him to reopen negotiations looking to "absolute control of the harbor" and the right to construct a drydock. The Secretary felt that nothing could be done during the crisis and managed to delay. After he resigned on June 4, 1892, there was another flurry of interest in Chimbote, and then that scheme was dropped.

Môle St. Nicholas was an excellent anchorage commanding the Windward Passage between Haiti and Cuba. In November, 1883, a bankrupt Haitian president, bedeviled by irate British creditors, tried to solve his fiscal woes by offering the site to the United States. The Arthur administration, however, had no desire for overseas possessions, and on February 1, 1884, Secretary Frelinghuysen informed his envoy at Port-au-Prince that the United States had never deemed it necessary "to maintain impregnable fortresses along the world's highways of commerce." In words that would infuriate Mahan he declared: "Even as simple coaling stations, such territorial acquisitions would involve responsibility beyond their utility." But the expansionist-minded Harrison did not hesitate to rush in where Arthur, and Cleveland after him, had feared to tread. In December, 1890, discussions began at Port-au-Prince for the lease of the Môle as a coaling station. On January 25, 1891, the commander of the North Atlantic squadron arrived and promptly resorted to bribery and a show of force. By February 9 three warships had anchored off the capital; six weeks later the number had risen to five. It is not surprising that these tactics caused Haiti to break off negotiations on April 22, 1891.

At the other end of the island lay Samaná Bay, strategically situated on the Mona Passage separating Haiti and Puerto Rico. After Grant's scheme to annex this outpost of the future canal had failed in 1870, little was heard of the spacious harbor until February, 1883. In that month the Dominican president, viewing with alarm and disgust the empty character of his treasury, tried to lease the anchorage to the United States. Not even by invoking the specter of European intervention could he attract the continental-minded Arthur and Frelinghuysen. In January, 1886, he used the same bait with Cleveland and Bayard, but neither of those traditionalists rose to the occasion. Harrison and Blaine, however, might be more receptive; and in January, 1892, President Ulises Heureaux proposed a defensive alliance by which the American navy would acquire Samaná Bay free of cost and gain the privilege of maintaining fortified stations in other Dominican ports. In return, the United States must promise to help its ally, should the latter make war on Haiti for reasons considered justifiable in Washington, to the extent of furnishing two naval vessels and a loan of $1 million. If the Dominicans captured Môle St. Nicholas in that conflict, they would hand the Haitian port over to the United States.

This offer was too much, even for Harrison and Blaine. With the Chilean crisis at its height, they did not consider the proposal seriously. But after Blaine resigned, Secretary Foster tried again. On August 6, 1892, he instructed his minister in Santo Domingo to lease Samaná Bay for ninety-nine years in exchange for the payment of $250,000 at once, $50,000 annually for the next five years, and $25,000 each year thereafter. Premature publicity hurt the plan, and by the end of 1892 Heureaux had obtained the money he needed on more favorable terms from financiers in New York. And by that time the voters had replaced Harrison with Cleveland, an adamant foe of overseas expansion.

With Cleveland in the White House, the quest for Caribbean bases had to originate on Capitol Hill. There Lodge supplied the leadership, and his objective was the Danish West Indies. Ever since the Senate had refused to act on Seward's treaty of October, 1867, the United States was more concerned with the sale of the islands to a European power than with annexing them itself. Lodge opened his campaign on January 3, 1896, with a vain attempt to direct the Foreign Relations Committee to inquire whether the group was still for sale under the terms of 1867 and, if not, whether Denmark intended to cede the islands to someone else. Six months later the Massachusetts Republican helped write into the party platform a plank calling for the acquisition of the Danish isles as "a much needed Naval station in the West Indies." But even the election of McKinley did not insure success for the expansionists. On March 31, 1898, Lodge reported from the Foreign Relations Committee a recommendation to appropriate $5 million for the purchase of St. Thomas, St. John, and St. Croix. An acrimonious debate the next day disclosed considerable bipartisan opposition, its arguments ranging from the heavy expenditure involved to the imminence of war with Spain. When some of McKinley's staunchest supporters joined the critics, the measure was shelved. Denmark, in all probability, would not have negotiated with a potential belligerent.

This intensified but unsuccessful quest for naval sites in the Caribbean reflected a simultaneous demand for the early completion of an American-controlled canal. Although the Clayton-Bulwer Treaty still obligated the United States to share equally with England in the construction and operation of any isthmian waterway, many public men argued that the agreement was obsolete. On March 8, 1880, President Hayes had told Congress that henceforth "the policy of this country is a canal under American control." Within two months committees in both houses virtually requested the executive to take steps to abrogate the pact. From 1881 to 1883 Blaine and Frelinghuysen tried by diplomacy to cancel the commitment, and on December 1, 1884, the latter signed with Nicaragua a treaty giving the United States the exclusive right to build a canal through that country. The vote in the Senate on January 29, 1885, was 32 to 23, five short of the needed two thirds. Before another ballot could be taken, the newly inaugurated Cleveland withdrew the document on March 13.

Cleveland's respect for treaty obligations and his opposition to government ownership forced the proponents of the Nicaraguan canal to fall back upon private enterprise. Although some digging began in October, 1889, American entrepreneurs quickly discovered what the

French had learned earlier in Panama—that public assistance was indispensable. Hence as progress faltered, bills were offered in Congress to guarantee the construction company's bonds up to $100 million; but despite two endorsements by Harrison and some Democratic support, the measures did not pass. The depression of 1893 bankrupted those financing the project, and the return of Cleveland to the White House meant another four years of a hands-off policy by the federal authorities. In their platform for 1896 the Republicans demanded a Nicaraguan canal to be "built, owned, and operated by the United States"; but when the War with Spain commenced, that goal was still in the future. Nevertheless, the debate over the canal, like that on the wisdom of obtaining Caribbean footholds, had turned the eyes of some Americans outward and thus helped to facilitate the triumph of imperialism when, under different conditions, the decision on colonies had to be made.

"PRACTICALLY SOVEREIGN ON THIS CONTINENT"

A swelling demand during the 1890's for an American-controlled canal was not the least of the nation's new pretenses in the New World. Just as the United States asked to be released from obligations it had gladly assumed in 1850, took the lead in promoting hemispheric conferences it had long ignored, and intensified the search for naval sites it had never wanted, so did it enlarge the meaning of the Monroe Doctrine. Indeed, a relatively insignificant dispute between Venezuela and British Guiana evoked from the normally cautious Cleveland administration on July 28, 1895, the unprecedented claim that "today the United States is practically sovereign on this continent, and its fiat is law upon the subjects to which it confines its interposition."

The decision of the government in Washington to inject itself into the Anglo-Venezuelan quarrel was long in the making.[1] As early as January 31, 1881, the Hayes administration told the Venezuelans that it could not be indifferent to forcible acquisitions by Great Britain in the New World, and two years later Frelinghuysen intimated to his envoy in Caracas that Arthur would press upon England the

[1] In the colonial period Spain and Holland had never agreed upon a clear demarcation between their South American possessions. When Venezuela declared its independence in 1810 and the western part of Dutch Guiana was ceded to England in 1814, the governments at London and Caracas inherited potential trouble. In 1840 the latter declined to accept a line drawn by Sir Robert Schomburgk, and the discovery of gold in the region soon afterwards complicated the problem. Although both sides inflated their claims, Venezuela was the more culpable of the two; and Great Britain's consistent refusal to arbitrate any territory east of the Schomburgk line reflected its justifiable fear that the arbitrator might simply split the difference between the two extremes. The United States had often avoided arbitration for that very reason.

desirability of an equitable settlement. The severance of diplomatic relations by the disputants prompted Cleveland and Bayard to extend their good offices on February 8, 1887, but to no avail. On April 11, 1888, the Senate dragged the issue into the open by calling for papers, but that request brought no action by the legislature or executive. It was Harrison who first referred to the controversy in a presidential message. On December 3, 1889, he voiced the hope for an amicable adjustment, and on December 9, 1891, he expressed disappointment that no solution had been reached. For a moment it seemed the Republicans might force a showdown, for on October 28, 1891, Blaine had informed his minister at Caracas that Harrison had decided upon an important step in behalf of Venezuela. The ensuing war scare with Chile pushed aside whatever may have been contemplated, and during the rest of 1892 and 1893 the administration had its hands full with the fur-seals dispute in the Bering Sea and the revolution in Hawaii.

Somewhat surprisingly, Cleveland the traditionalist brought the problem to a head. For the first two years of his second term he did not go beyond his predecessors, though on December 4, 1893, he mentioned to Congress the desirability of having the controversy submitted to arbitration. A year later, on December 3, he promised that he would seek to restore relations between the disputants and persuade them to arbitrate. Such initiative, he argued, accorded with "our established policy to remove from this hemisphere all causes of differences with powers beyond the sea." By 1895 the persistent refusal of England to arbitrate any land east of the Schomburgk line and the callous indifference of its leaders had aroused the stubborn President, with his instinctive sympathy for the underdog, while various domestic pressures had induced him to conclude that the time to force the issue had arrived.

For one thing, the Venezuelans had launched an effective propaganda campaign in the United States. In August, 1894, William L. Scruggs, a former minister at Caracas, printed a widely circulated pamphlet with the lurid title *British Aggressions in Venezuela, or the Monroe Doctrine on Trial.* In January, 1895, he secured the introduction of a joint resolution urging the President to recommend arbitration "most earnestly" to both sides. Adopted unanimously by the House, the resolution passed the Senate without debate and was signed on February 20. England chose that unpropitious moment to deliver an ultimatum to Nicaragua for past grievances, and on April 22, 1895, four hundred sailors and marines occupied the customs house at Corinto. Although the troops were soon withdrawn and although such punitive steps had never been forbidden by the Monroe Doctrine, this Corinto affair put Cleveland on the defensive.

He was accused of standing idly by while an Old World state

disciplined one in the New. Advocates of a vigorous diplomacy drew a deadly parallel between Nicaragua and Venezuela. They already disliked Cleveland for his attempt to restore the monarchy in Hawaii, for his wish to terminate joint rule in Samoa, and for his opposition to a government-constructed canal. In the *Forum* for March, 1895, Lodge had referred to "Our Blundering Foreign Policy," and he renewed his attack in *The North American Review* for June. His article entitled "England, Venezuela, and the Monroe Doctrine," concluded: "The supremacy of the Monroe Doctrine should be established and at once—peaceably if we can, forcibly if we must. It will be the duty and the privilege of the next Congress to see that this is done."

Before the legislature convened in December, 1895, the executive had assumed the initiative. Gresham's death on May 28 brought to the State Department the blunt-spoken Olney. Like the President, the new Secretary had swallowed the Venezuelan charges about the Monroe Doctrine. Almost alone he prepared a draft dispatch, carried it to Cleveland's summer cottage for minor changes, read the revised version to a rump cabinet in Washington, and on July 20, 1895, transmitted the finished product to Ambassador Bayard in London—all this after Congress had adjourned. The document in effect called upon England to submit the boundary dispute to arbitration immediately and requested an answer in time for the President to inform Congress when it met on December 2. In tone, if not in content, Olney's note was an ultimatum.

The British reply was too little and too late. The Marquess of Salisbury, who was both Prime Minister and Foreign Secretary, unhappily chose to combat an ingrained American prejudice with dialectical reasoning, and Bayard unwisely failed to impress upon Salisbury the extent to which popular passions in the United States were rising. Worst of all, the unyielding and supercilious rejoinder of November 26, 1895, was, in error, forwarded by mail instead of by cable, with the result that it had not arrived when Cleveland delivered his state of the Union message on December 2. With ill-concealed annoyance he informed the lawmakers of what he had done; with equally ill-concealed bias he embraced the Venezuelan cause. He virtually insisted that England arbitrate the area east of the Schomburgk line—something it had repeatedly refused to do and something the United States, under similar circumstances, would never have done.

On December 5, 1895, the President left Washington for a ten-day duck hunt. He authorized Olney in his absence to block out a second message to Congress as soon as Salisbury's answer was received. This the Secretary did without consulting a single person and by having the final copy typed at his Boston law office rather than at the State

Department. When he returned, Cleveland discussed the draft only with Olney and the Secretary of War. He did not seek the advice of Congress, the military, or the rest of the cabinet. He simply informed the last group of what he was doing a few hours before sending the message to Capitol Hill.

Cleveland began on December 17, 1895, by telling of England's refusal to arbitrate. He then recommended that Congress empower him to appoint a commission to determine the exact boundary. When that report was "made and accepted," the United States must be ready to uphold it, by force if necessary. He was "fully alive," he said, to "all the consequences that may follow"; but a great nation can invite no worse calamity than "supine submission to wrong and injustice." In an alarming display of bellicosity the Senate and the House created the commission at once. Indisposed to question whether a rank injustice was being perpetrated upon Venezuela or whether a hands-off policy by the United States constituted supine submission, Republicans vied with Democrats in passing unanimously a bill which the President signed on December 21. On January 4, 1896, the names of the five commissioners were announced.

Fortunately, that quintet never had to draw a line which the executive would be obliged to enforce. There was a little will to war on either side of the Atlantic, and the British soon grasped the gravity of the situation. Although international complications, such as German encouragement of the Boers in South Africa, may have improved their perception, most Englishmen would in any case have agreed with Colonial Secretary Joseph Chamberlain, who declared that an Anglo-American conflict "would be an absurdity as well as a crime." On February 11, 1896, Salisbury admitted to the House of Lords that "the mixture of the United States in this matter" might actually hasten a settlement.

The final solution was hardly rapid, but the crisis was past. After December 17, 1895, Cleveland and Olney exhibited exemplary patience and tact. Having awakened the lion, they abstained from irritating him further. It was Olney who hit upon a formula whereby England would accept arbitration, even for the area east of the Schomburgk line, without endangering its sovereignty over long-established settlements. On November 12, 1896, Olney and Pauncefote agreed upon a series of articles which the latter converted into a treaty with Venezuela on February 2, 1897. This pact set up an arbitral board, which included two justices from the Supreme Court. Its award of October 3, 1899, fell far short of Venezuela's claims and gave Great Britain most of what it had contended for. Because of these developments, the congressional commission refrained from carrying out the mission of defining "the true divisional line." Instead it submitted a brief report on February 27, 1897 with supporting documents and maps which proved useful to the court of arbitration.

Whether Cleveland's handling of the Venezuelan affair needlessly drove the English-speaking nations to the brink of war or enabled the Anglo-Venezuelan disputants to reach a satisfactory solution is still a matter of controversy; but there can be no doubt that it showed how the executive can monopolize the shaping of foreign policy. It also revealed a failure to coordinate diplomatic pretensions and military power. The President and his Secretary of State may have surmised that their demands would not lead to war, but they did nothing to alert the armed forces in case their assumption turned out to be wrong. Indeed, fewer preparations were made than in January, 1892, when Chile was the likely foe. To issue a virtual ultimatum under those circumstances was to conduct international relations in a vacuum. It is true that on land the overwhelming superiority of the British army was offset by distance, the Canadian hostage, and England's commitments elsewhere in the world. But at sea the disparity was frightening. In November, 1895, the Royal Navy had in commission fifty battleships, twenty-five armored cruisers, fifty-two protected cruisers, and thirty-four torpedo boats. The United States then possessed three battleships, one armored cruiser, thirteen protected cruisers, and one torpedo boat.

Less open to dispute, too, is the importance of the episode in the history of the Monroe Doctrine. Never before were the words of the fifth president so unanimously endorsed at home without distinction of party, even though they were stretched to cover a situation which neither Monroe nor Adams had envisaged. For Olney's note of July 20, 1895, added another corollary to the principles of 1823. It declared, in effect, that the refusal by a European power to settle by pacific and equitable means a boundary dispute with a nation of the New World would be considered by the United States an unfriendly act, dangerous to its peace and safety. The note implied—and Cleveland's message of December 17, 1895, made clear—that the government in Washington would decide what was equitable and would employ force, if necessary, to see that justice prevailed. Thus was the meaning of the Monroe Doctrine enlarged, as it had been by Polk and by the no-transfer and canal corollaries.

Finally, the reaction against a possible war over several thousand square miles in the Orinoco jungle accelerated forces already at work that were making for an Anglo-American friendship in world affairs. The British in particular realized as never before the international value of a well-disposed United States. Sensing belatedly that acceptance of the Monroe Doctrine was the key to the heart of Uncle Sam, John Bull beat a hasty retreat from Salisbury's arrogant reply of November 26, 1895. While several powers, notably Germany, were still spluttering over Olney's claim to being "practically sovereign on this continent," prominent Englishmen of all parties hurriedly reversed themselves and began to pay lip service to the American pretension. This change would become even more marked three years later, when the United States followed Great Britain down the path of empire.

14

➤➤➤-➤➤➤-➤➤➤-➤➤➤❮❮❮-❮❮❮-❮❮❮-❮❮❮

Armed Intervention in Cuba

NONE OF THESE new pretensions in the New World had such fateful consequences as the unprecedented armed intervention in the Cuban insurrection. By claiming a right, in the name of humanity and self-interest, to demand that Spain retire from its war-torn island in the Caribbean, ninety miles from the Florida shore, the United States set in motion a chain of events that culminated in the unexpected planting of the Stars and Stripes in the South China Sea some 6,000 miles from the California coast. The American government thereby departed from its vaunted course of not interfering in the internal affairs of other peoples and also abandoned its traditional antipathy to possessing colonies. This triumph of imperialism strengthened forces already at work which were making for the emergence of the republic as a world power.

CLEVELAND AND CUBA

Interest in Cuba, to be sure, was not new. As early as April 28, 1823, John Quincy Adams had called the island a natural appendage of the North American continent and warned that its transfer to another European power would be inimical to the security of the United States. Commencing on June 17, 1848, three Democratic presidents—Polk, Pierce, and Buchanan—tried in various ways to acquire it, while a Republican secretary of state—Seward—hoped for eventual annexation with Spain's consent. After 1865 American expansionists shifted their attention elsewhere, but a ten-year rebellion that began in 1868 strained to the utmost the forbearance of the Grant and Hayes administrations. With armed intervention barely averted in that decade, a deceptive calm descended upon Cuba until a new uprising exploded on February 24, 1895.

Cleveland was then in the White House and could be expected to maintain a hands-off attitude. He was already occupied with defending his self-denying course in Hawaii and reaching an equitable settlement in Venezuela. Acting cautiously, he issued on June 12, 1895, the customary proclamation of neutrality, admonishing American citizens to refrain from illegal assistance to either side and enjoining revenue officials to enforce the laws with due diligence. In his message of December 2, 1895, the President noted briefly how the fighting had upset normal trade, had aroused American sympathies, and had confronted the government with the difficult task of preventing its soil from being used by the insurgents for military purposes. While deploring the cruelty already manifest in the sanguinary struggle, he voiced his hope for an early peace and his determination to fulfill all international obligations.

After the war scare with England subsided, Congress became more restive over Cuba. In a concurrent resolution, adopted on February 28, 1896, by a vote of 64 to 6, the Senate favored granting belligerent status to the insurgents and employing good offices to win Spain's recognition of Cuban independence. Both recommendations were premature, but the House followed suit on April 6 by a margin of 246 to 27, after a motion to intervene by force had failed. The executive was free to ignore this concurrent resolution, but Olney decided to head off trouble in an election year by acting first. On April 6, he submitted to Enrique Dupuy de Lome, the Spanish minister, a friendly plea in which he argued that timely concessions were the best means of forestalling intervention. Noting that many high-minded Americans already believed it their duty to stop the bloodshed, he warned that his country "cannot contemplate with complacency another ten years of Cuban insurrection." Olney disclaimed any wish to annex the island or imperil Spain's sovereignty, and he urged that substantial reforms, perhaps autonomy, be instituted at once. This initial pressure had no visible effect in Madrid.

When Congress reassembled after the Republican victory at the polls, Cleveland's position was much weaker. His own party had virtually repudiated his administration, while his opponents had demanded in their platform that the United States "should actively use its influences and good offices to restore peace and give independence to the Island." Nor did the President's message of December 7, 1896, seem to justify his policy of watchful waiting. There was no progress toward peace in Cuba, and both sides were systematically destroying

American investments worth $40 million and an annual trade valued at $100 million. Spain had ignored Olney's overture and was insisting upon the unconditional surrender of the rebels as a prerequisite for reforms. The United States government was saddled with the arduous task of upholding its neutrality laws and collecting damages for its citizens. In short, the situation was getting worse, not better. Yet Cleveland spoke of patience. He did concede that there were limits to the nation's forbearance, but many lawmakers were ready to say that those limits had been passed. For Republicans especially, the incentive to act was irresistible. If the Cuban issue could be settled by March 4, 1897, it would spare McKinley difficult decisions and enable him to concentrate on domestic affairs.

This partisan aim produced a brief crisis over recognition. On December 18, 1896, while Cleveland was out of town, the Senate Foreign Relations Committee agreed to report favorably the Cameron resolution, directing the President to acknowledge the independence of Cuba and to employ his good offices with Spain. The move was made in spite of Olney's strenuous objections and only after Chairman Sherman had changed his mind. The next day, acting on his own responsibility, the Secretary asserted in the press that the recognition of new states was purely an executive function and intimated that Cleveland would ignore the joint resolution, even if it commanded a two-thirds majority in each chamber. The outcome of this episode and its significance in the struggle for the control of American foreign policy has been indicated above; here it is enough to say that Olney's maneuver halted any legislative interference with Cleveland's hands-off policy. The Secretary effectively prevented the Republicans from forcing the President to act before he left office.

THE MC KINLEY APPROACH

Paradoxically, the task of the triumphant McKinley, possessing sizable majorities in both houses, was more difficult than that of the repudiated Cleveland, a man without a party. The lame-duck Democrat might with impunity defy public and congressional opinion, since he could accomplish little more during his tenure. For Cleveland, a negative role was both desirable and possible. But the incoming Republican had to maintain party unity and to see Cuba in the light of his entire internal and external program. It would not do to endanger that unity or jeopardize other policies unless negotiations with Spain offered some hope of success. For McKinley, a prolonged course of watchful waiting was neither desirable nor possible. He had only so much time to resolve the problem before he became a victim of forces he could not or would not control.

Initially, the new administration was most discreet. In his inaugural address the President did not mention Cuba and lauded the cherished "policy of non-interference." He declared unequivocally: "We want no wars of conquest; we must avoid the temptation of territorial aggression." Early in March, 1897, McKinley told Cleveland and Olney that he would follow in their steps. Believing that skillful diplomacy could save the day, he spared no pains to find the best man for the post in Madrid. He offered it to five outstanding persons before he selected Stewart L. Woodford, a lawyer and former Union general. Nor was McKinley prepared to allow Congress to force his hand, as it had tried to do with Cleveland. When Morgan introduced a joint resolution to recognize Cuban belligerency, the President appealed to his followers to check the move lest it embarrass his conduct of foreign affairs. After the Senate passed the measure anyway on May 20, 1897, by a vote of 41 to 14, the administration successfully blocked consideration in the House during the session.

A similar moderation prevailed at the outset in dealing with Spain. Woodford's instructions did not differ materially from what Olney had asked of de Lome in April, 1896. They said that Cuba must be pacified promptly, that the American government stood ready to help, and that future intervention was not impossible. The tone was friendly. McKinley knew that threats would antagonize the Spaniards and delay the concessions needed to keep the peace. The President realized, too, that procrastination would strengthen the interventionists at home and bring about a war. Hoping to find the golden mean, he put the best face on the first reports from Woodford: the accession of a well-disposed Liberal ministry under Mateo Sagasta, the recall of Governor General Valeriano Weyler who was known as "The Butcher," the modification of the concentration-camp policy which had killed thousands of noncombatants, and the explicit promise of autonomous rule for the islanders. His message of December 6, 1897, also described proudly the steps taken to protect American interests and to extract Spanish concessions. It opposed recognition of Cuba's belligerency or independence. It pleaded for giving Spain "a reasonable chance" to carry out its promises. McKinley did not say what he would do if his hopes failed to materialize; but he warned that should the United States intervene by force, it must be because of "obligations to ourselves . . . and humanity" and with the "approval of the civilized world." Armed intervention must not lead to forcible annexation; that, the President said, "by our modes of morality, would be criminal aggression."

During the winter of 1897–8 events largely beyond McKinley's control crushed his hopes for peace. In Cuba, autonomy proved unsatisfactory to both sides. The rebels, confident of eventual intervention, constantly raised their demands until they would accept nothing less than independence—the one concession the crown could not grant. On January 12, 1898, short-lived riots in Havana put pressure on the administration to take some action. Until then, Consul Fitzhugh Lee had been vainly urging the stationing of warships in Cuban ports for the protection of American citizens. Both Cleveland and McKinley had held back, fearing inflammatory incidents. Suddenly the roles were reversed. Lee now discouraged the dispatch of naval craft, lest the move seem provocative. The State Department, on the other hand, told de Lome that an exchange of courtesy calls might signalize improving relations, and on January 24, with much misgiving, that hapless diplomat agreed to such a step. Without waiting to consult Lee or to prepare Cuban opinion, the President rushed the second-class battleship *Maine* to Havana. Why he proceeded so hastily and why he chose to employ one of the navy's eight armored vessels simply to show the flag has never been adequately explained. Certainly he and his cabinet bear some responsibility for the tragedy that followed.

Fifteen days after the *Maine* reached Havana, de Lome achieved a dubious fame that led to his recall amid angry recriminations. On February 9, 1898, the bellicose *New York Journal* printed a private letter, one conveniently purloined by a rebel sympathizer, in which the Minister spoke of the President in unflattering terms. Hardly had the interventionists exploited that opportunity to foment trouble when they received a much greater leverage for war. On the night of February 15 the *Maine* blew up at her mooring buoy with the loss of 260 lives. How she was destroyed remains a mystery today. An exclusively American naval court of inquiry concluded on March 21 that the vessel had been sunk "by the explosion of a submarine mine, which caused the partial explosion of two or more forward magazines." [1] Whether the mine was set off by a Spaniard, by a Cuban, or by accident the tribunal did not vouchsafe. Indeed, it was illogical to assume that any responsible Spanish official would have courted disaster by so rash a deed. It is more likely that a daring rebel, eager to embroil the two countries, or a proud Castilian, operating on his own, was to blame. Both Lee and the ship's captain acquitted the insular and peninsular authorities of being implicated, but the warmongers and sensational journalists at home were not that tolerant. To them the destruction of the *Maine* was a supreme act of Spanish treachery and the final justification for armed intervention in Cuba.

[1] When the United States refused to participate in a joint investigation, Spain undertook its own inquiry and found the explosion to have been internal. Until the hulk could be raised after the war, many people suspected that the Spanish officers were closer to the truth than the Americans; and that feeling has never entirely disappeared. A second American court in 1911 confirmed the findings of the first, after which the wreck was sunk in deep water beyond recall.

McKinley, however, exhibited commendable restraint. He handled the de Lome letter in a gentlemanly manner. He asked the public to suspend judgment on the *Maine* until the naval court had made its findings. He frowned upon the numerous resolutions before Congress demanding a legislative investigation of the disaster, calling for the recognition of Cuban belligerency, and directing that an ultimatum require Spain to quit the island. But the ground was fast being cut from beneath the moderates. Fifteen months had passed since Cleveland's warning that American forbearance could not last indefinitely. In Cuba peace seemed as remote as ever; in Spain discussions were at an impasse. On February 26, 1898, Woodford cabled that Sagasta could not yield further and still retain power. He wanted to avoid war, but he would accept one rather than take any steps that might imperil the monarchy.

Under these conditions McKinley felt he had no choice but to prepare for possible hostilities. On March 6, 1898, he appealed to the chairman of the House Committee on Appropriations for an immediate grant of $50 million with which to bolster the nation's defenses. He asked that the initiative come from Congress, lest the outside world dismiss his own diplomatic efforts as insincere. The President's winning charm and a full treasury did the trick. On March 8 the House gave him what he wanted by a vote of 331 to 0; the Senate followed suit the next day by a count of 76 to 0. This demonstration of legislative unity, of faith in the executive, and of a fiscal strength that could raise such a sum without new taxes or a bond issue stunned the Spaniards and convinced the insurgents that deliverance was at hand.

Still another fortnight slipped away. From March 10 to 24, 1898, indecision paralyzed diplomacy at Madrid, while in Washington the suspense of waiting for the report on the *Maine* became unbearable. On March 17 the Senate listened to Redfield Proctor, a conservative Republican from Vermont, known for his prudence and fairness. Skeptical of the atrocities reported from Cuba, Proctor had visited four provinces still controlled by Spain. In dispassionate terms, all the more terrifying because of their restraint, he described the appalling suffering of the 400,000 persons who had been crowded into concentration camps by Weyler and who were no better off since the recall of "The Butcher." The recent reforms, he concluded, were of little value; and although he did not favor annexation, he wished to deliver the island from "the worst misgovernment" he had ever known about. His words shocked the nation. With few exceptions, said *The Literary Digest,* the conservative press felt that Proctor's address had made intervention "the plain duty of the United States on the simple ground of humanity."

THE PRESIDENT PROPOSES

By March 25, 1898, McKinley knew the time for action had come. The report on the *Maine* was in, and Woodford needed new instructions. He had to inform Congress and Spain of the court's findings; more important, he had to lay down the conditions on which the Cuban problem could be settled. "Full self-government, with reasonable indemnity" were the cryptic words transmitted to Madrid early on March 26. The next day more elaborate terms followed. First, there must be an armistice until October 1, during which time negotiations for a peace would be carried on through the good offices of the President. Second, there must be an immediate end to the concentration camps and a relief of the needy, with the United States cooperating. Third, if possible, the President was to act as final arbiter between Spain and the insurgents should no settlement be reached by October 1. Even as that dispatch of March 27 was being sent, Woodford inquired as to the meaning of "full self-government, with reasonable indemnity." The answer of March 28 said: "Full self-government with indemnity would mean Cuban independence." [2]

It was this last demand which ultimately wrecked the negotiations. But even before that point was reached, Spanish procrastination threw away the best remaining chance to prevent armed intervention. With the concentration camps and the *Maine* disaster, there was no delay. The ministry revoked the *reconcentrado* order on March 30 and expressed a willingness to arbitrate the question of responsibility for the battleship's destruction. Sagasta would not, however, grant an immediate armistice or promise to accept McKinley's mediation should subsequent discussions with the insurgents fail. Rather, he insisted that the latter request a truce, and he left the long-range solution to the Cuban parliament which would not meet until May 4. Since the rebels dared not make that request and since McKinley would not resist congressional and party pressures for another five weeks, the Spanish reply of March 31 in effect rejected the American note of March 27. On April 9, to be sure, Sagasta proclaimed an end to hostilities without a rebel request, but he did not accept the President's future mediation and he did not promise eventual independence.

Meanwhile McKinley proceeded deliberately. His message of March 28, 1898, dealing with the *Maine*, was temperate. He did not doubt that Spain would offer adequate reparation. He infuriated inter-

---

[2] McKinley and Woodford were later blamed for not making absolutely clear to Spain that freedom for Cuba could alone avert intervention. The absence of such a statement among the three items in the telegram of March 27, 1898, has led to the widespread belief that Spain eventually conceded everything the United States demanded.

ventionists by advising restraint until the executive had advised the legislature of the outcome. When some impatient lawmakers introduced warlike resolutions, they received no support from the White House. Even the discouraging Spanish reply of March 31 did not quicken the President's pace. Rather, McKinley let it be known that he would lay the issue before both chambers on April 4. Postponed once until April 6, his statement was withheld a second time so that American citizens could be evacuated from Cuba. Not until April 11 did the President voluntarily surrender the initiative and leave to Congress the question of peace or war.

McKinley's message of April 11, 1898, opened with a historical survey. It listed the numerous occasions in the last fifty years when rebellion against misgovernment in Cuba had subjected the United States to great expense in enforcing its neutrality laws, had caused enormous losses to American trade and property, and had "offended the humane sympathies of our people." It then traced the present stalemate in war and diplomacy to the inescapable conclusion that neither side could prevail and that further negotiations were futile. The only practical way to restore peace to the island, the President said, was by "the forcible intervention of the United States." International law, he continued, justified such intervention on four grounds: first, to put an end to bloodshed and starvation which the combatants were unable to stop; second, to give protection to American citizens in Cuba which no government there could provide; third, to prevent a continuing serious injury to American trade and commerce; and fourth, to remove a constant menace to the peace of the United States and an enormous burden in discharging its neutrality.

The executive, McKinley concluded, had the power only to propose. Hence he asked the legislature, "in the name of humanity, in the name of civilization, in behalf of endangered American interests," to authorize him to end the war in Cuba, to secure a stable government in the island, and to use the armed forces for those purposes. "The issue," he warned, "is now with Congress. It is a solemn responsibility. I have exhausted every effort to relieve the intolerable condition of affairs which is at our doors. Prepared to execute every obligation imposed upon me by the Constitution and the law, I await your action."

On that note the message of April 11, 1898, was intended to close. The first draft had been approved by the cabinet a week earlier and did not take cognizance of the belated proclamation of an armistice. When word of that development reached Washington on April 9, Woodford was telling McKinley that all his demands, even independence, might yet be met. This last assertion was most questionable, but in any case, the President could no longer delay his report to Congress. Would he, in the light of this new information, revise drastically what he had already written or would he simply append a postscript? In May, 1846, Polk had entirely recast his message after learning of the attack on Taylor's troops, but that last-minute intelligence served to strengthen his case against Mexico. In 1898 the eleventh-hour advices encouraged further negotiation. Significantly, the patient and hitherto noninterventionist McKinley chose the second alternative. In noncommittal terms he merely alluded to the armistice and expressed confidence that Congress would give it careful attention in "the solemn deliberations" about to begin. If the truce was successful, he concluded, "then our aspirations as a Christian, peace-loving people will be realized. If it fails, it will be only another justification for our contemplated action."

Any appraisal of the message of April 11, 1898, must keep in mind the standard of conduct among nations in the nineteenth century. Armed intervention in a neighboring country to abate an indisputable nuisance or grievance, while never before resorted to on this scale by the United States, was a right clearly recognized by international law. Did the executive make a good case for exercising that right? There can be no doubt that the scorched-earth tactics of both combatants greatly injured a few American property holders, that the interminable conflict badly hurt some American merchants and shippers, and that the widespread suffering on the island grossly outraged the moral sensibilities of all the American people. Hence, although not every citizen was affected equally by what transpired in Cuba, the nation as a whole was; and it was this national interest which gave us, as McKinley put it, "the right and the duty to speak and to act." Nor could it be denied that the United States government had discharged faithfully and at great inconvenience its neutral duties, that neither belligerent could hope to triumph in the foreseeable future, or that, in intervening "in the name of humanity," the President had no thought of territorial gain. The only debatable points are whether further negotiations were futile and whether the concessions of April 9 warranted additional delay. We shall, of course, never know, and it is all too easy in retrospect to believe that something more could have been done. To contemporaries who had grown weary of broken promises and the inevitable Spanish *mañana,* the chances seemed slight. Unquestionably it would have been more statesmanlike to revise the message to Congress and display more prominently the belated news of the tardy armistice. But we must not exaggerate what Spain actually yielded or underestimate the overwhelming pressures—moral, political, economic, and personal—that beset the peace-loving man in the White House.

For the incitements to war in 1898 were much more powerful than those goading Madison in 1812, Polk in 1846, Wilson in 1917, or Roosevelt before December 7, 1941. The American people nursed a traditional dislike of the Spaniards and wanted them driven from the New World. Now, with a strong moral case to end atrocities and the prospect of a fairly painless struggle, the temptation to embark upon a humanitarian crusade was irresistible. Popular indignation was kept at boiling point by an irresponsible press whose disgraceful practices were not confined to any one city. Economic pressure for intervention came from those who benefited by increased circulation, from those who owned land in Cuba, from those who engaged in a once lucrative trade with the island, from those who would profit from army contracts, and from those who hoped a war might derange the currency and upset the gold standard. Yet it is easy to overemphasize these material forces. The business community as a whole eventually accepted but never desired a crusade to free Cuba, while there is no evidence that McKinley was greatly influenced by them.

Political pressures also affected the decision to intervene. The main impulse came not from a tiny coterie of such well-known expansionists as Lodge, Roosevelt, and Mahan, but from an almost united Democracy and a sizable segment of Republicans. It is sometimes assumed that because the anti-imperialists later drew their greatest numbers from the Democrats, that party advocated a hands-off policy in Cuba. Such was not the case, especially after McKinley took office. Then most of the noninterventionists who had remained loyal to Cleveland joined the majority of their colleagues in constant criticism of the new administration's efforts to maintain peace. The President's party was badly split. The so-called "old guard" supported his moderation because it feared that foreign adventures would imperil domestic prosperity. That group dominated the powerful Rules, Judiciary, and Appropriations Committees in the Senate and claimed the Speaker of the House. Opposed to it was a younger element that gained control of the Senate Foreign Relations Committee and persistently urged the executive to move faster than he wished to go.

In view of these alignments, political considerations did enter into McKinley's decision to ask Congress for authority to employ armed force in Cuba. That is not to say that the President sacrificed peace upon the altar of party unity or, in Roosevelt's much quoted gastronomical phrase, that he had the backbone of a chocolate éclair. On the contrary, he demonstrated surprising courage in holding out as long as he did; and if the Sagasta ministry had yielded more quickly and more completely, he might have held firm. But no chief executive has ever defied public sentiment indefinitely, and by April, 1898, national emotions were not what they had been in December, 1896, when even Cleveland conceded that patience could cease to be a virtue. McKinley was undoubtedly pleased to deprive the Democrats of an increasingly popular issue and to close the ranks in his own party; but he did not decide primarily for those reasons.

A final inducement to armed intervention was the favorable international setting. Not a single European power dared come to Spain's rescue. There was, to be sure, much sympathy on the Continent for the plight of the Queen Regent and considerable antipathy to the forcible expulsion of an Old World state by a New. The possibility of American territorial gains was foreseen and in some quarters dreaded. The Spaniards tried to exploit these feelings to obtain a joint mediation which might deter the government in Washington. One attempt was made in the summer of 1896 and another in the autumn of 1897, but both times the European chancelleries were understandably reluctant to antagonize the United States. Perhaps some of the foreign secretaries also realized that, in similar circumstances, they would not have tolerated the same sort of disturbance so close to their frontiers.

What actually transpired smacked of a Gilbert and Sullivan operetta. On April 7, 1898, after McKinley's message had been drafted but before it went to Capitol Hill, the envoys of Austria-Hungary, France, Germany, Great Britain, Italy, and Russia addressed an appeal to the "humanity and moderation of the President" in the hope that differences with Spain could be settled by peaceful means. In reply, the executive thanked the powers for their friendly interest and voiced the hope that they would understand his own "earnest and unselfish endeavors to fulfill a duty to humanity by ending a situation the indefinite prolongation of which has become insufferable." Perhaps encouraged by this response and by the failure of Congress to grant thus far McKinley's request, the six diplomats on April 15 drew up a second and sterner note. In censuring the United States for its unyielding attitude, this document went far beyond the wishes of the cautious home governments and was, therefore, never presented to the State Department. Thus ended Europe's feeble attempt to protect one of its own in the Western Hemisphere.

THE CONGRESS DISPOSES

While this contretemps was in progress, the legislative branch proceeded to exercise its constitutional prerogatives. "The issue is now with Congress," the President had warned, and there was no question about how it would act. But an unexpected delay did arise over a relatively minor point. Although virtual unanimity prevailed in wishing to drive Spain from Cuba, a disagreement arose over the wisdom of including in the joint resolution, which empowered the President to use armed force, an explicit acknowledgment of the insurgent government. In general, the extreme interventionists—Republican and Democratic—wished to recognize its independence, just as they had wanted to do for two years. But the administration doubted whether a nation worthy of that name actually existed on the island and opposed such a step. Hence the House, where McKinley's lieutenants were in control, passed a resolution without any encumbrance on April 13, 1898, by a count of 325 to 19. Three days later the less tractable Senate adopted by a margin of 67 to 21 a resolution specifying recognition. After a brief but heated struggle, McKinley's charm won over Republican extremists in the Senate, and a conference committee eliminated the clause acknowledging Cuba's independence. On April 19 the Senate approved the equivalent of the House version by the misleading tally of 42 to 35—misleading in that most of the negative votes came from Democrats who certainly wanted war. That same day the House endorsed the measure by a total of 311 to 6.

The joint resolution was signed on April 20, 1898. Its preamble declared that the "abhorrent conditions which have existed for more than three years" had so shocked the moral sense of the American people that they could no longer be endured. Congress, therefore, resolved: first, that the people of Cuba are and of right ought to be independent; second, that the United States demand Spain's withdrawal from Cuba; third, that the President be empowered to use the entire land and sea forces of the nation to carry out these resolutions; and fourth, that the United States disclaim any intention "to exercise sovereignty, jurisdiction, or control" over Cuba, except to insure pacification, but would, as soon as that is accomplished, "leave the government and control of the island to its people." This fourth article, renouncing annexation, was added at the last minute by Senator Henry M. Teller, Silver Republican of Colorado. It passed without debate or a recorded vote. There was little disposition in either house to acquire the land which the republic sought to liberate from misery and misrule.

Inexorably, the final moves followed. As soon as the President had signed the joint resolution, the Spanish minister asked for his passports. Simultaneously Woodford was instructed to secure compliance with the American demands by noon of April 23, 1898, or the executive would resort to the authority granted by the legislature. When the government in Madrid severed relations before that ultimatum could be delivered, Congress on April 25 enacted another joint resolution declaring that war with Spain had existed since April 21. Already on April 22 a blockade had been clamped on Cuba; the next day the first shots were fired. On April 24 Dewey was ordered to proceed forthwith from Hong Kong to the Philippines and to capture or destroy the enemy squadron there. Little did the American people or their elected representatives or even their military leaders realize, as they concentrated on the crusade to free Cuba, that Dewey's orders would soon confront the United States with the most momentous diplomatic decision since its quest for an independent foreign policy more than three quarters of a century earlier.

15

❯❯❯·❯❯❯·❯❯❯·❯❯❯❮❮❮·❮❮❮·❮❮❮·❮❮❮

The Decision on Colonies

BEFORE MAY 1, 1898, few, if any, Americans expected that armed intervention in Cuba would require a decision on colonies. The clash with Spain was humanitarian in origin, not imperialistic. The orders to Dewey spoke of destroying a fleet, not of capturing an archipelago. The Teller resolution intended to liberate Cuba, not annex it. The expansionists of the 1890's had not sought any part of the Spanish Empire. In retrospect, to be sure, it seems incredible that the administration did not foresee the territorial temptation a successful war would bring or the strategic dilemma a victory at Manila would pose. In light of the subsequent peace, McKinley's earlier talk of forcible annexation's being criminal aggression rings hollow, and it is easy to dismiss the President as a fool or a knave—a fool for not anticipating the consequences of a Spanish defeat, a knave for misleading the people about his true aims. But a sounder explanation of this controversial episode is that, like most of his countrymen, he was swept along by the logic of events, by a vague sense of duty and destiny, and by the belated realization that it was simpler to retain, at least temporarily, the lands that fell to American arms than to give them up immediately.

THE WAR WITH SPAIN

Foremost in diverting the War with Spain from a crusade to a conquest was McKinley's decision on May 2, 1898, to send army units to assist

Dewey. This step, which he took on the advice of his cabinet and military aides but without consulting Congress or awaiting Dewey's battle report, is revealing. If the President and his associates had intended from the outset to dismember the Spanish Empire, they would have perfected these arrangements before, not after, the triumph in Manila Bay on May 1. If Roosevelt and his strategy board, created in March, 1898, had meant from the beginning to obtain islands in the Western Pacific, they would not have concentrated exclusively on Cuba. Prior to this decision of May 2, there is no evidence that anyone gave thought to, much less drafted plans for, what would be done after Dewey fulfilled his mission.[1] Everything had to be improvised: mobilizing an expeditionary force, chartering commercial transports, selecting an army commander, finding a naval escort. This took time. Not until May 25 had the first three troopships and the cruiser *Charleston* left San Francisco; not until June 30 did they reach the Philippines. It took until July 31 to carry 15,600 soldiers to the Far East, and during that interval the mood of the American people and their leaders underwent an enormous transformation.

Dewey's sensational victory quickly broadened the horizons of the most ardent expansionists. Before May 1, 1898, the exponents of the new manifest destiny had not looked beyond Samoa; by May 5 they saw differently. Davis wrote that, because of developments in China, "we ought to have territory in the Asiatic Pacific," while Lodge asserted, in referring to the Philippines, "we must on no account let the Islands go." Surprisingly, the administration followed suit. Although Dewey requested only 5,000 men as a landing team, McKinley was ready to give him 20,000. On May 10, the captain of the *Charleston* was ordered to seize Guam. The next day the President chose Major General Wesley Merritt, the army's second-ranking officer, to head the expeditionary force. By May 24 he had approved sending to Manila two heavily-gunned harbor-defense vessels, which had to be towed across the ocean and were not likely to be brought back. Still more astonishing was McKinley's changed thinking about the peace. On May 7 the British asked Ambassador Hay in London whether the evacuation of Cuba was the sole condition for an armistice. Secretary Day took until June 3 to reply, and his answer would have been unthinkable five weeks earlier. He told Hay that, in addition to renouncing Cuba, Spain must cede, in lieu of an indemnity, Puerto Rico

---

[1] McKinley did not seriously consider having Dewey quit the Orient altogether. Since the Far Eastern ports, from which the Asiatic Squadron operated in peacetime, were closed under international law, the Commodore had no real alternative between remaining in the Philippines or returning to the United States. To do the former would require a landing force to defend his foothold at Cavite and, if necessary, to oust the Spaniards from the city of Manila.

and also grant one island in the Marianas with a harbor suitable for "a coaling station" and "one port and necessary appurtenances" in the Philippines.

Several other factors explain this shifting sentiment. First, an unbroken string of victories betokened a short war. The United States invaded Cuba on June 10, 1898; captured Guam on June 22; destroyed the Spanish squadron in the Caribbean on July 3; and landed in Puerto Rico on July 25. Second, incredible German blunders in Manila Bay helped to keep that harbor in the public eye. After May 1 the major nations rushed naval contingents there to protect the lives and property of their citizens. Germany, however, assembled a detachment out of all proportion to its interests in the islands, one which equaled in firepower and exceeded in armor that of the United States. Its commander, Vice Admiral Otto von Diederichs, had an uncanny knack of irritating Dewey by disregarding rules for identification and anchorage. On July 7 a crisis threatened when a German cruiser in Subic Bay openly aided the Spaniards in their fight against native insurgents. The eagerness of the Reich to annex the archipelago persuaded many Americans that it was valuable enough to be retained for themselves.

A third development which focused attention on the Philippines was the drama of a Spanish relief expedition. On June 16, 1898, Admiral Manuel de la Cámara left Cadiz with a force stronger than Dewey's and with transports bearing 4,000 men. If he reached Manila before the arrival of the two monitors and the last echelons of Merritt's command, the United States would be in for trouble. Hence, while the American people held their collective breath and as their own reinforcements slowly threaded their way across the Pacific, the Navy Department mounted two countermeasures to meet the danger. After the victory off Santiago on July 3, it ordered two modern battleships to pursue Cámara into the Mediterranean and the Suez Canal, while it dispatched an even more powerful task force on a diversionary sweep of the Spanish coast. The mere prospect of these operations caused a panic-stricken government at Madrid to recall Cámara from the Red Sea, but the Americans had their anxious moments as they pondered Dewey's exposed position in East Asia and the lack of bases for the fleet in the Pacific.

Finally, complications with the Filipinos led to an outcome none had foreseen. In March, 1898, fighting broke out anew on Luzon. At Singapore the American consul held unauthorized conversations with the exiled Aguinaldo and probably encouraged him to believe that a United States victory over Spain would mean independence for the Philippines. In any case, Dewey was persuaded to let Aguinaldo return to direct the resistance movement. On May 24 the Filipino suddenly formed a native government with himself as head, and four days later he defeated a Spanish column sent against him. Within a month he had taken 4,000 prisoners, won control of most of Luzon, laid siege to Manila, and issued a virtual declaration of independence. Although his activity helped divert the enemy while Dewey waited for Merritt's troops, the last pretension conflicted with that general's instructions to "establish supreme political control" over the inhabitants of the islands. Relations quickly deteriorated, and by July 26 Dewey reported Aguinaldo as "threatening towards our army." No major clash occurred before United States forces captured Manila on August 13, 1898, but by then the ill-concealed distrust and hostility on both sides made it extremely difficult, if not impossible, to hand the archipelago over to Aguinaldo after the war.

This changing attitude toward the Western Pacific helped to consummate the annexation of the Hawaiian Republic. Dewey's victory and the assistance the islanders rendered in servicing both the naval reinforcements and Merritt's transports wiped out much of the resistance on Capitol Hill to the joint resolution Davis had introduced on March 16, 1898. Under urging from McKinley and the plea of military necessity, the House approved the measure on June 15 by a margin of 209 to 91. The Senate gave its consent on July 6 by a two-thirds majority of 42 to 21. Democrats, Populists, and independents furnished most of the opposition to this long anticipated step. McKinley signed the bill on July 7, and on August 12, 1898, Hawaii became part of the American Union.

THE PARIS PEACE TREATY

By then Spain had sued for peace. On July 26, 1898, it announced a readiness to give up Cuba and requested the United States to suggest how the island might be disposed of. Spain said nothing about the rest of its empire in the Caribbean and Pacific, parts of which were falling to American arms. The United States replied four days later with terms formulated solely by the executive. McKinley did not call Congress back into session or pay much attention to the barrage of unsolicited advice he received from several prominent members. His demands, which Day had foreshadowed in his dispatch to Hay on June 3, astonished Spain by their imperialistic tenor, but the helpless cabinet in Madrid had to comply. Signed at Washington on August 12, 1898, the armistice protocol obliged Spain to renounce all claims to Cuba and to cede Puerto Rico and one of the Marianas, to be chosen later, to the United States. The West Indian islands had to be evacuated at once. As to the Philippines, the victor would "hold the city, bay and harbor of Manila" until a final settlement determined "the control, disposition and government" of the archipelago. Commissioners not

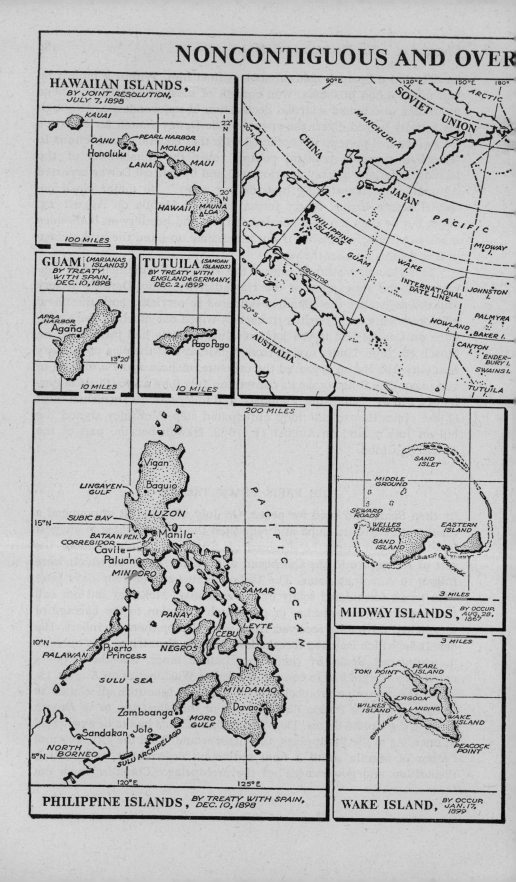

NONCONTIGUOUS AND OVER

HAWAIIAN ISLANDS, BY JOINT RESOLUTION, JULY 7, 1898

KAUAI
OAHU — PEARL HARBOR
Honolulu
MOLOKAI
LANAI
MAUI
HAWAII
MAUNA LOA
22° N
20° N
100 MILES

GUAM (MARIANAS ISLANDS) BY TREATY WITH SPAIN, DEC. 10, 1898

APRA HARBOR
Agaña
13°20' N
10 MILES

TUTUILA (SAMOAN ISLANDS) BY TREATY WITH ENGLAND & GERMANY, DEC. 2, 1899

Pago Pago
10 MILES

SOVIET UNION
ARCTIC
CHINA
MANCHURIA
JAPAN
PACIFIC
PHILIPPINE ISLANDS
GUAM
MIDWAY
WAKE
EQUATOR
INTERNATIONAL DATE LINE
JOHNSTON I.
HOWLAND
PALMYRA
BAKER I.
CANTON
ENDERBURY I.
SWAINS I.
AUSTRALIA
TUTUILA
90°E 120°E 150°E 180°
0°
20°S

PHILIPPINE ISLANDS, BY TREATY WITH SPAIN, DEC. 10, 1898

Vigan
Baguio
LINGAYEN GULF
LUZON
SUBIC BAY
BATAAN PEN.
CORREGIDOR
Manila
Cavite
Paluan
MINDORO
15°N
SAMAR
PANAY
LEYTE
CEBU
NEGROS
PUERTO Princess
PALAWAN
10°N
SULU SEA
MINDANAO
Davao
Zamboanga
MORO GULF
Sandakan
Jolo
NORTH BORNEO
SULU ARCHIPELAGO
5°N
120°E 125°E
PACIFIC OCEAN
200 MILES

MIDWAY ISLANDS, BY OCCUP. AUG. 28, 1867

SAND ISLET
MIDDLE GROUND
SEWARD ROADS
WELLES HARBOR
EASTERN ISLAND
SAND ISLAND
3 MILES

WAKE ISLAND, BY OCCUP. JAN. 17, 1899

TOKI POINT
PEARL ISLAND
WILKES ISLAND
LAGOON
LANDING
WAKE ISLAND
PEACOCK POINT
3 MILES

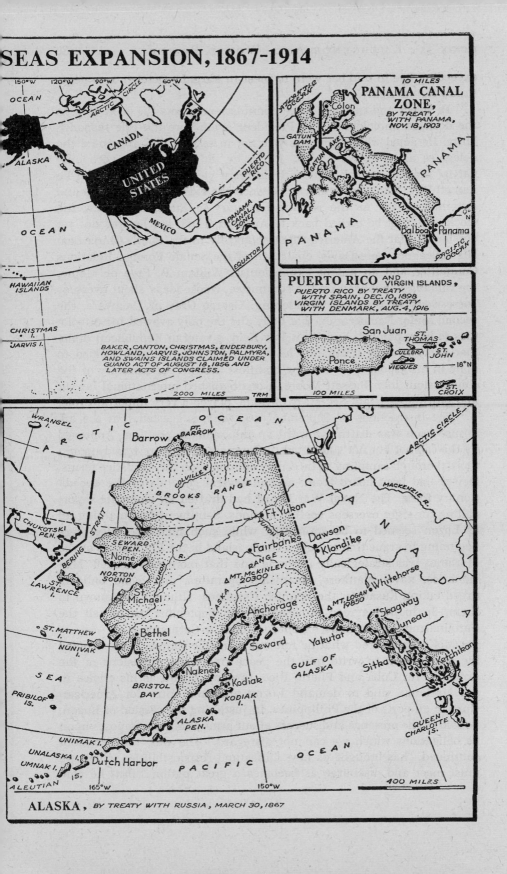

SEAS EXPANSION, 1867-1914

PANAMA CANAL ZONE, BY TREATY WITH PANAMA, NOV. 18, 1903

10 MILES

ATLANTIC OCEAN · Colon · PANAMA · GATUN DAM · GATUN LAKE · CANAL · PANAMA · Balboa · Panama · PACIFIC OCEAN

PUERTO RICO AND VIRGIN ISLANDS, PUERTO RICO BY TREATY WITH SPAIN, DEC. 10, 1898. VIRGIN ISLANDS BY TREATY WITH DENMARK, AUG. 4, 1916

San Juan · ST. THOMAS · CULEBRA · ST. JOHN · Ponce · VIEQUES · ST. CROIX · 18°N

100 MILES

150°W · 120°W · 90°W · 60°W · ARCTIC CIRCLE · OCEAN · CANADA · ALASKA · UNITED STATES · OCEAN · MEXICO · PUERTO RICO · PANAMA CANAL ZONE · EQUATOR · HAWAIIAN ISLANDS · CHRISTMAS I. · JARVIS I.

BAKER, CANTON, CHRISTMAS, ENDERBURY, HOWLAND, JARVIS, JOHNSTON, PALMYRA, AND SWAINS ISLANDS CLAIMED UNDER GUANO ACT OF AUGUST 18, 1856 AND LATER ACTS OF CONGRESS.

2000 MILES · TRM

WRANGEL I. · ARCTIC · OCEAN · PT. BARROW · Barrow · COLVILLE R. · BROOKS RANGE · MACKENZIE R. · ARCTIC CIRCLE · CHUKOTSKI PEN. · BERING STRAIT · Ft. Yukon · YUKON R. · Dawson · Klondike · SEWARD PEN. · Nome · Fairbanks · RANGE · MT. McKINLEY 20300 · Whitehorse · ST. LAWRENCE I. · NORTON SOUND · St. Michael · YUKON R. · ALASKA RANGE · Anchorage · MT. LOGAN 19850 · Skagway · ST. MATTHEW I. · Bethel · Seward · Yakutat · Juneau · NUNIVAK I. · GULF OF ALASKA · Sitka · Ketchikan · SEA · Naknek · Kodiak · BRISTOL BAY · KODIAK I. · PRIBILOF IS. · ALASKA PEN. · QUEEN CHARLOTTE IS. · UNIMAK I. · UNALASKA I. · UMNAK I. · IS. · Dutch Harbor · PACIFIC · OCEAN · ALEUTIAN · 165°W · 150°W · 400 MILES

ALASKA, BY TREATY WITH RUSSIA, MARCH 30, 1867

exceeding five in number were to meet in Paris by October 1 to negotiate a formal treaty.

To select and instruct those commissioners was the next step in
the decision on colonies. The President again bore the sole responsibility. He acted while Congress was not in session and appointed the
delegates as executive agents. McKinley did try, though with only
partial success, to pick men with different views. To be chairman he
named Day, who stood midway between the extreme imperialists and
anti-imperialists. As the retiring Secretary of State, Day knew the
clock could not be turned back to April 30, 1898, but he was not yet
persuaded that the American flag should fly in the South China Sea.
His colleagues were Davis, chairman of the Senate Foreign Relations
Committee and an ardent expansionist; William P. Frye of Maine,
the ranking Republican on the committee, whose ideas about overseas
possessions were rapidly broadening; George Gray of Delaware, the
second senior Democrat on that body and the only avowed foe of colonies to be appointed; and Whitelaw Reid, a veteran Republican diplomat and currently editor of *The New York Tribune*, who yielded to
none in his espousal of the new manifest destiny. As secretary of the
commission, John Bassett Moore, a distinguished international lawyer
and retiring Assistant Secretary of State, played a very important role.

The instructions of September 16, 1898, suggested that the administration was drifting toward an imperialistic position. Approved
by the cabinet but not submitted to Congress, they were based upon a
more thorough sampling of informed opinion than the armistice terms.
Dewey had been heard from, as had several generals of the expeditionary force. The Naval War Board had drafted an elaborate report
calling for eight overseas coaling stations. Sentiment for retaining all
of Luzon seemed to be spreading, while such men as Lodge were
beginning to argue that to hold a single island in the Philippines or the
Marianas was strategically unsound and that more was needed. Missionaries, naval planners, steamship operators, and cable builders
urged taking Kusaie in the Spanish Carolines, although, unknown to
them, Spain had agreed provisionally on September 10 to sell the
Caroline and the Marianas, except for Guam, to Germany.

McKinley steered what he felt was a middle course. He instructed
the commission to write into the peace treaty the provisions of the
armistice for Cuba and Puerto Rico, to name Guam as his choice in
the Marianas, and to demand Luzon and free entry for American
ships in all ports of the Philippines. In justifying the cession of Luzon,
he said: "The presence and success of our arms at Manila imposes upon
us obligations which we can not disregard." The war, the President
continued, "has brought us new duties and responsibilities which we
must meet and discharge as becomes a great nation." But, he con-

cluded, "we seek no advantages in the Orient which are not common to all."

This theme of duty and destiny, mingled with a concern for the equal treatment of trade in East Asia, appeared frequently during a two-week speaking tour which McKinley began on October 8, 1898. At first he was uncertain whether his demand for Luzon and free entry into Filipino ports went far enough. The delegates in Paris were divided, and as the President traveled to Omaha, he tried in some fifty-seven addresses to gauge the wishes of the people. His remarks were vague, commonplace, and platitudinous, but the popular reaction was unmistakable. Thunderous applause greeted his numerous allusions to the responsibilities, obligations, and opportunities that a successful war had thrust upon a now mature republic. By the time he returned to Washington on October 22, McKinley had made up his mind.

How McKinley reached his decision has often been retold in his own words. An intensely religious man, he informed some clergymen, over a year later, that he had never made any plans beyond Dewey's initial offensive. After the victory he sought advice about the Philippines from many leaders but remained puzzled. "I thought first we would take only Manila; then Luzon; then other islands, perhaps, also. . . . I went down on my knees and prayed Almighty God for light and guidance . . . and one night late it came to me. . . . (1) That we could not give them back to Spain—that would be cowardly and dishonorable; (2) that we could not turn them over to France or Germany—our commercial rivals in the Orient—that would be bad business and discreditable; (3) that we could not leave them to themselves—they were unfit for self-government . . . and (4) that there was nothing left for us to do but to take them all, and to educate the Filipinos, and uplift and civilize and Christianize them, and by God's grace do the very best we could by them."

If we discount the pious overtones inspired by the occasion, McKinley's explanation aptly summarizes the dilemma confronting many destiny-conscious and duty-minded Americans in 1898. It had been simpler to go into the Philippines than to get out. Not having thought through the implications of Dewey's orders or of collaborating with Aguinaldo, the policy makers were plagued by those acts at a moment when the popular appetite for territorial gain and business advantage was growing. Public sentiment did bar restoring the islands to Spain. It was diplomatically unwise to cede them to a foreign power; international rivalries in the Far East were too tense to permit that way out. Although the evidence is fragmentary and although it is always perilous for one people to sit in judgment on another, the fear that the Filipinos could not govern themselves without some apprenticeship and the danger that they would fall prey to a stronger nation were very real. Finally, if we forgive the President's oversight that most Filipinos were already Christians and if we accept his words at face value, the conclusion he reached was justifiable. To hold the islands as a temporary mandate, to train their inhabitants for self-rule and ultimate freedom, was a reasonable, though perhaps not ideal, solution to a very difficult and complex problem.

Whatever its merits, McKinley arrived at this decision none too soon. In Manila Dewey was warning that only the speedy creation of a stable government could avert bloodshed. In Paris the commissioners filed a gargantuan cablegram revealing their hopeless disagreement. Although the President had already settled with Hay the precise instructions to be forwarded, the time required to decode the long message and his own presence in Philadelphia caused a further delay. Hence it was not until October 28, 1898 that the momentous dispatch was sent. Endorsed by the whole cabinet save for one absentee, it directed the delegates to demand all of the Philippines. To leave any part to Spain, it argued, "would increase our difficulties and be opposed to the interests of humanity." Equally inadmissible was the archipelago's transfer to a third power or its disposition as a protectorate by the United States and others. Consequently, "grave as are the responsibilities and unforeseen as are the difficulties," there was only "one plain path of duty—the acceptance of the archipelago."

And so, spurred on by the heady enthusiasm of a successful war, by an understandable fear of foreign complications, by the seductive lure of business and missionary opportunities, by an oversimplified concept of sea power, and by a burgeoning sense of destiny and duty, McKinley cast the die. Feeling that there was no reasonable alternative, he extended American sovereignty, at least temporarily, over some 7,500,000 peoples possessing a different language and legal tradition, observing divergent social customs, and living only 600 miles off the coast of Asia. Once this decision was taken, the conferees at Paris slowly ground out the treaty of December 10, 1898. By its terms, Cuba was to be relinquished by Spain and to undergo American occupation for an unspecified period. Territorially, the United States obtained Puerto Rico and some tiny adjacent isles in the Caribbean, Guam in the Marianas, and all of the Philippines. Choosing to negotiate for the last item rather than to claim it as conquest, the victor paid the vanquished $20 million.

THE VOTES IN THE SENATE

Consent to this tradition-shattering settlement was by no means certain. Since the Alaskan treaty of March 30, 1867, the Senate had in one way or another blocked every expansionist treaty. If relatively small or nearby sites such as Samaná Bay, the Danish West Indies, and Hawaii failed to find favor, what would be the fate of a large archipelago 6,000 miles from San Francisco? The arguments against the pact were many: the threat to isolationism and other accepted policies, the difficulty of defending such distant outposts, the payment of $20 million for lands unconnected with the cause of the war, the danger of clashing with Filipino aspirations for freedom, the belief that the republic could not hold colonies without betraying its ideals. On the other hand, no peace treaty had ever been rejected. To defeat the present one would leave the country technically at war. Finally, the administration could count upon all but two of the forty-five Republican votes in the upper house and therefore needed only seventeen of the other forty-five distributed among the Democrats, Populists, Silver Republicans, and independents.

Whether it would obtain those seventeen depended largely on William Jennings Bryan, the titular leader of the opposition. The Nebraska pacifist had volunteered in the war and served as colonel. Not until December 13, 1898, three days after his discharge, did he make known his views on the peace. He was not averse to retaining "a harbor or coaling station" in both Puerto Rico and the Philippines, and he was willing to consider annexing the former if the inhabitants approved. But he was unalterably opposed to acquiring colonies in general and the Philippines in particular. Nevertheless, he would accept the treaty of Paris, lest rejection delay the coming of peace and encourage dangerous territorial clashes in East Asia.

From this position Bryan could not be budged. The anti-imperialists tried all manner of persuasion, for he commanded ten to twenty Senate votes. But the Great Commoner sincerely believed that a formal end of the war must precede final action on the Philippines and that such action must be taken by both houses of Congress. He objected to the two-thirds rule, which gave a minority the power to defeat so important a measure. Whether political considerations were joined to pacifist principles and constitutional scruples—whether Bryan planned at that date to make imperialism an issue in the election of 1900—is a point on which historians disagree. But certainly his refusal to fight the treaty was a valuable and unexpected boon to the administration.

When it reassembled on December 5, 1898, Congress had its first opportunity to participate in the decision on colonies. Although McKinley tactfully suggested that a discussion of the status of the new possessions be postponed until the peace treaty had been consented to, his critics refused to wait. On December 6 George G. Vest, Democrat of Missouri, offered in the Senate a resolution which challenged the President at every point. It denied that the Constitution empowered the government to acquire territory which might be held permanently as a dependency and argued that, except for small sites useful for coaling stations, all lands added to the Union must be organized ultimately into states and be admitted on a footing of complete equality. Since the Vest resolution would thwart McKinley's plan to effect annexation before deciding the issue of colonialism and since it denied the right to retain Guam and Puerto Rico as well as the Philippines as colonies, the Republican leaders did everything possible to prevent its being voted upon until the peace pact was disposed of. They succeeded, but at a price. The debate on a resolution, unlike that on a treaty, cannot be kept behind closed doors, and the speeches on the Vest motion not only stimulated anti-imperialist sentiment at home but also aroused Aguinaldo's followers abroad.

Two other resolutions disclosed the temper of the Senate. On January 11, 1899, Augustus O. Bacon, Democrat of Georgia, introduced one patterned on the Teller amendment. By its terms, the United States would have disclaimed any intention to exercise sovereignty over the Philippines and would have promised to leave control of the islands to their people as soon as a stable, independent government had been established. Bacon, however, was unable to bring his proposition to a vote until after the treaty had passed. The second, sponsored by Arthur P. Gorman, Democrat of Maryland, was intended to be an amendment to the treaty itself. Under his change Spain would relinquish the Philippines, but not cede them to the United States, while the latter would be responsible for their welfare only until a free regime had been set up. On February 6, 1899, the Gorman amendment was lost by a margin of 53 to 30.

While the Senate deliberated, dispatches from the Far East told of mounting tension between the Filipino and American forces. The tense situation of the previous August had grown worse. Open warfare was said to be but a matter of weeks. The President's decision of October 28, 1898, apparently surprised Aguinaldo; an order of December 21 extending military rule to the entire archipelago obviously angered him. Whether prompt passage of the Vest or Bacon resolutions would have averted the tragedy that followed is impossible to say; but on the night of February 4–5, 1899, just as Davis was bringing the treaty to a vote, an exchange of shots near Manila touched off an insurrection against the United States that lasted in one form or another until July, 1902.

This outbreak occurred too late to influence the balloting in the Senate. With great patience Davis had unified his own party and had reaped rewards from Bryan's attitude. With consummate skill he had kept the treaty free of amendments or declarations on the status of the new possessions. With supreme confidence he defied talk of a filibuster, for the Republican majority would be larger in the Senate which

McKinley could convene on March 4, 1899. Although the outcome was doubtful to the end, the tally of 57 to 27 on February 6 gave a two-vote margin of safety. A combination of forty-one Republicans, eleven Democrats, and five others defeated a coalition of two Republicans, twenty-two Democrats, and three others. Several of Bryan's followers insured victory for McKinley.

Approval of the Paris Treaty was the final step in the decision on colonies, but it did not constitute a clear endorsement of imperialism. Some lawmakers found it difficult to separate the question of retaining dependencies from that of ending the war, while many more preferred to stop with Puerto Rico, Hawaii, and the smaller islands. There was much opposition to keeping indefinitely the populous and distant Philippines, as two subsequent ballots attested. The Bacon resolution, promising independence as soon as a stable government had been installed, was finally brought up on February 14, 1899. With thirty-two Senators abstaining, the result was a tie of 29 to 29, and only the casting vote of the Vice President killed the resolution. That roll call disclosed that when early freedom for the Filipinos was distinguished from terminating the war, it enlisted the backing of nine men who had supported the peace treaty. Further evidence was the alignment the same day on a joint resolution introduced by Samuel D. McEnery, Democrat of Louisiana, whose last-minute decision to vote aye had helped muster the two-thirds margin eight days earlier. Less forthright than the Bacon proposal, the McEnery resolution explained that, in consenting to the Paris settlement, the Senate did not intend to annex the Philippines permanently but only temporarily, in order to train their people for self-rule and "in due time" to dispose of the group "as will best promote the interests of the citizens of the United States and the inhabitants of said islands." That declaration passed 26 to 22, with forty-two abstentions, but the House never acted on it.

How central the Philippines were to the battle over imperialism was illustrated when the McKinley administration, without causing a ripple of criticism, added two more Pacific islands to the American empire in 1899. One was the tiny, unoccupied atoll of Wake, lying 1,320 miles east of Guam. Although visited by explorers in 1841, Wake was forgotten until Dewey had to be reinforced; then every spit of land on the steamship route to Manila assumed significance. The general heading the second echelon of the expeditionary force had gone ashore on July 4, 1898, just long enough to make observations and raise the flag. On January 17, 1899, the commander of the gunboat *Bennington* proclaimed formal possession. No Senate approval was needed or asked. The second island was Tutuila in the Samoan group, which the United States obtained when it belatedly abandoned its opposition to partition. With the experiment in joint rule an obvious failure, Hay signed at Washington on December 2, 1899, a tripartite treaty which awarded Savaii and Upolu to Germany and placed Tutuila under American sovereignty. By a separate agreement, England, the third signatory, received compensation in the Solomon Islands. To this accord the Senate gave its consent on January 16, 1900, with almost no debate and without a recorded vote.

THE ELECTION OF 1900

Acquiescence in the annexation of Wake and Tutuila did not mark an end of opposition to colonies. On the contrary, the votes in the Senate ushered in a widespread debate over imperialism which kept the country aroused until the election of 1900 and which did not finally slacken until the initial laws for governing the dependencies had been enacted. Again, the wisdom and justice of retaining the Philippines lay at the center of the impassioned oratory. Both sides drew ammunition from the bloody insurrection in the archipelago, where brutal atrocities shocked the conscience of the nation, and from the dramatic events on the mainland, where the turmoil in China posed diplomatic, economic, and strategic problems for the new Far Eastern power. Indeed, the prolonged inquest compelled Americans to re-examine past assumptions about their place in world affairs and to consider future challenges to their cherished isolationism. There had been no similar probing of first principles in foreign policy since the early days of the republic; there would be nothing like it again until 1919 and 1920.

In the debate that raged until 1902, the imperialists presented a more homogeneous group than their rivals, but also a less literate and, in the retrospect of the 1960's, a less appealing one. Their hard core consisted of four major groups: political leaders, who had either advocated overseas expansion since the 1880's or staked their fortunes on the decision of 1898–9; naval officers and civilians, who had urged the acquisition of strategic sites; foreign missionaries and their domestic allies, who believed that new territory would aid in spreading God's word; and businessmen, who hoped for material gain from dependencies. Politically, the imperialists tended to be Republicans, and party lines hardened perceptibly as the debate progressed. The arguments they used did not differ markedly from those employed before the war, except that the economic justification loomed much larger. Contemporary developments encouraged also the call to duty, the appeal to destiny, and the idea of inevitability. Rudyard Kipling best described with prophetic insight and in haunting cadences the challenge of the white man's burden, but Beveridge spoke the same language when, after returning from a tour of the Philippines, he told the Senate on January 9, 1900: "We will not repudiate our duty in the archipelago. We will not abandon our opportunity in the Orient. We will not renounce our part in the mission of our race. . . . And we will move forward to our work, not howling out regrets like slaves whipped to their burdens, but with gratitude for a task worthy of our strength and thanksgiving to Almighty God that He has marked us as His chosen people."

To anti-imperialists, talk of duty, destiny, and inevitability smacked of unconscious rationalization or deliberate distortion in order to justify territorial rapacity, economic cupidity, and diplomatic lunacy. The nucleus of those opposed to colonialism can be identified in six groups: political leaders, who had long combatted the trend toward noncontinental possessions; pacifists, who saw no difference between the evils of militarism and of imperialism; free-silver advocates, who desired an enlargement of the nation's currency but not of its boundaries; certain immigrant stocks like the Irish- and German-Americans, who were motivated more by a dislike of England than of colonies; an amorphous bloc of reformers, who ran the gamut from patrician defenders of constitutional liberties through middle-class crusaders for social justice to self-tutored champions of the toiling masses; and a less diverse battery of scholars, novelists, and poets, who expressed eloquently the sense of outrage which many citizens felt at the thought of governing without the consent of the governed and of suppressing honest strivings for freedom by armed force. Politically, those foes of overseas dependencies were predominantly Democrats, Populists, and independent intellectuals.

The anti-imperialist indictment maintained that the new empire was unconstitutional, undemocratic, unprofitable, and unsafe. It was unconstitutional because neither President nor Congress possessed the authority to acquire territory and hold it indefinitely in a subordinate status. It was undemocratic because of the self-evident truth that governments derive their just powers from the consent of the governed. It was unprofitable because trade did not follow the flag. It was unsafe because colonies would drag the republic into the maelstrom of world politics and destroy the aloofness under which it had grown great. In general, the passing years have confirmed the first three indictments, but the abandonment of isolationism was four decades in the making and can be attributed only slightly to the triumph of imperialism.

By its very nature, this debate could not reverse the decision on colonies. It could, and did, strengthen an existing reluctance to embark upon further overseas expansion as well as lay the foundation for the retreat from empire twenty years later. But to translate their views into governmental policy, the anti-imperialists would have to elect in 1900 a president who would repudiate McKinley's course or write into the initial legislation for the dependencies a statement promising an early grant of autonomy and an ultimate bestowal of independence.

So far as the presidential canvass was concerned, the anti-imperialists had to combat the fact that no such contest had ever hinged upon a single issue, much less one in foreign policy. They had also to accept Bryan's refusal to convert his second battle with McKinley into a referendum on colonialism. The Democratic platform, to be sure, denounced the administration's action in Puerto Rico and the Philippines, deplored the "unnecessary war" which had placed the country in a "false and un-American position," and demanded a prompt fulfillment of the pledge to withdraw from liberated Cuba. It asserted that "no nation can long endure half republic and half empire" and warned that "imperialism abroad will lead quickly and inevitably to despotism at home." It even called imperialism "the paramount issue of the campaign." But having said so much, the platform proceeded to attack monopoly, condemn protectionism, laud the free-silver plank of 1896, censure the Gold Standard Act of 1900, and favor a bevy of progressive proposals. In short, the Democrats offered no haven for an anti-imperialist who was a conservative in domestic affairs, and Bryan's subsequent tactics only alienated such people.

McKinley's party, as might be expected, reversed the order in which it pointed with pride and viewed with alarm. It began by questioning the capacity of the Democrats to govern. It renewed its allegiance to the gold standard, re-endorsed high tariffs, and demanded a larger merchant marine for foreign trade. Only at the end, when praising the President's diplomacy, did the platform refer to imperialism. McKinley, it said, had been compelled to destroy Spanish control in the West Indies and the Philippines. He and the Senate had been wise to approve the peace treaty. The nation as a whole was obligated to establish order in the lands its troops had freed. The conclusion was clear: "Our authority could not be less than our responsibility; and wherever sovereign rights were extended it became the high duty of the Government to maintain its authority, to put down armed insurrection and to confer the blessings of liberty and civilization upon all the rescued people." Independence and self-rule were assured to the Cubans; for those areas actually annexed, the party pledged itself to confer "the largest measure of self-government consistent with their welfare and our duties."

During the campaign Bryan failed to weld a strong bipartisan opposition to colonialism. He saw his potential backing torn apart by divergent economic beliefs and conflicting party loyalties. Although he deepened those fissures by refusing to abandon free silver, it is doubtful whether any candidate could have kept so disparate a following united on the issue of empire. The leading Republican foes of dependencies either supported McKinley or sat on the sidelines. Cleveland declined to endorse Bryan, and some conservative Democrats openly fought him. The independents scattered their strength. Thus, when the ballots were counted in November, 1900, McKinley repeated his triumph of 1896 by slightly larger majorities in both the popular and the electoral vote, while Congress remained heavily Republican.

Victory at the polls enabled the McKinley administration to interpret the result as an approval of its record and a mandate to persevere along the path of empire. The anti-imperialists were powerless to reverse the President's policies or enact into law a pledge of early independence for any of the new possessions. Such a promise was not expected or even desired for Tutuila, Guam, or Wake, since those islands did not disturb deep-seated scruples. The annexation of Hawaii was also accepted as a *fait accompli;* like Alaska, it could hope to be a state some day. But Puerto Rico and the Philippines were different, as was occupied Cuba, and upon them the foes of dependencies in Congress concentrated. By the end of 1902 they had little to show for their efforts. The Foraker Act of April 12, 1900, gave a very limited amount of self-rule to Puerto Rico and said nothing about eventual freedom. The Platt Amendment to an army appropriation bill of March 2, 1901, authorized the President to withdraw American forces from Cuba only after relations for the future had been defined; and the treaty of May 22, 1903, severely curtailed Cuba's sovereignty at several points. As to the Philippines, the Civil Government Act of July 1, 1902, escaped all amendments which would have committed the United States to free the islands at a later date. At no time could the anti-imperialists muster 40 per cent of the vote in Congress, and that figure exceeded Bryan's 34.7 per cent in the electoral college.

Although it is hazardous to say what the American people thought on a specific issue of the past, it seems reasonable to conclude that at the time of the decision and debate on colonies a majority favored— some enthusiastically, more reluctantly—the acquisition of an empire. The reasons for this break with tradition are to be found in the events of the 1890's, which nurtured the strategic, economic, religious, and emotional roots of imperialism, and in the course and outcome of the War with Spain. The latter presented a temptation and an opportunity to follow the road of other world powers. It was hard, in an hour of triumph, to display the virtue of self-restraint and adopt the policy of abnegation. The United States did not, and it then discovered the difficulty of reversing the step just taken. But while facile notions of naval strategy and business needs made easier the acceptance of Guam, Tutuila, and Wake, and while the annexation of Hawaii and Puerto Rico appeared as the lesser of evils, the retention of the Philippines, even as a temporary mandate, troubled the nation's conscience;

and the sickening insurrection seemed to symbolize imperialism at its worst. Hence the impulse toward overseas expansion quickly subsided, and the amount of territory added after 1902 was surprisingly small. Indeed, even though the government of the dependencies was efficient and disinterested and even though the Philippines were set free before the wave of anticolonialism swept the rest of the globe, the people of the United States preferred to forget their own thrust into the so-called backward areas. Yet that experience accelerated forces already at work, making for their emergence as a world power, and influenced the evolution of American foreign policy.

16

➵➵➵➵➵➵⋘⋘⋘⋘⋘

Impact on Traditional
Policies and Attitudes

EARLY IN 1901 a foreign envoy remarked that, while stationed in Washington, he had known two different republics—the United States before the War with Spain and the United States after that conflict. Although the changes he witnessed seem less drastic to the historian than they did to the contemporary, the triumph of imperialism did leave its mark on traditional policies and attitudes. It led to unprecedented attention to colonial administration and military reorganization. It helped to erode somewhat the historic principle of isolationism and to expand further the elastic definition of the Monroe Doctrine. It contributed to a formula for dealing with China that lasted four decades. It caused the diplomats to view other colonial powers in a new light, one in which ancient foes loomed as potential allies and old friends as dangerous enemies.

COLONIAL ADMINISTRATION AND MILITARY REORGANIZATION

For the job of ruling the dependencies, the United States lacked both experience and machinery. In 1898 it had no established colonial policy, no trained colonial personnel, and no recognized colonial office. It did possess a well-tested system for creating self-governing territories and preparing them for statehood, but few believed that the process which had worked so well on the mainland could be applied to distant islands. Indeed, most imperialists admitted that the majority of the recent acquisitions could never become states in the Union.

At the outset, both President and Congress devoted much time to the new colonies. The former sent fact-finding commissions to Hawaii, Puerto Rico, and the Philippines and entrusted the inquiries in Guam and Tutuila to naval officers. He also studied the feasibility of having a single executive agency administer all the dependencies and weighed for some time the relative advantages of placing a Bureau of Insular Affairs in the State, War, or Interior Department. Both houses of the legislature created standing committees to handle the problems of empire. In the Senate three able men became chairmen: Lodge for the Committee on the Philippines; Foraker for the Committee on Puerto Rico and the Pacific Islands; and Orville H. Platt, Republican of Connecticut and an outstanding constitutional lawyer, for the Committee on Cuban Relations.

Legislation for the colonies was a necessity after the decision of 1898–9. Nothing had to be done for unoccupied Wake, while Guam and Tutuila were put under naval jurisdiction by executive order. Hawaii's experience in self-rule earned it immediate territorial status in an act of April 30, 1900. Puerto Rico was less fortunate. The Foraker Act of April 12, 1900, set up a government which, while more democratic than the one it supplanted, was less liberal than the type prevailing on the mainland. In addition to important economic clauses, it provided that the governor, the heads of the executive departments, and the members of the upper house be appointed by the president. Only in voting for the lower chamber of the assembly did the islanders gain a voice in their own affairs. In the Philippines the story was much the same, except that the insurrection delayed termination of the military regime until July 1, 1902. The Civil Government Act of that date gave the archipelago a highly centralized administration. A five man commission, chosen by the president, constituted the executive branch, with the chairman serving as governor and the other members as heads of departments. The commission was to exercise all legislative functions until two years after the completion of the first census. Then there would be a general election for delegates to the lower house, while the commission would act as the upper house. As in Puerto Rico, nothing was said about complete autonomy or eventual independence.

Although Cuba was not a colony, the law ending military rule had the most lasting influence of all these pioneer statutes. The Platt Amendment to the army appropriation act of March 2, 1901, the terms of which were embodied in a treaty of May 22, 1903, obligated the new Cuban Republic to accept several restrictions upon its freedom. It must continue the health projects commenced during the American occupation. It must assure the United States of the opportunity to lease or buy naval sites in specified areas. It must not negotiate agreements which would impair its independence or enable a foreign power to control any portion of the island. No public debt might be incurred unless it could be serviced out of ordinary revenues. Most important of all, the United States received "the right to intervene for the preservation of Cuban independence" and for the maintenance of a government adequate to keep order and discharge the obligations contained in the Paris peace treaty.

After 1902 there were fewer colonial statutes and less concern for colonial administration. In Puerto Rico the Foraker Act was not substantially changed until March 2, 1917, while in the Philippines a new organic law did not come until August 29, 1916. The Bureau of Insular Affairs, temporarily assigned to the War Department, remained there, the only supervisory agency and a very incomplete one at that. Talk of training a colonial service and founding a colonial office soon died out. This rapid dissipation of interest in both Washington and the country at large revealed the ephemeral nature of the imperialist impulse. Once the emotions which had been nurtured during the 1890's found release in the War with Spain and its immediate aftermath, a more sober approach to overseas possessions set in, one which reflected traditional attitudes and current realities. The subsequent lack of attention to dependencies deprived them in the next decade of new ideas and fresh programs, so that the hallmark of American colonial rule became not early autonomy and independence but rather material advantages in the form of new roads, good schools, improved sanitation, and modern hygiene.

The acquisition of colonies had a more enduring impact on the armed forces. As a world power with far-flung territorial outposts, the United States could no longer afford the nineteenth-century luxury of ignoring its military establishment in peacetime. The conflict with Spain, moreover, had laid bare glaring deficiencies in the army's antiquated organization, while the ensuing rebellion in the Philippines made unprecedented demands on both services and required a deployment of men and ships that would have been unthinkable a decade earlier.

Chagrined by wartime scandals which reflected upon his administration, McKinley appointed Elihu Root as Secretary of War on July 21, 1899. A leading corporation lawyer from New York, Root shifted units to suppress the Filipino uprising, charted a course for the larger colonies, and modernized the army itself. His far-reaching changes included an increase in the authorized strength of the ground forces, the abolition of permanent assignments to staff posts in Washington, the revival of the special service schools, the creation of an Army War College, the overhauling of an antediluvian militia system, and the replacement of the commanding general by a chief of staff. The last reform met the need for an officer whose primary duty was not to lead troops in the field but to draft plans for the nation's defense, maintain readiness, insure a speedy mobilization, and advise the secretary on all military matters. It was the institution of the General Staff Corps in February, 1903, that one of Root's successors called "the outstanding contribution made by any Secretary of War."

Having escaped both criticism and scandal during the war, the navy was less in need of administrative reorganization. Its main problems were the construction of new ships and their location, both of which impinged upon diplomacy. Thus, at the very moment the fleet's mission was enormously complicated by the annexation of colonies, the other major powers were rapidly enlarging their navies and eagerly seeking additional bases. Indeed, competitive building between Germany and Great Britain helped bring on the First World War, while the Kaiser's territorial ambitions in the Western Hemisphere did much to arouse American fears of a hostile Reich. The years from 1899 to 1905 witnessed a steady growth of the fleet and a continuing discussion on how to deploy it. Thanks to President Theodore Roosevelt, whose pride in modern vessels matched his grasp of military strategy, the United States by 1907 ranked second to England in total tonnage. But not even Roosevelt could persuade Congress of the imperative necessity of developing the new insular outposts into operating bases, nor could he prevent a revolution in naval architecture from making obsolete almost every battleship designed before the commissioning of HMS *Dreadnought* at the end of 1906.

One administrative innovation of this period was the General Board, which represented a compromise between Secretary Long's desire for professional military advisers and his fear that a general staff might weaken the principle of civilian supremacy. Instituted by a departmental order of March 13, 1900, it was composed of nine officers and presided over by the Admiral of the Navy, a rank recently revived for Dewey. The General Board's main function was to draft war plans, collaborate with the army, and counsel the secretary. It must also recommend where to locate new vessels and where to establish additional facilities. Its role was purely advisory. It issued no orders and, lacking legislative sanction, could be abolished by any future secretary. Yet with all its shortcomings, the General Board marked a step forward in military planning.

Despite the teachings of Mahan and the lessons of 1898, the return of peace saw the major units of the fleet again dispersed to the four quarters of the globe. This revival of prewar cruising squadrons was accentuated by the special needs of the Far East, where the navy played a key role in coping with the Filipino Insurrection and the

Boxer Revolt. But in June, 1902, this trend was reversed as orders went out to concentrate all battleships on the North Atlantic or Asiatic stations. It was then believed that the main threat to the nation's security lay along the Eastern seaboard and in the Caribbean and that a secondary area of danger was in the Orient. That estimate of the situation and that allocation of ships lasted until the middle of 1906, when changes in world conditions and the completion of a large number of far-ranging armored cruisers, which could be assigned to Asiatic waters, led to the decision to place all battleships in a newly formed Atlantic Fleet.

Overseas bases were not easily developed. Here the Congress, controlling the purse and responsive to pressures remote from national defense, was the chief obstacle. In this period, as in subsequent years, the legislators were more willing to appropriate funds for continental installations, where the money might benefit their constituents directly, than for insular outposts, where no votes could be garnered. The navy itself was also to blame for the indecision and delay. There was disagreement within the service as to which locations should receive priority and an inability to reconcile differences with the army. It was a sorry tale and one that would continue.

No adequate operating base was developed in the Caribbean before 1905. The annexation of Puerto Rico did not answer the navy's needs, for it lacked decent harbors. The tiny island of Culebra off its eastern shore could be employed as a temporary anchorage, but the fleet required something better. The United States was entitled to lease naval sites in Cuba, and a treaty of July 2, 1903, brought Guantanamo Bay under American jurisdiction; but congressional penury delayed any real use of that splendid facility until after 1914. A second attempt to buy the Danish West Indies failed when Denmark refused to approve the accord of January 24, 1902. In the Pacific there was no dearth of potential bases; the task was to choose between rival claimants and produce tangible results. This the navy failed to do before 1905. A running debate raged over the relative merits of Guam and the Philippines and, within the latter, between the advocates of Cavite on Manila Bay and of Olongapo on Subic Bay. Understandably, Congress procrastinated and did nothing.

ISOLATIONISM

It would be a mistake to see in the triumph of imperialism an end to the policy of isolationism. A willingness to negotiate permanent alliances and to participate continuously in the diplomatic affairs of other continents still lay in the future, but the acquisition of colonies did compel the United States government to pay increased attention to the world balance of power. Only a few citizens yet denied that the nation could reconcile forever the aloofness of a weak continental republic and the responsibilities of a strong colonial empire. The great majority still believed it possible to hold overseas dependencies and adhere to traditional principles.

Certainly isolationism encountered no direct challenge in the form of an alliance. Party platforms continued to pay tribute to the Farewell Address and Jefferson's first inaugural. Politicians were quick to condemn as dangerous entanglements everything from diplomatic collaboration with England to a joint military expedition for relieving the legations at Peking. The Senate scrutinized multilateral treaties drafted at international conferences and instituted the practice of appending reservations that disclaimed any intention to depart from custom. Thus, in giving consent on January 11, 1892, to the Brussels convention of July 2, 1890, dealing with the regulation of the slave trade and the liquor traffic in Africa, the upper house expressly denied that the United States had any interest in African colonies or protectorates and was not in any way approving of their "wisdom, expediency, or lawfulness."

Isolationism underwent its most publicized test in these years at the First Hague Conference of 1899. The spectacle of the United States attending in Holland a gathering of twenty-six nations for the purpose of minimizing the likelihood of war was distinctly novel, and the wonder is that the McKinley administration accepted with so little hesitation the Tsar's invitation of January 11, 1899. It is especially surprising because most informed persons recognized that Nicholas II had acted for selfish reasons and was less concerned with world peace than with Russia's difficulties stemming from the European alliance system.[1]

McKinley took pains to send a distinguished delegation to The Hague. The contrast with the unknowns who had represented the United States at Berlin in 1885 and at Brussels in 1890 was striking. Andrew D. White, prominent educator and veteran diplomat, headed a five-man group that included the president of Columbia University and Captain Mahan. Hay's instructions of April 18, 1899, however, undercut Russia's concern for armaments. The question of limiting or reducing the sea and land forces, the Secretary declared, was "so in-

---

[1] As an impetus to world peace, the Tsar invited the major nations to meet together in order to (1) agree not to increase existing armaments or budgets therefor; (2) examine in a preliminary way the means of reducing in the future both armed forces and appropriations needed to maintain them; (3) prohibit the use of destructive weapons, such as new explosives, submarines, and projectiles dropped from the air; (4) revise current rules on the laws and customs of war; and (5) accept in principle the right of any state to extend its good offices or mediation in a dispute between the signatories.

applicable to the United States" that it must be left entirely to the other great powers. As for eliminating destructive weapons, the Tsar's suggestions were "lacking in practicability" and to discuss them would do more harm than good. The United States, Hay continued, would be happy to help minimize the horrors of war but believed the most fruitful topic to consider was the employment of good offices, mediation, and arbitration. He enjoined the delegates to propose a plan for an international court to which would be submitted all disagreements not settled by ordinary diplomacy, except those relating to political independence and territorial integrity.

For more than ten weeks in 1899 the American people watched their representatives confer at The Hague with those of twenty-five other nations—twenty from Europe, four from Asia, and one from the New World. The amount of printed comment was out of all proportion to the tangible results, and the public was disappointed that a meeting called to foster peace should devote so much time to trying to humanize war. Of the four conventions and declarations signed on July 29, 1899, none furthered the reduction of armaments. One dealt with launching projectiles, one with applying the principles of the Geneva Convention of 1864 to maritime warfare, one with the laws and customs of land fighting, and one with composing differences among states. Only the last was significant.

The Convention for the Pacific Settlement of International Disputes assumed that an acceptance of arbitration and cognate processes must precede the limitation of military forces and budgets. It contained three main provisions. First, it entitled every signatory not a party to a dispute to extend its good offices and mediation to others. These steps were not to be regarded as unfriendly to either side. Second, it recommended commissions of inquiry for investigating the facts in any situation which threatened the peace. These commissions would act only when the controversy involved specific data and not broad questions of national honor. Their findings were not binding upon the disputants. Third, a Permanent Court of Arbitration was established. It was not a real court but only a panel of distinguished jurists whose services might be drawn upon. Arbitration itself was voluntary; no signatory was obliged to submit any type of controversy to the tribunal.

Compulsory arbitration was not one of Hay's goals. Indeed, White and his colleagues carefully avoided limiting America's freedom of action in any way. Before signing the convention on peace machinery, they inserted a provison declaring that nothing therein should be so construed as to require the United States to depart from its traditional policy of not entangling itself in the internal or external affairs of any foreign nation. Originally proposed by Mahan to make certain that no question affecting the Monroe Doctrine had to be referred to arbitration, the disclaimer had been broadened to cover isolationism. So satisfactory did the Senate consider the safeguard that it approved all four Hague agreements without dissent.

In the history of isolationism, the First Hague Conference was a portent of the future, not a break with the past. In the next six years the United States did not, as a result of the conference, offer mediation or employ a commission of inquiry; and even the Permanent Court might have died of inanition if Roosevelt had not insisted in 1902 that Hay dig up some unsettled controversy for the Hague panel to arbitrate. Actually, the real threat to isolationism came not from feeble governmental efforts at international cooperation or even from the agitation for an Anglo-American alliance that flared up briefly after the war. Rather, it lay in the minds of a few perceptive men who grasped the impact of imperialism on traditional policies. Two presidents and one former secretary of state admitted that the aphorisms of the past could not be applied in the new century. At Buffalo on September 5, 1901, William McKinley delivered his last address. Although he talked about the need for a reciprocal reduction of tariff duties, his words had a broader meaning. "Isolationism," he warned, "is no longer possible or desirable. . . . The period of exclusiveness is past." His successor, speaking at San Francisco on May 13, 1903, emphasized diplomacy, not commerce. "We have no choice," declared Theodore Roosevelt, "we the people of the United States, as to whether or not we shall play a great part in the world. That has been determined for us by fate, by the march of events. We have to play that part. All that we can decide is whether we shall play it well or ill."

But what of the Farewell Address, which neither McKinley nor Roosevelt mentioned? On March 2, 1898, just before the war, Richard Olney essayed an answer. In a lecture on "The International Isolation of the United States" he deplored the prevailing tendency to invoke the precepts of 1796 against legitimate moves on the world stage. Washington's great rule of conduct, he insisted, was narrower in scope than the interpretation currently given to it. A nation, like an individual, was a member of society, and that membership called for more than an attitude of abstention. The United States must "realize its great place among the Powers," Olney concluded, for "isolationism that is nothing but a shirking of the responsibilities of high place and great power is simply ignominious." Two years later he renewed the attack. Writing on the "Growth of Our Foreign Policy" in March, 1900, he rejoiced that the United States had "come out of its shell and ceased to be a hermit among the nations." Although opposed to retaining the Philippines, he favored closer ties with England. Of all the major powers, Great Britain was "most formidable as a foe and most effective as a friend." Thus Olney in 1900 reached the same conclusion Trescot had come to in 1849. International rivalries in the colonial areas, he believed, affected American security, and firm bonds with England could best promote the national interest. Thus did the acquisition of overseas possessions erode isolationism, not so much in the immediate acts of the government as in the minds of sensitive observers whose thinking would influence men in the future.

NEUTRALITY AND THE MONROE DOCTRINE

Upon the other two bases of nineteenth-century foreign policy—neutrality and the Monroe Doctrine—the triumph of imperialism had a contrasting impact. It did not bring any substantial change in neutrality. The government neither assumed new duties nor relinquished old ones. It clung to the traditional concept of neutral rights and at the Hague Conference persisted in its familiar quest to exempt from seizure in wartime all private property at sea. It did not anticipate the problems that might arise from changes in industrial technology and military weapons. Only after a major conflict had erupted in 1914 did the people begin to question whether in the new century aloofness from the struggles of other world powers was still possible or desirable.

On the other hand, the Monroe Doctrine underwent further change between 1898 and 1905. The forcible expulsion of Spain from Cuba and the retention of an overseas empire put a new face on an old problem. Many contemporaries, at home and abroad, regarded these developments as a violation of Monrovian principles. Had not the fifth president declared that there would be no interference with existing European colonies? Had he not implied that if Europe kept its hands off the Americas, the United States would confine itself to the New World? How did distant colonies conform to the idea of the two spheres? These were valid questions, but the anti-imperialists were unable to persuade their countrymen that a cardinal element in the republic's diplomacy was being transgressed.

Between 1898 and 1905 the meaning of the Monroe Doctrine was enlarged in several ways. The disclaimer in the Hague Convention of July 28, 1899, made sure that questions pertaining to the principles of 1823 did not have to be submitted to the Permanent Court of Arbitration. The Anglo-German blockade of Venezuela in December, 1902, revealed that public opinion in the United States would not tolerate, even if the government might, the use of force by European powers to collect debts owed them by New World republics. And finally, the Roosevelt Corollary of December 6, 1904, growing out of a plan to establish an American customs receivership in the Dominican Republic, converted the Monroe Doctrine from a concept of absolute nonintervention by Europe in the countries of the Western Hemisphere into one of precautionary intervention by the United States.

RELATIONS WITH OTHER WORLD POWERS

The impact of imperialism upon traditional policies and attitudes was most strikingly manifested in Anglo-American relations. In the space of a few years Great Britain was transformed from an ancient enemy into a valued friend, thus enabling diplomats to contemplate parallel policies which a decade before would have been unthinkable. Indeed, although much of the hatred and envy dating from the Revolution had died down by 1889, there were many in the United States who wished to keep antagonisms alive. The Irish-American vote tempted politicians to twist the Lion's tail on every opportune occasion. The silverites disliked England as the bastion of the gold standard, while the Populists, with their delusions of conspiracy, blamed many of the troubles on that kingdom. The advocates of an American-controlled canal fulminated at the British refusal to release the United States from its obligations under the Clayton-Bulwer Treaty. Even the expansionists, who used England's wealth and power as an argument for overseas colonies, were willing to raise the specter of Perfidious Albion to promote their cause in Hawaii. The last decade of the century witnessed constant bickering over several issues: the unsettled Alaskan frontier, the Bering fur seals, and the North Atlantic fisheries. In December, 1895, the two countries seemed to stand on the brink of war over the Venezuelan boundary; and although both drew back in horror at the prospect, an attempt to extract good from evil was thwarted when the Senate defeated the Olney-Pauncefote Treaty providing for compulsory arbitration in a few classes of disputes.

Then, in 1898, a temporary feeling of diplomatic isolation on each side of the Atlantic, together with well-timed words of mutual esteem, worked wonders for the cause of Anglo-American friendship. Still aloof from the rival alliance systems, the British were alarmed by French ambitions in Africa, Russian designs in Asia, German aspirations on the high seas, and their own threatened position in China. Although their overture of March 8, looking to a joint statement on equality of trade opportunity, failed to arouse an administration preoccupied with Cuba, leading statesmen and writers in England wooed American public and governmental opinion with talk of common racial ties and common diplomatic interests. Such expressions of unity were music to McKinley and his colleagues when they discovered that armed intervention in the name of humanity was regarded with suspicion and hostility everywhere in Europe except in the British Isles. Thus, when Ambassador Hay told a London audience on April 21 that there was "a sanction like that of religion which binds us in a sort of partnership in the beneficent work of mankind," Colonial Secretary Chamberlain replied in reassuring tones. "Terrible as war may be," he declared at Birmingham on May 13, 1898, "it would be cheaply purchased if in a great and noble cause the Stars and Stripes and the Union Jack could wave together over an Anglo-Saxon alliance." Exchanges of that sort encouraged in both nations the formation of leagues dedicated to achieving such an alliance.

More helpful, however, was the role played by the British government during and after the war. While the Germans annoyed an anxious Dewey at Manila, officers of the Royal Navy were models of tact and decorum. Unlike Germany, England evinced no desire to acquire the Philippines, and it quickly made clear that it welcomed annexation by the United States. The Foreign Office in London, again in contrast to Berlin, pursued no secret deals with Madrid for salvaging remnants of the Spanish Empire in the Pacific. Most European powers gloated when the Filipinos rebelled; but the British remained silent, and wisely so—within eight months they were engaged in an equally unpopular war with the Boer republics. Then Secretary Hay reciprocated by resisting in an election year the demands of German and Irish groups that some kind of aid be given the Boers.

This mutual cordiality and understanding made possible by 1905 a limited Anglo-American entente. Given the traditional policy of the United States, a formal alliance was out of the question, and both the McKinley and Roosevelt administrations felt obliged to issue disclaimers to that effect. But important progress was made in disposing of old quarrels and acting together, where possible, in world affairs. Thus the troublesome Clayton-Bulwer Treaty was finally abrogated in November, 1901; the vexing Alaskan boundary was referred in February, 1903, to a tribunal of jurists; and a new approach to compulsory arbitration was initiated in February, 1904. In the Pacific, England agreed in December, 1899, to leave the Samoan group to Germany and the United States. In East Asia, the two governments professed to support equality of commercial opportunity. In the Caribbean, the British paid further lip service to the Monroe Doctrine and eventually urged the United States to assume the thankless role of international policeman. In December, 1904, the Foreign Office applauded the promulgation of the Roosevelt Corollary; that same month the Admiralty, confronted by growing German might in the North Sea, began to transfer all heavy units from the West Indies to home waters. This reconcentration left the United States militarily supreme in the New World.

Although the burgeoning friendship with England marked a major shift in American policy, its immediate consequences can be exaggerated. There were still many difficulties to be resolved and obvious limits beyond which cooperation was not feasible. In some areas the identity of interests was more apparent than real. Thus, the closer England bound itself to Japan in East Asia, especially after 1905, the more complicated relations with the United States became. In forging ententes with France in April, 1904, and with Russia in August, 1907, Great Britain often alienated the men in Washington on specific points, a fact that the Algeciras Conference in January, 1906, and the Second Hague Conference in June, 1907, revealed. Yet when all qualifications are entered, the growth of Anglo-American friendship remains one of the most important diplomatic developments at the turn of the century.

If England was the chief beneficiary of the change which imperialism wrought in American foreign policy, Germany was the main loser. Like the United States, the Reich acquired colonies belatedly. Unlike Great Britain, it could not be indifferent to the raising of the Stars and Stripes in the Caribbean, the Pacific, or the South China Sea. Every territorial addition to the New World republic deprived Germany of an opportunity to catch up with its more forehanded European neighbors. German diplomacy, moreover, reflected the brusqueness and impetuosity of a parvenu. Before 1902 it showed, again unlike Britain, little concern for American public opinion. Consequently, the same events in this period which led the governments in Washington and London to take a common position in world affairs caused the United States and Germany to view each other as current rivals and future enemies.

Almost overnight, then, Germany replaced England as the main threat to the national interest. The German press excoriated the armed intervention in Cuba. Earlier it had said that new pretensions like the Olney Corollary must be curbed; now it raised the specter of a European move to protect Spain. During the war the blunders of von Diederichs in Manila Bay aroused fresh apprehensions. The image of a malevolent Reich gained additional credence when the Kaiser's government openly begrudged America's acquisition of the Philippines and secretly negotiated for the remainder of Spain's empire. The purchase of the Carolines and the Marianas, except for Guam, placed Germany athwart the line of communication between the California coast and the new outposts in the Pacific.

It was in the Western Hemisphere, however, that Germany seemed the greatest menace to American security. The appointment of Admiral Alfred von Tirpitz as Minister of Marine in June, 1897, and the passage of a six-year construction bill in March, 1898, ushered in a new era in German sea power. By June, 1900, the Reichstag had raised its original goal—a battleship fleet equal to France and superior to the United States—and provided for a navy so potent that even England could not engage it without serious risk. Simultaneously, Tirpitz embarked upon a quest for overseas bases. Although the Kaiser and the Foreign Office restrained him from challenging the United States in the sensitive Caribbean area, such men as Roosevelt, Hay, Root, and Lodge asserted that the Monroe Doctrine was in danger and cited the ill-concealed scorn which the German press poured upon that cherished principle. In 1901 the Navy Department publicized a pamphlet which described how the Imperial navy would crush the Atlantic Fleet in American waters and would thus pave the way for an invasion of the mainland by the Imperial army. And when on October 22, 1902, Denmark rejected a treaty ceding its West Indian islands to the United States, Hay and others wrongly blamed German pressure.

The nadir of German-American relations in this period came in the winter of 1902–3. To obtain redress for unrequited injuries suffered by their citizens in Venezuela, Germany and England—later joined by Italy—resorted to punitive measures. They acted with the full knowledge and tacit consent of the United States, which had never invoked the Monroe Doctrine to bar the forcible collection of debts so long as no acquisition of territory and no interference in domestic matters were contemplated. But American public opinion exploded unexpectedly when Venezuelan ships were sunk and a harbor was bombarded. This reaction prompted President Roosevelt to bring extreme pressure on both countries to suspend their naval demonstration and to submit their claims to the Hague Court. England was the more amenable—or, at least, more ready—to retreat from an embarrassing predicament. The Germans, perhaps less well served by their ambassador in Washington, procrastinated before reversing their course and thus compelled Roosevelt to send two stern warnings, one about December 8, 1902, to end the reprisals against Venezuelan shipping, the second about February 3, 1903, to terminate the blockade which had been imposed pending an agreement to arbitrate the unpaid claims.

Roosevelt's urgent messages to the Kaiser coincided with an impressive display of sea power in the West Indies. A year earlier the Navy Department had decided to hold its largest peacetime maneuvers during December, 1902, with Dewey in command. The President used this mobilization, which had been planned before the Venezuelan crisis broke, to bolster his diplomacy. Fortunately, Dewey never had to carry out his orders to open fire if necessary, but the episode left its mark upon a naval hierarchy already hostile to the Reich because of the events in Manila Bay. Henceforth American officers employed the German fleet as a yardstick when seeking bigger appropriations from Congress.

Both capitals viewed this mounting distrust with misgiving. Roosevelt was too much of a realist to want Germany as a diplomatic foe. He couched his warnings in firm but friendly tones, and he so carefully excluded these warnings from the official record that it has taken historians over fifty years to be certain that they were delivered. Wilhelm II also did not wish to drive the transatlantic giant into the camp of his enemies. In January, 1902, he requested permission to send his brother on a goodwill tour of the United States. A year later he recalled Ambassador Theodor von Holleben on the fictitious ground of bad health and replaced him with Baron Speck von Sternburg, a personal favorite of Roosevelt. He donated presents with a lavish hand —a medal for the President, a statue for the city of Washington, a museum for Harvard University. His efforts were seconded by the well-organized German-American groups, who attacked any collaboration with England as evidence of a secret alliance. But these countervailing measures did not help very much. Although it is as easy to exaggerate the spread of German-American distrust before 1905 as it is to overemphasize the growth of Anglo-American friendship, an important shift in traditional attitudes did occur, the full impact of which would become more apparent after August, 1914.

England and Germany were not the only world powers whose relations with the United States were affected by the decision on colonies. An old cordiality with both Russia and Japan disappeared when the republic entered the area of conflict in East Asia. Russia's cynical acts in Manchuria and North China after the Boxer Revolt, added to the well-publicized horrors of the Siberian prisons and the Jewish pogroms, drained the last vestige of American goodwill before 1905. Japan's threat to American security, together with the vexing issue of immigration, became clear only after that date. France alone of the major nations seemed unaffected by this reorientation in American foreign policy, and that was because its interests and those of the United States did not clash in the colonial sphere.

17

The Open Door Policy in Asia

ON DECEMBER 3, 1894, Cleveland told Congress that a war between China and Japan, then raging in Korea and Manchuria, endangered no policy of the United States. He carefully avoided taking part in the peacemaking that followed. Ten years later Roosevelt reacted in a completely opposite way to the Russo-Japanese conflict, also fought in Korea and Manchuria. More than any single person he was responsible for the peace negotiations that began at Portsmouth, New Hampshire, on August 10, 1905. This contrast in the attitudes of two presidents suggests how greatly American concern for East Asia had grown within a decade. That growth can be attributed partly to the forces making for imperialism and partly to economic desires which would have been voiced even if no colonies had been acquired. The most important consequence of that growth, aside from helping to modify traditional attitudes toward other world powers, was a restatement of the open door policy, a policy which shaped American diplomacy toward China and her neighbors from its announcement in September, 1899, to the triumph of communism in China fifty years later.

THE FIRST OPEN DOOR NOTES

Upon taking office in March, 1897, McKinley contemplated no new assertion of American interests in East Asia. Despite apprehensions among missionaries and a few businessmen about the future of the Manchu Empire, the incoming administration felt no sense of urgency. Even when the second round in the scramble for concessions began, Secretary Sherman blandly asserted that a partition of China would not hurt American markets. The British ambassador was informed on March 17, 1898, in reply to his inquiry about a joint statement, that while "the President is in sympathy with the policy which shall maintain open trade in China," all his advices indicated that there was "no foreign occupation which interferes with that trade or aims at exclusive commercial privileges."

To destroy such apathy in Washington, various cotton exporters, railroad promoters, and mining officials organized on January 6, 1898, the Committee on American Interests in China. This group tried to encourage chambers of commerce throughout the country to publicize by petitions the menace posed by the new European leaseholds and spheres of influence. A parallel endeavor struck at the concept of isolationism. Thus *The United States Investor* prophesied in April that commercial relations with Asia would lead to an abandonment of the Farewell Address, while four months later Brooks Adams argued in *Forum* that an alliance with Great Britain was needed to safeguard America's stake in the Orient. On June 9, 1898, the Committee changed its name to the American Asiatic Association and expanded its efforts. The enthusiasm of a successful war opened new vistas, as men such as Adams and Charles A. Conant developed the economic case for colonies. The desire for the Philippines and a concern for China became mutually supporting. Retention of the archipelago was demanded to offset European leaseholds on the mainland; increased profits and missionary activity on the Continent were advanced as arguments to annex the islands. Duty allied itself with dollars, and for many the white man's burden was bracketed with the businessman's opportunity.

McKinley, however, preferred to deal with the two problems separately. He did not decide to demand all of the Philippines until October 28, 1898. Before then he touched only tangentially upon equality of trade in China and not at all upon its territorial integrity. In his instructions to the peace commission on September 16, 1898, the President asserted that "incidental to our tenure in the Philippines is the commercial opportunity to which American statesmanship cannot be indifferent." But, he added, "we seek no advantages in the Orient which are not common to all. Asking only the open door for ourselves, we are ready to accord the open door to others." What was meant by the open door and how it might be upheld were questions which remained unanswered for another year. All McKinley did in the interim was to assure Congress on December 5, 1898, that American trade was not being discriminated against in Russian Port Arthur and Dairen, in German Kiaochow, or in British Weihaiwei and to recommend an investigation of "the opportunities for and obstacles to the enlargement of markets in China for the raw products and manufactures of the United States."

During that year pressures at home and abroad convinced the State Department that the time had come to act. On January 3, 1899, fifty-three cotton manufacturers and exporters warned in a petition that "unless a vigorous policy is pursued," the markets of North China and Manchuria would be lost. During February Lord Charles Beresford, representing the Associated Chambers of Commerce of Great Britain, made a much publicized transcontinental speaking tour in which he pleaded for an Anglo-American stand against the partition of China. On March 16, 1899, Minister Edwin H. Conger suggested from Peking that to keep the door open the United States must acquire a harbor on the mainland. Then, on April 28, the British astonished Secretary Hay by concluding an agreement which recognized the area north of the Great Wall as a Russian sphere for railroad construction and the Yangtze Valley as an English one. Hay had long been eager to join Great Britain in upholding the principle of equality of trade opportunity in China; now he had to devise some other formula.

In his search, Hay leaned heavily on two men. One was William W. Rockhill, who had served in the legations at Peking and Seoul before 1887 and had been Assistant Secretary under Olney. In May, 1899, Rockhill returned to Washington from Athens to be director of the Bureau of the American Republics and unofficial adviser to Hay on the Far East. He admired China's civilization and desired internal reforms that would make the Peking government strong enough to resist foreign encroachments. He was more interested in keeping the Manchu Empire territorially intact than in preserving equality of economic opportunity for the West. While Rockhill did not ignore the pressures upon the State Department, he was not primarily concerned with business and missionary enterprise. He was, moreover, suspicious of England and regarded it as great an offender as anyone else. On August 28, 1899, Rockhill incorporated his ideas in a memorandum which Hay had requested four days earlier.

The other influence on Hay was Alfred H. Hippisley, a British subject and longtime member of the Chinese Customs Service. While visiting his wife's family in Baltimore in June, 1899, Hippisley renewed his contacts with Rockhill, whom he had met in 1884, and the two explored together the situation in Asia. Because of his citizenship, Hippisley has often been regarded as upholding the English point of view; and some historians have called Hay's open door policy either a response to British prompting or a diplomatic deal by which the United

States, in return for supporting Britain in the Orient, gained a free hand in the Caribbean. Actually, the aims of the two governments were not identical. Hippisley, moreover, sought to benefit China, not England. He accepted as *faits accomplis* the spheres of influence already established and the exclusive railroad and mining concessions already granted, but he did wish to preserve the Chinese tariff, for the duties it yielded kept the Peking government solvent. He wanted the United States to obtain from all the powers, Britain included, assurances that the tariff would be applied uniformly throughout China, even in the leaseholds, and that treaty ports would not be interfered with. Much of the memorandum, but not all, that Rockhill sent to Hay on August 28 reflected Hippisley's thinking.

On September 2, 1899, McKinley and Hay met to dispose of the many diplomatic problems that had accumulated over the summer. Congress was not in session, and the President decided to act on his own. Until then he had been reluctant to intrude upon the Far Eastern turmoil; now pressure from the business and religious community plus the arguments of Hay, Rockhill, and Hippisley overcame his doubts. The views of Jacob G. Schurman, chairman of the Philippine Commission, were also instrumental. Just back from the Orient, Schurman told McKinley that Russian advances boded ill for the West and that America should stand with England and Japan in preventing the dismemberment of China. Accordingly, Rockhill drafted the necessary instructions on September 5. Polished by Assistant Secretary Alvey A. Adee, they went forth the next day under the signature of John Hay. As in 1823, the United States acted alone. Unlike the Monroe Doctrine, this new touchstone of American foreign policy was contained in a diplomatic dispatch, not in a presidential message.

These First Open Door Notes of September 6, 1899, requested the major powers to agree to three principles. First, within its "sphere of interest" or leased territory, no state would interfere with any treaty port or vested right. Second, within each sphere and leasehold, China's tariff would apply to the merchandise of every nationality shipped to those ports, except the free ones, and that the Chinese government would collect the duties. Third, within such spheres and leaseholds, no power would discriminate in favor of its own citizens with respect to harbor dues or railroad charges. In short, England, Germany, and Russia—subsequently, also France, Italy, and Japan—were asked to preserve equality of commercial activity within the areas they had recently wrung, or might hereafter extract, from China. Hippisley's recommendation that these spheres be accepted as *faits accomplis* was followed, as was his hope that China be permitted to gather duties from its tariff inside the leased areas. Rockhill felt this last point gave some recognition to China's sovereignty in those sectors, but unlike the later notes of July 3, 1900, this first set did not mention Chinese territorial and administrative entity. Nor did they insure equality of opportunity in mining and railroad concessions or in capital investments within the leaseholds. They said nothing about equality outside of the "sphere of interest" and they did not employ the words "open door."

Evasion characterized the replies of the powers. Hay asked for a statement of intentions, not a formal treaty. Even then each nation conditioned its acceptance of the three principles on the acquiescence of everyone else. The British response was the most satisfactory, the Russian the least. Indeed, Russia's was a thinly disguised rejection in that it avoided any commitment to the leased territory. Under these circumstances the McKinley administration resorted to wishful thinking and unwarranted assumptions. On December 5, 1899, before all the answers were in, the President assured Congress that in China "our commercial rights under existing treaties have been everywhere maintained during the past year, as they will be in the future." On March 20, 1900, Hay blandly announced that he had received adequate assurances from all six powers and that in each case the assent was "final and definitive." Yet it would be hard to determine what new legal safeguards either China or world trade had received from what Hay's biographer aptly calls "diplomatic prestidigitation." For the First Open Door Notes, as he observes, had not been put forward by a lawyer as a contribution to the law of nations but by a publicist to crystalize public opinion.

THE SECOND OPEN DOOR NOTES

Hay's stratagem undoubtedly aroused popular sentiment at home against the partition of China, but the rush of events during 1900 demonstrated that wishful thinking and unwarranted assumptions were not enough. In the three months after Hay accepted the assurances as "final and definitive," the situation in Asia deteriorated rapidly. Occidental cupidity threatened American trade despite the open door; Oriental terror endangered American lives on Chinese soil. The Boxer Revolt, a reactionary movement of secret societies, first opposed reforms within the empire and then turned its fury against foreigners. Beginning with assaults upon the missionaries and their converts in Shantung, the Boxers marched north to Peking. On May 30, 1900, Conger called for help, and the next day more than 300 British, Russian, French, Japanese, Italian, and American troops arrived to guard the legations. A larger column of 1,500 men was attacked between Tientsin and Peking on June 11 and was forced to turn back. On June 13, the Boxers entered the capital and severed all telegraphic connection with the outside world. Rioting ensued. The German minister was murdered, and the legations were besieged. To insure access to the railhead at Tientsin, the powers demanded the surrender of the Chinese forts off Taku. When this request was refused, all naval vessels present, except those of the United States, opened fire and captured the forts by force. A virtual state of war with China existed.

The Boxer Revolt confronted McKinley with two troublesome tasks. The first was to rescue Conger and his associates. This was achieved without serious domestic or foreign complications. Troops were lifted from the Philippines starting on June 27, 1900. Additional units were rushed from the United States to form the China Relief Expedition under Major General Adna R. Chaffee. On August 4 an allied detachment of 18,000 men, including 2,500 Americans, began to fight its way to Peking. Despite stiff opposition, it raised the siege ten days later. But that was as far as McKinley would go in an election year. He feared criticism of this unprecedented operation and was eager to get the army off the mainland. As early as June 10 Hay had warned Conger: "We have no policy in China except to protect with energy American interests, and especially American citizens. . . . There must be no alliances."

More difficult to resolve was the second task—to prevent the powers from exploiting the crisis and further partitioning China. Once again Hay turned to note writing. On September 6, 1899, he had requested the major nations to subscribe to three self-denying principles. That approach failed. In the Second Open Door Notes of July 3, 1900, he simply defined the policy of the United States toward China and set forth the grounds on which that unhappy nation could enjoy peace and safety. He envisaged no treaty and requested no reply. As before, the executive formulated an important policy while the legislature was in recess.

Like their predecessors, the Second Open Door Notes took the form of instructions to American envoys in major capitals. They began by proclaiming the adherence of the United States to a course of "peace with the Chinese nation" and of furthering lawful commerce "by all means guaranteed under extraterritoriality treaty rights and by the law of nations." The Boxers would be held to accountability for injuries done to American citizens, but the United States had only friendship for the Chinese people and for the provincial authorities who were seeking to maintain order. The President's purpose in the current crisis was to cooperate with other powers in rescuing the legations and checking the spread of violence. For the future—and this was the heart of the dispatch—the policy of the United States was "to seek a solution which may bring about permanent safety and peace to China, preserve Chinese territorial and administrative entity, protect all rights guaranteed to friendly powers by treaty and international law, and safeguard for the world the principle of equal and impartial trade with all parts of the Chinese Empire."

Thus was the preservation of China's territorial integrity made a cardinal goal in American foreign policy. The second circular notes went beyond the first. They no longer accepted spheres of influence and leaseholds as necessary and irrevocable evils. They would extend "equal and impartial trade" to all portions of the empire. They even hinted that the open door principle could be respected only if China remained a political and administrative entity. They did not, of course, promise to guarantee equality of economic opportunity or the independence of China, and they did not say how violations of those ideals would be met. The aims of Rockhill now took precedence over those of Hippisley. Although Hay consulted both men, as well as McKinley and Root, he was primarily responsible for the finished product. In its timing and phrasing the document was intended to forestall Democratic criticism and to present the powers with a set of objectives from which they could not, in all decency, dissent.

Nor did they dissent. Although no answer was required, Great Britain, Germany, Russia, France, and Italy expressed in different ways their general agreement with the second circular notes. Whatever they really thought, none was eager to parade publicly its opposition to the principle of equal commercial opportunity in a free and territorially inviolate China. It remained to be seen whether Hay was justified in telling England, as he did on October 29, 1900, that all the countries concerned held views similar to those of the United States.

Indeed, Hay's own allegiance to the Second Open Door Notes has been questioned. Ever since 1924 it has been known that on November 16, 1900, he directed Conger to investigate the possibility of acquiring on the Chinese coast opposite Formosa the exclusive use of Samsah Bay as a coaling station, with the stipulation that a twenty-mile perimeter not be ceded to anyone else. Why Hay acted so indiscreetly has never been satisfactorily explained. After the Boxer crisis erupted, the navy did renew its agitation for a site on the Asiatic littoral. It preferred the Chusan Islands at the mouth of the Yangtze in a traditionally British sphere. Hence it is possible that England, who concluded a vague agreement with Germany on October 16 reaffirming a belief in the open door, diverted the Americans southward. But Samsah Bay was in Fukien province, an area China had promised Japan it would never alienate to a third power. Conger suggested, therefore, that inquiries be made in Tokyo before he took any action. This was done, ironically, on December 7, 1900, and the Japanese reply was a masterpiece. The foreign minister reminded Hay not only of China's promise and the Anglo-German declaration but also of his own circular of July 3. He then intimated that China's territorial entity could best be maintained if all nations exercised self-restraint. There the matter ended. Since Hay was not a fool, we can only suppose, in the absence of conclusive evidence, that he yielded unthinkingly and unwisely to the importunities of the Navy Department.[1]

THE RUSSIAN MENACE

The importance of Hay's aberration over Samsah Bay can easily be exaggerated, but his suspicion and dislike of Russia cannot. His attitude, which Roosevelt shared, colored American diplomacy in East Asia from 1900 to 1905. Although Germany might shock with its gaucheries and saber-rattling, although France might annoy with a reluctance to offend its Slavic ally, and although England might be disappointingly inconsistent in trying to choose between Berlin and Tokyo, it was Russia who constituted the chief obstacle to a prompt liquidation of the Boxer incident and the main threat to the open door.

Russia's challenge to the open door angered the United States. Having extracted from China the right to build two railroads in Manchuria as well as the Kwantung leasehold in the Gulf of Chihli, the Tsar's government welcomed the Boxer uprising as an opportunity to improve its position in East Asia. The Russian Minister of War is reputed to have exclaimed: "This will give us an excuse for seizing Manchuria." With disorders along their right of way providing the justification, the Russians did exactly that. They also took over the Chinese customs house at Newchwang north of their leasehold and began to discriminate against the commerce of other nations. Even after the rebellion had been suppressed, they refused to hand back to China the civil administration of Manchuria unless they received permission to retain troops in Mukden and along the railroad linking Harbin and Dairen.

These Russian advances did not go unchallenged. Japan, as well as the United States and Great Britain, refused to acquiesce and did everything possible to stiffen Chinese resistance to the proposed terms of withdrawal. Despite an unmistakable infraction of the Open Door Notes, an American secretary of state had to concede, for the first time though not the last, that his countrymen would not fight to uphold those principles. Hay told the Japanese on February 1, 1901, that the United States was not prepared to enforce those views, "singly or in

[1] Agitation for a foothold on the mainland of Asia did not cease. On March 31, 1901, Conger urged a fresh approach to Japan, and on July 3, 1902, Rockhill, then in China, recommended a coaling station in Korea. The General Board continued to want the Chusans. It opposed anything further south as a duplication of facilities in the Philippines and anything further north as needless if Japan were an ally and untenable if it were a foe.

concert," by any act of hostility toward another nation. On April 28, 1903, he wrote to Roosevelt: "Russia knows as we do that we will not fight for Manchuria, for the simple reason that we cannot." Public opinion would not support such a policy, either with England and Japan or alone.

Under the circumstances Hay could do only two things. One was to bemoan his fate and castigate the Russians privately. Their promises, he wrote the ambassador to England in September 1900, "are as false as a dicer's oaths when treachery is possible." To Roosevelt he confided in May 1903: "Dealing with a government with whom mendacity is a science is an extremely difficult and delicate task." His other recourse was to harass the Russians with inquiries and protest openly. On April 20, 1901, for example, he requested additional assurances that the rights of American citizens would not be abridged in China or Manchuria by any treaty concluded at St. Petersburg or Peking. When it seemed that China might be compelled to grant to a Russian-dominated bank the sole authority to develop Manchuria, the United States declared on February 3, 1902, that it "could look only with concern upon any arrangement by which China should extend to a corporate concern the exclusive right within its territory to open mines, construct railroads, or exert other industrial privileges." If he had to choose, and it seemed that he might have to, Hay was prepared to subordinate the territorial integrity of China to insuring equality of economic opportunity within its borders. He was ready to recognize Russia's special rights in certain areas. "What we have been working for two years to accomplish," he told Roosevelt on May 1, 1902, "is that, no matter what eventually happens in northern China and Manchuria, the United States shall not be placed in any worse position than while the country was under the unquestioned domination of China." In short, American statesmen quickly learned they could not uphold by force or by diplomacy the territorial and administrative entity of China.

On April 8, 1902, Russia finally agreed to evacuate Manchuria within eighteen months and without onerous conditions. This decision was prompted less by protests from Washington than by the formation of the Anglo-Japanese alliance on January 30, 1902. Still unready to risk a showdown in East Asia, the Tsar's ministers agreed to curb their extreme pretensions until the last link in the Trans-Siberian Railroad was completed and until the international scene was more propitious.

THE COMING OF THE RUSSO-JAPANESE WAR

In their play for time the Russians failed. They failed partly because they underestimated the military and diplomatic power of Japan. They failed also because, like everyone else, they were puzzled by the cross-currents in international relations. That American statesmen fully understood all the forces at work in the Far East may be doubted, but the charge that they were outmaneuvered because of their ignorance cannot be substantiated. In every chancellery there was hesitation and uncertainty as the rival alliances jockeyed for advantage. Each side knew that the United States and Japan had to be reckoned with. England was actively searching for allies, but it was not yet clear with whom it would join. Anglo-German discussions dragged on fruitlessly from 1898 to 1901. Britain's bid for an Anglo-German-Japanese bloc to check Russia foundered on the Kaiser's unwillingness to challenge the Tsar in Manchuria. Hope for an Anglo-American-Japanese combination was ruled out by the policy of isolationism in the United States. An understanding between Germany and Russia was opposed by France. In the end, the only changes on the diplomatic chessboard were the Anglo-Japanese alliance of January 30, 1902, and the Anglo-French Entente Cordiale of April 8, 1904.

The former played a large role in American foreign policy. Its preamble proclaimed the allegiance of the signatories to the independence of China and Korea and to the maintenance of the open door. The text, however, recognized that England had special interests relating to China, while Japan, in addition to those it possessed in China, was "interested in a peculiar degree politically as well as commercially and industrially in Korea." Each might intervene to protect those vital concerns. If one of the signatories, in defending its interests, became involved in war with a third power, the other would remain neutral. But that neutrality must give way to armed assistance if the third power were joined by a fourth. That is, the defensive arrangement went into operation whenever either ally was faced by two foes. The treaty prohibited separate agreements by either party prejudicial to the other, provided for consultation, and set the duration at a minimum of five years.

Each side sought a different objective. Thinking mainly in global terms, the British wished to forestall a settlement between St. Petersburg and Tokyo which might free Russia to push forward in Asia or anywhere else. The Japanese, on the other hand, had their eyes fixed on the Far East, especially Korea. In Washington, where progress of the negotiations was not fully known, the published text was hailed as a useful check on Russian pretensions in Manchuria and North China.

One aftermath of the Anglo-Japanese alliance was Russia's promise to evacuate Manchuria. A second was Japan's attempt to reach a satisfactory arrangement with Russia over Korea. Having been denied a foothold on the mainland by Europe's intervention in April, 1895, and not having obtained a leased area during the scramble for concessions, Japan was determined to make Korea its sphere of influence. In

May, 1896, it would have divided Korea with Russia, but by August, 1903, it would not go that far. What Japan then proposed was a mutual recognition of China's sovereignty over Manchuria and a mutual acceptance of Russia's privileged position in Manchuria and of Japan's in Korea. The refusal of the Tsar's government to accept promptly those terms or their equivalent, together with its bad faith in not evacuating Manchuria by October 8, 1903, as it had promised, persuaded the rulers in Tokyo to substitute force for diplomacy. With the last link in the Trans-Siberian Railroad nearing completion, further delay could benefit only the Slav. Hopeful of a benevolent attitude in Germany and the United States, Japan severed relations on February 6, 1904. Two days later, without formally declaring war, its navy delivered a surprise torpedo attack on the Russian squadron at Port Arthur.

Fortunately, the Russo-Japanese War did not ignite a general conflagration. None of the powers was eager to join in. Since Japan was fighting only one foe, England was not obliged to come to its aid; inasmuch as the Triple Alliance was not involved, Russia could not count on French help. China also remained neutral, despite a secret defensive treaty of 1896 with Russia. As for the United States, there was certainly no reason to become a participant, especially since the Japanese quickly asserted their military superiority. As late as July 18, 1903, Roosevelt had described himself as "aroused and irritated" by Russian perfidy in Manchuria and confident that eventually the people "would back me in going to an extreme in this matter." To his son he wrote on February 10, 1904, on learning of Russia's initial defeats: "I was thoroughly pleased with the Japanese victory, for Japan is playing our game."

On February 11, 1904, the United States proclaimed its neutrality. More important than this traditional step was Hay's attempt to use the occasion to reaffirm the open door policy. After some preliminary discussions, especially with Germany, a note was addressed to China and the belligerents on February 10, with copies going to all signatories of the Boxer Protocol, expressing the earnest desire that, in the course of the military operations, "the neutrality of China and in all practicable ways her administrative entity shall be respected by both parties, and that the area of hostility shall be localized and limited as much as possible, so that undue excitement and disturbance of the Chinese people may be prevented and the least possible loss to the commerce and peaceful intercourse of the world may be occasioned."

As in September, 1899, and July, 1900, the response of the powers left much to be desired. France was puzzled by the words "administrative entity," and Russia saw in the omission of any reference to Korea an attempt to circumscribe its freedom in Manchuria while leaving the Japanese unfettered in the area they hoped to dominate.

Once again it may be doubted whether China derived any tangible benefits from this new appeal for the preservation of its independence and territorial integrity and for the maintenance of equal economic opportunity within its borders; but it is clear that by 1904 the open door, as embodied in those objectives, had become a symbol of American interests in the Far East.

The Russo-Japanese War also revealed the increased concern in Washington for the balance of power in Asia. Where Cleveland and Gresham had made no effort a decade before to prevent interference by the West in the fighting between China and Japan, Roosevelt and Hay were now eager to isolate the Russo-Japanese conflict from Europe's alliances and alignments. Whether the President actually warned France and Germany not to assist Russia, lest the United States intervene on the side of Japan—another instance in which historians have doubted, perhaps too hastily, Roosevelt's veracity—we shall probably never know. Certainly, such a move by the French and Germans in 1904 was most unlikely. But certainly, too, the American stake, territorial and economic, in the Far East had grown enormously in ten years; and the United States could no longer be indifferent, as it had been under Cleveland, to the kind of peace that would follow this war. Roosevelt was convinced that the national interest would be served best by a system of balanced antagonisms in East Asia; and when such an equilibrium was endangered by decisive Japanese victories early in the war, he was willing to essay the role of mediator. And it was his diplomacy that caused the peace treaty of 1905 to be written, not at Shimonoseki under Russian, French, and German pressure, but at Portsmouth under American good offices.

CHAPTER

18

❯❯❯-❯❯❯-❯❯❯-❯❯❮❮❮-❮❮❮-❮❮❮-❮❮❮

Hegemony in the Caribbean

IN THE nearby Caribbean, American foreign policy between 1898 and
1905 also revealed the new position of the United States as a world
power. But in contrast to distant Asia, the adjustments here were less
precipitate and more predictable, the diplomacy of Cleveland and Roosevelt having more in common, and the events representing a consummation rather than a change. The attainment of an American-controlled
canal, the choice of the Panama route, the extension of sovereignty
over the isthmus, and the novel interpretation of the Monroe Doctrine
justifying precautionary intervention by the United States were not
entirely unforeseen. It was the means, not the ends, which distinguished these years of culmination after the War with Spain from those
of preparation before it.

A CANAL UNDER AMERICAN CONTROL

An interoceanic canal was the key to American policy in the Caribbean
after 1898. For almost two decades that project had been considered
vital to the nation's economy and defense. Its pressing necessity had
been dramatized during the war by the sixty-six-day dash of the battleship *Oregon* around Cape Horn to join the fleet in the West Indies. The
annexation of Puerto Rico and the temporary occupation of Cuba
seemed to provide the necessary bases to command the eastern approaches to the canal. Only the prohibition in the Clayton-Bulwer
Treaty remained.

Early in December, 1898, Hay moved to rid the present of the dead hand of the past. The time appeared propitious. At home, McKinley told Congress on December 5 that building a canal was "now more than ever indispensable" and that its control by the United States was imperative. Abroad, the Salisbury cabinet had no objection to superseding the treaty of 1850, provided British vessels received the same treatment as American ships. By January 13, 1899, the Secretary, without consulting the Senate, had completed a draft treaty with Ambassador Pauncefote. At that point a delay occurred. Under pressure from Canada, the Foreign Office was obliged to link the canal question with the unsettled Alaskan boundary. Since Hay regarded the Canadian case as spurious, he refused to make a deal and shelved his *projet* for a year. Then, in January, 1900, he hurriedly picked up the broken threads. He feared the House might pass a bill authorizing the immediate construction of a canal in violation of the Clayton-Bulwer pact, and he believed that the Boer War compelled England to act without disposing of the Alaskan dispute. On this last point Hay was correct, but in his eagerness to press ahead he failed to make sure of the Senate's support.

The First Hay-Pauncefote Treaty, of February 5, 1900, modified but did not abrogate the Clayton-Bulwer agreement. It enabled the United States government, either by itself or through a corporation, to build, regulate, and manage an interoceanic canal. It retained the principle of neutralization provided for in 1850 but restated the specific requirements to accord with the Suez Convention of 1888. It also obligated the signatories to invite other nations to become parties to the treaty.

To Hay's astonishment, his work encountered savage criticism. The principal target was the denial to the United States of the right to fortify the canal in time of peace and to close it in time of war. Also under attack was the failure to abrogate the Clayton-Bulwer pact and the invitation for others to adhere. The former was denounced as an egregious blunder; the latter as an entangling alliance and a blow to the Monroe Doctrine. Many of these strictures were unfair. Some were politically inspired. Hay was correct in alleging that England had made substantial concessions for very little in return. Yet it would be a mistake to conclude, as most historians have done, that Hay's work was all good and that the objections stemmed from personal animosities and the Senate's concern for its prerogatives. The opposition cut across party lines, included some of Hay's friends, rested on several sound arguments, and went beyond the question of whether the Secretary had conferred in advance with the Foreign Relations Committee.

On March 9, 1900, that committee recommended approval of the treaty with but one change. After the furor of the previous month, the report was quite restrained. The amendment stipulated that the American government was free to employ its armed forces in the canal area "for the defense of the United States and the maintenance of public order." Such moderation pleased no one. Many Senators felt the amendment did not go far enough, while Hay regarded it as a personal rebuke. On March 13 he submitted his resignation, which McKinley wisely declined to accept. But with equal wisdom the President avoided an outright endorsement of the original version. A compromise was necessary, and it was decided to wait until after the presidential election.

Despite McKinley's victory, the Senate would not approve the agreement as signed. On December 13, 1900, it adopted by a vote of 65 to 17 the committee amendment of the previous spring. A week later it unanimously accepted two more additions. The first stated clearly that the Clayton-Bulwer Treaty was superseded; the second struck out the article inviting others to adhere. With these three amendments the Senate then gave its consent to the Hay-Pauncefote pact by a margin of 55 to 18. In view of the controversy that developed in 1912, it should be noted that the Senate did not approve another amendment which would have permitted the United States to discriminate against foreign shipping by charging lower tolls for American vessels engaged in coastal trade.

Although the Hay-Pauncefote Treaty as amended by the Senate did not conform to the wishes of the executive branch, neither McKinley nor Hay sought to withhold ratification. However much they preferred the original version and disliked asking England to accept a different text, they knew speedy action to be imperative. Pauncefote shared their views and recommended that his government acquiesce. But Lord Lansdowne, the new Foreign Secretary, ruled otherwise. While he knew that eventually there would be a canal under American control and while he was ready to concur in the hegemony over the Caribbean which the waterway would give to the United States, he argued that propriety and pride obliged him to reject the amended treaty and to start negotiations all over again.

Lansdowne's decision proved to be sound. In April, 1901, Hay resumed the discussions without newspaper publicity or congressional scrutiny. With the legislature not in session, the executive enjoyed a free hand. Many persons contributed to the final settlement: Hay, who now acted more adeptly; Pauncefote, who shuttled across the Atlantic; Ambassador Joseph H. Choate, who worked well with Lansdowne; and even Lodge, who talked with several British leaders during a summer visit to London. The assassination of McKinley did not hurt, for Roosevelt, a bitter critic of the original pact, had pledged himself to carry out the policies of his predecessor. On November 18, 1901, a new treaty was signed. Submitted to the Senate on December 4, it was consented to without change on December 16 by a vote of 76 to 6.

Under the Second Hay-Pauncefote Treaty, the United States was entitled to construct, either directly or through its citizens and by whatever route it deemed expedient, an interoceanic canal and to regulate and manage the same. The rules for neutralization, again adapted from the Suez Convention, were not the same as before. The most notable omissions were the ban on fortifications and the requirement that the canal be open to vessels of all nations in both war and peace. In return for these gains the American government now promised that conditions and charges affecting traffic in the canal would be "just and equitable." All in all, the United States emerged as the chief beneficiary. Sole control and complete freedom of action replaced joint control and the ban on colonization it had been compelled by weakness to accept in 1850. For this improvement the Senate deserves considerable credit, since such men as Davis and Lodge grasped better than McKinley and Hay the realities of world politics and world power. If the treaty constituted, as Hay hoped, the foundation of Anglo-American diplomatic friendship in the twentieth century, it also symbolized the passing of British dominance and the advent of American hegemony in the Caribbean.

THE BATTLE OF THE ROUTES

Even while the release from England was being won, a battle raged over the proper route. For years Nicaragua had been favored over Panama. Although longer—about 200 miles, as compared to 50—a canal there could use natural channels most of the way. As early as February 7, 1876, a commission appointed by Grant unanimously endorsed Nicaragua. The beginning of construction at Panama by a French company in 1881 compelled Americans to look elsewhere. Although they encountered difficulties in Nicaragua, the subsequent reports of the Ludlow Commission on October 31, 1895, of the First Walker Commission on May 9, 1899, and of the Second Walker Commission on November 16, 1901, continued to support the northerly route. The last document did stress the advantages of the isthmus, but pointed out that the New Panama Canal Company, heir of the original French enterprise, evaluated its property at $109,141,500, well above the figure of $40 million which the commission set as a fair value.

Transit rights had been obtained at both sites. In a treaty of December 12, 1846, Colombia—then named New Granada—promised that the right of transit across the isthmus of Panama, by "any modes of communication that now exist or that may be hereafter constructed," would be open on the same terms to American and Colombian nationals. In return, the United States agreed to guarantee Colombia's sovereignty over the isthmus as well as the neutrality of the isthmus with a view that traffic thereon would not henceforth be interrupted. Simi-

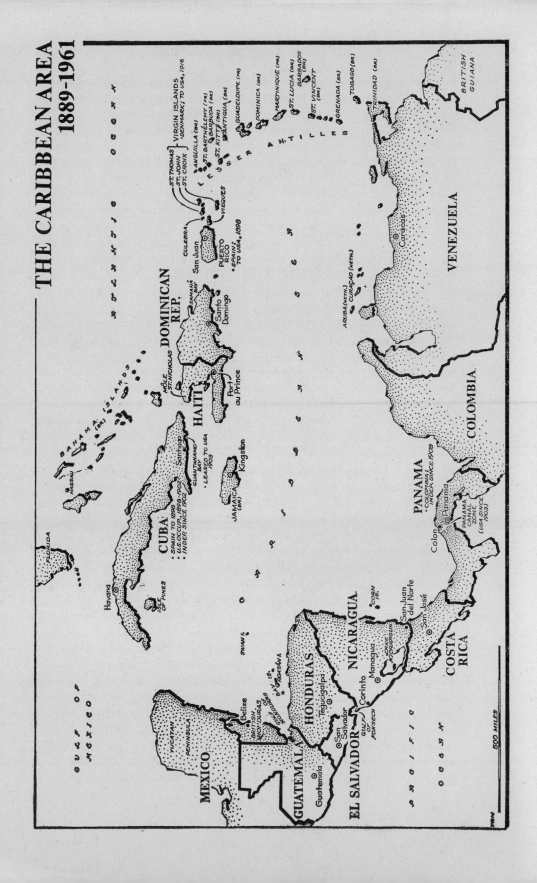

THE CARIBBEAN AREA
1889-1961

ATLANTIC OCEAN

BAHAMA ISLANDS (BR.)

Nassau

FLORIDA

GULF OF MEXICO

Havana

CUBA
- SPAIN TO 1898
- U.S.OCCUP. 1898-1902
- INDEP. SINCE 1902

ISLE OF PINES

Santiago

GUANTANAMO BAY
LEASED TO USA
1903

JAMAICA (BR.)
Kingston

HAITI

MÔLE ST. NICHOLAS

Port au Prince

DOMINICAN REP.

Santo Domingo

SAMANA BAY

San Juan

PUERTO RICO
- SPAIN; TO USA, 1898

CULEBRA
VIEQUES

ST. THOMAS
ST. JOHN   VIRGIN ISLANDS
ST. CROIX   DENMARK; TO USA, 1916

ANGUILLA (BR.)
ST. BARTHÉLEMY (FR.)
ST. MARTIN   BARBUDA (BR.)
ST. KITTS (BR.)
ANTIGUA (BR.)
GUADELOUPE (FR.)
DOMINICA (BR.)
MARTINIQUE (FR.)
ST. LUCIA (BR.)
BARBADOS (BR.)
ST. VINCENT (BR.)
GRENADA (BR.)
TOBAGO (BR.)
TRINIDAD (BR.)

LESSER ANTILLES

ATLANTIC OCEAN

CARIBBEAN SEA

SWAN IS.

CORN IS.

ARUBA (NETH.)
CURAÇAO (NETH.)

Caracas

VENEZUELA

BRITISH GUIANA

COLOMBIA

PANAMA
- COLOMBIA;
  INDEP. SINCE 1903

Colón
Panamá

PANAMA CANAL ZONE
(USA SINCE 1903)

COSTA RICA

San José

San Juan del Norte

NICARAGUA

Managua

Corinto

GOLFO DE FONSECA

HONDURAS

Tegucigalpa

BRITISH HONDURAS

Belize

YUCATAN PENINSULA

MEXICO

GUATEMALA

Guatemala

EL SALVADOR

San Salvador

GULF OF FONSECA

PACIFIC OCEAN

500 MILES

larly, in a treaty of June 21, 1867, Nicaragua granted to American citizens the same rights between the oceans that its own citizens enjoyed. Nicaraguan sovereignty over the route would be preserved, but the United States consented to protect the route and guarantee its neutrality.

With the publication of the Second Walker Commission's report on November 16, 1901, the uneven battle between Nicaragua and Panama entered a new phase. Two days later the Second Hay-Pauncefote Treaty removed all legal barriers to an American-controlled canal. On January 9, 1902, the House passed by a vote of 308 to 2 a bill appropriating $180 million to construct a Nicaraguan canal. Faced with defeat, the directors of the New Panama Canal Company agreed to sell their property and franchise to the United States for $40 million the exact value set by the Walker Commission. That price meant the Panama route would now cost $5,600,000 less than its rival.

This last-minute offer reached Washington on January 4, 1902. Roosevelt, once a champion of Nicaragua but now persuaded that recent engineering advances had made Panama more feasible, immediately reconvened the Second Walker Commission. In a supplementary report on January 18 that group reached the same conclusion as Roosevelt. Ten days later Senator John C. Spooner, Republican of Wisconsin, offered an amendment to the House bill which authorized the President to purchase the concession and property of the New Panama Canal Company for $40 million, provided a valid title was obtained; to acquire from Colombia perpetual control of a six-mile wide zone across the isthmus; to construct there a ship canal under a governmental commission; and to negotiate with Nicaragua if, within a "reasonable time," proper titles could not be procured from the French company or a satisfactory treaty could not be secured from Colombia. Thanks to the untiring efforts of Spooner and Mark Hanna, to the skillful propaganda of the New Company's agents, and to the timely and publicized eruption of a volcano in Nicaragua, the Senate accepted the substitute on June 19 by a margin of 42 to 34. The amended bill then carried by a count of 67 to 6; and although the House momentarily stood firm, it finally yielded on June 25 in a roll call of 260 to 8.

Two things remained to be done after the passage of the Spooner Act of June 28, 1902. First, the Attorney-General must rule that the New Panama Canal Company held a valid title to its concession and could legally transfer it to the United States. This Philander C. Knox did in an opinion of October 25, 1902. Second, the Secretary of State must negotiate with Colombia for perpetual control of a zone through which the canal would run. This John Hay did in a treaty of January 22, 1903. Hay's task was not easy. The unstable government of

President José M. Marroquín at Bogotá frequently changed envoys in Washington and rarely entrusted them with adequate powers. The agreement Hay hammered out with Tomas Herrán permitted the New Panama Canal Company to sell its property to the United States and granted the latter for one hundred years, renewable for similar periods, the sole right to build, operate, and control a ship canal though a strip of territory extending three miles on either side of the waterway. In that zone Colombia remained sovereign. The canal itself would be neutralized according to the Hay-Pauncefote Treaty. As compensation, the United States promised to pay a sum of $10 million at once and an annuity of $250,000 beginning in 1912.

In the United States Senate, the opponents of the Hay-Herrán Treaty fell into two groups. The champions of Nicaragua urged its defeat on the grounds that Colombia was in chaos, that Marroquín would soon be overthrown, that Herrán lacked authority to negotiate, and that the New Company had resorted to fraud. The nationalists, led by Spooner, Hanna, and Foraker, wanted more extensive rights for the United States in the canal zone. After a short fight, the treaty was approved without change on March 17, 1903, by a majority of 73 to 5.

Opposition in the Colombian Senate was rooted in patriotism, pride, greed, and politics. Many men sincerely believed that Colombian sovereignty over the isthmus was not fully protected. Others argued, with some justice, that the compensation was inadequate. These wished to assess the French company $10 million for transferring its property and to raise the initial American payment to $15 million. Hay reacted in the worst possible way to these belated demands. Contemptuous of all Latins, to whom he referred as "dagos," and irritated by the drawn-out negotiations, he yielded to the specious reasoning of William N. Cromwell, the talented lawyer for the New Panama Canal Company, and on April 28, 1903, he asserted that the Hay-Herrán Treaty estopped the government at Bogotá from imposing any levy on the cession of the French franchise. On June 9 he warned that if Colombia rejected the pact or delayed unduly, "the friendly understanding between the two countries would be so seriously compromised that action might be taken by the Congress next winter which every friend of Colombia would regret." That thinly veiled ultimatum had no effect, and on August 12, 1903, the Colombian Senate unanimously defeated the treaty. The next move was up to the Roosevelt administration.

THE UPRISING IN PANAMA

That move could take several forms. One was to negotiate anew with Colombia. That course would entail delay and probably larger payments. A second was to turn to Nicaragua, as the Spooner Act provided. That course would involve a more costly route and exposure to sharp bargaining by the government at Managua. A third possibility was to do nothing—to call Colombia's bluff, if such it was—until the lure of ready cash brought a reduction in its demands. That course could boomerang; for if no settlement was reached by October 31, 1904, the franchise of the New Panama Canal Company would expire. A fourth option was to take advantage of the disappointment on the isthmus, where there had been fifty-three rebellions in as many years and where as late as September 6, 1902, the authorities at Bogotá had appealed for American aid to maintain their control. Such a course might bring a canal at the earliest possible date, but it was fraught with danger for the good name of the United States and its policy of nonintervention.

The choice of the fourth option must be attributed to the personality and temperament of Theodore Roosevelt. A firm believer in the superiority of the Anglo-Saxons, he looked with scorn upon the less strenuous Latins. An ardent advocate of the white man's burden, he sincerely believed the United States to have an obligation to the world to prevent "contemptible little creatures" at Bogotá from exploiting the best canal route for their own gain. A staunch champion of the navy, he could not brook delay in a project vital to the nation's defenses, especially since it would double the striking power of the fleet and insure American hegemony in the Caribbean. Like Hay, Roosevelt failed to see that Marroquín and his associates were moved by more than monetary considerations. At a time when patience and understanding were called for, an impetuous and indignant man sat in the White House. At a moment when he most needed a restraining hand, the only men capable of providing it—Root and Lodge—were in London, serving on the Alaskan Boundary Tribunal.

Roosevelt, it must be insisted, did not instigate the uprising in Panama. The inhabitants of the isthmus, fearful lest the policy makers at Bogotá gamble away the great prize and encouraged by agents of the New Panama Canal Company, decided in September 1903 to secede. At that time the President was contemplating the possibility of constructing a canal without Colombia's assent. He thought he had found a justification in a memorandum prepared by John Bassett Moore, then a professor of international law at Columbia University. Moore argued that in the past only the United States had fulfilled the mutual obligations contained in the treaty of December 12, 1846. It had frequently landed troops to preserve Colombian sovereignty over the isthmus and to keep traffic there free and uninterrupted.[1] For its

---

[1] Prior to 1903 American forces had landed on the isthmus, under the treaty of 1846 or the general right to protect lives, on at least nine occasions. In each

part, Colombia had done nothing and was still bound to allow the American government or its citizens to use the right of way to build a canal. Moore argued that sovereignty had duties as well as rights and that Colombia could not break its word by closing for selfish purposes one of the great highways of world trade.

Nor did Roosevelt then intend to act without the consent of Congress. Early in October, 1903 he sketched a message he might send to that body when it met on December 7. In it he declared that he would not submit to "extortion" by men he had called elsewhere "the foolish and homicidal corruptionists of Bogotá." If Congress approved, he would buy the New Company's property and begin building without consulting Colombia. If the legislature disagreed, he would turn instead to Nicaragua.

Events on the isthmus forestalled this audacious scheme. Aided by funds from Philippe Bunau-Varilla, an agent of the New Panama Canal Company, and confident the United States would prevent Colombian troops from interrupting the freedom of transit, the secessionist leaders planned the uprising for November 3, 1903. They received no assurances, explicit or implied, from Roosevelt or Hay. They did not have to. Both men knew that a rebellion was brewing and that they could benefit from it without giving encouragement. Both had made it clear that American warships would be in the vicinity, ready to keep peace on the isthmus, even if it meant barring Colombian reinforcements. Naval movements were then fully reported in the press. To forecast American policy, one had only to read and listen.

Colombia was not ignorant of this secessionist plot. In the early hours of November 3, 1903, General Juan B. Tobar disembarked 400 men at Colon, on the Atlantic side, with the intention of crossing by rail to the rebel headquarters at Panama City. At first Commander John Hubbard, who had arrived in the gunboat *Nashville* the previous day, interposed no objections. With the success of the revolt hanging in the balance, the superintendent of the railroad acted. Alleging that he had only enough cars to take Tobar and his staff to the Pacific coast immediately, he promised to transport the main body the next morning. Twelve hours later those officers were under arrest in Panama City, and Hubbard had informed the superintendent that since "any movement of troops in the neighborhood must inevitably produce a conflict and interrupt the transit of the isthmus which the United States is pledged to maintain uninterruptedly," the further carrying of men be-

instance, except that of September 17, 1902, the consent of Colombia had been obtained in advance. Only in 1902, moreover, had the United States interfered with the free movement of Colombian troops, and on October 16 Hay disclaimed any intention to infringe upon Colombian sovereignty.

longing to either party was prohibited. With the main Colombian detachment thus isolated in Colon, the rebels in Panama City proclaimed
their independence on November 4. They then managed, by bribery
and by Tobar's stupidity, to persuade the Colombians to evacuate Colon. Thus on November 6 the insurgents held both ends of the route,
and the first phase of the revolution had succeeded.

There can be no doubt that if the United States had kept its warships away from the isthmus or had not subjected the treaty of 1846 to
a novel reading, the Republic of Panama would not have come into
being in November, 1903. Colombia had the man power and the will
power to suppress the uprising, but it was prevented from engaging
the rebels in battle. For the first time the American government interpreted its obligations of 1846 to the detriment of the other party. It
insisted upon keeping the route open, even if in the process it destroyed
Colombia's title to it. Without accusing the Roosevelt administration of
conspiring to overthrow Colombian rule on the isthmus, without minimizing the difficulties it had encountered in trying to resolve the problem by diplomacy, and without exonerating the irresolute and often
insincere men at Bogotá, we cannot escape the conclusion that the
events of November 3–5, 1903, reflect little credit upon the President
and his Secretary of State.

Subsequent developments did not put them in a better light. On
November 6, 1903, about forty hours after learning that a *de facto* government had been formed in Panama City, Hay instructed his consul to
enter into diplomatic relations with it. In moving with unseemly haste,
the Secretary contended that covenants ran with the land and that the
Republic of Panama and the United States inherited the mutual obligations contained in the treaty of 1846. That same day the Marroquín
cabinet offered to ratify the Hay-Herrán agreement by executive
decree, provided the United States sent troops to the isthmus to preserve Colombia's sovereignty. Hay ignored that act of desperation and
on November 9 informally received Bunau-Varilla as the minister
from Panama. Four days later he extended full recognition and on
November 15 began negotiations for a treaty. Two years to the day
after signing the second treaty with Pauncefote, Hay affixed his name
to another important document.

The treaty with Panama of November 18, 1903, improved upon
the Colombian agreement of January 22. The American government
now acquired in perpetuity, not for a hundred years, a strip of land
across the isthmus extending five miles, not three, on either side of
the proposed waterway, together with four small islands in the Bay of
Panama. Within that zone the United States could act "as if it were the
sovereign" and could build, maintain, and operate a canal. That facility
would be neutralized according to the Hay-Pauncefote Treaty, but the

American government retained the right to protect and defend it. Panama also agreed to other infringements upon its sovereignty, including the sale or lease of sites on both coasts suitable for naval stations. The compensation was the same as in the Hay-Herrán convention. Panama was to receive $10 million at once and annuities of $250,000 beginning in 1912. The only new obligation that the United States assumed was a promise to guarantee and maintain the independence of the Republic of Panama.

Totally dependent for survival upon their new friend, the Panamanians had no choice but to accept the treaty of November 18, 1903. The Senate was not so bound, and a vigorous debate ensued. Some members had not despaired of building the canal through Nicaragua and saw in this controversial espisode an opportunity to refight the battle of the routes. Others seized upon it to bolster a shaky Democratic cause in an election year. Finally, some lawmakers, without commitment to route or party, felt that the good name of the United States had been sullied. Roosevelt was not content to defend himself against these charges of inciting revolution, violating sovereignty, and damaging the nation's honor. In messages of December 7, 1903, and January 4, 1904, he placed the blame squarely on the blind and impotent men of Bogotá. He asserted that Colombia was unable to maintain control over the province of Panama; he insisted that Colombia had failed to discharge its obligations under the treaty of 1846; he "raised the question of whether Colombia was entitled to bar the transit of the world's traffic across the Isthmus." The President did not convince everyone, but the desire for immediate construction was widespread and the appeal for party unity compelling. On February 23, 1904, the treaty passed by a vote of 66 to 14.

Echoes of this controversy reverberated through the years. Criticism of Roosevelt persisted and grew louder once the Democrats won control of the House in 1911 and of the executive branch in 1913. Moves to mollify Colombia began during his tenure and continued under Taft, Wilson, and Harding. The administration's course, while legally defensible, was thought by many to be morally wrong; and some of Roosevelt's later boasts—such as "I took the Canal Zone and let Congress debate"—did not help his case. Although it was all too easy after the canal was built to minimize the frustrations of 1903 and to ignore what other nations, under similar circumstances, would have done, historians have been almost unanimous in condemning the President for not understanding the sensibilities of Colombia, for not considering the alternative of Nicaragua, for not delaying the recognition of Panama, and for not realizing that questionable means, even in a laudable cause, would cost the United States the goodwill of the weaker New World republics.

THE ROOSEVELT COROLLARY

The expulsion of Spain from the West Indies, the annexation of Puerto Rico, the curbs placed on a liberated Cuba, the termination of the Clayton-Bulwer Treaty, and the creation of a virtual protectorate in Panama were all part of the growth after 1898 of American hegemony in the Caribbean. By 1904 one last step remained—for the United States to assume the task of preserving stability in a region vital to its security. The Roosevelt Corollary to the Monroe Doctrine provided the justification for this role as international policeman; and although the gloss was hardly a logical deduction from the principles of 1823, it had important antecedents. These included Polk's message of April 29, 1848, questioning Yucatan's right to transfer its sovereignty to a European power, the abortive McLane-Ocampo agreements of December 14, 1859, permitting the United States to protect its citizens and their property in Mexico, the joint resolution of April 20, 1898, authorizing armed intervention to stop a bloody, costly, and interminable war in Cuba, and the more recent treaties with Cuba and Panama on May 22 and November 18, 1903, allowing the American government to employ military force to maintain order in and the independence of those infant republics.

In 1904 there was less precedent for intervention designed to end financial anarchy. Only once before had the United States considered such preventive action. On February 7, 1880, a delinquent Venezuela, fearing punitive measures by France, proposed to deliver in Washington certain monthly revenues for distribution to foreign creditors. On July 23, 1881, Blaine went so far as to warn the French that under certain conditions the United States might be obliged to administer Venezuela's customs houses, but he never carried out that threat. Actually, it was the Venezuelan Imbroglio of 1902–3 that did the most to shape the Roosevelt Corollary. The reaction at home to the Anglo-German blockade convinced the President that coercion by European nations in collecting debts from American republics must be avoided, yet his sense of fairness told him that legitimate claims could not go unredressed. The decision of the Hague Court on February 22, 1904, which in effect rewarded those creditors who had used force, persuaded him that the temptation to apply strong-arm methods must be removed. This could be done only if the United States supervised the collection and distribution of revenues in the unstable and impotent countries of the Caribbean.

The Dominican Republic was such a country. Chaos had reigned there ever since the assassination of Heureaux in July 1899. An impoverished land of 500,000 persons faced a staggering debt of $40 million. Bondholders from Belgium, England, France, Germany, Italy, Spain, and the United States clamored for payment. Roosevelt was not eager to intervene. The battle over the Panama Treaty still raged in the Senate; the Russo-Japanese War had begun; the election of 1904 loomed ahead. But the President believed the islanders were "utterly incompetent" to govern themselves. "Sooner or later," he wrote his son on February 10, 1904, we must "assume an attitude of protection and regulation in regard to all these little states." On February 23, the day he learned of the Hague Court's verdict, he told a friend: "I want to do nothing but what a policeman has to do in Santo Domingo. . . . I have about the same desire to annex it as a gorged boa constrictor might have to swallow a porcupine wrong-end-to."

Ten months later, after a triumph at the polls, Roosevelt set forth his corollary to the Monroe Doctrine. In a message on December 6, 1904, he denied that the United States sought additional lands in the New World. All it wanted to have was stable and prosperous neighbors. Those who kept order and paid their debts had nothing to fear. But, he warned, "chronic wrongdoing, or an impotence which results in a general loosening of the ties of civilized society, may in America, as elsewhere, ultimately require intervention by some civilized nation, and in the Western Hemisphere the adherence of the United States to the Monroe Doctrine may force the United States, however reluctantly, in flagrant cases of wrongdoing and impotence, to the exercise of an international police power."

Like Monroe's pronouncement, the Roosevelt Corollary was a statement by the executive branch. In 1904, as in 1823, the legislature did not endorse it; indeed, some Congressmen saw no connection between the two declarations. But it was not until the President attempted to translate theory into practice that he met opposition. On January 20, 1905, Minister Thomas C. Dawson signed a protocol in Santo Domingo. This executive agreement provided for a guarantee by the United States of the territorial integrity of the Dominican Republic, complete American control of the customs houses, and the payment of all outstanding Dominican debts from 55 per cent of the revenues thus collected. When the Senate learned of this document, it exploded with righteous indignation and injured pride. Already angered by the Panama affair, many members denounced this act as an invasion of senatorial prerogatives. To blunt the charge of presidential usurpation, Dawson was instructed to change the agreement to a treaty, which he did on February 7, 1905. He also altered the pledge to guarantee the territorial integrity of the Dominican Republic into a promise to respect it, and he inserted in the preamble a reference to the Monroe Doctrine. Thus transformed, the pact reached the Senate on February 15, but no vote was taken before adjournment. Roosevelt then called the upper house back into special session, but he was unable to overcome the opposition and muster the necessary two-thirds majority.

Roosevelt held one more trump. Convinced that he had diagnosed correctly the disease in the Dominican body politic and that he had prescribed the proper medicine, he prepared to treat the patient in still a third way. If an executive agreement aroused protest and a treaty could not be acted upon, he would initiate the customs control by a modus vivendi. This he did on April 1, 1905, in a temporary arrangement which embodied the essence of the abortive treaty. Actually the arrangement was not very temporary; for it took Root, who succeeded Hay on July 7, 1905, almost a year and a half to devise a new formula which satisfied both the Dominican government and the United States Senate.

By April, 1905, nonetheless, American hegemony in the Caribbean was an indisputable fact. Puerto Rico and the Canal Zone had been annexed. A naval site in Cuba had been leased. The right to intervene in Cuba and Panama had been gained. Administration of the Dominican customs houses was about to begin. The authority to build, operate, and defend a canal had been attained. The Monroe Doctrine had been again expanded and brandished. Germany had not won its coveted foothold while England was in the process of transferring all large warships from the West Indies to the North Sea. The United States was militarily supreme.

BOOK · III

THE FIRST TEST:
THE
GREAT CRUSADE

1905 – 21

*In which the American people intervene
reluctantly in a world war, rationalize
their participation as a great crusade,
but refuse to abandon isolationism.*

19

The Shaping of Foreign Policy, 1905–21

ALTHOUGH the United States emerged as a world power between 1889 and 1905, most Americans believed that this change did not require any basic modification of their foreign policy. It seemed to them possible—and in that period it was—to possess overseas colonies and still adhere to historic principles and practices. In the years from 1905 to 1921, however, the Great War challenged that belief and confronted the republic with the first test of its new international position. Responding to momentous developments in Europe and Asia, Wilson by 1917 urged the abandonment of isolationism and neutrality, but after a bitter debate and for a variety of reasons the country rejected his counsel. The outcome of this initial test was an unsatisfactory compromise between Wilson's ideas and traditional attitudes, one that shaped the character of American diplomacy from 1921 to 1939. Only after the beginning of the Second World War did the real break with the past occur.

THE PRESIDENTS

This first test of the United States as a world power revealed the president continuing to enjoy the initiative in the formulation and conduct of foreign policy and the constitutional division of authority continuing to provoke conflict between the executive and the legislature. All three occupants of the White House in this period held well-defined views on the presidency as the sole organ of the nation in its external relations. Each strengthened the methods for discharging the responsibility; each showed a greater awareness than the men on Capitol Hill of the new role the republic must play on the global stage.

Theodore Roosevelt was elected in his own right in November, 1904, and he dedicated himself to the task of making the Republican party progressive. But he never lost interest in foreign affairs, and his second administration was marked by novel efforts in the realm of world peace. If Roosevelt as president remained constant in his emphasis on military preparedness, his belief in paternalistic colonial laws, and his almost pathologic fear of instability in the Caribbean, he broke new ground in his experiment with compulsory arbitration, his support of a permanent court of international justice, his mediation in the Western Hemisphere, his good offices during the Russo-Japanese War, and his help in the Moroccan imbroglio of 1905. He never ceased to insist that the president could exercise all authority not explicitly entrusted to Congress or expressly denied to him. He always regarded himself as commander-in-chief. "In a crisis," he wrote in 1913, "the duty of a leader is to lead and not to take refuge behind the generally timid wisdom of a multitude of councillors." His personal correspondence with the European monarchs was unprecedented. His use of the press to focus attention on his work foreshadowed the future. His visit to the Canal Zone in November, 1906—the first time a president ever left the country during his incumbency—anticipated a mobility that would soon be taken for granted.

More than any of his predecessors, Roosevelt influenced foreign policy after quitting the White House. For ten years before his death in January, 1919, he spoke out frequently and freely, and his thinking evolved with the times. Always a staunch nationalist and an ardent believer in coordinating diplomacy with force, he toyed with the idea of a league of nations. Ever a realist, he quickly grasped the limitations of compulsory arbitration and of an organization based upon the principle of equality and universality. Under the impact of war he came to regard isolationism and neutrality as obsolete, but he also abandoned his concept of a league of big states for a defensive alliance with England and France. Out of office, Roosevelt grew dogmatic and irresponsible, and his attacks upon Wilson were often unfair and uncouth. He tended to pontificate without a firm grasp of the facts, and his views sometimes reflected individual antipathies, partisan prejudices, and personal frustrations. Yet when all this is said, Roosevelt did have an important message for those who would flee the realities of the twentieth century.

William Howard Taft, as Roosevelt's chosen successor, expected to carry on the same domestic and foreign policies. For that task the genial and gargantuan Ohioan seemed well equipped. After two years as solicitor-general under Harrison and eight years on the federal circuit court, he was named by McKinley in March, 1900, to head the Second Philippine Commission. He served as governor of the islands until January, 1904, and then replaced Root as Secretary of War. There he showed great talent as a troubleshooter, especially in Cuba, the Canal Zone, the Philippines, and Japan. Unfortunately, his temperament and political acumen did not match his travel and administrative experience. A kindly, well-intentioned man, Taft lacked Roosevelt's vigor and sense of drama; he also lacked Wilson's intellect and ability to inspire. Indecisive by nature, inept on the hustings, a judge at heart, he had an uncanny ability to antagonize those he wished to conciliate. Plagued throughout his term by an acrid intraparty struggle, he found himself by October, 1911, completely estranged from an embittered Roosevelt.

Although the diplomatic achievements of his administration were minimal, Taft never lost sight of the changed position of the United States. After his defeat for re-election, he devoted much of his last annual message to foreign policy. "We have emerged fully grown as a peer in the great concourse of nations," he told Congress on December 3, 1912. "We can not meet new questions nor build for the future if we confine ourselves to outworn dogmas of the past and to the perspective appropriate at our emergence from colonial times." Not surprisingly, in 1915 Taft became the champion of a league of nations. Nor did he fail, while in the White House, to make his contribution to the techniques of the presidency. In August, 1911, when the Foreign Relations Committee threatened to amend his cherished arbitration treaties, he took his case to the people. After delivering several speeches in behalf of the treaties along the Atlantic seaboard, he returned to the subject on a swing through the West and thus became the first president to appeal, even indirectly, over the head of the Senate on external problems.

Woodrow Wilson, unlike his two predecessors, had no first-hand contact with diplomacy before entering the White House. On leaving for Washington in March, 1913, he remarked: "It would be the irony of fate if my administration had to deal chiefly with foreign affairs." Intent on restoring equality of economic opportunity at home—in a program he called the New Freedom—Wilson was so absorbed with domestic reform that his inaugural address contained not a single reference to international issues. Yet, as a perceptive and articulate citizen, as a historian and political scientist, as President of Princeton University and Governor of New Jersey, he had not ignored the rise of the United States to world power. After initial misgivings, Wilson accepted overseas colonies as the inevitable consequence of American growth. "A new era has come," he wrote in March, 1901. "Our almost accidental possession of the Philippines has put us in the presence of forces which make the politics of the twentieth century radically unlike the politics of the nineteenth." Steadily his horizons broadened. "We are participants, whether we would or not, in the life of the world," he told a Washington audience in May, 1916. "What affects mankind is inevitably our affair."

Wilson also brought to the White House firm convictions on the nature of his office. In 1907, in a lecture at Columbia University, he warned that the president "can never again be the mere domestic figure he has been throughout so large a part of our history." In March, 1913, he thought of himself, not like Roosevelt as commander-in-chief, but as an American equivalent of the British prime minister. To strengthen executive control he revived the forgotten practice of delivering his messages to the legislature in person. In his first term he obtained a remarkably high percentage of the laws he proposed. During both terms he acted as secretary of state on all important matters, even typing key dispatches on his own machine. During both terms he frequently went on the stump to enlist popular support. Wilson's eloquence made him an inspiring war leader and a towering world figure.

In his impact on foreign policy, Wilson the president cannot be divorced from Wilson the man. All his political thought and action derived from his Presbyterian theology: his belief in a stern yet loving God, enthroned in a moral universe, whose laws governed nations as well as men. He was imbued with an idealism that subordinated material goals to ethical standards and with a democratic faith that blinded him to the capacity of Mexican peons and Russian peasants to operate American institutions. His diplomacy savored of the missionary spirit, for its aim was to serve humanity. Dedicated to the cause of freedom, Wilson was occasionally prepared to propagate it by the sword. Universal in outlook, he was sporadically pharisaical in his defense of specific proposals. Bold in vision, he was sometimes astigmatic in his choice of methods. Warm-hearted and generous, he could also be petty and vindictive. Desperate for intimate friends, he rarely treated his trusted advisers as equals. The right, he insisted, was more precious than peace, and he was confident that he knew intuitively what was right. A superb orator, a gifted writer, a courageous fighter, he was usually an effective leader; but when enlisted in a great cause, he could be dogmatic and inflexible. He understood the need for compromise in politics, but in a supreme crisis, involving basic principles, he would stand fast, feeling—like Luther—that he could do no other.

THE SECRETARIES OF STATE

Elihu Root was the first of several secretaries of state from 1905 to 1921 to contribute to the formulation and conduct of American foreign policy. Strong-willed and witty, he acted on the assumption, then tenable, that the main object of diplomacy was "to keep the country out of trouble." In contrast to Roosevelt, his chief, he was cautious by nature and judicious by training. He was skilled in the art of human relations and had a positive genius for reconciling the irreconcilable. Unlike Hay, Root got along well with the Senate and treated the South American ministers as his equals. As a former secretary of war, he knew at first hand the problems of military organization and colonial administration. As a student of international law, he tried to devise at The Hague a permanent court of arbitral justice. As a realist, he recognized the changed position of the United States but did not urge a sudden or wholesale renunciation of traditional policies. He worked closely with the President; and until they split over domestic issues in June, 1912, Roosevelt always called Root the ablest man in public life. Root was equally affectionate but could not resist deflating with banter his chief's extreme pretensions. He liked to credit Roosevelt with discovering the Ten Commandments and compared the repeated justification of his course in Panama to that of a man who had been accused of seduction and was proven guilty of rape.

Philander C. Knox of Pennsylvania served for four years under Taft and encountered all the frustration abroad and bickering at home which characterized that unhappy administration. Since the President gave him a relatively free hand, Knox was responsible for some of these difficulties. Lazy, testy, and supercilious, he was less fitted to deal with foreign envoys than he had been to handle legal problems as attorney-general from 1901 to 1904. His brusqueness antagonized the sensitive Latins, and he lacked the patience and attention to detail so essential in international relations. Although he had been in the Senate from 1904 to 1909, his cooperation with that body was less effective than Root's. To his credit, Knox undertook a long overdue reorganization of the State Department, but he is best remembered for trying to place American finance behind American diplomacy in underdeveloped areas, a policy often called "dollar diplomacy." A short, vain, but brainy man, Knox—like Root—helped shape foreign policy long after he left office.

William Jennings Bryan, the first of Wilson's three secretaries of state, is more difficult to categorize. Thrice a defeated candidate for the presidency, still a power at the Democratic convention in 1912, and a veteran spokesman for anti-imperialism and world peace, the Great

Commoner inspired intense loyalty and intense scorn. By some he was criticized for his provincialism, pacifism, and petty politics; by others he was revered for his idealism and insight into the true meaning of neutrality. Actually, Bryan was neither so ignorant as his detractors claimed nor so prescient as his admirers maintained. What he brought to the State Department was an untiring devotion to party, an unswerving loyalty to his chief, and an unfailing ability to sense the feelings of the rural South and West. With Wilson he shared a moralistic approach to diplomacy, a belief that international relations could be viewed in terms of immutable principles and that the mission of the United States was to spread the blessings of democracy. Given a free hand in only a few areas, Bryan's positive contributions were an agreement with Nicaragua, a statement on China in May, 1915, and the "cooling-off treaties." For ten months after August, 1914, he tried desperately to bridge a growing divergence from Wilson on neutrality, finally resigning on June 9, 1915.

Robert Lansing, his successor, was a very different man. An urbane and handsome New Yorker, he was the son-in-law of John W. Foster and a protégé of Elihu Root, both Republicans. Without any political standing but well trained in international law, Lansing had represented the United States before a number of arbitral boards. Selected to replace the eminent John Bassett Moore as Counselor on April 1, 1914, he made himself so useful in the State Department that he was chosen to succeed Bryan on June 23, 1915. Lansing was too independent in his thinking to follow Wilson slavishly and too reserved in his manner to fight for what he believed. As a result, the President consistently underestimated his talents and unwisely ignored him during the peace negotiations. This was unfortunate, for the Secretary's realistic approach to the problems bequeathed by the First World War deserved a fairer hearing than it received. Lansing's tenure ended in bitterness when in February, 1920, he was compelled to resign by an irate and irritable Wilson.

Bainbridge Colby, a New York lawyer and former member of the Republican and Progressive parties, acted as secretary of state during Wilson's final year in office. His qualifications for the post are hard to discover, and he is remembered, if at all, for a vigorous note of August 10, 1920, in which he assailed the Bolshevik regime and laid the foundation for the nonrecognition of Russia that lasted for thirteen years.

Edward M. House of Texas was in March, 1913, totally lacking in diplomatic experience and after that date never held an elective office or one subject to senatorial confirmation. Yet as an executive agent and the President's personal confidant, he wielded more influence than Bryan, Lansing, or Colby. This quiet, soft-spoken, almost mouselike man, whom Wilson called "my second personality," was the one individual to whom the President turned freely for sage counsel and objective appraisal. To House he could—and did—unburden his heart, confess his hopes, and entrust the most delicate missions. It was House who went to Europe as Wilson's "silent partner" on four occasions before the United States entered the war, who organized the experts known as The Inquiry to collect and collate data for the peacemaking, who negotiated the Pre-Armistice Agreement with Germany, and who stood second only to Wilson in the American delegation at Paris. Nor was this faith misplaced. More than any other man, House understood Wilson's complex temperament. A good listener and a loyal collaborator, the selfless Texan maintained his integrity and his independence. When the tragic break in this remarkable friendship finally came in April, 1919, it was over a fundamental question and one on which each remained true to himself.

THE CONGRESSIONAL LEADERS

Congressional opposition to the president's control of foreign affairs deepened during the prewar years and reached a climax over the Versailles Treaty. The chief actor in this drama and the chief protagonist for the legislature was Henry Cabot Lodge. Roosevelt confided freely in the Massachusetts Republican and Taft wanted him as secretary of state, but Wilson, after a brief period of cooperation, found him a bitter and unrelenting foe. Yet it would be misleading to forget Wilson's own hatred of Lodge or to dismiss the Senator as a blind obstructionist, motivated solely by personal and partisan considerations. Despite his haughty manner, colossal egotism, and uncharitable spirit, Lodge was the best-informed and hardest-working member of the Foreign Relations Committee, on which he had served since December, 1895, and of which he became chairman in May, 1919. Lodge shared many of the ideas of Roosevelt, Root, and Taft on colonial, hemispheric, and military problems. Like them, he was before 1916 more insistent than Wilson that the United States engage in positive endeavors for world peace. But he demanded that all new obligations be subjected to senatorial scrutiny, and he opposed the League of Nations for being too sharp a break with the past. The most influential Senator in the battle over the peace treaty, Lodge's devious course has left historians unable to say whether his reservations were intended to improve upon or to defeat the Wilsonian settlement.

No senator of either party rivaled Lodge as an authority on external affairs. Shelby M. Cullom, Republican chairman of the Foreign Relations Committee from 1901 to 1913, was an average politician who owed his position to seniority. Root might have matched Lodge in experience if he had not retired in 1915 after one term. Some of the best-known Republicans concentrated until 1917 upon domestic developments. After that date such men as Robert M. La Follette of Wisconsin, William E. Borah of Idaho, George W. Norris of Nebraska, and Hiram W. Johnson of California grew more concerned about foreign policy. Two years later these liberals joined with such extreme conservatives as Knox, Frank B. Brandegee of Connecticut, and George H. Moses of New Hampshire to crush Wilson's dream for American participation in a new world order. Until the Democrats won control of the Senate in March, 1913, they could do little but criticize. Even when they were entitled to name the chairman of the Foreign Relations Committee, they produced no statesman of distinction. Augustus O. Bacon of Georgia died in February, 1914, without leaving his mark, while William J. Stone of Missouri was often out of sympathy with Wilson's basic policies. Indeed, on April 4, 1917, Stone cast one of the six votes against the war resolution. He was succeeded in May, 1918, by Gilbert M. Hitchcock of Nebraska, who later, as minority leader, tried to carry out Wilson's wishes in the battle over the Versailles Treaty.

Neither party possessed in the House a spokesman who exerted much influence upon external affairs. The fault lay more with the constitutional system which denied to the lower chamber the advantages held by the Senate than in the quality of the members. Except as a strident critic or author of an unusual resolution, there was little opportunity for a representative to make a name for himself, and the best-known men were those who either carried out the administration's program faithfully or set themselves to obstruct it at all costs.

THE CONSTITUTIONAL CONFLICT

The first test of the United States as a world power revived and sharpened the historic conflict between president and Congress. Since it involved situations the framers of the Constitution had not foreseen and solutions the diplomats of the past had not sought, it threatened to upset the familiar distribution of authority between the executive and the legislature. Each branch reacted as might be expected, and the clash was particularly intense over the treaty-making process and the control of the armed forces.

Appointments to the cabinet and major missions abroad continued to enjoy immunity from senatorial vetoes. As before 1905, the main source of tension was the use of executive agents, especially by Wilson, under the name of personal representatives and unofficial observers. Once again, most objections stemmed from the policies of these agents, not from their constitutional status. Yet the legislature tried twice to prevent this alleged invasion of its prerogative. On March

4, 1913, it passed a bill requiring the president henceforth not to accept or extend an invitation to participate in an international conference unless he had been specifically authorized to do so. On November 15, 1919, the Senate stipulated, in the seventh reservation to the Versailles Treaty, that Congress must provide by statute for the appointment of United States representatives to the Council, the Assembly, or any committee of the League of Nations. Wilson ignored the first as an encroachment upon his rightful powers; the second never went into effect.

Tension over appropriations and the call for documents, at least on constitutional grounds, was largely absent from 1905 to 1921. One reason may be that Congress utilized more fully than ever before its investigatory function. For the first time hearings dealt extensively with external affairs. The most spectacular was held on the Versailles Treaty by the Foreign Relations Committee from July 31 to September 12, 1919. Another example was the probe into Roosevelt's part in the Panama uprising which the Democrats launched as soon as they won control of the House in 1910. When Bryan negotiated a treaty with Colombia on April 6, 1914, which expressed regret and offered reparation for past action, the former President demanded an opportunity to state his views before a legislative committee. Thus this period laid the foundation for the current practice of making every important treaty run the gauntlet of friendly and unfriendly, informed and uninformed witnesses.

Recognition in the years from 1905 to 1921 was more significant for the additional criteria imposed than for the clash between president and Congress. By the twentieth century most commentators agreed that recognition was largely an executive function. Thus John Bassett Moore's *Digest of International Law* concluded in 1906 that in every case of recognizing a new regime or a belligerent, the question was determined "solely by the Executive." In acknowledging the independence of a new state, on the other hand, the president frequently, though not invariably, "invoked the judgment and cooperation of Congress." In a lecture in 1913 former President Taft asserted that the authority to recognize lay completely within the discretion of the man in the White House, while another State Department digest in 1940 declared that "in every instance in which recognition has been accorded by the United States since 1906, the act has been that of the President, taken solely on his own responsibility." Surprisingly, Congress did not challenge these views. When Senator Bacon urged the outgoing Taft administration to recognize the new republic in China, he did not dispute Knox's reply that the executive was supreme in that sphere. When Senator Albert B. Fall, Republican of New Mexico, proposed on December 3, 1919, that recognition of the existing regime in Mexico be withdrawn, he bowed to Wilson's protest that he was encroaching upon the province of the presidency.

This period witnessed a shift of emphasis in recognizing new rulers in established states. For over a century Jefferson's dictum—that the type of government was not a determining factor—had been adhered to. Stability and faithfulness in discharging its duties were the main criteria employed. On September 8, 1900, Assistant Secretary David J. Hill defined more precisely the policy the United States must pursue after a successful revolution. It would defer recognition of the new regime, he said, "until it shall appear that it is in possession of the machinery of the state, administering government with the assent of the people thereof and without substantial resistance to its authority, and that it is in a position to fulfill all the international obligations and responsibilities upon a sovereign state under treaties and international law."

Taft gave some weight to constitutional legitimacy as a prerequisite for recognizing new governments, but Wilson placed it at the forefront of his policy. We can have no sympathy, he declared one week after his inauguration, for those who seize power to promote their own ambitions. Intercourse among states depended upon mutual respect, and the American government chose as friends "those who act in the interest of peace and honor, who protect private rights, and respect the restraints of constitutional provision." In Mexico, Wilson refused to recognize President Victoriano Huerta even when he exercised *de facto* control, because he was implicated in the murder of his predecessor. "It is the purpose of the United States," the State Department said on November 24, 1913, "to discredit and defeat such usurpations wherever they occur." Wilson frowned upon similar revolutionary rises to power in Cuba, Ecuador, Haiti, and the Dominican Republic, while he continued to apply the test of constitutionality in Central America where it rested on a treaty Roosevelt had sponsored but not signed on December 20, 1907. The nonrecognition of Bolshevik Russia was the result of additional factors, but neither in that case nor in the others did a departure from traditional policy provoke a clash between president and Congress.

The treaty-making process had always produced conflict, and the period from 1905 to 1921 was no exception. Although the Senate earned its reputation for obstructionism in these years, the scope of the struggle actually contracted. Congress no longer tried to compel a president to conclude a treaty against his wishes. The president no longer sought a formal commitment from the Senate during the negotiations, as Polk had done over Oregon in 1846, although Wilson might have been wise to ask for a prior vote on the modifications desired in the Versailles Treaty. The House no longer balked at implementing agreements in which it played no part. The president was left free to ratify or not ratify, as he saw fit. With one exception, the termination of treaties caused no trouble. The single attempt of the legislature to force the executive's hand concerned a commercial convention with Russia, but Taft thwarted that move, the result of domestic pressures, by giving the required notice on December 17, 1911, four days after a 300-to-1 vote in the House but before the Senate acted. In short, tension over the treaty-making process grew out of the Senate's tendency—for good reasons or bad—to alter, reject, or refuse to vote on the agreements submitted to it.

Very few major treaties were approved without change between 1905 and 1921. This contrasted sharply with the formative years of the republic. Those that won unqualified consent included two from the Third Inter-American Conference (August 13, 1906); nine signed at the Second Hague Conference (October 18, 1907); twenty-four of Root's bilateral arbitration pacts (February 10, 1908—March 13, 1909); a reparation accord with Colombia (January 9, 1909), which the government at Bogotá rejected; the Declaration of London (February 26, 1909), which died in the House of Lords; a quadripartite settlement of the sealing controversy in the Pacific (July 7, 1911); eighteen of Bryan's Treaties for the Advancement of Peace (December 18, 1913—October 13, 1914); the renewal in 1913–14 and 1918–19 of several of Root's arbitration pacts; and the convention creating the protectorate in Haiti (September 16, 1915).

Other major treaties cleared the Senate hurdle only after changes had been made. Amendments or actual alterations in the text were insisted upon four times: in the customs receivership for the Dominican Republic (February 8, 1907); in the Taft-Knox arbitration agreements with England and France (August 3, 1911), which the President declined to ratify; in ten of the Treaties for the Advancement of Peace (August 7, 1913—July 24, 1914); and in the Bryan-Chamorro convention for a Nicaraguan canal (August 5, 1914). Reservations or statements giving the Senate's interpretation of a clause were resorted to with growing frequency. They were appended to the Act of Algeciras (April 7, 1906); to three of the Hague conventions (October 18, 1907), one of which never went into effect; to a Panamanian treaty designed to foster friendship with Colombia (January 9, 1909), an arrangement the latter did not accept; to an agreement with England submitting the North Atlantic fisheries dispute to the Hague Court (January 27, 1909); to the abortive Taft-Knox treaties (August 3, 1911); and to the purchase of the Danish West Indies (August 4, 1916).

Only one outstanding treaty was voted down, but its fate has colored the entire period. On November 19, 1919, the Versailles Treaty failed to muster a simple majority either with or without reservations, and in a second ballot on March 19, 1920, on a version with reservations, it fell victim to the two-thirds rule. On all other occasions the Senate defeated treaties indirectly by requiring unacceptable changes or by refusing to act. It used the first method with the Taft-Knox arbitration agreements of August 3, 1911; it employed the second in nine cases. These embraced loan conventions with Honduras (January 10, 1911) and with Nicaragua (June 6, 1911); a canal agreement with Nicaragua (February 8, 1913); "cooling off" treaties with Panama (September 20, 1913) and with the Dominican Republic (February 17, 1914); the Treaty of Bogotá with Colombia (April 6, 1914); and three documents signed at Versailles on June 28, 1919— the French assistance pact, a convention on the occupation of the Rhineland, and a measure to protect minorities in Poland.

Evasion of the treaty-making process by executive agreements became more frequent after 1905 but did not create much friction with the legislature. Congress itself authorized the wartime financial arrangements with the Allied governments in the Liberty Loan Act of April 24, 1917; it also approved on July 26, 1911, an accord Taft had reached earlier with Canada for a reciprocal reduction of tariff duties. The Gentlemen's Agreement with Japan, a series of notes exchanged in 1907–8, was cast in that form because a treaty settling the immigration question would have taken too long to complete. The Root-Takahira Agreement of November 30, 1908, and the Lansing-Ishii Agreement of November 2, 1917, were not altogether successful attempts to dispel mutual suspicion between two former friends, to reaffirm their general attitude toward China, and to define their specific interests in the Pacific and East Asia. Root voluntarily submitted his accord to the Senate for its information and was even willing to ask for a vote, but Lansing had to conceal in a secret protocol, not printed until 1938, some of the curbs which Japan then recognized on its freedom of action. Lastly, there were executive agreements which may be considered a logical extension of the president's power as commander-in-chief. The Pre-Armistice Agreement of November 5, 1918, laid down the broad conditions of a definitive peace, but like the one concluded by McKinley on August 12, 1898, it was not submitted to the Senate. Neither were the arrangements Wilson made at Paris on April 9, 1919, providing for a temporary Anglo-American truce on naval construction, and on May 8, 1919, disposing of Germany's merchant marine. There were no objections on Capitol Hill to any of these.

Joint control of the armed forces did not, from 1905 to 1921, paralyze the conduct of foreign policy or embroil president and Congress. In the one declared war of the period, the constitutional machinery operated as the framers had intended. Following a prolonged controversy with Germany, extending two months past the time when diplomatic relations had been broken, the executive asked the legislature to recognize that the status of a belligerent had been thrust upon the republic. The response was overwhelming, but in the postwar disillusionment both President and Congress were blamed for yielding too readily to interventionist sentiment. The people, it was then argued, were against entering the European struggle, and that belief led to proposals to amend the Constitution by requiring a popular referendum before Congress could declare war.

On numerous occasions the military was used without specific congressional authorization. These familiar police measures ranged from a brief show of strength against rioters to an extended demonstration of power against revolution. In the Caribbean, where such interventions occurred most often, the president might invoke treaty rights, as he did in Cuba and Haiti, or the Roosevelt Corollary, as he did in Nicaragua and the Dominican Republic. In Mexico, Wilson was reluctant to act without the prior consent of Congress. On April 20, 1914, after the Tampico incident, he asked a joint session for approval to employ the armed forces "in such ways and to such an extent" as might be necessary to make Huerta respect American rights. The House responded the same day with a much vaguer statement saying he would be justified in directing the army and navy to secure compliance with his demands. Before the Senate voted, Wilson ordered the customs house at Veracruz to be seized, so as to prevent a shipment of munitions from reaching Huerta. A more serious complication arose when Wilson ordered Brigadier General John J. Pershing to pursue Pancho Villa on Mexican soil. This Punitive Expedition crossed the border on March 15, 1916, two days before Congress passed a joint resolution endorsing such a move. Not until February 5, 1917, did the last of Pershing's troopers return to the United States.

Customarily the president deploys men and ships without consulting Congress. Roosevelt alone decided in June, 1907, to send the battleship fleet on a cruise to the Pacific and then bring it home by encircling the globe. When warned that the legislature might not vote appropriations for such a venture, he is alleged to have said that he had enough money to move the vessels to the West Coast, and it would then be up to Congress to insure their return. Wilson, on the other hand, leaned over backward on February 26, 1917, when he sought legislative sanction for placing gun crews on American merchantmen in the Atlantic. He freely admitted that he already possessed the authority to act, but he wished to associate Congress with himself in so important a step. When, however, a filibuster blocked his request, the President gave the necessary orders on March 12 to install the armed guards.

During the war, of course, the executive's commands were not questioned; but after hostilities had ceased, the legislature tried to reassert its authority over the army and the navy. It displayed that attitude in its pressure to bring the boys home, in its demand to pull out of North Russia and Siberia, in its opposition to a mandate over Armenia, and in its refusal to consent to the Versailles Treaty without reservations. The battle over Article 10 revealed that the lawmakers were determined not to surrender to the League of Nations or to the executive one iota of their control over the armed forces.

In the historic struggle between president and Congress for the direction of external affairs, the years from 1905 to 1921 were important for the restrictions imposed by the legislature. As in the past, the executive took the initiative, performed such planning as existed, and made most of the vital decisions. Only occasionally did the Senate or House formulate a specific policy, as the former tried to do on August 12, 1912, in adopting the Lodge Corollary to the Monroe Doctrine. The negative role of the legislature was evident in its veto of presidential proposals to enlarge the area of compulsory arbitration and in its refusal to permit a fuller participation in global politics. Men will long debate whether the abstention of the United States from the League of Nations was wise, but they cannot deny that in a critical hour of the world's history the Senate exerted, for better or for worse, a decisive influence upon the course of American foreign policy.

20

The Caribbean Lifeline

ONCE THE United States became a world power, it had to pay greater attention to threats to the peace of Asia and Europe; but the Caribbean remained until August, 1914, the area of primary interest. Most citizens believed that the nation's security hinged upon the proposed canal and stability in the lands close to it. The diplomats, ever fearful of European intrusion, reflected this concern for the Caribbean lifeline as they planned the future of the waterway, established protectorates in nearby countries, strove for hemispheric cordiality, and faced revolution and counterrevolution in Mexico.

THE CANAL AND AMERICAN SECURITY

The canal itself did not open until August 15, 1914. Although traffic would be repeatedly interrupted in the next three years, the construction was a magnificent feat and owed much to technical ingenuity, medical science, and individual heroism. Yet the building also revealed difficulties which would plague relations with Panama, whose main cities lay within the Canal Zone. With its special privileges, the United States could imperil the economic life of the new nation, and there were continuing controversies over sovereignty, customs receipts, and the war against tropical disease.

Construction of the canal also posed problems for the navy. The navy was responsible for defending the isthmus until 1911, when it handed the task to the army. It maintained a Caribbean Squadron of older vessels, suitable for coping with minor disturbances; but it did not develop any operating base in the West Indies, mostly because the best site at Guantanamo received only $89,000 in congressional appropriations before 1914. Exaggerated fears in Washington of a German menace led to the concentration of all battleships in the Atlantic beginning in 1906, and that deployment still prevailed when the First World War broke out. Until the canal was completed, there could be no thought of diverting part of the battle line to face Japan in East Asia. So strongly did Roosevelt feel on this point that he made it the subject of a "closing legacy" in his last letter as president. "Under no circumstances divide the battleship fleet between the Atlantic and Pacific Oceans prior to the finishing of the Panama Canal," he wrote Taft on March 3, 1909. "I should obey no direction of Congress and pay heed to no popular sentiment, no matter how strong, if it went wrong in such a vital matter as this."

As that completion drew near, the Taft administration stumbled into a controversy with Great Britain. A statute of August 24, 1912, provided that "no tolls shall be levied upon vessels engaged in the coastwise trade of the United States." While the bill was pending, Root and others warned that this exemption violated the Hay-Pauncefote Treaty, but Taft and Knox interpreted the promise in 1901, to treat all nations equally, to apply to all foreign nations. Congress agreed, and the measure passed the House by a voice vote and the Senate by a margin of 47 to 15. England withheld its protest until after the presidential election, in which the Democrats and Progressives advocated discriminating in favor of American shippers. The ensuing discussions were marred by the quibbling of Knox and the inconsistency of Taft who, as a champion of arbitration, refused to submit this dispute to that procedure even though it fell clearly within a category covered by an existing treaty.

Only after delay and difficulty did Wilson extricate the republic from its false position. As a candidate, he had endorsed the exemption, but reflection convinced him that the nation's honor required a repeal of the offending clause. Since the canal was not yet open, he waited until he had enacted part of his domestic program before broaching the subject to the Foreign Relations Committee on January 26, 1914. He rested his case on duty and the need for British aid in dealing with Mexico. On March 5 he asked Congress for an unconditional repeal, hinting that such a step was necessary to avert a larger crisis. With help from Root and Lodge in the Senate, the President prevailed. The House yielded by a count of 247 to 162 on March 31, and the Senate followed suit on June 11, 1914, by a tally of 50 to 35.

Of lesser importance was a second canal. The choice of Panama in 1903 did not end American interest in Nicaragua. That route offered a useful supplement, and it might tempt ambitious European powers. In a treaty signed at Managua on February 8, 1913, the United States secured, in return for $3 million, an exclusive option on the Nicaraguan route, a ninety-nine year lease of Great Corn and Little Corn Islands in the Caribbean, and the right to establish a naval base on the Gulf of Fonseca, a strategic site on the Pacific touching Nicaragua, Honduras, and El Salvador. The Senate never voted on this convention, which it received less than a week before Taft left office; but Bryan signed another, containing almost identical terms, on August 5, 1914. The Senate did not give its consent—and when it did, only subject to a reservation—until February 18, 1916.

THE PROTECTORATE POLICY

By the time Wilson became president, the protectorate policy was an integral part of American diplomacy in the Caribbean. Designed originally for Cuba, which the United States had barred itself from annexing, it was resorted to with increasing frequency as the acquisition of colonies lost popular appeal. Even the anti-imperialistic Bryan felt obliged to adopt it. Protectorates might differ in their legal basis and outward trappings, but the essential ingredients were a diminution of sovereignty for the nation protected and the assumption of special privileges and responsibilities by the United States. To justify such action, Roosevelt added his corollary to the Monroe Doctrine on December 6, 1904.

Cuba was the first protectorate. Under a treaty of May 22, 1903, the United States had the right to intervene for the preservation of independence and a government adequate to maintain order. Such a government ceased to exist on September 28, 1906. Faced with a two-month-old rebellion and a reluctance in Washington to help him, President Tomas Estrada Palma suddenly resigned, and the inability of the Cuban congress to agree on a successor plunged the island into chaos. Much against his wishes, Roosevelt hustled Taft to Havana to avert catastrophe and then accepted the Secretary of War's advice to assume temporary control. Actually, the provisional regime thus installed lasted until January 28, 1909, and its accomplishments were many. It not only restored order but also instituted reforms in administration, finance, and sanitation. Most important of all, however, was the fact that the United States did not convert a protectorate into a colony. As in 1902, many observers predicted Cuba would never recover the right to rule itself.

Once more before 1914 did American troops land in Cuba. An uprising in May, 1912, challenged the regime of José M. Gomez and so endangered foreign property that Taft sent eight battleships and 2,000 marines to the island. Most of the latter were kept at Guantanamo, but between June 10 and 19 small detachments went ashore at El Cuero and Nipe Bay. The rebellion collapsed a few days later, when the insurgent chieftain died, and by August this interposition ended without the United States' having had to take over the government. Wilson and Bryan also managed to escape that step prior to the outbreak of the First World War.

Panama was the second protectorate. The sovereignty of that nation was diminished by the inclusion within its territory of the Canal Zone, by the obligation in the treaty of November 18, 1903, to sell or lease sites suitable for naval stations, and by the right of the United States to maintain order in cities when the Panamanians were incapable of doing so. The American government also guaranteed the independence of the country. Down to 1914 the United States did not exercise its option on naval sites, nor did it occupy Panamanian soil. It abstained, too, from meddling in local affairs. Secretary Root avoided involvement in isthmian politics and twice refused to permit American citizens to assist in Panama's elections, lest they seem to disparage its sovereignty. Knox was less cautious and, at the urging of the two major parties, agreed in June, 1912, to supervise the forthcoming presidential contest. The result was not altogether happy. During the canvass one candidate withdrew, complaining of unfair treatment by the American officials.

The Dominican Republic became the third protectorate by placing its customs houses under an American receiver general. For almost two years the position of the United States rested on the modus vivendi of April 1, 1905, by which 55 per cent of the revenues went to foreign creditors and the rest to governmental expenses. Under this arrangement the Dominican treasury fared better than when it had been entitled to the entire receipts, and by July 31, 1907, its cash assets had risen from zero to $3 million. In that same period Root regularized the procedure by casting it into treaty form. His accord of February 8, 1907, gave the United States no right to intervene and no option on strategic sites, but it did continue the successful receivership and placed some restrictions on the authority of insular officials to increase the public debt and to modify import duties without American consent. Financial solvency was paralleled by political stability until the assassination of President Ramon Cáceras ushered in a new era of chronic wrongdoing and impotence. In September, 1912, Taft dispatched a peacemaking commission and 750 marines, but the resignation of the provisional executive on March 31, 1913, upset the temporary settlement and dumped the Dominican dilemma into the laps of the incoming Democrats.

Initially, Wilson and Bryan tried to substitute friendly advice for imposed solutions. More particularly, they sought to persuade the Dominicans that the proper road to office was by the ballot box, not by armed force. They warned the contending factions on October 2, 1913, that "revolution would never again bring a government into power," but that appeal to constitutionalism went unheeded. As civil war began, Wilson sent another commission in August, 1914, with instructions to install a provisional executive and then supervise the election of his successor. Once this was done, the document said, the United States would "insist that revolutionary movements cease" and that all subsequent changes" be effected by the peaceful processes provided in the Dominican Constitution." Thanks to the marines, a truce was effected, but within two years the Democratic critics of the Roosevelt Corollary would be intervening on a scale that would put the Republicans to shame.

Nicaragua was the fourth protectorate to be created near the Caribbean lifeline before August, 1914. There the Taft administration's course is often regarded as the classic example of "dollar diplomacy" or the frank enlistment of finance to bolster foreign policy. Actually, Nicaragua differed from the other protectorates. It had long been independent, and its indebtedness, while substantial, had not aroused demands for foreign intervention. Rather, it was a revolution, long overdue, against the dictatorial José S. Zelaya, who had balked Roosevelt's peace efforts in the region and who had encouraged rumors of canal cessions to European countries, which gave Knox the opportunity in December, 1909, to hasten his downfall. The Secretary refused to recognize a hand-picked successor, and in the ensuing chaos troops were landed on May 19, 1910, to protect American life and property. Then, on June 6, 1911, the United States moved into the economic sphere. In the Knox-Castrillo convention, Nicaragua promised to refund its entire debt through a loan obtained from American bankers and secured by revenues from imports. The nation agreed to put the administration of its customs houses under an officer nominated by the bankers and approved by the President of the United States. Because it helped remove "conditions of turbulence and instability," Taft praised the document as a bulwark of peace and a complement to the Monroe Doctrine; but the Senate, suspicious of favors to the financial community, twice refused to bring it to a vote.

This rebuff did not deter the New York investment houses whose loan of $15 million depended upon approval of the Knox-Castrillo agreement. They advanced emergency funds, and on December 16, 1911, their designate assumed his duties as collector general of customs. Further confusion occurred on July 29, 1912, when a rebellion broke out against President Adolfo Díaz. Unable to insure the safety of foreign property, Díaz asked for help, and by September 19 some

2,400 sailors and marines had gone ashore. Their presence hastened the end of the uprising. By January, 1913, all American forces had withdrawn except a legation guard at Managua and a naval vessel at Corinto. Yet, for the second time, the United States had intervened decisively, in the name of protecting its citizens, to determine which faction should rule in Nicaragua.

Such was the situation when the Democratic critics of "dollar diplomacy" took office. Although Wilson and Bryan abhorred protectorates, they followed in the path of their predecessors and would eventually outdo them. In Nicaragua the main problem was the insolvency of the Díaz regime and the need of a foreign guarantee to float a loan. The canal route was the sole asset. Hence on June 11, 1913, Nicaragua proposed a new convention in which it would be prohibited from impairing by treaty its independence and territorial integrity and in which the United States would be permitted to intervene for the preservation of that independence and the maintenance of a government capable of keeping order. Twice Bryan tried to win prior senatorial consent, and twice the Foreign Relations Committee refused to extend the Platt Amendment to Nicaragua. As a result, on August 5, 1914, Bryan signed with Emilio Chamorro a treaty that omitted all mention of intervention, protection, and customs control. In exchange for $3 million, the United States received in perpetuity exclusive propriety rights to construct a canal by any route it wished. To help the American government protect the Panama Canal and other rights, Nicaragua also granted renewable ninety-nine-year leases on the two Corn Islands and on a site, to be selected, for a naval base on the Gulf of Fonseca.

Costa Rica, Honduras, and El Salvador promptly charged that their safety was endangered. Those protests, together with pressures from the war and objections by anti-imperialists, delayed senatorial action until February 18, 1916. Then, subject to a reservation that there was no intention to impair the rights of those three states, the upper house gave its consent by a vote of 55 to 19. Yet the protectorate thus established did not rest on the same broad treaty rights as pertained in Cuba and Panama. But the customs houses were supervised, as in the Dominican Republic, and a few marines remained. By successive loans, moreover, the New York bankers came to dominate the economic life of Nicaragua in a way not matched elsewhere in Central America.

THE QUEST FOR HEMISPHERIC CORDIALITY

Vital as the protectorate policy was to the security of the Caribbean lifeline, it aroused hostility elsewhere in the New World. Root may have been correct in 1934 when he remarked that "you cannot understand the Platt Amendment unless you know something about the character of Kaiser Wilhelm," but to people below the Rio Grande the United States seemed a more immediate peril. Hence, even as the protectorates were being established, a parallel move sought to banish fear of Yankee imperialism and to promote a feeling of hemispheric cordiality. It was pursued by every administration and assumed many forms, but the point of departure in each case was to appease Colombia for the wrong allegedly done during the Panama uprising in November, 1903.

Progress toward a settlement began in June, 1906, under Secretary Root. Earlier, Hay had rejected Colombia's suggestion that the Hague Court decide whether the United States had acted in accordance with its obligations under the treaty of 1846. Hay argued that the question of a nation's culpability was not a proper subject for arbitration. Root's goal was a tripartite arrangement which would also liquidate all outstanding differences between Colombia and Panama, but it took thirty-one months before he signed on January 9, 1909, three interlocking and interdependent treaties. By the first, the United States agreed to commence its annual payments to Panama in 1908 instead of in 1913, and the latter undertook to transfer the first ten of these annuities to Colombia as its share of the national debt incurred before secession. In the second, Colombia acknowledged Panama's independence and submitted a disputed frontier to arbitration. Under the third, the United States granted to Colombia free transit through the Canal Zone for troops and warships, while both countries promised to bring the treaty of 1846 up to date. Panama approved these pacts immediately, and the United States Senate gave its consent on February 24 and March 3, 1909, but in Colombia national pride combined with political alignments to overthrow the government and kill the treaties.

Without reparation and an apology, the Colombians would not be satisfied; and while Roosevelt lived, no Republican president could go that far. The Democrats were not so bound, and on the basis of instructions drafted by Wilson, a new treaty was signed at Bogotá on April 6, 1914. The preamble frankly indicated that the purpose was to repair the damage done in 1903. The United States expressed "sincere regret that anything should have occurred to interrupt or to mar the relations of cordial friendship that had so long subsisted between the two nations." Colombia received an indemnity, though it was not called one, of $25 million and certain privileges in the Canal Zone. In return, it promised to recognize the independence of Panama and, through the good offices of the United States, establish diplomatic contacts with that country.

As was anticipated, these clauses drew a pungent protest from Roosevelt. He at once branded them a reflection on the nation's honor and his own integrity, then demanded to be heard by the Foreign Relations Committee, and finally published a series of articles denouncing "the blackmail treaty." Actually, Wilson had wished simply to restore the moral prestige of the United States in the New World; but idealism could not be kept separate from politics, and the Treaty of Bogotá encountered rough sledding in the Senate. Although submitted to that body on June 16, 1914, it was not reported until February 2, 1916, and then with an amendment which made the expression of regret mutual and reduced the payment to $15 million. To Roosevelt's friends, this version was no more palatable than the original, and further delay followed. In February, 1917, after the break with Berlin, Wilson tried vainly to persuade the Senate that prompt approval was needed to counteract German influence at Bogotá, but on March 23 Lansing told him the pact could never pass. The war soon pushed the matter into the background, and it was not until April 20, 1921, under changed conditions, that the Senate approved a very different treaty.

In the quest for hemispheric cordiality, assurances that the United States did not seek more land in the New World ranked second only to assuaging Colombia's grievance. Every president and every secretary of state gave such pledges. After preaching his annual sermon on December 5, 1905, about the duty of his Latin neighbors to maintain order and pay their debts, Roosevelt added that "under no circumstances will the United States use the Monroe Doctrine as a cloak for territorial aggression." Under him, between July and September, 1906, Secretary Root made an unprecedented goodwill tour of seven South American countries. Taft repeated the disavowal, and under him Secretary Knox paid official visits to ten Caribbean countries from February to April, 1912. But it remained for the Democrats to issue the loftiest statements. "One of the chief objects of my administration," Wilson declared on March 11, 1913, "will be to cultivate the friendship and deserve the confidence of our sister republics." At Mobile on October 27, 1913, he promised: "The United States will never again seek one additional foot of territory by conquest."

How sincerely were these words translated into deeds? For one thing, the United States did not enlarge its limits at the expense of its New World neighbors. For another, it participated actively in periodic meetings. The First International Conference of American States had been held in Washington from October 2, 1889, to April 19, 1890. A second had sat at Mexico City between October 22, 1901, and January 31, 1902. Its accomplishments were four: a reorganization of the Bureau of the American Republics, set up in 1890; a protocol enabling those governments which had not been present at The Hague in 1899 to adhere to the conventions adopted there; a treaty requiring, under certain conditions, the arbitration of all claims for pecuniary losses which could not be adjusted through ordinary diplomatic channels; and a resolution to meet again within five years.

The Third International Conference of American States assembled at Rio de Janeiro from July 23 to August 27, 1906. Besides extending the claims convention of 1902, the delegates adopted three main proposals. One recommended that each government instruct its representatives at the next Hague Conference to work for a general treaty of compulsory arbitration. A second invited that conference to examine the whole question of collecting public debts by force. A third established a commission of jurists to prepare a code of international law. Although the Senate consented with reasonable speed and a minimum of debate to these treaties, many of the Latins began to display a perverse habit of signing but not ratifying. For example, the claims convention of January 30, 1902, did not go into force until March 24, 1905, and then for only nine of the seventeen signatories; its renewal, adopted on August 13, 1906, was not proclaimed until January 28, 1913, by which time twelve of the nineteen parties had given final approval. Hence the Fourth International Conference at Buenos Aíres directed most of its efforts from July 12 to August 30, 1910, to consolidating and supplementing the labors of its predecessors. A fifth conference would have been held at Santiago, Chile, in November, 1914, if it had not been for the outbreak of the war.

Another means of demonstrating hemispheric unity was to include the Latin American nations in the activities at The Hague. Only Mexico and the United States had been present in 1899, but partly as a result of Root's efforts, twenty countries from below the Rio Grande were invited in 1907, and eighteen actually attended. Indeed, one reason for delaying the Second Hague Conference for a year was to avoid a conflict with the inter-American gathering at Rio de Janeiro in July, 1906.

Of all the ideas for promoting hemispheric cordiality, the most ambitious was the Wilson administration's for mutual cooperation and nonaggression among the republics of the New World. Beginning in 1910 a series of books and articles discussed the desirability of transforming the Monroe Doctrine, which had become identified with intervention and "dollar diplomacy," from a unilateral defense policy of the United States into a multilateral obligation of the entire hemisphere. In 1911 the House Committee on Foreign Affairs reported favorably a resolution endorsing an agreement among the New World states "for the mutual guarantee of their sovereignty and territorial integrity," but no action followed. The next year Colombia proposed an inter-American declaration proscribing the acquisition of territory by conquest. During 1914 Wilson and House developed a four-point Pan-American pact, guaranteeing the territorial integrity of the signatories, requiring the amicable settlement of all pending boundary disputes, making obligatory the use of arbitration or inquiry in certain types of controversies, and experimenting with an arms embargo; but the World War intervened before the pact took final shape.

More limited in scope but more concrete in results were the moves made by Roosevelt and Root to preserve peace in Central America. With Mexico's aid, a truce between El Salvador, Guatemala, and Honduras was mediated aboard the cruiser *Marblehead* on July 20, 1906. This was followed by the Treaty of San José of September 25, by which the three nations agreed to submit differences among themselves to the presidents of Mexico and the United States. The next year the meddling of Zelaya led to new hostilities, and again the northern neighbors cooperated to end the fighting. A Central American Peace Conference was held under their auspices in Washington from November 14 to December 20, 1907. Although the United States and Mexico did not sign, they supported the three agreements reached. The first created a Central American Court of Justice to which all disputes, not settled by ordinary diplomacy, could be referred. The second was a ten-year treaty of peace and amity. The third was a pledge not to recognize any government within the five republics that gained power by a *coup d'état* or by a revolution against the established regime. The last became the basis of the State Department's policy in Central America from 1907 to 1934. Much was expected of the Court of Justice, but it died prematurely in March, 1918, partly because the Wilson administration failed to heed the protests of Nicaragua's neighbors against the Bryan-Chamorro Treaty.

REVOLUTION AND COUNTERREVOLUTION IN MEXICO

Such success as was achieved in the quest for hemispheric cordiality after 1905 owed much to the collaboration of the United States and Mexico. Ever since Porfirio Díaz began his long rule in 1877, major controversies between the two nations had been conspicuously absent, and in the new century the atmosphere became exceptionally amicable. During this period American investments in mining, smelting, and oil lands increased enormously; by 1908 almost half of Mexico's wealth was owned by United States citizens and 80 per cent of the railroads were in Yankee hands. Unlike his Caribbean neighbors, Díaz was not guilty of chronic wrongdoing or impotence in his foreign relations; perhaps that is why the property-conscious Roosevelt, Root, Taft, and Knox were not appalled by his tyranny. Yet with the middle class

inducement he could offer and scoffed at every threat he dared make. The general broke off the discussions on August 26 with a blistering attack upon this intrusion into Mexico's internal affairs. The next day Wilson went before Congress to tell what he had done. Since he would not thrust his good offices upon an unwilling neighbor, he was prepared to pursue a course of watchful waiting after reimposing the arms embargo on both sides in the civil war.

For the moment tensions subsided. With the threat of American intervention removed, Huerta announced he would not succeed himself and called for elections on October 26, 1913. But neither he nor Wilson reckoned with Carranza, who derided talk of free voting and continued his drive southward. His rapid advance prompted Huerta, on the ground of disloyalty, to arrest 110 members of the legislature and then, on the ground of national emergency, to assume dictatorial powers. Stung by this reversal, Wilson abandoned his hands-off policy. He now felt it "his duty to force Huerta's retirement." Toward this end he contemplated a blockade of the major Mexican ports and a military line across the northern provinces, but, upon reflection, he held back for the moment.

Instead, Wilson tried to isolate Huerta diplomatically. He brought pressure on England to withdraw its recognition, saying it was important "to teach the South American Republics to elect good men." Belatedly he sought to cooperate with Carranza. At Nogales in November, 1913, Hale suggested ways in which the United States might aid the Constitutionalists, but Carranza asked only that American forces be kept out of Mexico and he be recognized as the legitimate ruler. None too pleased by this show of independence, Wilson did nothing; but when Carranza was halted in January, 1914, he tried to help by lifting the arms embargo.

To Wilson's consternation, raising the arms embargo on February 3, 1914, did not get rid of Huerta. On the contrary, this favor to Carranza caused the counterrevolutionists to resist more stubbornly. Fearing intervention to be inescapable, the President chose the pettiest of incidents to justify it. That was the mistaken arrest of eight American sailors on April 9, 1914, at Tampico, where the Huertistas were repelling a Constitutionalist siege. The affair could have ended with the profuse regrets accompanying the immediate release of the men if Rear Admiral Henry T. Mayo, the senior officer present, had not insisted upon a public apology. A contest of protocol and ultimatums ensued. Seeing a golden opportunity to deprive Huerta of key ports, Wilson backed Mayo to the hilt. On April 15 he told committees of the Senate and House that unless Huerta complied with his demands, he would—with prior congressional approval—occupy Tampico, seize

lacking in commercial opportunity, the mestizos deprived o
the workers brutalized by exploitation, and millions living in p
a social upheaval was only a matter of time. On May 25, 191
was finally overthrown.

Taft promptly recognized Francisco I. Madero, who too]
on November 6, 1911. When Madero's reforms led to new distur
the President obtained from Congress on March 14, 1912, as a
of discouraging revolution, authority to prohibit the export of
tions to any country of the New World. On March 25 Taft trans
the embargo into a discriminatory measure by permitting the
ment to buy arms in the American market and denying that p
to the rebels. But even this advantage did not halt the c
revolution headed by General Victoriano Huerta. Madero was c
on February 18, 1913, and shot four days later while allegedly t1
escape. With only a week of his term remaining, Taft left to
the problem of recognizing Huerta.

Wilson was shocked by the murder of Madero. His conc
moral principles and constitutional procedures quickly broug
into conflict with diplomatic realities and legal precedents. He b
that to recognize Huerta would encourage government by assass
throughout the hemisphere. He was not moved by argument
his ambassador in Mexico or the financial community in Ne1
that only Huerta could save the country from anarchy. He w
impressed by the prompt recognition accorded by England, Ge
France, and Japan. He was not convinced by citations of past
or the words of Counselor John Bassett Moore. "We regard §
ments as existing or not existing," Moore said. "We do not requir
to be chosen by popular vote." But in his zeal for upholding the
cratic process, Wilson exaggerated the average Mexican's fam
with the ballot and underestimated the far-reaching social eff
the revolution.

On March 13, 1913, Wilson announced that he would
recognition. He had a valid excuse, for Huerta was being chal
in the north by Venustiano Carranza, leader of the so-called
stitutionalists, and in the south by Emiliano Zapata, champion
radicals. In June, Wilson sent William Bayard Hale, a literai
laborator, to investigate; and while Hale's reports confirmed t]
favorable judgment of Huerta, they did not depict accurate
strength and aims of Carranza. Then, in August, 1913, the Pre
dispatched former governor John Lind of Minnesota as his pe
representative to propose a four-point settlement: immediate ces
of fighting, a free and early election, a pledge that Huerta wou
be a candidate, and a promise that all parties would abide l
result. Lind failed. Angered by nonrecognition, Huerta spurned

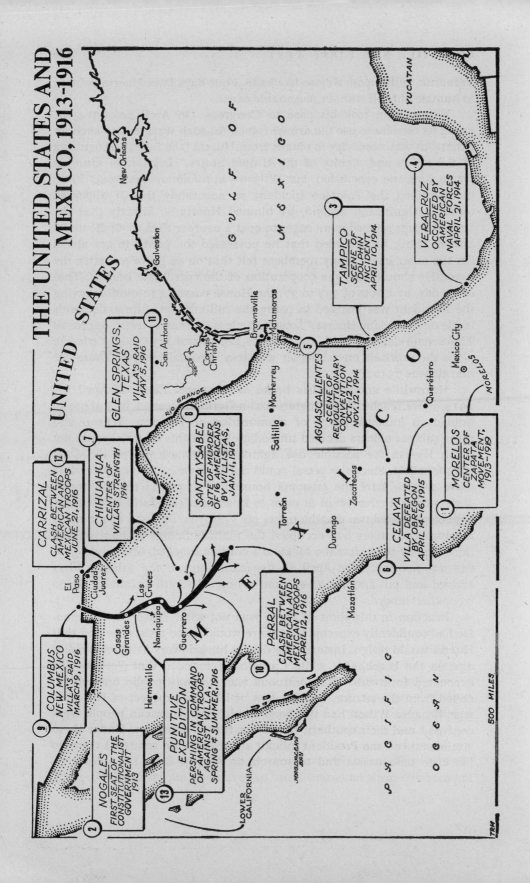

THE UNITED STATES AND
MEXICO, 1913-1916

UNITED STATES

12 CARRIZAL
CLASH BETWEEN
AMERICAN AND
MEXICAN TROOPS
JUNE 21, 1916

7 CHIHUAHUA
CENTER OF
VILLA'S STRENGTH
1916

11 GLEN SPRINGS,
TEXAS
VILLA'S RAID
MAY 5, 1916

8 SANTA YSABEL
SITE OF MURDER
OF 16 AMERICANS
BY VILLISTAS,
JAN. 11, 1916

9 COLUMBUS
NEW MEXICO
VILLA'S RAID
MARCH 9, 1916

2 NOGALES
FIRST SEAT OF
THE CONSTITUTIONALIST
GOVERNMENT
1913

13 PUNITIVE
EXPEDITION
PERSHING IN COMMAND
OF AMERICAN TROOPS
AGAINST VILLA,
SPRING & SUMMER, 1916

10 PARRAL
CLASH BETWEEN
AMERICAN AND
MEXICAN TROOPS
APRIL 12, 1916

6 CELAYA
VILLA DEFEATED
BY OBREGON
APRIL 14-16, 1915

1 MORELOS
CENTER OF
ZAPATA
MOVEMENT,
1913-1919

5 AGUASCALIENTES
SCENE OF
REVOLUTIONARY
CONVENTION
NOV. 12, 1914

3 TAMPICO
SCENE OF
DOLPHIN
INCIDENT
APRIL 10, 1914

4 VERACRUZ
OCCUPIED BY
AMERICAN
NAVAL FORCES
APRIL 21, 1914

GULF OF MEXICO

New Orleans

Galveston

Corpus Christi

Brownsville

Matamoros

Monterrey

Saltillo

Zacatecas

Torreón

Durango

Mazatlán

Hermosillo

El Paso

Ciudad Juarez

Las Cruces

San Antonio

Casas Grandes

Namiquipa

Guerrero

RIO GRANDE

M E X I C O

LOWER CALIFORNIA

Querétaro

Mexico City

MORELOS

YUCATAN

PACIFIC OCEAN

500 MILES

JOROLONGZAPA 1919

TRH

Veracruz, and impose a close blockade. Four days later Huerta refused to humble himself without reasonable cause.

Wilson then took his case to Congress. On April 20, 1914, he asked its consent to use the armed forces "in such ways and to such an extent" as was necessary to obtain from Huerta "the fullest recognition of the rights and dignity of the United States." Legislative sanction was a foregone conclusion, but Wilson's arguments were weak. First, he described the Tampico incident so accurately that it appeared totally insignificant. Second, he blamed Huerta so directly that the United States seemed more eager to oust a usurper than to vindicate its honor. Third, he conceded that he possessed the power to act alone. On the other hand, many members felt that on so grave a matter the executive should seek the cooperation of the coordinate branch. That same day, by a vote of 337 to 37, the House passed a resolution saying the President was justified in using the military "to enforce demands made on Victoriano Huerta," something less than an outright approval. The Senate delayed until April 22, as Lodge and Root vainly tried to place the reprisals on a broader and less personal ground. There the margin was 73 to 13.

Meanwhile another crisis broke at Veracruz. Early on April 21, 1914, news reached Washington that a German steamer was about to unload an immense cargo of ammunition at Veracruz. Wilson and three cabinet officers decided immediately that this matériel must not reach Huerta for possible use against the Americans or the Constitutionalists. Since the vessel could not be touched, the only feasible move was to seize the customs house and impound the shipment. Orders to that effect went at once to Rear Admiral Frank F. Fletcher, who commanded two dreadnoughts off Veracruz. By noon about 1,000 marines and sailors had occupied the main buildings without opposition. Shortly thereafter the Mexicans counterattacked, and naval gunfire was necessary. On April 22 five battleships of the Atlantic Fleet arrived and put another 3,000 men ashore. By April 30 almost 6,700 troops had landed.

Reaction to this show of force was not what Wilson anticipated. He had confidently expected that there would be no resistance and that Huerta would resign. Instead, the despot hurled every available soldier against the beachhead, while Carranza demanded that Veracruz be evacuated forthwith. More ominous was the way public opinion recoiled from the seizure, with its loss of life and prospect of full-scale war. Because Wilson had not been candid, the American people were confused and their southern neighbors feared the worst. Under these circumstances, the President quickly drew back. He scrapped plans to blockade both coasts and to march on Mexico City. He quietly reimposed the arms embargo. Most important of all, on April 25, 1914, he accepted the mediation of Argentina, Brazil, and Chile. Pressure from England, France, and Germany caused Huerta to do likewise, and on April 30 a sort of armistice went into effect. Delegates from the five nations conferred at Niagara Falls from May 20 to July 2. The final accord was vague and, because Carranza refused to be bound by it, meaningless. Huerta was to resign and the United States was to recognize a provisional successor. The furor over Tampico and Veracruz was ignored. In short, the mediation was significant because it enabled Wilson to escape gracefully from an untenable position, not because it provided any permanent settlement.

For Mexico's future would be determined on the battlefield, not at the peace table. In April, 1914, the Constitutionalists were poised for an assault on the capital, and Huerta's resistance was crumbling. He finally abdicated on July 15. During the next month a temporary president arranged successfully to surrender his office to Carranza, while Wilson strove vainly to win from that chieftain an assurance that there would be no wholesale executions and confiscations. Carranza's entry into Mexico City on August 20, a fortnight after the World War had begun, gave Wilson scant reason to rejoice. A tyrant had been removed, but the President had failed utterly to steer the revolution into democratic channels or to insure respect by the victors for foreign property and investments. He had intervened by force in the affairs of a neighbor, tarnishing thereby his ideal of friendship and equality in the hemisphere. He had not strengthened the Caribbean lifeline in any way, and by modifying the traditional policy of recognition, he had opened a veritable Pandora's box of troubles. Lastly, Huerta's downfall did not bring to a close Mexico's ordeal. It was only the end of the beginning.

CHAPTER

21

✻≫≫-≫≫-≫≫-≫≫≪≪-≪≪-≪≪-≪≪

A New Balance of Power

in Asia

SECOND ONLY to the Caribbean lifeline as the chief diplomatic concern of the United States from 1905 to 1914 was the Far East. Just as the security of the Panama Canal depended upon stability in nearby lands, so did the safety of the Philippines and Guam rest on a balance of power in Asia. But where the republic in those years realized increasingly its vital objectives in the region close at hand, it met with growing frustration in the one beyond the Pacific. In the Caribbean it was able to minimize the striking force of Europe and achieve both a military supremacy and an economic domination. In the Orient it was checkmated by a Russo-Japanese combination and failed to satisfy either its strategic requirements or its commercial ambitions. In one area the configuration of power was favorable; in the other it was not.

THE PEACE OF PORTSMOUTH AND AFTER

By the spring of 1905 Japan was eager to end a war in which it had gained every advantage. Beginning with the surprise attack on Port Arthur on February 8, 1904, the Japanese had won an unbroken string of victories on land and sea. By mid-March they had thrown 100,000 men into Korea; by May 1 they had crossed the Yalu into Manchuria. Dairen fell on May 30, as did Port Arthur on January 2, 1905. Driving north from that fortress, Japanese troops encircled Mukden on March 10, while the well-trained navy annihilated the Russian Baltic Squadron in Tsushima Strait on May 27–8, 1905. These impressive triumphs, however, virtually exhausted the nation's resources and obliged the civilian and military leaders to seek an early termination of hostilities.

Japan found in Roosevelt a willing peacemaker. Although the President had said in 1904 that the Japanese were "playing our game," he was concerned essentially with protecting American interests by preserving an equipoise in the Orient. While his main motive, as he wrote Eugene Hale on October 27, 1906, "was the disinterested one of putting an end to the bloodshed, I was also influenced by the desirability of preventing Japan from driving Russia completely out of East Asia." Roosevelt had a firm grasp of *Realpolitik,* but it did not negate a sincere wish to have the United States play well, rather than ill, its part as a world power.

It was the need for good offices, when neither side would make the first open bid for peace, that Roosevelt supplied. On May 31, 1905, the Japanese minister in Washington asked him, "of his own motion," to invite the belligerents to come together for direct negotiations. The President was amused by this suggestion and likened it to requests of officeholders during elections for a voluntary contribution. Nonetheless, he went ahead and skillfully gained Russia's consent, so that, when he formally extended his good offices on June 9, 1905, he knew in advance they would be accepted. The United States was not, of course, solely responsible for the outcome. Fearful lest a revolution sweep the Romanovs from their throne, the Kaiser exerted pressure in St. Petersburg, while bankers in London, Paris, and New York were reluctant to float the additional loans needed to carry on the war. Yet it was Roosevelt who, during the next two months, helped to arrange the details of the forthcoming conference at Portsmouth, tried vainly to secure an immediate armistice, welcomed the delegates at his summer residence, and then stood ready to aid as the negotiations got under way on August 10, 1905.

In the peace treaty of September 5, 1905, Russia acknowledged that Japan possessed in Korea paramount political, economic, and military interests, and it agreed not to obstruct any measures Japan deemed it necessary to take there. Subject to China's consent, Russia transferred to Japan the Kwantung leasehold, including Port Arthur and Dairen, and the branch of the Chinese Eastern Railroad below Changchun, soon renamed the South Manchuria. Both powers promised to evacuate within eighteen months all of Manchuria except the leased area and to restore it to China. They reserved, however, the right to station guards along the railways they controlled. Russia disavowed any desire for territorial arrangements or exclusive concessions which might impair China's sovereignty or contravene the principle of equality of opportunity. In lieu of a war indemnity, Russia ceded to Japan the southern half of Sakhalin.

The peace of Portsmouth had profound implications for Japan, Russia, China, and Korea, as well as for the United States. It made Japan the dominant power in the Orient, able to thwart American aims, and it should have satisfied all but extreme nationalists. Actually, the treaty disappointed the Japanese people, and they came to blame the United States for its alleged shortcomings. This indignation, with its tragic consequences, need not have arisen if in the spring of 1905 the cabinet of Taro Katsura had told the man in the street candidly how urgent it was to stop the fighting and how unreasonable it was to expect a huge indemnity from the enemy.

Russia's strength in East Asia declined after the war, but not to the point of being ignored. To be sure, it had suffered grievously in men and ships, had been deprived of its warm water ports, and had lost face in Oriental eyes. In Europe, moreover, a mutiny in the armed forces and numerous strikes culminated on December 22, 1905, in a bloody uprising, the precursor of the great revolution twelve years later. But Russia still held the Maritime Province and part of Sakhalin, dominated the economic life of northern Manchuria, and controlled the Chinese Eastern Railroad and its branch between Harbin and Changchun. Either alone or in concert with Japan, Russia could endanger the open door policy.

China seemed in a stronger position after the Treaty of Portsmouth, at least on paper. The belligerents had promised to evacuate Manchuria, except for the leasehold, and to return the administration to China. Both had spoken in favor of the open door, Japan's pledge being the price it paid for Roosevelt's good offices. In fact, however, China faced a bleak future. Japan had replaced Russia as the main threat to its independence and integrity. Japan had gained paramountcy in Korea and exclusive privileges in Manchuria. On December 22, 1905, Japan forced China to sign a treaty approving the transfers arranged at Portsmouth and allowing Japan to operate for fifteen years a military railway from Mukden to Antung on the Korean frontier. In a secret protocol the Peking government presumably promised not to build any lines parallel to or competing with the South Manchuria. The legality of this document has long been disputed, but it did reveal a determination in Tokyo to forge a railroad monopoly in the new sphere of influence. To check Japanese ambitions, China could not count on the United States, for Roosevelt was contemptuous of its weakness and alienated by a wave of anti-American boycotts that began in 1905.

For Korea, the Portsmouth settlement meant temporary extinction as a nation. The Japanese were determined to absorb the backward kingdom, and they faced no real opposition. They took the first step on February 23, 1904, by promising to guarantee the independence and territorial integrity of Korea in return for the right to intervene against "the aggression of a third power or internal disturbances." Roosevelt stood idly by, believing that Korea, like Nicaragua and the Dominican Republic, needed the guidance of a more virile people. "We can not possibly interfere for the Koreans against Japan," he told Hay on January 28, 1905. "They couldn't strike one blow in their own defense." Hence the President endorsed an "agreed memorandum" of a conversation in Tokyo on July 27, 1905, between Secretary of War Taft and Prime Minister Katsura, in which the former declared that "the establishment by Japanese troops of a suzerainty over Korea to the extent of requiring that Korea enter into no foreign treaties without the consent of Japan was the logical result of the present war and would directly contribute to permanent peace." Japan won a similar approval from England in renewing their alliance on August 12, 1905, and from Russia at Portsmouth on September 5, 1905. It kept up a pretense of freedom for five more years and then annexed the country on August 22, 1910. The United States did not protest. "It was better for the people of Korea," Root wrote to Lodge on February 26, 1916, "who were not governing themselves, to be incorporated in the liberal and progressive Empire of Japan than to remain puppets of their absurd, old opera bouffe emperor."

EAST ASIA AND AMERICAN SECURITY

This new balance of power in Asia affected the security of the United States. The problem was partly diplomatic, for a triumphant Japan was linked to England by an alliance and, after 1907, to Russia by a marriage of convenience. The value in the Far East of the Anglo-American *rapprochement* diminished as Great Britain forged tighter bonds with Tokyo and St. Petersburg.[1] The problem was partly economic, for the new Russo-Japanese bloc sought in Manchuria and

---

[1] On August 12, 1905, England and Japan broadened their alliance to promise mutual military aid in cases where either party was attacked by a single nation—not by two, as provided for in 1902. As Japanese-American relations worsened after 1905, experts in Washington and London feared the alliance might lead to an Anglo-American war. To lessen that possibility, the renewal of July 13, 1911, stipulated that its terms did not apply to countries with whom the signatories had a general treaty of arbitration. On July 30, 1907, Japan and Russia signed a secret treaty recognizing southern Manchuria and Inner Mongolia as a Japanese sphere of influence and northern Manchuria and Outer Mongolia as a Russian one. On August 31, 1907, Great Britain and Russia negotiated an entente in an attempt to settle all outstanding differences between them in the colonial world.

North China special privileges, not equality of commercial and investment opportunity. How to define and defend the open door was a
perplexing question for Roosevelt, Taft, and Wilson. Lastly, the problem was partly strategic, for the United States was in no position to
protect its outposts in the Western Pacific.

At the close of the Russo-Japanese War, American planners had
cause for alarm. The lessons of that conflict seemed to undermine
their fundamental policy in the Far East. They had assumed that, in
case of hostilities in that area, the Asiatic Squadron would fight a
delaying action and then take refuge in a protected anchorage to await
rescue by the main fleet. Now the Japanese had shown again their
ability to capture enemy strongholds on hostile shores. Their rout
of the Russians in Tsushima Strait had exposed the folly of depending
upon reinforcements from distant ports, especially when those units
lacked a safe base in which to replenish before battle. It was unmistakably clear that Japan could, whenever it wished, seize the
Philippines and Guam and that the obstacles to reconquest were almost
insuperable.

One reason for this gloomy prospect was a failure to develop in
those islands the advanced operating base that the expansionists of
1898 had envisaged. The army and navy continued to quarrel over
whether the facility should be placed at Manila or Subic Bay. Even
Roosevelt began to doubt the wisdom of retaining the islands he had
eagerly desired after the War with Spain. "The Philippines form our
heel of Achilles," he wrote Taft on August 21, 1907. To keep them
"without adequately fortifying them and without building up a navy
second only to that of Great Britain would be disastrous in the extreme." Irked by the vacillation of his advisers, he requested the
Joint Army-Navy Board on February 11, 1908, to turn its attention
from the Philippines and determine whether Pearl Harbor or Honolulu
should be improved by dredging, a dry dock, shore installations, and
local defenses. The outcome was a recommendation on November 8,
1909, that no major base be established in the Pacific west of Hawaii,
that the lion's share of the annual appropriations be spent on Pearl
Harbor, and that Subic Bay be restricted to a repair station without
military value in wartime. Three days later President Taft approved
that important decision.

Long before the navy abandoned plans for a major base in the
Western Pacific, it had stripped down its striking force in that area.
By July, 1906, it had transferred all battleships to the Atlantic to help
guard the Caribbean lifeline. It replaced them with four new armored
cruisers, larger in size and faster in speed, though slighter in firepower and armor belt. These vessels seemed well suited for long-
range scouting in the vast reaches of that ocean; but following the war

scare with Japan over immigration, they were withdrawn to the West Coast in August, 1907. During the next seven years no modern ships of any strength were permanently stationed in Asiatic waters.

TWO CRISES WITH JAPAN

Before the first crisis with Japan in October, 1906, the United States continued to look with favor on its former protégé. In early 1905 Roosevelt enthusiastically approved the proposed renewal of the Anglo-Japanese alliance. On July 29 he endorsed a memorandum of a conversation held in Tokyo two days earlier between Taft and Katsura. This exchange did not stem from the President's fear that a victorious Nippon might seize the Philippines, but from the Premier's wish to discuss three points. First, Katsura assured Taft that any apprehension over the Philippines was unwarranted, for his nation did not "harbor any aggressive designs" on the archipelago. Second, Katsura believed that the best means of preserving peace in East Asia would be "to form a good understanding between the three governments of Japan, the United States and Great Britain"; to which Taft replied that "without any agreement at all the people of the United States were so fully in accord with the policy of Japan and Great Britain in the maintenance of peace in the far East that whatever occasion arose appropriate action of the Government of the United States, in conjunction with Japan and Great Britain, for such a purpose could be counted on by them quite as confidently as if the United States were under treaty obligations." Third, Taft accepted the Japanese protectorate over Korea as the logical result of the war then ending. This routine memorandum was neither an unofficial alliance nor a secret bargain, as some have called it; rather, it indicated the mutual goodwill still existing in July, 1905.

Almost immediately a reaction set in. The outcry in Tokyo against the peace treaty disturbed the President. On February 23, 1906, the State Department issued its first complaint about discrimination against American trade in occupied Manchuria and the Kwantung leasehold. Meanwhile Roosevelt watched uneasily the growth of anti-Japanese feeling on the Pacific coast until it culminated on October 11, 1906, in a decree by the San Francisco School Board that henceforth all Japanese children must attend segregated institutions.[2] This order produced angry denunciations in Japan, where extremists demanded

[2] Racist sentiment, manifested against the Chinese in the 1860's, did not turn upon the Japanese until the 1890's, when the number of immigrants multiplied twelvefold. In a vain effort to halt protests, Japan promised in August, 1900, to withhold passports from all laborers going to the mainland, but Hawaii was not included in the ban.

reprisals. Although Roosevelt did not yield to the war hysteria, he understood how sensitive the proud, bellicose Japanese could be and how difficult the complex federal system made the conduct of diplomacy. It was imperative to have a definite policy toward Japan, he told Senator Hale on October 27, 1906, "a policy of behaving with absolute good faith, courtesy and justice to her on the one hand, and on the other, of keeping our navy in such shape as to make it a risky thing for Japan to go into war with us." That same day he asked the acting secretary of the navy for a comparison of the two fleets and a report on the plan of operations envisaged by the General Board in event of a conflict. As he left Washington to inspect the work at Panama, he directed Root in his absence "to use the armed forces . . . to protect the Japanese in any portion of this country if they are menaced by mobs."

For the next two years Roosevelt spoke softly and carried a big stick. Eager to remove grievances, he would not bow to Japanese bluster. Since the government of Prince Kinmochi Saionji remained conciliatory, the President's main task was to persuade the San Francisco authorities to rescind the segregation order. In February, 1907, he brought the mayor and members of the school board to Washington, where he pointed out the dangers arising from their action and gave assurances that, in return for its repeal, the federal government would check the influx of immigrants. On March 13, 1907, the obnoxious decree was revoked.

The negotiations with Japan took longer. They were conducted by Root and led to a new promise that the government in Tokyo would deny passports to laborers bound for the continental United States. It also waived objections to American restrictions upon coolies entering from Hawaii, Mexico, or Canada. This so-called Gentlemen's Agreement was a series of notes exchanged between February, 1907, and February, 1908. It represented an indirect approach, for Root knew that an outright exclusion law would needlessly offend and that a formal treaty could not be passed in time to liquidate the current controversy. The solution, of course, was not ideal. Japan retained too much control, and Congress resented the denigration of its authority. The Senate later made certain that no dispute over immigration would ever be submitted for settlement to arbitration or a league of nations. Yet the Gentlemen's Agreement did achieve its main purpose without sacrificing Japanese goodwill.

Despite these negotiations, the tensions created in October, 1906, did not subside quickly. Although both governments proceeded with caution and cordiality, there was violence and talk of war in both lands. Roosevelt insisted throughout that military power be coordinated with foreign policy, and eventually he took steps to exemplify his maxim about speaking softly and carrying a big stick. In December, 1907, he started sixteen battleships on an extended practice cruise from the Atlantic to the Pacific. He was confident that Prime Minister Saionji would not be offended, and he was correct. When it was revealed on March 13, 1908, that the fleet, then at Magdalena Bay in Lower California, would return home by way of Australia, the Philippines, and the Suez Canal, the Japanese ambassador hastily requested that his country be included in the itinerary. The result was a triumphant goodwill tour of the Far East that ended on February 22, 1909, shortly before Roosevelt left the White House. With pardonable pride and characteristic exaggeration he wrote in 1913: "In my own judgment the most important service that I rendered to peace was the voyage of the battle fleet around the world."

Less spectacular but equally useful were Root's moves to reduce Japanese-American hostility. After completing the Gentlemen's Agreement in February, 1908, he negotiated on May 5 a treaty requiring the arbitration of certain classes of disputes. Although this pact did not cover major controversies, it had some symbolic value. More important was a joint declaration of policy for China and the Pacific. By an exchange of notes with Ambassador Kogoro Takahira on November 30, 1908, the two governments affirmed their desire "to encourage the free and peaceful development of their commerce on the Pacific Ocean." They disavowed "any aggressive tendencies" in that area and "resolved reciprocally to respect the territorial possessions belonging to each other in said region." By "all peaceful means" they would support "the independence and integrity of China and the principle of equal opportunity for commerce and industry of all nations in that Empire." Thus they pledged themselves to nonaggression with respect to their Pacific holdings and to a reaffirmation of the open door concept as defined by Hay on July 3, 1900. They also promised that if the *status quo* or equality of economic opportunity were menaced, they would "communicate with each other in order to arrive at an understanding as to what measures they may consider it useful to take."

This executive agreement has been criticized as a meaningless gesture, as a blow to China, as a surrender to Japan, and as an evasion of the treaty-making process. The vagueness of the language, the pledge to respect rather than to guarantee, and the absence of any enforcement machinery caused some to regard the document as a pious hope. Others considered the failure to specify Manchuria in the clauses relating to China as a tacit admission that equality of commercial opportunity no longer prevailed in those provinces. Still others read into the notes a deal whereby the United States granted Japan a free hand in Manchuria in return for additional assurances that the Philippines would not be attacked. Actually, Root had no desire to appease, bargain,

or evade. The broad terms in which he couched his ideas were intended
to conciliate, not conceal, and he was ready to ask the Senate for its
consent. Root did not fear for the safety of the colonial outposts, nor
were they in danger. What he wished was to leave office with some
token of restored cordiality. He was too realistic to think that mere
words would halt a Japan bent on conquest, but he trusted the regime
then in power. Hence he saw no harm and some good in a mutual
subscription to general principles.

During the Taft administration there was less talk of war and
less trouble over immigration. To be sure, on August 2, 1912, the
Senate adopted a Lodge resolution aimed at rumors that Japan was
interested in Magdalena Bay. It attempted to stretch the Monroe Doctrine to cover "any harbor or other place in the American continents"
so situated that occupation by a foreign government for "naval and
military purposes might threaten the communications or safety of the
United States"; but since neither the House nor the President concurred, the Lodge Corollary remained simply an expression of opinion
by the Senate. Indeed, the major difficulties from 1909 to 1913 were
economic, as Taft and Knox tried to assist business enterprise in Asia
and to bolster foreign policy there with the support of the financial
community.

"Dollar diplomacy" in the Far East centered upon the railroads in
Manchuria. As early as July 15, 1909, Taft had made an unprecedented
personal appeal for the admission of American bankers to a pool which
the British, French, and Germans had formed to build a railway in
central and southern China. In no wise discouraged by the cool reception abroad and the obvious apathy at home greeting that move,
Knox on November 6, 1909, forwarded to London a startling suggestion. He proposed to challenge the economic supremacy of Japan and
Russia in Manchuria by enabling the Peking government to buy the
Chinese Eastern and the South Manchuria lines. While China was re-
paying the loan it would need to make the purchase, the powers
lending the money would administer the railroads. The plan required
the cooperation of China, Russia, and Japan. Knox professed to believe
that the last two, "desiring in good faith to protect the policy of the
open door and equal opportunity in Manchuria and wishing to assure
to China unimpaired sovereignty," would welcome this chance to shift
their responsibilities to a disinterested group of nations. If, however,
this attempt to neutralize the commerce of Manchuria was unacceptable, the United States was prepared to join with England in sponsoring
a new line running north from Chinchow, near the head of the Gulf of
Liaotung, to Aigun on the Amur River.

It is hard to imagine a scheme more calculated to antagonize
Japan and Russia, to embarrass Great Britain, or to expose the weak-

ness of China. The first two were not interested in maintaining the open door in Manchuria or the unimpaired sovereignty of the Peking government. On July 30, 1907, they had signed two treaties. The published one endorsed generally Hay's principles; the secret one agreed that southern Manchuria and Inner Mongolia should be a Japanese sphere of influence and northern Manchuria and Outer Mongolia a Russian sphere. For Japan the South Manchuria Railroad and for Russia the Chinese Eastern line were the key to their economic and military position in the northeastern provinces. They did not welcome a chance to get rid of these responsibilities, and they regarded the Chinchow-Aigun project as a threat to their paramountcy. Knox could never obtain their cooperation, nor was he likely to get that of France and England. The former was an ally of Russia and in a treaty of June 10, 1907, had recognized Japan's special interests in Manchuria and Mongolia. The latter was an ally of Japan and in an accord of August 31, 1907, had settled with Russia many long-standing differences. Under these circumstances the Knox plan did more than fail; it drove Russia and Japan closer together. On July 4, 1910, they concluded another pair of treaties. The printed one, in contrast to the public assurances of July 30, 1907, was silent on the integrity of China and on equality of opportunity. The unpublished one reaffimed the line of 1907 separating their spheres of influence, allowed each party to safeguard his interests therein by appropriate measures, and promised to pursue a common course against a third nation threatening those interests. Thus did a new balance of power in Asia affect adversely American objectives there.

Under Wilson, the immigration issue touched off a second crisis with Japan. Diplomacy became entangled again in federal-state relations, and California was again the troublemaker. Although the Gentlemen's Agreement had checked the flow of newcomers and although Japanese residents held only 17,000 acres, on May 3, 1913, the legislature passed a bill restricting land ownership to aliens eligible for citizenship. The law was intended to prevent the Japanese, as Governor Hiram W. Johnson put it, "from driving the root of their civilization into California soil." Frankly discriminatory, it drew a strong protest from Ambassador Sutemi Chinda.

Wilson and Bryan were not ideally fitted to deal with the controversy. Both took a very narrow view of the federal government's authority; both shared to some degree the prejudices of the West Coast citizens; both conceded the right of a state to legislate as it wished on land tenure; both expected the Californians to be influenced by personal appeals and the Japanese to be assuaged by friendly professions. The President ignored the Supreme Court's ruling that the nation's treaty-making power overrode the state's police power, and he shrank from using the armed forces to protect foreigners from mobs. Then, too, the crisis broke while the new administration was absorbed in pushing through its domestic program.

Within those limits, the President and the Secretary made a sincere attempt to avoid a rupture. First, Wilson tried to convince friendly California congressmen that the same ends could be achieved without patent discrimination. Next, he appealed through Bryan to Governor Johnson, reminding him of the repercussions local laws might have on foreign relations. Finally, he sent Bryan to Sacramento to plead with the state legislature. When all these steps failed, the two men turned to mollifying Japan and discouraging war talk at home. On May 13, 1913, Wilson and his cabinet discussed Chinda's protest, while the next day the Joint Board urgently recommended the transfer of three gunboats from river-patrol duty in China to harbor-defense work at Manila. On May 14 the Aid for Operations told Secretary Josephus Daniels that Japan might strike without warning and that, in his opinion, "war is not only possible, but even probable." Wilson rejected the Joint Board's advice; and when its members asked him to reconsider, he said that another such presumptuous request would lead to the abolition of the organization.

Bryan's dealings with Chinda were not too successful. On May 18, 1913, he had to admit he could not give any assurance of remedial action by the United States. When asked if that reply was final, the Secretary responded: "There is nothing final among friends." Goodwill, however, was not enough. The cabinet of Gombei Yamamoto rightly called the California statute discriminatory and "disregardful of the national susceptibilities of the Japanese people." Disappointed by the inability of the federal government to give satisfaction, Japan proposed in August, 1913, to negotiate a new treaty, one which would accept the present law, confirm land titles acquired before its enactment, and require future laws to apply equally to all aliens. Again Bryan had to tell Chinda that the President could not impose his will on a state and that the Senate would not approve such a treaty. The issue was still unresolved when a more aggressive cabinet replaced Yamamoto's on April 16, 1914.

THE PROBLEM OF CHINA

The whirligig of time, with its new perspectives and benefit of hindsight, can easily mislead the present-minded. In a century which has seen the rise and fall of the Japanese Empire, the eclipse and revival of Russia as a Far Eastern power, and the transformation of an enfeebled China into a communist monolith, it is tempting to indulge in might-have-beens and to accuse the diplomats of betting on the wrong horse. Yet no amount of second-guessing can obscure the fact that between 1905 and 1914 Japan replaced Russia as the chief threat to American interests in Asia, that Russia preferred a marriage of convenience with Japan to closer ties with the United States, and that China commanded less respect among the policy makers than any nation in the Orient.

It is true that dreams of a vast Chinese market had not faded from the minds of American businessmen. It is true that missionaries had made many Americans kindly disposed toward the Chinese in Asia. It is also true that the territorial integrity of the country and equality of economic opportunity within its borders had become bywords in the State Department, though Hay, Root, Knox, and Bryan each interpreted their meaning differently. Yet to Roosevelt's generation, the Chinese government seemed guilty of the same chronic wrongdoing and impotence which led the United States to play a policeman's role in the Caribbean and to acquiesce in the extinction of a sovereign nation in Korea. As Roosevelt wrote Taft on December 22, 1910, an "alliance with China, in view of China's absolute military helplessness, means of course not an additional strength to us, but an additional obligation which we assume." Hence it is ironical that the first sign of an awakening nationalism in China came during his presidency and was anti-American in nature.

During this period the open door continued to characterize the policy of the United States toward China, but its definition often varied. Hay's original pronouncement of September 6, 1899, accepted foreign leaseholds as *faits accomplis* and asked only for equality of commercial opportunity within them. On July 3, 1900, Hay talked of preserving the territorial and administrative entity of the empire and of extending equal and impartial trade to all parts of the realm. Subsequent haggling with Russia caused him to retreat to the more limited concept, to acquiesce in the abridgment of China's sovereignty, and to settle for equal treatment of American business within Russian-occupied Manchuria. Initially, Root inflated the principles. On March 30, 1906, he intimated that equality of investment opportunities must be insisted upon; but by the time of the Takahira notes on November 30, 1908, he had shifted his emphasis to opposing any further encroachment on China's sovereignty. Root steered a middle course and refused to allow his subordinates to convert the open door into an anti-Japanese crusade.

Knox yielded to that temptation and enlarged the meaning to include equality of investments. His scheme for wresting the Manchurian railroads from Russian and Japanese control failed completely and led Roosevelt to make some prophetic remarks. "The 'open door' policy in China," he told President Taft on December 22, 1910, "was an excellent thing, and will I hope be a good thing in the future, so far as it can be maintained by general diplomatic agreement; but as has been proved by the whole history of Manchuria, alike under Russia and under Japan, the 'open door' policy, as a matter of fact, completely disappears as soon as a powerful nation determines to disregard it, and is willing to run the risk of war rather than forego its intention." Knox disagreed and argued that there was an "alternative between silently renouncing our historic policy in China whenever it may cross the interest of another power and being prepared to go to war in defense of that policy," but he was unable to discover that alternative in his attempt to loosen the grip of Japan and Russia on Manchuria's economy from 1909 to 1913.

Wilson and Bryan were inclined to define the open door as Hay had done on July 3, 1900. In the matter of equality of investment, they revealed a commendable unselfishness together with a profound distrust of both the major powers and their Republican predecessors. Without consulting the appropriate members of the State Department or informing the other participants, the President publicly withdrew his government's approval of a six-power consortium that would enable China to build railroads south and west of Hankow. "The conditions of the loan," he declared on March 18, 1913, "touch very nearly the administrative independence of China." It was, therefore, inconsistent with the American policy of maintaining "the open door—a door of friendship and mutual advantage . . . the only door we care to enter."

In recognizing the new Chinese Republic, Wilson also broke away from the cooperative course pursued by Taft. In October 1911, Sun Yat-sen's followers began a rebellion that led to the overthrow of the Manchu dynasty on February 12, 1912. In accordance with their policy on loans, Taft and Knox wanted the powers to act jointly in extending recognition. But the demands of Japan and the European nations for a prior confirmation of their special privileges frustrated Taft's wishes, and the matter was still pending when he left the White House. On March 28, 1913, Wilson told his cabinet that the United States could best help China by standing alone and forcing others to divulge their selfish designs. He did yield to Bryan's plea that one more attempt be made to secure action by all eighteen nations having treaty relations with China, but that failed. On May 2, 1913, the United States recognized the regime of President Yüan Shih-k'ai, accompanied by Brazil, Mexico, Peru, and Cuba.

Sincerity and disinterestedness was Wilson's solution for the problem of China before August 1914. He combined a high moral purpose with a suspicion of power politics that would reappear during the World War. But China needed something more than idealism and goodwill. There was a job of building and modernizing to do. In retrospect, it is clear that the United States, by keeping hands off, made it easier for Japan to improve its economic and administrative position on the mainland, especially after the other great nations became absorbed in the war in Europe.

22

Prewar Strivings for Peace

OF SOMEWHAT less urgency to American diplomats than the Caribbean lifeline and a new balance of power in Asia was the quest for world peace. The lower priority assigned to that goal in the years from 1905 to 1914 does not denote an indifference to the evils of war. The triumph of imperialism had convinced most Americans that they would have to cooperate more fully with other countries in reducing international tensions and establishing machinery for the pacific settlement of disputes. Their government responded to this sentiment and after 1905 paid greater attention to the problem than ever before. If in retrospect the achievements seem minimal, it is because the statesmen had to move within narrow limits imposed by traditional principles and practices. It would take the first test, the Great Crusade, to change the pattern.

LIMITING FACTORS

Any realistic appraisal of these prewar strivings for peace must begin with an analysis of those limits. The historic policies of isolationism, neutrality, and the Monroe Doctrine still influenced popular thinking, and it was widely assumed that war in Europe or Asia, however far-reaching its repercussions might be, need not directly involve the United States. Within that conceptual framework, an American contribution to global peace represented the freewill offering of an enlightened bystander, not the imperative sacrifice of an endangered nation. Once that fact is grasped, we can understand more easily why this generation was content to experiment with measures of restricted usefulness. We can appreciate better why it emphasized compulsory arbitration and periodic Hague Conferences rather than a network of defensive alliances or a system of collective security. We can then comprehend why, when the First World War enveloped Europe and much of the colonial world, almost all Americans were confident that they could remain aloof.

Before 1889 the United States had frequently used arbitration to settle a disputed boundary or determine the amount of a claim. It had occasionally accepted the friendly mediation of a third party, and by the 1890's sentiment had developed for treaties requiring the arbitration of a carefully defined list of controversies. Prejudice against agreements in which there were more than two parties had disappeared, and attendance at international conferences dealing with economic and social problems had become frequent. Yet those gatherings did not lead to binding diplomatic commitments or the forsaking of basic policies. At the First Hague Conference in 1899 the American delegates specifically disclaimed any intention to abandon isolationism or the Monroe Doctrine, and that formula was followed in all joint strivings for peace before 1914. In consenting to the Act of Algeciras, which liquidated a crisis in Morocco, the Senate on December 12, 1906, appended a reservation stating that the purpose of the convention was to increase American trade and protect American citizens, not to relinquish "the traditional American foreign policy which forbids participation . . . in the settlement of European questions which are entirely European in their scope." At the Second Hague Conference in 1907 the American representatives repeated verbatim the disclaimer of 1899, and the Senate incorporated those words into a formal reservation when it gave its approval on April 2, 1908.

In short, the American people were not prepared to renounce the time-honored precepts of foreign policy. Isolationism, neutrality, and the Monroe Doctrine were looked upon as being compatible with the status of a world power. Permanent alliances were regarded as beyond the realm of practical politics; membership in an international organization was not seriously considered. It was generally believed that abstention from a global conflict was both possible and desirable. In attempting to define more clearly the rights and duties of neutrals at The Hague in 1907 and at London in 1908, the discussion centered on old problems. No attention was paid to new weapons, such as the submarine, which might make past notions obsolete. Although some critics urged that the Monroe Doctrine be made the responsibility of all republics in the Western Hemisphere, that view was still a minority one. More typical was the Lodge Corollary of August 2, 1912, which would stretch the principles of 1823 to cover threats undreamed of a century before.

One other view circumscribed these prewar strivings for peace. It was an optimism that great wars, like those of the Napoleonic era, were a thing of the past. In spite of bitter rivalries and intermittent alarms, no similar holocaust had ravaged Europe for a century, and some observers concluded that modern warfare had grown too costly and destructive to wage. Not everyone subscribed to that opinion, but almost all predicted that future conflicts would be brief. It is not surprising, therefore, that men insulated by two oceans refused to believe that to enjoy peace they must take unprecedented steps to stamp out war.

THE CHIMERA OF ARBITRATION

These limiting factors made arbitration appear, in the decade before 1914, the most feasible way for the United States to promote peace for itself and for the world. The idea was widely endorsed in theory; the task was to discover a formula that would render it usable in practice. Although that quest showed arbitration to be a chimera, the accompanying debates went to the root of a government's willingness to settle major controversies by pacific means and thus persuaded a later generation to seek a more ambitious and comprehensive method.

The first attempt to find such a formula was the Olney-Pauncefote Treaty of January 11, 1897. This agreement was the product of a congressional resolution in 1890, of a favorable response by the House of Commons, of conversations begun by Secretary Gresham but interrupted by the Venezuela crisis, and of Lord Salisbury's desire to benefit from the expressions of friendship following that war scare. By its terms, three types of disputes, not adjusted by direct negotiation, had to be submitted to arbitration. First, pecuniary claims up to £100,000 would go to a board of three, consisting of one jurist of repute nominated by the United States, one by England, and one by the arbiters already chosen. Second, pecuniary claims exceeding that sum and all other disputes not involving territory would go to the same kind of board, but the decision had to be unanimous. Third, territorial disputes would go to a board comprised of three justices of the United States Supreme or Circuits Courts and three from the highest British tribunals. In those cases the award must be concurred in by five of the arbiters.

However logical it may have seemed to launch the experiment in compulsory arbitration with Great Britain, it was tactically unwise. In 1897 the currents of Anglophobia still ran deep. The alleged bullying of Venezuela was not forgotten. Silverites saw in England the chief bastion of the gold standard; canal men resented the refusal to abrogate the Clayton-Bulwer Treaty; politicians feared the Irish vote. Hence, delay, amendment, and eventual defeat became the fate of the Olney-Pauncefote agreement. Cleveland sent it to the Senate on January 11, 1897, but it was not reported until March 17. Although McKinley also gave it his blessing, the treaty was revised in several ways. First, no dispute had to be arbitrated which, in the judgment of either party, affected its honor, its territorial integrity, and its governmental policy or which involved the question of whether a treaty was still in force. Second, claims against individual American states were exempted, thus protecting those in the South which had repudiated their Civil War debts. Third, every *compromis,* or special agreement defining the exact issue to be arbitrated, must be approved by the Senate. Finally, every arbiter nominated by the United States under the treaty had to be confirmed by the upper house. Even those changes failed to satisfy two thirds of the senators present. The roll call on May 5, 1897, stood at 43 to 26, three votes short of the necessary majority.

Seven years passed before another attempt was made to negotiate compulsory arbitration treaties. Some encouraging events occurred in that period. In 1899 the First Hague Conference created a panel of available arbiters. It also proclaimed that arbitration was the most effective and equitable way of settling questions of a legal nature and those pertaining to the interpretation of treaties. In May, 1902, Roosevelt rescued the misnamed Hague Court from inactivity by referring to it a controversy with Mexico. The next year he provided more employment by persuading England, Germany, and Italy, then blockading Venezuela, to submit their grievances to the Hague Court. So loudly did the pacifists acclaim his deeds that he incautiously promised during the election to sponsor a series of bilateral pacts requiring arbitration in certain classes of disputes. That fictitious commentator, Mr. Dooley, was amused by this transformation of a war hero into an advocate of peace and told an incredulous friend that he was authorized "to deny th' infamous rayport that th' Prizidint was iver at San Joon Hill. At th' time iv this gloryous an' lamintable performance, th' good man was down with measles conthracted at th' Internaytional Peace Convintion."

Secretary Hay followed up Roosevelt's pledge by signing eleven bilateral treaties between November 1, 1904, and February 11, 1905. Five major powers—France, Germany, England, Austria-Hungary, and Japan—were included; only Russia held aloof. The new formula stipulated that differences of a legal nature and those relating to the interpretation of treaties would be referred to the Hague Court, if they did not "affect the vital interests, the independence, or the honor of the two contracting states" or concern "the interests of third parties." In each case the signatories would conclude a special agreement clearly defining the point at issue, the powers of the arbitrators, and the manner of proceeding. This second formula was less sweeping than the first in 1897, but again the Senate balked, this time insisting on a single amendment. On February 11, 1905, it adopted by a vote of 50 to 9 a recommendation by the Foreign Relations Committee to substitute the word "treaty" for "special agreement." By this change the Senate made sure that the *compromis* in every arbitration would be submitted to it. This amendment was inserted in the treaties with England and France; both were then consented to on February 11 without a roll call.

This one amendment, in Roosevelt's opinion, destroyed the value of the treaties. What sense did it make, he asked, for the United States to promise to arbitrate all disputes of a certain type if each time it tried to keep its word, the Senate might interpose a veto? Convinced that the amendment nullified his purpose, he warned that he would not exchange ratifications if it were added. When the Senate went ahead in spite of this threat, or perhaps because of it, the President refused to complete any of the conventions. Other factors, however, help explain this mutual intransigence. Hay had again bungled his attempt to win senatorial approval in advance, and the lawmakers were outraged by Roosevelt's simultaneous attempt to establish the Dominican receivership by an executive agreement. Although the President was thwarted in that bid momentarily, he had needlessly aroused fears in the upper house that its prerogatives in the treaty-making process were in jeopardy.

Early in 1908, while Roosevelt was still in the White House, Secretary Root made a third bid for compulsory arbitration treaties. He believed that avoidable mistakes and an unfortunate concatenation of events had foiled the previous attempt. The Senate's amendment, he felt, should have been foreseen. That body had insisted in 1897 upon approving the *compromis;* it would do so again. Root was willing to take half a loaf rather than none at all. Could he convince the President to do the same? Three years earlier Roosevelt had denounced the Senate's change as a fraud. Now, thanks to Root's persuasiveness, he reversed himself. Perhaps the readiness of the other nations, signified in advance, to accept the amendment helped; perhaps the award of the Nobel Peace Prize for his role in ending the Russo-Japanese War played a part.

Between February 10, 1908, and January 23, 1909, Root signed twenty-four bilateral treaties, all but three of which were eventually ratified. Every major power save Russia and Germany was included. The formula was almost identical to the amended version of 1905.

Differences of a legal nature and those relating to the interpretation of treaties, which could not be settled by diplomacy, would go to the Hague Court for a decision. Disputes affecting the vital interests, independence, or honor of the signatories and those involving third parties were again exempted. In each case the special agreement defining the scope and procedure of the arbitration had to be approved by a two-thirds vote of the Senate. To save face, the words "special agreement" were retained, but the requirement that the *compromis* be made by the President with the consent of the Senate gave the legislators the substance of what they had demanded in February, 1905. Designed to run for five years, the Root treaties were promptly and overwhelmingly approved.

Would the republic ever be willing to arbitrate differences involving vital interests? To answer that question, Taft and Knox in 1911 renewed the search for a usable formula and, in so doing, precipitated the most revealing debate of the prewar years. The President was determined to enlarge the categories of arbitrable disputes, and he believed public opinion was on his side. Certainly the peace societies were most articulate, but many pacifists were more interested in vague principles than in specific details. Such a person was Andrew Carnegie, the retired steel magnate, whose millions swelled the coffers of peace organizations. In February, 1908, Carnegie told Root that he did not care what was in an arbitration treaty; the main thing was to have one on the statute books.

On August 3, 1911, Secretary Knox concluded two new arbitration treaties with England and France. They were designed as models for many more. They omitted the familiar exclusion of disputes affecting vital interests, honor, or independence. Now "all differences" in which the signatories were concerned by a claim of right under a treaty or otherwise and which were "justiciable in their nature" must be submitted to the Hague Court or some other arbitral tribunal. Justiciable questions were those "susceptible of decision by the application of principles of law or equity." Doubts as to the justiciability of a dispute would be resolved by a joint commission of six members, which might also serve as a board of inquiry. Five of the six commissioners must concur before a controverted matter was ruled justiciable. As in 1908, the *compromis* had to be approved by the Senate.

These model pacts were never ratified. They reached the Senate at the end of a session, too late for action, while a last-minute change antagonized the very lawmakers Knox had consulted. Worse yet, they split the Republicans, already divided over domestic issues, into four groups. Taft wanted an unqualified approval; Roosevelt called for a complete rejection; Lodge favored substantial amendments; Root could be satisfied with explanatory reservations. Among the Democrats, some were eager to discredit the administration; others, mostly from the South, insisted that arbitration of repudiated state debts be ruled out. On August 15, 1911, Lodge reported the treaties from the Foreign Relations Committee with amendments, the most important of which transferred the authority to decide which disputes were justiciable from the joint commission to the Senate. In a minority report on August 21, Root recommended approval subject to an understanding that the treaties did not authorize the arbitration of questions concerning the Monroe Doctrine or other governmental policies. Meanwhile, the President had taken his case to the people in a series of speeches in Maryland, New Jersey, New York, Connecticut, and the Mississippi Valley, but a groundswell of popular support never materialized. With the election of 1912 just ahead, arbitration attracted less attention than the trusts, the tariff, and the banking sysetm.

In the next session Root's approach offered the best prospect of success. Thus, on January 11, 1912, Lodge presented from the committee a new formula, a reservation which let the joint commission stand but which stipulated that its verdict must be approved by the Senate. Even that compromise did not prevail. By a margin of 42 to 40 an amendment eliminated the main function of the commission. By a count of 46 to 36 the Senate added a reservation expressing its understanding that the agreements did not authorize the arbitration of such questions as the admission of aliens into the country, the acceptance of immigrants in public schools, the alleged indebtedness of individual states, the Monroe Doctrine, or any "purely governmental policy." With these changes, the treaties were consented to on March 7, 1912, by a vote of 76 to 3.

Like Roosevelt in 1905, Taft refused to ratify the amended treaties. He believed they were no better than the Root conventions, and he was correct. But it would be wrong to regard the episode as a blow to world peace or attribute the Senate's action solely to a concern for party advantage and legislative pride. Although politics, personalities, and prerogatives did enter in, there was a basic issue at stake. What were the feasible limits of the arbitral process? Could it be used in disputes of major importance? Roosevelt, Root, and Lodge did differ as to the best way to handle the Taft-Knox project, but they agreed that its terms committed the republic to a procedure it would not dare employ when vital interests were in jeopardy. All three argued that the cause of peace was not well served when governments made sweeping promises in a moment of calm which they would not fulfill in an hour of crisis.

A conviction that the Taft formula had gone beyond the proper scope of arbitration shaped the action of the Wilson administration. First, it was content to renew many of the Root treaties when they

expired in 1913 and 1914, although those with England and Japan
aroused some opposition. Next, Bryan sought to supplement the arbitral process by his so-called Treaties for the Advancement of Peace.
These embodied inquiry, a procedure which the United States had endorsed at the First Hague Conference in 1899. One of the conventions,
to which the Senate had then consented, had recommended that international commissions, drawn from a permanent panel of names, be
used "as far as circumstances permit," to investigate "differences of
opinion on points of fact." Differences involving vital interests and
national honor were specifically excluded, and the report did not bind
the signatories. The Bryan plan proposed to transform the *ad hoc* commission into a permanent body, ready for use when a crisis should
break; to enlarge its authority to cover all disputes, even those affecting
vital interests, territorial integrity, and national honor; to allow a
year for the investigation, during which time both parties would refrain from fighting; and to keep the purely advisory character of the
fact-finding report. The "cooling off" period was his peculiar contribution.

From August 7, 1913, to October 13, 1914, Bryan concluded
thirty bilateral Treaties for the Advancement of Peace. They were with
sixteen states in the New World, twelve in Europe, and two in Asia.
Those who did not sign, for obvious reasons, were Colombia, Japan,
and Mexico, while Germany held back lest it sacrifice its unmatched
power to strike instantaneously. The terms were much the same, except for the first few which prohibited any increase in armaments
while the investigation was being conducted. The treaties ran for five
years but would be renewed automatically unless a notice to abrogate
was given. The contracting parties agreed to refer all disputes not
settled by ordinary diplomacy to a permanent commission which would
have one year in which to investigate and report on the facts in the
case. In that period neither side could begin hostilities; but once the
report was in, the signatories recovered their freedom of action and
could do what they pleased.

Bryan needed all his political acumen to prevail. He explained
his plan carefully in advance to the Foreign Relations Committee, the
diplomatic corps, and the public. Before sending the first treaty to the
Senate on July 24, 1914, he let twenty others accumulate. In spite of
the gathering storm in Europe, or perhaps because of it, the moment
was propitious. The administration had won great prestige by enacting
most of its original domestic program and had not yet been rebuffed
on a major foreign issue. A potential critic, Lodge, was abroad, re-
cuperating from an operation. There was no long inquest and little
partisan debate. The main problem was a quorum. The first treaty to
be approved was by a vote of 44 to 5, with almost half the members

absent or abstaining. By October 22, 1914, twenty-eight had been consented to, ten with amendments, and two had been tabled. In all,
twenty were ratified.

The importance of Bryan's work can easily be exaggerated. It was
more impressive on paper than in practice. Only ten commissions
were organized; none ever investigated a dispute. A later generation
would experiment further, but inquiry, like arbitration, remained a
chimera in the prewar strivings for peace. The appeal of both methods
to men at the time provides ammunition for today's realists, who
scoff at an idealism that believed in the sanctity of treaty obligations
and the pledged word of nations. Without agreeing entirely with such
criticism, we must admit that from 1905 to 1914 the United States
resorted to arbitration in only two major controversies. On January 27,
1909, it agreed to arbitrate with England the Newfoundland fisheries
question and on June 24, 1910, it agreed to arbitrate with Mexico the
disputed Chamizal tract. On the other hand, it refused to settle in that
way the alleged wrongs suffered by Colombia in 1903, the interpretation of the Hay-Pauncefote Treaty in the quarrel over tolls in 1912, or
the many differences with Huerta in 1913–14. In short, the limits of
the arbitral process had been clearly revealed before the outbreak of
the First World War.

THE HAGUE CONFERENCE IDEA

A second goal in America's prewar strivings for peace also relied on
paper agreements rather than on military sanctions. The Hague Conference idea was rooted in the premise that war might be rendered less
likely through periodic gatherings to discuss the reduction of armaments, the creation of a permanent court, and the codification of international law. Implicit in the idea was a belief that nations, like individuals, could be made to respect the collective opinion of mankind.
There was no intention to establish a world federation or a suprana-
tional parliament. In contrast to the bilateral emphasis in compulsory
arbitration, the Hague Conferences represented a multilateral approach to peace.

Multilateral efforts were not entirely new in 1905. The United
States had participated in inter-American meetings in 1889 and 1902
as well as in the initial effort at The Hague in 1899. Despite the meager
achievements of the last, a sequel was quickly demanded. On September 24, 1904, Roosevelt publicly proposed one; but nothing could be
done until the end of the Russo-Japanese War, and then the President
permitted the Tsar to issue the formal call. Invitations went out on
April 3, 1906, but Root obtained a year's delay so as not to conflict

with the Third Inter-American Conference. Joseph H. Choate, former ambassador to England, headed a competent, though not outstanding, delegation.

Root's instructions of May 31, 1907, indicated the limits of the Hague Conference idea. He stressed the need for unanimity and warned that if states were forced to yield under pressure, they would not respect their pledges or attend future meetings. He reminded the delegates "to avoid entangling alliances and to refrain from any interference or participation in the political affairs of Europe." The reduction of armaments, he feared, was then an idle dream, nor did the United States wish to be fettered while its army was tiny and its navy weakened by the advent of the dreadnought. America's goals were an agreement to limit the use of force in collecting contract debts owed to the citizens of one country by the government of another, the extension of arbitration, the immunity of all private property at sea except contraband and that on ships running a blockade, revision of the rules of land warfare adopted in 1899, and a clearer definition of the rights and duties of neutrals.

The Second Hague Conference met on June 15, 1907. Forty-four nations attended—a gain of eighteen since 1899. It adjourned on October 18 after adopting thirteen conventions, one declaration, two resolutions, and five recommendations. Although eight of the conventions dealt with fighting at sea, none touched the key problems of contraband, blockades, and immunity of private property. The three conventions relating to hostilities on land did little to reduce the likelihood of war, while the one on armaments simply expressed concern. A twelfth revised slightly the convention of 1899 for the pacific settlement of international disputes. A final convention forbade recourse to armed force by one government for the recovery of contract debts owed to its citizens by another, but the prohibition was not absolute. The United States and the European nations did not think the ban should apply when the debtor refused to arbitrate or when, having agreed, it failed to abide by the award, and they wrote that exemption into the treaty. The American republics, for whom Root had designed the pact, wished to outlaw force under all circumstances, and they subsequently rejected the accord.

Arbitration was the subject on which the United States came closest to success. Although a multilateral treaty requiring the arbitration of certain types of disputes was lost for want of unanimity, the conference did adopt a resolution endorsing the principle and saying that differences over the interpretation and application of treaties should be submitted to that procedure. But Root wanted more than a general statement. He believed that one reason why arbitration was not widely used was the tendency of arbiters to base their decisions on diplomatic considerations instead of on judicial reasoning. What was needed was a truly permanent court of justice, not the panel of available names set up in 1899. There was strong support for such a tribunal in 1907, but Root's hopes were dashed when no acceptable method of selecting the judges could be worked out. Not until the League of Nations came into existence in 1920 was machinery avail-able to resolve that problem.

To many Americans the Second Hague Conference seemed to be much ado about nothing. They were unimpressed by the gains and disappointed by the failures. Mr. Dooley expressed a popular view when he complained that most of the time was spent discussing "how future wars shud be conducted in th' best inthrests iv peace." The Senate was more tolerant. It gave its consent to the one declaration and to ten of the eleven conventions submitted for approval. To three of the latter, however, it appended reservations reaffirming the principles of isolationism and the Monroe Doctrine and requiring that in all arbitra-tions held under those conventions, it must first pass on the *compromis*.

Minimal as were the results at The Hague in 1907, they did not deter dedicated men from further efforts. The leading maritime powers met in London on December 2, 1908, and produced a comprehensive statement on blockades and contraband; but this Declaration of London of February 26, 1909, which the Senate endorsed on April 24, 1912, was lost in the House of Lords. Plans for a third Hague Confer-ence in 1915 were thwarted by the Great War. A small but articulate group led by Hamilton Holt, editor of *The Independent*, advocated world federation and developed a scheme for a legislature to enact in-ternational statutes, a court to adjudicate disputes, and an executive to enforce the laws passed and the decisions rendered. There were other blueprints for peace. Carnegie, speaking in October, 1905, envisaged a five-nation league, which would act through economic sanctions and not through military might. Roosevelt, in accepting the Nobel Prize in May 1910, declared: "It would be a master stroke if those great powers honestly bent on peace would form a League of Peace, not only to keep peace among themselves, but to prevent, by force if necessary, its be-ing broken by others." On June 25, 1910, Congress empowered Taft to appoint a commission to explore means of reducing armaments and of combining the navies of the world into an "international force for the preservation of peace," but nothing came of the resolution. Roose-velt refused to serve as chairman; Root feared it might upset the nor-mal channels of diplomacy; soundings abroad drew discouraging re-plies. Yet with all its shortcomings, the Hague Conference idea shaped one school of thinking during the world settlement of 1919–20.

MILESTONES TO ARMAGEDDON

One other approach was available to American diplomats in their pre-war strivings for peace. In any crisis they could extend their good offices which, if accepted, might lead to mediation. They could act alone, as Roosevelt did in June, 1905, in his moves to end the Russo-Japanese War, or they could collaborate with other nations, as was done with Mexico in checking trouble in Central America in 1906 and 1907. In 1905 Roosevelt made another major contribution by cooperating with the great powers, on an *ad hoc* basis, to forestall a war over Morocco.

The Moroccan controversy was a product of Europe's rivalries. By the Entente Cordiale of April 8, 1904, France had obtained from England a free hand in that North African region, and Foreign Minister Théophile Delcassé intended to use it to humiliate Germany. The Kaiser's government responded in kind. Fearful lest Britain be drawn into the Dual Alliance, it took advantage of Russia's preoccupation with Japan and tried to check the Anglo-French combination at the outset. Germany did this by posing as the champion of the open door in Morocco and as the defender of her independence. Since the United States had treaty rights in the sultanate under a fourteen-power convention of July 3, 1880, the Kaiser hoped to gain the President's support for a general conference. Roosevelt was loath to become involved. He had just begun his peace efforts in East Asia and was embroiled with the Senate over the Dominican receivership and the arbitration treaties. The American economic stake in North Africa, in contrast to the Far East, was slight. Moreover, he was uncertain where the national interest lay. He had no desire to break up the new entente; he did not wish to see Germany humiliated. When he finally agreed to act behind the scenes, it was because he felt that the republic had an obligation as a world power to exert its influence in behalf of peace whenever this could be done with safety.

As in the preliminaries to the peace of Portsmouth, Roosevelt acted with skill and modesty. By June, 1905, he had agreed with Germany that a conference was necessary. His first task was to overcome French opposition and to weaken England's support of its partner on that point. He did this by giving assurances on June 6 that the United States would not attend any gathering to which France did not acquiesce. Delcassé's resignation that day helped, and by June 23 France's sole condition was that the agenda be worked out in advance at Paris and Berlin. The President then turned to Germany and received from its ambassador on June 28 a promise that the Kaiser would, in event of irreconcilable differences during the conference, accept the solution which the United States deemed fairest. Whether the envoy accurately translated what his monarch had in mind later became a disputed point, but for the moment his assurances enabled Roosevelt to sweep away all Anglo-French hesitancy and through his good offices bring about a meeting of thirteen powers at Algeciras, in Spain, on January 16, 1906.

What happened at Algeciras can be quickly told. Its problems, except where they touched world peace, did not greatly concern the United States. Control of the Moroccan police and bank was largely a matter of prestige for France and Germany. The important fact was that an American president helped arrange the conference, that he aided in deciding where the delegates would meet and what they should discuss, that he offered to mediate at a critical juncture on February 19, that he broke a deadlock a month later by reminding the Kaiser of his ambassador's promise, and that—in spite of bitter Democratic criticism—he authorized two American diplomats not only to participate in the proceedings but also to sign the resulting treaty of April 7, 1906. In consenting on December 12, 1906, to this Act of Algeciras, the Senate appended a reservation insisting that the sole purpose of the agreement was to benefit American trade and disclaiming any intention to settle questions entirely European in their scope; but this bow to tradition could not conceal the fact that at a tense moment in history the United States had cooperated with other great powers to avert a possible catastrophe.

Not until 1914 did a president again try to prevent a general war. In September, 1908, new trouble flared up in Morocco, when a German consul attempted to help deserters from the French Foreign Legion, but that controversy was referred to the Hague Court without American assistance. A third crisis erupted in 1911 when Germany, fearing that France was about to depose the Sultan, demanded territorial compensation. By sending the gunboat *Panther* to Agadir on July 1, the Reich alarmed the British and led to blunt warnings that they would resist any German bullying. By November, 1911, the war scare was over, but it is significant that President Taft took no important step to aid in the solution. And when Italy and Turkey clashed over Tripoli in September, 1911, soon to be followed by the Balkan Wars, Taft assured Congress that the United States had no direct interest in the conflicts.

On the eve of Armageddon, President Wilson authorized Edward M. House to undertake one of the boldest missions in American diplomacy to that time. On December 12, 1913, he agreed to let the Texan go abroad and try to draw England, France, and Germany into an informal entente with the United States to preserve peace. House reached Berlin on May 26, 1914, and his reaction to the situation on the Continent was one of horror. "It is jingoism run stark mad," he reported to the President. "Unless some one acting for you can bring about a different understanding, there is some day to be an awful cataclysm. No one in Europe can do it." House did what he could in talking to the civilian and military leaders, the Kaiser included, to reduce fear of England. On June 2 he proceeded to London where, in a month of conversations, he discovered an intense desire to put Anglo-German relations on a better footing. Foreign Secretary Edward Grey urged him to convey that fact to the Kaiser, but House's letter of July 7 did not reach Wilhelm until July 27. By then, time had run out. On June 28, the heir to the Habsburg throne was assassinated by a Serbian nationalist at Sarajevo in the Austrian province of Bosnia. Europe shuddered with alarm and then relaxed during a deceptive calm before the storm. On July 21 House sailed for home. Two days later the Austrian government delivered an ultimatum to Serbia and thus set in motion the chain of events which precipitated the First World War.

It has been fashionable to scoff at House's self-styled "Great Adventure" and to depict him as an unwary novice among the iniquitous diplomats of the Old World. Actually, his efforts offered some hope of success, and with more time Wilson in 1914 might have won as much of a respite as Roosevelt did in 1906. Yet in retrospect, the importance of the House mission is not that it failed but that it was undertaken at all. There had been nothing like it before. It was a worthy climax to these prewar strivings for peace which, with all their shortcomings, left the American government better prepared than it had been in 1905— although not so well equipped as it needed to be—for the testing of the World War and the negotiations in Paris that followed.

23

❯❯❯-❯❯❯-❯❯❯❯❯❮❮-❮❮❮-❮❮❮

The Breakdown of Neutrality

THE WAR OF 1914–18, known to contemporaries as the Great War, constituted a watershed in Western civilization. In Europe, it brought to a close the nineteenth century—a century of progress, of hope, and of relative peace. In the United States, the conflict confronted the government with the severest external challenge since the days of the French Revolution. Although the people and their leaders instinctively assumed that the republic could remain aloof by taking refuge in a traditional neutrality, they slowly came to realize the inadequacies of that cherished policy and to face the question of whether isolationism was possible or desirable when large parts of the world were at war. The decision of April, 1917—to intervene in a stalemated struggle, in behalf of American maritime rights—was, paradoxically, both a vindication and a repudiation of neutrality. It was also something more. Intervention laid bare the forces that were eroding an ancient opposition to permanent alliances and to involvement in the diplomatic affairs of other continents.

THE FIRST WORLD WAR

Austria-Hungary's determination to settle scores with Serbia following the murder of Archduke Franz Ferdinand at Sarajevo caught most Americans by surprise. Although the people were not so provincial as they are sometimes depicted, even the best-informed expected that this crisis, like so many in the past, would end peacefully. Hence the initial reaction of almost all citizens was to heave a sigh of relief that the United States was physically separated from Europe. In the weeks that followed, these citizens were amazed by the magnitude of the first German victories and shocked by the callous German violation of Belgium's neutrality. Only gradually did they sense that trench warfare portended a long and bloody battle of attrition.

During the last days of peace the United States government did little. The time for action was too short, the means at hand too feeble, and the odds against success too great. As late as July 27, 1914, Ambassador James W. Gerard cabled from Berlin his belief that "matters will be arranged without general European war." The next day the Austro-Serbian conflict began, and pressure upon Wilson to take some step mounted. On July 28 Bryan inquired of Ambassador Walter H. Page in London whether the good offices of the United States, if extended under the Hague Convention of 1899, "would be acceptable or serve any high purpose." It took Foreign Secretary Sir Edward Grey until July 31 to answer, and then he simply expressed gratitude and asked whether the same offer had been made in Vienna, St. Petersburg, or Berlin. By July 31 Russia had mobilized, while France and Germany would follow suit the next day. Wilson, however, moved with excruciating slowness and only on August 4 said he would be happy to act in the interest of peace at that moment or subsequently. By then, Germany had declared war on Russia and France, had invaded Belgium, and had received a British demand to withdraw at once from the kingdom whose neutrality the powers had guaranteed in 1839. By then, Grey had stared into the gathering London dusk and murmured: "The lamps are going out all over Europe; we shall not see them lit again in our lifetime." Five hours after the American offer had been sent, England's ultimatum expired and the First World War began.

If Wilson seemed dilatory and defeatist in facing the impending catastrophe abroad, he acted with dispatch and decision in preparing for neutrality at home. When prices on the New York Stock Exchange plummeted on July 30, 1914, Secretary of the Treasury William G. McAdoo instantly made available a large amount of emergency currency provided for by a recent statute. On July 31 the President conferred with congressional leaders on the need for prompt legislation to expand the merchant marine, and by August 3 the Senate had passed a bill authorizing the use of naval vessels as commercial cargo carriers. The next day the customary proclamation of neutrality was issued, setting forth the traditional restrictions on Americans and belligerents. But Wilson was not content to adhere blindly to the past. Worried lest a nation of such diverse peoples become divided against

itself, on August 19 he made an unprecedented appeal to his countrymen. "Every man who really loves America," he declared, "will act and
speak in the true spirit of neutrality, which is the spirit of impartiality
and fairness and friendliness to all concerned." The United States, he
asserted, "must be neutral in fact as well as in name . . . impartial
in thought as well as in action." It must keep itself "fit and free to do
what is honest and disinterested and truly serviceable for the peace of
the world."

THE INADEQUACY OF NEUTRAL DUTIES

By asking the American people to be impartial in thought and in action, Wilson went beyond the requirements of international and domestic law. Even without his request, the neutral duties the United
States had to observe in 1914 were not the same as those of 1793 or
1817. New weapons had raised new problems. Fighting along the borders was not expected. The republic was no longer a puny infant whose
survival depended on abstention from Europe's strife. Now its economic and military power could spell the difference between victory
and defeat for one of the alliances. Hence, Wilson was not worried lest
American citizens on American soil recruit for the combatants or
launch expeditions against friendly neighbors or convert cargo vessels
into privateers. There was still the question of warships hovering beyond territorial waters and of admitting armed belligerent merchantmen into American ports; but the novel difficulties, for which familiar
concepts proved to be inadequate, had to do with the granting of loans
and the sale of munitions.

With respect to loans, international law distinguished between
money lent by neutral governments and by citizens of a neutral state.
It did not forbid, nor did American domestic statutes so forbid, individuals to float loans or to extend short-term credits for facilitating
trade. Such a prohibition was not needed in the Napoleonic era when
the young republic lacked financial reserves. During the Civil War, the
Union borrowed extensively from Prussian bankers; during the Russo-
Japanese struggle, New York investment houses aided Japan. Although the Hague Conferences had taken no stand on the matter, many
Americans—Bryan among them—came to believe by 1914 that unless
some curbs were imposed, the operations of private financial institutions might undermine American neutrality.

Actually, the administration's first pronouncement was a surprise.
On August 15, 1914, Bryan, with respect to a French plan to float a
bond issue of $100 million with J. P. Morgan & Company, declared
that loans to belligerents by American bankers "were inconsistent with
the true spirit of neutrality." Money, he had told Wilson five days

earlier, was "the worst of all contrabands because it commands everything else." The Secretary argued that public subscriptions intensified
emotions and would destroy the very impartiality the President sought,
and on that point Bryan may have been right. But there were much
sounder reasons why huge loans to combatants should be discouraged
in August, 1914. The war had unsettled the entire American economy.
The security markets were disorganized and the gold reserves endangered. To ban loans as unneutral merely confused the problem. If
the export of dollars was to be forbidden as contraband, why should not
the outflow of other contraband items also be stopped? Bryan did not
go that far, and it is not clear whether his concept was designed to keep
the country out of war, to offset the advantage held by the Allies, or to
promote the material well-being of the United States. If persisted in,
however, his policy would have led to serious economic dislocation,
since within a few months British sea power made a prosperous foreign trade possible with only England and France.

Because it was commercially unsound and strategically unwise,
this opposition to loans was gradually relaxed and ultimately abandoned. But to save Bryan's pride and to avoid offending German
sympathizers, the return to tradition was not candidly explained, with
the result that many people at the time and in later years regarded it as
a conspiracy against the Secretary and proof of the pro-Allied bias of
the administration. On October 15, 1914, the Department privately
conceded that loans stood on the same ground as the shipment of other
contraband and did not violate American neutrality. On October 23
Lansing secretly assured two investment houses that it was proper to
extend commercial credits to the belligerents. Bryan assented, but he
insisted on maintaining a distinction between credits—which banks
could grant quietly to promote trade that was valuable to the whole
country—and loans—whose bond rallies might arouse popular passions and divide the American people. By March 31, 1915, it was publicly acknowledged that short-term credits were not barred by the statement of August 15, 1914. The statement itself was never openly
repudiated; but the President tacitly renounced it on September 7,
1915, when he agreed to permit a group of New York bankers to float
a $500 million bond issue which England and France desperately re-
quired if they were to continue their substantial war purchases in this
country.

Thus ended in failure the first attempt by the United States to include among neutral duties a proscription on loans by its citizens to
belligerent governments. It failed because it seemed inconsistent to
halt the export of dollars as contraband and not to halt the shipment
of other kinds. It failed because it seemed unfair to deny the Allies
access to American banks to carry on a mutually profitable commerce

just because Germany had no comparable trade to finance. But it failed primarily because such a ban, while beneficial to the nation's economy in August, 1914, had the opposite effect a year later. The influence of Wall Street or fear of a German victory had nothing to do with the reversal. There was no expectation in September, 1915, that the Allies would be defeated or that the United States would enter the struggle.

The sale of munitions posed a more difficult problem. Again, there was nothing in international or domestic law to stop American manufacturers from selling guns and shells to belligerent governments. Secretary of State Jefferson admitted as much on May 15, 1793, while forty-four nations declared at The Hague on October 18, 1907, that a neutral was not obliged to prevent the export of weapons. The only limiting factor was that, as contraband, those materials could be confiscated by the belligerents wherever found. In theory, then, the United States had no authority to halt the arms traffic, and Germany had no grounds to protest. But in practice, many Americans were disturbed by the deaths which the products of their factories inflicted almost wholly on the Central Powers. The Germans, caught in the grip of the British navy, had to rely on propaganda and their kinsmen in the New World to try to check that trade in the name of humanity and fair play.

Once again Wilson faced a dilemma. To stop the flow of munitions would penalize the Entente for its command of the sea at the very moment when its foes had shown themselves more powerful on land. To permit the traffic to go unimpeded would antagonize Germany and perhaps invite retaliation. Neither traditional neutrality nor a new interpretation of its duties fully protected the national interest. Hence, the President refused to interdict the sale of guns and shells, arguing that it would be more unneutral to alter the rules after hostilities had commenced, especially to compensate one side for its inferiority, than it would be to adhere to precedent. But because the arms traffic obviously helped the Allies more than it did their rivals, because it aroused humanitarian sentiment, and because it seemed easier to eliminate by legislative fiat, the administration met with a stiffer challenge than on the loan issue. Resolutions empowering the executive to impose an arms embargo were introduced into both houses and found strong support among idealists, pacifists, Anglophobes, and German sympathizers. Bryan agreed with Wilson on this matter and tried to stem the agitation on January 25, 1915, by a public defense of the President's policy. On February 18 the Senate tabled by a margin of 51 to 36 an embargo contained in an amendment to another bill. Although the campaign for a ban on arms shipments was renewed in the next session, no other vote was taken.

For a second time a move to widen the duties of a neutral lost. Once again it failed early in the war, before relations with Germany were embittered by the submarine controversy and before it was felt imperative to save the world from Prussian autocracy. Once again it failed because it ran counter to Wilson's definition of the national interest. Superficially, of course, an arms embargo seemed to insure greater impartiality; actually, it would have been an attempt to offset an advantage possessed by one belligerent. Superficially, too, it looked as if the continuation of the munitions traffic was dictated by economic considerations; actually, Wilson did not make up his mind on that ground.

THE DILEMMA OF NEUTRAL RIGHTS

A breakdown of traditional concepts in a twentieth-century war was even more apparent with neutral rights. It was also more dangerous. Since the Hague Conferences had not defined precisely acceptable belligerent practices on the high seas, the United States became embroiled with England once that country tried to strangle Germany by a long-range blockade. The introduction of the submarine precipitated an even more violent controversy with Germany which, two years later, led to intervention on the Allied side. Yet that decision came only after the most agonizing soul-searching, for Wilson saw the dilemma of neutral rights and the paradox of going to war to vindicate principles designed to preserve peace.

As in the Napoleonic era, the United States discovered that neutral rights involved a compromise between the belligerent's desire to cut off his foe from all commerce with the outside world and the neutral's wish to deal uninterruptedly with all combatants and other neutrals. As in the period 1793–1812, the British tolerated some neutral trade lest they add the United States to their list of enemies, while the American government endured some interference as a lesser evil than going to war. But there were also important differences. From 1914 to 1917 no impressment issue or territorial ambitions complicated the problem. The dependence of the Allies on American exports gave Wilson, if he had chosen to use it, a more effective means of retaliation than Jefferson's embargo, whereas the American people and their leaders grew emotionally more involved in this conflict than Madison and his contemporaries had been in theirs. Nor did the Wilson administration seriously contemplate fighting England over infringements of neutral rights. As to Germany, the differences were not the same as those with France before 1812. In the First World War the right of American citizens to travel in safety on the high seas was challenged for the first time. Germany's violation of maritime rights, moreover, meant the loss of human lives, not simply of property. Logically, the difficulties with the two sets of belligerents cannot be separated, but for a clearer analysis we must deal first with one and then with the other. Yet chronology should be kept in mind, for the timing of the German depredations often permitted the British to escape from troubles created by their own.

From August 20,1914, to March 28, 1915, England was the chief transgressor of neutral rights. On the first date Britain rejected, as was its prerogative, Bryan's plea of August 6 to accept the rules of naval warfare contained in the unratified Declaration of London of February 26, 1909. Instead, the British issued an order-in-council defining contraband in terms much less favorable to nonbelligerents. Steadily thereafter they built up a system of controls intended to deny the Central Powers all sources of oil, copper, cotton, food, and other raw materials. The British mined the North Sea, extended the contraband list, interfered with mails, exercised sweeping powers of search, intercepted shipments to neutral ports, detained neutral vessels, and confiscated neutral goods—though compensation was promised. They justified these acts by citing Northern precedents from 1861 to 1865 and by insisting upon the changed character of modern warfare. The United States declined to acquiesce in these practices and repeatedly complained that they went beyond international law and recognized belligerent rights. But Wilson was reluctant to retaliate, to break off diplomatic relations, or to go to war to uphold the freedom of trade. Neither side wanted a showdown. The American government was content to enter protests and recover damages later. England's objective, as Grey put it, was "to secure the maximum of blockade that could be enforced without a rupture with the United States."

Grey's task was not easy. What seemed in Washington a legitimate move to promote American interests was often viewed in London as a sinister plot to help Germany. The attempt to provide more bottoms for farm exports in the Ship Registry Act of August 18, 1914, and in the subsequent abortive Ship Purchase bill were regarded in England as unneutral in fact and in spirit. The ban on loans, imposed for domestic reasons, was also misunderstood. On the other side, German sympathizers tried to push Wilson into challenging the long-range blockade. To offset Allied propaganda on atrocities in Belgium, they resorted to comparable fabrications. They blamed Britain's restrictive measures for the alleged starvation of women and children in the Reich. Food supplies were actually adequate, but these reports marshaled popular support behind an American proposal of February 20, 1915, which, if accepted, would have destroyed the British blockade on the importation of food and raw materials into Germany.

Tension with England over neutral rights was alleviated by the simultaneous submarine controversy with Germany and by the burgeoning prosperity which the war trade brought to almost all Americans. Over the years Wilson has been severely criticized for allowing those two factors to outweigh Britain's questionable maritime practices. His acquiescence has been attributed to the influence of the munitions makers and of Wall Street, to an allegedly pro-Allied bias, and to a failure to heed his own counsel. Yet Wilson tried desperately to be neutral; but his efforts were nullified by the fact that complete neutrality, in the sense of absolute impartiality, had been made impossible for the United States by its importance in the world's economy and by the nature of modern warfare. Whatever the republic did or failed to do benefited one side and, at least indirectly, injured the other. To insist on nineteenth-century standards would hamper England and perhaps lead to war. To forego ancient privileges would hurt Germany and perhaps lead to war. Such was the dilemma of neutral rights from 1914 to 1917. Wilson believed that to accept British restrictions was less of a strain on traditional concepts than to deny it the advantages of superior sea power. This conviction did not stem from ignorance, propaganda, or bad advice but rather from his own notion of what was best for the United States. To be sure, his decision created an intricate web of economic ties with the Allies and a dangerous resentment with the Central Powers, but it did not make intervention inevitable. That was brought about by the submarine, a weapon Germany would have used no matter what England did or Wilson believed.

THE SUBMARINE CONTROVERSY

Four things should be said at once about the submarine question. First, it stirred passions to fever pitch. The initial havoc wrought by the U-boats in 1915 shocked and outraged most people in the United States. Second, the submarine killed American citizens. This fact shaped Wilson's determination to insist upon some traditional rights and to forego others. Third, the submarine killed American citizens under varying circumstances—on American vessels, on belligerent passenger liners, on unarmed belligerent cargo ships, and on armed belligerent merchantmen. This distinction is noteworthy because, prior to the break with Berlin on February 1, 1917, only three American lives were lost on American ships. Fourth, the submarine controversy was not primarily responsible for Germany's fateful decision in January, 1917, to defy American opinion. Military considerations dictated that decision.

Germany's proclamation of a war zone around the British Isles on February 4, 1915, first raised the submarine issue. Beginning on February 18, Germany announced, every enemy vessel found in the area would be sunk and, because of England's abuse of neutral flags, nonbelligerents would also be in danger of destruction. Only six months had passed since the first underwater torpedo had been fired in battle, but already the U-boat had proved itself against naval craft. The justification for turning this terrifying weapon upon unarmed vessels, passenger and cargo, was the food situation in Germany. In reality, the move was intended to frighten the British into relaxing their economic pressure. The Germans had enough to eat but not enough submarines to maintain an effective patrol. As a military measure, the counterblockade was unimportant at first; as a source of diplomatic bickering, it quickly became extremely significant.

In Washington, the German announcement drew a prompt response. Aided by Counselor Lansing, Wilson drafted a paper that spoke in general terms of attacks on American ships. He argued that no belligerent had a right to destroy any vessel without first determining its nationality and the character of the cargo. That could be done only by visit and search, a device which also prevented the misuse of neutral flags. The United States, the President concluded, must hold the Imperial Government to "strict accountability" for the illegal destruction of any American lives or ships. Since nobody foresaw the deadly power of the U-boats, this note was dispatched on February 10, 1915, without any dissent or a full realization of its implications. The same day a complaint was hurried to London because the passenger liner *Lusitania,* on approaching Ireland five days earlier, had hoisted the Stars and Stripes as a *ruse de guerre.*

Not until March 28, 1915, did Wilson have to interpret the meaning of strict accountability. On that date the *Falaba,* an unarmed British liner en route to Africa, was sunk in the Irish Sea with the loss of 103 lives, one American. Bryan and Lansing offered conflicting advice. The latter contended that to destroy a passenger or cargo ship, neutral or belligerent, without providing for the safety of those aboard was "a practice unwarranted by international usage." The former believed that, under existing conditions, an American sailing on an English liner or merchantman was guilty of "contributory negligence." Lansing did not admit the legality of the submarine blockade; Bryan would bar all citizens from traveling in the war zone. Wilson sided with Lansing. On April 22 he outlined a protest based "not on the loss of this single man's life, but on the interests of mankind." The proposed note was never sent because the President was not sure of his ground and hoped that an open confrontation with Germany could be avoided.

Then, on May 7, 1915, the eastbound *Lusitania,* unarmed but carrying contraband, was torpedoed off the tip of Ireland and sunk in eighteen minutes with the loss of 1,198 souls, 124 of them Americans. This mass drowning in broad daylight gripped the nation with horror. Initially it was branded as sheer murder, but subsequently the complexities of international law and alleged extenuating circumstances blunted that judgment. A few indignant Americans talked of entering the fray, but the vast majority did not believe such a step was wise or necessary. Wilson took that view. He was confident Germany would not persist in these inhumane tactics, and at Philadelphia on May 10 he pleaded for calm. "There is such a thing," he declared, "as a man being too proud to fight. There is such a thing as a nation being so right that it does not need to convince others by force that it is right." Hence he turned to diplomacy to win an apology, a reparation, and a promise of future good behavior.

Wilson began by asking for a complete abandonment of submarine attacks on all vessels, on the ground that U-boats could not operate under traditional rules of cruiser warfare. The first note of May 13, 1915, rested mainly on moral considerations and implied the right of Americans to travel anywhere at sea. Although Bryan dissented from that idea and disliked the stern tone, he signed the document. The German reply of May 28 was argumentative and evasive. For ten months a correspondence dragged on without outwardly reconciling deep-seated differences. Germany maintained throughout that the submarine, because of its design and because of British countermeasures, could not be expected to conform to nineteenth-century practices. To rise to the surface for visit and search was patently dangerous; to take aboard the passengers and crew of a victim was manifestly impossible. The enemy, Germany argued, had obliterated all distinctions between merchant and war vessels by arming cargo carriers and instructing them to take offensive action. The United States denied that changed conditions entitled one combatant to ignore universally accepted rules, especially at the expense of human lives. In a second note on June 9, Wilson continued to press for a renunciation of U-boat warfare; this time Bryan heeded the call of conscience and resigned.

Behind the scenes, however, the crisis slowly eased. Chancellor Theobald von Bethmann Hollweg had no desire to add the United States to his list of foes. Although he could not, and did not, apologize for the *Lusitania* or publicly disavow the attack, he expressed regret and privately tried to prevent a recurrence. On June 1 and 6, 1915, the Admiralty issued secret orders to spare all American vessels and large passenger liners of every nationality. More important, as opinion at home recoiled against a break with Berlin on this issue, Wilson narrowed his demands. The third note of July 21 insisted that a belligerent, in retaliating against an enemy, must not harm neutrals; and it warned that the destruction of another *Lusitania* might compel a rupture in diplomatic relations. But the key paragraphs, in effect, accepted the use of submarines if they adhered to traditional rules, confined America's concern to the safety of unarmed liners, and left to the future the security of belligerent merchantmen and of United States citizens traveling thereon. Since U-boat commanders had already been ordered to give immunity to large passenger vessels, a momentary accommodation seemed possible.

That hope was shattered on August 19, 1915, by the sinking off southern Ireland of the unarmed British liner *Arabic*, westbound and without contraband. Forty-four persons died, including two Americans. A bitter clash followed between Bethmann Hollweg and extremist admirals, who wanted a free hand in underwater operations, but the Kaiser decided in favor of the civilian leader. On September 1 Ambassador Johann von Bernstorff assured Lansing for the first time that "liners will not be sunk by our submarines without warning and without safety of the lives of non-combatants," provided they did not try to escape or resist. For another month tension remained high over the meaning of this Liner Pledge and a disavowal of the *Arabic* incident, but by October 15 Wilson had gained his more limited objective and Germany had drastically curtailed the submarine warfare it had envisaged on February 4, 1915.

Undeniably, Wilson had won a substantial victory, but the controversy was not over. The immunity of belligerent merchantmen remained, and again outmoded concepts of neutrality plagued the diplomats. On September 19, 1914, in a routine circular, the State Department had announced it would continue to distinguish between offensively armed and defensively armed cargo carriers. This meant that merchantmen which mounted guns ostensibly for self-protection would not be classified as warships but might enter American ports at will and stay indefinitely. The ruling was not intended to penalize Germany, but it had that effect. It conferred advantages and immunities on vessels which could cope with submarines almost as easily as units of the fleet or naval auxiliaries. Within a year Lansing realized the mistake, and on September 12, 1915, he recommended that henceforth all armed merchantmen be treated as warships. The President hesitated to change the rules after hostilities had begun, but by 1916 a decision was imperative. The British had started to place guns on passenger liners, on whose decks American citizens, according to Wilson, had a right to travel with impunity.

To escape from this trap the United States proposed on January 18, 1916, a modus vivendi under which England would disarm all merchant craft, passenger and cargo, in return for Germany's promise to operate submarines according to customary principles of visit and search. In effect, Lansing suggested extending the Liner Pledge of September 1, 1915, to freighters. If accepted, the plan would remove much of the danger inherent in the asserted right of Americans to travel anywhere at sea and would extricate the United States from its untenable distinction between types of armed vessels. The scheme impaled the British on the horns of a cruel dilemma. If they acquiesced, all their imports might be cut off; if they said no, they might alienate the Wilson administration, with equally disastrous consequences.

Germany capitalized at once on the British predicament. On February 10, 1916, it announced that, beginning on February 29, U-boats would attack without warning armed belligerent merchantmen. In the next few days Wilson and Lansing began to have second thoughts. From London, where he was engaged in discussions looking toward American mediation to end the war, House protested strongly against the modus vivendi. In the Senate, Republican spokesmen insisted that illegal submarine activity should not be tolerated. Then on February 15 Lansing told reporters that while he believed the plan served the best interests of humanity, his government would not force a change in the conventional rules.

This abrupt about-face was followed by an incipient revolt in Congress. The administration's stand on the right of travel and rumors of imminent intervention combined with Lansing's sudden reversal to produce the only concerted uprising against Wilson's neutrality policy between August, 1914 and April, 1917. On February 21, 1916, three ranking Democrats went to the White House to discover what the President would do if American lives were lost on armed belligerent merchantmen. Wilson reiterated his determination to hold Germany to strict accountability and his refusal to proceed with the modus vivendi. The trio left, greatly worried lest such a course drag the country into war, and their fears were deepened by a simultaneous statement in Berlin that the unrestricted campaign would be adhered to. The next day a veritable panic swept Capitol Hill. On February 17 Jeff: McLemore, Democrat of Texas, had introduced in the House a resolution warning American nationals against sailing on armed belligerent ships, and there seemed little doubt that it would pass. In both chambers other resolutions were in the making to deny passports to travelers going into the war zone and to bar armed vessels from entering American ports.

Wilson met head-on this challenge to his conduct of diplomacy. In a public letter on February 24, 1916, he promised to do "everything in my power to keep the United States out of war." But he would not allow one nation to alter or disregard principles agreed upon by all, and he would not consent to any abridgment of American rights. "Once accept a single abatement," he warned, and "the whole fine fabric of international law might crumble." But Wilson had to do more than restate his position. He must demonstrate to the country and the world who directed foreign policy, the president or Congress. On February 29, therefore, he sought immediate action on the McLemore resolution and a similar one offered in the Senate by Thomas P. Gore, Democrat of Oklahoma. Reports of divided counsels in Washington, he asserted, had confused other governments and were impeding his most delicate negotiations. By invoking the prestige of his high office and his influence as party leader, Wilson prevailed. Republican critics such as Lodge rallied to his side in opposing any curtailment of American rights. Many Democrats rebelled, arguing that a defensively armed merchantman was a warship and that a theoretical freedom to travel at sea should be suspended temporarily. After several amendments, some of which nullified the original intent of the resolutions, the controversial measures were tabled. The vote in the Senate on March 3 was 68 to 14; that in the House on March 7 was 276 to 142.

Meanwhile, Germany was preparing to commence on April 1, 1916, a campaign against all armed merchantmen. Even liners would be attacked if they mounted guns. On March 24, however, a new crisis arose when the unarmed *Sussex,* with 380 passengers aboard, was torpedoed in the English Channel. Although the small French steamer kept afloat, over fifty persons were killed and several Americans wounded. Lansing and House urged stern action after this breach of faith, but Wilson hesitated to take any action that might hasten intervention. After three agonizing weeks he agreed to denounce the destruction of commerce by submarines as incompatible with the principles of humanity and the rights of neutrals. A note of April 18, 1916, concluded by warning that unless Germany abandoned immediately its war against liners and cargo ships, the United States would have no choice but to sever diplomatic relations. On April 19 the President told Congress in person of the stand he had taken, but a vote of confidence was neither asked nor given.

In Germany, a similar period of soul-searching ensued. Wilson was widely condemned for trying to deprive the Central Powers of the one weapon by which they could gain speedy victory. Once again the civilian and military leaders debated the alternative of hobbling the U-boats and thus appeasing the United States or permitting them to wreak havoc and perhaps driving the republic into the struggle. Once again the Kaiser sided with the diplomats. Unlike the admirals, he did not believe there were yet enough submarines to guarantee the defeat of England before American military might could be brought to bear. Thus, the German reply of May 4, 1916, met Wilson's minimum demand by announcing that henceforth no merchant vessels would be torpedoed, in the war zone or elsewhere, without warning or providing for the safety of those aboard. This major concession was somewhat vitiated by a begrudging tone and a condition imposed at the very end. The Foreign Office called upon the United States to "demand and insist that the British Government shall forthwith observe the rules of international law," as accepted before 1914 and as outlined by Bryan and

Lansing since then. Should these American efforts fail, "the German Government would then be facing a new situation in which it must reserve to itself complete liberty of decision."

Eager for peace and thankful for a surrender on the main point, Wilson declined to make an issue of this condition. Despite Lansing's references to a "gold brick" swindle, the President accepted the German concession. His note of May 8, 1916, warned, however that friendly relations would depend on a scrupulous observance of this latest promise and insisted that a respect by German naval authorities for American rights on the high seas was in no way contingent upon the conduct of other governments. "Responsibility in such matters," the document concluded, "is single, not joint; absolute, not relative."

Like the Liner Pledge of September 1, 1915, the *Sussex* Pledge of May 4, 1916, represented a triumph for Wilson's diplomacy. Whatever qualifications were made at the time and whatever dangers lurked in the future, it liquidated a serious crisis and ushered in more than eight months of relative calm in German-American relations. Not until January, 1917, would the submarine controversy again threaten to drag a reluctant United States into war. Until then the critical problems resulting from the breakdown of neutrality would be with England, not Germany.

The long-range significance of Wilson's victory, however, escaped most of his grateful and peace-loving countrymen. It was not due to the moral prestige of the United States or to an acceptance of its views on neutral rights. The German verdict in May, 1916, like that in August, 1915, was based on military considerations. When its leaders became convinced that the unrestricted use of the submarine could win the war, no amount of diplomatic protest, not even the certainty of American intervention, held them back. By May, 1916, then, save for an unlikely reversal of Wilson's policy, the question of American participation was in the hands of the Kaiser, not the President—unless, of course, the latter could bring about peace before the fateful decision would be reached.

24

✦✦✦✦✦✦✦✦✦✦✦

Complications at Home
and Abroad

No ACCOUNT of Wilson's endeavors to find a viable neutrality would be complete without reference to the many simultaneous complications at home and abroad. No summary of his dogged determination to keep the nation at peace can do justice to the numerous other problems, foreign and domestic, that crowded in upon him from August, 1914, to April, 1917. The Great War could not monopolize his thoughts. He had a reform program to develop, a party unity to maintain, a public opinion to guide, and a second term to win. In East Asia, there was the European struggle to reckon with, an aggressive Japan to restrain, and an impatient Philippines to satisfy. In the Caribbean, there was unfinished business with Colombia, Nicaragua, Puerto Rico, and the Danish West Indies; with Haiti and the Dominican Republic; and, above all, with Mexico.

AMERICAN OPINION AND THE WAR

Despite all that has been written about the influence of Allied propaganda and economic pressures, only one generalization is possible regarding American sentiment between August, 1914, and April, 1917: it was overwhelmingly noninterventionist. The people and their representatives were virtually unanimous in a desire and a belief that the United States should and could remain aloof. Only when it seemed that forces beyond the nation's control would drive it into war did the belief crumble. Yet the desire persisted. Hence the final step was taken reluctantly, because the republic's own interests were at stake and because, as Wilson put it, "God helping her, she can do no other."

To say that public opinion was preponderantly against intervention is not to deny that many Americans held strong views about the Great War. A majority undoubtedly favored the Entente, but to that conclusion two qualifications must be added. First, the intensity of the pro-Allied feeling was markedly less than it was to be from 1939 to 1941. In 1914, Anglophobia was more rampant, while among citizens of German descent there existed an affection for the Fatherland that was largely absent with regard to Hitler's Reich. Second, favoring England and France did not denote a wish or willingness to fight for their cause. Unlike the pessimism that gripped the American people after the fall of France in 1940, only a negligible few ever believed that the Kaiser's forces would win.

A comparable generalization can be made for Wilson. Until January 31, 1917, the President had no desire to intervene, unless it were to mediate a peace. Even after the rupture in relations with Germany, he continued to hope that a renewal of unrestricted submarine operations would not produce the overt act which would make war inescapable. On the very eve of asking Congress to recognize the status of a belligerent that had been thrust upon the United States, he was tortured by misgiving and doubt that had not plagued Madison in 1812, Polk in 1846, or McKinley in 1898. Of course, Wilson was never completely impartial. He reflected his past training and present convictions. He was instinctively drawn to Great Britain by its intellectual legacy and its political structure. He was an avid reader of English literature and an unabashed admirer of the parliamentary system. It was not difficult for him to regard the Allies, Russia excluded, as the defenders of democracy. Nor is it hard to extract sentences from unguarded letters and vague recollections that seem to indicate a determination to thwart a German victory. But concrete deeds are more revealing than isolated words, and the evidence is irrefutable that Wilson steered a course which was dictated solely by what he thought, rightly or wrongly, to be best for America.

Within Wilson's circle there was much diversity of opinion but little relish for war. At one extreme, until he resigned, stood Bryan. The Great Commoner saw no difference in the moral position of the belligerents; as a pacifist, he opposed any step which might drag the nation into the European bloodbath. At the other extreme was his successor. Lansing seems to have become convinced by July, 1915, that a German triumph would imperil the security of the United States; henceforward he shaped his advice with the likelihood of intervention in mind. Secretary of War Lindley K. Garrison, until he resigned over the issue of preparedness in February, 1916, shared some of Lansing's fears, while Secretary of the Navy Josephus Daniels was essentially in accord with Bryan. In London, Page was often realistic in his appraisals but always too Anglophile in presenting them; his influence can easily be exaggerated. House came nearest to approximating Wilson's position, but with one difference: after his three missions to Europe before 1917 his thinking was less rooted in purely national considerations. It need only be added that while Wilson listened to many people, he made all the vital decisions himself.

These decisions aroused increasing criticism. At first, very little fault was found at home with Wilson's policies. Then, on November 8, 1914, Theodore Roosevelt began an attack, in which Lodge and Root later joined, on the President's failure to protest under the Hague Conventions against Germany's violation of Belgian neutrality. These strictures were not wholly candid or accurate. The agreements of 1899 and 1907 gave the United States no rights beyond extending its good offices, which Wilson did, while in August, 1914, the same Republicans had not proposed to do more. After the sinking of the *Lusitania* the President's course evoked louder objections. Some felt he was going too far; others argued that he was not going far enough. Roosevelt voiced the second view. An apostle of the strenuous life, he was infuriated by the phrase "too proud to fight." He deplored a reliance on note writing to gain apology and reparation. Although he did not openly advocate entering the war, his demands, if followed, would have led to that step. But even in his own camp Roosevelt was an extremist. More typical were Lodge and Root. Pro-Allied in their sympathies, they did not come out for intervention until after the break with Berlin on February 1, 1917. They did much, however, to foster the idea that the European conflict was a struggle between decency and barbarism, between liberty and absolutism. They castigated the President for weakness in defending American lives and property at sea and in Mexico; they assailed his opposition to preparedness.

Statistically, more Americans criticized Wilson for being too outspoken in upholding the nation's interest than for being too lax. That opinion was strongest in the rural South and West; it was equally divided between the major parties. Bryan was the most prominent exemplar, but it had eloquent supporters in Congress. Many in this group favored a ban on loans and an embargo on munitions; most were willing to renounce temporarily the right to travel on armed belligerent ships. Above all, they disliked Wilson's supposed double standard in dealing with infractions of American neutral rights. They could not see why England should be permitted in the long-range blockade to violate traditional maritime practices on the ground that the nature of warfare had changed, while a similar plea by Germany to justify the submarine activity was rejected.

Two other problems relating to American opinion remain to be noticed. One is the imponderable influence of propaganda; the other, the unmeasurable enticement of economic forces. Both sets of belligerents undertook a carefully planned campaign to shape American thinking. The Entente effort was undoubtedly more successful, but that of the Central Powers had some impact. The Allies won out, not because they controlled the media of communication—that control was never complete—but because concrete facts bolstered their abstract arguments. If German atrocities in Belgium were greatly distorted, the occupation of that kingdom was a brutal reality. Sympathy for the alleged starvation in Germany resulting from England's blockade was quickly forgotten when one U-boat claimed 1,198 on the *Lusitania* alone. Prussian schemes for world conquest may have been an Allied fabrication, but the inept German spying and reckless sabotage carried on in the United States during 1915 was something the man in the street understood. Then, too, many of the best propagandists for the Entente were American citizens who had, independently, grasped the meaning of the conflict and the role the republic must play.

Economic factors were more important than propaganda in molding American opinion. Prosperity at home overshadowed the fighting abroad. Even Wilson was not immune to these pressures. His rulings on the extension of loans and the sale of munitions were dictated partly by their effect on the nation's economy, while the difference in his handling of the various infractions of American neutral rights stemmed from both humanitarian and material considerations. That is not to say, as did the noninterventionists in 1917 and the disillusioned after 1929, that the United States went to war at the behest of the munitions makers and the international bankers. Wilson instinctively suspected the leaders of finance capitalism; his concern was for the country as a whole. Nor should it be forgotten that the most effective single lobby was the southern farmer, whose need for finding an outlet for the cotton he normally exported to Central Europe produced nightmares in both the White House and the British Foreign Office. Everyone's pocketbook was affected to some degree. Yet, when intervention came in 1917, the economic argument carried more weight in Berlin than in Washington.

EAST ASIA AND THE PACIFIC

The global nature of the First World War became apparent at once. On August 7 and 11, 1914, Bryan tried vainly to persuade the belligerents to avoid hostilities in China and the Pacific Ocean. Japan was the chief stumbling block, for England had called upon it to help cope with enemy commerce raiders in that area. Foreign Minister Takaakira Kato was loath to embark upon a limited war for limited objectives, but he would gladly enter the fray for such goals as Germany's leasehold in Shantung province and the colonies in the Marshalls, Carolines, and Marianas. Grey did not wish to invoke the alliance, but he was desperate and had to bow to Kato's wishes. On August 17 an ultimatum flashed from Tokyo to Berlin demanding, in the interest of peace in the Far East, the immediate withdrawal of all armed vessels from the region and the delivery to Japan within a month of Kiaochow "with a view to eventual restoration of the same to China." The Kaiser's government, as was expected, refused to comply, and the next few weeks witnessed an Anglo-Japanese assault on all of Germany's weakly held holdings in East Asia and the Pacific. The most publicized battle was the siege of Tsingtao, and the surrender of that base on November 7 gave Japan a temporary foothold in China proper as well as railway rights and economic concessions in Shantung.

Fighting on the Asiatic mainland touched a sensitive nerve in American diplomacy. On August 17, 1914, a House resolution directed the secretary of state to inform Japan that the United States viewed with concern the forcible transfer of any Chinese territory to a foreign power. Two days later Bryan instructed his minister in Tokyo to note with satisfaction the assurance, contained in the ultimatum to Germany, regarding the eventual return of Kiaochow to China. Wilson accepted the promises at face value, although the rejection of the ultimatum gave Japan a legal excuse to ignore them. On October 8, he said that the Japanese conquest of Tsingtao and the German islands north of the equator did not imperil American interests. Yet two months later Kato told the Diet that his government had no obligation to restore Kiaochow to China and had given no guarantees regarding the captured German colonies.

Actually, Japan was preparing to improve its position in southern Manchuria and northern China. It knew that the Kwantung lease would expire in 1923; it had seen the efforts to obtain railroad and mining concessions below the Great Wall thwarted by President Yüan Shih-k'ai. The preoccupation of Europe with the war gave the expansionist-minded cabinet of Shigenobu Okuma the opportunity.

On January 18, 1915, the Japanese ambassador at Peking presented to Yüan Shih-k'ai in strictest secrecy a paper containing twenty-one demands, arranged in five groups. The first group dealt with Shantung. It demanded that China assent to any future agreement between Tokyo and Berlin disposing of the German concessions in the province, that China promise not to lease or cede any part of the province to a third power, and that China approve Japanese railway construction in the province. The second group concerned southern Manchuria and Inner Mongolia. It demanded that China extend from twenty-five to ninety-nine years the lease of Port Arthur, Dairen, the South Manchuria Railroad, and the Antung-Mukden line; that China permit Japanese subjects to farm, mine, and own land in southern Manchuria and Inner Mongolia; and that China ask Japan's consent before granting to a third party economic privileges in those two regions. The third group referred to the Yangtze Valley. It demanded that China create there a Sino-Japanese mining monopoly. The fourth group spoke of the non-alienation of Chinese territory. It demanded of Peking a pledge "not to cede or lease to any Power any harbour or bay on or any island along the coast of China." The fifth group, termed "desires," stipulated that China employ Japanese military and financial advisers, that the two nations police jointly certain troubled areas, that China buy half of its armaments in Japan, and that Fukien province be regarded as its sphere of influence.

Washington reacted slowly to these demands. On November 4, 1914, Acting Secretary Lansing had written to the minister in Peking that while his government would be glad to promote the welfare of the Chinese people by peaceful means, "it would be quixotic in the extreme to allow the question of China's territorial integrity to entangle the United States in international difficulties." When the first reports of Japanese pressure arrived, Bryan refused to be alarmed, for Kato was disclaiming any intention to impair China's freedom or the rights of other countries. Even Wilson conceded on February 8, 1915, that interposition in China's behalf at that time might do more harm than good. Without full knowledge of the facts, Bryan on March 13 dispatched a badly worded note which reaffirmed his nation's concern for China's territorial integrity and for the equality of economic opportunity therein. He objected to converting Fukien into a sphere of influence, but with the demands affecting Shantung, southern Manchuria, and Inner Mongolia he recognized that "territorial contiguity creates special relations between Japan and those districts." The note denied any wish to obstruct Japan or encourage China during their negotiations.

Within two months the United States took a firmer stand. By judicious leaks the Peking government shed light on what had hitherto been obscure. Kato, it grew apparent, had not told the whole truth but was pressing as hard for the "desires" as for the "demands." It became clear that Bryan had spoken of "special relations" when he should have said "special interests." Japan was obviously using his passiveness to beat down China's resistance. In mid-April, 1915, Wilson assumed control of the correspondence and injected a more resolute tone. A note of May 7 flatly stated that the administration had no idea of surrendering any treaty rights or asking China to do so. England's simultaneous objection to the fifth group enabled the Elder Statesmen to persuade Kato to omit the last group from an ultimatum that was given China on May 9. Although China had to yield, Bryan went on record two days later, in identic notes to Tokyo and Peking, declaring that his government could not recognize any agreement "impairing the treaty rights of the United States and its citizens, the political or territorial integrity of the Republic of China, or the international policy relative to China commonly known as the open door." [1] The effect of this caveat was to cast doubt on Bryan's earlier statement of March 13, 1915, to encourage Japan to seek fresh assurances from Secretary Lansing in November, 1917, and to create a precedent for the Hoover-Stimson nonrecognition doctrine in January, 1932.

One other East Asian problem called for action during the World War. Ever since 1900, Wilson's party had demanded greater autonomy and eventual independence for the Philippines, and he had been elected on a platform calling for a declaration of purpose. An attempt in October, 1914, to abolish the old commission form of government and to make elective both houses of the assembly ran afoul of the Senate, where Root and Lodge still thought in terms of the McKinley era. The battle was resumed on February 4, 1916, when a new Senate adopted by a vote of 52 to 24 a bill which enlarged self-rule and promised full freedom by March, 1921. This last feature drew such violent criticism from the Catholic church, which feared a confiscation of property, and from former Presidents Roosevelt and Taft, who spoke of a betrayal of trust, that the House struck it out on May 1. As approved on August 29, 1916, the Jones Act ended the outmoded commission, gave the voters the right to choose both houses of the legislature, and proclaimed that independence would be granted as soon as a stable government could be established.

MEXICO AND THE CARIBBEAN

In the Caribbean, as in East Asia, the Wilson administration faced unfinished business, some of which was only slightly affected by the war but all of which intruded upon the debates over neutrality. With Colombia, the Treaty of Bogotá remained unacted upon; as late as February, 1917, Wilson strove vainly to win approval. With Nicaragua, the Bryan-Chamorro agreement required consent, and that took from August 5, 1914, to February 18, 1916. In Puerto Rico, a second Jones Act

[1] In various treaties and notes signed on May 25, 1915, China extended the Kwantung leasehold to ninety-nine years, while enlarging other Japanese privileges in southern Manchuria; recognized Shantung as a Japanese sphere of influence, while stipulating that Kiaochow be returned to it after the war; and granted Japan the right to be consulted when China required foreign capital for railway or harbor construction in Fukien.

of March 2, 1917, modified the Foraker law by dissolving the link between the executive and legislative branches, by making elective both
chambers of the assembly, and by giving United States citizenship to
the islanders. In the Danish West Indies, Lansing succeeded where
Seward and Hay had failed because he was able to take advantage of
wartime fears. In negotiations which culminated in a treaty on August 4, 1916, the Secretary told the Danes that his government wanted
the group mainly to deny them to a future enemy and that it might
seize them in self-defense if the struggle in Europe made annexation by
Germany likely. The United States paid $25 million for St. Thomas, St.
John, and St. Croix; subject to a minor reservation, the Senate consented to the transaction by a majority of 6 to 1.

A year earlier the United States had added the republic of Haiti to
its list of protectorates. Periodic revolutions racked that debt-stricken
land. Between August, 1911, and March, 1915, there were seven different presidents, one having been removed by poison and another having been blown up in his executive mansion. The need for some form
of customs control was so obvious that Bryan made several moves in
that direction, even threatening to deny recognition unless a new regime promised in advance to sign a treaty. But no decisive step was
taken until an irate mob invaded the French legation on July 28, 1915,
and hacked to pieces a fugitive president who had just executed 167
political prisoners. That same day sailors and marines under Rear Admiral William B. Caperton went ashore at Port-au-Prince to restore order, and additional troops soon followed. Caperton's task was twofold.
First, he had to crush the power of the mercenaries who fomented rebellions in Haiti and the Dominican Republic. It required a virtual war
of extinction to do that. Second, he had to find a government willing to
accept a customs receivership. On August 12 he persuaded the National Assembly to elect Sudre Dartiguenave as president, but even
the pro-American Dartiguenave had little relish for the agreement he
was asked to negotiate and did so only when Lansing warned that he
would be replaced by a more amenable puppet.

By the treaty of September 16, 1915, the United States set up in
Haiti a more comprehensive customs control than that in the Dominican Republic. The pact also went beyond the provisions of the Platt
Amendment. Haiti was not allowed to increase its debt except by previous agreement with the American government. Haiti promised not to
sell, lease, or otherwise surrender any territory to a foreign power or to
enter into any treaty impairing its independence. The United States received the right to take all steps necessary to attain the objectives of
the treaty and to maintain a government capable of keeping order. The
constabulary and all sanitation projects were to be directed by Americans. The agreement was to last ten years and might be extended for

another decade. A modus vivendi put it into effect immediately, while the Senate gave its consent without much opposition on February 28, 1916. The war against the mercenaries continued, claiming 3,000 lives by 1921, and the last marine did not withdraw until August, 1934.

As negotiations over the *Sussex* reached a climax in May, 1916, Wilson broadened the protectorate in the Dominican Republic. The customs control under the convention of February 8, 1907, was not working well, and a new uprising had begun. When the rebels seized Santo Domingo, Admiral Caperton ordered them to lay down their arms, and on May 15, 1916, he sent sailors and marines into the capital. Other landings were made in the north, but there was no bitter war, as in Haiti. On June 26 Caperton announced his troops would stay until all revolutionary movements had been suppressed and the reforms needed for the country's welfare had been adopted. It took eight years to achieve that goal. Unlike the case in Haiti, American authority did not rest on a treaty, for no native leader was willing to act as a figurehead. Thus, Wilson approved on November 26, 1916, "with the deepest reluctance" and as "the least of the evils in sight," the creation of a military regime. Rear Admiral Harry S. Knapp discharged the functions of the president and the assembly; other officers ran the executive departments. In Washington, Knapp was regarded as a trustee for the Dominican Republic, but his orders came from the secretary of the navy. His rule was efficient and disinterested, yet the islanders never reconciled themselves to the loss of independence. Not until December 4, 1920, were steps taken to return the government to the Dominicans; not until September, 1924, did the last marine depart.

The most serious complication abroad to distract Wilson during his search for a viable neutrality was Mexico. Although Huerta had been overthrown, the victors quarreled among themselves and plunged the country into three more years of bloodshed. The real troublemaker was the ambitious and illiterate Francisco Villa, one of Carranza's most popular generals. Born a peon and hating all landowners, Villa had received a good press in the United States and was depicted as the champion of the downtrodden masses. Where Carranza had been coolly independent and thus incurred Wilson's dislike, Villa had astutely conveyed the impression he would work with the President. On August 16, 1914, Villa promised to cooperate with the United States in establishing a constitutional government, after which he would retire. On September 23, however, he declared war on Carranza and in November gained control by the very unconstitutional means of a convention at Aguascalientes, called to select a new president. Carranza regarded the choice of a Villa follower as rank usurpation and declined to accept the verdict. Full-scale fighting then broke out.

Faced with renewed civil war, Wilson blundered badly. Instead of remaining impartial and realizing that Carranza was the stronger and more responsible man, he threw his moral support behind Villa, only to discover he had erred. Between January and April, 1915, the Carranzistas, ably led by Álvaro Obregón, inflicted a series of crushing defeats on Villa's army and sent him reeling northward to his native province of Chihuahua. Carranza's mounting victories and the knowledge that German agents in the Americas were trying to embroil the two neighbors caused Wilson to reverse himself. Lansing, who on August 6, 1915, was convinced Carranza must be eliminated, argued two months later that he should be recognized *de facto*. That step was taken on October 19 in conjunction with Argentina, Brazil, Chile, Uruguay, Bolivia, and Guatemala. That same day an embargo on the export of arms was proclaimed and so administered as to discriminate against Villa.

Villa then showed his true colors. Hoping to drive a wedge between Wilson and Carranza, he tried to goad the United States into intervening. On January 11, 1916, his men in cold blood murdered sixteen Americans taken from a train in Chihuahua. The massacre was a boon to Roosevelt and Roman Catholic leaders who, for different reasons, had been castigating the President for not protecting adequately American lives and property. For the moment the administration blocked a resolution in Congress designed to force its hand, but Villa was not through. On March 9 the New Mexican border town of Columbus was raided and left with nineteen dead. After that atrocity Wilson could not stem the cry for action, and the next day orders went out to assemble a Punitive Expedition under Brigadier General John J. Pershing. On March 13 Lansing concluded a protocol with Carranza's ambassador-designate empowering either nation in the future to pursue bandits into the territory of the other. With this apparent sanction and with strict instructions not to commit aggression against Mexican sovereignty or Carranza's forces, 6,000 men crossed the frontier on March 15, 1916. Two days later Congress adopted a resolution approving what the President had done.

Pershing faced insuperable odds. It was impossible to find Villa and difficult to disperse his followers. The further the Americans drove southward, the more likely they were to clash with the troops of Carranza. The latter denied having permitted so large an operation on Mexican soil and pressed for an early termination. On April 13, 1916, he demanded an immediate withdrawal in view of a fracas the previous day at Parral, some 340 miles south of the border, in which two American and forty Mexican soldiers had died. Then Villa struck again. A raid on May 5 at Glen Springs in Texas killed four persons. As the halls of Congress rang with shouts to occupy northern Mexico, Carranza tried to compel a showdown. In a note delivered on May 31 he accused the United States of provoking a conflict, challenged it to prove otherwise by recalling Pershing, and said he would repel the Yankee invader by force if necessary. A few days later he instructed his commanders to stop any new crossing of the frontier and to resist any new advance of the Punitive Expedition.

In June, 1916, the republic teetered on the brink of a second war with Mexico. The arrest of American naval officers and the firing on a boat crew at Mazatlán on June 19 made the Tampico incident look like a minor offense. Lansing rejected Carranza's demand for an immediate withdrawal and on June 20 warned that attacks on the Punitive Expedition "would lead to the gravest consequences." On June 21, twelve of Pershing's men were killed and twenty-three captured when they charged a Carranzista post near Carrizal, about 85 miles south of El Paso. Two days later Congress authorized the President to call the National Guard into federal service. On June 25, acting on erroneous reports of the Carrizal affair, Wilson prepared to ask the legislature for powers to impose order along the border. He never did. The next day he learned an American captain had been responsible for the fighting at Carrizal, and on June 28 Carranza released the captives. With popular sentiment overwhelmingly for peace, Wilson gladly pleaded its cause. "Do you think," he asked rhetorically in a speech on June 30, that "the glory of America would be enhanced by a war of conquest in Mexico?" Carranza was impressed, and on July 4, 1916 he suggested a renewal of negotiations.

So long as the Punitive Expedition remained on Mexican soil, those discussions were bound to fail. Yet both leaders welcomed a respite from tension. As for Wilson, the talks would please public opinion at home and blunt Republican criticism during his forthcoming bid for a second term. As for Carranza, they would allow him to go ahead with his plans for a new constitution and a new election. Hence, on July 28, 1916, a joint commission was created to investigate all phases of Mexican-American relations. It deliberated from September 6, 1916, to January 15, 1917, without agreeing on a settlement or a plan for evacuating Pershing's forces. Yet by its very existence it provided a breathing spell at a critical moment in both countries and, in neutralizing the Mexican issue during the campaign of 1916, it contributed indirectly to Wilson's victory. When the commission finally broke up, the situation in Europe was so menacing that the administration had no alternative but to retreat.

By January 15, 1917, the danger of American involvement in the First World War was very great. Wilson's effort to mediate a peace before the United States was drawn in had been fruitless. At any moment Germany might commence unrestricted submarine operations. Indeed, unknown to the President, that decision had been made six days earlier. On January 18 Pershing was told he would soon be ordered back into Texas; within nine days the retirement had begun. On February 5 the new Mexican constitution was promulgated, and on March 13, 1917, the United States finally recognized *de jure* the recently elected President Carranza.

PREPAREDNESS AND THE ELECTION OF 1916

If Mexico was the most serious problem abroad to complicate Wilson's quest for neutrality, his re-election had by 1916 become the chief distraction at home. In retrospect, we are likely to forget how uncertain was his return to office. The country was still preponderantly Republican. Not since Andrew Jackson had a Democrat served two consecutive terms, and in 1912 the party had polled less than 42 per cent of the popular vote. If the Republicans could bury their differences and win back those who, four years earlier, had either bolted with Roosevelt or defected to Wilson, there would be a change in administration just as the war was about to take a decisive turn.

Essentially, the President's success depended on the answers to three questions. First, would his domestic program, which had moved steadily from its original objectives to the broader aims laid down by Roosevelt in 1912, secure the ballots of the progressive-minded? Second, did his foreign policy, especially in Europe and Mexico, seem more likely to keep the nation at peace than that of his Republican rival, Charles Evans Hughes, a former reform governor of New York, who had just resigned from the Supreme Court? Third, could he resolve the issue of preparedness, which by 1916 he could not ignore, without arousing latent fears of intervention by doing too much and without exposing himself to charges of blindness by doing too little? The first two of these hurdles were the more easily cleared. The numerous accomplishments in agriculture, labor, vocational education, and highway construction caused progressives, irrespective of party, to back Wilson. Farmers, workingmen, humanitarians, and intellectuals all felt that the President, despite frequent mistakes and occasional intransigence, offered a better prospect for avoiding intervention in Europe and Mexico than did his opponent. The average citizen yearned for peace, and nowhere more so than in the rural South and West or among the working class and immigrant stock of the big cities. Their vote went to Wilson.

More divisive, and therefore more dangerous, was the problem of preparedness. Should the armed forces be modernized and enlarged? To some, such a step was necessary to uphold American rights during the present conflict and to safeguard the nation at its close. To others, such a step was an entering wedge for the sort of militarism that had produced the holocaust abroad and would imperil the recent social gains at home. To still others, such a step was a prelude to intervention.

As early as December, 1914, the advocates of preparedness began to speak out. In a weekly magazine Roosevelt played countless variations on his favorite theme, while on Capitol Hill, Lodge and others questioned the adequacy of the defense establishment. A National Security League undertook to publicize the possibility of a war with Germany. To Wilson, with his intense passion for neutrality and his inherent suspicion of the professional soldier, this agitation was annoying, and he did all he could to minimize the alarm it was intended to arouse. Yet by midsummer of 1915 events at home and abroad compelled him to modify his stand. Without lessening in any way his devotion to peace, he asked Secretaries Garrison and Daniels on July 21 to recommend new programs for the army and navy. On November 4 he openly urged preparedness for the first time. His speech provoked a strident counterattack from such pacifist groups as the League to Limit Armament and from such popular figures as Bryan and La Follette. After some hesitation, Wilson carried his case to the people. From January 27 to February 4, 1916, he made a whirlwind tour of the Middle West, during which he pleaded for a Continental Army, a modern reserve force to replace the old National Guard. He also spoke of a bigger fleet and at one point, with unintended zeal, called for "incomparably the greatest navy in the world."

The congressional battle lasted until August, 1916. It began with a defeat for the President—the abandonment of the Continental Army scheme and the resignation of Garrison, its champion. But this strategic defeat enabled Wilson to score in the National Defense Act of June 3, 1916. That measure increased the peacetime strength of the army from 105,029 to 219,665, expanded the National Guard, and put the latter under stricter federal supervision. Its naval counterpart on August 29, 1916, represented a triumph for an orderly enlargement of the fleet. It committed the nation to a three-year building program of ten battleships, six battle cruisers, and ten scout cruisers. It also stipulated that four units in each category be laid down within twelve months—the first time since the introduction of the dreadnought in 1906 that Congress had authorized more than two battleships in any one year.

Despite his impressive record of progressive legislation, despite a lull in the controversies with Germany and Mexico, despite his attainment of a moderate preparedness program, Wilson's re-election was in doubt to the very end. Fortunately for him, Hughes waged an equivocating campaign in which Roosevelt, who destroyed valid arguments with unpardonable taste, proved more of a hindrance than a help. The

President's margin in the electoral college was the smallest since the disputed Hayes-Tilden contest of 1876, and he could not be certain of victory until a few days after the polls had closed.

Victory under any conditions would have carried with it a terrifying responsibility, but one aspect of the canvass added to Wilson's mental anguish. At the Democratic convention the keynote speaker and the permanent chairman had discovered, almost by accident, a surging pacifism among the delegates. Playing upon this deep-seated emotion, they had coined the phrase "He kept us out of war." That slogan was exploited to the full in the months ahead. Voters were reminded: "You are working—not fighting!" They saw in newspaper advertisements the alternatives of "Wilson and peace with honor?" or "Hughes with Roosevelt and war?" The President was not happy with that approach, although he used it indirectly. It implied a promise he would not make and could not keep. Better than anyone else he knew that the question of war would be decided in Berlin, not Washington. He preferred to seek re-election on the basis of his domestic achievements; and when he spoke of foreign affairs, he stressed that part of the Democratic platform which referred to America's changed position in the world and its duty as a major power to aid in formulating a just peace. That was the challenge he would later offer in the Great Crusade, but in November, 1916, the people were not interested in making the world safe for democracy. They did not want to intervene and were glad that Wilson, thus far, had kept the nation at peace.

25

➤➤➤-➤➤➤-➤➤➤-➤➤➤❮❮❮-❮❮❮-❮❮❮-❮❮❮

The Decision for War

WITH FOUR MORE YEARS in the White House ahead, Wilson tackled with renewed determination the problems of the war. He still wished to keep America out, but rather than rely on an outmoded neutrality, he now sought to terminate the struggle before acts by the belligerents compelled the United States to intervene. Yet by the time he repeated his oath of office on March 4, 1917, the picture had changed drastically. The first three months of 1917 marked the climax of a drama that possessed the qualities of a Greek tragedy. The denouement which the President had long feared and had striven to avoid was indeed the result of his own past decisions and of forces beyond his power to control.

PEACE EFFORTS

Wilson's eagerness to assist in ending the war was not new. He had long hoped to marshal the moral strength and diplomatic prestige of the United States behind an equitable settlement. In extending his good offices on August 4, 1914, he spoke of "the opportunity to act in the interest of European peace, either now or at any other time." On September 7 Bryan instructed Gerard to investigate whether the Kaiser would accept American mediation; the next day he directed a similar inquiry to London and Paris. In each case the reply was the same: let those who started the fighting sue for an armistice; any move on our part would be looked upon as a sign of weakness. Three months later Wilson tried again. The initial blows aimed at a quick victory had failed, and the belligerents were settling down to a contest of attrition. In December, 1914, he asked House to go abroad again as his personal representative, not to negotiate a peace, but rather to discover what sort of a peace might be negotiated. By the time House debarked at Liverpool on February 6, 1915, his task was greatly complicated by the proclamation two days earlier of a submarine blockade of the British Isles. Nowhere in government circles did he find much eagerness to stop hostilities. France, emboldened by the miracle on the Marne, dreamed of revenge. England was engrossed in plans for the Dardanelles campaign. Germany, confident of success, outlined terms only a defeated alliance could accept. Even neutral Italy was about to desert the Central Powers and enter the war on the Entente side.

Despite these ill omens, House canvassed the situation in a leisurely fashion. He spent over a week in Berlin, more than a fortnight in Paris, and about two months in London. He talked about disarmament, the freedom of the seas, the indemnification of Belgium, and a future international organization to maintain peace. The longer the colonel remained, the more antagonistic to Germany he became. Yet his mission failed primarily because neither coalition was yet prepared to concede that it could not win on the battlefield. Failure under those conditions is not to be wondered at, but it did have one fateful result. Never again after the spring of 1915 did Germany regard American diplomacy as disinterested. Once the submarine controversy commenced, Wilson's alleged double standard on infractions of neutral rights fed suspicions which his sincere endeavors to bring about a just peace could not dispel.

House's next mission in December, 1915, differed in purpose and spirit. This time he was not to discover what sort of a peace could be procured but to threaten Germany with American intervention on the Allied side if it did not accept the President's mediation. This second effort was prompted by Grey's assurance that England would agree to a negotiated peace, provided the United States joined a postwar league of nations, and by Wilson's fear that the U-boats would provoke a fresh crisis in spite of the Liner Pledge. Again House was authorized to talk in general terms about a territorial settlement based on the *status quo ante*, reductions in defense establishments, the freedom of the seas, and an international agency to halt future aggression. Should either coalition acquiesce in these terms, he was to employ the entire moral and diplomatic strength of the United States to force its opponent to the council table.

The outcome was the House-Grey Memorandum of February 22, 1916. Drawn up in London after the colonel had again visited Berlin and Paris, it stipulated that Wilson, on hearing from England and France that the moment was opportune, would propose a peace conference along the lines House had been suggesting. If the Allies agreed to negotiate and the Central Powers declined, "the United States would probably enter the war against Germany." How accurately the text reflected the President's views has long been a disputed point, but the important factor is that the memorandum led to no concrete results.[1] Within a month the torpedoing of the *Sussex* precipitated a new crisis with Berlin, and by the time it was liquidated, the summer offensives in Europe had ended all talk of peace.

In the middle of 1916 Wilson's chief difficulties over neutrality were with England. For almost eight months after the *Sussex* Pledge a relative calm prevailed in relations with Germany. During that same period the President's feelings toward Great Britain so hardened that by November 15 he could seriously talk of a possible war with the Allies. One reason for this change was the intensification of British curbs on maritime commerce. In a supreme effort to strangle Germany, England ended all distinctions between absolute and conditional contraband, seized parcels in American mails, blacklisted American firms suspected of trading with the Central Powers, and denied coaling facilities to American owners unless they accepted stringent rules for the operation of their vessels. A second reason was the persistent refusal of the cabinet of Herbert Asquith to carry out the House-Grey Memorandum. Although that agreement had left to the Allies the decision on when to invite American mediation, Wilson was eager to get on with the job. His campaign for re-election had disclosed a deep-seated yearning in America for peace, yet he knew that the only guarantee against involvement was to end the fighting before one of the belligerents goaded the United States into intervening. Hence, when Grey told House on August 28, 1916, that a conference such as they had envisaged was impossible in the near future, the President grew so resentful that he considered forcing his mediation on the Entente, just as six months earlier he had been prepared to impose it on the Central Powers. But he held back until after his bid for a second term was over, not even using the retaliatory laws that Congress enacted on September 7–8, 1916.

It was under these circumstances that Wilson made a final peace effort. This time he acted through diplomatic channels, not indirectly

[1] Neither Wilson nor House contemplated armed intervention at that time. Both were persuaded that diplomatic pressure would be sufficient; both believed that the United States was more likely to be drawn into the war by a failure to mediate than by the memorandum House signed; both wished to justify American involvement, if it had to come, on the need for an equitable peace rather than on a defense of neutral rights. On the other hand, House undoubtedly conveyed to the French the idea that in a dire emergency they could count on American assistance. The use of the word "probably" had been insisted upon by Wilson on October 18, 1915, when House was engaged in a preliminary correspondence with Grey.

through House. An appeal to the combatants, remarkably impartial, was still being drafted when Chancellor von Bethmann Hollweg anticipated him by announcing on December 12, 1916, that Germany was ready to join in a conference to end the war. He said nothing about specific terms, but with the military situation on the Continent in their favor, the Central Powers intended to ask what the undefeated Allies could never grant. In no way deterred by the prompt Entente refusal to enter a conference without knowing what the enemy would settle for, Wilson dispatched his own proposal on December 18. In its final form, it abandoned the notion of having all belligerents and interested neutrals meet together. It did not offer mediation or propose terms. It was primarily a call upon both sides to define the objectives for which they were fighting.

The response to this modest plea disappointed the would-be peacemaker. As Wilson expected, the Allies and their American sympathizers bitterly accused him of playing Germany's game. On December 30, 1916, the Entente governments spurned Bethmann's original bid, and their reply to the President on January 12, 1917, left no doubt of their determination to exact huge reparations from the Central Powers and to destroy Prussia's military machine. What Wilson had not foreseen was the intransigent attitude in Berlin which, while willing to use him to bring England and France to the conference table, was adamant in opposing his presence there. Publicly and privately the new Secretary of State for Foreign Affairs, Arthur Zimmermann, was disturbingly evasive about his nation's minimum objectives, but he was blunt enough in barring any American collaboration until after the peace had been written. Only then, so Bernstorff was finally allowed to tell House secretly on January 15, would Germany join the United States in plans to prevent future wars through disarmament, arbitration treaties, and a league of nations.

For Wilson this was not enough. He believed that stability in the postwar era depended upon a nonvindictive and nonpunitive settlement. With a definition of belligerent war aims still not received, he went before Congress on January 22, 1917, to plead for "a peace without victory." Disclaiming any desire by the United States to shape the exact details, he promised that his country would "help guarantee peace and justice throughout the world." No peace, Wilson asserted, could endure without the cooperation of the Western Hemisphere. The future, he continued, "must be made secure by the organized major force of mankind." It must rest on a peace without victory, without reprisals, without humiliations. It must rest on the principle of the equality of nations, "for only a peace between equals can last."

This call to rise above the past and its hatreds evoked divergent reactions at home and abroad but did not affect the outcome of Wil-

son's peace efforts. On January 26, 1917, aware that a vital decision
had been taken regarding the submarine, the British informed House
privately they were ready to open discussions, provided the enemy
really desired a reasonable peace. On January 31 the final word came
from Berlin. The Germans were willing to negotiate on the basis of territorial acquisitions in Eastern Europe, an enlarged colonial empire, a
return to France of occupied areas but under reservations respecting
strategic frontiers and financial compensation, the restoration of Belgium but under guarantees assuring Germany's safety, indemnification
for injuries to German corporations and citizens, and the freedom of
the seas. The last item sounded ironic when Bernstorff accompanied
the note with an announcement that, starting the next day, all ships—
belligerent and neutral—would be sunk without warning in a zone
around the British Isles, France, and Italy, as well as in the eastern
Mediterranean. As a token of goodwill, one American passenger ship
would be permitted to sail weekly in each direction to and from Fal-
mouth in southwest England, provided it was painted a certain color,
arrived and departed on a specified date, and carried no contraband.

THE BREAK WITH BERLIN

Germany's decision to resume unrestricted submarine operations was
long in the making and was reached without much reference to Wilson's peace efforts. Several times since the U-boat blockade was first
proclaimed on February 4, 1915, the Kaiser, Bethmann, and the General Staff had restrained the navy from fully exploiting the underwater
torpedo. Secret orders on June 6, 1915, spared large passenger liners,
and on September 1 that immunity was extended to unarmed liners re-
gardless of size. The *Sussex* Pledge of May 4, 1916, subject to a proviso
Wilson rebuffed, promised that no merchant ships—passenger or
cargo, armed or unarmed, in the war zone or outside—would be attacked without warning or caring for those aboard. Each time the admirals had to yield because they lacked enough submarines to guarantee a British defeat before the military might of the United States could
be brought to bear. In August, 1916, the navy again pressed its case.
The number of U-boats at sea, in dock, or under repair had risen from
twenty-seven in February, 1915, to seventy-four. Still the margin of
safety had not been reached, and the army, poised for an invasion of
Rumania, again compelled the Kaiser to say no.

By December, 1916, the situation was different. The conquest of
Rumania had been a spectacular success. The conditions contained in
the *Sussex* Pledge had been a miserable failure. The number of submarines to be available in February, 1917, was estimated at 103. The
army chiefs now supported their naval colleagues in saying that, if the

Sussex Pledge were withdrawn, England could be knocked out of the war by the middle of 1917. The Emperor yielded to this prospect of victory, even though he realized that unleashing the U-boats would probably cause Wilson to intervene. Bethmann still demurred, and on December 8 it was agreed he might try once more for a favorable negotiated peace. The prompt rejection of his bid of December 12 and the obvious futility of Wilson's note of December 18 convinced almost every German leader that the hour to strike had come. They argued that the United States as a belligerent could not provide greater aid to the Entente than it had as a neutral and that its man power would be too late to save Britain from certain disaster. On January 9, 1917, it was decreed that "unrestricted submarine war be launched with the greatest vigor" on February 1 and that care be taken to conceal this intention from both enemies and neutrals.

The nature and timing of Germany's decision left Wilson no room to maneuver and no alternative to suspending official intercourse. The announcement of January 31, 1917, did not distinguish between neutral and belligerent commerce, between passenger ships and cargo carriers, or between armed and unarmed merchantmen. The submarines would destroy all of them at once. The U-boats were even then on station, and American vessels which had left port days ago with assurances of safety might now be attacked. The resigned manner in which Bernstorff convoyed the news to Lansing showed that American intervention was expected in Berlin.

A break with Berlin did not have to mean war. Wilson refused to regard the renewal of unrestricted operations as a reason in itself for taking up arms. On February 3, 1917, after recalling Gerard and handing Bernstorff his passports, the President addressed Congress on the course he proposed to follow. While deploring the sudden renunciation of a pledged word, he could not believe, he said, the Germans intended to carry out their threat to destroy American lives and ships. There must be overt acts to convince him. If he were wrong, he would come back to seek legislative authority to protect by every available means all citizens engaged in lawful errands on the high seas. Wilson professed friendship for the German people and denied hostility toward their rulers. His sole aim was to vindicate the indisputable rights of American nationals. God grant, he concluded "we may not be challenged to defend them by acts of wilful injustice on the part of the Government of Germany!"

Wilson's restraint mirrored the sentiments of his countrymen. The vast majority believed it to be impossible to ignore a threat to sink American ships and kill American lives, but for the moment they were content to wait on Germany. Thus the Senate endorsed the executive's action by a vote of 78 to 5 on February 7, 1917. One immediate problem, however, the President could not ignore. It was the paralysis which gripped the Atlantic and Gulf ports in the wake of the German warning. Although in February only two American vessels fell victim to the U-boats and no deaths occurred, goods piled high in coastal warehouses and cargo carriers lay idle at their wharves. When on February 7 the administration rejected a plea that the navy convoy passenger ships through the war zone, one major company canceled the sailings of its largest liners. More important, however, was the arming of American merchantmen, a matter on which the cabinet divided sharply. On February 6 the President said that it was all right for owners to mount on their vessels whatever ordnance they felt was needed, but he would not sanction the use of naval gun crews without a vote of Congress. On February 23 he still remained unwilling to embark upon a policy of armed neutrality.

Two days later Wilson was shocked into changing his mind. On February 25, 1917, he received from Page a telegram which the British had intercepted on January 19 and had subsequently decoded. It contained instructions from Zimmermann to the German minister in Mexico City. In event of war with the United States, he was to propose to the Carranza government a formal alliance whereby Mexico would enter the conflict and receive not only generous financial support but also compensation in the form of "the lost territory in Texas, New Mexico, and Arizona." More than that, Carranza should be asked to mediate between Germany and Japan, who were officially at war, and then invite Japan to join the coalition. Although the Zimmermann message was fully justified as a war measure, its transmission in peacetime disillusioned Wilson as to Germany's real motives. He reacted to this piece of intelligence by deciding to seek legislative authority at once for arming American merchantmen.

On February 26, 1917, Wilson again addressed Congress. His tone was temperate, and he did not mention the Zimmermann note. He still hoped for peace and admitted that no overt act had yet occurred. But the absence of sinkings, he feared, was the result of good luck on the part of American seamen, not goodwill on the part of the German government. At any moment conditions might change; and since Congress would adjourn in six days and might not reconvene for nine months, he believed it wise to obtain approval in advance to place naval crews on American merchant ships and to employ other means for protecting maritime rights. By implication, he conceded, the Constitution allowed him to take those steps; but in the present circumstances, he continued, "I wish to feel that the authority and the power of the Congress are behind me in whatever it may become necessary for me to do."

To Wilson's dismay and disgust, Congress adjourned on March 4,

1917, without granting the authority he sought. The difficulty arose not over arming American merchantmen—a majority could have been secured in both chambers for that—but over his vague request "to employ any other instrumentalities or methods" that might be needed "to protect our ships and our people in their legitimate and peaceful pursuits on the seas." This last sounded like waging an undeclared war, and it aroused extremists on both sides. Interventionists such as Lodge, though ready for strong moves, distrusted Wilson and wanted the legislature on hand to scrutinize his acts. Noninterventionists such as La Follette, opposed even to armed neutrality, wished to stop the President from going to war. The former was prepared to filibuster so that appropriations and other key bills could not pass; the latter were willing to do so to kill the armed-ship plan. If these tactics succeeded, Wilson would have to call a new Congress into special session before its scheduled meeting in December.

Bitterness filled the closing hours of the old session. On March 1, 1917, Wilson had published the text of the Zimmermann note. A wave of anger swept the nation such as had not been felt since the *Lusitania* went down two years earlier. That very day the House passed the armed-ship bill by a vote of 403 to 13 but withheld the broader authority Wilson desired. When administration leaders in the Senate, supported by Lodge, tried to empower the President to engage in defensive operations at sea, eleven die-hards, led by La Follette and Norris, talked the measure to death. Thoroughly aroused, Wilson issued a public statement on March 4 deploring "a situation unparalleled in the history of the country" in which "a little group of willful men, representing no opinion but their own" had rendered the government of the United States "helpless and contemptible."

"NEUTRALITY IS NO LONGER FEASIBLE OR DESIRABLE"

"There may be no recourse," Wilson warned Congress on February 26, 1917, "but to armed neutrality." When the legislature was prevented by eleven determined men from authorizing the placing of naval gun crews on American merchant ships, the President decided to use his powers as commander-in-chief to install that protection. He did so on March 9, 1917, and that same day he summoned a special session to meet on April 16.

This last recourse short of war took place during a month when the submarine commenced to levy its toll of American lives on American ships and when the hitherto solid phalanx of opposition to entering the European conflict began to crumble. Although noninterventionists strove desperately for peace, forces beyond their control were assuming command. As Lodge said of Wilson on March 2, 1917, he did not want war but "he is in the grip of events." The Zimmermann note awakened those regions remote from the Atlantic seaboard to the possible dangers of a German victory. For the first time, interventionists struck a responsive chord among the people at large; and although only a few were yet ready to agree with Roosevelt that "Pacifism and Pro-Germanism are Siamese twins," belief grew that involvement was inescapable. On March 8, 1917, came the first rumblings of the Russian Revolution; within a week the Tsar had abdicated in favor of a liberal provisional government. Thus fell the last barrier to depicting the war as a contest between the democracy of the Entente nations and the autocracy of the Central Powers.

But it was the submarine that tipped the scale toward intervention. On March 14, 1917, word came that the eastbound *Algonquin* had been sunk off Land's End, England, though without loss of life. She was the third unarmed American merchantman to be destroyed since the unrestricted campaign was renewed, but the first to be attacked without warning. Since that resumption, eighteen Americans had died on belligerent or other neutral ships, bringing the total, beginning with the *Falaba*, to 194. Grimmer news, however, arrived on March 18 with the sinking of three additional unarmed American cargo carriers and the drowning of six more citizens. Here were the overt acts Wilson had dreaded. After three days of self-torture and soul-searching, he made up his mind. On March 21 he advanced the date on which Congress was to meet to April 2, in order that it might receive a message "on grave questions of national policy which should be taken immediately under consideration."

Wilson did not want war but was, as Lodge said, in the grip of events. It mattered little now that seven Americans were killed on an American tanker off neutral Holland on March 21, 1917, or that on April 1 twelve more died off the French coast on the *Aztec*, the first armed American merchantman to be lost. The decision for war had been taken. On March 24 diplomats in occupied Belgium were recalled; that same day Daniels was told to initiate plans for coordinating naval operations with England. The quest for neutrality was over because, as Wilson had conceded on October 26, 1916, "the position of neutrals sooner or later becomes intolerable." On April 2, 1917, he would confess to Congress that "armed neutrality is no longer feasible or desirable where the peace of the world is involved." Yet to the very end he was beset by gloomy forebodings. On April 1 he warned a friend that to enter the war "would overturn the world we have known." Germany would be beaten, but the result would be a dictated peace, not a peace without victory. "Once lead this people into war," the President continued, "and they'll forget there ever was such a thing as tolerance. To fight you must be brutal and ruthless, and the spirit of ruthless brutality will enter into the very fibre of our national life." In the depths of despair he exclaimed: "If there is any alternative, for God's sake let's take it."

"THE RIGHT IS MORE PRECIOUS THAN PEACE"

It was drizzling on the evening of April 2, 1917. That morning crowds had gathered on Capitol Hill, while Wilson tried to relieve an overwrought mind in golf. At eight thirty he entered the House chamber amid a stirring ovation and turned at once to the unpleasant business at hand. He declared "the recent course of the Imperial German Government to be in fact nothing less than war against the government and people of the United States" and advised the joint session to accept formally "the status of belligerent which has thus been thrust upon it." Quietly, without any obvious appeal to emotion, the President developed his case. He let the record of broken pledges and wanton destruction speak for itself. He underlined the distinction between the loss of lives and of property. The traditional safeguards of noncombatants having failed, he said, "we have seen the last of neutrality under such circumstances." He reminded his listeners that there were "many months of fiery trial and sacrifice ahead." Intervention would require close cooperation with the Allies, the grant of liberal credits to them, the mobilization of the nation's material resources, and the addition to the armed forces of at least 500,000 men, chosen on the principle of universal liability to service.

Thus far, the vast majority of his audience and his countrymen would have concurred, in varying degrees, with Wilson's sentiments. Nor would they have objected when he disclaimed any quarrel with the German people and branded the Kaiser's government as "this natural foe to liberty." Sabotage, espionage, the treatment of Belgium and, above all, the submarines and the Zimmermann note had robbed the Reich of the goodwill it had initially possessed in the United States. Only when the President moved on to delineate the shape of the postwar world did he elicit considerable dissent. Only when he attempted to sublimate a war in defense of American rights into a Great Crusade for all mankind did he arouse misgivings among those who had already split with him after his endorsement of a league of nations. Only when he proclaimed the end of isolationism as well as of neutrality did he open a quarrel between himself and numerous Americans who were having enough difficulty adjusting their thoughts to entering a war against a distant foe who had not yet set foot and did not threaten to set foot on American soil.

For what purpose did Wilson ask America to give her blood and her might? We shall fight, he declared "for the ultimate peace of the world and for the liberation of its peoples, the German peoples included: for the rights of nations great and small and the privilege of men everywhere to choose their way of life and obedience. The world must be made safe for democracy." We have no selfish ends to serve, he went on. "We desire no conquest, no dominion. We seek no indemnities for ourselves, no material compensation for the sacrifices we shall freely make. We are but one of the champions of the rights of mankind."

In the face of German aggression, Wilson vowed, "we will not choose the path of submission." With imperishable prose the President held out the vision of a just and lasting peace. "It is a fearful thing," he said in a tone that ill concealed his mental anguish, "to lead this great peaceful people into war, into the most terrible and disastrous of all wars, civilization itself seeming to be in the balance. But the right is more precious than peace, and we shall fight for the things which we have always carried nearest our hearts,—for democracy, for the right of those who submit to authority to have a voice in their own Governments, for the rights and liberties of small nations, for a universal dominion of right by such a concert of free peoples as shall bring peace and safety to all nations and make the world itself at last free. To such a task we can dedicate our lives and our fortunes, everything that we are and everything that we have, with the pride of those who know that the day has come when America is privileged to spend her blood and her might for the principles that gave her birth and happiness and the peace which she has treasured. God helping her, she can do no other."

The effect was electrifying. A deafening roar swept the hall. The applause was virtually unanimous. As Wilson left the chamber, Lodge shook his hand and exclaimed: "Mr. President, you have expressed in the loftiest manner possible the sentiments of the American people." But La Follette, his face grimly set and his arms folded conspicuously across his chest, stood silent. His sardonic smile was a reminder that the nation was not yet at war. Congress still had to be heard from.

Actually, the outcome was never in doubt. The next day—April 3, 1917—the Senate Foreign Relations Committee reported a joint resolution endorsing Wilson's arguments and giving him the powers he requested. Only chairman Stone dissented. Because of La Follette, the measure was postponed for a day, but it passed on April 4 by a vote of 82 to 6. All six were from "the little group of willful men" who, a month earlier, had blocked the armed-ship bill. Three were Republicans and three Democrats. In the House the debate lasted from the morning of April 5 to the small hours of April 6. There the count stood 373 to 50. The minority consisted of thirty-two Republicans, sixteen Democrats, one Socialist, and one independent. Of these, one came from the Northeast, nine from the South, and six from Nevada and the Pacific Coast. The remaining thirty-four were from the Middle West, with the heaviest concentration proportionately in Wisconsin, South Dakota, and Illinois.

The advocates of intervention, except for William E. Borah, added little to what Wilson had said, and none stated the case more meaningfully than the President. Lodge insisted that party lines must be forgotten in the struggle against barbarism, but his speech was more significant for its silences. In summarizing the purposes for which the United States was fighting, the veteran from Massachusetts talked much about preserving free institutions, upholding the Monroe Doctrine, and waiving territorial conquests, but he never mentioned "a concert of free peoples" that might bring peace to all nations. Senator Warren G. Harding, Republican of Ohio, was more concerned with vindicating American rights than spreading the cause of democracy. But it remained for Borah to separate explicitly the quarrel with Germany from membership in a future league of nations. There can be, the Republican from Idaho told the Senate, "but one sufficient reason for committing this country to war, and that is the honor and security of our own people." He joined no crusade, he went on, "I seek or accept no alliances; I obligate this Government to no other power. I make war alone for my countrymen and their rights."

The opponents of intervention had their innings. La Follette alone spoke for over four hours. They bitterly accused Wilson of using a double standard for infractions of American neutral rights. They blamed him for not holding the Allies to the same strict accountability he exacted of Germany and for requiring the U-boats to operate in a way that robbed them of their effectiveness. Some argued that since the British blockade also took lives, submarine attacks were a justifiable retaliation. La Follette dismissed the distinction between human rights and property rights as irrelevant and untenable. Others emphasized the supposedly nefarious influence of the bankers and munitions makers. "We are going into the war upon the command of gold," shouted Senator Norris. "We are about to put the dollar sign upon the American flag." Much was made of a widespread reluctance to fight. "The truth of the matter," said Representative Fred A. Britten, Republican of Illinois, "is that 90 per cent of your people and mine do not want this declaration of war." Hence he proposed amending the resolution to restrict overseas duty to volunteers until Congress directed otherwise. Senator James K. Vardaman, Democrat of Mississippi, wanted a popular referendum before the lawmakers acted; others wished to substitute purely defensive measures for full-scale hostilities. None of these suggestions passed.

With the aid of hindsight, we can see more clearly than contemporaries did two fundamental facts affecting the decision for war. First, Wilson had no real alternative. Any course he pursued, once traditional neutrality had broken down, conferred a benefit on one set of belligerents and thereby injured, sometimes indirectly, the other. Each side could have charged that he was adhering to a double standard. To have changed the rules on selling munitions and floating loans or to have insisted upon nineteenth-century concepts of contraband and the blockade would have compensated Germany for its weakness at sea, something the American government had no obligation to do. It would also have led to either a victory of the Central Powers or an open clash with the Entente. Those outcomes would not have served the national interest better than did the Great Crusade. An Allied triumph was preferable to a German one, and there was no likelihood of a drawn war once the submarine was unleashed. In short, although the Versailles Treaty had many faults, it was a more reasonable settlement for the entire world, including the United States, than the kind the Reich would have imposed. The terms given to defeated Russia at Brest-Litovsk in March, 1918, demonstrate that fact.

Second, while intervention was made more likely by Wilson's own previous judgments and warnings, it became inescapable only when Germany undertook unrestricted submarine operations. If in January, 1917, the Kaiser and his advisers had been willing to adopt a middle course between the tactics pursued by the U-boats after the *Sussex* Pledge of May 4, 1916, and the all-out campaign begun on February 1, 1917, there is reason to believe that the President would have been content—for the time being, at least—with armed neutrality. If, after the break with Berlin, American vessels had been spared or if the attacks without warning had been confined to armed belligerent ships, even to all belligerent craft except unarmed passenger liners, the entry of the United States into the deadlocked struggle might have been delayed and possibly averted. For in February, 1917, Wilson was more impartial than ever before, and it is not likely that he would have again insisted on the right of American citizens to travel on armed belligerent ships in the war zones. But the Prussian High Command was dazzled by the prospect of a quick triumph through unleashing the submarine completely. It did not seem to realize that, even under current restrictions, the U-boats were taking a catastrophic toll of Allied tonnage. It did not seem to foresee a revolution that would force Russia out of the war. It is conceivable that those two developments—a paralysis in Allied seaborne commerce and the freeing of countless German divisions from the Eastern Front—might have broken the stalemate before the United States ever intervened.

And so America went to war. There were no crowds in the street shouting "On to Berlin!" as there had been in Paris in August, 1914.

There was no violent rage, as there would be in December, 1941. There was no thought of territorial gain, as there had been in some quarters in June, 1812 and May, 1846. There was no expectation of an easy victory, as there had been in April, 1898. The American people had not wanted this war and did not relish it any more than the English people would wish to oppose Hitler over Poland in September, 1939. Both cases were marked by a calm resignation over the seemingly inevitable, by a reluctant conviction that there was no honorable alternative, and by a grim determination to get a dirty job over with as quickly as possible.

26

❯❯❯-❯❯❯-❯❯❯-❯❯❯❮❮❮-❮❮❮-❮❮❮-❮❮❮

Wartime Diplomacy

Participation in the First World War was a novel experience for the United States. Not since its birth, and then under very different circumstances, had the nation fought as a member of a coalition. Never had its troops been in combat on European soil. The problems of planning, logistics, and coordination were unprecedented. Could they be resolved within the framework of the Constitution and within the limits of isolationism? Could the republic in its first test as a world power reconcile military goals and diplomatic aims so that it might gain not only victory on the battlefield but also security at the peace table?

MILITARY OBJECTIVES

Victory on the battlefield was the primary objective between April 6, 1917, and November 11, 1918. Very few Americans distinguished total from limited war; fewer still had heard of the dictum that war was simply a continuation of political intercourse by other means. For all too many, the defeat of the Central Powers was an end in itself, not a means to some broader diplomatic design.

Even if this had not been so, there were three reasons for the United States to concentrate on military objectives. One was the belief that only a herculanean effort could break the stalemate on the Western Front. A second was the havoc the U-boats were wreaking on the British merchant marine—a toll which was not revealed until April 10, 1917. Unless these staggering losses could be checked—and no solution was in sight—England would be compelled to surrender by the

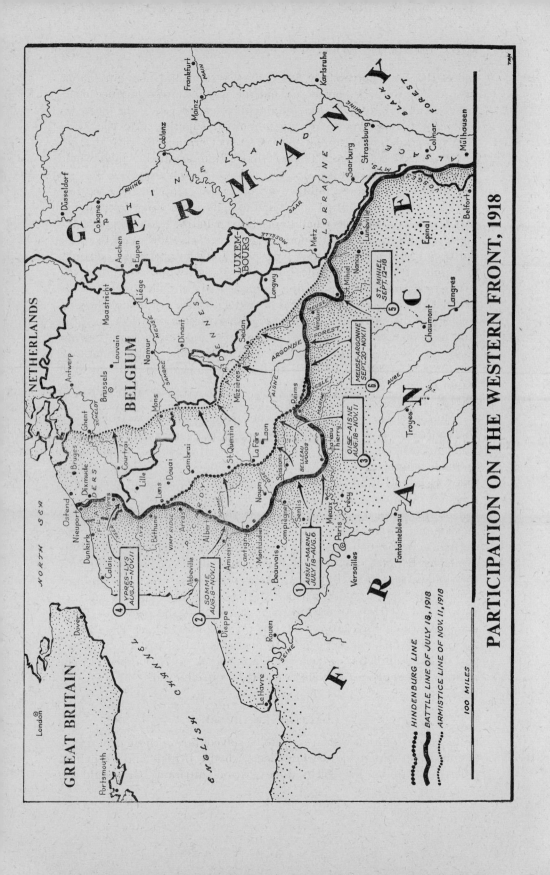

PARTICIPATION ON THE WESTERN FRONT, 1918

end of the year. Fortunately, the convoy system and new antisubmarine devices won the war at sea, but the war on land remained deadlocked. Thus, a third reason for drastic measures was the need for American man power to restore numerical superiority to the Allies after Russia defected, to halt the last great German offensive that began in March, 1918, and to launch the counterattack which would make the enemy sue for peace.

Attainment of these military objectives was simplified by the fact that in 1917–18 the United States had to fight on only one front and in only one ocean. The navy had to organize a Patrol Force to guard the Western Atlantic, a Special Squadron to protect the flow of oil from the Caribbean, and a Cruiser and Transport Force to carry 927,000 men to Europe. It also hurried destroyers to British waters to aid in the struggle against the submarine, assigned six dreadnoughts to the Grand Fleet at Scapa Flow so as to reduce Germany to hopeless inferiority in the battle line, stationed another three in southwestern Ireland as a precaution against ocean raiders, and laid a mine barrage across the North Sea to hamper U-boat operations. Unlike the situation during the Second World War, the navy engaged in no major fleet action but concentrated on the dangerous job of antisubmarine duty and the dull task of logistical supply.

More decisive was the role of the army, which grew from about 200,000 men on April 6, 1917, to over 3,600,000 on November 11, 1918. As early as June 13, 1917, Major General John J. Pershing set up the headquarters of an American Expeditionary Force at Paris; but this was largely a gesture to bolster morale. The influx of doughboys was only beginning on March 21, 1918, when Germany, freed from a war on the Eastern Front, dealt a shattering blow at the British along the Somme. From then until mid-July the question was whether the Germans could crush their foes before American man power was fully available. By May 29 General Erich Ludendorff's forces stood only forty miles from Paris. But the Yanks were coming: 50,000 in January, 100,000 in April, 250,000 in May. During June, Ludendorff's advance was slowed as fresh American troops poured into the trenches; at the second battle of the Marne on July 15–17 he was halted. Then began the counterattack which pushed the enemy out of much of France and part of Belgium before an armistice was signed on November 11. The military defeat of the Central Powers had been achieved.

COALITION WARFARE

Problems of coalition warfare had to be solved during these operations. Should American troops be brigaded with the British and French in order to fill ranks thinned by three years of attrition? Or should the

Expeditionary Force be constituted as a separate army and be given responsibility, when trained and equipped, for its own sector of the Western Front? To Pershing, there could be but one answer, and his wishes prevailed. So far as the strategic situation permitted, the soldiers of the United States fought under their own flag, were led by their own officers, and were provisioned by their own supply corps.

Another problem of coalition warfare concerned command relationships among the nations fighting the Central Powers. No real coordination had been achieved before April, 1917, and little progress was made immediately thereafter. Even within the American forces friction arose between the men in Europe and those in Washington, while interservice unity was hindered by the lack of a body like the Joint Chiefs of Staff during the Second World War. England, France, and Italy created a Supreme War Council on November 7, 1917, which the United States quickly approved. Although too cumbersome to devise a basic strategy which the field commanders could develop, modify, and implement, the Council helped smooth the way for the appointment on April 14, 1918, of General Ferdinand Foch as commander-in-chief of the Allied armies in France.

With regard to diplomatic coordination, Wilson kept in mind three considerations. First, the United States was not allied to its cobelligerents, and the President always referred to it as an Associated Power. Second, he carefully kept his nation clear of the secret treaties by which England, France, Russia, Italy, and Japan had agreed earlier to divide their conquests. Third, in spite of what he had told Congress on April 2, 1917, Wilson hoped to defeat Germany with his country's doing little more than supplying money, ships, arms, food, and a token number of men. During April and May he encouraged the European governments to send delegations to arrange for immediate economic assistance; later, permanent British and French missions were established in Washington. On August 24 Secretary McAdoo agreed to set up in the American capital an Allied Purchasing Commission. But none of the early steps solved the problem of coordinating Allied demands with American supplies. To improve matters, Wilson consented on October 13 to send House and several key figures from the warmaking agencies to examine conditions abroad. In addition, House was to represent the United States at an eighteen-nation conference in Paris on November 29. This conference was called to consider the deteriorating situation in Russia.

House and his colleagues reached England on November 7, 1917, when Entente fortunes were at a low point. The Italian rout at Caporetto a fortnight before had compelled a hasty transfer of much needed troops from the Western Front. That very day the Bolsheviks in Petrograd overthrew the provisional regime and set in motion a train of events that would take Russia out of the struggle with Germany. Against this gloomy background the Americans conferred in London for two weeks and then crossed the Channel for discussions with the French. The Inter-Allied Conference sat from November 29 to December 3 and made some important decisions in economic warfare and military dispositions; but the coordination was mostly at the technical level, through councils dealing with finance, munitions, transportation, and food. There was no statement of war aims and no solution to the Russian question.

While in France, House and General Tasker H. Bliss, a former chief of staff, attended at Versailles on December 1, 1917, the first meeting of the Supreme War Council. The initial impression on both men was unfavorable, and henceforth Wilson was wary in seeking diplomatic coordination through that body. He permitted Bliss to serve as the permanent American military member beginning in January, 1918, but did not appoint civilian counterparts to the prime ministers and foreign secretaries of England, France, and Italy. This decision was unfortunate, for the main value of the Supreme War Council turned out to be as a meeting place for the heads of government to discuss the broader issues of the war and the peacemaking, not as a planning agency for specific military campaigns. When, however, the Council had to approve Wilson's armistice negotiations in October, 1918, the President hurried House back to Paris to act as his personal representative.

Two other factors tended to lessen diplomatic coordination with the wartime associates. One was the slowness of transportation. If air travel had been feasible, Wilson might have conferred in person with Prime Minister David Lloyd George of England and Premier Georges Clemenceau of France. As it was, neither the President nor the Secretary of State left the country until after the armistice. The other factor was Wilson's attitude toward the peace, which made him appear more like an arbitrator between the combatants than as a member of one coalition. Fearful lest the Allied war aims not coincide with his, he was content to go his separate way. As a result, when the fighting came to a sudden halt on November 11, 1918, there was no agreement among the victors on the territorial settlement or the future league of nations.

EAST ASIA AND THE PACIFIC

In East Asia and the Pacific, Japan posed problems for American wartime diplomacy that were only partly related to the European conflict. After their initial attacks on Germany's possessions in 1914 and their successful inroads on China's sovereignty in 1915, the Japanese turned their attention to problems which would arise with the peace. By April, 1917, they were eager for an understanding with the United States on two matters. One was China. The Japanese were disturbed by the growing number of loans that American bankers, with Wilson's blessing, were floating for railroads and other public works on the mainland, and they were suspicious of the influence American diplomats continued to exert in Peking. The second was the future of the German Empire in the Orient. By providing much-needed naval assistance to the Allies in the eastern Mediterranean, Japan gained assurance in February and March, 1917, that England, France, Russia, and Italy would support its claim to German rights in Shantung and the captured islands north of the equator.

This eagerness led to the choice in June 1917 of Kikujiro Ishii, a former foreign secretary, to head a mission to the United States. Ostensibly, it was intended to promote cooperation in the common war against the Reich, as delegations from other cobelligerents were doing. Actually, Ishii's primary objective was to clarify the American government's stand on Japan's special position in China and to reconcile, if possible, the apparent discrepancy between Bryan's notes of March 13 and May 11, 1915. If at the same time he could remove some of Wilson's suspicions engendered by the Twenty-One Demands and if he could win American backing for the Japanese claims to the economic concessions in Shantung and to the Marshalls, Carolines, and Marianas, so much the better. In none of these aims did Ishii succeed. American fear of future trouble with Japan could not be uprooted; an understanding on China could be reached only by burying divergent views in ambiguity.

By an exchange of notes, or executive agreement, on November 2, 1917, Lansing and Ishii endorsed the principle that "territorial propinquity creates special relations between countries" and that consequently the United States recognized that "Japan has special interests in China, particularly in the part to which her possessions are contiguous." Nevertheless, the document continued, "the territorial sovereignty of China remains unimpaired"; and the United States accepted Japan's assurances that it had no desire to discriminate against the trade of other nations or to disregard the commercial rights previously granted them by China. Finally, the two governments mutually disclaimed "any purpose to infringe in any way the independence or territorial integrity of China" and promised to adhere to "the so-called 'open door' or equal opportunity for commerce and industry in China." To placate the United States without embarrassing Japan, the two men simultaneously signed a secret protocol, not printed until 1938. It declared that in their discussions they had also committed their countries not to take advantage of the war to seek special privileges in China that would abridge the rights of friendly states. They explained that this pledge was omitted from the official text as being "superfluous" and liable to create an "erroneous impression in the minds of the public."

The Lansing-Ishii Agreement created as many difficulties as it solved. It was impossible for the United States and Japan to proclaim repeatedly their allegiance to the ideal of the territorial integrity of China and the equality of economic opportunity without arousing suspicion that one or the other was betraying its word. Ambiguous phrases, such as "territorial propinquity creates special relations," fostered doubts as to their true meaning. Worse yet, Japan prematurely disclosed to the uneasy Chinese the fact that notes had been exchanged, and it persuaded them, as well as many Americans, that special interests meant paramount interests. Lansing insisted that he had done more than Hay in 1900 or Root in 1908 to protect China from external aggression, but his was essentially a temporary measure. In November, 1917, the Wilson administration was concentrating on the defeat of the Central Powers. Until that was accomplished, the President avoided a showdown.

THE RUSSIAN REVOLUTION

Unlike such issues as Shantung and Germany's Pacific islands or the expansion of Japan in East Asia, the Russian Revolution was an immediate problem for American diplomats. Upon the course of that convulsion could depend the outcome of the war. Without an eastern front to hold, Germany might win in the west before American man power reinforced the French and British, bled white by staggering losses in 1916 and by ill-advised offensives in 1917. All too often, Wilson's Russian policy is judged solely in relation to the future of communism, whereas his major concern was to keep that country in the war. Military considerations, not blind reaction to a vast social upheaval, dictated the decisions made in Washington.

Maintaining Russia as a belligerent did not seem to Wilson in April, 1917, to be an insuperable task. He believed a democratic nation would emerge from the wreckage of the Romanovs. He was encouraged by the determination of Prince George Lvov's provisional government, which the United States had been the first to recognize, to continue in the war. He was confident that by sending to Petrograd some prominent citizens he could demonstrate American goodwill, discover the needs of the new regime, and counteract the peace propaganda emanating from Germany. To head that mission and to underscore its bipartisan nature, the President chose an outstanding Republican elder statesman, Elihu Root.

Actually, Wilson's assumptions about the Russian Revolution were mistaken. The Tsar's downfall did not produce a stable democratic leadership, capable of prosecuting the war with vigor. The middle-class liberals under Prince Lvov lacked both political strength and popular support, while the common soldier had lost all enthusiasm for fighting and all obedience to his officers. As early as April 16, 1917, Vladimir I. Lenin and other Bolsheviks had returned from exile with German aid, and through the Petrograd Soviet, a council of workers' and soldiers' deputies, they began to destroy the provisional government. A premature coup on July 16 failed, but it did force the replacement of Prince Lvov by Alexander F. Kerensky, his Socialist minister of war. The latter soon found himself caught in a cross fire between the radical Bolsheviks, who gloated over the breakdown of the summer offensive, and the conservative element, who condemned his softness in dealing with Lenin. In September, he managed to suppress a threat from the right but, in so doing, had to give more and more authority to the Petrograd Soviet. Hence, when the Bolsheviks made their second bid for power on November 7, 1917, they succeeded. Under these conditions, the Root mission could accomplish nothing.

Bolshevism's triumph confronted Wilson with staggering problems. Should the new regime be recognized? If not, could it be influenced through informal contacts? How should the numerous counter-revolutionary groups, eager to resist the usurpers in Petrograd, be treated? What course might best keep Russia in the war? This last consideration was uppermost in the President's mind. Like the vast majority of his countrymen, he was instinctively hostile to the Bolshevik notions of class struggle, the overthrow of capitalism, and the dictatorship of the proletariat. Like them, he readily believed that Lenin was a German agent, returned for the purpose of demoralizing the armed forces, inciting civil strife, and agitating for peace. The first acts of the Communists confirmed these beliefs. On November 8, 1917, they called for an immediate peace of no annexations or indemnities and the end of colonial rule. On November 20 they ordered the commanding general to propose to the Germans a three-month armistice and removed him when he disobeyed. The next day Leon Trotsky, Commissar for Foreign Affairs, accused Wilson of going to war at the behest of Wall Street and of covertly betraying the Allies. In an obvious bid to embarrass the Entente, Trotsky began publishing the secret treaties concluded by the Tsar with England, France, and Japan. Finally, on November 28, it was announced that military operations had been halted and that truce talks with Germany would commence on December 2, 1917.

In Washington these developments produced consternation and resentment. Prompt recognition of the Lenin faction was now out of the question, and on December 6, 1917, Ambassador David R. Francis was told to avoid direct communication with the Bolshevik government. This course could be justified by the obvious inability of the men in Petrograd to control the entire nation. On the other hand, Wilson refrained from acts likely to drive the Communists deeper into the enemy camp. He hoped the Russo-German negotiations might fail, and he tried to hurt them by outlining on January 8, 1918, a fourteen-point basis for a moderate peace. But the Bolsheviks were not deterred. Internally, they persisted in measures obnoxious to the capitalist mind: repudiation of the public debt, confiscation of church property, nationalization of the land. Externally, they bowed to relentless German pressure, and on March 3 they signed the Treaty of Brest-Litovsk. By it, Russia was stripped of Finland, the Baltic provinces, Poland, and the Ukraine. Its army had to be demobilized, and it was to desist from all propaganda in the lands of the Central Powers.

Thus was Russia lost to the coalition opposing Germany. Those who nursed hopes that it might yet seek help were gradually disillusioned. Nonrecognition hardened into a basic American policy, and even informal contacts with the Bolsheviks were broken off. When, for security reasons, Lenin transferred his capital to Moscow on March 9, 1918, Francis had already gone to Vologda, 180 miles to the north. Deaf to entreaties from Trotsky, he moved still further away, and on August 9 he reached Archangel on the White Sea. The ambassador was confident that the Communists could not survive and that watchful waiting, with perhaps surreptitious encouragement to the counterrevolutionary White Russians, was called for. Many in Washington shared his views. But Wilson saw the problem primarily from the standpoint of the European war, and it was that emphasis which led him in June and July, 1918, to consent reluctantly to American participation in Allied landings in North Russia and Siberia.

The underlying cause of these interventions was the desperate need of the Entente to open a second front on Russian soil and thus ease the pressure from the great German offensive in France. The problem was simpler in Europe than in East Asia. In the former the chief task was to prevent the Central Powers from advancing through Finland to seize an immense quantity of arms and supplies that lay at Murmansk, an ice-free port on the Barents Sea, and at Archangel, a harbor open only in summer. It was also desirable to block German plans for a submarine base in that area and to encourage the residents to resist an enemy incursion. On February 21, 1918, Francis cabled that it was imperative to keep the two ports in friendly hands and hinted of strong anti-Bolshevik sentiment at both. On March 7 the British landed a small detachment at Murmansk, and in the next three

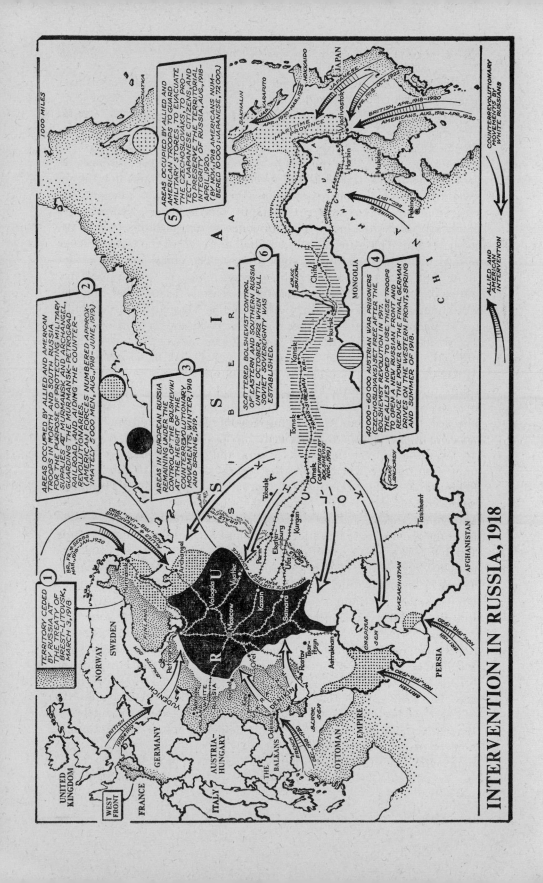

INTERVENTION IN RUSSIA, 1918

1000 MILES

① TERRITORY CEDED BY RUSSIA AT THE TREATY OF BREST-LITOVSK, MARCH 3, 1918.

② AREAS OCCUPIED BY ALLIED AND AMERICAN TROOPS IN NORTH AND SOUTH RUSSIA FOR THE PURPOSE OF PROTECTING MILITARY SUPPLIES AT THE MURMANSK AND ARCHANGEL, GUARDING THE MURMANSK-PETROGRAD RAILROAD, AND AIDING THE COUNTER-REVOLUTIONARY MOVEMENTS. (AMERICAN FORCES NUMBERED APPROX-IMATELY 5,000 MEN, AUG., 1918-JUNE, 1919.)

③ AREAS IN EUROPEAN RUSSIA REMAINING UNDER THE CONTROL OF THE BOLSHEVIKI AT THE HEIGHT OF THE COUNTERREVOLUTIONARY MOVEMENTS, WINTER, 1918 AND SPRING, 1919.

④ 40,000-60,000 AUSTRIAN WAR PRISONERS RELEASED AFTER THE BOLSHEVIST REVOLUTION IN 1917. THE ALLIES HOPED TO USE THESE TROOPS TO OPEN A NEW RUSSIAN FRONT AND REDUCE THE POWER OF THE FINAL GERMAN DRIVES ON THE WESTERN FRONT, SPRING AND SUMMER OF 1918.

⑤ AREAS OCCUPIED BY ALLIED AND AMERICAN TROOPS TO GUARD MILITARY STORES, TO EVACUATE THE CZECHOSLOVAKS, TO PRO-TECT JAPANESE CITIZENS, AND TO PRESERVE THE TERRITORIAL INTEGRITY OF RUSSIA, AUG., 1918-APR., 1920. (BY NOV., 1918 AMERICANS NUM-BERED 10,000; JAPANESE, 72,000.)

⑥ SCATTERED BOLSHEVIST CONTROL OF EASTERN AND SOUTHERN RUSSIA UNTIL OCTOBER, 1922 WHEN FULL SOVIET SOVEREIGNTY WAS ESTABLISHED.

COUNTERREVOLUTIONARY WHITE RUSSIANS

ALLIED AND AMERICAN INTERVENTION

months Wilson encountered increasing pleas to send naval vessels and ground forces to those strategic sites.

A more complex situation prevailed at Vladivostok, the Pacific terminus of the Trans-Siberian and Chinese Eastern Railroads. There the question was not simply one of taking precautionary war measures but of filling the vacuum created by the temporary eclipse of Russia as an East Asian power. The Lenin government was too busy holding its own in Moscow to be able to administer the Trans-Siberian line, guard a large number of Austrian prisoners in central Siberia, control the stores at Vladivostok, or exercise influence in northern Manchuria. Already several White Russian leaders had emerged in the Orient, eager to oust Lenin but needing foreign support. The chaos in Siberia and along the Chinese Eastern's right of way, moreover, encouraged five nations to intervene, though for different reasons. France and England were interested in preserving the matériel at Vladivostok, in mobilizing a westward thrust against Germany, and in keeping open the Trans-Siberian road, so that aid could be sent to anti-Bolsheviks fighting in the Ukraine and the Caucasus. China believed the time had come to regain some of its authority in Manchuria. Japan saw an opportunity to end forever the threat to its flank from the Maritime Province. The United States feared that unless the men in Tokyo were checked, the open door in Manchuria would be imperiled and the balance of power in East Asia destroyed.

As those nearest the scene, China and Japan were best able to move into Russian territory. At the request of the Allied ministers in Peking and at the invitation of the railroad manager at Harbin, a holdover from the Tsarist regime, the Chinese sent 3,500 men into Manchuria and by the end of 1917 had expelled all Bolshevik forces from the province. Meanwhile, France and England were encouraging Japan to lead a joint expedition to protect the stocks at Vladivostok and to take charge of the Trans-Siberian Railroad. The cabinet of Masatake Terauchi seemed willing to oblige but insisted on the approval of the United States. On January 28, 1918, therefore, the British suggested that the coalition ask Japan to serve as its mandatory. The American reply of February 8 was an emphatic no. Wilson thought the time inopportune and declared that if intervention became unavoidable later, it should be undertaken jointly and not with one country acting for the others. He did allow, however, an aged armored cruiser to supplement the one British and four Japanese warships at Vladivostok. On March 5 the President reaffirmed his stand, but events forced his hand. Both England and Japan landed small detachments on April 7, and in agreements signed at Peking on May 16 and 19 the Terauchi government gained the right to station troops in northern Manchuria.

Beyond a doubt, Wilson was loath to interfere in Russia's internal affairs. On practical as well as on moral grounds he was averse to involving the United States in the civil strife then raging on many fronts. However abhorrent were the ideals of the Bolsheviks, he had no desire to dismember their country. The President may have been naive in his faith in the latent democracy of the uneducated peasants, and he was obviously mistaken in his estimate of Lenin's ability to survive; but he expressed his innermost convictions when he declared at Paris in 1919 that "trying to stop a revolutionary movement by troops in the field is like using a broom to hold back a great ocean." His final surrender must be attributed to his belief that there was no alternative, that intervention was imperative as a war measure, and that the interests of all peoples—the Russians included—would be best served by American participation.

Wilson yielded first at Murmansk. With the railhead imperiled and German submarines active in the area, an old cruiser was added to the Allied warships off that port on May 24, 1918. On June 1 the President agreed, at the request of the Supreme War Council and pending approval by General Foch, to divert a contingent from France but under orders to do no more than guard military stores and "render such aid as may be acceptable to the Russians in the organization of their own self-defense." Fifty-four sailors formed part of the joint force that occupied Archangel on August 2; a month later transports brought in about 4,800 soldiers. These operations drew sharp protests from Moscow, but they were ignored. Limited intervention, however, turned out to be difficult to conduct. There was considerable interference in local affairs and some fighting within 300 miles of Petrograd. Although no more troops were sent, getting out of North Russia proved harder than getting in, and the armistice found the Americans still there. Not until June, 1919, did the last doughboy depart from the Archangel-Murmansk region.

Meanwhile, a development in the heart of Russia helped undermine Wilson's opposition to intervening in Siberia. This was the anabasis of the Czechoslovaks, a detachment of over 60,000 men who had fought against the Germans on Russian soil. After the Treaty of Brest-Litovsk they were eager to go to the Western Front, and on March 26, 1918, they received permission from Lenin's regime to start eastward along the Trans-Siberian Railroad for evacuation at Vladivostok. On May 25, when only 12,000 had reached the Pacific terminus, the men in Moscow changed their mind, a reversal that touched off severe fighting in central Siberia between the Czechoslovaks and the local Bolsheviks. On June 29 the advance group seized control of Vladivostok, appealed to the Allies for help, and marched inland to rescue their beleaguered brethren.

Here was a moral argument to overcome Wilson's scruples, and the Supreme War Council made one last plea. On July 2, 1918, it asked the United States to participate in a Japanese-led expedition of 100,000 men for the threefold purpose of rebuilding a second front, enabling Russia to expel the German oppressor, and succoring the Czechs. On July 6 Wilson decided to invite Japan and the Allies to join in a more limited enterprise. He rejected as impractical the establishment of a new Eastern Front, and he did not want a large Japanese army deployed on the mainland. But he did respond to the plight of the Czechoslovaks. Hence he proposed to supply them with arms at once and to occupy Vladivostok with a force from the Allied warships already there. Later he would assemble at that port about 14,000 men—half Japanese and half American, each commanded by their own officers—to protect the rear of the Czechs marching westward. In making this proposal, Wilson wished to underscore the solidarity of the Allies at a critical moment in Europe, but he was not unmindful of the encouragement it might give to "friendly Slavs everywhere." He insisted that all statements clearly show that the intervention was intended to safeguard the Czechs, not jeopardize Russia's independence or territorial integrity.

Japan's ambitions on the mainland also persuaded Wilson to act. He felt that a joint expedition was best calculated to restrain Japan and preserve the open door in northern Manchuria. Like everyone else at the time, the President exaggerated the unity in Tokyo on the question of continental expansion. Despite extremist pretensions in Siberia, the moderates won acceptance of the American invitation in almost the very form it was extended. In giving its consent on August 2, 1918, the Terauchi cabinet abandoned several of its demands, including a pointed reference to Japan's special position in East Asia and an explicit recognition of the right to send troops into the Maritime Province and the area beyond Lake Baikal. Terauchi promised that the initial contingent would not exceed 12,000 men, but he reserved the question of sending additional troops "to Vladivostok or elsewhere" until circumstances made it necessary to do so.

American soldiers from the Philippines reached Vladivostok on August 16, 1918. They were reinforced on September 1 by the arrival of Major General William S. Graves and detachments from the United States to bring their total number, by the time of the armistice, to a little under 10,000. With exemplary faithfulness Graves adhered to his instructions not to become involved in the Russian civil war, and he was the only Allied commander not to manifest extreme hostility to the Bolsheviks. He refused to incite counterrevolutionary activity but stuck to his unpleasant and dangerous task of guarding the Trans-Siberian Railroad and protecting the rear of the Czechs. Neither before nor after November 11, 1918 did his men engage in fighting with the Communists.

The associates of the United States were not so restrained. The Czechoslovaks easily overcame the perils that beset them, and by mid-September, 1918, they could have reached Vladivostok. Instead, they joined the anti-Bolshevik factions in western Siberia and participated in the spreading civil war. The British general seemed to think it his mission to stamp out Bolshevism. The Japanese quickly enlarged the scope of their operations. Before the armistice, their forces numbered over 72,000 men, and they had taken up key positions in northern Manchuria, the Amur River basin, and the Lake Baikal area. These developments did not please the State Department any more than they did the Soviet leaders, and from August, 1918, on, Lansing was embroiled in an increasingly acrid controversy with Russia on one hand and with Japan on the other.

In short, what had begun as a wartime expedient to rescue the Czechoslovaks and demonstrate the unity of the coalition against Germany, had become by the armistice a diplomatic headache of monumental proportions. Intervention, moreover, had not prevented Allied interference in Russia's internal affairs, nor had it curbed Japan's advance on the mainland. Once the guns were stilled on the Western Front, Congressmen pressed for the removal of all troops from Russian soil. But at Vladivostok, as at Archangel and Murmansk, it had been easier to go in than to pull out. The last American soldier did not leave Siberia until April 1, 1920, while the Japanese lingered on until October, 1922. Before then, however, the world had turned to peacemaking, and among the weaknesses of the settlement at Paris was the failure to deal adequately with the problems posed by the Russian Revolution and the vacuum created by the temporary eclipse of Soviet power in East Asia.

27

❯❯❯·❯❯❯·❯❯❯·❯❯❯·❮❮❮·❮❮❮·❮❮❮·❮❮❮

Preparations for Peace

IF MILITARY OBJECTIVES remained uppermost in the minds of the American people from April 6, 1917, to November 11, 1918, that concern did not preclude a discussion of the type of world in which they would live after the guns fell silent. If the diplomats subordinated to winning the war the long-term solution of the questions raised by the Russian Revolution and by Japanese ambitions, they nonetheless undertook more preparations for peace than the United States had attempted during any previous conflict. In retrospect, their efforts must be judged inadequate, both within the triumphant coalition and between the executive and legislative branches of the American government, but that failure does not alone explain the disappointments that followed the Great Crusade.

DIPLOMATIC OBJECTIVES

The difficulties facing the peacemakers were overwhelming. Injustices rooted in the past could not be deracinated overnight. Mercy, tolerance, and the wisdom of a Solomon could not be exercised by those who had stood for over four years in the shadow of death. Perfection, even a pale facsimile thereof, could not be expected. Aside from specific issues—such as the evacuation of Belgium, the restoration of Alsace-Lorraine, the disposal of conquered colonies, and the indemnification for appalling damages—four general problems had to be resolved. First, there was the problem of ending the war. Should unconditional surrender be demanded or should the fighting be halted at the earliest possible moment? Second, there was the question of the future of Germany. Where was the golden mean between a lenient peace that permitted Germany to renew the battle in a few years and a harsh settlement that carried within itself the seeds of another tragedy? Third, there loomed the war aims of the coalition. Could the realism of the secret treaties among the Triple Entente, Italy, and Japan be reconciled with the idealism of Wilson's peace without victory? Fourth, there was the dilemma of proposed international organization. What restrictions would sovereign states accept to establish an instrumentality for checking aggression?

Although Wilson's was the dominant voice in defining the diplomatic objectives of the United States, he was neither original in his thinking nor the first to advocate a specific program. Like most Americans after 1914, he was convinced that the Great War had been caused by militarism, imperialism, nationalism, and alliances. He and his countrymen held the rulers less responsible for the cataclysm than the race in armaments, the competition for colonies, the maltreatment of minorities, and the reliance on a balance of power. Hence, they believed an enduring peace must rest on a reduction of armies and navies, a liberation of subject races, an acceptance of self-determination, and a substitution of a concert of nations for the alliance system. Above all, foreign affairs must be democratized. They must cease to be the plaything of allegedly sinister autocrats and be responsive to the supposedly pacific instincts of the people. Secret diplomacy must give way to open covenants, openly arrived at.

Until October, 1918, when unconditional surrender became a pressing issue, the main topic dividing those preparing for peace was a league of nations. Before 1914 only Hamilton Holt and a small band of world federationists talked of such an organization, but with the advent of the war the principle elicited support from such men as Roosevelt, Taft, and Lodge. The most systematic agitation came from the League to Enforce Peace, a private group that was nonpartisan in its operations but Republican in its leadership. Founded on June 17, 1915, and headed by Taft, Holt, and President A. Lawrence Lowell of Harvard University, the League adopted a platform calling upon the United States to join a universal league which would bind its members to submit justiciable questions to a judicial tribunal, to employ conciliation for nonjusticiable disputes, to codify international law through periodic conferences, and to use economic and military sanctions under certain circumstances. Although Root held aloof and Roosevelt remained hostile until 1918, Lodge briefly endorsed the group's aims in May, 1916; but the great triumph was the addition of Wilson to its ranks in that same month.

It was before the League to Enforce Peace that the President first publicly proposed that the United States enter a league of nations. At the annual meeting in Washington on May 27, 1916, he followed Lodge to the rostrum. "We are participants, whether we would or not, in the life of the world," he asserted. "What affects mankind is inevitably our affair as well as the affair of the nations of Europe and Asia." He assured his listeners that the republic would become "a partner in any feasible association of nations." The details of the treaty ending the present conflict were for the combatants to decide, he said; "our interest is only in peace and its future guarantees." Wilson envisaged a universal league, not one confined to great powers, which would secure the freedom of the seas and prevent any war to be begun either contrary to treaty covenants or without warning and a full submission of the causes to world opinion.

Wilson's espousal of a league of nations was no impulsive act. Ever since 1914 he had toyed with a Pan-American pact by which the states of the New World would mutually guarantee their boundaries and independence and then develop effective machinery for settling disputes among themselves. In November, 1915, he had permitted House to assure Grey that he believed an international organization must be set up after the war and that his country would join. Encouraged by the reception given his address on May 27, 1916, the President had inserted in the Democratic platform the assertion that it was the duty of the United States to enter any reasonable association which would protect small nations, promote self-determination, and uphold neutral rights. After his re-election Wilson told Congress in his peace-without-victory speech that a new community of power must replace the old balance of power. As if to forestall criticism over abandoning the principles of isolationism and James Monroe, he concluded on January 22, 1917, by saying: "I am proposing, as it were, that the nations should with one accord adopt the doctrine of President Monroe as the doctrine of the world" and that "all nations henceforth avoid entangling alliances." There can be, he said, "no entangling alliances in a concert of power."

By his peace-without-victory address Wilson provoked the first substantial criticism of his diplomatic objectives. Although he had spoken in generalities, attacks came from three sides. First, there were those like Roosevelt, who saw no substitute for victory on the battlefield and demanded unconditional surrender. Second, there were those like Borah, who revered isolationism and deplored any settlement forsaking it. Third, there were those like Lodge, who wavered on a league of nations but disliked discussing it with a war to be won. But Wilson was not discouraged and returned to his theme on April 2, 1917. Again he spoke of the disinterested nature of American war aims and a new era in international relations. "The world must be made safe for democracy," he asserted, and the surest way was through "a concert of free peoples as shall bring peace and safety to all nations." This formula again drew objections from those who would later oppose the Versailles Treaty.

After the United States became a belligerent, Wilson had to reconcile diplomatic with military objectives. His most notable attempt was a fourteen-point sketch on January 8, 1918, of how the globe could be made a fit place to live in. He began by listing five general points: the end of secret diplomacy, the freedom of the seas in war and peace, the removal where possible of all trade barriers, guaranteed reductions in armaments to the lowest level consistent with domestic safety, and an impartial adjustment of colonial claims giving equal weight to the interests of the people concerned and the claims of their governments. Points Six through Thirteen dealt in broad strokes with territorial matters. Russia, Belgium, and France must be evacuated, with the first being allowed to develop under institutions of its own choosing and the last regaining Alsace-Lorraine. Italy's frontiers should be adjusted along recognizable lines of nationality, while the peoples of Austria-Hungary should enjoy an opportunity for autonomous development. Rumania, Serbia, and Montenegro were to be free, and the Balkan states would make treaties insuring their independence. The Turkish portion of the Ottoman Empire might retain its sovereignty, with the Dardanelles permanently open to all, but the other nationalities were to be accorded a chance for a separate existence. An independent Poland, with access to the sea, was to be erected under international guarantees. The fourteenth point called for "a general association of nations" which would safeguard the political independence and territorial integrity of great and small nations alike.

Wilson timed this address to Congress to take advantage of a momentary rupture in the Russo-German peace talks. The point dealing with Russia was the longest of all, but the Bolsheviks ignored the appeal and accepted the harsh terms of Brest-Litovsk on March 3, 1918. Wilson was then disillusioned as to the ability of the German civilians to curb the military. Henceforth it must be "force without stint or limit," he said on July 4, and he warned "the blinded rulers of Prussia" that they had unleashed powers that would overwhelm them. Yet in saying that "no halfway decision would be tolerable," the President was not abandoning his dream of a just peace. On the contrary, during the rest of the war he reiterated and refined in countless speeches the purposes for which Americans were dying. In thirteen additional points he insisted that people must not be bartered about, that the German military machine had to be destroyed, that the future league should check "every invasion of right" through "the combined power of free nations," and that no special alliances would be permitted to exist in that organization.

In thus proclaiming his diplomatic objectives, Wilson omitted two vital steps. One was his failure to obtain congressional sanction for these war aims. At no time did he ask the legislature to endorse the Fourteen Points or express an opinion on the wisdom of joining a league of nations. The second was his failure to commit the cobelligerents to a firm acceptance of his ideas before the coalition fell apart after the armistice. Not until a week before that event did the Allies adopt as a basis of negotiating the generalities he had set forth on January 8, 1918. Undoubtedly the President's fear of disrupting wartime unity at home and abroad helps explain these miscalculations, but the true reason goes deeper. Wilson was already convinced that only he was sufficiently disinterested and impartial to bring about an enduring peace. He believed that the pressure of world opinion, his own prestige, and the financial dependence of both victors and vanquished upon the United States would enable him to prevail.

THE ARMISTICE NEGOTIATIONS

Between March 21 and July 15, 1918, Germany bent but did not break the Allied line on the Western Front. In spite of four major victories, it was unable to destroy the enemy in the field, and with the counterattack of July 18 the initiative passed to the coalition. From August 8 to September 26 Foch mounted four offensives. The last of these coincided with the imminent collapse of Turkey and Bulgaria and an Austrian appeal to Wilson for an informal discussion of peace terms.

At this juncture the German High Command lost its nerve. Ever since the appointment of Field Marshal Paul von Hindenburg as chief of staff on August 29, 1916, the army had virtually ruled the Reich, and behind Hindenburg's imposing façade stood his dynamic quartermaster-general, Erich Ludendorff. It was Ludendorff who directed the last great advance in 1918 and who began to suspect in the late spring that Germany could not win the war. Not until August 14, however, did he reveal his misgivings to the civilian leaders, and even then he was confident he could keep his forces intact on French soil. But on September 29 he suddenly demanded that the diplomats obtain an immediate armistice. No delay was permissible. "Today the troops are holding their own," he said. "What may happen tomorrow cannot be foreseen." The Chancellor-designate, Prince Max of Baden, wanted a few days in which to prepare the ground, but he yielded when Hindenburg declared "the situation is daily growing more acute." On October 3, 1918, therefore, he asked Wilson to take steps to end hostilities at once and to initiate peace negotiations on the basis of the Fourteen Points and his subsequent addresses.

Actually, there was no imminent disaster, and Ludendorff had no intention of ending the war at that time or under those conditions. The advancing Allies were still deep in France, and no alien foot stood on German soil. What the High Command wished was to secure temporary relief from enemy pressure and to regroup its tired armies in a more advantageous position. Wilson detected the danger in the overture and skillfully thwarted Ludendorff's stratagem. After consulting House and Lansing but not the Allied leaders, he replied on October 8, 1918, that he could not propose an armistice until he was assured that the Fourteen Points were accepted in their entirety, that France and Belgium would first be evacuated, and that the Chancellor spoke for a legitimate civilian government. This insistence disturbed both the High Command and the Foreign Office, for they were still thinking of gaining a breathing space in which to negotiate as an equal or to fight on. Not yet acknowledging defeat, their answer on October 12 contained an unqualified acceptance of the Fourteen Points and an unequivocal claim that Prince Max spoke in the name of the German people; but instead of agreeing to pull out of France and Belgium immediately, it suggested the appointment of a mixed commission to arrange for that operation.

Once again Wilson outmaneuvered his adversary. He steered cautiously between the twin perils of sacrificing the present strategic advantage to his desire for an early peace on the one hand and of delaying that peace by driving too hard a bargain on the other. He bluntly rejected the idea of a mixed commission and declared that the details of the evacuation must be left to the Allied generals. His note of October 14, 1918, ruled out any armistice which did not maintain the existing military supremacy of the coalition. Nor could there be a cessation of hostilities without a prompt abandonment of submarine attacks on passenger ships and the overthrow of the men who had hitherto guided the destinies of the Reich and disturbed the peace of the world.

In Germany, Wilson's second note produced a sense of impending doom. The Kaiser was confronted with abdication, the generals with defeat, and the diplomats with surrender. His gambit having failed, Ludendorff now wanted to fight to the finish, while Hindenburg argued that even with a total rout the terms could not be harsher. But the High Command did not face reality. Morale on the home front had cracked. The mere talk of peace released an overwhelming desire for it. Desertions in the army multiplied; mutterings of a naval mutiny began to be heard. Ludendorff had set in motion forces he could not check. His contradictory predictions had cost him the confidence of his associates, and at long last the civilians grasped control of the government from the discredited military. On October 20, 1918, after a week of confusion and indecision, Germany accepted the conditions laid down by Wilson.

The President turned next to persuading the Allies to grant an immediate armistice and to negotiate a treaty based on the Fourteen Points and his subsequent speeches. The first goal was easier to attain. With the situation on the battlefield brightening steadily, only Pershing wished to fight on, and he received no support from Wilson, Lloyd George, Clemenceau, or Foch. The second task was not so readily accomplished. Although the European leaders could endorse many of America's objectives, their approach differed. First, England, France, Italy, and Japan were bound by treaties, no longer wholly secret, to divide among themselves parts of the German, Austrian, and Turkish Empires. Wilson knew of these pacts but had chosen to ignore them. Second, Lloyd George and Clemenceau did not wish to tie their hands by entering into a contract with the foe. Wilson felt that unless that were done, his peace without victory would degenerate into a victors' peace. Third, the Allies wanted an interpretation of some of the Fourteen Points. Wilson had purposely kept them general, and there was a need to be more specific.

To reconcile these divergences, Wilson sent House to Europe on his fourth wartime mission. The President had handled the bid for an armistice in Washington, but the exact manner in which Germany laid down its arms and gave guarantees of good behavior during the peacemaking had to be settled in France. On October 26, 1918, House joined the Supreme War Council to hammer out the military and naval provisions of the proposed armistice. These obligated Germany, among other things, to withdraw its armies to the east bank of the Rhine, leaving all stores behind; to pull its troops out of Russia, Rumania, and Turkey; to halt all fighting in East Africa; to surrender large numbers of guns, locomotives, and rolling stock as well as 2,000 airplanes and 160 submarines; to send to Allied ports for internment the bulk of its fleet, including ten battleships and six battle cruisers; and to disarm all other surface craft. If these stipulations were complied with, Germany would be unable to renew the war, no matter what happened at the peace conference.

These same inter-Allied discussions witnessed a battle over the Fourteen Points. Lloyd George refused to endorse the freedom of the seas, lest England be deprived of the blockade in future wars. Clemenceau insisted that French civilians be compensated for damage done to their property. Prime Minister Vittorio E. Orlando demanded territory on the east shore of the Adriatic for Italy. The last two men seemed out of sympathy with the league idea and opposed incorporating it in the peace treaty. On October 30, 1918, House warned that if the Allied leaders persisted, Wilson would go before Congress, divulge the terms his associates wished to impose, and ask the legislature whether the United States must continue to fight for those ends. The threat of a

separate American peace was not an idle one, and it resulted in a compromise on November 4. In two brief paragraphs the Allies declared
explicitly that, subject to two qualifications, they were willing to make
peace on the terms laid down in Wilson's address of January 8, 1918,
and the principles enunciated in his later speeches. The first concerned
the freedom of the seas. Since that phrase was open to various interpretations, all parties reserved a right to define it at the peace conference. The second involved reparations. The European statesmen
wanted it understood that Germany's obligation to restore all occupied
territory meant that it would make compensation "for all damage
done to the civilian population of the Allies and their property by the
aggression of Germany by land, by sea and from the air."

Shortly after five o'clock on the morning of November 11, 1918, in
a railway car in the forest of Compiègne, a German delegation signed
the document which ended the Great War. Six hours later the guns fell
silent. Thanks to Wilson, this boon came a year earlier than most experts had anticipated. Thanks to him, Germany did not surrender unconditionally, although the terms of the armistice left it unable to
insure respect for the safeguards the victors had promised. And it is
appropriate to dispel here two myths, one Allied and one German, that
gained wide credence after the war. First, Wilson did not impose a
premature peace upon his associates and thereby deprive them of total
victory. The Allies were free, when on October 23, 1918, they received
word of the enemy's acceptance of Wilson's conditions, to reject a cessation of hostilities. All that the President's diplomacy did was to make
possible an end to the fighting sooner and with fewer casualties than if
the Allies had relied on purely military measures. Second, neither Wilson nor Prince Max's government betrayed the German army. There
was no stab in the back by the civilians, as the Nazis later maintained.
It was the High Command that lost its nerve and set in motion a process which it later could not stop. Unfortunately, Ludendorff made it
appear that the Chancellor was responsible for proposing a needless
armistice while the men at the front still stood unconquered on French
and Belgian soil.

CONGRESS AND THE ELECTION OF 1918

At home, Wilson's handling of the armistice negotiations drew considerable criticism. As in Europe, the initial German overture was
widely regarded as a ruse, and the President's ready response led to
loud cries for unconditional surrender. Many citizens, surfeited with
heavy doses of propaganda, had lost all tolerance. A spirit of ruthless
brutality had entered the country's fiber, as Wilson had predicted.
Congress, moreover, was restive under the President's domination. For

a year it had been content to investigate the conduct of the war on the home front; now the legislature prepared to challenge the executive's control of foreign affairs. On Capitol Hill a series of resolutions, which never passed, opposed a cessation of hostilities until the foe had been disarmed and attempted to prevent any American official from talking peace with Germany prior to an unconditional surrender. Roosevelt joined in these efforts to block Wilson. Blind in one eye and failing in health, embittered and frustrated because he was not allowed to fight in France, grief-stricken over the death in battle of his youngest son, Roosevelt attacked the President unmercifully. On October 14, 1918, he called upon the Senate to repudiate the Fourteen Points. Ten days later he sent a public telegram to three Republican leaders. "Let us dictate peace by the hammering guns and not chat about peace to the accompaniment of the clicking typewriters," it read. "Let us clearly show that we do not desire to pose as the umpire between our faithful and loyal friends and our treacherous and brutal enemies."

Roosevelt could not deter Wilson from paving the way for an armistice and a treaty based on the Fourteen Points, but he did help to lure him into a false step which endangered his subsequent peacemaking. With the congressional elections in the offing and the party in power being criticized for high taxes, the cost of living, and the dislocations of the war, Democratic leaders desperately sought a presidential blessing for their candidates. On October 25, 1918, one day after Roosevelt's telegram, Wilson issued a blanket endorsement. While denying that any party was paramount in patriotism, he did call the Republican minority prowar but antiadministration. Since divided counsels ought not to be risked in such parlous times and since the capture of either chamber would be interpreted in Europe "as a repudiation" of his leadership, he begged the voters to express themselves unmistakably "by returning a Democratic majority in both the Senate and the House of Representatives."

Wilson's October appeal was a blunder. Although neither unjustified nor unprecedented, it was both unnecessary and unwise. With propriety and safety the President might have asked for the election of anyone, irrespective of party, who had supported him in the past and who shared his hopes for the future; but it was extremely dangerous to stake his leadership on the outcome of almost five hundred separate contests, most of which would be determined by local issues. In that course he had little to gain and everything to lose. And lose he did. On November 5, 1918, as he rejoiced in word of the Pre-Armistice Agreement, he was saddened by the verdict at the polls. Exceeding their most sanguine expectations, the Republicans captured both houses of Congress with a margin of 240 to 190 in one and of 49 to 47 in the other. The first represented a gain of about thirty seats; the second, seven. Had the Democrats lost one less senatorial seat, they could have retained control of that body and provided the President with a more sympathetic chairman of the Foreign Relations Committee than Henry Cabot Lodge.

Did the American people in early November, 1918, favor Wilson's peace plans? The mid-term election does not give the answer. But it is clear that on the eve of the Paris Conference, when Lloyd George and Clemenceau were receiving votes of confidence, the President suffered a grievous blow to his prestige. Whether or not it was true, his critics could say, as Roosevelt did on November 26, that "our allies and our enemies and Mr. Wilson himself should all understand that Mr. Wilson has no authority whatever to speak for the American people at this time. His leadership had just been emphatically repudiated by them."

THE PEACE COMMISSION

Among the last preparations for peace was the selection of five commissioners to draft a treaty. Although numerous experts would advise the Paris Conference on technical matters, public attention focused on the top officials. Unless these men were considered to be outstanding and representative, the peacemaking would be conducted under a hostility at home which might jeopardize the final outcome.

From the outset, Wilson was determined to head the American delegation. This decision, so widely criticized at the time and so divergently appraised since, was eminently sound. No one could argue his case more effectively than the President. No one better embodied the aspirations of the war-weary masses everywhere. No one was more trusted by the vanquished or more feared by the victors. This does not mean that his attendance was without danger or harm. Thrust directly into the bargaining arena, subjected to countless personal pressures, deprived of an opportunity for reflection, and cut off from contact with the American people and their lawmakers, Wilson would lose the power that comes with distance and detachment. In Paris, he was simply one of many; a public protest by him would be dismissed as the complaint of a thwarted and disappointed negotiator. In Washington, he could act as the arbiter of freedom; if his commission was balked in matters he deemed vital to a just peace, he could go before Congress and invoke the conscience of all mankind. His decision to attend was a calculated risk, but he took it knowingly and the Versailles Treaty, with all its faults, emerged as a fairer document because he participated directly.

The four other appointments went to Robert Lansing, Edward M. House, Tasker H. Bliss, and Henry White. The first three were logical choices; and although partisan critics dubbed them "Wilson's errand boys," each had a potential contribution to make. As Secretary of State, Lansing was familiar with all phases of foreign policy; his realistic thinking and independent mind could have been of great value—if only he had spoken freely and Wilson had consulted him. As the President's alter ego on four wartime missions, House had more close contacts with leading diplomats abroad than any living American; his skillful negotiation of the Pre-Armistice Agreement had just enhanced his prestige. As permanent military representative on the Supreme War Council, Bliss stood second only to House in firsthand knowledge of conditions in Europe; as former chief of staff, he could speak for the armed forces on matters of security. On the other hand, the selection of White, the sole Republican, astonished Wilson's supporters and outraged his foes. White had served the nation ably in London, Rome, and Paris as well as at Algeciras, where he headed the American delegation. Roosevelt had called White "the most useful man in the entire diplomatic service" during his presidency, while Lodge and Root claimed him as a close friend. But White had been retired since 1909 and wielded no influence in Congress or his party. Many disinterested observers thought that a more prominent Republican, perhaps a senator, should have been picked.

Such advice was easier to give than to follow. The use of senators on the peace commission in 1898 had aroused sharp protests. A more compelling objection for Wilson was that he could not avoid Lodge if he named a Republican senator. A bitter feud between the two men had already developed; each regarded the other as unscrupulous and untrustworthy. Outside of the Senate there were Roosevelt, Taft, Hughes, and Root. Even if the first had not been failing in health, Wilson could not have ignored the vitriol which Roosevelt had aimed at him ever since 1914. The President, moreover, considered Taft as ill-fitted by temperament for diplomacy and Hughes as too inexperienced. Those objections could not be leveled at Root, whose towering reputation, wise counsel, and skill in the art of human relations would have made him a pillar of strength, not only in Paris, but also in Washington when the treaty was before the Senate. But Wilson disliked Root and called him "a hopeless reactionary" whose appointment "would discourage every liberal element in the world." Instead, he first offered the one Republican position to Associate Justice William R. Day, who had not dealt with foreign affairs since 1898, and after his refusal, to White.

With an equal lack of wisdom Wilson ignored the Senate in his final preparations for peace. Although one session of Congress did not end until November 21, 1918, and another began on December 2, the President made no attempt, formal or informal, to solicit advice from his partner in the treaty-making process. He did not even seek its consent for his commissioners but appointed them as executive agents. To be sure, McKinley had done the same thing in 1898 and his own nomination would have raised unprecedented questions, but Wilson seemed not to grasp that the Senate in general and its Republican members in particular were determined to have a hand in the peacemaking. Thus Senator Knox, Taft's secretary of state, asserted on October 28 that Congress alone had a mandate from the people to declare war and to define war aims. Knox was no isolationist. He was prepared to form alliances and join some kind of a league, but on December 3 he introduced a resolution which struck at the heart of Wilson's proposed course of action. Since the war, it said, had been fought to vindicate maritime rights and to destroy the menace of Germany, the peacemakers should confine themselves to those purposes and leave the creation of an international organization to a future conference of all states, belligerent and neutral. Neither that resolution nor another proposing to send a watchdog committee to Paris had been acted upon when Wilson sailed for France the following day, but the tone and temper of the Senate boded ill for the fulfillment of his cherished dream.

28

❯❯❯·❯❯❯·❯❯❯·❯❯❯·❮❮❮·❮❮❮·❮❮❮·❮❮❮

The Treaty of Versailles

SHORTLY AFTER noon on December 13, 1918, as the sun slanted through leaden skies, Wilson landed at Brest to begin a triumphant four-week tour of France, Italy, and England. To the delirious crowds that jammed the streets of ancient cities and ravaged villages he seemed to be the one leader with vision and courage, backed by the vast resources of the dynamic democracy beyond the sea, who was capable of creating a just peace. His mere presence, the first American while president to stand on European soil, presaged a new era in international relations.

THE PARIS PEACE CONFERENCE

It was a new Europe, too, that confronted Wilson. All around, proud dynasties were tumbling, familiar boundaries dissolving, and independent countries emerging. The mighty German Empire, which for four years had held at bay the greatest coalition since the days of Napoleon, lost its Kaiser and succumbed to revolution. In the disintegrating Austrian Empire the Czechoslovaks, Yugoslavs, and Hungarians proclaimed their freedom; the Habsburgs followed the Hohenzollerns into exile; and a republic came into being in Vienna. In Russia, out of whose spacious domains the new nations of Finland, Estonia, Latvia, Lithuania, and Poland had been carved, a bloody civil war raged. In the amorphous Ottoman Empire the Sultan's power in Mesopotamia, Syria, and southeastern Europe was fast ebbing, and it appeared that the last remnant of Turkish sovereignty would be confined to Anatolia.

Harried by these fast-moving events, the statesmen assembled at

Paris early in January, 1919, with many of the vital problems of procedure and organization unresolved. In all countries preparations had been concerned primarily with the contents of the forthcoming treaty, not the methods by which it would be written. Machinery for inter-Allied action did exist, but it had been forged to win a war, not to negotiate a peace. Immediate answers had to be found to numerous perplexing questions. Who should attend the conference? Were all participants to have an equal voice and vote? How much publicity should be risked? Which topics should be handled first? Above all, what kind of a treaty was wanted? Would it be a preliminary draft, to serve as a basis for discussion and negotiation with the Central Powers? Or would it be a final version, to which the defeated foe must consent without change?

In the broadest sense, the Paris Peace Conference lasted from January 12, 1919, until August 10, 1920. It produced five treaties with nations to whom an armistice had been granted, and they were signed as follows: with Germany at Versailles on June 28, 1919; with Austria at St. Germain on September 10, 1919; with Bulgaria at Neuilly on November 27, 1919; with Hungary at Trianon on June 4, 1920; and with Turkey at Sèvres on August 10, 1920. The United States shared in negotiating all except the last, but only the first was submitted to the Senate. Since every issue essential for understanding American foreign policy was contained in the Versailles Treaty, we shall confine our analysis to it.

Prior to May 7, 1919—the date on which the Preliminary Peace Conference technically became the Peace Congress—the participants were of four types. First were the belligerent powers with general interests—England, France, Italy, Japan, and the United States—also known as the Principal Allied and Associated Powers, who attended all sessions. Next came the belligerent powers with special interests—Belgium, the British Dominions, China, Greece, Rumania, Serbia, and thirteen others who had declared war against Germany and its associates—who attended sessions at which questions concerning them were discussed. Third were the powers who had broken diplomatic relations with the foe—four in South America—who attended sessions at which questions interesting to them were taken up. Lastly, there were the neutral nations and states in the process of formation who could be summoned for questions in which they were directly concerned. Only beginning on May 7, 1919, were the so-called enemy powers allowed to take part, and then under severe restrictions.

The work of the Paris Peace Conference was conducted at many levels. The plenary sessions, of which there were fourteen, were formal in character and did little more than ratify decisions already reached. The most dramatic occurred on May 7, 1919, when the Germans appeared to learn the provisions of the treaty, and on June 28, 1919, when the official signing took place. The main labors were carried on in a plethora of councils, commissions, and committees. There were general commissions for labor, reparations, and the League of Nations; there were permanent and *ad hoc* committees to deal with territories, colonies, prisoners, and drafting. But the real source of authority lay in the councils, the first of which—the Supreme Council—was formed on January 12, 1919, by eliminating the military members of the Supreme War Council. The civilian leaders of the United States, England, France, and Italy then agreed to hold informal conversations on matters of substance and procedure before meeting with the lesser powers in the Preliminary Peace Conference. On January 13 representatives from Japan joined the Supreme Council, thereafter known as the Council of Ten. Until March 23 every important decision of the conference had to pass through the Council of Ten.

After Wilson returned from a brief visit to the United States to attend the close of a congressional session, a more expeditious manner of proceeding was devised, and on March 24, 1919 the Council of Four came into being. It was composed of heads of government: Wilson; Lloyd George, the brilliant, dynamic, mercurial, and opportunistic Prime Minister of Great Britain, a master of improvisation; Clemenceau, the aged, blunt, tenacious, and realistic Premier of France, appropriately called "The Tiger"; and Orlando, the amiable, cultured, eloquent, and legalistic Premier of Italy, the only one who could not speak English. The Council of Four reserved to itself the most controversial problems, but it was aided by the foreign ministers, grouped into a Council of Five.

Chronologically, the Paris Peace Conference can be divided into several distinct periods. At the second plenary session on January 25, 1919, it was agreed to incorporate the constitution of an international organization in the treaty itself; from that date until February 14, when the Covenant of the League of Nations was adopted provisionally, that topic claimed most of the attention. Between February 15 and March 14 no major steps were taken. Wilson was absent on his trip to Washington, while Clemenceau was convalescing after an attempt on his life. From March 28 to April 30 the problems of the Rhineland, reparations, the Saar, Fiume, Shantung, and the revised Covenant created a rift within the coalition. During those tense days members of the Council of Four exchanged recriminations, walked out in disgust, and—in the case of Wilson—appealed to the Italian people over Orlando's head. In this period, when stricken with influenza, Wilson made or approved many of the compromises for which he was later so savagely criticized.

With their own deep-seated differences barely reconciled, the victors presented the "Conditions of Peace" to the vanquished on May 7, 1919, the fourth anniversary of the sinking of the *Lusitania*. The day of reckoning had come, and the surly behavior of Foreign Secretary Count Ulrich von Brockdorff-Rantzau destroyed what little chance remained for modifying the harsh terms. In a defiant diatribe, Brockdorff-Rantzau completely alienated not only Wilson, who regretted that this was not a peace without victory, but also Lloyd George, then suffering qualms over the misery the blockade was still causing in Germany. Nor were his manners improved when Brockdorff-Rantzau returned on May 29 to offer an official protest, in the course of which he accused the Allies of violating the Fourteen Points and condemning millions of women and children to death. As a consequence, only minor concessions had been granted when Clemenceau replied on June 16. The unrepentant attitude of the German delegates, he said, showed an utter failure to understand the helpless position of their country and the judgment passed upon it by mankind. There could be no further debate. The foe must signify within five days his readiness to sign the pact as it stood; in default of such a declaration, the armistice would be terminated and the victors would take steps to enforce their terms.

A week of suspense followed. As the Germans hesitated, Foch was instructed on June 20, 1919, to march toward Berlin if no affirmative answer was received by 7:00 P.M. on June 23. That same day the ministry of Philipp Scheidemann resigned rather than give its approval. On June 23, fearing an imminent surrender, the commander of the interned fleet ordered the sea cocks opened; whereupon nine dreadnoughts, five battle cruisers, and many smaller ships sank beneath the icy waters of Scapa Flow. In Berlin, however, there was no relish for dramatic and futile gestures. Crowds surged through the streets with banners saying, "We have had enough; peace, for God's sake." Accordingly, a new cabinet agreed just before the time limit expired to accept the treaty.

On June 28, 1919, exactly five years after the murder at Sarajevo, the final ceremonies occurred at Versailles. This time there was no audible protest and only a brief speech by Clemenceau, but the day was pregnant with meaning for the world in the next two decades. It also marked a milestone in the foreign policy of the United States. On that day Wilson signed not only the Versailles Treaty, envisaging American membership in the League of Nations, but also a defensive alliance with England and France, promising immediate Anglo-American assistance to the French in the event of unprovoked aggression by Germany.

THE MILITARY SETTLEMENT

The French Assistance Treaty, seemingly an incongruous relic of the old order, can be understood only in the light of the total military and territorial settlement at Paris. The Versailles Treaty required that Germany be disarmed so as to make possible "the initiation of a general limitation of the armaments of all nations." Its army could not exceed 100,000 men or employ airplanes, tanks, and poisonous gas. The general staff, historic planning agency and custodian of the Prussian tradition, was to be dissolved. The navy was confined to six predreadnought battleships, six small cruisers, and twelve destroyers. It had to surrender all modern capital ships and do without submarines. The manufacture of munitions was closely restricted.

Of equal importance to France were the provisions intended to curb Germany's power to invade Western Europe. Both Foch and Clemenceau believed the only safe device was to draw a new boundary that would deprive the Reich of Alsace-Lorraine, covered by the Fourteen Points, and the Rhineland. To avoid conflict with the principle of self-determination, the German population west of the Rhine would be constituted into an autonomous buffer state. This plan satisfied neither Wilson nor Lloyd George. After a bitter argument, the last two persuaded Clemenceau not to dismember Germany but to accept instead a fifteen-year occupation of the Rhineland and a treaty of mutual assistance. Just in case the Senate rejected the treaty, France was given the right to extend the occupation period.

Other measures sought to quiet the French passion for security. The entire Rhineland was demilitarized, as was the east bank of the river to a depth of thirty miles. During the occupation period the Allies would hold bridgeheads at Cologne, Coblenz, and Mainz. The Saar basin, adjacent to Lorraine, was entrusted to the League of Nations for fifteen years, with France free to exploit its coal. At the end of that time a plebiscite would determine whether the inhabitants wished to be part of Germany or France. Foch, for one, regarded these precautions as futile. Within a decade the annual flood of German youths reaching military age would be double that in France. Only the broad, swift-flowing Rhine, held by a mighty army, could provide a shield behind which Frenchmen might live in comparative safety. When overruled, the general warned in June 1919: "This is not Peace. It is an Armistice for twenty years."

Where Wilson invoked the principle of self-determination to keep France from dismembering Germany, he looked to the freedom of the seas to check England's interference with the rights of neutrals. An Anglo-American struggle over the second of the Fourteen Points did not materialize at Paris because Wilson came to hope that the League

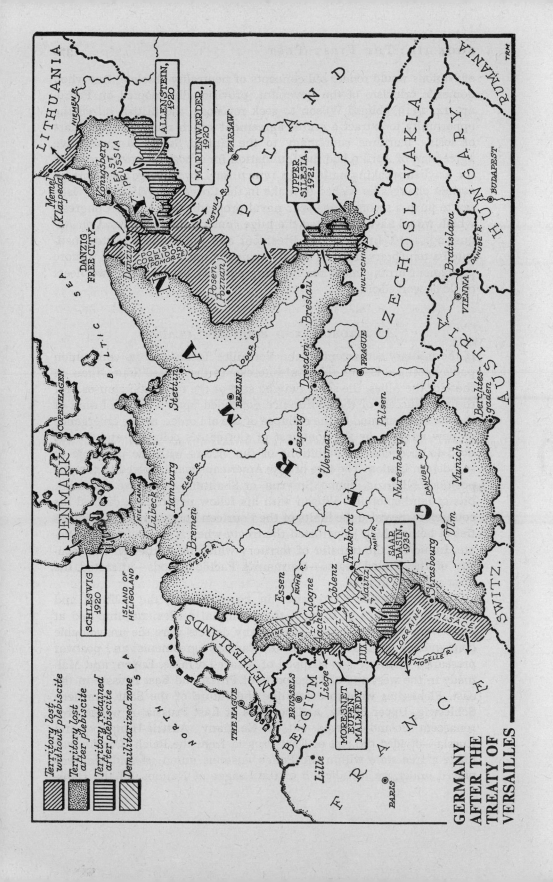

GERMANY
AFTER THE
TREATY OF
VERSAILLES

Territory lost
without plebiscite

Territory lost
after plebiscite

Territory retained
after plebiscite

Demilitarized zone

LITHUANIA

ALLENSTEIN, 1920

MARIENWERDER, 1920

UPPER SILESIA, 1921

POLAND

WARSAW

Memel
(Klaipeda)

Königsberg
EAST
PRUSSIA

NIEMEN R.

VISTULA R.

ODER R.

DANZIG
FREE CITY.

POLISH
CORRIDOR
POMORZE

Posen
(Poznań)

Danzig

BALTIC SEA

Stettin

Breslau

Dresden

HULTSCHIN

CZECHOSLOVAKIA

PRAGUE

Pilsen

RUMANIA

HUNGARY

BUDAPEST

Bratislava

VIENNA

DANUBE R.

AUSTRIA

Berchtes-
gaden

Munich

Danube R.

Ulm

Nuremberg

MAIN R.

Strasbourg

ALSACE

LORRAINE

MOSELLE R.

SAAR BASIN, 1935

DENMARK

COPENHAGEN

SCHLESWIG 1920

ISLAND OF
HELIGOLAND

KIEL CANAL

Lübeck

Hamburg

Bremen

WESER R.

ELBE R.

BERLIN

Leipzig

Weimar

Frankfort

Essen

RUHR R.

Cologne

Aachen

Coblenz

Mainz

RHINE R.

NORTH SEA

NETHERLANDS

THE HAGUE

BELGIUM

BRUSSELS

Liège

Lille

LUX.

MORESNET
EUPEN
MALMEDY

SWITZ.

FRANCE

PARIS

TRM

of Nations would render old concepts of neutrality obsolete. But when domestic criticism of the Covenant, provisionally adopted on February 14, 1919, obliged Wilson to seek revisions, the British seized the opportunity to extract a secret agreement which removed their fears of losing maritime supremacy to the United States. An executive agreement of April 9 laid the foundation for a postwar parity between the English-speaking nations. In return for Lloyd George's support on certain changes he wished to make in the Covenant, Wilson promised not to push a second three-year naval program, then before Congress, which would have duplicated the huge construction authorized on August 29, 1916. In effect, the President and the Prime Minister instituted a temporary truce in naval expansion until a time when a more permanent arrangement for insuring equality between the two fleets could be worked out.

TERRITORIAL AND ECONOMIC CLAUSES

If the military settlement in the Versailles Treaty and its companion pacts impinged less on the vital interests of the United States than on those of the Allies, the same may be said of the territorial clauses. Yet the very success of the conference depended upon a wise solution of the problems created by the collapse of the old order, by the emergence of new nations, by the conquest of Germany's colonies, and by the need to reconcile the ambitions of the victors with the principle of self-determination. The fate of few Americans was involved in the disposition of Danzig, Fiume, Smyrna, or Shantung; but these and other bits of land embroiled Wilson with his fellow negotiators, divided his counselors, revealed the limits of the Fourteen Points, and fed animosities at home which jeopardized the treaty when it was before the Senate. Ironically, the transfer of territory which most affected the security of the United States—Germany's Pacific islands—attracted the least attention in 1919.

Given the wide discrepancy in 1914 between the political and ethnographic maps of Europe, the territorial settlements imposed at Paris were remarkably fair. Their many defects were the unavoidable consequences of ancient injustices, wartime agreements, and postwar pressures. Germany was stripped of Alsace-Lorraine, Eupen, and Malmédy in the west and of large parts of Posen and East Prussia in the east. Plebiscites were to determine the future of the Saar, northern Schleswig, Upper Silesia, and portions of East Prussia. A wedge of a renascent Poland—carved out of Germany, Austria-Hungary, and Russia—divided the rest of East Prussia from the Reich; Danzig was made a free state within the Polish customs union; and Memel was placed under the jurisdiction of the League of Nations. Of the Habs-

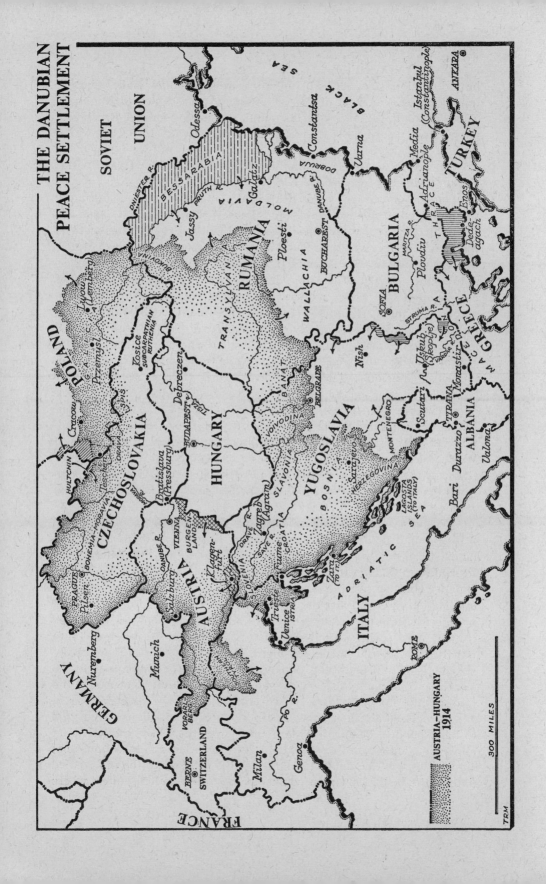

THE DANUBIAN
PEACE SETTLEMENT

GERMANY

FRANCE

SWITZERLAND
BERNE

Nuremberg
Munich
Milan
Genoa
ROME

ITALY

POLAND
Cracow
Lwow
(Lemberg)
Przemysl
GALICIA
SPIS

CZECHOSLOVAKIA
HULTSCHIN
Kosice
Teschen
BOHEMIA
MORAVA
ORAVA
PRAGUE
Pilsen
SUBCARPATHIAN RUTHENIA

AUSTRIA
Debreczen
TISZA
BUDAPEST
Bratislava
(Pressburg)
DANUBE
VIENNA
BURGEN-
LAND
Salzburg
VORARL-
BERG
Klagen-
furt

HUNGARY

RUMANIA
BUKOVINA
TRANSYLVANIA
BANAT
Ploesti
BUCHAREST
WALLACHIA
VOJVODINA
BELGRADE

MOLDAVIA
Jassy
PRUTH R.
DNIESTER R.
BESSARABIA
Galatz
DANUBE R.
DOBRUJA

SOVIET

UNION

Odessa
Constantsa
Varna

BLACK
SEA

BULGARIA
SOFIA
Ploudiv
MARITZA R.
STRUMA R.
Nish

YUGOSLAVIA
Zagreb
(Agram)
CROATIA
SLAVONIA
DRAVE R.
SAVE R.
SLOVENIA
Fiume
Trieste
ISTRIA
Venice
Klagenfurt
BOSNIA
HERZEGOVINA
Sarajevo
MONTENEGRO
Zara
(TO ITALY)
LAGOSTA
ISLAND
(TO ITALY)
ADRIATIC
SEA
Bari
Durazzo
Valona
ALBANIA
TIRANA
Scutari
Monastir
Uskub
(Skoplje)
VARDAR R.
GREECE
MACEDONIA

TURKEY
ANKARA
Istanbul
(Constantinople)
Media
Adrianople
Enos
Dede-
agach
THRACE

AUSTRIA—HUNGARY
1914

300 MILES

TRM

burg dominions, Austria and Hungary were reduced to small, separate, landlocked states; most of the remainder were assigned to Rumania, Yugoslavia—an enlarged Serbia—and the newly formed Czechoslovakia. Italy received the Trentino, the southern Tyrol—a clear violation of self-determination—Istria, and Trieste. Bulgaria ceded its Aegean littoral to Greece; Rumania received Bessarabia from Russia; Turkey yielded Thrace to Greece.

Outside of Europe, fewer territorial transfers occurred. Germany was deprived of all its colonies and Turkey of all its non-Turkish domains; but because of Wilson and several Britons, these lands went to the victors temporarily as mandates of the League of Nations, not permanently as conquests. Mandated territories were of three types. Class A mandates consisted of communities which had reached a stage of development where they required only slight supervision by the mandatory. Of these, Syria and Lebanon became French wards; Iraq, Palestine, and Trans-Jordan the responsibility of Great Britain. Class B mandates comprised lands in Central Africa, where an outsider had to guarantee religious freedom, halt the slave trade, and exercise considerable supervision. All of these were former German colonies, over which Belgium, England, and France assumed control. Class C mandates embraced areas which, owing to their small size, sparse population, or contiguity to the territory of a mandatory could best be administered as part of the latter's domains. In this group, German South West Africa was assigned to the Union of South Africa; parts of New Guinea, the Solomons, the Samoa plus the Bismarck Archipelago, to Australia and New Zealand; the Marshalls, Carolines, and Marianas, to Japan.

Wilson was not entirely pleased by these arrangements. He had wanted small neutrals, such as Holland, to serve as mandatories for lands still unready for self-government. Instead, the distribution conformed roughly to that envisaged by the secret treaties. He knew that Japan would control the islands lying across America's line of communication to Guam and the Philippines. But short of force, he could not eject it from the strategic sites it had conquered, and he had to be content with promises that the islands would not be developed into naval bases. Nor was the President happy over the solution to the vexed question of Shantung. Japan had demanded and obtained in the Versailles Treaty all of Germany's concessions in that province. In the Council of Four on April 30, 1919, and in a press release on May 5, Japan declared an intention to retain only the economic privileges and to hand back to Peking full sovereignty over the leased area at Kiaochow Bay. This sort of restitution angered the Chinese, who would not sign the treaty. The unofficial nature of the pledge and the unspecified date of the restoration aroused suspicions in the United States, where the whole issue was badly distorted. But Wilson could do no more. He had incorporated the League of Nations in the Paris settlement. He had defied France on the Rhineland and Italy on Fiume. He had thwarted Japan's bid for a statement in the Covenant on racial equality; if rebuffed again, Japan might refuse to join the League. In short, the President could say no only so many times. Actually, Japan did live up to its promises, although belatedly; by a treaty of February 4, 1922, control of the Kiaochow leasehold passed to China.

These inescapable compromises on territorial matters cost Wilson dearly in prestige, health, and friendships. In the eyes of many contemporaries, his dream of a peace without victory was tarnished by his abandonment of self-determination in the southern Tyrol, by his alleged desertion of China over Shantung, and by his ostensible cynicism in trying to mask an old-fashioned division of spoils by idealistic talk of trusteeships for backward peoples. His nervous system, weakened by influenza early in April, 1919, was subjected later that month to a strain from which it never fully recovered. A rift in his remarkable collaboration with House appeared simultaneously. Yet the President sincerely believed that whatever shortcomings were inherent in these decisions could be mitigated or eradicated in the future by the League of Nations.

Faith in the unborn League also explains Wilson's acquiescence in the harsh economic clauses of the Versailles Treaty. They required Germany to pay reparations in kind: to give the victors vast numbers of livestock and the bulk of its merchant marine; to build for them 200,-000 tons of shipping annually for five years, and to deliver large quantities of coal for a decade. They bound Germany to bear the costs of the armies of occupation. Most intolerable of all was Article 231 and the monetary reparations that followed. "The Allied and Associated Governments affirm," stated the article which the Nazis later exploited, "and Germany accepts the responsibility of Germany and her allies for causing all the loss and damage to which the Allied and Associated Governments and their nationals have been subjected as a consequence of the war imposed upon them by the aggression of Germany and her allies."

If this "war guilt" clause was an obvious historical exaggeration—more obvious, however, to a later generation than to the one whose sense of justice had been deadened by suffering and propaganda—the financial burdens that came next were sheer economic folly. Yielding to the pleas of Lloyd George, Clemenceau, and Orlando, who had led their countrymen to expect that Germany would shoulder the entire cost of the war, Wilson reluctantly retreated from his determination not to saddle the vanquished with a huge indemnity, such as Prussia extracted from France in 1871. He consented to interpret Germany's liability under the Pre-Armistice Agreement—about $15 billion, according to American estimates, for all damage done to civilians and their property—to include the pension and separation allowance that the Allies would give their veterans. This concession doubled Germany's bill and made it doubtful whether Germany could ever pay. The logic of Wilson's reasoning was not easy to follow; but in a moment of exasperation on April 1, 1919, when caught in a cross fire between his technical experts and the Allied premiers, the President blurted out: "Logic! Logic! I don't give a damn for logic."

Wilson's surrender on two other points made this regrettable decision even more disastrous. His advisers pressed upon him the necessity of fixing in the treaty the total amount of Germany's liability and the exact time period in which it must be met. They argued that the specific figure should be based on the nation's capacity to pay, not the Allied claims, and that the number of years should not exceed thirty. As one of his experts put it: "The enslavement of one generation is enough." But the French and British preferred not to settle those two items at the moment; for, according to Clemenceau, no matter how much he obtained for France, the people would demand twice that sum and call him a traitor. So the questions of the total liability and the exact time period were left to a Reparation Commission, provided for in the treaty and on which the United States would have a representative. Wilson, of course, could not foresee that the Senate's veto would keep an American from sitting on that commission, but he was confident that the League of Nations, as the executor of the Versailles settlement, would minimize and eliminate the inequities which the peacemakers at Paris were unable to avoid.

THE LEAGUE OF NATIONS

What was this League of Nations in which Wilson had sublime faith? Its constitution, or Covenant, formed Part One of the Versailles Treaty and consisted of twenty-six articles. Its purpose, according to the preamble, was to promote international cooperation, preserve peace, and provide security. This was to be done by accepting obligations not to resort to war, by establishing international law as the rule of conduct among governments, and by respecting treaty commitments. Membership was open to any fully self-governing state, dominion, or colony which agreed to the stipulations in the Covenant and was approved by two thirds of the Assembly. A member could withdraw two years after announcing its intention, providing it had met all its obligations. A member could be expelled by the Council for violating its pledges. The original members were the twenty-seven nations, excepting Germany, and the five British Dominions which signed the Versailles Treaty.

Thirteen neutrals were invited to join; Russia, Mexico, and the other Central Powers were not.

The chief organs were the Assembly, the Council, and the Secretariat. The first two were empowered to deal with "any matter within the sphere of action of the League of Nations or affecting the peace of the world." In the Assembly, each member had an equal vote but might appoint as many as three delegates. The Council comprised only nine states. Five permanent seats were allotted to the United States, Great Britain, France, Italy, and Japan. Four temporary seats were filled from the Assembly, which could also enlarge the size of the Council. Except where otherwise provided in the Covenant, decisions in the Council and Assembly required the assent of all members present. The rule of unanimity, however, did not apply to procedural matters or the appointment of investigating committees. The Secretariat was located in Geneva and was headed by a secretary-general. The Council could at any time designate another seat. The Council was also entrusted with formulating plans for a Permanent Court of International Justice, which would decide disputes of an international character submitted to it by the parties involved and which would render an advisory opinion on questions referred to it by the Council or Assembly. There was also to be a permanent commission to advise on military problems and another to examine the reports of the mandatory nations.

Members of the League had to register all treaties with the Secretariat for immediate publication. They might be advised by the Assembly to reconsider old agreements that had become inapplicable or whose continuance endangered the peace. Acceptance of the Covenant abrogated automatically all obligations inconsistent with its provisions, but the Covenant did not affect "the validity of international engagements, such as treaties of arbitration or regional understandings like the Monroe doctrine, for securing the maintenance of peace." Members promised to work for more humane conditions of labor and better industrial relations, for the just treatment of backward peoples under their jurisdiction, for the improvement of health, and for freedom of communication and travel. The League was to supervise the opium traffic, the white slave trade, and the sale of munitions to countries where international control was needed. The Covenant recognized that "the maintenance of peace requires the reduction of national armaments to the lowest point consistent with national safety." To that end the members undertook a full exchange of information about their land, sea, and air programs, while the Council was to draft plans for a mutual reduction of the armed forces.

For the actual settlement of international disputes and the prevention of war, Articles 10 through 17 were of paramount importance. Article 10, which Wilson called "the heart of the Covenant" and without which, he said, "the League would hardly be more than an influential debating society," stated:

> The Members of the League undertake to respect and preserve as against external aggression the territorial integrity and existing political independence of all Members of the League. In case of any such aggression or in case of any threat or danger of such aggression the Council shall advise upon the means by which this obligation shall be fulfilled.

Wilson saw in those words a guarantee, though not an absolute one, for small states against external aggression. But since the Council could only advise upon the means by which the guarantees be made good and since no nation not involved in the dispute could be bound to a policy of reprisals against its will, the President believed he had preserved both the freedom of action of the United States and the power of the Congress to declare war.

Article 11 declared that any war or threat of war was the concern of every member, whether or not that state was immediately affected. By its terms, each member had a right to bring to the attention of the Assembly or Council any circumstance likely to disturb the peace. In an emergency the secretary-general could be requested to summon an extraordinary session of the Council. This article did not, however, obligate members of the League to take positive action.

Articles 12 and 13 provided machinery for inquiry and arbitration, while Article 14 looked toward a Permanent Court of Internationl Justice. Under the first, the Council might be used for both inquiry and arbitration. In the case of inquiry, the Council was required to make its report within six months after receiving the dispute, and the parties were bound not to resort to war until after another cooling-off period of three months. Article 13 defined the kinds of disputes suitable for arbitration: the interpretation of treaties; questions of international law; the existence of a fact which, if established, constituted a breach of an obligation; the nature of the reparation to be made for any such breach. It also required that members carry out in good faith the award rendered and not make war on a member who complied with the award.

Article 15, one of the most complex in the Covenant, attempted to deal with disputes which were not referred to arbitration or the Permanent Court. Such threats to peace would ordinarily be handled by the Council, but they could be sent to the Assembly. If the Council did not succeed in effecting an agreement, it would nevertheless submit a report and make recommendations. If the report was unanimous, except for the parties to the dispute, then the members of the League were obligated not to go to war with whichever one abided by the recommendations of the Council. If, however, the report was not unanimous, the members were free to take such action as they considered necessary to maintain right and justice. This was the so-called "gap in the Covenant" through which members of the League could pass in order to make legal war against each other.

Article 16, the "sanctions article," was intended to deal with members who resorted to war in disregard of their obligations under Articles 12, 13, or 15. Such a state would be regarded as having committed an act of war against all members, and these would at once sever all trade and financial relations with the Covenant-breaking country. In cases of that sort the Council had the duty to recommend what land, sea, or air forces should be contributed by each member to protect the authority of the League. Members were pledged to support one another in imposing these economic sanctions and to permit the passage through their territory of the armed forces of other members engaged in carrying out the recommendations of the Council. The word "sanction," which does not appear in the text, came to mean penalties or coercive measures inflicted collectively to punish violations of the Covenant. They could be economic or military. By 1939 some observers felt that it had been a mistake to oblige members to employ their economic and, if necessary, military power to stop unlawful wars. In 1919, however, most supporters of the league idea thought Article 16 did not go far enough, for it lacked assurances that the members would follow the Council's recommendations to use armed force against an offending state.

Lastly, there was the problem of disputes between members of the League and states outside the organization. Article 17 was intended to cope with aggression by nonmembers and provided machinery whereby they could be invited to accept the obligations of membership in the League for the sole purpose of composing a specific controversy. If such an invitation was accepted, the provisions of Articles 12 through 16 would be applied to the case with whatever modifications the Council deemed wise. If the nonmember rejected the invitation and resorted to war against a League member, then the sanctions contemplated in Article 16 might be invoked against it.

As finally adopted at Paris, the League of Nations represented a compromise between the wishes of Clemenceau and his colleagues on the one hand and those of Wilson, Lloyd George, and their associates on the other. The French wanted it to be an agency to execute and enforce the Versailles Treaty, a sort of continuation with additional members of the Supreme War Council. The Anglo-American statesmen desired a concert of free nations dedicated to promoting international cooperation and preventing war. Both sides recognized that complete equality within the League was impossible and that the smaller states must play a lesser role. Both were prepared to admit Germany and Russia to membership and permanent seats on the Council at a later date, when the first was purged of its lust for world domination and the second of its goal of world revolution. Clemenceau would have preferred a league that possessed its own army, navy, and air force; Wilson and Lloyd George, realizing that such a grant was a political impossibility, argued that the Covenant could be made effective if it commanded wholehearted support and cooperation of the leading members.

Only time could tell how this structure on paper would function in practice, but two things were apparent in 1919. First, the League of Nations could not succeed if two potentially great powers, Germany and Russia, were long excluded. Second, it could not operate as its founders envisaged without a continuing unity, trust, and mutual forbearance among the members of the victorious coalition. Any defection, in body or in spirit, would strike a paralyzing blow, perhaps even a fatal one.

29

A World in Turmoil

IN SINGLING OUT the many shortcomings and injustices of the Treaty of Versailles, critics at the time and since have minimized the obstacles with which the peacemakers had to cope. Neither the Covenant nor the settlement with the Central Powers could be devised in an atmosphere of calm detachment. Hunger, hatred, and revolution stalked through the lands of Europe and Asia. Far-reaching decisions had to be made hastily, often with an imcomplete knowledge of the facts and sometimes with the disturbing realization that another course was wiser but impossible. Before analyzing the defection which hobbled the League of Nations at its birth and helped perpetuate the worst features of the Versailles Treaty, we must describe a world in turmoil from June 28, 1919, when Wilson left Paris, firm in his convictions and confident of victory at home, until March 4, 1921, the day he quit the White House in defeat, broken in body and embittered in spirit.

EUROPE

The signing of the treaty with Germany did not bring peace to Europe or end the work of the conference. Companion pacts with Austria, Hungary, Bulgaria, and Turkey remained to be completed, while unfinished business in reparations and mandates had to be disposed of. On July 1, 1919, the Council of Four became the Council of Heads of Delegations, and the United States participated officially until December 9. By then the Senate had refused for the first time to approve the Versailles Treaty and the Wilson administration had begun to cut its ties with the victorious coalition. This withdrawal occurred just as the League started to function. The initial meetings of the Council and Assembly, the drafting of the World Court Statute, and the organization of permanent Reparation and Mandates Commissions all took place before March 4, 1921.

Ferment was already the order of the day in Western and Central Europe. By promptly ratifying the Versailles Treaty, Germany did on July 12, 1919, secure an end of the wartime blockade and a release of millions from the shadow of starvation. But the Weimar Republic was assailed from both left and right, and on March 13, 1920, a monarchist coup in Berlin forced its ministers to flee to Stuttgart. Communism threatened to engulf truncated Austria and Hungary. In the former, a moderate socialist regime survived to conclude a peace treaty on September 19, 1919, and to place the republic on a reasonably firm footing. In the latter, the Bolsheviks under Béla Kun had seized power in March 1919; not until a year later did conservative elements regain control and restore the monarchy with a vacant throne. The rich new state of Czechoslovakia—formed out of Bohemia, Moravia, and Slovakia—enjoyed a fairly placid existence, except for a border dispute with Poland. The same could not be said of Yugoslavia, the kingdom of the Serbs, Croats, and Slovenes. It had absorbed Montenegro against the will of the ruler and was embroiled in a bitter and sometimes bloody controversy with Italy over Fiume.

Eastern Europe was also in a state of flux. There the trouble maker was newly independent Poland, whose re-creation Wilson had sponsored in order to right old wrongs, to placate domestic groups, and to satisfy France's desire for a friendly nation between Germany and Russia. Although the Versailles Treaty defined Poland's western boundaries, it left the eastern ones undrawn; and Allied suggestions in December, 1919, of a line based on ethnographic considerations failed to meet with favor in Warsaw or Moscow. On April 25, 1920, after direct negotiations had broken down, Poland invaded the Ukraine to settle the matter by force.

RUSSIA AND EAST ASIA

This Russo-Polish War was only one phase of the fighting which convulsed the former empire of the Tsars after November, 1918. Germany's surrender had not eased the plight of Lenin, whose authority to speak for Russia was challenged in every direction. In the Archangel area a Provisional Government of the North Region had been established under Nicholas V. Chaikovsky and was supported by Allied and American troops. From Estonia a White army under General Nicholas N. Yudenich was pushing toward Petrograd. In the south, where the independence of the Ukraine and the Caucasus had been proclaimed, General Anton I. Denikin was driving into the Don and Volga basins, while the French occupied Odessa. Most serious of all was the situation in Siberia, where Admiral Alexander V. Kolchak had assumed control at Omsk and seemed likely to fuse all anti-Bolshevik forces east of the Urals into a single army.

At Paris, Wilson's efforts to deal with the Russian problem had ended in failure. After the armistice he could no longer maintain the convenient fiction that the Bolsheviks were simply tools of the German army, and he realized that the original aim of the Allied intervention in North Russia and Siberia could be perverted into a device for aiding the counterrevolutionaries. Unlike Clemenceau, who thought Lenin's downfall could be accomplished by refusing to deal with him and by imposing an economic blockade, Wilson and Lloyd George urged more positive steps to halt the fighting and to heal a running sore that was poisoning Europe and Asia. On January 21, 1919, the President suggested in the Council of Ten that every faction, spanning the spectrum from Red to White, meet with representatives of the Allies and the new Baltic States at some place other than Paris; and the next day it was agreed to hold such a conference on February 15 at Prinkipo Island off Constantinople. Its sole purpose was to gather information, not negotiate. No formal invitation was sent to Moscow, but the proposal was broadcast by wireless. On February 4, Georgi V. Chicherin, Commissar for Foreign Affairs, accepted in terms which envisaged an immediate cessation of hostilities, but the refusal of the White leaders to sit down with the Reds, together with misgivings in Paris, caused that approach to fail.

Although Wilson acquiesced in excluding the Bolsheviks from the peacemaking, he tried to avoid an intransigent policy. On February 14, 1919, after listening to Winston Churchill ask the Supreme Council to hurry more volunteers and munitions to the counterrevolutionaries, the President urged that all foreign troops be pulled out of Russia. He then sent William C. Bullitt on an unofficial mission to Moscow to gather data on which a more realistic course might be based. Bullitt's report, which reached Paris on March 17, contained a plan by Lenin for an immediate armistice and amnesty on all sides, a prompt Allied withdrawal and stopping of aid to the Whites, and an early lifting of the blockade and discussion of Russia's external debt. Bullitt declared that Lenin was in firm control, that intervention had caused other socialists to rally to his banner, and that the counterrevolutionaries were wholly dependent on outside help. He was convinced that the Communists wanted peace and that this plan should be accepted as a basis for negotiation. Bullitt's plea won some adherents in Anglo-American circles, but the Council of Four never seriously considered the Bolshevik proposals.

Several factors explain why Lenin's offer was ignored. By the end of March, 1919, the conference had entered the crisis stage, and Wilson was more concerned with the revised Covenant, the Rhineland, reparations, Fiume, and Shantung than with pacifying Russia. Béla Kun's seizure of power in Hungary raised the specter of communism in Central Europe, while Admiral Kolchak's advance west of the Urals led wishful thinkers to feel he might soon reach Moscow or join the Whites around Archangel. Wilson was gradually persuaded to give material aid to Kolchak, who had the advantage of being both anti-Bolshevik and anti-Japanese. The President did insist upon prior guarantees that the admiral, once in control, would call a freely elected constitutent assembly, recognize the Tsarist debt, seek Russian membership in the League, and adjust all boundaries by peaceful means. Kolchak's vague compliance with these stipulations was accepted in Paris on June 12; immediately thereafter orders went out to speed guns and munitions to the government at Omsk. The question of extending recognition was held in abeyance.

Actually, the Allied move was too little and too late. Kolchak had reached his furthest point west of the Urals in May, 1919, and was then retreating into Siberia. Men alone could save him, and there Wilson drew the line. Indeed, all American troops had left North Russia by June; and when the British followed suit, the Bolsheviks recovered Archangel. Elsewhere the Red Army checked the forward progress of Denikin in the Ukraine and of Yudenich before Petrograd. In November it drove Kolchak out of Omsk. As the admiral's forces melted away and the Bolsheviks pushed east of Lake Baikal, a clash with the Americans guarding the Trans-Siberian Railroad became a distinct possibility. Then, on January 9, 1920, Washington announced that a complete withdrawal would soon begin and by April 1 the last doughboy had sailed from Vladivostok.

Thus ended the dual intervention which was to embitter Soviet-American relations for years to come. To the Russian propagandist, the landings at Archangel and Vladivostok and the material help to Kolchak would always look like a capitalist plot to strangle communism at its birth. Wilson, of course, was not so motivated, though some of his subordinates were; but except to deny Murmansk to the Germans, the operations did no good and much harm. The rescue of the Czechoslovaks turned out to be a farce. The steps to aid Kolchak were belatedly taken and inadequately implemented. The hope that joint action might restrain Japan was not realized. Particularly in Siberia, American policy fell between two stools, although, given the origins of the undertaking and the more pressing problems elsewhere, it is hardly surprising. The dilemma was aptly summarized by a contemporary who remarked that "some might have liked us more if we had intervened less, that some might have disliked us less if we had intervened more, but that, having concluded that we intended to intervene no more nor no less than we actually did, nobody had any use for us at all."

Opposition to recognizing Russia hardened during 1920. The invading Poles, at first uniformly victorious, were driven back in August to Warsaw and then saved only by substantial French aid. A treaty of October 12 drew a preliminary boundary. Freed from external threats, the Bolsheviks stamped out the last pocket of counterrevolutionary resistance in the Crimea, and on November 14 the great civil war ended. Acceptance of the Lenin regime, however, did not follow. Already on August 10 Secretary of State Colby had set forth, in words replete with friendship for the Russian people and hostility toward their rulers, a three-point policy. First, the United States would oppose all foreign interference in Russia's domestic affairs. It would not help reactionary movements, but it did expect the Bolsheviks to be overthrown from within. Second, it would continue to uphold the territorial integrity of Russia. It believed that, save for Finland, ethnic Poland, and Armenia, Russia was entitled to the frontiers of 1914. Third, the United States would not enter into diplomatic relations with the dominant group in Moscow. That Lenin and his associates governed without the consent of the people, Colby said, was "an incontestable fact." They represented "the negation of every principle of honor and good faith, and every usage and convention, underlying the whole structure of international law." So long as the Bolsheviks were "determined and bound to conspire against our institutions," Colby concluded, there could be no recognition.

With Japan, the tensions generated at Paris were fed by fresh irritants. The most publicized question was of whether the island of Yap in the western Carolines should be included in Japan's mandate. Because Yap was a junction point on one of the two transpacific cable routes, Wilson had urged that it be placed under international control, but his proposal was not made part of the record when the Allies named Japan as the mandatory of the Caroline group. Hence the American protest of November 9, 1920, entered a month before the Council of the League approved the assignment, was legally weak; but it created friction for another fifteen months. The most troublesome issue, however, was Japan's slowness in restoring Kiaochow to China and in evacuating its troops from Russian soil. No sooner had the last American left Siberia than the Japanese military exploited two incidents to justify occupying key points in the Maritime Province and Sakhalin, from which they did not withdraw until October, 1922, and May, 1925, respectively.

THE MIDDLE EAST AND THE NEW WORLD

During these years of turmoil some Americans realized for the first time the importance to them of the Middle East—that vast area stretching from Egypt and Turkey to India.[1] Although the United States did not declare war against the Ottoman Empire and thus did not sign the Treaty of Sèvres, it was concerned with the fate of the Sultan's domains. Recent experience had shown the importance of petroleum to industry and the fleet. The oil-rich lands of Persia, Mesopotamia, and the Arabian Peninsula assumed a new significance. Already refiners and the navy were bringing pressure for a more active diplomacy in a region which hitherto had interested only missionaries and archeologists. Then, too, Wilson had tentatively endorsed the Balfour Declaration of November 2, 1917, favoring the establishment in Palestine of a national home for the Jewish people. Finally, the formation of Transcaucasian republics along the Turkish frontier and the fighting which took place there in 1918–19 revealed the strategic link between the Middle East and the Soviet Union.

The United States did not participate in choosing mandatories for the Middle East. The distribution of Class A mandates was agreed upon at San Remo on April 25, 1920, where the American ambassador to Italy was present simply as an observer. That same day the victorious coalition invited the United States to accept a mandate over the new republic of Armenia, which Colby had just recognized. Although Wilson asked Congress on May 24 to empower him to undertake the trust, the Senate denied him the authority on June 1 by a vote of 52 to 23.

Closer to home, relations with the nations of the New World were comparatively placid between 1919 and 1921. The United States continued to keep troops in Nicaragua, Haiti, and the Dominican Republic and to maintain its special position in Cuba and Panama. The treaty with Colombia was still pending, but the death of Roosevelt on January 6, 1919, improved its chances for passage. Sixteen of the twenty states in the Western Hemisphere decided to join the League of Nations, but that fact did not seem likely to complicate the inter-American peace machinery.

Only Mexico posed a serious diplomatic problem at the moment the Versailles Treaty was before the Senate. The source of trouble was an article in the constitution of 1917 which reserved to the state all subsoil resources. The question for foreign owners of petroleum and mineral deposits was whether the rule applied retroactively and, if so, whether there would be expropriation with compensation or outright

---

[1] As used today, the Middle East refers to the nations of Turkey, Egypt, Syria, Lebanon, Israel, Jordan, Iraq, Iran, Saudi Arabia, Yemen, and the sheikdoms of the Persian Gulf.

confiscation. President Carranza's equivocation on the issue disgusted Lansing and led the expanding oil interests, speaking through Senator Albert B. Fall, Republican of New Mexico, to demand protection. The kidnaping of an American consul in November, 1919, revived talk of intervention, and on December 3 Fall introduced a resolution requesting Wilson to withdraw the recognition previously accorded to Carranza. Six days later the ailing President replied, vigorously opposing the measure as an encroachment on the powers of the executive. He had no relish for further adventures below the Rio Grande, and the release of the consul caused the crisis to subside. Fresh difficulties soon arose. In May, 1920, Carranza was killed after a revolution begun by three of his aides. The Wilson administration refused to recognize Adolfo de la Huerta as the provisional successor, on the ground that he had gained office by illegal means. It also left to the Harding cabinet the question of recognizing Álvaro Obregón, who was elected president on September 5, 1920.

THE AMERICAN SCENE

From such a world in travail the American people turned to more immediate tasks at home. The question of accepting the Versailles Treaty was only one of many pressing problems they had to resolve between June, 1919, and March, 1921. The sudden end of a war which had been expected to last another year necessitated a hasty demobilization of men, industry, agriculture, and spirit. The first of these was the easiest to effect. The demobilization of industry led to canceled contracts, unchecked inflation, a brief boom, and a sharp depression that by late 1920 caused widespread unemployment. The demobilization of agriculture and the consequent withdrawal of supports sent prices tumbling, led to the accumulation of surpluses, and resulted in the end of two decades of prosperity on the farm. The demobilization of emotions meant the relaxation of wartime passions, which resulted in turning hatreds marshaled against the foe upon alleged enemies at home. Economic uncertainty, labor unrest, race tension, and mass hysteria provide the background for the battle in America over the peace settlement.

For the Senate, the period from Wilson's departure for Paris on December 4, 1918, to the tentative approval of the Covenant on February 14, 1919, was one of watchful waiting. It could do little to influence events, but its criticism of the President mounted steadily. Originating in the sweeping wartime powers wielded by the executive, its resentment fed upon his unprecedented action in attending the conference, his unforgivable slight in not consulting the upper house before he left, and his unexpected decision in remaining abroad as the negotiations dragged on. Hostility was clearly evident during his return to the United States from February 24 to March 4, 1919. A dinner at the White House on February 26 for the Foreign Relations Committee failed to effect a meeting of minds. Borah refused to be present lest his freedom be restricted by any confidential information divulged there. Lodge thought Wilson's report was "anything but good," while the outspoken Brandegee told reporters he felt that he had been "wandering with Alice in Wonderland" and had "had tea with the Mad Hatter." Such remarks did not encourage Wilson to seek cooperation or to offer concessions.

How sharply lines were drawn was revealed before the President sailed again for France. Late on March 3, 1919, as the old Congress was dying, Lodge presented a resolution or "round robin" which Brandegee had suggested. Signed by more than a third of the senators who would deal with the treaty subsequently, it declared that the Covenant, in its present form, "should not be accepted by the United States." It further demanded that peace with Germany be concluded before any more attention was paid to the League. For this challenge to his basic strategy Wilson had a prompt and fighting reply. Speaking in New York the next day, just before embarking, he promised that when the treaty came back the Covenant would be in it and tied by so many threads "that you cannot dissect the covenant from the treaty without destroying the whole vital structure." The peace structure would not be vital without the League of Nations, he concluded, "and no man is going to bring back a cadaver."

Despite this bravado, Wilson realized that some changes in the Covenant were imperative. From March 14, 1919, when he resumed talks with Lloyd George and Clemenceau, until April 28, when a revised version was adopted by the conference, the President strove to meet some of the objections raised by such moderate Republicans as Taft, Root, and Hughes. Root became the spokesman of the group. Although he believed Wilson should have called the Senate into special session to discover precisely what amendments it desired, he yielded to the pleas of Henry White to put his own thoughts on paper. On March 26, 1919, Root suggested that the Covenant be altered to insure revision after five years, to give more prominence to arbitration, to emphasize the codification of international law, and to place the Monroe Doctrine and other domestic policies beyond the authority of the League. Most important of all, Root advised that the obligation under Article 10 be limited in duration, so as not to freeze the territorial settlement. Some of these ideas Wilson tried to follow, but he would not modify Article 10. The changes he did obtain failed to satisfy even the moderates who, not being on the scene, grossly underestimated the President's difficulties.

On May 19, 1919, as the revised Covenant was still being scrutinized, the new Congress assembled. Thanks to their two-vote margin in the Senate, the Republicans could make Lodge chairman of the Foreign Relations Committee. The League issue, however, cut across party lines, and by the time Wilson returned four groups were discernible. First, there were those who would accept the treaty without change. This group, later known as the Non-Reservationists, consisted of forty Democrats and one Republican—Porter J. McCumber of North Dakota. Its spokesman was Hitchcock of Nebraska, former chairman of the Foreign Relations Committee. Second, there were those who would accept the treaty with only minor changes. This group, later known as the Mild Reservationists, consisted of thirteen Republicans. Its guide was Frank B. Kellogg of Minnesota, a future secretary of state. Third, there were those who professed to favor the treaty but asked for major changes. This group, later known as the Strong Reservationists, consisted of twenty-one Republicans and four Democrats. It looked to Lodge for leadership and included Harding. Historians still debate whether Lodge and others in this bloc really wanted the treaty to pass, even with substantial modifications, or whether they supported reservations in order to kill the treaty. There was no doubt, however, where the fourth group stood. The Irreconcilables, as they were called, consisted initially of fourteen Republicans and three Democrats. They opposed the treaty in any form so long as it contained the Covenant. The most effective Republicans were Borah, Knox, Brandegee, and Johnson; the most effective Democrat was James A. Reed of Missouri.

In organizing the Foreign Relations Committee, Lodge neglected the second group. The Republican majority was entitled to ten seats, six of which were held by incumbents. Of these, one was a Strong Reservationist, one a Non-Reservationist, and four were Irreconcilables. Of the four newcomers, two were Strong Reservationists and two were Irreconcilables. No Mild Reservationist was named. Of the seven Democrats, six were Non-Reservationists and one a Strong Reservationist.

It is impossible to say with scientific accuracy how the people stood in June, 1919, on the Versailles Treaty. A few generalizations can be made. Then, as later, attention focused on the Covenant. For the idea of a league of nations there was widespread enthusiasm. Wilson and Taft had persuaded many educators, clergymen, editors, and other articulate groups that only through an international organization could future wars be prevented. The man in the street was emotionally prepared by recent experience to accept American membership; but the break with tradition must be made quickly, without prolonged debate, lest the spirit of sacrifice engendered in 1917–18 disappear. Yet a close examination of the League's structure was the very thing Wilson had avoided before 1919, and the pioneer Covenant was vulnerable to both distortion and legitimate criticism. Furthermore, as it became known how often the President had been compelled to compromise at Paris on the military, territorial, and economic clauses, there was a reaction among his liberal supporters who saw in the articles on reparations, mandates, and boundaries and in the French Assistance Treaty a perpetuation of prewar evils. On politics, this fact should be kept in mind. Although many Republicans were angered by Wilson's monopoly of the peacemaking, partisan opposition was not foreordained. After all, the Republicans had guided the nation through its emergence as a world power, and before 1914 they had been more favorable to international cooperation than the Democrats.

Actually, in June, 1919, the Republicans were badly split. To Lodge fell the difficult task of holding together the divergent views of Borah and Knox on one extreme and of Taft and McCumber on the other. A frontal attack on the treaty would destroy party unity, yet the critics must be satisfied. In his predicament Lodge called upon Root to devise a plan which all could support, and this was done in Washington that same month. Realizing the impossibility of securing further changes at Paris, Root proposed that the Republican senators approve the treaty subject to certain reservations. That is, instead of asking Wilson to obtain additional amendments and thus reopen controversies twice compromised, he would have the upper house, in giving its consent, simply express its understanding of obscure passages in the text and disclaim an obligation to honor objectionable articles. By this approach —the same Root had advocated for dealing with Taft's arbitration agreements in 1911—the concurrence of the other signatories could be assumed unless they entered a formal protest during the process of ratification.

Root's reservations were three in number. One was intended to clarify the procedure for quitting the League. A second was designed to place the Monroe Doctrine and other purely American questions beyond the jurisdiction of the Council and Assembly. The third would free the United States from any commitment under Article 10. Root believed that the "heart of the Covenant" was undesirable because the American people were not yet ready to honor it in time of crisis. He incorporated these three reservations in an open letter, which he drafted with the aid of Lodge, Knox, and Brandegee. Published on June 22, 1919, it declared that the revision of the Covenant had gone far enough. Since, however, that document contained undesirable features and since time did not permit further negotiations, the Senate should accept the Versailles Treaty with these safeguards. Root hoped his recommendations might provide a common ground for all Republicans. Whether they would and how Wilson might view them were two momentous questions.

To answer to the second came first, and very quickly. On June 25, 1919, a cablegram from the President called ratification with reservations the equivalent of rejection. Wilson was probably correct in regarding two of Root's proposals as amendments rather than reservations, but whether he was wise in taking a stand publicly before sampling opinion in America was another matter. Taft, who wished him well, thought he had "better wait until he gets home before he attempts to decide what course is best." But even before leaving Paris on June 28, Wilson had decided. His mood was grim and unyielding. Obviously he regretted some of the concessions he had made at the conference; rightly or wrongly, he blamed House for many of them. The latter, he felt, had been too eager to sacrifice everything for the League of Nations. Hence, when the colonel bade him farewell at the railroad station and urged him to meet the Senate in a conciliatory spirit, the President replied pointedly, his jaw set: "House, I have found one can never get anything in this life that is worth while without fighting for it." The two old friends shook hands and parted, never to meet again.

30

The Battle in America

ON JULY 10, 1919, Wilson laid before the Senate the Treaty of Versailles. Confident of success, he avoided a detailed exposition but offered instead to meet with the Foreign Relations Committee at any time. The League of Nations, he did say, had become a "a practical necessity"; and while the treaty was "not exactly what we would have written," its compromises violated no basic principles. The real issue was whether the United States could refuse to accept the moral leadership of the world. "The stage is set, the destiny disclosed," he concluded. "We cannot turn back. We can only go forward, with lifted eyes and freshened spirit. . . . America shall in truth show the way. The light streams upon the path ahead, and nowhere else."

THE FIRST VOTE IN THE SENATE

The Senate's handling of the peace treaty was as novel as the document itself. Various sections had been openly discussed while the President was still in Paris. The text was inserted in the *Congressional Record* prior to the signing at Versailles. The French Assistance pact was printed without anyone's waiting for Wilson to send it in. For the first time in the history of treaties the Foreign Relations Committee examined witnesses in public hearings.

A majority of that committee wished to delay action as long as possible. A prompt vote on the broad issue posed by the peace settlement would undoubtedly be more favorable than one taken after each article had been subjected to what Lodge called "pitiless publicity." Those desiring substantial changes in the Covenant or a complete rejection hoped that an extended inquest might uncover discrepancies or obscurities, reveal differences within the American delegation, and pander to disgruntled interest groups in the United States. For that reason Lodge had the 264-page document read word by word beginning on July 14, 1919. Certainly, it was imperative that the Senate deliberate fully before breaking so sharply with tradition, but to spend a fortnight in such a way was not the wisest use of its time. Worse yet, the prevailing attitude, as one observer put it, was not of "men intent upon a sympathetic examination" of the Covenant but rather like "a body of the Inquisition hunting through an Erasmian pamphlet for heterodox utterances, or a gimlet-eyed church committee bent upon convicting the parson of heresy."

Six weeks of public hearings opened on July 31, 1919. Wilson and Lansing were the most prominent witnesses; the other commissioners were still in France. The Secretary's testimony on August 6 hurt the President, for it made clear that he had been ignored both before and during the conference and that he disliked the Shantung solution and much of the Covenant. The questioning which Wilson eagerly sought took place at the White House on August 19. It centered on Article 10 and Japan's prior commitments from the Entente. Although the executive spoke mostly with candor and in good temper, he persuaded no skeptics and did lie about the time when he learned of the secret treaties. Most of the men heard, however, were more intent on inflaming passions outside the Senate than on shedding light within. For political reasons, if no others, Lodge and his colleagues listened to witnesses who pleased German-Americans by deploring violations of the Pre-Armistice Agreement, who delighted Italian-Americans by denouncing Wilson's refusal to yield on Fiume, and who aroused Irish-Americans by condemning his failure to free Erin.

As the hearings dragged on, Wilson realized that he was losing ground. The initial sympathy for the League lessened. The opposition held the initiative and monopolized the headlines. From the White House it was difficult to explain the Covenant to the man in the street and to combat the endless stream of distortions. Although he had conferred with individual Mild and Strong Reservationists and had told the Foreign Relations Committee he would accept purely interpretive reservations that did not require the consent of the other signatories, the President feared that he lacked a two-thirds majority. But he had one recourse—a direct appeal to the people. Once properly informed, he believed, they would rise in righteous wrath to smite the forces of selfishness and evil. To be sure, his appeal of October 25, 1918, had backfired and his health, undermined at Paris, might not withstand an arduous speaking tour. In fact, his doctor warned that he could endanger his life. But such arguments only strengthened his determination to stump the country. What consideration was more important than the League? What was one man's survival compared to the millions who would perish in a future war?

Leaving Washington on September 3, 1919, while the Foreign Relations Committee spun out its hearings, Wilson headed into the upper Mississippi Valley, worked his way through the northern Great Plains, crossed the Rockies into the Pacific Northwest, traveled down the California coast, and started homeward through Nevada, Utah, and Colorado. In twenty-two days he covered over 8,000 miles, delivering thirty-two major addresses and eight minor ones. Everywhere he spoke, enormous crowds responded to his impassioned oratory which, for sheer emotion, fervor, and imagery, surpassed anything he had said before.

Three basic ideas pervaded these speeches. One was the value of Article 10, the clause on which his critics concentrated and which some would eliminate. A second was the impact of League membership on the American constitutional system. The last was the indispensability of that membership for world peace. Article 10, Wilson said at St. Louis on September 5, 1919, was the "logical center of the whole system." It would not involve the United States in perpetual wars to keep the peace; on the contrary, it would greatly reduce, though not entirely prevent, disputes among nations. Recent experience had shown that the republic would be dragged into any major conflict, whether or not it belonged to a league. As to minor hostilities which did not directly concern the American people, the Council would call upon members nearest the scene of trouble. "If you want to put out a fire in Utah," the President argued at Salt Lake City on September 23, "you do not send to Oklahoma for a fire engine." The President did not deny that membership in the League would impinge upon the Constitution, but he repeatedly attacked the notion that Congress would lose the power to declare war. In disputes to which the United States was not a party, he reminded his listeners, it could veto in the Council motions to use armed force. If the United States was a disputant, it was always free to defend itself. In short, the legislature's chief prerogative remained unimpaired.

Wilson emphasized how vital American participation was to the League. Without support from every great power, the organization would be unable to curb aggressors. Yet the United States also needed the League's system of collective security. Peace in the twentieth century was indivisible. Nations could no longer live unto themselves. Each must make sacrifices, but they were trifling compared to what another war would entail. Should the Covenant be rejected, Wilson warned on September 5, 1919, the "nightmare of dread" which lay upon the nations in the past would return; "and there will come sometime, in the vengeful Providence of God, another struggle in which, not a few hundred thousand fine men from America will have to die, but as many millions as are necessary to accomplish the final freedom of the peoples of the world."

Fearful of losing the initiative, the committee finally released three reports on September 10, 1919. Nine Republicans—three Strong Reservationists and six Irreconcilables—recommended that the treaty be approved with forty-five amendments and four reservations. They decried the need for haste; no other major power had yet ratified. They denied that amendments were impractical; the peace conference was still sitting. "The other nations," they asserted, "will take us on our own terms, for without us their League is a wreck." Six Democrats submitted a minority report urging consent without change. They praised the settlement, argued that Germany was not obliged to accept a revision, and accused the majority of trying to kill the treaty by subterfuge. One Democrat would not sign any report, while McCumber drafted his own. Abandoning the Non-Reservationists—a straw in the wind—the North Dakota Republican wanted to pass the treaty with six interpretive reservations. He flayed the majority for its ill-concealed hostility to the President and the minority for its ill-advised loyalty. He asked both sides to place the noble purposes of the League above politics and personalities.

The issue was now joined, but how a battle fought along those lines would have ended we shall never know. Three weeks of grueling campaigning had drained Wilson's last reservoir of stamina. Visibly tired and blinded by recurring headaches, he spoke at Pueblo, Colorado on September 25, 1919, and concluded by promising that the truth of justice and liberty was "going to lead us, and through us the world, out into pastures of quietness and peace" such as had never been dreamed of before. That night his exhaustion was so apparent that the remainder of the tour had to be canceled, and he was rushed back to Washington. Four days after his return he suffered a severe stroke that paralyzed the left side of his face and body. His life hung in the balance for two weeks; later his recovery was only partial. Never again would his voice sway audiences by its inspired eloquence; never again would he be physically able to steer his program through the Congress.

With one partner in the treaty-making process felled, the other carried on. Between October 2 and November 6, 1919, a combination of Non-Reservationists and Mild Reservationists defeated every motion to alter the text of the Versailles Treaty. The margin was usually about fifteen, but on one occasion it was a scant two. Amendments having been ruled out, the Senate turned to reservations and by November 15 it had placed fourteen of these, plus a preamble, in the resolution of ratification. This was done by votes ranging from 48 to 59. Ominously, no reservation received the support of two thirds of the Senators present.

Of the fourteen reservations, only two dealt with the treaty as distinct from the Covenant. One withheld American consent from the Shantung settlement (No. 6); the other permitted United States citizens to press certain claims against Germany (No. 12). As to the Covenant, three reservations were intended to clarify the process of withdrawal (No. 1), the exclusion of domestic legislation from the jurisdiction of the League (No. 4), and the immunity of the Monroe Doctrine from interpretation by or reference to the Council (No. 5). Three asserted the right of the United States to rearm if invaded, a League agreement notwithstanding (No. 10); to allow its citizens, under some conditions, to trade with those of a nation against whom sanctions had been imposed (No. 11); and to refuse to be bound by an action of the Council or Assembly in which Great Britain and its dominions cast more than one vote (No. 14). The remaining six sought to safeguard the authority of Congress. Thus the legislature alone could decide whether the United States should accept a mandate (No. 3), provide by law for the appointment of representatives to the Council and Assembly (No. 7), permit the Reparation Commission to check German-American trade (No. 8), vote funds for carrying on the work of the League (No. 9), and determine whether the country should join the International Labor Organization (No. 13).

These thirteen reservations maintained prerogatives, removed uncertainties, and stated the obvious. Some were unnecessary, others were harmless, a few may have been helpful. All reflected the Senate's insistence upon sharing in the peacemaking and its fear the Covenant had gone too far. Those likely to cause trouble with other signatories were numbers five, six, and fourteen. Actually, the spirit, not the substance, made most of these interpretations objectionable—the querulous, suspicious, and begrudging terms in which they were couched. This spirit was most manifest in the preamble and the second reservation. The latter limited Article 10 by disclaiming an obligation to preserve the territorial integrity or political independence of any country or to employ the armed forces of the United States under any article in the treaty unless Congress in a particular case "shall by act or joint resolution so provide." Thus the legislature's war-making authority remained inviolate. As to the preamble, it required acceptance of the reservations by three of the four Principal Allied Powers through an exchange of notes, not silent acquiescence, before the treaty could go into effect.

But the preamble and second reservation did more than depart from the spirit of the Covenant. They differed basically in substance and were, therefore, unacceptable to Wilson. Article 10, he believed, was vital to the League and must not be watered down. The preamble now contained a requirement which even Root had not envisaged in June. The President did not oppose interpretive reservations, as distinct from amendments in disguise, and before leaving on the western tour, he had drafted four of his own. Three covered the same ground— though not in the same language—as numbers 1, 4, and 5. Wilson's version of the second, however, did not disclaim an obligation to uphold Article 10, but rather made it clear that a Council vote to use armed force was only a recommendation which left each member free to act as it saw fit. These four, which did not need explicit consent by the other parties, might have been acceptable to all of the Mild and some of the Strong Reservationists if they had been offered before those senators had agreed to the fourteen sponsored by Lodge. The reason for the delay was Wilson's illness, which imposed insuperable obstacles on his floor leader. Only twice did Hitchcock see the President before the first vote on November 19, 1919, and he feared to tell his stricken leader the whole truth. Yet Hitchcock must share with Wilson the responsibility for risking a defeat of the treaty with reservations in the hope that a wave of popular indignation would bring about an unencumbered treaty. In the Democratic caucus he echoed Wilson's argument that the fourteen reservations would nullify and stultify the Versailles settlement.

On November 19, 1919, the Senate voted. Four futile ballots were held. First, the Versailles Treaty with the fourteen reservations lost by a count of 39 to 55. Thirty-five Republican Reservationists—including Lodge, Harding, Kellogg, and McCumber—and four Democratic Reservationists could not muster even a simple majority against thirty-nine Democratic Non-Reservationists and sixteen Irreconcilables, all but three of whom were Republicans. Next, a motion to take up the Hitchcock reservations was defeated by a tally of 41 to 50. Then, the treaty with the fourteen reservations was beaten again by a margin of 41 to 51. Save for three more Democrats joining the Reservationists, the ranks stood firm. Finally, the treaty without reservations failed to pass, the tally being 38 to 53. Only thirty-seven of the forty-seven Democrats and one of the forty-nine Republicans—McCumber— went on record for the treaty as drafted. With the Non-Reservationists and the Reservationists being about equally divided, the Irreconcilables held the balance of power. Unconditionally opposed to the League, they voted against the treaty with reservations and against the treaty without reservations. When it was clear that a two-thirds majority could not be obtained for the treaty in either form, the Senate adjourned until the new session on December 1.

THE SECOND VOTE IN THE SENATE

The battle was not over. The articulate public seemed to want the League, even if modified. Over four fifths of the senators had voted for one of the versions, and throughout the land a cry went up for reconsideration and compromise. Most of the demands for concessions were directed to Wilson. They came from such Democratic friends of the League as Hitchcock, Bryan, and House, and from such Republican champions as Taft, Lowell, and Holt. Nor was Lodge immune from this pressure. Root disapproved of the preamble and warned that crippling reservations might be self-defeating. From England came hints that a League in which the United States played a qualified role was better than no League at all.

Was compromise possible? The conflict cut deep. It was not, as often depicted, between isolationism and collective security. It was not between abstention from and participation in world affairs. The Irreconcilables were a small minority. The real clash was between two groups, each eager to aid in preventing war but disagreeing on how far the United States should commit itself in advance. The long wrangling over the exact wording of the reservations was not simply legislative quibbling, partisan jockeying, or personal preening. The differences were very much more than those between Tweedledum and Tweedledee.

On the one hand, Wilson wanted collective security, a phrase not yet widely used. He envisaged a system of international organization in which all nations recognized an obligation to combine against those guilty of aggression, as determined by procedures in the Covenant. He believed that an unprovoked attack upon one country must be regarded as an attack on all and that each government must trust its safety to collective rather than to independent action. On the other hand, Lodge, Root, Taft, Hughes, and Kellogg—to name only a few—argued that the American people, and perhaps the world, were not yet ready for such a system. They insisted that Wilson's program involved too sharp a break with American diplomatic tradition and imposed too heavy a burden on American constitutional practice. In varying degrees they questioned the wisdom of any promise to employ armed force against treaty breakers, and they preferred a league which concentrated on the development of inquiry and arbitration, the reduction of armaments, the establishment of a world court, and the codification of international law. These men were not isolationists—some favored an alliance with England and France—but their views on international collaboration were not Wilson's.

Compromise was not made easier by the attitude of the only two men able to break the log jam. It is undeniable, of course, that the consuming hatred with which Wilson and Lodge regarded each other was a major obstacle to mutual concessions, but the problem transcended conflicting personalities. The President felt it was immoral, cowardly, and futile to retreat from principle. He clearly recognized the disparity between his position and that of sincere Reservationists. Nor can his intransigence be blamed on illness. Although he was still paralyzed and unable to provide physical leadership to his cause, his mind was keen and his contacts with the outside world were increasing. He knew exactly what he was doing on January 8, 1920, when he reiterated his opposition to the fourteen reservations and argued that the Senate did not reflect popular sentiment. "If there is any doubt as to what the people of this country think on this vital matter," he wrote to a Democratic gathering, the way out would be "to give the next election the form of a great and solemn referendum, a referendum as to the part the United States is to play in completing the settlements of the war and in the prevention in the future of such outrages as Germany attempted to perpetrate."

Lodge's aim in January, 1920, was fourfold. He wished to avoid obligations a later generation might not honor, to protect the constitutional rights of Congress in foreign affairs, to preserve Republican unity, and to place the blame for a defeated treaty on the President. In seeking these ends, he rarely acted like a devoted friend of the League and frequently worked with the Irreconcilables, yet he did remain true to his beliefs. He had always championed senatorial prerogatives, set great store by party responsibility, and kept an eye on the judgment of history. Although willing to enter the League conditionally, he would not give up an iota of sovereignty. Indeed, he much preferred the old balance of power system, in which nations allied for specific purposes but otherwise maintained their freedom of action.

After December 1, 1919, frantic negotiations failed to find a common ground on which Wilsonians and Reservationists could stand. The stumbling block was the interpretation of Article 10. Therefore, the Senate resumed consideration of the treaty on February 10, 1920, and in the next weeks revised and expanded the fourteen reservations to include a fifteenth, one linking a profession of sympathy for Irish independence with the principle of self-determination. The sole significant change came in the preamble. No longer was it necessary for three of the four great powers to give their assent by an exchange of notes. Now the mere absence of protest meant acquiescence. But this concession was offset by another clause giving minor signatories a veto that would prevent the Versailles Treaty from going into force. In any case, Wilson was not placated. On March 8, before those modifications were completed, he appealed to his supporters again to oppose the treaty with reservations.

By March 19, 1920, the Senate was ready to vote for the second time. There was only one ballot. It would have been futile to consider the treaty without reservations or with the Hitchcock interpretations. The Non-Reservationist position had become untenable; the real question was whether enough Democrats would defy Wilson to enable the Reservationists to carry the day. The answer came quickly. On a motion to consent to the Versailles Treaty with fifteen reservations, the Senate divided 49 to 35. Twenty-eight Republicans, including Lodge, combined with twenty-one Democrats to put the pact seven votes short of the requisite number. Twenty Democrats out of the original thirty-nine Non-Reservationists, heeding Wilson, joined fifteen Irreconcilables in blocking a two-thirds majority. As on November 19, 1919, a small minority of Irreconcilables was able to produce a negative result. The Senate did not act again on the Versailles settlement nor did it take up the French Assistance Treaty.

It is idle to speculate on what would have happened if seven other Democrats had been less loyal to Wilson or less fearful of his ire. In all probability the President, eager for the solemn referendum in November, 1920, would not have completed ratification of a treaty which contained reservations he regarded as ignoble and stultifying. It is equally fruitless to apportion blame for the inconclusive outcome. Personalities, politics, provincialism, and sincere conviction all entered in. Neither Wilson nor Lodge would compromise—the former preferring to be a prophet rather than a statesman, the latter placing party harmony above a possible boon to mankind. The Irreconcilables can be censured for a shameless distortion of the peace settlement and some Democrats for a needless fealty to a stubborn leader. Yet in the end, the Wilsonians, the Reservationists, and the Irreconcilables were all true to themselves; for the Versailles Treaty posed a challenge—a first test for the United States in world affairs—to which men responded in different ways.

THE ELECTION OF 1920

Passionate controversy often confused the battle in America, and obfuscation characterized the election of 1920. Wilson injected unreality into the campaign by terming it a referendum on the League of Nations, although he knew that no presidential contest had ever hinged on a single issue of foreign policy. The Republicans misled the voters by adopting an ambiguous platform that won the endorsement of such diverse leaders as Taft, McCumber, Kellogg, Lodge, and Borah. Root was the chief author; but it did not contain, as he wished, a clear pledge to accept the Versailles Treaty with suitable reservations. Instead, it rebuked Wilson for faulty peacemaking and lauded the Senate

for resisting executive tyranny. It promised to promote peace through a
permanent court, periodic conferences, and an ill-defined association
of nations. The Democratic plank was more forthright. It called the
present League, not a future association, the only practicable means
of preventing war. It advocated immediate approval of the Versailles
Treaty "without reservations which would impair its essential integrity" but, if necessary, with those which made "clearer or more specific
the obligations of the United States." It praised the President for his
vision, condemned the Senate for its hostility, and branded a separate
peace as disgraceful.

In the ensuing campaign neither party was wholly candid, but on
the League issue the Democrats were less guilty of equivocation. Their
candidate, Governor James M. Cox of Ohio, carried on, albeit reluctantly, Wilson's fight. Harding, the Republican nominee, wandered
amiably from one side of Root's capacious platform to the other. At
first he seemed to favor American membership in an association of
nations. Whether this was to be the League, with the Covenant purged
of collective responsibilities to use force, or a new organization he did
not say. Probably he did not know and thought it wiser not to be too
specific. Then he talked as if the World Court, whose statute Root was
then helping to draft at The Hague, would be enough. As the speech
making progressed, Harding appeared to yield to the Irreconcilables.
His hostility to the existing League increased, and at Des Moines on
October 7, 1920, he criticized the commitments inherent in Article 10.
"I do not want to clarify those obligations," he was quoted as saying,
"I want to turn my back on them. It is not interpretation, but rejection
that I am seeking."

These words delighted the Democrats and distressed Republican
Reservationists. The former felt the issue was now clearly joined,
while the latter feared a covert abandonment of their platform. To
eliminate uncertainty among the voters and to remind the candidate of
his millions of pro-League supporters, on October 15, 1920, thirty-one
prominent Republicans released a statement asserting that "the true
course to bring America into an effective league to preserve peace" was
to elect Harding. Describing themselves as men "who desire that the
United States shall do her full part in association with the other civilized nations to prevent war," the thirty-one declared that the question
was not one of the League or no league. Rather it was "whether we
shall join under an agreement containing the exact provisions negotiated by President Wilson at Paris, or under an agreement which omits
or modifies some of the provisions that are very objectionable to great
numbers of the American people." The most offensive, the document
continued, was Article 10. Since Cox was committed to retaining it,
his election would perpetuate the existing deadlock. Harding, on the

contrary, was pledged to accept the best and reject the worst of the Versailles Treaty. Only he was free to call on the other members to remove obnoxious items from the Covenant.

Drafted mainly by Root, this statement was endorsed by one future president—Herbert Hoover—and two future secretaries of state—Charles E. Hughes and Henry L. Stimson. Taft would have signed but could not be reached in time. Significantly, no senator appended his name. Although often regarded as a last-minute act of desperation to save Harding from defeat, the paper had a very different purpose. By October, 1920, all evidence pointed to a decisive Republican victory. What such men as Root wanted was to prevent the Irreconcilables from becoming spokesmen for the party. They did not seek to deceive the voters but to remind Harding that total abstention from world affairs had not been the practice under McKinley, Roosevelt, and Taft.

Harding's overwhelming election on November 2, 1920, did not result from a great and solemn referendum on the Versailles Treaty. The Republican landslide represented the accumulated grievances against eight years of Wilson—including the progressive legislation, the war resolution, and the suppression of free speech after April, 1917. Hostile businessmen, apprehensive farmers, disgruntled laborers, frightened Negroes, and disillusioned liberals deserted the winning coalition of four years earlier and produced the most one-sided tally since Monroe's return to office in 1820. The League issue was too blurred to be meaningful; and the ultimate fate of that organization, so far as the United States was concerned, would be determined not by the expressed will of the voters at the polls but by the interpretation the victors subsequently chose to put upon their triumph.

THE SEPARATE PEACE

That judgment would not be rendered until after Wilson had left the White House, but well before then the inexorable march toward a separate peace began. After the second defeat of the treaty on March 19, 1920, Congress debated, amended, and passed a joint resolution ending a technical state of war with Germany. Still hopeful of a referendum on the League, Wilson responded on May 27, as his foes had anticipated, with a ringing veto. Thus on the eve of the party conventions the Republicans could chant: "He kept us out of peace."

Nothing more was done until after Harding's inauguration. On July 2, 1921, the new president approved another joint resolution that not only repealed the declarations of war but also reserved to American citizens all the rights to which they would have been entitled under the

Treaties of Versailles, St. Germain, and Trianon. The second proviso foreshadowed the nature of the agreements reached with Austria on August 24, Germany on August 25, and Hungary on August 29, 1921. The German pact, for instance, simply re-established friendly relations and obligated the Weimar Republic to recognize "all the rights and advantages stipulated for the benefit of the United States in the Treaty of Versailles," just as fully as if that nation had ratified it. Lest any doubt remain that the American government was thereby demanding all the privileges of the peace settlement while disavowing all the responsibilities, pertinent sections of the Versailles Treaty were carefully enumerated. Thus the convention signed at Berlin was an "index-treaty," for it could not be understood without a copy of the Versailles text at hand. In such a churlish manner did the Great Crusade end in a separate peace.

The repercussions of the battle in America were felt long after Wilson's death on February 3, 1924. The passions aroused by the Versailles Treaty exercised a continuing influence and did much to shape the climate of opinion on foreign affairs from 1921 to 1945. To some, the outcome was a triumph of traditional America, a second Declaration of Independence that kept the republic at peace for two decades. To others, the result was a supreme tragedy, a great betrayal which required another struggle twenty years later to make the world again safe for democracy. The truth lies somewhere between those extremes. The defection of the United States dealt the League of Nations a paralyzing blow, but it did not make the Second World War inevitable. We do not know how Wilson's grand design, as he planned it, would have functioned, but the trials of the United Nations suggest some of the difficulties that would have been encountered. On the other hand, we do know that the interwar compromise which was erected as a substitute for membership in the League proved incapable of coping with an aggressive totalitarianism after 1931.

With the benefit of hindsight, we can see that the separate peace was a reaction to Wilson's attempt to break too sharply with the past. For all his broad vision and generous idealism, the President had gone too far. The American people were not prepared to assume the moral leadership of the world; the other great powers were not willing to accept the type of collective security that he envisaged. But the consequences of this first test of the United States in global politics were not entirely negative. The republic remained a world power and, as a result of wartime financing, became the world's creditor as well. The death of over 50,000 soldiers, sailors, and marines—while infinitesimal when compared with European losses—was not forgotten, and many grateful Americans were determined that the sacrifice should not be in vain. Nor could the Irreconcilables, with all their incantation of traditional dogmas and all their exploitation of xenophobic prejudices, conceal the fact that they constituted a tiny minority in the Senate and that they dreamed of an America whose ability to keep aloof from the affairs of Europe and Asia was gone, never to return.

BOOK IV

INTERLUDE:
THE INTERWAR
COMPROMISE

1921–39

*In which the American people vainly
seek a foreign policy based upon a compromise between traditional principles
and Wilsonian ideals.*

31

⟫⟫-⟫⟫-⟫⟫-⟫⟫-⟪⟪-⟪⟪-⟪⟪-⟪⟪

The Shaping of Foreign Policy, 1921–39

IN ITS FIRST TEST as a world power, the United States intervened in the Great War, contributed to the military victory, participated at the peace table, and then sought to return to a more familiar and limited role in international affairs. But it was no more able in 1921 to regain the golden age of aloofness than it had been in 1914 to ignore the conflict overseas. Its flag still flew over distant Pacific outposts. Its merchants pressed for assistance not only in the old markets of East Asia but also in the new oil-rich regions of the Middle East. Its economic welfare was linked to German reparations and Allied war debts; its defense establishment was influenced by naval building in England and Japan. More than ever before, American citizens were aware that trouble in any part of the world might affect them.

Torn between Wilson's warning that a concert of free peoples alone could bring peace and safety to all nations and the opposing argument that such a break with the past was not yet necessary, the molders of foreign policy after 1921 settled for a compromise between two widely divergent views. One was the desirability of disengagement from all diplomatic entanglements and obligations so that the United States could promote unfettered its own interests and not sap its strength in every last quarrel in Europe, Asia, and Africa. The other was the indispensability of cooperation with all democratic countries and even the League of Nations so that the United States could throw its weight behind the champions of law and thus help prevent another major war. Each side was convinced its plan would best contribute to the security of the republic and the peace of the world. The first reflected the pull of tradition and the resurgence of nationalism; the second rested on a belief that the United States could not avoid being drawn into a global conflict. Both found support for their program after 1921, though in different ways, from the constant bickering abroad, the acrimony engendered by the war debts, and the growing disillusionment with the Great Crusade.

THE PRESIDENTS

Warren G. Harding is important in American foreign policy only because of the separate peace. His nomination was engineered by senatorial colleagues who expected to dominate him and thus recover some of the power Wilson had exercised as war leader. If, as Walter Lippmann wrote in 1920, Harding was "distinguished by the fact that nothing distinguishes" him, he was the type of executive the Republican party and the American people wanted that year. The editor of a small-town newspaper in Ohio, he had served in the state legislature and as lieutenant governor before entering the Senate in 1915. There he voted with conservatives on most issues, including the war resolution of 1917. Although he had demonstrated neither interest nor competence in external affairs, in May, 1919, he was placed on the Foreign Relations Committee, where he demanded that adequate safeguards be appended to the Versailles Treaty. During the campaign of 1920 he barely managed to please both Reservationists and Irreconcilables, and he gave his backers many uneasy moments. They had been advised "to keep Warren at home"; for, as one veteran warned, "if he goes out on a tour somebody's sure to ask him questions, and Warren's just the sort of damned fool that will try to answer them."

As president, Harding did not surrender the prerogatives of his office. He did ostentatiously soothe senatorial sensibilities long irked by Wilson's tactics, but his deferential treatment of Congress served a good purpose. He stood firm, however, when the lawmakers asked him to submit for their scrutiny confidential data bearing upon the negotiation of a treaty. What Harding yielded, and then only to Secretary of State Hughes, was the formulation of foreign policy. Sincerely humble, the President knew his own shortcomings. He was not an imaginative or deep thinker. His meandering words might occasionally capture, as McAdoo once said, "a straggling thought and bear it triumphantly, a prisoner in their midst, until it died of servitude and overwork." He envied those who possessed the college education he lacked. He was certain that answers to everything could be found in books; and if he did not know where to look, he felt that Hughes would. Even before his inauguration Harding told reporters they must go to the State Department, not the White House, to discover what his diplomacy would be. Betrayed by dishonest friends, he died suddenly on August 2, 1923, just before Congress uncovered the worst scandals in high government places since the days of Grant.

Calvin Coolidge differed from Harding in almost every respect save one—his lack of interest in foreign affairs. An undemonstrative and acidulous Yankee, he was the epitome of frugality, parochialism, and a vanishing rural America. Where Harding was humble, handsome, polite, gregarious, hedonistic, and confusingly verbose, his successor was smug, dour, rude, solitary, abstemious, and pretentiously curt. Harding was easily swayed; even his father allegedly remarked that it was well Warren was not a girl, for he could not say no. Coolidge was stubborn, rigid, and almost defiant when crossed. A lawyer by profession, he had risen steadily in Massachusetts politics, to become governor in 1918. The next year he gained national prominence by declaring during the Boston police walkout that "there is no right to strike against the public safety by anybody, anywhere, any time." His nomination in 1920 can be attributed to a burst of independence by a convention which, having accepted a third-rater for the top spot, was determined to have a vice-presidential candidate who was not connected with the party bosses on Capitol Hill.

Like Harding, Coolidge gladly left foreign affairs to his Secretaries of State, Hughes and Kellogg. Rather than utilizing his vast executive powers to enlighten and lead the people, he diverted public attention from the outstanding issues of the day. To quote Lippmann again, writing in May, 1926: "There have been Presidents in our time who knew how to whip up popular enthusiasm. There has never been Mr. Coolidge's equal in the art of deflating interest." A poorly read man, almost wholly lacking in ideas, he did little to improve his mind or work at his job. Congenitally lazy, he spent more than a fair share of most afternoons taking a nap. Overseas trade was one of the few matters that excited him, and his best-remembered saying had to do with the reason war debts should be paid in full. It was: "They hired the money, didn't they?"

Herbert Hoover was quite unlike his two predecessors. A poor farm boy from Iowa, he quickly climbed the ladder of success and wealth in a career that could have come from the pages of Horatio Alger. As a mining engineer, he traveled widely and learned at first hand about other continents. The Great War deepened his experience. From August, 1914, to May, 1917, he headed one government commission to aid Americans stranded in Europe and a second to feed Belgians suffering under the German yoke. Then Wilson placed him in charge of the wartime Food Administration, where he won fame as an efficient humanitarian. Although Hoover advised Wilson at Paris in 1919, he joined Root, Hughes, and Stimson in signing the statement of the thirty-one during the campaign of 1920. As Secretary of Commerce under Harding and Coolidge, he untiringly promoted business enterprise abroad and diplomatic compromise at home. Elected overwhelmingly in 1928, he made a preinaugural tour of Central and South America, the only portion of the globe he had never previously visited.

Despite experience and intelligence, Hoover turned out to be a disappointing president. He did not possess the spark of leadership. In large groups he was cold and diffident. He lacked the light touch and never relaxed tensions at cabinet meetings by telling a joke. His timing was bad; too often he said the right thing at the wrong moment. When he spoke in public, he droned; when he wrote, his prose was like a thick fog moving across a bleak landscape. He was unable and unwilling to dramatize himself and his cause. To be sure, Hoover served during the depth of the Great Depression, a calamity that focused attention on domestic issues, led to pared budgets of the armed forces, and fostered rancors against foreigners, especially delinquent debtors. It also destroyed a Republican control of Congress, and the President proved incapable of coping with the harassments of an opposition which scented victory in 1932. Bitter and discredited, Hoover was defeated that year by a man he never fully trusted.

Franklin D. Roosevelt did not offer a new deal in diplomacy. Like Wilson before him, he hoped to concentrate on internal reform, for that had been the staple of his electoral campaign. Yet he did enter the White House with some knowledge of external problems. A distant cousin and ardent admirer of his Republican namesake, he too had served as Assistant Secretary of the Navy. In that post from 1913 to 1920 he cultivated his love for ships, imbibed Mahan's doctrine of sea power, saw the Caribbean protectorates at their ugliest, and bolstered an interest in China inherited from ancestors engaged in the Asiatic trade. After a losing battle for the Covenant as vice-presidential candidate in 1920, he said little about foreign policy for several years. Crippled forever by poliomyletis, he did not re-enter public life until 1928, when he won the first of two terms as governor of New York. Judged by their speeches in 1932, Hoover and Roosevelt did not disagree on the role that the United States should play in world affairs, and the latter did not advocate the abandonment of neutrality and isolationism until after 1939.

As a person and as a president, Roosevelt differed greatly from Hoover. He was gay, witty, sanguine, and often superficial where his predecessor was sober, humorless, apprehensive, and always painstaking. Despite his privileged upbringing, Roosevelt had the common touch. He coined catchy phrases that inspired his fellow men. A superb speaker with a mellifluous voice, he developed the medium of radio with effective fireside chats. A skilled actor with a flair for the dramatic, he gave the impression of moving forward while sometimes standing still. He used his press conferences as a sounding board for steps not yet taken. In contrast to Harding and Coolidge, he and Hoover worked hard, though not in the same ways. Roosevelt was the poorer administrator of the two but understood better the potential of the presidency. To him it was a place to exert both moral and political leadership. He also grasped, as Hoover never did, its responsibility for correlating foreign policy and military might. Yet before 1940 Roosevelt hesitated to act as boldly abroad as he did at home. He believed that priority must be given to relief, recovery, and reform. He was cowed by the resurgence of isolationist feeling that accompanied the collapse of the interwar compromise. He was appalled by his inability to awaken the people to the dangers he felt beset them. "It's a terrible thing," he later told a friend, "to look over your shoulder when you are trying to lead—and to find no one there."

THE SECRETARIES OF STATE

Charles Evans Hughes was the first of the four men to serve as secretary of state from 1921 to 1939. He occupied the post under both Harding and Coolidge, resigning on March 4, 1925. A former governor of New York and associate justice of the Supreme Court, he had narrowly lost the presidency to Wilson in 1916. As a private citizen, in July, 1919, he advocated appending mild reservations to the Versailles Treaty; as one of the thirty-one prominent Republicans, in October, 1920, he asserted that the election of Harding was the best way to insure American membership in a league. Picked with Hoover to give distinction to an ill-starred cabinet, Hughes received a free hand in foreign affairs. An assiduous worker with a keenly analytical mind, he extracted the best from his subordinates and appeared to be an ideal incumbent. If the handsome and debonair Harding looked like a president, the dignified and bewhiskered Hughes seemed the epitome of a diplomat, a judge, and even a deity. In spite of relative inexperience in international negotiations, he scored a resounding success in his first effort, the Washington Conference on armaments and China. Although he was timid on matters affecting the League of Nations and never made good his assurances to the voters in 1920, he built wisely on Root's Good Neighbor ideal and brought prestige to his department. His relations with Harding, in view of divergent temperaments and interests, did credit to both men.

Frank B. Kellogg was the least successful of the four. By the time

Coolidge transferred him to the State Department from the London embassy, the former Rooseveltian and leader of the Mild Reservationists had lost much of his progressivism and daring. Irascible and explosive, he never inspired his colleagues as Root and Hughes had done. Short of stature and white of hair, he had a harried look that may explain the soubriquet of "Nervous Nellie." To be sure, he labored for a president who was usually uninformed and unwilling to admit it, but a more sensitive and less ponderous secretary might have avoided the public stalemates, open disagreements, and mutual recriminations that marked Kellogg's diplomacy. Ironically, he accepted the antiwar pact which bears his name most reluctantly and only because he was driven to it by a wave of uncritical popular opinion.

Henry L. Stimson is the most difficult of the four incumbents to appraise. A patrician by training and a soldier by inclination, he had worked as a young man with Theodore Roosevelt and Root, and he carried into his mature years the enthusiasms and values of the era before 1914. He had been a successful New York lawyer, secretary of war under Taft, an artillery colonel in France, and a signer of the statement of the thirty-one, before Coolidge sent him to Nicaragua as a trouble shooter and to the Philippines as Governor General. Little known to Hoover and supposedly the fourth choice to head the cabinet, Stimson differed from his chief in many ways. He was readier to support diplomacy with armed force and to maintain peace through consultative treaties. He believed that economic sanctions could restrain an aggressor, while Hoover feared they would precipitate hostilities. The President was cautious, circumspect, and keenly alive to domestic pressures; the Secretary was bold, forthright, and deeply concerned with foreign problems. Even in manner and appearance they presented a contrast. Hoover was urbane, deliberate, and cherubic; Stimson was brusque, hasty, and gaunt. The first was slow to anger and slower to forget; the second was quick to blow up and quicker to forgive. Each inspired intense loyalty, but not from the same people. For two years they worked in harmony and then drifted steadily apart.

Cordell Hull had little experience in foreign affairs before 1933, but as representative and senator from Tennessee, he showed himself to be a staunch Wilsonian, a champion of freer trade among nations, and a judicious party counselor. Roosevelt picked him as an elder statesman who was reputed to be influential on Capitol Hill. Dignified and courtly, except when extreme irritation released a stream of picturesque profanity, the silver-thatched democrat shared Wilson's concern for morality in international relations; but platitudinous reiteration of obvious truths robbed his words of their effectiveness. Hull's mind worked slowly, and it was not easy for him to keep abreast of his nimble-witted chief who relished improvisation and repartee. It was even more difficult for this essentially conservative spokesman of the rural South to feel at ease in the mixture of liberal, urban, and intellectual reformers who thronged the White House in the early days of the New Deal. Hull's loyalty to the mercurial Roosevelt was his most commendable trait, and he was often ill rewarded when the President dealt directly with subordinates in the State Department or in the embassies abroad. Yet until 1940 the two men usually worked together effectively and held each other in high esteem.

THE CONGRESSIONAL LEADERS

Congressional challenges to the president's control of foreign policy persisted after 1921 along the lines drawn during the battle over the Versailles Treaty. Except for Harding's brief tenure, the executive branch was in the hands of those who had been willing in 1919–20 to accept that settlement as drafted or with mild reservations. Hughes, Hoover, and Stimson had signed the statement of the thirty-one; Roosevelt and Hull had supported Wilson; Coolidge had hoped for a compromise. By contrast, Irreconcilables continued to dominate both the Senate and its Foreign Relations Committee, and those men were determined to veto moves toward undue international collaboration. Lodge remained chairman until his death in November, 1924, but gradually he edged from his position as a Strong Reservationist into the camp of the Irreconcilables.

William E. Borah succeeded Lodge and was the most powerful senatorial spokesman on external problems during the interwar years. A member of the Foreign Relations Committee since 1911, he had voted for the war resolution in 1917, resisted the peace treaty in every form, criticized the protectorate policy without stint, and urged a drastic reduction of naval armaments. An inveterate isolationist, he believed that engagements to use force could never prevent wars. A combination of sincere humility and colossal egotism, the leonine Idaho Republican was universally respected on Capitol Hill but, save by Hoover, generally disliked in the White House. More prone to oppose than to favor, he allegedly prompted Coolidge to express amazement, when seeing him on the bridle path, that horse and rider were going in the same direction. An eloquent orator and a man of great integrity, Borah came to regard his committee as the peer of the State Department. Even when in the minority after March, 1933, he exercised tremendous influence. He died in January, 1940, during the early stages of the war which, six months earlier, he had predicted would not come in 1939.

Hiram W. Johnson, the squat, leather-lunged Irreconcilable from California, stood foursquare with Borah in upholding isolationism.

Named to the Foreign Relations Committee in May, 1919, he had attacked the Covenant unmercifully and despite the whirligig of time was, on his deathbed in July, 1945, one of the three senatorial foes of the new United Nations. Less likable as a person than Borah, Johnson was equally effective as a speaker and delighted in exposing what he called the secret machinations of the State Department to forge alliances abroad. A staunch nationalist, he sponsored a rigid immigration law in 1924 and ten years later a bill to punish friendly governments which had defaulted on their war debts.

Among the Democrats during their years as a minority, no one senator can be regarded as leader. In March, 1933, Key Pittman of Nevada became chairman of the Foreign Relations Committee and remained so until his death in November, 1940. First appointed to that body in 1916, he had been one of the Non-Reservationists who deserted Wilson on the final vote of March 19, 1920. A dignified but dull man, Pittman grew ever more timid and irresolute, and rather than buck the resurgence of isolationist sentiment during his tenure, he tried vainly to temporize and compromise. By 1938 he was a most ineffective spokesman for the administration.

In the House neither party produced an outstanding leader in the realm of foreign policy, but the same difference in emphasis between the executive and legislature prevailed. Indeed, this divergence helps to explain the diplomatic ambivalence from 1921 to 1939. But a contrast between the two ends of Pennsylvania Avenue should not obscure the fact that nobody responsible for shaping foreign policy in those years openly advocated a prior commitment to employ armed force to keep the peace.

THE CONSTITUTIONAL CONFLICT

Paradoxically, the battle over the Versailles Treaty, which so influenced the nature of American diplomacy after 1921, did not sharpen the constitutional conflict between president and Congress. Save where the charter of 1787 was silent or ambiguous and save where it purposely provided for sharing authority, there was relatively little controversy over which branch of the federal government should act. In the interwar years men divided more over the wisdom of steps to promote the national interest than over their constitutionality.

Appointments to the cabinet and missions abroad had become a routine matter. Nominations were rarely challenged or even debated. The persistent use of executive agents, however, still rankled, and on October 18, 1921, the Senate appended to the separate peace with Germany a reservation which fulfilled the intent of one offered by Lodge on November 15, 1919. It stipulated that no person should represent the United States on any agency or commission under the treaty until Congress so authorized in each specific case. Although this understanding made Harding cautious about any matter related to the peace settlement, he and his successors used unofficial observers for reports on the League and executive agents as official delegates to international conferences.

Appropriations for the conduct of external affairs created few tensions between president and Congress. A foe of protectorates might occasionally try to insert in a money bill a rider prohibiting the use of those funds for troops stationed on foreign soil, but such diversions were not significant. The legislature, in words that recalled Lodge's ninth reservation, did insist upon its prerogative to fix the liability incurred in any joint action with an international body. One condition imposed by the Senate on January 26, 1927, for membership in the World Court was that Congress should determine and appropriate the expenses to be borne by the American government. The power of the purse enabled the lawmakers to force the hand of the executive indirectly, as they did with some presidents in limiting armaments by multilateral agreement.

Calls by the legislature for papers in executive hands were frequent from 1921 to 1939, but almost all acknowledged the right of the president to withhold documents whose transmittal would be against the public interest. Both Harding and Hoover exercised that prerogative when the Senate professed to be searching for secret commitments in treaties. On February 20, 1922, the former denied that the Four-Power Pact contained any hidden obligations and declined to divulge the substance of conversations held during the negotiations. He deemed it improper to inform Congress of "tentative suggestions or informal proposals" so indispensable to reaching international agreements. On July 11, 1930, Hoover balked at supplying all dispatches bearing upon the naval treaty recently concluded at London. He, too, argued that needless publicity would hamper the conduct of foreign relations, but to dispel suspicion he offered to show in private to any senator all the records in executive hands.

Investigations and hearings, designed to elicit information for approving treaties and enacting laws, became the rule after 1921. The long inquest over the Versailles settlement led to the examination of witnesses concerning the Kellogg Pact in 1928 and the London Naval Treaty in 1930. Other inquiries dealt with the occupation of Haiti, the lobby against disarmament, the sale of foreign securities, and the subversive activities of Communists and Fascists. A select Senate committee under Gerald P. Nye conducted a sensational probe into the ramifications of the munitions industry, but the only constitutional issue raised was the dissemination of documents not yet cleared by foreign governments.

Recognition after 1921 was less a question of prerogative than of criteria. Congress never waived its power to bring pressure on the president, but it grew reconciled to the fact that the final decision in acknowledging the existence of a new state, in exchanging envoys with a new government, or in according status to a new belligerent was to be reached in the White House, not on Capitol Hill. The recognition of recently independent nations raised no problems in the interwar years, but the manner of dealing with newly installed regimes was modified. Wilson's emphasis on constitutional legitimacy was minimized, and after a wave of revolutions swept South America, Stimson set forth on February 6, 1931, three basic criteria. First, the new government must be in *de facto* control and without active resistance to its rule. Second, it must make clear its intention to fulfill all international obligations. Third, it must hold elections in due course to regularize its status.

The major innovation affecting recognition from 1921 to 1939 had to do with territory seized by force and in violation of existing treaties. Foreshadowed by Bryan's note of May 11, 1915, during the crisis over the Twenty-One Demands and by Hughes' warning to Japan on May 31, 1921, regarding some troops in Siberia, it was set forth as the Hoover-Stimson Doctrine on January 7, 1932. In identic notes to Nanking and Tokyo the United States declared that it could not admit the legality of any situation in Manchuria or recognize any solution which infringed upon the open door principle or upon American treaty rights in China. Nor would it recognize any settlement of current Sino-Japanese differences that was brought about by means contrary to the Kellogg Pact. Solely the work of the executive branch, this new cornerstone in American diplomacy aroused no opposition in the legislature.

One surprising aftermath of the separate peace was a lessened tension over the treaty-making process. Although no president revived the practice of consulting the Senate formally before or during actual negotiations, all profited from Wilson's experience and proceeded with caution. There were no unpopular agreements to raise the thorny issue of who decides whether a treaty should be terminated. No president felt compelled to withhold ratification, and no House refused to implement an accord fashioned by the president and Senate. More than in previous years, the impetus for treaties came from Capitol Hill, but even in the most notable instance, the Kellogg Pact, a doubting secretary did not try to combat legislative and popular opinion.

Most important treaties signed from 1921 to 1939 were approved without change. These included four emanating from the Washington Conference and all dated February 6, 1922—the Five-Power, the Nine-

Power, and the two regulating submarine warfare and China's tariff. Others were the Yap settlement with Japan (February 11, 1922); the Gondra Treaty for the use of inquiry by the American republics (May 3, 1923); the Dominican agreement on troop withdrawals (June 12, 1924); the Kellogg Pact (August 27, 1928); the General Convention of Inter-American Conciliation (January 5, 1929); the agreement with Cuba to abrogate the Platt Amendment (May 29, 1934); the agreement with Panama to end certain privileges (March 2, 1936); the second London Naval Treaty (March 25, 1936); and four conventions from the Inter-American Conference at Buenos Aires (December 23, 1936). The votes were usually overwhelmingly favorable or there was no roll call at all.

Even where major treaties were consented to with change, the alterations generally took the form of reservations, not amendments. The separate peace with Germany was approved on October 18, 1921, with the understanding that Congress must so designate before the United States could be represented on any commission to execute its terms. The Senate consented to the Four-Power Pact on March 24, 1922, only after expressing the opinion that it contained no alliance or commitment to use armed force—points on which Harding had already given assurances. With the first London Naval Treaty, suspicious legislators insisted upon placing in the resolution of ratification on July 21, 1930, an acceptance of Hoover's pledge that no secret agreements or hidden files in any way affected the published text.

In a few cases reservations prevented a treaty from going into effect. It took ten years before a qualified consent could be won for an arms traffic convention of June 17, 1925; by then the other parties had lost interest. The General Convention of Inter-American Arbitration was approved on April 1, 1935, after a delay of six years, with the understanding that the *compromis* in any agreement reached under its provisions be in treaty form. In consenting on June 15, 1934, to the Convention on the Rights and Duties of States, signed at Montevideo on December 26, 1933, the Senate appended as a reservation Hull's statement safeguarding the right of the United States to intervene in accordance with existing international law. The most far-reaching reservations were those added to the World Court Protocol on January 27, 1926, for they caused a long delay and the ultimate defeat of the project.

No major treaties were decisively beaten from 1921 to 1939, but three fell victim to the two-thirds rule. On January 18, 1927, the poll on an agreement to restore relations with Turkey, signed on August 6, 1923, was six short of the requisite margin, 50 to 34. The St. Lawrence Seaway Treaty of July 18, 1932, even with precautionary reservations, received only a bare majority of 46 to 42 on March 14, 1934. But

the most publicized example came on January 29, 1935, when supporters of the World Court, balloting on the revised Protocol, missed
their long-sought goal by seven votes, 52 to 36. Statistics on the small
number of treaties defeated in the interwar years, however, do not tell
the whole story. By their very presence, the surviving Irreconcilables
and their younger associates forestalled the negotiation of agreements
which might have been vetoed by the Senate.

Evasion of the treaty-making process after 1921 came mostly
through executive agreements, but not all of these circumvented the
Constitution or created friction between president and Congress. Some
were authorized by statute, such as those concluded under the World
War Foreign Debt Commission Act of February 9, 1922, or the reciprocal Trade Agreements Act of June 12, 1934. Others lacked that sanction, but almost all were made public at once. These included the war
claims agreement of May 19, 1927, with England; the understanding of
August 7, 1933, expediting the withdrawal of marines from Haiti; the
letters of March 24, 1936, reaffirming Anglo-American naval parity;
and the exchange of notes of February 1, 1939, clarifying the text of
the Panamanian treaty of March 2, 1936. A minor type of evasion was
a tendency to place multilateral declarations of policy in resolutions
rather than in treaties. The Washington Conference of 1921–2 put one
of its important decisions in a resolution creating a commission to
study the problem of extraterritoriality in China. A summary of past
agreements was cast at Buenos Aires on December 21, 1936, into the
Declaration of Principles of Inter-American Solidarity. At the Lima
Conference in December, 1938, resolutions replaced treaties entirely.
In the Americas, this practice was not intended to deceive or conceal,
for treaties dealing with hemispheric affairs had always passed the
Senate with little debate and overwhelming support.

Joint control of the armed forces did not lead to any serious constitutional clash between president and Congress in this period. That
fact can be explained partly by the peace which the United States enjoyed during this interlude and partly by the modification of its protectorate policy in the Caribbean. The republic did not fight any wars,
declared or undeclared, and there was a marked reduction in the sort
of police action that had been frequent before 1921. Nor did the deployment of ships and men lead to congressional charges of presidential warmongering, as was the case after 1939. On one point the legislators continued to agitate. At every session, amendments to the
Constitution were proposed to alter the war-making clauses. The most
frequent were designed to halt profiteering, to bar using conscripts outside the continental United States, to require that a declaration of war
pass each house by a three-fourths vote rather than a simple majority,
and to hold a popular referendum, except in cases of invasion, before a

congressional decision to go to war could take effect. The only change
to muster even a roll call was the Ludlow resolution dealing with a
referendum, but a motion to bring it out of committee was lost on
January 10, 1938, by a count of 188 to 209.

In the familiar contest between president and Congress for the control of foreign policy, the interwar years saw the legislature exert a
positive and negative influence. Helped by two weak men in the White
House and several strong ones on the Foreign Relations Committee and
also aided by public opinion, Congress provided much of the impetus
for the reduction of naval armaments, the renunciation of war, the
liberation of the Philippines, the modification of the protectorate system, the penalizing of delinquent debtors, and the passage of new neutrality laws. In a negative way, senatorial opposition killed Harding's
association of nations and blocked membership in the World Court.
The executive bore the primary responsibility, however, for the formulation and conduct of policy. If Borah campaigned for a curb on naval
construction, Hughes drafted the specific plan. If Borah and his colleagues crusaded to end the Caribbean protectorates, Coolidge and his
successors decided how it should be done. If Congress tried to insulate
the nation from war, it left the President free to determine when a state
of hostilities existed and how much trade should be curtailed. The very
names underline the role of the executive: the Kellogg Pact, the Hoover
Moratorium, the Stimson Doctrine, the Roosevelt Good Neighbor Policy, the Hull Reciprocal Trade Program. Yet no president, not even
Roosevelt after his sweeping re-election in 1936, could ignore opposition on Capitol Hill, and the strength and weaknesses of the interwar
compromise reflect the effect of divided counsels upon American
diplomacy.

The Aftermath
of the Separate Peace

WHEN HARDING took the oath of office on March 4, 1921, the future of United States foreign policy was wrapped in obscurity. By the time he died twenty-nine months later, that uncertainty had dissipated; and the compromise which characterized American diplomacy during the interlude between the two World Wars had begun to emerge. Starting in 1921, leaders of both political parties sought a viable middle ground between traditional practices and Wilsonian principles. Working within limits circumscribed by the bitter battle over the Covenant and the continuing influence of the Irreconcilables in the Senate, they tried to have their cake and eat it too. They wanted the United States to enjoy the advantages of collective security without renouncing in the slightest its freedom of action and without committing itself to use armed force or economic sanctions against an aggressor. While they were willing to push beyond the prewar strivings for peace, they clung to the historic bases that had served the republic so long and so well. Isolationism must be maintained; neutrality must be revived; the Monroe Doctrine must remain the unilateral responsibility of the United States. In this judgment the great majority of the American people concurred.

AN ASSOCIATION OF NATIONS?

Harding waited almost six weeks to clarify the ambiguous stand he had taken on the League during the campaign. After some vague remarks at his inauguration, he met the issue in an address to Congress on April 12, 1921. "In the existing League of Nations, world-governing with its superpowers, this Republic will have no part," he said. "There will be no betrayal of the deliberate expression of the American people in the recent election." Having thus put his own questionable construction on the Covenant and what the voters had meant in 1920, he argued that the high purpose of the former had been defeated by linking it to the Versailles Treaty. No society of nations should combine "the dual functions of a political instrument of the conquerors and of an agency of peace." The time had come, the President went on, for the United States to end the technical state of war with the Central Powers. While blaming Wilson for vetoing the joint resolution as well as negotiating the most important treaty in history without consulting the Senate, he warned against swinging to the "equally objectionable" other extreme whereby the legislature usurped the prerogatives of the executive.

But what of the association of nations? Harding referred many times to such an organization and the principles on which it must rest. "In the national referendum to which I have adverted," he recalled, "we pledged our efforts to such an association, and the pledge will be faithfully kept." Yet what followed were glittering generalities. The American people cordially applauded "the aim to associate nations to prevent war, preserve peace, and promote civilization." Their aspiration was for "an association of nations, based upon the application of justice and right, binding us in conference and cooperation." In rejecting the Covenant, the President asserted, "we make no surrender of our hope for an association to promote peace"; yet he offered no suggestions on how and where to begin. Talk of America's obligation to aid in "effecting European tranquillity" was coupled with a reminder that "helpfulness does not mean sponsorship for treaty commitments which do not concern us."

Two developments during 1921 pushed the association-of-nations idea to the background and sealed its fate. One was the decision of the administration, announced on July 11, to hold a conference in Washington for the purpose of limiting naval armaments and of reaching "a common understanding with respect to principles and policies in the Far East." Until its deliberations were completed on February 6, 1922, Harding was justifiably reluctant to raise any issue which might jeopardize its success. The second was the Senate's handling of the separate peace with Germany of August 25, 1921. Although that agreement stipulated that the United States was not bound by the Covenant or other enumerated articles of the Treaty of Versailles, the upper house insisted upon a reservation. By a vote of 66 to 28 on October 18, the Senate made clear that the United States would not be represented,

under its terms, on any commission unless Congress specifically provided for it by law. This was a blunt notice that in dealing with Germany there must be no furtive collaboration with the League and an
implied hint that an association of nations which infringed upon the
prerogatives of the legislature would revive the kind of struggle in
which Wilson had gone down to defeat.

Thus warned, the new regime deferred any move to form an association of nations, even though it exposed some Republicans—especially the thirty-one—to the charge of misleading the voters in 1920.
The alignment in the Senate, however, left no real choice. Of the eighteen Irreconcilables who had voted against the Versailles Treaty on
March 19, 1920, twelve Republicans and two Democrats remained in
the upper house. They did not want America to join any sort of international organization. Of the twenty Democrats who had stood by Wilson in rejecting that settlement with reservations, fifteen were still
members. Their opposition to the separate peace with Germany indicated their intention to snipe at Republican foreign policy. Then there
were at least a dozen Strong Reservationists, led by Lodge, who were
barely distinguishable from the Irreconcilables. They refused to have
anything to do with the League and demanded that consideration of the
alternative be postponed. In short, it was clear that a two-thirds majority could not be mustered to support American membership in an
association of nations.

Finally, it may be doubted whether such an association was ever a
practical solution. Even if Harding had been more sincerely devoted to
the plan or had possessed a clearer grasp of what it required, members
of the existing League would not have agreed to scrap a going concern
for an unformed rival. If in June, 1919, the French had demanded an
Anglo-American guarantee to supplement Articles 10 and 16, they were
not likely to be satisfied with less in March, 1921. Although contemporaries could not be certain, it is evident in retrospect that Harding had
to choose between the League and no association at all. When he rejected the former on April 12, the die was cast. Yet even this second
victory of the Irreconcilables was not complete. If the pressures of national politics barred America from joining the League, the facts of international life forced the United States into ever closer collaboration
with it. This mingling of diverse tendencies was typical of the interwar
compromise in foreign policy.

FIRST CONTACTS WITH THE LEAGUE

One aftermath of the separate peace was the intense hostility it engendered toward the League of Nations. So deeply had passions been
stirred by the battle over the Versailles Treaty that many citizens felt

committed to assail the infant organization long after the Senate vote
had passed into history. Not content with the abstention of the United
States, these people wished to thwart the operations at Geneva in every
way. This animus gradually diminished during the 1920's, but it colored the Harding administration and placed the question of American
membership outside the realm of practical politics.

When Secretary Hughes took office, the League had been functioning for over a year. His predecessor had received thirty-three communications, of which some—such as those on mandates—held much interest for the United States. Fifteen had not been answered, and that
number increased during the summer of 1921, when a minor official in
the State Department was allowed to place all such correspondence in a
dead-letter file. Although Hughes later disavowed any knowledge of the
procedure and claimed to have removed the offender as soon as he discovered the facts, he acted only after the newspapers had publicized
this display of bad manners.

Similar to the mail episode was the embarrassment caused by a
request for nominations to the World Court. The Statute of that tribunal had been approved on December 13, 1920. To obtain a list of names
from which the Council and Assembly could choose fifteen justices, the
judges of the old Hague Court were asked to submit suggestions. The
invitations to the four American members—Elihu Root, John Bassett
Moore, Oscar S. Straus, and George Gray—were sent on June 4, 1921,
as an act of courtesy, via the State Department. There they were
buried, and it was not until August 14 that the Secretary-General cabled the four men directly. Root and his colleagues were eager to comply but bothered by a question of propriety. Since they were asked to
act in an official capacity, not as private citizens, and since they had
been appointed to the Hague Court under a treaty to which the Senate
had consented, could they assist the League after the upper house had
rejected the Covenant? Might they not hurt Harding on the eve of the
Washington Conference by arousing the Irreconcilables? The situation
was further complicated when Root learned that he was to be one of
the American delegates to that gathering.

Under the circumstances, Root consulted Hughes before acting. On
September 8, 1921, the Secretary told him that since the Hague judges
held presidential appointments, any actions they took would be interpreted as governmental policy. In the popular mind, the Court was the
judicial arm of the League, and Hughes hoped no nominations would
be made. Root and Moore agreed readily to respect his wishes; Straus
and Gray did so reluctantly. In mid-September the four men notified
the Secretary-General that they could not make the nominations and
apologized for the delay. To some Americans, this extreme caution was
disappointing.

On several other occasions the Harding administration balked at cooperating with the League. It refused to allow an International Health Organization, created by the Assembly, to absorb the International Office of Public Health, established in December, 1907, by the United States and twelve other powers. On May 12, 1921, Hughes explained that such a departure from the original treaty would require the sanction of the Senate, and he obviously did not wish to ask for it. He also declined to proceed with an arms-traffic convention, signed with twenty-two countries on September 10, 1919. This pioneer attempt to curb trade in weapons of war was defective in several ways, and it is understandable that the Secretary and his successors were loath to submit it to the Senate. Less justifiable was Hughes' churlish refusal to answer two inquiries from Geneva in 1921 as to why his government was unwilling to go ahead. It took him until September 12, 1923 to transmit a bill of particulars, the chief of which was the bond between the convention and the League.

Among the League's early activities, none affected the United States more than the mandates question. Although under the Covenant the Council was to define the degree of control exercised by the mandatory, the allocation of the former German colonies and Turkish possessions was the prerogative of the Principal Allied and Associated Powers, operating through the Supreme Council. Wilson had been present on May 7, 1919, when the Class B and C mandates were distributed; but after the second defeat of the Versailles Treaty by the Senate, he declined to send a formal representative when the Supreme Council assigned the Class A mandates on April 25, 1920. Almost at once Secretary Colby engaged in a heated controversy with England over its alleged denial of equal trade opportunities in the oil fields of Mesopotamia and Palestine. The United States also objected to the inclusion of Yap in Japan's mandate, and on February 21, 1921, Colby declared that the American government had a right to approve both the assignment and the provisions of each mandate.

Colby's protest reached the League Council after a Permanent Mandates Commission had been set up. Among the nominees was W. Cameron Forbes, a former Governor of the Philippines. This attempt to elicit American cooperation was foiled when Forbes declined to serve. Nevertheless, the Council did its best to enable the State Department to have a voice in fixing the terms under which mandatories would discharge their trusteeship. On March 1, 1921, it postponed further action on Class A mandates and invited the United States to participate in the discussion at its June session. Hughes did not even reply to this bid. Rather than dealing with all the mandatories collectively at Geneva, he tried to protect American interests by negotiating with each separately.

CARRYING OUT THE PEACE SETTLEMENT

If the Harding administration chose to treat the League with studied hostility, it was not obligated thereby to desert the republic's wartime associates in carrying out the peace settlement. It was one thing to reject the Covenant lest it impair America's freedom of action; it was something else to desert the coalition which alone could make good the military and economic aims of the victors. The United States had a stake in the reconstruction of Europe, and it did not have to quit the Supreme Council simply because it refused to join the League.

Wilson began the process of reducing the American role in the later stages of the peacemaking. On December 9, 1919, after the first Senate vote, he recalled the remaining commissioners and restricted the presence at the Supreme Council of his ambassador to France to that of an unofficial observer. Members of the Reparation Commission and the Rhineland High Commission, two agencies in which the United States had a considerable interest, were placed in the same category. Even these informal contacts were broken off in the next two months.

At the urgent request of the Allied premiers on May 6, 1921, Harding resumed the practice of using unofficial observers. The new envoy to England was instructed to act as the President's representative at the deliberations of the Supreme Council whenever they touched upon "matters of world wide importance" but to abstain when they dealt with those of "distinctly European concern." He was also informed on May 11 that his government was most interested in "economic questions growing out of the war" and that he should exert his influence for "recognition of the open-door policy of equal opportunity." On the other hand, the United States wished to maintain "its traditional policy in political matters of European concern" and not become involved in them. As an example, Hughes declined to send a delegate to a twenty-nine-nation conference at Genoa in April, 1922, because the agenda was more political than economic. Yet so eager was the Secretary for a firsthand account of the proceedings that he had his ambassador to Italy move temporarily to Genoa, ostensibly to keep in touch with the Foreign Ministry, and permitted a minor functionary on the Reparation Commission to travel there incognito, ostensibly to vacation at the Italian seaport.

Hughes' policy enabled the United States to watch closely without participating fully as England and France tried to solve urgent postwar problems, not at the League, but in a series of conferences attended by premiers and foreign secretaries. Twenty-three of these gatherings served, however, only to lay bare the gulf separating the French passion for security and the British desire for conciliation. The British believed that a true peace must rest, not on the dominance of the victors, but on a speedy return of the defeated and outcast states into the comity of nations. The French were persuaded that security should precede conciliation; they had no faith in either the Treaty of Versailles or the Covenant. Thwarted in their bid for the Rhine frontier and deprived of the Anglo-American guarantee, they sought to check future German aggression by a ring of alliances and a strict enforcement of the reparations clauses. This last issue wrecked Anglo-French unity in 1923 and caused the focus of European diplomacy to shift from the Supreme Council to the League of Nations.

France's resort to military sanctions when Germany defaulted on reparation payments hastened the withdrawal of the American army from its occupation duty in the Rhineland. In carrying out this phase of the peace settlement, the War Department steadily reduced the size of the detachment in the Coblenz area, but it was not until the day before the French entered the Ruhr that the last contingent of 1,000 men was ordered home. In January, 1923, the Stars and Stripes were lowered over the fort at Ehrenbreitstein, where they had flown for four years and where they would be raised again in March, 1945.

In the Middle East, a region to be of paramount importance thirty years later, the United States did little to carry out the peace settlement. Since Congress had not declared war on the Ottoman Empire, Wilson and his colleagues did not share in drafting the Treaty of Sèvres of August 10, 1920. The punitive terms imposed there upon the Sultan were rejected by nationalists under Mustapha Kemal. A three-year war for revision ended with the abolition of the sultanate and a new treaty. At Lausanne on July 24, 1923, a republic renounced all non-Turkish territory lost in the war, recovered eastern Thrace and Constantinople, and demilitarized the Straits. The last were to be open to all nations in peacetime and if Turkey was neutral, in wartime. The United States sent unofficial observers to Lausanne; their chief concern was to preserve the open door, protect minorities, and free the Dardanelles.

THE SURVIVAL OF TRADITIONAL POLICIES

A final aftermath of the separate peace was the survival of the traditional bases of American foreign policy—isolationism, neutrality, and the Monroe Doctrine. The persistence of the first and the last was foreshadowed by the battle over the Versailles Treaty. With the defeat of Wilson's "concert of free peoples" and the failure to act on the French Assistance Treaty, permanent alliances were clearly ruled out; and the impulse in Washington was to disengage from Europe and East Asia, not to participate more actively in the affairs of those continents. Similarly, the pronouncement of 1823 remained inviolate, to be interpreted solely by the United States. To be sure, Secretaries Kellogg and Stimson attempted to separate the Roosevelt Corollary from the Monroe Doctrine, but most of their fellow citizens regarded the words of the fifth president as sound and timeless. Only slowly did the idea grow of transforming a unilateral responsibility to defend the Western Hemisphere into a multilateral one.

What of neutrality? Was it "no longer feasible or desirable," as Wilson had declared, "where the peace of the world is involved"? Had the United States "seen the last of neutrality under such circumstances"? The answer was no. Even for members of the League, a neutral status was still possible, while five important nations—Germany, Mexico, Russia, Turkey, and the United States—were not bound by the Covenant at all.

After the separate peace the American government did not itself assume any additional neutral duties, nor did it impose new restrictions on the wartime activity of its citizens. During the ensuing decade of relative calm little thought was given to the problems that had emerged in 1914—the sale of munitions to belligerents and the extension of loans and credits. The presidents did continue the practice, begun in 1905, of using arms embargoes to discourage revolution. Under authority granted by Congress, they prohibited the export of war materials by private firms to China and several countries of Latin America. Sometimes the ban was against both sides, sometimes only against the rebels. Occasionally surplus stocks from government arsenals were sold to regimes faced with insurrection. This was done for Mexico in January, 1924, and for Nicaragua in February, 1927. As to the international traffic in munitions, Harding refused to send to the Senate the Treaty of St. Germain of September 10, 1919. A revised version was signed at Geneva on June 17, 1925, but it was not approved until June 6, 1935, and then it never went into effect.

The issue of neutral rights also persisted beyond the separate peace, although the absence of large-scale wars permitted a respite from the sort of controversies that led to American intervention in 1917. Wilson had included the freedom of the seas—a vague term at best—in his Fourteen Points, but the Paris Conference took no action on it. How far a future administration would go in insisting upon the right of American citizens to travel on armed belligerent ships in dangerous waters remained unanswered during the 1920's. So did the question of whether the United States would carry on trade with a country against whom the League of Nations had applied economic sanctions.

Some attempts were made to clarify the rules of war at sea. In Washington on February 6, 1922, the United States, England, Japan, France, and Italy signed a treaty requiring submarines, when operating against surface vessels, to conform to the traditional custom of visit and search and to provide for the safety of passengers and crew. The Senate gave its consent unanimously on March 29, but the French declined to ratify. The same principles were written into Article XXII of the London Naval Treaty of April 22, 1930; and these were accepted by the United States, England, and Japan on October 27, 1930; by France and Italy on November 6, 1936; and by more than thirty other nations—including Germany and Russia—by 1939. On February 20, 1928, the Sixth International Conference of American States concluded at Havana an agreement on maritime neutrality which sought to bring the Latin American countries into accord with the Hague Conventions of 1907, but up to 1939 that document had been ratified by only the United States and five other signatories.

Perhaps the most significant postwar development in the realm of neutral rights was the virtual abandonment by the American government of claims for losses suffered by its citizens from 1914 to 1917 as a consequence of British belligerent practices. Before entering the conflict, Wilson had argued that the taking of American lives by German submarines required immediate reparation but that England's destruction or confiscation of American property could await monetary compensation at the close of hostilities. After the armistice it was widely felt that the principle of the freedom of the seas would be vindicated by having these claims arbitrated, and several times between January, 1921, and June, 1926, the Senate prodded the executive with requests for information on the progress of negotiations. Both Hughes and Kellogg were reluctant to press the issue, partly because the moral force of the earlier neutral protests had been blunted by subsequent wartime practices and partly because England had been angered by the terms imposed on the funding of its war debts. Furthermore, a State Department examiner reported on November 9, 1926 that only eleven claims out of more than 2,600 possessed conspicuous merit. Warning that in a future war the United States might wish to restrict neutral maritime commerce by the same measures employed by the Royal Navy, he advised that nothing be done which could "later hamper our freedom of action in case of emergency." Accordingly, on May 19, 1927, the United States and Great Britain signed an executive agreement providing in effect that neither would press diplomatically for or demand arbitration of the war claims of its citizens.

Without, then, departing from its isolationism, neutrality, or the Monroe Doctrine, after the separate peace the United States evolved a series of agreements and policies which formed the interwar compromise. First, there was the Pacific treaty system, designed to preserve the *status quo* in that ocean and in East Asia. Second, there was the limitation of armaments, particularly of naval tonnage. Third, there was cooperation with the League of Nations, initially confined to economic and social matters but later intruding on diplomatic affairs. Fourth, there was to be a qualified membership on the World Court. Fifth, there was the Kellogg Pact, a simple renunciation of war as an instrument of national policy and a promise by over fifty nations to settle disputes among themselves by peaceful means. Sixth, there was the Good Neighbor ideal, an attempt to promote hemispheric solidarity against threats to peace from within and without. This interwar compromise was not, of course, a tightly integrated security system, but rather an alternative to one. It was a jerry-built structure, lacking a consistent design and standing unfinished when subjected to its first challenge along the South Manchuria Railroad in September, 1931.

33

❯❯❯-❯❯❯-❯❯❯-❯❯❯❮❮❮-❮❮❮-❮❮❮-❮❮❮

The Pacific Treaty System

FIRST TO EMERGE as an element in the interwar compromise was the Pacific treaty system. It consisted of three interrelated agreements, negotiated at the Washington Conference between December 13, 1921, and February 6, 1922. Although Harding and Hughes had called that gathering primarily to check a costly race in capital ship construction, they soon discovered that the only way to reach their goal was to attack simultaneously certain diplomatic problems of East Asia and the Pacific. Their willingness to do so revealed once again that the United States entered into regional understandings more readily in the Orient than in Europe. Alliances and commitments to use force were barred in both areas, but the new Pacific treaty system, in dealing with China and Japan, built upon the older and more limited work of Hay, Root, Bryan, and Lansing.

THE WASHINGTON CONFERENCE

A large volume of unfinished business in the Far East faced the incoming Harding administration. China still lacked a central government strong enough to keep order and uphold its territorial integrity. Ever since the death of Yüan Shih-k'ai in June 1916, presidents and premiers had followed each other in rapid succession. A clique of conservative war lords, claiming constitutional legitimacy, ruled in the north, with their capital at Peking. In the south, a pseudo-liberal regime at Canton under the leadership of Sun Yat-sen, the apostle of revolution, tried to maintain its hold against provincial leaders and bandits. Most of Manchuria was under alien control, and the German concessions in Shantung, seized by Japan, had not been returned. The outside world conducted its diplomacy through Peking, but no group spoke for China, and the question might arise whether a nation really existed. Asiatic Russia was in equal turmoil. The authority of the Bolsheviks ended at Lake Baikal, and a separatist republic functioned at Chita. Japanese troops had not yet left the Maritime Province or northern Sakhalin.

Much uncertainty prevailed regarding the American possessions. In his last annual message Wilson had reminded Congress of the promise in the Jones Act to grant the Philippines independence whenever a stable government had been set up; but the return of the Republicans, long the conservative party in colonial matters, and the appointment of Leonard Wood as Governor, made unlikely an early relinquishment of American sovereignty. As to Guam, naval strategists revived plans to convert that island into a Gibraltar of the Western Pacific, but those dreams were jeopardized by a growing legislative revolt against military spending. Yet a new order of sea power was confirmed on June 4, 1921, when it was announced that the decision, taken two years earlier, of dividing the United States Fleet between the Atlantic and the Pacific would be carried further by basing the newest and largest units on the West Coast.

The most pressing problems, however, were with Japan. In the first place, the United States had run into a stone wall in its efforts to prod the Japanese into returning the Kiaochow leasehold to the authorities at Peking, into removing their soldiers from along the Chinese Eastern right of way, and into evacuating all Russian soil. Secondly, a deadlock had been reached on the territories mandated to Japan at the Paris Peace Conference and later confirmed by the League of Nations. Wilson had fought against the inclusion of Yap in the Class C mandates, and Hughes broadened the issue on April 2, 1921, by challenging the legality of any distribution of the former German colonies without American consent. A third source of trouble was the rampant nationalism which swept the United States after 1918 and fed the demand for more stringent immigration laws. A revision of the Gentlemen's Agreement was long overdue, and the question of alien land ownership again agitated California. Finally, a smoldering naval rivalry had flared up as both countries embarked upon an ambitious construction program.

Any expansion and relocation of American sea power affected England as well as Japan. Britannia still ruled the waves with the world's largest fleet, but her current building was confined to a handful of auxiliaries and converted vessels. Burdened by debts, England had no desire for more capital ships, yet it could not ignore the challenge from across the Atlantic. In the face of changed global conditions, the Brit-

ish were prepared to abandon the two-power standard they had insisted on before 1914 and concede, in theory at least, equality or parity
to the United States navy. But that problem was linked to the Anglo-
Japanese Alliance, a bond which had outlived the needs it had filled in
1902 and which was now intensely disliked in the United States and in
some of the Dominions. Yet the cabinet of Lloyd George was loath to
give up the historic safeguard without substituting another, and it
wondered how to dispel suspicions in Washington without hurting feelings in Tokyo.

Two events in the summer of 1921 enabled England to resolve the
dilemma. One was an Imperial Conference at London, where Canada
persuaded Lloyd George to terminate the Anglo-Japanese Alliance
when the third renewal expired in July. The second was an overture
from the United States on July 8 to participate in a three-power conclave at Washington for the limitation of armaments. The Foreign Office promptly suggested an enlargement to include all countries with
interests in East Asia; for if other nations also attended, it might be
possible to replace a bilateral defensive pact with a more general accord. Under the circumstances, Hughes readily agreed to expand the
gathering and broaden the agenda.

In picking the delegates to the Washington Conference, Harding
consciously avoided the path Wilson had trod in 1918. He confined his
own role to a welcoming address and made certain that both the Senate
and the opposition party were properly represented. The chairman and
guiding spirit was Secretary of State Hughes. Root, the dean of the Republicans, provided prestige and perspective. From the Senate the
President chose Lodge, head of the Foreign Relations Committee, and
Oscar W. Underwood of Alabama, the Democratic floor leader. He thus
made sure that Lodge's power was on his side, while Underwood's vote
on the German treaty showed that, unlike many Wilsonians, he would
not allow bitterness over the loss of the Covenant to prejudice him
against a new effort to promote peace.

Equal care was taken by the other powers. Arthur J. Balfour, a
former Prime Minister, headed England's delegation, which also included the First Lord of the Admiralty, the ambassador to the United
States, and ranking Dominion officials. Foreign Minister Aristide
Briand spoke for France, and Senator Carlo Schanzer for Italy. Japan
named an imperial prince but transacted most business through Tomo-
saburo Kato, Minister of the Navy, and Kijuro Shidehara, Japan's envoy in Washington.

THE FOUR-POWER AND FIVE-POWER TREATIES

At the opening session on November 12, 1921, Hughes astounded the
Washington Conference with a detailed plan to limit the battle fleets of

the United States, Great Britain, Japan, France, and Italy. Specific vessels, built and building, were earmarked for decommissioning; and a
hush prevailed while the Secretary sank more British battleships, as
one observer put it, "than all the admirals of the world had destroyed in
a cycle of centuries." Despite initial enthusiasm for his proposal, it
soon became evident that scrapping hulls and discarding blueprints
were not enough. The nations accepting curbs on their navies required
some assurance that these would not imperil their safety. Thus while
public attention focused on the limitation of armaments and the future
of China, the two chief items on the agenda, Hughes searched quietly
for a formula that would stabilize the Pacific by ending the Anglo-Japanese bond, by settling the mandates question, and by providing security
for the insular possessions of all the signatories. Fearful of the Senate,
he declined to join any alliance or make any commitment to use force.
Wary of a tripartite agreement which might leave the United States in
a minority, he hit upon the idea of including France. The result was the
Four-Power Treaty of December 13, 1921, an indispensable preliminary to the Five-Power Treaty on armaments and the Nine-Power
Treaty on China.

This nonaggression pact substituted a quadripartite promise to
consult for a bilateral obligation to fight. By its terms, the United
States, England, France, and Japan agreed to respect their mutual
rights "in relation to their insular possessions and insular dominions in
the region of the Pacific Ocean." Should a controversy arise between
two of the four "out of any Pacific question and involving their said
rights," which could not be settled by direct negotiation, then they
would invite the other two to a conference at which the dispute might
be adjusted. If the rights of any signatory were threatened by an outsider, the four nations would communicate with each other as to "the
most efficient measures to be taken, jointly or separately, to meet the
exigencies of the particular situation." The treaty was to last ten
years; after that period, it was to remain in effect until one of the parties gave a twelve-month notice to end it. Upon the pact's going into
force, the Anglo-Japanese Alliance would lapse.

Almost at once uncertainty arose. The secrecy with which the
Four-Power Treaty had been negotiated bred suspicion and false
charges. Did it constitute an alliance? Was the promise to respect territory a polite way of expressing a pledge to guarantee it? What were
the rights and which were the insular possessions that each signatory
was bound to leave inviolate? Were the Japanese home islands—
Honshu, Hokkaido, Shikoku, and Kyushu—and the mandates assigned
to Japan—the Marshalls, Carolines, and Marianas—covered by the
pact? Hughes had tried to follow Root's example of 1908 and avoid any
semblance of an alliance. He left China to be dealt with in a separate

treaty. He was willing to allow the Japanese to decide whether metro-politan Japan should be included, but their delegates had a hard time making up their minds. Nor was his task simplified when, on December 20, 1921, Harding gave to the press an interpretation of the agreement that was diametrically opposed to Hughes' own. Eventually the President corrected himself, but the damage was done.

Some clarification was, therefore, necessary before the Four-Power Treaty could go to the Senate. Upon signing, Hughes formally declared that it was the intent of the contracting parties to apply its terms to the Pacific mandates but that the United States did not thereby accept arrangements previously made without its consent. He stipulated further that the controversies mentioned in the text did not embrace questions which, under international law, lay exclusively within the jurisdiction of sovereign states. These disclaimers protected American rights on Yap and elsewhere; they also made it clear that congressional restrictions on immigration could not be brought before a four-power conference. On February 6, 1922, Hughes concluded a supplemental pact in order to meet the latest wishes of the Japanese delegates and to silence the continuing protests of the senatorial critics. It specified that the insular possessions of Japan, referred to in the original treaty, were Formosa, the Pescadores, the mandated islands, and the southern half of Sakhalin.

Of all the settlements reached at Washington, the Four-Power Pact encountered the severest opposition in the Senate. Unlike the Five-Power Treaty, which satisfied an overwhelming demand to reduce naval expenditures, and the Nine-Power Treaty, which embodied the traditional open door policy, it lacked popular support. The man in the street never understood that, without it, there would have been no agreements on armaments and China. He looked upon it as an entangling alliance and the product of secret diplomacy. Since the other treaties would fail if the four-power accord were rejected, Lodge insisted that the Senate vote on it first and persuaded Harding to present it in person. On February 10, 1922, the President flatly asserted: "There is no commitment to armed force, no alliance, no written or moral obligation to join in defense." But his words did not quiet the fears of a noisy minority which cut across party lines and which tried without success to compel the executive to make available all papers bearing upon the negotiations.

Attempts to defeat or amend the Four-Power Treaty failed. Senators who called the agreement "treasonable and damnable" or "a war breeder" had to be content with a reservation sponsored by Brandegee, a former Irreconcilable. This disclaimer, which had the backing of both Harding and the Foreign Relations Committee, stated that the Senate, in giving its consent, understood that the pact contained "no commitment to armed force, no alliance, and no obligation to join in any defense." With this stipulation the upper house approved the treaty on March 24, 1922, by a five-vote margin of 67 to 27. The close tally suggests that, although the obligations of the United States were minimal and did not differ markedly from some of those contained in the Root-Takahira exchange of notes in 1908, the Four-Power Pact would not have mustered the requisite majority if the Senate had not been eager to secure the benefits of the Five-Power and Nine-Power Treaties.

Hughes' quest for stability in the Pacific took him beyond the Four-Power Treaty. Although he rejected Holland's plea to be included in the nonaggression pact, he did persuade the other three signatories to join with him on February 3, 1922, in assuring the Netherlands through identic notes that they would respect Dutch rights in the oil-rich East Indies. In a bilateral agreement with Japan on February 11, 1922, the Secretary gave his approval to the mandates north of the equator in return for explicit promises that the rights of American citizens would be recognized. As a result, Yap dropped out of the headlines. Still more important was Article XIX of the Five-Power Treaty of February 6, 1922, the other provisions of which will be discussed in the next chapter. By this clause the United States, England, and Japan agreed not to fortify further or build new naval bases in most of their insular possessions in the Pacific. More precisely, the American government promised not to augment the defenses of the Aleutians, Midway, Wake, Tutuila, Guam, and the Philippines, but it reserved the right to develop Hawaii and the islands adjacent to its continental shores, including Alaska and the Canal Zone. The British accepted the principle of non-fortification for all parts of their Pacific empire except Singapore, Australia, New Zealand, and the islands along the Canadian coast. The Japanese—who were already barred from using for military purposes their mandates in the Marshalls, Carolines, and Marianas—renounced their freedom to strengthen the Kuriles, the Bonins, the Ryukyus, Formosa, and the Pescadores. The home islands and southern Sakhalin were not covered by Article XIX.

THE NINE-POWER TREATY

The Nine-Power Treaty of February 6, 1922, on China wrote into international law the concept of the open door which the United States had advocated since Hay's first circular notes on September 6, 1899. It was designed to supplement those parts of the Root-Takahira Agreement of November 30, 1908, which had not been covered by the Four-Power Pact and to eliminate all ambiguities arising out of the Lansing-Ishii exchange of November 2, 1917. While it fell far short of what China wished and, like every agreement reached at Washington, relied for enforcement on the pledged word of the signatories, it did represent a promise by the United States, Great Britain, France, Japan, Italy, Portugal, Belgium, and the Netherlands to give the Chinese people an opportunity to put their house in order. It must also be judged in the light of the other understandings relating to China which were concluded either in the conference itself or by some of the participants independently.

Although the Chinese delegates to the Washington Conference came from a land torn by internal strife, they were unanimous in the goals they sought. They wanted something more than renewed assurances that Japan and the West would respect China's territorial integrity and administrative entity or maintain the equality of economic opportunity therein. They hoped to eliminate the century-old system which had enabled other countries to carve leaseholds out of Chinese lands, to station troops on Chinese soil, to impose limitations on Chinese tariffs, and to exempt their citizens from Chinese justice. An attempt to remove these infringements of sovereignty had been thwarted at Paris in 1919. Now, at Washington, in 1921, they would try again.

Article I constituted the core of the Nine-Power Treaty. In it the contracting parties, other than China, agreed:

> (1) to respect the sovereignty, the independence, and the territorial and administrative integrity of China; (2) to provide the fullest and most unembarrassed opportunity to China to develop and maintain for herself an effective and stable government; (3) to use their influence for the purpose of effectually establishing and maintaining the principle of equal opportunity for the commerce and industry of all nations throughout the territory of China; (4) to refrain from taking advantage of conditions in China in order to seek special rights or privileges which would abridge the rights of subjects or citizens of friendly States and from countenancing action inimical to the security of such States.

In return, China promised not to alienate or lease any portion of its territory or coastline to any power and not to discriminate in any way against any of the powers on any of the railways under its control. Most of the other articles spelled out in more detail these general principles, but the seventh provided for full communication among the signatories "whenever a situation arises which in the opinion of any of them involves the application of the stipulation of the present Treaty." Other governments which had been recognized by the signatories and which had treaty relations with China might be invited to adhere. No provision was made for terminating the pact, and no time limit was written into the text.

Unwilling to place in the Nine-Power Treaty the full range of

China's aspirations, the delegates at Washington dealt with some of them in supplementary resolutions and agreements. A customs convention, also signed on February 6, 1922, by the same nine nations, provided for an immediate 5 per cent increase in duties on imports, for subsequent additions in the next few years, and for an early review of the entire problem; but this welcome gain in revenue did not constitute the tariff autonomy the Chinese envoys sought. Similarly, a demand for terminating all special privileges which derogated from Chinese sovereignty went largely unheeded. The most that could be obtained was a resolution, adopted on December 10, 1921, creating a commission to investigate current practices in extraterritoriality and in the judicial system generally. As with tariff autonomy, inquiry turned out to be delay, not prompt reform. Still other resolutions looked to the withdrawal of foreign troops from Chinese soil, the reduction of China's own forces, and the publication of all obligations incurred by China to the great powers.

Little was done by the arms conference itself to re-establish China's territorial integrity, but several steps taken independently and simultaneously worked to that end. On February 1, 1922, Great Britain offered to restore Weihaiwei. Three days later, after protracted negotiations under Anglo-American good offices, Japan and China signed a separate treaty by which the former handed back the Kiaochow leasehold; but the final arrangements enabled Japan to retain for another fifteen years control of the Tsinan-Tsingtao Railway. At the same time Hughes strove for a mutual abrogation of the Lansing-Ishii notes, arguing that they had been superseded by the Nine-Power Treaty; but not until December 27, 1922, when confronted with a threat to publish the secret protocol, did the government at Tokyo yield. It was adamant, however, in refusing to renounce any of the concessions in southern Manchuria which it had wrung from Russia at Portsmouth in 1905 and which it had confirmed in May, 1915, in a series of treaties with China following the presentation of the Twenty-One Demands. The Secretary did elicit from Shidehara on January 23, 1922, a public pledge that Japan would withdraw at an early date from Russian territory in eastern Siberia and northern Sakhalin.

Unlike the quadripartite nonaggression pact for the Pacific, the Nine-Power Treaty on China was received with great enthusiasm in the United States. There were no unexpected negotiations to explain and no secret commitments to fear. A joint subscription to general principles, not a pledge to use force, had become the customary method for upholding American interests, economic and diplomatic, in East Asia. Hence, the Senate gave its consent on March 30, 1922, by a vote of 66 to 0. The customs convention was approved the same day by a count of 58 to 1. Ratification by the other signatories soon followed. Even in

Japan, where the reduction of naval armaments and the end of the alliance with England encountered considerable objection in the Diet, the legislators acquiesced silently in the Chinese settlement.

THE TREATY SYSTEM IN OPERATION

We should not render final judgment on the Pacific treaty system until we have analyzed, in the next chapter, the related question of arms limitation. The initial consequences, however, can be appraised here, at least as they pertain to relations with Japan and China. With the former, tensions subsided. The race in capital ship construction was checked; and although competitive building soon resumed in cruisers, efforts were made to curb that too. The development of naval bases in a potential theater of war was also suspended. The cancellation of the suspicion-breeding Lansing-Ishii Agreement, the removal of the emotionally charged Shantung issue, and the ultimate withdrawal of the Japanese troops from Russian soil, all helped to clear the air. Indeed, a cordiality reminiscent of the pre-Portsmouth era was reached when the American people and their government gave generous monetary and material assistance after an earthquake devastated Tokyo in September, 1923.

Much of this gain was nullified in May, 1924, by a legislative affront to a proud race. The wave of xenophobia which gripped the United States in 1919–20 revived opposition to Oriental immigration and alien land ownership. Given time, the diplomats might have devised a satisfactory solution, but in the fetid atmosphere of the Great Red Scare, neither patience nor tolerance was in large supply. Beginning in 1921, some fourteen states joined California in enacting laws to restrict the ownership or leasing of land by foreigners, and on November 13, 1922, the Supreme Court ruled that Japanese subjects could not become American citizens by naturalization. Although on May 19, 1921, Congress passed emergency legislation embodying the quota principle—which would have reduced the inflow to a trickle—that approach was too moderate for the Japanophobes. Complete exclusion was their goal.

Hughes sensed the danger and moved to forestall it. He warned the House Committee on Immigration on February 8, 1924, that such a law would destroy the goodwill produced by the arms conclave and urged that instead Japan be placed under the quota system. If that were done, no offense could be taken; and the number of Japanese eligible for annual admission would be only 246, considerably fewer than those entering under the Gentlemen's Agreement. But the committee was troubled by the meaning of that agreement and reported a bill calling for exclusion. Hughes then suggested that Ambassador Masanao Hanihara draft a letter setting forth his government's understanding of the notes exchanged in 1907–8. The resulting document, dated April 10, disavowed any desire to interfere in the right of the United States to regulate immigration. Hanihara thought that a diplomatic solution, agreeable to both sides, could be reached easily; but he feared that unless some concession was made to Japanese pride, the pending statute might have "grave consequences" upon the happy relations then existing. Hughes concurred in these sentiments and promptly sent the correspondence to Congress.

There the Secretary's stratagem boomeranged. Ignoring all explanations, the House passed the exclusion bill on April 12, 1924, by an overwhelming majority of 323 to 71. In the Senate, Lodge and others tore the words "grave consequences" out of their friendly context and insisted that the United States must not yield to such veiled threats. In vain did Hughes and Hanihara deny that any intimidation had been intended. On April 15 an administration amendment to recognize the Gentlemen's Agreement as still binding was rejected, and a variant of the House bill was then adopted by a margin of 71 to 4. While a conference committee was ironing out the differences in the rival measures, Coolidge tried to win a two-year postponement in applying the exclusion clause; during that time a treaty might be negotiated to achieve the same purpose. After being twice rebuffed by his own party leaders, the President signed the new immigration law on May 26, 1924, declaring that, if it had been possible, he would have vetoed the article aimed at Japan.

Congressional intransigence itself had grave consequences. The danger, as Hughes wrote a friend on April 24, 1924, was "not one of war but of the substitution of antagonism for cooperation in the Far East." Certainly the first fruits of the exclusion law were baneful. Crowds picketed the American embassy in Tokyo and voiced threats to boycott American goods. Hanihara resigned in humiliation, and on May 31 the Japanese government formally protested. In time the agitation subsided, and the two nations managed to collaborate in the diplomatic arena until 1931; but the affront was not forgotten, and it served as a convenient pretext for Japanese extremists who, as the decade closed, began to chafe under the Pacific treaty system.

As for China, the aftermath of the Washington Conference was most disappointing. The studies of tariff autonomy and of extraterritoriality did not produce any immediate results. Arrangements for the British restitution of Weihaiwei were not settled until April 18, 1930; and although the Japanese withdrew from Kiaochow and from along the Chinese Eastern right of way, they retained control of the Tsinan-Tsingtao Railway and refused to discuss revising the treaties of May, 1915. Worse yet, there was no progress in the quest for unity. China was not putting its house in order. There was a constant overturn of war lords in Peking, and their clashes with the followers of Sun Yat-sen in Canton continued to bleed the land. Manchuria remained virtually autonomous, and the Soviet Union, its civil war ended, tried to draw all of China into the Russian orbit.

This turbulence and threat of communist infiltration disturbed the signatories of the Nine-Power Treaty. On June 7, 1923, Hughes told the Chinese minister that since the Washington Conference the situation had grown worse, not better. It was idle, he said, to talk about China's sovereignty and territorial integrity when China lacked a government able to exercise authority throughout its domain and competent to discharge its international obligations. On December 6, 1927, Coolidge described China as an unhappy country, "torn by factions and revolutions which bid fair to last for an indefinite period." Yet never, apparently, did American diplomats consider revising or abandoning the Pacific treaty system. The United States avoided taking sides in the civil strife and, despite attacks upon its citizens and their property, declined to join the other Western powers or Japan in reprisals and degrading demands.

Actually, 1927 marked a small turning point in China's destiny. In April, Chiang Kai-shek, leader of the conservative wing of the Kuomintang or National People's party, broke with the Communists whom Sun Yat-sen had welcomed into the fold before his death in March, 1925. Chiang established his capital at Nanking, purged his ranks of Russian agents, and drove their native disciples into the mountains of Kiangsi in South China. On June 8, 1928, he occupied Peking, and on July 25 the United States recognized him as the rightful ruler of China by concluding a treaty which at long last granted tariff autonomy. On paper, the unification of China, so ardently desired at the Washington Conference and so vital to the Pacific treaty system, seemed complete. In fact, however, the next years were not ones of peace and independence but of continued war and ultimate armed intervention by Japan.

34

The Limitation of

Armaments

SIMULTANEOUSLY with the forging of the Pacific treaty system at Washington in 1921–2, the United States laid the foundation for the second element in the interwar compromise. This was the limitation of armaments, mainly naval armaments—the most popular policy of the period. A reluctance to maintain large military forces was rooted deep in the traditions of the republic, and after 1918 few Americans doubted that peace would be promoted by scrapping obsolete vessels afloat, abandoning modern dreadnoughts on the ways, and curtailing future capital ship construction. The Five-Power Treaty of February 6, 1922, embodying those ideas, and the supplemental London Treaty of April 22, 1930, which placed curbs on smaller craft, were hailed as major diplomatic triumphs, and it was widely regretted that similar reductions could not be effected on land and in the air. That verdict was not challenged until after Pearl Harbor, when criticism of these interwar restrictions was as sweeping and unreasonable as the earlier praise had been lavish and unreasoning.

THE PROBLEM OF ARMAMENTS

The problem of armaments in the preatomic age was infinitely simpler than today. In the era of conventional weapons, the force-in-being counted for much less than the industrial plant. From 1921 to 1939 there was still time to gird for battle after the shooting had started, although the democracies gambled recklessly with survival by indulging too freely in that luxury. But technology was then relatively stable, and a country planning an attack could not easily conceal its preparations. Changes in the tools of war came slowly, as civilian leaders attempted for fiscal reasons to extend the life of those on hand. Only the developments in air power injected an element of flux and uncertainty. Compared with the present, the task of arms control in those years now seems deceptively easy.

Yet even then the obstacles to limitation were formidable. The American people were not prepared for the task by experience or temperament. It was not until Wilson's wartime demand that future armies and navies be reduced to the lowest point consistent with national safety and until Congress' postwar revolt against military spending that the issue received full attention. Optimistically, the man in the street in 1921 hoped for a prompt and comprehensive solution. Illogically, he failed to distinguish between single weapons and the total potential of a nation. He did not understand that industrial capacity, raw materials, financial resources, scientific research, and sheer man power were much more significant items than a few additional tanks, ships, and men. He did not see how senseless it was to separate, as isolationism required, curtailments in armaments from commitments in diplomacy. Security depends on many variables, and only the impotent will give up their freedom to arm without assurances that such concessions will not endanger their very existence. The average citizen did not grasp how impossible it was to equate the needs of all countries by one yardstick. Each sets different values upon and each preferred different components within land, sea, and air power.

However inadequately the American people envisaged the task of disarmament, they unmistakably demanded that something be done. Congress rather than the president responded first. It encouraged a speedy demobilization. It cut back the bloated wartime army to the small peacetime cadre of professionals. It refused to authorize any new ships and it threatened to halt construction on those provided for in the act of 1916. On December 14, 1920, Borah introduced a resolution requesting that Great Britain and Japan be invited to discuss joint measures for reducing naval estimates over the next five years by up to 50 per cent. The notion of an arms conference caught the public fancy. At first the Harding administration hesitated, as Lodge and other big-navy adherents warned against the menace of Japan. But the legislature found the appeal of a tax cut irresistible, and the executive discovered that a conclave in Washington, broadened to include problems of East Asia, was an excellent escape from the blind alley into which it had wandered with campaign talk about an association of nations. An amended Borah resolution of July 12, 1921, passed the Senate by 74 to 0 and the House by 352 to 4.

One other development in the summer of 1921 bolstered the cause of naval limitations. That was the highly publicized and controversial bombing tests off the Virginia Capes conducted by the airplanes of Brigadier General William L. Mitchell on a group of anchored warships, some of them already obsolete against surface craft. Although one may doubt that much was proved by repeated runs over vessels that could not take evasive action and which lacked both antiaircraft guns and fire-control crews, some observers hastily concluded that the days of the battleship were numbered. Thus, the Five-Power Treaty was the product, not only of an idealistic reaction against war and of a realistic concern for the taxpayer, but also of an incipient misgiving about the nature of future conflicts and the vulnerability of traditional fleets.

THE FIVE-POWER TREATY

Signed on February 6, 1922, by the United States, Great Britain, Japan, France, and Italy, the Five-Power Treaty represented the first voluntary acceptance by large nations of restrictions on their liberty to possess weapons of war. Basically the work of Hughes and his civilian advisers, it rested on two principles. First, navies should be limited in a ratio calculated on their existing strength. Second, specific tonnage quotas for different categories would be met by scrapping vessels afloat, by halting construction on the ways, and by regulating building in the future. No attempt was made to deal with land or air forces; and as it was not feasible to place curbs on every type of warship, attention was centered on the most powerful. Since it was equally impossible to gain assurances on armaments without touching broader aspects of foreign policy, this agreement was closely interrelated with the Four-Power nonaggression pact for the Pacific and the Nine-Power Treaty on China.

Capital ships were the primary concern of the negotiators. Whatever role air power might play in the years ahead, the heavily gunned battleship and battle cruiser still had to be regarded as the backbone of the fleet. It was in that category that nations had concentrated their efforts before 1914; it was in that class that competitive building was most marked in 1921; it was in that area that the conference effected the most substantial savings.[1] After long discussion, the delegates

[1] As of November, 1921, the capital ship strength in dreadnoughts was as follows. In commission: United States, 18 (all battleships); Great Britain, 43 (33 battleships, 10 battle cruisers); Japan, 10 (6 battleships, 4 battle cruisers). Under construction: United States, 15 (9 battleships, 6 battle cruisers); Great Britain,

agreed: first, to abandon current capital ship programs; second, to accept a maximum tonnage quota that would require the scrapping of capital ships already in commission; third, to prohibit new construction in capital ships for ten years; and fourth, to define the size of capital ships so that none would exceed 35,000 tons or mount guns with calibers of more than sixteen inches. The tonnage quotas were set as follows:

United States	525,850 to be distributed among 18 ships
Great Britain	558,950 to be distributed among 20 ships
Japan	301,320 to be distributed among 10 ships
France	221,170 to be distributed among 10 ships
Italy	182,800 to be distributed among 10 ships

The text of the treaty contained the name of every vessel to be retained or given up and a schedule of replacements through 1942. When those replacements were completed, the tonnage quotas would be 525,-000 for the United States and Great Britain; 315,000 for Japan; and 175,000 for France and Italy—a ratio of 5 : 5 : 3 : 1.67 : 1.67. The exact sacrifices each signatory had to make are indicated below.

	United States	Great Britain	Japan	France	Italy
Tonnage	843,380	447,750	192,751	none	none
Pre-dreadnoughts	15	9	8	0	0
Dreadnoughts	2	13	1	0	0
Ships under construction	13*	0	6*	0	0
Ships authorized	0	4	8	0	0
Spent on ships building	$277,695,000	169,936,000	106,796,000	none	none

* two additional vessels converted to aircraft carriers

Aircraft carriers, then in the experimental stage, were also restricted by the Five-Power Treaty. Again the tonnage quota system was used, and a maximum of 135,000 was allotted to the United States and England, 81,000 to Japan, and 60,000 to France and Italy. Again the upper limits in size and armament were defined. No carrier could exceed 27,000 tons or mount guns of more than eight inches. For the

0; Japan, 7 (3 battleships, 4 battle cruisers). Authorized but not begun: United States, 0; Great Britain, 4 (all battle cruisers); Japan, 8 (4 battleships, 4 battle cruisers). Each nation also possessed many obsolete predreadnoughts which had little or no combat value.

sake of economy, each signatory was permitted to convert to this category two capital ships, built or building, and these might be as large as 33,000 tons. This concession was extremely valuable for the United States, for Congress had refused to authorize any new carrier construction. Thus two battle cruisers, begun under the act of 1916 and earmarked for scrapping, were redesigned and joined the fleet at the end of 1927.

Cruisers, destroyers, and submarines were not placed under a tonnage quota at Washington. France had accepted the curbs on capital ships and aircraft carriers with the utmost reluctance, and it would not tie its hands on smaller craft. The United States could not bargain on auxiliaries, for it had no huge building program to give up. Hence the sole limitation in the Five-Power Treaty affecting cruisers sought to prevent pocket battleships from masquerading in an unrestricted category. It provided that no cruiser could weigh more than 10,000 tons or carry guns of more than eight inches. Another agreement, also signed on February 6, 1922, tried to govern the operation of submarines and thereby eliminate one argument for additional escort craft; but that treaty, as we have seen, was not ratified by France.

Other clauses in the Five-Power Treaty deserve mention. As has been noted above, Article XIX restrained the United States, England, and Japan from enlarging existing fortifications or starting new bases in most of their insular possessions in the Pacific. The treaty was to last until the end of 1936 and as long thereafter as desired, but beginning on December 31, 1934, anyone could give a two-year notice to terminate. Each signatory could also request a new conference whenever it believed that changed conditions were endangering its security. In any case, a new conference had to be held after eight years. Lastly, a signatory at war had the right to suspend for the duration all but two minor articles. In such cases, the others would consult as to their own courses of action.

From the diplomatic point of view the Five-Power Treaty was a substantial achievement. It offered a heartening example of great states settling their problems by discussion and compromise. It fostered better relations among the major Pacific nations and halted a dangerous race in capital ships. From the domestic point of view the pact had comparable advantages. It restored to America some of the moral leadership that had been lost with the separate peace. It met the prevailing demand for less military spending, and the prompt consent which the Senate gave on March 29, 1922, by a vote of 74 to 1 testified to its popularity. But from the strategic point of view the agreement was more open to criticism, and the admirals did not hesitate to denounce it as a blow to American sea power. More specifically, they deplored losing a golden opportunity to gain a two-ocean fleet.

throwing away millions already spent on vessels from 4 to 76 per cent completed, and giving up the means of defending the outposts in the Western Pacific.

Actually, the sacrifices which aroused the navy's ire were more apparent than real. None of the predreadnoughts that were scrapped would ever have steamed again in the battle line, while most of the leviathans then building under the act of 1916 would probably have been abandoned in a few years for want of funds. Ever since 1899 Congress had refused to erect a Far Eastern Gibraltar in Guam or the Philippines. The Washington Conference accepted a situation; it did not create one. Article XIX was a tacit admission that two decades of indecision and neglect had allowed control of the Western Pacific to pass to Japan. Nor can one say with assurance that the United States could have achieved the world's greatest navy. To attain supremacy it would have needed the building program of 1916 and still more; and there is no reason to suppose that England, as yet unmindful that its Victorian grandeur was ebbing away, would have relinquished its cherished trident without a struggle.

This initial attempt was a partial success. It did not cover every class of warship, and it left unsettled the submarine issue which had driven the United States to war in 1917. It failed to establish beyond cavil the principle of Anglo-American parity. It ignored Germany and Russia, potential maritime nations. It revealed the difficulty of using tonnage quotas as the sole basis of calculation. It made clear that diplomatic agreements must accompany military concessions. To be sure, the consequences of the Five-Power Treaty were not all beneficial, but it would be unfair to dismiss the pact as a typical example of American idealism, naive in its reliance on paper promises. Rather, it was a tentative and partial first step in grappling with an enormously complex question, and its framers were realistic enough to understand the art of the possible. They had only begun an experiment; others would have to continue, reappraise, and—if need be—abandon it.

THE QUEST FOR FURTHER LIMITATIONS

Further limitations could be of three kinds. The tonnage quota system might be applied by the five powers to all naval craft. Similar restrictions might be extended to other maritime nations, great and small. Or attention might be focused on land and sea units. Only the first of these was realized, and rather incompletely, before the initial challenge to the interwar compromise occurred in September, 1931.

As might be expected, the United States left to the League of Nations the initiative in dealing with guns, tanks, and planes. Hughes believed that the American army and air corps were too small to burden

the taxpayer or menace the peace, and he argued that the reduction of
ground forces was essentially a European problem. Nor was he disposed to take the lead in securing the adherence of other European
countries to the principles of the Five-Power Treaty. The Western
Hemisphere was another matter. Under the auspices of the Harding
administration, the Central American republics signed on February 7,
1923, a comprehensive convention which limited, but did not reduce,
the size of their land, sea, and air components. Less success attended
Hughes' efforts at the Fifth Inter-American Conference, which opened
at Santiago on March 25, 1923, and the Secretary had to be content
with a meaningless recommendation that all New World states should
adhere to the prohibition against battleships of more than 35,000 tons
and aircraft carriers of more than 27,000 tons.

Even the extension of the tonnage quota system to the smaller warships of the five powers ran into serious obstacles. In England the idea
of parity was not accepted wholeheartedly. In Japan the desire for a
higher ratio in auxiliary vessels became a matter of pride. France
grew reluctant to discuss navies apart from security pacts, while Italy
began to fear the building programs of other Mediterranean countries.
In the United States, Congress encouraged the president on January 22, 1923, May 28, 1924, and February 11, 1925, to call a new conference, but this popular enthusiasm was tempered by the few who
realized America's glaring deficiency in fast, modern cruisers.

Indeed, the question of cruisers provoked most of the controversy
from 1922 to 1930. Those vessels varied considerably in size, speed,
armament, and duties; and since different nations used them for different missions, their value to the fleet was less easy to measure than
that of the costlier battleship. In 1921 the United States had none in
commission and ten on the ways. England, on the other hand, had
thirty-four in service and six building, while Japan owned seven with
six under construction. In 1922, 1923, and 1924 the British laid down
five additional vessels and the Japanese ten. The expected response
came on December 18, 1924, when Congress authorized the president
to undertake, prior to July 1, 1927, the construction of eight 10,000-
ton cruisers, each mounting eight-inch-caliber guns. This bill stimulated further building abroad, and by October, 1926, the race looked as
follows.

	United States		Great Britain		Japan	
Built	10	75,000	40	194,000	19	102,000
Building and appropriated	5	50,000	14	138,000	6	54,000
Total	15	125,000	54	332,000	25	156,000

To attain the same ratio established at Washington for capital ships, the United States would have to build twenty-one more cruisers while its rivals virtually stood still. Clearly such an expansion did not accord with the popular desire for reductions or the Coolidge gospel of economy, and the best hope for parity lay in reaching some new international agreement. Consequently the United States sponsored a three-power conference which met at Geneva from June 20 to August 4, 1927.

Poorly conceived and badly executed, the Geneva Conference was a dismal failure. France and Italy would not participate. The delegates were able but second-rank figures. No prime minister or foreign secretary attended, and unlike Hughes in 1921, Kellogg was unable to devise a dramatic opening move behind which public opinion could mobilize. His instructions contained nothing more than a plan which had been rejected in 1922; when it was turned down, a deadlock over cruisers ensued. The United States and Great Britain drifted far apart, as each tried to protect the type which best met its own strategic needs. The former desired a small number of large vessels with eight-inch guns; the latter preferred a large number of small vessels with six-inch guns. In contrast to their situation at Washington, the Americans negotiated from weakness. They had no nearly complete ships on the ways to scrap, and they were not prepared to offer a diplomatic assurance such as the Four-Power Treaty.

Failure at Geneva in 1927 brought Anglo-American cordiality to the lowest point in a decade. The cruiser race entered a new phase when Congress, on February 13, 1929, authorized the president to construct fifteen more 10,000-ton vessels and one aircraft carrier before June 30, 1931. This statute, combining the largest building program since the act of 1916 with a request for another arms conference, helped pave the way for eventual agreement by showing the British that the American demand for parity must be taken seriously. The final opportunity came in the spring of 1929, when Hoover, a firm believer in cooperation with England, replaced Coolidge in the White House and Ramsay MacDonald, a staunch advocate of disarmament, succeeded Stanley Baldwin at 10 Downing Street.

Under these favorable conditions the cruiser deadlock quickly broke up. The United States removed one cause when on April 22, 1929, it announced at Geneva that it was not committed to the concept of a single tonnage quota for each class of warship. MacDonald eliminated a second cause three months later by telling the House of Commons that he accepted the principle of parity in all categories. There then remained the task of drafting some formula which would place a ceiling on cruiser tonnage and still permit each navy to build, within defined limits, the type best suited to its needs. That goal was attained after a summer of intensive talks, and in the autumn MacDonald climaxed this resurgence of harmony by visiting America. On October 7 invitations went out for a new five-power gathering at London, with the dual purpose of extending the tonnage quota system to smaller vessels and of fulfilling the injunction in the Washington Treaty to hold another conference after eight years.

THE LONDON TREATY

Determined to avoid the fiasco of 1927, Hoover spared no effort to duplicate at London the diplomatic triumph of 1922. He persuaded a reluctant France and a doubting Italy to attend. He picked a delegation consisting of Secretary of State Stimson, Secretary of the Navy Charles F. Adams, two influential senators—one from each party— and three highly competent ambassadors. He encouraged the other participants to send equally distinguished men, and they responded favorably. Exploratory conversations smoothed out all Anglo-American differences and assured acceptance of the request by Japan for slightly higher ratios. The one pitfall was France's determination that a security pact accompany any further limitation in armaments; and on that point the conference, which met from January 21 to April 22, 1930, almost collapsed.

What France demanded was an Anglo-American promise to consult should it be endangered, as a consequence of now naval restrictions, by Germany or in the Mediterranean. Foreign Minister Briand did not care how this pledge was given, but it had to go beyond the Four-Power Pact. Stimson feared a refusal would drive France from the conference, yet he knew that acquiescence might be repudiated at home. Torn by conflicting emotions, he wavered and even contradicted himself. He was rescued from his predicament by Hoover's unwillingness to sanction any consultative agreement, lest it bring defeat to the naval treaty in the Senate. The British also decided to avoid the sort of commitment which had taken them into war in 1914. Rebuffed on two sides, France would not accept any extension of the tonnage quota system, and its attitude led Italy to follow suit. This failure to solve the French security problem caused the five-power negotiations to end in a tripartite settlement.

By the terms of the London Treaty of April 22, 1930, existing restrictions on capital ships were modified in three ways. First, the ten-year holiday in the construction of battleships and battle cruisers was extended to December 31, 1936. Second, the tonnage allowance in this category was revised downward, so that the United States and Great Britain dropped from 525,000 to 464,300 and 474,500 respectively while Japan fell from 315,000 to 272,000. These new quotas, still in a 5 : 5 : 3 ratio, necessitated scrapping or demilitarizing three American capital ships, five British ones, and one Japanese. Third, the number of vessels of this type was set at fifteen, fifteen, and nine.

The cruiser settlement was complicated. For the first time a tonnage quota was imposed in this category, but it required altering the capital ship ratio and distinguishing two types of cruisers. Vessels mounting guns with calibers of more than 6.1 inches, henceforth known as heavy cruisers, were limited in both numbers and total tonnage. Those carrying ordnance with a caliber of 6.1 inches or less, subsequently called light cruisers, were restricted only in total tonnage. Although the United States was given several options, it chose to build as many of the 10,000-ton heavy cruisers as possible, and the following tabulation shows how the problem was ultimately solved.

	United States		Great Britain		Japan	
Heavy cruisers	18	180,000	15	146,800	12	108,400
Light cruisers		143,500		192,200		100,450
Total tonnage		323,500		339,000		208,850

Under this arrangement, the light cruiser ratio was 10 : 10 : 7; that in heavy cruisers was, on paper, 10 : 10 : 6. To satisfy Japan, however, Stimson promised not to complete three of the eighteen American units before 1936, 1937, and 1938. Thus a ratio of 10 : 10 : 7 in heavy cruisers would exist for all but one year in the life of the London Treaty.

For the first time, too, destroyers and submarines received a tonnage quota. Japan's existing strength in those categories justified an improvement in the capital ship ratio. In destroyers the allotment of 150,000 tons to the United States and England and of 105,000 to Japan meant a relative standing of 10 : 10 : 7. In submarines the Japanese achieved parity as each fleet received 52,700 tons. As to aircraft carriers, the limitations fixed at Washington were left unchanged.

Among the other provisions, Article XXII forbade submarines to attack without warning or without caring for the safety of those aboard when operating against merchant shipping. A comparable agreement in 1922 had never gone into effect because the French had reneged. This time all five powers ratified the prohibition; unlike the rest of the London Treaty, which expired on December 31, 1936, this article was without a time limit. Since, however, it was the only important section in which France and Italy concurred, escape clauses had to be inserted for the United States, England, and Japan. Each was left free to increase its tonnage in cruisers, destroyers, and submarines whenever any one of them deemed its security to be jeopardized by the building activities of nations not covered by the quotas.

In spite of obvious shortcomings, the London Treaty was well received at home. Major criticism came from only two sources. One was the big-navy bloc in Congress, which, along with most high-ranking officers, deplored the narrowing superiority over Japan. Unable to persuade the public that restrictive agreements were unwise, these men attacked concessions made in heavy cruisers. The other source was those senators who opposed any commitment to use force. Suspicious of consultative pacts and mindful of the disclaimer appended to the Four-Power Treaty, they asked the executive for all confidential memoranda bearing upon the negotiations. Hoover refused to comply, but on July 11, 1930, he assured the lawmakers that nothing had been concealed. Still dissatisfied, the upper house gave its consent on July 21 by a vote of 58 to 9, but with the express understanding—embodied in a reservation—that there existed no hidden files or secret agreements which affected the published text.

Japan ratified the treaty only after a bitter internal battle. Scorning the improved ratios accorded smaller craft, extremists insisted upon complete parity for the Imperial Navy, and it took all the prestige that Prime Minister Yuko Hamagachi and Foreign Minister Kijuro Shidehara could muster to get the agreement approved. The subsequent murder of the Premier seemed to many a warning against deferring to the Occident.

Any final judgment on the London Treaty and its predecessor must take into account the general temper of the times and the specific objectives of the framers. The interwar quest for limiting armaments was very popular in the United States, and in 1930 there was still reason to hope for beneficial results. The admirals were understandably hostile, charged as they were with defending the republic, but to fly in the face of public opinion required more foresight and courage than the political leaders of the 1920's possessed. Harding, Coolidge, Hoover, Hughes, Kellogg, and Stimson—as well as all defeated presidential candidates—favored arms cuts, and Stimson's stand is revealing. A firm believer in preparedness, he shared the pacifistic Hoover's enthusiasm for the work accomplished at London.

Given these attitudes, the American goal in 1930 was to insure naval parity with England and to keep a 30 per cent superiority over Japan without having to embark on a huge building program. This could be achieved best by extending the quota system to cruisers, destroyers, and submarines and by fixing the total tonnage in each category at a figure which would check the race the Five-Power Treaty had diverted to lighter craft. That goal was attained at London, but at a price. The agreement was confined largely to three nations and filled with escape clauses. It might not last more than six years; its reception in Japan suggested it would not. It was clear that no further meaningful reductions could be made without diplomatic concessions to those countries limiting their armaments, yet the men in Washington hesitated to take that step.

Was the price of partial success at London too high? Was it wise for the United States and Great Britain to restrict each other when in the decade ahead they would face danger from a common foe? The answer in 1930 could well differ from that of today. Then there was good cause for optimism. Then the paralyzing hand of the depression had not yet been fully felt. Germany, freely accepting the western boundaries imposed at Versailles, had joined the League. Russia seemed more interested in domestic reconstruction than in world revolution. Italy was still seeking its aims by peaceful means; Japan's record since 1922 had been exemplary. All the great powers had recently signed the Kellogg Pact renouncing war as an instrument of national policy; all would soon attend the long-awaited World Disarmament Conference. The latter's task would be greatly facilitated by a partial solution of the naval problem.

All in all, American diplomats had little choice in 1930 but to try to limit armaments by international agreement. The London Treaty was the best they could obtain so long as a policy of isolationism obliged them to keep arms reductions separate from other collaborative efforts to promote peace. The baneful consequences of the naval treaties of 1922 and 1930 were not the specific restrictions on warships but the general attitude they fostered. Like other elements of the interwar compromise, they lulled people into a false sense of security and a rigid way of thinking. They made Americans unwilling before 1936 to build the quotas permitted and reluctant after that date, when the pacts expired, to rearm in the face of obvious peril. In short, to experiment with limitations from 1922 to 1930 was not a mistake, but to persist in it after world conditions had changed profoundly was sheer folly.

35

❯❯❯·❯❯❯·❯❯❯·❯❯❯❮❮❮·❮❮❮·❮❮❮·❮❮❮

The League, the Court, and the Kellogg Pact

THE NEXT three elements of the interwar compromise in foreign affairs can be considered together. They consisted of a cautious but growing cooperation with the League of Nations, a prospective but ultimately abortive membership on the World Court, and an enthusiastic but often frustrating sponsorship of the Kellogg Pact. By collaborating with an international organization in most of its economic and social endeavors but few of its diplomatic ones, by seeking a qualified adherence to an international tribunal, and by advocating in a multilateral treaty the renunciation of war as an instrument of national policy, the United States went well beyond its prewar strivings for peace. To the historian that fact is significant, even though the half-measures—shaped to accord with the principle of isolationism and a prohibition against commitments to use force—seem minimal today.

COOPERATION WITH THE LEAGUE OF NATIONS

America's first contacts with the League had been marred by needless discourtesy and ill-concealed hostility, but that phase, which reflected the bitterness aroused by the battle over the Covenant, soon passed. In April, 1923, Harding could bring himself to say that the institution at Geneva was helping the Old World but, he hastily added, "it is not for us." Throughout the decade the executive branch insisted that the

question of membership had been decided once and for all. In this the
legislature concurred. Indeed, to join the League was not politically
possible. No presidential nominee in 1924, 1928, or 1932 dared propose such a step. Although the Republicans grew less hostile and by
1932 boasted of the Hoover administration's contribution to the World
Disarmament Conference, they continued to warn against alliances
and foreign partnerships. As heirs of Wilson, the Democrats were
often ambivalent but regarded talk of membership as unwise.

Outside the political arena the League was widely discussed in
books, essays, and lectures. The treatment was highly emotional. Belief in or opposition to the fledgling at Geneva became for most citizens an article of faith, not a reasoned conviction. The way in which
membership could help or hurt American foreign policy was rarely
analyzed with precise knowledge or logical thinking. Whether the
United States could find security outside the Covenant was seldom
probed realistically.

From 1921 to 1931 cooperation with the League occurred at three
levels. One was formal correspondence through diplomatic channels.
The Council, the Assembly, and the Secretariat could communicate
with Washington by means of the American minister at Berne or the
consul at Geneva, and the United States was fortunate in having at the
Swiss capital in these years men of exceptional ability—Joseph C.
Grew, Hugh Gibson, and Hugh R. Wilson. A second level was informal
discussions with officers and members of the League and unofficial
participation in some of its functions. Here discretion was necessary;
at the outset it was not safe for Grew to be seen in League buildings,
even on social calls. The first unofficial observers were not chosen
from the diplomatic corps, and Grew had to wait until February, 1924,
before being allowed to attend a League meeting in that role. The third
level was official participation in the work of the League. This began
in November, 1924, with very minor matters, but by 1926 Gibson and
others were aiding in preparations for the World Disarmament Conference. So far as the men in Geneva were concerned, however, this
growing cooperation was no substitute for American membership.
Without the United States the League was sorely handicapped in both
its normal functions and its repeated attempts in the 1920's to supplement and improve its basic structure. These efforts, it is now clear,
were institutionally the most meaningful of the decade.

A Draft Treaty of Mutual Assistance on September 29, 1923, was
the first move to strengthen the Covenant, especially Articles 10 and
16. If adopted, it would require every signatory to render immediate
military aid to any signatory that was attacked. It empowered the
Council to designate the aggressor within four days, to determine what
troops and ships each party should provide, and to appoint a com-

mander of the combined operations. This vast authority was subject
to two restrictions. No state was compelled to send its armed forces
outside its own continent and none could claim benefits from the treaty
until it had complied with a plan the Council was to devise for limiting armaments. As might have been expected, the United States declined on June 16, 1924, to have anything to do with this League-
sponsored project. Its sweeping obligations were also too much for the
British Dominions and the Scandinavian countries, who wanted to curtail, not enlarge, the demands of the Covenant. The deathblow came
from the Labour cabinet of Ramsay MacDonald, which argued that
the guarantees afforded did not warrant reducing armaments.

As an alternative, on October 2, 1924, Anglo-French leaders offered the Protocol for the Pacific Settlement of International Disputes.
Known as the Geneva Protocol, this document tried to define aggression and close the gap in the Covenant under Article 15. To do so, it
relied heavily on arbitration. It required the signatories to adopt the
optional clause in the World Court Statute and thereby bind themselves to refer to that tribunal all disputes of a certain type. It broadened the authority of the Council in those controversies submitted to
it. It provided for a conference on disarmament at Geneva in June,
1925. If substantial cuts were agreed upon then, the sections dealing
with arbitration and security would go into effect at once; otherwise
they would not. Hughes refrained from giving his blessing to this new
approach, and the British Dominions were openly hostile. Ever since
the abstention of the United States, many parts of the Empire had
lost their enthusiasm for the League. As one Canadian put it: "We live
in a fire-proof house, far from inflammable materials." Under these circumstances, the Conservative cabinet of Stanley Baldwin rejected the
Geneva Protocol on March 12, 1925, and killed the proposed arms
parley in the process.

Regional arrangements obligating only those nations directly concerned proved to be the best solution to the problem of supplementing
the Covenant. Gustav Stresemann, the German Foreign Minister, had
made that suggestion on January 20, 1925, in advancing a perpetual
four-power guarantee of the boundary with France. The British liked
the idea; and after some delay, caused by futile attempts to deal in a
similar fashion with Germany's eastern limits and by successful efforts to bring the Weimar Republic into the League, a series of interlocking treaties was initialed at Locarno on October 16, 1925. Under
the most important—the Treaty of Mutual Guarantee—Germany,
France, and Belgium promised to keep inviolate their frontiers drawn
at Versailles as well as the demilitarized zone west of the Rhine. They
vowed never to attack each other and to settle all disputes by the procedures envisaged in the Geneva Protocol. England and Italy joined in

enforcing the guarantee. To supplement this five-power Rhineland pact, Germany negotiated arbitration conventions with France, Belgium, Poland, and Czechoslovakia, while France concluded mutual-assistance agreements with the last two. This was the most hopeful moment on the European scene of the interwar years.

There was no thought of drawing the American government into the Locarno guarantees, nor would an attempt have succeeded. Secretary Kellogg declined to advise Germany during the preliminary conversations, and on June 5, 1925, he warned his minister in Poland "that the United States could not in any way associate itself with a Security Pact." A month later Coolidge publicly advocated the regional approach for those nations directly affected and on December 8 told Congress somewhat smugly: "These recent Locarno agreements represent the success of this policy which we have been insisting ought to be adopted, of having European countries settle their own political problems without involving this country."

Thus far and no further did the United States go before 1931 in cooperating with the League of Nations. Today the contribution may seem negligible, but it did mark a substantial advance over the prewar years. Whether full partnership in the 1920's might have averted the tragedies of the next decade is impossible to say, but we must not assume that it would have. To be a member was not the same as fulfilling the obligations of membership. That is the point Grew made in his diary upon leaving Berne in March, 1924. "We are not yet ready for membership," he wrote, "or for participating in the political activities of Europe—I don't know that we ever shall be. We have too many discordant elements in our own country, and an American member of the Council and the Assembly could never properly represent the country as a whole. Every position he might take with regard to European politics would infuriate some national element at home, the Italians or the Irish, the Germans, Poles, or Jews. This is the real and practical reason for our not joining."

MEMBERSHIP ON THE WORLD COURT?

If after 1921 joining the League of Nations was politically impossible, membership on the World Court seemed to be a feasible goal. The American people had a deep-rooted faith in legal processes, and they took pardonable pride in their Supreme Court. At the Second Hague Conference in 1907 their government had proposed to create and to participate in an international tribunal. Wilson had envisaged such a judiciary in 1919, Root had helped bring one into being in 1920, and Moore had become one of the judges in 1921. From 1923 to 1935 four successive presidents, representing both political parties, recommended conditional adherence to this Permanent Court of International Justice, even though it was also the judicial arm of the League.

Since political questions went to the Council, the Court dealt with legal issues. Its work was of two sorts. First, it might prepare advisory opinions upon the request of the Council or Assembly. Second, it could decide all cases which members voluntarily referred to it either by special agreements or general conventions. An optional clause enabled states wishing to do so to promise in advance to submit all disputes involving the interpretation of a treaty, a question of international law, the existence of a fact which—if established—would constitute a breach of an international obligation, and the extent of the reparation to be made for such a breach. In arriving at their decisions, the judges were to apply international conventions, judicial findings, legal principles recognized by civilized states, and teachings of qualified publicists. A majority of the justices present must concur in all verdicts.

On February 23, 1923, Harding asked the Senate to adhere to the Protocol and Statute of the World Court. He also transmitted a letter in which Hughes argued that the tribunal was independent of the League and that its decisions were "not controlled or subject to review" by it. Of course, nonmembership in the League posed problems, and Hughes urged that his government join subject to four conditions. First, adherence was not to imply a legal relationship with the League or an assumption by the United States of any obligations under the Covenant. Second, the United States was to be permitted to participate in those proceedings of the Council and Assembly in which the judges were chosen. Third, the United States was to pay its share of the Court's expenses through appropriations by Congress. Fourth, the Statute of the Court was not to be amended without the consent of the United States. The Secretary also advised that his government reject the optional clause for compulsory jurisdiction.

With only ten days left before adjournment, the Senate was not likely to heed Harding's plea for prompt action. But no one foresaw a delay of three years. First Lodge and then Borah kept the matter buried in the Foreign Relations Committee, where old Irreconcilables still held sway. The Court, like the League, was anathema to them. Meanwhile, Coolidge subscribed to his predecessor's plan on December 6, 1923. In the election of 1924 both party platforms endorsed the Court. On December 3, 1924, Coolidge renewed his appeal, but this time he added a fifth condition saying that the United States would not be bound by advisory opinions rendered without its express consent. On March 3, 1925, by a margin of 301 to 28, the House approved the President's recommendations, asserting that it was ready to enact whatever supplementary laws were needed.

Before a final vote came, the problem of advisory opinions was blown up into a major issue. Coolidge had noted with concern that the Court advised the Council and Assembly on the legality of acts still in contemplation; and although such opinions did not bind anyone, the President feared that they might be embarrassing. This idea was developed by Judge Moore, who warned that his tribunal might discuss in an advisory opinion the Monroe Doctrine or control of immigration, two policies most American citizens felt were not subject to international adjudication. Moore argued that members of the League had an unfair advantage in that they could in the Council or Assembly oppose a call for advisory opinions on topics distasteful to themselves. These apprehensions led the Senate to demand an expanded fifth condition, permitting the United States to block advisory opinions on matters in which it claimed an interest. The Senate also enlarged Hughes' fourth condition to include a right to withdraw at any time. Not content with these safeguards, the upper house added two more reservations. One stipulated that the United States, in resorting to the Court, must do so by treaties and thus obtain senatorial approval. The other declared that adherence to the Court should not be construed as a departure by the United States from its policies of isolationism and the Monroe Doctrine. With these understandings, the Senate gave its consent on January 27, 1926, by a bipartisan majority of 76 to 17.

But that was not the end. Although the fifth condition was not intended by most of its backers as a device to kill the Court plan, it succeeded in doing so. Normally, reservations do not require positive action by the other parties, but in this instance the Senate asked that each of the forty-eight members acquiesce separately. Several, including England, believed that some of the reservations were ambiguous; and on March 18, 1926, the Council invited the United States to a conference at Geneva to discuss them. Kellogg rejected the bid, saying he had no authority to deviate from the procedure laid down by the Senate. Meeting alone, most of the signatories agreed on September 23 to accept four and a half of the conditions but balked at permitting the American government to veto advisory opinions on subjects in which it claimed an interest but was not directly involved. That would give the United States a right the others did not possess. Again they suggested mutual negotiations to iron out the remaining differences.

In an extraordinary display of bad manners, Coolidge refused to continue the discussion or even to reply. Kellogg warned indirectly that the Senate would not be asked to modify its stand, and Coolidge declared publicly on November 11, 1926, that the United States would not join the Court unless all the reservations were fully accepted. With the same stubbornness he was to manifest after the Geneva naval fiasco in 1927, the President dropped the Court plan and concentrated on the Kellogg Pact. But popular interest did not slacken. Prominent leaders kept the idea alive, even though the party platforms failed to endorse qualified membership in 1928, as they had in 1924. Former Secretary Hughes helped by agreeing in June, 1928, to fill the vacancy on the tribunal caused by Moore's resignation, and a Senate resolution, calling upon the President to resume negotiations, was scheduled for debate in December. That month the Council decided the time had come to re-examine the Statute of the Court and invited a group of experts to Geneva for that purpose. When Root, then almost eighty-four, agreed to attend, many hoped that he could hammer out a compromise to satisfy the Senate's fifth condition.

Acting as a private citizen, Root was successful on two counts. First, with the committee of jurists he revised the Statute he had helped draw up in 1920. Second, he was largely responsible for a report on March 18, 1929, which formed the basis for a new Protocol designed to comply with the Senate's conditions. The vital part, often called "the Root formula," set up machinery whereby the American government could protest against a request for an advisory opinion on questions in which it claimed an interest. If after this opposition a majority of the Court's members still asked for an opinion, the United States might then quit the tribunal "without any imputation of unfriendliness or unwillingness to co-operate generally for peace." This cumbersome procedure did not remove all senatorial objections, nor did it quiet men such as Borah, who wished to get rid of advisory opinions altogether. But the legendary reputation of Root, the towering prestige of the incoming Hoover, and the glowing optimism engendered by the Kellogg Pact silenced critics momentarily; and when the revised Statute and the new Protocol of Accession were accepted by almost every member of the Court, the United States appended its own signature on December 9, 1929.

Again victory proved elusive. Although Hoover favored joining the World Court, he considered limiting armaments a more pressing need. Hence he gave priority to the London Treaty, and by the time the Protocol reached the Senate on December 10, 1930, the problems of the depression were gaining ascendancy in men's minds. Wary of endangering their recovery programs with divisive foreign issues, both Hoover and Roosevelt procrastinated until it was too late. Not until January 29, 1935, and then in a very different climate of opinion, did the Senate act, and the vote fell seven short of a two-thirds majority. Disappointing as this outcome was to many Americans, it may be doubted whether membership on the World Court in the 1920's would have materially altered the course of international relations. A secondary bulwark of peace at best, the tribunal was more important as a symbol of the willingness of the United States to play an increasingly prominent role in global affairs.

THE MULTILATERAL RENUNCIATION OF WAR

While cooperation with the League of Nations was being narrowly circumscribed and membership on the World Court repeatedly delayed, public opinion forced upon the Coolidge administration a simpler approach to national security. This was the Kellogg Pact, a multilateral renunciation of war. The background of this treaty, a seemingly quixotic gesture of pure idealism, is to be found in the work of three groups with very different aims—one to outlaw war, a second to promote collective action, a third to improve Franco-American relations. The first followed the lead of Salmon O. Levinson, a Chicago businessman, who was also generously endowed with persistence, salesmanship, and money. He was aided by John Dewey, the philosopher and educator; by Charles C. Morrison, editor of *The Christian Century;* and—belatedly —by Borah. The second group took its cue from President Nicholas M. Butler and Professor James T. Shotwell of Columbia University, two disappointed adherents of the League. Unlike Levinson's coterie, the Butler-Shotwell bloc regarded the multilateral renunciation of war as only the first of many steps in building a systematic peace structure. The third group found its spokesman in French Foreign Minister Aristide Briand, who wished to remove the bitterness recently created over the funding of war debts and the limitation of naval armaments. Using a draft prepared by Shotwell, Briand addressed an open letter to the American people on April 6, 1927—the tenth anniversary of the Great Crusade—in which he proposed a bilateral treaty to outlaw war and renounce it as an instrument of national policy.

To this unprecedented scheme, presented in such an unorthodox manner, the Coolidge administration was understandably cool. If left alone, Kellogg would have done nothing; but he was not granted the luxury of inertia. Butler gave publicity to Briand's appeal in a letter to *The New York Times.* Levinson stirred up a popular outcry for compliance in some form. Borah made it clear that the Foreign Relations Committee was interested. Seldom has a reluctant diplomat been so compelled to act against his wishes; seldom has grass-roots sentiment so prompted the legislature to prod the executive into formulating foreign policy. Yet Kellogg's own ideas also shaped the finished product. In the next seventeen months he succeeded—often over Briand's objections—in enlarging the project into a multilateral one, in avoiding commitments to consult or use force, in ruling out machinery for punishing violators, and in persuading the signatories and the Senate not to impair the simplicity of the text with amendments or reservations.

The resulting Kellogg-Briand Pact was signed at Paris on August 27, 1928, by fifteen nations, including the United States, Great

Britain, France, Germany, Japan, and Italy. It was a brief document of only three articles, in which the contracting parties renounced war as an instrument of policy, promised to settle all disputes among themselves by peaceful means, and invited the rest of the world to adhere. It contained no time limit, no provision for termination or change, no clause for carrying out or enforcing its terms. The word "outlaw" did not appear. Presumably the renunciation embraced conflicts of every sort; actually, such was not the case. Everyone agreed that defensive wars had not been renounced, yet no attempt was made to define them. France insisted on the right to fight in fulfillment of its obligations under the Covenant and postwar alliances; England argued that protection against attack in "certain regions of the world" was "a measure of self-defense." Kellogg accepted these disclaimers without protest, but he ruled that they were qualifications and interpretations, not formal reservations.

By the same kind of legerdemain the Senate was persuaded to approve the Kellogg Pact without change. Many lawmakers considered it vague and meaningless. Others demanded the customary reservations which would disavow any obligation to use force or any intention to sacrifice traditional policies. But the administration was determined to obtain an unfettered treaty, and displeased though he was over the omission of all references to outlawry, Borah agreed to cooperate. Only one concession was made to the Irreconcilables. On January 15, 1929, the Foreign Relations Committee presented a report giving its own interpretation of the text. It specifically stated that the right of self-defense was not curtailed and that under that prerogative the power to uphold the Monroe Doctrine was not abridged. It also declared that "the treaty does not, either expressly or impliedly, contemplate the use of force or coercive measures." No vote was taken, and Borah denied that the report was in any way a reservation. With these assurances, the Senate gave its consent that very day by a margin of 85 to 1.

It is easy to scoff at the Kellogg Pact, and it has long been fashionable to do so. A generation that survived the Second World War and lives in dread of a nuclear apocalypse may be excused if it regards the renunciation of 1928 as sheer idiocy. But to the historian it is important. By 1934 sixty-four nations, including Russia, had endorsed its provisions, and they represented the victors, the vanquished, and the neutrals of 1914–18. There were those at the time who called the Pact "an international kiss" and "worthless, but harmless." Other contemporaries disputed the harmless aspect. They argued that the multilateral instrument, like all elements of the interwar compromise, too easily satisfied the conscience of the American people and lulled them into false security. On the other hand, many intelligent citizens saw the

Kellogg Pact as marking the dawn of a new era in international relations; and while it did not do so, it played a prominent role in American diplomacy from 1929 until the Nuremberg trials of 1945–6.

THE KELLOGG PACT: END OR BEGINNING?

Even before the Kellogg Pact was proclaimed on July 24, 1929, two suggestions were being offered to insure its effectiveness. The one, contemplating a rewriting of the old arbitration and inquiry agreements, elicited no dissent. Did not the new treaty call upon the signatories to settle all disputes among themselves by peaceful means? What could be more logical than to overhaul existing machinery? The second, envisaging mutual consultation, discriminatory arms embargoes, and nonrecognition of territorial conquest, aroused protest. From the outset Borah and Levinson had opposed putting teeth into the Pact, while Butler and Shotwell had wished to do so. Thus, to some, the renunciation of war was an end in itself; to others, it was simply a beginning.

Revision of the existing machinery added little new to American foreign policy. As of December, 1927, the United States had in force thirteen bilateral arbitration conventions—identical to those negotiated by Root in 1908–9—eighteen bilateral treaties for the advancement of peace—the ones designed by Bryan in 1913–14—and two multilateral conciliation agreements pertaining to the Americas; but some were about to expire. The time had come for bringing up to date those much-publicized but little-used instruments. Accordingly, between February, 1928, and February, 1931, the State Department signed and the Senate subsequently approved twenty-seven bilateral treaties dealing with arbitration and nineteen with inquiry. All were nations outside of the Western Hemisphere.

The Kellogg-Stimson arbitration treaties of 1928–31 departed from the Root version in defining the type of questions falling within their purview. In 1908, differences of a legal nature and those relating to the interpretation of a treaty were considered proper subjects for arbitration; in 1928, an attempt was made to apply the test of justiciability, first proposed by Taft in 1911. In 1909 the exceptions were disputes that "affect the vital interests, the independence, or the honor of the two Contracting Parties, and do not concern the interests of third Parties." In 1928 compulsory arbitration was deemed unsuitable for four types of controversies: those involving obligations under the League Covenant, those pertaining to the Monroe Doctrine, those falling within the domestic jurisdiction of the signatories, and those bearing upon the interests of third parties. Otherwise these conventions were much the same as before, with the Senate still having to consent to each *compromis* setting forth the scope of the arbitration and the procedure to be followed. The inquiry agreements were more clearly worded than Bryan's pioneer efforts. Worthwhile as these changes may have been, the new treaties aroused much less enthusiasm than those before 1914. By 1931 the limitations of arbitration and inquiry were better understood.

Meanwhile three novel methods of supplementing the Kellogg Pact were under discussion. In the spring of 1929, with the aid of Shotwell, Hoover drew up two possible additions to the text. Both sought to cope with those who waged war in violation of their pledge. In one case the President would have the other signatories set up an impartial commission to investigate, conciliate, and—if the violator remained recalcitrant—withdraw diplomatic recognition. The alternative was a declaration by all signatories that they would not recognize any territorial or other gains resulting from conquest and that they would sever diplomatic relations with aggressors. Neither version got beyond the talking stage.

Other Americans saw in an arms embargo a second means of supplementing the Kellogg Pact. If Congress could authorize the president, as it had done for over twenty years, to prohibit at his discretion the export of guns and munitions to Latin America in order to discourage revolution, then surely the same device might be used to deter offensive wars. Such a ban against treaty breakers had been proposed in the House before 1928, and on February 11, 1929, Senator Arthur Capper, Republican of Kansas, introduced a resolution which would impose an arms embargo on any country which the president identified as having violated the Kellogg Pact. That suggestion also failed to bear fruit.

Thirdly, there were those who looked to consultation as the simplest way to make the Kellogg Pact workable. The three main treaties concluded at Washington in 1921–2 had obliged the signatories under different conditions to confer with each other in case of trouble. No such provision was included at Paris in 1928, and Kellogg's successor quickly regretted the omission. During the Sino-Russian clash over the Chinese Eastern Railroad in 1929, Stimson discovered how difficult it was to use the Pact effectively, and he gave much thought thereafter, to strengthening it. He toyed with a conciliation commission, as Hoover had done in 1929; and he explored the possibility of a consultative pledge at the London Conference in 1930. Reluctant or unable to link consultation with disarmament, Stimson looked again at the text and decided that consultation was implicit in the Pact. Indeed, by October 26, 1932, after three frustrating years, Stimson asserted that consultation was not only implied but also obligatory. But he could never persuade the other signatories that such was the case.

From the moment the signatures were affixed, many Americans argued that the Kellogg Pact should be the beginning, not an end. Only time would tell whether their appraisal was wiser than that of Borah and Levinson. But one fact is clear. Even those who wished to supplement the Pact did not urge doing so by armed force. As late as August 8, 1932, Stimson admitted that the treaty contained no sanctions but depended for its enforcement on the will of the people. In short, the multilateral renunciation of war in 1928 can be understood only in the light of a persistent American faith in the pledged word of nations and in a decent respect for the opinions of mankind. That faith did credit to the nation's heart but revealed a legalistic approach to international relations which characterized the entire interwar compromise and which was to prove inadequate to cope with the challenges of the future.

36

⇢⇢⇢-⇢⇢⇢-⇢⇢⇢-⇢⇢⇢-⇠⇠⇠-⇠⇠⇠-⇠⇠⇠-⇠⇠⇠

The Good Neighbor Ideal

THE LAST ELEMENT of the interwar compromise, the Good Neighbor ideal, was hardly new. In contrast to Europe and East Asia, the Western Hemisphere was an area in which the United States had long been concerned with preserving peace. Although alliances were barred there also, the United States had engaged in mediation and arbitration, regional conferences, goodwill tours, preventive arms embargoes, reciprocal trade treaties, territorial disclaimers, and plans for nonaggression pacts. The task in 1921 was less to reconcile traditional principles with the Wilsonian dream than to eliminate festering sores. This could be done best by modifying the protectorate policy, reappraising recognition procedures, separating the Roosevelt Corollary from the Monroe Doctrine, improving machinery for settling inter-American disputes, treating the sensitive Latins as equals, and not compelling them to choose between their recently forged bonds with Geneva and their more familiar ties with Washington.

NEW PERSPECTIVES IN THE NEW WORLD

Progress along those lines was facilitated by new perspectives after the First World War. That struggle had destroyed the German navy which, ever since 1898, alarmists had regarded as the chief threat to American security in the Caribbean. Neurotic fears for the safety of the Panama route could now subside. That conflict had also fed the reaction against imperialism, and an articulate segment of the American people demanded not only abandoning the protectorates but also

ending the practice of interfering in the internal affairs of New World
states. Finally, the postwar era brought another instrument for peace
into the hemispere. By March, 1921, sixteen of the Latin American
countries—all except Argentina, Ecuador, Mexico, and the Dominican
Republic—were members of the League.

Younger men in Washington helped liquidate older grievances.
Neither before nor after Roosevelt's death had Wilson been able to win
senatorial approval for the Treaty of Bogotá of April 6, 1914, and
thereby to appease Colombia. On March 9, 1921, Harding tried again,
and some Republicans who had looked upon a Democratic solution as
a partisan maneuver were now disposed to yield. It was widely charged
at the time that the petroleum interests, eager for concessions in Colombia, exerted strong pressure; but it is likely that the treaty would
have passed anyway. In its final form, it obligated Colombia to recognize Panama but also granted the Colombians $25 million and certain
rights in the canal area. The United States did not apologize for alleged
wrongdoing in the past but promised to employ its good offices for restoring diplomatic relations between Colombia and Panama. Subject
to a reservation that Colombia might not use the waterway for ships
and troops in wartime, the Senate gave its consent on April 20 by a
bipartisan majority of 69 to 19.

With Wilson gone, a fresh attempt could also be made to unravel
snarled relations with Mexico, where a far-reaching social revolution
was clashing with American business activity. The controversy over
Article 27 of the constitution of 1917 or, more precisely, over the compensation which alien property owners would receive for subsoil rights
and lands expropriated by the government, had not been settled, while
Wilson had left to Harding the decision on recognizing President
Álvaro Obregón. Before extending recognition, Hughes tried unsuccess-
fully to extract from Obregón a promise not to interfere with subsoil
holdings acquired by American citizens prior to 1917. Only after the
Mexican Supreme Court affirmed that there could be no retroactive
application of the nationalization decree where the owner had performed some positive act, such as drilling a well, was a compromise
reached on August 15, 1923, in the Bucareli agreements. Two of these
were subsequently embodied in treaties, but Obregón's pledge to respect foreign subsoil rights antedating 1917 had to be put in an executive agreement. Thus satisfied, Hughes granted full recognition on
August 31. For two more years relations were cordial; and when an
insurrection threatened in January, 1924, the Coolidge administration not only permitted Obregón to purchase arms from private manufacturers, while denying that privilege to the rebels, but also allowed
him to buy surplus stocks from government arsenals.

Despite this token of friendship, the controversy over subsoil resources broke out again when Obregón's successor, Plutarco E. Calles, declined to be bound by the Bucareli agreements. In December, 1925, the Mexican legislature limited to fifteen years the ownership of oil rights acquired before 1917. Calles also refused to cooperate with the United States in attempts to discourage revolution in Nicaragua. On January 10, 1927, in a message to Congress, Coolidge accused the Calles regime of shipping arms to rebels there, and two days later Kellogg told the Foreign Relations Committee that Russian agents had been active in Mexico "during the past few years." But neither the clamor of businessmen nor the specter of communism could shake the anti-interventionist sentiment on Capitol Hill. By a vote of 79 to 0 on January 25, the Senate passed a resolution urging arbitration of the so-called confiscations of American property.

Almost at once Coolidge's policy softened. On April 25, 1927, he expressed hopes for an amicable settlement, and on September 21 he named Dwight W. Morrow as ambassador. Morrow's success was spectacular. Aided by goodwill tours of two popular heroes, Charles A. Lindbergh, the aviator, and Will Rogers, the humorist, and guided by his own common sense, he quickly won the confidence of President Calles. Another decision by the Mexican Supreme Court and a revision of the petroleum code by the Mexican Congress paved the way for a solution which in effect rested on the Bucareli agreements. On March 27, 1928, the State Department declared that, because of steps taken by the Mexican government, the ten-year-old differences were over.

New perspectives also led to a reappraisal of the criteria for extending recognition. The Wilsonian test of constitutional legitimacy, intended to discourage revolutions in the Western Hemisphere and prevent political adventurers from gaining office by assassination, had not worked well. Many Latin Americans regarded it as a subtle form of intervention. There was much truth in that objection, for the willingness or refusal of the United States to enter into diplomatic relations with a newly formed government could spell the difference between survival and downfall. Except in Central America, Hughes and Kellogg did not emphasize the aspect of legality, while Stimson, as we have seen, made no reference to it in the three criteria he set forth on September 6, 1931. In Central America, however, the United States still respected the treaty of December 20, 1907, by which Costa Rica, Guatemala, Honduras, Nicaragua, and El Salvador agreed not to recognize any government among themselves which gained power by a *coup d'état* or a revolution against the established regime. When those nations reaffirmed and strengthened that principle in a treaty at Washington on February 7, 1923, the State Department had no choice but to adhere to the same policy so far as the five were concerned. Only when the Central American countries abandoned the concept did the United States announce on January 26, 1934, that it, too, would no longer be so bound.

MODIFYING THE PROTECTORATE POLICY

More important than the foregoing in promoting the Good Neighbor ideal was the modification of the protectorate policy. When Harding took office, American troops were stationed in Nicaragua, Haiti, and the Dominican Republic. A naval officer ruled the last. In Cuba and Panama, as well as in Haiti and the Dominican Republic, the United States enjoyed a privileged position, thanks to treaty rights. But the time had come for a change. Protectorates had been resorted to as an alternative to colonies when the latter seemed to be an anachronism in a democracy. After the First World War there was the same popular reaction against the substitute as there had been after 1902 against the original. During the next decade a flood of books and articles stressed the arbitrary and predatory nature of the insular regimes. The very titles disclosed their message: *Dollar Diplomacy, Our Cuban Colony, The Bankers in Bolivia, The Capitalists and Colombia, Dollars for Bullets*, and *Machine Gun Diplomacy*.

This agitation stirred Congress. On April 11, 1921, the Senate created a select committee to inquire into conditions on the island of Haiti. Other useful investigations followed. Legislative proddings did much to speed the recall of American forces, which withdrew first from the Dominican Republic. Actually, the process of restoring local rule there had begun under Wilson, but it proceeded slowly and was not completed until July, 1924. After eight years the Stars and Stripes were lowered, and the last marine departed. Yet not every vestige of the occupation disappeared. The customs receivership was continued by a new treaty of December 27, 1924, replacing that of February 8, 1907, and was intended to last until all outstanding bond issues had been retired. In that period the public debt must not be raised without American consent.

The next withdrawal was short-lived. In Nicaragua a deceptive six-year calm encouraged the United States to propose on November 14, 1923, an early termination of the legation guard at Managua, and the withdrawal was carried out on August 1, 1925. A revolt on October 25, however, touched off one of the most violent civil wars in Nicaragua's bloody history. Within thirteen months, four different men held the presidency. The State Department declared that it would adhere to the Central American treaty and not recognize claimants who resorted to force, but Mexico refused to be so bound or to cooperate in imposing an arms embargo. A few marines went back in May and August, 1926; many more soon followed.

To justify this much-criticized move, Coolidge reminded Congress on January 10, 1927, that the government had proprietary rights in the canal route and solemn obligations to protect the investments of its citizens. Disclaiming any desire to interfere in Nicaragua's domestic affairs, he warned that he would use the powers of the executive to uphold the nation's interests "whether they be endangered by internal strife or by outside interference." In a more conciliatory step, he sent Henry L. Stimson, then retired to private life, as his personal representative with full authority to effect a settlement. Stimson reached Managua on April 17, and by May 11, 1927, he had concluded the Peace of Tipitata. Taking advantage of the military stalemate and war weariness, he persuaded both sides to lay down their arms and abide by the outcome of an election to be supervised by the United States. It was agreed to enlarge the existing regime of Adolfo Díaz with elements of the opposition and to train the native constabulary with American officers. Except for Augusto C. Sandino, all the rebel chieftains complied with these terms.

Stimson's plan made possible the second withdrawal of troops from Nicaragua. The election of 1928 was fairly administered and ended in a victory for the former rebel general, José M. Moncado. The same was true in 1932 when Moncado's party triumphed again. The marines proceeded to train the Guardia Nacional; and if it had not been for the guerrilla warfare waged by Sandino, Nicaragua might well have ceased to be in the news. On February 13, 1931, Secretary of State Stimson announced that all combat forces would be recalled within a few months; and even when a fresh wave of banditry broke out, he made it clear that his government could not protect its citizens in the interior. On January 2, 1933, the command of the Guardia was turned over to native officers and the last contingent of marines left for home. Except for the customs receivership set up in November, 1911, by private agreement and the canal rights granted in August, 1914, by the Bryan-Chamorro Treaty, the United States ceased to hold a privileged position in Nicaragua.

Elsewhere in the Caribbean, the protectorate policy was modified more slowly. In Panama the United States waited until March 2, 1936, to replace the pact Hay and Bunau-Varilla had signed on November 18, 1903. In Cuba the Platt Amendment was not abrogated until May 29, 1934, though, strictly speaking, it was not invoked after 1921. That self-denial was sorely tested during a revolution in August, 1933, when the Roosevelt administration did rather more than mediate between rival candidates and actually withheld recognition from those it did

not trust; but no troops landed. In Haiti the American government had
been deeply involved since September, 1915, but in spite of many criti-
cisms, the Senate investigating committee recommended on April 20,
1922, that the occupation be continued. In 1930, after much material progress, Hoover began to restore independence. A treaty of September 3, 1932, provided for the Haitianization of the American-
officered constabulary, the withdrawal of all marines, and the
maintenance of limited financial control until the existing bonded
indebtedness had been liquidated. The last item caused the insular
legislature to reject the pact, but its terms were largely incorporated
in an executive agreement negotiated under Roosevelt on August 7,
1933. Although a year would pass before this protectorate was terminated officially, the necessary arrangements were complete.

From 1921 to 1933 this modification of the protectorate system
was supported by words as well as by deeds. Every president and secretary of state proclaimed, as their predecessors had done since the days
of Root, that the United States did not covet a single inch of additional
territory in the New World or wish to interfere in the domestic concerns of other American republics. They sought to divest the Monroe
Doctrine of all obnoxious connotations and to separate it from the
Roosevelt Corollary. Hughes opened this campaign in 1923, but it was
Kellogg who asked Under Secretary of State J. Reuben Clark to prepare an historical exegesis to show that Roosevelt's message of 1904
was not logically derived from Monroe's of 1823. In a long memorandum of December 17, 1928, Clark concluded that "the Doctrine states
a case of United States *vs.* Europe, not of United States *vs.* Latin America. Such arrangements as the United States has made, for example,
with Cuba, Santo Domingo, Haiti, and Nicaragua, are not within the
Doctrine as announced by Monroe. They may be accounted for as the
expression of a national policy which, like the Doctrine itself, origi-
nates in the necessities of security or self-preservation."

This Clark Memorandum, published in March, 1930, by Stimson,
did not repudiate the Roosevelt Corollary or the practice of intervention. It simply separated the former from the Monroe Doctrine and
justified the latter as an attribute of sovereignty. But neither the separation nor the justification satisfied the sensitive Latins, and the Good
Neighbor ideal had to be buttressed by an endorsement of the principle of nonintervention. Thus Hull agreed at Montevideo on December 26, 1933, subject to a single reservation, that no state had the right
to intervene in the internal or external affairs of another. Two days
later Roosevelt asserted that "the policy of the United States from now
on is one opposed to armed intervention." By adhering to the Argentine Anti-War Treaty of Nonaggression on April 27, 1934, and by accepting unconditionally a protocol on nonintervention at Buenos Aires

on December 23, 1936, the American government would soon give, as fully as words could, assurances that the era of protectorates was over.

THE INTER-AMERICAN MOVEMENT

In seeking to realize the Good Neighbor ideal after 1921, the United States continued to support the inter-American movement but encountered many difficulties. In the first place, the United States must not be too prominent. It had to emphasize the concept of equality and avoid any trace of condescension. Second, it must see that the conferences did not become a medium for attacks on Yankee imperialism. Grievances had to be appeased in advance, and controversial subjects eschewed. Third, it had to make the results of the gatherings more meaningful than other results had been in the past. The negotiation of vague treaties, which many parties did not ratify, had become frustrating. If this element of the interwar compromise was to promote hemispheric peace, then the safeguards it erected must be realistic in conception and universal in application.

Before the First World War, four International Conferences of American States had been held. A fifth was scheduled to meet at Santiago, Chile, in November, 1914, but it did not assemble until March 25, 1923. Once again the tangible results were few. A Commission of Jurists, created in 1906 to draft a code of public and private law, was reorganized. Increases in armaments beyond normal requirements were condemned, and adherence to the limitations on capital ships and aircraft carriers, contained in the Five-Power Pact of Washington, was recommended. The most ambitious undertaking was a Treaty to Avoid or Prevent Conflicts among the American States, signed on May 3, 1923, by sixteen nations and eventually in force between eight, the United States being one. Known as the Gondra Treaty, it required the use of inquiry in all disputes not settled by diplomacy or submitted to arbitration. It set up machinery for choosing the investigatory commissions whose authority was limited to examining the facts and making a report. As in the Bryan conventions of 1913–14, there was a cooling-off period but no provision for conciliation.

Dissatisfied with these minimal achievements and disappointed by a persistent Yankeephobia to the south, the Coolidge administration put its best foot forward at the Sixth International Conference in Havana from January 16 to February 20, 1928. The President participated in the opening ceremonies and Hughes came out of retirement to head a distinguished delegation. The two most important treaties, concluded on February 20, dealt with Maritime Neutrality and the Duties and Rights of States in Event of Civil Strife. The first attempted to bring the Latin American countries into accord with the Hague Convention of 1907; it was signed and ratified by the United States—along with five others up to 1939—subject to a single reservation affecting armed merchantmen. The second prohibited the export of war materials by neutrals under certain conditions; it too was signed and ratified by the United States, along with twelve others up to 1941, subject to a minor understanding. One resolution, adopted on February 18, anticipated the Kellogg Pact in condemning war. Another pledged the signatories to settle all inter-American disputes by peaceful means. A third directed a special conference to assemble at Washington within a year to give conventional form to those principles.

On December 10, 1928, the International Conference of American States on Conciliation and Arbitration, summoned at Havana, met and by January 5, 1929, had hammered out two treaties. The General Convention of Inter-American Conciliation supplemented the Gondra Treaty by clothing the commissions of inquiry with powers of conciliation. That is, the commissions could now go beyond simply investigating the facts and making a report in all controversies that were not settled by diplomacy or by arbitration. Henceforth, after finishing their report, they would submit a concrete solution and work actively with the disputants to win their approval. In a companion pact, the General Convention of Inter-American Arbitration, the United States accepted compulsory arbitration in all differences of a justiciable character, among which were those involving the interpretation of a treaty, a question of international law, the existence of a fact which—if established—would constitute a breach of an international obligation, and the nature of the reparation to be made for such a breach. Exempted from compulsory arbitration were questions which lay within the domestic jurisdiction of a disputant and those which affected the interests of or referred to the action of a nonsignatory. The Senate gave its unqualified consent to the conciliation convention on February 20, 1929, but it did not approve the arbitration agreement until April 1, 1935, and then only with the customary reservation that the *compromis* must be in treaty form.

A Seventh International Conference of American States met at Montevideo from December 3 to 26, 1933. It was the first to be held during the presidency of Franklin D. Roosevelt who, in his inaugural address nine months earlier, had dedicated the nation to "the policy of the good neighbor." It was also the first to deal with nonintervention. Because the protectorate policy had been modified and the Roosevelt Corollary separated from the Monroe Doctrine, Hull could sign the Convention on Rights and Duties of States on December 26. It asserted that "no state has the right to intervene in the internal or external affairs of another" and bound the signatories "not to recognize territorial acquisitions or special advantages which had been obtained by force." The Secretary did, however, reserve for the United States the right to act in accordance with international law as then accepted. The other important treaty at Montevideo was an Additional Protocol to the General Convention of Inter-American Conciliation, which placed on a permanent basis the commissions of inquiry and conciliation provided for in 1923 and 1929.

THE PROBLEM OF PEACE IN THE AMERICAS

By the end of 1933 the United States had done much to eliminate from Latin American minds the caricature, which had grown since the turn of the century, of a predatory Colossus of the North; but it had not yet developed effective machinery for maintaining peace in the hemisphere. The State Department rarely used the agreements which emerged from the inter-American movement in trying to compose regional differences but tended to rely on the familiar tools of negotiation, good offices, and mediation. To bring stability to a turbulent area, the United States sponsored a special conference on Central American affairs in Washington from December 4, 1922, to February 7, 1923, and in 1929 it played a helpful role in ending an ancient quarrel between Chile and Peru over Tacna-Arica. But it still shrank from embracing the principle of joint consultation or negotiating a treaty of reciprocal assistance, and it was understandably reluctant to welcome into the New World the irenic efforts of the League of Nations.

Two boundary disputes at the end of the period under review threatened to bring war to the Americas and simultaneously posed the question of what role, if any, the League might play in preserving peace. In June, 1932, the long-smoldering clash between Paraguay and Bolivia for control of the Chaco, a vast tract of worthless jungle, erupted into full-scale hostilities. Three different agencies were soon striving to check the fighting. One was a Commission of Neutrals— Colombia, Cuba, Mexico, Uruguay, and the United States—set up in January, 1929, under inter-American auspices. This body sponsored an appeal to the belligerents on August 3, 1932, in which nineteen New World republics pledged themselves not to recognize any territorial gains resulting from the conflict. A second group consisted of Argentina, Brazil, Chile, and Peru, all of whom bordered on the Chaco or the disputants. Argentina's ambitions for hemispheric leadership caused this quartet to work at cross-purposes with the Commission of Neutrals. The third was the League of Nations. Out of courtesy to Washington, the men in Geneva stayed in the background at first; but when two members threatened to violate the Covenant, the Council appointed a Committee of Three to follow the case.

Although the United States had never claimed under the Monroe Doctrine that European governments could not mediate, arbitrate, or use their good offices in the New World, it had frowned upon such practices. During the 1920's it was very sensitive about the League and repeatedly opposed that body's participation in inter-American conferences. Thus, Assistant Secretary of State Francis White, chairman of the Commission of Neutrals, was politely discouraging when the Committee of Three urged sending investigators to the scene and imposing an arms embargo. The League, he implied, need not be concerned. Even when his group virtually gave up on December 31, 1932, it turned the problem over to Argentina, Brazil, Chile, and Peru on the ground "that the nations of America working in common accord can preserve peace in this hemisphere."

During 1933 the League's efforts to halt the Chaco War were viewed more favorably in Washington. On June 24 White announced that the Commission of Neutrals was dissolving so that negotiations could be concentrated at Geneva. In December, Hull told the Montevideo Conference that the committee of inquiry recently appointed by the Council was the only body with a real mandate to act, while Roosevelt publicly commended the League's endeavors. Also indicative of this change were requests by Hoover and Roosevelt to Congress for discretionary power to restrict the export of munitions. Hoover did not conceal his intention "to join with other nations" in preventing a shipment of arms to the scene of battle. Although the legislature declined to grant such broad authority to the executive at that time, the next year it did permit a nondiscriminatory ban which Roosevelt imposed on May 28, 1934, with the full knowledge that the League was taking parallel action.

Similar cooperation with the League for preserving peace in the Americas occurred when Peru on September 1, 1932, seized the Colombian village of Leticia, a tiny jungle settlement some 3,000 miles from the mouth of the Amazon. At the request of Colombia and after conferring with the ambassadors of the major powers in Washington, Stimson reminded Peru on January 25, 1933, of its pledges in the Kellogg Pact. When this appeal failed to stem the drift toward war, the Council instructed its Committee of Three to work out a formula. The United States acquiesced in that procedure and on February 27 endorsed the specific plan proposed. Nor did Hull end this collaboration. The new Secretary did feel unable to accept an invitation to appoint a representative on an Advisory Committee to assist the Council, but he directed Minister Wilson to participate in its deliberations as a nonvoting member. The assassination of the Peruvian dictator the next month led to a lessening of tension and a retrocession of the disputed territory on June 19, 1934.

The Chaco War and the Leticia dispute had made it clear by the end of 1933 that, however far the United States had gone in realizing the Good Neighbor ideal, the machinery for preserving peace in the Americas was still imperfect. There were serious limitations to the conventions of arbitration and conciliation; there was no provision for joint consultation. The League of Nations might be helpful, but as a nonmember, the United States would always find effective collaboration difficult. The Kellogg Pact had been tried and found wanting. Hence much remained to be done if this element of the interwar compromise was to prevent wars in the New World and protect the Western Hemisphere from external attack.

37

The Problem of Germany and Russia

WITH THE benefit of hindsight, one is struck by the relatively slight attention paid to Germany and Russia in the interwar compromise. At the time the reasons for the neglect seemed compelling. In 1921 and for some years thereafter the Weimar Republic was materially prostrate and militarily helpless, while the Soviet Union was racked by domestic turmoil and threatened with internal collapse. In East Asia, the major problems of the United States were with Great Britain and Japan, who alone could compete with American sea power, challenge the open door in China, or menace the security of the Philippines and Guam. In Europe, France and England were dominant, as the former strove to maintain the advantages won at Versailles and the latter to adjust its imperial role to a changing world. In Washington, neither the economic plight of Germany nor the social upheaval in Russia appeared as important as the Pacific treaty system, the limitation of armaments, the Good Neighbor ideal, or the evolution of the League, the Court, and the Kellogg Pact.

THE ECONOMIC CONSEQUENCES OF THE PEACE

Before Hitler, the tangled question of reparations and war debts caused the American people to think of Germany as an economic problem, not as a potential foe. The Versailles Treaty had made the Reich responsible for all damage done to the civilian population of the victors, and this was interpreted to include not only real and personal property but also pensions and separation allowances. The total indebtedness and the time of repayment were left to a Reparation Commission to decide. On its recommendation, the Supreme Council approved on May 5, 1921, a schedule by which the Weimar Republic would pay $33 billion over many years. That figure did not embrace obligations in kind, the cost of the Allied occupation, or certain funds owed to Belgium. The receipts were to be distributed according to the following percentages: France, 52; the British Empire, 22; Italy, 10; Belgium, 8; Japan and the lesser powers, 8. Two installments were met in 1921, but no cash was remitted in 1922. As the value of the mark plummeted, the government in Berlin asked for a moratorium, but in vain. On January 11, 1923, one week after the Reparation Commission had declared Germany in default, French and Belgian troops began a twenty-two-month occupation of the heavily industrialized Ruhr Valley east of the Rhine.

This resort to sanctions aroused grave misgivings in America. "The prosperity of the United States," Hughes declared in June, 1921, "largely depends upon the economic settlement which may be made in Europe"; while Coolidge reminded Congress in December, 1923, that "we have a direct interest in the economic recovery of Europe." These warnings reflected the fact that the First World War had transformed the mature republic from a debtor to a creditor nation. Between August, 1914, and January, 1920, the foreign indebtedness of American citizens totaling $3,686,000,000 had been wiped out and replaced by a favorable balance of nearly $3 billion. This momentous shift resulted from the liquidation by Anglo-French holders of almost 70 per cent of their American securities and from the rise in private loans to foreigners by Americans. In addition, various governments owed the United States about $10,351,000,000. Of this amount, $7,100,000,000 had been lent in cash before the armistice and were spent largely in purchases in the United States. After the cessation of hostilities another $2,501,000,000 had been borrowed in cash, and some $750,000,-000 were taken in the form of supplies. These last two items were not used for fighting but to relieve the civilian population and to rehabilitate the credit of the Allied governments. Not included in these statistics were the claims, as yet unawarded, of American citizens against the Central Powers for damages suffered from 1914 to 1917. These claims were later referred to arbitration under an executive agreement of August 10, 1922.

Prospects for recovering such huge sums were not bright. In Europe there were devastated lands to rebuild and disrupted economies to restore. For the well-disposed, the opportunity to gain dollar credits through sales in the American market was restricted by the enactment on September 19, 1922, of the Fordney-McCumber Tariff, the rates of which in many instances were higher than those of 1913. But the chief obstacle was the reparations riddle. If it were solved on Allied terms, Germany might remain prostrate for years. If it were not so solved, the victors could plead an inability to meet their indebtedness to the United States.

After the armistice, suggestions were made that the war debts owed the American government be either lumped with the reparations due to the Allies or canceled altogether. The argument for the first course was that it would entail less dislocation of the international exchange and fewer burdens on the normal channels of trade. The justification for the second was that the loans had benefited the American economy, that the money had been spent in a common cause, and that the European members of the coalition had made a costlier sacrifice in human lives. A few people argued that the debtors could not pay and that insistence would lead only to bitterness. But the Wilson administration rejected both suggestions. The Secretary of the Treasury cabled the delegates on December 19, 1918: "Congress believes the loans are good and should be collected." At Paris the President spurned all pleas to discuss the problem in relation to the entire peace settlement. Twice in 1920 the British, who had lent to others more than they borrowed from the United States, proposed the forgiveness of all inter-Allied debts, in order to promote European recovery; twice they were rebuffed. The American government replied that, having gained no territory or material advantage from the war, it could not ask its citizens to bear the heavier taxation that cancellation would require. From that stand no political leader dared to deviate.

On June 22, 1921, Harding requested Congress to empower the secretary of the treasury to negotiate with some twenty nations for funding the debts owed the United States. The authority, as granted on February 9, 1922, created a World War Foreign Debt Commission to convert these obligations within three years into bonds bearing not less than 4.25 per cent interest and maturing not later than June 15, 1947. From June, 1923, to May, 1926, the Commission reached agreements with thirteen countries, and two more agreements were later negotiated by the Treasury Department. A total of $22,259,040,056 was funded anew at an average interest of 2.1 per cent. In every case the arrangement was below the minimum set by Congress; in each case a special exemption had to be secured. In theory, no part of the principal was canceled; actually, the amount of forgiveness ranged from 19 to 75 per cent. England, the first to settle, received the harshest terms. On a principal of $4,600,000,000, the British paid an interest of 3.3 per cent and had 19.7 per cent of the whole scaled down.

The French, who signed reluctantly, paid 1.6 per cent on $4,025,000,-000 and had 52.8 per cent of the whole canceled. The equally hesitant Italians paid 0.4 per cent interest on $2,042,000,000; their write-off was 75.4 per cent.

Although Hughes, like Wilson, barred linking war debts and reparations, he did what he could to reach a sensible solution of the latter. Convinced of the need for a businesslike appraisal of Germany's capacity to pay, he suggested publicly on December 26, 1922, that the Allies invite from all countries "men of such prestige, experience, and honor" that their findings on a schedule of payments "would be accepted throughout the world as the most authoritative expression obtainable." Distinguished American financiers, he added, would be willing to serve without government appointment. A year later, when the folly of occupying the Ruhr became self-evident, the Reparation Commission took the hint, and on November 30, 1923, it set up a commission of experts to consider means of balancing the German budget and stabilizing the currency. On April 9, 1924, under the chairmanship of Charles G. Dawes, a Chicago banker, that group made a report designed to achieve those aims and the withdrawal of the French troops. Although accepted in principle by the Allies and endorsed in general by Coolidge, this document had to be implemented at a fifteen-power conference in London that summer. Outwardly the United States held aloof from the gathering and permitted Ambassador Kellogg to join in discussing only the few matters directly affecting his government. Yet Hughes chose that very moment to attend a meeting of the American Bar Association in the British capital; he was thus able to urge, personally and successfully, that the experts' proposal be put into operation on September 1, 1924.

The Dawes Plan did not solve the reparations problem. It left unchanged the total compensation required of Germany and unsettled the date of completion. But it did arrange a rational schedule of payments, starting at once and rising in scale as the Reich's economy regained its health. It provided also for an immediate loan of $200 million, an Agent General to receive remittances, and an inter-Allied Transfer Committee to convert marks into foreign currencies. American citizens, acting in a private capacity, filled some of these posts.

For a few years reparations ceased to be a major irritant in European diplomacy. With its credit restored, the Weimar Republic met the schedule of the Dawes Plan by borrowing abroad, not by drawing upon resources at home. American investors purchased German bonds in vast quantities, and these funds, in part, enabled the vanquished to fulfill their obligations to the victors. The Allies, in turn, paid some of the annual installments on their war debts with money obtained from Germany, although not without considerable grumbling about Uncle

Shylock. Hughes and his successors did not object to this lending but
continued to argue, under congressional pressure, that reparations
and war debts were wholly unrelated. They regarded foreign investments as evidence of a sound economy and classified only a few kinds
of loans as undesirable. These were ones made to governments not
recognized by the United States, to governments which failed to maintain their obligations to this country, and to governments whose budgets were unbalanced because of low taxes. Also frowned upon were
loans for increasing armaments abroad and aiding foreign monopolies harmful to the American consumer. Lending to Germany did not
fall into those categories, and the flow of dollars in the 1920's greatly
strengthened industry and transportation in the postwar Reich.

By September, 1928, it seemed time for a definitive settlement of
the reparations question. Not only had Germany faithfully discharged
its financial commitments; it had also accepted the Locarno guarantees, joined the League of Nations, and signed the Kellogg Pact.
Berlin now asked the victors to withdraw from the Coblenz and
Mainz zones as they had earlier from the Cologne area. At Geneva,
England, France, Italy, Belgium, and Japan agreed to handle the two
problems simultaneously. A new committee of experts was convened,
and their report was ready by June 7, 1929. It was approved by seventeen nations at The Hague on January 20, 1930, and went into effect
on May 17. Although an American, Owen D. Young, was chairman, the
attitude of the United States had not changed. It refused to nominate
one of its citizens to serve with the experts or allow one of its diplomats to participate in the negotiations. It did not object, however, to
the selection of Young, a New York industrialist and member of the
Dawes panel, by the joint action of the Reparation Commission and the
Weimar Republic.

The Young Plan revised Germany's bill for reparations downward
and set a date for its liquidation. Germany's liability for the next fifty-
nine years was placed at $9 billion, of which it was to pay annual in-
stallments of about $153 million from 1929 to 1966 and of about $180
million from 1966 to 1988. Even after adding the accumulated interest, this figure was still some $6 billion below that fixed by the Su-
preme Council in 1921. The experts intentionally proportioned the
German remittances to cover the yearly amount owed by the Allies to
the United States, and they provided that any reduction in war debts
would be followed by a further scaling down of reparations. The
American government was not a party to this arrangement and persisted in viewing the two matters as unrelated. The Young Plan also
led to the final evacuation of the Rhineland. All foreign troops left the
Coblenz area on December 14, 1929, and the Mainz sector on June 30,
1930.

With Russia, the economic consequences of the peace were less important than the political. Wartime trade restrictions were lifted on July 7, 1920, except in materials used by the Bolshevik armies. In such commerce as followed, the balance was highly unfavorable to the Soviets. They imported large amounts of cotton, rubber, farm machinery, and semi-finished goods, but they exported little. The United States discouraged public credit operations and prohibited the importation of gold. Only by stimulating a demand for recognition were these economic factors significant in Russian-American diplomacy from 1921 to 1933.

THE POLITICAL CONSEQUENCES OF THE PEACE

So far as Germany was concerned, the United States viewed with equanimity the political consequences of the peace. Having renounced all responsibility for carrying out the Versailles settlement, it refused to become involved in the reparations riddle, the mandates question, or the Locarno guarantees. It benefited from the disappearance of German territorial ambitions in the New World and competitive naval building. Both countries signed the Kellogg Pact; for different reasons, each wanted other great powers to reduce their armaments. The controversies which marred the relations of the United States with France, England, Japan, and Russia after 1921 were conspicuously absent with the Weimar Republic. In such an atmosphere the diplomats were able on May 5, 1928, to conclude a compulsory arbitration treaty and a convention providing for inquiry. Whereas in 1919 American opinion was divided over the terms handed the defeated foe, ten years later there was widespread sympathy for the needless humiliation and ruinous inflation Germany had endured. In the disillusioned aftermath of the Great Crusade many Americans talked about the Versailles *Diktat* and the folly of the victors.

In the case of Russia, the United States was not so indifferent to the political consequences of the peace. The war left in its wake a government whose deeds and words were anathema to the capitalistic democracies and whose strength or weakness affected American interests, especially in East Asia. As early as August 10, 1920, Colby had expounded the case for nonrecognition, stressing the Soviet Union's dedication to world revolution and its repudiation of the obligations of the preceding governments. The confiscation of church wealth and the nationalization of land were domestic matters, not subject to foreign complaints, but the United States could protest against the sequestration of American-owned properties amounting to $336,691,000, against the cancellation of bonds bought by American citizens under the Tsars totaling $106,884,000, and against the invalidation of Treas-

ury credits to the sum of $187 million advanced to the Provisional
Government between May and November, 1917.

Hughes was not disposed to reverse the policy of his Democratic
predecessor. He endorsed Colby's objections to renewing diplomatic
relations and insisted that recognition would not bring a mutually
profitable commerce. Investment in a Communist country, he warned,
was a hazardous undertaking, and there was nothing to show that
those who acknowledged the Bolshevik regime fared better in trade
than those who did not. The United States, Hughes said, was not concerned with legitimacy. It accepted the right of revolution and of people to choose their own form of government. But the men in the Kremlin must first fulfill their international obligations by assuming the
debts of the Tsarist and Provisional authorities, by compensating
American citizens for confiscated property, and by ending support of
the United States branch of the Communist party, whose pernicious
activities sought the "overthrow of the existing political and social order." Coolidge supported these demands when he told Congress on
December 6, 1923: "I do not propose to barter away for the privilege
of trade any of the cherished rights of humanity."

Recognition of Russia remained political dynamite for another
ten years, but as the decade wore on, support slowly grew. It became
increasingly difficult to dismiss the Bolsheviks as adventurers who
would soon be ousted. By January, 1925, Germany, England, Italy,
France, and Japan had established formal relations, although the British broke them again for two years in May, 1927. Russia's adherence
to the Kellogg Pact marked another step along the road back. Yet the
implacable opposition of religious and patriotic groups so tied the
hands of party leaders that only a few courageous mavericks such as
Borah dared to urge a restoration of diplomatic intercourse. With the
onset of the depression late in 1929, the economic argument won new
adherents, even in conservative circles, but it was not until the Japanese strengthened their hold in Manchuria in 1931–2 that American
statesmen began to see the Soviet Union as a useful element in the
balance of power in East Asia.

Despite a consistent refusal to recognize the Bolsheviks, the
United States tried to act as the friend of the Soviet people. In the terrible famine of 1921 the government aided private charities and diverted funds to relief agencies independent of Moscow. Before, during,
and after the Washington Conference, Hughes posed as the defender
of Russia's territorial integrity. On May 31, 1921, he warned Japan
that the United States would never accept any arrangement which
jeopardized that integrity. On September 17, 1921, he told the authorities at Chita that the conference would serve as the trustee of
"legitimate Russian interests" in Asia. On January 23, 1922, he wrung

from the Japanese a promise to withdraw from Siberia and Sakhalin at the earliest opportunity. In Europe, Hughes waited until July 27, 1922, to acknowledge the independence of Estonia, Latvia, and Lithuania, but he coupled that step with the reminder that the Baltic States, like Poland and Finland, were exceptions to Wilson's wartime pledge to uphold Russia's antebellum boundaries.

INTERNATIONAL COMMUNISM IN EAST ASIA

However friendly to the Russian people American statesmen professed to be, they were not so regarded by the men in the Kremlin. Talk of defending the territorial entity of the Soviet Union was dismissed as either a reactionary scheme to incite a new civil war or a capitalistic plot to despoil the working class. Memories of Archangel and Vladivostok and a prolonged nonrecognition fostered a suspicion and hatred which Communist dogma inflated. The Commissar for Foreign Affairs found no help in Washington for his moves to restore Russia's prestige in Europe and to regain its prewar influence in the Orient.

Even while utterly helpless in the darkest days of the counter-revolution, the Bolsheviks had as a goal the promotion of international communism in East Asia. Although their initial bid for China's friendship failed in July, 1919, the next four years saw a steady accretion of Russian power. During that period the Lenin regime won back control over Outer Mongolia, reincorporated the separatist republic at Chita, watched the Japanese leave Vladivostok, and formed a Communist party at Shanghai. Skillfully exploiting the division between the northern and southern warlords, they forged important ties with Sun Yat-sen's Kuomintang in Canton and the feeble rulers in Peking. In August, 1923, Chiang Kai-shek, one of Sun's ablest lieutenants, went to Moscow to obtain arms and other assistance for the campaign to unify China. Two months later Michael Borodin, a Comintern organizer, reached Canton to serve as a political adviser to Sun.

A convention restoring official relations with the Peking government followed on May 31, 1924. In it, Russia abandoned its extraterritorial rights, surrendered its concessions at Hankow and Tientsin, accepted Chinese suzerainty over Outer Mongolia, and conceded that China was sovereign in the railroad zone through northern Manchuria. The future of the Chinese Eastern was to be determined by the two parties alone; the management would be joint. The same railway clauses were put into a pact of September 30, 1924, with Chang Tso-lin, the war lord of Manchuria and a favorite of Japan. Further evidence of Russia's re-emergence as a Far Eastern power came in a treaty signed at Tokyo on January 20, 1925. It renewed diplomatic intercourse and secured the evacuation of northern Sakhalin.

From 1924 to 1927 the red star shone brightly in the China sky. The Kuomintang admitted members of the Communist party and patterned many of its activities after its Russian model. Soviet agents were active from Mukden to Canton. Russian instructors staffed the military school where Chiang Kai-shek trained his Nationalist army. When he launched his drive for unification on July 9, 1926, he was accompanied by high-ranking Soviet officers. But this collaboration did not survive his subsequent victories as he swept northward and established his capital at Nanking. The rupture came in April, 1927, when radicals within the Kuomintang and their Bolshevik mentors sought a show of strength. Rallying the conservative elements and employing superior military force, Chiang purged the party of Russian influence and expelled the native Communists. When the latter used the Soviet consulate in December, 1927, in an attempt to seize Canton, he broke off relations with Moscow for another five years.

Although the United States watched these developments closely, the threat of international communism did not seem to contemporaries the paramount problem in East Asia. The Coolidge administration showed more outward concern for the defense of its nationals, the granting of tariff autonomy, and the abolition of extraterritoriality. To be sure, there was displeasure in Washington when Peking recognized the Bolsheviks in 1924 and approval when Chiang ousted them in 1927. But Manchuria had long been the focus of American interests, and it was there in 1929 that a dispute over the Chinese Eastern Railroad startled the diplomats.

The Sino-Russian controversy stemmed from the same resurgence of Chinese nationalism which two years later helped precipitate a more serious crisis in southern Manchuria. Flushed with success, Chiang Kai-shek and his associates were eager to extend their authority to the Three Eastern Provinces, where Japan and the Soviet Union possessed extensive railway rights. In 1929 it was easier to challenge the latter on both legal and military grounds. To justify what followed, the Nanking government cited the subversive activities of Soviet consulates in Manchuria, which had remained open after those in China proper had been closed. A raid on the one at Harbin led to the arrest of many Russian citizens, the removal of the Soviet railroad manager, and the virtual seizure on July 10, 1929, of the entire line. A strong protest from Moscow was met by charges of prior transgressions and the assertion that "the solidarity of the Chinese nation" was at stake. By July 19 discussions had been broken off, and both sides were mobilizing what few troops they could muster near their common frontier.

News of these events was received with dismay in Washington. A ceremonial proclamation of the Kellogg Pact was to take place on

July 24, 1929, and it was feared that two of the signatories might then be at war. Secretary Stimson was understandably eager to find a quick solution, and the multilateral renunciation seemed the most appropriate instrument. Since he could not communicate directly with the Commissar for Foreign Affairs, Stimson asked the major powers on July 18 to remind the disputants of their promise to settle differences by peaceful means. This was done at Paris, London, and Tokyo with varying degrees of enthusiasm. When, however, the Secretary proposed a conciliation commission to study the problem, he could not win support from England, France, Germany, or Japan. All argued that the plan would fail; all warned of Russian resentment. None was ready to force a settlement on Moscow or Nanking. The Japanese were particularly sensitive to any international action in Manchuria, where their interests were so vital. Hence Stimson's suggestion died at birth, but not without a leak that enabled the Soviet press to accuse the United States of selfish designs on the railroad. For the next three months the dispute simmered as German attempts at mediation failed.

By November, 1929, however, there were reports of bombings and invasions. Although no severe fighting occurred, the Kellogg Pact was being violated. On November 26 Stimson again asked the great powers to call to the attention of Russia and China their pledge of 1928. Four days later he went further. He told England, France, Japan, Germany, and Italy that, having received their generally favorable comments— actually, more general than favorable—on invoking the Kellogg Pact, he would send the correspondence directly to Nanking and through Paris to Moscow and eventually publish it. He hoped the other signatories would do the same. But the American approach found little favor in other capitals, and the response was lukewarm. Outside of Washington, there was reliance on a direct settlement, and this came to pass on December 3, before the effect of Stimson's *démarche* could be felt. A provisional peace provided for the termination of hostilities, the evacuation of territory, the release of prisoners and arrested citizens, and a reorganization of the railway to insure the joint control envisaged by the treaty of 1924.

Two lessons could be learned from the incident. One was the ineffectiveness of the Kellogg Pact. It lacked machinery for punishing violators; it did not even authorize a signatory to invoke it during a crisis. The other was the handicap of nonrecognition. Moscow did not ignore the clumsy device to which Stimson had to resort. In a stinging rebuke on December 3, 1929, Russia accused the United States of assuming powers under the Kellogg Pact which it did not possess, in order to bring pressure on one side while negotiations were in progress. With ill-concealed sarcasm, the note expressed astonishment that a government which did not entertain official relations with the Soviet Union "should find it possible to address to [the] latter advice and recommendations."

THE ONSET OF THE GREAT DEPRESSION

While China's bid to curb Russian power in northern Manchuria was failing, developments on the New York Stock Exchange warned of a fateful downturn in the American economy. The onset of the Great Depression late in 1929 did not at first markedly affect the foreign policy of the United States; but by September, 1931, when Japan moved to protect its own lifeline in southern Manchuria, the diplomats in Washington and every Western capital were fettered by domestic difficulties.

So far as Germany and Russia are concerned, only two matters linked to the depression need be mentioned here. One was the financial crisis which threatened the Reich with bankruptcy, hastened the rise of Hitler, and halted the payment of reparations. That suspension affected the remission of war debts. No longer could the relationship be denied. Moreover, unless relief were granted, Germany would be compelled to default on the huge volume of bonds held by American banks and investors. Such a catastrophe would exacerbate the grinding process of liquidation in the United States. Faced with a choice of evils, Hoover announced on June 20, 1931, that, subject to congressional confirmation, his country would waive all intergovernmental debts for one year, provided other nations did the same. This step, one of the few daring and popular acts of an unhappy administration, was eventually accepted, though not before further damage was done. France withheld approval until July 6, while the legislature, in giving its consent in December, rejected the executive's plea to re-examine the entire debt situation. As a consequence of French procrastination, Europe's monetary structure was needlessly weakened; as a result of congressional intransigence, the insoluble problem of reparations and debts continued to bedevil relations among the wartime associates even as the dictators began to march.

For Russia, the prospect of winning recognition improved as economic conditions deteriorated. Just as American taxpayers opposed any relief to foreigners that would add to their own burden, so did American businessmen seek any outlet overseas that might stimulate their own sales. The lure of trade with the Soviets became a major argument for renewing diplomatic relations with a regime which had lasted over a dozen years. In retrospect, it is clear that all too many were impressed by that will-o'-the-wisp and all too few realized that the basic problem of peace and security could not be solved while

Russia was treated as a pariah. Recognition did come on November 16, 1933; but when two years previous to that date the United States faced in southern Manchuria the first challenge to its interwar compromise in foreign policy, the Soviet Union, like the Weimar Republic, had not been properly fitted into that compromise.

38

❯❯❯-❯❯❯-❯❯❯-❯❯❯❮-❮❮❮-❮❮❮-❮❮❮

The First Challenge:
Manchuria

HISTORIANS have long asserted that the chain of events leading to the Second World War began in Manchuria in September, 1931. There and then the Japanese army, defying its civilian superiors, manufactured an incident at Mukden, fanned out from the zone guarding the South Manchuria Railway, pushed northward beyond the Chinese Eastern line, and drove the local defenders below the Great Wall. There and then the League of Nations suffered a blow from which it never recovered, as its inability to check this resort to force encouraged other dissatisfied governments to violate the Covenant and subvert the Versailles settlement. There and then the interwar compromise in American foreign policy underwent its first real challenge; the Mukden incident put to test almost every element—the Pacific treaty system, the Kellogg Pact, the limitation of armaments, and cooperation with the League. The response of the United States to Japan's actions merits the closest scrutiny, for the experience of 1931 not only profoundly affected relations with that country down to Pearl Harbor but also indirectly shaped decisions respecting Berlin in 1948, Korea in 1950, Formosa in 1955, and Lebanon in 1958.

THE CRADLE OF CONFLICT

Dangerous to peace as were the Japanese moves in Manchuria, they must not be set down as wholly naked acts of aggression. A few observ-

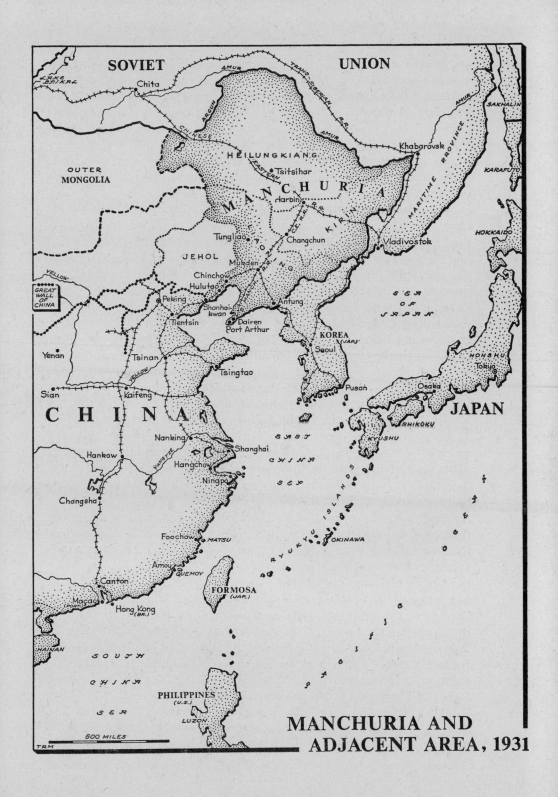

MANCHURIA AND ADJACENT AREA, 1931

ers pointed out at the time—though most Americans and much of the world forgot in the emotional turmoil of the ensuing years—that Japan possessed far-reaching legal rights in the Three Eastern Provinces of Liaoning, Heilungkiang, and Kirin. Some of these extraordinary powers had been gained, of course, through military conquest and diplomatic pressure, but China and the West had accepted them for years. It was a threat, real or alleged, to that privileged position which explains the army's coup of September 18, 1931, and the ultimate acquiescence in it of the moderate cabinet of Reijiro Wakatsuki.

That privileged position dated back to 1905. It included the Kwantung leasehold, an area of 1,300 square miles at the tip of the Liaotung Peninsula; the South Manchuria Railway, connecting Port Arthur and Dairen on the Yellow Sea with Changchun 400 miles to the north; the stationing of military guards, fifteen to a kilometer, in a narrow zone paralleling the South Manchuria; the Antung-Mukden line, providing a link with Korea which had been annexed in 1910; and broad concessions to Japanese citizens to reside, rent land, and engage in business outside the leasehold. The South Manchuria Railway, however, was the key to Japanese operations on China's soil. Organized in 1906 as a private corporation, it was in fact a governmental enterprise. It offered many services other than transportation, such as schools, libraries, and agricultural depots. It financed the construction of branch lines and exerted great influence in small towns. It enabled Japan to control certain taxes, public utilities, and law enforcement agencies. A League of Nations commission in 1932 aptly remarked: "There is probably nowhere in the world an exact parallel to this situation, no example of a country enjoying in the territory of a neighboring State such extensive economic and administrative privileges."

Such conditions were not to China's liking. Especially galling was the use of railway guards which, the Chinese charged, infringed upon their sovereignty and exceeded Japan's treaty rights. Some countermeasures had been attempted in the 1920's. One was a plan to make the harbor of Hulutao a rival of Dairen. Another was the building of new railroads to compete with the South Manchuria. A few modern lines were operating by 1928, and others were under way. Against these alleged violations of the protocol of 1905 the government in Tokyo protested, but in vain. Several developments late in the decade further alarmed those who looked upon Manchuria as a Japanese satrapy. In November, 1928, Chang Hsüeh-liang, the war lord whose father had been pro-Japanese, recognized the nominal authority of the Nanking regime. In July, 1929, a surge of nationalist feeling led to a premature assault on Russia's joint control of the Chinese Eastern Railway. Early in 1931 the Kuomintang was permitted to organize in

Manchuria for the first time. A minor clash on July 1 near Changchun was headlined in the Tokyo press as a massacre of Korean farmers. A fatal shooting by Chinese soldiers of a military spy in northwestern Heilungkiang was seized upon in Japan by patriotic societies as a deliberate provocation which required immediate reprisals.

There is every reason to believe that Wakatsuki and Foreign Minister Shidehara wished to avoid trouble in Manchuria. A delegate to Washington in 1921 and twice head of the Foreign Office, Shidehara argued that Japan could best realize its aims in East Asia by conciliating China. But civilian control had been weakened the previous year by the murder of Prime Minister Hamaguchi, who had sponsored the London Naval Treaty. How far extremists dominated the army's general staff was noted by one of the Emperor's chief advisers when he wrote in his diary four days after the Mukden incident: "The determination of military circles toward Manchuria is so strong that it is feared that orders given by the central authorities may not be thoroughly carried out."

THE MUKDEN INCIDENT

Shortly after ten o'clock on the evening of September 18, 1931, an explosion north of Mukden allegedly caused a gap in the rails of the main line of the South Manchuria. Since a southbound express negotiated the rupture several minutes later, since officials refused for five days to show newsmen the exact spot, and since the whole story rested on the word of a Japanese patrol, most contemporaries regarded the incident as a fabrication. Evidence presented at the Tokyo war crimes trial in 1946 divulged that it was indeed part of an elaborate plot devised by the Kwantung Army to bring about the conquest of all Manchuria. Claiming Chinese provocation, some 10,400 troops—about half of them railway guards—moved simultaneously and with clocklike precision along the entire right of way against an estimated 200,000 men commanded by Chang Hsüeh-liang. Within twenty-four hours they had captured Mukden and Changchun. By September 22 they had occupied towns seventy miles east of the latter and well west of the South Manchuria's tracks. Casualties were light, for the Chinese retreated without resistance. All operations were executed without the knowledge or approval of the Wakatsuki cabinet.

No better time could have been chosen for escaping external restraints. At Nanking, Chiang Kai-shek was unable to give armed aid to Chang Hsüeh-liang. For almost two years Chiang had been alternately buying off and suppressing rebellious war lords, and in July, 1931 he moved south to deal with the resurgent Communists. Since the end of that campaign coincided with fresh troubles in Canton, the most Chiang could do was to undertake a diplomatic offensive in London, Washington, and Geneva.

England, however, was being rocked by a domestic crisis. Under mounting financial difficulties the second Labour government gave way to a coalition cabinet on August 25, 1931. But the weakening of the pound continued, and on September 21 the gold standard was abandoned. Six days earlier, as a protest against pending pay cuts, 15,000 sailors had refused to muster aboard five warships at Invergordon. Between those two events, symbolizing Britain's declining maritime supremacy and monetary stability, came vague reports of fighting around Mukden.

In the United States, the paralyzing hand of the depression lay heavy on the land. Banks were closing on an average of seventy-five a week; unemployment figures were nearing seven million. Congress had not yet approved Hoover's moratorium, and on September 16, 1931, Secretary Stimson found the President "very blue and pessimistic." Even if there had been a disposition to contain Japan by armed force— and there was none—the means were lacking. At Cavite the Asiatic Fleet's striking power consisted of one heavy cruiser. The Battle Force, based on the West Coast, had available eleven battleships, two aircraft carriers, but no cruisers. Against this array, Japan could marshal in home waters eight battleships, three carriers, and fifteen cruisers. In Washington, however, no thought was given to mobilization. On the basis of fragmentary reports, the State Department considered the clash a localized incident and permitted the ambassador in Tokyo to depart for home on leave.

At Geneva, the Council was to convene the very day that word of the Mukden explosion arrived. The Assembly was already in session, but men's minds were not on East Asia. Besides pressing economic problems, the chief topics of conversation were the recent ruling of the World Court banning the proposed Austro-Germans customs union and the long-awaited World Disarmament Conference, scheduled to open in February, 1932. In any case, it was difficult to act promptly without more accurate information from the other side of the world.

Initially, then, caution prevailed in Geneva and Washington. On September 21, 1931, China called simultaneously upon the League to act under Article 11 and upon the United States, as sponsor of the Kellogg Pact, to take steps to uphold "the principle of peaceful settlement of international disputes." The next day the Japanese member asked the Council to delay on the ground that his government was dealing with the controversy. Meanwhile Secretary-General Sir Eric Drummond, who had already inquired of Stimson whether the pact of 1928 was involved, posed two additional questions. Would the United

States cooperate in sending a commission of inquiry to Manchuria, and would it join in appealing to the disputants through identic notes? Sensitive over his experience in 1929, Stimson hesitated to invoke the Kellogg Pact, but he told the Japanese ambassador that "this situation is of concern morally, legally, and politically to a considerable number of nations." Stimson felt it unwise to appoint a commission of inquiry if Japan objected, and he so informed Drummond on September 23. To restore peace, the Secretary advised direct negotiations first, then the machinery of the Covenant, and lastly—should all else fail—consultation under the Nine-Power Treaty or such action "as may be practicable" under the Kellogg Pact.

Until December 11, 1931, Stimson believed that the Wakatsuki cabinet could curb the army and bring the affair to a speedy close. Any outside pressure, he felt, either from the League or from America, would only hinder the civilians and inflame the extremists. That was the ground on which he opposed a commission of inquiry on September 23. His problem, as he wrote in his diary that day, was "to let the Japanese know that we are watching them and at the same time to do it in a way that will help Shidehara who is on the right side, and not play into the hands of any nationalist agitators." This, too, was the ground on which the Council reached its first decision on September 30. With the assent of both disputants, it adopted a resolution which accepted Japan's assurances that it would withdraw its troops into the railway zone as soon as possible, which called upon the two sides to prevent any extension of hostilities, and which postponed further discussion until October 14.

Such promises the Japanese diplomats were not able to honor. The officers in the field decided what was to be done; the general staff in Tokyo supported them, and the war minister beguiled the cabinet with false pledges. Each day Wakatsuki was shown maps with lines beyond which the troops were not to go; but, as he later explained, "almost daily the boundary line was ignored and further expansion was reported, but always with assurances that this was the final move." The commander of the Kwantung Army refused to recognize Chang Hsüeh-liang's authority in any part of Manchuria, and to emphasize the point, on October 8, 1931, Japanese planes bombed Chang's temporary capital at Chinchow, 130 miles southwest of Mukden and far distant from the main railroad line.

THE AMERICAN RESPONSE

This attack confirmed the worst fears of men who had suspected Japan from the start. Alarmed lest the conquest of all Manchuria was in the making, Stimson deluged Drummond with admonitions and suggestions. His concern encouraged members of the Council to seek closer American support. On October 10, 1931, Stimson persuaded Hoover to allow Consul General Prentiss B. Gilbert to sit with the Council when it assembled three days later. Over Japanese objections, an invitation was extended, and on October 16 Gilbert took a seat at the horseshoe table. Although he was permitted to speak only when the Kellogg Pact was being discussed, it was still the first time in the eleven-year history of the Council that a representative of the United States had participated officially. Heartened by this gesture, France, England, Italy, Germany, and Spain the next day formally reminded Japan and China of their promises made in August, 1928. This was the step Stimson had taken alone two years earlier, during the Sino-Russian quarrel. Now, responding to a French request, he cabled Tokyo and Nanking that the United States, having "cooperated with the League in its efforts to secure a peaceful settlement," wished to join the other signatories of the Kellogg Pact in calling its obligations to the attention of Japan and China. Four days later the Council renewed its bid for a pacific solution, suggested how this might be done, and expressed the hope that Japan would have withdrawn its troops into the railway zone by the time of the next session on November 16.

Again the diplomats were thwarted by the military. Even as the Council broke up, the Kwantung Army started to advance northward. Using as an excuse the destruction of bridges on a Japanese-financed line, it crossed the Chinese Eastern on November 19, 1931, and occupied Tsitsihar, 250 miles beyond Changchun. At the same time trouble in Tientsin aroused fears that the fighting might spread below the Great Wall. Hence it was an uncertain and discouraged Council that reassembled in Paris. This time Stimson used the ambassador to Great Britain, Charles G. Dawes, as the contact man, but Dawes was not to sit with the Council. The issue was whether the League would dare to impose economic sanctions now that an appeal to the Kellogg Pact and a resort to Article 11 had failed. On this point Hoover was firm. He told his cabinet on October 19 that while the Japanese affront was outrageous, the Nine-Power and Kellogg treaties were "solely moral instruments," enforceable only by "the moral reprobation of the world." He was prepared to cooperate with the League "in every field of negotiation or conciliation," but he would not engage in "sanctions either economic or military, for those are the roads to war." Stimson's own feelings were mixed, but he loyally warned Dawes not to participate in any discussion of Article 16. The most he would allow was for Dawes to hint that if the League should act, his government would not interfere and some citizens might voluntarily stop trading with Japan.

Sanctions were not debated at Paris. On November 21, 1931, Japan revived the plan for a commission of inquiry, and everyone except the

Chinese member heaved a sigh of relief. To be sure, that move gave no assurance of peace, and the Kwantung Army would still be free to continue its advance. But it was the best that could be hoped for, and the Council unanimously resolved on December 10 to dispatch a five-man group to the scene to report on all circumstances of an international character which threatened good relations between China and Japan. As a fact-finding commission, it had no authority to halt military movements or to make recommendations for solving the dispute. That same day Stimson publicly praised the Council's work and pledged American support.

Hopes that this commission might freeze the *status quo* in the Three Eastern Provinces quickly faded. Its members were not chosen until January 14, 1932, and did not reach Mukden until April 21. By then the Kwantung Army had attained most of its objectives. On December 11, 1931, a day after the Council's action, the irresolute Wakatsuki cabinet resigned. Unable to stem the downward economic spiral at home or to curb the independent military faction abroad, it handed the reins over to the rival party. The new regime promptly approved plans to occupy all of Manchuria and the adjacent province of Jehol. On January 3, 1932, Japanese troops captured Chinchow, and four days later they entered Shanhaikwan at the Great Wall. Except for two disorganized detachments north of Harbin, all of Chang Hsüeh-liang's soldiers had been cleared out of Manchuria.

Indignant but puzzled, Stimson reviewed his policy. What else could he do? With military and economic sanctions ruled out, only two weapons remained in his armory, a disavowal comparable to Bryan's of May 11, 1915, and the Nine-Power Treaty of February 6, 1922. During the negotiations over the Twenty-One Demands, Bryan had told China and Japan that his government could not recognize any agreement impairing the treaty rights of the United States and its citizens in China, or the political and territorial integrity of that republic, or the open door policy generally. This had been a unilateral declaration, as had been Hughes' note to Tokyo on May 31, 1921, warning that the Harding administration would not recognize any claim or title growing out of the occupation of Russia's Maritime Province. When on November 9, 1931, Hoover suggested a similar disclaimer as the best way out of the Manchurian dilemma, Stimson enlarged the idea to include other countries with interests at stake and treaties not in existence in 1915. He also waited until the fall of Chinchow to act.

The Stimson Doctrine—or the Hoover-Stimson Doctrine, as it is now called—was embodied in identic notes transmitted to Nanking and Tokyo on January 7, 1932. After remarking on the destruction of the last remnant of Chinese authority in southern Manchuria and ex-

pressing hope that the commission of inquiry would "facilitate an ultimate solution of the difficulties," the document warned that the American government could not admit the legality of any situation or
recognize any agreement between the disputants "which may impair
the treaty rights of the United States or its citizens in China, including
those which relate to the sovereignty, the independence, or the territorial and administrative integrity of the Republic of China, or the
international policy relative to China, commonly known as the open
door policy." Nor did the United States intend to recognize any situation or agreement "brought about by means contrary to the covenants
and obligations of the Pact of Paris."

At the last moment Stimson abandoned the multilateral approach.
The French and British ambassadors were not told of the nonrecognition declaration until two days before the notes were dispatched.
They were asked only to inform their governments. No joint action was
sought; none was withheld. To be sure, the Secretary hoped that other
signatories of the Kellogg Pact might follow suit, but England did not
decline to cooperate, as was later alleged. What was annoying was a
carelessly worded Foreign Office communiqué of January 9, 1932,
which emphasized Japan's promise to respect the open door in Manchuria, omitted all mention of the Kellogg Pact or Nine-Power Treaty,
and failed to make clear that Great Britain, while approving Stimson's
note, was obliged as a member of the League to proceed differently.
Two days later the influential London *Times* applauded the cabinet's
refusal to adhere to America's policy and denied that the "administrative integrity" of China existed in 1922 or in 1932. Unhappily for
Anglo-American relations, Japan's reply of January 16 seemed to echo
the *Times* editorial. Unhappily for the Pacific treaty system, the note
came close to challenging the binding character of the Nine-Power accord, by asserting that "the present unsettled and distracted state of
China is not what was in the contemplation of the high contracting
parties at the time of the Treaty of Washington."

Eventually, the Hoover-Stimson Doctrine was endorsed at Geneva.
Thanks to the efforts of Sir John Simon, the British Foreign Secretary,
the Assembly resolved on March 11, 1932, that "it is incumbent upon
the members of the League of Nations not to recognize any situation,
treaty or agreement which may be brought about by means contrary to
the Covenant of the League of Nations or to the Pact of Paris." But
before this was done, another resort to force by Japan obliged Stimson
to bring forth his last available weapon, the Nine-Power Treaty.

In Shanghai, 700 miles south of Mukden, a second undeclared war
erupted on January 28, 1932. Again it was provoked by the local Japanese commander, not by the government at Tokyo. An effective boycott in reprisal against the conquest of Manchuria had created an

inflammable situation, and mob violence was imperiling the lives and property of Japanese citizens. Despite a last-minute acceptance by municipal authorities of his ultimatum, Rear Admiral Koichi Shiozawa sent Imperial Marines from their station in the International Settlement into adjacent Chapei, where they clashed with units of the 19th Route Army. This time the Chinese resisted gallantly and, for the moment, successfully in the face of heavy aerial bombardment and steady naval gunfire. To the chagrin of the admirals, who had hoped to win some of the cheap laurels the generals had reaped in Manchuria, reinforcements were needed; and eventually, 70,000 troops went ashore. China appealed to the League under Articles 10 and 15. Once more Geneva was the scene of heated debates and hesitant decisions. On-the-spot neutrals extended their good offices; and by March 3, their immediate objectives gained, the Japanese began to pull out. In the armistice of May 5, 1932, they did not obtain any territory.

American opinion, like world opinion, was shocked by the events at Shanghai. Indiscriminate bombing of large cities was not yet the rule. At once demands were voiced in the United States for a boycott of Japanese goods, and Stimson was asked not to interfere with whatever sanctions the League imposed. But in February, 1932, such views were in a minority. Even the Secretary, no matter what he later said or thought, was doubtful about the wisdom of economic reprisals, and well he might be. Not only was Hoover adamantly opposed, as he had been the previous autumn; but, as the depression reached its nadir and the election loomed ahead, the President said, in effect, that he would like "to get out" of international affairs temporarily and concentrate on domestic problems. And at Geneva there was no inclination to apply Article 16.

Given these conditions, Stimson first tried to end hostilities through a multilateral appeal. On February 2, 1932, the United States, Great Britain, France, and Italy offered simultaneously in Nanking and Tokyo a five-point plan for stopping the fighting. When Japan rejected it, the Secretary turned to an Anglo-American proposal for a conference under Article VII of the Nine-Power Treaty. That clause did not require such a gathering or oblige any signatory to attend; rather, it provided for frank communication among the nine nations whenever one of them felt that a situation had arisen involving the treaty. For a week beginning on February 9, Stimson vainly sought British cooperation along that line. On this occasion he gave the Foreign Office plenty of time to make up its mind. Unlike his *démarche* in January, he now emphasized the Nine-Power Treaty, not the Kellogg Pact. As before, Simon argued for prior action by the League. Whether he really favored a bilateral invocation of the Washington agreement is not clear, but his dilatory tactics persuaded Stimson to go forward alone.

How to do this posed a problem. Stimson's purpose was to "put the situation morally in its right place," but without compelling Japan to reply. He wished to express his views on the open door without having to back up words with deeds. He dared not refer to the Nine-Power Treaty in diplomatic correspondence, for fear, as he wrote in his diary, "of the yellow-bellied responses" he would get from some countries. The device he finally used was an open letter to Borah. Dated February 23, 1932, and released the next day, it was a temperate, comprehensive, and legalistic review of the policy pursued by the United States in East Asia since the time of Hay. Reaffirming the principles contained in the nonrecognition notes of January 7, it paid particular attention to the Nine-Power accord and thus answered the Japanese implication of January 16 that the Washington treaty might no longer be valid. But the key section was an explicit reference to the interdependence of all the agreements concluded in 1921–2 and an implicit threat that further Japanese violations of China's territorial integrity and political independence could free the United States from the restrictions of the naval treaty.

Writing in 1936, Stimson declared that his letter to Borah was intended for "five unnamed addressees." It was designed "to encourage China, enlighten the American public, exhort the League, stir up the British, and warn Japan." It probably did not achieve any of those purposes. China remained torn by internal dissensions, and Chiang Kaishek was able to give little assistance to the defenders of Shanghai. Not many Americans cared about the interrelationship of the Washington treaties; fewer still wanted to enlarge the navy or fortify the Pacific outposts to relieve China's plight. The League did endorse the principle of nonrecognition and the British can claim credit for that move, but neither in Geneva nor in London was there enthusiasm for another nine-power conference. As to Japan, its decision to halt the operations at Shanghai was reached before Stimson's document could be digested, and its leaders divined that the threat to abrogate the Five-Power Treaty was a bluff. They knew only too well that Hoover disliked big navies and would not use armed force to uphold world peace. In short, the immediate consequences of the letter to Borah, like those of the nonrecognition doctrine, were negligible. A notice was filed, the record was kept straight, another chapter was added to the history of the open door. The true significance of the paper was that it revealed the interwar compromise to be in jeopardy.

THE INTERWAR COMPROMISE IN JEOPARDY

By the end of February, 1932, less than six months after the Mukden incident, almost every element of the interwar compromise had been tested and found wanting. Cooperation with the League had been closer than ever before, but it was evident that there were limits beyond which the United States would not go and loyalties which the members inevitably put first. The Kellogg Pact had proved again to be a frail reed on which to lean; no action had been taken to make it more effective. The Pacific treaty system had not protected China's territorial integrity or the open door policy of the United States. The wisdom of reducing armaments and refraining from fortifying further bases in the Philippines and Guam could be questioned—even if the nation had desired it—in view of the navy's inability to muster any force in Japan's home waters capable of curbing the expansionist pretensions on the mainland.

Stimson had tried to bolster the interwar compromise by making Bryan's disclaimer of 1915 a cardinal element in American diplomacy. But this nonrecognition doctrine did not halt the Japanese. One week after the Secretary issued his identic notes, Japan captured Tungliao, an important railway junction near the Jehol border. On February 5, 1932, it occupied Harbin, long regarded as in Russia's sphere of influence. Then, on February 18, the governors whom the Kwantung Army had installed in each of the Three Eastern Provinces declared their independence of both Chang Hsüeh-liang and Chiang Kai-shek. They proclaimed a republic with the capital at Changchun and invited the last Manchu emperor to be the executive. By March 12 they had created the new nation—a puppet state—of Manchukuo.

Considering the jerry-built nature of the interwar compromise and the reluctance of its architects to use armed force to carry out its purposes, it is not surprising that the first challenge in Manchuria went unchecked. There was still time, however, at the end of Hoover's term and the beginning of Roosevelt's tenure to strengthen the machinery for peace. Would the United States grasp that opportunity? For the real issue posed by Japan's action, as some contemporaries sensed, was not an outmoded Occidental defense of trade and investments but a vindication of the Washington treaties, the Kellogg Pact, and the League Covenant on which the safety of the West and the hopes of China depended. It was not a question of denying to a "have-not nation" new outlets for its products and population or new sources of raw materials for its factories. Rather, it was whether one country could unilaterally abrogate obligations it had voluntarily assumed nine years earlier by international agreement. If the problem put that way sounds today excessively legalistic and lacking in realism, that is the form in which it appeared to a generation taught to respect the pledged word of nations. Whether the American people were prepared after the experience of 1931–2 to go beyond the interwar compromise and resort to military and economic sanctions to maintain peace would depend on the leadership they received and the judgments they made on later events at home and abroad. The answer was not long in coming.

39

The Resurgence of

Isolationism

THE ANSWER to the question of whether the United States was ready to adopt stronger measures was no. Conditions in 1932 were not conducive to more diplomatic activity or further international cooperation. The land was still gripped by depression. A chastened Hoover resolutely opposed economic and military sanctions. An unruly Congress, increasingly bitter over unpaid war debts, scrutinized suspiciously any plan to punish treaty violators by multilateral action. Indeed, as the situation deteriorated in Europe and Asia, a resurgence of isolationist sentiment helped undermine the interwar compromise and compel the nation's leaders to fall back on unilateral measures for insuring peace.

MOTIVATING FACTORS

As a sentiment, isolationism was not dormant after 1921, and as a policy, it was never abandoned. The interwar compromise did involve a more active concern than ever before in the diplomatic affairs of other continents, but it stopped short of alliances, permanent or temporary. To speak of resurgence, then, is merely to denote rising pressures growing out of recent disappointments and current apprehensions. The long economic dislocation fostered fear, mistrust, and acrimony. The people wanted scapegoats for their afflictions and singled out ungrateful associates abroad and men of wealth at home. They resented huge military spending by those who did not pay their debts and blamed their own plight on bankers and munitions makers, now accused of having fomented intervention in 1917. Popular writers revised old judgments and denied that the right was more precious than peace. The failure of the World Disarmament Conference, the revival of a vengeful Germany, the expansion of a bold Japan, and the decline of a weakened League portended another war, from which, it was argued, America must insulate itself at all costs.

Both branches of the government and both political parties held that view. Differences were of degree, not of kind. Although the executive was more sensitive to foreign perils, neither Hoover nor Roosevelt was prepared to clash head-on with a resurgent isolationism. In his diary Stimson often deplored the absence of strong measures; in practice his only additions to the interwar compromise were the nonrecognition doctrine and the contention that consultation was implicit in the Kellogg Pact. Hull frequently condemned breaches of treaties, but at no time did he advocate stern reprisals against those faithless to their pledged word. Congressional attitudes were much the same. As the depression produced budgetary deficits, appropriations for the army and navy were slashed. It made little difference whether these economies interfered with the efficiency of the fleet or the modernization of battleships on which rested superiority over Japan. Borah shared Hoover's abhorrence of sanctions and declared five days after the Mukden incident that he would never "support any scheme of peace based upon the use of force." Always fearing clandestine cooperation with the League, the Senate quickly called for papers on Manchuria and deliberately omitted the customary proviso exempting those whose publication would not be in the national interest.

Significant for the future was the Senate's refusal to grant either Hoover or Roosevelt discretionary power to prohibit the export of arms and munitions. Although such a ban had been imposed in the past to discourage revolution, Congress was averse to employing it against treaty violators. But increasing criticism of the munitions traffic and heavy fighting in the Chaco prompted Hoover on January 10, 1933, to request authority to forbid at his judgment the export of guns and shells to any place in the world and in cooperation with other arms-producing nations. The President's message referred generally to "recent events" which showed the need for such legislation, while an enclosed letter from Stimson argued that "the day is gone when the spread of a conflagration is easily confined to any continent." To take this step, the Secretary said, "would give momentum to the struggle for world peace."

At first the lawmakers seemed favorably disposed. On January 11, 1933, Borah reported a resolution empowering the president to declare illegal, in conjunction with other nations, the sale of arms whenever he felt it would discourage international strife. On January 19 the Senate passed the measure without debate or dissent, but charges of unneutrality the next day caused the matter to be dropped. In the House, Hamilton Fish, Republican of New York, successfully insisted on restricting any bill to the Western Hemisphere, so that the executive could not use the authority in the Sino-Japanese dispute. Thus Hoover never obtained the powers he sought. Roosevelt persisted in asking for an arms embargo against aggressors. On April 17, 1933, the House adopted the original Senate version by a vote of 254 to 109. But qualified assurances by American delegates at the World Disarmament Conference that, under certain conditions, the United States would not interfere with sanctions levied by the League enabled Johnson and others to kill the bill by changing its purpose. An amendment required the provisions to apply equally to all belligerents. For the first time but not the last, Congress revealed its distrust of an unfettered presidential arms embargo.

Also reflecting this resurgent isolationism was the Johnson Act of April 13, 1934, which closed the chapter on what Stimson later called those "damn debts." In June, 1932, the Hoover Moratorium expired, and the Treasury Department expected payments of $150 million to be resumed on December 15. At Lausanne on July 9 the former Allies agreed to forgive Germany about nine tenths of the remaining reparations, provided they received comparable relief in Washington. There nothing could be decided until after the election, and in the four-month interregnum Hoover and his successor were unable to unite on what should be done. The former was convinced that Roosevelt would sabotage any plan so as to heap discredit on the outgoing administration, while the President-elect felt that Hoover wished to ensnare him in policies which had just been repudiated. As a result, the defaults began on December 15, 1932; within six months only Finland, who alone had a favorable trade balance, was paying in full.

Such delinquency infuriated Johnson. Eager to punish those who had defaulted and to make impossible a repetition of the financial ties forged during 1914–17, he introduced a bill to outlaw within the United States all bonds issued by governments then in arrears on their war debts. Protests from Hull against such *ex post facto* legislation caused some delay and amendment; but when England and others resorted to token payments in 1933, Johnson's revised measure passed both houses with little debate. Signed by Roosevelt on April 13, 1934, it forbade American citizens from making loans in the future, by the sale of bonds or other means, to any government in default on its debts to the United States. A subsequent ruling by the attorney general implied that the remission of token payments did not secure exemption from the prohibitions of the law. Hence when June 15, 1934, arrived, England and five other nations, all of whom had made partial payments since June, 1932, joined France and seven others, who had paid nothing since then, in default. The unpaid principal and back interest totaled about $11,842,500,000.

If the Johnson Act revealed a bitterness against the fruits of an earlier involvement with Europe, the Nye Committee investigation of the munitions industry convinced many Americans that intervention in 1917 had been a ghastly mistake. Throughout the interwar years there had been a concern over the nefarious influence which manufacturers of armaments supposedly exerted upon the foreign policies of all nations, and in the United States several laws were proposed for taking the profits out of war. But it was not until 1933 and 1934 that these alleged evils were widely publicized in books with such lurid titles as *The Bloody Traffic, Merchants of Death,* and *Iron, Blood and Profits.* In such an atmosphere, the Senate created a special committee to explore the activities of those engaged in the production and sale of munitions and to report on the adequacy of existing laws and treaties for regulating that trade. By chance the chairmanship fell to Gerald P. Nye, Republican of North Dakota, and his approach differed greatly from that of Roosevelt, who had urged the Senate on May 18, 1934, to perform the task with a "thoroughness commensurate with the high importance of the questions at issue."

Nye and his colleagues were convinced that America need not have gone to war in 1917, and the effect of the hearings they conducted and the reports they compiled from September, 1934, to June, 1936, was to stimulate the resurgence of isolationism. With an astonishing display of oversimplification and a remarkable disregard for causality, the committee argued that the United States had entered the Great War to protect the arms traffic and to save the bankers. After a theatrical examination of prominent financiers and an amateurish probe into records of the government and private investment firms, it concluded that Wilson had pursued a false neutrality with respect to the sale of munitions, the granting of loans, the operation of submarines, and the right of Americans to travel on belligerent ships. Its findings were calculated to leave the impression that the United States blundered badly, that the Allies lied skillfully, and that the Germans suffered unfairly.

Many historians and journalists had reached the same conclusion before that inquest. Wilson's case for intervention had been challenged in 1917, and it was only natural that his critics returned to the fray as wartime emotions subsided, as disillusionment with the Great Crusade grew, and as new documentary evidence became available. The private papers of Page, House, and Lansing disclosed intense sym-

pathy for the Allies as well as Wilson's own doubts and soul-searching.
While not all scholars agreed with this revisionist view that the United
States had fallen a victim to Allied propaganda, economic pressures,
and its own diplomatic ineptitude, the man in the street was impressed
by the argument that his government could have escaped involvement
if it had been truly neutral from 1914 to 1917. In short, by 1935, millions of Americans believed they must insulate themselves from future wars and that this could be done if the obligations of the interwar
compromise were curtailed, not extended, and issues containing the
seeds of conflict were yielded, not upheld.

THE RETREAT FROM EMPIRE

One issue was the retention of the Philippines. Ever since Theodore
Roosevelt ruefully conceded on August 21, 1907, that the islands were
an Achilles heel, many strategists had urged that the United States re-
deem its promise of freedom before a war with Japan broke out. In
such a struggle, they said, neither the archipelago nor Guam could be
held, although both might be recaptured before the fighting ended. On
grounds of national security as well as national honor, a retreat from
empire seemed desirable to a large number of Americans.

The retreat had begun many years earlier. The debate over imperialism had revealed an antipathy to permanent dependencies, and
the zeal for overseas possessions evaporated well before 1914. Near
the Caribbean lifeline an alternative was developed, but that protectorate policy had also been drastically modified by 1934. To be sure,
there was little disposition to renounce the smaller Pacific holdings—
Midway, Wake, Tutuila, and Guam—or even Hawaii, which some
hoped might eventually become a state. Puerto Rico was too close to
the canal to cast adrift hastily, and responsible insular leaders realized
that independence could spell economic suicide. But the more remote
Philippines were different. Their annexation had been an accident,
their value a disappointment, and their inhabitants a source of constant bickering. In the Jones Act of August 29, 1916, the United States
had promised to withdraw as soon as a stable government was established.

For eighteen years that pledge had remained unfulfilled. After
1921 there was a succession of able and dedicated governors, but none
of them advocated liberation. Not until the depression did native agitators gain new allies on the mainland who had more influence than
the old ones—the anti-imperialist Congressman and the editors of the
liberal *Nation* and *New Republic*. As prices declined, American sugar,
cotton, dairy, and cordage interests demanded protection from competing Philippine products; as unemployment rose, West Coast labor

leaders decried the influx of Filipinos. Placing the archipelago outside the tariff and immigration walls might be one answer. Thus did cupidity combine with conscience to hasten a belated act of justice, and after the conquest of Manchuria the element of caution entered the picture. Why tempt Japan? Why present an exposed and indefensible flank to a potential enemy?

Out of this complex of motives emerged a series of bills to free the Philippines. By December 29, 1932, Congress had passed the Hare-Hawes-Cutting Act, which permitted the islanders to attain independence after a ten-year transition period. In a veto of January 13, 1933, Hoover denounced the measure for leaving the archipelago liberated but without economic self-sufficiency and for leaving the United States responsible but without adequate authority. He denied that the mandate, assumed in 1898, had been discharged, and he warned that premature action would invite internal chaos and external aggression. Deaf to these admonitions, the House and Senate overrode the veto, but with more wisdom than consistency the Philippine legislature rejected the offer on October 17, 1933. It gave as reasons the unfavorable provisions on trade and immigration and the undue influence the United States might still wield through the power of the High Commissioner and the retention of military bases.

But the pressure for freeing the Philippines was too strong to be resisted. On March 2, 1934, Roosevelt recommended passage of an amended Hare bill with the provisions for army and navy bases eliminated. The former, he said, should be given up altogether; the latter could be settled by direct negotiations. The resulting Tydings-McDuffie Act was adopted in the House without a roll call and in the Senate by a vote of 68 to 8. Signed on May 24, 1934, it converted the islands for ten years into a self-governing commonwealth. During that decade the United States was to conduct foreign affairs, protect the islands, and maintain order if necessary. Complete independence was scheduled for July 4, 1946.

THE DEFEAT OF THE WORLD COURT

Another manifestation of a resurgent isolationism was the final defeat of the World Court. Four years of delay and relative unconcern preceded that unexpected outcome. Hoover sent the revised Statute and Protocol of Accession to the Senate on December 10, 1930. Borah kept them in committee until June 1, 1932, when a bare majority agreed to a report. No vote was held in the remaining fortnight of the session. Although both parties endorsed conditional adherence, the Court played no role in the election; and Roosevelt did not press the issue until January 16, 1935. Even then his brief message was hardly an impassioned plea. The President reviewed the facts, assured the nation there would be no diminution of its sovereignty, and declared that "when every act is of moment to the future of world peace, the United States has an opportunity once more to throw its weight into the scales."

The response to this challenge was disappointing. Pittman, the chairman of the Foreign Relations Committee, was lukewarm. Borah and Johnson received help from two Democratic xenophobes, Huey P. Long of Louisiana and Robert R. Reynolds of North Carolina. Old arguments were marshaled again, but in an atmosphere laden with fears about the trend in world affairs. The Court was alleged to be a creature of the discredited League. Membership would lead to a cancellation of the war debts, an end to the Monroe Doctrine, the abolition of immigration restrictions, and the ruin of the tariff. Reynolds scented danger in the fact that only two of the judges spoke English. "What chance would we poor Americans have," he asked, "with some fellows there speaking five or six languages?"

Despite this criticism, the Court plan might have won if it had not been for an overweening confidence inside the administration and an overwhelming pressure outside Congress. Roosevelt believed he had made the necessary concessions. Besides the Root formula, he had accepted a committee reservation that the tribunal would not render an advisory opinion on any question in which the United States claimed an interest. The President also acquiesced in two other reservations: that adherence must not be construed as abandoning isolationism or the Monroe Doctrine, and that recourse to the Court by the American government must be in treaty form. What Roosevelt did not foresee was the storm whipped up by a hostile Hearst press and a demagogic Catholic priest. Using the radio as his medium, Father Charles E. Coughlin attacked the Court as a "Frankenstein, raised by the international bankers," and prophesied that it would pilfer $12 billion from the American people. An avalanche of telegrams frightened wavering Senators into opposition, and on January 29, 1935, the vote for adherence was 52 to 36, seven short of victory.

"THE NEW NEUTRALITY"

Resurgent isolationism appeared most characteristically in the neutrality laws of 1935, 1936, and 1937. Those statutes embodied a new concept of neutrality, one intended to keep the republic out of war rather than guide its conduct while other nations fought. They enlarged traditional duties and restricted historic rights. Rooted in the experience of 1914–17, they tried to prevent a repetition of what had happened then.

The first law passed hastily at the end of a long legislative session. By August, 1935, the hearings of the Nye Committee had been in progress for several months, and a clash between Italy and Ethiopia was imminent. The State Department had completed studies on licensing the sale of armaments in peacetime, but the ferment in Congress forced it to draft a more comprehensive law authorizing the president, at his discretion and in time of war, to ban the export of arms, to prohibit their transportation in American vessels, to forbid the granting of loans, and to withdraw the government's protection from those citizens traveling on belligerent ships. Roosevelt approved the plan on July 21, but Congress balked again at investing him with such broad discretionary powers. After a month of wrangling, a compromise was adopted without a roll call in the House and by a vote of 79 to 2 in the Senate. Exultingly, Johnson called the outcome a triumph for those who supported isolationism and a defeat for those who preached the false gospel of internationalism.

This act of August 31, 1935, required the president to proclaim, upon the outbreak of or during a war between two or more foreign states, that hostilities existed. His proclamation automatically imposed two embargoes: one on the export of arms and munitions from the United States to any belligerent, the second on the transportation of such materials by American vessels to belligerent ports or, if consigned further, to neutral ports. This much was mandatory. As an added device to keep the nation at peace the president was given discretionary power to take three more steps. First, he might by proclamation extend the arms embargo to other countries entering the war. Second, he might by proclamation close American ports and territorial waters to foreign submarines. Third, he might by proclamation warn American citizens not to travel on belligerent ships. Another section set up a National Munitions Control Board to register persons doing business in armaments and to issue licenses for exports. The law was to expire on February 29, 1936.

To this temporary measure, which tied his hands in some matters and permitted him wide discretion in others, Roosevelt gave his qualified approval. As an expression of the nation's wish to escape war, he said, the law was "wholly excellent" and would contribute to that end. But in the mandatory arms embargo, which allowed no distinction between the aggressor and victim of aggression, the President saw a rigidity which might "drag us into war instead of keeping us out." No legislature or executive, he argued, could anticipate all contingencies; history was "filled with unforeseeable situations that call for some flexibility of action." Although the United States desired to avoid "any entanglements" which could lead to conflict, it also wanted "by every peaceful means and without entanglement to cooperate with other similarly minded Governments to promote peace." The President suggested that Congress re-examine the problem at its next session.

Before that recommendation could be carried out, Italy invaded Ethiopia. Although war was not declared, Roosevelt proclaimed at once that a state of hostilities existed and thus brought into effect on October 5, 1935, the embargo on the export of arms and the ban on their transit in American vessels. That same day he issued two proclamations. The first defined arms and munitions; this the President was required to do. The second admonished American citizens to refrain from traveling on belligerent ships; this was an exercise of his discretionary power. In another statement Roosevelt tried to discourage transactions not specifically prohibited by law and warned that individuals engaged in them at their own risk. Nevertheless, a profitable though legal traffic grew up in commodities useful for war but not in the category of arms. Hence the President again went beyond what he was required to do and on October 30 asked his countrymen to keep such trade within normal peacetime limits. When this plea proved ineffective, Hull on November 15 appealed for a voluntary embargo on oil, copper, trucks, scrap iron, and scrap steel. Excessive exports in those items, he asserted, were contrary to the policy of the government and the spirit of the neutrality statute.

Such was the situation when Congress reconvened on January 3, 1936. The administration was ready with a bill to replace the one due to expire in eight weeks. Roosevelt and Hull would have liked the authority to discriminate against treaty violators by banning arms shipments to them, but they knew it could not be obtained. Hence they concentrated on writing into law the voluntary embargo on commodities helpful in war. As Roosevelt said in his annual message: "We seek to discourage the use by belligerent nations of any or all American products calculated to facilitate the prosecution of war over and above our normal exports to them in time of peace." But a hopeless disagreement between the executive and the legislature led to another last-minute compromise.

The act of February 29, 1936, extended until May 1, 1937, the statute of August 31, 1935, with only four changes. It retained the automatic embargo on the export of arms and the compulsory ban on their transportation in American vessels. It left untouched the president's discretionary power to warn citizens not to travel on belligerent ships and to close the nation's ports to foreign submarines. The first change transferred from the discretionary category to the mandatory the clause extending the arms embargo to new countries entering the war. The second change added a prohibition on the traditional right of private citizens to grant loans and credits to belligerent governments. The third change exempted from the application of the act an American republic at war with a non-American nation. The fourth change involved putting the law into force. In 1935 the President had been required to proclaim the existence of a war. In 1936, he was given the discretion to determine whether a state of hostilities existed, and the prohibitions of the statute did not become operative until he so proclaimed.

Four months later the Italian conquest of Ethiopia was over. On June 20, 1936, as Congress adjourned, the President lifted the arms embargo and withdrew the warning against travel. A month later another crisis exposed a flaw in the attempt to legislate a "new neutrality." On July 18 a bitter and prolonged civil war began in Spain, one which aroused passionate feelings in America. Yet the statute of 1936 said nothing about civil wars, and in the past the United States had often permitted governments in power to purchase arms in this country while denying that privilege to the rebels. With Mexico in 1924 and Nicaragua in 1927 surplus stocks had been sold directly from federal arsenals. Whichever course the Roosevelt administration chose, criticism was certain. Its task was not made easier when Spain became a testing ground for the Second World War as a result of the assistance that Italy and Germany gave to the nationalist elements in rebellion and that Russia provided for those loyal to the existing government.

Faced with this dilemma, Roosevelt and Hull decided to invoke a voluntary embargo on the export of arms. On August 22, 1936, the State Department released its reply to a manufacturer who had inquired about selling bombers to the Loyalist regime. While conceding that the law did not cover civil wars, this letter declared that, "in conformity with its well-established policy of non-interference with the internal affairs of other countries," the United States would refrain from "any interference whatsoever" in Spain; and it concluded that the sale of airplanes "would not follow the spirit of the Government's policy." For a few months this voluntary embargo was generally observed, but by December licenses to export weapons were being requested. On January 6, 1937, Roosevelt asked the newly assembled Congress for "an addition to the existing Act to cover specific points" raised by the fighting in Spain. That day the Senate voted 81 to 0 and the House 406 to 1 to forbid the export of arms to both sides.

After this emergency resolution of January 6, 1937, need for a permanent neutrality law remained. The act of February 29, 1936, was due to expire on May 1. Although the executive wanted broader discretionary powers, especially with respect to the arms embargo, than the legislature was willing to grant, the administration was in no position to press the issue; for it was then embroiled in controversies over the Supreme Court and strikes. Both President and Congress were attracted by a "cash-and-carry" provision which would prohibit American ships from transporting all goods, not just weapons and munitions, to the belligerents even if they had been paid for and even if their title had changed hands. Champions of "the new neutrality" hoped that under this plan such commodities as oil, cotton, copper, and steel could be exported with great profit to the American economy and with no danger to American security. Roosevelt and Hull saw in it an opportunity to regulate the flow of goods useful for carrying on war and perhaps to control it for the benefit of victims of aggression. A composite bill containing mandatory and permissive features cleared the Senate by a vote of 63 to 6 and the House by a count of 376 to 13 and was signed by the President on May 1, 1937.

The act of May 1, 1937, was intended to be permanent except for the "cash-and-carry" section. It became operative whenever the president proclaimed that a war existed between two or more foreign states. At once it became illegal for American citizens to commit six actions: to export arms and munitions to any belligerent, to export the same to either side in a civil war, to transport those materials on an American vessel, to travel on belligerent ships, to sell bonds or extend credit to belligerent governments, or to arm merchantmen engaged in trade with warring nations and with those where civil strife existed. As in 1936, the executive was required to extend the arms embargo to any country entering the war; and he could, at his discretion, close American ports and waters to foreign submarines and armed cargo ships. As before, an American republic at war with a non-American state was exempted from the application of the law. The registering and licensing functions of the National Munitions Control Board were continued. The most novel article, expiring on May 1, 1939, empowered the president to prohibit, except on a "cash-and-carry" basis, the export of articles other than arms and munitions whenever he deemed such additional curbs conducive to the peace of the United States. In such cases, he would enumerate those commodities which might not leave the country until the title had changed and then only in non-American vessels. Lastly, the operation of the law could be terminated at the discretion of the executive.

Twenty months after the first attempt to legislate "the new neutrality," a reasonably comprehensive and presumably permanent law was on the statute books. By extending traditional duties and curtailing historic rights, the United States sought to insulate itself from future wars. Through mandatory features, Congress tried to limit the president, who, according to the Nye Committee and revisionist writers, had in the past favored one of the belligerents. Yet even on May 1, 1937, the executive retained much freedom. If he could not use an arms embargo to halt signatories violating the Kellogg Pact and the

Washington treaties or to support sanctions imposed by the League upon members breaking the Covenant, he alone possessed the authority to place in effect the statutory prohibitions and to decide whether essential war materials, other than weapons and munitions, should be placed on a "cash-and-carry" basis.

40

The Collapse of
the Interwar Compromise
in Europe

WHILE A resurgent isolationism at home was coming to dominate American foreign policy, swift-moving developments made a shambles of the interwar compromise in Europe. The years from 1932 to 1937 witnessed the collapse of those half-way measures, as the World Disarmament Conference reached an impasse on June 12, 1934; as the Senate rejected the World Court on January 29, 1935; as Italy ignored the Kellogg Pact in Ethiopia on October 3, 1935; as Germany broke the Locarno pledge in the Rhineland on March 7, 1936; and as the League proved helpless in Spain beginning on July 18, 1936. By 1937 a revived Germany had upset the balance of power established in 1919, and in the United States there was little disposition to take positive steps to combat that ominous change.

THE WORLD DISARMAMENT CONFERENCE

Throughout its troubled life the World Disarmament Conference was bedeviled by the German problem. After six years of preparation it met on February 2, 1932, under the most inauspicious circumstances.

The Draft Convention, drawn up by a commission of League members and nonmembers, pleased no one. In northern Manchuria, Japan advanced unchecked; in Shanghai, fighting raged. The diplomats would have gladly postponed the conference, but they dared not disappoint the popular demand for action or ignore Germany's plea to modify the restrictions imposed at Versailles. Unless the Weimar Republic could end the inequity in armaments, it might be destroyed by internal forces. In September, 1930, Adolf Hitler's National Socialist Party jumped from 12 seats in the Reichstag to 107. As true socialists left the fold, Hitler allied himself with extreme nationalists and received subsidies from industrial and financial magnates who were unwilling, under existing circumstances, to tolerate longer the workings of a parliamentary democracy.

Hoover and Stimson were not reluctant to participate in this League-sponsored conference. Hugh Gibson and others had been helping with the agenda since 1925. But the basic American attitude had not changed. The limitation of naval armaments was still paramount. The reduction of land forces was still a European matter, in which the United States was only remotely concerned. Even after the experience at London in 1930, disarmament and security were kept in separate compartments. When Pierre Laval, the French Premier, told Hoover at the White House on October 23, 1931, that the best hope for success lay in a consultative pact and a promise not to impede sanctions levied by the League, the President said that his government would not enter into any agreement which might lead to military consequences. On November 18 he explained to the Italian Foreign Minister that the average American, after adding up the forty billions spent during the war, the ten billions lent after the armistice, and the one billion going annually to disabled veterans, "wanted to keep out of the whole business."

From the start, the fifty-nine-nation Disarmament Conference found itself badly divided. The French asked for an international police force and evaded the German problem. England and the United States urged the limitation or elimination of weapons designed for offensive warfare; both ignored the French emphasis on security and the German insistence on equality. The Reich called for reducing all armies and navies to the levels of the Versailles Treaty. Italy supported Germany's position, rejected France's notion of additional guarantees, and advocated a total prohibition of capital ships, aircraft carriers, bombing planes, and tanks. Japan favored abolishing aircraft carriers and, initially, maintaining the restrictions imposed at Washington and London. Russia would accept anything from partial to complete disarmament.

Once hostilities had ended at Shanghai, Stimson attempted by personal diplomacy to break the deadlock at Geneva. He tried to do this by promoting Franco-German talks. As he told Premier André Tardieu in Paris on April 15, 1932, the United States felt the arms parley to be "more in the nature of a European peace conference" than anything in which America had "a direct responsibility." To Heinrich Bruening, the moderate German Chancellor, he confessed that the world situation seemed like "the unfolding of a great Greek tragedy, where we could see the march of events unfold and know what ought to be done" and yet were powerless to avert the "grim conclusion." Bruening pleaded for concessions that might save his cabinet and perhaps democracy in Germany, but Stimson could give him little aid. The Secretary had pointed out the proper approach but was hobbled by his belief that the negotiations related to questions which were "purely European and political." Hence, as he reported to Hoover upon his return in May, while it was helpful to get the conversations started, he would have felt out of place conducting them once they did start.

Stimson's hopes did not materialize. Private talks between Tardieu and Bruening never occurred. The former was defeated; the latter resigned. The British turned to a simultaneous conference at Lausanne and frightened Hoover into thinking England, France, Belgium, Italy, and Japan might offer a package deal combining reparations and armaments. Irritated by delay and eager to act before the Democratic Convention opened, the President sprung a surprise comparable to his moratorium of the previous year. Overriding some advisers and without fully briefing the other delegations at Geneva, he proposed a simple plan on June 22, 1932, which fitted arms limitations into a mathematical formula, ignored the French demand for security, and barely recognized the German insistence on equality. Hoover argued that the Kellogg Pact had committed all nations to using arms solely for defense and suggested that offensive weapons—tanks, bombers, and large mobile guns—be prohibited altogether. He would then cut land forces by about a third, reduce the tonnage quota and number of battleships by 33 per cent, decrease the tonnage quota of aircraft carriers, cruisers, and destroyers by 25 per cent, and restrict all countries to forty submarines totaling 35,000 tons.

This dramatic gesture was too superficial to win acceptance. Italy, Russia, and Germany warmly favored it; England was politely noncommittal; France and Japan strongly objected. Until the great powers settled their differences, little could be done, and on July 23, 1932, a two-month recess was voted. The reaction in Berlin was immediate; the elections of July 31 gave the Nazis 230 seats in the Reichstag, the most of any party. On September 15 Franz von Papen's tottering government warned that it would not return to Geneva unless the principle of equal military forces was conceded. Although this threat was not carried out, developments in the next nine months killed almost all hope of success. On January 30, 1933, Hitler became Chancellor and quickly obtained the dictatorial authority which transformed the Weimar Republic into the Third Reich. On February 24 Japan announced its withdrawal from the League after the Assembly had accepted an incriminating report by the committee investigating the Mukden incident. In desperation, European statesmen advanced all sorts of ideas to save the conference.

In Washington the new Roosevelt administration drafted a plan to link arms reductions with promises of nonaggression and consultation. More realistic than Hoover's approach, it showed, nonetheless, the bounds beyond which the United States would not go. On May 16, 1933, the President appealed directly to the heads of state in fifty-four countries, asking them to support a new British program at Geneva and to refrain for the time being from increasing their armaments beyond existing treaties. He envisaged the negotiation—once land, sea, and air units were limited—of a multilateral nonaggression pact which would bind each signatory, so long as the disarmament pledge was observed, not to send military forces across their frontiers. On May 22 Norman H. Davis, the chief American delegate, supplemented this appeal. Davis promised that if satisfactory reductions were effected by international agreements, the United States would consult with other nations for the purpose of averting war. Should the nations conferring determine that a power had broken the peace in violation of its obligations and then take measures against that power, Davis said, the United States would, if it concurred in that judgment, "refrain from any action tending to defeat such collective effort." That is, once armaments had been cut, the American government would consult with others to keep the peace and, provided it agreed that sanctions had been rightly imposed, would do nothing to impair their efficacy.

Roosevelt's appeal and Davis' promise were too little and too late. In 1928 a pledge to consult might have given substance to the Kellogg Pact. In 1930 it might have enabled France and Italy to sign all of the London Treaty. Even a year earlier it might have saved the Disarmament Conference from futility. But by May, 1933, the moderates had lost control in Germany, and France bristled in the face of a new danger across the Rhine. In the United States a resurgent isolationism caused the Senate to hesitate and then deny the President's request for power to use an arms embargo against treaty violators. When a further deadlock developed at Geneva, therefore, it was decided to adjourn until October 16. Although most delegates were resigned to failure, a few hoped that a world economic conference, about to open in London, might by its success breathe life into their own moribund proceedings.

As early as June 1, 1932, Hoover had agreed to England's desire for a multilateral attempt to steady commodity prices. He stipulated, however, that there be no discussion of war debts or reparations. Two committees, one of diplomats and one of experts, laid the groundwork that autumn, and after March 4, 1933, the new Democratic regime carried on the preliminaries with enthusiasm. In his appeal of May 16 Roosevelt coupled the forthcoming economic parley with the arms conclave as indispensable to "the happiness, the prosperity, and the very lives" of men and women everywhere. It must, he added, "establish order in the place of the present chaos by a stabilization of currencies, by freeing the flow of world trade, and by international action to raise price levels." Hull headed a distinguished but diverse delegation.

Despite these preparations, the Monetary and Economic Conference which sat at London from June 12 to July 27, 1933, was a complete fiasco. The United States was as much to blame as anyone; many would say that it was more blameworthy. The New Deal was in its formative stage, and Roosevelt, having registered initial gains, refused to tie the dollar to foreign currencies. This decision, taken after Hull had sailed, and announced on July 3, repudiated the aims proclaimed on May 16. The Secretary was dumbfounded and later wrote he had never seen "such bewildering movements and utterances" made "without a moment's notice to anyone." For thus sacrificing foreign policy to domestic needs Roosevelt has been severely censured, perhaps too severely, but the unhappy episode remains a classic example of how not to conduct diplomacy.

There can be no doubt that the tactics pursued at London in July, 1933, contributed to the collapse of the Disarmament Conference in the autumn. Still, the demise of that gathering was probably inevitable. The French held the key to any solution, and they faced a difficult choice. If they granted concessions, they could not be sure Hitler would be deterred from subverting the entire settlement of 1919. If they did not, Germany would rearm openly and at an accelerated pace. Worst of all, it was clear that neither France nor England would fight to uphold the disarmament clauses of the Versailles Treaty. Consequently, reason yielded to emotion, and the French adopted a course that was certain to offend the Germans. They disclosed their position on October 14, 1933; within minutes came word of Germany's withdrawal from the conference. Later that day Hitler let it be known that he was also ending Germany's eight-year membership in the League.

During the next nine months the World Disarmament Conference reached a dead end. No progress of any sort was made, nor did the American position change. Hull deplored Germany's rearming but would not try to stop it. "We are willing," Davis said at Geneva on

May 29, 1934, "in connection with a general disarmament convention to negotiate a universal pact of nonaggression and to join with other nations in conferring on international problems growing out of any treaties to which we are a party." But the United States would not make "any commitment whatever to use its armed forces for the settlement of any dispute anywhere." Thus, without technically adjourning, the conference turned on June 12, 1934, to the lesser problem of curbing the munitions traffic.

THE REVIVAL OF GERMANY

Henceforth the rapid growth of German military might was the salient fact in European diplomacy. Germany had always evaded the Versailles restrictions to some extent. The general staff disappeared only in name. The 100,000-man army became an efficient cadre of professionals for a vastly expanded force. The fleet was slowly rebuilt around three pocket battleships. The future Luftwaffe benefited from novel designs in commercial aircraft. The ban on producing munitions was violated by setting up factories in Sweden and Russia. Ties were forged between the Reichswehr and the Red Army which permitted training on Soviet soil. In April, 1934, Hitler tore off the wraps of secrecy by announcing that for the following year military expenditures would be 90 per cent above those for the previous twelve months.

After several false starts, the revival of German power led to portentous changes on the international scene. The initial attempt to create a Rome-Berlin Axis was upset by an abortive Nazi coup in Austria on July 25, 1934, which pushed Benito Mussolini back into the Anglo-French camp. But in a plebiscite conducted by the League on January 13, 1935, nine out of ten inhabitants of the Saar voted to return that coal-rich territory to the Reich. Then, on March 16, 1935, one week after admitting the existence of a forbidden air force, Hitler ripped up the disarmament section of the Versailles Treaty by reinstituting compulsory military service and calling for an army larger than France's. The feeble response of England, France, and Italy on April 11 did not deter the Nazis, while the British virtually condoned the Führer's action by signing a naval accord on June 18. In it, Germany promised to restrict its tonnage in every category except submarines to 35 per cent of England's. Although granted parity in principle for underwater craft, Germany agreed to adhere to a quota of 45 per cent for the time being.

In the United States, the Nazis were heartily detested. Their blood purges, concentration camps, economic warfare, race theories, and brutal anti-Semitism shocked all Americans. The new regime was appraised accurately in the State Department. "If this Government remains in power for another year," read a report from Berlin on June 26, 1933, "it will go far towards making Germany a danger to world peace for years to come." Some leaders, it said, were "psychopathic cases"; others were capable of acts which should "outlaw them from ordinary intercourse." As early as May, 1934, the military attaché mentioned accumulating evidence of "unusually close and friendly relations between Germany and Japan even to the extent of a possible alliance." But while Hull publicly condemned Hitler's attacks on the Versailles Treaty, he privately assured the ambassador in Moscow on May 7, 1935, that America's "first concern is with relations in the Pacific" and that any interest in German naval building was for the effect it might have on Great Britain.

Perhaps the decisive moment came when a revived Germany reoccupied the Rhineland on March 7, 1936. This step violated both the Versailles Treaty and the Locarno Pact. The Reichswehr opposed the gamble and had orders to retreat if its advance was resisted. But Hitler was confident that England and France, at odds with Italy over Ethiopia, would not fight, and he was correct. At a critical juncture the British faltered, and the French gave up easily a point on which they had been adamant in 1919. As for the United States, Hull called the episode "a European development in which we were not involved," one requiring no action in Washington. On March 9 the Secretary told the President that American treaty rights had not been infringed. The next day he rejected a French plea that Roosevelt condemn publicly on moral grounds the unilateral repudiation of international commitments. Hull would not even let the chargé in London attend a meeting of the League Council as an observer. The time was still distant when the Roosevelt administration was prepared to devise extraordinary measures to halt the spread of Naziism.

THE RECOGNITION OF RUSSIA

Just as the failure of the World Disarmament Conference marked the crumbling of the interwar compromise in Europe and the revival of Germany undermined the Versailles settlement, so did the recognition of Russia on November 16, 1933, remove another element in American foreign policy dating from the Great Crusade. Although the resumption of diplomatic intercourse with the Soviet Union seemed a belated act of common sense, it did not confer many benefits. Although the change coincided with Russia's adherence to the League of Nations and Japan's and Germany's withdrawal, it did not bring a realignment of forces which might have preserved the superiority of the victors of 1918.

By the end of Hoover's term the arguments for recognition were difficult to refute. The Communists had held power for fifteen years and were accepted as the legitimate rulers by every major country. Lenin's successor, Josif V. Stalin, had emerged by 1927 as the supreme dictator. Absorbed in a five-year industrialization plan at home, he needed peace abroad. Hence he ostensibly abandoned the doctrine of world revolution and argued for coexistence among socialist and capitalist nations. As the depression deepened in the United States, business groups voiced the need for a change. Diplomatically, Americans and Russians had worked side by side at Geneva since 1927, and both had signed the Kellogg Pact. By April, 1932, Stimson was coming to favor recognition, but his superior dissented and, in any case, caution was necessary in an election year.

Harbingers of a new approach were manifest soon after Roosevelt took office, but not until October 10, 1933, did the President invite the Soviets to send to Washington an envoy with whom he could explore all outstanding questions. The phraseology suggested there would be no resumption of ties without a prior agreement on the adjustment of mutual claims, the cessation of Communist propaganda in the United States, and the protection of the rights of Americans in Russia. Discussions began on November 8 with Maxim Litvinov, the Commissar for Foreign Affairs; and it required all the charm of the President, all the caution of the State Department, and all the enthusiasm of William C. Bullitt, a special adviser, to reach an accord on November 16. That accord consisted of eleven letters, one memorandum, and a "gentlemen's agreement." All but the last were as satisfactory as paper pledges could be. Russia promised unequivocally to refrain from subversive activities in the United States and, in effect, bound the Comintern—an organization in Moscow for promoting communism abroad—to do likewise. The religious and civil rights of American residents in the Soviet Union appeared to be safeguarded. An exact settlement of claims was left to the future. In the poorly drafted "gentlemen's agreement" Litvinov said he would advise his government to pay $100 million, while Roosevelt expressed confidence that Congress would accept $150 million.

On nondiplomatic grounds, recognition quickly proved to be a disillusioning experience. The debt question remained unsolved. The "gentlemen's agreement" gave Russia the loophole it needed and may have wanted; by January 31, 1935, the subsequent negotiations had broken down amid mutual recriminations. The results of a trade agreement of July 13, 1935, were disappointing. During 1937 American exports averaged only one third more than the amount for 1930. Evidence of Soviet bad faith came with a disclosure in July, 1935, that the Comintern had not ceased its subversion in the United States. A strong protest on August 25 met with a flat denial that Litvinov had ever bound that organization to do so.

Disillusioning, too, was the diplomatic aftermath. It was well to be on speaking terms with Soviet officials, even if they often lapsed into name-calling, and to have a listening post in Moscow. But collaboration for peace was difficult, if not impossible. Stalin's support of the Chinese Communists ran counter to American policy, and he could not be depended upon to take a strong stand against Japan. On July 19, 1935, Ambassador Bullitt wrote: "To think of the Soviet Union as a possible ally of the United States in case of war with Japan is to allow the wish to be father to the thought." She would wait, he prophesied, "until Japan has been thoroughly defeated and would then merely use the opportunity to acquire Manchuria and Sovietize China." As for Europe, on December 31, 1934, Hull rejected Litvinov's plan to convert the expiring Disarmament Conference into a permanent body for upholding the Kellogg Pact. Russia's interference in the Spanish Civil War in August, 1936, coinciding with the first of the state trials which rocked Stalin's regime to its foundations, showed Roosevelt that the Soviet Union was not a disinterested or dependable partner for peace.

ETHIOPIA AND SPAIN

Italy's conquest of Ethiopia, which began on October 3, 1935, revealed how far the interwar compromise in Europe had disintegrated. Unlike Japan's assault in Manchuria, this second undeclared war surprised no one. Mussolini had decided early in 1933 to expand his African empire at the expense of Haile Selassie's kingdom, and he had tried for a year to provoke incidents that would ostensibly justify an attack. The League had discussed the matter intermittently starting in December, 1934, but these warnings did not prompt the United States to act. Its economic and diplomatic stake in East Central Africa was slight, and it had there no Pacific treaty system to maintain.

Ethiopia did touch two elements of the interwar compromise. The Kellogg Pact was one. On July 3, 1935, Haile Selassie asked the American government "to examine means of securing Italy's observance" of that pledge. Hull did not relish handling the request, and his response two days later expressed a gratification that the League was studying the matter and a confidence that both signatories would respect their word. When Mussolini's propagandists called the reply evidence that Kellogg's treaty was dead, the Secretary declared publicly on July 13 "that the Pact of Paris is no less binding now than when it was entered into." He repeated that sentiment on several occasions, but obviously the Roosevelt administration was placing less reliance on the

Kellogg Pact than its predecessor had done in July, 1929, or September, 1931.

Cooperation with the League was the second element challenged by this new attack on the peace. Here, too, there was less collaboration than after the Mukden incident. The reasons went beyond a resurgent isolationism at home. England and France worried more about the revival of German power in Europe than the threat of Italian expansion in Africa, and they handled Mussolini gently lest they push him into Hitler's arms. On September 10, 1935, Foreign Secretary Sir Samuel Hoare and Premier Laval ruled out such measures as a naval blockade or closing the Suez Canal, and the later efforts of the League to punish a flagrant breach of the Covenant only angered Mussolini without restraining him. By October 11 the Council and Assembly had condemned Italy for violating Article 12, but not until November 18 did they impose partial sanctions consisting of an arms embargo, a ban on Italian exports, a prohibition on financial transactions, and a curb on a small number of exports to Italy, from which oil was omitted. Hoare and Laval were more concerned with a speedy peace, even at Ethiopia's expense, than with a vindication of the principle of collective security. They agreed privately on December 8 to offer the Duce almost everything he wanted. An aroused public in England did kill that deal, but hopes for the vital oil embargo died when Germany reoccupied the Rhineland on March 7, 1936. The Italians entered Addis Ababa on May 5, and four days later Ethiopia became part of their empire.

This second defeat suffered by the League stemmed more from the irresolution of England and France than from lack of cooperation by the United States. To be sure, uncertainty over American exports, if sanctions were applied, made for timidity in Paris and London, but the failure to deny oil to Mussolini should not be blamed on Roosevelt and Hull. They did what they could, by parallel rather than by joint action, to support the League. The arms embargo was invoked on October 5, 1935. When traffic in commodites useful for war but not forbidden by law increased markedly, Roosevelt asked his countrymen on October 30 to keep such trade within normal peacetime limits. After that plea failed, Hull on November 15—three days before the League's sanctions went into force—requested a voluntary embargo on oil, copper, scrap iron, and scrap steel. How effective his appeal was is not clear, but certainly it would have been felt more if the members of the League had themselves refrained from exporting oil. In short, although no American sat with the Council in this crisis and although Hull carefully kept his policies separate, the episode reveals at most a lessening faith by the United States in the League, not a fatal sabotage of its endeavors.

A more widespread loss of faith was revealed when the Spanish Civil War began on July 18, 1936. From the outset Italy and Germany gave substantial help to the rebels, or Nationalists, while Russia aided the government, or Loyalists. Fearful lest this internecine strife, with its ideological implications, touch off an international struggle between fascism and communism, France forbade the export of war materials to both sides. On August 8 it proposed that the other powers follow the same course. Twenty-six nations—including Germany, Italy, and Russia but not the United States—eventually agreed, and a Non-Intervention Committee was established at London on September 9 for the purpose of exchanging information on how those pledges were being fulfilled. The work of this body was greatly hampered by the bad faith of Italy and Germany and by their premature recognition of the rebel regime of General Francisco Franco on November 18. But the significant fact was that England and France, in deference to Hitler and Mussolini, were attempting to cope with a threat of war outside the machinery of the League.

To Hull's relief, France did not invite the United States to serve on the Non-Intervention Committee. The Secretary wished to pursue a course of parallel rather than one of joint action. He desired, in the interest of hemispheric solidarity, to avoid any semblance of interfering in the domestic affairs of other countries. Then, too, the Spanish war turned upon religious as well as political beliefs, and in an election year it was wise not to alienate Catholic voters who accused the Loyalists of communist leanings and anticlerical practices. Thus the administration discouraged the sale of munitions to both sides until it secured from Congress on January 6, 1937, a resolution extending the arms embargo to civil wars.

However tragic American policy in Spain may seem today—and many believe it emboldened the dictators in their drive to dominate Europe—it was probably the only one feasible at the time. The United States could not undercut the Anglo-French plan to localize the fighting and to deny weapons to Loyalists and Nationalists alike. Nor could it sit in judgment on the failures of the Non-Intervention Committee on which it did not wish to serve. If the United States reversed a traditional policy of permitting governments in power to buy arms in American markets while denying that privilege to insurgents, that change seemed minor when it was enlarging its neutral duties and curtailing its neutral rights. Lastly, while the ultimate victory of Franco was another advance for fascism, that outcome did not of itself make the Second World War inevitable. Nor was it certain at the end of 1936 that the struggle, which lasted until March 28, 1939, would result in the triumph of the Nationalists.

CHAPTER

41

◆◆◆-◆◆◆-◆◆◆-◆◆◆≪≪≪-≪≪≪-≪≪≪-≪≪≪

The Collapse of
the Interwar Compromise
in Asia

STEADY PRESSURE by Japan upon the Pacific treaty system from 1932 to 1937 brought a simultaneous collapse of the interwar compromise in Asia. The Nine-Power Treaty was virtually abrogated by unilateral action. The Five-Power Treaty and the London supplement were terminated, upon request from Tokyo, at the earliest possible date. The Four-Power Treaty remained in effect but no longer provided realistic protection for the signatories. As for the Kellogg Pact and League Covenant, the former had failed twice in Manchuria prior to 1932, while the latter ceased to apply when the Japanese delegates stalked out of the Assembly in 1933. What, then, caused this sharp reversal in Japan's policy in the 1930's and shaped a course which led directly to the attack on Pearl Harbor?

JAPAN AND THE NINE-POWER TREATY

Externally, three forces were at work. One was the slow growth of Chinese nationalism, which threatened Japan's privileged position on the mainland. This sentiment had been fed by the resistance at Shang-

hai and the rape of Manchuria. A second was the gradual build-up of
Soviet military might in Siberia and the active concern of the Comintern for communism in East Asia. The resumption of Sino-Russian
diplomatic relations on December 12, 1932, seemed ominous in Tokyo,
where a government spokesman asserted that "the elements most disturbing to the peace of the world have now joined hands." Third, after
quitting the League and feeling isolated on the international scene,
Japan turned to the other totalitarian states, Germany and Italy, which
had also defied that organization. Yet the identity of interests among
the future members of the Tripartite Pact is easily exaggerated. What
Japan wanted at this time was the consent of the Western powers to
its hegemony in the Orient. Only when this could not be obtained did
Japan sound a Pan-Asiatic note about a "New Order" in which it alone
decided what was best for China.

Internally, two influences were decisive. The first was the economic imperatives of an insular empire: supplies of raw materials,
outlets for surplus population, markets for industrial exports. Some of
these needs were more immediate than others; all were proclaimed to
be equally pressing. The second was the political trend away from
party government toward the traditional primacy of the armed forces.
Parliamentary democracy in Japan had been a superficial phenomenon
of the 1920's. The Kwantung Army's defiance of its civilian superiors
in 1931 was only the start of a series of coups and assassinations
which left the generals able to overthrow any cabinet they disliked.
Although factional differences between and within the two services
prevented their complete domination of Japanese diplomacy, no foreign minister after 1935 could carry out his policies without the acquiescence of the military.

Japan's unilateral abrogation of the Nine-Power Treaty began with
the reply of January 16, 1932, to the Hoover-Stimson Doctrine. In that
note Japan asserted that China's unsettled state nullified the purpose of
the agreements concluded at Washington in 1921–2. Then and later
the Japanese implied that China could not be considered an organized
nation and that the time for putting its house in order had run
out. They called Stimson's letter to Borah, with its emphasis on the
interrelated character of the Washington treaties, "distinctly provocative." But it was Japan's response to the report of the commission of
inquiry, headed by the Earl of Lytton and dated September 4, 1932,
which fully revealed the course it would pursue toward the Nine-
Power Treaty.

Read today, the Lytton report seems a model of impartiality.
Objective in tone and comprehensive in coverage, it described frankly
China's unsatisfactory administration in Manchuria and Japan's legiti-
mate complaints. It denied, however, that the latter had been justified

in the steps to redress the grievances, and it exploded the claims that the Kwantung Army had acted in self-defense and that Manchukuo had come into existence by a spontaneous movement for independence. Yet the main recommendations of the report—the re-establishment of China's sovereignty in Manchuria, while safeguarding Japan's rights—was unacceptable in Tokyo. Hence, even before that document was debated at Geneva, Japan formally recognized Manchukuo and signed an alliance with it. On February 21, 1933, the new allies invaded adjacent Jehol, the easternmost province of Inner Mongolia. Three days later the Assembly, voting that Manchuria belonged to China, indirectly condemned Japan's violation of the Covenant. At that point Japan's delegates strode from the hall, never to return.

Faced with an imminent breakdown in one element of the Pacific treaty system, the incoming Roosevelt administration followed the path of its predecessor. Like Stimson, Hull insisted that international agreements be lived up to, and he applied the nonrecognition doctrine to Manchukuo. But if the Democrats did not retreat from the open door policy, the government in Tokyo would no longer respect the political independence and territorial integrity of China or equality of economic opportunity therein. The last was shown by the establishment on February 21, 1934, of the monopolistic Manchurian Petroleum Company, a forerunner of other favored commercial enterprises in Manchukuo. To repeated Anglo-American protests of discrimination, the Foreign Office answered that nations refusing to recognize the new state forfeited all claims to equal treatment within its borders. In short, the closed door in Manchukuo was both a reply to the Hoover-Stimson Doctrine and a repudiation of one aspect of the Nine-Power Treaty.

Equally disturbing was an assault by words and deeds upon the other objectives of that agreement. On April 17, 1934, a Foreign Office spokesman argued that Japan's "mission" and "special responsibilities in East Asia" compelled it to oppose technical, financial, and military aid to China by the West. He also said that China must not "avail herself of the influence of any other country to resist Japan." When Hull asserted that this claim to exclusive control contravened American rights, the spokesman was removed but not disavowed. Japanese diplomats, moreover, referred increasingly to their own Monroe Doctrine for the Orient, but the United States refused to recognize such a principle. On May 19, 1934, Hull declined to endorse a joint declaration assigning primary responsibility for preserving law and order "in the eastern Pacific regions" to the United States and "in the western Pacific regions" to Japan.

Of more immediate danger to American interests were Japan's persistent efforts to subvert the authority of Chiang Kai-shek in North

China. Japan's aim was to create an autonomous buffer state out of
Hopei, Chahar, Suiyan, Shansi, and Shantung provinces—an area
equal in size to Manchuria and containing half of China's coal resources and cotton crop. Adjacent to Manchukuo and Jehol, this zone
would constitute a tempting field for economic exploitation, a natural
barrier to Russian influence in Outer Mongolia, and a strategic basis
for further penetration south of the Yellow River. After an easy conquest of Jehol in March, 1933, Japan's next move, in June, 1935, was
to force the dissolution of the Kuomintang in Hopei and Chahar and
the removal of all Chinese troops from those provinces. Three months
later a field commander publicly called for a regime independent of
Nanking, but without immediate results. Although Hull protested on
December 5 that this separatist agitation imperiled American rights,
Japan did not desist. By September, 1936, it was formulating demands
for the autonomy of the five northern provinces; but by then the unilateral abrogation of the Nine-Power Treaty had merged with other
problems leading to an undeclared war with China.

THE END OF NAVAL LIMITATIONS

Unlike the repudiation of the Nine-Power Treaty, Japan threw off the
naval limitations in a legal manner. The Five-Power Treaty and its
London supplement could be terminated on December 31, 1936, whenever a signatory expressed such a wish. It had been apparent since the
assassination of Prime Minister Hamaguchi in November, 1930, that
Japan would either make that request or demand an upward revision
in the ratio of tonnage quotas. The navy was determined not to bow
again to the civilians, as it had done in the case of the London Treaty.
Its resolution was bolstered by the army's successful defiance in 1931
and the accelerated pace of American construction in 1933.

Not a single warship had been authorized under Hoover. In fact
only eight of the fifteen cruisers included in the act of February 13,
1929, were begun, and progress was so slow that by March, 1933, the
American fleet was approximately 65 percent of treaty strength, while
Japan's stood at 95 per cent. The advent of Roosevelt brought a
change. A devotee of sea power, he was ready to use shipbuilding as a
means of fighting the depression. Accordingly, he had written into the
National Industrial Recovery Act of June 16, 1933, a proviso that
money could be allotted for naval construction within existing treaty
limits. Roosevelt apportioned $238 million for the fleet at once, and
orders were soon placed for two aircraft carriers, five cruisers, and
many smaller craft. A supply bill of March 15, 1934, allowed four
more cruisers to be started, while the Vinson-Trammell Act of
March 27 established a policy for the future. Although it did not ap-

propriate funds for a single vessel, it empowered the executive to bring the fleet to full treaty strength by 1942.

By 1942 there would be either different treaty limits or none at all, if Japan had its way. On December 29, 1934, Japan gave notice of a desire to renounce existing curbs. Subsequent talks with the United States and England disclosed a hopeless divergence over retaining the present ratios and tonnage quotas. The Japanese demanded full parity for their fleet and an end to limiting tonnage by categories. The Americans refused to concede equality and proposed to cut all quotas by 20 per cent; but they also wanted each nation to be free to build, within treaty limits, the type of craft best suited to its own needs. The British did not concur in either view, but faced with a choice of evils, they elected to stand with the United States. All three were aware that France, Italy, and Germany had laid down the keels of the first capital ships to be undertaken since the holiday decreed at Washington in 1922. Under most inauspicious circumstances, therefore, the signatories of the Five-Power Treaty met at London on December 9, 1935. Two of the five, England and France, had recently imposed partial sanctions on a third, Italy, because of the fighting in Ethiopia. A fourth, Japan, had already quit the League; on January 15, 1936, it was to walk out of this conference also.

Given the situation, the United States, Britain, and France agreed to abandon all tonnage quotas. Henceforth each was at liberty to construct as many vessels as it wished in any category. On March 25, 1936, the three powers did sign a second London Treaty which contained three restrictions and one requirement, all of them binding until December 31, 1942. First, no eight-inch-gun cruiser could be built for six years, and the same prohibition applied to six-inch-gun cruisers weighing over 8,000 tons. Second, no battleship was allowed to exceed 35,000 tons or mount guns of more than fourteen-inch caliber. Third, aircraft carriers were limited to 23,000 tons in size and 6.1-inch guns in armament. Fourth, information on construction programs must be exchanged annually. Escape clauses allowed the signatories to renounce those curbs in war or in peace if they deemed it vital to their security, while the fourteen-inch maximum in capital ship guns depended on the concurrence of Japan and Italy. By identical letters on March 24, 1936, the United States and Great Britain reaffirmed the principle of Anglo-American parity and promised to refrain from competitive building. Perhaps these meager results were responsible for the Senate's giving its consent on May 18 without any opposition, enthusiasm, or roll call.

Little can be said for this pretense of naval limitations. The hope that Italy, momentarily obdurate because of sanctions, would adhere eventually to all or part of the treaty and that England could bring in Germany and Russia through bilateral agreements proved to be illusory. Even as this face-saving accord was being completed, the Reichswehr reoccupied the Rhineland. Furthermore, Japan rejected the restriction on capital ship guns, and its refusal to divulge whether it was building 45,000-ton battleships forced the signatories to invoke an escape clause on June 30, 1938. Yet despite the breakdown in this important element of the interwar compromise and Japan's assertion that it felt free to fortify the mandated islands, public opinion in the United States kept Roosevelt for almost two years from asking Congress to expand the fleet beyond the old treaty limits or to strengthen the insular outposts in the Western Pacific.

CONFLICT IN CHINA

No adequate substitute for the interwar compromise in Asia had been found by July, 1937, when Japan and China clashed again. That conflict, which Chiang Kai-shek had avoided as long as he could, did not catch the world by surprise. For several years the government in Tokyo had watched with obvious concern the increase of Russian power in Siberia and the failure of its own separatist schemes in North China. To cope with the former, it had signed the Anti-Comintern Pact with Germany on November 25, 1936. As published, that treaty provided simply for an exchange of information on the dangers of Communist subversion. But a secret protocol stipulated that if one signatory was attacked by Russia without provocation, the two would consult together and the second would do nothing to help the Soviets. At the same time those Japanese leaders who had counted on the compliance of Chiang to enable them to realize their goals on the mainland grew less certain he could be trusted, especially after he reached an understanding with the Chinese Communists. By September 28, 1936, the Foreign Office was saying matters must not be allowed to drift indefinitely; on June 9, 1937, General Hideki Tojo urged that the fate of North China be settled while Russia was staggering under treason trials and the execution of high ranking officers in the Red Army.

A chance skirmish near the Marco Polo Bridge west of Peking on July 7, 1937, precipitated a full-scale but undeclared war. Provocative measures by a Japanese garrison stationed along a strategic railway touched off the explosion, and commanders on the spot fanned the flames. On this occasion, however, the fighting could have been stopped if Prime Minister Fumimaro Konoye had shown more courage or if Chiang Kai-shek had repeated his hands-off tactics. But civilian leaders in Tokyo were weaker than they had been six years earlier, while the Nanking regime had to resist or be overthrown. After a fortnight in which a settlement seemed possible, hostilities roared out of control. By the end of July, Peking was in Japanese hands, and the capitals of Chahar and Suiyan soon fell to the invader. On August 13 the conflict spread south to Shanghai.

Generally speaking, the United States acted more cautiously and more independently in 1937 than it had in 1931. Quite apart from the resurgent isolationism at home, it would have been sheer folly to look again to Geneva or the Kellogg Pact. On July 15 the French Foreign Minister told the American ambassador that it would be "disastrous" if China called on the Council and thus demonstrated "the absolute impotence of the League." Nor was an appeal to the Nine-Power Treaty likely to be more effective. Hull seemed to rule out close Anglo-American collaboration when he replied on June 1 to a British feeler: "It is the traditional policy of this country not to enter into those types of agreements which constitute or suggest alliance." The Secretary believed, rather, in consultation "followed by procedure on parallel lines and concurrently." Suspicious of any bilateral or tripartite solution, Hull warned that the eventual settlement must not deviate from the principles to which the interested powers were committed by existing treaties.

During the first weeks of the Sino-Japanese conflict Hull operated within that narrow range of possibilities. On July 12, 1937, he rejected China's plea to mediate because, as an aide said, it was "premature and ill-advised," likely to hurt rather than help. The next day he informed the British he would not join in sending messages to Tokyo and Nanking since "cooperation on parallel but independent lines" aroused less antagonism. On July 16 Hull fell back on a device he dearly loved and often employed—a statement of broad principles, which to him were "as vital in international relations as the Ten Commandments in personal relations." Declaring that war anywhere in the world was bound to affect every country and urging a respect for the sanctity of treaties, he managed to combine in one sentence the earnest desire of the United States to promote peace by every "practicable means" with its steadfast determination "to avoid entering into alliances or entangling commitments." He did not even refer directly to the Nine-Power Treaty. On July 21 the Secretary turned down a suggestion that the United States, England, and France recommend to Japan and China that all troop movements be suspended. He did permit Ambassador Grew in Tokyo to extend his good offices on August 10, but they were declined.

Would the United States do more? Would it impose sanctions? Would Roosevelt invoke the Neutrality Act? Would Hull seek a conference under the Nine-Power Treaty? The answer to the first was

clear. The mere announcement on August 17, 1937, that 1,200 marines were being sent to Shanghai from San Diego to safeguard American interests excited fears in Congress, where resolutions disclaimed
any responsibility by the government to protect citizens or their property in the war zone. Nor was the navy able to act. The Asiatic Fleet
remained a token unit, helpless in the face of a Japanese advance. The
battle line, still deficient in cruisers and based in California, could not
match Japan's striking power in Asiatic waters. Actually, there was
no thought of mobilizing. Neville Chamberlain had prophesied correctly four years earlier that, short of an attack on Hawaii, the United
States would make no promise to England to resist Japan by force.

Roosevelt's decision was less predictable. To proclaim that a state
of hostilities existed would harm China, not help. It would justify
Japan's blockading the entire coast, something Japan had not done.
A resort to the "cash-and-carry" section would work to Chiang Kai-
shek's disadvantage since he lacked the funds and ships to buy and
transport oil, scrap iron, and raw materials. Japan had both. Hence the
best way of helping China—and it accomplished very little—was for
the President to exercise his discretionary power not to invoke the
Neutrality Act of May 1, 1937. Accordingly, he announced on September 14 that although government-owned merchantmen would not be
permitted to carry implements of war to either belligerent and although privately owned cargo vessels flying the American flag did so
at their own risk, the question of applying the statute remained "on a
24-hour basis." This decision drew some criticism from the champions of "the new neutrality"; but since most citizens sympathized
with China, there was no disposition to force the hand of the executive.

As to a conference under the Nine-Power Treaty, Hull let the
League assume the initiative. When China appealed to Geneva, its
case went to an advisory committee that had been set up in 1933 and
on which the United States was represented. The American observer,
however, was the epitome of caution and contributed little to the final
report. On October 6, 1937, the Assembly endorsed a document which
found that Japan had violated its pledges under the Nine-Power
Treaty and the Kellogg Pact, that China was entitled to all moral support, and that a conference ought to be called under the Nine-Power
Treaty. That same day Hull said his government was "in general accord" with these conclusions, and he censured Japan in similar words.
Anglo-American efforts quickly paved the way for a parley. Belgium
agreed to act as host and on October 16 sent invitations to all the signatories and all nations with interests in East Asia. England insisted
that Germany and Russia be included. The expressed purpose was to
examine the situation in China and to consider "friendly methods" for
ending the current conflict.

THE BRUSSELS CONFERENCE

Like so many conferences of this period, the one which opened at Brussels on November 3, 1937, faced certain failure. Japan refused to attend, ostensibly because it had been condemned in advance, actually because it no longer wanted to recognize the binding character of the Nine-Power Treaty. It also persuaded Germany to decline and agreed only reluctantly that Italy's presence as its spokesman might serve a useful purpose. The Soviet Union, with whom China had recently signed a nonaggression pact, talked big but was prepared to do little. The United States, England, and France did not even think in large terms. The reaction at home to Roosevelt's so-called "Quarantine Speech" of October 5 (to be analyzed below) did not encourage the President to engage in collective measures to punish an aggressor. On October 12 he emphasized publicly the friendly purpose of the Brussels Conference. Nine days later Prime Minister Neville Chamberlain told the House of Commons that it was a mistake to talk about economic sanctions, for the British aim was to bring peace, not to extend the fighting.

It is unnecessary to review the dreary details of the Brussels Conference. On the third day Italy announced its adherence to the Anti-Comintern Pact. On November 7, 1937, another invitation was sent to Japan. After this was rebuffed, the major powers seemed more eager to avoid the responsibility for failure than to prevent it. England, as the ambassador in Washington said on November 13, "was tied by the leg to Europe" and would run the risk of war in East Asia only if "assured in advance that it would receive military and naval support from the other signatories." France would not undertake positive steps against Japan unless it obtained a joint guarantee to defend its exposed colony of Indochina. Hull complained on November 17 that the delegates at Brussels wished to place the blame for the fiasco on the United States. The only agreement reached, and that with Italy dissenting, was a strong reaffirmation of the Nine-Power Treaty and a feeble warning that Japan's course would compel the conferees "to consider what is to be their common attitude" when one party to an international agreement maintains against the views of all the others that its actions do not fall within the scope of that agreement. On November 24 the delegates recessed, presumably to reconvene when conditions were more favorable. That day never arrived.

For the Brussels Conference, it soon became clear, was worse than a fiasco. It was a disaster. It encouraged China, already buoyed by support the Communists now gave the beleaguered Nationalist regime; it stiffened Japan, already angered by the condemnation of the League and the United States. While it sat, the tide of battle began to run against Chiang Kai-shek and thus dissipated the last slender hope that a long war might be averted. Because of the conference, China would not even discuss early in November, 1937, the unofficial peace terms which had been shown in Tokyo to the British ambassador. A month later, when defeat made Chiang less unbending, he discovered that the victorious generals had compelled the Konoye cabinet to raise the price. As for the United States, we can sympathize with Roosevelt's domestic distractions and applaud his willingness to consult for the first time under the Nine-Power Treaty. But again it was too late. What might have been a useful expedient in 1931 had become a futile gesture in 1937. By then the Pacific treaty system had crumbled, and a new course of action was imperative. Yet there was no agreement at home or abroad as to what it should be, and in the two years left before the outbreak of the Second World War, the President and Congress would grope for a viable policy in Europe and in Asia.

42

Groping for a Policy

AGAINST THE BACKDROP of a recession in the economy at home and the menace of a war abroad, the American people continued to debate the wisdom of their diplomacy. As the world careened once more toward disaster, they argued and accused, beseeched and bemoaned, warned and wavered. But from September, 1937, when Roosevelt left open the question of applying the neutrality law to the Sino-Japanese conflict, to September, 1939, when the Nazi legions burst into Poland, no consistent policy emerged. Whatever the President may have wished to do, he did not break with a traditional isolationism and a reinforced neutrality until it was evident that the Second World War would not follow the course of the First.

WHITHER NATIONAL SECURITY?

To Americans in 1937 it was not clear in which direction their security lay. The interwar compromise had collapsed. Nonrecognition of territorial conquest had not saved Manchuria or Ethiopia; for it was like saying, as one wag put it, "though we will not lift a finger to prevent your being attacked, be of good cheer; after you have been killed, we shall refuse to admit you are dead." The attempt to insulate the nation by "the new neutrality" had raised as many problems as it had solved, and the efficacy of the laws remained to be proven. An overwhelming majority of citizens wanted to stay out of another European war no matter how disturbing were the deeds of the dictators. In a poll conducted in April, 1937, 70 per cent of those with an opinion replied that intervention in 1917 had been a tragic mistake. Yet a sizable number feared the loss of democracy everywhere unless the march of totalitarianism were halted, in Europe and in Asia. What arguments, then, did the two groups, too easily tagged isolationists and internationalists, have to offer?

The so-called isolationists sought security in unilateral action. They were confident that the United States could keep aloof from any major conflict, and they were convinced that no amount of collaboration with other countries could prevent the recurrence of European wars. Many felt certain that Hitler simply wished to redress the injustices of the past, that Germany, Italy, and Japan would fall prey to internal weaknesses, and that England and France had the capacity to preserve the balance of power established in 1919. All demanded that the neutrality statute be carried out fully. Some wished to eliminate the president's discretionary power to determine when a state of war existed and whether the "cash-and-carry" section should be invoked. They opposed as futile and dangerous efforts to distinguish between an aggressor and his victim. There were those who favored amending the Constitution so as to require, except in cases of invasion, a popular referendum before Congress could declare war. On rearmament the group was divided. The pacifist segment fought the move as a harbinger of involvement; the nationalist element endorsed it as a safeguard to peace.

The so-called internationalists sought security in independent and parallel action but envisaged possible collaboration with the nontotalitarian countries of Western Europe and China. They also opposed commitments in advance to use force. Unlike their rivals, however, they believed the United States could not escape being embroiled in a major struggle and thus must do everything, within customary limits, to bolster those with whom it might later have to align itself. Specifically, they urged modification of the neutrality law. Since total repeal was out of the question, they concentrated on rescinding the arms embargo. This group argued that the ban encouraged aggressors by assuring them that weapons would be withheld from their victims. The group also endorsed expanding land, sea, and air units, insisting that to do so was not provocative.

Such were the arguments the diplomats had to ponder as war drew closer. Late in 1937 two leaders groped for the answer as to how the United States might stem the tide. At Chicago on October 5 Roosevelt delivered his "Quarantine Speech," which has often been said to denote a change in his foreign policy. There he inserted into a routine address the assertion that "war is a contagion" and that "it can engulf states and peoples remote from the original scene of hostilities." The figure had been used many times before, but Roosevelt did not propose to "quarantine the aggressor" as has been frequently alleged. He merely declared that "the epidemic of world lawlessness is spreading" and reminded his audience that "when an epidemic of physical disease starts to spread, the community approves and joins in a quarantine of the patients in order to protect the health of the community." While he portrayed vividly the deteriorating world situation, the President was vague in his recommendations. He asked "the peace-loving nations" to make "a concerted effort" to uphold basic principles and called for "a return to a belief in the pledged word, in the value of a signed treaty." Although he warned that there could be no escape "through mere isolation or neutrality" and no complete protection "in a world of disorder," he was determined to keep the nation out of war and said he was adopting measures for that purpose.

These words heralded no new departure. That they seemed unduly significant at the time can be attributed to the mention of "positive endeavors to preserve peace" and to the League's censure of Japan the following day. But there was no connection between events in Chicago and Geneva. Roosevelt was simply sending a trial balloon aloft to gauge the winds of popular sentiment, and the reaction was what he probably expected. From irate isolationists came harsh criticism and cries of warmongering; from hopeful internationalists came lavish praise and pleas to aid the Chinese Nationalists and Spanish Loyalists. But the President had no intention of sponsoring sanctions at the Brussels Conference or working against the Non-Intervention Committee. He did not retreat from his "Quarantine Speech" because he had barely advanced in it.

How pale Roosevelt's generalities were was seen when Stimson published his solution on October 7, 1937. Out of office, he could speak more freely than the President and even accuse specific nations. Shocked and outraged by Japan's actions, he proposed to ban the export of all commodities useful for war to countries violating the Kellogg Pact or the Nine-Power Treaty. He disavowed any desire to send American troops to fight China's battles, but he did not wish to assist Japan by selling it materials needed to run its military machine. Noting that the Japanese depended on the United States and the British Empire for 75 per cent of their oil, rubber, cotton, and iron ore, Stimson pleaded for a return to the precept that the right is more precious than peace.

Roosevelt, however, was grasping for straws in another direction. He had toyed with the idea of meeting with the heads of the major European states, and in May 1937 Mussolini virtually invited him to take the initiative. But not until after the fruitless "Quarantine Speech" did the President and Under Secretary of State Sumner Welles develop a variant of the plan. They considered assembling the diplomatic corps on November 11, 1937, to hear Roosevelt suggest an agreement for resolving current economic problems, revising inequitable treaties, and redefining standards of international conduct. Actual drafting would be entrusted to the small states who might pave the way for a later summit meeting. Hull's objections to this "pyrotechnical plan," as he called it, was an obstacle during October; and when the scheme was revived in January, 1938, Chamberlain's opposition killed it once and for all.

Meanwhile two events had occurred which revealed the popular mood. On December 12, 1937, Japanese bombers intentionally sank the American gunboat *Panay* in the Yangtze River near Nanking. Two sailors were killed, and survivors were strafed as they swam to safety. Unlike the sinking of the *Maine* in 1898, this incident provoked no cry for reprisals. Most citizens felt the government had no business protecting Standard Oil tankers in the battle zone, and many congressmen called for withdrawing all ships from Chinese waters. Since the Konoye cabinet apologized and offered reparation, the matter was dropped, but not before a significant vote in the House on the Ludlow Amendment.

That proposal forbade Congress to declare war, except in cases of invasion, until the people had approved in a special referendum. Many such resolutions had been presented since 1914, but none had been acted upon. To get his bill out of committee, Louis L. Ludlow, Democrat of Indiana, filed a petition on February 26, 1936, which, when it obtained 218 names, would require the House to take up the measure. One day after the *Panay* sank the requisite number was secured, and the voting was set for January 10, 1938. The administration moved heaven and earth to kill the scheme. On January 6 Roosevelt declared that "the proposed amendment would be impracticable in its application and incompatible with our representative form of government." Hull warned two days later that it would "impair disastrously" his peace program. Thus despite pleas to let the mothers of the country decide whether their boys should fight, the motion to bring the Ludlow Amendment to the floor lost by a count of 188 to 209. It was close, but a two-thirds majority in both houses was needed to send a constitutional amendment to the states for approval.

THE RIDDLE OF REARMAMENT

As Roosevelt groped for a positive policy to prevent the war into which, he feared, the United States would be drawn, he tried to bolster the nation's defenses. His initial concern was for the navy and its overseas bases. The authorized strength of the fleet was still at the figure set by the defunct Washington and London Treaties and would not be reached until 1942. The Philippines and Guam were as vulnerable as they had been under the nonfortification clause, which had also lapsed. With Japan, Germany, and Italy embarked on large building programs, the President could not ignore the possibility of a two-ocean war, and for that contingency the sea arm was woefully inadequate. Indeed, it could not even cope with Japan in Asiatic waters. On January 28, 1938, therefore, he recommended a 20 per cent increase in the size of the navy and the immediate construction of two additional battleships and cruisers.

The violent opposition to this request disclosed the anxiety afflicting the country and the distrust of the President. Many Americans read into the "Quarantine Speech" attitudes he never intended; others feared an abuse of his discretionary powers under the neutrality law. A disclosure that the head of the navy's War Plans Division had visited London in December, 1937, lent color to rumors of a secret alliance with England, and resolutions on Capitol Hill sought to discover the nature of the agreement and the extent to which the State Department was "controlled by the British Foreign Office." After an acrimonious debate, the bill passed by a vote of 56 to 28 in the Senate and 294 to 100 in the House. Roosevelt signed it on May 17, 1938.

Eight months later the navy sought funds to develop twelve bases. One was Guam, and its importance was enhanced by the impending liberation of the Philippines. There was no intention of converting the island into a fortified Gibraltar, but only of enabling long-range planes to operate from Apra harbor. To dredge a channel and build a breakwater, $5 million was asked for, but the House eliminated the item on February 23, 1939, by a count of 205 to 168. Such improvements, it was said, might provoke Japan into an attack; thus, according to Fish, the House action was "a direct vote for peace." Rearmament had indeed become a riddle when defensive measures were defeated lest they lead to war.

By early 1939 Roosevelt was also alive to the pressing needs of land-based air power. On January 12 he asked Congress for $525 million beyond the regular annual appropriations for the armed services and earmarked $300 million for military aircraft. That sum represented about half of what the air corps had received in the past fourteen years and would have given it a minimum of 5,500 planes. The legislature responded in the act of April 3, 1939, but only after a battle. A crash of the newest type of bomber divulged that the French were buying such planes, something not prohibited by law. But the President made the mistake of shrouding these purchases in secrecy; and when they became known, he was accused of forging entangling alliances. To explain why such sales promoted the nation's security, he briefed a Senate committee about the world situation on Janu-

ary 31 and offered confidential evidence for his belief that war was
imminent. But the fat was in the fire again when he was quoted as
placing the American frontier in France or along the Rhine. Although
he denied having made the remark, the publicity hurt his drive for
rearmament and for a revision of the neutrality law.

STRENGTHENING HEMISPHERIC TIES

In only one area was Roosevelt able to formulate a policy which produced tangible results and elicited universal support. Having dedicated
the nation in his inaugural address to being a good neighbor and having demonstrated his sincerity at Montevideo later that year, he and
Hull strove after 1933 to strengthen hemispheric ties. On January 26,
1934, the United States joined the five Central American governments
in returning to *de facto* recognition. On April 27 it adhered to the Anti-
War Treaty of Nonaggression and Conciliation sponsored by Argentina. On May 29 it abrogated the Platt Amendment; on August 15 the
last of the marines left Haiti. The first reciprocal reduction of duties
under the Trade Agreements Act of June 12, 1934, was concluded with
Cuba on August 24. By a treaty of March 2, 1936, replacing the one
signed by Hay and Bunau-Varilla, the United States gave up its guarantee of Panama's independence, its right to intervene, and its power
of eminent domain.

Alarmed by the ambitions of the European dictators, Roosevelt
and Hull decided in 1935 to seek a special hemispheric gathering to
deal with the totalitarian menace in the New World. Although the
Nazis were busy indoctrinating the 1,500,000 Germans resident in
Latin America, the President had to await the end of the Chaco War
before he could propose a meeting in Buenos Aires on December 1,
1936, designed to promote peace by ratifying treaties previously
signed, by amending those already ratified, and by creating new machinery. Hull again headed a distinguished delegation, while Roosevelt himself addressed the opening session.

Five main treaties, all dated December 23, 1936, emanated from
this Inter-American Conference for the Maintenance of Peace. The
first contained an unqualified pledge of nonintervention. Going beyond
their promise of 1933, the signatories declared that it was inadmissible to interfere directly or indirectly in the internal or external affairs
of each other. The second provided for consultation whenever the
peace of the Western Hemisphere was menaced, whenever war or a
virtual state of war arose between New World nations, and whenever
a conflict originating elsewhere endangered the American republics.
But consultation was not obligatory unless the signatories so desired,
and Argentina blocked Hull's plan for a permanent Inter-American

Consultative Committee. The third and fourth treaties supplemented existing methods for utilizing good offices and mediation. The last dealt with the tendency of these inter-American conclaves to negotiate agreements which the home governments never ratified. It sought to coordinate, extend, and assure the fulfillment of commitments under a number of earlier treaties.

Two years later in Peru, at the Eighth International Conference of American States, Hull again sought an effective procedure for consultation. Nazi propaganda, he believed, threatened the New World with external aggression and internal subversion, and even as he spoke German agents tried to disrupt the conference. Accordingly, the twenty-one republics approved on December 24, 1938, the Declaration of Lima. It renewed a determination to defend their republican institutions and principles of international law against "all foreign intervention or activity." It provided that "in case the peace, security, or territorial integrity" of a signatory was menaced, they would proclaim their common cause and consult as to what steps each might take. Consultation would be through the foreign ministers, any one of whom could call a meeting. Hull did not get a permanent committee, but the Declaration plugged the gap left in 1936 and covered subversion from within as well as invasion from without.

THE LAST YEARS OF PEACE

It is not easy to summarize the complex events leading to the Second World War, but the successive triumphs of Germany, Italy, and Japan were aptly described in 1940 by a writer who used the verbal images of the total state. "All through 1936, all through 1937, and all through 1938," he said, "if not by God's grace then somehow or other, these three militant nations held to their appointed courses. They left in their wake a litter of statisticians who perished in the act of proving that the German—Italian—or Japanese economy had already bogged down. They thumbed their noses at sociologists who calculated that the home front of the totalitarian countries was about to crack up. . . . They picked up the apostles of law and order by the scruff of the neck, took them for a ride, and threw them gasping on the dump heap. They 'purged,' they burned, they stole, they lied. They worked their bloody pleasure on Ethiopians, Chinese, and Jews. They made a mockery of Christianity, they chased the terrified democracies under the bed. They ripped the *status quo* from hell to breakfast, and they sat on the top of the world."

In China, the Japanese bombed indiscriminately and pillaged unmercifully. Despite a few setbacks from the united Nationalists and Communists, they captured Shanghai, ravaged Nanking, and overran

Shantung by the end of 1937. During 1938 Chiang Kai-shek lost his major ports and was forced to move his capital first to Hankow and then to Chungking far in the interior. Japan set up puppet regimes in Nanking, Peking, and Inner Mongolia, but total victory eluded that country. On November 3, 1938, Konoye announced a New Order in East Asia. A modern version of the Twenty-One Demands and a final repudiation of the Nine-Power Treaty, it required China to recognize Manchukuo, to join the Anti-Comintern Pact, to permit foreign troops on Chinese soil, and to accept economic vassalage.

Appalled by these developments, the American people could not bring themselves to stop them. When Chiang Kai-shek begged for help in January 1938, he had to be told the United States was doing everything possible to promote peace. To the Japanese this meant, as they informed the Germans, that Roosevelt "had declined to intervene in any way." The Treasury Department did provide some help by buying silver, and in mid-1938 Hull started down the road of economic retaliation. To Konoye's talk of a New Order in East Asia the Secretary replied that if Japan felt the Nine-Power Treaty to be outmoded, it must negotiate anew, not abrogate unilaterally. He was well aware, he wrote on December 30, 1938, that the situation had changed since 1922, but his government did not concede the right of any one nation to prescribe the conditions of a "new Order" in areas not under its sovereignty. But by 1939 the world's attention was riveted on Europe, and Japan enjoyed a relatively free hand. This it exploited by seizing on February 10 the Chinese island of Hainan, which commanded the approaches to Indochina, and by annexing on March 31 the disputed Spratly Islands, which lay astride the invasion route to British Malaya, the American Philippines, and the Dutch East Indies.

Halfway around the world the Spanish Civil War brought victory to Franco. The Non-Intervention Committee failed to curb outside interference. Three members—Italy, Germany, and Russia—openly violated their pledges, but for geographic and other reasons the aid given the Loyalists by the Soviets could not match that reaching the Nationalists from Rome and Berlin. In the Iberian Peninsula, civilians were bombed without warning. In the Mediterranean, German warships shelled undefended towns and Italian submarines sank unsuspecting ships. Roosevelt referred to these atrocities at Chicago on October 5, 1937, but the administration continued to prohibit the export of arms to both sides. On January 24, 1939, Stimson publicly urged that the ban against the government be lifted and warned that a law, intended to keep America at peace, was imperiling the country by easing the path of the dictators. But Hull, like the leaders in London and Paris, believed the most he could do was to prevent the conflict from touching off a major war. He maintained a scrupulous impartiality to the end, and on April 13, 1939, he recognized, as England and France had already done, the triumphant Franco regime.

The German problem was not so easily solved. By 1938 Hitler was ready to risk war to obtain his goals in Central and Eastern Europe. On July 11, 1936, he had pledged himself to respect the independence of Austria. After thus calming Italian fears, on October 25 he formed the Rome-Berlin Axis, a loose nonmilitary arrangement inspired by resentment against the *status quo*. On November 6, 1937, Italy joined the Anti-Comintern Pact and on December 12 quit the League. Then, as Mussolini was being courted by Chamberlain with promises of recognizing the conquest of Ethiopia, Hitler stirred up trouble in Austria and on March 12, 1938, proclaimed it to be part of the Third Reich. His next victim was Czechoslovakia; his excuse, the alleged mistreatment of 3,500,000 persons of German descent in the Sudetenland. But the government at Prague under Edvard Benes was a tougher nut to crack. It had a strong army, a defensible frontier, and a military alliance with France and Russia. If Benes stood firm, general war might ensue. His failure to do so stemmed mainly from Chamberlain's belief that, by dismembering Czechoslovakia, he could appease Hitler. By ignoring an enigmatic Russia and by persuading a frightened France, Chamberlain was able to sign at Munich on September 29, 1938, a four-power settlement with Hitler, Mussolini, and French Premier Eduoard Daladier, which left Benes no alternative but to yield.

Appeasement failed at Munich, and this traditionally legitimate move in foreign affairs has since become a dirty word in diplomatic usage. The disillusioned have also charged that Roosevelt played a part in the deal that sacrificed Czechoslovakia. Actually, his role was a minimal one. On September 26, 1938, he appealed publicly to Hitler, Benes, Chamberlain, and Daladier to seek a pacific solution. On September 27 he privately urged Mussolini to aid in the attempt. That same day, in response to Hitler's reply, the President told the Führer he could render "an outstanding service to humanity" by exercising moderation; but he did not threaten, or suggest a settlement, or offer to take part in the discussions. Roosevelt clearly stated that his country would not assume any obligations. On September 28 he did pat Chamberlain on the back with a "good man" message, but his two-word cablegram was designed to keep the deliberations alive, not endorse the specific terms reached. On September 30 Hull declared that his government would not pass on the merits on the Munich Pact. Lacking a viable policy of its own, the United States acquiesced in the judgment of England and France, but under the nonrecognition doctrine, it refused to approve the fruits of conquest.

If Roosevelt's share in the appeasement of Germany has been distorted, the capitulation at Munich did compel him to grope anew for a policy that might yet avert the war he dreaded. Hope that Hitler would be satisfied with recent concessions was dissipated late in 1938 by an obvious intention to destroy what was left of Czechoslovakia and to even scores with Poland. Sickened by a fresh wave of anti-Semitism in the Reich and motivated, perhaps, by a slackening momentum in the New Deal at home, the President placed a stern warning in his message of January 4, 1939. "Events abroad have made it increasingly clear," he said, "that dangers from within are less to be feared than dangers from without." Those democracies which respected the sanctity of treaties had learned they cannot be indifferent to lawlessness anywhere in the world. As for the United States, he concluded, "the mere fact that we rightly decline to intervene with arms to prevent acts of aggression does not mean that we must act as if there were no aggression at all. Words may be futile, but war is not the only means of commanding a decent respect for the opinions of mankind. There are many methods short of war."

"Methods short of war"—here was a phrase Roosevelt was to use with increasing frequency down to the eve of Pearl Harbor. What did he mean by it in January, 1939? Hull's list of feasible measures included the recall of the American ambassador from Berlin, the reassertion of the Hoover-Stimson Doctrine, the speeding up of rearmament, the application of countervailing duties to imports from Germany, and the revision of the neutrality statute. This last was what the President had in mind, for he candidly told Congress on January 4: "We have learned that when we deliberately try to legislate neutrality, our neutrality law may operate unevenly and unfairly—may actually give aid to the aggressor and deny it to the victim. The instinct of self-preservation should warn us that we ought not to let that happen any more."

From January 4 to July 18, 1939, Roosevelt and Hull did what they could to persuade Congress to alter the Neutrality Act of May 1, 1937. Seeking what was possible rather than desirable, they did not ask for its repeal or even for the power to discriminate against treaty breakers. Their plan was to extend the "cash-and-carry" section, which expired on May 1, to cover arms and munitions. If this were done, any belligerent could purchase implements of war, as well as vital commodities, provided he paid for the goods and transported them in his own ships. Since Anglo-French control of the sea was likely, this change would enable the democracies to cope more effectively with the rearmed totalitarian states and, perhaps, thereby deter Hitler from taking the step which would plunge the Continent into war.

What that step would be was clear by April, 1939. Violating the assurances given at Munich, Hitler annexed the rest of Czechoslovakia

on March 15–16. Like a jilted suitor, Chamberlain precipitately abandoned appeasement. When the Führer elaborated within a week his
demands on Poland and Lithuania, England and France extended
sweeping—some would say reckless—pledges of aid in treaties with
Poland on April 6, with Greece and Rumania on April 13, and with
Turkey on May 12. On May 22 Germany and Italy concluded a military alliance to which Japan was expected to adhere. The United States
did not play a part in these developments, and there is no evidence
that Roosevelt encouraged England and Poland to take an irrevocable
stand. His sole move was to ask Hitler and Mussolini on April 14,
1939, to stipulate that for ten years their troops would not attack certain countries, thirty-one in all, stretching from Ireland and Norway
to Egypt and Iran. The President was willing to obtain similar engagements from the thirty-one and, after such covenants were exchanged,
to bring the United States into multilateral discussions for the purpose
of reducing armaments and opening avenues of trade.

The dictators could well afford to spurn that slight offer, for Congress was in the process of refusing to revise the neutrality law. As a
floor leader, Pittman again proved to be hopelessly vacillating and
easily discouraged. On May 8, 1939, he gave up in despair, even
though a public-opinion poll had just disclosed that 57 per cent of
those responding favored a change to permit the sale of munitions to
Great Britain and France. An alternative bill was introduced in the
House; but when it passed on June 30, it contained the old arms embargo and a new right of the legislature, as well as the executive, to
decide whether a state of war existed. Roosevelt then turned back to
the recalcitrant Senate, but on July 10 the Foreign Relations Committee voted by a margin of 12 to 11 to defer consideration of all neutrality legislation until January, 1940.

Convinced that war was imminent and that it was being hastened
by these congressional rebuffs, Roosevelt made one last effort. Hoping
that the full Senate might override the Foreign Relations Committee,
he invited leaders of both parties to the White House on the evening of
July 18, 1939. He reviewed with them the dangers abroad and the conditions on Capitol Hill. After a long and brutally frank exchange, he
was persuaded he could not win. As Vice President John N. Garner
supposedly told him: "Captain, we may as well face the facts. You
haven't got the votes." Roosevelt and Hull accepted their defeat in
good grace. They had discharged their duty, and the Senate was both
willing and eager to take credit for the postponement. What infuriated
the two men was Borah's arrogance in declaring that he found his
sources of information more reliable than the State Department's.
When Hull pointed out that every report from overseas indicated an

explosion within the near future, Borah continued to insist there would
be no war in Europe that year.

Six weeks later, on September 1, 1939, Hitler's armored divisions
crashed into Poland. The Second World War had begun.

BOOK · V

THE SECOND TEST:
THE
STRUGGLE FOR
SURVIVAL

1939–53

*In which the American people survive
a dangerous challenge, abandon historic
policies, and begin to learn to live with
crisis.*

43

⤜⤜⤜⤜⤜⤜⤜⤜⤛⤛⤛⤛⤛⤛⤛

The Shaping of Foreign
Policy, 1939–53

WHERE THE Great War of 1914–18 provided the first test of the United States as a world power and involved a crusade to insure the safety of democratic institutions, the global conflict of 1939–45 provided the second test and involved a struggle to insure the survival of the republic itself. If in their hour of victory in 1919–20 the people and their leaders chose to return to what they hoped would be a limited role in international affairs but were compelled to seek a middle way between the traditional concept of independent action and the Wilsonian ideal of collective security, that choice and that compromise were not open to them in 1945. Then there seemed no alternative to abandoning their historic isolationism and neutrality, to adjusting the Monroe Doctrine to changed conditions, and to marshaling their economic and military strength to prevent everywhere the triumph of totalitarian tyranny. Nor did this second test end with the defeat of fascism in Germany, Italy, and Japan, for almost immediately the menace of Russian communism became apparent. From 1945 to 1953 Americans learned for the first time they must live with continual, as opposed to periodic, threats to their existence and way of life.

THE PRESIDENTS

This abandonment of traditional policies was executed, in many cases, by men who had held office during the interlude of the interwar compromise. Even before Germany invaded Poland, Franklin D. Roosevelt began to subordinate internal reform to external danger; after that date he stepped up the urgency of his warnings and the scope of his activity. In his quest for extraordinary powers, the President usually secured legislative sanction; but when he doubted his ability to gain prompt approval on Capitol Hill, he might resort to executive agreements or stretch his prerogatives as commander-in-chief. Despite his election in 1940 to an unprecedented third term, he grew increasingly sensitive to criticism of his diplomacy and several times acted as if the people could not be told the truth. If he was occasionally guilty before December 7, 1941, of being something less than candid in his speeches and something more than devious in his tactics, he did not usurp the functions of Congress or mislead the nation about the perils enveloping it.

During the war Roosevelt drew upon traits which had helped win the domestic battles of the 1930's. His ability to speak persuasively, to inspire confidence, to transmit enthusiasm, and to dramatize his cause never flagged. He relished his role in the coalition fighting the Axis. He was fascinated by military matters and aided in shaping strategy. In waging the war he relied heavily on the Joint Chiefs of Staff, often to the neglect of the State Department. By intimate correspondence with Winston S. Churchill he established a warm friendship such as Wilson never enjoyed with his opposite numbers; and while it is now clear that Roosevelt was less successful than he thought in binding Stalin to future cooperation with the capitalistic states, he did overcome skillfully numerous obstacles to wartime unity. Yet for all his breadth of vision Roosevelt could be petty, as he evidenced in dealing with Charles de Gaulle; and for all his dedication to democracy, he could be callous to the rights of small nations, as he showed in handling Poland. Power tended to corrupt his moral standards, but it does not follow that he won the war at the price of losing the peace or betrayed the hopes of the free world by failing to see the ambitions of international communism. Certainly his health deteriorated rapidly just before his sudden death on April 12, 1945, but that does not mean that the decisions he made at Yalta were affected by physical or mental incapacity.

Harry S. Truman inherited problems which would have taxed the wisdom of a Solomon, and he was ill-prepared to cope with them. As a Democratic Senator from Missouri beginning in January, 1935, he had been a consistent but inconspicuous supporter of Roosevelt's policies at home and abroad. After Pearl Harbor he strove to gain congressional approval for membership in a new international organization, but he was best known as chairman of a committee to investigate the defense program. Partly as a result of that work, in 1944 he received the vice-presidential nomination, but he was never one of Roosevelt's inner circle. Hence he was not privy to the accords reached at Yalta, to the subsequent difficulties with Russia, or to the fast-changing situation in the Pacific. Indeed, he did not even know of the project to develop the atomic bomb.

Initially, Truman leaned on Roosevelt's advisers, but he soon revealed those qualities which characterized his eight-year tenure. Independent, self-confident, and straightforward, he was unwilling and unable to dissemble. Easily moved to anger, he was quick to forgive and forget. Blunt, forthright, and sometimes coarse in manner and speech, he had a strong sense of duty and a keen awareness of the potential of his office. As a writer and orator, he was colorless. His commonplace prose suffered in contrast to Wilson's eloquence; his nasal twang compared unfavorably with the vibrant voice of his predecessor. But he had the courage to dare and the will to do. A captain in the First World War, he did not hesitate to remove General Douglas MacArthur in 1951. A student of history, he chose to meet head-on the communist challenge in order to save South Korea from the fate of Manchuria and the United Nations from that of Wilson's League. A controversial figure, whose decisions have shaped the modern era, the man from Independence demonstrated anew the vast authority of the presidency and the awesome truth of the words upon a card standing on his desk—"The buck stops here."

THE SECRETARIES OF STATE

Cordell Hull was secretary of state longer than any man in history. Despite differences in temperament and tastes, he and Roosevelt usually collaborated effectively, though by 1941 strains in their relations began to appear. Hull disliked the third term, resented the access to the White House enjoyed by Under Secretary Welles, and was hurt by the President's growing reliance on the Joint Chiefs of Staff and personal envoys. For his gradual exclusion from some areas of decision making, however, Hull was partly to blame. Since he had refused before Pearl Harbor to regard war planning as within his domain, it is not surprising that Roosevelt consulted him less and less on grand strategy once hostilities had commenced and did not take him to high-level parleys abroad. Still, until compelled by health to resign on November 27, 1944, Hull exerted great influence on such matters as the extended negotiations with Japan in 1941, the tortuous wooing of Vichy France and Franco Spain, and the successful preparations for the United Nations. To the end the courtly Tennessean remained forthright, loyal, tenacious, and sanctimonious.

Edward R. Stettinius, Jr., his successor, was the son of a Morgan partner and former chairman of the board of the United States Steel Corporation. A man of personal charm and business acumen, he had no experience in foreign affairs until he was named Lend-Lease Administrator in August, 1941, but his record in that post led to his becoming Under Secretary of State in September, 1943. Although he intended to concentrate on reorganizing the department, he was obliged by Hull's failing health to play a major role in negotiating a draft Charter of the United Nations. His choice to replace Hull evoked surprise; but since Roosevelt obviously intended to deal directly with Churchill and Stalin, the Senate did not object. Serving only from December 1, 1944, to June 27, 1945, Stettinius could accomplish little. His presence at Yalta was hardly felt. He attended an inter-American gathering in Mexico City which laid the groundwork for a treaty of reciprocal assistance, but that document did not come into being until after he had left office. Perhaps his main contribution was preserving harmony in the delegation at the United Nations Conference in San Francisco. Immediately thereafter he resigned, a little reluctantly, to make room for Truman's known preference.

James F. Byrnes of South Carolina was secretary of state from July 3, 1945, to January 21, 1947. A representative and senator for almost thirty years, he had gone on the Supreme Court in July, 1941, only to leave it fifteen months later to run the Office of Economic Stabilization and War Mobilization. Popularly known as the "Assistant President," he saw at first hand the problems of coalition diplomacy. Present at Yalta, he discovered only later all that had transpired. Byrnes brought to his job an ability to deal with people and to find a middle ground. He had the admiration of Truman, the goodwill of Congress, and the respect of the country. He helped build a bipartisan foreign policy in a critical era; he was partly responsible for the shift from trying to get along with the Russians to acting tough with them. The first steps in containment came during his tenure. Unfortunately, he grew so engrossed in negotiating the minor peace treaties that he sometimes neglected larger issues. Unfortunately, too, frequent absences from Washington strained the close bond with Truman, who was gradually alienated by Byrnes' secretiveness and by his cockiness that bordered on conceit.

George C. Marshall, the man most responsible for the strategy of victory against the Axis, followed Byrnes. A professional soldier who never questioned civilian supremacy, Marshall lacked formal diplomatic experience, but his record as chief of staff from September, 1939, to November, 1945, offered abundant proof of his capacity for keen analysis, sound judgment, and inspiring leadership. A person of quiet dignity, absolute integrity, and utter selflessness, he surrounded himself with talented subordinates and encouraged them to speak out.

He created a Policy Planning Staff and put it in charge of George F. Kennan, an extremely gifted career officer. But while Marshall insisted upon a full discussion, he never shrank from his duty to render a decision. Indeed, duty was more to him than an obligation; it was a way of life. Three times after he had retired with honor he yielded to Truman's plea to serve his country anew: in November, 1945, to undertake the thankless mission to strife-torn China; in January 1947 to head the State Department for two years; and in September, 1950, to guide the Defense Department during the darkest weeks of the Korean War.

Dean G. Acheson, who succeeded Marshall on January 21, 1949, was the brainiest of Truman's four secretaries of state. Blessed with an acute, logical, and incisive mind, he could cut quickly to the heart of a problem and present his opinions cogently and compellingly. He had left a lucrative law practice to become Under Secretary of the Treasury in 1933, but he soon quit in disgust over the fiscal heresies of the New Deal. He returned in February, 1941, as Assistant Secretary of State, first for economic affairs and then for congressional liaison. He was Under Secretary from August, 1945, to July, 1947, by which time he had shown traits which plagued him during his turbulent secretaryship. His aristocratic mien, his impeccable dress, his clipped accent, and his neatly trimmed mustache personified the professional diplomat, whom legislators tend to distrust. Acheson did not suffer fools gladly and was unable to conceal the fact; to many his intellectual prowess appeared as intellectual arrogance. Nobody could doubt his technical competence or political courage, but one might question his discretion and timing. On two important occasions he stated his views so tersely that they were misconstrued at home and abroad; on another he rashly defied public opinion by speaking charitably of Alger Hiss, a former State Department officer who had at that time just been convicted of perjury. Yet Acheson's place in history must not be obscured by these personal shortcomings or by the torrent of criticism that often hobbled his endeavors. Keenly appreciative of the relation of power to diplomacy, he did much to persuade the President to take steps in moments of crisis which revealed to the world that the United States could and would act the role befitting a great nation.

Harry L. Hopkins was never secretary of state, but from May, 1940, until his death in January, 1946, he wielded more influence in certain areas of foreign policy than Hull or Stettinius. A social worker from Iowa, he had administered the New Deal's welfare programs and then served briefly as secretary of commerce. A lean, disheveled, nervous man, he had a knack of getting quickly to the heart of problems and setting forth a course of action. A doer rather than a thinker, he was utterly lacking in diplomatic experience when Roosevelt entrusted him with the most delicate missions to Churchill and Stalin. "Harry is the perfect Ambassador for my purposes," Roosevelt once said, for "he doesn't even know the meaning of the word 'protocol.' " Although the uninformed objected to the powers exercised by this new Colonel House, wartime leaders on each side of the Atlantic regarded him as indispensable. Unlike House, Hopkins never professed to know what the President was thinking when he did not; hence there was no tragic break in the friendship. But like House, he filled a role that Roosevelt described to Willkie after 1940. If you ever sit in the White House, he told his late rival, you will find that every caller wants something for himself. You will then learn "what a lonely job this is, and you'll discover the need for somebody like Harry Hopkins who asks for nothing except to serve you."

THE CONGRESSIONAL LEADERS

From 1939 to 1953 congressional leaders displayed a growing appreciation of the revolutionary changes in American foreign policy. The old distinction between internal and external affairs diminished, and new areas of concern emerged. Committee members spent much time investigating conditions abroad; individual lawmakers went as delegates to many international conferences. These duties fostered a sense of responsibility and reduced the appeal to legislative prerogative, partisan advantage, and xenophobic prejudice which had once prevailed on Capitol Hill.

Two senators wielded an influence in this period in the manner of Lodge and Borah. One was Tom Connally, Democrat of Texas, who sat in the House from 1917 to 1929 and in the upper chamber from 1929 to 1953. Appointed to the Foreign Relations Committee in 1931, he became chairman a decade later and, save for an interlude of Republican control in 1947–8, remained in that post until his retirement. A striking figure with flowing hair, and a florid orator of the old school, Connally used his parliamentary skill and personal warmth to persuade his colleagues to abandon isolationism and embrace a bipartisan working arrangement with the executive branch. Not a man of deep ideas, he left his mark by championing the Roosevelt-Truman policies, by playing a key role in the formation of the United Nations, and by placing a restrictive reservation in the resolution of August, 1946, by which the United States accepted the compulsory jurisdiction of the new International Court of Justice.

Arthur H. Vandenberg, Republican of Michigan, was the more important of the two because of his past record and party label. A former journalist with an amiable disposition and the common touch, he served in the Senate from 1928 until his death by cancer in 1951.

Named to the Foreign Relations Committee in 1929, he followed at first the lead of the Irreconcilables. He endorsed the findings of the Nye Committee, favored "the new neutrality," and opposed Lend-Lease. The impact of war modified his thinking, and in a widely publicized address on January 10, 1945, he sought to atone for the past by advocating full membership in the United Nations and close collaboration with the Soviet Union. Like Connally, he was instrumental in framing the Charter and cementing bipartisanship; but he had a more difficult task in convincing his Republican associates that they must replace the negativism of the 1930's with a modern approach to external affairs. Vandenberg cooperated faithfully with the Democrats in developing the Truman Doctrine, the Marshall Plan, and the mutual defense assistance program, while his resolution in June, 1948, paved the way for negotiating the North Atlantic Treaty. Bipartisanship, however, he regarded as a two-way street, and in 1949 he criticized the administration for its policy in China. Yet he always voiced his disagreement with moderation and fairness.

Robert A. Taft, senator from Ohio since 1939, succeeded Vandenberg as the Republican spokesman on foreign policy. The son of a former president and a disciple of Hoover in the First World War, he was a man of high principles, keen intelligence, austere manners, intense pride, and undeviating party loyalty. If he lacked his father's personal charm and sense of humor, he understood better the political process. Like Vandenberg, he was an admitted isolationist before Pearl Harbor and had fought most of Roosevelt's measures. Like Vandenberg, his ideas were affected by the struggle for survival, but the transformation was less complete. Although he supported membership in the United Nations, he tried to insure congressional control over the American delegates. He accepted reluctantly the European Recovery Program but voted against the North Atlantic Treaty and the Mutual Defense Assistance Act. He attacked on constitutional grounds the president's decision to defend South Korea and to station additional troops in Europe. In his bitterness against these alleged executive usurpations, he encouraged the Republican vendetta led by Senator Joseph R. McCarthy of Wisconsin. Ever a staunch defender of legislative prerogatives, Taft nonetheless changed with the times, and by 1953 his position was closer to Truman's than to his own of 1941.

Despite the enhanced prestige of the House because of huge appropriations for national defense, mutual aid, and scientific research, no congressman rivaled Connally, Vandenberg, or Taft. Ranking members did represent the United States at international gatherings, but the shorter term, the curb on debate, and the size of the chamber lessened opportunities for unusual contributions. So did the rapid

turnover in the chairmanship of the Foreign Affairs Committee, where
only one man held that post for more than two years between 1939
and 1953.

THE CONSTITUTIONAL CONFLICT

During the struggle for survival, the constitutional conflict sharpened.
At first, Roosevelt felt constrained to proceed cautiously, even where
his right to act was indisputable. As the crisis deepened in 1941, he
grew bolder and obtained emergency powers. After Pearl Harbor the
pendulum swung still further as the executive's role in dealing with
other countries became inseparable from his position as commander-
in-chief. Nor did the end of hostilities bring the traditional reaction.
Profiting from the lessons of history, Roosevelt and Truman promoted
a fruitful collaboration with the Senate and House which lasted until
the disaster in China, the conflict in Korea, and the removal of Mac-
Arthur revived questions of prerogative and partisanship. Then Congress reasserted its rights and endeavored to hobble the president by
plans to curtail his constitutional authority.

Appointments were more difficult to confirm after 1939. The votes
against Acheson as secretary of state and Marshall as secretary of
defense in 1949–50 were unusually high. There was substantial opposition to Edward J. Flynn as ambassador to Australia in 1943 and to
Chester Bowles as ambassador to India in 1951. Controversial nominations to the United Nations General Assembly included Francis Biddle
in 1947 and Philip C. Jessup in 1951. Although the Senate did not reject any of these men directly, excessive delay or adverse sentiment
in committee kept Flynn, Biddle, and Jessup from being confirmed.

Appropriations grew larger in an era of global wars and mutual-
aid programs, but constitutional clashes were rare. The presidents
knew who held the purse strings and realized that the scrutiny of
money bills was unavoidable. Congress understood that modern diplomacy is too complex to allow 500 individuals to pass on every detail.
Thus, although the executive received $30,697,498,000 under the
Lend-Lease Act of March 11, 1941, and its supplements, he was required to submit an accounting four times a year. Periodic reports
were also obligatory under the mutual aid bills, and in each instance
the legislature voted twice. First it determined what sum should be
authorized; later it decided how much ought to be appropriated. Congress might also stipulate that economic assistance be withheld from a
particular country. In short, the president's discretion in spending was
circumscribed in many ways.

Calls by the legislature for diplomatic papers in executive hands
were frequent from 1939 to 1953, but the expanding use of the in-

vestigatory power forestalled major constitutional controversies. Almost every treaty, appropriation, or military bill was subjected to one or more committee hearings. These probes normally helped Congress to discharge intelligently its proper functions, but occasionally they were undertaken to embarrass the president or reap partisan advantage. The three most publicized inquests of the period involved the circumstances surrounding the attack on Pearl Harbor, the recall of General MacArthur, and the alleged Communist infiltration into the Institute of Pacific Relations, a private research organization.

Recognition had become by 1939 a potential rather than an actual source of friction between president and Congress. There was no disagreement between the two branches on the question of entering into formal relations with Communist China, East Germany, or North Korea. On the first, perhaps, the executive was less rigid, but any disposition to acknowledge the legitimacy of the Peking regime after the defeat of Chiang Kai-shek was killed by the intervention of Mao Tsetung's forces during the assault on South Korea. In the recriminations that followed it was politically impossible for Truman to recognize Communist China or tolerate its admission to the United Nations.

The treaty-making process provoked fewer clashes between the executive and legislature than in the past. Both presidents and most senators cooperated to exclude politics and prerogatives from the consideration of the United Nations Charter and other postwar agreements. Yet before the Axis was conquered, it had occasionally been necessary to bypass constitutional procedures designed for an age which did not have to live with crisis, and the result was proposals to curb the use of executive agreements. The circle was completed when the president complained that his authority over external affairs was being invaded.

Legislative initiation of treaties, a practice long dormant, returned in this period. A joint resolution in June, 1940, encouraged Hull to conclude at Havana a month later a convention for the provisional administration of European colonies in the Americas. The Fulbright and Connally Resolutions in the fall of 1943 provided congressional sanction for membership in a new world organization. The Vandenberg Resolution in June, 1948, gave assurance in advance that the Senate would approve the North Atlantic Treaty.

Consent without change was the normal lot of treaties after 1939. They included the convention on European colonies (July 30, 1940), the treaty relinquishing extraterritorial rights in China (January 11, 1943), the United Nations Charter (June 26, 1945), the peace pacts with Bulgaria, Hungary, Italy, and Rumania (February 10, 1947), the Inter-American Treaty of Reciprocal Assistance (September 2, 1947), the North Atlantic Treaty (April 4, 1949), the Mutual Defense Treaty with the Philippines (August 30, 1951), the Security Treaty with Australia and New Zealand (September 1, 1951), the Security Treaty with Japan (September 8, 1951), and the Protocol to the Treaty Constituting the European Defense Community (May 27, 1952).

Even when the Senate declined to pass treaties without change, it used reservations rather than amendments. Furthermore, the effect of those appended to the Charter of the Organization of American States on August 28, 1950, to the Japanese Peace Treaty on March 20, 1952 and to the Bonn Convention on July 1, 1952 was relatively slight. The one vital alteration was in the resolution accepting the compulsory jurisdiction of the International Court. On August 2, 1946, the Senate exempted three classes of disputes and then followed Connally in reserving to the United States the sole right to define which were domestic in nature.

More significant than these minimal modifications was the fact that the Senate did not defeat any major treaty from 1939 to 1953. As a result, there was little complaint over the two-thirds rule or excluding the House from the treaty-making process. Other problems which had once generated friction between the executive and the legislature were largely absent. The president did not refuse to ratify treaties; Congress did not balk at implementing them. Nor did the termination of unpopular or outmoded accords produce difficulties.

If the declining mortality rate was the most important single development in the treaty-making process during this period, then the increased use of executive agreements ranks second. These phenomena do not, however, represent cause and effect, since the motivations for and the consequences of evading the constitutional provision varied greatly. Those concluded before Pearl Harbor dealt mainly with defense and were published at once. Among them were the Inter-American Declaration of Reciprocal Assistance of July 30, 1940, the Ogdensburg Agreement of August 18, 1940 with Canada, the Destroyers-Bases Agreement of September 2, 1940 with England, the notes exchanged on April 9 and July 1, 1941, about Greenland and Iceland, and the Atlantic Charter of August 14, 1941, proclaimed by Roosevelt and Churchill. After hostilities began, secrecy was inevitable, especially in matters relating to military operations. Outlines of the future peace appeared in executive agreements, but most of them were common knowledge. Such was the case with the United Nations Declaration of January 1, 1942, the communiqués issued at Casablanca, Moscow, Cairo, and Tehran in 1943, and part of the understandings reached at Yalta and Potsdam in 1945. It was not possible to place all of those decisions in treaties, and we must not suppose the Senate would have defeated them if they had been. Lastly, executive agreements were widely used after the war to carry out the various mutual aid programs.

This vast power wielded by Roosevelt and Truman provoked a reaction in the form of proposals to amend the Constitution. Many people argued that modern diplomacy had upset the balance between president and Congress established in 1787. They were supported by those who hated the two Democrats, by those who feared the economic and social goals of the United Nations, and by those who blamed the perils of the Cold War on the decisions made at Casablanca, Tehran, Yalta, and Potsdam. While not every suggestion was aimed at executive agreements, as the limitation of presidents to two terms shows, the much publicized scheme of Senator John W. Bricker, Republican of Ohio, dealt with the treaty-making process in a way very different from the plans of the interwar years.

First introduced on September 14, 1951, the Bricker Amendment had been revised by February 7, 1952 to seek three goals. One was to prevent any treaty or executive agreement from abridging the rights of individual citizens or altering federal statutes and state laws. A second was to block any treaty which might enable the United Nations to intrude upon domestic matters or convert that body into "an instrument of world government." The third was to circumscribe the president by providing that "executive agreements shall not be made in lieu of treaties." Unless terminated sooner, such agreements would automatically expire one year after the term for which the president who had concluded them was elected. He might, however, ask Congress to extend them. All agreements must be published, except where secrecy was imperative; in those cases the text would be submitted to the proper committees of Congress for information. Although backed by fifty-eight senators, the Bricker Amendment did not reach the floor until Truman had left the White House.

Clashes over the control of the armed forces were frequent after 1939. They arose from divergent views on how to meet the threat of fascism or communism and from different solutions for adapting the war-making machinery to changing times. Actually, the United States fought three wars in this period, two of them undeclared. The first was confined to sea and air hostilities with Germany in the Atlantic from September 11 to December 11, 1941. It was begun by a presidential order which Congress was told about but never asked to implement. The second was the global struggle against the Axis and its satellites from December 7, 1941, to August 14, 1945. Here the legislature fulfilled its constitutional function and yet simply ratified a *fait accompli*. The third was the contest in Korea which started on June 27, 1950, as a supposedly brief police action and ended on July 27, 1953, as a seemingly interminable limited war. Congress never adopted a declaration but strongly supported the steps taken by the president, at least in the beginning.

Despite the criticism leveled against Roosevelt and Truman, no move was made to amend the war-making clauses of the Constitution. This restraint, all the more surprising in the face of the new alliances, can be explained on several grounds. One was the care exercised by the executive, when drafting the United Nations Charter and other postwar treaties, to avoid absolute commitments to use armed force. The power of Congress to declare war was preserved—on paper. A second was the end of the old practice of landing troops on foreign soil to protect lives and property without obtaining legislative authorization. A third was the realization on Capitol Hill that, in an era of push-button warfare, the president must have latitude to act in an emergency.

Nor were curbs imposed on the president's powers as commander-in-chief. Congress was loath to deny the right of the executive to deploy men, ships, and planes or to decide how a war should be fought. What it tried to do was forestall moves which might provoke hostilities. A rider to a law of June 28, 1940, prohibited the president from disposing of military equipment until his top uniformed aides certified the matériel was not essential to the nation's defenses. The Lend-Lease Act of March 11, 1941, said that it did not empower American naval vessels to escort foreign merchantmen. The bluntest challenge to the prerogatives of the executive occurred in January, 1951, when Congress questioned Truman's order to send additional regiments to Europe; the most dramatic came three month's later when Truman removed MacArthur from his command. Despite a resolution expressing the sense of the Senate in the first case and loose talk of impeachment in the second, the period closed with the authority of the commander-in-chief unimpaired.

By 1953 the historic conflict between president and Congress was being overshadowed by the question of whether the constitutional system could meet the needs of coalition diplomacy and the thermonuclear age. More than ever before the initiative rested with the executive, and his powers as commander-in-chief were at the heart of every controversy.

44

❯❯❯-❯❯❯-❯❯❯-❯❯❮❮❮-❮❮❮-❮❮❮-❮❮❮

The Abandonment of Neutrality

TWENTY-FIVE YEARS after the Kaiser's infantry and cavalry had poured into Belgium, Hitler's armored divisions and dive bombers launched the conquest of Poland. In September, 1939, as in August, 1914, almost all Americans rejoiced in their geographic and diplomatic detachment. Like Wilson, Roosevelt promptly proclaimed his government's neutrality and publicly promised to remain at peace. Confident that the earlier experience would enable them to avoid the alleged mistakes of 1914–17 and hopeful that the recent laws would insulate them from the conflict, the people settled back, expecting the Second World War to follow the pattern of the First. To their astonishment and dismay, it did not. After seven months of deceptive calm in the West, Germany unleashed a devastating offensive which quickly crushed five neutrals, overran France, and left England apparently helpless to resist invasion. Convinced the republic was in dire peril, Roosevelt began to abandon neutrality in June, 1940, by promising to extend to the foes of Hitler all aid short of war. A final break with historic policies was at hand.

THE SECOND WORLD WAR

In September, 1939, the people and the government were better informed about the gathering storm than had been the case in August, 1914. Repeated crises since 1931 had made the man in the street fully aware of the totalitarian menace. Since the days of Munich, newscasts had brought a sense of urgency into every home. Roosevelt's administration was more alive to the portents of disaster than Wilson's had been. Ambassadorial and consular reporting were infinitely superior in 1939, while the President did not wait until the last days to offer his services for peace. Another significant difference was the greater dislike in the United States of Hitler's Reich than of the Kaiser's and the greater distrust in Berlin of Roosevelt than of Wilson. From the outset the former was regarded as committed to the cause of the so-called democracies.

Yet it cannot be said that the United States played a decisive role in the final crisis which began with the signing of the Nazi-Soviet Pact of August 23, 1939. This marriage of convenience between regimes that seemed ideologically irreconcilable freed Hitler from the nightmare of a two-front war and gave Stalin time to prepare for eventual trouble with Germany and Japan. The published terms stated that for ten years neither party would attack the other or join a bloc aimed against the other. A secret protocol defined mutual spheres of influence, should "a territorial and political rearrangement" become necessary. The German orbit embraced western Poland and Lithuania; the Russian, eastern Poland, Latvia, Estonia, Finland, and Bessarabia.[1] Already Stalin foreshadowed his intention to protect the Soviet Union with a ring of buffer states in the West and to advance its interests in Central Europe and the Balkans.

This ominous *rapprochement* was foreseen more clearly in Washington than in London or Paris, but there was little the United States could do. On August 1, 1939, Roosevelt warned Stalin that if he joined Hitler, the latter "would turn on Russia" as soon as he conquered France. The men in the Kremlin may have agreed, but they also knew the American government would not help them in Europe or Asia. Failing to dissuade the Soviets, the President asked the King of Italy on August 23 to offer proposals for settling the worsening German-Polish crisis, but the answer was a polite negative. On August 24 an appeal went to Hitler and the Polish executive, although one of the drafters expected it to have "about the same effect as a valentine sent to somebody's mother-in-law out of season." The suggestions were familiar, direct negotiation and arbitration. As in April, Roosevelt said he would bring the United States to a conference for reducing armaments and freeing trade; now he added he stood ready to act as a conciliator. When the Poles jumped at the idea, he rushed their acceptance to Berlin on August 25. Hitler responded with routine thanks on Au-

[1] An agreement of September 28, 1939, assigned Lithuania to Russia's sphere.

gust 31, but his real reply came the next day with the invasion of Poland.

Feeble and futile as America's endeavors may have been, they went beyond anything attempted before. Different, too, was Roosevelt's radio address of September 3, 1939, a document to be compared with Wilson's appeal of August 19, 1914. Again the emphasis was on neutrality; again no belligerent was singled out for blame. But by condemning recent resorts to force, the President pointedly criticized Germany. Nor did he ask the people to be impartial in thought and action. "This nation," he said, "will remain a neutral nation, but I cannot ask that every American remain neutral in thought as well. Even a neutral has a right to take account of facts. Even a neutral cannot be asked to close his mind or his conscience." Roosevelt disclaimed any desire to intervene and pledged that as long as he could prevent it, "there will be no black-out of peace in the United States." Yet he warned his countrymen that the conflagration could reach them. "Passionately though we may desire detachment," he declared, "we are forced to realize that every word that comes through the air, every ship that sails the sea, every battle that is fought, does affect the American future."

NEUTRAL DUTIES AND NEUTRAL RIGHTS

Roosevelt possessed, as Wilson had not, two devices designed to keep the United States out of war. One was an up-to-date neutrality law. Thus on September 5, 1939, he not only issued the customary proclamation announcing America's abstention, but also imposed on individual citizens the restrictions contained in the act of May 1, 1937. The second device was the machinery for consultation among the American republics set up at Lima in 1938. On September 3 Hull sounded out Argentina and others regarding an immediate meeting of the foreign ministers. Upon receiving favorable replies, he persuaded Panama to invite the delegates to consider the rights and duties of both neutrals and belligerents, the precautions necessary to preserve the hemisphere free of fighting, and the steps required to safeguard the economic stability of the New World nations. The conference met at Panama from September 23 to October 3, 1939, with Under Secretary Welles representing the United States.

Three important measures were adopted. The General Declaration of Neutrality set forth certain standards of conduct, such as denying to belligerents the right to mount combat operations or establish radio stations on American soil. The Declaration of the Transfer of Sovereignty stipulated that if a change in sovereignty of territory belonging to a European power should endanger the security of the Western Hemisphere, a consultative meeting would be held immediately. The Declaration of Panama drew a 300-mile zone in both oceans around the continental and insular possessions of the Americas, extending from the southern boundary of Canada to Cape Horn. Within that area belligerents were expected to refrain from hostile acts, while neutral patrols might be undertaken, individually or collectively, to see that those waters were not violated. This restriction, justified as self-protection, had no precedent in international law and was ignored by both sides.

With much less enthusiasm, Roosevelt faithfully fulfilled the obligations of the Neutrality Act of May 1, 1937. He was determined to renew the battle against the arms embargo and called Congress into special session for that purpose. He regretted, he told that body on September 21, 1939, having signed the original law and warned that the present statute could lead to war. A burgeoning and unrestricted trade in vital raw materials might draw the republic into the conflict now that the "cash-and-carry" clause had expired. He asked, therefore, for a return to traditional practices in the sale of munitions and suggested that they and other essential commodities be placed on a "cash-and-carry" basis. He did not seek changes in existing prohibitions against loans and credits, travel on belligerent ships, or arming merchantmen. While the President was consistent in this message, he was not entirely candid. His reason for wishing to repeal the arms embargo was not to restore a historic neutrality but to promote national security, and it would have been more straightforward had he based his case on that ground.

After a stiff battle, Congress revised the neutrality law. The task was not easy. Many legislators feared that a lifting of the arms embargo would start anew the cycle of 1914–17. The reaction to the torpedoing of the *Athenia* on September 4, 1939, was symptomatic. Although this westbound British liner was sunk without warning and with the loss of 128 lives, twenty-eight of them American, there was no popular outcry, as there had been after the destruction of the *Lusitania*. Americans were so suspicious of propaganda that many believed the Nazi lie about England having staged the slaughter in order to drag the United States into the war. In spite of opposition from Hoover, Borah, and Nye, public-opinion polls in October showed that 62 per cent of those responding supported the President, as against 57 per cent in April. By a vote of 63 to 30 in the Senate and 237 to 177 in the House, Roosevelt finally prevailed.

Under the Neutrality Act of November 4, 1939, the president had the power to decide whether a state of war existed and thus to bring the law into operation. Congress could also do so by concurrent resolution. Once the step was taken, by either executive or legislative initiative, a proclamation was to be issued identifying the belligerents. Thereafter it became illegal for American ships to carry passengers or goods to those nations. Exports to them, whether tools of war or other commodities, had to be paid for in cash and transported from the United States in foreign vessels. If he chose, the president might set up combat zones into which no American craft could go, even to trade with other neutrals. These clauses differed from the act of 1937, but some old prohibitions reappeared. American citizens were still forbidden to travel on belligerent ships, to arm merchantmen engaged in commerce with warring countries, or to extend loans and credits to belligerent governments. At his discretion the president could still close American territorial waters to foreign submarines.

For twelve months after the repeal of the arms embargo neutral rights and duties ceased to be a pressing matter. So long as the Allies could pay for their purchases, control the Atlantic, and contain Germany in Europe, the United States had no cause for alarm. Until the blitzkrieg in May, 1940, the British and French kept their orders small and their dollar reserve intact, anticipating a long war. So long as American ships were not sunk or lives lost, the administration had no reason to protest. Presidential action at home and restraint abroad eliminated most of the problems which had plagued Wilson. By defining the combat areas as the waters around the British Isles, the North and Baltic Seas, and the Bay of Biscay, Roosevelt could bar American vessels from belligerent ports. There were a few complaints when the Royal Navy reinstituted the long-range blockade and control system of the First World War, but it was obvious from the outset that England would not permit such controversies to create the bitterness they had from 1914 to 1917. Similarly, Hitler shackled his U-boats so effectively that they did not claim their first American victim until May 21, 1941.

Meanwhile, neutrality underwent an unexpected test when Russia invaded Finland on November 30, 1939. Soviet stock in the United States was at its nadir. The Nazi pact of August 23 was widely condemned as a green light for Hitler and a death knell for Poland. It had led also to the virtual extinction of the Baltic States and brusque demands for parts of Finland. Roosevelt did what he could to avert the Russo-Finnish clash but frankly admitted that "his influence in Moscow was just about zero." Once the fighting had begun, he found himself in a dilemma. Public opinion was violently anti-Russian, and there were frenzied pleas to help Finland in its heroic resistance. Yet Roosevelt and Hull, reasoning that Stalin was mainly interested in bolstering his western defenses, were reluctant to take any action which might drive him irrevocably into Hitler's arms. Hence they did not invoke the neutrality act, and Congress did not object. The President denounced Russia as the aggressor, while the Secretary asked for a voluntary embargo on the export of airplane parts to the Soviet Union. But they withstood pressure to break off relations and escaped having to stand up and be counted when the League of Nations for the first time expelled a member who had violated the Covenant.

Yet the Russo-Finnish struggle, which ended in the inevitable Soviet victory of March 13, 1940, was a temporary diversion. The fate of Europe would be decided in the West, where an uneasy calm fed hopes for an early peace. After crushing Poland in three weeks, Hitler had bade England and France to quit, but they refused. Still nothing happened. Borah described the situation as a "phony war"; others labeled it a "sitzkrieg." During the lull Roosevelt asked Congress on January 3, 1940, to increase military appropriations slightly, but he was ignored. In this lull Welles undertook a fact-finding mission in Rome, Berlin, Paris, and London, but he reported upon his return on March 29 that there was little prospect of a negotiated peace.

THE FALL OF FRANCE

Then on April 9, 1940, the storm broke in full fury. Overnight the sitzkrieg became a blitzkrieg. Neutral Denmark submitted under protest to German "protection" and was occupied at once. Neutral Norway resisted and was beaten in a month. On May 10 the Nazi juggernaut hurtled into neutral Holland, Belgium, and Luxembourg, compelling the surrender of the Dutch in four days and the Belgians in seventeen. On May 13 a breakthrough at Sedan enabled the Germans to cut off the British Expeditionary Force in Flanders, and by May 29 the desperate evacuation at Dunkirk began. On June 14 Paris fell. Unable to stop the Wehrmacht and attacked in the rear by Italy, France sued for peace. On June 22, in the same railroad car at Compiègne where Foch had accepted the capitulation twenty-two years before, an armistice was signed.

Only one who lived through those terrifying days can appreciate the impact of this disaster. The fall of France marked the end of an era and destroyed for most Americans the notion that neutrality automatically protected them against involvement. The fate of Scandinavia and Holland, whose impartiality in 1914–17 had often been contrasted with Wilson's alleged double standard, was not lost on a people who had believed that domestic laws could insulate them from foreign peril. The seemingly inevitable defeat of England foreshadowed a control of the Atlantic and all Europe by totalitarian nations. Would the New World be immune from interference or invasion? To be sure, there was an understandable tendency in June, 1940, to exaggerate the power of the Nazis on land and in the air, together with the threat they posed to the Western Hemisphere; but the existence of the British navy had so long influenced the framers of American foreign policy that they were not prepared on psychological or military grounds to consider a situation in which it was absent.

Whither national security? In this hour of decision, as the familiar configuration of power disintegrated, two answers were heard. One argued that the outcome in Europe did not vitally affect the United States so long as the nation remained aloof and friendly with both sides. It contended that the neutrality law, with all its shortcomings, was still the most reliable guide. The second insisted that a Europe dominated by dictators would constitute a perpetual economic and military menace to American democracy. It maintained that neutrality should be abandoned and all aid short of war be extended to those nations fighting Hitler. On two points, however, these divergent analyses agreed. One was the imperative necessity of expanding the armed forces to cope with future contingencies; the other was the pressing need of taking steps to insure the safety of the Western Hemisphere.

Roosevelt had no difficulty in winning congressional consent to a rapid build-up of land, sea, and air units. The tanks, ships, planes, and men which had occasioned bitter battles in 1938 were now his for the asking. As conditions deteriorated abroad, the President appealed for extraordinary appropriations: on May 16, 1940 for $1,182,000,000, on May 31 for $1,281,000,000, and on July 10 for $4,848,172,000. What this meant for a single service can be seen when one naval expansion bill on June 14 enlarged the fleet by 11 per cent and another on July 19 by about 70 per cent. On July 29, Roosevelt requested authority to activate the National Guard for a year; by August 27 the Senate had voted 71 to 7 and the House 342 to 33 to give him that power, subject only to calling men without dependents and assigning them to duty in the Western Hemisphere or the possessions of the United States. The most striking recognition of the peril came in the Selective Service Act of September 14, 1940. In spite of prophesies that conscription would destroy civil liberties and hasten intervention, the bill passed the Senate by a count of 47 to 25 and the House by 232 to 134.

President and Congress also cooperated in warning Germany to keep hands off the New World possessions of its European victims. At Hull's urging, the Senate and House adopted a resolution on June 17–18, 1940, saying the United States would not recognize the transfer of territory in the Western Hemisphere from one non-American country to another. If a cession appeared likely, joint consultation would follow at once. Although the Nazis scoffed at the assertion, they witnessed an impressive display of unity when the foreign ministers met promptly at Havana from July 21 to 30. A Declaration of Reciprocal Assistance stipulated that an attack by a non-American state upon an American nation was to be regarded as aggression against all the signatories and that consultation would ensue. The Act of Havana set forth a scheme of collective trusteeship. It authorized an emergency committee, composed of one member from each country, to administer provisionally any European colony in the New World that was in danger of being bartered away. In urgent cases requiring a decision before the committee could assemble, one republic might act alone. A convention giving permanency to these resolutions was signed on July 30 and consented to by the Senate unanimously on September 27. Although it did not enter into force until 1942, it gave the United States the sanction it desired to move instantaneously against any German intrusion into the possessions of France or the Netherlands.

Not unexpectedly, Roosevelt encountered much more difficulty in marshaling popular sentiment to abandon neutrality. His task was facilitated, however, by British heroism and courage. On May 10, 1940, Churchill replaced Chamberlain as Prime Minister, and he stiffened the national backbone with his indomitable spirit and eloquent words. "I have nothing to offer but blood, toil, tears, and sweat," he told Parliament on May 13. "We shall never surrender," he vowed on June 4, but will continue to fight on the beaches and in the streets. With mounting admiration the American people watched the English in "their finest hour." The cause, which seemed hopeless when Churchill coined that phrase, miraculously survived because the land-minded Germans lacked plans and equipment for an immediate cross-channel invasion and because the Royal Air Force beat back the Luftwaffe in September. Yet the margin was close, and the agony persisted as fire bombs gutted London, as submarines sank vital shipping, as the swastika flew unchallenged from the North Cape to the Pyrenees, and as Britain stood alone.

Spurred on by these events, Roosevelt slowly developed his case for abandoning neutrality. "The American people," he told Congress on May 16, 1940, "must recast their thinking about national protection." Ten days later in a fireside chat he emphasized how air power rendered dangerous and futile any "retiring within our continental boundaries." Although he believed England's survival was indispensable to American security, the President hesitated to make any definite pledge. Then on June 10, the day Italy entered the war, Roosevelt promised at Charlottesville that "we will extend to the opponents of force the material resources of this nation; and, at the same time, we will harness and speed up the use of those resources in order that we ourselves in the Americas may have the equipment and training equal to the task of any emergency."

Here was the commitment, though not a military one, which would take the United States from neutrality to nonbelligerency. It was made openly and for the purpose of enabling England to repel Germany. It also coincided with a swiftly changing public opinion. But proclaiming a principle is easier than implementing one, and at every stage henceforth there would be debate over what proper measures short of war were. As Churchill described them to Roosevelt on May 15, 1940, Britain's most urgent needs were a loan of fifty old destroyers and several hundred new aircraft. After Dunkirk he added equipment for the routed Expeditionary Force. Some of these demands could be met under a statute of June 15, 1917, which allowed the government to sell surplus stocks to private firms even if they were later resold to belligerent states. The new Republican Secretaries of War and Navy—Stimson and Frank Knox, whom Roosevelt appointed on June 19 in a bid for bipartisan support—employed the law freely to empty arsenals of materials dating back to 1918. But there were limits to this solution, for the generals and admirals were reluctant to part with even obsolete weapons until modern ones were available. The naval bill of June 28, moreover, contained a rider forbidding the disposal of military equipment unless the chief of staff or the chief of naval operations certified it was "not essential to the defense of the United States."

THE DESTROYERS-BASES AGREEMENT

As the summer of 1940 lengthened and the invasion of England appeared imminent, Roosevelt could no longer evade Churchill's request for a loan of fifty overage destroyers. The vessels were desperately needed for convoy duty and defense of the home islands. The United States could spare the ships without danger—most of them had been decommissioned for years—provided the British fleet did not fall into Nazi hands. But a transfer seemed to violate domestic and international law, and it was unlikely that new authority could be legislated or a treaty be approved in time to meet the crisis. The President was loath to take the step in an election year unless the rival candidate, Wendell Willkie, concurred; for without Willkie's endorsement the Republicans in Congress would vote against the scheme and denounce its sponsor.

On August 1, 1940, a group of New York lawyers offered a way out. They proposed to trade the destroyers for selected sites in the Western Hemisphere and thus be able not only to justify the exchange as a contribution to national defense but also to silence those who had long demanded such cessions in payment for war debts. When this plan won the outspoken support of the aged Pershing and the tacit approval of Willkie, Roosevelt decided on August 11 to resort to an executive agreement. Some delay ensued as he and Churchill bickered over details and until the chief of naval operations certified that, in view of the strategic sites acquired, the ships released were not essential to the nation's security.

The Destroyers-Bases Agreement of September 2, 1940, consisted of two letters between Hull and the British ambassador. It contained no secret clauses and was transmitted to Congress at once for information, though not for consent. It provided that, in return for the immediate transfer of fifty destroyers and certain unspecified weapons, England would lease without charge and for ninety-nine years six sites in the Caribbean suitable for air and naval stations. In addition, Great Britain granted without compensation the right to develop similar facilities in southern Newfoundland and eastern Bermuda. Simultaneously but independently, Britain pledged that its fleet would never be allowed to fall to Germany.

Not since the Louisiana Purchase, as Roosevelt told Congress on September 3, 1940, had a more advantageous step been taken to bolster the nation's defenses. Nor did he exaggerate when he declared: "The value to the Western Hemisphere of these outposts of security is beyond calculation." Air power had placed the Americas within ten hours of flying time from Greenland, the Azores, and West Africa. From these new bases search planes could spot an approaching enemy long before he was able to strike the continental United States. From their harbors an undersized navy could guard more effectively the approaches to the Panama Canal and discharge more efficiently its duties under the neutrality patrol. On purely strategic grounds, the President's case was unassailable.

Constitutionally, Roosevelt was more vulnerable. Never before had an executive agreement been used to annex territory. When the treaty-making process was evaded in 1845 for Texas and in 1898 for Hawaii, a joint resolution involving both the Senate and House had been employed. Now Congress, which had been in session for months, was presented with a *fait accompli* and for an obvious reason. Legislative debate would be too slow and uncertain to meet the needs, or what the President thought were the needs, of modern warfare and diplomacy. A decade later the people might agree; in 1940 they were shocked by this reflection on their form of government. Many citizens were offended also because the attorney general's opinion, on which Roosevelt relied to overcome the domestic statutes, was a tortured one, based partly on the location of a single comma. Since, however, the agreement was patently beneficial to the United States, its reception was enthusiastic on both Capitol Hill and Main Street. The minority who still insisted that the war in Europe could not touch the country were, of course, outraged and talked of the unscrupulous dictator in the White House.

Yet on one point Roosevelt's critics were correct. The exchange of destroyers for bases was incompatible with international law. It violated the traditional neutrality, which Wilson had championed from 1914 to 1917, and "the new neutrality," which Congress had enacted from 1935 to 1937. The transfer was so unneutral, Churchill conceded in 1949, that "according to all the standards of history," Germany would have been justified in declaring war. Roosevelt was too realistic to speak of neutrality in his message to Congress. Rather he argued that the agreement was not inconsistent with "our status of peace. Still less is it a threat against any nation. It is," he insisted, a "far-reaching act of preparation for continental defense in the face of grave danger."

Roosevelt was wise to rest his case on the ground of security. Neutrality had always been a means to an end, and the end was the national interest. No nation is obliged to be neutral when its safety is menaced. Every sovereign state has the right, Root once said, "to protect itself by preventing a condition of affairs in which it will be too late to protect itself." Hitler's kind did not respect the rights of neutrals, as the fate of Denmark, Norway, Holland, and Belgium attested. Traditional codes could not be relied upon when dealing with dictators, as events since 1931 had showed. The Destroyers-Bases Agreement should be judged not on whether it was consonant with nineteenth-century international law but on whether it was conducive to the security of the state. Certainly this strengthening of the defensive perimeter was sound unless it goaded Germany into declaring war. Roosevelt had to guess it would not, and he was right. To be sure, he took a calculated risk, as statesmen often must, and it was but the first of others yet to come.

45

❯❯❯—❯❯❯—❯❯❯—❯❯❯❮❮❮—❮❮❮—❮❮❮—❮❮❮

From Nonbelligerency
to Undeclared War
in the Atlantic

WITH THE Destroyers-Bases Agreement of September 2, 1940, the
United States ceased to be a neutral in the sense it had used the term
since 1776. Yet another year would elapse before the American government began an undeclared war with Germany in the Atlantic and
another fifteen months before it became a full participant against the
Axis powers and Japan. Its anomalous status, similar to Italy's before
June 18, 1940, is best defined as nonbelligerency. In rejecting absolute
impartiality and returning to the seventeenth-century distinction between just and unjust wars, Roosevelt believed, as his attorney general said on March 27, 1941, that "a system of international law which
can impose no penalty on a law-breaker and also forbids other states to
aid the victim would be self-defeating."

THE LEND-LEASE ACT

In abandoning neutrality, Roosevelt and Hull did not regard total
belligerency as inevitable. On the contrary, they believed that to give
all aid short of war to those fighting Germany was the best way to

\ escape involvement. Although they failed to foresee every form that | such assistance would take, they did recognize that in attempting to | avoid hostilities they ran the risk of provoking them. Yet they were heartened by multiplying signs that their course was what the country wanted.

\ Did the decision to give England all aid short of war command popular support? The evidence available suggests that in the autumn of 1940 three Americans out of five, perhaps two out of three, approved. An important force in marshaling favorable sentiment was the Committee to Defend America by Aiding the Allies, founded in mid-May after Germany had invaded the Low Countries. Its guiding spirit was William Allen White, a respected Republican editor from Kansas; its membership was nationwide but heavily sprinkled with eastern lawyers and college professors. Its original purpose was achieved by March, 1941, with the passage of the Lend-Lease Act; thereafter its backers tended to divide over the question of full participation in the war. To counter the influence of White's group in July, 1940, General Robert E. Wood, a Kansas-born West Point graduate and chairman of the board of Sears Roebuck, helped a Yale law student to form a frankly noninterventionist organization, initially called the Emergency Committee to Defend America First. Public announcement of this America First Committee, as it came to be known, was made on September 4, 1940, one day after Roosevelt informed Congress of the Destroyers-Bases Agreement. It too drew from all parts of the country but was popularly regarded as centered in the Middle West. Its leaders, among whom were prominent industrialists and Charles A. Lindbergh, Jr., the air hero of the 1920's, continued their crusade right down to December 7, 1941.

In the summer of 1940 the platforms of both parties endorsed the decision to give England all aid short of war. This approbation was dependent, however, upon assurances that such assistance did not require armed intervention. The Republicans were "firmly opposed to involving this nation in foreign war," while the Democrats vowed not to send the armed forces "to fight in foreign lands outside of the Americas, except in case of attack." Roosevelt and Willkie later gave solemn covenants on this point, but the former was usually more explicit in restricting his pledge to cases where the United States was not hit first. His one lapse came in Boston on October 30, 1940, when he told the parents of America what he had said "again and again and again," that their boys were "not going to be sent into any foreign wars." On this occasion he omitted the proviso, presumably because he felt his position was sufficiently clear. Three days later he stated that it was his intention to keep the country out of war, to keep war as far away as possible from the Western Hemisphere, and to give "all possible material aid to the nations which still resist aggression." The President was not guilty of duplicity on the hustings; he was careful not to tie his hands or promise the impossible.

After his re-election Roosevelt faced a new crisis. To be sure, the panic that had swept the United States in June, 1940, had subsided. The defeat of England or the loss of the Royal Navy had not materialized. Thanks to the fifty destroyers, the staggering blows to vital shipping had eased a little. Yet once American resources were fully harnessed to its needs, Britain's dollar reserve sank alarmingly. "The moment approaches," Churchill warned Roosevelt on December 2, "when we shall no longer be able to pay cash." Since floating loans was prohibited by the Johnson and Neutrality Acts, the President had to find a novel solution.

At a press conference on December 17, 1940, Roosevelt talked of a man whose house was imperiled by fire in an adjacent building and who lent his garden hose to the owner, asking not payment in advance or afterward but return of the hose. Here was the germ of the Lend-Lease idea which the President explained further in a fireside chat twelve days later. Recognizing the danger implicit in the recent alignment of Japan, Germany, and Italy, he declared there need be no fear of attack "anywhere in the Americas while a free Britain remains our most powerful naval neighbor in the Atlantic." What England needed were weapons, not men, and to meet its demands the republic must become "the great arsenal of democracy." On January 6, 1941, he specifically asked "for authority and for funds sufficient to manufacture additional munitions and war supplies of many kinds, to be turned over to those nations which are now in actual war with aggressor nations." The United States would be compensated after the war "in similar materials, or, at our option, in other goods of many kinds, which they can produce and which we need."

This concept of nonbelligerency was developed with full publicity and submitted to Congress for enactment. Both the Senate and the House held hearings on H.R. 1776, as it was denominated, and the opposition had ample opportunity to be heard. Some disagreed with the basic policy of rendering all aid to England short of war; others considered the specific measure unsound. The latter objected particularly to the vast powers conferred on the executive and the likelihood that American warships would be needed eventually to insure safe delivery of the leased goods. After a two-month debate the bill passed the House by a vote of 317 to 71 and the Senate by a margin of 60 to 31.

The Lend-Lease Act of March 11, 1941, drove the final nail into the coffin of neutrality. A more drastic departure from that historic policy than the Destroyers-Bases Agreement, it aimed to promote American security by supplying material aid to nations fighting the potential foes of the republic. It empowered the President to have manufactured, to the extent Congress provided funds, "any defense article for the government of any country whose defense the President deems vital to the defense of the United States." Such articles he could "sell, transfer title to, exchange, lend, lease, or otherwise dispose of" to those governments. Factories could be erected; naval craft could be repaired; guns, tanks, and planes could be built. Shipments from existing stocks were limited in value to $1,300,000,000 and needed the consent of the service chiefs, but goods produced from future appropriations were not restricted. The terms upon which foreign governments received this assistance were "those which the President deems satisfactory," but the executive did have to report to the legislature every three months on operations under the law. The statute expressly noted that it did not authorize American warships to escort foreign vessels or permit American merchantmen to enter the combat areas set up under the neutrality law.

Hitler's reply was to push his blockade of the British Isles west to the thirty-eighth parallel, thereby placing a further strain on the escort facilities of the Royal Navy. If this reaction was milder than many had expected, it was because the Führer's primary concern at that time was Russia, which he had decided to invade, and the Balkans. He had made satellites of Hungary, Rumania, and Bulgaria, but Yugoslavia and Greece still held out. On April 6, 1941, the German army unleashed a powerful offensive against the two recalcitrants and compelled them to surrender in three weeks. These victories threatened England's position in the Middle East, especially in Syria and Iraq, while a simultaneous catastrophe loomed in North Africa where General Erwin Rommel, rescuing the disorganized Italians, launched a counterattack with the objective of driving the British back to the Nile.

PATROLS AND CONVOYS

These disasters, coming on the heels of the Lend-Lease Act, called for still bolder action in Washington. "The decision for 1941," Churchill had warned Roosevelt on December 2, 1940, "lies upon the seas." There and in defense plants the United States could best play its part as a nonbelligerent. Production was moving into high gear, but delivery of the goods had not been assured. Tonnage losses in Allied and neutral shipping rose from 320,048 in January 1941 to 653,960 in April. To cope with the peril, the President opened American dockyards to damaged British naval craft and transferred ten coast guard cutters for operations out of Iceland. On March 30, sixty-five interned Axis and Danish vessels were seized for eventual requisition by the government, and on April 9 an executive agreement with the Danish minister in exile placed Greenland under the temporary protection of the United States and permitted the construction of air and naval bases there. Yet none of those measures went to the heart of the problem. American merchantmen were forbidden by law to enter belligerent ports. The Royal Navy was unable to provide adequate protection for the convoys of British and neutral freighters carrying Lend-Lease materials. The United States Fleet was restricted to patrol duty inside a 300-mile belt around the Western Hemisphere and did little to guarantee the safety of cargoes destined for England.

Roosevelt shrank from the most effective remedy: the use of American warships to escort convoys made up of belligerent and neutral merchantmen. He had reason to hesitate. During the Lend-Lease debates administration spokesmen had implied, even if they did not explicitly state, that such a step would not be necessary. An amendment to forbid the navy from escorting foreign vessels was barely avoided. Hence, the President temporized with half-measures. Beginning on April 24, 1941, patrol operations were extended eastward to a line running from Denmark Strait west of Iceland to a point about 700 miles off the easternmost tip of Brazil. Since patrols, as then conducted, were the equivalent of scouting, this enabled American naval craft to aid the British escorts of Atlantic convoys by warning them of the presence of German submarines, even in the war zone proclaimed by Hitler. The army's counterpart of this extended patrol was an order to the Caribbean Defense Command on May 12 to resist the forces of any belligerent, other than those holding territory in the New World, which threatened to attack a British colony on which the United States had an air or naval facility.

Even these precautions—some would call them provocations—did not seem enough as England's position in the Mediterranean and Middle East deteriorated. After much vacillation, on May 13, 1941, Roosevelt transferred one aircraft carrier, the three most modern battleships, and four of the newest light cruisers from the Pacific Fleet to the East Coast. Ten days later the giant battleship *Bismarck* broke into the Atlantic and tied up half the Royal Navy before being sunk. Fearful that Hitler might strike next at the approaches to the New World, the President began preparations on May 24 to land 25,000 men in the Azores and canceled the operation only when Portugal hesitated to ask for that protection. With two cabinet members demanding escorts for convoys of foreign ships and two more arguing for immediate intervention, the executive tried in a fireside chat of May 27 to prepare the people for the worst.

"It is unmistakably apparent," Roosevelt began, that "unless the advance of Hitlerism is forcibly checked now, the Western Hemisphere

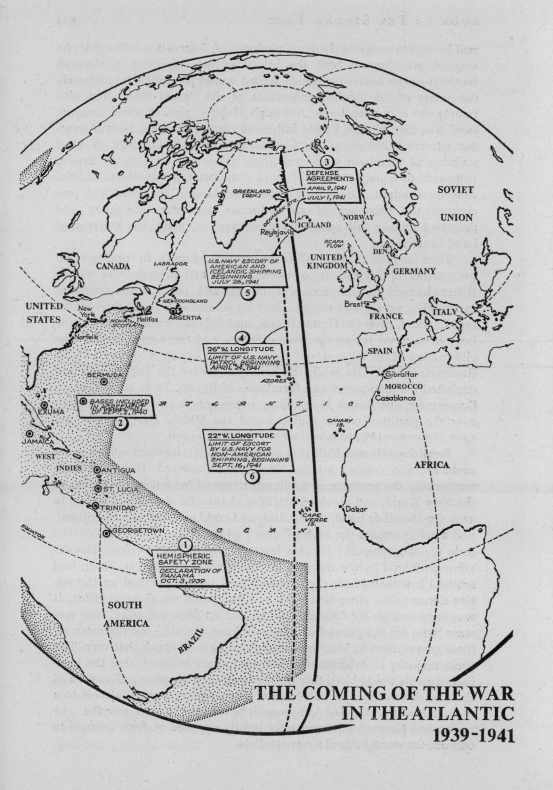

GREENLAND
(DEN.)

③ DEFENSE
AGREEMENTS
APRIL 9, 1941
JULY 1, 1941

NORWAY

SOVIET

UNION

DENMARK STR.

ICELAND
Reykjavik

SCAPA
FLOW

UNITED
KINGDOM

DEN.

GERMANY

CANADA

LABRADOR

U.S. NAVY ESCORT OF
AMERICAN AND
ICELANDIC SHIPPING
BEGINNING
JULY 26, 1941
⑤

NEWFOUNDLAND
ARGENTIA

Brest

FRANCE

ITALY

UNITED
STATES

New York
NOVA
SCOTIA
Halifax

Norfolk

④ 26° W. LONGITUDE
LIMIT OF U.S. NAVY
PATROL BEGINNING
APRIL 24, 1941

SPAIN

Gibraltar

MOROCCO
Casablanca

AZORES

BERMUDA

② BASES INCLUDED
IN AGREEMENT
OF SEPT. 2, 1940

EXUMA

A T L A N T I C

O C E A N

CANARY
IS.

22° W. LONGITUDE
LIMIT OF ESCORT
BY U.S. NAVY FOR
NON-AMERICAN
SHIPPING, BEGINNING
SEPT. 16, 1941
⑥

AFRICA

JAMAICA

WEST

INDIES

ANTIGUA

ST. LUCIA

TRINIDAD

CAPE
VERDE
IS.

Dakar

EQUATOR

GEORGETOWN

① HEMISPHERIC
SAFETY ZONE
DECLARATION OF
PANAMA
OCT. 3, 1939

SOUTH

AMERICA

BRAZIL

THE COMING OF THE WAR
IN THE ATLANTIC
1939-1941

will be within range of the Nazi weapons of destruction." The war, he warned, was "approaching the brink" of the Americas. A German foothold in the Azores or French Africa would jeopardize immediately the safety of the insular possessions of the United States and ultimately the entire continent. Although Hitler's "plan of world domination" was then blocked by his failure to control the seas, he was nearing success. "The blunt truth" was that the present rate of Nazi sinkings of merchant ships was three times the capacity of British shipyards to replace them and more than twice the combined Anglo-American output. Confronted with that danger, the President proclaimed the existence of an unlimited national emergency and promised to take "all additional measures" to insure the delivery of Lend-Lease goods.

Then on June 22, 1941, Germany invaded Russia. In turning upon his partner of August, 1939, as Roosevelt had predicted he would, Hitler changed the complexion of the war and, perhaps, the course of history. His motive was simple. Only by smashing Russia could he defeat England, deter the United States, and defy the world. Britain's sole hope of survival lay in the United States and the Soviet Union. The elimination of the latter would also embolden Japan, who might divert Roosevelt in East Asia, while the Reich conquered the British Isles and exploited the man power and farmlands of Russia. To be sure, Foreign Commissar Vyacheslav M. Molotov overreached himself in haggling over the partition of the Balkans and the Middle East, but in any case, Hitler would have launched his massive assault.

For Roosevelt and Hull this momentous development solved some problems and created others. By driving eastward, Hitler lessened temporarily the pressure on England, removed for a time the threat to the New World, and provided briefly a chance for the United States to arm. On the other hand, the sinking of Lend-Lease cargoes continued, and a policy toward the Soviet Union had to be formulated. There was little popular sympathy for this latest victim of Nazi perfidy. The devious path trod by the Russian Communists since August, 1939, had aroused intense hatred; the obstructionist tactics pursued by the native Communists since that date had hampered the defense effort. It was easy enough for Churchill to declare on June 22, 1941, that any state "who fights against Nazidom will have our aid," but the more remote government in Washington did not have to speak that way. The great majority of Americans hoped, and many believed, that the ideological rivals would bleed themselves white in a gigantic stalemate and thus rid the world of a double curse. The military experts, almost to a man, argued that the Red Army would be crushed in three months. The unchecked German advance, only lightly opposed at first, seemed to confirm the worst fears of the specialists.

Under these conditions, Roosevelt moved cautiously. Prior to the invasion, which intelligence officers had predicted, he had promised Churchill to support publicly any welcome given by England to its new ally, but the statement released by Welles on June 23, 1941, was vague. Three days later it was announced that the neutrality law would not be invoked against Russia because the security of the United States was not imperiled by the conflict. Slowly steps were taken to facilitate purchases of American goods, and on July 26 the President authorized Harry Hopkins to fly to Moscow as his personal representative to discover just what Stalin needed. As the staying power of the Red Army became evident, the United States promised on August 2 "to give all economic assistance practicable for the purpose of strengthening the Soviet Union in its struggle against armed aggression." Not until November 7, however, did Roosevelt declare the defense of Russia vital to the security of his own country and thus make it eligible to receive Lend-Lease materials.

Aid to Russia was not the paramount problem facing Roosevelt in the summer of 1941. The continuing expansion of Japan in Southeast Asia, the impending dissolution of the new army at home, and the heavy toll of Lend-Lease shipments in the Atlantic claimed precedence. The occupation of southern Indochina on July 25 brought to a climax, as we shall see below, the economic retaliation against Japan begun in June 1938. At the same time, the government had to consider how it would act when the one-year training period for the men drafted under the act of September 16, 1940, expired. The War Department wanted to extend the duty by twelve months and rescind the prohibition against using conscripts outside the New World, but such changes were politically impossible. Hence it was forced to settle for a six-month extension, and that was obtained by only the narrowest of margins. In the Senate the vote on August 7 was 45 to 30; in the House on August 12 it was 203 to 202.

Most important of all was the decision to occupy Iceland. As soon as Germany invaded Russia, Stimson and Knox urged the President to exploit its preoccupation in the East by ordering American warships to escort convoys of foreign vessels bound for England through the Western Atlantic. As in April, 1941, Roosevelt wavered, reversed himself, and finally chose a less extreme measure. On July 7, he informed Congress that, under an executive agreement six days earlier, the United States had assumed protection of Iceland and that troops were then arriving to supplement and eventually replace the British garrison. He justified the move as one denying the Nazis an outpost from which they could mount "an eventual attack against the Western Hemisphere," from which they could menace "all shipping in the North Atlantic," and from which they could threaten "the steady flow of munitions to Britain," a policy laid down by the legislature. As commander-in-chief, he had ordered the navy "to insure the safety of communications in the approaches between Iceland and the United States." Translated into an operation plan effective July 26, this meant that the Atlantic Fleet could escort Icelandic and American vessels to Iceland and destroy any hostile interloper en route.

THE ATLANTIC CONFERENCE

How far the United States had traveled from nonbelligerency to undeclared war was revealed when Roosevelt and Churchill met for the first time and issued a declaration dealing with the peace. This Atlantic Conference was held on August 9–12, 1941 off Argentia, Newfoundland, close by the site included in the Destroyers-Bases Agreement. Originally the President wished to talk alone with the Prime Minister, but later he consented to bring along his military and diplomatic advisers. There was no agenda, and most of the exchanges were informal. The chief topics discussed were measures to restrain Japan, economic aid to Russia, England's war with Germany, and the so-called Atlantic Charter.

Twice before in 1941 top-ranking officers of the army, navy, and air corps had engaged in staff conversations with the British. At Washington from January 29 to March 29 and at Singapore, with the Dutch present, from April 21 to 27 studies were made concerning basic strategy and tactical collaboration in case the United States were drawn into war against Germany or Japan or both. It was agreed that in a two-ocean conflict the defeat of Germany should have priority, but at no time did Roosevelt allow the generals and admirals to make binding commitments or infringe upon the power of Congress to declare war. Now at Argentia he was willing to caution the government in Tokyo not to attack the possessions of England and Holland but refused to give that warning jointly. Nor would he promise to fight if Japan ignored his words. Unlike Churchill, he wished to delay as long as he could a showdown with the Japanese. One concession he did make. In the near future British cargo ships might join convoys of Icelandic and American freighters bound for Iceland and thus be protected by American naval escorts.

Highly publicized but of less immediate consequence was the eight-point declaration of "common principles" on which the two leaders based their hopes for the postwar world. The Atlantic Charter was a by-product of the conference, not a primary objective. Neither Roosevelt nor Churchill was eager to draw too specifically the outlines of the future, but the agreements reached by Russia with England in July, 1941, aroused fears in Washington that secret treaties like those of 1914–18 were in the making. To allay apprehensions both statesmen disavowed any desire for territorial aggrandizement, reaffirmed the principle of self-determination, and pledged themselves to promote freer channels of commerce and fuller access to sources of raw materials. They envisaged a world liberated from Nazi tyranny in which men might live without fear and traverse the seas without hindrance. Lastly, they urged that force be abandoned and, "pending the establishment of a wider and permanent system of general security," that armaments be drastically reduced.

Two years earlier, loud protests would have greeted the president of a nonbelligerent republic conferring secretly with the prime minister of a belligerent empire on the problems of war and peace. In Wilson's day it would have been unthinkable. Yet by August, 1941, most Americans looked upon the event as a logical consequence of the policy of giving all aid to England short of intervention. Because of the noble aspirations of the Charter and of prompt publicity, Roosevelt's statement of what had transpired was widely accepted at face value. Those who had always opposed the commitment of America's resources to the enemies of Germany were, of course, indignant. Suspecting a hidden meaning, they charged that the nation had been bound unwisely and unconstitutionally to send an expeditionary force to Europe. Actually, Roosevelt assumed very few obligations at Argentia, but he touched a responsive chord at home by emphasizing the ideals of peace rather than realities of war.

SHOOT ON SIGHT

By September, 1941, fifteen months had passed since Roosevelt had pledged material support to the opponents of Hitler. His calculated risk that the Führer would not retaliate with force against a nonbelligerent had proven sound, but the danger of a sudden change remained. Indeed, the President's own attitude, according to some of his associates, shifted at this time. He now sought, they contend, to defeat Germany, not simply to prevent the conquest of England. Unwilling to accept a statemate, so they argue, he desired intervention as the sole means of safeguarding the republic. This question can never be answered satisfactorily, but the evidence available suggests that Roosevelt continued to hope and expect that the nation could survive without full participation.

Yet the long-delayed solution to the convoy problem indicates that Roosevelt was willing, if not eager, to engage in a limited and undeclared war in the Atlantic. Having consented to allow United States warships to protect British freighters between Newfoundland and Iceland, provided they joined American and Icelandic cargo carriers un-

der escort, he wished to enlist popular support for that perilous step.
His desire explains, but does not excuse, the distorted account he publicized of an encounter on September 4, 1941, between the destroyer
Greer and the *U-652* about 175 miles southwest of Iceland. While proceeding to Reykjavik, the *Greer* was informed by a British patrol plane
of a submerged U-boat ahead. The destroyer changed course to locate,
trail, and report the submarine's position. After a few hours of harassment the German commander fired a torpedo and missed; whereupon
the *Greer* dropped depth charges without effect. One more torpedo
went wide of the mark, and the action was then broken off. It was this
exchange which Roosevelt described the next day, before all the
facts were in, as a deliberate assault on a United States warship in
American waters. It was this incident that he exploited to justify new
rules on convoys and new orders to shoot on sight.

"When you see a rattlesnake poised to strike," the President told
the nation on September 11, 1941, "you do not wait until he has struck
before you crush him." Nazi U-boats and commerce destroyers were
such rattlesnakes, and Roosevelt cited three other attacks on vessels
flying the Stars and Stripes. Accusing the *U-652* of firing without warning, he called the episode part of a German plot to control the Atlantic and invade the New World. Therefore, he announced, "in the
waters which we deem necessary for our defense, American naval vessels and American planes will no longer wait until Axis submarines
lurking under the water, or Axis raiders on the surface of the sea,
strike their deadly blow—first." The United States Navy would henceforth "protect all merchant ships—not only American ships but ships
of any flag—engaged in commerce in our defensive waters." There
would be "no shooting unless Germany continues to seek it." But the
warning was clear. "From now on," he said, "if German or Italian vessels of war enter the waters, the protection of which is necessary for
American defense, they do so at their own peril."

Despite its lack of candor, or perhaps because of it, Roosevelt's
speech was well received. His appeal to the freedom of the seas, a principle which all Americans cherished but few understood, had been persuasive. Popular sentiment was running in his favor. A public-opinion
poll on October 5, 1941, would reveal that some 70 per cent of those
consulted thought it more important to defeat Germany than to keep
the country out of war. The decision to shoot on sight, moreover, did
not precipitate a crisis. Hitler was intent on the Russian campaign
and declined to make an issue of the order. Expecting to capture Moscow by the end of October, he instructed his admirals to avoid trouble
with the United States for the time being.

The decision to provide naval escorts for all belligerent and neutral merchantmen between Newfoundland and Iceland and the order to

shoot on sight any Axis warships in those waters made obsolete parts of the Neutrality Act of November 4, 1939. Hence Roosevelt asked Congress on October 9, 1941, to repeal that section which prohibited arming cargo carriers engaged in foreign commerce. Originally written into the law of May 1, 1937, this clause made no sense at a time the Atlantic Fleet was authorized to fire in protection of these unarmed vessels. The President suggested that other modifications were advisable but withheld explicit recommendations. Disclaiming any desire to enter the war, he argued that he wished only to return to traditional practices respecting the freedom of the seas, to insure the safe delivery of Lend-Lease goods, and to keep control of the Atlantic out of German hands.

Six weeks elapsed before Congress gave the President what he requested, but the result was never in doubt. While the people and their representatives would have rejected overwhelmingly a declaration of war on Germany, they were ready, perhaps inconsistently, to adopt almost any measure to encompass Hitler's defeat. During this period the legislature appropriated $5,985,000,000 for Lend-Lease and killed an amendment forbidding the use of those funds to aid Russia. During this period a German submarine off West Africa sank the third American cargo vessel to be lost in the war. During this period the shooting occurred in the Atlantic. On October 17, 1941, the destroyer *Kearny* was torpedoed with the loss of eleven lives while protecting a convoy southwest of Iceland, but she made port. On October 30 the naval tanker *Salinas* was hit by two torpedoes about 700 miles east of Newfoundland, but there were no casualties and she did not sink. The next day, some 600 miles west of Iceland the destroyer *Reuben James*, also engaged in escort duty, took 100 men to the bottom when struck by a torpedo. It was in response to attacks like these that Roosevelt declared in an address on October 27: "The shooting has started. And history has recorded who fired the first shot." We Americans are pledged, he said, "to pull our own oar in the destruction of Hitlerism" and for that purpose we "have cleared our decks and taken our battle stations."

During this period, too, the critics of the administration had their innings. Although a minority on Capitol Hill and in the nation, they fought doggedly to the end. In speeches and tracts they more than matched Roosevelt's own lapses in candor and historical accuracy, but they failed to carry the day. On October 17, 1941, the House voted by 259 to 138 to rescind the prohibition against arming cargo ships. The Senate went further. By a count of 50 to 37 it repealed on November 7 not only the section on armed merchantmen but also the two which forbade American vessels to enter combat zones or touch at belligerent ports. The House approved this expanded bill four days later, but extraneous domestic factors reduced the earlier comfortable margin to a mere 212 to 194. Thus, the Neutrality Act of November 17, 1941, retained only the National Munitions Control Board, the ban on travel by American citizens on belligerent ships, and the restrictions on loans and credits. Even the last was of minor significance under Lend-Lease. The important fact was that American freighters were now free to transport any type of goods, to deposit cargoes anywhere in the world, and to receive protection from American and British escorts and from their own gun crews.

Little has to be said about the undeclared war after November 17, 1941. On December 2 the navy placed its first armed guard aboard a merchant vessel; the next day another American freighter was sunk. Still determined to take Moscow despite the onset of winter, the Germans launched a new offensive on December 4, but it quickly ground to a halt. Absorbed, almost hypnotized by the Russian campaign, Hitler persisted in his refusal to convert the shooting in the Atlantic into a full-scale conflict. Roosevelt, too, was content. Britain had survived. Germany was being checked. Public opinion was favorable. And on the other side of the world a crisis with Japan demanded his full attention.

46

The Coming of War
to the Pacific

AMERICAN POLICY toward Asia before December 7, 1941, would have
been very different if there had been no prospect of an Axis victory in
Europe. But once Hitler upset the balance of power in the Old World
and seemed to menace the security of the New, every move in the
Pacific had to be weighed for its impact in the Atlantic. Roosevelt and
Hull quickly abandoned thoughts of stopping the Führer by traditional diplomacy but to the end hoped to restrain Japan by negotiation
and economic pressure. In retrospect, it is clear that after the fall of
France they exaggerated the Nazi peril and underestimated the danger from Nippon.

EAST ASIA AND THE WAR

Japan's decisions were also shaped by the interrelationship of events
in Europe and Asia. In strengthening the New Order Japan could move
in three directions: against China on the mainland, against Russia in
Siberia, and against the British, French, Dutch, and American colonies
to the south. Closer ties with Germany and Italy might aid in gaining
all three objectives, but Hitler had shown little interest in the war
against Chiang Kai-shek or in the bloody border clashes against the
Red Army at Changkufeng in July, 1938, and at Nomonhan in August,
1939. The Konoye cabinet was eager to convert the Anti-Comintern

Pact into a military alliance against the Soviet Union but reluctant to direct it also against England, France, and the United States. The army was willing, but the navy, the diplomats, and the industrialists were not. Internal dissension, along with the stalemate in China, caused Konoye to resign on January 4, 1939, but Kiichiro Hiranuma, his successor, was not able to harmonize interservice differences. Then the impact of Europe on Asia was demonstrated when Hitler, in flagrant violation of his pledge to Japan, came to terms with Stalin on August 23. The Nazi-Soviet accord caught Tokyo by surprise and led to Hiranuma's overthrow. The new Prime Minister, General Nobuyuki Abe, suspended negotiations on a tripartite agreement with Germany and Italy, obtained a cease-fire with Russia along the Manchurian frontier, and concentrated on ending the conflict in China. After the invasion of Poland, Abe pursued a policy of impartial aloofness.

Before the fall of France the war did not unduly affect Japanese-American relations. The United States began belatedly to make Pearl Harbor an operating base by organizing a Hawaiian detachment of the fleet on September 28, 1939. It extended slightly the voluntary embargo on exports and on January 26, 1940, permitted the trade treaty of 1911 to lapse. But that was all. In Tokyo, however, Abe resigned, and on January 16, 1940, Admiral Mitsumasa Yonai headed the fourth cabinet in thirteen months. Although Yonai opposed a military alliance with Germany and was friendly to the West, Hull did not trust him. Fearing Japan would exploit Hitler's victory in Norway, the Secretary demanded publicly on April 17 that the *status quo* be maintained in the Pacific. To bolster that request Roosevelt on May 1 ordered the United States Fleet, then in Hawaii for maneuvers, to remain there until further notice. This move, more diplomatic than naval in purpose, was opposed by Admiral James O. Richardson who argued he could train the force more efficiently at its California ports. The President overruled the protest, but he also ignored Churchill's plea to send some vessels to Singapore and refused to say what he might do if British or French possessions were attacked.

In Tokyo there was more concern over the progress of the blitzkrieg than with the deployment of the American fleet. The surrender of the Netherlands on May 14, 1940, left the future of the East Indies in doubt; and when England and France agreed to protect the Dutch islands in the Caribbean, Japan had a perfect excuse to occupy Java, Sumatra, and Borneo with their rich supplies of oil, rubber, and ore. Reluctant to antagonize the West, Yonai waited until France's capitulation seemed to leave no doubt that Germany would win the war. With the army blaming the cabinet for betting on the wrong side, Yonai had to demand concessions from a defeated France, a helpless Holland, and an imperiled Britain. He asked the first to permit a military mission

THE COMING OF THE WAR
IN THE PACIFIC, 1939-1941

to be stationed in northern Indochina to see that no aid reached Chiang Kai-shek by that route. He requested the second to give assurances that the flow of raw materials from the Indies would not stop. He threatened the third with war unless it withdrew its troops from Shanghai, halted traffic from Hong Kong to the mainland, and closed the Burma Road linking Chungking with the outside world. By July 12 most of his demands were met.

Dissatisfied with these gains, the Japanese army brought down the Yonai cabinet, and on July 22, 1940 Konoye returned as Premier with Yosuke Matsuoka as Foreign Secretary and General Tojo as War Minister. The last two were staunch advocates of an alliance with Hitler; and since Konoye lacked the will to oppose them, prospects for the tripartite pact brightened. On July 27 the new leaders summed up their aims: political combination with Germany and Italy; stronger measures against Indochina, Hong Kong, and foreign concessions in China; and vigorous diplomacy toward the East Indies. They expected a Nazi triumph in Europe to keep the United States quiescent, if not acquiescent.

MOVES AND COUNTERMOVES

With Konoye back in power, Roosevelt's objective was to avoid a further weakening of the Anglo-French-Dutch position in Asia while he shored up British strength in Europe. Thus relations with Japan became a series of moves and countermoves, closely related to German successes, in which the United States remained largely on the defensive for a year. The Americans did impose new commercial restrictions late in July, 1940, while Ambassador Grew, whose faith in Japanese reasonableness had until then caused him to oppose economic sanctions, conceded in his so-called "green light" dispatch of September 12 the need for "a show of force." But Japan was not deterred. In August, that country asked France for the right to station units in northern Indochina and Holland for increased quotas of crude oil. On September 19, the top civilian and military leaders defined the territorial limits of the New Order as "the former German islands under mandate, French Indo-China and Pacific Islands, Thailand, British Malaya, British Borneo, Dutch East Indies, Burma, Australia, New Zealand, India, etc. with Japan, Manchuria, and China as the backbone." The "etc." was a euphemism for the Philippines. On September 22 the army obtained key positions in northern Indochina; and although Roosevelt retaliated four days later with an embargo on all grades of iron and steel scrap, Japan proceeded to sign the Tripartite Pact in Berlin.

As published, the German-Italian-Japanese treaty of September 27, 1940, combined a joint recognition of spheres of leadership with a defensive alliance. It made Germany and Italy custodians of postwar Europe, without specifying boundaries, and assigned to Japan a similar hegemony in Asia. Article III was the heart of the pact. In it the three parties undertook "to assist one another with all political, economic and military means" if they were attacked "by a Power at present not involved in the European War or in the Chinese-Japanese conflict." Since Article V stipulated that those terms did not affect relations between the signatories and the Soviet Union, the agreement was obviously aimed at frightening the Roosevelt administration from going too far in aiding England and China. Three secret understandings were embodied in an exchange of notes. The first permitted questions about the applicability of Article III to be decided by consultation. The second promised Japan full German aid in event it went to war with England. The third assured to Japan the mandated islands which had once belonged to Germany.

It is easy to see why Hitler liked the pact. Even if Article III never became operative, it stood as a threat to Great Britain in Asia and as a deterrent to the United States in Europe. The benefits to Japan are not so evident. If it fought America in the Pacific, Germany and Italy could not provide effective military support; if Russia attacked Japan, the Reich could remain neutral under the Nazi-Soviet accord. Yet for different reasons Konoye, Matsuoka, Tojo, and some moderates desired a bond with the Axis. It would insure a triumphant Hitler's assent to the New Order in East Asia and nullify any territorial ambitions he had there. It offered a chance that, through the Führer's good offices, Stalin might be persuaded to stop his supplies to Chiang Kai-shek and thus end the stalemate in China. Finally, once its northern flank was secure and Nationalist resistance overcome, Japan could turn south against the weakly defended colonies of England, France, and Holland.

Japan's hopes under the Tripartite Pact never materialized. Germany did not triumph. China did not surrender. Hitler's invasion of Russia meant that there would be no accord with Moscow through Berlin. Most important of all, the United States was not intimidated. Far from ending aid to England and China, Roosevelt and Hull moved from nonbelligerency to undeclared war. Furthermore, the Axis alliance tarred the Japanese with the Nazi brush and underlined the world-wide totalitarian threat to democracy. After September, 1940, there was a perceptible hardening of American attitudes toward Japan.

Yet there were still limits to what the United States would do. Eager to keep things quiet in Asia, Roosevelt gave Richardson to understand on October 8, 1940, that he would not act if Thailand, Malaya, or the East Indies were attacked. Although he rejected the admiral's pleas to return the battle line to California, he again ignored Churchill's requests to station American warships at Singapore. The President allowed joint staff talks, as we have seen, but withheld his approval of the agreements drafted in March and April, 1941. He was ready to map in advance a common strategy, but he kept in his own hands control of the armed forces. He had not yet accepted a Pacific war as inevitable, and his countermoves were designed to restrain Japan, not incite it.

After June 22, 1941, Roosevelt felt freer to stand firm in Asia. The invasion of Russia took some pressure off England and exposed some strains in the Tripartite Pact. In March, Hitler had been unable to persuade Japan to attack Singapore and unwilling to reveal his own plans. On April 13 Matsuoka signed in Moscow a five-year neutrality treaty that outraged the Nazis, displeased his own government, and contributed to his downfall. Yet this disunity did not preclude a Japanese ultimatum to France on July 12 demanding the right to occupy airfields in southern Indochina and to use Saigon harbor and Camranh Bay for their fleet. Unlike the concessions obtained in June, 1940, these sites could not be justified as vital to the blockade of Chiang Kai-shek. They portended rather a drive south against the Anglo-Dutch possessions.

This new advance spurred Roosevelt and Hull into action. On July 24, 1941, the President proposed that the United States, England, Japan, and the Netherlands agree to keep hands off Indochina, but the suggestion was not seriously considered. On July 25 the commanders at Hawaii and other Pacific outposts were told that economic sanctions were imminent and that they should take "appropriate precautionary measures." That same day Douglas MacArthur was recalled to active duty and placed in charge of a new Far Eastern force. On July 26 an executive order froze Japanese assets in America, subjected Japanese commercial transactions to government control, and barred Japanese vessels from the Panama Canal. Oil exports were drastically curtailed, and a total ban seemed likely.

Such was the climax to the trade restrictions begun in June, 1938. Roosevelt's advisers were split. Some felt economic retaliation to be the sole weapon the United States could wield in the Pacific while it was preoccupied in the Atlantic. Others feared that so sweeping an embargo might precipitate the clash it was designed to avert. Public and congressional opinion were overwhelmingly favorable. There were almost no complaints of executive usurpation or warmongering. The President knew that the step involved some risk, but he believed that Japan could be checked for a little more time by economic pressure. He was eager to win that respite, since he shared MacArthur's view that the Philippines, long considered indefensible, could now repel a Japanese assault if they had a requisite number of the new type of heavy bombers.

DIPLOMATIC IMPASSE

Despite the Tripartite Pact, Japan wavered during 1941 between accommodation and defiance of the West. Preferring to gain their ends by negotiation, its leaders engaged in conversations at Washington from February through November in order to devise a formula for settling long-standing differences with the United States. Although these were pursued in good faith, the military prepared simultaneously for an armed resolution of the conflict should a diplomatic impasse occur.

No brief account can summarize properly the many proposals and counterproposals. The most it can do is to analyze the basic issues and to describe the three periods into which the talks fell. The United States viewed the problem in global terms. It deplored aggression in the Orient but was more concerned with the world balance of power. Japan was not unmindful of Europe but focused its attention on Asia. The American government asked for a complete reversal of past policy; the Japanese were ready to yield only enough to escape an immediate clash. The Roosevelt administration pressed rigidly for a comprehensive solution based on broad principles; the Konoye cabinet maneuvered flexibly for a partial accord in the light of existing conditions. Hull preached idealism and demanded a disavowal of past misdeeds; Ambassador Kichisaburo Nomura stressed expediency and sought a retreat from past mistakes. Both sides refused to yield on fundamental issues, and time was not on the side of peace. The men in Washington were willing to stall until a verdict was rendered in Europe; those in Tokyo needed an agreement before their golden opportunity vanished.

At the outset, three main points divided the diplomats. One was Japan's obligation under the Tripartite Pact. Hull argued that the Lend-Lease Act and the Atlantic patrols should be interpreted as defensive measures beyond the scope of Article III, while the Japanese, who did not intend to help Hitler in Europe, refused to repudiate openly their vague commitment. The second point was the termination of the war in China. Konoye wanted a free hand, even American cooperation, in bringing Chiang to terms; and he envisaged, as a minimum, the recognition of Manchukuo, the stationing of troops on Chinese soil, and the retention of a privileged economic position on the mainland. The State Department clung to the past and wished to restore the open door and the sanctity of treaties. The third point was Southeast Asia. Hull feared a Japanese assault on that region, while Nomura worried about the American countermoves aimed at preventing it. This initial phase ended late in July, 1941, with the occupation of southern Indochina and the freezing order.

The second period lasted from early August to mid-October, 1941. The tensions from the Tripartite Pact lessened, but the future of China, the safety of Southeast Asia, and the traffic in oil continued to plague the negotiators. With Russia surviving through raw courage and England recovering through Lend-Lease, the American attitude stiffened. This became evident when Konoye sought to break the diplomatic deadlock by a meeting with Roosevelt. His idea for a summit Pacific Conference was broached on August 6, just before the Atlantic Conference with Churchill, and its rejection can be attributed mainly to Hull. Distrusting Konoye, the Secretary persuaded the President to require some preliminary understanding before accepting—the very circumstance Konoye did not want. The Prime Minister could say only so much in advance, lest he alienate his militant supporters at home and his military allies abroad. He hoped to pave the way for an enduring settlement by convincing Roosevelt in private of his sincerity. Many historians have regretted that the United States did not afford him the opportunity in September, 1941, but we must not conclude that, in refusing, Roosevelt intentionally blocked a path to peace.

Nor can we be certain that the two leaders could have produced an agreement, especially on China, that would have satisfied the Japanese army and the State Department. Indeed, an impasse at the summit might have exacerbated relations and hastened the resort to arms. All we know is that the ensuing delay sealed the fate of the Konoye cabinet. On July 2, 1941, an Imperial Conference decided on southward expansion even if it meant war with Great Britain and the United States. After Konoye's idea had been declined, a similar gathering defined on September 6 Japan's minimum objectives, though in less sweeping terms than on September 19, 1940, and set a time limit for their attainment.[1] If by early October, the document read, there was no reasonable hope of gaining those demands, "we shall immediately make up our minds to get ready for war against America (and England and Holland)." After further fruitless talks and a futile attempt to

---

[1] These obliged the United States and England to halt all aid to China and not obstruct a direct Sino-Japanese settlement; to avoid threats to Japan's security from bases in Russia, China, Thailand, or the East Indies; and to restore normal trade while helping Japan gain access to raw materials in Southeast Asia. Japan would restrict its use of Indochina to operations against, China, evacuate that land when hostilities ended, withdraw from China at the close of the war all forces save those needed to combat communism, and refrain from attacking Russia so long as the Soviets respected the treaty of April 13, 1941. Japan was also ready to promise that there would be no changes in executing its obligations under the Tripartite Pact.

rescind that decision, Konoye resigned on October 16 in favor of War Minister Tojo.

Konoye's downfall edged the two nations closer to war, but with shooting having begun in the Atlantic, Roosevelt still tried to keep things quiet in the Pacific. He hoped "to baby the Japanese along" until the Philippines were adequately manned with B-17 bombers. The first nine arrived on September 12, 1941, but a second echelon of twenty-five did not touch down until November 6. In Washington, time was a precious commodity, but in Tokyo, Tojo was determined to break the deadlock, by diplomacy or force, before the end of the year. The weather was growing less suited to amphibious landings, and the oil reserves were dwindling. On November 5 an Imperial Conference agreed to wage war against the United States and Great Britain if the conversations in Washington failed to produce results by November 25. Before that date two proposals, A and B, would be offered. The former contained a broad settlement in line with the minimum objectives of September 6; the latter was a stopgap measure. Should both be declined, the Japanese would ask their Axis allies to enter the fray; but they were prepared to go it alone.

Thanks to its breaking the Japanese diplomatic code, the American government learned at once of this deadline. Chief of Staff George C. Marshall and Chief of Naval Operations Harold R. Stark urged Roosevelt to play for time and on November 5, 1941, asked that "no ultimatum be delivered to Japan." They reminded him that Germany's defeat was the primary objective and argued against fighting in case the Japanese invaded Russia from Manchukuo, China from northern Indochina, or eastern Thailand from southern Indochina. They said war in Asia was justified only if the United States and its dependencies or certain areas essential to their security were attacked. Those areas were the British Empire and its mandates, the Dutch Indies, Thailand west of the hundredth meridian and south of the Kra Isthmus, Portuguese Timor, and French New Caledonia. Roosevelt endorsed this estimate but made no promise of any sort.

A diplomatic impasse was reached at the end of November, 1941. When Hull quickly rejected Plan A as offering nothing new, Nomura— joined dramatically by a special envoy, Saburo Kurusu—pressed frantically for acceptance of Plan B before the revised deadline expired on November 29. Presented on November 20, Plan B ignored the Tripartite Pact. It bound both governments to forego further advances in Southeast Asia, to restore trade relations as they had been on July 25, and to cooperate in getting from the East Indies the resources each needed. The Japanese undertook to evacuate Indochina when a general peace was established; meanwhile they would withdraw from the southern sector. The United States was obliged to supply Japan with "a required quantity of oil" and to desist from actions prejudicial to terminating hostilities in China. The last meant no more diplomatic and economic support for Chiang Kai-shek.

Hull dismissed Plan B as "preposterous." Not content with a curb on their southward drive, he insisted that the Japanese abandon their four-year campaign against China and all gains made at China's expense since 1931. To please Marshall and Stark, however, he drew up on November 25, 1941, a counteroffer, a three-month modus vivendi. It required Japan to get out of southern Indochina at once, to reduce its forces in northern Indochina, and to renounce expansion in any direction. In return, the United States would admit Japanese imports and allow limited exports in cotton and oil, the latter for civilian use only. Tojo probably would have balked at the oil item, but he never had the opportunity. From London a not fully informed Churchill warned against weakening Chiang's regime; from Manila came reports of troop movements which suggested Japan was not negotiating in good faith. Worried by charges of appeasement at home and cries of protest in Chungking, Hull reversed himself that evening and decided to answer Plan B in another way.

His resulting ten-point note of November 26, 1941, proposed in effect to turn back the hands of the clock to September, 1931. It called for the complete evacuation of Indochina and its joint protection by the United States, Great Britain, Japan, China, Holland, and Thailand. These six nations, plus the Soviet Union, would also sign a nonaggression pact. As to China, Japan would have to withdraw all its troops— thereby forsaking Manchukuo—to deal only with Chiang—thereby deserting its puppets—and to join the United States in giving up extraterritorial rights. For its part, the American government would lift restrictions on Japanese trade, conclude a new commercial convention, and stabilize the dollar-yen rate. Nomura and Kurusu realized immediately that the men in Tokyo would not—indeed, could not—accept those terms. A task force of six aircraft carriers had already sailed from the Kuriles with orders to bomb Pearl Harbor unless recalled. On December 1 an Imperial Conference ratified the decision for war, and the next day Vice Admiral Chuichi Nagumo was instructed to proceed with the attack on December 7.

Since 1945 this ten-point note has been widely criticized in terms ranging from a humiliating ultimatum which fanned the flames of war in Japan to a regrettable blunder which killed the hopes of peace in the United States. Certainly the American retreat to the high ground of principle and morality convinced doubters in Tokyo that a diplomatic settlement was impossible. It made a dangerous situation much worse. Yet these facts hardly excuse Japan's launching an air raid without warning. Certainly Hull's stand was unnecessarily rigid and utterly unrealistic. He ignored Japan's economic plight, forgot the Oriental need to save face, and closed the door to a temporary compromise. Yet in passing that judgment, we must not conclude that Hull intentionally goaded the enemy into firing the first shot or that Plan B and the modus vivendi contained a permanent solution. Hull simply did not trust the Japanese assurances on Southeast Asia, while a satisfactory agreement on China was as distant as ever. If Hull erred, and many think he did, it was in assuming that economic pressure would not bring armed reprisal and that a slight postponement of hostilities was not worth the price of delaying a solution on China.

Roosevelt was more flexible than Hull and more concerned with strategic factors, yet he approved the reply of November 26, 1941. The decision was an agonizing one. It did not stem from unwarranted optimism or devious diplomacy but rather from a conviction that material and moral support for Nationalist China must be continued at all costs. The President had no desire to enter the European war by the back-door of Asia, and he knew that Japan was poised to strike at Southeast Asia. It was the absolute certainty of that threat, not the remote possibility of a raid on American soil, that monopolized his attention as Nomura's deadline expired. How should he answer Anglo-Dutch pleas for armed assistance against imminent invasion? What should he do if the Philippines were by-passed? Could he act without legislative sanction? Compared to those difficult questions, it seemed almost routine to alert the island commanders by a "war warning" on November 27 that negotiations in Washington had collapsed and that an offensive against Thailand, Malaya, and perhaps Java was expected momentarily.

DAY OF INFAMY

At no time had Roosevelt committed the United States to defend non-American lands in Asia. He felt only Congress could make that pledge and hesitated in asking it to do so. On November 28, 1941, however, the cabinet agreed that he must inform the lawmakers that if Japan occupied Singapore or the East Indies, the security of the United States would be endangered. Stimson and Knox also wanted to warn Tojo immediately that any southward advance would be met with force. The President demurred and decided to appeal first to Emperor Hirohito. This personal message, the drafting of which dragged on for a week, emphasized that the evacuation of Indochina, not a final solution in China, was the key to peace. During that period Roosevelt also prepared to address Congress on December 8 or 9 should this bid fail. After many false alarms the dispatch went to the Emperor on Saturday, December 6—too late to be of help.

That same Saturday evening almost all of a long Japanese reply to the note of November 26, 1941, was intercepted. It confirmed what had been anticipated, a refusal to consider Hull's ten points. No clue was given to the next move, but early Sunday morning cryptanalysts learned that Nomura and Kurusu would deliver the answer at one o'clock. With all eyes glued on Southeast Asia, where the blow was expected to fall, few noticed that the hour coincided with dawn in Hawaii. Last-minute warnings were issued, some fumbling in nature but none urgent in tone. At noon on December 7 Nomura requested a slight delay. At 1:50 incredulous operators in the Navy Department plucked from the air waves the astounding news that Pearl Harbor was under aerial attack.

The day, which Roosevelt later said "will live in infamy," has become so weighted with controversy and so encrusted with myth that a bare statement of the facts will seem a defense of the administration. Although the military catastrophe lies beyond the scope of this volume, it is relevant to inquire whether the leaders in Washington helped bring on the disaster, withheld vital information from the island commanders, and exposed the fleet to destruction so the United States might enter the war without legislative opposition or popular protest.

Actually, the administration had everything to gain by avoiding hostilities with Japan. Its main aim was to check Germany, and fighting in the Pacific would only divert attention from the Atlantic. As each month passed, the unity of the Axis allies diminished and the bomber strength in the Philippines increased. The United States was unready for a two-ocean war and uncertain of its course if Japan invaded non-American soil in Asia. Hence Roosevelt's dilemma was not how he could maneuver the Japanese into firing the first shot but whether he could secure congressional authority to defend Thailand, Malaya, or the East Indies. Those countries were the main targets of Japan's opening campaign, while the raid on Pearl Harbor was simply a move to paralyze the Pacific Fleet. Policy makers in Washington, like those in Berlin, guessed wrong when they ruled out a carrier operation as too dangerous to undertake, yet in the long run they proved to be right. Japan tried too much with too little; and although the events of December 7, 1941, brought an unexpectedly decisive triumph, they also insured an ultimate defeat.

Why had the Japanese caught Hawaii by surprise? The officers in charge, Admiral Husband E. Kimmel and Lieutenant General Walter C. Short, insisted later they had not been fully alerted to the impending danger. They had not read the intercepted dispatches; and assuming that internal subversion and not external aggression was the major threat, they guarded mainly against sabotage. They reported to Washington what they had done; and since neither Marshall nor Stark urged different measures, the latter must bear some of the blame for what

happened. But to contend, as Kimmel has done, that important facts
and adequate matériel were withheld so as to insure the success of the
attack is sheer nonsense. Pearl Harbor was the best-equipped of the
overseas bases, and the data from the intercepts was restricted only to
prevent Japan from knowing its code was cracked. There was no other
motive. Since Kimmel and Short did not utilize fully the information
they possessed, it may be doubted whether they would have done much
better if they had seen all the secret files on the mainland.

To say this is not to impugn the intelligence of Kimmel and Short
but to suggest how little exact knowledge anyone had. The Foreign
Office never told its ambassadors where or when the lightning would
strike. The last order to Admiral Nagumo was never deciphered. After
the bombs had fallen, a more leisurely perusal of the instructions to
the consul at Honolulu revealed a special concern for vessels in port,
but those papers had a lower priority than the messages to Nomura
and may not have been seen in time. Despite exhaustive investigations, there is no convincing evidence that Roosevelt and his advisers
knew of the coming attack.

Should they have foreseen it? Today, it seems incredible that they
did not. Planners had frequently assumed that Japan might begin a
war with the United States by a surprise raid on Hawaii. On January 27, 1941, Grew reported, though skeptically, rumors of such preparations. Several times in the next months the insular outposts were
told to be on guard, but the admonitions tended to be routine and lacking in conviction. The danger was widely accepted in theory but not
translated into policy. It seemed more logical for Japan to advance in
Southeast Asia where the United States might not fight. But the Japanese defied logic and succeeded beyond their most sanguine expectations because of skillful planning, superb execution, and unbelievable
good luck.

Few Americans, save those under fire, showed to best advantage in
the Pearl Harbor tragedy. The failure was universal. At every level,
from the White House to the destroyer patrolling the harbor entrance,
there were mistaken judgments and errors of omission. Not everyone
was later judged by the same standards, but sympathy for the scapegoats must not lead us to accept their charges that a military disaster
was staged in order to escape from a diplomatic impasse. Similarly,
the ungracious refusal of officials in Washington to assume some of
the blame must not cause us to conclude they had a despicable plot to
hide. There was no treason in high quarters in 1941; there is no mystery surrounding Pearl Harbor. The true explanation of the debacle lies
in the realm of human frailty; and since no one saw the portent clearly
at the time, it behooves a later generation not to be omniscient after
the event.

47

The United Nations
and the War

THE DISASTER at Pearl Harbor unified the American people and made almost superfluous a declaration of war. Even as the President prepared his recommendation, reports poured in of attacks on Midway, Wake, Guam, and the Philippines and of landings on non-American soil in an arc stretching from Hong Kong to Malaya. Faced with heavy losses in men and ships, Roosevelt was brief in addressing Congress on December 8, 1941. Speaking for only six minutes, as compared with Wilson's thirty-two, he accused the Japanese of unparalleled infamy in striking while the diplomats sought peace. He did not have to convince anyone. Within an hour a joint resolution recognizing that war had been thrust upon the United States was adopted by a vote of 82 to 0 in the Senate and 388 to 1 in the House. Three days later, after Hitler had announced he was joining his Oriental ally, Congress passed unanimously a similar resolution for Germany and Italy.

FORGING THE WARTIME COALITION

"There is no blinking at the fact," Roosevelt told Congress on December 8, 1941, "that our people, our territory, and our interests are in grave danger." Here was a struggle for survival, not a crusade for democracy. American possessions had been invaded; American waters were imperiled. One enemy dominated Europe; the other Asia. Although the republic did not fight alone, the problems of coalition warfare were very different from 1917. Now there were numerous fronts to man, divergent strategies to reconcile, and mutual suspicions to dispel. The intense hatred of communism, the lingering vestiges of Anglophobia, and the grim memories of Wilson led one observer to note: "There are some patriotic citizens who sincerely hope that America will win the war—but they also hope Russia will lose it; and there are some who hope that America will win the war, but that England will lose it; and there are some who hope that America will win the war, but that Roosevelt will lose it."

To demonstrate the unity of those resisting the Axis, a joint declaration of cooperation and purpose was quickly drawn up. On January 1, 1942, the United States, England, Russia, China, and twenty-two other signatories subscribed to the principles of the Atlantic Charter. They also promised to employ all their resources against those members of the Tripartite Pact with whom each was at war and not to make a separate peace. Although Churchill later called the wartime coalition "The Grand Alliance," Roosevelt carefully avoided that traditionally suspect word and the circumlocution of "Associated Powers" Wilson had employed. He contributed the phrase "United Nations" and that was the title given the Declaration. The President did not regard the document as a treaty but merely a group of principles set forth under his authority as commander-in-chief. It was a well-publicized executive agreement, free from secret articles and designed to bolster morale in a dark hour. It contained neither a plan for winning the war nor a blueprint for writing the peace.

Cooperation with England inside the wartime coalition was easy to achieve. The basic strategy of defeating first Germany and then Japan had been settled in March, 1941. Under Lend-Lease the facilities of the United States had been opened without stint to Great Britain. Roosevelt and Churchill had corresponded incessantly since September, 1939, and had met once. After Pearl Harbor the Prime Minister promptly made good his earlier pledge that "the British declaration will follow within the hour" and a fortnight later arrived for the first of the ten conferences he would hold with the President. From the outset close coordination prevailed in handling munitions, shipping, raw materials, and military planning. The Combined Chiefs of Staff—a small group of top officers from both countries—determined broad operational schedules and watched the execution by different theater commanders.

Such mutual trust was not possible with Russia, to whom the West always remained a potential foe. The men in the Kremlin also remembered the years of intervention, nonrecognition, and futile collaboration; the West recalled repudiated debts, religious persecution, and relentless subversion. The Nazi-Soviet Pact had revealed how easily Stalin could forsake ideology for territorial gain; its demise disclosed the enormity of his ambitions. After June 22, 1941, however, Churchill instantly and Roosevelt gradually concluded that the cause of freedom required cooperation with Russian totalitarianism. The decision was not easy to reach or implement, but by December 7 the die had been cast. Few Americans then wanted it otherwise, and many wished the Soviets to join the war against Japan or make available bomber bases in Siberia. Yet it was a difficult task to create the image of a trustworthy, democratic Russia. The personal contacts enjoyed by the Anglo-American leaders were largely absent; Stalin met with Roosevelt and Churchill only twice and not before November, 1943. The Muscovite suspicion of foreigners persisted, and the Red generals were never part of the Combined Chiefs of Staff.

China's role in the coalition was an anomalous one. Despite misgivings by Churchill and Stalin, Roosevelt treated China as one of the four great powers.[1] How far his policy was based on sentiment and how far on strategy is difficult to say; but if the purpose was to fill the vacuum left by the destruction of the Japanese Empire, he failed utterly. Perhaps success was impossible. Never in this century had China been unified at home or listened to abroad. By 1942 Chiang Kai-shek's regime had been sapped by four years of resistance to Japan and was patently incapable of making a major contribution to the United Nations cause. The fall of Burma in April cut off all reinforcements by land until January, 1945. During that period inflation and corruption robbed the Nationalists of popular support. At the same time the Kuomintang and the Communists eyed each other suspiciously, each reserving its best troops for the eventual showdown rather than sending them against a common foe. The United States never assigned sufficient men, planes, and ships to the China area to make it a primary theater of the war.

Between January 1, 1942, and June 30, 1945, the adherents of the United Nations Declaration increased from twenty-six to forty-five. Besides the Big Four, that number included nineteen American republics —all but Argentina; five members of the British Commonwealth— Australia, Canada, India, New Zealand, South Africa; nine states of Europe—Belgium, Czechoslovakia, France, Greece, Holland, Luxembourg, Norway, Poland, Yugoslavia; three of Africa—Egypt, Ethiopia, Liberia; and five of Asia—Iran, Iraq, the Philippines, Saudi Arabia, Turkey. Actually, France and nine others did not sign until 1945, but only France's absence was felt.

---

[1] To emphasize this attitude the United States surrendered its extraterritorial rights by treaty on January 11, 1943, and ended its exclusionist policy by statute on November 17, 1943.

After June, 1940, the United States dealt with the government of Marshal Henri Philippe Pétain. Although his authoritarian regime at Vichy was heartily disliked in America, Roosevelt and Hull believed that they derived strategic benefits by maintaining formal relations. Critics of the "Vichy gamble" argued that it discouraged the resistance movement headed by Charles de Gaulle. Cold, vain, and enigmatic, but supremely dedicated and superbly confident, this junior general had fled to England from which he rallied part of the overseas empire to the Free French banner. He was less successful in gaining the support of Roosevelt and Churchill. The former disliked him, underestimated his following, and preferred his rival, General Henri Honoré Giraud, until well into 1943. But de Gaulle was the guiding genius, first of the Committee of National Liberation and then of the Provisional Government of the French Republic, which the United States finally recognized on October 23, 1944. Earlier that month it was decided at Dumbarton Oaks that "in due course" France would become a permanent member of the Security Council of the new international organization to be known as the United Nations.

Except for Vichy France, fascist Spain was the most potentially dangerous neutral. Bound to the Axis by treaty and ideology, Franco's government shifted in June, 1940, to a nonbelligerency which threatened to deprive England of Gibraltar, cut the British lifeline to the Middle East, and open a highway to Africa for the Nazis. Indeed, if Hitler had agreed in October, 1940, to pay the exorbitant price Franco was asking, Spain would have joined the fray. But the Führer demurred, turned on Russia instead, and did not concentrate on the Mediterranean until after Pearl Harbor. For another year Franco teetered, but his failure to interfere with the North African invasion in November, 1942, indicated he had lost faith in an Axis victory. With the surrender of Italy in September, 1943, he slowly reduced his assistance to Germany; by the close of hostilities in Europe he had become benevolently neutral to the Anglo-American cause. But Spain never signed the United Nations Declaration and was later judged to be unfit for membership in the new world organization.

THE WAR AGAINST GERMANY

No matter how many countries opposed the Axis, the bulk of the fighting fell to the United States, Great Britain, and the Soviet Union. The strategy pursued by those three powers strained the wartime coalition and influenced the postwar settlement. Yet on one point there was no disagreement. Germany was the most dangerous foe and must be conquered first. For Russia, at peace with Japan and reeling under the full weight of the Wehrmacht, a choice did not exist. Nor did England ever waver in its purpose to crush Hitler at the earliest moment, despite the rapid loss of Hong Kong, Malaya, and Burma. But in the United States conflicting emotions were at work. When the Hawaiian catastrophe was followed by the heart-rending but futile defenses at Wake, Bataan, and Corregidor, many Americans demanded that Japan be punished at once. German mastery of Europe, they contended, made it impossible to aid the beleaguered Red Army directly.

Roosevelt refused to heed such counsel. He assured Churchill at the end of 1941 that "Germany is still the prime enemy" and reversed the argument of those who feared, perhaps hoped, that Russia might not survive. The very plight of the Soviets made it imperative, he insisted, that American troops engage the Nazis in 1942. The President knew that Stalin regarded the immediate opening of a second front in Europe as the acid test of Anglo-American sincerity. Until it became a reality, the man in the Kremlin would always suspect the democracies of holding back until the two totalitarian states exhausted themselves.

But it was easier to talk about a second front than to open one in 1942, as the Combined Chiefs of Staff soon discovered. The Joint Chiefs of Staff—General George C. Marshall, Admiral Ernest J. King, General Henry H. Arnold, and Admiral William D. Leahy—wished to exploit the unsurpassed logistical facilities and staging areas of Great Britain to mount a massive cross-channel invasion that would strike at the heart of Germany through France. They believed that the necessary force could be put ashore successfully with a new type of landing craft and concentrated air power, though casualties on the beaches would be heavy. They wanted to drive deep into the Reich, partly to assist Russia and partly to avoid Wilson's alleged mistake of not dictating the peace in Berlin. The British agreed that the decisive battle must be fought in Europe but thought an immediate assault suicidal. They recalled the failure at Gallipoli in 1915 and the ghastly toll of lives taken by frontal attacks on the German lines in France in 1914–18. Until the United States had fully mobilized its man power and resources, they preferred to confine their activities to bombing the Ruhr industrial complex and to jabbing at the periphery of the Continent so as to keep Hitler off balance, threaten his satellites, and uncover his weaknesses.

These differences produced grave tensions within the coalition. On April 14, 1942, Marshall and Hopkins won acceptance in London of a plan calling for a cross-channel attack in 1943 and a possible emergency landing in France late in 1942. Churchill approved the first part, known as ROUNDUP, but procrastinated on the second, known as SLEDGEHAMMER. It would have been better to say no at once, for he was compelled to do so in July after the setbacks in North Africa. Disappointment was keen in Washington, where the future of ROUNDUP seemed in jeopardy. On July 10 the Joint Chiefs of Staff recommended

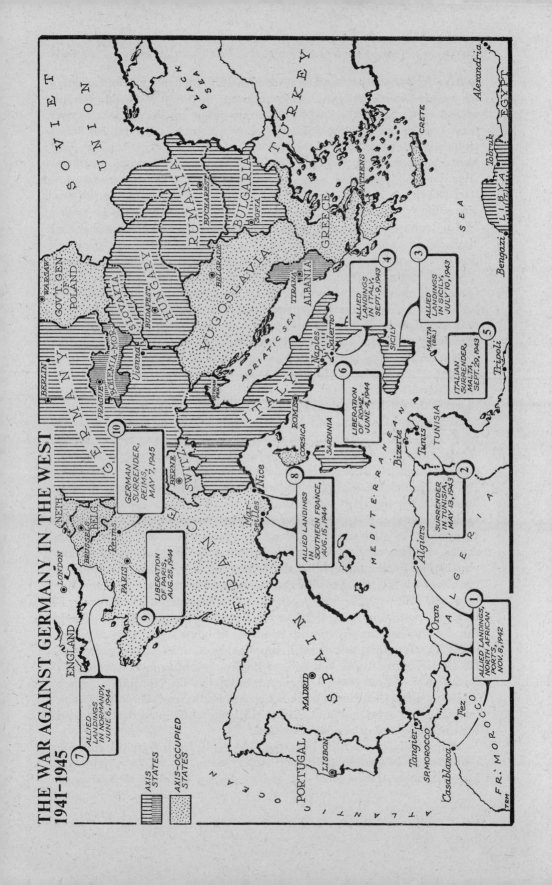

THE WAR AGAINST GERMANY IN THE WEST
1941–1945

AXIS STATES

AXIS-OCCUPIED STATES

SOVIET UNION

ENGLAND

LONDON

NETH.

BRUSSELS

BELG.

PARIS

Reims

F R A N C E

Marseilles

Nice

SWITZ.

BERNE

GERMANY

BERLIN

PRAGUE

BOHEMIA-MOR.

Vienna

SLOVAKIA

GOV'T GEN. OF POLAND

WARSAW

HUNGARY

BUDAPEST

AUSTRIAN PROV.

ISTRIAN PROV.

RUMANIA

BUCHAREST

YUGOSLAVIA

BELGRADE

BULGARIA

SOFIA

ALBANIA

TIRANA

GREECE

ATHENS

TURKEY

BLACK SEA

ADRIATIC SEA

I T A L Y

ROME

Naples

Salerno

SARDINIA

CORSICA

Bizerte

Tunis

TUNISIA

Algiers

Oran

A L G E R I A

SICILY

MALTA (BR.)

Tripoli

Bengazi

LIBYA (ITAL.)

Tobruk

Alexandria

EGYPT

CRETE

SEA

MEDITERRANEAN SEA

PORTUGAL

LISBON

SPAIN

MADRID

Tangier

SP. MOROCCO

Casablanca

Fez

FR. MOROCCO

ATLANTIC OCEAN

① ALLIED LANDINGS, NORTH AFRICAN PORTS, NOV. 8, 1942

② SURRENDER IN TUNISIA, MAY 13, 1943

③ ALLIED LANDINGS IN SICILY, JULY 10, 1943

④ ALLIED LANDINGS IN ITALY, SEPT. 9, 1943

⑤ ITALIAN SURRENDER, MALTA, SEPT. 29, 1943

⑥ LIBERATION OF ROME, JUNE 4, 1944

⑦ ALLIED LANDINGS IN NORMANDY, JUNE 6, 1944

⑧ ALLIED LANDINGS IN SOUTHERN FRANCE, AUG. 15, 1944

⑨ LIBERATION OF PARIS, AUG. 25, 1944

⑩ GERMAN SURRENDER, REIMS, MAY 7, 1945

TRM

to Roosevelt that if the British were unwilling to strive wholeheartedly
for a cross-channel operation in 1943, the United States should turn its
attention in 1942 to the Pacific, where the first offensive against Japan
was about to begin in the Solomon Islands. In one of the fateful decisions of the war and one of the few times he overruled his military advisers, Roosevelt rejected the suggestion. If SLEDGEHAMMER is impossible, he said, "then we must take the second best—and that is not the
Pacific." Hence he sent Marshall, King, and Hopkins to London to devise some scheme that would pit Americans against Germans in 1942.
The outcome was an agreement on July 25 to hold to ROUNDUP for
1943 but to launch within four months operation TORCH, the occupation of Morocco and Algeria on "the soft underbelly" of the Axis.

Anticipating Stalin's anger over the scrapping of SLEDGEHAMMER,
Churchill flew to Moscow on August 12, 1942 to break the news in person. There he listened as the Soviet leader bitterly accused the democracies of breaking their promise on a second front in Europe and
scathingly compared their inability to land six divisions in France with
Russia's capacity to engage 280 German divisions all the way from the
White Sea to the Black. The Briton heatedly denied any breach of faith
and asserted that a victory in North Africa would help the Red Army
more than a debacle in Normandy. Eventually Stalin appeared to be
mollified, but his resentment influenced the Anglo-American chieftains
when they next met together at Casablanca on January, 14–25, 1943.

By then the Axis forces had been cleared out of Libya, Algeria,
and Morocco, but the surrender in Tunisia did not come until May,
1943. Although this delay in completing TORCH threatened to disrupt
ROUNDUP, the conferees were reluctant to call off the cross-channel invasion for 1943. But they were badly split on alternatives. Roosevelt
stressed Stalin's desire for a landing in France. Churchill advocated an
attack on Sicily and a drive up the Italian boot. King preferred to emphasize the Pacific rather than the Mediterranean. Marshall wanted to
proceed with ROUNDUP at all costs. Compromise was in order, and the
principal military decisions reached at Casablanca, omitting those affecting Japan, were to reaffirm the priority of a German defeat, to check
the submarine menace in the Atlantic, to bomb the Reich day and
night, to strengthen Russia with supplies, to complete the conquest of
North Africa, to invade Sicily immediately thereafter, and to assemble
forces in England for a late-summer descent on Normandy. Since
Stalin would be infuriated by the date and nature of this tenuous commitment, the President and Prime Minister proclaimed as their goal
the unconditional surrender of the Axis.

Not until five months later did Roosevelt and Churchill concede
there would be no cross-channel attack in 1943. At Washington on
May 25, 1943, they set the target date for an invasion of France at

THE WAR AGAINST GERMANY IN THE EAST, 1941-1945

Territory acquired by the U.S.S.R., 1939-1941

Territory acquired by Hungary, 1938-1940

THE DATES NEAR THE CAPITAL CITIES ARE THE DATES OF FINAL CAPTURE

——— Soviet-Axis frontier on June 22, 1941
•••••••• German advance up to Dec., 1941
•••••••• German advance up to Nov., 1942
═══════ Battle line on Aug. 12, 1943
•••••••• Battle line in the spring of 1944

TRM

May 1, 1944, and agreed to follow up the assault on Sicily with such measures as might best cause the surrender of Italy and best contain the maximum number of Nazi troops. Operations in the Mediterranean, however, would not be allowed to interfere with the landings in Normandy, now called OVERLORD. These decisions apparently caught Stalin by surprise, and he reacted angrily. Again he accused the West of breaking promises; as a sign of displeasure he canceled a tentative meeting with Roosevelt in July and recalled his ambassadors from Washington and London. Indeed, there is evidence that in June, 1943, he explored the possibility of a negotiated peace with Germany. But Hitler was not interested, and the opening of the summer campaign on July 5 marked the end of these soundings.

Shortly thereafter the extreme tensions subsided. The invasion of Sicily on July 10, 1943, led to the downfall of Mussolini and the surrender of his successor in September. Although the battle for Italy was not over, the Führer had to immobilize more and more troops there. In the East the Red Army gained the upper hand. It repulsed the Nazi offensive and then began an advance which did not stop until it reached Berlin in May, 1945. Heartened by these events, Stalin cast aside thoughts of a separate peace and cleared the way for a conference of foreign ministers at Moscow on October 18 and a meeting of heads of government at Tehran on November 28. The first was concerned primarily with postwar problems; the latter with the strategy for defeating Germany and Japan.

OVERLORD was the key to that strategy. From August 14 to 24, 1943, Roosevelt resisted at Quebec all of Churchill's suggestions to delay or modify the Normandy landings in order to exploit opportunities in the Adriatic and Aegean created by Italy's collapse. The sole addition was a supplementary invasion of southern France, so that a column driving north in the Rhone Valley could join the main body fanning eastward from the Cotentin Peninsula. Operation ANVIL would thus use men and ships already in the Mediterranean and secure a much needed port at Marseilles. At Tehran the Briton again urged other preliminary probings, but Stalin joined the Americans in opposing a dispersal of forces. The Soviet chief promised to launch a major attack in the East to coincide with OVERLORD.

Churchill made one more vain effort to alter the campaign planned for 1944, and that attempt has caused much misunderstanding. He did not seek to abandon OVERLORD, though he remained flexible regarding the date and apprehensive concerning the pitfalls. He did not propose, as some uncritical admirers claim, to mount a large-scale invasion of the Balkans for either diplomatic or military reasons. Rather, Churchill tried to substitute for ANVIL a landing at the head of the Adriatic on the Istrian Peninsula and a push through the Ljubljana Gap into

Austria and Hungary. This maneuver was logistically more difficult and tactically more dangerous; as such, it was rejected. Even if successful, the scheme would not have achieved Churchill's aims. It would have been too late to precede the Russians into Central Europe; it would have been too little to draw many German divisions from the major fronts.

Between June 6, 1944, when the greatest amphibious force ever assembled stormed ashore in Normandy, and February 4, 1945, when the most controversial of the wartime conferences began at Yalta, the doom of the Third Reich was sealed. The coalition's sound strategy, superbly executed under General Dwight D. Eisenhower, was convincingly demonstrated. Neither saturation bombings nor dispersed attacks could have done so much so quickly, and in view of the rapid development of missiles and jet aircraft by Hitler's scientists, a failure to wrest control of Western Europe in 1944 might have been disastrous. Thus the military phase of the Yalta deliberations, so far as they touched Germany, gave no trouble. They produced a vast pincers movement which crushed the Wehrmacht and led to the surrender in a Reims schoolhouse on May 7, 1945.

THE WAR AGAINST JAPAN

Compared with the war against Germany, the conquest of Japan did little to divide the coalition. Once it was decided to defeat Hitler first, only two big questions remained. What specific steps should be taken, with limited men and equipment, to roll back the Japanese tide? What specific steps could be taken, in view of its neutrality pact, to bring Russia into the struggle? The first was for the Combined Chiefs of Staff to decide. They framed the broad directives which enabled the United States to dominate the Pacific war. The second had to be dealt with at the highest level and only when victory in Europe seemed certain. Stalin gave no firm assurances until November, 1943, and did not present an itemized bill until February, 1945.

To defeat Japan, most strategists believed, American soldiers would have to fight their way to Tokyo itself. Although well-selected advances eventually reduced its bloated empire and although submarine depradations and bomber raids gradually destroyed its strained economy, Japan's fanatical resistance on Guadalcanal, Tarawa, Saipan, and Iwo Jima suggested that the end would not come until the last defender had been killed in the home islands and on the mainland. To reach Tokyo, only two routes were feasible. One began from New Caledonia in the South Pacific and climbed up the Solomons and New Guinea to the Philippines; the other started from Hawaii and pushed through the Marshalls, Carolines, and Marianas to Formosa. Both were pursued in part, with agonizing slowness in 1942–3 and with amazing rapidity in 1944–5.

As the war neared Japan's home islands and Hitler faced defeat in Europe, the question of Soviet participation came to the fore. After Pearl Harbor, with the Nazis deep on Red soil and the Japanese unchecked in Asia and the Pacific, Stalin would not talk of intervening. In August 1942, however, he hinted for the first time that Russia would eventually fight in the Orient. On October 30, 1943, he surprised Hull by saying in confidence but without prodding that he was waiting only until Germany had been beaten before helping to crush Japan, and he volunteered the same information in plenary session at Tehran on November 28. These assurances delighted the United States, for as late as the conference at Yalta in February, 1945, every responsible American leader, civilian and military, believed that Soviet aid was indispensable. The Pacific front had not yet passed Luzon, and the bloody battles on Iwo Jima and Okinawa lay ahead. The Japanese still had a million men in Korea and Manchukuo, where the supposedly élite Kwantung Army was expected to make a last-ditch stand, and an equal number in China. Estimates of the casualties the United States would suffer on invading Kyushu in November, 1945, and Honshu in March, 1946, ran as high as a million. These considerations and the realization that Stalin was determined to come in for the final kill were responsible for the negotiation at Yalta of the much criticized Far Eastern Agreement, to be described in the following chapter.

Five months of swift-moving developments rendered obsolete this pre-Yalta thinking. By mid-July, 1945, the navy was convinced that aerial bombing, submarine sinkings, and surface gunfire would induce Japan to yield without an invasion. The air corps was equally optimistic, but the army dissented. So did the State Department, which doubted that the cabinet's desire for peace was shared by the generals. A few key officials knew that the ultimate weapon was being perfected, yet the first nuclear explosion did not light up the New Mexico desert until July 16. Worsening relations with Russia injected another new element. The spirit of cooperation, so painfully built up, quickly disintegrated before the inspired coup in Rumania, the incipient quarrel over Germany, and the insoluble problem of Poland. With difficulty a conference at San Francisco produced a United Nations Charter on June 26, 1945, and with uncertainty Truman, Churchill, and Stalin met at Potsdam on July 17. By then the future peace overshadowed the current conflict, but the question of Russia's participation remained. By then many Americans had come to feel that step would be unnecessary and unfortunate.

Actually, only an immediate collapse of Japan could keep Stalin from intervening. He had already ignored pleas from Tokyo to arrange

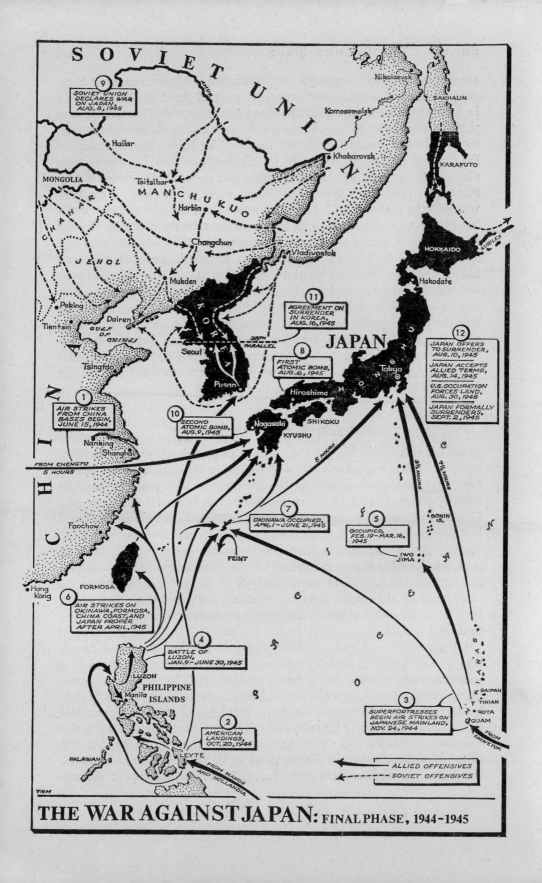

THE WAR AGAINST JAPAN: FINAL PHASE, 1944-1945

an armistice, a fact not known in Washington, and now sought at Potsdam an excuse to break the neutrality pact of April 13, 1941, which had nine months to run. Truman was loath to provide that excuse and perhaps hoped the atomic bomb would end hostilities before the Red Army marched, but his touch was unsure. The badly phrased Potsdam Declaration of July 26, 1945, in which the United States, Great Britain, and China called for an immediate and presumably unconditional surrender, may have persuaded Japan to resist further. A vaguely worded note to Stalin on July 31, in which the President suggested citing the Charter and other United Nations documents to justify moving against Japan, was open to misinterpretation. It is possible that the sudden use of the bomb at Hiroshima on August 6 caused Stalin to go ahead more quickly than he had intended. Late on August 8 Molotov notified the Japanese ambassador that his government was responding to proposals for hastening the end of the fighting and would enter the war the next day. On August 9 a second bomb was dropped on Nagasaki, the Russians crossed into Manchukuo, and an Imperial Conference began the process leading to surrender. The official proclamation came on August 14, and the formal proceedings occurred aboard the battleship *Missouri* in Tokyo Bay on September 2, 1945.

THE LIMITATIONS OF VICTORY

From the military point of view, American diplomacy during the Second World War was undeniably successful. In the dark days of December, 1941, no one expected the United Nations to defeat Germany in forty-one months and Japan in forty-four. As late as July, 1945, the Combined Chiefs of Staff assumed that the fighting in the Pacific would last until November. Yet despite some mistakes and frequent tensions, the coalition destroyed the Axis with amazing speed. Today, however, that achievement seems tarnished by the fact that decisions vital to triumph on the battlefield led to tragedy at the peace table. Later we shall consider the conflict between wartime goals and peacetime aims; here we shall indicate those limitations of victory stemming from the nature of war itself.

Wars rarely end exactly as the victors wish, and the end in 1945 was no exception. In both Europe and Asia the enemy collapsed at a moment when the Red Army was advantageously located to influence later events. By mid-April the Soviet Union controlled the Baltic States, Poland, Hungary, Rumania, Bulgaria, and most of Austria, Czechoslovakia, and Yugoslavia. Eisenhower's divisions could have beaten the Russians to Prague and might have preceded them to Berlin, but the Allied Commander lacked instructions to do so and did not know of the diplomatic deterioration since Yalta. Even if he had captured those two capitals, the outcome probably would have been the same, for after V-E Day Churchill urged Truman not to pull back units from that part of Germany earmarked for Russian occupation until the status of Berlin was clarified and earlier Soviet promises were carried out. But the new President, guided by men preoccupied with the Pacific war, refused to break with Stalin at that time and on those grounds. On June 12, 1945, he ordered all troops withdrawn into the American zone.

An even less satisfactory situation existed in Asia. On August 14, 1945, the Americans had not yet landed in Japan, but the Russians were overrunning Manchukuo and Korea. Chiang Kai-shek's men, long since pushed back from the coast into South and Central China, were in no position to assert Nationalist authority in North China or Manchuria. The Communists at Yenan were better placed for disarming the Japanese and joining hands with the Russians. The facts of geography favored the Soviet Union, and the most the United States could do was to hasten its own occupation of Japan and keep the Red Army above the thirty-eighth parallel in Korea.

Would a different wartime strategy have prevented this postwar disadvantage? There is no reason to believe that crushing Japan before Germany or delaying the cross-channel invasion would have produced better results, while the baneful consequences of the unconditional surrender policy have been grossly exaggerated. Actually, no matter which military course was pursued or which diplomatic goal was proclaimed, the triumph of the United Nations meant the destruction of greater Germany and Japan and the consequent flow of Soviet power into the vacuum. The logic of total war made that outcome inescapable. It is easy enough after the event to argue that the United States should have fought for limited goals, but the record of the past indicates how difficult, if not impossible, it is for a single member of a coalition to select the exact moment, before the pendulum swings too far, for checking his own headlong advance and dealing leniently with the foe.

The use of the atomic bomb eventually became another limitation of victory. The decision to employ this terrible device did not go unchallenged among the few who knew it existed. Some scientists responsible for its development hoped it might not be needed; others urged that it first be detonated, as a warning to Japan, on some remote and barren island. But from the outset the policy makers had assumed the bomb must be resorted to if it could shorten the war and save American lives. Thus after full reflection Truman and his advisers rejected the notion of a prior demonstration and warning because the supply of bombs was limited to two and because the risk of failure, after Japan had been alerted, was substantial. It is doubtful whether the bombs were dropped so as to end the fighting before Russia entered the war, though Truman would have been pleased if such had been the result. The determination to go ahead was essentially a military one, based unfortunately on inadequate intelligence respecting Japan's will to resist. Later, when the true facts became known and it was realized that the horrors of Hiroshima and Nagasaki had been needless, the conscience of many Americans grew troubled. Still later, when the true dimensions of the thermonuclear age became clear and it was evident that man had fashioned a weapon of self-destruction, thoughtful citizens regretted that their country had been the one to open a Pandora's Box, the contents of which were frightening to contemplate.

History suggests a final limitation of victory. However complete the triumph on the battlefield and however judicious the settlement at the peace table, there must still be a will to uphold the verdict when the guns are stilled. Roosevelt wanted the great powers, as the dominant states in the new world organization, to act as international policemen, but he feared a hasty demobilization at home. Thus he told Stalin at Tehran that while American naval and air forces could be relied upon to help keep the peace, Russia and England must supply the land armies. At Yalta the President said he could not keep ground troops in Germany for more than two years after the Nazis surrendered. Had he lived, Roosevelt might have thought in bolder terms, especially when the wartime unity dissipated rapidly; but the experience of his successor from 1945 to 1950 showed that the republic had not yet grasped the price it must pay for preserving what it had won in the struggle for survival.

48

⋙⋙⋙⋙⋘⋘⋘⋘

The United Nations
and the Peace

"WE ARE GOING to win the war," Roosevelt assured the nation on December 9, 1941, "and we are going to win the peace that follows." Yet although American diplomacy from 1941 to 1945 helped to end the fighting in very short time and with very few casualties, it has been widely criticized for sacrificing diplomatic goals to military strategy. More specifically, the Roosevelt administration has been charged with needlessly creating a divided Germany in Western Europe, with wantonly abandoning liberty in Poland and Eastern Europe, and with stupidly—if not treacherously—losing to the enemy China and other parts of East Asia. The triumphant struggle for survival, it is alleged, simply replaced the fascist brand of totalitarianism with the communist. Before accepting these strictures, we should subject them to historical analysis.

GERMANY AND WESTERN EUROPE

Except for the new international organization (whose formation will be described in the next chapter), the most important question facing the United Nations as they prepared for peace was the future of Germany. Twice within a generation that country had upset the balance of power on the Continent and come perilously close to defeating an impressive coalition of foes. On other matters—Poland, Eastern Europe, the

Middle East, or the Orient—the victors might vary in the intensity of their concern, but all were equally determined that the German people pay a heavy penalty for past crimes and relinquish a vast potential for future wrongdoing.

Men differed on how this was to be accomplished. None doubted that Hitlerism must be extirpated, that boundaries must be rectified, that a long occupation must be imposed, and that demilitarization must be scrutinized. They were less certain about reparations, after the experience of the 1920's, but the real disagreement came over dismemberment. Stalin favored an independent Austria and Bavaria, the transfer of East Prussia to Poland, and the detachment of the Rhineland, Ruhr, and Saar. The State Department's Advisory Committee on Post-War Problems opposed partition, while Roosevelt and Welles felt that, to prevent a revival of militarism, Prussia must be isolated from the rest of the Reich. Hull wavered, fearing that solution might sow the seeds of future trouble; eventually Churchill and Foreign Secretary Anthony Eden concurred.

This indecision was evident at Moscow in October, 1943, when the foreign ministers first took up the problems of peace. Two Declarations were issued on November 1, one promising freedom to Austria, the other threatening punishment for atrocities. The matter of dismemberment was referred to a three-power European Advisory Commission which would sit permanently in London. To that body was entrusted the task of dividing Germany into three zones of occupation and of defining a joint zone for Greater Berlin. Everyone agreed that past conquests must be renounced, but East Prussia was the only territorial change mentioned.

The next year was one of confusion. At Tehran in November, 1943, Roosevelt talked of partitioning Germany into five nations The State Department resisted dismemberment. The European Advisory Commission haggled over the occupation zones. The American member wanted a specific accord on access to Berlin in the Soviet zone, but the army preferred to settle the matter itself at a later date. Secretary of the Treasury Henry Morgenthau, Jr., seeking to remove Germany's warmaking capacity forever and to bolster England's weakened economy, proposed to strip the Reich of its industrial complex and convert it into a country primarily agricultural and pastoral in character. Despite strenuous objections from Hull, Stimson, and Hopkins, Roosevelt and Churchill initialed this project at Quebec on September 15, 1944, but unfavorable publicity and sober second thoughts caused them to cast it aside.

Germany was a major topic for deliberation at Yalta in February, 1945. The surrender terms there drafted vested supreme authority in the United States, Great Britain, and Russia and stipulated that they could "take such steps, including the complete disarmament, demilitarization and dismemberment of Germany as they deem requisite for future peace and security." The heads of government decided to study dismemberment longer and referred the punishment of war criminals to the foreign ministers for a future report. They assigned an occupation zone to France but carved it out of an area already allotted to the West. No decision was reached on boundaries, and nothing was done to spell out the right of access to Berlin. Reparations received a thorough airing. The victors agreed that Germany must "pay in kind for the losses caused by her to the Allied nations in the course of the war" with priority to those who "have suffered the heaviest losses and have organised victory over the enemy." Three categories of reparations in kind were to be exacted: removal for two years of capital goods, "chiefly for the purpose of destroying the war potential" of the nation; annual deliveries of goods from current production, for a period to be fixed; and the use of German labor. A three-power reparation commission in Moscow was to work out a detailed plan based on these principles. It would take as a basis for discussion a total sum of $20 billion, half of which was to go to Russia.

When the Potsdam Conference met on July 17, 1945, Hitler was dead and unconditional surrender was a reality. The victors had assumed supreme authority in Germany amid growing signs of distrust. Still, they managed to reach three major decisions. First, they adopted a set of controls for the initial occupation. These were hardly Carthaginian in spirit and stressed the need of developing local responsibility. The country was to be treated as a single economic unit; and although there would be no central government for the time being, dismemberment was not mentioned. Second, they approved a plan for reparations. It permitted each occupying power to remove property from its zone, with Russia compensating Poland out of its share and the Anglo-American powers doing the same for France and other claimants. Since German industry lay largely outside the Soviet zone, Russia was to receive from the West 10 per cent of its portion of capital equipment outright and another 15 per cent in exchange for raw materials. Third, the conferees agreed upon a few boundaries. They endorsed Stalin's claim to the northern part of East Prussia and accepted Poland's temporary occupation of the territory east of a line marked by the Oder and Neisse Rivers.

POLAND AND EASTERN EUROPE

If the problem of Germany became the most dangerous of the postwar era, the future of Poland was the most troublesome during the fighting itself. The members of the coalition felt an equal stake in the first but not in the second. Although five million Americans of Polish descent might demand that the nation, re-created by Wilson, remain independent, the United States did not regard Eastern Europe as an area of vital concern. Poland, as Hopkins told Stalin in May, 1945, was mainly important as "a symbol of our ability to work" with the Soviet Union. For England, Poland was something else. In April, 1939, the British had promised—perhaps unwisely but probably unavoidably—to defend the land from Nazi aggression. Their interest, as Churchill put it at Yalta, was one of honor; they could accept no settlement which did not leave the Poles free and sovereign.

For Russia, Poland was much more than a symbol or a point of honor. The Soviets' very security was involved. Twice in a quarter of a century Germany had used Poland as an invasion route. The Poles themselves had tried to seize the Ukraine in 1920. Anxiety over his western frontier helps explain Stalin's tortuous diplomacy in 1939–40. He refused to join an anti-Hitler bloc unless he was permitted, as a precaution, to station Red troops in Poland and the Baltic States. The unwillingness of England and France to ask such terms of the countries affected led to a breakdown in negotiations and the conclusion of the Nazi-Soviet Pact on August 23, 1939. Following that deal, Russia was able to absorb Estonia, Latvia, and Lithuania as well as to push its boundary west of the Curzon Line, an ethnographic demarcation proposed by Great Britain at Paris in 1919. When Hitler turned upon his accomplice in June, 1941, the hammer and sickle flew over half of Poland, whose government was functioning in exile at London.

During the next four years Stalin missed no opportunity to insure a favorable position in postwar Poland. When Eden visited Moscow in December, 1941, one of the darkest hours in Soviet history, he found Stalin eager to discuss future boundaries, and only pressure from Washington prevented an agreement then or at the signing of an alliance on May 26, 1942. By late 1943, however, the advance of the Red Army and the rupture with the government in exile over an unexplained earlier massacre in the Katyn Forest made Hull withdraw his opposition to reaching a territorial understanding while the fighting raged. The Secretary feared that Stalin might recognize as the legitimate rulers the Union of Polish Patriots, a Communist group organized in Russia. At the Foreign Ministers Conference on October 29 he and Eden urged the restoration of relations with the London exiles, now headed by Stanislaw Mikolajczyk, but Molotov replied that he favored an independent Poland only if its government was friendly to the Soviet Union. At Tehran on December 1 Stalin resisted all pleas that he resume diplomatic ties with Mikolajczyk. He did offer to accept the Curzon Line as a western boundary if he obtained the Königsberg sector of East Prussia. Churchill did not object, since the Poles could be compensated at the expense of Germany up to the Oder River, while Roosevelt suggested an exemption of the predominantly Polish districts of Lwow and Galicia. But no accord was concluded at that time.

Between Tehran and Yalta the future of Poland was determined by the advancing Red Army. On January 4, 1944, Soviet troops crossed the prewar frontier and launched a big offensive to coincide with the Normandy landings five months later. In the interim Churchill warned the stubborn exiles that the Curzon Line was the best they could hope for, but not until July and only at Roosevelt's behest did Mikolajczyk set out to talk with Stalin. By then the Russians had reached the Vistula and had handed over the lands west of the Curzon Line to a rival provisional government, the Committee on National Liberation. Efforts to merge the two groups failed, and on August 15 the Committee proclaimed Lublin to be the temporary capital. New tensions were created by a premature uprising in Warsaw, where anti-Communist Poles were wiped out by the Germans as Red Army units stood idly by; and on October 9 Churchill went to Moscow with Mikolajczyk in another attempt to reconcile Anglo-American desires for a free Poland with the imperatives of coalition warfare. That mission also failed. Molotov interpreted Roosevelt's words at Tehran as an approval of the Curzon boundary, and neither Churchill nor Ambassador W. Averell Harriman dared endanger Big Three harmony on that issue. On November 24, 1944, Mikolajczyk gave way to a more intransigent successor; on January 5, 1945, Stalin recognized the Lublin government. Within a month Soviet forces were inside Germany and only forty-five miles from Berlin.

At Yalta the Polish agenda consisted of boundaries, elections, and the formation of a single provisional government. The first was the easiest to settle. The Protocol of February 11, 1945, stipulated that the eastern frontier would follow the Curzon Line with slight digressions in favor of Poland. The western border would be drawn at the future peace conference but with "substantial accessions of territory" for the Poles. The Lublin regime was to be "reorganized on a broader democratic basis" by including leaders at home and abroad. Molotov and the Anglo-American ambassadors in Moscow would consult with the parties concerned to achieve that aim. When properly formed, this Provisional Government of National Unity would be recognized by all three powers. It would then hold "free and unfettered elections as soon as possible on the basis of universal suffrage." As a statement on paper, these clauses sounded reasonable, but they lacked the safeguard Roosevelt and Churchill had wished—for the ambassadors to observe the balloting. Harriman had warned on December 28, 1944, that the Russian meaning of "independent governments" and "democratic elections" was very different from the American.

These fears were justified. Poland, as Churchill later wrote, was the first of the great issues which caused the breakdown of wartime unity. Neither he nor Roosevelt was happy about the agreements reached at Yalta, for they seemed to violate the Atlantic Charter and were disavowed by the exiles in London. As it became evident that there would be no genuine reorganization of the Lublin regime, the Prime Minister urged the President to join in a protest to Moscow, and one of Roosevelt's last acts was to complain to Stalin that the Crimean pledges had not been kept. After his death the situation grew worse. A separate treaty of mutual assistance with the Lublin group on April 21, 1945, strengthened the impression that in Poland, as in Eastern Europe, the Kremlin had adopted a unilateral policy. When the drafting of the United Nations Charter hit a snag, Truman sent Hopkins to talk with Stalin; and from May 26 to June 5 the two men ranged over all aspects of Russian-American relations. They reached a procedure for establishing a government which would include Mikolajczyk and others not associated with the National Committee. On receiving assurances that diplomats and journalists would be allowed to observe the impending elections, the United States and Britain recognized the new regime on July 5, 1945.

At Potsdam, Poland was a less troublesome problem than Germany or Japan. In the Protocol of August 1, 1945, the three powers expressed their pleasure at the formation by "representative Poles" of a provisional government and their expectation that free and unfettered elections would soon be held. They reaffirmed their belief that the western boundary must await the definitive peace settlement, and they agreed that until then the area east of the Oder-Neisse line should be administered by Poland. Yet it soon became clear that the Russians and the Poles considered the demarcation to be a permanent one, while in the next months over six million Germans either fled or were transferred, under a stipulation in the Potsdam Protocol, to the area west of the Oder and Neisse Rivers. That flow of population was not likely to be reversed.

Elsewhere in Eastern Europe, Russia's military triumphs and passion for security jeopardized the kind of self-determination envisaged by the Atlantic Charter. Stalin regarded the annexation of the Baltic republics as final and spurned Roosevelt's wish for a postwar plebiscite. In October, 1944, he was not averse to recognizing temporarily British predominance in Greece, but only if Churchill agreed that Russia had a greater influence in Rumania and Bulgaria and an equal one in Hungary and Yugoslavia. Hull disliked such measures, even as wartime expedients, for they seemed to revive the evils prevailing before 1914; and at Yalta, in the Declaration of Liberated Europe, Roosevelt gained approval of the principle that the three victors would collaborate in aiding the peoples formerly under Nazi rule to establish democratic governments of their own choosing. Actually, however, the United States could hope to realize its aims only in France, Belgium, and Holland and perhaps in Italy, Germany, Austria, and Greece; elsewhere in Europe it would have to rely on the strength of the United Nations and the goodwill of the Soviet Union.

JAPAN AND EAST ASIA

In planning peace, as in waging war, the United States paid more attention to Europe than to Asia. In the latter the task seemed simpler. After Japan had surrendered unconditionally, it would be shorn of the lands it had wrested from its neighbors since 1894 and be guided into democratic ways during a period of occupation. China would receive belated justice and take its place among the great powers. Russia would regain its traditional position in the Orient. Korea would recover its freedom, perhaps after a few years of tutelage. Members of the coalition would retrieve their colonies, though some liberation was anticipated. As the chief architect of the Pacific war, the United States expected to be solely responsible for the occupation of Japan.

Not until late 1943 were these objectives set forth publicly. Roosevelt and Churchill met with Chiang Kai-shek for the first time at Cairo on November 22–6 and then, since Russia was not at war with Japan, talked with Stalin at Tehran. Returning to the Egyptian capital, they issued the Cairo Declaration of December 1. It asserted that the United States, Great Britain, and China were fighting to punish aggression and coveted no gains for themselves. They proposed to strip Japan of all the Pacific islands it had seized since 1914 and to restore to China all the territories Japan had stolen, "such as Manchuria, Formosa, and the Pescadores." They also intended to expel the Japanese from other lands taken by violence and to see that "in due course Korea shall become free and independent." They were less explicit on Japan's other possessions. The future of the Ryukyus was left in doubt. The United States might claim the Marshalls, Carolines, and Marianas or serve as their trustee. Stalin divulged at Tehran his desire for the Kuriles and southern Sakhalin as well as the use of the Manchurian railways, and he welcomed Roosevelt's suggestion that Dairen be made a free port.

No publicity followed the discussions at Tehran on Russia's role in dismembering the Japanese Empire, since the Soviet Union was still neutral. For the same reason the Far Eastern Agreement, signed at Yalta on February 11, 1945, but not part of the Protocol, was classified as top secret. That controversial document—negotiated by Roosevelt, Stalin, Harriman, and Molotov without the full knowledge of either the State Department or the Joint Chiefs of Staff and without Churchill's participation until the very end—became so important in the postwar era that it must be quoted in its entirety.

THE LEADERS of the three Great Powers—the Soviet Union, the United States of America and Great Britain—have agreed that in two or three months after Germany has surrendered and the war in Europe has terminated the Soviet Union shall enter the war against Japan on the side of the Allies on condition that:

1. The *status quo* in Outer-Mongolia (The Mongolian People's Republic) shall be preserved;

2. The former rights of Russia violated by the treacherous attack of Japan in 1904 shall be restored, viz.

(a) the southern part of Sakhalin as well as all the islands adjacent to it shall be returned to the Soviet Union,

(b) the commercial port of Dairen shall be internationalized, the preeminent interests of the Soviet Union in this port being safeguarded, and the lease of Port Arthur as a naval base of the USSR restored,

(c) the Chinese-Eastern Railroad and the South-Manchurian Railroad which provides an outlet to Dairen shall be jointly operated by the establishment of a joint Soviet-Chinese Company it being understood that the preeminent interests of the Soviet Union shall be safeguarded and that China shall retain full sovereignty in Manchuria.

3. The Kuril islands shall be handed over to the Soviet Union.

It is understood that the agreement concerning Outer-Mongolia and the ports and railroads referred to above will require concurrence of Generalissimo Chiang Kai-shek. The President will take measures in order to obtain this concurrence on advice from Marshal Stalin.

The Heads of the three Great Powers have agreed that these claims of the Soviet Union shall be unquestionably fulfilled after Japan has been defeated.

For its part the Soviet Union expresses its readiness to conclude with the National Government of China a pact of friendship and alliance between the USSR and China in order to render assistance to China with its armed forces for the purpose of liberating China from the Japanese yoke.

Such were the provisions of the most bitterly denounced step in Roosevelt's entire wartime diplomacy. The President's action has been attacked as unnecessary, unconstitutional, irresponsible, and immoral —the aberration of a dying and feeble-minded man. It has been called unnecessary because Russian aid was not needed to defeat Japan without invading the home islands. It has been termed unconstitutional because it by-passed the treaty-making process. It has been branded irresponsible because its provisions were kept secret from men entrusted with the conduct of American diplomacy. It has been condemned as immoral because it was negotiated in the absence of China and infringed upon certain promises in the Cairo Declaration. In short, say the critics, by this blunder the United States lost the fruits of victory in Asia and made the Soviet Union the predominant element in the balance of power there.

Some of those strictures are justified; yet, as with everything concerning the Yalta Conference, they must be explained and qualified. Roosevelt was ill but mentally alert; he knew in advance exactly what Stalin would ask for, and he bargained within the limits set by coalition warfare. The President was not alone in failing to foresee in February, 1945, that Japan might be vanquished without Soviet participation; every high-ranking statesman and officer agreed then that he dare not risk the casualties that going it alone entailed. To have cast the accord in treaty form would have ignored the wartime precedents of McKinley and Wilson, on lesser matters to be sure, and would have been an unwarranted gamble with security, given the frequency of senatorial leaks to the press. The absence of Chiang Kai-shek was understandable, in view of Russia's neutrality, and it is unlikely that China would have fared better with the Generalissimo present. Finally, even without this convention the Soviets would have entered the war whenever they chose and would have played a prominent role in the Orient after hostilities had ceased.

Yet the Far Eastern Agreement was deficient on several counts. The phrasing sounded too much like a bribe. Stalin had already promised to engage in the Pacific war, and it was to his long-range interest to do so. The historical justification for some of the territorial changes was faulty, even if it seemed analagous to the principle behind the Cairo Declaration. Japan did get the Kwantung leasehold, the railroad rights in Manchuria, and southern Sakhalin by conquest in 1904–5, but Russia had extracted the first two items from China in 1896–8 by threats of force. The protection afforded the absent Chiang was more apparent than real. His consent meant little; for while the clauses on Outer Mongolia, the ports, and the railways required his approval, the next sentence said that the Soviet claims must be fulfilled unequivocally. A determined Russia might have secured without Roosevelt all it obtained at Yalta, but his acquiescence lent an air of legality. And his zeal for secrecy later fastened needless opprobrium on a vital diplomatic expedient.[1]

The Far Eastern Agreement was a response to the imperatives of coalition warfare and must be appraised in the light of Roosevelt's belief that big power unity was as indispensable in peace as in battle. He went to Yalta determined to manifest trust in the Soviet Union and to secure its cooperation in fighting Japan and founding the United Nations. It would be naive to think that he could have solved perfectly all the complex issues of the Orient. The result was a product of give and take. Stalin obtained four things exactly as he wished: the annexation of the Kuriles, the cession of southern Sakhalin, the naval base at Port Arthur, and the maintenance of the *status quo* in Outer Mongolia. His desire to lease Dairen and to control the Chinese Eastern and South Manchuria lines did not fully materialize, the port being placed under international jurisdiction and the railways under joint operation. Roosevelt gained his three objectives in the form he proposed: Russian participation in the Pacific war, Stalin's promise to support the Chinese Nationalists, and the necessity to procure Chiang's consent to the articles on Manchuria and Mongolia. Thus, while men will speculate endlessly on the wisdom and the justice of the agreement, they ought not to label it a "sell-out" or blame it for the subsequent disasters in China and Korea.

After Yalta, two steps remained in planning the peace for Asia. One was for the United States to inform Chiang Kai-shek of the accord and to win his approval; the other was for China to negotiate with Russia an alliance embodying the points agreed upon in the Crimea. As the weeks passed, both posed unexpected difficulties. The American government was distressed by multiplying signs of Soviet duplicity, while the American military was impressed by increasing evidence of its ability to defeat Japan alone. The men in the Kremlin, on their part, demanded concessions from China that the Far Eastern Agreement did not include and a voice in the occupation of Japan that their contribution to the Pacific war did not warrant. Truman rejected these last pretensions, but on June 15, 1945, he told Chiang, through Ambassador Patrick J. Hurley, of the decisions at Yalta. The Generalissimo seemed disappointed but not upset.

The Sino-Soviet Treaty of Friendship and Alliance of August 14, 1945, provided for wartime cooperation against the common foe and bound the parties to peacetime collaboration "according to the principles of mutual respect for their sovereignty and territorial integrity and of non-interference in the internal affairs of the other." Equally

---

[1] The Far Eastern Agreement was not mentioned in the communiqué on the Yalta Conference of February 12, 1945, or in Roosevelt's report to Congress on March 1. It was first published on February 11, 1946.

important were the supplementary accords defining the new status of Dairen, Port Arthur, and Manchuria. In these the Russians recognized explicitly China's full sovereignty over Manchuria, renounced any intention of intruding in Sinkiang, and promised to deal solely with the Nationalists as the legitimate central government. They thus repudiated the Chinese Communists under Mao Tse-tung. In return, Chiang Kai-shek agreed to an independent Outer Mongolia if a plebiscite expressed that wish. He made Dairen a free port and exceeded the Yalta obligations in transferring half of the harbor facilities to Soviet control. Port Arthur was to be a naval base for both nations; again Chiang went further than the United States liked, but not so far as the Russians wanted, in opening most of the Liaotung Peninsula to Soviet use. The consolidated Chinese Eastern and South Manchuria Railways were to be operated jointly for thirty years, the same time limit as that governing the ports. Lastly, the Red Army could administer Manchuria as long as it remained a zone of military operations; thereafter the Nationalists would assume full authority.

With one exception and one proviso, the Sino-Soviet Treaty was a good bargain for Chiang Kai-shek. The exception was that Manchuria, for the foreseeable future, would be under Soviet military and economic domination, even though China was technically sovereign. The proviso was that Stalin would have to honor his word. If he faltered and secretly helped Mao Tse-tung, then the outlook would be bleak, for the abrupt end of hostilities gave the Communists a geographic advantage. Yet even the most confirmed pessimist would not have predicted in August, 1945, the agony China was to undergo in the next few years—an agony which upset American peace plans for Asia and the world.

DIPLOMATIC GOALS AND MILITARY STRATEGY

Tehran, Yalta, and Potsdam symbolize in the popular mind the failure of American statesmanship to achieve a just settlement after the triumphant struggle for survival. An earlier generation blamed Wilson's alleged blunders and the Senate's ostensible blindness for the lost peace of 1919. Today it is widely believed that Roosevelt's subordination of diplomatic goals to military strategy cost the nation the fruits of victory even before a treaty could be drafted. His return to the secret negotiations which Wilson had condemned has been particularly deplored.

Undeniably, major decisions affecting American security were made after 1941 without being divulged to Congress or the people. This was inevitable. A commander-in-chief does not broadcast his intentions to the enemy, and the gatherings at Tehran, Yalta, and Potsdam dealt with vital military matters, though in descending order. The first concentrated on wartime problems; the second divided its time between peace and war; the third occupied itself mostly with peacetime issues. Strategic alternatives were easier to resolve than diplomatic legacies, and the area of disagreement widened as the coalition faced the supreme test—the ability to maintain unity once the common foe had been vanquished.

Should not Roosevelt and Churchill, two students of history, have known the fate of past coalitions? Were they wise—and here the President was more optimistic than the Prime Minister—in counting so heavily on the continued friendship of the Soviet Union and the future effectiveness of the United Nations? Today, the answer seems obvious; in 1945, the choices open to them were limited. Victory on the battlefield was not assured before Yalta, and Roosevelt understandably declined to risk that triumph or the formation of a new world organization on matters where only the use of American troops—perhaps against the Russians—gave any promise of success. Regrettable as was the absorption of the Baltic States, the mockery of democracy in Eastern Europe, and the delay in restoring to Chiang a Manchuria he had never ruled, it is hard to see how those developments could have been avoided.

All of this is not to say that in planning peace the Roosevelt administration was consistently sound in its thinking or faultless in its judgment. The President placed his stamp of approval too readily on what he could not prevent. It would have been better to defeat Germany and Japan without crushing them, but the alleged lessons of 1918, the accumulated hatred of the Nazis and the Japanese, and the demands of coalition warfare precluded moderation. It would have been sounder to correlate the advance of Eisenhower's armies with the decline in Yalta's harmony, but the newly installed Truman could not be expected to break with Stalin over the zones of occupation while the assault on Japan lay ahead. It would have been wiser to terminate the Pacific war before the Soviets intervened, but none of these alternatives was attainable. Admittedly, the United States acted upon faulty intelligence regarding the strength of the Kwantung Army and the steadfastness of the Japanese people. Its policy makers were also dangerously divided on China, which turned out to be much weaker than anyone supposed; and they gave insufficient thought to filling the power vacuum created in the Orient by the destruction of Japan. Indeed, there were many parts of the world—Africa, the Middle East, Southeast Asia—where the global conflict had released a surging tide of anticolonialism, and the State Department was not equipped to cope with these nationalistic passions in areas hitherto unimportant.

Yet in 1945 war-weary men everywhere hoped, as others had hoped in 1918, that any imperfections in the coming peace could be minimized and even eliminated through an association of nations designed to provide security and promote justice. But there was this difference: when the guns were stilled this second time, the Charter of the United Nations had been drafted, the overwhelming consent of the Senate had been voted, and the ratification of the United States had been deposited.

49

❯❯❯-❯❯❯-❯❯❯-❯❯❮-❮❮❮-❮❮❮-❮❮❮

The Abandonment of

Isolationism

"WE MUST BEGIN the great task that is before us," Roosevelt told the nation on December 9, 1941, "by abandoning once and for all the illusion that we can ever again isolate ourselves from the rest of humanity." Thus did the President proclaim the abandonment of isolationism as a diplomatic policy. Just as the terrifying months from the fall of France to the enactment of Lend-Lease had witnessed the repudiation of neutrality, so did the agonizing years from the attack on Pearl Harbor to the surrender in Tokyo Bay mark the beginning of permanent alliances. Such engagements, traditionally banned as a means of promoting the national interest, became a reality as the republic first joined the United Nations and later signed a network of security treaties and executive agreements embracing the New World, the North Atlantic, the Pacific, Southeast Asia, and the Middle East.

THE LESSONS OF HISTORY

Seldom has past experience played so large a role in shaping foreign policy as it did in marshaling popular sentiment for membership in the United Nations. The lessons of history, real or alleged, operated at every level from the White House and Capitol to the city and farm. Grossly oversimplifying complex events, an articulate group of commentators maintained—most of them after December 7, 1941, but some before—that the refusal of the United States to enter the League of Nations had condemned that body to a futile existence, incapable of checking aggression. The weakness of the League, so the argument ran, made the Second World War inevitable, and for that tragedy the American government and people were partly to blame. To atone for past sins and to avoid future catastrophes, the analysis concluded, the republic must take the lead in building a new world-wide system of collective security.

Roosevelt drew heavily on a study of Wilson's tactics. He quickly decided that the new covenant should be kept out of the peace treaty, that its provisions should be publicized while in the drafting stage, and that its adoption should be sought before the end of the war dissipated the unity of the coalition abroad and the Congress at home. He determined to win legislative sanction for his proposal before translating general principles into specific clauses. He wished to avoid the baneful influence of party politics and the inescapable jealousy of executive prerogatives by having the Charter framed by delegates from both parties and both houses of Congress. Roosevelt revealed his own ideas very slowly, not wishing to get too far ahead of public opinion and, perhaps, not wanting to allow diplomatic goals to intrude upon military strategy. He did oppose resurrecting the League because of its aura of failure, and he was convinced that the preservation of peace must depend on the armed might of the great powers. Not until the Foreign Ministers Conference at Moscow did he permit a four-power declaration on November 1, 1943, to assert "the necessity of establishing at the earliest practicable date a general international organization, based on the principle of the sovereign equality of all peace-loving states, and open to membership by all such states, large and small, for the maintenance of international peace and security."

At home, the political climate encouraged hopes that the bitterness of 1919–20 might not recur. On March 16, 1943, a bipartisan Senate team of two Republicans and two Democrats offered a resolution advising that the United States take the initiative in forming an organization of the United Nations with machinery to settle disputes and force to insure obedience. On June 15 J. William Fulbright, Democrat of Arkansas, introduced a similar measure in the House, but voting was held up over the summer so as to muster impressive majorities. Support came from speeches by Hull and other Democrats, from the phenomenal sales of Willkie's book entitled *One World,* and from leading Republicans assembled at Mackinac Island. Led by Vandenberg and Governor Thomas E. Dewey of New York, both isolationist rivals of Willkie in 1940, the group advocated participation in a postwar body of sovereign states in order "to prevent military aggression and to attain permanent peace." On September 21 the Fulbright Resolution passed

the House by a margin of 360 to 29. In the Senate, Connally presented
a version which embodied key clauses of the Moscow four-power declaration and which stressed the need to adhere to constitutional procedures and the treaty-making process. On November 5, 1943, the Senate adopted the Connally Resolution by a count of 85 to 6.

By the summer of 1944 Roosevelt and Hull had turned the lessons
of history to good use. They had committed the British and the Russians, the Senate and the House, the Republicans and the Democrats,
to a system of collective security and to American participation therein.
By May 29 the Secretary had gone over a draft charter with the Foreign Relations Committee. The next step was to gain Stalin's consent
to discuss the American text. This was done on July 9, and talks began
at the Dumbarton Oaks estate in Washington on August 21, 1944. Because of Soviet neutrality in Asia, China attended only from September 29, the day the Russians departed, until October 7, when the proceedings closed.

Experience with the League of Nations had taught the diplomats
what to retain and what to discard. The League's structural soundness
was attested to by prompt agreement on the need for a Security Council, a General Assembly, a Secretariat, and an International Court of
Justice. Four weaknesses of the League were examined: the requirement of unanimity for every important move, the omission of obligations binding members to definite action, the exclusion of nonpolitical
problems from its direct jurisdiction, and the unavailability of armed
forces to carry out its rulings. The conferees concluded that unanimous
votes should not be mandatory to reach decisions in the Council or in
the Assembly, although each of the Big Three wanted to possess a veto
in the former and assumed that there must be unanimity among themselves on important moves. They agreed that all signatories must
pledge in advance to accept and act upon the findings of the Security
Council and to put at its disposal contingents of their armed forces.
The delegates concurred in the principle of creating an Economic and
Social Council. They split, however, on the matter of membership. The
United States wished to admit several Latin American countries not at
war with the Axis; Russia acquiesced providing every one of the sixteen Soviet republics be represented in the Assembly. This scheme
contravened the basic concept of the United Nations, an organization
of independent states, and caused Stettinius to object. The Russians
withdrew the plan but reserved the right to raise it again at a later
date.

Nor could the veto issue be worked out at Dumbarton Oaks. There
was no disagreement over the right of permanent members to prevent
the Security Council from taking any action against themselves to
which they objected. The United States felt as keenly on that point as

the Soviet Union. But were they entitled to exercise that prerogative in disputes in which they were not directly involved? If so, at what stage might they interpose their veto: before the Security Council discussed the controversy, before it made recommendations, or before it voted to require compliance? On these questions the Americans and Russians parted company and viewed the world organization very differently. Stalin regarded it as a device whereby the Big Three would maintain their wartime supremacy and, when necessary, impose their will on the small nations. Roosevelt also looked upon the great powers as policemen charged with keeping the peace, but he was reluctant to favor the large states on purely procedural matters. Hull thought of the United Nations as a talisman which, in itself, would heal quarrels between peoples and obviate the need for alliances.

The United Nations was the name chosen at Dumbarton Oaks for the proposed organization. Many matters were settled, but four had to be left for the heads of government to solve. One was the voting procedure in the Security Council. A second was the membership. A third was the jurisdiction of the International Court. The fourth was the status of dependent territories, such as the former German islands in the Pacific mandated to Japan. The official communiqué of October 9, 1944, declared that, after further study, a full United Nations Conference would be held as soon as possible. The same day Roosevelt expressed satisfaction that "so much could have been accomplished on so difficult a subject in so short a time." On November 6 Stalin added: "The surprising thing is not that differences exist but that there are so few of them."

Meanwhile, the presidential campaign got under way. Although both parties endorsed the same general principles—the Republicans the Mackinac Declaration, the Democrats the Connally Resolution— there was room to bicker over details. Already two problems of the past reappeared. Could the president put American troops at the disposal of the Security Council by executive agreement and thus evade the treaty-making process? Could the American representative on that Council send units into action without authorization from Congress and thus infringe upon the war-making process? To clarify these points and to avoid misunderstanding in the critical weeks ahead, Hull met from August 23 to 25, 1944, with John Foster Dulles, who was advising Dewey, the Republican candidate, on foreign affairs. Hull and Dulles worked out means for keeping the Republican leaders informed of developments and for enabling them to offer suggestions. The machinery was not perfect, but it reduced partisan sniping in the ensuing election.

At Yalta in February, 1945, the heads of government discussed the matters left unsolved at Dumbarton Oaks. Since the United Nations had to compete for attention with the assault on Germany, the reconstruction of Europe, and the war in Asia, the results must be judged as part of a larger diplomatic and military settlement. On the whole, Roosevelt obtained much of what he sought. Before conceding a single point to the Russians, he won their consent on February 7 to his formula for voting in the Security Council. Procedural matters were to be decided under this arrangement by seven of the eleven members. On other issues—the most important one being to determine that a threat to peace existed and to frame measures for curbing it—the seven must include all permanent members. But when the Council was investigating in a preliminary way to bring about a voluntary settlement, any member who was a party to the dispute would abstain. In short, the veto was to be used in those cases where a great power was most directly concerned: the obligation to apply sanctions against aggressors or a threat by others to discipline it. If this meant that world peace depended upon a unanimity among the United States, Russia, and Britain, then the men at Yalta were simply recognizing the facts of modern international life.

Stalin yielded to Roosevelt on other points. He agreed to fix a date for a conference to draft the Charter, to accept San Francisco as the site, and to define the qualifications of the participants. The last were those countries who had signed the United Nations Declaration by February 8, 1945, or had entered the war by March 1. The Red leader also withdrew his earlier demand that each constituent state of the Soviet Union be seated in the General Assembly, but he did insist on special treatment for two of the sixteen. The President hesitated and then, using the false analogy of the British Commonwealth, said he would support at San Francisco a plan to admit Byelorussia and the Ukraine to membership. In return, he secured the right to claim two additional seats for his government, a claim he never carried through. Although Roosevelt's acquiescence was unwise, neither the United States nor Russia would have gained any substantial advantage by possessing two more votes in a chamber which debated rather than decided. The chief damage resulted from a futile attempt to conceal for the moment what he had done; for when the facts leaked out on March 29, they bred fears that other secret concessions had been made at Yalta.

THE SAN FRANCISCO CONFERENCE

The United Nations Conference on International Organization met in San Francisco on April 25, 1945, as the Third Reich crashed in ruins in a spectacular *Götterdämmerung*. Despite Roosevelt's death, his plans were carried out. The new security system was formed before the

war ended. Its constitution was kept out of the peace treaty. Cooperation between the executive and legislature was maintained. Secretary
Stettinius headed a delegation which drew no complaints. It included
Connally and Vandenberg from the Senate; the ranking members of
the House Foreign Affairs Committee—Sol Bloom, Democrat of New
York, and Charles A. Eaton, Republican of New Jersey; Harold E. Stas-
sen, a disciple of Willkie and former governor of Minnesota; and Virginia C. Gildersleeve, a long-time crusader for peace and dean of Bar-
nard College. Within the coalition, however, tensions had been rising
since Yalta. On March 29 Russia announced ominously that Molotov
would not attend, even though most delegations were to contain the
foreign minister. But Ambassador Harriman finally persuaded Stalin to
indulge in a friendly gesture to the incoming Truman, and Molotov was
ordered to be present.

Fifty nations gathered at San Francisco for the purpose of discussing, amending, and adopting the Dumbarton proposals as supplemented or interpreted by the Yalta Protocol. For the first time the
smaller powers had an opportunity to criticize the grand design of the
Big Three. Three additions and several changes were made. First, a
preamble to the Charter set forth in idealistic, almost millennial terms
the goals of peace, justice, and toleration. Second, a group of articles
provided for dependent territories a kind of trusteeship which satisfied
both empires, such as England and France, and the champions of colonial peoples, such as China and Russia. The exact lands to be placed in
trust were left for a later decision. Third, the jurisdiction of the International Court of Justice was settled. A committee of jurists had produced in Washington from April 9 to 20, 1945, a draft Statute which,
with modifications, was accepted by the Conference. Among the
changes, one enlarged the role of the General Assembly. It could now
make recommendations to the members or the Security Council on any
subject, save when the latter was exercising the functions assigned to
it. Unrestricted freedom of debate thus provided a forum in which the
complaints of anyone could be heard.

Defining the powers of and procedures in the Security Council provoked the most controversy, for Russia insisted on being untrammeled
in that body. The Dumbarton draft forbade the members to enforce
peace "under regional arrangements or by regional agencies without
the authorization of the Security Council." This pleased neither the
Soviet Union nor the United States. For the former it would have
nullified the recent mutual aid pacts with Poland, Czechoslovakia, and
Yugoslavia; for the latter it would have interfered with the hemispheric
defense envisaged by the Act of Chapultepec of March 6, 1945. Since
the American delegates wished to avoid a fracas over the Monroe Doctrine like that of 1919, they sponsored the following sentence, which

became part of Article 51: "Nothing in the present Charter shall impair the inherent right of individual or collective self-defense if an armed attack occurs against a Member of the United Nations, until the Se- curity Council has taken the measures necessary to maintain inter- national peace and security."

More difficult to dispose of was the exact meaning and specific ap- plication of the voting formula hammered out at Yalta. The Protocol had not defined "procedural" questions and had left distressingly vague the scope of "all other matters" on which permanent members must concur. Would a decision on whether a question was procedural be subject to a veto? Was the right of the Security Council to discuss and investigate, as distinct from to act and enforce, fully protected? Ap- prehensions on this last point, latent during the opening weeks, erupted into angry protests on May 27, 1945, when Ambassador Andrei A. Gromyko, who had succeeded Molotov as head of his delegation, let it be known that the veto did apply to decisions on whether a question was procedural. On June 2 he almost broke up the Conference by claiming that a dispute could not even be discussed by the Security Council unless every permanent member voted to place it on the agenda. This flatly contradicted the American interpretation of the Yalta Protocol.

In desperation, Truman appealed to Stalin to alter the Russian stand. Harriman and Hopkins, who was in Moscow for talks on Poland and other issues driving the Big Three apart, added their opinions, and on June 6, 1945, the Red leader yielded. The next day the big powers closed ranks on the voting formula. They conceded that "no individual member of the Council can alone prevent consideration and discussion by the Council of a dispute or situation brought to its attention" and that parties to a controversy had the right to be heard. But they dis- tinguished between procedural and substantive questions, without de- fining either, and they kept a complete veto on the latter. They also reserved to permanent members, who promised not to abuse the au- thority, the right to veto any decision on whether a question was pro- cedural or substantive. The great powers argued that unless they were in agreement, the Security Council could not function and, further, that the proposed machinery was less objectionable than that in the League Covenant. Except for one concession regarding amendments, therefore, they overrode all opposition and placed in the Charter as Article 27 these controversial and rather unclear sentences.

By June 26, 1945, the United Nations Charter was ready for signing. Truman solemnized the occasion with a cautiously optimistic speech in which he said that the preponderant sentiment of the Ameri- can people and their senators favored immediate ratification. Churchill called the work of the Conference "an invaluable contribution." Stalin did not comment publicly, but the official organ of the Communist Central Executive Committee described the Charter as "the best possible at present" and a vast improvement over previous ones. Newspapers on both sides of the Atlantic spoke in a similar vein but with a difference in emphasis. The Russian press emphasized the need of unanimity among the great powers; the British dwelt upon the abandonment of isolationism by the United States and the Soviet Union; the American accented the triumph of Wilsonian principles and the opportunity to achieve a reign of moral law.

THE UNITED NATIONS CHARTER

What was the United Nations to which Americans now looked for security instead of to traditional isolationism? Its constitution, or Charter, consisted of nineteen chapters broken down into 111 articles. Its purpose was much the same as the League's: to maintain peace and security, to take collective measures for preventing war and aggression, to settle disputes among nations, to develop friendly relations based on the principle of equal rights and self-determination, and to promote cooperation in handling international problems. These aims were to be achieved by resolving all controversies through peaceful means, by refraining from threats against the territorial integrity and political independence of other countries, and by collaborating with the United Nations in its acts of prevention and enforcement. The original members were those states which participated in the San Francisco Conference or, having subscribed earlier to the Declaration of January 1, 1942, now signed and ratified the Charter. Membership was also open to "all other peace-loving states" that accepted the obligations contained in that instrument and were judged able and willing to fulfill them. Admission was effected by the decision of the General Assembly upon recommendation by the Security Council. A member against whom preventive or enforcement action had been taken could be suspended by the Security Council; a member which violated the principles of the Charter persistently might be expelled by the Assembly upon the recommendation of the Council.

The United Nations' principal organs were a General Assembly, a Security Council, an Economic and Social Council, a Trusteeship Council, an International Court of Justice, and a Secretariat. All members were represented in the Assembly, and each had a single vote. Decisions on important questions were to be made under a two-thirds rule; all others by a simple majority. The Assembly was to meet in annual sessions; special sessions might be convened by the Secretary-General at the request of the Security Council or of a majority of the members. The powers of the General Assembly were deliberative, supervisory, financial, elective, and constituent. Deliberative functions were performed by discussing any matter within the scope of the Charter and by recommendations to the Security Council or the total membership. Supervisory functions were fulfilled by grants of authority to regulate the activities of other agencies. Financial functions covered approving the budget of the organization and apportioning expenses among the members. Elective functions had to do with choosing nonpermanent members of the Security Council and all or some of the other principal organs. The constituent function found expressions in admitting new members and amending the Charter.

As the body primarily responsible for maintaining peace, the Security Council consisted of eleven members. Five were permanent: the United States, the United Kingdom, the Soviet Union, France, and China. Six were elected by the General Assembly for a two-year term with due regard for geographical distribution and the contribution of individual countries to the organization. The Council was to meet periodically and be so constituted as to operate continuously. The voting procedure—the subject of long debate at Dumbarton Oaks, Yalta, and San Francisco—was outlined with deceptive simplicity in Article 27. Each member had one vote. Decisions on procedural matters were by an affirmative ballot of seven. All other business required a majority of seven including every permanent member, except that a motion to bring a dispute to the attention of the Council could not be vetoed or be voted on by one of the disputants. The members of the United Nations agreed to accept and carry out the judgment and orders of the Security Council.

To deal with threats to peace or acts of aggression, the Council was given broad powers. It could investigate, admonish, and recommend. It determined when a breach had occurred and what action should be taken. It might call upon members to impose partial or complete economic sanctions. In more urgent cases it could employ "air, sea, and land forces as may be necessary to maintain or restore international peace and security." For this last task all members undertook to place troops, ships, and planes at the disposal of the Council through special agreements defining the numbers and types of forces. They were also obliged to hold air units in readiness for instantaneous use. A Military Staff Committee, consisting of the chiefs of staff, or their representatives, of the permanent members, was to advise and assist the Security Council. Until that body acted, each member retained the right to defend itself individually or collectively. "Regional arrangements and agencies" could deal with threats to peace, according to Article 51, provided their principles were consistent with those of the United Nations. Under Articles 52 and 53, the Security Council was to encourage the settlement of disputes by such groupings and to utilize their facilities for its own enforcement action.

Compared with the Covenant, the Charter was more detailed and less demanding. Unlike its predecessor, it was not part of a peace treaty. In 1919 the Council and the Assembly had been made equally responsible for preventing war; in 1945 the Security Council was given the more prominent role. Yet what distinguishes the second venture from the first is not the structural framework and basic purposes but the manner in which the functions of the organs and the commitments of the members are defined. The most striking difference is the absence of anything like Articles 10 and 16. The obligations of the United States under the Charter resemble more closely those it would have assumed under the Lodge reservations. Wilson intended the League to be a coercive type of body, in which members were pledged to apply sanctions automatically and come to the immediate defense of each other. Through his second reservation Lodge sought to transform the League into a noncoercive organization, in which the absolute promise to aid a victim of aggression was subordinated to the less demanding processes in Articles 11 to 15.

A true system of collective security embodies an international organization possessing authority to determine when a resort to force is illegitimate and to require states to collaborate, under its direction, in suppressing such a use of force. The men at San Francisco endorsed the ideal but provided for its operation in rather limited instances. For minor breaches of the peace the collective force of the United Nations might come into play; but in major cases, affecting the interests of the great powers, the veto could block any attempt to determine if aggression had occurred, to designate the guilty party, and to decide whether sanctions, military or otherwise, should be imposed. The veto represented the antithesis of Wilson's ideal; its insertion in the Charter meant that the new organization should not and could not be drawn into efforts to implement the principle of collective security in opposition to a permanent member. Indeed, the existence of Article 51, proclaiming the inherent right of individual and collective self-defense, is a virtual invitation to return to the old balance of power concept to deal with threats of attack by nations possessing the veto.

THE VOTE IN THE SENATE

There was never any doubt the Senate would approve the Charter. The choice, Truman told that body on July 2, 1945, "is not between this Charter and something else. It is between this Charter and no Charter at all." It embodied, he added, the lessons of history, the "experience of a world where one generation has failed twice to keep the peace." The historic policies of isolationism and neutrality did not meet the needs of mid-century. This time there must be no half measures, no compromise between the past and the present. As a universal organization with fixed obligations but firmly rooted in natural law, the United Nations aimed to perpetuate the victory in the struggle for survival. With such qualities and qualifications it appealed to Americans burdened with a wartime guilt over their abstention a quarter-century before and burgeoning with a wartime hope for their participation in the critical era ahead. Roosevelt and Truman had done an effective job; their message had fallen on fertile soil. With the battle against Japan still raging, senators found it impossible to ignore the obvious wishes of the people and both parties.

The contrast with 1919 was striking. The Senate did not divide into staunch supporters, fluctuating reservationists, and irreconcilable foes. Indeed, the opposition was minimal. The hearings began on July 9, 1945, and lasted five days, not six weeks. On July 16 the Foreign Relations Committee made one report, not three. It recommended consent without change, not forty-five amendments and four reservations. The debate on the floor commenced on July 23 and occupied six days, not eight months. Where two decisive tests had to be held in November, 1919, and March, 1920, a single vote sufficed on July 28, 1945. The count was 89 to 2. The dissenters were both Republicans—William Langer of North Dakota and Henrik Shipstead of Minnesota. Of the five abstaining, the sole opponent was the unreconciled Hiram W. Johnson, then on his deathbed.

Only a few questions disturbed the general agreement. Still in doubt was the power of the United States delegate on the Security Council to commit American armed forces without specific authorization by Congress. Also unresolved was the nature of the special agreement in Article 43 by which members placed military components at the disposal of the Council. Was it to be by formal treaty, joint resolution, or executive action? Connally and Vandenberg believed the first method had been intended at San Francisco, but they preferred to handle the issue as a domestic one, to be settled subsequently, rather than as an international one, to be clarified immediately by a reservation. The desire to avoid any amendment or interpretation which might mar the pristine Charter contrasted sharply with attitudes in Lodge's day. Truman eliminated this problem without determining the legal aspect when he cabled from Potsdam on July 27, 1945, that he would seek congressional approval for all future military arrangements.

Two roll calls after July 28, 1945, throw further light on this abandonment of isolationism. One was on the United Nations Participation Act of December 20, 1945, which passed the Senate by 65 to 7 and the

House by 344 by 15. The Senate made no change, except to require its consent to the appointment of delegates to the General Assembly and the various commissions as well as to the Security Council. Several amendments which would have required the president to seek permission from Congress every time American troops, ships, and planes were used in behalf of or by the United Nations were decisively rejected.

The other roll call involved the Connally Reservation which the Senate added when on August 2, 1946, it accepted the optional clause of the Statute of the International Court of Justice. By joining the United Nations, the American government became automatically a member of the new tribunal whose jurisdiction extended to all cases specifically referred to it and all matters explicitly provided for in the Charter and in other treaties. Signatories might, if they chose, recognize as compulsory the Court's adjudication of all legal disputes concerning the interpretation of a treaty, any question of international law, the existence of a fact which—if established—would constitute a breach of an international obligation, and the nature of the reparation to be made for that breach. In giving its consent by a vote of 60 to 2, the Senate exempted from this compulsory jurisdiction three classes of disputes: those which existing or future treaties required to be settled by some other tribunal; those arising under a multilateral pact, unless all signatories were parties to the case or the United States agreed especially to the submission; and those pertaining to matters which were essentially within the domestic jurisdiction of the United States "as determined by the United States." These six words, added by Connally, were inserted by a vote of 51 to 12. The question of whether one of its disputes was domestic in nature was for the United States to decide, not for the Court. Although its effect has been more intangible than demonstrable, the Connally Reservation marked one limit to the overwhelming sentiment for abandoning isolationism so evident in the roll call on the United Nations Charter.

CHAPTER

50

❯❯❯-❯❯❯-❯❯❯-❯❯❮❮❮-❮❮❮-❮❮❮-❮❮❮

The Abortive Joint Peace

EIGHTEEN MONTHS after joining the United Nations the American people realized that a new era of justice and stability had not dawned. During the protracted struggle for survival they had vowed not to repeat the alleged mistakes of an earlier generation. This time surrender would be unconditional. This time a league would be created before the victorious coalition disintegrated. This time demobilization would be cautious and slow. This time there would be no separate peace. Yet in spite of these intentions, a joint peace proved to be as elusive from 1945 to 1947 as it had been from 1919 to 1921. Now, however, the defection came from abroad. Apparently Stalin decided that Russia had less to gain from continued collaboration with its capitalistic associates than from unilateral action in Europe, the Middle East, and the Orient. As a consequence, a hopeful start in peacemaking collapsed, the wartime unity vanished, and the United Nations emerged in practice a very different organization from the one the American people had anticipated.

THE BEGINNINGS OF PEACEMAKING

Like every cataclysm in history, the Second World War left in its wake a perplexing tangle of nationalistic aspirations, territorial inequities, and political anarchy. Rulers had been toppled, populations uprooted, economies disrupted. The totality of the global conflict, the extent of the physical devastation, the horror of the planned genocide, and the inescapable cry for retribution made the task of reconstruction more difficult in 1945 than in 1919. The revolt of the colonial peoples in Asia and Africa and the trial of the war criminals at Nuremberg and Tokyo are two other examples of the difference.

Mindful of the charge that the Versailles Treaty perpetuated wartime hatreds and that the League Covenant froze an imperfect peace, the Americans again tried to apply the lessons of history. At Potsdam they succeeded in deferring a formal conference until passions had cooled and set up instead a Council of Foreign Ministers from the United States, England, Russia, France, and China to do the preparatory work. The Protocol of August 1, 1945, stipulated that the Big Three alone should lay down the principles governing the settlements with Bulgaria, Hungary, and Rumania. France would join in discussing the Italian pact; the British and the Soviets would handle Finland. The Council might be used later for dealing with Germany and Japan. The treaties thus drafted, Truman hoped, would be submitted eventually to a general conference of all the United Nations for adoption.

Three sessions of the Council of Foreign Ministers were needed from September, 1945, to December, 1946, to reach a peace settlement with Italy and the Axis satellites. Secretary Byrnes attended all, using as advisers Connally and Vandenberg from the Senate and Dulles from the Republican camp. After unexpected difficulties and exasperating delays a twenty-one nation conference met in Paris from July 29 to October 15, 1946. Unlike the one envisaged by Truman at Potsdam, it was confined to those countries which had waged war with substantial forces against the European members of the Axis. Its purpose was to offer recommendations on the decisions which the Council of Foreign Ministers had tentatively agreed upon; the final texts were drafted by the Big Four in New York and signed at Paris on February 10, 1947.

Except for additions to the Soviet Union, these treaties altered the map of Europe very little. Finland's earlier transfer to Russia of Petsamo province and the Karelian Isthmus was confirmed. Hungary gave to Czechoslovakia a few villages across the Danube from Bratislava. Rumania had previously relinquished southern Dobruja to Bulgaria and both northern Bukovina and Bessarabia to the Soviets; these too were ratified. Italy was compelled to make a free territory of the area surrounding Trieste, to cede eastern Venezia Giulia to Yugoslavia, to surrender the Dodecanese Islands to Greece, and to accept minute border adjustments with France. Italy renounced title to its colonies— Libya, Eritrea, and Somaliland; their future was to be determined by the United States, Britain, Russia, and France, or, should the four powers disagree, by the General Assembly. These changes were in addition to the cession by Poland to Russia of western Byelorussia and the western Ukraine in a treaty of August 16, 1945, the renunciation by Czechoslovakia to Russia of Subcarpathian Ruthenia in a treaty of June 29, 1945, the transfer to Soviet administration of the Königsberg area by the Potsdam Protocol of August 1, 1945, and the annexation by Russia of Estonia, Latvia, and Lithuania, the legality of which annexation the United States did not admit.

These peace treaties made the best of a bad situation. The installation of one-party Communist regimes in Eastern Europe nullified the Yalta promises of free elections and aroused bitter resentment in the United States. But the reality of Soviet military power in that region and the haste of American demobilization precluded any effective retort. Reluctantly, the Truman administration accepted the facts of international life and recognized the Hungarian government on September 29, 1945, the Rumanian on February 4, 1946, and the Bulgarian on October 1, 1947. In doing so, it disclaimed any intention of condoning the suppression of democratic institutions in those countries. On June 5, 1947, the Senate consented to the Italian pact by a vote of 79 to 10 and then approved the satellite treaties without a roll call.

Two other peace settlements were delayed for several years and the most important one never materialized. The Japanese treaty, to be discussed below, was signed at San Francisco by forty-nine nations on September 8, 1951. The Senate gave its consent with reservations on March 20, 1952, by a margin of 66 to 10. It took even longer to reach an accord on Austria. The United States, the United Kingdom, the Soviet Union, and France instituted a joint control, each with a separate zone, on July 9, 1945, and this temporary arrangement lasted ten years. Not until May 15, 1955 did the foreign ministers sign a treaty at Vienna which the Senate approved on June 17 by a count of 63 to 3.

Germany, as was expected, posed the most difficult problems, and no peace treaty could be negotiated. In June, 1945, the victors began the occupation and five months later moved to punish surviving top-ranking Nazis. An International Military Tribunal sat at Nuremberg from November 14, 1945, to October 1, 1946, and tried twenty-three men accused of conspiring to wage aggressive war in violation of established treaties and of perpetrating crimes against humanity. Three of the defendants were freed, seven were jailed for extended terms, and eleven were hanged. Two took their lives, one during the trial and a second after being sentenced to death. At the time and since the legality of these proceedings has been hotly debated. To some, they represented a logical culmination of attempts to outlaw war initiated by the Kellogg Pact and the commencement of a new era in international morality. To others, they constituted an *ex post facto* judgment, set dangerous precedents, and smacked of hypocrisy in overlooking comparable atrocities committed by the Russians in Poland and the Baltic States. Like the

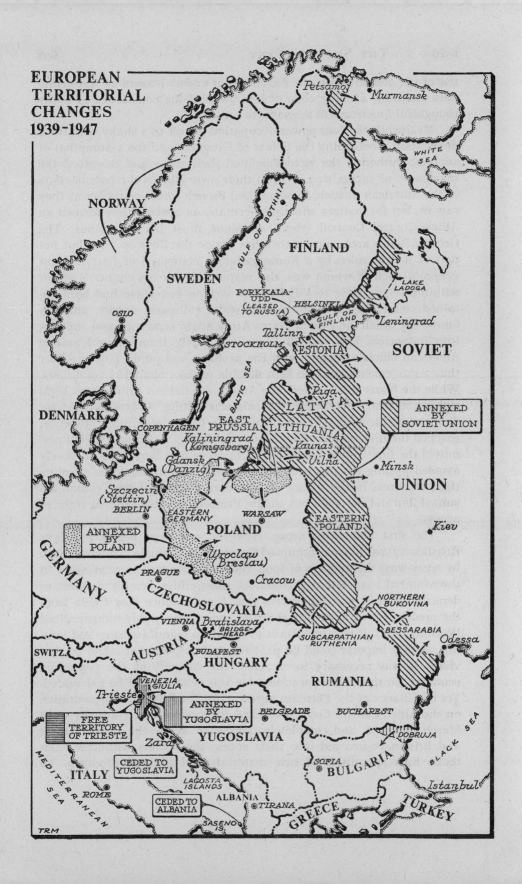

EUROPEAN TERRITORIAL CHANGES 1939-1947

NORWAY

SWEDEN

FINLAND

Petsamo •Murmansk

WHITE SEA

GULF OF BOTHNIA

LAKE LADOGA

PORKKALA-UDD (LEASED TO RUSSIA)

•OSLO

HELSINKI

GULF OF FINLAND

•Leningrad

Tallinn
•STOCKHOLM

ESTONIA

SOVIET

DENMARK

BALTIC SEA

Riga

LATVIA

EAST PRUSSIA

•COPENHAGEN

LITHUANIA

Kaliningrad (Königsberg)

Kaunas

Vilna

•Minsk

UNION

ANNEXED BY SOVIET UNION

Gdansk (Danzig)

Szczecin (Stettin)
•BERLIN

EASTERN GERMANY

WARSAW

POLAND

EASTERN POLAND

•Kiev

GERMANY

ANNEXED BY POLAND

Wroclaw (Breslau)

•PRAGUE

•Cracow

CZECHOSLOVAKIA

NORTHERN BUKOVINA

Vienna

Bratislava

BRIDGE-HEAD

BESSARABIA

SUBCARPATHIAN RUTHENIA

•Odessa

SWITZ.

AUSTRIA

•BUDAPEST

HUNGARY

RUMANIA

•BUCHAREST

Venezia Giulia

Trieste

ANNEXED BY YUGOSLAVIA

•BELGRADE

BLACK SEA

FREE TERRITORY OF TRIESTE

Zara

YUGOSLAVIA

DOBRUJA

CEDED TO YUGOSLAVIA

ITALY

•SOFIA

BULGARIA

MEDITERRANEAN SEA

•ROME

LAGOSTA ISLANDS

•Istanbul

CEDED TO ALBANIA

ALBANIA

•TIRANA

GREECE

TURKEY

SASENO IS.

TRM

use of the atomic bomb, the execution of enemy leaders as war criminals under the existing code of law troubled the conscience of many thoughtful Americans in the years to come.

Meanwhile the four-power occupation got off to a shaky start. In a declaration proclaiming the defeat of Germany and the assumption of supreme authority, the victors defined their zones and described the machinery of supervision. Within their own spheres the commanders of the American, British, Russian, and French forces could act as they saw fit, but for matters affecting Germany as a whole they formed an Allied Control Council where decisions must be unanimous. The Greater Berlin area, some 110 miles inside the Russian zone but not part of it, was ruled by a Kommandatura composed of four resident generals, each of whom was also responsible for his country's sector within the city. Prior to V-E Day, no written guarantee had been obtained concerning the routes—highways, railroads, canals, and airlanes—by which the United States Army might send men and supplies into its sector. This omission resulted partly from discord among American officials dealing with the problem and partly from a belief that arrangements must be kept flexible to meet changing conditions. While the Nazis still resisted, the Americans did not think about legal rights and their importance in a cold-war setting. As late as June 29, 1945, when Lieutenant General Lucius D. Clay, the military governor, reached the understanding with Marshal Georgi K. Zhukov which permitted the first United States troops to move into Berlin, he purposely avoided putting too much in writing, lest he jeopardize the absolute right of access in the future. At Potsdam a month later Truman assumed, but did not spell out in the Protocol, an unrestricted right of access.

The first difficulties arose, however, not over Berlin but over Russia's refusal to treat occupied Germany as a single economic unit. In many ways the problem of food, fuel, and jobs was more pressing in the winter of 1945–6 than boundaries, indemnities, demilitarization, or denazification. It was imperative that farm produce flow freely from the predominantly agricultural Soviet zone to the highly industrialized Western zones. It was important to speed up manufacturing and mining, so that imports could be paid for and employment could be provided. It was necessary to establish the capacity of the peacetime economy, so that the reparations due the victors could be calculated. Yet in defiance of the Potsdam agreements, the Russian representative on the Allied Control Council blocked these processes, gradually until March 26, 1946, and completely thereafter. While the United States and Britain poured aid into their zones, the Soviets withdrew from theirs huge quantities of raw materials and finished products. To continue the dismantling of industrial plants in the Anglo-American zones for delivery to Russia, while it defaulted on food deliveries to the West, would constitute, as Clay later said, indirect payments to the Soviet Union.

In the face of these difficulties, Byrnes waited until April 25, 1946, before proposing that the Council of Foreign Ministers name deputies to draft a German peace treaty. To quiet French and Soviet fears of a renascent Reich, he offered to sign a twenty-five-year alliance to insure the disarmament of that country. The pact would provide for full inspection and commit the parties to use force in case of violations. Molotov's curt dismissal of the plan, which Byrnes had been led to believe Stalin favored, coincided with the decision of the United States on May 3 to halt temporarily all reparation deliveries to the Soviet zone, pending the treatment of Germany as a single economic unit. These two events marked the end of any pretense of a common Russian-American policy.

For another year the Truman administration tried to prevent the growing division of Germany. It was especially eager to stop the Soviets from pillaging their zone. At Paris on July 11, 1946, Byrnes offered to merge the American zone with any or all others. Russia and France declined. Then at Stuttgart on September 6 he renewed his scheme for a four-power alliance to keep Germany disarmed and extended the period to forty years. He accused the Communists of breaking their Potsdam pledge by claiming excessive reparations, and he asked for the early establishment of a provisional government. The time had come, he said, when zonal limits should designate areas to be occupied for security purposes, not self-contained economic or political units. Lest there be any doubt, he asserted: "We are staying here. As long as there is an occupation army in Germany, American armed forces will be part of that occupation army."

Byrnes' firmness produced a brief ray of hope. At New York on December 12, 1946, Molotov acquiesced in appointing deputies to commence work on a German peace treaty and in putting its consideration on the agenda for the meeting of the Council of Foreign Ministers in Moscow on March 10, 1947. By then Marshall had replaced Byrnes, and Molotov had imposed another obstacle. Russia would not agree to treat Germany as an economic unit unless it received $10 billion in reparations and joint control over the Ruhr industries in the British zone. The West refused to meet those conditions. A similar stalemate ensued over the four-power alliance, boundaries, and a peace treaty. After six weeks of fruitless haggling, the Council adjourned on April 24. The end of wartime unity was clearly evident and the prospect of a divided Germany painfully obvious.

THE END OF WARTIME UNITY

The future of Germany was only one reason for the rift between the Soviet Union and the West. The marriage of convenience consummated in 1941 flew in the face of deeply rooted historical antagonisms, fiercely competing economic systems, and sharply conflicting political philosophies. A common peril had driven the incompatibles together. During the crisis mutual suspicions were, of necessity, allayed; once the struggle was won, centrifugal forces began to work again. With its addiction to secrecy, its mistrust of foreigners, and its fear of espionage Russia assumed that deadly hostility was the basis of international relations and that peaceful settlements were merely temporary truces before the next battle. Nor could Stalin resist the temptation to push forward in Eastern Europe, the Middle East, and East Asia when he found the West weary of war and eager for continued collaboration with the Soviets.

Another cause for the end of wartime unity was the power vacuum left by the destruction of Hitler's Reich and Japan's New Order. Into the void flowed an irresistible Russian tide which no modern Canute could hold back. Neither England nor China was strong enough to play the role Roosevelt had expected. The British Empire was not only a pale shadow of its Victorian grandeur but also a feebler version of the weakened state that emerged from the First World War. With its colonial ties snapping, its maritime supremacy vanished, and its economic health imperiled, England ceased to be the decisive weight in the global equilibrium. China counted for even less. Beset with the accumulated burdens of an eight-year war—inflation, corruption, and obsolescence—and faced with a resolute Communist rival at home, the Nationalists were unable, without outside help, to reclaim their own.

Certainly the United States had enough reasons in 1945 to be disillusioned. The ruthless imposition of a Communist regime in Rumania in March presaged the extinction of democracy in Eastern Europe. The vile accusations about American motives in seeking an armistice in Italy that same month foreshadowed trouble elsewhere. The struggle in April at San Francisco was a prelude to difficulties over voting in the Security Council. The separate mutual assistance pact with the Lublin group, also in April, was a foretaste of the Soviet-dominated treaty system in Eastern Europe. The demands made upon the Chinese in July at Moscow went beyond the terms of the Far Eastern Agreement at Yalta. The Control Council in Berlin got off to a bad start, and the initial session of the Council of Foreign Ministers at London in September and October broke up over differences in handling the minor peace treaties. Yet given the course of events since 1941 and the pull of wartime emotions, most Americans still wished "to get along with the Russians."

As Soviet-American relations steadily worsened during 1946, that desire ebbed. In January the opening meetings of the United Nations laid bare the disunity of the great powers. On February 9 Stalin spoke of an irreconcilable conflict between communism and capitalism. On March 5, with Truman in the audience, Churchill declared at Fulton, Missouri, that "from Stettin in the Baltic to Trieste in the Adriatic an iron curtain has descended." This was not, he said, "the liberated Europe we fought to build up." The Soviets in reply compared the Briton to Hitler. In April the Red Army withdrew from most of Manchuria, but not before stripping the province of vast quantities of industrial equipment and allowing the Chinese Communists to fall heir to large numbers of Japanese guns. Later that month Mao Tse-tung, whether on orders from Moscow or in defiance of them, broke a truce with the Nationalists which the United States had arranged. At Paris in May, Byrnes, Vandenberg, and Connally told Molotov there would be no more unilateral American concessions or, as Vandenberg said, "our 'surrender days' are over." Simultaneously Clay suspended the dismantling of plants in the American zone for reparations to the Soviets. A turning point had been reached, and Truman's dismissal in September of Secretary of Commerce Henry A. Wallace simply underlined the administration's determination "to get tough with Russia."

Looking at the other side of the estrangement, we cannot be sure of all factors that motivated the men in the Kremlin to engage in acts which progressively eroded the goodwill of the democracies. Did Stalin excite opposition at home by his concessions at Yalta? Did he raise the bogey of external threats so as to stifle internal divisions? Did he recoil in alarm at America's atomic monopoly? Final answers to those questions cannot be given, but it is clear that the Soviets deprived the West of a voice in the realignment of Eastern Europe, ignored a promise of free elections in Poland, spurned a four-power alliance to keep Germany disarmed, boggled over a Lend-Lease settlement, and violated their Yalta pledge for Asia. Undoubtedly some acts of the United States were misinterpreted, and such problems as the termination of economic aid, the supervision of Japan's surrender, the extent of Korea's freedom, the administration of the Italian colonies, and the procurement of German reparations did not appear the same in Moscow as in Washington. The Russians anticipated a struggle for supremacy between capitalism and communism; in so far as they acted upon the notion that ideological differences breed implacable hatreds, they helped foment greater hostility.

A desire for expansion and a passion for security thus led the

Soviets consciously to jeopardize big power unity. By renouncing certain objectives in Eastern Europe, the Middle East, and East Asia, they might have retained Anglo-American friendship, but thinking in terms of conventional, preatomic weapons, they considered the price too high. Russia's strategists apparently argued that its best protection was not membership in an untested league or an alliance with its wartime partners, but rather a divided Germany, together with absolute control over a broad band of territory along Germany's eastern frontier. If there could not be in Germany, then there must be in Finland, Poland, Czechoslovakia, Hungary, Rumania, and Bulgaria—even in Yugoslavia, Greece, Turkey, and Iran if possible—rulers who were not merely friendly but subservient. The paramountcy of this aim, as Arnold Toynbee has suggested, was the rock on which the coalition split; for in most of the countries in question the only kind of government that could be trusted completely was one which local Communists dominated. Yet that was the very kind which would never be chosen in a truly free election. This fact was disclosed in Poland, rightly regarded as the acid test of Soviet good faith. No regime acceptable to Stalin could be democratic in Anglo-American terms, and any which met the standards of Roosevelt and Churchill would not have been favorably disposed toward Russia. There lay the tragedy which turned wartime friends into peacetime foes.

THE UNITED NATIONS IN OPERATION

Since unanimity among the great powers was its basic concept, the United Nations in operation differed markedly from what most Americans had expected. At first all went well. The required number of ratifications was met by October 24, 1945, and the principal organs began to function in January, 1946. A month later Trygve Lie, a former Norwegian foreign minister, became Secretary-General. Although the League of Nations had transferred its properties to the new organization, there was little wish to make Geneva the permanent site. A preparatory commission recommended the United States, and in December, 1945, Congress tendered the necessary invitation. In February, 1946, the General Assembly voted to establish interim headquarters in New York City and permanent ones in the northern suburbs. After a brief stay at Hunter College in the Bronx, the Assembly was placed in a World's Fair building on Flushing Meadow, while the Secretariat and Council were installed in the Sperry gyroscope plant at Lake Success. When the residents of Westchester and Fairfield counties protested the future invasion of their privacy, John D. Rockefeller, Jr. offered $8,-500,000 to purchase a six-block area along the East River on Manhattan Island. To that convenient location, with its handsome edifices and housing headaches, the United Nations moved early in 1951.

More difficult to solve were problems of membership, armaments, and threats to peace. In most instances the rift between East and West impeded a solution. Thus during 1946–7 only six of seventeen applications for membership were approved. Of those rejected, five fell victim to the Soviet veto. From the outset Russia tended to reject any country likely to vote against its interests. The United States began by favoring the admission of all applicants but then switched to opposing those candidates—Albania, the Mongolian People's Republic, Hungary, Rumania, and Bulgaria—who had violated their treaty pledges and international obligations or who had not yet demonstrated true independence. In no case, however, did the American delegate cast a veto.

Differences among the big powers also produced a stalemate in armaments. They could not agree under Article 43 to put specific military units at the disposal of the Security Council. A similar impasse was reached in the Atomic Energy Commission, established by the General Assembly on January 24, 1946. Speaking for the United States, which then possessed a monopoly of the new bomb, Bernard M. Baruch on June 14 presented a comprehensive plan—a realistic choice, he said, "between the quick and the dead." It called for creating an international Atomic Development Authority to which would be confided ownership of "all atomic energy activities potentially dangerous to world security." This body would license and promote nonmilitary investigations in the field, and its supervision over hazardous research was to be exclusive. It would have unlimited power to inspect all phases of production and employ sanctions against nations violating their obligations under a proposed atomic-control treaty. If the plan were adopted, the United States stood ready to hand over to the Authority its technical knowledge of fissionable materials and, gradually, its stockpile of destructive weapons. To make sure that this relinquishment did not imperil America's safety, Baruch asked every signatory to forego the right of veto in enforcing the treaty.

Although the Soviets disliked inspection, their main objection was to the last stipulation. On June 19, 1946, they offered two alternative accords, one providing for the demolition of existing atomic bombs and a second forbidding their future manufacture. They refused, however, to abandon the principle of unanimity among the permanent members of the Security Council. Thus from the start the two nations diverged on three issues: the renunciation of the veto in enforcing atomic-control pacts, the right of unrestricted international inspection in carrying out such treaties, and the question of whether existing bombs should be retained pending the conclusion of a pact, as the Americans wished, or be destroyed as a condition of negotiation, as the Russians desired. This deadlock caused the Commission to vote on May 17, 1948, to suspend operations.

Lack of progress was also the story with debates on other weapons. The General Assembly resolved on December 14, 1946, that an early reduction of armaments and armed forces was necessary and recommended that the Security Council give the problem prompt attention. The latter responded on February 13, 1947, by setting up a Commission for Conventional Armaments and entrusted it with the responsibility for drafting specific measures. Again big-power rivalry proved to be an insuperable obstacle. On August 12, 1948, the Commission admitted defeat and warned that until mutual confidence was restored, nothing could be done. That atmosphere might be attained, it suggested, by negotiating military agreements under Article 43, establishing an international control of atomic energy, and concluding peace treaties with Germany and Japan.

In failing to curb armaments, the United Nations revealed a disunity which plagued its attempts to cope with threats to peace. The first of these came before the Security Council on January 19, 1946—the day after it had been organized—when Iran accused Russia of meddling in its internal affairs. During the next year seven more charges were aired: against England by the Ukraine for keeping troops in Indonesia; against England by Russia for maintaining soldiers in Greece; against England and France by Syria and Lebanon for not evacuating their armed forces; against Spain by Poland for the danger posed by Franco's regime; against England by the Ukraine for aiding the persecution of minorities in Greece; against Albania, Bulgaria, and Yugoslavia by Greece for inciting guerrillas in Greece's northern provinces; and against Albania by England for mining international waters and firing on British vessels. Although the Council helped somewhat in the Iranian episode because its discussion spotlighted the source of trouble and in the Indonesia case because its instrumentalities provided mediation, it was sorely hampered by internal bickering, propaganda oratory, and obstructive vetoes. Within a year the Soviet delegate had cast eight vetoes and set the pattern for stalking from the chamber when he was unable to choke off debate.

Thus the United Nations in operation was not the system of security its founders had envisaged. The Court of International Justice heard no cases. The lack of agreements under Article 43 and the virtual demise of the Military Staff Committee wrecked the potential police force Roosevelt had emphasized. Discord among the permanent members of the Council threatened that body with paralysis and robbed it of prestige. Yet despite a sharp reaction from the bright expectations of 1945, the American people and their government did not repudiate the commitments they assumed at San Francisco but turned to modifying the organization in the light of changed conditions. By late 1947 two trends were apparent. One was to enhance the role of the General Assembly; the other, to stress regional arrangements for collective defense. The former was manifested when the United States proposed on September 17 to create a standing body for investigating, while the Assembly was in recess, disputes impairing friendly relations. Established on November 13, 1947, by a vote of 41 to 6, with 6 abstaining, this Interim Committee was opposed by Russia, ostensibly because it usurped the duties of the Security Council, actually because it deprived Russia of a veto. The second tendency was seen in the Inter-American Treaty of Reciprocal Assistance of September 2, 1947, and in the North Atlantic Treaty of April 4, 1949.

ARMAMENTS IN THE ATOMIC AGE

Even if it had not been for the abortive joint peace, the end of wartime unity, and the changed nature of the United Nations, the problem of armaments in the atomic age would have taxed the ingenuity of the wisest leaders. Now that man had developed the means of destroying himself, could he control his fearful product? How long might the United States hope to maintain its nuclear monopoly? Did the new bomb spell the doom of conventional weapons? Had air power made ground and naval units obsolete? These and other questions set off an acrimonious debate over strategy for the postwar era that was still raging when an explosion of fissionable materials in Siberia in September, 1949, and the eruption of limited war in Korea in June, 1950, forced yet another reappraisal.

Sole possession of nuclear devices strengthened the hands of those who championed air power and those who advocated reduced spending. If, as many argued in 1945, the atomic bomb was the ultimate weapon, it was folly to waste the taxpayer's money on infantry divisions and surface fleets. Believing that land-based planes must deliver the decisive blow, air enthusiasts demanded the lion's share of the defense budget. "More bang for the buck" was the inelegant phrase that appealed to economy-minded legislators. Against such reasoning the army could not prevail. Its trained troops were hastily demobilized, and the end of selective service on March 31, 1947, badly curtailed the army's future resources. The navy fought back tenaciously. The admirals were not ready to admit they had no role to play in the atomic age. Insular outposts, they contended, were useful for tactical bombing. Aircraft carriers offered mobility and dispersal in mounting nuclear attacks. Submarines might launch ballistic missiles. Marines were needed for brush-fire wars. With these arguments the navy was allowed to place its mighty armada in "moth balls," retain important bases in the Pacific and Atlantic, and plan supercarriers capable of operating jet-propelled aircraft armed with atomic warheads.

Some of the problems posed by armaments in the postwar era came to the fore in the legislative battles over the control of atomic energy, the unification of the armed forces, and the budget for the fiscal year 1947–8. Ever since the first bomb fell on Hiroshima, Truman intended to make the manufacture and use of atomic power a governmental monopoly. Few dissented, but men differed on how completely civilians should take over a project begun under the army. In the Atomic Energy Act of August 2, 1946, Congress set up a five-man civilian commission with absolute authority over research and production in fissionable materials. It was to be assisted in scientific matters by a General Advisory Commission and in strategic applications by a Military Liaison Committee. An eighteen-man congressional body, nine from each house, would watch over the entire enterprise which was transferred to the Atomic Energy Commission on December 31, 1946.

Unification of the separate services seemed in 1945 a cardinal lesson of the Second World War and an absolute prerequisite for the atomic age. Integration under a single theater commander had proven wise in the field, but no similar fusion had occurred at high administrative levels in Washington. Although a single uniform, a single purchasing agency, and a single chain of command appealed to civilians on grounds of efficiency and economy, they flew in the face of desirable service traditions and undesirable vested interests. The National Security Act of July 26, 1947, attempted to compromise irreconcilable views. It set up a military establishment consisting of three departments—army, navy, and air force. Each had its own secretary, but all were subordinate to a newly created Secretary of Defense. The latter was the president's main counselor in this area; he alone held cabinet rank. The law gave statutory authority to the Joint Chiefs of Staff and provided for a National Security Council whose function was "to advise the President with respect to the integration of domestic, foreign, and military policies." Its members were the President; the Secretaries of State, Defense, Army, Navy, and Air; the chairman of the National Security Resources Board; and such others as the President determined. To aid the Council and to replace the wartime Office of Strategic Services, a Central Intelligence Agency was instituted. Time would reveal defects in this law, but it was a step forward in protecting the republic from the perils of the atomic age.[1]

[1] An act of August 10, 1949, established a separate Department of Defense, created the post of chairman of the Joint Chiefs of Staff, made the Joint Chiefs the military advisers to the National Security Council, and named as members of the Council the President, the Vice President, the Secretaries of State and Defense, the chairman of the National Security Resources Board, and such others designated by the President with the approval of the Senate.

One benefit expected from the National Security Act was an end to interservice rivalry for legislative appropriations and a realistic approach to military expenditures. Ironically, the budget for 1947–8, which passed at the same time, saw the navy and air force locked in a titanic bid for additional support. It also witnessed the triumph of the economy-minded in the Republican-controlled Eightieth Congress and in the Democratic-dominated Bureau of the Budget. All of this occurred in the face of an alarming situation abroad (to be described below) and at a time when the readiness of the armed forces left much to be desired. Yet the demand for retrenchment, the monopoly of the bomb, and the addiction to extreme doctrines of air power blinded both the executive and legislative branches to the kind of modern weapons and trained men needed to meet the growing menace of communism in Europe and Asia.

51

✈✈✈✈✈✈✈✈✈✈✈✈✈

The Containment
of Russia in Europe

DISAPPOINTING as was the abortive joint peace of 1945–7, it differed from the separate peace of 1919–21 in that the United States met the ensuing challenges from abroad with fortitude and determination. But where the first test of the interwar compromise did not arise until thirteen years after the armistice in the railway coach at Compiègne, the initial battle in the renewed struggle for survival came less than two years after the surrender in the schoolhouse at Reims. It came as international communism probed for weaknesses in the free world along a perimeter stretching from Western Europe through Greece and Turkey to East Asia. By a variety of measures—the Truman Doctrine, the Marshall Plan, the Berlin airlift, the North Atlantic Treaty and its Organization, and the Mutual Assistance and Security programs—the American government was able to contain Russia in Europe but, in doing so, diverted pressures to less defensible areas in the Middle and Far East.

THE TRUMAN DOCTRINE AND THE MARSHALL PLAN

Since communism thrives on misery and want, Truman began early to persuade Congress that the economic well-being of Europe was essential to the safety of the United States. Although Lend-Lease was terminated on August 21, 1945, generous appropriations enabled the United

Nations Relief and Rehabilitation Administration to carry on its wartime work.[1] The legislature also consented to the Bretton Woods Agreement Act of July 31, 1945 by which the United States and forty-three other countries created an International Monetary Fund and an International Bank for Reconstruction and Development. Even more significant was the Anglo-American Financial and Trade Agreement of December 6, 1945, which granted the United Kingdom a line of credit of $3,750,000,000 drawable through 1951 and payable in fifty annual installments at 2 per cent. When the Senate approved this loan on May 10, 1946, by a vote of 46 to 34 and the House followed suit on July 13 by a count of 219 to 155, they took the first of many steps to insure fiscal stability in a key area.

But even men properly fed, clothed, and employed might not be able to stand alone against external aggression or internal subversion. In the State Department a theory of containment, not wholly novel, was elaborated by George F. Kennan, formerly Counselor in Moscow, whom Marshall picked in February, 1947, to head a new Policy Planning Staff. Kennan traced Soviet conduct to the belief of Stalin and his circle in an irrepressible conflict with capitalism, their imperviousness to Western diplomacy and reasoning, and their preference for indirect methods which would not jeopardize the triumph they confidently expected. To cope with this antagonist, he argued, there must be "a long-term, patient but firm and vigilant containment of Russian expansive tendencies." Because the West was superior in economic potential and armed strength, it could and should apply counterforce at "a series of constantly shifting geographical and political points, corresponding to the shifts and maneuvers of Soviet policy." Kennan felt that communism contained the seeds of its own decay and that the United States might by its acts influence internal developments within Russia and the Communist movement. The question was: would Americans accept the "responsibilities of moral and political leadership that history plainly intended them to bear?"

Five months before those words appeared anonymously, the Truman Doctrine gave the answer in a ringing affirmative. By 1947 Communists held key offices in Yugoslavia, Czechoslovakia, Poland, Albania, Hungary, Rumania, and Bulgaria. A harsh winter enabled them to make impressive gains in Italy and France. Further east, Greece, Turkey, and Iran had managed—thanks to their own courage, to assistance from the United Kingdom, and to support from the United States on such matters as the Straits question and Russian intrigue in

[1] The United States spent over $50,596,000,000 on Lend-Lease—England receiving about $31,392,000,000 and Russia about $11,298,000,00. Negotiations for liquidating accounts with the former were concluded in July, 1948; those with the latter were begun in April, 1947, and are still pending.

Azerbaijan—to withstand strong Soviet pressure, but a crisis was at hand. Great Britain could no longer play its traditional role in the Middle East. On February 21 its envoy told the State Department that, as of March 31, England would have to end all economic and military aid to Greece, then racked by Communist-fomented civil strife, and that its more limited help to Turkey would soon cease.

Abrupt as this notice was, the Truman administration responded quickly. On March 12, 1947, a grim-visaged President told Congress that Greece was about to succumb to an armed minority and that not even the United Nations could save it. Its downfall, moreover, would have an "immediate and serious effect" on Turkey, would spread "confusion and disorder" throughout the Middle East, and would discourage those peoples of Europe who were "struggling against great difficulties" to retain their independence. "Totalitarian regimes," the President asserted, "imposed upon free peoples, by direct or indirect aggression, undermine the foundations of international peace and hence the security of the United States." Thus he came to the core of his message, the part later known as the Truman Doctrine. "I believe," he said, "that it must be the policy of the United States to support free peoples who are resisting attempted subjugation by armed minorities or by outside pressures. I believe that we must assist free peoples to work out their own destinies in their own way." Feeling that help should be primarily economic, he asked not for authority to use armed force but for an appropriation of $400 million with which to aid both Greece and Turkey until June 30, 1948. He also requested permission to send civilian and military personnel, if solicited, to supervise reconstruction and training.

Congress eventually gave the President what he wanted, but only after a full inquest. Stunned by the sweep of the Truman Doctrine, which in its opposition to totalitarianism reminded some of the Holy Alliance's determination to uproot republican governments everywhere, critics warned that it would bankrupt the United States, weaken the United Nations, and provoke the Soviet Union. Defenders stressed the cost of not acting, the inability of the new league to cope with the problem, and the certainty that Russia would decide for itself the time and place of the next war. They denied that the President was embarking on an ideological crusade of global proportions; they were encouraged when an amendment by Vandenberg stipulated that the program would cease whenever the recipients so desired, whenever the United Nations took steps rendering it unnecessary, or whenever the executive found that its purpose had been fulfilled or was incapable of being fulfilled. The final version—authorizing the expenditure of $100 million in military aid to Turkey and of $300 million for Greece, equally divided between economic and military assistance—was signed on May 22, 1947, after being approved in the Senate by a vote of 67 to 23 and in the House by a count of 287 to 107.

The Greek-Turkish Aid Bill was a tacit admission, grudgingly given by some, that security for the United States in the atomic age required more than membership in the United Nations. Although hastily improvised to meet a particular crisis, the Truman Doctrine had profound implications. The American government stood ready to replace a faltering Britain as the chief antagonist of international communism. In January, 1939, Roosevelt had raised a storm of protest by suggesting that America's frontier lay in France or along the Rhine; eight years later his successor persuaded Congress that the ramparts to watch were the Dardanelles and the mountains of Thrace. For the first time in its history the republic adopted peacetime military assistance as a regular tool of diplomacy. And this, needless to say, was only the beginning.

Next to demand attention was the plight of Europe. Truman's advisers, notably Under Secretary Acheson, realized that in helping Greece and Turkey they were dealing with a flooded tributary, not the rampaging main stream. At his initial meeting of the Council of Foreign Ministers in Moscow in April, 1947, Secretary Marshall talked with Stalin and came away convinced that the Soviet leader viewed with equanimity the collapse of Europe's economy. As several democratic nations careened toward disaster during the eight-week debate on the Truman Doctrine, the State Department laid the groundwork for the next move in its policy of containment. Aware that even kindly disposed legislators such as Vandenberg had been offended by the handling of the Greek crisis, when congressional support was asked for a decision already made, the executive branch carefully prepared the way at home and abroad. Two speeches—one by Acheson at Cleveland, Mississippi, on May 8, the other by Marshall at Cambridge, Massachusetts, on June 5—expressed a willingness to cooperate with those nations which agreed to coordinate their efforts for recovery. "It is logical," Marshall argued, for the United States "to assist in the return of normal economic health in the world, without which there can be no political stability or assured peace." American policy was not directed against any country or designed to be imposed on the continent. "The initiative," he asserted, "must come from Europe." The program was to be "a joint one, agreed to by a number, if not all, European nations." The enemy was "hunger, poverty, desperation, and chaos."

Anglo-French enthusiasm for what became known as the Marshall Plan was unrestrained, but Soviet comment was unfavorable. On June 27, 1947, Foreign Ministers Ernest Bevin and Georges Bidault joined Molotov in Paris, where Russia refused to participate in the scheme on the ground that it constituted meddling in internal affairs.

In no wise discouraged, Bevin and Bidault invited all the states of Europe—except Spain, and Germany, which had no government—to discuss common moves for stimulating recovery. The eight within the Soviet orbit declined, some reluctantly. Delegates from the other fourteen—Austria, Belgium, Denmark, Greece, Iceland, Ireland, Italy, Luxembourg, the Netherlands, Norway, Portugal, Sweden, Switzerland, and Turkey—met in Paris on July 12 with those from England and France. Speaking as the Committee of European Economic Cooperation, they estimated on September 22 that they could achieve self-sufficiency and stability by 1951 with $19,300,000,000 from the American Treasury and $3,100,000,000 from the International Bank.

While the sixteen nations deliberated, the United States began studies to determine how far it could embark on a large-scale foreign aid program without endangering the domestic economy. The President named three groups to appraise America's resources, and the House dispatched to Europe a nineteen-man committee headed by Christian A. Herter, Republican of Massachusetts. Armed with the fruits of these investigations, Truman recommended on December 19, 1947, that Congress authorize an appropriation of $17,000,000,000—$6,800,000,000 to be spent before June 30, 1949 and $10,200,000,000 in the following three years. The purpose, he insisted, was permanent recovery, not temporary relief. Such collaboration, he added, would prove "that free men can effectively join together to defend their free institutions against totalitarian pressures."

This proposal required courage in an election year. Confident of victory in 1948, the Republicans planned to campaign on a platform of a balanced budget and reduced spending. Russian tactics, however, eased the task of the Democratic President. The curt rejection of Marshall's offer in July, 1947, showed how completely the Kremlin had come to control the diplomacy of eight ostensibly independent states, while the formation of the Cominform (Communist Information Bureau) in September revealed how illusory had been the wartime hope that the Soviets might abandon their goal of world revolution. But it was the bloodless coup of February 25, 1948, in Czechoslovakia, where a new Communist-dominated coalition assumed power, that provoked fears for the future of France and Italy. In this gloomy atmosphere the Senate passed the administration's measure by a vote of 69 to 17 and the House by a margin of 329 to 74. Signed by the President on April 3, 1948, the Foreign Assistance Act authorized the expenditure of $5,-300,000,000 during the first twelve months. Much still had to be done in actual appropriations, but by the rapid enactment of the Greek-Turkish Aid Bill and the European Recovery Program, President and Congress demonstrated that, in an emergency, they could overcome the normal restraints of timidity, partisanship, and provincialism.

WEST GERMANY AND THE BERLIN BLOCKADE

By April, 1948, Europe was split into "Marshall Plan countries"—those engaged in a cooperative economic endeavor with the United States—and the "iron curtain bloc"—those promoting communism with the Soviet Union. This division killed what slight chance remained for the early negotiation of a German peace treaty after the Council of Foreign Ministers failed at Moscow in April, 1947, and became deadlocked at London in December. The Truman administration decided, therefore, to hasten a process begun when the Anglo-American zones were merged for mutual material benefits on January 1, 1947. Ignoring Russia's protests, on the ground Russia had violated the Potsdam pledge to treat Germany as a single economic unit, the ambassadors of the United States, England, France, Belgium, Holland, and Luxembourg met in London and on March 6, 1948, announced an agreement in principle on closer economic integration of the Western zones, formation of a federal government in Germany, participation by Germany in the European Recovery Program, and association of the so-called Benelux nations with the Western Big Three on matters pertaining to the late foe. Further talks led to recommendations on June 1 for convening a constituent assembly at Bonn to establish a West German republic, placing the Ruhr under an International Authority, keeping existing curbs on Germany's armed forces, and delaying the withdrawal of Anglo-American troops until a secure peace had been made and France had been consulted. During this period Britain, France, and the Benelux countries signed a treaty of collective self-defense at Brussels on March 17, 1948.

Some Russian riposte was anticipated. In February, 1948, after surveying the meager units ready for combat duty, Marshall had said: "We are playing with fire while we have nothing with which to put it out." On March 5 Clay cabled from Berlin that "within the last few weeks" he had detected "a subtle change" in the Soviet attitude which made him feel that war "may come with dramatic suddenness." These forebodings were justified, but they presaged a new kind of conflict—a cold war, not a shooting war. On March 20, Marshal Vassily Sokolovsky walked out of the Allied Control Council in protest against the six-power parley and the steps taken in the Western zones. On March 31 and April 1 regulations were issued requiring that passengers and baggage on military trains entering the Russian zone be checked at the border and decreeing that no rail freight could leave the capital without the permission of the Soviet authorities. The Berlin blockade had begun.

On June 24, 1948, the Russians halted all surface transportation between Berlin and the Western zones. The final squeeze grew out of a dispute over what kind of currency should circulate in the former capital and who should control it. Actually, Stalin's primary objective was to prevent the establishment of a separate West German government and to disrupt the contribution of its people to the European Recovery Program. He failed in both aims and for two reasons. The first was the sacrifice and courage of the West Berliners, who refused to crack under the ordeal. The second was the ingenuity and daring of the Anglo-American fliers, who improvised a gigantic airlift. At its peak their planes were bringing in more supplies daily than the preblockade traffic by rail and water. The airlift, together with countermeasures banning shipments into the Soviet zone, made the Russian *démarche* unprofitable, all the more so since it did not stop the constitution-making at Bonn or the success of the Marshall Plan. On May 8, 1949, a Parliamentary Council adopted the Basic Law of the German Federal Republic, and on May 12 the Western Military Governors gave it their approval. That same day the blockade ended.

Liquidating the Berlin crisis was a difficult problem. American diplomats had always insisted that the supreme authority assumed by the United States and the other conquerors of Hitler on June 5, 1945, embraced an unrestricted right of access to the capital. They also cited Clay's oral agreement with Zhukov on June 29. Unfortunately, there was no specific guarantee on paper; but it would not have made any difference if one had existed. The Russians possessed the means of sealing off the city on the ground, and they used the currency controversy as an excuse to apply them. On September 23, 1948, the aggrieved powers referred the matter to the Security Council as a threat to peace, but a Soviet veto on October 25 precluded any settlement in that arena. Only when Stalin shifted his policy did a solution come through direct negotiations. On May 4, 1949, after private talks at the Secretariat, representatives of the four nations agreed to end simultaneously the blockade and the countermeasures and then hold a meeting of the Council of Foreign Ministers. The sixth session of that ill-starred body, the first since December, 1947, and the last until January, 1954, wrangled in Paris from May 23 to June 21, with only a confirmation of the agreement of May 4 to show for its efforts. As Secretary Acheson remarked: "At the end of four weeks of talks, it is agreed that the blockade shall not be reimposed. That is something, not much, but it is something."

Although the restoration of access to Berlin removed a threat of war, it did not improve the legal position of the United States. The communiqué issued by the foreign ministers on June 21, 1949 did not provide an ironclad pledge against future interference. It simply obliged the occupation authorities "to take the measures necessary to insure the normal functioning and utilization of rail, water, and road

DIVIDED
GERMANY
AND
AUSTRIA

BERLIN'S CHANNELS TO THE WEST

DIVIDED
GREATER BERLIN

transport." Nor did the lifting of the blockade solve the German problem. That issue was the focal point in the clash between East and West, and there could be no relaxation of tensions while it remained unsettled. Yet in 1949 a treaty for a unified Germany was impossible. Hence, as the Cold War grew more menacing in Asia too, the Truman administration saw no alternative to the early inauguration of the Federal Republic and its prompt integration in the European Recovery Program. Civil rule began in West Germany on September 21, 1949, as the three zones merged, as an Allied High Commission replaced the military regime, and as Konrad Adenauer became Chancellor. The occupying powers, however, maintained troops on West German soil and reserved to themselves not only the conduct of foreign relations but also the supervision of disarmament and the Ruhr industries. In a not unexpected move, the Soviet Union created the German Democratic Republic in East Germany on October 7, 1949.

THE NORTH ATLANTIC TREATY AND NATO

To contain Russia in Europe, the United States had resorted by 1949 to the Truman Doctrine, the Marshall Plan, the Berlin airlift, and the organization of a friendly West German government. These moves were successful as far as they went. The continental economy showed signs of revival, while the Communists suffered heavy losses in the French and Italian elections. Yet the coup in Prague and the blockade of Berlin suggested that economic recovery, if not backed by military capability, might still leave individual democracies at the mercy of the totalitarian colossus. A regional arrangement for collective self-defense, as provided for in the United Nations Charter, seemed the way out; and precedents existed in the Inter-American Treaty of Reciprocal Assistance, signed by the United States and eighteen New World republics at Rio de Janeiro on September 2, 1947, and in the Western Union, signed by France, England, and the Benelux countries at Brussels on March 17, 1948.

On that last date Truman expressed his confidence to Congress that the United States would "by appropriate means" help the free nations of Europe to protect themselves. Already there was much support, some of it Republican, for supplementing the Marshall Plan with military aid or a promise to the Western Union to go to war if any member was attacked. But nothing could be done until the Foreign Assistance Act was signed on April 3, 1948. Then Under Secretary of State Robert A. Lovett and Vandenberg went to work on a resolution that bore the Senator's name. Introduced on May 11 and passed by a vote of 64 to 4 on June 11, it recommended that the United States associate itself, "by constitutional process, with such regional and other collective arrangements as are based on continuous and effective self-help and mutual aid." A similar declaration, approved by the Committee on Foreign Affairs, was not acted upon by the House before it adjourned on June 19. Enough legislative backing had been obtained, however, to encourage the administration to proceed with the next bulwark of containment, the North Atlantic Treaty of April 4, 1949.

No act better exemplified the abandonment of isolationism than this alliance. In order to insure peace in a specified region, the United States and eleven other nations—England, France, Canada, Belgium, Italy, Holland, Luxembourg, Iceland, Denmark, Norway, and Portugal —undertook to develop by self-help and mutual aid "their individual and collective capacity to resist armed attack." They promised to consult together whenever the territorial integrity, political independence, or security of any of the signatories were threatened. Most importantly, they agreed in Article 5 that an armed attack against one of them in Europe or North America should be considered an attack on all and that in those instances each would assist the victim "by taking forthwith, individually and in concert with the other Parties, such action as it deems necessary, including the use of armed force." These measures would be reported to the Security Council at once and be terminated when that body had acted to restore peace. The treaty had to be ratified "and its provisions carried out by the Parties in accordance with their respective constitutional processes." It was to last ten years and could be adhered to by any other European state that was invited unanimously to do so.

As a barrier against a Russian invasion of Western Europe with conventional weapons, the North Atlantic Treaty was generally popular. By withholding an absolute guarantee of armed assistance to members under attack, the framers had preserved the legislative prerogative to declare war. In spite of Truman's scathing assault on the Republican-controlled Congress in the recent election and his sudden sponsorship of Point Four at his inauguration,[2] the postwar emphasis on bipartisanship in foreign affairs persisted. Acheson removed one fear when he incautiously told the Foreign Relations Committee on April 27, 1949, that there was no plan to send substantial numbers of new troops to Europe. Taft and two other Republicans, Kenneth S. Wherry of Nebraska and Arthur V. Watkins of Utah, vainly urged three reservations. One disclaimed any obligation on Congress to declare war if a signatory was attacked. A second required legislative

[2] Without prior consultation, the President recommended on January 20, 1949, that Congress embark upon a bold new course for making the benefits of American science and industry available to lesser-developed areas. This was the final item in a four-point foreign policy—the other three being support of the United Nations, extension of the European Recovery Program, and conclusion of regional arrangements for collective self-defense.

approval before American units were assigned to participate in joint defense efforts. A third denied that the United States was bound, legally or morally, to furnish weapons or equipment to its allies. No more than twenty-one votes could be mustered for any of the reservations, and the Senate gave its unqualified consent on July 21, 1949, by a count of 82 to 13.

Out of this document eventually grew a complex structure known as the North Atlantic Treaty Organization or NATO. The process began with the formation at Washington on September 17, 1949, of the North Atlantic Council, the supreme policy-making body provided for in Article 9. Normally meeting once a week to supervise the work of its numerous committees, the NATO Council later arranged for two sessions a year attended by the foreign ministers and at which the heads of government might be present. Next came the drafting of plans for defending the North Atlantic area and an integrated military force. On December 19, 1950, Eisenhower, then President of Columbia University, was appointed Supreme Commander of the Allied Forces in Europe with headquarters near Paris. In February, 1952, at Lisbon, the NATO Council reorganized the civilian structure by creating a Secretary-General—a post held first by Lord Hastings L. Ismay of Britain and then by Paul-Henri Spaak of Belgium—and by obtaining the appointment of Permanent Representatives to the Council at Paris. Lastly, new members were added. On September 20, 1951, the NATO Council recommended that Greece and Turkey be invited to join, and they did so in a protocol of October 17 which extended the area covered by Article 5 to those countries and to the men, ships, and aircraft of the signatories while they operated in the eastern Mediterranean. The Senate gave its consent on February 17, 1952, by a vote of 73 to 2. Another protocol, signed on May 27, 1952, would have linked the German Federal Republic to NATO through a new European Defense Community, but French opposition to that approach delayed West German membership until October 23, 1954.

THE MUTUAL ASSISTANCE AND SECURITY PROGRAMS

In itself, the North Atlantic Treaty was a diplomatic gesture rather than a military bulwark. The commitment to employ force was not ironclad; and even if the United States did retaliate against a Russian drive westward by bombing the Soviet Union, liberation would be a long and perhaps futile process. Thus the strategic corollary of the pact was a mutual assistance policy, designed to arm the new allies to a point where they had some prospect of containing the invader if he relied on conventional weapons. Although an all-out assault by the Red Army would be unstoppable, NATO's troops were expected to provide a thin line of protection until America's air force, operating from bases at home and abroad, hit back at Russia with atomic warheads.

Congressional authorization for peacetime military assistance was difficult to obtain. The successful collaboration between the executive and legislative branches and between the Democratic and Republican leaders, which had eased the passage of so many key measures commencing with the United Nations Charter, was ending. Bipartisanship could hardly survive the Republican disappointment in 1948, the disaster in China in 1949, and the administration's lack of candor when the North Atlantic Treaty was before the Senate. At the very time its spokesmen were denying an obligation to send arms abroad, planners were estimating that it would cost $30 billion to equip the new allies. Such a sum, twice that to be spent in over four years under the Marshall Plan, was not possible to contemplate, and even Vandenberg regarded as "too big" Truman's request of July 25, 1949 for $1,450,000,000 to cover twelve months. Thus many harsh words were spoken before the measure cleared the Senate by a margin of 55 to 24 and the House by a tally of 223 to 109. Even then the amount would have been less if it had not become known five days before the key vote that Russia had exploded a nuclear device.

The Mutual Defense Assistance Act of October 6, 1949, authorized the expenditure by June 30, 1950 of $1,341,010,000 in military aid. The NATO countries received $1,000,000,000; Greece and Turkey, $211,370,000; Iran, Korea, and the Philippines, $27,640,000; and the "general area" of China, $75,000,000. Materials could be transferred and equipment bought as best suited the needs of the beneficiaries, but all transactions must be governed by bilateral executive agreements. Both the president and Congress were empowered to terminate the assistance whenever its continuance was found to be inconsistent with the interests of the United States or its obligations to the United Nations. To insure a prompt carrying out of the North Atlantic Treaty, only $100,000,000 of the $1,000,000,000 allocated to the NATO countries could be used until the president approved the Council's recommendations for an integrated defense of the area. That step was taken on January 27, 1950; shortly thereafter the necessary executive agreements were concluded.

Prior to June, 1950, military aid was subordinate to economic assistance in American foreign policy. For the fiscal year ending that month, $100,000,000 was spent for the former and $3,400,000,000 for the latter. With the invasion of South Korea and the end of the atomic monopoly, the emphasis shifted. In each of the next four years appropriations for military help averaged about $4,500,000,000, while those for economic rehabilitation declined to less than $2,000,-000,000. This change was reflected in the Mutual Security Act of

October 10, 1951, which combined under one program and one agency the purposes and activities initiated by the Foreign Assistance Act of April 3, 1948, the Mutual Defense Assistance Act of October 6, 1949, and the Act for International Development of June 5, 1950, the last of which put Point Four into practice. In general, the new law sought the same strategic goals as had its predecessors and left the executive with broad authority to negotiate bilateral agreements on matters once dealt with in treaties. It was, however, a more complex statute and revealed a growing distrust of the State Department, a lessening enthusiasm for Point Four, and a more critical attitude toward the NATO countries.

Before the President signed the Mutual Security Act of October 10, 1951, an angry debate broke out over another aspect of the military assistance program. The frustrations of the Korean War were primarily to blame, but a subsidiary cause was Acheson's assurances to the Foreign Relations Committee on April 27, 1949, that the United States was not expected to send additional troops to Europe under the North Atlantic Treaty. In spite of a drastic change in the world situation seventeen months later, many Republicans regarded his words as a binding pledge and objected indignantly when Truman announced on September 9, 1950, that, on the advice of his chief civilian and military aides, he was ordering "substantial increases in the strength of the United States forces" in Western Europe. The aged Hoover fired the opening gun on December 20, contending that the protection of Europe was the responsibility of the allies, who had yet to demonstrate their unity or purpose. He would give priority to building up the air and sea power of the United States and to transforming the New World into a "Gibraltar of Western Civilization." Taft concurred, although he disagreed with "those who think we can . . . rely solely on the defense of this continent." In a speech of January 5, 1951, he opposed committing more divisions to Europe and denounced what he termed executive usurpations and deceptions. Three days later Wherry introduced a resolution expressing the opinion of the Senate "that no ground forces of the United States should be assigned to duty in the European area for the purposes of the North Atlantic Treaty pending the formulation of a policy with respect thereto by the Congress."

Thus was joined at a critical hour in the history of the free world the perennial battle for control of American foreign policy. The executive was intent on exercising his prerogative as commander-in-chief to station units where he saw fit; the legislature was insistent that its war-making power not be curtailed. But enough people believed in NATO to permit a face-saving compromise. The President, as Republican Senator H. Alexander Smith of New Jersey said, "needs Congress and public opinion behind him and the way to get it is to have Congress share in the decision." Two distinguished generals lent their support. On February 1, 1951, Eisenhower, just back from an inspection tour, secretly asked the lawmakers for a flexible approach; a fortnight later Marshall, recently recalled to be secretary of defense, publicly stated that only four divisions would go to Europe, a number considerably smaller than some being bruited about. Thus on April 4 the Senate adopted by a vote of 69 to 21 a resolution sponsored by John L. McClellan, Democrat of Arkansas, which approved the designation of Eisenhower as Supreme Commander, urged that the military and other resources of West Germany, Italy, and Spain be utilized for the defense of Europe, and recommended that the President consult in these matters with the appropriate congressional committees as well as with his civilian advisers and the Joint Chiefs. It also endorsed the present plan to dispatch four divisions abroad but maintained that, "in the interests of sound constitutional processes, and national unity," no additional troops should be deployed under the North Atlantic Treaty without further congressional authorization.

During the four years separating the Truman Doctrine of March 12, 1947, and the McClellan Resolution of April 4, 1951, the containment of Russia in Europe met with some success. The westward surge of the Red Army had been checked. The airlift had preserved part of Berlin from being submerged in the surrounding Soviet sea, while the German Federal Republic had developed into a potential buffer. The Marshall Plan had revived the economy of free Europe, and the North Atlantic Treaty was being gradually transformed from a diplomatic gesture into a military alliance. The Mutual Assistance and Security programs had given hope that the alliance might eventually be effective. But all was not gain. By the close of 1949 the atomic monopoly had ended, continental China had fallen to the Communists, and the Republic of Korea was in peril.

52

Disaster in China

IN THE incessant struggle for survival which has characterized American diplomacy since 1939, the most unexpected calamity was the disaster that overtook China in 1949. The loss to the free world at so critical a moment of a country with untapped resources and untold man power was a major catastrophe. Together with the agonies and frustrations of the limited war in Korea that began in 1950, it was largely responsible for the bitter recriminations which divided the American people as the Roosevelt-Truman era closed and which obscured the many constructive and successful policies of those years.

POSTWAR JAPAN

Any appraisal of America's postwar record in East Asia must note the nation's part in turning an autocratic, bellicose Japan into democratic, peaceful ways. Although the coalition had defined at Cairo, Yalta, and Potsdam the territorial losses the vanquished must suffer, it had given little attention to the problem of occupation. Not until August 11, 1945, did the United States propose to England, Russia, and China that General Douglas MacArthur be designated Supreme Allied Commander and be empowered to coordinate the Japanese surrender. Moving with dispatch and aided by the fact that only American troops had landed in the home islands, MacArthur launched there a regime which made the Emperor subject to his will and the United States the spokesman for the nations fighting Japan.

Stalin disliked this beginning. He had expected Russia to have a zone of occupation, but Truman wished to keep full control in American hands. After four months of bickering, the foreign ministers of the Big Three reached an agreement on December 26, 1945. It called for an eleven-nation Far Eastern Advisory Commission and a four-power Allied Council for Japan. The former—composed of representatives of the United States, England, Russia, China, France, Australia, Canada, India, New Zealand, the Netherlands, and the Philippines—had headquarters in Washington and was responsible for shaping policy and reviewing acts of the Supreme Commander. The Commission could not deal with military operations or territorial adjustments, and the delegates of the first four countries had to concur in every decision. The Allied Council—limited in membership to the United States, the British Commonwealth, the Soviet Union, and China—sat in Tokyo and exercised purely advisory functions. Although MacArthur was supposed to consult the Council on matters of substance, "the exigencies of the situation permitting," he attended only one session.

MacArthur brought to his task a unique personality and a dedicated spirit. Regal in bearing, imperious in manner, versed in Asia's history, and convinced of his destiny to rebuild the empire he had helped crush, the general combined in one being the twentieth-century war hero, the nineteenth-century proconsul, and the ninth-century Mikado, the Viceroy of Heaven on earth. Physical destruction and territorial losses were serious obstacles to recovery, but MacArthur found the Emperor cooperative, the extremists discredited, and the people reconciled to defeat. The average citizen freely admitted the collective guilt of the nation; unlike his German counterpart, he did not place all the blame on dictatorial rulers. He was truly grateful to the American soldier who brought not only food but also pity. The contrast with the atrocities committed by the Japanese military after the capture of Nanking in 1937 and Bataan in 1942 could not be ignored.

The occupation wrought vast changes in three areas: demilitarization, democratization, and social organization. Japan was stripped of its empire and confined to the four home islands. The armed forces were disbanded and the war-making potential diminished. The Emperor disavowed his divinity; the older leaders were purged and, in some cases, tried as war criminals.[1] These steps did much to promote democracy; further help came from the dissolution of patriotic organizations and the police in charge of thought control. Also important was the constitution that went into effect on May 3, 1947. An amalgam of American and British practices, it bore the imprint of MacArthur's thinking and of Japanese desires. The document renounced war "for-

[1] The International Military Tribunal for the Far East, composed of members from eleven nations, sat in Tokyo from May, 1946, to November, 1948. It decreed death for seven of the twenty-eight persons tried.

ever" and denied the right to maintain an army, navy, and air corps. It declared that sovereignty rested with the people, not with the Emperor. It incorporated a detailed bill of rights and a judicial system resembling that of the United States. As in England, however, the legislature, or Diet, was supreme. In the social and economic sphere the occupation broke up huge commercial combines, encouraged labor unions, restricted the holdings of landlords, and drastically reduced farm tenancy. Whether these changes would be permanent remained to be seen, but the transformation of Japan's society and government was regarded in Washington and much of the free world as an initial success.

Concluding a peace treaty was more difficult. As with Germany, Byrnes wanted a prior accord on disarmament and demilitarization. He sought a twenty-five-year agreement that gave England, Russia, China, and the United States the right of inspection and obliged them to take action if Japan broke its word. Although Stalin seemed favorably disposed in December, 1945, Molotov brusquely rejected the scheme seven months later. On July 11, 1947, therefore, the United States suggested that the eleven nations represented on the Far Eastern Advisory Commission discuss peace terms, but the Soviets objected. Arguing that the wartime conferences had reserved that task for the Big Four, they proposed to refer the matter to the Council of Foreign Ministers. Because that Council had not been able to agree on a German or Austrian settlement and because Japan's future was important to others—notably to Australia and the Philippines—Truman refused. For two more years he hesitated in the face of a cruel dilemma. To sign a Japanese peace treaty without the Soviet Union would expose the United States to the charge of violating its pledges; to attempt one on Soviet terms, including the veto, might destroy all the benefits accomplished in the islands.

By December, 1949, a decision was imperative. The occupation had achieved its primary goals, and the time had come to see whether Japan could stand alone as a peaceful member of society. Retaining an alien administration over the Japanese government was costly and hurt the economy. External pressures were also at work. The loss of China to communism and the tensions of the Cold War indicated that, as in Germany, a former foe might be helpful against an erstwhile friend. The invasion of South Korea in June, 1950, injected another element. Strategic considerations, always present, became paramount. Control of the bases in Japan must be continued, for they were vital arteries through which men and matériel flowed to the battlefield. The airstrips there and on Okinawa constituted privileged sanctuaries from enemy attack. In September, 1950, the President instructed John Foster Dulles, then a consultant to the State Department, to begin negotiations in earnest, despite protests from Moscow, for a treaty that would preserve America's favored position. The intervention of Communist China against the United Nations in Korea won support for Dulles' endeavors, but the key to his success was the concession that representatives from neither Tapei nor Peking be invited to participate, thus permitting Japan to determine later with which of the two Chinas it would deal. Under those conditions Britain consented to cosponsor a general conference.

On September 4, 1951, delegates from fifty-two nations met in San Francisco to ratify, in effect, what had already been agreed upon. The chief absentees were India, Yugoslavia, Burma, and the two Chinas. Although the Russians had declined to collaborate in the preliminary drafting, they attended—along with Poland and Czechoslovakia —in a vain effort to defeat or amend the work Dulles had done so well. But the latter, ably supported by Acheson and Assistant Secretary Dean Rusk, overcame all obstructionist maneuvers, and on September 8 the Japanese peace treaty was signed, with the Soviets abstaining. The result was a victory for bipartisanship in American foreign policy.

It was also a triumph for magnanimity. Only in the loss of territory did Japan fare badly. It was obliged to renounce all claims to Formosa, the Pescadores, the Kuriles, southern Sakhalin, and the mandated islands; to recognize Korea as independent; to accept the decision of the Security Council in placing the Marshalls, Carolines, and Marianas under a United States trusteeship; and to concur in a future move to do the same for Okinawa and the Bonins. Japan also had to acquiesce in a temporary American occupation of those two groups. The treaty declared Japan to be free and sovereign, with a right to enter into regional arrangements for collective defense. All occupation forces must be withdrawn in ninety days, but the government in Tokyo could retain foreign troops on its soil through agreements with one or more of "the Allied powers." Membership in the United Nations was to come in time. Japan also gave up all special privileges in China and assented to the judgment of the International Military Tribunal. As to reparations, the treaty stated that Japan lacked the capacity to pay, but it committed the country to negotiating with those victors who desired compensation for damages.

Six years earlier, such terms would have been unthinkable; but the onset of the Cold War, the loss of China, and the fighting in Korea made a rearmed Japan seem a desirable outpost of the free world. In Asia some neighbors disliked the leniency, but the Senate did not. On March 20, 1952, it gave its consent by a vote of 66 to 10. The one reservation was aimed at Russia. It declared that nothing in the treaty was to be interpreted as ceding to the Soviet Union the right of Japan to the Kuriles, southern Sakhalin, or any other territory held by it on December 7, 1941, and that senatorial approval did not imply American recognition of the provisions of the Far Eastern Agreement of February 11, 1945.

At San Francisco the United States concluded two other treaties to fortify its position in the Orient. On September 1, 1951, it entered into a defense pact with Australia and New Zealand, similar to one signed with the Philippines in Washington on August 30. In both documents the parties recognized that an armed attack in the Pacific on any one of them was dangerous to the peace and safety of the others, and they agreed to consult whenever their territorial integrity, political independence, or security was threatened. Each promised "to meet the common danger in accordance with its constitutional processes," but no commitment to use armed force was required. On September 8 a security treaty with Japan supplemented the peace settlement of that date. Conceived of as a temporary measure, it granted the United States exclusive rights to dispose its land, sea, and air forces "in and about Japan" so as to maintain order in East Asia and protect the Japanese against attack from without or disturbance from within. Aid against internal riots, however, had to be specifically requested. The treaty would expire when the United Nations or regional pacts provided for Japan's safety. Executive agreements would determine the conditions governing the deployment of American troops, ships, and planes; one was signed on February 28, 1952. The Senate regarded all three measures as an integral part of the Far Eastern peace settlement, and on March 20 it approved the Philippine treaty by 66 to 10, the Japanese treaty by 58 to 9, and the ANZUS treaty without a vote.

THE CHINESE CIVIL WAR

More decisive in the Cold War than the rapid metamorphosis of Japan from foe to friend was the sudden reversal of China from associate to antagonist. It is easy to argue today that, in a world of bipolar power, the Chinese Communists would inevitably receive support from the Soviet Union and the Nationalists from the United States—that every move should have been based on that premise. Yet in 1945 many intelligent and loyal men thought another outcome possible. They did not regard an armed clash between the followers of Chiang Kai-shek and Mao Tse-tung as inescapable. They hoped the wartime partnership might continue, and in wishing to broaden the base of the Kuomintang government, they were not trying to promote communism. They knew the difficulties which beset that unhappy land, and only a few called the Communists agrarian reformers. They did not discount Russia's ambitions in East Asia or rule out its repudiation of past pledges. But they can hardly be blamed for not predicting on V-J Day that Stalin would shift his support to Mao. As late as December 6, 1945, Ambassador Hurley, a bitter critic of the Far Eastern specialists, told the Foreign Relations Committee that the Chinese Communists were not getting help from Moscow.

Actually, there was little disagreement among the policy makers in September, 1945, as to how the United States should proceed. It had three options. One was to let China settle its internal problems without external interference. A second was to insure Nationalist supremacy by extending unlimited aid. The third was to mediate between the factions. Each course had its merits, but only the last was feasible, given the military situation in Asia and the climate of opinion in America at the time Japan surrendered. Immediate withdrawal would satisfy the demand to bring the boys home and avoid involvement in a civil war, but it would handicap Chiang Kai-shek in his race to occupy North China before the Communists did so. Full-scale backing of the Generalissimo was impossible because of the magnitude of the commitment; no president could use troops for such a purpose when confronted with pressure for speedy demobilization. A mediation designed to avert strife and to promote rehabilitation would, if successful, rescue the United States from its predicament and enable China to play its role as a great power.

If successful—that was the nub of the issue. Today it is widely believed that the task was hopeless and, therefore, should never have been attempted. Such was not the contemporary appraisal. There was indeed a profound divergence of views among Foreign Service officers stationed in Asia as to the democratic nature of Chinese communism and the reactionary character of the Kuomintang, but there was no thought in Washington of substituting Mao for Chiang. Hull, Stettinius, and Byrnes all hoped to forge a coalition, and even Hurley sought that goal. He brought the rival chieftains together for friendly talks before he left for a short leave on September 22, 1945. On November 26 he suddenly resigned, and shortly thereafter hostilities erupted on the mainland.

What had gone wrong? Probably neither side negotiated in good faith, although we cannot be sure. Perhaps each counted on outside help, but again evidence is lacking. What is clear is that mutual suspicions were aroused in Washington and Moscow, as well as in Chungking and Yenan, by a plethora of problems ranging from the occupation of Japan and the surrender of the Kwantung Army to America's role in the race for North China and Russia's part in the seizure of Manchuria.

MacArthur's order of August 17, 1945, specifying the forces to which the Japanese must capitulate, ignored the Communists. Their field general, Chu Teh, vainly protested and then flatly disobeyed a directive to remain in Shantung and Chahar. Fanning northward, his men disarmed the Japanese and made contact with the Red Army in Manchuria early in September. Meanwhile Lieutenant General Albert C. Wedemeyer, commanding the China Theater, had been instructed to use all means at his disposal to airlift the Nationalists to key cities and junctions. South of the Yangtze and along the coast, he had no trouble; in the north some 50,000 marines had to be landed to help Chiang reoccupy Peking, Tientsin, and Tsingtao. By October, Mao's followers were complaining that "American intervention" was aiding their rivals.

Russia's actions in Manchuria also contributed to the growing tension. The Red Army accepted the Japanese surrender as arranged but did not in September, 1945, begin the evacuation Stalin had promised. His generals quickly perverted the intention of both the Yalta agreement and the Chinese treaty. Industrial centers were stripped of machinery under the guise of war booty; prisoners were sent to Siberia instead of being repatriated. Chu Teh's forces were allowed to filter into the southern sector, while Chiang's envoys were harassed and compelled to leave. Worst of all, the Generalissimo was denied use of the Dairen gateway; and when transports bearing his troops were diverted to Hulutao and Yingkow, at a Soviet request, they found those ports in Communist hands. As a result, Chiang's soldiers had to march overland to Manchuria, and Chu Teh's attempts to halt that advance in mid-November threatened to touch off a full-blown civil war.

Three months after V-J Day the Truman administration had to reassess its China policy. In doing so, it considered several incisive analyses written by Wedemeyer from November 14 to 23, 1945. The general stated bluntly what might be expected of Chiang Kai-shek. By introducing thorough reforms, Chiang could control South and Central China, but he was too weak to extend his rule to North China without an agreement with the Communists or into Manchuria without the permission of the Red Army. Wedemeyer suspected Stalin's intentions, doubted whether Chiang and Mao could be reconciled, and advocated a three-power trusteeship over Manchuria until the rest of China was stabilized. He warned that if the United States wanted the country unified under the Nationalists, it must undertake the task of enlarging its forces there, run the risk of a clash with the Soviet Union, and accept the possibility of involvement in civil war. Truman could not contemplate that solution. Trained troops were not available; and if they were, neither sound strategy nor public opinion would permit their use. His problem was to get the marines out of China, not to send the army in. Since it was impossible to withdraw completely, the most logical course was still pacification and unification. To accomplish that most difficult task, the President called upon General George C. Marshall, who had just retired as chief of staff.

Marshall's instructions received close scrutiny from Truman, Byrnes, the Joint Chiefs, and the general himself. As formulated on December 15, 1945, they sought to develop a united, democratic China and to assure its sovereignty over Manchuria. The first steps were to secure a truce in the north and to call a national conference representing all shades of opinion. The marines would remain for the time being, and additional Chinese troops and matériel would be transported in American vessels to Manchurian ports. Loans, military advisers, and technical assistance might be promised, but Chiang was to be told that substantial American aid would not go to a strife-torn land. In a public statement the same day Truman asked for an end to hostilities but insisted that the Chinese must solve their domestic quarrels without foreign interference. He would continue to recognize Chiang's regime as the legitimate one, but he saw no prospect of real peace until its base had been broadened.

At first the Marshall mission prospered. Interference with the movement of Chiang's forces into Manchuria stopped. Mukden and Changchun were in Nationalist hands by December 12, 1945. Outwardly Stalin seemed cooperative, although he had probably begun to support Mao Tse-tung, at least indirectly. Less than three weeks after arriving in Chungking, on January 10, 1946, Marshall helped arrange a cease-fire, during which no troops were to shift positions except the Nationalists advancing into Manchuria. The same day a conference of all parties and nonparty groups opened and there Chou En-lai, speaking for the Communists, acknowledged the leadership of Chiang Kai-shek and disavowed any desire to establish a separate government. Provisions were made on January 31 for drafting a new constitution, commencing on May 5, and for a coalition to replace the Kuomintang cabinet until that charter went into effect. On February 25 Marshall won promises for a gradual reduction and redistribution of the rival armies which, by September, 1947, would leave the Nationalists with fifty divisions and the Communists with ten.

This bright outlook soon faded and then vanished. On March 11, 1946, Marshall flew to Washington to report to the President. During his absence a hasty and perhaps calculated withdrawal of the Red Army from Manchuria led to clashes between Nationalists and Communists. Four days before he returned on April 8, Mao Tse-tung repudiated the cease-fire order. With great difficulty Marshall patched up another truce on June 6 and made slight gains in reweaving the tangled threads of agreement. But he now faced an increasingly angry Mao and a recklessly confident Chiang. On June 24 the former demanded the evacuation of all American troops from the mainland and the termination of all economic aid to his rival. In September the latter permitted his men to attack towns in North China held by the Communists for over a year. Extremists on both sides ignored public appeals by Truman, and pressure in the form of an arms embargo did not work. As the Nationalist tide reached its flood, the Communists cast aspersions on Marshall's impartiality. Chou En-lai's return to Yenan on November 19, 1946, in effect, brought the mediation to a close. Sensing that his services were no longer wanted, the general asked to be recalled. That step was announced on January 6, 1947, and the next day the President nominated him to be secretary of state.

THE COMMUNIST TRIUMPH ON THE MAINLAND

Once again the American government had to reappraise its China policy. Once again Truman affirmed his determination to work through the Nationalist regime, to seek an end to domestic strife, and to refrain from intervening in a civil war. Marshall voiced a plague on both sides and blamed his failure on reactionaries within the Kuomintang and on doctrinaires among the Communists. Actually, neither he nor the President was ready to try a new approach, and during 1947 the course of the United States was largely one of drift. This invitation to disaster can be explained on several grounds. First, there was no sense of urgency. Although Marshall had warned Chiang he could never prevail by force, few Americans expected the Communists to win. This feeling was especially strong early in 1947. Second, there was the legacy of failure. For the first time in a distinguished career Marshall had been unable to cope with a complex problem. Quite naturally he preferred to concentrate on other areas. Third, there was the immediacy of graver issues. One month after taking office Marshall was swept up in the chain of events that led to the Truman Doctrine, the Greek-Turkish Aid Bill, and the European Recovery Program. To him Europe seemed, as it had since 1939, the more dangerous front in the struggle for survival.

Not everyone shared the administration's views. As 1947 wore on, Republican leaders urged greater military and economic assistance to Chiang Kai-shek. If the Truman Doctrine was intended to strengthen free peoples resisting armed minorities and outside pressures, and if Greece and Turkey were getting substantial aid, then surely, Vandenberg and Dulles argued, a loyal wartime associate was entitled to more help. But the most important challenge came from General Wedemeyer, whom Truman sent to China during the summer to survey conditions and make recommendations. Like Marshall, Wedemeyer deplored the corruption of the Kuomintang and warned Chiang he could never crush his rivals by force, but in his report of September 19 he emphasized what was good for the United States, not what was wrong with the Nationalists. The defeat of the latter would imperil American security. The fighting, Wedemeyer said, must be ended at once; and since Russia was uncooperative, he would refer the problem to the United Nations. He also felt that in Manchuria, China must temporarily accept a five-power guardianship or a United Nations trusteeship. For its part, the United States must mount a bold program of military and economic support, lasting at least five years. It should be contingent upon Chiang's promise to initiate sweeping political and social reforms.

Wedemeyer's confidential report presented Truman with a difficult choice. Mediation to avert war and broaden the base of the Kuomintang government had failed. So had a limited program of military and economic aid, for it had helped the Nationalists just enough to antagonize Mao's followers and the Russians and yet not enough to consolidate Chiang. In September, 1947, Wedemeyer thought—perhaps he simply hoped—that there was still time to save the day short of full-scale armed intervention by the United States—with all its risks of a clash with the Chinese Communists or the Red Army. In retrospect, it is clear that only a wholesale commitment stood any chance of success; but with the situation in Europe worsening and trained man power unavailable, neither the President nor the Joint Chiefs dared embrace it. Still, the executive branch showed an astonishing lack of leadership. It did little to ward off the impending disaster or prepare public opinion. It did almost nothing to seek the collaboration of those Republican leaders who had demonstrated their allegiance to a bipartisan foreign policy. As a consequence, the moves to avert catastrophe were haphazard and futile.

Attempts to do more for Chiang Kai-shek became evident late in 1947. The Generalissimo lent encouragement by telling visiting congressmen on October 11 that if he were defeated, it would not be because of the Russians or Communists but because the United States had withheld vital assistance in his hour of peril. This charge was unfair, but on November 5 Dewey denounced Truman for trying to impose a coalition on the Nationalists and subordinating the needs of Asia to those of Europe. When the administration sought interim aid for France, Italy, and Austria until the Marshall Plan went into operation, the House insisted upon including China in the law of December 17, 1947. The Foreign Assistance Act of April 3, 1948 contained a sum of $338 million for China, of which $125 million was for the purchase of arms. Because of unavoidable delays, only $60 million worth of military equipment was shipped during the rest of 1948, and most of it did not arrive until November.

By then, however, the Nationalists were paying the price for disregarding sound tactics. Against the advice of every American general since 1945, they had isolated their best troops and newest weapons in the cities of North China and Manchuria, at the end of tenuous supply lines that ran through hostile territory. A Communist offensive, which started slowly in the spring of 1948, gathered momentum in the autumn. Chinchow, a main depot for the forces in Manchuria, fell on October 15. Changchun and Mukden were next. By early November the Communists controlled all Manchuria and had overcome their inferiority in numbers and equipment. The Nationalists had lost about 400,000 men and most of their American-made guns and cannon. They had also lost the will to fight.

In Washington the debacle of the Kuomintang was watched with mixed emotions. The administration refused to be stampeded into military intervention and thereby risk touching off the Third World War. In reply to Chiang's frantic appeals, Truman said on November 13, 1948, that all possible aid was being rendered, but Vandenberg disagreed. Learning that the National Security Council had recommended halting a shipment of arms lest it fall into Communist hands, he begged the President on February 9, 1949, to let the China question be settled "*by China* and *in China* and not by the *American government in Washington.*" He saw no chance of stopping the Red tide, but he declined to be responsible for giving Chiang "the final push into disaster." Others demanded more positive action, and fifty senators endorsed a plan to provide $1,500,000,000 in economic and military assistance. Acheson, who had succeeded Marshall, opposed the idea. The Nationalists, he wrote Connally on March 10, had lost no battles in the past year for want of ammunition and equipment. To reverse the current trend, he warned, would require "an unpredictably large American armed force in actual combat" and direct "involvement in China's fratricidal war." The mammoth aid measure never passed.

Chiang's situation was beyond redemption. Widespread desertion and wholesale surrender caused his defenses to collapse like a house of cards. In January, 1949, the Communists captured Peking and destroyed the main Nationalist force north of the Yangtze. Flushed with victory, Mao spurned peace feelers, demanding unconditional surrender and the trial of Chiang as a war criminal. His armies burst across the Yangtze on April 20, overwhelmed Shanghai on May 25, engulfed Canton on October 14, and reached Chungking on November 30. On December 8, Chiang fled to Formosa. Ten weeks earlier, on October 1, 1949, the People's Republic of China had been proclaimed at Peking with Mao Tse-tung as President and Chou En-lai as Foreign Secretary.

THE NATIONALIST GOVERNMENT ON FORMOSA

Post-mortems on the disaster in China were inevitable, but the bitterness they assumed in 1949–50 must be attributed to politics, to personalities, and to revelations of past Soviet espionage in government circles. The Republicans had never been fully associated with decisions affecting Asia; hence they were free to criticize as they would not have been if a similar setback had occurred in Europe. Acheson was less to blame for the China policy than Byrnes or Marshall, but he was a more vulnerable target. His desire to set the record straight also drew protests. On August 5, 1949, even before Chiang quit the mainland, the Secretary released a volume of documents selected from the Department's files and known as "The White Paper." It contained a prefatory letter and a historical summary in which Acheson reviewed the events of the last five years, charged the Kuomintang with corruption and ineptitude, and defended the Truman administration to the hilt. "Nothing that this country did or could have done within reasonable limits of its capabilities," he concluded, "could have changed the result." The Communist victory "was the product of internal Chinese forces, forces which this country tried to influence but could not."

History will probably confirm that contemporary verdict; but as Nationalist China crashed in ruins, the self-righteous tone offended many Americans, especially those who saw in Chiang, with all his faults, the best hope of halting communism in Asia. Acheson's refusal to admit that any real mistake had been made since V-J Day, or even at Yalta, stung the Republicans. Some accused the Democrats of bad judgment; others, of virtual treason. On February 9, 1950, Senator Joseph R. McCarthy began to develop his thesis that subversion in high places was responsible for the loss of China and the nuclear monopoly. Two widely publicized trials made his unsubstantiated charges credible to many citizens. On January 20 Alger Hiss, a former State Department officer who had played a prominent but unimportant role at Yalta, was convicted of perjury growing out of a denial that he had acted as a Soviet spy in the 1930's. On February 3 it was learned that Klaus Fuchs, a German-born physicist, had passed top-secret information to Moscow while working in the United States during the war on the atomic-bomb project.

Quarrels with the past rarely solve problems of the present, and late in 1949 a new China policy had to be devised. The White Paper offered no clue to the administration's thinking, except to underline an earlier Acheson statement that one could not act wisely "until the dust had settled." But the Republicans wanted action. The moderate Senator

H. Alexander Smith of New Jersey, after touring the Far East, recommended on December 1 that the United States, with Chiang's permission, occupy Formosa. The more bellicose Senator William F. Knowland, Republican of California, joined Hoover on January 2, 1950, in urging naval protection, if needed, for the Nationalists on Formosa and the Pescadores. Taft concurred in that view, although Vandenberg dissented.

Truman and Acheson also disagreed. Both the National Security Council and the Joint Chiefs of Staff warned against moves for which men and equipment were not available. The President stated unequivocally on January 5, 1950, that Chiang's refuge would not be converted into an American base. The government did not intend, he added, to pursue a course which might lead to involvement in the Chinese civil war or require military aid to the Nationalists on Formosa. On January 12 Acheson explained this reasoning in detail before the National Press Club. Claiming that China's interests in the Orient differed from Russia's, he argued that the proper policy was to avoid deflecting Chinese hostility from the Soviet Union to the United States. Sound military strategy, he went on, did not include defending Formosa, for the perimeter vital to the nation's security in the Pacific ran along the Aleutians through Japan and the Ryukyus to the Philippines.

The other question to be settled in the dreary winter of 1949–50 was whether to recognize the People's Republic. Even before Mao Tse-tung had established his government, Knowland had sought assurances that the President would not desert the Nationalists to deal with the Communists. On July 1, 1949, Acheson wrote Connally that the Foreign Relations Committee would be consulted on the matter. On October 12 the Secretary outlined the traditional criteria—control of the country, support by the people, fulfillment of international obligations—and implied that Mao's regime met none of them. The arrest later that month of the American consul at Mukden and the outrageous treatment of him and his staff seemed to kill any thought of early recognition.

How long nonrecognition would have lasted, if it had not been for ensuing events, is impossible to say. Control of the mainland by the People's Republic grew stronger each month. Russia extended recognition on October 2, 1949, and England followed on January 5, 1950. By June 25, 1950, the Peking government enjoyed diplomatic relations with three more NATO partners, six Soviet satellites, and seven other countries. Yet to regard Mao Tse-tung rather than Chiang Kai-shek as the rightful ruler of China would, in the opinion of most Americans, run counter to historic friendship, common decency, and national security. It would appear as a base desertion of a faithful wartime associate, an undoubted benefit to a potential peacetime foe, and a needless endorsement of a dangerous alien ideology. In short, the situation was still fluid when the outbreak of limited war in Korea and the intervention of Communist China therein froze the policy of the United States into an adamant refusal to recognize the government in Peking.

53

Limited War in Korea

IF THE DISASTER in China was the most unexpected calamity in the continuing struggle for survival, the limited war in Korea was the most frustrating. Although the episode involved a gallant response to an attack upon the interests of the United States and the entire free world, it left behind extremely bitter memories and undeservedly tarnished reputations. Its importance cannot be exaggerated. From the military point of view it exposed the folly of relying so heavily on atomic bombs, showed the need of rearming quickly with conventional weapons, and laid bare the difficulty of enlisting popular enthusiasm for a peace without victory. From the constitutional point of view it revealed again the historic contest between president and Congress over the war-making process. From the diplomatic point of view it was a vindication for the United Nations, a setback for Communist China, a windfall for Nationalist China, and an inducement to bring West Germany and Japan into the system of security designed to contain international communism.

THE EMERGENCE OF TWO KOREAS

Korea seemed in 1945 an improbable battle site. Unlike China, Japan, and the Philippines, the rugged peninsula had never figured prominently in American foreign policy. Blaine did not look beyond saving shipwrecked seamen or opening ports to external trade; Roosevelt did not object to an impotent regime's being absorbed by Japan; Wilson did not pay any attention at Paris to an exiled leader named Syngman

Rhee. After Pearl Harbor, Korea attracted attention mainly because it belonged to the Japanese and was a conquest which must be taken from them. At Cairo on December 1, 1943, Roosevelt, Churchill, and Chiang Kai-shek declared that "in due course Korea shall become free and independent," a sentiment Stalin endorsed at Potsdam on July 26, 1945. The key words were "in due course." None of the four men thought that a people without experience in self-rule could stand alone; all felt some kind of tutelage was imperative. But no details had been worked out before Japan capitulated.

A routine military operation in August, 1945, did much to bring about the unexpected emergence of two Koreas. The sudden collapse of Japan required a quick decision on who would accept the surrender of its troops and disarm them. The United States had only enough ground forces in the forward area to take care of the home islands, and its contingents from Okinawa did not reach Honshu until August 30. By then the Russians had occupied every major city in Manchuria and, having entered Korea from the northeast on August 12, were in a position to overrun the entire peninsula. As a protective device, therefore, the Joint Chiefs directed MacArthur to specify in his order of August 17 that the enemy should submit to the Red Army north of the thirty-eighth parallel and to United States elements south of it. On September 8 the first American soldiers, transported from Luzon, went ashore at Inchon, and the advance Soviet units dutifully withdrew to their assigned sector.

This temporary division, intended only to facilitate surrender, froze into a permanent demarcation under the chilling blasts of the Cold War. Yet that outcome was not foreseen, and it developed slowly. At Moscow on December 26, 1945, Byrnes, Bevin, and Molotov agreed that a Joint Commission, representing the American and Soviet commands, should assist the Koreans in establishing a single provisional government which, after a five-year four-power trusteeship, would gain full independence. But difficulties arose almost immediately thereafter. As in Germany, the Red generals looked upon their zone as an area to exploit and communize. As in Germany, they refused to treat the nation as an economic unit. The result was that the thirty-eighth parallel became an impediment to both political unification and economic rehabilitation. The northern part of the country contained most of the heavy industry and supplied the rest of the peninsula with 70 per cent of its electric power. The southern portion was predominantly agricultural but possessed the main communication centers. A hermetically divided Korea would leave each half unhealthily dependent on outside resources.

Little is to be gained by tracing the breakdown of the Moscow agreement during 1946 and 1947. The dissipation of wartime cordiality was partly to blame; so was the inability of the Joint Commission to decide which political groups should participate in forming the new government. When unification by bilateral action proved impossible and when on September 4, 1947, Molotov rejected a quadrilateral approach, the Truman administration took the problem to the United Nations. On September 17 Secretary Marshall proposed in the General Assembly that each occupying power hold an election in its zone, that a United Nations commission be present to observe the balloting and to aid in forming a central government, and that the new regime arrange with the United States and the Soviet Union for an early withdrawal of their troops. A vituperative Russian reply argued that Korea was a question for the Big Four alone. Thus the Soviet bloc abstained when the Assembly voted 41 to 0 on November 14 to hold legislative elections throughout Korea on March 31, 1948, and to create a Temporary Commission to oversee the proceedings.

As was expected, Russia and the satellites boycotted the Commission. The Ukrainian member declined to serve; the Red Army commander refused access to his zone. After another sharp debate, the Interim Committee of the General Assembly instructed the Commission to execute its mission in those areas open to it. The elections in the American sector on May 10, 1948, certified as valid by the observers, led to the adoption of a constitution on July 12, the choice of Syngman Rhee as President on July 20, and the launching at Seoul of the Republic of Korea on August 15. In the north the elections of August 25 were not watched by the Temporary Commission, and on September 9 a Democratic People's Republic began to function at Pyongyang under Kim Il Sung. Since each government professed to speak for all Korea, denounced its rival as traitorous, and vowed to unify the peninsula by its own efforts, the outlook for peaceful coexistence was dim.

With two Koreas in being, the United States had to decide when to remove its troops, how to provide economic aid, and whether to rely on the United Nations to protect Rhee's republic. On the first issue the Russians enjoyed an advantage. With their zone closed to outsiders, they could claim to have withdrawn their forces when they had not, and in any case, they had systematically trained and armed the North Koreans. The Americans operated in the full glare of publicity and had erred on the side of underequipping the South Koreans lest the volatile Rhee be tempted to carry out his promise to unify the land by the sword. On December 25, 1948, the Soviets announced that the Red Army had been evacuated. Since both MacArthur and the Joint Chiefs preferred to have their limited man power in Japan rather than on the mainland, Truman and Acheson decided to heed the admonitions of the General Assembly, and they removed the last occupation units on June 29, 1949.

Substantial material support was needed to make the Republic of Korea's economy viable. The United States had already spent vast sums on relief, rehabilitation, and surplus arms. Now the administration tried to do for Korea what the Foreign Assistance and Mutual Defense Assistance Acts were doing for Europe. On June 7, 1949, the President requested an appropriation of $1,500,000,000 for the period ending June 30, 1950, and Acheson told a closed session of the House Foreign Affairs Committee that without economic aid Rhee's government would fall within three months. Truman got only a part of what he had asked for, since many congressmen were disgruntled by his decision not to defend Formosa and argued that it was senseless to waste money on the more vulnerable peninsula. But even if the executive and legislature had made greater efforts, time did not remain for insuring the defenses or the prosperity of the new republic.

For a year before June, 1950, an uneasy calm, broken by periodic border violations, hung over the rugged land. As Kim Il Sung's army was bolstered by regiments returning from service with the Communists in the Chinese civil war, it became evident that an ordeal by battle was only a matter of months. Although the Defense and State Department foresaw an invasion from the north, they had—like the Roosevelt administration concerning a raid on Pearl Harbor—accepted the danger in theory without providing for it in practice. As early as March 1, 1949, MacArthur had told a British journalist that America's defensive perimeter did not include Korea but extended from the Philippines through the Ryukyus, Japan, and the Aleutians to Alaska. On June 8 the State Department said of South Korea, in explaining the withdrawal of the occupation forces: "It is only through continued support by the entire community of nations to which that republic owes its existence that the security and stability of this new nation can be assured." Thus it was not a novel prescription that Acheson offered the National Press Club on January 12, 1950. Obliged to justify the President's refusal to make Formosa an American outpost, the Secretary drew the same defense line that MacArthur had, one which excluded both Chiang's island refuge and Rhee's mountainous domain. He did not imply that the United States was indifferent to the fate of Korea or would not heed a Communist assault. In case of aggression, Acheson asserted, "the initial reliance must be on the people attacked to resist it and upon the commitments of the entire civilized world under the Charter of the United Nations." How far the North Koreans, or their Russian mentors, viewed his words as a green light, we do not know, but this faith in the United Nations to respond instantaneously and with arms to a breach of the peace was about to be put to the test.

THE DEFENSE OF SOUTH KOREA

Saturday, June 24, 1950, found Washington in the middle of a summer week end. Truman was in Missouri and Acheson in nearby Maryland. Although the Central Intelligence Agency had charted a steady build-up of North Korean forces along the thirty-eighth parallel, the cablegram that arrived from Seoul at 9:30 in the evening caught most people by surprise. At dawn the army of Kim Il Sung had begun to drive south in what appeared to be "an all-out offensive." Still, the situation resembled that of September 18, 1931, more closely than that of December 7, 1941, and, like Stimson, Acheson had to be make sure the attack was not simply a localized, unauthorized raid. He dissuaded the President from flying home that night, but he alerted Trygve Lie, who realized at once the larger meaning of the incursion. "My God," he exclaimed, "this is war against the United Nations."

In a sense Lie was correct. The United Nations had brought the Republic of Korea into being; its demise would constitute an irreparable loss of prestige. Yet the steps Truman subsequently took were not aimed solely at preventing a repetition of the fate which befell the League in Manchuria. The United States had additional reasons for wanting to check the assault; its own interests coincided with the need for preserving the organization created five years earlier. Thus the defense of South Korea was more than a vindication of the abstract principle of curbing aggressors. It is unlikely that the American government would have responded the same way if Rhee's forces had been the ones to cross the thirty-eighth parallel. In short, the ensuing limited war was also a phase of containment, another attempt to stem the surge of Russian power. It was undertaken, too, to convince the NATO partners that if a similar crisis arose in Europe, they would not stand alono.

Was the invasion of June 25, 1950, a Soviet probe for soft spots in the free world? Who made the decision to drive south? At first, it was widely assumed that the North Koreans had acted under orders from the Kremlin, and that the Truman administration's insistence on meeting the challenge with limited means and for the limited purpose of repelling the invaders reflected a fear of being diverted from the more vital European front. Later it was suggested that the absence from the Security Council at so critical a moment of Yakov A. Malik, who was then boycotting that body for its refusal to unseat Nationalist China, indicated that the Soviets were caught by surprise and that Kim Il Sung unexpectedly pulled the trigger of the gun others had loaded. Still later, after Communist China had intervened, some argued that Mao Tse-tung was responsible for the move. Actually, although the evidence is not complete, the decision originated in Moscow, not in Pyong-

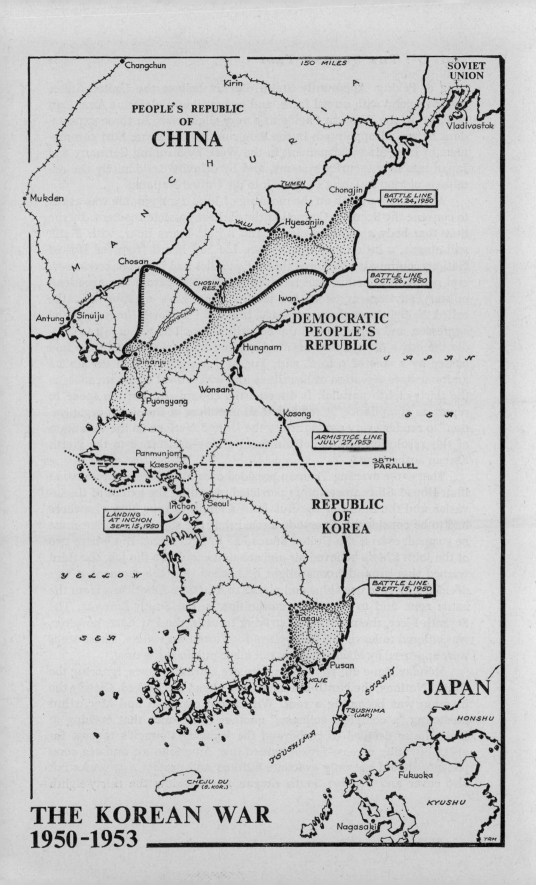

Changchun

Kirin

150 MILES

SOVIET
UNION

Vladivostok

PEOPLE'S REPUBLIC
OF
CHINA

M · A · N · C · H · U · R · I · A

TUMEN

Chongjin

BATTLE LINE
NOV. 24, 1950

Mukden

YALU

Hyesanjin

Chosan

CHOSIN
RES.

BATTLE LINE
OCT. 26, 1950

Iwon

Antung · Sinuiju

YALU

CHONGCHON

DEMOCRATIC
PEOPLE'S
REPUBLIC

J · A · P · A · N

Sinanju

Hungnam

Wonsan

Pyongyang

Kosong

S · E · A

ARMISTICE LINE
JULY 27, 1953

Panmunjom
Kaesong

38TH
PARALLEL

YELLOW

Inchon · Seoul

REPUBLIC
OF
KOREA

LANDING
AT INCHON
SEPT. 15, 1950

BATTLE LINE
SEPT. 15, 1950

Taegu

S · E · A

Pusan

KOJE
I.

TSUSHIMA STRAIT

JAPAN

HONSHU

TSUSHIMA
(JAP.)

TSUSHIMA

CHEJU DU
(S. KOR.)

Fukuoka

KYUSHU

THE KOREAN WAR
1950-1953

Nagasaki

TRM

yang or Peking. Apparently Stalin did not believe the United States would respond with armed force, and he hoped to undermine American defenses in the Western Pacific at a very slight risk. In these expectations he was disappointed; in the long run the adventure hurt communism by hastening rearmament in the West, by bringing Germany and Japan into new security systems, and by delaying indefinitely the admission of Mao Tse-tung's regime into the United Nations.

About three o'clock on the morning of June 25, 1950, Lie was asked to convene the Security Council at the earliest possible moment. By the time that body assembled eleven and a half hours later, with Malik still absent, a little more was known. Lie had heard from the United Nations commission in Korea that the parallel had been pierced at several points; MacArthur had received frantic pleas from the American military advisers at Seoul for ammunition. Lie's opening remarks called the fighting a threat to peace, branded the North Koreans as the aggressor, and denominated the Security Council as the organ to handle the crisis. By six that evening a revised American resolution had passed by a vote of 9 to 0, with Yugoslavia abstaining. It demanded an immediate cessation of hostilities and withdrawal of the invaders to the thirty-eighth parallel. It directed the commission on the scene to report on compliance. It requested all members of the world organization "to render every assistance to the United Nations in the execution of this resolution and to refrain from giving assistance to the North Korean authorities."

That same evening Truman presided over a top-level conference at Blair House. Since uncertainty persisted regarding the extent of the invasion and the intent of the Russians, a simultaneous blow elsewhere had to be considered. Everyone agreed that the southward drive must be stopped, even if the United States had to fight alone. But where two of the Joint Chiefs believed air and sea units could do the job, the third warned that ground troops might be needed. For the moment it was decided simply to use ships and planes to evacuate Americans from the battle zone and to dispatch ammunition to the South Koreans. The Seventh Fleet, the main naval striking force in the Far East, however, was ordered to leave the Philippines for Formosan waters. These steps were approved by MacArthur but not made public at the time.

Monday, June 26, 1950, brought more alarming news. Ignoring the United Nations, the North Koreans drove ahead unchecked. Clearly the invasion was becoming a rout. With Seoul captured and MacArthur predicting "a complete collapse," another conference that evening at Blair House decided to go beyond the Security Council's request for aid in effecting a cease-fire. It agreed that American air and sea components should not only evacuate citizens and protect exit routes but also cover and support South Korean forces below the thirty-eighth parallel. The Seventh Fleet was to be ordered to insulate Formosa and to prevent attacks in either direction. All these decisions anticipated authorization by the United Nations or Congress. The next morning Truman briefed the legislative leaders and issued a statement to the press. The reaction was gratifying. Dewey telegraphed his approval, while the Republican New York *Herald-Tribune,* in praising the President's "magnificent courage," said "it was time to draw a line—somewhere." The House broke into applause on hearing the news. There was some grumbling in the Senate about the war-making power, but Knowland asserted that Truman deserved bipartisan backing.

On Tuesday evening, June 27, 1950, the Security Council passed an American proposal. Malik rejected Lie's bid to return, and hence there was no veto when the vote stood 7 to 1, with Yugoslavia opposed and India and Egypt abstaining. The text recommended that members of the United Nations furnish such assistance to the Republic of Korea as was needed to repel armed attack and restore peace in the area. Thus the purpose of the sanctions was to end the fighting, not to unify the peninsula.

As the initial excitement subsided, the inevitable criticism arose. The extension of the defensive perimeter to include Formosa seemed to reverse the Truman-Acheson argument of five months before, and many Republicans on Capitol Hill called upon the Secretary to resign. The champions of Chiang Kai-shek objected to insulating his island refuge and demanded that his veteran regiments be utilized in Korea or elsewhere on the mainland. The fact the Congress had not declared war—indeed, had barely been consulted—bothered others. In the Senate on June 28, 1950, Taft questioned the President's right to order troops into battle without legislative authorization, even in support of the United Nations. But he blamed the method, not the move, and said he would have voted for armed intervention if that issue had been presented. The next day Truman brushed aside as partisan the call for Acheson's resignation and insisted the country was not at war. It was trying, he said, to suppress a bandit raid. He then accepted as accurate a reporter's description that the United States was engaged in "a police action under the United Nations."

But the navy and air force was unable to halt the North Korean advance. Late on June 29, 1950, the National Security Council considered a limited use of the army—service troops to maintain transportation and communication lines, combat troops to guard docks and airstrips at Pusan, a key port on the southwestern tip of the peninsula. Truman hesitated; then, encouraged by Acheson's estimate that Russia did not intend to act, he gave his consent. He also approved a plan to allow ships and planes to hit military targets above the thirty-eighth parallel. But this was not enough. At dawn on June 30 the President

received from MacArthur, who found Rhee's forces "completely disintegrated," a request for permission to land one regimental combat
team in Korea immediately and two divisions as soon as possible. Truman agreed to the first step but for the second preferred to employ
Chiang's veterans rather than the green occupation units in Japan.
Acheson and the Joint Chiefs persuaded him, however, of the logistic
difficulties and diplomatic dangers he ran by injecting the Chinese Nationalists into the fray. Thus by early afternoon MacArthur had been
empowered to put two divisions into Korea at once and subsequently
to utilize all ground forces under his command. Simultaneously a naval
blockade was clamped upon the peninsula's long, indented coastline.

That decision of June 30, 1950, turned a police action into a war.
Yet it was a limited war in that it was fought for limited goals and with
limited means. The experience was a new one for the American people,
and a further novelty consisted in the fact that the government was
waging its first war as a member of the United Nations. There was no
formal declaration. Individual lawmakers were consulted, but Congress as a whole was not asked to exercise its cherished prerogative. It
is easy to understand why Truman hesitated on Monday to magnify
what might be only a border skirmish. The gradual commitment of
troops during the week demonstrated his antipathy to embarking hastily on all-out hostilities. It is also simple to comprehend why he did
not, as late as Friday, June 30, 1950, request the customary joint resolution. The pace of modern warfare had outrun the leisurely procedure
of the Constitution. With each hour vital to success, the President may
be forgiven for wishing to avoid a protracted discussion on Capitol Hill.
But no one has explained satisfactorily why, in the ensuing weeks, the
executive did not seek legislative approval for his *faits accomplis*. He
could have had it for the asking, all the more easily because the critics
of his Asian policy would have been silenced by MacArthur's recommendations. Perhaps the President hoped to discourage Russian intervention by not acknowledging that a war existed, but thereby he stored
up trouble for the future.

THE INTERVENTION OF COMMUNIST CHINA

The next five weeks were a nightmare. Outmanned, outgunned, and
often outfought, the inexperienced Americans and poorly armed South
Koreans were pushed back steadily until they held only a small perimeter around Pusan. Reservists were mobilized; reinforcements dispatched; rearmament speeded up. Marshall was again called from retirement, now to be secretary of defense. But the embattled defenders
did not fight alone. The Security Council—by a vote of 7 to 0 on
July 7, 1950, with Russia absent and three abstaining—recommended

that members make military contributions to a unified command under the United States and requested the American government to designate a commander of the combined operations. The following day Truman appointed MacArthur. By September 15 Australia, Belgium, Canada, France, Greece, the Netherlands, New Zealand, the Philippines, Thailand, Turkey, the Union of South Africa, and the United Kingdom had responded. The United States and the Republic of Korea did supply most of the man power, but Britain and France were then combatting international communism in Malaya and Indochina.

Retreat into the Pusan beachhead ended on August 6, 1950. As fresh levies arrived from home, plans were matured for a counterattack in the form of a two-pronged pincers movement. On September 15, the X Corps landed behind the enemy's lines at Inchon and slashed eastward to Seoul. The next day the Eighth Army broke out of the perimeter and drove northward, making contact on September 26. By October 1 Rhee was back in his capital, the North Koreans lacked an organized force below the parallel, and MacArthur was issuing an appeal to the foe to lay down his arms.

Should the United Nations carry the war into North Korea? On that question there were widespread differences. Some saw in the turn of the military tide a golden opportunity to unify the peninsula. Others warned that to give the aggressor time to recover behind the frontier would bring further assaults. Still others feared that Communist China would intervene rather than see the North Koreans crushed or the fighting approach China's border. On September 15, 1950, the Joint Chiefs authorized ground operations north of the thirty-eighth parallel provided there were no large concentration of Russian or Chinese Communists there. South Korean units pierced the line with impunity on October 1. Six days later the General Assembly adopted a resolution which created a new committee on unification, recommended means of insuring stability, and mentioned three times that the aim of the United Nations was to establish "a unified, independent and democratic government." This, ostensibly, was a mandate for MacArthur's command to move forward. The resolution passed by a count of 47 to 5, with 7 abstentions. The next day American patrols ventured for the first time beyond the old frontier, and on October 10 Truman announced that he was flying to Wake Island to confer with MacArthur. On October 11 the Peking radio quoted Chou En-lai as saying that his country would not stand idly by while a neighbor was wantonly invaded.

Thus the stage was set for a dual tragedy, the breach between Truman and MacArthur and the intervention of Communist China. Although the general endorsed the President's decision to defend South Korea, he abhorred the notion of fighting for limited goals with limited means. "The object of war," he often asserted, "is victory"; and there could be no victory until the foe was defeated. Asia-minded since his youth, MacArthur disliked the priority given to Western Europe in American diplomacy. Suspecting alien and even Communist influences in the State Department, he bridled at administration orders to keep silent on policy issues. Eventually he came to believe that Marshall, Acheson, and Truman were conspiring against him; but until he tasted defeat, he managed to suppress those emotions. At Wake on October 15, 1950, MacArthur assured the President that resistance would end in Korea by Thanksgiving. He did not think the Chinese Communists would intervene; but if they did, they could not put more than 60,000 men into North Korea.

His estimate was fallacious on both counts. Ever since August, 1950, Chou En-lai had been accusing the United States of instigating the Korean War and of menacing the Peking regime by armed aggression in the Formosa Strait. He had warned that his government would act if the thirty-eighth parallel was breached, and during October veterans of the civil war crossed the Yalu for a secret build-up that numbered 200,000. But to MacArthur the battle seemed won. Pyongyang was captured on October 19. The X Corps was put ashore on the east coast. By October 26 advance elements of the Eighth Army were just short of the mouth of the Yalu, while a few South Koreans actually reached that stream to the northeast. Simultaneously, however, the presence of Chinese "volunteers" was discovered in many places in the northern mountains.

MacArthur was annoyed by this disclosure but not dismayed. On November 5, 1950, he claimed publicly that the war had been won until the Chinese Communists, in one of the most lawless acts in history, had moved without any notice of belligerence into Korea from "behind the privileged sanctuary" of adjacent Manchuria. Privately, he demanded in Washington authority to bomb the Yalu bridges, but it was denied. The Joint Chiefs, confused by his contradictory statements, were content to hold a defensive position along the Chongchon River–Chosin Reservoir line. The State Department, intent on securing a condemnation of Communist China in the General Assembly, was eager to avoid alienating delegates already worried by MacArthur's flamboyant utterances. Their apprehensions proved to be well founded. The Supreme Commander's communiqué of November 24 announced the start of a "massive compression envelopment" of "the new Red armies" in northern Korea. It described glowingly a pincers movement which, if successful, "should for all practical purposes end the war." Two days later, as the Eighth Army moved up the west coast, it was hit by an overwhelming Chinese counterattack. The next day the X Corps in the east ran into forces so obviously superior in size that retreat became imperative. On November 28 MacArthur declared that "an entirely new war" had begun, one posing issues which lay beyond the scope of his command and which "must find their solution within the councils of the United Nations and the chancelleries of the world."

Again disaster had struck. Again casualties mounted. Again retreat became a daily event. But this time the American troops were not inexperienced; they had simply encountered an adversary of equal skill, who was willing to trade lives for miles. The Eighth Army fell back on Pyongyang and abandoned it on December 5, 1950. The X Corps broke out of a gigantic trap to reach the port of Hungnam but evacuated it on December 24. Two days later the Chinese crossed the thirty-eighth parallel and on January 4, 1951, retook Seoul. Not until January 25 was Lieutenant General Matthew B. Ridgway, the new commander of the Eighth Army, able to hold a firm line across the peninsula, about sixty miles below the parallel and eighty-five north of the Pusan perimeter.

Meanwhile Acheson moved to have Communist China condemned as an aggressor. Chou En-lai's arrogance facilitated his task. From Peking came the demand on December 22, 1950, for the withdrawal of all foreign troops from Korea, the removal of all American forces from the Formosa area, and the admission of the People's Republic to the United Nations. Still, the Secretary encountered caution when he emphasized on January 17, 1951, that the Chinese had "no intention of ceasing their defiance" of the world organization. The Asian-Arab bloc felt that formal censure would hinder a negotiated peace. Others feared that the imposition of sanctions could, in view of the Sino-Soviet alliance of February 14, 1950, lead to a general war. Hence, despite cries on Capitol Hill for prompt action, Acheson agreed to delay in applying sanctions, pending efforts by a new Good Offices Committee. The resolution adopted on February 1, 1951, found Communist China guilty of aiding those who had committed aggression and of being an aggressor itself. It called again for a termination of hostilities and a withdrawal of troops; it reaffirmed the purpose of the United Nations to meet force with force. The vote was 44 to 7. India and Burma joined the Soviet bloc in the negative; Sweden, Yugoslavia, and seven Asian-Arab states abstained.

FRUSTRATIONS AND RECRIMINATIONS

One reason for caution in dealing with Communist China was a deep distrust in the United Nations of its military commander. Almost every member believed that the war in Korea must be a limited one. The goal should be a restoration of the situation on June 25, 1950, in the hope that peaceful unification might ultimately follow. To persuade the Chinese to retire beyond the Yalu, there must be no bombing of Manchuria and no invasion from Formosa. Truman, Acheson, and Marshall concurred in that view. They preferred a temporarily divided Korea to the risk of provoking Russian intervention. They were convinced that international communism posed a greater threat to the free world in Europe than in Asia. They wished to restrict the fighting, not enlarge it, and to disengage with peace and honor if possible. To become involved in a major struggle on the mainland would, in the words of General Omar N. Bradley, chairman of the Joint Chiefs of Staff, be waging "the wrong war, at the wrong place, at the wrong time, and with the wrong enemy."

Such ideas had never found favor with MacArthur, and after his disastrous November offensive, they became anathema to him. Yet the ensuing clash was not between the civil and the military, for the Joint Chiefs agreed with Truman and Acheson. Rather, it raised the question of whether the man charged by the Constitution with control of diplomacy and the armed forces could tolerate open disagreement by a theater commander. For the general's complaints about not being allowed to bomb Communist China or use Chiang's veterans became public knowledge, and to a people frustrated by a novel limited war, the privileged sanctuary of Manchuria and the idle regiments on Formosa became symbols of a conflict which an inept or cowardly administration could not or did not wish to win.

MacArthur, then, insisted upon seeking total victory. The argument that Korea was not the place to fight a major war fell on deaf ears. He did not know of or care about the dangers in other areas which, according to Marshall, made it foolhardy to commit the bulk of America's ground forces to the Orient. On December 30, 1950, MacArthur asked for authority to blockade the China coast, destroy its industrial capacity by aerial attack and naval gunfire, and release Chiang's garrison for diversionary action on the mainland. When his request was denied, he warned that he might have to pull out of the peninsula unless his policy was adopted. Then on January 25, 1951, Ridgway undercut his argument by starting a slow advance that inflicted heavy casualties on the foe and recaptured Seoul on March 7.

As the battle again neared the thirty-eighth parallel, Truman decided to join other members of the United Nations in a new bid for a cease-fire before invading North Korea. MacArthur not only dissented but also sabotaged the forthcoming White House move with a manifesto of his own on March 24, 1951. By anticipating the President and antagonizing the enemy, he transformed a tentative offer to negotiate into a stern demand to submit. Truman now knew he had no choice but to remove the general, yet he wavered until MacArthur wrote to the Republican leader in the House, in a letter published on April 5, saying: "It seems strangely difficult for some to realize that here in Asia is where the Communist conspirators have elected to make their play for global conquest . . . that here we fight Europe's wars with arms while the diplomats there still fight it with words." Having thus criticized the administration's policy of giving priority to Europe and of limiting the war in Korea, he concluded sententiously: "There is no substitute for victory."

Nor was there an alternative to what followed. No president could longer endure these deliberate attempts to thwart his decisions and to encourage his political opponents to reverse them. Yet it took pluck to subject a deservedly popular war hero to humiliation and to expose an already much-criticized administration to further abuse. But the nettle was grasped. On rereading the record, Marshall said that MacArthur should have been ousted earlier. The Joint Chiefs argued that, from a military point of view, it was imperative to have a "more responsive" theater commander. Efforts to cushion the blow failed, and word of his dismissal from his United States and United Nations commands reached MacArthur, rather brutally, in a newscast on April 11, 1951.

The general's triumphant return to the United States, the emotional outpouring that greeted him, and his poignant address before Congress on April 19, 1951, lie beyond the scope of this account. So do the highly publicized but largely inconclusive hearings by the Foreign Relations and Armed Services Committees of the Senate that laid bare the divergent prescriptions for coping with aggression in Korea. Although the testimony produced much ammunition for critics of the administration, it generated no pressure to alter the present course. Far from insisting upon MacArthur's idea of victory, the people acquiesced in Truman's policy of limited war. They listened to the general with affection but did not endorse his solution. It was too expensive in lives, too barren in results, too likely to invite catastrophic retaliation.

Such slight attraction as MacArthur's recipe may have had was destroyed by other events as the Senate hearings drew to a close. Ever since March, 1951, the pendulum of battle had swung in a decreasing arc on either side of the thirty-eighth parallel. Ridgway's advance had carried him ten miles beyond that line when, on April 11, he was named to replace MacArthur. On April 22 the Chinese counterattacked, recrossed the frontier, and almost reached Seoul. After a month their momentum was spent, and Ridgway's successor quickly liberated all but a tiny portion of South Korea and occupied a slightly larger amount of North Korean soil. That was the situation on June 23 when Malik intimated that a cease-fire might be possible. The next day Lie declared that Ridgway was empowered by the Security Council to conclude an armistice which left political matters for later discussion. After a delay caused by differences on where to conduct the negotiations, talks got under way on July 10 at Kaesong, a few miles below the thirty-eighth parallel in Communist-held territory.

Two years were to elapse before the United States got the kind of truce it could accept. Many lives would be lost in that time, but the nature of the fighting changed. The goal was neither Rhee's unification by armed force nor MacArthur's victory at any cost. It was simply a cessation of hostilities. The Chinese dropped as a *sine qua non* the withdrawal of foreign troops from Korea, the removal of American units from the Formosa area, and the entry of their government into the United Nations. The main issues in dispute were the location of the cease-fire line, the enforcement of the armistice terms, and the repatriation of war prisoners. After frequent interruptions, the talks were suspended on October 8, 1952, and not resumed until Truman had yielded the White House to a Republican. Yet the eventual settlement conformed to the limited objectives for which his administration had fought a limited war.

What had been accomplished? It is too early to render a final judgment, but the historically minded President offered one when he told Congress on January 8, 1951: "If the democracies had stood up against the invasion of Manchuria in 1931, or the attack on Ethiopia in 1935, or the seizure of Austria in 1938 . . . as the United Nations has done, the whole history of our time would have been different." Scholars may disagree over the validity of the comparison or the soundness of the conclusion, but the eight years beginning in 1953 did witness a renewed faith in the United Nations and an increased reliance on its machinery.

54

New Areas of Concern

and Old

As THE Truman administration drew to a close, new areas and old demanded attention. While the containment of Russia in Europe and the solidarity of the Americas remained primary concerns, the Korean War demonstrated how unexpected events could bring to the fore lands which had not previously been important in United States foreign policy. In South Asia, Southeast Asia, and the Middle East, the Second World War had stimulated the desire for liberty in the empires long ruled by Britain, France, and the Netherlands. The Communists after 1945 encouraged the agitation for freedom and tried to turn nationalist movements to their own advantage. Regions once denominated as "backward" and still called "underdeveloped" suddenly became vital stakes in the Cold War.

SOUTH AND SOUTHEAST ASIA

This trend toward independence and the international problems it posed was evident in South and Southeast Asia.[1] The priority that the United States gave to the more familiar zone of conflict in Western

---

[1] The terms "South Asia" and "Southeast Asia" are of relatively recent origin. In August, 1945, the former consisted of Afghanistan, India, Ceylon, and Nepal. The latter comprised the Philippines, Indochina, Thailand, Burma, the Malayan States, the British East Indies, the Dutch East Indies, and Portuguese Timor.

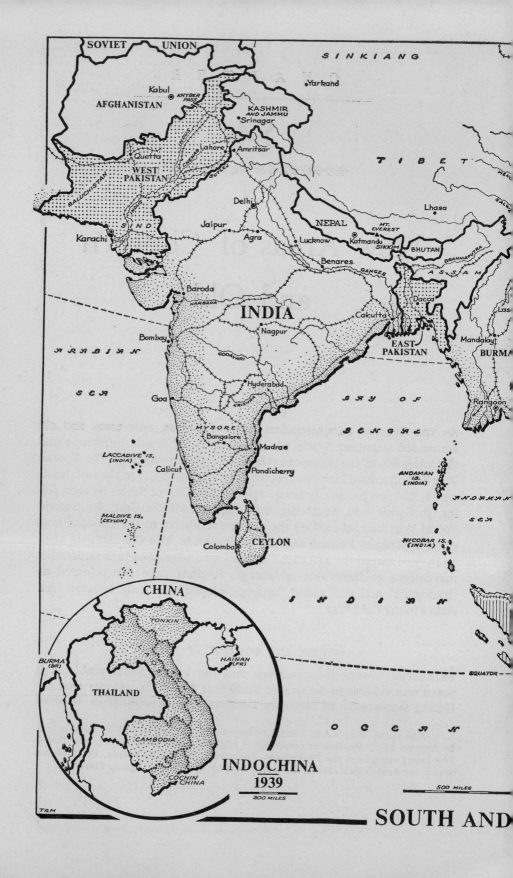

SOUTH AND

SOUTHEAST ASIA, 1961

Europe and its reluctance to see impaired the man power and resources of its North Atlantic allies caused many emerging nations to doubt modern America's allegiance to Jefferson's principles of 1776. Certainly there was a fear of change after 1945 among a people whose birthright was identified with revolution. And certainly the government in Washington, bound diplomatically and economically to the colonial powers, often saw the initiative pass in these new areas to those who professed to glory in insurgency and to speak for the common man.

One exception was the Philippines. Although independence had been granted on May 24, 1934, a ten-year transition period was still in effect when Japan overran the archipelago in December, 1941. Sovereignty was formally relinquished on July 4, 1946, and a treaty defining the future relations of the two republics was signed the same day. Those connections were understandably close. The United States helped train the Filipino army and donated surplus matériel left from the Pacific War. On March 14, 1947, it obtained the right to use for ninety-nine years a number of bases for its armed forces. That agreement barred any third power from utilizing those facilities without the consent of the signatories, although the United Nations might do so by special permission. A bilateral defense pact was concluded, as we have seen, on August 30, 1951. Congress appropriated liberally for relief and rehabilitation in the postwar years and, beginning in 1949, included its former ward in the various mutual security acts. In short, the imperial tie was cut much too belatedly, but with honor and generosity.

With the peaceful freeing of India, Pakistan, Ceylon, and Burma during 1947–8 and the incorporation of all but the last in the British Commonwealth, the United States had little to do. Relations with India were less cordial than might be expected, partly because the government at New Delhi avoided taking sides in the Cold War and partly because the government at Washington remained impartial in India's dispute with Pakistan over Kashmir. As a member of the Security Council, the United States became involved, beginning July 30, 1947, in the bloodshed that accompanied the birth of Indonesia. Its representatives served on two United Nations commissions which strove to obtain a cease-fire and insure the orderly transfer of sovereignty from Dutch authorities. Quite unjustly, many in the new republic felt that the Americans were more interested in preserving the strength of the Netherlands in the North Atlantic area than in promoting the independence of Indonesia in Southeast Asia.

Of all the crumbling empires in South and Southeast Asia, that of France in Indochina raised the greatest threat to the United States. The danger arose from the capture of the nationalist movement in

Vietnam by the Communists under Ho Chi Minh. After feeble attempts by both sides at accommodation, the Viet Minh—League for the Independence of Vietnam—launched a savage attack on the French garrison at Hanoi on December 19, 1946, and began a bloody civil war that did not end until after Truman had left office. While it was in progress, France matured slowly, too slowly, plans for unifying Vietnam and making it along with Laos and Cambodia an autonomous state whose diplomacy and defense would still be controlled from Paris. In the kingdoms of Laos and Cambodia this concession was sufficient, but in Vietnam the regime of Bao Dai aroused less enthusiasm than that of his Communist rival. Worse yet, by the time the three nations came into being on February 2, 1950, Ho Chi Minh could look to the adjacent Chinese People's Republic for supplies and "volunteers."

The Associated States of Vietnam, Laos, and Cambodia thus became problems for Truman and Acheson in the same agonizing winter which saw the search for a viable policy toward revolutionary China, beleaguered Formosa, and divided Korea. The Communist peril was real, and there were strong economic and strategic reasons for preventing Southeast Asia from being sucked into the Soviet orbit. So long as France was bogged down in a war that engaged 140,000 troops and consumed a tenth of the national budget, it could not fill the role of a key member of NATO. Yet to support France's antiquated colonialism against a movement with wide popular appeal would seem to place the United States in the reactionary camp. The dilemma was solved on February 7, 1950, eight days after Russia recognized Ho Chi Minh's insurgent regime, when the American government entered into diplomatic relations with Vietnam, Laos, and Cambodia. Then, on May 8, Acheson declared that, because Soviet imperialism endangered nationalism and democracy in Indochina, the United States was prepared to extend economic aid and military assistance to the three emerging nations and to France. The President subsequently allocated $15 million in military help to the French under the act of October 6, 1949, and a program of material and technical assistance was drawn up.

The invasion of South Korea caused Truman to bolster America's defenses throughout Asia. In ordering on June 27, 1950, that air and sea units cover Rhee's forces and that the Seventh Fleet bar an attack on Formosa, he also promised additional military assistance to France and the Associated States of Indochina. On October 17 the State Department said that, in view of the importance of operations in Indochina, a major part of the supplemental sums then being asked of Congress would be used to combat the Viet Minh. A mutual defense assistance agreement with France, Vietnam, Laos, and Cambodia was signed on December 23; by the end of the month light bombers, small arms, and other supplies were on their way. But until the end of the

Korean War in July, 1953, enabled Communist China to shift its forces elsewhere, the United States held back from a regional arrangement for the collective defense of Southeast Asia.

Economic and technical aid continued to grow. The American government endorsed the Colombo Plan, a movement initiated on January 14, 1950, within the British Commonwealth for the development of South and Southeast Asia. Starting on February 12, 1951, it participated with other non-Commonwealth states in the work of the Consultative Committee. Southeast Asia was also an important target for the Point Four program. Launched with much fanfare by Truman on January 20, 1949, but conceived of by the State Department in more modest terms, Point Four aimed at rendering technical assistance—in the form of physicians, engineers, agronomists, health experts—to underdeveloped areas. Its purpose was not to build power dams or irrigation projects but to export specialized knowledge and administrative skills. Congressional appropriations rose steadily from the initial figure of $26,900,000 on September 6, 1950, but they were always a small fraction of the total foreign aid. Thus the approximate amounts for Asia and the Pacific in the fiscal year ending June 30, 1953 were: military aid, $540 million; economic assistance, $203 million; Point Four program, $68 million.

THE MIDDLE EAST

Like Southeast Asia, the Middle East became a major area in American diplomacy only after 1945. The reasons for the new importance of the two regions were much the same: the possession of rich natural resources, the opportunity for extensive economic development, and the dissolution of once powerful European empires. Geographically, the territory stretching from Turkey and Egypt through the Levant and Iran to the gates of India was tricontinental. It linked Europe, Asia, and Africa and could be approached by large bodies of water—the Persian Gulf and the Mediterranean, Black, Caspian, Arabian, and Red Seas. Economically, its potential wealth was fabulous. Two thirds of the world's known oil supply lay beneath its soil. Racially, it was a tinderbox. A rampant Arab nationalism collided with Jewish hopes for a Western-backed homeland in the British mandate of Palestine. Strategically, it was a danger zone in the Cold War. Steady Russian pressure on Turkey and Iran brought the protagonists into closer contact than in Southeast Asia.

During the nineteenth century American interests in the Middle East were confined to missionary activities, educational institutions, archaeological excavations, and commercial enterprises. It took the Second World War to transform the area into one of vital concern to

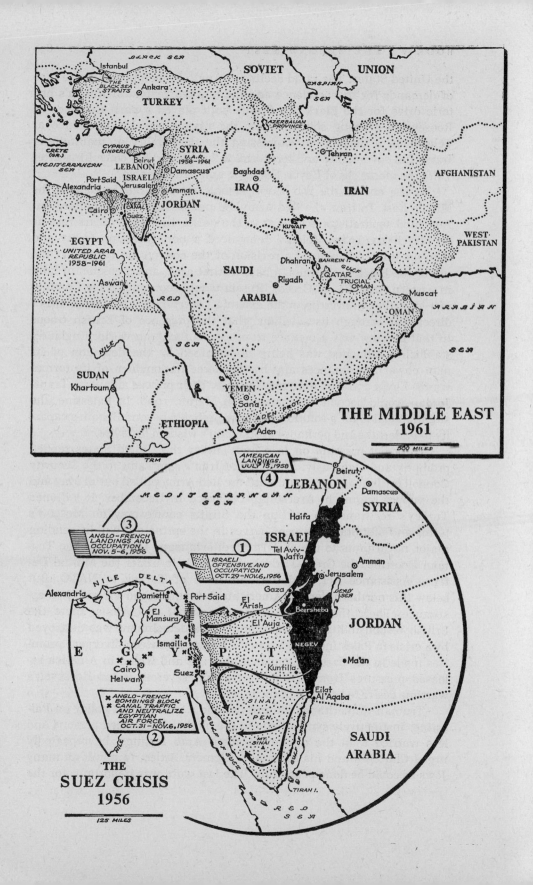

THE MIDDLE EAST
1961

THE
SUEZ CRISIS
1956

the United States. The rapid decline of Anglo-French power in the face of demands for independence and the marked revival of Russia's historic drive for the Black Sea Straits both played a part. Evidence of Roosevelt's growing solicitude for the region was his insistence at Tehran on a declaration expressing the desirability of maintaining Iran's full sovereignty and territorial integrity and his consulting after Yalta the monarchs of Egypt, Ethiopia, and Saudi Arabia.

At the end of the war storm signals were flying throughout the Middle East. In Iran, the Red Army did not withdraw as promised but fomented separatist movements in the north. In Turkey, fears rose as on March 19, 1945, Molotov denounced a nonaggression treaty and then on June 7 demanded a revision of the convention regulating the use of the Black Sea Straits, a base in that area, and a cession of land in eastern Anatolia. In Greece, Russia would soon encourage Communist guerrillas to overthrow the existing government and assert, either directly or through its satellites, that the presence of British troops in that country was a menace to peace. In the Arab world, England's stabilizing influence was being undermined by the depletion of its man power and finances and by the fierce nationalism of its former wards. Egypt and Iraq were restive under their prewar alliances; Trans-Jordan would become independent in March, 1946. In Palestine, the situation called for a solution that was probably beyond Britain's capacity to undertake and perhaps beyond man's wisdom to devise.

To Soviet pressure on Iran and Turkey the United States replied promptly and vigorously. It supported Iran's complaint to the Security Council on January 19, 1946, until the Red Army pulled out in May and the puppet regime in Azerbaijan collapsed in December. It stiffened Turkey's resistance to settling the Straits controversy on Moscow's terms and met Stalin's war of nerves in the spring of 1946 by sending major naval units to the eastern Mediterranean. Then came the Truman Doctrine, the Greek-Turkish Aid Bill, help under the Mutual Defense Assistance Act, and the admission of Turkey to NATO. But below this northern tier the American government moved with less assurance. There the Russian menace was not so obvious; there the British responsibility was traditional. This detachment was destroyed by a crisis in Palestine, which caught England between divergent promises made in the past to Zionists and Arabs and which in America released pressures from Jewish voters that severely tested Roosevelt's wartime desire to keep out of the issue.

Truman's inheritance did not include a well-defined policy on Palestine. Instinctively sympathetic to the plight of displaced persons and less worried than the diplomats about Arab feelings, he repeatedly urged Churchill and his successor, Clement Attlee, to admit as many Jews as could be done peacefully. The last word was important, for the

Arabs were determined to keep out those who had fled Hitler's persecution or cheated his gas chambers. Like most Americans, the new President approached the problem from a humanitarian rather than from a strategic point of view. He had no intention of using the armed forces of the United States to suppress any violence that might erupt from unrestricted immigration. The British were not oblivious to human values, but they were very aware of the explosive situation throughout the Middle East. They also felt they were receiving a maximum of advice and a minimum of assistance from across the Atlantic. Ultimately the two nations agreed to set up a Committee of Inquiry. It recommended on April 20, 1946, the immediate entry of 100,000 immigrants, the early transfer of the British mandate to a trusteeship under the United Nations, and the eventual creation of a state belonging to neither Jews nor Arabs but one guarding the rights of all faiths. Extremists on both sides rejected that solution.

On February 14, 1947, the Attlee cabinet decided to take the problem to the United Nations. As in Greece and Turkey, Great Britain acknowledged it could no longer play the prewar role in the Middle East. For seven months, beginning on April 28, the General Assembly and its committees wrestled with what Churchill once described as "the second riddle of the Sphinx." The outcome was a plan of partition, adopted on November 29 by a vote of 33 to 13, with 10 abstentions. It called for the termination of the mandate and the withdrawal of British troops by August 1, 1948, the formation of two independent Jewish and Arab states, plus Jerusalem to be administered separately by the Trusteeship Council; the establishment of a United Nations Commission on Palestine; and assistance from the Security Council to prevent forcible disruption of the scheme.

Peaceful partition proved impossible. The Arab delegates left the Assembly, vowing they would not be bound by the vote. Within days Palestinian Arabs, aided by neighboring kinsmen, were attacking Palestinian Jews. On December 17, 1947, the Arab League—consisting of Egypt, Iraq, Saudi Arabia, Lebanon, Syria, Trans-Jordan, and Yemen —proclaimed its determination to stop the division at all costs. Matters grew worse when the United States imposed an embargo on the export of arms to all belligerents, while England continued to sell them to Egypt, Iraq, and Trans-Jordan under old treaties. Attlee then moved to end the mandate on May 15, 1948. In Washington, the policy makers wavered. Having supported partition and encountered difficulties, they now tried to postpone that solution. This ostensible reversal in the Security Council on March 19 aroused astonishment and dismay, but a special session of the General Assembly was convened to explore a possible temporary trusteeship. Debate was still in progress when the Palestinian Jews announced on May 14 the birth of the state of Israel. The President extended *de facto* recognition at once, thus killing his own trusteeship idea.

Fighting in the Holy Land now roared out of control. Showing surprising strength, the Israelis outfought the Arab League and occupied territory which, under the partition plan, lay beyond their boundaries. The Security Council repeatedly sought to obtain a cease-fire, but except for short interludes, the struggle continued until November 30, 1948. Even then hostilities ceased largely because the permanent members, badly embroiled over Berlin, did not want war in Palestine and because the United Nations mediators displayed extraordinary skill. Separate armistice agreements were signed by Israel and its neighbors between February and July, 1949, but it was impossible to convert them into a peace treaty. This situation left Israel possessing most of Palestine, except for the central area west of the Jordan River, the coastal strip of Gaza in the southwest, and the eastern portion of Jerusalem. Egypt held on to the Gaza Strip, while Trans-Jordan— known as Jordan after April, 1949—irritated its jealous allies by making good a claim to the central sector. No permanent settlement had been reached with regard to boundaries, the status of Jerusalem, or the relocation of refugees.

The United States now had to reassess its policy in the Middle East. Torn between humanitarian, economic, and strategic considerations, it had been neither sufficiently favorable to Israel to please the pro-Zionists nor sufficiently sympathetic to the Arabs to satisfy the ardent nationalists. Its concern for the oil of the region had grown rapidly, and from Saudi Arabia it had gained the right to operate an airfield at Dhahran near the Persian Gulf. Yet its ability to block Russian penetration was slight, and England's military position had deteriorated alarmingly. The British could no longer use Palestine as a base, and attempts to extend their privileges in Egypt and Iraq failed. To be sure, the men in the Kremlin still showed little interest in the Middle East, but the poverty of the area made it a fertile field for Communist propaganda and the hostility of the Arabs against the West over the emergence of Israel made them a likely prospect for Soviet blandishments.

Stability and a combined command was the goal Truman and Acheson sought in the lower tier of states. They began on May 25, 1950, by joining England and France in a declaration designed to halt an Arab-Israeli arms race. The three governments also voiced their opposition to the use of force in the area and their readiness to act together, within or outside the United Nations, should the armistice lines or frontiers be violated. Then on May 24, 1951, the President urged Congress to include the entire Middle East in the pending Mutual Security Act, citing the peril from Soviet subversion and underdeveloped economies. But the chief innovation was the proposed Middle East Command. Sponsored by the United States, Britain, France, and Turkey, it was intended to protect all the countries in the region from external aggression. Because of its geographic position, its leadership in the Arab League, and, perhaps, its current difficulties with England, Egypt was invited on October 13, 1951, to become an original member. Iran was not asked, in view of the storm it had stirred up in nationalizing foreign oil companies, while it was felt that the other Arab states would take their cue from Cairo. As part of the arrangement, Egypt was to furnish the Command with facilities which might, in peace and war, help defend the Middle East. The British base at Suez would thus become an allied holding with full Egyptian participation in its administration, and all British forces not allocated to the Command would be withdrawn.

The Middle East Command never materialized. The government in Cairo was committed to ejecting the British and would not consider an international defense of its prized waterway. Russia formally protested, while its propagandists depicted the plan as benefiting solely the West. Many American leaders doubted the wisdom of a regional enterprise which contained only one Middle Eastern nation; others feared that England was trying to win support for a hopeless, if not bankrupt, Suez policy. Yet if nothing came of the project, it did foreshadow the more ambitious schemes of the Eisenhower-Dulles era after 1953.

THE NEW WORLD

Compared with Southeast Asia and the Middle East, the problems confronting the United States in the New World after 1945 have a familiar ring. The quest for hemispheric solidarity, the devotion to nonintervention, the improvement of consultative machinery, and the exclusion of alien ideologies had all been faced before. So had the divided loyalties of the American republics between a regional association and a world organization. New were the shrinking role the Western Hemisphere played in a diplomacy of global proportions, and the danger that its people might be taken for granted.

Except for Argentina, the New World republics followed the lead of the United States in the war against the Axis with varying degrees of enthusiasm. But the leaders in Buenos Aires, traditionally jealous of the government in Washington and steeped in an authoritarian philosophy, harbored enemy agents, suppressed free speech, persecuted Jews, and courted the fascist dictators. Argentina did not become a belligerent until March 27, 1945, and it never signed the United Nations Declaration. Tempers were already frayed when a revolution in

the summer of 1944 brought to power an extremist group headed by
General Edelmiro Farrell and Colonel Juan D. Perón. Both the United
States and Britain withheld recognition.

Understandably, Argentina was not invited to a special Inter-
American Conference on Problems of War and Peace which met at
Mexico City from February 21 to March 8, 1945. Secretary Stettinius
headed the United States delegation. The main achievement of the
gathering, known as the Act of Chapultepec, went beyond the Declaration of Reciprocal Assistance enunciated at Havana in July, 1940, by
asserting that an act or threat of aggression against one American state
by any country, American or non-American, was an act or threat
against all. Until the end of the war each nation would repel such acts,
within the scope of its constitutional framework, by measures ranging
from the recall of ministers to the use of military force. The measure
also recommended that, at the conclusion of hostilities, the New World
republics negotiate a treaty establishing procedures to carry out this
principle. Another resolution at Mexico City made it possible for Argentina to accept the foregoing and adhere to the policies of the United
Nations, which it did on April 4. Five days later, the United States
granted recognition and then succeeded, despite Russian protests, in
winning the recalcitrant neighbor an invitation to attend the San Francisco Conference.

Continuing antagonism between the United States and Argentina
delayed negotiation of the reciprocal assistance treaty envisaged by the
Act of Chapultepec. The Farrell government did not abandon its authoritarian ways, but the efforts of Spruille Braden, first as ambassador
and then as assistant secretary of state, to expose its iniquities served
only to insure the triumph of Perón in the election of February, 1946.
Not until Braden resigned in June, 1947, did new efforts pave the way
for the Inter-American Conference for the Maintenance of Continental
Peace and Security at Rio de Janeiro from August 15 to September 2.
Secretary Marshall headed a delegation which included the two ranking senators on the Foreign Relations Committee, the minority leader
of the House Foreign Affairs Committee, and the ambassador to the
United Nations. Their labor produced the first regional arrangement
for collective self-defense as permitted by Articles 51 and 52 of the
Charter.

Under the Inter-American Treaty of Reciprocal Assistance of September 2, 1947, an armed attack upon one American state was considered an attack on all, whether the offender came from within or outside the hemisphere. Each signatory promised to assist in meeting such
attacks, as well as other forms of aggression that did not resort to overt
force. The precise type of aid in each case was to be determined by an
Organ of Consultation, which was to assemble without delay and which

was empowered to adopt various measures ranging from severance of diplomatic relations through economic sanctions to military reprisals. The decisions of the Organ were to be by a two-thirds vote of all contracting parties, except that no state could be required to use armed force without its consent. The Senate offered no trouble. With Vandenberg calling it "the greatest advance ever made in the business of collective peace," the treaty was approved on December 8, 1947, by a vote of 72 to 1. It went into effect a year later, when the requisite number of signatories had exchanged ratifications; eventually all twenty-one republics completed that process.

Next came the Ninth International Conference of American States, which met at Bogotá from March 30 to May 2, 1948. Its primary tasks were to consider economic issues, purposely deferred at Rio the previous year; to define the duties of the various hemispheric institutions, such as the Organ of Consultation; and to coordinate and extend existing agreements for the peaceful settlement of disputes. Marshall again led the United States delegation which, in view of the emphasis on finance and trade, included the secretaries of the treasury and of commerce. With the Truman administration embarked on the European Recovery Program, the southern neighbors expected some sort of assistance for their own postwar adjustments. Communist parties, then bidding for power in France and Italy, were also active in the New World, and riots attributed to them disrupted proceedings for several days beginning on April 9.

Following past patterns, the delegates at Bogotá accomplished more in devising institutional machinery than in stimulating material growth. Two documents received particular attention. One was the Pact of Bogotá, a comprehensive treaty dealing with the pacific settlement of disputes and so intricate that seven of the signatories, including the United States, appended reservations. The other was the Charter of the Organization of American States, which gave a new name to and described fully the agencies of the inter-American system. The Inter-American Conference was "the supreme organ" of the OAS and was to convene every five years. The Meeting of Consultation of Ministers of Foreign Affairs—the lineal descendant of the body established at Lima in 1938—was "to consider problems of an urgent nature" and to serve as the Organ of Consultation under the Treaty of Reciprocal Assistance. An Advisory Defense Committee was to help in the military sphere. The Council of the OAS was the executive branch and handled the day-to-day routine at Washington. In a crisis, before the foreign ministers could assemble, it might operate provisionally as the Organ of Consultation. The Pan American Union formed the secretariat of the new dispensation.

The Organization of American States came closer to the ideal of the New World leaders than did the United Nations. Equality reigned. It contained no great-power veto and no privileged group, such as permanent members of the Security Council. Everyone was represented on all major organs; everyone had a single vote. Yet as had been the case so often before, the treaties looked better on paper than in practice. The OAS Charter did not go into effect fully until December 13, 1951, when two thirds of the signatories completed ratification, while the Pact of Bogotá still lacked the requisite majority when Truman left office.[2]

No Inter-American Conference took place during the remainder of Truman's term, but the outbreak of the Korean War led Acheson to convene a Meeting of Consultation of Ministers of Foreign Affairs in Washington from March 26 to April 7, 1951. Already the OAS Council had declared on June 28, 1950, its support of the action taken by the United Nations the previous day; by August, seventeen republics had pledged token contributions to MacArthur's command. But with a Soviet attack in the Americas seemingly remote, the diplomats were not disposed to transform the Rio pact of 1947 into another NATO. The platitudinous resolutions they adopted were more useful as a show of continental unity than as a means of strengthening the defenses of the free world.

WESTERN EUROPE

Of all areas of concern, new and old, Western Europe remained the most important to the outgoing Truman administration. The President's most far-reaching decision there after June 25, 1950, was to rearm the Federal Republic of Germany. Like the insulation of Formosa, this move involved a reversal of a past stand. From a purely military point of view the use of West German soldiers in NATO's forces had always been desirable, but before the invasion of South Korea, that consideration was overborne by sole possession of the atomic bomb and recent memories of Hitler's Reich. It took the loss of the nuclear monopoly and the lessons of a limited war to emphasize the continuing need for conventional weapons and to restore the infantry to its proper place in strategic thinking.

France and its neighbors concluded more slowly that German man power was indispensable for containing Russia in Europe. To talk of raising divisions beyond the Rhine before their own armies had been bolstered by the Mutual Defense Assistance Program seemed sheer

[2] A resolution allowed the new organs of the OAS to start functioning before ratifications were completed. In giving its consent to the Charter on August 28, 1950, the Senate insisted on a reservation disclaiming any construction which would enlarge the powers of the federal government or diminish those of the several states.

folly. Nor were they prepared for so abrupt a shift in the American position. Hence, when Acheson first proposed to Bevin and French Foreign Minister Robert Schuman on September 12, 1950, that German contingents be used by the new alliance, he met stubborn resistance. The ensuing NATO Council session of September 15–26 voted to establish at once an integrated military force, under a centralized command, sufficient to protect Western Europe. It also instructed the NATO Defense Committee to study means by which Germany might be able to contribute to that build-up. A simultaneous communiqué of the Big Three on September 19 proclaimed their intention to treat any attack against the Federal Republic or Berlin as one upon themselves, but it also asserted that "the re-creation of a German national army would not serve the best interests of Germany or Europe."

For the next three months, and longer, the allies wrangled over how they might tap Germany's military potential without creating a Frankenstein. Prime Minister René Pleven urged a European Defense Community, linked to NATO, in which units supplied by Adenauer's government would be merged with those from the rest of the continent. Acheson wanted the West Germans in uniform as quickly as possible, and he finally persuaded the French to allow their ancient foe to re-arm while the Pleven Plan was being perfected. On December 19, 1950, the NATO Council approved the participation of the Federal Republic in the defense of Western Europe. Thus did events in Korea hasten a fateful step which the United States took precipitately, England hesitatingly, and France fearfully.

Russia, as was expected, protested. On October 20, 1950, it held at Prague a gathering of satellites which denounced remilitarization and demanded an immediate peace settlement in accordance with the Potsdam Protocol. On November 3 Russia suggested that the Council of Foreign Ministers, which had not met since June, 1949, be assembled for that purpose. This overture led to exploratory discussions that were finally broken off on June 21, 1951. The Western powers were willing to negotiate but not at the expense of NATO, the pending European Defense Community, or the rearming of the Bonn regime. They pointed to the utter inability of the Council in the past to agree on treaties for Germany and Austria. They insisted that the issue of German rearmament could not be separated from the general question of armaments, on which no progress had been made since 1945 in limiting either conventional or atomic weapons. Lastly, they disagreed with the Soviets on procedure. They believed that the formation of an all-German government on the basis of free elections must precede a peace treaty with the wartime coalition. Russia contended that the treaty should come first, and it was unwilling to hold the kind of elections which would satisfy the democracies.

While these fruitless notes were being exchanged and the Pleven Plan was being worked out, the United States, Britain, and France moved to restore full sovereignty to the Bonn regime. On March 6, 1951, they authorized it to establish a ministry of foreign affairs. On September 14 they reaffirmed their intention to include a democratic Germany in any European defense organization but warned that the danger from a continued division into West and East Germany would compel them to keep troops in the former. On October 19 Congress officially terminated the war by a joint resolution. Finally, after Russia had vainly held out as an alternative the hope of early unification, there was signed at Bonn on May 26, 1952, a Convention and Related Agreements between the Three Powers and the Federal Republic of Germany. Designed to make the latter an equal partner in the community of nations, it gave the Adenauer government almost full control over its internal and external affairs, abolished the Allied High Commission, provided for an exchange of ambassadors, and declared that the sole mission of the foreign troops remaining on German soil was to defend the free world of which the Federal Republic and West Berlin were a part. The Convention also pledged the four powers to seek a unified Germany and a definitive peace. But no part of the accord could become operative until the Pleven Plan entered into force.

Attention now shifted to Paris, where on May 27, 1952, the Treaty Constituting the European Defense Community was signed by France, Belgium, the Netherlands, Luxembourg, Italy, and West Germany. The political, economic, and military clauses of the pact need not be analyzed, for they never went into effect. But supplementing the pact were a protocol defining the relations between the European Defense Community and NATO, a special guarantee by Great Britain to the former, and an Anglo-American-French declaration. The first, the only one submitted to the Senate, extended the obligations of NATO respecting resistance to armed attack to the members of the European Defense Community and vice versa. The second in effect made Italy and West Germany part of the Brussels Treaty Organization. The third reassured France that the United States and England would maintain their interest in the success of the European Defense Community and keep their troops in West Germany and Greater Berlin.

All of this interlocking machinery came to naught. The Senate interposed no obstacles. On July 1, 1952, it consented to the Bonn Convention and Related Agreements by a vote of 77 to 5 and to the Paris Protocol linking NATO and the European Defense Community by a count of 72 to 5. Its one objection to the first was taken care of in a reservation which pointed out that any military implementation of the provisions by the United States must be authorized by Congress. The misgivings of the French were not so easily disposed of. They had never liked the idea of rearming the Federal Republic so quickly. They had yielded to Acheson in 1950 only because the invasion of South Korea seemed to portend a Soviet offensive in Europe. That threat had not materialized. Indeed, by 1952 Russia was talking of a four-power conference to settle the German question. If that could be done, the optimists reasoned, there would be no need to strengthen NATO with man power from a quondam enemy.

Truman and Acheson did not deny the inherent danger in their policy, but they were prepared to take a calculated risk. They knew that a proud people could not be disarmed permanently, and they felt it wise to extend freely what later might be extorted unwillingly. The two men realized that the containment of Russia, of which rearming West Germany was a part, was the preliminary to eliminating the underlying sources of tension. They were not granted the opportunity, however, of writing that second chapter. Time was running out. The administration was caught, moreover, in the backwash of disillusionment over the triumphs of 1941–5, of frustrations over a limited war in Korea, and of hysteria over the recall of MacArthur and the recklessness of McCarthy. The abuse heaped upon the executive branch and its bitter battles with the legislature over the direction of American foreign policy dismayed the NATO allies and encouraged dissident elements abroad to postpone final action on the Treaty Constituting the European Defense Community until they discovered who would occupy the White House after January 20, 1953.

BOOK VI

THE CONTINUING TEST: NEITHER PEACE NOR WAR

1953–61

In which the American people remain suspended between peace and war, undertake unprecedented commitments, and dwell in dread of a nuclear apocalypse.

55

The Shaping of Foreign Policy, 1953–61

AFTER TWENTY YEARS of Democratic rule, the Republicans regained the presidency in January, 1953, and with it, control of Congress. The time seemed ripe for reversing policies which Roosevelt and Truman had pursued in the struggle for survival. Most Americans had discounted long ago the military victory over the Axis and had come to believe that diplomatic blunders had lost the peace. The outgoing administration, despite its success in containing Russia in Western Europe and its courage in meeting aggression in East Asia, had encountered mounting criticism. For various reasons, some of them valid, men were questioning the effectiveness of the new alliances, the cost of mutual security, and the probity of their own officials. Shocked by the Communist triumph in China, frustrated by the limited conflict in Korea, confused by the charges of treasonous subversion, and fearful of the horrors of nuclear destruction, they looked to new leaders to restore internal unity and external strength. Yet the next eight years, in which the nation remained suspended between peace and war, saw no real departure from the course already charted; instead, the assumption of global commitments went beyond those of the Democratic era.

THE PRESIDENT

One reason for this unexpected continuity was the character of the new president. Dwight D. Eisenhower was a moderate, fair-minded man, who had already demonstrated an ability to quiet discord and to inspire harmony. Texas born, he had grown up in mid-America and graduated from West Point. He was in charge of the War Plans Division when Marshall chose him to head the European Theater of Operations and direct the North African and Mediterranean landings in 1942–3. Later he became Supreme Commander of the Allied Expeditionary Force that conquered Germany from the west in 1944–5, chief of staff upon Marshall's retirement in November, 1945, and President of Columbia University beginning in February, 1948. He took a leave of absence from that last post in December, 1950, to set up the defense structure envisaged by the North Atlantic Treaty, and he was commanding the NATO forces in April, 1952, when he decided to seek his first political office. His nomination in July represented a triumph for the so-called internationalist faction of the Republican party.

Because he was identified with the strategy that had crushed Germany and with many of the instrumentalities forged after 1945 to halt Russian expansion, Eisenhower could be expected to respect the postwar revolution in American diplomacy. There would be no return to isolationism, no withdrawal from the United Nations, no abandonment of NATO. To be sure, he often sounded like Taft on such issues as unnecessary waste in overseas spending, executive abuse in treaty making, and Communist infiltration in government, but in his campaign speeches he stressed the need to end the debilitating dissension at home and the unpopular war abroad. His assurance on October 24, 1952, that, if elected, he would go to Korea was the most persuasive thing he said during the entire canvass.

To the presidency Eisenhower brought a capacity for reconciling diverse views, choosing able subordinates, and winning public affection. A halting speaker and a poor writer, he managed with a captivating smile, devoted aides, and television techniques to project his warm personality and simple faiths to millions of his countrymen and to calm their fears by expressions of confidence and goodwill. His was a soothing influence, one which was desperately needed at the outset but which, after a time, tended to deaden the average mind to unpleasant facts and perilous situations. He also brought to the executive chair a restricted conception of its power that reflected his innate modesty, intellectual limitations, and nonpolitical background. He never worked hard at the job, and three serious illnesses made him conserve his strength. He relied heavily on brief digests and staff work to keep informed. Eisenhower wanted Congress to reassume its role as a coordinate shaper of foreign policy, and he leaned over backwards to avoid clashes with senators of his own party, such as Taft, Bricker, and McCarthy. He wished the State Department to act again as the nation's voice on external affairs; save for a belated and reluctant resort to summit diplomacy, he left even top-level negotiations to the secretary. This was particularly true with the first incumbent, who wielded an authority which few, if any, of his predecessors had possessed.

THE SECRETARIES OF STATE

John Foster Dulles was well fitted by inheritance and training to be secretary of state. A grandfather and an uncle had held the post before him, and his own diplomatic career stretched from his attendance as a mere observer at the Second Hague Conference in 1907 through his participation as a legal adviser on reparations at Paris in 1919 to his contribution as a chief draftsman of the Japanese peace treaty at San Francisco in 1951. A Republican international lawyer from New York, he had believed in the late 1930's that the United States should insulate itself from Europe's wars and not resist inflexibly Japan's expansive tendencies. Only after Pearl Harbor did he, along with Vandenberg and Dewey, join Willkie in championing bipartisanship and an active role in global affairs. Lastly, his intimate association with Hull, Stettinius, Byrnes, Marshall, and Acheson—as well as his frequent presence at international conferences and the General Assembly—made it unlikely that, once in authority, he would evade the commitments undertaken since 1945.

Yet Dulles was an independent thinker, with deep convictions on the evil of communism and the proper methods of combating it. In his emphasis on morality and his strong Presbyterianism he resembled Wilson. An impressive, vigorous man, blessed with an agile and retentive mind, he was always self-assured and often self-righteous. An inveterate phrase maker, he indulged in striking but deceptive slogans that both aroused enthusiasm and bred uncertainty. "Massive retaliation" and "agonizing reappraisal" are but two; and his denunciation of the Roosevelt-Truman era in the platform of 1952—with its promise to end "neglect of the Far East," to repudiate all "secret understandings," and to replace "the negative, futile and immoral" policy of containment—led people to expect changes that never materialized. It was Dulles who popularized the idea of liberating the captive nations of Eastern Europe and of unleashing Chiang Kai-shek to harass the Asiatic mainland. Three times before January, 1956, he claimed, he had gained his objectives by daring to take the country to the brink of war. Although many observers regarded this "brinksmanship" as bad diplomacy, it revealed Dulles' deep-seated belief that most wars result from miscalculation. Peace is best preserved, he argued, when a nation makes clear in advance, even at considerable risk, exactly what it will do. Ironically, he often engaged in a deliberate ambiguity that kept both friend and foe guessing.

Dulles dominated the Department as few secretaries have. His subordinates rarely did more than serve as his mouthpiece. The Policy Planning Staff declined in importance as Dulles relied on improvisation or on his own prodigious knowledge. He forced into temporary retirement George F. Kennan, one of the few Russian experts in the Foreign Service, and ostentatiously transferred Charles E. Bohlen, another Soviet specialist with whom he disagreed, from Moscow to Manila. Often called "the man in the airplane," he probably traveled abroad more than all his predecessors combined. His total mileage has been computed at 479,286; the countries visited at forty-six. Envoys might joke that they could always escape a function by saying "The Secretary may drop in"; but to those who believed in the dignity of ambassadorships, the itinerant Dulles was no laughing matter. Foreign reaction to him varied. In Bonn he was regarded as the champion of the free world; in London he was disliked by all shades of opinion. Certainly he never inspired the confidence among his allies that Acheson had held. On the other hand, profiting from Acheson's troubles, he successfully avoided antagonizing congressional and public opinion, though sometimes at the cost of ruffling feelings abroad.

Christian A. Herter succeeded the cancer-stricken Dulles on April 22, 1959. A former congressman from and Governor of Massachusetts, he had been Under Secretary since February 21, 1957. A soft-spoken, tall, considerate man—compelled by arthritis to use crutches—he could not hope in the time that remained to stamp his personality upon American foreign policy or to develop the intimate relationship with Eisenhower that Dulles had enjoyed. Indeed, deprived of the secretary on whom he had leaned for six years, the President began at once to play a much more active part on the diplomatic stage. Thus Herter took office with everything to lose and little to gain. If matters went wrong, people would say that Dulles could have done better. If matters went right, they would give the credit to Eisenhower. Certainly all too little went right in Herter's twenty-one-month incumbency, but it is too early to say how much he or circumstances beyond his control were to blame.

THE CONGRESSIONAL LEADERS

No congressional leader wielded the power in external affairs after 1953 that Connally, Vandenberg, Borah, and Lodge had held in the preceding half-century. Many of the President's own party differed with him, and in any case, except for the first two of Eisenhower's eight years, the Democrats controlled both houses of the legislature. Taft's premature death on July 31, 1953, removed the most influential Republican spokesman on Capitol Hill, while Alexander Wiley of Wisconsin proved rather ineffectual as chairman of the Foreign Relations Committee from 1953 to 1955. Knowland and Bricker were too closely identified with extreme positions and ended their careers in 1958, the former by choice and the latter by defeat. McCarthy's nuisance value diminished markedly after his censure by the Senate on December 2, 1954.

Walter F. George of Georgia, a conservative Democrat, did much during Eisenhower's first term to restore vitality to a bipartisanship that had been weakened by the disaster in China and the events in Korea. Like Vandenberg, he had shed his prewar isolationism during the struggle for survival, and by the time he became chairman of the Foreign Relations Committee in January, 1955, he was a sort of senatorial patriarch with a towering reputation for integrity, independence, and oratory. Commanding in appearance and courtly in manner, he brooked little opposition once he had set his course. He insisted on granting the executive the authority it sought in the crisis over Quemoy and Matsu in January, 1955, and he helped persuade the President to attend a summit conference at Geneva in July, 1955. Neither of his Democratic successors, Theodore F. Green of Rhode Island or J. William Fulbright of Arkansas, exercised a similar influence after George retired in January 1957.

THE CONSTITUTIONAL CONFLICT

Throughout Eisenhower's two terms his amazing personal popularity and cautiously invoked leadership kept the historic clash between the president and Congress in a minor key. Although the executive branch did not hesitate to stretch its prerogatives to the utmost, it rarely encountered legislative resistance. Indeed, it frequently disarmed the opposition by soliciting and obtaining collaboration in advance, as was the case with the Formosa and Middle East Resolutions in January, 1955, and March, 1957. Occasionally there was trouble in the traditional areas of conflict. Senatorial criticism forced Clare Boothe Luce to resign as ambassador to Brazil on May 1, 1959, three days after being confirmed by a vote of 79 to 11. McCarthy's demands in 1954 for privileged records of cabinet discussions caused Eisenhower to reassert the president's right to withhold confidential papers from needless publicity on Capitol Hill. When the Senate and House seemed unlikely to authorize the use of air power in Indochina to aid the beleaguered French in April, 1954, the administration did not make a specific request. The wonder is not that differences arose between the two branches, but that they were so few.

Treaties generated little friction from 1953 to 1961. Ten major pacts were signed: the Security Treaty with the Republic of Korea (October 1, 1953); the Southeast Asia Collective Defense Treaty (September 8, 1954); the Protocol on Termination of the Occupation Regime in the Federal Republic of Germany (October 23, 1954); the Protocol to the North Atlantic Treaty on the Accession of the Federal Republic of Germany (October 23, 1954); the Security Treaty with the Republic of China (December 2, 1954); the Treaty of Mutual Understanding and Cooperation with Panama (January 25, 1955); the Austrian State Treaty (May 15, 1955); the twelve-nation Treaty Guaranteeing Non-militarization of Antarctica and Freedom of Scientific Investigation (December 1, 1959); the second Security Treaty with Japan (January 19, 1960); and the fourteen-nation Convention Establishing the Organization for Economic Cooperation and Development (December 14, 1960). None of these was defeated; only the Korean and Chinese pacts had reservations appended by the Senate. All were approved with less than seven negative votes, except the two dealing with Panama and Antarctica; they mustered fourteen and twenty-one respectively.[1] The dwindling mortality rate of treaties had characterized the period from 1939 to 1953, but Dulles went further than his predecessors in employing executive agreements to do the work formerly expected of treaties.

Against this background, Bricker resumed his efforts to restrict the scope of treaties and the use of executive agreements. Much of his support came from those who deplored Roosevelt's wartime by-passing of the Senate or feared a United Nations peacetime infringement of American sovereignty. The version Bricker introduced on January 7, 1953, with the blessing of sixty-two members of both parties, omitted some of his old curbs, but Dulles quickly criticized it as a serious blow to the president's powers in general and to the treaty-making process in particular. The Secretary was willing to abandon plans for protecting human rights by international action, thus calming fears for the sanctity of domestic affairs, but he balked at a new "which clause" that would require the concurrence of both houses and all forty-eight states to make valid such common treaties as those on extradition and migratory birds.[2] On July 20 the administration threw its weight behind a Knowland substitute that eliminated the "which clause" and all legislative regulation of executive agreements. Instead, it empowered the courts to review the constitutionality of treaties and international agreements, required a roll call when any treaty was voted upon, and gave the Senate explicit authority, upon consenting to treaties, to stipu-

[1] The treaty establishing the OECD was not approved until March 16, 1961. The vote was 72 to 18, and the Senate insisted on a guarantee that the accord did not lessen the powers of president or Congress.

[2] As reported on June 19, 1953, the so-called "which clause" provided that a treaty could become effective as internal law "only through legislation which would be valid in the absence of treaty."

late that they should not go into force without appropriate legislation by Congress. Neither amendment was passed before the session ended on August 4, 1953.

Bricker renewed his agitation in the next session. His strong backing in and out of Congress—he had the support of such groups as the American Medical Association, the Daughters of the American Revolution, and an organization of "housewives and mothers of boys overseas" called the Vigilant Women for the Bricker Amendment—frightened the administration. On January 25, 1954, Eisenhower publicly warned against a revived isolationism and said he was "unalterably opposed" to the amendment, not only because it "would make it impossible for us to deal effectively with friendly nations for our mutual defense" but also because it would serve notice "that our country intends to withdraw from its leadership in world affairs." On February 25 the resolution, as amended, was lost by a count of 42 to 50, not even by a simple majority. Bricker's followers then lined up behind a substitute offered by George. It also declared that a provision in a treaty or executive agreement conflicting with the Constitution was invalid; it too required a roll call on the question of consenting to treaties. But in place of the controversial "which clause," it simply stated that an international agreement, other than a treaty, could become effective as internal law "only by an act of Congress." On February 26, 1954, a vote of 60 to 31 left the George substitute one short of the necessary two-thirds.

In each of the next four sessions Bricker presented variants of his scheme, but none came close to passing. As he watered them down to vague generalities that could be interpreted in different ways and to procedural matters that could be effected by changing the Senate rules, it became evident that his zeal was of more consequence in justifying himself and the Republican platform of 1952 than in safeguarding the nation and the individual states. With the President resolutely opposed to a diminution of his powers, the Republicans in 1956 kept silent on the proposed amendment, while Bricker's defeat at the polls in 1958 virtually guaranteed that there would be no tinkering with the Constitution in the delicate area of foreign affairs before Eisenhower quit office.

56

>>>->>>->>>->>>*<<<-*<<<-*<<<-*<<<*

Trends in the Cold War

BY JANUARY 1953 the Cold War was a familiar phenomenon. The competing political philosophies, rival economic systems, and divergent diplomatic objectives, which had torn asunder the victorious coalition, had long since hardened into a deadly and protracted conflict between the forces of freedom and communism. The front was everywhere—on the ground and in the air, on the farm and in the factory, on the rostrums of the United Nations and in the minds of the uncommitted peoples. In this struggle totalitarianism gave the Russians one advantage—the ease with which they could mobilize their man power, marshal their resources, expand their research, and sacrifice their citizens. To survive, the United States had to attain a similar unity of purpose and action, one it had traditionally reserved for brief moments of crisis. But now the nation had to maintain that unity indefinitely in a period that was neither peace nor war.

THE DEATH OF STALIN

Barely six weeks after Eisenhower's inauguration, the death of Stalin on March 5, 1953, injected a new element into the Cold War. The undisputed ruler of Russia for twenty-five years, he had grown increasingly more secluded, more suspicious, and more sadistic, while even his intimate associates lived in fear. At first his power was divided. His heir apparent, Georgi M. Malenkov, became Premier, but five others shared supreme authority. They were Molotov, who returned to the Foreign Office he had headed from 1939 to 1949; Lavrenti P. Beria,

Minister of Internal Affairs; Nikolai A. Bulganin, Defense Minister; Lazar M. Kaganovich, minister without portfolio; and Nikita S. Khrushchev, First Secretary of the Central Committee of the Communist Party. Before the summer ended, Beria had been shot as a traitor. On February 8, 1955, presumably for domestic reasons, Malenkov gave way to Bulganin, and the Defense Ministry went to Marshal Zhukov, a war hero. For another three years the benign-looking and goateed Bulganin ranked nominally at the top of the Soviet hierarchy, but the real control rested in the hands of the bull-like and tenacious Khrushchev.

Khrushchev did not assume Stalin's mantle in name until March 27, 1958. Molotov resigned on June 1, 1956, to be succeeded eventually by Gromyko. On July 3, 1957, Malenkov, Molotov, and Kaganovich were ousted from the Central Committee and assigned minor posts in the hinterlands. In that struggle Khrushchev owed his survival to Zhukov, and he moved quickly to eliminate that dependence. In an astonishing reversal, Zhukov himself was forced off the Central Committee on October 26, 1957, and was replaced as Defense Minister by Marshal Rodion Y. Malinovsky. Finally, Bulganin stepped down five months later, and Khrushchev became Chairman of the Council of Ministers, or Premier.

Despite this internal conflict, all participants seemed to believe that Russia's interest would be served best in the next few years by a more friendly and less provocative diplomacy. The reasons for this shift in attitude, which did not denote a change in objectives, are still shrouded in mystery, but some of the factors at work can be surmised. Stalin's death provided an opportunity for stock-taking and for shedding unproductive ideologies. To denounce the dictator as a bloody tyrant and to repudiate his views on the inevitability of war, as Khrushchev did on February 24, 1956, was domestically wise; it might also persuade the West to modify the firmness with which it had met the challenges of the Cold War. Far from retreating into isolationism, the United States had supported the United Nations and had forged an alliance to protect Western Europe. It had shown in Korea that it would defend certain peripheral regions with conventional arms. It was maintaining a deterrent force of intercontinental bombers and a ring of bases along the Soviet perimeter. Capitalism had not collapsed; rather, it was underwriting a global program of mutual assistance.

Marx and Lenin had taught, however, that time was on the side of communism. Hence Stalin's successors were content to probe for soft spots, such as the Middle East, and to court the uncommitted peoples of Asia and Africa. With shameless hypocrisy they posed as champions of self-determination. With messianic fervor they predicted that their industrial output would soon surpass that of the United States. With blandishments and appeals to national safety they sought to induce the European members of NATO to deny their soil to American planes, to limit their contributions to collective defense, and to demand a discontinuance of nuclear experiments. They knew their scientists were rapidly closing the gap in atomic and hydrogen bombs; perhaps they foresaw their own superiority in launching missiles. They could afford to wait.

THE TEST OF SUMMIT DIPLOMACY

With the advent of new leaders in Washington and Moscow, men sought fresh approaches to old problems. By 1960 the most novel of these was the resort to summit diplomacy. It was also the most unexpected, for in 1952 the Republicans had castigated Roosevelt's secret wartime dealing with Stalin. Like Truman before him, Eisenhower initially turned a deaf ear to suggestions which Churchill, certainly no optimist in Russian affairs, had been urging since February, 1950. In phrases not unlike Hull's objections to a Roosevelt-Konoye confrontation in August, 1941, the President insisted that there must be some reasonable assurance of success and some positive indication of Soviet good faith. The last could be shown by ending hostilities in East Asia, by freeing the captive peoples of Eastern Europe, and by concluding peace treaties with Germany and Austria. To expedite the third aim, the United States invited Russia on July 15, 1953, to a four-power meeting of the foreign ministers, and after much haggling, Russia gave its consent on November 26.

Three times in the next two years the foreign ministers took steps which cleared a path to the summit. At Berlin from January 25 to February 18, 1954, they failed to settle the Austrian and German treaties but did agree to discuss subsequently the more immediate danger in Asia. At Geneva from April 26 to June 15, 1954—along with other interested parties, including Communist China—they went through the motions of trying to unify Korea; later they accepted as unavoidable a partition of Vietnam at the seventeenth parallel. At Vienna on May 14–15, 1955, they drafted a document restoring Austria's freedom and providing for a withdrawal of all occupation forces. This last achievement fostered hopes that, under Premier Bulganin, the Soviets genuinely desired to relax tensions. It went far to pave the way for a summit conference.

At Geneva from July 18 to 23, 1955, the heads of government met for the first time in a decade. Although the NATO allies frequently held top-level discussions, no American president had talked directly to a Russian premier since Potsdam. The participants were Eisenhower, Eden, Bulganin, and Edgar Faure of France, each accompanied by his foreign minister. Also present in the Soviet delegation was

Khrushchev. The goals were modest. A solution of basic problems was
not anticipated; rather, the heads of government would try to formulate the issues and agree upon the methods to be followed. They were
to give direction to the foreign ministers, who would then seek substantive answers to the main controversies. The proceedings would
thus be in two stages. Although the first was not the intimate, secluded
type that Churchill had called for, it did establish a bridgehead for
negotiations and engender a transitory goodwill referred to as "the
spirit of Geneva."

As defined by the heads of government, the paramount needs were
German reunification, European security, disarmament, and fuller
contacts between East and West. The first was to be achieved by free
elections "carried out in conformity with the national interests of the
German people and the interests of European security." The second
was to be sought in several ways, but particularly in a treaty which
would embrace all or part of the Continent and obligate the signatories
to eschew force as well as deny aid to an aggressor. The third was to be
pursued through the United Nations and its newly created Disarmament Subcommittee, but attention was called to suggestions made at
this conference—notably the Eisenhower proposal to promote mutual
confidence by exchanging blueprints of military installations and allowing aerial photographs of each other's territory. The fourth was to
come through the progressive elimination of barriers in the flow of
people, ideas, and goods.

Since the foreign ministers were unable, at their meeting in Geneva
from October 27 to November 16, 1955, to translate that directive into
concrete agreements, this first test of summit diplomacy must be put
down as a failure. Some gains were made. The Kremlin leaders smiled
and talked politely, rather than glowering and threatening annihilation. Eden came away with a deeper understanding of their genuine
fear of a rearmed Germany, while Eisenhower's sincere disavowal of
belligerent intentions seemed to be believed. Both sides realized, as the
President said on his return, that "nuclear warfare, pursued to the ultimate, could be practically race suicide." For the first time Russia
agreed that German unification was indissolubly linked to European
security. Still, neither antagonist made any vital concession, and such
matters as freedom for Eastern Europe and recognition of Communist
China could not even be discussed publicly. Khrushchev spoke the
truth when he told some East Germans on September 17, 1955: "We
are in favor of a détente, but if anybody thinks that for this reason we
shall forget about Marx, Engels, and Lenin, he is mistaken. This will
happen when shrimps learn to whistle."

Hopes for a détente remained bright for another year. If there was
no thought of a second summit meeting, there was likewise no return

to the harsh epithets of the Stalin era. Instead, on September 19, 1955, Bulganin initiated an extraordinary public correspondence with Eisenhower in which he explored many of the subjects taken up at Geneva. Thirteen letters were exchanged before the end of 1956. Designed as an appeal to world opinion rather than as an overture to diplomatic accord, they were nonetheless couched in polite and cordial terms that gave the illusion of two well-disposed gentlemen searching for a common ground. Then in October, 1956, the picture changed drastically. Poland and Hungary rocked with rebellion. Israel invaded Egypt, and this action was quickly followed by Britain's and France's encroachment on Egypt. To check the ominous drift toward a general war, Switzerland proposed that India join the Big Four in a heads-of-government conference. Although Bulganin endorsed the plan guardedly on November 17, Eisenhower replied that the United Nations was the proper organ to handle the crisis.

Late in 1957 the Kremlin leaders revived their agitation for a meeting at the summit. Capitalizing on the successful launching of the first earth satellite and exploiting a universal desire for ending the Cold War, the Russians compelled Eisenhower and Dulles to yield against their better judgment. Nothing in the Bulganin correspondence, which stretched into 1958, suggested an accord on the basic issues of reunification for Germany, self-determination for Eastern Europe, or a foolproof system of inspection and control for nuclear weapons and their testing. On the contrary, Russia's aim was the dissolution of NATO and America's withdrawal from all foreign territory without a comparable Soviet sacrifice. Yet such was the pressure of public opinion that on March 31, 1958, the United States, England, and France accepted in principle a heads-of-government conference. They stipulated, however, that it be preceded by four-power conversations, first at the ambassadorial level and then among the foreign ministers, to iron out numerous procedural details.

When Khrushchev replaced Bulganin on March 27, 1958, a harsher note crept into Russian diplomacy, and with it those frequent reversals that have baffled the West ever since. His release of confidential memoranda and his public reproaches of Eisenhower's actions seemed by June 16 to kill any hope for a summit meeting. Then, a month later, after the revolt in Iraq and the American landings in Lebanon, the Soviet leader turned about and demanded an immediate heads-of-government conference, to which Prime Minister Jawaharlal Nehru of India and Secretary-General Dag Hammarskjold of the United Nations would be invited. On July 22 Eisenhower countered by suggesting that since the Security Council was already dealing with the problem, the heads attend the sessions of that body. The Charter explicitly authorized such a course, but it had never been tried. After additional acrimonious exchanges, which boded ill for the future, the President promised on August 1 to represent the United States at a special meeting of the Security Council about August 12. Again Khrushchev committed an about-face. Following a hasty consultation with Mao Tsetung in Peking, he declared on August 5 that the entire Middle East question should be referred to the General Assembly; and it was there that the crisis was finally liquidated.

The supreme test of summit diplomacy began on November 10, 1958, when Khrushchev challenged the West's rights in Berlin. His demand that new arrangements be negotiated within the next six months led to a series of top-level visits and the first gathering of the foreign ministers since they broke up in failure in November, 1955. Khrushchev again preferred to go right to the summit, but the ailing Dulles refused to do so without some prospect of success. The Foreign Ministers Conference at Geneva, which lasted with one interruption from May 11 to August 5, 1959, hardly gave that assurance, yet tension eased when the six-month deadline expired without incident and an exchange of official visits by the President and Premier was announced. Following his checkered American tour, Khrushchev dropped the time limit for a Berlin settlement, while Eisenhower consented to a heads-of-government meeting without further specific agreements. From September, 1959, to February, 1960, a spirit of cordiality seemed to prevail; then it became apparent that two irresistible objects were about to collide. Although some progress had been made in narrowing differences over the suspension of nuclear tests, none had been registered on the broader aspects of arms control, the reunification of Germany, or the future of Berlin. Under these circumstances the summit conference, scheduled to open at Paris on May 16, 1960, held little hope of success even before an American reconnaissance plane was shot down deep inside Russia on May 1 and the government did not disavow the pilot.

Khrushchev's refusal to confer at Paris without an apology for violations of Soviet air space and his tirades against the American President spelled the end of summit diplomacy until Eisenhower left office. This outcome persuaded many citizens that the United States should return to traditional methods—the patient, unobtrusive, point-by-point negotiation at the ambassadorial level. These men argued that the president should not be exposed to the risk of personal failure or to the pressure of heads of government to whom the normal restraints of international intercourse are alien. Certainly the summit is a perilous place to bargain. It can be used more profitably in coordinating peacetime aims of trusted allies and in harmonizing military operations in coalition warfare. Yet while its suitability as a site for reconciling deep-seated differences in a cold war remains to be demonstrated, the trend of the times suggests that there will be further tests.

THE ROLE OF THE UNITED NATIONS

The inability of the United Nations to settle differences stemmed from the very nature of that organization. The efficient working of the Security Council depended upon unanimity among the permanent members, and its absence produced two baneful consequences. One was a failure to implement Article 43, which sought to maintain peace by placing military components at the disposal of the Council. The other was the frequent use by Russia of the veto, a device which often blocked action on nonprocedural matters even when seven or more parties voted in favor. By January 20, 1961, the Soviet Union had cast ninety-two vetoes, thirty-eight of them while Eisenhower was president; whereas France had exercised the privilege four times, the United Kingdom twice, and the United States never. Not all of Russia's vetoes, to be sure, abused the prerogative. Almost half dealt with the admission of new members, an issue that both camps exploited for tactical purposes. A few safeguarded the country's vital interests. The remainder, however, did go beyond what the framers of the Charter had expected; they severely crippled the Council's mediatory role and prevented it from checking major breaches of the peace or settling basic controversies threatening that peace.

This partial paralysis of the Security Council led to moves to enhance the authority of the General Assembly. Two steps had been taken under Truman. On November 13, 1947, an Interim Committee was set up to act between sessions, and for a couple of years it met frequently. The experience of the Korean War brought a more ambitious move. A four-point "Uniting for Peace" resolution, urged by Acheson and adopted on November 3, 1950, invested the Assembly with responsibility for handling breaches of the peace when vetoes hamstrung the Council. First, it provided in such cases for emergency sessions of the General Assembly on a day's notice if seven members of the Security Council or a majority of all members of the organization so requested. Second, it established a fourteen-member Peace Observation Commission for use by the Security Council, General Assembly, or Interim Committee to report on conditions in any area where international tensions imperiled the peace. Third, it invited all members to maintain units in their armed forces trained for special United Nations duty. Fourth, it created a Collective Measures Committee to suggest ways of improving existing security arrangements.

Although the "Uniting for Peace" resolution was hailed in 1950 as a major advance, it proved to be of limited usefulness. A single recommendation from the Collective Measures Committee has gone unheeded. Military components have not been regularly assigned to the United Nations, although a substantial force was hastily assembled in July 1960 to keep order in the liberated Belgian Congo. The Peace Observation Commission functioned only once; on December 7, 1951, the Assembly named a group to watch conditions in the Balkans. On four occasions an emergency session of the General Assembly has been convened: on November 1, 1956, to cope with the invasion of Egypt; on November 4, 1956, to deal with the suppression of the Hungarian uprising; on August 8, 1958, to consider the danger to Lebanon and Jordan; and on September 17, 1960, to continue the policy of aiding the Republic of the Congo. In the first and third instances the Assembly helped settle the crisis; in the second it accomplished nothing; in the fourth it adopted a resolution endorsing the course already charted but one which the Soviet Union opposed.

Although it was well for the veto-free General Assembly to gain this new responsibility for maintaining peace, a rapid expansion of membership offset some of the benefits Acheson had anticipated in shifting the center of influence from the veto-ridden Security Council. When the "Uniting for Peace" resolution passed, only nine countries had been added to the fifty-one who had signed the Charter. Thanks to the twenty Latin American nations and its thirteen NATO allies, the United States could normally muster an impressive majority on most issues of the Cold War. Then between December, 1955, and January, 1961, thirty-nine new members were admitted. Of these, twenty-eight came from the neutralist continents of Asia and Africa, while four others lay behind the Iron Curtain. As a result, the Eisenhower administration was no longer sure of a two-thirds margin on controversial questions, and it tended to play down the mediatory and peacemaking function of the General Assembly.

Perhaps the most important role of the United Nations in the Cold War after January, 1953, was the service rendered by the Secretary-General. The first incumbent, Trygve Lie of Norway, deliberately tried to provide leadership, and in June, 1950, he encouraged the Security Council to brand North Korea as an aggressor. In so doing, he antagonized the Russians who boycotted his endeavors and virtually forced him to resign. Dag Hammarskjold of Sweden succeeded him on April 10, 1953, and quickly gained the confidence of both East and West by his skill as a negotiator and his impartiality as an administrator. He preferred the quiet type of diplomacy and exploited the opportunities for informal discussion that his headquarters afforded. His personal contributions to reducing tensions were numerous. They included securing in August, 1955, a release by Communist China of

American fliers held in violation of the Korean armistice; persuading in April, 1956, the Arabs and Israelis to respect a cease-fire; planning in November, 1956, a United Nations Emergency Force to supervise the termination of hostilities in Egypt; organizing in June, 1958, a United Nations Observation Group in Lebanon to check alleged infiltrations from Syria; expediting in August, 1958, the withdrawal of Anglo-American troops from Jordan and Lebanon; and investigating in November, 1959, the explosive situation in Laos. In almost every case he acted at the request of the Council or Assembly, both of which showed a growing tendency on thorny issues "to let Dag do it."

Overnight the picture changed completely. After supporting on July 14, 1960, a plan by which the Secretary-General would create a peace force to aid the shaky Congolese government, Russia turned on Hammarskjold and accused him of favoring the "NATO colonialists." This reversal in reality reflected fear in Moscow that Hammarskjold's work would curb Communist infiltration into the troubled area and would demonstrate the capacity of the world organization to cope with similar threats to peace. Khrushchev wanted no such precedents set, and in the General Assembly on September 23 he demanded that the Secretary-General be replaced by a three-man directorate representing the East, the West, and the neutralist bloc. Hammarskjold refused to quit under fire, saying he would serve as long as the small powers wished him to do so. But it became increasingly evident during the winter of 1960–1 that his influence was declining, that his re-election was impossible, and that his successor—if one could be agreed upon—must come from Asia or Africa. It was also clear that in attacking the man and his office, the Soviet Union was trying to transform the character of the United Nations.

Ever since 1946 proposals had been offered to change the world organization by amending the Charter. The functioning of the Security Council, many persons felt, had been fatally weakened by the unrestrained use of the veto and the failure to place military components at its disposal. Others argued that the membership did not properly reflect the rise of new states after 1945. The Truman administration had discouraged wholesale change during the formative years but had supported attempts to strengthen the General Assembly and to forge regional arrangements for collective defense. Article 109 stipulated, moreover, that a call for a General Conference to review the Charter be put on the agenda for 1955 if such a gathering had not by then been held. In anticipation, the Senate set up on July 28, 1953, a subcommittee to prepare studies on key issues and to tap public opinion in several cities. The State Department favored review, as distinct from revision, but the Soviets opposed both. Hence an Assembly resolution of November 21, 1955, passed by a vote of 43 to 6, with 9 abstentions, merely recognized the desirability of re-examining the Charter periodically, agreed that a conference should meet at an appropriate but unspecified date, and established a large preparatory committee. Little has been done since then. Russia's refusal to serve on the committee and its ability to veto any amendment rendered unlikely any formal change in the foreseeable future.

Despite its unrectified flaws, the United Nations received from the Eisenhower administration the same wholehearted backing it had known under Truman. Although extremists in the Republican ranks might talk of diminished financial support or of withdrawal from the organization if it acted against their wishes, the President refused to countenance such blackmail. America, he told a group of recalcitrant congressmen in May, 1953, simply could not live alone in the atomic age. Thus even when the Eisenhower-Dulles policies operated outside of the Council and Assembly—as with the landings in Lebanon, the later arms negotiations, and the resort to summit diplomacy—the executive remained convinced, as he said on October 31, 1956, "that the United Nations represents the soundest hope for peace in the world." He lived up to that belief during the Suez crisis by placing loyalty to the Charter above loyalty to the chief NATO allies. Yet as Eisenhower left office, the institution to which he had been steadfastly true was about to undergo its severest ordeal.

THE NUCLEAR STALEMATE

Of all the problems spawned by the Cold War none exceeded in peril or perplexity the control of armaments. Man had indeed stolen the fire of the gods, and he must now learn to live with the horror of his achievement. Weapons of appalling power made it possible to destroy in hours a civilization built up over centuries. The frightening consequences of atomic warfare led optimists to argue that nations dared not embark upon it. This mutual deterrent, this balance of terror, this nuclear stalemate, they hoped, would compel statesmen in the 1950's to succeed where their predecessors had failed in dealing with the simpler issues of the 1930's. Yet that decade had showed that there could be no real disarmament without security and no security without faith in the pledged word of governments. The lesson of the recent past, in Czechoslovakia and Korea, warned the diplomats not to forget internal subversion and conventional forces while attempting to damp the fires of Prometheus.

Certain considerations shaped the Eisenhower administration's views on armaments. First, it did not trust Russia. The Kremlin, the President told Congress on March 13, 1959, was the center of "a fanatic conspiracy," and he repeatedly asked that Moscow's desire for peace be manifested by deeds, not words. Second, the United States had lost its monopoly in both fission and fusion bombs. Fifty months had elapsed between the first American atomic detonation in July, 1945, and the Soviet counterpart in September, 1949; only nine separated the initial hydrogen blast at Eniwetok in November, 1952, and the pioneer thermonuclear explosion in Siberia in August, 1953. Third, Communist scientists made sensational strides in rockets after Stalin's death. They launched an intercontinental ballistic missile in August 1957, fifteen months before the United States did so; they anticipated the Americans by three months in sending up an earth satellite in October, 1957. Fourth, the "nuclear club" was expanding. The British set off their first atomic device in October, 1952, and their first hydrogen bomb in May, 1957, while the French conquered fission in February, 1960. Lastly, the Republicans returned to office intent on equating military needs with material resources. They wished to reduce the defense budget by obtaining "more bang for the buck" and to free individual enterprise by removing government controls.

This great equation pointed to a new look in military planning and to massive retaliation in strategic thinking. The former stressed nuclear weapons at the expense of conventional arms; the latter justified that emphasis in the light of the Korean deadlock. The United States, according to Dulles, must not exhaust itself in wars of attrition in peripheral areas nor allow the size of its ground and sea forces to stunt its economic growth. Nations along the Sino-Soviet borders could mass sufficient troops to suppress internal subversion and to repel external attack, at least momentarily. America's might should be mustered to inhibit danger at its source by threatening nuclear annihilation. "Local defenses must be reinforced by the further deterrent of massive retaliatory power," the Secretary explained on January 12, 1954. "The way to deter aggression is for the free community to be willing and able to respond vigorously at places and with means of its own choosing." Some experts read the lessons of Korea differently and others contended that the nuclear stalemate had made massive retaliation impracticable, but the President adhered to the equation until the first sputnik orbited in outer space. Even then he denied that budgetary ceilings had cost the country superiority in the missile field or that a concern for thermonuclear wars had left it unfitted to cope with brushfire conflicts.

From the outset Eisenhower and Dulles strove to end the seven-year impasse on arms control. They worked initially through the United Nations which had established on January 11, 1952, a single commission to discuss both atomic and conventional weapons. When that body failed to register progress, it requested the five powers principally concerned—the United States, Britain, Russia, France, and Canada—

to seek a solution in private. Thus came into being the United Nations Disarmament Subcommittee which held 157 meetings between April 23, 1954, and September 6, 1957. Three topics dominated the conversations. One was an effective system of inspection to control the new weapons. This had been a primary American goal since 1946, but it became more pressing when technological change made impossible the complete elimination of fissionable materials. The second was a dependable method of preventing surprise attacks. The most publicized suggestion was the President's "open skies" plan offered at Geneva on July 21, 1955. The third was an immediate ban on testing nuclear and thermonuclear devices. First advanced by Nehru on April 2, 1954, when the terrifying results of the initial hydrogen bomb were discovered, it seemed to most of the world an attainable and indispensable beginning.

Neither of the first two topics appealed to Russia. Everything in the Communist commitment to a closed society militated against permitting outsiders to inspect, photograph, and control. Instead, the Soviets continued to advocate an immediate and total abolition of all atomic and hydrogen bombs, omitting, however, any meaningful guarantees; the complete withdrawal of American troops from foreign bases, emasculating thereby the North Atlantic alliance; and the drastic reduction of conventional arms and armies, preserving nonetheless their existing superiority. They used the moratorium on testing to embarrass the United States, especially after Eisenhower in June, 1954, and June, 1955, opposed the idea unless it contained adequate safeguards and was part of a larger settlement. They also fished in troubled waters during the presidential campaign in which Adlai Stevenson, the Democratic candidate, vainly urged his countrymen to take the initiative in halting further experiments.

After the election Russia renewed its agitation for suspending nuclear tests and on March 31, 1958, announced its intention to act alone, while reserving the right to resume if others did not follow suit. The United States countered on April 28 with a plea for technical studies to determine the feasibility of that approach. The Soviet Union consented, provided the inquiry was not conducted by the Disarmament Subcommittee, on which its satellites were poorly represented. Accordingly, two groups convened at Geneva in 1958. One sat from November 10 to December 18 and examined measures which might be helpful in preventing surprise attacks. It broke up in failure. The other, a panel of scientists, addressed itself from July 1 to August 21 to the possibility of detecting violations of an agreement on the suspension of nuclear tests. It was a partial success. Its report was so constructive that the American and British governments offered conditionally to halt testing and agreed to meet with Russia in a conference to draft a three-power treaty. That gathering opened on October 31, 1958, and at first made substantial progress, but during 1960 it bogged down on such issues as the number of on-site inspections, the length of the moratorium on testing, and the need for joint efforts to improve detection methods. After 273 sessions, it recessed on December 5 to await the inauguration of President John F. Kennedy.

This Conference on the Discontinuance of Nuclear Weapons Tests influenced and was influenced by developments in the broader area of disarmament. The encouraging start prompted the foreign ministers of the United States, the United Kingdom, the Soviet Union, and France to decide on September 7, 1959, to hold a ten-nation parley the next spring outside the United Nations. That same month, while in America, Khrushchev offered a four-year plan for total disarmament and two less sweeping alternatives. These were on the agenda when delegates from the United States, Britain, France, Canada, Italy, Russia, Czechoslovakia, Poland, Bulgaria, and Rumania assembled at Geneva on March 15, 1960. There the Soviet bloc concentrated on a three-stage scheme, to be completed in four years, in which the reduction of conventional forces and the elimination of foreign bases preceded a prohibition of nuclear weapons and the establishment of full supervisory machinery. The West also proposed a three-stage project, but it was gradual in development and specific in controls. On inspection the two sides were far apart, yet they deliberated in good temper for six weeks, almost next door to the group seeking a treaty to ban nuclear tests. On April 29 the ten-nation conference recessed in the hope that the summit meeting, scheduled to begin on May 16, could break the deadlock.

The fiasco at Paris killed those hopes, and the atmosphere was bleak when the talks resumed on June 7, 1960. In the light of the plane incident and in an effort to split the NATO allies, Khrushchev shuffled his formula and placed the destruction of nuclear weapons carriers in the first stage. This change compelled the chief American envoy to return to Washington for consultations. By June 27 he was back and ready to present a revised plan, which emphasized measures to guard against surprise attacks and to reduce the danger of missile warfare. Before he could speak, the Russian delegate announced that his country was interrupting participation in the conference because the United States and its associates had not negotiated in good faith. Declaring that the Soviets would refer the problem to the next session of the General Assembly, he stalked out of the chamber, followed by the representatives of the four satellites, without waiting to hear the American report.

Such was the situation as the Eisenhower administration ended. The ninety-nine-member Assembly was not a proper forum for handling complex and technical issues, and the session that opened on

September 20, 1960, did little but afford Khrushchev a platform from which to trumpet his appealing but deceptive plea for total and immediate disarmament. With mutual trust conspicuously absent, it was impossible to agree on either the restricted matter of weapons testing or the broader questions of reducing conventional forces, prohibiting missiles, curbing delivery systems, averting surprise attacks, controlling outer space, or creating inspection machinery. Torn between an abhorrence of renewing thermonuclear experiments, thereby polluting the atmosphere with fall-out, and a fear of trusting Russian assurances, thereby risking the chance of deception, the American people fervently hoped that the incoming Democrats could make a fresh start in removing the shadow of destruction that hovered over all mankind.

Europe: The Aftermath
of Containment

WHEN IN JANUARY, 1953, Eisenhower and Dulles surveyed the various fronts of the Cold War, they found Asia the most immediately dangerous; for the truce negotiations in Korea had dragged on interminably and the French position in Indochina had deteriorated alarmingly. The Middle East remained explosive, as the Arabs vowed to destroy Israel and extirpate the last vestiges of colonialism; but two years would elapse before Russia concentrated on that area. Europe was momentarily quiet, as both sides awaited final action on Pleven's Defense Community in which a rearmed Federal Republic would play a part; yet even if that hurdle was cleared, an early solution had to be found for three sources of trouble—a divided Germany, an exposed Berlin, and the captive peoples behind the Iron Curtain. In 1952, the Republicans had promised a positive and dynamic policy in Europe, condemning containment as negative and futile.

LIBERATION AND THE CAPTIVE NATIONS

Liberation of the Soviet satellites became a primary goal of the new administration. Like many slogans coined by Dulles, it soon had to be toned down. Yet it was an understandable response to a very real problem: the repudiation by Russia of its pledge at Yalta to cooperate in forming broadly representative governments and holding early free elections not only in Poland but also in all countries rescued from Nazi tyranny. This betrayal had been consummated by 1948, and Truman's second term witnessed in Eastern Europe the harassment of diplomatic missions and the flouting of legal rights. Religious bodies having ties with the West were persecuted; individual Americans were imprisoned for alleged espionage; the ministers to Bulgaria and Hungary were asked to leave the country. On November 3, 1950, the General Assembly condemned those two nations and Rumania for a "wilful refusal" to observe the peace treaties of 1947, but that reprimand did not loosen the Russian grip nor satisfy the American people.

How could liberation be effected? In 1951 Taft spoke vaguely of using exiles and intelligence agents for infiltration and subversion. In 1952 Dulles talked of "a beacon light of hope" that would produce unrest among the captive peoples and make their rulers impotent to pursue "their monstrous ways." Liberation, the 'Secretary-designate told the Foreign Relations Committee on January 15, 1953, could be accomplished by processes short of war. One of these Eisenhower revealed on February 20 when he asked Congress to declare that the United States rejected any interpretation of wartime agreements "which have been perverted to bring upon the subjugation of free peoples" and to express hope that victims of Soviet despotism would yet enjoy the right of self-determination promised in the Atlantic Charter. The resolution that emerged pleased neither the Republicans critical of Roosevelt nor the Democrats loyal to his memory, and no action was taken. Actually, as Dulles soon realized, to repudiate the Yalta understandings would destroy the main legal prop for American protests against Soviet absolutism in Eastern Europe. Moreover, the outbreak of antigovernment riots in East Berlin and East Germany on June 17, 1953, caught the advocates of liberation without any practical means of aiding those who were rebelling against Russia's puppets. Dulles could only claim that the Soviets had overextended themselves, while Eisenhower had to be content to offer food to the populace of the former capital. Congress did no more than resolve that the heroism displayed in Germany would aid the cause of freedom in all Communist-enslaved nations.

By 1955 it was difficult to tell the new Republican policy of liberation from the old Democratic one of containment. References to Eastern Europe grew fewer as Dulles had to cope with crises in Southeast Asia, the Formosa Strait, and the Middle East. The administration, to be sure, did not accept the existing situation as final or stop encouraging nations behind the Iron Curtain, and at the summit meeting in Geneva Eisenhower talked informally about the satellites. But he was unwilling to wreck the conference on that issue, and most Americans felt the same way. A month earlier, when Senator McCarthy tried to

EUROPE

1961

AREAS OF GERMANY PLACED
UNDER SOVIET AND POLISH
ADMINISTRATION, 1945

500 MILES

T.R.MILLER

insist upon a settlement at Geneva, his resolution was reported adversely by the Foreign Relations Committee and was then beaten on June 22 by a vote of 77 to 4. In 1956 the candidates and platforms of both parties were relatively subdued. The Democrats simply blamed their rivals for broken promises; the Republicans quietly voiced confidence that "peaceful policies, resolutely pursued," would restore freedom to oppressed peoples.

Shorn of partisanship and bombast, liberation remained a legitimate goal of the United States, but many Americans thought of it in overly simple terms. They envisaged the withdrawal of Soviet troops and the holding of free elections, confident that those steps would bring the overthrow of the unrepresentative satellite regimes. They forgot that many of the countries lacked a tradition of western democracy and that some might be willing to settle, as did Yugoslavia under Josip Broz-Tito, for a Communist state independent of the Kremlin. These differences were revealed in the revolutions that began in Poland on October 21, 1956, and in Hungary two days later. Both reflected Khrushchev's denunciation of Stalinism; both were directed against the tyranny of native party bosses and the power of the Russians in local affairs. But where the Poles were able to install a nationalist Communist government under Wladyslaw Gomulka and to inaugurate a new deal in relations with Moscow, the Hungarians pushed too far and tried to break out of the Soviet orbit entirely.

Thus the Hungarian revolt became an international issue. Begun on October 23, 1956, as a student protest against the Stalinist policies of Ernö Gerö, First Secretary of the Worker's Party, it sought the return as Premier of Imre Nagy, a moderate Communist. When Gerö invoked martial law and summoned Russian aid, he fanned the spark into a conflagration. Within a week Nagy had taken office, János Kádár had succeeded Gerö, and two high ranking envoys from the Kremlin had promised an immediate evacuation of all soldiers from Budapest and a later examination of all phases of Russia's military and economic position in Hungary. Whether these assurances of October 30 were made in good faith we do not know, but Nagy's followers carried him beyond a point the men in Moscow could tolerate. By November 1 a reversal had set in. As fresh Red troops crossed the border, Nagy proclaimed his country's neutrality between East and West and appealed to the United Nations for help in maintaining that status. By November 4 it was all over. Soviet tanks had stamped out resistance in the capital; hundreds of Hungarian youths lay dead in the streets. Kádár headed a new puppet government; Nagy had taken refuge in the Yugoslav embassy.

Russia's decision to crush the Hungarian insurrection by force resulted from a fear that its protective ring in Eastern Europe might crumble and from the opportunity that a simultaneous crisis in the Middle East afforded. On October 29, 1956, Israel invaded the Sinai Peninsula; two days later England and France opened air operations against Egypt. The Security Council was unable to halt these three resorts to arms because of Anglo-French vetoes on October 30 and a Russian one on November 4. In all cases the controversy was referred, under the "Uniting for Peace" machinery, to Emergency Sessions of the General Assembly. On November 5, with Dulles hospitalized by surgery and the popular mind riveted on the presidential election, Bulganin proposed joint Russo-American military action to bring peace to the Suez area. At once Eisenhower dismissed the suggestion as "unthinkable" and "an obvious attempt to distract world attention from the Hungarian tragedy." He looked to the United Nations to restore order in the Middle East and in Central Europe; he asked the Soviet Union to respect the decisions of that organization.

Neither the United States individually nor the United Nations collectively could save Hungary. The only weapon the former could employ was the bomb, and that, too, was unthinkable. So except for expressions of sympathy and appropriations for relief, the American government sat by helplessly. The United Nations could only appeal. Four times from November 4 to December 4, 1956, did the General Assembly call upon the Kremlin leaders to remove their troops and allow a representative cabinet to be formed. Four times it urged the Soviet Union to permit observers, designated by Hammarskjold, to enter Hungary and report their findings. Each time it was rebuffed. Hence on December 12, by a vote of 55 to 8 with 13 abstentions, the Assembly formally condemned Russia for violating the Charter and depriving the Hungarians of their independence.

One doubt gnawed at American consciences as Russia reasserted its control over Hungary. Had the policy of liberation led the freedom fighters in Budapest to expect armed assistance from the West? Did the United States bear some responsibility for their futile sacrifices? The government's Voice of America had certainly labored through broadcasts to keep the spirit of liberty alive behind the Iron Curtain, while the privately financed Radio Free Europe had been even less inhibited. Since the line between encouragement and incitement is shadowy at best, we shall never know the answers; but the episode did prompt the Eisenhower administration to rephrase its views on the captive nations. The President declared on November 14, 1956: "The United States doesn't now and never has advocated open rebellion by an undefended populace against force over which they could not possibly prevail." Yet he thought it would be a terrible mistake for the free world to accept as permanent the enslaved satellites and urged it to see that all men "live under governments of their own choosing." Accordingly, the United

States kept the issue of Hungary before the General Assembly and obtained from that body frequent reprimands of Russia's obstruction of justice.

While Eastern Europe was not the primary source of difficulty in the Cold War after 1956, it remained a constant irritant. On July 17, 1959, for example, in pursuance of a congressional resolution, Eisenhower proclaimed "Captive Nations Week." To Vice President Richard M. Nixon, then touring Russia, Khrushchev exploded with unusual vehemence and accused the United States of blocking a relaxation of tensions. Nor will television viewers forget the Soviet leader's rage on September 16, 1959, when he replied in Washington to a question about Hungary by likening it to a "dead rat" stuck in the throat of the American people.

THE EVOLUTION OF NATO

If by 1961 the times required a reappraisal of both liberation and containment, the same could be said of the North Atlantic Treaty Organization. Born of the fear that gripped Europe after the coup in Czechoslovakia in February, 1948, it became the central arch of Truman's foreign policy and continued little altered under Eisenhower save for the addition of West Germany on May 6, 1955. As an instrument of collective defense, NATO had succeeded to the extent that for a decade no aggression had been attempted against its members in the North Atlantic area. This respite can be attributed only in part to its military strength. Hobbled by competing strategic theories and changing weapons systems, NATO never possessed the thirty-five divisions set as a provisional goal for December, 1953, or the thirty described as a minimum in April, 1958. Neither the United States nor its allies were willing to pay the price of an integrated force-in-being that would counterbalance the Soviet bloc's ground troops on the Continent. They were content to maintain a protective shield, sufficient to deter limited probing actions and to slow down a major land attack until retaliatory bombing could be brought to bear. The United States Strategic Air Command, with bases in mid-America and in a wide arc around Russia's frontiers, constituted a striking sword for annihilating any aggressor. Yet as the decade passed, the Soviet Union's rapid strides in thermonuclear weapons led to a mutual deterrent which undermined the concept of massive retaliation.

Over the years the Kremlin leaders strove desperately to minimize the effectiveness of NATO. They played upon past enmities and current fears. They warned that any future war would hurt the European members the most; they proposed disarmament schemes calculated to deprive the United States of its forward bases. They tried desperately to keep the Federal Republic at Bonn out of the organization; and when they failed, they created their own regional grouping. The Warsaw Pact of May 14, 1955, bound Albania, Bulgaria, Czechoslovakia, East Germany, Hungary, Poland, and Rumania to the Soviet Union; it was almost a copy of the North Atlantic Treaty. Subsequently the Russians talked of merging the two alliances into a single European security system, from which the United States would be excluded. Russia reaped rich dividends when the Suez War in October, 1956, drove the chief Atlantic partners into opposite camps. But perhaps the most telling blow it dealt NATO was perfecting an intercontinental ballistic missile, for this achievement compelled Western planners to rethink their mission.

The gravity of the situation was underscored at the twentieth session of the North Atlantic Council in Paris on December 16–19, 1957. The heads of government attended for the first time and reached important military decisions. To offset Russia's lead in rockets, they agreed to train allied forces in the use of tactical atomic weapons, to stockpile nuclear warheads in Western Europe, and to emplace intermediate-range missiles in countries that would accept them. Thus they hoped to counter Soviet intercontinental missiles, aimed at the United States, with a shorter version that could travel the 1,500 miles from England to Moscow.

These agreements did not solve the problems troubling NATO. If anything, its difficulties multiplied in the ensuing months. First the weakness of France in the dying days of the Fourth Republic and then its intransigence under President Charles de Gaulle bade fair to reduce the contribution of a key member. Except for England, no nation consented to install launching sites for intermediate-range missiles until March, 1959; then only Italy and Turkey were willing. Prosperity dispelled the sense of urgency that had prevailed earlier in the decade, and the cost of nuclear arms tended to deprive NATO of an effective conventional capacity. The new Bundeswehr haunted those with long memories and caused some to wonder whether, in the missile age, it was not more of a provocation than a protection. Why not, some Europeans asked, recognize Russia's apprehension on this score and give up the rebuilding, in exchange for concessions from Moscow? Why not consider suggestions for establishing a demilitarized zone in Central Europe from which both nuclear and conventional weapons would be barred? Why not try disengagement in that area where a clash seemed most likely? Needless to say, Communist propaganda made the most of these misgivings, as it alternated blandishment with threats and called for total disarmament while warning of thermonuclear destruction.

There were no easy remedies for the ills that beset the North Atlantic Treaty Organization. Conceived in one phase of the Cold War, it had to adjust to the challenges of another. It had grown from a purely military alliance to a nerve center of coalition diplomacy. The containment of Russia in Europe remained a paramount objective, but it had to be attained without the atomic and hydrogen superiority the United States once enjoyed. This meant not only closing the missile gap which the Soviets had opened up but also preparing for limited wars with conventional weapons. It also meant that the European partners must contribute more in man power and industrial might as well as exercise a larger voice in the conduct of affairs. They were no longer the weaklings of 1948, while America's global commitments had expanded since that date. The toughest nut to crack was de Gaulle, whose evident capacity for leadership in the alliance was offset by his unilateral course on nuclear testing and his continued insistence that the United States, Britain, and France act as a *directoire* within the organization. Yet for all its weaknesses, NATO had a symbolic as well as a military value. After ten years of its semiannual ministerial meetings, its numerous planning committees, its periodic war games, and its extensive headquarters, America seemed a century removed from its traditional isolationism.

GERMANY: THE ELUSIVE TREATY

In seeking a peace treaty for Germany, Eisenhower and Dulles followed the path of Truman and Acheson. The latter, unable to reach an agreement with Russia on unification through open elections, had decided to make the Federal Republic part of the free world. They exploited the fears aroused by the Korean War to persuade England and France to end the joint occupation, grant the Bonn regime broad authority in internal and external affairs, guarantee its territory, and permit limited rearming. They had encouraged a European Defense Community, linked to NATO, which won the approval of the old Democratic Senate and the new Republican president. But France held back, reluctant to trust an ancient foe, while political instability brought into office eight different cabinets during the four years after Pleven had proposed his plan.

French hesitancy caused deep misgiving in Washington. Although Dulles knew that prospects were poor and that other arrangements might be devised, he fought doggedly for the European Defense Community. At two meetings of the Big Three foreign ministers in July and October, 1953, and at a three-power heads-of-government conference in December he refused to discuss a substitute. Eisenhower attempted to quiet French fears by promising on April 15, 1954, to keep American troops in Europe indefinitely and to regard a threat to the Community as one to the United States. Meanwhile, Dulles tried to frighten the French into acceptance. On January 27, 1953, he warned that if France, Britain, and West Germany did not act together, "it would be necessary to give a little rethinking to America's own foreign policy." On December 14 he told the NATO Council that the defeat of the European Defense Community "would compel an agonizing reappraisal" in the United States of fundamental principles. Congress did what it could to support the executive in threatening to suspend mutual security aid to any country which, by the end of 1954, had failed to ratify the pending treaty or an acceptable alternative.

Neither pressure nor promises prevailed, and on August 30, 1954, France killed the European Defense Community. This "major setback," as Eisenhower termed it, following the disunity revealed in Indochina, might have destroyed the alliance if Eden had not quickly hit upon a new idea. While Dulles was busy at Manila framing the Southeast Asia Treaty Organization, the British Foreign Secretary proposed to enlarge the Western Union created at Brussels on March 17, 1948. He would have Germany and Italy join the original members—England, France, Belgium, Luxembourg, and the Netherlands—while parallel provisions were made for admitting the Federal Republic to NATO and securing assurances from the United States. The details were agreed upon at London between September 28 and October 3, 1954. There Dulles held out the hope that the United States would keep in Europe enough troops to constitute a fair share of the men needed for the joint defense of the North Atlantic area, and Eden committed Great Britain to maintaining four divisions on the Continent until a majority of the Brussels Pact powers agreed to their withdrawal.

Four documents were signed at Paris on October 23, 1954. One restored full sovereignty to the Bonn regime and ended the occupation. A second provided for West Germany's adherence to the North Atlantic Treaty and membership in NATO. A third set up a seven-nation Western European Union. The fourth dealt with the Saar and Franco-German cooperation. The United States was a party to only the first two, and those the Senate approved on April 1, 1955, by a vote of 76 to 2. Three weeks earlier the President had repeated his pledge to retain a sizable defensive force in Europe. Although this declaration could not bind his successor, it went far to reassure France and to revitalize the Atlantic alliance.

The admission of West Germany to NATO attained only one goal of the Eisenhower administration. A second was to hold free elections as a first step toward unification and a definitive peace. Russia opposed that procedure. Fearful lest the Democratic Republic, with a population of 18,000,000 be swamped in a countrywide poll by the Federal Republic, numbering 53,500,000, Russia urged instead direct negotiations between East and West Germany while the occupying powers concentrated on a treaty. Because of these differences there had been no four-power talks since June, 1949, although Acheson had tried in September, 1952, to revive them. His bid was still unanswered when the Republicans took over. Soon afterward the death of Stalin and the agitation of Churchill encouraged the West to test the Malenkov regime. A joint note to Moscow on July 15, 1953, suggested that the foreign ministers meet, preferably in Switzerland, to consider the German and Austrian questions. It took four months for Russia to acquiesce in such a gathering, to be held at Berlin.

Nothing came of the Berlin Conference, which met from January 25 to February 18, 1954, except an agreement to discuss Asian matters at Geneva in April. The West wanted unification. In his opening remarks Dulles warned that the existing division "cannot be perpetuated without grave risks." A stable Europe required a free and united Germany. Eden then offered a simple five-stage plan by which all Germans, their choice safeguarded by international supervision, would elect a constituent convention. The resulting government would undertake to conclude a peace treaty with all nations that had been at war with the Nazis. But Russia was less interested in unification than in keeping the Federal Republic out of NATO and in forcing the United States off the Continent. To that end Molotov proposed an all-European security pact which would exclude the American government and replace both the European Defense Community and the North Atlantic Treaty. This scheme was unacceptable to the West, but it revealed the Soviets' intention to make German unity depend on a regional system in which Moscow, not Washington, would have the decisive voice. In short, the United States must choose between a divided Germany or dismantling the bulwarks of containment.

A second attempt to unify Germany occurred at the Geneva summit meeting on July 18–23, 1955. Russia's unexpected concessions in signing an Austrian peace treaty and its oft-expressed desires for a relaxation of tensions kindled hopes that never materialized. To be sure, Bulganin retreated a little in acknowledging that free elections in Germany were linked with European security and in agreeing to seek a solution on that basis. But when the foreign ministers met from October 27 to November 16, the old stumbling block reappeared. Molotov could not risk having the communistic Democratic Republic absorbed by the capitalistic Federal Republic lest he undermine the ring of satellites in Eastern Europe.

For the next three years all efforts to gain the elusive peace treaty foundered on Russia's insistence that the two Germanies negotiate directly. The Soviet stand reflected a relinquishment of earlier hopes that the Communists would dominate a unified Germany. Having failed to prevent the Federal Republic from rearming or joining NATO, the men in the Kremlin were determined to maintain their grip on East Germany and to build up its economic and military power. For the moment they would accept the zonal boundaries as the westernmost limit of Russian influence but reject any proposal that might sacrifice the German Democratic Republic. The frontier between East and West Germany, Khrushchev declared in July, 1959, "divides the world of socialism and the world of capitalism, and we will defend this frontier with all our strength."

During this period the idea of disengagement entered the discussion of the German problem. In the General Assembly on October 2, 1957, Adam Rapacki, the Polish Foreign Minister, advocated a ban on the production and stockpiling of atomic and hydrogen weapons by anyone in the two Germanies, Poland, and Czechoslovakia. Although George F. Kennan, as a private citizen, declared that reunification was impossible until all troops had been withdrawn from the heart of the Continent and a demilitarized zone had been established there, the United States rejected the Rapacki Plan. A note of May 3, 1958, called the scheme too limited to serve as a basis of European security and totally lacking in any control over the source of a thermonuclear attack.

Then in November, 1958, Khrushchev pushed the peace treaty into the background by precipitating a new crisis over Berlin. While that fuse sputtered dangerously, both sides had to set forth their position on unification. Russia submitted on January 10, 1959, a draft treaty to be considered at a conference in Warsaw or Prague within two months. This document recognized the existing boundary between East and West Germany, renounced all German claims to lands east of the Oder-Neisse line, and prohibited a reunited Germany from joining any alliance that did not number the four occupying powers among its members. The draft treaty also restricted Germany's right to possess armaments and required the withdrawal of all foreign troops from its soil within a stipulated period. The Western plan, presented at the Foreign Ministers Conference in Geneva on May 14, called for a committee of 25 members from West Germany and 10 from East Germany to frame an electoral law and the holding of elections to an all-German assembly within thirty months. The government thus formed would negotiate a peace treaty, and questions of removing armed forces from Germany must await that development. In short, Russia wanted to separate the issue of reunification from the peace treaty; the West insisted that no peace treaty was possible without reunification.

Actually, the emphasis at the Foreign Ministers Conference and in the preliminaries to the abortive summit meeting at Paris on May 16, 1960, was on disarmament, nuclear testing, and Berlin. The collapse of

top-level conversations raised anew the possibility that Khrushchev
would carry out his oft-repeated threat to sign a separate peace treaty
with East Germany. That step in itself might not be disastrous, but it
could lead to a situation which threatened the freedom of West Berlin
and the rights of the United States in that city.

BERLIN: THE SPUTTERING FUSE

Where a divided Germany was diplomatically frustrating, an exposed
Berlin was militarily dangerous. With the former, the United States had
learned to live over the years; with the latter, it had since the days of
the airlift done nothing to improve its position. Indeed, the situation
had worsened since May, 1949. Just as the zonal boundaries had
hardened into a frontier between capitalism and communism, so had
the sector lines within Berlin become more rigid. When the German
Democratic Republic was formed on October 7, 1949, it took East
Berlin as its capital. After that date, four-power control of the city was
virtually nonexistent. More ominous was an exchange of letters on
September 20, 1955, in which the Soviets made the East Germans
responsible for supervising civilian traffic and freight on the communication routes linking Berlin with the Federal Republic. Though this
move left in Russian hands the checking of men and supplies destined
for the Anglo-American-French garrisons, it provided the East German
regime, which the Western powers had not recognized, with the means
of disrupting life in Berlin. The United States, Britain, and France
warned that Russia would be held accountable for any infringements
of their rights in or leading to Berlin.

Such was the situation on November 10, 1958, when Khrushchev
told a Moscow audience that the four-power occupation of Berlin was
outdated. Brazenly accusing the West of violating the Potsdam Protocol
and thus forfeiting its rights, he announced that Russia would hand
over its functions in the former capital to the Democratic Republic and
urged the other three governments to do likewise. If they refused, they
must deal henceforth with the regime nominally headed by Prime
Minister Otto Grotewohl but actually ruled by party leader Walter
Ulbricht. Khrushchev gave no details on when or how the transfer
would be effected, but he said any resort to force by the West would
be met with force. In replying to this challenge, the United States and
its associates asserted that their authority in Berlin rested on the victory over the Nazis, not on the Potsdam accord. Their occupation rights
ran until the completion of a peace settlement with a unified Germany,
of which Berlin would be the capital. They had promised to protect the
residents of the Western sectors; they did not intend to violate that
pledge.

Khrushchev, however, was deadly serious. He could no longer endure an island of capitalism and prosperity in a sea of communism and want. So long as free Berlin stood in their midst, East Germans would not reconcile themselves to a Soviet type of police state. So long as the sector borders could be crossed, much-needed technicians and specialists would employ that escape hatch to freedom. So long as the Democratic Republic remained unstable, the entire satellite system was in jeopardy. The showcase of liberty must be destroyed, and Khrushchev was confident that, in time, he could oust its protectors. A decade earlier the West Berliners had been accustomed to austerity and their industry had been crippled; now the citizens waxed fat on profits and their factories were booming. A repetition of the aerial miracle of 1948–9 would be difficult, if not impossible. On the ground, the allied garrison of 11,000 was no match for the Red divisions encircling it. In short, conditions were ideal for applying pressure, and the possible rewards ranged from razing a Western outpost to gaining recognition for the East German regime.

On November 27, 1958, Khrushchev formally notified the three powers that Russia considered null and void its wartime consent to their presence in Berlin and their access to the city. Continued occupation of West Berlin, he argued, was abnormal and a threat to the security of the German Democratic Republic, the Soviet Union, and the entire Communist bloc. The controls hitherto exercised by the Red Army, he said, would be transferred to Grotewohl's government. Khrushchev preferred to unite the two Berlins and absorb them into East Germany, but as an alternative he would allow the Western sectors to be consolidated as a "free city." This separate political entity must be neutralized, disarmed, and barred from conducting subversive activities against its neighbors. The Premier concluded by saying that if an orderly solution were not forthcoming in six months, Russia would sign a peace treaty with East Germany.

The West stood firm. It denied Russia's right to renounce obligations unilaterally; it refused to abandon 2,250,000 West Berliners to communism. It was willing to negotiate, but not under an ultimatum and only within the framework of the broader German question. It set forth these views in a communiqué of the Western foreign ministers on December 14, 1958, in a declaration of the NATO Council two days later, and in notes to Moscow at the end of the year. None of these documents disclosed any new ideas for resolving the controversy on terms acceptable to both sides, and there ensued, on the surface at least, a war of nerves during which Eisenhower and Khrushchev speculated on what might happen if access to Berlin was severed. Yet even as men wondered whether an interrupted truck convoy might touch off a general war, the crisis eased. On his American tour in January, 1959,

First Deputy Premier Anastas I. Mikoyan ridiculed talk of an ultimatum; in February, British Prime Minister Harold Macmillan flew to Moscow to talk with Khrushchev; in March, French President de Gaulle implied that the Oder-Neisse line might be made permanent. Ultimately it was decided to reverse the procedure of 1955 and approach the summit through a meeting of the foreign ministers. Eisenhower was not eager for a heads-of-government confrontation, but he said he would attend if progress could be achieved at the lower level.

No real progress was made by the foreign ministers at Geneva from May 11 to August 5, 1959. Actually, Khrushchev did not want success, lest his insistence on the need for a summit meeting be disproved. He was satisfied when he obtained the attendance of the East Germans as observers. Although Secretary Herter and his colleagues concentrated on a package plan in which Berlin was only a part, they did make a few concessions. They talked of an interim agreement for Berlin which would ban atomic weapons or missiles in the city, limit the size of the Anglo-American-French forces there, and impose mutual restraints on propaganda activities. But a deadlock ensued over the Soviet refusal to acknowledge that the West's juridical position would remain unchanged at the end of the interim period and over the West's determination to stay in Berlin until a final settlement had been made for both Germany and the capital. This impasse was hardly surprising and, for the moment, not serious; for as the two sides talked, the Russian deadline of May 27 passed.

Indeed, Khrushchev seemed ready to forego his demand for both a prompt Berlin solution and an early summit meeting if he was invited to the United States. With Dulles dead, Eisenhower embarked upon a course of personal diplomacy. On August 3, 1959, he announced an exchange of official visits with the Soviet Premier, and on August 26 he flew to Bonn, London, and Paris to coordinate Western strategy. Khrushchev reached Washington on September 15 and ended his tour with two days of private conversations with the President. The two men wetted down the sputtering fuse by declaring that disarmament was the most important issue facing the world and that all outstanding international questions should be settled by peaceful means. As to Berlin, they agreed that negotiations should be reopened and that, while they must not be prolonged unduly, no time limit should be imposed. This formula removed any semblance of an ultimatum and permitted Eisenhower to accept a summit meeting which, like his visit to Russia, was later postponed until the spring of 1960.

Berlin may have been the rock on which that much-anticipated gathering was wrecked. Between September, 1959, and May, 1960, the two sides failed to close the gap which separated their solutions for the divided capital. If anything, lines tended to harden. Russia still demanded the withdrawal of allied troops; the three powers still insisted on the right to remain until Germany was unified. Khrushchev talked about converting West Berlin into a free city but shied away from including East Berlin in the arrangement. Many prominent Americans argued that the United States should not negotiate at all, that the existing situation was better than anything the Kremlin leaders might concede. In March, the Soviet Premier learned from conversations with de Gaulle in Paris and from announcements by Adenauer and Eisenhower in Washington that his hopes were not going to materialize, and perhaps he began to suspect he had mistaken the President's geniality for weakness. Simultaneously the ten-nation conference on disarmament at Geneva reached a deadlock. In short, it is likely that Khrushchev had written off the summit as a place to solve the Berlin riddle even before the fateful U-2 flight on May 1, 1960, gave him an opportunity to place the blame for the disruption of the heads-of-government conference on the United States.

As the Eisenhower administration drew to a close, the fuse was still sputtering in Berlin. How long it could do so without detonating an explosion was a point on which experts disagreed. Some argued that an iron nerve and the *status quo* offered the best hope. Khrushchev showed unexpected restraint following his tirades in Paris and stated that he would wait until after the American election before signing a separate peace treaty with East Germany. On October 18, 1960, he set April, 1961, as a new deadline. At the same time he seemed to give Ulbricht free rein to engage in nuisance tactics, just so long as there was no showdown. The Soviet Premier also used the threat of such a treaty as pressure upon the West to accept his ideas on disarmament. For he realized that of all the problems confronting the men in Washington, Berlin was the least susceptible of a satisfactory outcome. Militarily the Atlantic alliance could not withstand a determined assault upon its position there, yet it dared not retreat from pledges to hold firm. To escape from this *cul de sac*, the United States had to seek accommodation on other troublesome issues in the hope of reducing tensions and avoiding a crisis until the larger German question was resolved. Berlin thus remained a thermometer of the Cold War, a symptom of the disease but not the actual cause.

58

❯❯❯-❯❯❯-❯❯❯-❯❯❯≺≺≺-≺≺≺-≺≺≺-≺≺≺

East Asia: The Duel
with Communist China

FOREMOST AMONG the danger zones in which the Republicans might be expected to reverse Democratic policy was East Asia. Unlike Europe, where sustained attacks on containment barely antedated the election of 1952, partisan differences over China, Formosa, and Korea had grown ever since the collapse of the Marshall mission in 1947. By 1953 the Truman administration stood accused of having suffered in China the most disastrous diplomatic defeat in recent years, of having removed in MacArthur the most glamorous military hero of the twentieth century, and of having retained in Acheson the most criticized secretary of state of all time. Worse yet, it seemed unable to curb Communist China, the most difficult foe ever encountered in the Orient, or to end the Korean War, the most unpopular appeal to arms since Madison's ill-starred venture in 1812.

THE KOREAN TRUCE

Whatever else the triumphant Eisenhower might wish to do after January 20, 1953, halting the fighting in Korea claimed top priority. No act in the presidential campaign aroused more enthusiasm than his promise to go personally to the scene of hostilities, a step he took in December, 1952. On his way back, he reached two decisions for breaking the log jam in the cease-fire conversations, which had begun on

July 10, 1951, and had bogged down on October 8, 1952 over repatri-
ating prisoners. One was to strive for an honorable truce within the
framework set by his predecessor rather than launch an offensive
against Communist China along the lines advocated by MacArthur.
The other was to let Peking know that if the discussions dragged on
interminably, the United States might resort to tactical atomic weapons in Korea.

Slowly the new administration felt its way along a path fraught
with peril. For domestic consumption, Eisenhower encouraged raising
new South Korean divisions, but he angered Rhee by barring unification of the peninsula by force. To keep the foe guessing, Eisenhower
announced that the Seventh Fleet would no longer neutralize Formosa
Strait, yet he alarmed his allies in the process. Somewhat ostentatiously, jet fighters were added to the Far Eastern Command, and
nuclear missiles were moved to Okinawa. Most important of all, Dulles
impressed upon Nehru while in New Delhi on May 21–2, 1953, his
government's determination to end the war promptly—by negotiation
if possible, by arms if necessary. He was sure that information would
reach Peking quickly, and it did.

These tactics produced results. At Panmunjom on March 28, 1953,
the Red commanders suddenly reversed themselves and agreed to exchange the sick and wounded before concluding an armistice. They
also proposed to resume the parleys interrupted five months earlier.
Like Truman, Eisenhower held fast to the principle that no captive who
had turned against communism should be sent back to his native land
involuntarily. On May 25 the United Nations delegate suggested that
all prisoners who chose not to be repatriated should be placed in neutral custody for a definite period, during which time they would be informed about the choices open to them. Ten days later, a fortnight after
Dulles spoke to Nehru, the Chinese and North Koreans accepted those
terms. But the long-awaited cease-fire was not yet a reality. In Washington, Knowland and Taft called the prospective truce dishonorable
and a threat to American interests in East Asia. In Seoul, Rhee freed
27,000 anti-Communist North Koreans in his custody and vowed he
would ignore any order to halt the fighting.

Dulles learned of Rhee's catastrophic behavior on June 18, 1953,
at two in the morning. He telephoned Eisenhower immediately, and together they discussed what should be done if the Communists used the
incident as a pretext to break off, or even prolong, the negotiations at
Panmunjom. By his own account, the United States stood on the brink
of a new war and had to decide what strategy to pursue if the worst
came to pass. The President and the Secretary apparently felt they had
no choice but to fight with every resource at their disposal, including
tactical atomic bombs. Dulles never claimed that this decision caused

Mao Tse-tung or Chou En-lai to avoid a rupture, but he did argue that the administration carried the day by maintaining a resolute front and making clear its general intentions. Whatever the reason—the most likely being a realization that the Republicans would neither intensify the conflict nor abandon nonrecognition—Peking chose the path of peace.

The armistice signed by the field commanders on July 27, 1953, called for a cease-fire and drew a demarcation line where the front had been stabilized. It established a demilitarized zone four kilometers deep, prohibited the introduction of reinforcements, provided for an exchange of prisoners as outlined above, and set up a neutral commission to insure compliance. The new dividing line ran irregularly in a northeasterly direction from a point just below the thirty-eighth parallel on the Yellow Sea to a point thirty miles above it on the Sea of Japan, thus adding to Rhee's domain, after three years of fighting, some 1,500 square miles. To "a political conference of a higher level" were entrusted such unanswered questions as the ultimate withdrawal of troops and the eventual unification of the peninsula. Scheduled to meet within ninety days, that body never assembled because of disagreements over its composition.

To bolster the truce, Dulles took two steps. First, he won from the sixteen participants in the United Nations Command on July 27, 1953, a pledge to resist promptly any breach of the armistice and a warning that, "in all probability," a renewal of hostilities could not be confined "within the frontiers of Korea." Second, he initialed at Seoul on August 8, 1953, the draft of a mutual defense treaty by which the United States and the Republic of Korea agreed to consult together whenever, in the opinion of either, the independence or security of either was threatened by "external armed attack." They recognized that such an attack in the Pacific area in territories then under their administrative control would imperil the peace, and each promised "to meet the common danger in accordance with its constitutional processes." In addition, South Korea granted the United States the right to station land, air, and sea forces on or about its soil. In general, the terms followed the spirit and the wording of the pacts concluded with Australia, New Zealand, and the Philippines in 1951 and represented a less automatic commitment to render military aid than the North Atlantic and Inter-American Treaties. The signing took place in Washington on October 1, 1953, and the Senate gave its consent on January 26, 1954, by a vote of 81 to 6. The upper house did append a reservation which expressly limited America's obligation to defending the territory below the armistice line.

Despite evident shortcomings, the Korean truce marked the first major East-West agreement since the lifting of the Berlin blockade in May, 1949. It encouraged the foreign ministers on February 18, 1954, at the end of the futile Berlin Conference, to seek at Geneva a twofold reduction of tensions in Asia. First the participants in the Korean War would try to dispose of unfinished business; then the Big Four and Communist China would discuss with "other interested states" the restoration of peace in Indochina. By the time the delegates assembled on April 26, the French collapse in northern Vietnam cast a pall over the proceedings. The Communists were confident and uncompromising; the Western allies were confused and divided. The former's plan for unifying Korea was almost identical to that advanced in 1950. There was no guarantee that countrywide elections would adhere to democratic standards, no assurance that the more populous non-Communist section would be given a larger voice, no recognition of the fact that a mutual withdrawal of troops meant a short distance for Russia and China but a long one for the United States. Since the Red leaders insisted on excluding the United Nations from the settlement, the sixteen countries that had fought under its banner had no choice but to break off negotiations on June 15, 1954.

In 1954 a solution to the Korean problem was no nearer than it had been in 1947. If anything, the opposing positions had hardened with the growth of separate economic and political institutions. After the fiasco at Geneva, no concerted attempt was made to promote unity. The subject has been raised periodically in the General Assembly, and loose talk of forcible unification has been heard in Seoul and Pyongyang. The truce terms have been grossly violated, but the line remains intact. No one liked the situation, and many realized its dangers, yet the alternative seemed too high a price to pay. On the other hand, continued support of the autocratic Rhee regime was also costly. The violent student riots which toppled the aged leader on April 27, 1960, were a sharp reminder that not every anti-Communist is a reliable and useful ally in a battle that transcends any one nation and affects uncommitted peoples everywhere.

THE TWO CHINAS

Although a divided Korea posed the initial problem in East Asia for the Eisenhower administration, the existence of two Chinas proved to be the most persistent. The first required ending a bloody limited war and enduring an uneasy cease-fire. The second led to continued backing of a weak fugitive government that symbolized a discredited past and continuing opposition to a strong revolutionary movement that promised a bright future. Where the Korean truce was followed by years of relative calm, the crises over Nationalist and Communist China grew more frequent. Indeed, the duel with the People's Republic permeated all of American diplomacy and raised the question of the West's ability to survive in the Orient.

By January, 1953, implacable hostility existed between Peking and Washington. The causes were many. Quite apart from its economic and social doctrines, Mao Tse-tung's regime had confiscated American property, had imprisoned American citizens, and had humiliated American officials. It had entered into a thirty-year alliance with Russia and had become its partner in the Cold War. It had thwarted an American victory in Korea and had defied the United Nations. It accused the United States of aggression in the Formosa Strait and of germ warfare in the Korean Peninsula. It vowed to liberate the islands held by Chiang Kai-shek; it gave substantial aid to the anti-French rebels in Vietnam. It maintained a steady stream of vilification against everything American. On their side, the Chinese Communists hated the United States for arming the Nationalists during the civil war, for protecting the Generalissimo after his flight, and for withholding a recognition that many had accorded. They saw in Washington a malevolent, reactionary spirit that constituted the main obstacle to their present admission to the United Nations and their future expansion in South and Southeast Asia.

It was easy for the incoming Republicans to shape their policy on Nationalist China. They decided, as Truman had done, to regard Chiang Kai-shek as the legitimate ruler of the Chinese people, to strengthen his defenses with arms under the Mutual Security Act, and to postpone a decision on the legal status of Formosa. They would continue to endorse Chiang's envoy as the rightful occupant of the permanent seat on the Security Council. But after promising on the hustings to end Democratic "neglect of the Far East," they must do something more. Hence they tried to encourage Nationalist hopes for recovering the mainland and to provide additional safoguards for American interests in East Asia.

On February 2, 1953, Eisenhower told Congress that the Seventh Fleet would "no longer be employed to shield Communist China." Changed conditions, he said, justified reversing Truman's order of June 27, 1950, for the navy to patrol Formosa Strait and to inhibit military moves in either direction. Like many statements of the new administration, this one was dramatically presented and seemed more important than it was. Widely heralded as "unleashing Chiang Kai-shek" —although the President had not used those words—it conveyed the impression that a Nationalist offensive was imminent. Actually, no such undertaking was possible, and the men in Peking were less frightened than America's friends in Europe and Asia, who had little love for the Generalissimo and his cause.

More important was the mutual defense pact of December 2,

1954. With the Philippines, Australia, New Zealand, Japan, and Korea already cared for, some assurances had to be given China. For various reasons, Dulles waited to complete the Southeast Asia Collective Defense Treaty on September 8, 1954, before dealing with the Nationalists alone. By then he was more interested in stabilizing the Pacific along existing lines than in exacerbating tensions by talk of "unleashing." His chief objective was a pledge by Chiang not to use force without American consent; his formula was a ten-article pact, similar to those with the countries named above, and an exchange of letters spelling out that commitment. Under the first, each party recognized that "an armed attack in the West Pacific Area" against the territory of either would imperil its own safety, and each promised "to meet the common danger in accordance with its constitutional processes." Formosa and the adjacent Pescadores were defined as the Nationalist soil thus covered; nothing was said about the lesser offshore islands. American land, air, and sea forces might be stationed "in and about" Formosa and the Pescadores. Because these terms left Chiang free to attack the mainland and thereby start hostilities which could involve the United States, Dulles eliminated that possibility by an exchange of letters. The Senate gave its consent on February 9, 1955, by a vote of 64 to 6, but appended three reservations. The most significant restricted the obligations of the parties to cases of "external armed attack" and required that military operations by either, from territories held by Nationalist China, be undertaken only after joint agreement.

Less easy to devise was a positive policy toward Communist China. The negative course of withholding recognition commanded wide popular approval. A few men argued that it was sterile and unrealistic, serving only to alienate friends—Chiang excepted—and antagonize foes. But Dulles was convinced it was morally sound and strategically wise. He insisted that so long as the People's Republic violated the Korean truce, threatened to employ force in the Formosa Strait, imprisoned American citizens, and heaped calumny upon the United States, it must be kept beyond the pale. To do otherwise would dishearten millions of Chinese on the mainland, break faith with a loyal ally, weaken free Asia's resistance to pressure by Peking, and vitiate the United Nations as an instrument of peace. As late as December 4, 1958, he warned that recognition would be "a well-nigh mortal blow to the survival of the non-Communist governments in the Far East."

Admission to the United Nations was the second problem posed by the two Chinas. Dulles could count on powerful support at home for barring a regime which the General Assembly had condemned for aggression in Korea. Some congressmen were ready to deny funds to, even to withdraw from, that organization if the Communists were seated. On at least six occasions after January, 1953, the Senate and House, or one of them, formally voiced disapproval and by overwhelming margins. On the other hand, the Secretary saw his backing abroad steadily declining. Each autumn, starting in 1950, the United States delegate moved to postpone action on Peking's bid for membership. Each year the motion prevailed, but the majority of affirmative ballots dropped from 78.5 per cent in 1953 to 42.8 per cent in 1960. On the last occasion, the verdict would have been reversed if nine of the twenty-two abstainers had voted with the minority.

Restrictions on trade with Communist China constituted a third aspect of the new administration's policy. Ever since December, 1950, the United States had maintained a total embargo on economic transactions with the People's Republic and had tried to preserve among its allies the curbs on strategic materials recommended by the General Assembly on May 18, 1951. As the exigencies of the Korean War receded, many European countries wished to relax those shackles and replace them with the sort imposed on other members of the Soviet bloc. Dulles fought hard to keep the differential, and Congress for a while made its continuation a prerequisite for assistance under the Mutual Security Act. By May, 1957, however, the British were willing to risk American displeasure by paring the forbidden items to those denied Russia and its satellites. The State Department expressed keen disappointment, but there was no reprisal.

None of the foregoing attitudes precluded Dulles from dealing directly with Communist China when American interests might be advanced, but he tried to confine such contacts to subordinates. Only once, during the abortive Geneva Conference on Korea in April, 1954, did he consent to sit across the table from Premier Chou En-lai. His goal, shorn of its frequently confusing verbiage, was to limit the material prosperity and military capacity of a dangerous foe by moral disapproval, diplomatic isolation, and economic pressure. Feeling that Mao's regime would eventually collapse, he sought to restrict its territorial expansion and to keep alive a rival government. Knowing that "face" meant power in the Orient, he strove to prevent the People's Republic from playing a major role on the world scene. He repeatedly rebuffed Soviet attempts to convert the Big Four into a Big Five, but the men in Peking grew constantly bolder and twice threatened America with war over the offshore islands.

THE OFFSHORE ISLANDS

Quemoy and Matsu became the best known of the offshore islands, a chain that parallels the Asiatic coast a hundred miles west and northwest of Formosa. They had a particular nuisance value because Que-

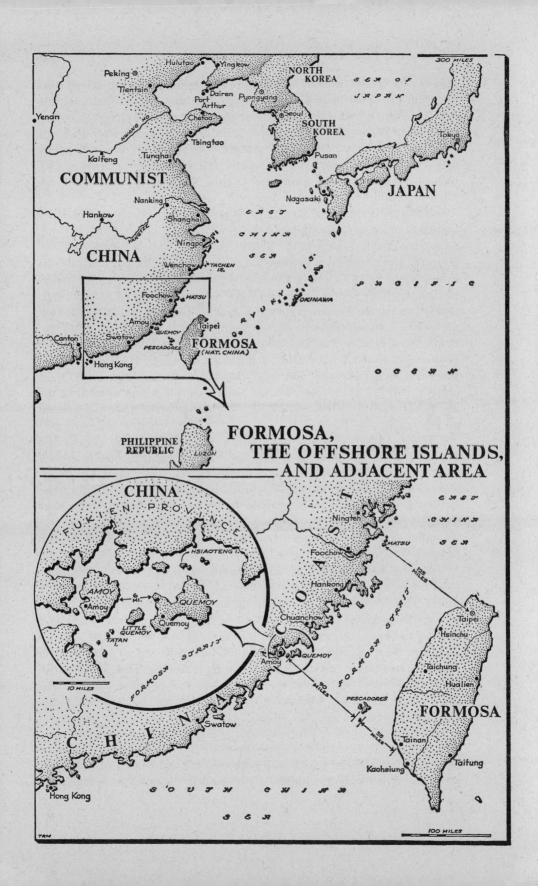

FORMOSA,
THE OFFSHORE ISLANDS,
AND ADJACENT AREA

moy lay barely six miles from the port of Amoy and Matsu less than ten from the coast near Foochow. None of these offshore islands had ever been in Communist hands, but that fact did not deter Mao Tse-tung, after December, 1949, from claiming sovereignty over them as well as over Formosa and the Pescadores. He branded Chiang Kai-shek as a traitor and accused his American protectors of meddling in China's internal affairs. He promised to oust the Generalissimo and his alien supporters.

Not until two other threats of war had been eliminated did the United States and Communist China clash in the Formosa Strait. First, as we have seen, there was the fighting in Korea, where Eisenhower on June 18, 1953, considered using tactical atomic bombs if the talks at Panmunjom broke down. Second, as we shall see, there was the struggle in Indochina, where Dulles on April 3, 1954, proposed armed intervention to rescue the beleaguered French. After the partition of Vietnam and the conclusion of a cease-fire in that area on July 20, 1954, the Peking government was free to probe Chiang's defenses. Chou En-lai proclaimed an early liberation of Formosa, to which the President replied that an invasion "would have to run over the Seventh Fleet." Discretion dictated, therefore, testing American intentions regarding the lesser outposts, and the first heavy bombardment of Quemoy opened on September 3, 1954.

This peril split Eisenhower's advisers. Some felt that the United States must pledge itself to defend the offshore islands; others argued for a flexible policy. The President chose the latter by deferring a decision until an assault materialized and it could be seen whether the landing was limited in scope or preliminary to one on Formosa. He thus followed the treaty of December 2, 1954, which brandished a determination to defend Formosa but masked a design for Quemoy and Matsu.

After several weeks of intermittent shelling, the Communists tried to pierce this ambiguity. On January 18, 1955, they captured one of the Tachen Islands, the northernmost group in the chain. Eisenhower then decided the remaining two Tachens were dispensable and ordered the navy to cover the evacuation of 11,000 Nationalist soldiers stationed there. At the same time he attempted to warn Chou that the United States might resist an attack on other offshore islands. On January 24 he asked Congress to supplement the pending treaty with Chiang by authorizing him to employ armed force "to assure the security of Formosa and the Pescadores" and, if need be, other "closely related localities" which he did not identify. Like Wilson during the Veracruz episode, he admitted he had the power to act; but he felt that if the executive and the legislature joined in a clear notice of firm purpose, the Chinese Communists would be less disposed to "precipitate a major crisis which even they neither anticipate nor desire." In short, he wanted to avoid the mistake he believed Truman and Acheson had made on the eve of the Korean War.

Congress responded promptly. The House the next day and the Senate on January 28, 1955, granted him authority to protect against armed attack not only Formosa and the Pescadores but also "such related positions and territories of that area now in friendly hands." He was empowered to take any additional measures that he judged appropriate, and the resolution was to remain in effect until the president decided that peace had been secured. Despite huge majorities—409 to 3 in the House and 85 to 3 in the Senate—there was much misgiving on Capitol Hill. Few felt the retention of Quemoy or Matsu was worth a war; many preferred, as did the European allies, to hold a line that was militarily less vulnerable and diplomatically more acceptable. Knowland and others, however, were quick to assail any retreat as a "Far Eastern Munich." What worried most legislators was the uncertainty; yet an amendment confining the authorization to Formosa and the Pescadores was defeated by a vote of 74 to 13. Democratic Senator George was determined to give the President exactly what he wanted, and he succeeded in doing so.

Gradually this first crisis over the offshore islands subsided. On February 3, 1955, Chou En-lai rejected a Security Council invitation to discuss a cease-fire. He called it intervention in China's domestic affairs and demanded that both the Nationalists and the United States get out of Formosa. In Tapei leaders claimed American backing for holding Quemoy and Matsu, while Chiang said he expected "material and logistical support" for his reconquest of the mainland. Dulles denied such assurances had been given, and Eisenhower asserted that his country "was not going to be a party to an aggressive war." Then on April 23 Chou suddenly offered to negotiate directly for a relaxation of tensions. Whether he was impelled to do so by troubles at home, by pressure from the new Bulganin-Khrushchev regime, by advice from Asian diplomats at the Bandung Conference, or by firmness in American policy, we still do not know. Dulles, for one, maintained that his willingness for the third time to go to the brink of war was primarily responsible. In any case, Quemoy and Matsu dropped out of the headlines for almost three years.

When they reappeared, it was in the midst of a crisis over the Middle East and on the heels of a Khrushchev visit to Peking. Again, the historian cannot say with confidence why the Communists resumed shelling Quemoy on August 23, 1958. Perhaps they wished to divert attention from domestic difficulties; perhaps they hoped to influence the United Nations in the annual vote on membership; perhaps they expected to find American resistance weaker. In the last, they were quickly disillusioned. Dulles cautioned them not to assume that an invasion of the offshore islands could be "a limited operation." On September 4, 1958, he noted that the authority contained in the resolution of January, 1955, might be used to cover Quemoy and Matsu and that those sites "have increasingly become related" to the defense of Formosa. To newsmen he spoke off the record of possible retaliatory bombing of the mainland if the Communists landed on Quemoy. A week later Eisenhower asserted that the current offensive was part of a plan to "liquidate all of the free-world positions in the Western Pacific." Decrying the folly of appeasement, he asked the nation to uphold the principle that armed force may not be employed to effect political change. Meanwhile the navy furnished escorts for Nationalist convoys to Quemoy, and warships hurried to Asiatic waters from distant stations. Khrushchev responded with a blunt warning that in a clash with the United States, the People's Republic could count on Russian aid. The Soviet Premier also demanded that the President end American intervention in China's internal affairs, recall the Seventh Fleet from the Formosa Strait, and evacuate all men and planes from Chiang's insular refuge.

The public interpreted the administration's cryptic statements as a hardening of its earlier stand. Combined with the serious situation in the Middle East and the dire threats of the Moscow press, they brought an outburst of domestic disapproval. Why, critics asked, was Chiang allowed since 1955 to commit a third of his best troops to Quemoy and Matsu? Why should the United States underwrite such folly? Was refusal to do so appeasement? On September 5, 1958, former Secretary Acheson spoke of "drifting, either dazed or indifferent" toward "a war without friends or allies" over issues which were not worth "a single American life." In Europe there was consternation at Eisenhower's apparent insistence that Quemoy, like Berlin, represented a test of the West's resolution to halt Communist aggression. In Washington congressional sources reported a heavy volume of adverse mail, while a State Department official estimated that 80 per cent of the letters received had found fault with or expressed apprehension over American policy.

Then on September 30, 1958, Dulles began to modify that policy, while denying he was doing so. First, he stressed that the United States had no commitment to protect the offshore islands or to help recover the mainland. Second, he conceded that "it was rather foolish" for Chiang to have put so many men on Quemoy and agreed that they could be removed if a dependable cease-fire were arranged. Third, he indicated that a *de facto* cease-fire fell into that category. Fourth, he intimated that once the shelling had stopped, he would urge the Generalissimo to reduce his force on the outposts. Only a day earlier Under Secretary Herter had called the offshore islands "not strategically defensible in the defense of Formosa" and described the Nationalist devotion to them as "almost pathological." On October 1 the President said much the same. Here certainly was a new emphasis, if not a new departure, and in Tapei, Chiang termed it "incredulous" and "incompatible with our stand."

But this shift hastened the end of a profitless Red venture. Thanks to American aid, Nationalist ships and planes enabled Quemoy not only to survive but also to grow stronger. Accordingly, the Communists announced on October 6, 1958, that "out of humanitarian considerations" they would halt for seven days the bombardment of the offshore islands. Supplies might be brought in freely, provided there were no American escorts. A week later they extended the respite for a fortnight, during which time Dulles flew to Tapei. On October 23 he and Chiang reaffirmed their solidarity, but for the first time the latter conceded that his rule on the mainland would not be restored by force. Two days later the Communists proclaimed that they would refrain from shelling Quemoy on even-numbered days, reserving the right to do so on odd-numbered ones. Foolish as this sounded, it was a retreat; and Dulles could boast that his policy of firmness, always dangerous and often ambiguous, had been vindicated again.

Yet Eisenhower left office with the problem of Communist China much as it had been in 1953. He had rejected the idea of accepting two separate states. He had withheld recognition of the Peking regime. The majority in the General Assembly opposed to admitting the People's Republic had dwindled alarmingly. The offshore islands remained a source of danger. The shelling of Quemoy went on spasmodically, except for a heavy barrage during the President's visit to Tapei in June, 1960. On the mainland, Mao had become firmly entrenched and was rapidly converting a once dormant giant into a major power. Self-imposed travel restrictions, however, hampered an intelligent assessment of these developments in the United States. Indeed, an air of unreality marked American thinking about the Oriental colossus. There were, to be sure, no easy solutions; but an agonizing reappraisal of policy was long overdue.

THE JAPANESE BASTION

Of all the prizes at stake in the duel with Communist China, Japan ranked first. In contrast to Rhee's Korea and Chiang's Formosa, it offered assets of the highest order. Strategically located, it possessed a mature industrial economy, an abundant labor supply, and a strong military potential. Like West Germany, Japan had been transformed by the Cold War from an enemy to a friend and had proved its worth during the Korean conflict. By the time Eisenhower took office, the original plan to neutralize and disarm the islands had given way to a decision to incorporating them in a regional system of collective defense. This was done in the bilateral security pact, signed the same day as the fifty-one nation peace treaty of September 8, 1951. Thereafter Japan stayed basically in Western camp, although its leaders were sensitive to the Afro-Asian revolt against colonialism abroad and the deep-seated desire for neutralism at home. They recognized Nationalist China and undertook a program of rearming which enabled the last American ground troops to leave in February, 1958.

Both Russia and Communist China tried by cajolery, threats, and subversion to divide Japan from the West. The Soviets overplayed their hand at first by intransigence, economic reprisals, and four vetoes in the Security Council against Japanese membership. In 1956 they shifted tactics and agreed on October 19 to negotiate a peace treaty, resume diplomatic relations, repatriate war prisoners, renounce reparations, and support Japan's admission to the United Nations. This helped somewhat, though the treaty did not materialize. The Chinese Communists followed a harsher line. They exploited fully Japan's desire to recover captives still held on the mainland and markets that had once been a source of lucrative trade. By May, 1958, the People's Republic had embargoed all commerce with Japan and had persuaded Socialists in that country to demand the abrogation of treaty ties with both Washington and Tapei.

Sino-Soviet efforts to deprive the United States of its Pacific bastion benefited from several troublesome issues in Japanese-American relations. The governments in Tokyo and Seoul bickered frequently over a variety of matters, and Dulles had to be careful not to offend one ally or the other. The Secretary did not like Japan's attempts to expand its business with Communist China or the reduction in July, 1957, by the friendly cabinet of Nobusuke Kishi of the ban on strategic commodities. Pentagon planners thought Japanese rearmament was too slow, but leaders in Tokyo had to reckon with a growing opposition. The use of land near a major American installation on Okinawa was a constant irritant. The Japanese were understandably aroused over the horrors of nuclear warfare and repeatedly urged a suspension of weapons testing in the Pacific. After 1958 Khrushchev effectively played upon their fear that his intercontinental ballistic missiles could hit foreign bases on their soil. Thus American bases in Japan appeared to be not only a source of acute danger but also a symbol of inferior status.

Revision of the security treaty of 1951 was, therefore, in order. Japan was too vital an element in the East Asian balance of power to lose to the Communist or neutralist bloc. Premier Kishi, a Liberal-

Democrat, visited Washington in June, 1957, and won consent to draft a new agreement. On October 4, 1958, with the crisis over Quemoy still raging, negotiations opened in Tokyo and continued for fifteen months. Khrushchev again warned that Japan's only safe course lay in cutting all ties with the United States, a view in which perhaps a third of the Nipponese people concurred. Since native Communists were relatively few, anti-American sentiment centered in the Socialist party and in various labor, teacher, and student groups.

Four questions puzzled the treaty makers. First, should Japan have the right to be consulted on how the United States deployed its forces in the islands? No such right was granted in 1951. Second, should Japan have the power to ban nuclear weapons on its soil? That problem was ignored in 1951. Third, should Japan be obligated to defend American bases if they were attacked? The responsibility in 1951 had been unilateral. Finally, should any new restrictions on America's freedom of action be extended to the Ryukyus and the Bonins? In 1951 those islands had been consigned to a special category. The answers given indicate the high value the United States placed on the Japanese bastion, for the new pact differed markedly from the old in limiting American rights and in putting the signatories on a more equal footing.

Signed in Washington on January 19, 1960, the Treaty of Mutual Cooperation and Security permitted the United States to maintain armed forces in Japan so as to promote Japan's safety and international peace. The privilege was restricted to the duration of the treaty which, unlike its predecessor, could be abrogated after ten years. It was also limited by a special agreement which obliged the United States to consult Japan before bringing new units into the islands or transferring those there to some other part of East Asia. Many Americans thought this arrangement gave the Japanese a veto on such delicate matters as missile sites and reconnaissance flights. Another article, a change since 1951, stipulated that "an armed attack" against either signatory "in the territories under the administration of Japan" would imperil both and that each would act to meet the common danger according to its constitutional processes. This wording, similar to that in the security treaties with Australia, New Zealand, the Philippines, South Korea, and Nationalist China, applied only to the four home islands. Nothing was said about the Ryukyus and the Bonins, but an accompanying agreement expressed mutual concern for their safety and promised, in case of aggression, that the United States and Japan would consult together and explore ways by which the latter might aid in defense of those islands.

For Japan the new treaty, in content and tone, represented a remarkable advance over the previous pact and a substantial concession to its sensibilities. Nevertheless, some opposition was bound to arise, for neutralism's appeal was mounting and Kishi's popularity was declining. How far the protest was increased by the U-2 incident, by the revelation that three such planes were then on Japanese runways, by the collapse of the summit meeting at Paris, and by the subsequent deterioration in East-West relations cannot be determined now. But the chronology is clear. Ignoring a boycott by Socialist members, Kishi pushed the treaty through the lower house of the Diet on May 20, 1960. Mammoth street demonstrations broke out immediately and kept Tokyo in a turmoil for the next month. As a result, the cabinet felt compelled to cancel on June 16 an official visit by Eisenhower scheduled to begin three days later. But the treaty survived this blow to American prestige. Kishi defied demands that he resign; instead, he kept the Diet in session for the period required to make ratification effective even without a vote in the House of Councillors. This goal he achieved on June 18; four days later the Senate approved the treaty without change by a count of 90 to 2. Only when this process was completed did Kishi step down.

Coming on the heels of Rhee's overthrow in Korea, the turbulent events of June, 1960, in Tokyo required the United States to re-examine its policy in East Asia. For nine years the Japanese bastion had been the pivot of American diplomacy in that area. Could the bases in the islands be maintained? Should they be retained if the people there wished to be free of a military alliance? Did they so desire? A partial answer came in November, 1960, when an election returned Kishi's Liberal-Democratic party to power under his successor, Hayato Ikeda. Ikeda pledged himself to carry out the treaty, but the minority Socialists, who also registered gains, refused to give up the fight. Thus, as Eisenhower left office, the United States was challenged to manifest understanding and self-restraint if it hoped to keep Japan as an ally in the continuing duel with Communist China.

59

The Rest of Asia, Africa, and the Americas

THE DUEL with Communist China was not limited to East Asia. In South and Southeast Asia the revolt against colonialism exposed to the ambitions of the People's Republic lands rich in natural resources, weak in military capacity, and deficient in political training. It was not easy to save those areas for the free world. The United States had little experience in dealing with them. Its armed might counted for less than it did in Europe. Its North Atlantic allies, themselves symbols of imperialism, were often a liability. And Dulles too often showed impatience with the neutralism of peoples more concerned with the attainment of national goals than with the menace of international communism.

THE WAR IN INDOCHINA

Symptomatic of the dilemmas confronting American diplomacy in Southeast Asia was the seven-year war in Indochina. France's tardiness in freeing Vietnam, Laos, and Cambodia enabled Communist China to exploit nationalist aspirations for its own gain. Truman and Acheson had recognized that the struggles in Korea and Indochina were related, and they responded with such generous economic and military aid that by 1952 the United States was bearing a third of the cost of the fighting in Southeast Asia. Eisenhower and Dulles proceeded on the same as-

POPULATION
DENSITY

PERSONS
PER SQUARE MILE

UNDER 5
5-100
101-250
OVER 250

SOVIET

NORWAY
SWEDEN
FINLAND

SPITZBERGEN
(NOR.)

FRANZ JOSEF
LAND
(USSR)

BARENTS
SEA

NOVAYA
ZEMLYA

KARA
SEA

Archangel

Vorkuta

Igarka

Moscow

Kuibyshev

Sverdlovsk

Omsk

Tomsk

Istanbul

BLACK
SEA

Ankara

Astrakhan

Karaganda

LAKE
BALKHASH

TURKEY

CYPRUS

Batum

CASPIAN
SEA

Baku

ARAL
SEA

Urumchi

LEBANON
ISRAEL

SYRIA

Bukhara

Tashkent

SINKIANG

SUEZ CANAL

Cairo

JORDAN

Bagdad

IRAQ

Teheran

IRAN

AFGHAN-
ISTAN

Kabul

JAMMU
AND
KASHMIR

EGYPT

KUWAIT

Basra

TIBET

SUDAN

RED SEA

Mecca

SAUDI

BAHREIN

PERSIAN GULF

QATAR

PAKISTAN

INDUS R.

Karachi

Delhi

NEPAL

GANGES R.

ARABIA

Riyadh

ERITREA

YEMEN

FR.
SOMALILAND

Djibouti

ADEN PROT.
(BR.)

Aden

INDIA

Calcutta

Bombay

ETHIOPIA

BR.
SOMALILAND

SOCOTRA
(BR.)

ARABIAN

SEA

Goa
(PORT.)

Hyderabad

Madras

Pondichéry

BAY

SOMALIA

EQUATOR

LACCADIVE IS.
(INDIA)

Colombo

CEYLON

BENG

MALDIVE IS.
(BR.)

ASIA, 1961

THE DARKER AREAS ARE THE STATES
RECOGNIZED AS INDEPENDENT
AFTER WORLD WAR II

1000 MILES

T.R.MILLER

sumption and with the same largesse. The former asserted on April 16, 1953, that a Korean truce which released Red armies to attack elsewhere would be a "fraud"; the latter warned on September 2 that "a second aggression" in Asia would have "grave consequences which might not be confined to Indochina." Actually, armed intervention by Mao Tse-tung's veterans was not necessary. The French were incapable of winning by themselves, and the United States had little taste for full-scale participation.

Dulles hoped to use the Foreign Ministers Conference at Berlin in January, 1954, to bring peace to Indochina. But the most he could gain there was an agreement that the matter be discussed with Chou En-lai at Geneva after Korea had been disposed of. Before that point was reached, the Vietminh surrounded France's best troops at Dienbienphu near the Laotian border. On March 20 the United States was told that only an immediate air strike against the besiegers and their supply lines could prevent disaster. Hence on April 3—a raw, windy Saturday—Dulles met privately with a bipartisan group of senators and representatives. Also present were Admiral Arthur W. Radford, chairman of the Joint Chiefs of Staff, and top Defense Department officials. The Secretary asked for a resolution authorizing the President to employ air and naval power in Indochina. Unlike the appeal Eisenhower would make openly in January, 1955, to protect Formosa, nothing was said about ground forces. What Dulles and Radford envisaged was a massive raid from two aircraft carriers in a last-minute attempt to save Dienbienphu. After a couple of hours of questioning, in which it turned out that England had not been approached and that no other chief of staff sided with Radford, the alarmed legislators advised the President not to send such a request to Congress until Dulles had rounded up some allies.

This response halted a desperation move at Dienbienphu, yet something had to be done. Eisenhower likened Indochina to a domino whose fall could upset a row of free-world positions from Malaya to Japan. He sent Dulles to discuss with Eden a Southeast Asian equivalent of NATO, but the two men failed to agree. The American wanted to form at once an anti-Communist coalition in the region, while the Briton wished to wait until after the Geneva Conference and then include neutralist countries, such as India. A communiqué of April 13, 1954, glossed over these differences by stressing the need to explore with other interested governments a system of collective defense; but what followed bred a mutual distrust that culminated in the Suez tragedy two years later. Upon returning to Washington, Dulles convened the ambassadors from Britain, Australia, New Zealand, France, the Philippines, Thailand, Vietnam, Laos, and Cambodia to begin studying the project. This was exactly what Eden had opposed, and he forbade his envoy to attend. Churchill was also appalled by the Secretary's tactics. When Dulles suddenly proposed to send token Anglo-American forces to Indochina, the Prime Minister said he was being asked "to assist in misleading Congress into approving a military operation" which might lead to "a major war."

Talk of American intervention in Indochina ended with the fall of Dienbienphu on May 7, 1954, and the diplomats then managed to bring the fighting to a close. The armistice agreements of July 20–1 left Laos and Cambodia nominally independent and territorially intact, but both had to promise not to join a regional alliance, not to allow foreign bases on their soil, and not to solicit outside military aid. Vietnam was divided at the seventeenth parallel into the northern Democratic Republic of Vietnam and the southern Republic of Vietnam, with unification depending upon an election in 1956. An international commission was to oversee the cease-fire arrangements. All participants at Geneva, except the United States and South Vietnam, pledged themselves to respect the independence and territorial integrity of the Indochinese nations, to refrain from interfering in their domestic affairs, and to consult on all questions raised by the truce commission. A fuller guarantee was blocked by Dulles' refusal to be bound to uphold Communist rule in North Vietnam, but his representative gave assurances that the American government would do nothing to disturb the armistice. Eisenhower conceded publicly that much of the Geneva settlement was unsatisfactory, while Knowland called it "one of the greatest victories for Communism in a decade." But with France eager for peace and the Vietminh strong enough to draw a boundary further south, Dulles had no alternative but to acquiesce. In doing so, however, he avoided a direct endorsement of the terms and served notice that the United States was not going to stand idly by and see all of Southeast Asia overrun by international communism.

SEATO AND LAOS

Almost at once Dulles resumed his quest for a regional system of collective defense. He knew he had little to work with and that the ANZUS Pact of 1951, not the North Atlantic Treaty of 1949, must serve as a model. Nehru was not interested because he felt that colonialism was more of a threat to South and Southeast Asia than communism. Burma, Ceylon, and Indonesia followed India's course of nonalignment, while Laos, Cambodia, and South Vietnam were forbidden to enter an alliance. Thus only Pakistan, the Philippines, and Thailand, among the Asian countries, attended the eight-nation conference which opened at Manila on September 6, 1954. There the Secretary of State candidly admitted that the free world could not match the huge armies the Communists were able to muster in the area and that its best deterrents were unity of purpose, a mobile striking force, and strategically located reserves.

The outcome was the Southeast Asia Collective Defense Treaty, signed on September 8, 1954, by the United States, Great Britain, France, Australia, New Zealand, Pakistan, the Philippines, and Thailand. Each signatory recognized that "an armed attack in the treaty area against any of the Parties or against any State or territory which the Parties by unanimous agreement may hereafter designate, would endanger its own peace and safety." Each promised to act, in meeting the common danger, "in accordance with its constitutional processes." Should the threat stem from subversion, the signatories would consult immediately. The British insisted upon a paragraph which forbade action in the specially designated state or territory except upon invitation by the government concerned; the United States appended an understanding which restricted its obligation to aggression of Communist origin. The treaty area was carefully defined. The eight nations also undertook to strengthen free institutions, to cooperate economically, to develop their capacity to resist armed attack and subversive activity, and to establish a Council ready to meet instantly. The treaty was to remain in force indefinitely but could be terminated by a year's notice. Other states able to contribute to the security of the area might accede to the pact if all parties agreed.

Two additional documents were signed at Manila. One was the Pacific Charter, a set of generalities regarding equal rights and self-determination, intended to remove any stigma of colonialism. The other was a protocol, designed by Dulles, to throw "some mantle of protection" over Cambodia, Laos, and South Vietnam. It did so by making those three countries eligible to share in the economic benefits of the pact and by including their domains in the defined treaty area. Some neutralists believed this protocol to violate the spirit, if not the letter, of the Geneva armistice; some strategists feared it might require fighting in an area where all the advantages lay with the enemy.

An Asian defense treaty more than half of whose signatories came from outside of that continent never could achieve the importance of the North Atlantic original. In England there was criticism of the understanding which limited America's obligation to resisting only armed attacks launched by Communists. Thailand and the Philippines regretted that no land or air units had been earmarked for the area. But in the United States the reception was generally favorable. Dulles called it the capstone of a comprehensive system of regional security in the Pacific. He claimed that it dealt more fully with indirect aggression than any earlier treaty, contributed substantially to preserving freedom in Southeast Asia, and checked effectively the on-

rush of communism into a region vital to the security of the United
States. In that appraisal the Senate concurred. It voted during the first
crisis over the offshore islands. Having just authorized the president
to protect Formosa by armed force and being about to approve the
bilateral agreement with Nationalist China, the upper house on February 1, 1955, consented to the Southeast Asia Collective Defense Treaty
by a margin of 82 to 1.

Three weeks later Dulles and envoys from the seven other powers
gathered at Bangkok to transform the Manila Pact into the Southeast
Asia Treaty Organization. By February 25, 1955, they had set up a
Council that was to meet in the treaty area once a year or more often
if necessary, with the foreign ministers or their alternates in attendance. The Council's duties were to promote the economic and social
welfare of the region and to prevent invasion and subversion. Its decisions had to be unanimous. Its permanent seat was in the Thai capital, where each member assigned for liaison a Council Representative
and a Military Adviser. SEATO, as it came to be known, had no armed
force of its own and no equivalent of the Supreme Allied Commander
in Europe. To repel attacks it had to rely on the mobile striking
power of the United States. In time it acquired a Secretary-General and
a Military Planning Office, but these additions still left it a very different organization from NATO.

For four years the Southeast Asia Treaty Organization did not
have to face armed aggression in its area. The reason was not its own
forbidding defenses but, rather, a shift in Communist tactics from
open threats of force to covert penetration. The significance of this
changed approach, first revealed in April, 1955, at the Afro-Asian Conference in Bandung, was grasped by the SEATO Council, which devoted much attention to countering subversion and raising the standard
of living in the treaty area. "While holding the bully off with one stiff
arm," explained a State Department spokesman on March 5, 1959, "we
use the other, under the mutual security program, to help the struggling new nations to develop conditions of inner strength." Yet at no
time was the United States prepared to undertake for the SEATO
area a program like the one Marshall offered to Europe in June, 1947.
Such a job, it felt, could be done better in South and Southeast Asia by
the Colombo Plan partners.

It was Laos, however, that laid bare the weakness of SEATO and
the obstacles to Dulles' policy there. That landlocked kingdom was important strategically because it shielded Cambodia and Thailand from
the Chinese People's Republic and North Vietnam as well as adjoining
two other targets of communism, Burma and South Vietnam. Under
the armistice of July, 1954, the country was to avoid association with
and assistance from both East and West, while an International Con-

trol Commission was to keep out foreign influence. The chief domestic problem was to integrate the pro-Communist Pathet Lao group which controlled two northeastern provinces and continued to receive aid from North Vietnam. It took four years for Prince Souvanna Phouma, the neutralist Premier during most of that period, to pacify the Pathet Lao and to bring its political and military leaders into a government of national unity. Having achieved that goal by July, 1958, he asked the International Control Commission to cease its labors and then tendered his own resignation.

Beginning in August, 1958, the political pendulum in Laos swung steadily to the right. Souvanna Phouma's neutralism had pleased neither the Communists nor the United States. The former stepped up their pressure during the second crisis over the offshore islands. The latter expanded its program of military and economic assistance until the per capita rate exceeded that of any other country. The new Premier, Phoui Sananikone, was a middle-of-the-road figure, but he excluded all Communist-led elements from his cabinet. Granted increased power on January 14, 1959, he moved to subdue the irate Pathet Lao and imprisoned one of its leaders, Prince Souvannouvong, a half-brother of Souvanna Phouma. The predictable riposte came from North Vietnam, and guerrillas of some sort crossed into Laos. On July 30, the royal government at Vietiane announced that the Pathet Lao, with alien support, was endangering the kingdom.

For help Laos turned to the United Nations, not to SEATO. On September 4, 1959, it accused North Vietnam of aggression and asked that an emergency force be sent to the scene. Since no such unit existed, the United States proposed that the Security Council appoint a subcommittee to investigate. Only Russia opposed that plan when a vote was taken on September 8, and it was thwarted in its use of the veto by a ruling of dubious legality. Over Soviet protests, representatives from Japan, Italy, Argentina, and Tunisia flew to Vietiane for an on-the-spot check, but they were permitted to examine only the Laotian side of the border. Their report of November failed to corroborate the presence of Vietnamese regulars on Laotian soil but confirmed that the rebels had been trained in, and supplied from, North Vietnam. This inquiry and an inspection by Secretary-General Hammarskjold from November 12 to 19 helped to reduce the tempo of the fighting but not to remove the underlying danger.

During 1960 the internal struggle in Laos set the stage for an international crisis in 1961. On January 1 Sananikone was forced out by General Phoumi Nosavan, a pro-Western strong man. The new Premier, Tiao Somsanith, aligned the nation more closely with the United States and rigged the elections against the Communists. These tactics led to his ouster by a military coup on August 9 under Captain Kong

Le. Initially, Le had no ties with the Pathet Lao, and his revolt returned Souvanna Phouma to power. Although Phoumi first agreed to serve in the new cabinet, he soon changed his mind and launched a counter-revolution in the south. The subsequent events are too recent for the historian to pass judgment upon, but clearly the Eisenhower administration did not share Souvanna Phouma's belief that only a government composed of all factions could bring peace. It sent Assistant Secretary of State J. Graham Parsons to Vietiane in mid-October to persuade the Premier to reverse his course, and it ineptly tried to use the military aid program as a lever. Eventually the United States gave full backing to General Phoumi. In the ensuing three-way contest among pro-American, neutralist, and pro-Communist Laotians, Souvanna Phouma lost out. On December 9, 1960, still recognized by Russia as the rightful Premier, he fled to Cambodia. After a bloody battle in Vietiane, Phoumi's army installed Prince Boun Oum on December 1, while the defeated Kong Le went over to the Pathet Lao.

Although these developments gave the United States a favored position with the new regime, they galvanized the Sino-Soviet leaders into intervening on a massive scale. Airlifts from North Vietnam dropped military equipment in numbers the Americans could not or would not match. As the year ended, the tide turned against Boun Oum, and Eisenhower frantically sought the neutralist solution he had rejected before. But from exile Souvanna Phouma blamed Washington for the impending disaster, while on the scene the victorious Pathet Lao spurned compromise. By the time Kennedy entered office, it seemed unlikely that a divided SEATO or a hesitant United States could save Laos short of risking a major war.

THE EMERGING CONTINENT

In Africa, as in Asia, the United States faced the question of whether the spread of communism must accompany the growth of independence. Would the attainment of nationhood on that vast continent be vitiated by an ideology that could turn its people and resources against the free world? There, as in the other new areas of diplomatic concern, the American government had to tread warily through pitfalls engendered by apathy, ignorance, prejudice, colonialism, and the Cold War.

Neither the Truman nor the Eisenhower administration devised a truly imaginative and dynamic policy for Africa. Until 1960 the men in Washington regarded that continent, or most of it, as mainly Europe's responsibility. They permitted a favorable image of America held by some African leaders to be marred by discriminatory practices against Negro citizens at home and by qualified enthusiasm for Negro

spokesmen abroad. As a report to the Foreign Relations Committee on
October 23, 1959, put it, the United States wrote too many prescriptions for self-rule. It exhorted the Africans to be patient, avoid extrem-
ism, eschew violence, renounce chauvinism, and adopt Western political and economic institutions. It ignored Kwame Nkrumah's reminder
that Africa was not an extension of Europe or any other continent. We
want, the Premier of Ghana said on April 15, 1958, to develop "an
African personality. Others may feel they have evolved the very best
way of life, but we are not bound, like slavish imitators, to accept it
as our mold."

To be sure, the policy makers faced formidable obstacles. The
vastness of the continent meant that Subsaharan problems differed
from those in the north, and the State Department had all too few
trained personnel. Not until 1958 was a separate Bureau of African
Affairs created. Much as the United States favored full freedom for all
peoples, it could not endorse wholesale grants of independence to those
obviously unprepared to govern themselves. Yet the pressure for
change was intense as the number of independent nations jumped
from five in December, 1955, to twenty-seven in January, 1961. Then
there was the difficulty of reconciling sympathy for African aspirations
with loyalty to the NATO partners, notably England, France, Belgium,
and Portugal. The first two tended to pursue an enlightened and progressive policy; the others, a reactionary or erratic one. The United
States tried to judge each case on its merits but sometimes ended by
displeasing all parties and thus providing the Communist and anti-
colonialist bloc with an issue to exploit.

In North Africa, Algeria headed the list of perplexing problems.
Beginning late in 1954, a bloody civil war racked that French colony
and presented the United States with a difficult choice. Should it advocate self-determination for the Muslims, and thereby antagonize a key
Atlantic ally, or should it consider the revolt a domestic matter, and
thus seem to condone imperialism? Until the struggle was ended,
France's contribution to NATO would be curtailed and its repression
of Algerian nationalists would seem to Afro-Asians indistinguishable
from Russia's course in Hungary. Faced with a choice of evils, the
Eisenhower administration tried to promote compromise and to prevent debate in the General Assembly. It reaped the reward of peacemakers by satisfying neither side. This was particularly true in adjacent Tunisia, where President Habib Bourguiba gradually swung from
being the most outspoken African friend of the West to a most eloquent champion of neutralism and nonalignment.

Bourguiba's influence made relations with Tunisia important.
Equally desirable were a well-disposed Libya and Morocco. The former had signed on September 9, 1954, a sixteen-year lease for the giant

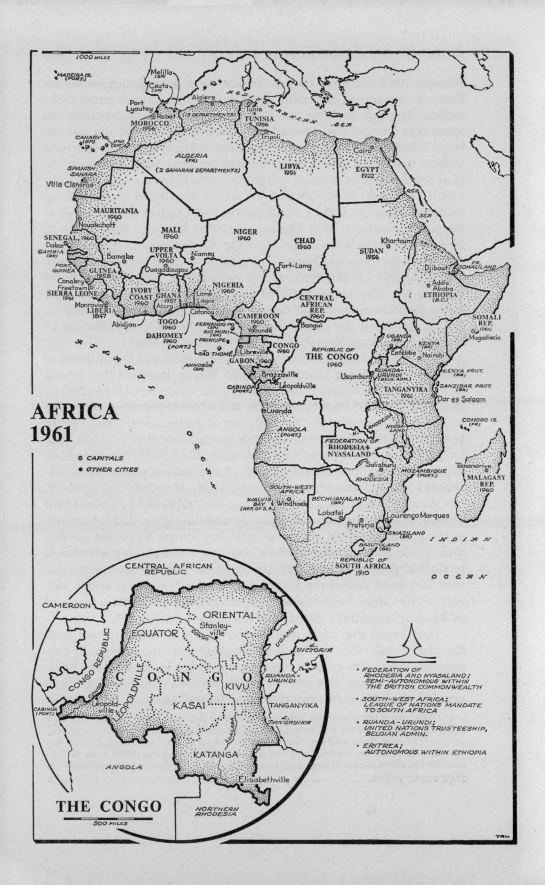

AFRICA
1961

○ CAPITALS
● OTHER CITIES

1000 MILES

MADEIRA IS.
(PORT.)

Melilla
(SP.)
Ceuta
(SP.)
Port
Lyautey
Rabat
Algiers
(13 DEPARTMENTS)
Tunis
TUNISIA
1956
Tripoli

MOROCCO
1956

CANARY IS.
(SP.)
IFNI
(SP.)

SPANISH
SAHARA

Villa Cisneros

ALGERIA
(FR.)

(2 SAHARAN DEPARTMENTS)

LIBYA
1951

Cairo
EGYPT
1922

MAURITANIA
1960
Nouakchott

SENEGAL 1960
Dakar
GAMBIA
(BR.)
PORT.
GUINEA
Conakry
Freetown
GUINEA
1958
SIERRA LEONE
1961
Monrovia
LIBERIA
1847
Abidjan

MALI
1960

Bamako

UPPER
VOLTA
1960
Ouagadougou

NIGER
1960

Niamey

CHAD
1960

Fort-Lamy

SUDAN
1956

Khartoum

Djibouti
FR.
SOMALILAND

Addis
Ababa
ETHIOPIA
(B.C.)

IVORY
COAST
1960

GHANA
1957
Accra
Lomé
TOGO
1960
Cotonou
DAHOMEY
1960

NIGERIA
1960

Lagos

CENTRAL
AFRICAN
REP.
1960

SOMALI
REP.
1960
Mogadiscio

FERNANDO PO
(SP.)
RIO MUNI
(SP.)
PRINCIPE
(PORT.)
SÃO THOMÉ
ANNOBÓN
(SP.)

CAMEROON
1960
Yaoundé

Bangui

UGANDA
(BR.)
Entebbe

KENYA
(BR.)
Nairobi

CONGO
1960
Libreville
GABON 1960

REPUBLIC OF
THE CONGO
1960

RUANDA-
URUNDI
(BELG. ADM.)
Usumbura

KENYA PROT.
(BR.)

Brazzaville
Léopoldville
CABINDA
(PORT.)

TANGANYIKA
1961

ZANZIBAR PROT.
(BR.)
Dar es Salaam

Luanda

RHODESIA

NYASA-
LAND

COMORO IS.
(FR.)

ANGOLA
(PORT.)

FEDERATION OF
RHODESIA &
NYASALAND
N.
RHODESIA
Salisbury
S.
RHODESIA

MOZAMBIQUE
(PORT.)

Tananarive

MALAGASY
REP.
1960

SOUTH-WEST
AFRICA

WALVIS
BAY
(REP. OF S.A.)
Windhoek

BECHUANALAND
(BR.)

Lobatsi

Lourenço Marques

Pretoria

SWAZILAND
(BR.)

BASUTOLAND
(BR.)

REPUBLIC OF
SOUTH AFRICA
1910

INDIAN

OCEAN

ATLANTIC OCEAN

MEDITERRANEAN SEA

RED SEA

ERITREA

THE CONGO

CENTRAL AFRICAN
REPUBLIC

CAMEROON

ORIENTAL

Stanley-
ville

EQUATOR

CONGO
REPUBLIC

C O N G O

KIVU

UGANDA

L. VICTORIA

CABINDA
(PORT.)

LEOPOLDVILLE

Leopold-
ville

KASAI

RUANDA-
URUNDI

TANGANYIKA

LUALABA

L.
TANGANYIKA

KATANGA

ANGOLA

Elisabethville

NORTHERN
RHODESIA

500 MILES

• FEDERATION OF
RHODESIA AND NYASALAND;
SEMI-AUTONOMOUS WITHIN
THE BRITISH COMMONWEALTH

• SOUTH-WEST AFRICA;
LEAGUE OF NATIONS MANDATE
TO SOUTH AFRICA

• RUANDA-URUNDI;
UNITED NATIONS TRUSTEESHIP,
BELGIAN ADMIN.

• ERITREA;
AUTONOMOUS WITHIN ETHIOPIA

TRH

Wheelus Air Force base outside Tripoli. As a jet training center for European squadrons, that field amply justified an annual rental of $4 million. By 1959, however, the Libyans began to complain about the terms that dropped the amount to $1 million for each of the last ten years. Negotiations to revise the figure upward dragged on during 1960 without reaching a new arrangement or arousing bitter animosity. In Morocco, nationalist pressures were stronger. There the end of French rule led to demands to cancel rights which the United States had acquired in 1950–1 to build a naval base at Port Lyautey and air bases at Benguérir, Nouaseur, Sidi Slimane, and Ben Slimane. Since some of these were major links in the Strategic Air Command's global deterrent, there was much reluctance to relinquish them before intercontinental ballistic missiles replaced manned aircraft. But it was doubtful whether the Moroccans could be induced to wait for that change; hence Eisenhower promised during a visit to Casablanca on December 22, 1959, that the United States would relinquish Ben Slimane by March 31, 1960, and the other four by December 31, 1963.[1]

Below the Sahara the spawning of new nations and the outburst of pan-African emotions brought the Cold War to a region that Russia had previously left untouched. Starting in 1958, Russia continually identified the West with imperialism and white supremacy. When the United States hesitated for a month, out of deference to French pride, before extending recognition to Guinea on November 1, 1958, and longer before offering economic assistance, the Soviet bloc stepped in with military equipment and a credit of 140 million rubles. But Khrushchev's real opportunity came in July, 1960, when Belgium's precipitate grant of independence to the Congo was followed by mutiny in the army, looting in the cities, fighting among the tribes, and separatism in the provinces. With understandable but unwise haste the government in Brussels reinforced the 2,000 troops it had been allowed to retain and thereby touched off new violence. On July 10 Premier Patrice Lumumba cabled the United Nations for immediate armed support to repel alleged external aggression. Playing on Western fears, he said he would seek help elsewhere if his plea went unheeded.

Thus began the crisis which kept the Congo in a turmoil until Eisenhower left office and exposed the danger of communism in Subsaharan Africa. The conflict raged at several levels: as a bloody battle between rival tribes, as a power struggle between ambitious men, as a genuine clash between centralism and federalism, as a false contest

[1] The loss of the Moroccan bases was offset by the completion in 1960 of a new complex in Spain. Under a bilateral defense agreement of September 26, 1953, and at a cost of over $400 million, the United States built four major air bases—one near Seville, one near Madrid, and two near Saragossa—a huge naval base at Rota near Cadiz, three minor depots, and seven radar sites, all linked by a 485-mile underground pipeline.

between independence and colonialism, and as a major campaign between East and West. Lumumba's dream of a unified state was thwarted by the secession on July 11, 1960, of the copper-rich province of Katanga under Moise Tshombe and on August 9 of the mining area of South Kasai under Albert Kalonji. In the ensuing dispute, Tshombe courted Belgian support; Lumumba had the backing of Ghana, Guinea, and eventually of Russia. The last secretly supplied aircraft and military equipment; along with Czechoslovakia, it hurried a large number of technicians to Léopoldville. On September 5 President Joseph Kasavubu dismissed Lumumba as a pro-Communist troublemaker; and when the parliament voted him back into power, the army took over. Colonel Joseph D. Mobutu disbanded the recalcitrant legislators, imprisoned the ousted Premier, ordered home the Soviet and Czechoslovak diplomatic missions, and sought an accord with the secessionists. Khrushchev continued to regard Lumumba as the rightful Premier, while Lumumba's followers organized their own separatist movement in Oriental and Kivu provinces, thus reducing the Congo to virtual chaos.

Equally frustrating were attempts by the United Nations to deal with the situation. On July 14, 1960, by a vote of 8 to 0, the Security Council asked Belgium to withdraw all troops and authorized the Secretary-General to establish a peace force to assist the Congolese government. The United States and the Soviet Union supported the motion, but this show of unity was deceptive. Khrushchev had wanted a stronger resolution and was already accusing NATO of seeking to reimpose colonialism in the new republic. Fervently he proclaimed his readiness to combat Western imperialism. A false rumor that Eisenhower was planning to transfer one division from Germany to the troubled area brought blunt warnings from both Moscow and Washington about keeping hands off the Congo.

In carrying out the directive of July 14, 1960, Hammarskjold initially used mostly African contingents and at no time sought aid from the major powers. But Lumumba's threat to request Russian troops, actually a device to hasten Belgium's withdrawal, raised the specter of the Red flag flying in the Congo. To forestall that development the Security Council on July 22 called upon Belgium "to implement speedily" the resolution of July 14 and then recommended that all states refrain from any action which might impede the restoration of order or "undermine the territorial integrity and political independence of the Republic of the Congo." The last clause temporarily quieted Lumumba's fear of losing Katanga and may have encouraged him to feel he could employ the United Nations force to extend his authority there. With Tshombe refusing to permit the entry of the United Nations command and with Russia and Ghana threatening to use their forces against him, the Security Council passed a third resolution on August 7. It declared that the entry of the United Nations force into Katanga was necessary but reaffirmed that the troops must not be used to advance the cause of any party in the internal quarrel.

Actually, the 20,000-man force could not establish peace and order without indirectly helping some faction. Khrushchev's vitriolic attack on Hammarskjold and his office before the General Assembly on September 22, 1960, reflected his belief that the Secretary's policy had hurt Lumumba. He was further aroused when the Assembly voted on November 22, by a count of 53 to 24 with 19 abstaining, to seat Kasavubu's delegates, not Lumumba's. But although the West was able to limit Soviet influence in the Congo, it appeared early in 1961 that the victory might be a Pyrrhic one. Russia's stubborn refusal to pay its share of the costly operation menaced the organization with bankruptcy. The imminent withdrawal of troops by several dissatisfied African states threatened the force with impotency. The continued bloodshed within the country foretold a long period of anarchy. Certainly the undertaking had from the start strained the resources of a divided United Nations, for the task of coping with internal chaos and external meddling in the Congo was much more formidable than the earlier joint enterprises to keep peace in Suez in 1956 and in Lebanon in 1958.

THE NEGLECTED CONTINENT

If by 1960 the diplomats had to deal with new countries and new problems in distant continents, they were on familiar ground when they turned to the Americas. Such issues as revolution and reaction, recognition and nonintervention, economic development and canal rights, the Monroe Doctrine and hemispheric solidarity all struck a responsive chord. Yet since 1945 the New World—hardly an appropriate term by mid-century—had been regarded in Washington with less and less urgency. The North Atlantic Treaty Organization, not the Organization of American States, was the major alliance. The Marshall Plan, the Mutual Security Act, and Point Four had Europe, Asia, and Africa as their primary goals. Novel doctrines bearing presidential names proclaimed a determination to defend free peoples in Greece and the Middle East. Small wonder that the southern neighbors looked upon theirs as the neglected continent.

What awakened the United States to the consequences of this neglect was the upsurge of communism in Latin America and the Soviet attempt to extend the Cold War to the Western Hemisphere. Despite precursors in Guatemala in 1954, it took an assault by Communist-directed mobs on Vice President Nixon in Peru and Venezuela in May,

1958, to underline the danger. Russia's subsequent success in exploiting the social revolution in Cuba and its warning of nuclear retaliation in case of military intervention there revived as nothing else, not even the Fascist challenge of the late 1930's, ever had, the clash of ideologies which inspired the declaration of James Monroe and John Quincy Adams.

So long as the United States held Puerto Rico and the Virgin Islands as colonies, leased without limit of time Guantanamo Bay, and exercised sovereign rights in the Canal Zone, it was an easy target for anti-imperialist attacks. To be sure, neither the Puerto Ricans nor the Virgin Islanders demanded independence, and the Cubans were content before 1959 to leave unchanged the treaty of May 29, 1934. That pact, continuing the grant of 1903, was to remain in force until both parties agreed to abrogate it or until the United States abandoned the naval station on the site. Hay's treaty with Bunau-Varilla of 1903 had undergone two substantial changes. On March 2, 1936, the United States had renounced its guarantee of Panama's independence, its authority to intervene, and its power of eminent domain. It had also increased the annual payment to $430,000. A second revision on January 25, 1955, raised the annuity to $1,930,000, returned certain lands, surrendered many sanitary controls, and shared more equitably the economic benefits of the transit route. In that treaty, which the Senate approved on July 29 by a vote of 72 to 14, Dulles gave more than he received, but concessions did not silence criticism. Egypt's nationalization of the Suez Canal on July 26, 1956, encouraged extremists to seek the same solution, spurred moderates to demand fuller recognition of Panama's sovereignty, and led idealists to propose putting the waterway under the aegis of the OAS.

Communism also benefited from a wave of revolutions which swept across Latin America after 1952, ousting the old-style caudillo-general and his demagogic counterpart. Ironically, the United States often lost rather than gained from these social upheavals. Because Truman and Eisenhower adhered rigidly to nonintervention, these triumphs over authoritarianism were won without help from Washington. Because Acheson and Dulles set great store by hemispheric solidarity, they felt compelled to deal with despots even at the price of antagonizing popular leaders of the future. Occasionally the State Department went too far in praising such tyrants as Rafael L. Trujillo of the Dominican Republic. Frequently it acted too slowly in suspending arms shipments which were used, under mutual defense pacts, to bolster dictators. Certainly it waited too long to promote boldly the economic welfare of the southern neighbors.

It was in backward Guatemala that the Eisenhower administration first grappled with communism in the New World. The long-overdue social revolution began there in 1944 and veered markedly leftward in 1950 after the election of Jacobo Arbenz. Within three years the Communist party, numbering 4,000 in a population of 3,000,000, controlled most key posts in the government, launched a campaign to expropriate foreign assets, and began spreading the gospel to neighboring countries. Dulles countered by asking the Tenth Inter-American Conference, which met at Caracas from March 1 to 28, 1954, to go on record as opposing the spread of communism to the Western Hemisphere. Respect for the concept of nonintervention and fear for the progress of reform kept the republics from doing much. They were not willing to enlarge their treaty obligations or to get rid of Arbenz by joint action. Dulles had to be content with a Declaration of Solidarity which, in phrases reminiscent of 1823, avowed "that the domination or control of the political institutions of any American State by the international communist movement, extending to this Hemisphere the political system of an extracontinental power, would constitute a threat to the sovereignty and political independence of the American States, endangering the peace of America, and would call for a Meeting of Consultation to consider the adoption of appropriate action in accordance with existing treaties." Guatemala voted in the negative, while Argentina and Mexico abstained.

Later events minimized what little advantage the United States gained at Caracas. During May, 1954, Guatemalan labor leaders fomented crippling strikes in adjacent Honduras just as a large supply of military equipment arrived in clandestine fashion from Czechoslovakia. Fearful that Honduras and even Nicaragua might be earmarked for external attack or internal subversion, the United States flew weapons to those countries under recently concluded mutual defense pacts. On May 25 Dulles accused Guatemala of planning aggression and pilloried its government as the only one in the Americas that had failed to ratify the Rio Treaty of 1947, that had voted against the anti-Communist resolution at Caracas, and that had obtained "a massive shipment of arms from behind the Iron Curtain." On June 8 Arbenz invoked martial law, stating that he was the victim of a foreign plot to unseat him. Ten days later a small force of exiles in Honduras crossed the border, joined with dissident army units, and compelled Arbenz to resign. How far the Central Intelligence Agency directed the invasion cannot be determined now, but there is no doubt that the uprising was more than a purely Guatemalan affair, that the rebels would not have acted without the sympathy of Washington, and that the United States received a bad press in Latin America and much of the free world.

The incident led to an angry debate in the United Nations. On June 19, 1954, Guatemala demanded emergency meetings of both the

Security Council and the Inter-American Peace Committee.[2] Charging that Honduras and Nicaragua had committed aggression "at the instigation of certain foreign monopolies," Guatemala asked that the two countries be called upon to restrain the mercenaries who were violating neutral soil and that an observation team be sent to the scene. The United States denied responsibility for the invasion and supported a motion to refer the matter to the Organization of American States. Russia objected on the grounds that immediate action was needed and that the OAS was controlled by Washington. Ambassador Henry Cabot Lodge, Jr., bluntly told the Soviet delegate on June 20 "to stay out of this hemisphere" and not to hatch "your conspiracies over here." When veto number sixty killed the motion, the Council passed unanimously a French resolution calling for an instant cessation of hostilities and of acts likely to cause bloodshed.

On June 25, 1954, the Security Council met again at the request of Guatemala and Russia. Both argued that since the earlier resolution had not been complied with, the United Nations must take further action. By a margin of 5 to 4 and over a Soviet protest, the Council decided to wait until the Inter-American Peace Committee had completed an investigation. Before that was done, Arbenz had fled. The United States then moved that the OAS Council cancel its call of June 26 for a special meeting of the foreign ministers to examine the Guatemalan situation. As it did so, the Senate with one dissenting vote and the House unanimously recommended that the OAS be supported in whatever steps seemed necessary "to prevent any interference by the international Communist movement in the affairs of the States of the Western Hemisphere."

Six years passed before another American republic was lured into the Communist camp. During that period fear of infiltration subsided. Attention shifted to economic cooperation, regional marketing, and an Inter-American Development Bank. During that period Eisenhower tried his hand at personal diplomacy. He attended a conference of presidents at Panama in July, 1956, and undertook a tour of the southernmost countries in February, 1960. During that period the United States realized again the value of Canada and Latin America, not only as friends in the United Nations but also as contributors to foreign trade. During that period the advent of intercontinental ballistic missiles transformed the whole nature of hemispheric defense.

A new Communist peril emerged in Cuba on January 1, 1959, with the triumph of Fidel Castro's social revolutionary movement. In his

[2] The Inter-American Peace Committee was created at Havana on July 30, 1940, but did not formally meet until September 9, 1948. It is a five-man group, chosen from members of the OAS Council, and has operated as a mediatory body, with the consent of the disputants, in about ten cases down to 1960.

six-year battle against the corrupt and cruel regime of Fulgencio Batista, Castro had shown some antipathy toward Washington but no love for Moscow. He felt, with justification, that the United States had been too tolerant of Latin dictators, Batista included, and too tardy in halting the flow of arms which were then turned upon the champions of liberty. He knew that his land-reform program would arouse foreign investors. Some difficulty was anticipated, therefore, despite prompt recognition of his regime, but no one was prepared for Castro's intense hostility toward the United States, his alarming complaisance toward his Communist associates, and his obvious determination to unseat forcibly all leaders, even the moderate ones, whom he disliked in the New World.

Almost at once Cuba became a breeding ground for invasion and subversion. Exiles from other Caribbean countries hastened to the island to mount attacks against their homelands. Communists from other nations flocked to a haven where they could store weapons, train cadres, and provoke strife. Observation teams from the Organization of American States reported the landing of armed expeditions, and the turmoil brought about at Santiago, Chile, on August 12–18, 1959, the Fifth Meeting of Consultation of Ministers of Foreign Affairs. This key organ under the Treaty of Reciprocal Assistance had not met since April, 1951, and Herter hoped to obtain from it new machinery to check the imminent invasions. Yet in the end he had to settle for two resolutions. The rather general Declaration of Santiago condemned totalitarianism and reaffirmed certain principles of democracy. The more specific directive to the Inter-American Peace Committee provided for a study of the unrest in the Caribbean and a report to the Eleventh Inter-American Conference scheduled to open six months later.

Castro's contempt for the Santiago meeting gave no hope that the Caribbean storm would abate. His abuse of the United States drove relations to a new low. By December, 1959, Herter confessed that it was impossible to communicate with the Cuban government, let alone compose differences. The reasons were obvious. Castro blamed the Eisenhower administration for harboring his enemies, inciting sabotage, plotting counterrevolution, and tolerating air raids from Florida. The United States was exasperated by confiscatory expropriations and libelous accusations. It also worried about the impact of the quarrel on the inter-American system and the East-West struggle. To remain passive in the face of Castro's provocations might encourage other Latin demagogues to sequester American property, yet to strike back economically—a military strike was then unthinkable—would arouse cries of dollar diplomacy. In the General Assembly that adjourned in December, 1959, the Cubans abandoned the hemispheric bloc and pursued an ostensibly neutralist course that actually coincided with the

Soviet position. On February 13, 1960, Castro signed a five-year trade agreement which could establish a Russian enclave for commerce and propaganda in the New World. There was even talk of a defensive alliance that might make Cuba a military outpost for the Kremlin. Still, Eisenhower hesitated to get tough, hoping Castro's excesses would alienate the rest of the Americas.

By June 27, 1960, patience ceased to be a virtue. In a memorandum to the Inter-American Peace Committee the United States accused Cuba of deliberately increasing tensions in the Caribbean and of engaging in a "systematic and provocative campaign of slander." Two days later Castro ordered the $25 million refinery of the Texas Company seized for refusing to process crude oil from Russia. By July 3 some $1 billion worth of American investments had suffered the same fate, and the President responded by cutting sugar imports, for which Cuba was paid more than the world price. This decision not to buy from an unfriendly neighbor and thereby deprive it of an income of $90 million led Cuba to complain to the Security Council of economic aggression and reprisals harmful to hemispheric peace. On July 9 Khrushchev entered the dispute by warning that "Soviet artillerymen can support Cuba with rocket fire" should the United States intervene with armed force. In Havana there was loud applause.

Not content to threaten nuclear destruction, Khrushchev flouted a cherished principle of American foreign policy, "We consider that the Monroe Doctrine has outlived its time," he told a news conference on July 12, 1960, and having died "a natural death," it should be buried so as not to "poison the air by its decay." The State Department's reply of July 14 was categorical. "The principles of the Monroe Doctrine," a spokesman asserted, "are as valid today as they were in 1823." They had been embodied in the Rio Treaty and the OAS Charter. Any Russian attempt to extend its system to the Western Hemisphere would be considered "dangerous to our peace and safety." A similar stand was taken in the Security Council, which heard Cuba's complaint on July 18. When the Soviet delegate depicted the Doctrine as a cloak for Yankee territorial greed, Lodge turned to him and declared: "Do not touch us; do not touch those with whom we are tied; do not seek to extend Communist imperialism." The next day, acting as it had in the Guatemalan case six years earlier, the Council referred the controversy to the Organization of American States.

Never before had the OAS been subjected to such strains. The Sixth Meeting of Consultation of Ministers of Foreign Affairs, sitting at San José, Costa Rica from August 17 to August 21, 1960, condemned the Dominican Republic for "acts of aggression and intervention" against Venezuela and agreed, by a vote of 19 to 0 with 2 abstentions, both to break off diplomatic relations and to impose partial economic sanctions. The Seventh Meeting, which lasted from August 22 to August 29, condemned "the intervention or the threat of intervention, even when conditional, by an extracontinental power in the affairs of the American republics," declared that the acceptance of such a threat by an American nation jeopardized the "solidarity and security" of the hemisphere, and rejected "the attempt of the Sino-Soviet powers to make use of the political, economic, or social situation of any American state." This second resolution—adopted by a count of 19 to 0 with two absences, the delegates of Cuba and the Dominican Republic having left San José—was at best an indirect indictment, for the name of Cuba was nowhere mentioned and the imposition of sanctions at no time contemplated. The simple fact was that the social objectives of Castro's revolution commanded wide sympathy throughout Latin America; and although many leaders deplored his welcome of Russian military assistance in a New World controversy, they were reluctant to accept completely the position of the United States.

Castro was equally reluctant to renounce the protection of his Sino-Soviet friends, and during the remainder of Eisenhower's tenure the situation went from bad to worse. On September 8, 1960, Russia tried to get the Security Council to exercise its legal right to review the acts of regional organizations; and although it abandoned this attempt in the face of strong opposition, the move portended future intrusions upon the affairs of the OAS. On October 19 the State Department imposed an embargo on all exports to Cuba except food, medicine, and medical supplies. On November 17 the president ordered the navy to set up a Caribbean patrol for preventing an invasion of Nicaragua or Guatemala by Castro's forces, and the operation was not suspended until December 7. Finally, on January 3, 1961, after an impossible and provocative demand to reduce in forty-eight hours the staff of the Havana embassy from eighty-seven to eleven, the United States formally severed relations. Six days later *The New York Times* fully revealed that American personnel were training anti-Castro elements at Retalhuleu, a secret camp in Guatemala.

The crisis over Cuba rocked the very foundations of American foreign policy. By January, 1961, the United States had to accept the fact that the Cold War had come to the New World. Differences among members of the OAS caused repeated postponements of the Eleventh Inter-American Conference which should have met in 1959. The Eisenhower administration had begun through the Central Intelligence Agency to aid the Cuban exiles in preparations for a military assault on the island, a fact unknown to the public and a course fraught with peril. And in time President Kennedy would have to decide whether the existing machinery for collective defense safeguarded the republic or whether he would have to fall back on the sort of unilateral action envisaged by the original Monroe Doctrine.

60

❯❯❯·❯❯❯·❯❯❯·❯❯❮❮❮·❮❮❮·❮❮❮·❮❮❮

The Middle East:

Battleground and Prize

EVEN BEFORE Russia extended the Cold War to Subsaharan Africa and the Western Hemisphere, it found the Middle East a fruitful area to exploit. Increasingly during the Eisenhower years that strategic sector attracted the attention of the Soviet Union and the United States. The former saw in the grinding poverty of the masses, the inflamed nationalism of the leaders, the bitter memories of colonialism, and the mortal conflict of Arab and Jew a golden opportunity to advance communism. The latter tried by conciliation and economic aid, by a new doctrine and an additional alliance, by support of the United Nations and reliance on its own power to save this battleground and prize for the free world.

THE ARAB-ISRAELI IMPASSE

Foremost among the Middle East problems inherited by the Republicans was the Arab-Israeli impasse. Although the Jewish state had entered the United Nations and been recognized by over forty governments, Egypt, Saudi Arabia, Iraq, Lebanon, Syria, and Jordan denied its right to exist. They blamed Truman and his associates for creating the state and vowed ultimate destruction even if it meant violating the Charter and the Anglo-American-French pledge of 1950 to uphold the armistice lines. There could be no long-range peace in the Holy Land while that attitude persisted.

Related to the Arab-Israeli feud was the Middle East Command
with which Acheson had hoped to forestall Russian penetration of the
region. Dulles regarded such a device as only a future possibility and
instead used his influence to promote an Anglo-Egyptian *rapprochement*. By a treaty of October 19, 1954, England gave up its rights to
maintain a base at Suez and to station troops in the canal zone, rights
which Egypt had abrogated unilaterally on October 15, 1951. It also
promised to evacuate all armed forces within twenty months. In return, Egypt agreed to keep in constant readiness the principal combat
installations at Suez and to allow the re-entry of British contingents if
any outside power attacked one of the Arab states or Turkey.

Although the Suez settlement weakened Western defenses, Dulles
and Eden believed it might lead to cooperation with the new Egyptian
head of state, Gamal Abdel Nasser. They wanted Nasser's assistance
in breaking the Arab-Israeli impasse and in building a Middle East defense organization. Both hopes died in 1955. The signing on February 24 of the Baghdad Pact—first restricted to Turkey and Iraq, but
later enlarged by England, Pakistan, and Iran—infuriated Nasser who
saw in it a blow to Egypt's primacy in the Arab world and a betrayal of
Anglo-American assurances that Cairo would be the center of any regional system of collective defense. Then a raid into the Gaza Strip by
Israeli soldiers on February 28 revealed the inferiority of Nasser's military forces and pushed him along a path which ran counter to Washington's prescription for keeping peace in the Middle East. Ever since
the tripartite declaration of 1950, the United States had tried to prevent an arms race in the area. Its Anglo-French partners were often
lukewarm, but the real danger lay in the Soviet bloc. Nasser cleverly
capitalized on Russia's ire over the Baghdad Pact, obtained a mammoth cotton-for-arms barter agreement with Czechoslovakia, and announced it to a startled world on September 27, 1955.

A vicious circle was now complete. Arab nationalists, bent on the
eventual annihilation of the Jewish state, found in Nasser a daring and
ambitious leader who promised to strengthen their military capability
so that they could stand up to Israel and assert themselves against the
West. Israel's existing superiority and its loose talk of a preventive war
provided an excuse, with the American market closed, to tap the limit-
less supply of Communist armaments. The Israelis, in turn, felt that
they had to act. They were no more willing than their antagonists to
compromise differences, and they had met raid with counterraid. That
they should now move to anticipate their foes, to strike while the advantage lay with them, was as understandable as it was deplorable; but
before their plans had fully matured, developments in Egypt transformed the incipient Arab-Israeli clash into a possible world war.

THE SUEZ DEBACLE

Nasser's success in exploiting East-West rivalries to procure arms for the destruction of Israel led him to employ the same tactics for the reconstruction of Egypt. He dreamed of building a dam on the Nile at Aswan, 800 miles south of Cairo, which would increase the nation's arable land by a third, permit two additional crops a year in many places, and stimulate a vast expansion of electricity and industry. Nothing could better glorify his rule than to enlarge the production of food and goods in a traditionally famine-stricken and poverty-ridden country. And nothing could be more beyond Egypt's resources. Since it was obvious that Cairo must look abroad for assistance and since it was unthinkable that Moscow should score another triumph, the Eisenhower administration joined the Eden cabinet in a trial offer of aid. It involved an initial grant of $70 million, of which the United States would contribute 80 per cent, to defray expenses for five years and a promise of $130 million at a later date. These assurances would enable the World Bank, after the opening phase was completed, to advance $200 million at 5 per cent, repayable in forty years. The combined Anglo-American and World Bank figure of $400 million for a work costing about $1,300,000,000 provided the decisive amount in foreign exchange.

Courting disaster, Nasser played one side against the other. In January, 1956, he rejected the conditions of the Anglo-American offer as threatening Egypt's independence and hinted that he could do better in Moscow. It also became evident that his zeal for weapons to deter Israel exceeded his desire for funds to develop Aswan. He supported the Algerian rebels against France and plotted against the British faction in Iraq and Jordan, while the controlled Cairo press and radio reviled the West, praised the Soviets, and proclaimed the doom of Zionism. Finally, inspired rumors in June, 1956, of a twenty-year loan of $1,120,000,000 by Russia at 2 per cent led Dulles to take a fateful step. On July 19 he told the Egyptian ambassador that it was "not feasible in present circumstances" for the United States to participate in the Aswan project. He gave as some of the reasons the failure of Egypt to gain the approval of the riparian countries affected by the dam and to insure the success of the enterprise by devoting enough of its resources to it. Since this decision was not reached on the spur of the moment, since the timing and manner were particularly galling to Nasser, and since another approach was possible, it is pertinent to ask why Dulles acted as he did.

Certainly the Aswan scheme had by July, 1956, become financially unsound, diplomatically untenable, and domestically unwise. By then

Nasser had virtually mortgaged his economy to the Soviet bloc for arms and thus raised doubts of his ability to meet his share of construction costs. By then his blatant hostility to Anglo-American policies had made such pro-Western countries as Turkey and Iran ask why they had not received the same massive help. By then congressional opinion had turned against the wisdom of wooing Egypt, and on July 16 a Senate committee recommended that no appropriations under the Mutual Security Act be used for the proposed dam. By then, too, Dulles felt the time had come to call the Kremlin's bluff. Irked by Russia's practice of holding out to the uncommitted nations vague promises of economic aid, he was confident that Russia would not make good in this case. Whether he also hoped to topple Nasser's regime or compel him to reverse course is not clear.

Did Dulles make the right move in the wrong way? Was a public rebuke preferable to a private denial? Could the blow have been better timed? Why humiliate an impetuous dictator at the moment he was meeting with two neutralist leaders, Tito and Nehru? Would not the departure of the last British troops from Suez on June 13, 1956, and Nasser's overwhelming election as President ten days later encourage a bold counterstroke? Should not Dulles have consulted more fully with Eden, so that the Briton might have had an opportunity to comment before the step was taken and to coordinate measures in event of a prompt response? Today the answers seem obvious.

On July 26, 1956, Nasser replied by expropriating the assets of the Universal Suez Maritime Canal Company, whose concessions to operate the waterway would expire in 1968. That lucrative enterprise netted annual profits of over $25 million and, in Nasser's possession, would be invaluable in financing the Aswan Dam. The seizure, while high-handed, was probably justifiable legally, though much would depend on how adequately the shareholders were compensated for the loss of their property. The company held an Egyptian charter and was subject to Egyptian law. The canal it administered lay in Egyptian territory and was recognized, even by England, as "an integral part" of Egypt. Its status, as a private corporation, differed from that of the United States government which in Panama received in perpetuity the authority to act as if it were the sovereign. The company was an international agency upon whose experienced operations rested the material well-being of Europe. In 1955 the canal accommodated over 107 million tons of cargo, three fifths of which was oil destined for NATO countries. Thus the question was not so much an assault upon a single company but the functioning of a facility to which the international economy was geared. On this point Nasser quickly stated that he would not interfere with the free navigation, guaranteed all nations in peace and war by the Constantinople Convention of October 29, 1888.

England and France refused to accept that assurance. They did not trust a man who had already shown scant respect for his international obligations. Might he not bar their shipping from the canal, as he had that of Israel since 1950, in spite of protests from the Security Council? They doubted whether the Egyptian government could retain the skilled personnel to carry on efficient operations and whether it would devote the financial proceeds to carry out planned improvements. They saw in Nasser's response an act of defiance that boded ill for the future. As Eden said, a man with his record must not be allowed "to have his thumb at our windpipe." They also saw historical parallels. They recalled Hitler's unopposed reoccupation of the Rhineland and were determined to stop Nasser before it was too late. In London, unrestricted use of the canal was looked upon as one of the few remaining symbols of Britain's prestige in the Middle East; in Paris, the seizure was regarded as another blow to a pride wounded in Indochina and Algeria. On July 27, 1956, Eden cabled Eisenhower that he and his colleagues were convinced that they "must be ready, in the last resort, to use force."

In Washington, a sense of urgency was not apparent. The United States was less dependent on the canal and more hopeful of negotiation. Although the administration's thinking was colored by a concern for its posture in the coming election and by a desire to stand aloof from Anglo-French colonialism, the President sincerely believed the West would lose more by fighting than by talking. Hence he ordered Dulles to fly to London, where a common policy was belatedly formulated on August 2, 1956. The Secretary agreed with Eden that it was intolerable for any single power to have unfettered control of the canal, but he hoped to mobilize world opinion behind international supervision. A way had to be found, he said, "to make Nasser disgorge." He did not exclude force but favored it only if all else failed. He would begin with a conference of the signatories of the Constantinople Convention and of those countries whose tonnage and trade gave them a vital interest in the waterway.

Between August 16 and October 13, 1956, three attempts to settle the Suez controversy by diplomacy collapsed. The first was a twenty-two-nation conference at London, which recommended on August 23 that the canal be entrusted to an international board. Russia, India, Indonesia, and Ceylon dissented; Nasser bluntly said no. The second was a scheme by Dulles to organize a Suez Canal Users Association for maintaining the route, hiring pilots, and collecting tolls—a portion of which would go to Egypt. Nasser again objected; and although fifteen governments gave their consent by October 1, the project never went into effect. The third was a set of six principles worked out by the French, British, and Egyptian foreign ministers under Hammar-

skjold's mediation. They called for a canal open to all without discrimination, insulation of its operations from the internal affairs of any
country, respect for Egyptian sovereignty, joint fixing of tolls by Egypt
and the users, allocation of revenues for improvements, and arbitration of all disputes between the canal company and the Egyptian government. These represented some concession by Nasser, but the absence of sanctions that would compel him to fulfill his obligations left
them short of Eden's demand that no single nation possess unfettered
control. To insure his compliance, England and France brought to a
vote in the Security Council on October 13 a two-part resolution. The
first half, embodying the six principles, passed unanimously. The second half, outlining the guarantees, had the support of nine members
but was killed by Russia's seventy-eighth veto.

As these efforts ended in futility, the Atlantic allies drifted dangerously apart. Contradictory statements and personal shortcomings
on both sides were partly to blame, but a basic difference did separate
the Anglo-French and American positions. To the former, a principle
involving their very existence was at stake; to the latter, only the unhampered use of the canal seemed important. Britain was prepared to
fight rather than be left at the mercy of Nasser; the United States was
persuaded that extreme measures were unnecessary. Dulles and Eden
reversed in 1956 the stand they had taken in 1954. During the siege of
Dienbienphu the American had vainly urged armed intervention lest
defeat in Indochina lead to the loss of all Southeast Asia. During the
Suez crisis Eden advocated force lest a bloodless victory by Nasser
bring about Arab domination of the Middle East. On both occasions
the other man demurred. Whatever Dulles may have said on August 2,
1956, about not ruling out military measures, he made it clear on September 13 that "the United States did not intend itself to try to shoot
its way through the Canal." Eisenhower himself had declared two days
earlier, when asked whether he would join England and France in preventing a closure of the canal, "I am not going to be a party to aggression if it is humanly possible." Wise or unwise, these statements played
into Nasser's hands. They revealed an ineptitude in coalition diplomacy and go far to explain the blackout in news from London and Paris
after October 13, 1956.

That blackout was intentional. Eden and Premier Guy Mollet had
felt from the start that only military might could make Nasser disgorge. They had agreed on August 2, 1956, to try other means, partly
to obtain American cooperation but mainly because they needed six
weeks to mount an attack. As negotiations dragged on fruitlessly and
as Dulles grew less sympathetic, they regretted not having gone ahead
in mid-September. By October 13 they were convinced they had been

cozened, confused, and contradicted by the Secretary of State and his cautious chief. They were in no mood to be deterred from doing what had to be done. Yet by concealing their plans, they antagonized the United States and lost any chance of winning its support for a maneuver that was atrociously timed, speciously justified, clumsily executed, and irresolutely pursued.

For the appeal to arms in Suez was not an isolated incident. It occurred simultaneously with the satellite uprising which broke out in Eastern Europe on October 21–3, 1956, and the preventive war which Israel launched against Egypt on October 29. How much collusion existed between London, Paris, and Tel Aviv is still disputed, but there can be no doubt that France had materially strengthened Israel's military establishment in previous months. It is clear that Premier David Ben-Gurion ordered the invasion of the Sinai Peninsula, in spite of assurances to the United Nations, to stop terroristic raids originating there, to open the canal to Israeli shipping, and to insure free passage to the Gulf of Aqaba. It is also clear that the Anglo-French aerial bombardment of Cairo and the canal zone, which began on October 31, offset in Afro-Asian eyes Russia's ruthless repression of the Hungarian rebellion and quickly converted Nasser from a menace to peace into a victim of aggression. When Eden and Mollet justified these drastic measures as a device to keep the Sinai War away from the canal and when their troops required a week to secure key points, during which time Egypt blocked the waterway by scuttling ships, it became evident that a colossal blunder had been committed.

At this critical moment the American people were about to go to the polls. Eisenhower's campaign had stressed peace and prosperity. His policy in the Middle East had been to exclude Russia from the area, keep the canal controversy separate from the Arab-Israeli feud, and uphold the tripartite declaration of May 25, 1950. The last obligated the United States, Britain, and France to take prompt action, within or outside the United Nations, to check any breach of the armistice lines. On April 9, 1956, the President had gone further in promising "to support and assist" any country in the region that was attacked. Now the Anglo-French move flouted every item in that policy. Dulles had repeatedly warned Eden that seizure of the canal would not destroy Nasser but would, rather, lead to a guerrilla war from which the Soviets alone could benefit. Hence there was little hesitation, though much regret, in taking a stand against the NATO partners. "There can be no peace without law," Eisenhower said on October 31 to a nationwide audience appalled by events in Hungary and Suez. "There can be no law if we work to invoke one code of international conduct for those we oppose and another for our friends." Thus he placed the ideals of collective security above the realities of collective defense, even if he jeopardized the alliance designed to provide the safeguards which the United Nations, in practice, had not furnished.

On October 30, 1956, Lodge offered a resolution in the Security Council calling upon all members to refrain from using force in Egypt and upon the Israeli troops to withdraw. Russia gave its backing, but England and France objected because they had already sent a twelve-hour ultimatum to Cairo and Tel Aviv in which they demanded an end to the fighting, the evacuation of all military units to a distance of ten miles from the canal, and Egypt's permission to occupy temporarily positions along the route so as to separate the belligerents and insure freedom of transit. With Australia and Belgium abstaining, Lodge's motion mustered seven votes, but it was lost when the British cast their first veto and the French their third. A Russian draft, similar in nature but omitting the injunction against interference by others, met the same fate. The next day the Council convened an emergency session of the General Assembly under a procedure designed in 1950, ironically, to circumvent Soviet vetoes. On November 2 that body adopted by a vote of 64 to 5 with 6 abstentions an American resolution urging all parties to observe a cease-fire and to pull back behind the armistice lines of 1949.

The next five days were agonizing. On November 3, 1956, Dulles underwent surgery for cancer. That same day England and France refused to accept a cease-fire until certain conditions were met; Egypt continued to sink ships in the canal; and saboteurs in Syria cut off Britain's oil supply from Iraq. A second emergency session met on November 4 to deal with Hungary, while the first renewed its appeal to the belligerents in the Sinai Peninsula. On November 5 the Assembly created a multinational Emergency Force "to secure and supervise the cessation of hostilities"; and while several weeks elapsed before these contingents could take the field, the invaders were able to retire without complete loss of face. But at the moment this gain was offset by Bulganin's warning that his country stood ready "to crush the aggressors and restore peace in the East through the use of force." His proposal for a joint Russo-American military action to end the fighting was rejected by Eisenhower, but talk in Moscow of recruiting "volunteers" to serve in Egypt conjured up memories of Korea. On November 6, election day, the President ordered a global alert of the armed forces, but by evening the worst was over. Having seized all of the Gaza Strip, most of the Sinai Peninsula, and two islands in the Gulf of Aqaba, the Israelis agreed to halt. Although the Anglo-French occupation of the canal zone was only starting and another seventy-two hours might put it entirely out of Nasser's grasp, Britain followed suit. Bereft of full support at home, deserted by Canada and the United States abroad, condemned by most newspapers throughout the world, and faced with an interruption of traffic at Suez, Eden stopped too soon a venture he began—if it was to be undertaken at all—too late.

Much still had to be done, but the task of evacuating troops, clearing debris, and maintaining order with the United Nations Emergency Force need not be recounted. The aftermath is significant mainly because Nasser emerged stronger than before, because Russia persuaded the Arab world that it had compelled "the colonialist aggressors" to desist, because the problem of Israel and the control of the canal remained unsolved, and because the Atlantic alliance bore deep and permanent scars. Somehow it seems, at least with the benefit of hindsight, that the whole affair could have been handled more deftly in Washington and in London.

THE EISENHOWER DOCTRINE AND LEBANON

The Suez debacle patently called for a reappraisal of American policy in the Middle East. The events of November, 1956, marked a new low in Anglo-French prestige and a further penetration of Soviet power. The next months would see Arab leaders generally and Nasser particularly step up their agitation against France's rule in Algeria and Britain's primacy in Iraq and Jordan. Allied disunity and Russian eagerness convinced the men in Washington that some new step must be taken. Already they had told Bulganin on November 5 that the entry of Red troops into the region, except under a United Nations mandate, would be opposed. On November 29 the State Department announced that a threat to the territorial integrity or political independence of Iran, Iraq, Turkey, or Pakistan would be viewed "with the utmost gravity." With Dulles averse to joining the Baghdad Pact it seemed best to bolster earlier presidential declarations on the Middle East with congressional action. That was what had been done to make the administration's intentions clear in the Formosa Strait.

Eisenhower's message of January 5, 1957, called a doctrine by the press, requested a grant of authority in advance to halt Communist aggression, direct or indirect, in the Middle East. After a stormy two-month debate, most of what he sought was contained in a joint resolution that passed the Senate on March 5 by a vote of 72 to 19 and the House on March 7 by a margin of 350 to 60. It first empowered the president to help develop the economic strength of and enter into military assistance programs with any nation or group of nations in the area which desired such aid. For this purpose he could before June 30, 1958, draw upon $200 million in mutual security funds already appropriated. It next asserted more clearly than any previous document that "the United States regards as vital to the national interest and world peace the preservation of the independence and integrity of the nations of the Middle East." What constituted the Middle East was not specified. It finally declared that if the president deemed it necessary, the United States was prepared "to use armed forces to assist any such nation or group of nations requesting assistance against armed aggression from any country controlled by international communism," provided that employment be consonant with the treaty obligations and the Constitution of the United States. The Congress could, by concurrent resolution, terminate that authority.

Several points in the resolution of March 9, 1957, should be underlined. First, it did not deal with the Arab-Israeli impasse or the Suez Canal; those controversies were left to the United Nations. Second, the promise to use American troops, ships, and planes covered only armed aggression from a country controlled by international communism; there would be no involvement in quarrels between Middle East neighbors. Third, military support against a Communist-dominated aggressor would be given only upon request; the United States would not act unilaterally. Fourth, the new grant of authority was of little value against indirect aggression; subversion must be fought by enabling friendly governments to protect themselves. Fifth, the resolution aroused more opposition than the one on Formosa did in 1955. Some of the criticism can be traced to the administration's disingenuous treatment of foreign affairs in the recent election and some to its confusing course during the Suez debacle. There were also legitimate questions which had not been fully answered. Was Russian armed aggression the real danger in the Middle East? Should not more emphasis be placed on coping with subversion? How could one determine a country "controlled by international communism"? Yet it was generally agreed at home that the United States must play a larger role in the region and fill the power vacuum left by England and France.

Foreign reaction to the Eisenhower Doctrine varied. Bulganin called it "gross interference" in the Middle East's internal affairs, and Khrushchev predicted it would end on "the garbage heap of history." The pro-Western nations of the northern tier—Turkey, Iran, Iraq—expressed a pleasure that could have been exceeded only if the United States had joined the Baghdad Pact. The professedly neutralist but actually Soviet-aligned governments of Egypt and Syria denounced it as "a plot engineered by the imperialists and fed by Zionism." The real test came in Lebanon, Saudi Arabia, and Jordan. The Lebanese foreign minister described the American move as "good and timely," while King Saud extended the Dhahran lease for five years. On April 10, 1957, plucky young Hussein of Jordan, who had acquiesced in cutting traditional ties with Britain, suddenly ousted his anti-Western, pro-Nasser cabinet and appealed to the loyal Bedouin tribes to protect his throne. For a moment his kingdom—perhaps the possibility of a general war—hung in the balance. Determined to prevent the chaos that Russia hoped to exploit, Eisenhower announced on April 24 that he regarded the independence of Jordan as "vital." The next day the Sixth Fleet sailed hastily from France for the eastern Mediterranean, and this display of support temporarily bolstered Hussein's shaky position.

Tensions, however, remained high. A midsummer alarm in Syria, whose Communist-dominated government charged the American embassy with plotting its downfall, was followed in October, 1957, by the gravest crisis since Suez. Early that month Khrushchev accused the United States of inciting Turkey to attack Syria, and he threatened Ankara with rockets if it yielded to American urging. On October 16 Syria asked the General Assembly to send a commission to investigate. In endorsing the request, Foreign Minister Gromyko warned that Russia would assist Syria militarily in halting aggression. Lodge's reply alleged that the Kremlin had fabricated a war scare for the purpose of embroiling the Middle East nations, whose independence it sought to destroy. Thanks to King Saud's mediation, the Assembly did not have to vote, but Syria continued to be a source of trouble. On February 1, 1958, it virtually compelled Nasser to merge the two countries in a United Arab Republic. From that time on, Cairo and Damascus served as headquarters for ill-concealed attempts to subvert the pro-Western regimes in Iraq, Jordan, and Lebanon.

In the half-Christian, half-Muslim republic of Lebanon a revolt began on May 9, 1958, against President Camille Chamoun, who had approved the Eisenhower Doctrine and wanted to stay in office when his term ended in September. Although internal in origin, the insurrection drew heavy support from adjacent Syria and was led by Lebanese who shared Nasser's anti-Western brand of Arab nationalism. On May 22 Lebanon complained to the United Nations that massive interference in its domestic affairs by Egypt and Syria was endangering the peace. After a delay, while Chamoun's government also appealed to the Arab League, the Security Council on June 11 voted unanimously, with Russia abstaining, to send investigators to probe charges of border violations. Within a fortnight Hammarskjold had placed in Lebanon a ninety-four-member United Nations Observation Group, drawn from eleven small non-Communist countries outside the Middle East. But its arrival did not stop the fighting. It was too small to seal the Syrian frontier, and it was barred from areas in rebel hands. Hence its reports, in Chamoun's opinion, grossly underestimated the infiltration of men and materials. Since neither the United Nations nor the Arab League seemed to offer protection, the Lebanese President decided to seek aid from a major power and cited the right of individual or collective self-defense guaranteed by Article 51 of the Charter. Eisenhower did not relish the request. He was loath to have American ground forces clash with Arabs; he knew that the action might lead to Russian counterintervention.

Suddenly a bloody revolution in Iraq changed the picture. On July 14, 1958, the pro-Western King and his Premier were brutally murdered in an uprising headed by Brigadier General Abdel Karim al-Kassim. Although nationalist in origin, this development had international ramifications. Iraq was the sole Arab member of the Baghdad Pact. If it fell prey to Nasser—and Kassim's principal aide was an ardent admirer of the Egyptian dictator—or if it swung into the Soviet orbit, it might carry Jordan, Lebanon, and Saudi Arabia with it. Thus the events of July 14 created a panic in Beirut and Amman. Chamoun cabled Eisenhower that his government could survive only if American troops were sent at once; and Hussein, who had watched the last British contingents depart on July 4, 1957, frantically begged London and Washington for help.

Eisenhower had three choices and only hours in which to decide. The first was to take no action of any kind. This carried the least danger at the moment; eventually it might be disastrous. The second was to throw troops into Iraq, so as to keep it aligned with the West. This would anger most of the Arab world and probably provoke Soviet counterintervention. The third was to comply with appeals to shore up the defenses of Lebanon and Jordan. The last course could be justified legally, but it certainly would bring protests, perhaps something more, from Moscow. It could lead to a clash with Arab nationalists or Russian "volunteers." Much depended on the timing of the operation and the reaction of the Kremlin.

The timing, from a military point of view, was perfect. Word of the Iraq coup and Chamoun's plea reached the White House early on July 14, 1958. The President conferred with the National Security Council and then with Nixon and Dulles alone. That afternoon he briefed selected senators and representatives. In the Mediterranean, all shore leaves were canceled, and that evening the Joint Chiefs of Staff ordered the Sixth Fleet, with its three carriers and their atomic-armed planes, to rendezvous off Lebanon and deploy for an amphibious landing. The next morning the White House announced that Chamoun's request had been met so as to protect American lives, encourage the Lebanese government to uphold its sovereignty, and demonstrate the concern of the United States for a country whose independence was "vital to the national interest and world peace." At that moment 1,700 marines were streaming across the beaches at Beirut—unopposed. By July 19 the United States had put into Lebanon almost 8,000 of the

14,300 men eventually sent, while Britain, answering Hussein's appeal, airlifted 3,000 fighters from Cyprus to Jordan.

The reaction, from a diplomatic point of view, was ominous. Most neutralist and some Western leaders deplored the move. The enraged Nasser flew to Moscow. Russia denounced the "aggression" and warned that it could not be indifferent to a menace so close to its borders. On July 19, 1958, Khrushchev sent letters to Eisenhower, Macmillan, de Gaulle, and Nehru asserting that the world tottered on "the brink of disaster" and could be saved only by a prompt end of "the present military conflict." He proposed a meeting of the four addressees, Hammarskjold, and himself at Geneva three days later. On July 22 Eisenhower replied: "I am not aware of any factual basis for your extravagantly expressed fear." The real danger, he said, came from those who would start a general war because Lebanon was helped to maintain its freedom. The President then suggested that the heads of government represent their countries at the Security Council, which had already begun to discuss the matter.

Lodge had reported to the Council on the Lebanon landings the day they occurred. He argued that Chamoun's request for support from a member of the United Nations was consistent with the Charter. Washington had acted, he avowed, only because no one else could at that time prevent outside interference in an internal revolt, and the responsibility would be gladly surrendered as soon as the world organization wished to assume it. But Moscow was determined, for propaganda purposes, to block that transfer. On July 18, 1958, the Soviet delegate—in the face of nine favorable votes and one abstention—vetoed an American resolution which sought additional United Nations measures to halt the infiltration across the Lebanese frontier. On July 22 he vetoed a milder Japanese request that the Security Council take steps that would stabilize the situation and enable the United States forces to withdraw. This time the count was ten to one. Yet a Russian motion calling upon the United States and Great Britain to get out of Lebanon and Jordan "immediately" mustered on July 18 only one favorable vote with eight opposing and two abstaining.

Faced with these vetoes, Lodge asked for an emergency session of the General Assembly. Action was delayed a fortnight to see whether the heads of government would meet, but after a visit to Peking during that interval Khrushchev abandoned the summit approach and turned to the Assembly with its large number of Afro-Asian neutralists. By the time the special session opened on August 8, 1958, the outlook had brightened. Despite tough talk, Russia had not sent regulars or "volunteers" to the troubled area. The United States had recognized the Kassim regime, thus removing fears that it might also intervene in

Iraq. In Lebanon bloodshed had been avoided, a new president acceptable to all factions had been found, and a few marines had been pulled
out. With the Assembly split over a Soviet demand that the Anglo-
American forces be ordered out and a Dulles proposal that indirect aggression be condemned, the Arabs themselves provided the solution.
On August 21 Iraq, Jordan, Lebanon, Libya, Morocco, Saudi Arabia,
Sudan, Tunisia, the United Arab Republic, and Yemen sponsored a resolution that passed unanimously. It accepted assurances that members
of the Arab League would "abstain from any action calculated to
change established systems of government," called upon members of
the United Nations to avoid interfering in the domestic affairs of other
states, and requested the Secretary-General to take steps to vindicate
in Lebanon and Jordan the principles of the Charter, thereby facilitating the "early withdrawal of foreign troops from the two countries."

Hammarskjold's efficient arrangements made possible the removal
of the American forces by October 25, 1958, the departure of the British units by November 2, and the break-up of the United Nations Observation Group by December 10. Although the United States had accomplished its purpose of preventing the subversion of Lebanon and
Jordan, the aftermath offered little cause for satisfaction. In the former
country, Chamoun's pro-Western policy gave way to neutralism; in the
latter land, Hussein's throne remained in jeopardy. The military operation had revived memories of Suez and had provided propagandists in
Moscow with a field day. The Eisenhower Doctrine had proved incapable of coping with either indirect Communist aggression or regional
nationalist rivalries. And Nasser's influence was greater than ever. He
controlled Egypt and Syria. Saudi Arabia no longer contested his leadership. Iraq and Lebanon had deserted the Western camp. And on December 27, 1958, Nasser accepted Russia's offer of $100 million, repay-
able in twelve years at 2.5 per cent, to finance the first steps in his
cherished Aswan Dam project.

THE CENTRAL TREATY ORGANIZATION

One consequence of the events of July, 1958, was the transformation of
the Baghdad Pact alliance into the Central Treaty Organization. From
the outset Dulles worried about the northern tier of nations next to
Russia. He helped bring into being on February 24 and October 25,
1955, a treaty between Turkey, Iran, Pakistan, Iraq, and Great Britain.
Although the first four were Muslim states, only Iraq belonged to the
Arab world. The American government did not join, ostensibly to
avoid antagonizing Israel and its neighbors, but it was already linked
with England and Turkey in NATO and with England and Pakistan in
SEATO. It had also signed mutual defense assistance pacts with Iran

on May 23, 1950, with Iraq on April 21, 1954, and with Pakistan on May 19, 1954, though none of these involved obligations to give armed aid or contained grants for American bases.

As a diplomatic symbol opposing Russia's penetration into the Middle East, the Baghdad Pact had some value. As a military barrier, it was a frail reed. Like SEATO, but unlike NATO, it possessed no unified command or specific forces of its own. Turkey had allocated its strength to defending Europe's eastern flank and could contribute little. Iran and Iraq were woefully weak. Pakistan lay on the fringes of the Middle East and was geographically bifurcated. The last three had joined more from a desire to obtain American arms than out of a devotion to the cause of regional security. Britain adhered because of Iraq, where leases on its two remaining Middle East bases would soon expire. Lastly, Iraq's inclusion angered the other Arab states, who branded Iraq a traitor, and India, who accused the West of bringing the Cold War to South Asia.

Despite these defects, or maybe because of them, Dulles edged ever closer to full participation in the Baghdad Pact without outright membership. He sent an observer to an organizational meeting in November, 1955, when a headquarters was set up in Baghdad and a Secretary-General appointed. At Tehran on April 19, 1956, the United States agreed to serve on committees dealing with economics and subversion and to maintain liaison with one on military affairs. After the Suez debacle had turned the Muslim members against England and left Russia to pose as the savior of the Arab world, Dulles went out of his way to stress American support of the pact. "A threat to the territorial integrity or political independence of the members," he said on November 29, 1956, "would be viewed by the United States with the utmost gravity." During 1957 the pact was overshadowed by the Eisenhower Doctrine, but some progress could be claimed with the decision of the United States to serve on the military committee and with the formation of a joint planning staff.

Then came the revolution in Iraq and its defection to the neutralist camp. Militarily the loss was slight, but Iraq had given the alliance its name and seat, had been the only Arab member, and had provided the sole rail link between Iran and Turkey. To soften the blow, Dulles told the Baghdad Pact Council on July 28, 1958, that, "in the interest of world peace and pursuant to existing Congressional authorization," his government was ready to spell out the commitments it had under the mutual security laws and the Eisenhower Doctrine. Later, on March 5, 1959, the American ambassador at Ankara signed identical executive agreements with Turkey, Iran, and Pakistan. These documents stipulated that in case of aggression and at the request of the other party, the United States would take appropriate action, "in accordance with the Constitution," including the use of armed force as might be jointly decided and as was envisaged in the resolution of March 9, 1957. Aggression was not defined, and the obligation resembled SEATO's rather than NATO's.

Iraq quit the Baghdad Pact on March 24, 1959, and the alliance became the Central Treaty Organization on August 18 with its seat at Ankara. The name can mislead, for the United States still held aloof. Actually, only NATO is a full multinational military combination; SEATO and CENTO are merely symbols of America's desire to keep Southeast Asia and the Middle East in the camp of the free world. To underscore the symbolism, Herter agreed to hold the seventh session of the CENTO Council in Washington on October 7–9, 1959, thus anticipating by several months the initial meeting of the SEATO Council in the United States. The delegates listened to laudatory speeches by Eisenhower and Nixon and even set up a permanent group of military deputies to explore a single CENTO command, but they heard no pledge of American membership. At Tehran on April 29, 1960, Herter assured the CENTO foreign ministers that they would be consulted before decisions affecting their countries were reached at the impending summit conference. Such was the state of the Middle East alliance as the Eisenhower administration drew to a close.

During 1960 the Middle East remained tense but, compared to the preceding years, relatively quiet. The Arab-Israeli impasse had not been broken. Nasser continued to be a disruptive force, but his neutralism had lost its Russian tinge. In Iraq, Kassim tried to find a safe channel between the Scylla of communism and the Charybdis of Nasserism; in Jordan, Hussein still sat on a shaky throne. With Africa emerging as a new source of conflict between East and West, the world of Islam lost a little of its importance. The discovery of large reserves north of the Sahara promised an alternative supply of oil which could lessen Europe's dependence on Iraq, Iran, Saudi Arabia, and the sheikdoms of the Persian Gulf. Yet for many years to come the Middle East will be both a battleground and a prize.

61

❯❯❯-❯❯❯-❯❯❯-❯❯❮-❮❮❮-❮❮❮-❮❮❮

American Foreign Policy Today

AMERICAN FOREIGN POLICY today would be unrecognizable to the informed citizen of 1939. A single generation has witnessed a revolution in the principles and practices of diplomacy, and that fact was clearly evident as the Eisenhower administration ended. The extensive travels of the executive, the intense concern for alliances, the revitalized debates in the United Nations, the harrowing dread of thermonuclear war, the widespread reverberations of developments in areas unthought of two decades earlier, and the deep significance attached to the ability of presidential candidates to perform on the world scene demonstrated the importance external affairs had assumed in the life of the United States.

THE SCOPE OF FOREIGN POLICY TODAY

Certainly the scope of American foreign policy today would astonish the practitioners of the past. In 1905 Secretary Root could write that "the main object of diplomacy" was "to keep the country out of trouble." Today that negative approach would be suicidal. A positive quest for security is indispensable. For twenty years the republic has engaged in a struggle for survival under various names—nonbelligerency, total war, limited war, cold war. In meeting the totalitarian challenge, Fascist and Communist, the government has embarked upon new activities, created new agencies, joined new organizations, and literally explored new space. In January, 1939, Roosevelt shocked the nation by suggesting that its frontier lay along the Rhine; in April, 1957, Eisenhower excited no one in asserting that the independence of tiny, distant Jordan was vital to the security of the United States.

The State Department remained the center of American diplomacy, but under Herter it bore little resemblance to the one Hull presided over in 1940. In that year its personnel numbered 971, and its appropriations were less than $3,000,000. The top officers consisted of a Secretary, an Under Secretary, a Counselor, and four Assistant Secretaries. The day-to-day work was handled in four Divisions: Far Eastern Affairs, European Affairs, Near Eastern Affairs, and the American Republics. By 1960 the Department had about 7,000 employees within the continental limits and 16,000 overseas. The budget for the fiscal year was $207,900,000, a sum that did not include the $1,925,800,000 allocated to the International Cooperation Administration under its jurisdiction. The roster of key officials had almost tripled. In addition to the Secretary and the Under Secretary, there was a second Under Secretary for Political Affairs, two Deputy Under Secretaries—one for Administration and one for Political Affairs—a Counselor, and twelve Assistant Secretaries. The last ruled over Administration, Economic Affairs, Policy Planning, Public Affairs, Congressional Relations, Security and Consular Affairs, European Affairs, African Affairs, Near Eastern and South Asian Affairs, and Far Eastern Affairs. A Director of the International Cooperation Administration supervised the nonmilitary parts of the mutual security program.

Familiarity with the enlarged functions of the State Department is only an introduction to the many instrumentalities which shape foreign policy today. The president, of course, is paramount. He must initiate, educate, conciliate, sometimes negotiate, and always decide. For help in these duties, he has built a group of White House advisers. He relies, too, on the National Security Council, which, in turn, obtains data from the Central Intelligence Agency. As a department, Defense ranks second only to State. The assistant secretary for international security affairs controls the military assistance efforts; several of his colleagues oversee the contribution of science to a rapidly changing weapons system. The Joint Chiefs of Staff, whose statutory authority was broadened on August 6, 1958, and whose assigned personnel rose to 400, devise strategy for war and peace. The Senate and House still share with the executive responsibility for the conduct of foreign policy and periodically review its accomplishments. Under Eisenhower their committees operated much the way they had in recent years. Probably the most striking innovation by 1960 was the prominence of the vice president. Henry A. Wallace received novel assignments during the war, but Richard M. Nixon undertook more diplomatic tasks than any of his predecessors. In addition to serving on the National Security Council and making ceremonial visits to England, Brazil, and the Philippines, he embarked upon major goodwill tours, with the State Department's blessing, to the Far East and Middle East in 1953, to Central America and the Caribbean in 1955, to Africa in 1957, to South America in 1958, and to Russia and Poland in 1959. Indeed, Nixon's exchange with Khrushchev before a television camera in Moscow made him the leading presidential candidate in subsequent public-opinion polls.

Even without additional problems of military defense, economic assistance, and scientific investigation, the scope of foreign policy today is staggering. By January, 1961, the United States maintained abroad ninety-two embassies and legations, whereas in 1940 the number had been forty-nine. It also staffed a permanent mission to the United Nations in New York, the European Economic Community in Brussels, the International Atomic Energy Agency in Vienna, and the European Regional Organizations in Paris. It was represented on the ANZUS Council and the Council and committees of NATO, SEATO, CENTO, and the OAS. A calendar of the international conferences and meetings which the United States proposed to attend from August 1 to October 31, 1960, contained seventy-three entries.

Perhaps the taxing nature of American foreign policy today can best be understood in personal terms. During Eisenhower's first six and a half years in office, he received official visits from about sixty heads of state but went abroad only four times—to confer with the Anglo-French prime ministers at Bermuda in December, 1953; to attend the summit conference at Geneva in July, 1955; to commemorate Bolivar's congress at Panama in July, 1956; and to participate in a NATO Council meeting at Paris in December, 1957. In the next twelve months his schedule included a goodwill visit to West Germany, England, and France from August 26 to September 9, 1959; a reception for Khrushchev in the Washington area from September 15 to 27; a goodwill tour to Italy, Turkey, Pakistan, Afghanistan, India, Iran, Greece, Tunisia, France, Spain, and Morocco from December 3 to 22; a Western summit meeting in Paris on December 19–21; a goodwill mission to Brazil, Uruguay, Argentina, and Chile from February 22 to March 7, 1960; the preliminaries of the abortive summit conference at Paris from May 14 to 20; and a final goodwill venture in the Philippines, Formosa, and South Korea from June 12 to 26. That same year Secretary Herter, who spent 156 of his first 414 days in office out of the country, participated in the Foreign Ministers Conference at Geneva, attended the Fifth Meeting of Consultation of Ministers of Foreign Affairs at Santiago, acted as chief American observer at the CENTO

Council meetings in Washington and Tehran, sat with the ANZUS Council in Washington, took part in the NATO Council sessions at Paris and Istanbul, and served as host for the SEATO gathering in Washington.

THE PRINCIPLES OF FOREIGN POLICY TODAY

For over a century and a half the principles of isolationism, neutrality, and the Monroe Doctrine determined the course of American diplomacy. Lesser policies—nonintervention in the domestic affairs of other countries, the right of self-determination, the recognition of *de facto* governments, the peaceful settlement of international disputes, and equal opportunity for trade and investment—also played a part. But it was upon the first three that the safety of the United States was thought to rest. In the dozen years before Eisenhower took office, those familiar landmarks disappeared or were drastically transformed. Isolationism —in the sense of avoiding permanent alliances and minimizing involvement in the rivalries of other continents—had long been eroded by changes in technology, communication, and warfare; it could not survive in the face of dangers which compelled the republic to join the United Nations, participate in NATO and other regional defense systems, underwrite bilateral assistance pacts, embark upon a costly program of mutual security, and build fleets of intercontinental bombers. Neutrality—in the sense of abstaining from wars of other states, while fulfilling certain duties and enjoying certain rights—had been abandoned before Pearl Harbor; it was not likely to be revived when every victory of communism seemed to threaten the national interest. The Monroe Doctrine—a complex of ideas assuming the separation of the hemispheres and barring territorial aggrandizement, armed intervention, and internal subversion by non-American nations in the New World—had been modified; no longer did the United States always choose to be alone responsible for its interpretation and enforcement.

In none of these areas did the Republicans after 1953 turn back the clock. Dulles extended the network of alliances begun by the Democrats. To the OAS, NATO, the ANZUS Pact, and the bilateral security treaties with Japan and the Philippines, he added SEATO, association with CENTO, and defensive ties with South Korea, Nationalist China, Turkey, Iran, and Pakistan. Eisenhower referred repeatedly to "our allies" in tones that must have sent Borah, Johnson, and Taft spinning in their graves. Some critics have said Dulles used a collector's approach to alliances, the more the better. Certainly two of them, SEATO and CENTO, were militarily negligible. The West just could not match the enemy in Southeast Asia and the Middle East in mustering huge armies or employing guerrilla tactics. Diplomatically, SEATO and

CENTO brought mixed returns. On the one hand, they antagonized the Communists and alienated the nonaligned without adding materially to the strength of the beneficiaries; on the other, they heartened the weak and symbolized American concern for freedom in areas once considered of little interest. Association with the Baghdad Pact was highly irregular. The Senate was never asked to approve the relationship which began on November 21, 1955, or the agreements with the Muslim members of CENTO that were signed on March 5, 1959.

A steadfast devotion to the United Nations also characterized the Republican regime. By January, 1953, much of the original enthusiasm for this second venture in world organization had subsided, and the frustrations of the Korean War dampened whatever ardor the action of June, 1950, had rekindled. Indeed, as Truman left office, Senator McCarthy and others were attacking the institution as a hotbed of spies. Nonetheless, Eisenhower based his diplomacy squarely on the principles of the Charter and eagerly supported the decisions of the Security Council and the General Assembly. The administration did not order a single veto. Occasionally it favored independent action, as with disarmament from 1957 to 1960, in Lebanon in 1958, and at the summit in 1955 and 1960. But it showed its real faith during the Suez debacle by relying on the United Nations to restore peace, even if that meant voting with enemies against allies. Nor is it without significance that the Republican convention in July, 1960, nominated for the vice presidency the grandson of Henry Cabot Lodge, mainly because of his work as ambassador to the United Nations. In politics isolationism was dead, though its spirit lingered among a few strategists who argued that thermonuclear weapons enabled the United States to defend itself without allies and without stationing troops overseas.

If isolationism had by 1960 become a dirty word, neutrality was a forgotten one. The ancient disputes over neutral rights seemed relics of a bygone age, while the training given Cuban exiles on American soil to reconquer their homeland ignored existing laws on neutral duties. On the other hand, the concept of neutralism emerged in Asia and Africa to test the republic's tolerance and understanding. Neutralism appealed to nations that wished to stay aloof from the Cold War. Most had just cast off a colonial status; few practiced the American brand of democracy. They viewed the East-West struggle much as the United States had looked upon the wars of the French Revolution and Napoleon. Yet in his zeal for building regional alliances, Dulles often ignored that sentiment. The strained relations with India can be attributed to his demands that it take sides and to Nehru's opposition to Cold War alliances in Southeast Asia and the Middle East. Some neutralist leaders, such as Nasser in 1955 and Lumumba in 1960, tried to make Washington and Moscow outbid each other, but their excesses must not obscure a genuine spirit that will grow as the capability of missiles brings every land within range of annihilation.

The Monroe Doctrine received in 1960 renewed attention as a principle of American foreign policy, thanks to Khrushchev's exploitation of the Cuban crisis. His contemptuous allusion to its demise obliged the State Department to assert on July 14 that it was as binding in 1960 as it had been in 1823. Yet Monroe's edict had lost some of its original meaning, for only in extreme cases would the United States resort to unilateral action. In most instances it would rely on the Inter-American Treaty of Reciprocal Assistance, while reserving the right to go it alone when others failed to agree that their safety was threatened. Of course, in an age of push-button warfare armed invasion of the Western Hemisphere is unlikely. The real danger, aside from nuclear destruction, is internal subversion, and the Doctrine does not prohibit an American republic from changing its form of government. Semifascist dictators have been common; and although the Declaration of Solidarity at Caracas avowed on March 28, 1954, that "domination and control of the political institutions of any American State by the international communist movement" would constitute a menace to the Americas, little can be done to cope with an indigenous dictatorship of the proletariat. At a news conference on August 10, 1960, Eisenhower expressed doubt that any people would freely choose communism; but if they did, he said, "I don't see how the United States could properly object." Nonintervention had long been a sacred principle of inter-American diplomacy; and if it served to protect a Trujillo in the Dominican Republic, it can afford similar immunity to a Castro in Cuba.

Two other doctrines bearing presidential names also undergird American foreign policy today. The Truman Doctrine is not frequently mentioned, for it is thought of in connection with a specific crisis, when the United States aided imperiled Greece and Turkey. Yet Truman's message of March 12, 1947, was sweeping in its commitment "to support free peoples who are resisting attempted subjugation by armed minorities or by outside pressures." To prevent aggression, direct and indirect, from facilitating the spread of totalitarianism, the American government embarked upon a system of far-flung alliances and a program of massive economic and military assistance. The Eisenhower Doctrine was more restricted in space and scope. If Monroe saw America's safety endangered by European intervention in the Western Hemisphere and Truman saw it menaced by the subversion of freedom anywhere in the world, Eisenhower limited himself to an undefined Middle East where the preservation of independent nations was vital to the interests of the United States. To forestall Russian penetration, however, he was willing to use American men, ships, and planes only upon the request of a government threatened with actual armed attack by a Communist-controlled country.

Another cardinal feature of American diplomacy today is mutual security, often called foreign aid. From July, 1945, to July, 1960, the United States committed for spending abroad a total of $84,090,800,-000—$56,900,000,000 in economic grants and credits, $27,100,000,-000 in defense assistance. For the fiscal year ending June 30, 1960, Congress appropriated $3,226,000,000. This was broken down as follows: $1,300,000,000 for military equipment and training in nearly fifty countries, most of which were joined in regional security organizations such as NATO and SEATO; $695,000,000 for the economic support of twelve nations—Nationalist China and South Vietnam are examples—whose own resources do not permit the sort of defensive posture needed by the free world; $245,000,000 for "special assistance," which included contributions to the United Nations Emergency Force and to the stability of countries that had become "new outposts of freedom"; $181,000,000 for technical cooperation, a portion of which went to the United Nations Expanded Program for Technical Assistance and to similar work under the Organization of American States; $550,000,000 for the Development Loan Fund, which had been established on August 14, 1957, to provide capital in newly independent and economically backward countries for long-term projects; $100,-000,000 for the United Nations Children's Fund and other programs; and $155,000,000 for unforeseen needs.

Such vast appropriations required frequent justification, especially when the outlay for nuclear submarines and ballistic missiles was staggering. In supplementing our defenses, Eisenhower told Congress on May 21, 1957, "the tested and proven mutual security program gives the American people more security per dollar invested than any other expenditure they make." On February 16, 1960, he said that the money allocated to mutual security was just as vital to the nation's protection as that spent on the armed forces. To the various assistance programs since 1947 he attributed the freedom of Greece, Turkey, Iran, Vietnam, Laos, Korea, and Formosa. Although this view was widely accepted by the people and by the lawmakers, criticism of the cost, focus, and execution of the program remained constant. Indisputable cases of waste were cited; countless suggestions for economy were offered. As Eisenhower completed his second term, there were demands that the purpose be defined more positively, that the facilities of the United Nations be used more fully, and that the common burden be shared more equitably with the now prosperous NATO partners. Yet the marked increase in grants and credits by the Sino-Soviet bloc to less developed areas made any sharp cutback dangerous. From mid-1955 to the end of 1960 Russia and its allies exceeded the West in commitments to Cuba, Yugoslavia, Ethiopia, Ghana, Guinea, the United Arab Republic, Iraq, Yemen, Afghanistan, Nepal, and Indonesia.

Conspicuously absent in 1960 were several familiar elements in American foreign policy. The Kellogg Pact had been shelved, though the necessity of curbing wars was more urgent than ever. Compulsory arbitration of international disputes reflected the faith of a still earlier generation; it saw use in only the most minor controversies. The open door was largely forgotten. Concern for the independence and territorial integrity of China lost its purpose with the triumph of the Communists, while the concept of equal opportunity for trade and investment collided with the trend toward expropriation in countries emerging from a colonial status. Membership in the International Court of Justice proved to be disappointing. Some supporters blamed the Connally Reservation, by which the United States retained the right to decide, under the optional clause, what were domestic matters; but several attempts to repeal it failed, the last on March 29, 1960, when the president, vice president, and chairman of the Foreign Relations Committee, all opposed the reservation.

Still prominent as principles of American foreign policy today are nonintervention, self-determination, and disarmament. The first has usually been adhered to, as required in the United Nations and OAS Charters, but the inroads of communism in Guatemala and Cuba made restraint difficult. The second has meant prompt recognition of new states in Asia and Africa; only when *de facto* governments, such as the one in Peking, refused to carry out their obligations or defied the United Nations has official intercourse been withheld. The third has assumed proportions which would dumbfound the men who gathered hopefully at The Hague in 1899 or at Washington in 1921. As late as 1939, the contribution that arms control could make to a nation's security, as distinct from its military budget, was marginal. In the pre-atomic age the industrial potential was much more important than the force-in-being. It was possible to suffer an initial defeat by being caught unprepared and still win eventual victory by mobilizing resources after the fighting had begun. Today the advantage of surprise is overwhelming, and the striking power available at the outset may be decisive. Since a total abolition of thermonuclear weapons is unlikely to occur, a rigid system of inspection becomes the key to the armaments riddle. The number of men, ships, planes, cannon, and even missiles is irrelevant so long as one country is free to launch the few deadly bombs still in its hands. Since inspection undercuts the very basis of the closed society which characterizes the monolithic Communist state, this aspect of arms control constitutes the great challenge of the 1960's.

THE PRACTICES OF FOREIGN POLICY TODAY

If the scope and principles of American foreign policy today differ markedly from those of 1939, the same is true with regard to the practices. More than ever before, the president dominates the scene. The vast range and infinite complexity of modern diplomacy, the major role played by military capability and scientific achievement, the extreme discretion required in intelligence operations and coalition endeavors, the imperative need for prompt decisions and clear accountability, and the obvious value of personal contacts abroad and personal leadership at home have combined to thrust upon the one man elected by all the people, who is also commander-in-chief of the armed forces, the supreme responsibility for guiding the republic in a world of unending crises.

Congress, of course, has not been reduced to a cipher. So long as appropriations are needed for the armed forces, mutual security, and scientific research, the legislature can, in effect, veto many important proposals. So long as appointments must be approved and treaties consented to, the Senate can, in fact, do the same. The huge bureaucracy administering foreign affairs requires periodic checks, and probes by the two houses may be helpful. The hand of the president can be strengthened in dealing with allies and antagonists by joint resolutions expressing the sense of the lawmakers. Finally, although 537 men, representing diverse constituencies and divergent needs, are not well equipped to engage in day-to-day decision making, they do possess means to handle long-range questions. Thus the Senate on July 31, 1958, instructed the Foreign Relations Committee to make "a full and complete study" of American foreign policy and more particularly the concepts governing the relations of the United States with the principal nations and geographic areas of the world, the present state of those relations, and the many overseas programs. Entrusting the task mainly to scholars, the Committee published in 1959 and 1960 fifteen valuable analyses of current problems.

One perplexing aspect of American diplomatic practice today is the contribution undercover missions or unconventional warfare can make to attaining national objectives. Locked in mortal conflict with an enemy for whom espionage, subversion, and guerrilla tactics are familiar tools, the United States has difficulty conducting clandestine operations in an open society. The press is enterprising, imaginative, and hostile to censorship. The public is inquisitive, demanding, and suspicious of secrecy. The government is inexperienced and ill at ease. We do not know—perhaps we should not know—whether the Central Intelligence Agency or other groups actually had a hand in the overthrow in 1953 of Mohammed Mosaddeq, the anti-Western premier of Iran, or in 1954 of Jacobo Arbenz, the pro-Communist president of Guatemala. But it is clear from the ill-fated reconnaissance flight over Russia in May, 1960, and the ill-starred exiles' invasion of Cuba in April, 1961, that a closer coordination of intelligence and diplomacy must be attained in the years ahead.

THE CHALLENGES OF FOREIGN POLICY TODAY

After eight years of Republican rule, American foreign policy seemed little altered from what it had been under the Democrats. Despite the fierce denunciation of 1952, Eisenhower and Dulles followed, for the most part, the course charted by Truman and Acheson. Changes there were, but the similarities were more striking than the differences. In some ways this continuity was helpful; in others, harmful. For the world in January, 1961, was not the same as when the Senate voted to join the United Nations, when Marshall moved to revive Europe's economy, when Vandenberg proposed to defend the Atlantic community, when Acheson began to develop mutual security, when Truman decided to repel the North Korean invader, when Dulles started to adumbrate the doctrine of massive retaliation, and when Eisenhower first agreed to deliberate at the summit. And since the disparities will increase with each passing year, the task of the 1960's is to define clearly the purposes the United States wishes to achieve. Hence one challenge of foreign policy today is flexibility.

Flexibility is imperative in many areas. NATO was created a decade ago, and the assumption on which it was based has disappeared. No longer is a westward drive of the Red Army the chief threat to Western Europe. Mutual security is just as old, and friends are no longer won by military and economic assistance alone. A new credo for foreign aid is urgently needed. Reliance on air bases along the perimeter of the Soviet Union is obsolete. The objections of countries whose soil has been used and the potentialities of missiles whose range has been lengthened have made the old strategy unfeasible and undesirable. Nonrecognition of China has hardened from an unavoidable necessity into a frozen policy, the merits of which are seldom soberly discussed. Yet the Communist regime is not going to disintegrate, and other ways of dealing with Peking merit consideration. In Japan, Korea, and Laos—in the Middle East, Subsaharan Africa, and Latin America—the United States must adapt to new situations. Its citizens must learn to live with crisis and renounce forever the notion that there are complete solutions to the dangers that beset them. Some understanding has been gained since the ordeal in Korea.

Understanding is a second challenge of foreign policy today. It is not enough to admit that the world is changing. The American people have to understand the aspirations of millions who inhabit distant places and inherit different cultures. They must shed their parochialism, even their European-centered training, and familiarize themselves with names which are often unpronounceable and attitudes which are often incomprehensible. The nation born of revolution must learn to tolerate rebels; the republic which once welcomed the oppressed of other continents must keep in mind that, by solving its own problems of race relations and social justice, it will profoundly influence those who remain uncommitted to either the Western brand of liberty or the Soviet gospel of communism. And this understanding has to encompass allies as well as neutralists, the processes of foreign policy as well as its goals. The United States needs to become more adept in coalition diplomacy; its citizens need to cultivate more respect for competency in the conduct of external affairs.

Competency in the conduct of external affairs is a third challenge of foreign policy today. The nation must train more specialists who can speak the language, gauge the economy, and value the culture of the countries to which they are sent. The Foreign Service cannot endure another round of the antiprofessionalism that disgraced the McCarthy era. Envoys must be encouraged to analyze and recommend without fear they may later be proven wrong and that mistaken ideas will be considered disloyal deeds. The State Department cannot afford another secretary, no matter how intelligent or dedicated, whose constant travels usurp the work of ambassadors and disrupt the process of planning. On the other hand, the province of the secretary must not be encroached upon by the White House, the Pentagon, the Central Intelligence Agency, or the Bureau of the Budget. Negotiations by the president ought to be kept to a minimum, and the overlapping authority that bedeviled the U-2 flight in May, 1960, has to be eliminated. It is obvious that the National Security Council has not fulfilled the hopes of its founders; it is fortunate that the Senate has suggested methods for coordinating more successfully the decision-making procedure and the vast operations overseas. Yet the diplomats cannot do the job alone. They depend upon the good taste of every American who journeys abroad and upon the good sense of every Congress to provide a strong military establishment that precludes negotiating from weakness.

A strong military establishment is a fourth challenge of foreign policy today. The republic cannot withstand atomic blackmail if its citizens subordinate defense requirements to balanced budgets and lower taxes. Yet in an age of scientific breakthroughs, volatile technology, rapid obsolescence, and staggering costs it is not easy to build a balanced weapons system that can cope with everything from a brushfire border incident to an all-out nuclear holocaust. Deep-seated convictions within the separate services, divergent approaches within the executive departments, and mutual suspicions between the civilian and the military impose handicaps in a democracy that are less troublesome in a dictatorship. Certainly large expenditures must be borne and a great variety of armaments must be supported, yet under modern conditions the most awesome and flexible array of military might cannot achieve a genuine victory. No real peace, no real safety can be hoped for without arms control.

Arms control is a fifth challenge of foreign policy today. But arms control must be properly meshed with diplomatic and military aims. Never before has the interaction of strategy, warfare, and foreign affairs been so crucial. It is not enough to maintain a strong military establishment in the customary sense or competency in the conduct of external relations as traditionally conceived. Never before has so much depended on military policies that have to be devised on insufficient knowledge about the effects of the weapons employed. Never before have two so completely antagonistic societies possessed the wherewithal to destroy each other and all mankind. How far this situation has transformed the very nature of diplomacy is still but imperfectly grasped. Old concepts in governmental processes and international intercourse must be re-examined. The basic issues now are arms control, not disarmament, and the management of power, not its elimination. The answers cannot be supplied wholly by Foreign Service officers, top-ranking military men, or prize-winning physicists; the nation must also draw upon the brains of social scientists and humanists. For the triumph of the free world, if it is to triumph, will come from creative intelligence, not from overwhelming might.

Creative intelligence is a final challenge of foreign policy today. The United States must deal courageously with the problems of the Cold War and still see beyond them; it cannot afford to let short-range considerations hobble long-term objectives. The struggle for men's minds will be won by those who articulate a dynamic, relevant, and compelling system of values for a world that can either lapse into barbarism or advance to heights yet unscaled. In that contest, the American people can succeed if they mobilize their material and spiritual resources; if they sacrifice some of their debilitating luxuries; if they exhibit courage, tolerance, and compassion; if they do not attempt to remake mankind in their own image. But for that victory to be meaningful, the same creative intelligence must find a way to live with the fire of the gods and spare humanity from a nuclear apocalypse.

APPENDIX

BIBLIOGRAPHICAL ESSAY

INDEX

APPENDIX

The Presidents, the Secretaries of State, and the Chairmen of the Senate Foreign Relations Committee [1]

PRESIDENTS	DATES OF SERVICE	PARTY	SECRETARIES OF STATE	DATES OF SERVICE	CHAIRMEN, FOREIGN RELATIONS COMMITTEE	PARTY	DATES OF SERVICE
1. George Washington	Apr. 30, 1789—Mar. 4, 1797	Federalist	1. Thomas Jefferson	Mar. 22, 1790—Dec. 31, 1793			
			2. Edmond Randolph	Jan. 2, 1794—Aug. 20, 1795			
			3. Timothy Pickering	Dec. 10, 1795—			
2. John Adams	Mar. 4, 1797—Mar. 4, 1801	Federalist	"	—May 12, 1800			
			4. John Marshall	June 6, 1800—Feb. 4, 1801			
3. Thomas Jefferson	Mar. 4, 1801—Mar. 4, 1809	Dem.-Rep.	5. James Madison	May 2, 1801—Mar. 3, 1809			
4. James Madison	Mar. 4, 1809—Mar. 4, 1817	Dem.-Rep	6. Robert Smith	Mar. 6, 1809—Apr. 1, 1811			
			7. James Monroe	Apr. 6, 1811—Sept. 30, 1814			
			"	Feb. 28, 1815—Mar. 3, 1817	1. James Barbour, Virginia	Anti-Dem.	1816— -1818
					2. Nathaniel Macon, North Carolina	Democrat	1818-19
5. James Monroe	Mar. 4, 1817—Mar. 4, 1825	Dem.-Rep.	8. John Quincy Adams	Sept. 22, 1817—Mar. 3, 1825			

President	Dates	Party	Secretary of State	Dates	Party	Chairman, Foreign Relations Committee	Party	Years
						3. James Brown, Louisiana	Democrat	1819-20
						4. James Barbour, Virginia	Anti-Dem.	1820-1
						5. Rufus King, New York	Federalist	1821-2
						6. James Barbour, Virginia	Anti-Dem.	1822-5
6. John Quincy Adams	Mar. 4, 1825— Mar. 4, 1829		9. Henry Clay	Mar. 7, 1825— Mar. 3, 1829	Dem.-Rep.	7. Nathaniel Macon, North Carolina	Democrat	1825-6
						8. Nathan Sanford, New York	Democrat	1826-7
						9. Nathaniel Macon, North Carolina	Democrat	1827-8
						10. Littleton W. Tazewell, Virginia	Democrat	1828-
7. Andrew Jackson	Mar. 4, 1829— Mar. 4, 1837	Democrat	10. Martin Van Buren	Mar. 28, 1829— May 23, 1831	Democrat		"	-1832
			11. Edward Livingston	May 24, 1831— May 29, 1833		11. John Forsyth, Georgia	Democrat	1832-3
			12. Louis McLane	May 29, 1833— June 30, 1834		12. William Wilkins, Pennsylvania	Democrat	1833-4
			13. John Forsyth	July 1, 1834—		13. Henry Clay, Kentucky	Whig	1834-6
8. Martin Van Buren	Mar. 4, 1837— Mar. 4, 1841 —Mar. 3, 1841	Democrat	"			14. James Buchanan, Pennsylvania	Democrat	1836-
						" "	"	-1841

¹ This table is based largely on tables in William Barnes and John Heath Morgan *The Foreign Service of the United States: Origins, Development, and Functions* (Washington, 1961), pp. 333-6 and in Eleanor E. Dennison, *The Senate Foreign Relations Committee* (Stanford, 1942) pp. 162-96.

The Presidents, the Secretaries of State, and the Chairmen of the Senate Foreign Relations Committee (Continued)

PRESIDENTS	DATES OF SERVICE	PARTY	SECRETARIES OF STATE	DATES OF SERVICE	CHAIRMEN, FOREIGN RELATIONS COMMITTEE	PARTY	DATES OF SERVICE
9. William Henry Harrison	Mar. 4, 1841—Apr. 4, 1841	Whig	14. Daniel Webster	Mar. 6, 1841—			
10. John Tyler	Apr. 6, 1841—Mar. 4, 1845	Whig	"	—May 8, 1843	15. William C. Rives, Virginia	Democrat	1841-2
					16. William S. Archer, Virginia	Whig	1842—
			15. Abel P. Upshur	July 24, 1843—Feb. 28, 1844			
			16. John C. Calhoun	Apr. 1, 1844—Mar. 10, 1845			—1845
11. James K. Polk	Mar. 4, 1845—Mar. 4, 1849	Democrat	17. James Buchanan	Mar. 10, 1845—Mar. 7, 1849	17. William Allen, Ohio	Democrat	1845-6
					18. George McDuffie, South Carolina	Democrat	1846
					19. Ambrose H. Sevier, Arkansas	Democrat	1846-8
					20. Edward A. Hannegan, Indiana	Democrat	1848-9
12. Zachary Taylor	Mar. 5, 1849—July 9, 1850	Whig	18. John M. Clayton	Mar. 8, 1849—July 22, 1850	21. Thomas H. Benton, Missouri	Democrat	1849
					22. William R. King, Alabama	Democrat	1849-50
13. Millard Fillmore	July 10, 1850—Mar. 4, 1853	Whig	19. Daniel Webster	July 23, 1850—Oct. 24, 1852	23. Henry S. Foote, Mississippi	Democrat	1850-1

Presidents			Secretaries of State		Presidents of the Senate pro tem.		
14. Franklin Pierce	Mar. 4, 1853— Mar. 4, 1857	Democrat	20. Edward Everett	Nov. 6, 1852— Mar. 3, 1853	24. James M. Mason, Virginia	Democrat	1851—
15. James Buchanan	Mar. 4, 1857— Mar. 4, 1861	Democrat	21. William L. Marcy	Mar. 8, 1853— Mar. 6, 1857	"	"	
			22. Lewis Cass	Mar. 6, 1857— Dec. 14, 1860	"	"	
			23. Jeremiah S. Black	Dec. 17, 1860— Mar. 5, 1861			—1861
16. Abraham Lincoln	Mar. 4, 1861— Apr. 15, 1865	Republican	24. William H. Seward	Mar. 6, 1861—	25. Charles Sumner, Massachusetts	Republican	1861—
17. Andrew Johnson	Apr. 15, 1865— Mar. 4, 1869	Union	"	—Mar. 4, 1869	"	"	
18. Ulysses S. Grant	Mar. 4, 1869— Mar. 4, 1877	Republican	25. Elihu B. Washburne	Mar. 5, 1869— Mar. 16, 1869	"	"	
			26. Hamilton Fish	Mar. 17, 1869— Mar. 12, 1877	26. Simon Cameron, Pennsylvania	Republican	1871-7 —1871
19. Rutherford B. Hayes	Mar. 4, 1877— Mar. 4, 1881	Republican	27. William M. Evarts	Mar. 12, 1877— Mar. 7, 1881	27. Hannibal Hamlin, Maine	Republican	1877-9
					28. William W. Eaton, Connecticut	Democrat	1879-81
20. James A. Garfield	Mar. 4, 1881— Sept. 19, 1881	Republican	28. James G. Blaine	Mar. 7, 1881—	29. Ambrose E. Burnside, Rhode Island	Republican	1881
21. Chester A. Arthur	Sept. 20, 1881— Mar. 4, 1885	Republican	"	—Dec. 19, 1881	30. George F. Edmunds, Vermont	Republican	1881

The Presidents, the Secretaries of State, and the Chairmen of the Senate Foreign Relations Committee (Continued)

PRESIDENTS	DATES OF SERVICE	PARTY	SECRETARIES OF STATE	DATES OF SERVICE	CHAIRMEN, FOREIGN RELATIONS COMMITTEE	PARTY	DATES OF SERVICE
21. Chester A. Arthur			29. Frederick T. Frelinghuysen	Dec. 19, 1881—Mar. 6, 1885	31. William Windom, Minnesota	Republican	1881-3
					32. John F. Miller, California	Republican	1883—
22. Grover Cleveland	Mar. 4, 1885—Mar. 4, 1889	Democrat	30. Thomas F. Bayard	Mar. 7, 1885—Mar. 6, 1889		"	—1886
					33. John Sherman, Ohio	Republican	1886—
23. Benjamin Harrison	Mar. 4, 1889—Mar. 4, 1893	Republican	31. James G. Blaine	Mar. 7, 1889—June 4, 1892		"	—1893
			32. John W. Foster	June 29, 1892—Feb. 23, 1893			
24. Grover Cleveland	Mar. 4, 1893—Mar. 4, 1897	Democrat	33. Walter Q. Gresham	Mar. 7, 1893—May 28, 1895	34. John T. Morgan, Alabama	Democrat	1893-5
			34. Richard Olney	June 10, 1895—Mar. 5, 1897	35. John Sherman, Ohio	Republican	1895-7
25. William McKinley	Mar. 4, 1897—Sept. 14, 1901	Republican	35. John Sherman	Mar. 6, 1897—Apr. 27, 1898	36. William P. Frye, Maine	Republican	1897
			36. William R. Day	Apr. 28, 1898—Sept. 16, 1898	37. Cushman K. Davis, Minnesota	Republican	1897—
			37. John Hay	Sept. 30, 1898—			—1900
					38. William P. Frye, Maine	Republican	1900—1

President	Party	Term	Secretary of State	Term	Chairman	State	Party	Term
26. Theodore Roosevelt	Republican	Sept. 14, 1901— Mar. 4, 1909	John Hay	—July 1, 1905	39. Shelby M. Cullom,	Illinois	Republican "	1901— —1913
			38. Elihu Root	July 19, 1905— Jan. 27, 1909				
			39. Robert Bacon	Jan. 27, 1909— Mar. 5, 1909				
27. William H. Taft	Republican	Mar. 4, 1909— Mar. 4, 1913	40. Philander C. Knox	Mar. 6, 1909— Mar. 5, 1913	40. Augustus O. Bacon,	Georgia	Democrat	1913-14
28. Woodrow Wilson	Democrat	Mar. 4, 1913— Mar. 4, 1921	41. William Jennings Bryan	Mar. 5, 1913— June 9, 1915	41. William J. Stone,	Missouri	Democrat	1914—
			42. Robert Lansing	June 24, 1915—	42. Gilbert M. Hitchcock,	Nebraska	Democrat	—1918 1918-19
			43. Bainbridge Colby	—Feb. 13, 1920 Mar. 23, 1920— Mar. 4, 1921	43. Henry Cabot Lodge,	Massachusetts	Republican	1919—
29. Warren G. Harding	Republican	Mar. 4, 1921— Aug. 2, 1923	44. Charles E. Hughes	Mar. 5, 1921—			"	—1924
30. Calvin Coolidge	Republican	Aug. 3, 1923— Mar. 4, 1929	45. Frank B. Kellogg	—Mar. 4, 1925 Mar. 5, 1925— Mar. 28, 1929	44. William E. Borah,	Idaho	Republican "	1924—
31. Herbert Hoover	Republican	Mar. 4, 1929— Mar. 4, 1933	46. Henry L. Stimson	Mar. 28, 1929— Mar. 4, 1933			"	—1933

The Presidents, the Secretaries of State, and the Chairmen of the Senate Foreign Relations Committee (Continued)

PRESIDENTS	DATES OF SERVICE	PARTY	SECRETARIES OF STATE	DATES OF SERVICE	CHAIRMEN, FOREIGN RELATIONS COMMITTEE	PARTY	DATES OF SERVICE
32. Franklin D. Roosevelt	Mar. 4, 1933— Apr. 12, 1945	Democrat	47. Cordell Hull	Mar. 4, 1933— —Nov. 30, 1944	45. Key Pittman, Nevada	Democrat	1933–40
					46. Walter F. George, Georgia	Democrat	1940–1
					47. Thomas T. Connally, Texas	Democrat	1941—
			48. Edward R. Stettinius	Dec. 1, 1944—			
33. Harry S. Truman	Apr. 12, 1945— Jan. 20, 1953	Democrat	"	—June 27, 1945	"	"	—1947
			49. James F. Byrnes	July 3, 1945—	48. Arthur H. Vandenberg, Michigan	Republican	1947–9
			50. George C. Marshall	Jan. 21, 1947—	49. Thomas T. Connally, Texas	Democrat	1949–53
			51. Dean G. Acheson	Jan. 20, 1949— Jan. 20, 1953			
34. Dwight D. Eisenhower	Jan. 20, 1953— Jan. 20, 1961	Republican	52. John Foster Dulles	Jan. 21, 1953— Apr. 22, 1959	50. Alexander Wiley, Wisconsin	Republican	1953–5
					51. Walter F. George, Georgia	Democrat	1955–7
					52. Theodore F. Green, Rhode Island	Democrat	1957–9
			53. Christian A. Herter	Apr. 22, 1959— Jan. 20, 1961	53. J. William Fulbright, Arkansas	Democrat	1959—
35. John F. Kennedy	Jan. 20, 1961—	Democrat	54. Dean Rusk	Jan. 21, 1961—	"	"	

Bibliographical Essay

THIS ESSAY attempts to provide a critical commentary on the materials available for the kind of study of American foreign policy developed in the text. It makes no pretence of being a complete bibliography of American diplomatic history. Most titles are secondary works of book length. Except in the first section, the essay lists primary sources and periodical articles only when they contain essential information not found elsewhere. It includes a few volumes in foreign languages for the same reason. To save space, subtitles which do not describe the contents of the book have been omitted, as have the names of series to which some entries belong. Abbreviations have been used for frequently-cited journals as follows:

AHR	*American Historical Review*
AJIL	*American Journal of International Law*
APSP	*American Philosophical Society Proceedings*
APSR	*American Political Science Review*
IC	*International Conciliation*
IO	*International Organization*
JHI	*Journal of the History of Ideas*
JMH	*Journal of Modern History*
MVHR	*Mississippi Valley Historical Review*
PHR	*Pacific Historical Review*
PSQ	*Political Science Quarterly*
RP	*Review of Politics*
USNIP	*United States Naval Institute Proceedings*
WMQ	*William and Mary Quarterly*
WP	*World Politics*
YR	*Yale Review*

A. GENERAL AIDS

1. Bibliographic Tools. Although useless for events since the First World War, Samuel F. Bemis and Grace G. Griffin, eds., *Guide to the Diplomatic History of the United States, 1775–1921* (1935) remains the most extensive appraisal of books and articles published through 1934 and the most satisfactory introduction to the printed sources then available. Oscar Handlin and others, eds., *Harvard Guide to American History* (1954) lists without comment books and articles appearing before 1951 and a few items after that date. George F. Howe and others, eds., *The American Historical Association's Guide to Historical Literature* (1961) is more selective but wider in scope. It evaluates tersely books issued through 1960, though the coverage is not systematic after 1956. Donald Mugridge and Blanche P. McCrum, eds., *A Guide to the Study of the United States of America* (1960) contains the fullest annotations, but for only a limited number of books on foreign policy. William L. Langer and others, eds., *Foreign Affairs Bibliography* (3 vols., 1933–55) brings together brief notes on books printed from 1919 through 1952 for the period beginning with the First World War. Laurence F. Schmeckebier and Roy B. Eastin, eds., *Government Publications and Their Use* (2d ed., 1961) is the most up-to-date treatise on United States documents.

2. Larger Documentary Collections. The chief documentary record of American foreign policy, culled mostly from the State Department's archives, is *Foreign Relations of the United States: Diplomatic Papers*. Published regularly by the State Department since 1861 under slightly different titles and organized mainly by calendar years, the series numbered 206 volumes in July, 1961, and had reached 1942. In addition, four volumes dealing with the Cairo, Tehran, Yalta, and Potsdam Conferences had appeared. For the years before 1861, comparable material can be found in less scholarly government compilations, such as Francis Wharton, ed., *The Revolutionary Diplomatic Correspondence of the United States* (6 vols., 1889); *The Diplomatic Correspondence of the United States* (7 vols., 1833–4), for the period 1783–9; and Walter Lowrie and Matthew St. Clair, eds., *American State Papers. Class I: Foreign Relations* (6 vols., 1832–59), for the period 1789–1828. Three privately sponsored collections, splendidly edited by William R. Manning, are: *Diplomatic Correspondence of the United States: Canadian Relations, 1784–1860* (4 vols., 1940–5); *Diplomatic Correspondence of the United States concerning the Independence of the Latin-American Nations* (3 vols., 1925); and *Diplomatic Correspondence of the United States: Inter-American Affairs, 1831–1860* (12 vols., 1932–9). For the period since 1941, a highly selective group of papers, all previously published, may be found in *A Decade of American Foreign Policy: Basic Documents, 1941–49* (1950), prepared at the request of the Senate Foreign Relations Committee; and in two compilations of the State Department: *American Foreign Policy, 1950–1955: Basic Documents* (2 vols., 1957) and *American Foreign Policy: Current Documents*. Volumes for 1956 and 1957 in the last series appeared in 1959 and 1961. John Bassett Moore, *A Digest of International Law* (8 vols., 1906) and Green H. Hackworth, *Digest of International Law* (8 vols., 1940–4) are indispensable.

The best edition of treaties is Hunter Miller's copiously annotated *Treaties and Other International Acts of the United States* (8 vols., 1931–48), but it stops in July, 1863. William M. Malloy and others, eds., *Treaties, Conventions, International Acts, Protocols, and Agreements between the United States and Other Powers, 1776–1937* (4 vols., 1909–38) goes to January, 1938. For the years 1938 through 1949 the texts must be sought in the separate prints of the *Treaty Series*. A new compilation, *United States Treaties and Other International Agreements*, begins with 1950. Eleven volumes in twenty-seven parts have appeared by July, 1961.

Presidential statements—be they letters, speeches, or press releases—are as important for a study of foreign policy as diplomatic notes and treaty texts. It is impossible to list for each incumbent the many excellent collected works now available or in preparation, but attention should be called to James D. Richardson, ed., *A Compilation of the Messages and Papers of the Presidents, 1789–1897* (10 vols., 1897) and its commercial supplements. Because of incompleteness and imperfections, this once useful collection of communications to the Congress needs to be replaced by a more extensive, scholarly, and up-to-date edition.

Documents from the archives of foreign governments help toward an understanding of American foreign policy. The more important printed collections, omitting the names of the editors, are: *British Documents on the Origins of the War, 1898–1914* (11 vols., 1926–38); *Documents on British Foreign Policy, 1919–1939,* of which twenty-seven volumes in three series have appeared since 1947; *Documents Diplomatiques Français (1871–1914),* of which forty volumes in three series have appeared since 1929; *Die Grosse Politik der Europäischen Kabinette, 1871–1914* (40 vols., 1922–7); *Documents on German Foreign Policy, 1918–1945,* of which fourteen volumes for the period starting in 1933, the only portion now to be published, have appeared since 1949; *I Documenti Diplomatici, 1861–1943,* of which fifteen volumes in nine series have appeared since 1952; and *Dokumenty Vneshnei Politiki SSSR,* of which four volumes for the period from November, 1917, through December, 1921, have appeared since 1957. For a judicious appraisal of the problems involved in handling these materials, see Bernadotte E. Schmitt, " 'With How Little Wisdom . . . ,' " *AHR,* LXVI (1961), 299–322.

3. *Serial Publications.* The Department of State periodically issues data on recent events. In addition to the new annual volumes on current documents, cited in the previous section, the following are helpful: *U.S. Participation in the U.N.,* the president's annual report to Congress, beginning with 1946; *Background: Highlights of Foreign Policy Developments,* a yearly summary published since 1956; and the weekly *Department of State Bulletin,* begun on July 1, 1939.

The Council on Foreign Relations has sponsored since 1931 *The United States in World Affairs,* an annual one-volume survey (there are none for 1941–4 and only a single volume for 1934–5 and for 1945–7), which normally appears in June following the year with which it deals. The Council took over in 1952 from the World Peace Foundation the very useful *Documents on American Foreign Relations,* issued annually since 1938.

A similar enterprise has been carried on by the Royal Institute of International Affairs. Its annual *Survey of International Affairs,* usually one volume to a year but occasionally more, began in 1925 with a volume covering 1920 to 1923. Eleven volumes deal with the period 1939–46 topically. The volume for 1947–8 resumed the chronological treatment; the latest to be printed is the one for 1955–6. A companion series begun in 1928, *Documents on International Affairs*, has reached 1957, although some installments for the war years are missing.

4. *One-Volume Surveys and Interpretations.* The best full-length surveys of American foreign policy are Julius W. Pratt, *A History of United States Foreign Policy* (1955); Samuel F. Bemis, *A Diplomatic History of the United States* (1936; 4th ed., 1955); Thomas A. Bailey, *A Diplomatic History of the American People* (1940; 6th ed., 1958); Richard W. Van Alstyne, *American Diplomacy in Action* (1944; 2d ed., 1947); and Nelson M. Blake and Oscar T. Barck, Jr., *The United States in Its World Relations* (1960). The best shorter surveys are Robert H. Ferrell, *American Diplomacy* (1959); Samuel F. Bemis, *A Short History of American Foreign Policy and Diplomacy* (1959); and L. Ethan Ellis, *A Short History of American Diplomacy* (1951). Jules Davids, *America and the World of Our Time* (1960) is confined to the twentieth century and emphasizes the years since 1921.

Scholarly interpretations of American foreign policy vary in quality and treatment. Worth examining are Dexter Perkins, *The American Approach to Foreign Policy* (1952); J. Fred Rippy, *America and the Strife of Europe* (1938); Nicholas J. Spykman, *America's Strategy in World Politics* (1942); Malbone W. Graham, *American Diplomacy in the International Community* (1948); Louis J. Halle, *Dream and Reality: Aspects of American Foreign Policy* (1959); Hans J. Morgenthau, *In Defense of the National Interest* (1951); and Ernest W. Lefever, *Ethics and United States Foreign Policy* (1957). Interpretations of twentieth-century foreign policy include Foster R. Dulles, *America's Rise to World Power, 1898–1954* (1955); Robert E. Osgood, *Ideals and Self-Interests in American Foreign Relations* (1953); William A. Williams, *The Tragedy of American Diplomacy* (1959); George F. Kennan, *American Diplomacy, 1900–1950* (1951); and Kenneth W. Thompson, *Political Realism and the Crisis of World Politics* (1960). Some excellent essays and some marginal ones appear in Alexander DeConde, ed., *Isolation and Security: Ideas and Interests in Twentieth-Century American Foreign Policy* (1957) and in George L. Anderson, ed., *Issues and Conflicts: Studies in Twentieth Century American Diplomacy* (1959).

Thomas A. Bailey, *The Man in the Street* (1948) is a pioneering attempt to trace the impact of public opinion on foreign policy. Walter Millis, *Arms and Men* (1956) and Samuel P. Huntington, *The Soldier and the State* (1957) analyze the role of the military in American life. Percy E. Corbett, *Law in Diplomacy* (1959) is a novel and important contribution.

B. MAJOR POLICIES, 1775–1961

1. *Isolationism.* There is no full-length history, though useful studies of particular periods exist. On the foundations, see Felix Gilbert, *To the Farewell Address: Ideas of Early American Foreign Policy* (1961); J. Fred Rippy, *The Historical Background of the American Policy of Isolation* (1924); Alexander DeConde, *Entangling Alliance: Politics & Diplomacy under George Washington* (1959); Samuel F. Bemis, "Washington's Farewell Address: A Foreign Policy of Independence," *AHR*, XXXIX (1934), 250–68; and Albert K. Weinberg, "Washington's 'Great Rule' in Its Historical Evolution," in Eric F. Goldman, ed., *Historiography and Urbanization* (1941), 109–38. Arthur P. Whitaker, *The United States and the Independence of Latin America, 1800–1830* (1941); Merle Curti, *Austria and the United*

States, 1848–1852 (1926); and the same author's "Young America," published in 1926 and reprinted in his *Probing Our Past* (1951), 219–45, help a good deal for the period from 1815 to 1889.

Selig Adler, *The Isolationist Impulse: Its Twentieth-Century Reaction* (1957) is fullest for the modern era. There are suggestive insights in Alexander DeConde, "On Twentieth-Century Isolationism," in Alexander DeConde, ed., *Isolation and Security* (1957), 3–32; in Albert K. Weinberg, "The Historical Meaning of the American Doctrine of Isolation," APSR, XXXIV (1940), 539–47; and in Norman A. Graebner, *The New Isolationism: A Study in Politics and Foreign Policy since 1950* (1956).

2. *Neutrality.* There is no adequate history of the American policy of neutrality. Most studies concentrate on the Napoleonic and World Wars. The digests by Moore and Hackworth, cited in Section A2, help locate the major landmarks, as do Carlton Savage, ed., *Policy of the United States toward Maritime Commerce in War* (2 vols., 1934–6) and Francis Deák and Philip C. Jessup, eds., *A Collection of Neutrality Laws, Regulations, and Treaties of Various Countries* (2 vols., 1939). Charles G. Fenwick, *American Neutrality: Trial and Failure* (1940) is a good, brief introduction. Philip C. Jessup and others, *Neutrality: Its History, Economics and Law* (4 vols., 1935–6) is not restricted to the United States. Julius Stone, *Legal Controls of International Conflict* (2d ed., 1959) contains an excellent analysis of contemporary trends.

On neutral duties down to 1914, see Charles S. Hyneman, *The First American Neutrality* (1934), covering the period 1792–1815; Charles M. Thomas, *American Neutrality in 1793* (1931); and Charles G. Fenwick, *The Neutrality Laws of the United States* (1913). A. L. Burt, *The United States, Great Britain, and British North America* (1940) contains the best treatment of neutral rights from 1783 to 1815. The literature for the years from 1914 to 1941 is hortatory and polemical. Descriptive material can be found in Alice M. Morrissey, *The American Defense of Neutral Rights, 1914–1917* (1939); in Nils Orvik, *The Decline of Neutrality, 1914–1941* (1953); and in Elton Atwater, *American Regulation of Arms Exports* (1941).

3. *The Monroe Doctrine.* Dexter Perkins, *A History of the Monroe Doctrine* (1955) is a model treatment. First published in 1941 under the title *Hands Off,* it has been brought up to date and, for seven of the eleven chapters, draws upon the more detailed studies of the author—*The Monroe Doctrine, 1823–1826* (1927); *The Monroe Doctrine, 1826–1867* (1933); and *The Monroe Doctrine, 1867–1907* (1937). John A. Logan, Jr., *No Transfer: An American Security Principle* (1961) is the only history of a corollary, although various books dealing with the Caribbean and the practice of intervention discuss the Roosevelt Corollary. J. Reuben Clark, *Memorandum on the Monroe Doctrine* (1930), compiled in 1928, is a key document.

4. *Nonintervention.* Most books consider this policy under the heading of isolationism, neutrality, and the Monroe Doctrine. Exceptions are D. A. Graber, *Crisis Diplomacy: A History of U.S. Intervention Policies and Practices* (1959) and Ann Van Wynen and A. J. Thomas, Jr., *Non-Intervention: The Law and Its Import in the Americas* (1956).

5. *The Open Door.* Although much attention has been given to the drafting of the notes of 1899–1900 and to the relations of the United States with China and Japan, there is no systematic coverage of the open door as a policy. A. Whitney Griswold, *The Far Eastern Policy of the United States*

(1938) and Paul A. Varg, *Open Door Diplomat: The Life of W. W. Rockhill* (1952) are useful points of departure, but we need more analyses like Raymond A. Esthus, "The Changing Concept of the Open Door, 1899–1910," *MVHR*, XLVI (1959), 435–54, and Charles Vevier, "The Open Door: An Idea in Action, 1906–1913," *PHR*, XXIV (1955), 49–62.

6. *Collective Security and Defense.* Again there is no complete study of these policies, the first of which is often loosely applied. Except for Willard N. Hogan, *International Conflict and Collective Security* (1955), the most suggestive writings are essays. See, for example, Richard N. Current, "The United States and 'Collective Security': Notes on the History of an Idea" and Kenneth W. Thompson, "Isolationism and Collective Security: The Uses and Limits of Two Theories of International Relations," in Alexander DeConde, ed., *Isolation and Security* (1957), 33–55, 159–83; Roland N. Stromberg, "The Idea of Collective Security," *JHI*, XVII (1956), 250–63, and "The Riddle of Collective Security, 1916–1920," in George L. Anderson, ed., *Issues and Conflicts* (1959), 147–70; Robert E. Osgood, "Woodrow Wilson, Collective Security, and the Lessons of History," *Confluence,* V (1957), 341–54; and the essays in Arnold Wolfers, ed., *Alliance Policy in the Cold War* (1959).

C. THE CONSTITUTIONAL CONFLICT, 1789–1961

There is no full history of this topic. Most of the work has been done by political scientists who concentrate on the period after 1933. A brief but useful beginning is Daniel S. Cheever and H. Field Haviland, *American Foreign Policy and the Separation of Powers* (1952). Quincy Wright, *The Control of American Foreign Relations* (1922) is good on the conduct of foreign affairs in the nineteenth century, while Elmer Plischke, *Conduct of American Diplomacy* (2d ed., 1961) is an up-to-date analysis of the present problem.

1. *The Executive Branch.* Edward S. Corwin has written extensively on the powers of the president in foreign affairs. His latest exposition is *The President: Office and Powers* (4th ed., 1957). Elmer Plischke, *Summit Diplomacy: Personal Diplomacy of the President of the United States* (1958) is a preliminary sketch. The role of the cabinet in foreign policy needs further investigation. Henry B. Learned, *The President's Cabinet* (1912) emphasizes structural growth, while Richard F. Fenno, Jr., *The President's Cabinet* (1959) analyzes functions and relationships from Wilson to Eisenhower.

The president's chief adviser and the department over which he presides are discussed in Graham H. Stuart, *The Department of State: A History of Its Organization, Procedure, and Personnel* (1949). Don K. Price, ed., *The Secretary of State* (1960) considers developments since Stuart wrote. Still useful despite its age is Samuel F. Bemis, ed., *The American Secretaries of State and Their Diplomacy* (10 vols., 1927–9). A sequel, dealing with incumbents from Kellogg through Dulles, is in preparation. Meanwhile Norman A. Graebner, ed., *An Uncertain Tradition: American Secretaries of State in the Twentieth Century* (1961) will serve a useful purpose. William Barnes and John H. Morgan, *The Foreign Service of the United States: Origins, Development, and Functions* (1961) and Warren F. Ilchman, *Professional Diplomacy in the United States: A Study in Administrative History* (1961) supersede earlier accounts.

2. *The Legislative Branch.* On the influence of Congress as a whole, see Robert A. Dahl, *Congress and Foreign Policy* (1950), which deals with only

the period 1933–48, and George L. Grassmuck, *Sectional Biases in Congress on Foreign Policy* (1951), which is limited to the years 1921–41.

The Senate of the United States (2 vols., 1938) by George H. Haynes has valuable chapters on the constitutional conflict. Eleanor E. Dennison, *The Senate Foreign Relations Committee* (1942) contains useful information on membership; David N. Farnsworth, *The Senate Committee on Foreign Relations* (1961) covers the period from 1947 to 1956. Joseph P. Harris, *The Advice and Consent of the Senate* (1953) discusses appointments; Henry R. Wriston's encyclopedic *Executive Agents in American Foreign Relations* (1929) analyzes a parallel topic.

The House of Representatives in Foreign Affairs (1958) by Holbert N. Carroll deals almost exclusively with the period after 1945. Albert C. F. Westphal, *The House Committee on Foreign Affairs* (1942) is thin on the historical side. Claims set forth by the House before 1900 to handle foreign affairs can be found in Asher C. Hinds, *Precedents of the House of Representatives* (8 vols., 1907–8). Lucius Wilmerding, Jr., *The Spending Power: A History of the Efforts of Congress to Control Expenditures* (1944) is of help for the question of appropriations.

3. *The Treaty-Making Process.* Samuel B. Crandall, *Treaties: Their Making and Enforcement* (2d ed., 1916) is still the fullest analysis for the period it covers. W. Stull Holt, *Treaties Defeated by the Senate* (1933) is by far the best of the many books on the topic, but it does not go beyond 1920. A more sympathetic account, Royden J. Dangerfield, *In Defense of the Senate* (1933), stops in 1928. R. Earl McClendon, "The Two-Thirds Rule in Senate Action upon Treaties, 1789–1901," *AJIL*, XXVI (1932), 37–56, is an important article. Elbert M. Byrd, Jr., *Treaties and Executive Agreements in the United States: Their Separate Roles and Limitations* (1960); Myres S. McDougal and Asher Lans, "Treaties and Congressional-Executive or Presidential Agreements: Interchangeable Instruments of National Policy," first published in 1945 and reprinted in Myres McDougal and Associates, *Studies in World Public Order* (1960), 404–717; and Wallace McClure, *International Executive Agreements* (1941) deal with a related problem.

4. *Control of the Armed Forces.* Despite the interest aroused by recent events, the best works on this subject are out of date. See, however, James G. Rogers, *World Policing and the Constitution: An Inquiry into the Powers of the President and Congress* (1945); Clarence A. Berdahl, *War Powers of the Executive* (1922); and Howard White, *Executive Influences in Determining Military Policy in the United States* (1924). Ernest R. May, ed., *The Ultimate Decision: The President as Commander in Chief* (1960) contains case studies on selected presidents from Madison to Eisenhower. Elias Huzar, *The Purse and the Sword* (1950) discusses congressional control of the army through military appropriations for the period 1933–1950.

D. THE FORMATIVE YEARS, 1775–1889

1. *Personalities.* The following books are useful on the contribution to foreign policy of the first twenty-two presidents: Douglas S. Freeman and others, *George Washington* (7 vols., 1948–57); Stephen G. Kurtz, *The Presidency of John Adams* (1957); Irving Brant, *James Madison* (6 vols., 1941–61); Samuel F. Bemis, *John Quincy Adams* (2 vols., 1949–56); Robert J. Morgan, *A Whig Embattled: The Presidency under John Tyler* (1954); Eugene I. McCormac, *James K. Polk* (1922); Holman Hamilton, *Zachary*

Taylor: Soldier in the White House (1951); Robert J. Rayback, *Millard Fill-more* (1959); Roy F. Nichols, *Franklin Pierce* (1931); James G. Randall and Richard N. Current, *Lincoln the President* (4 vols., 1945–55); George F. Howe, *Chester A. Arthur* (1934); and Allan Nevins, *Grover Cleveland* (1932). There are no adequate books on the foreign policy of Presidents Jefferson, Monroe, Jackson, Van Buren, Buchanan, Johnson, Grant, or Hayes, though in some cases a monograph or work on the secretary of state fills the gap.

George Dangerfield, *Chancellor Robert R. Livingston* (1961) and Frank Monaghan, *John Jay* (1935) are good on the two secretaries for foreign affairs before 1789. For the work of certain secretaries of state, see Dumas Malone, *Jefferson and His Time* (2 vols., 1948–52), which stops in December, 1792; Brant, *James Madison*, IV; Bemis, *John Quincy Adams*, I; William B. Hatcher, *Edward Livingston* (1940); Richard N. Current, *Daniel Webster and the Rise of National Conservatism* (1955); Charles M. Wiltse, *John C. Calhoun* (3 vols., 1944–51); Ivor D. Spencer, *The Victor and the Spoils: A Life of William L. Marcy* (1959); Allan Nevins, *Hamilton Fish: The Inner History of the Grant Administration* (1936); Chester L. Barrows, *William M. Evarts* (1941); and Charles C. Tansill, *The Foreign Policy of Thomas F. Bayard, 1885–1897* (1940). Studies of Secretaries Pickering, Clay, Van Buren, Forsyth, Buchanan, and Seward are badly overdue.

Books on congressional and other leaders important in these years include Gerald Stourzh, *Benjamin Franklin and American Foreign Policy* (1954); John C. Miller, *Alexander Hamilton* (1959); Bernard Mayo, *Henry Clay: Spokesman of the New West* (1937), which stops in June, 1812; Raymond Walters, Jr., *Albert Gallatin* (1957); J. H. Powell, *Richard Rush* (1942); Martin B. Duberman, *Charles Francis Adams, 1807–1886* (1961); Fred H. Harrington, *Fighting Politician: Major General N. P. Banks* (1948); and Edward Younger, *John A. Kasson* (1955).

2. *The Quest for Independence.* On the break with England, see Samuel F. Bemis, *The Diplomacy of the American Revolution* (1935) and Vincent T. Harlow, *The Founding of the Second British Empire, 1763–1793* (1952). The two monographs by Bemis—*Jay's Treaty: A Study in Commerce and Diplomacy* (1923) and *Pinckney's Treaty: A Study of America's Advantage from Europe's Distress* (1926)—throw light on postwar problems, as do A. L. Burt, *The United States, Great Britain, and British North America from the Revolution to the Establishment of Peace after the War of 1812* (1940); Arthur B. Darling, *Our Rising Empire, 1763–1803* (1940); Arthur P. Whitaker, *The Spanish-American Frontier, 1783–1795* (1927); and R. W. Van Alstyne, *The Rising American Empire* (1960).

The impact of the European conflict after 1793 can be traced in the works on isolationism and neutrality cited in Sections B1 and B2; in Bradford Perkins, *The First Rapprochement: England and the United States, 1795–1805* (1955); in Albert Z. Carr, *The Coming of War* (1960); and above all in Henry Adams, *History of the United States during the Administrations of Thomas Jefferson and James Madison* (9 vols., 1889–91). On the undeclared wars, see Marshall Smelser, *The Congress Founds the Navy, 1787–1798* (1959); Ray W. Irwin, *The Diplomatic Relations of the United States with the Barbary Powers, 1776–1816* (1931); and Louis B. Wright and Julia H. Macleod, *The First Americans in North Africa* (1945).

The reasons why the United States went to war in 1812 have been analyzed in many books and articles. Warren H. Goodman appraises that literature through 1939 in "The Origins of the War of 1812: A Survey of Changing Interpretations," *MVHR*, XXVIII (1941), 171–86. Burt's study, mentioned above, and the fifth volume of Brant's life of Madison are the most important books published since Goodman wrote, while Norman K. Risjord, "1812: Conservatives, War Hawks, and the Nation's Honor," *WMQ*, XVIII (1961), 195–210, mentions articles appearing since then. The manner in which the United States went to war in 1812 has attracted less attention. Henry Adams still provides the best account.

Works on the decade after 1815 are numerous. See, among others, Whitaker, *The United States and the Independence of Latin America* and Perkins, *The Monroe Doctrine, 1823–1826*, both cited in Section B3; also, George Dangerfield, *The Era of Good Feelings* (1952); Samuel F. Bemis, *The Latin American Policy of the United States* (1943); Charles C. Griffin, *The United States and the Disruption of the Spanish Empire, 1810–1822* (1937); William W. Kaufmann, *British Policy and the Independence of Latin America, 1804–1828* (1951); William S. Robertson, *France and Latin-American Independence* (1939); Philip C. Brooks, *Diplomacy and the Borderlands: The Adams-Onís Treaty of 1819* (1940); and Frederick Merk, *Albert Gallatin and the Oregon Problem* (1950).

3. *Continental Expansion.* R. W. Van Alstyne, *The Rising American Empire* (1960) is concerned with territorial growth in the nineteenth century and argues that the republic has been an imperialist power since colonial times. Albert K. Weinberg, *Manifest Destiny* (1935) and Edward McN. Burns, *The American Idea of Mission* (1957) analyze the arguments used by contemporaries to justify the expansion of the United States.

Ray A. Billington, *The Far Western Frontier, 1830–1860* (1956) and Norman A. Graebner, *Empire on the Pacific* (1955) are excellent introductions to expansion in the 1840's. For the acquisition of Texas, see William C. Binkley, *The Texas Revolution* (1952); Joseph W. Schmitz, *Texan Statecraft, 1836–1845* (1941); and Justin H. Smith, *The Annexation of Texas* (1911). Melvin Jacobs, *Winning Oregon* (1938) and Frederick Merk's many articles cited in Billington's bibliography are best on the partition of Oregon. Billington lists also the main articles on the Frémont episode on which see also, Allan Nevins, *Frémont: Pathmarker of the West* (1939).

A balanced account of the Mexican War is badly needed. The sketch by Graebner in *Empire on the Pacific* is good. Also to be consulted are Justin H. Smith, *The War with Mexico* (2 vols., 1919); Eugene I. McCormac, *James K. Polk* (1922); and John D. P. Fuller, *The Movement for the Acquisition of All Mexico, 1846–1848* (1936). On the Gadsden Purchase, see J. Fred Rippy, *The United States and Mexico* (2d ed., 1931) and James M. Callahan, *American Foreign Policy in Mexican Relations* (1932).

4. *Internal Crisis and External Adjustment.* There is no adequate study of United States foreign policy during the Civil War. Except for Jay Monaghan's melodramatic *Diplomat in Carpet Slippers: Abraham Lincoln Deals with Foreign Affairs* (1945), the best works focus their attention on the South or on foreign governments. These include Frank L. Owsley, *King Cotton Diplomacy: Foreign Relations of the Confederate States of America* (1931); Ephraim D. Adams, *Great Britain and the American Civil War* (2 vols., 1925); Donaldson Jordan and Edwin J. Pratt, *Europe and the American Civil War* (1931); and Robin W. Winks, *Canada and the United States: The Civil War Years* (1960). Perkins, *The Monroe Doctrine, 1826–1867* is

very full on the French intervention in Mexico. The biographies of Lincoln and Adams by Randall and Duberman help greatly, as does Allan Nevins, *The War for the Union* (2 vols., 1959–60), which has now reached April, 1863. Norman A. Graebner's essay entitled "Northern Diplomacy and European Neutrality," in David Donald, ed., *Why the North Won the Civil War* (1960), 49–76, is very perceptive.

On the postwar settlement with England and further attempts at territorial expansion, see the biographies of Fish and Banks by Nevins and Harrington; Lester B. Shippee, *Canadian-American Relations, 1849–1874* (1939); Thomas A. Bailey, *American Faces Russia* (1950); and two works by Charles C. Tansill—*The United States and Santo Domingo, 1798–1873* (1938) and *The Purchase of the Danish West Indies* (1932).

E. EMERGENCE AS A WORLD POWER, 1889–1905

Thomas A. Bailey, "America's Emergence as a World Power: The Myth and the Verity," *PHR*, XXX (1961), 1–16, is a stimulating essay, the conclusions of which differ somewhat from those in this volume. A general survey of the diplomacy of the period 1885–1909 can be found in Foster R. Dulles, *The Imperial Years* (1956).

1. Personalities. For the presidents from Harrison to Roosevelt, see Allan Nevins, *Grover Cleveland* (1932); Margaret Leech, *In the Days of McKinley* (1959); John M. Blum, *The Republican Roosevelt* (1954); William H. Harbaugh, *Power and Responsibility: The Life and Times of Theodore Roosevelt* (1961); and Howard K. Beale, *Theodore Roosevelt and the Rise of America to World Power* (1956). There is no good study of Harrison in the White House, but A. T. Volwiler, "Harrison, Blaine, and Foreign Policy, 1889–1893," *APSP*, LXXIX (1938), 637–48, is a helpful introduction.

The work of the secretaries of state is revealed in Alice F. Tyler, *The Foreign Policy of James G. Blaine* (1927) and Tyler Dennett, *John Hay: From Poetry to Politics* (1933). The existing biographies of Gresham, Olney, and Sherman are inadequate; there are none of Foster or Day.

Books on congressional and other leaders who influenced foreign policy include John A. Garraty, *Henry Cabot Lodge* (1953); Everett Walters, *Joseph Benson Foraker* (1948); William E. Livezey, *Mahan on Sea Power* (1947); and Claude G. Bowers, *Beveridge and the Progressive Era* (1932). There are no biographies of Senators Morgan, Davis, or Cullom.

2. East Asia and the Pacific. William L. Langer, *The Diplomacy of Imperialism, 1890–1902* (2 vols., 1935) is still the best introduction to international rivalries in Europe, Asia, Africa, and the Middle East.

For nineteenth-century American policy in China, Japan, and Korea, Tyler Dennett, *Americans in Eastern Asia* (1922) remains a reliable guide. More specialized are John K. Fairbank, *Trade and Diplomacy on the China Coast: The Opening of the Treaty Ports, 1842–1854* (2 vols., 1953); Earl Swisher, *China's Management of the American Barbarians: A Study of Sino-American Relations, 1841–1861* (1953); and Payson J. Treat, *Diplomatic Relations between the United States and Japan, 1853–1905* (3 vols., 1932–8).

There is no work on American policy during the Sino-Japanese War. A. Whitney Griswold, *The Far Eastern Policy of the United States* (1938) describes the scramble for concessions. It is very good on the writing of the open door notes but should be supplemented by Varg's biography of Rockhill and Charles S. Campbell, Jr., *Special Business Interests and the Open Door Policy* (1951). For the turbulent events from 1900 to 1904, see Dennett's life of Hay; Chester C. Tan, *The Boxer Catastrophe* (1955); Fred H. Harrington, *God, Mammon, and the Japanese: Dr. Horace N. Allen and Korean-American Relations, 1884–1905* (1944); Edward H. Zabriskie, *American-Russian Rivalry in the Far East* (1946); and Andrew Malozemoff, *Russian Far Eastern Policy, 1881–1904* (1958). The last emphasizes the causes of the Russo-Japanese War.

For the growth of American interests in Hawaii, there is Ralph S. Kuykendall, *The Hawaiian Kingdom* (2 vols., 1938–53), which goes only to 1874, and Sylvester K. Stevens, *American Expansion in Hawaii, 1842–1898* (1945). William A. Russ, Jr., *The Hawaiian Revolution, 1893–1894* (1959); the same author's *The Hawaiian Republic (1894–98) and Its Struggle to Win Annexation* (1961); and Julius W. Pratt, *Expansionists of 1898* (1936) are good on the developments of the 1890's. George H. Ryden, *The Foreign Policy of the United States in Relation to Samoa* (1933) is the best account of American activity in those islands, but Tansill's study of Bayard is also useful.

3. *The New World.* The role of the United States in the inter-American movement after 1889 merits further investigation, as does the war scare with Chile. Thomas F. McGann, *Argentina, the United States, and the Inter-American System, 1880–1914* (1957) embodies the best scholarship on the first topic; Volwiler's article, cited in Section E1, is the most satisfactory account of the second. On the Venezuelan boundary dispute, consult Perkins, *The Monroe Doctrine, 1867–1907;* the biographies of Cleveland and Bayard by Nevins and Tansill; and Walter LaFeber, "The Background of Cleveland's Venezuelan Policy: A Reinterpretation," *AHR,* LXVI (1961), 947–67.

The quest for an American-controlled canal has attracted many writers. The best of these are Wilfrid H. Callcott, *The Caribbean Policy of the United States, 1890–1920* (1942); Gerstle Mack, *The Land Divided: A History of the Panama Canal and Other Isthmian Canal Projects* (1944); Dwight C. Miner, *The Fight for the Panama Route: The Story of the Spooner Act and the Hay-Herrán Treaty* (1940); Miles P. DuVal, *Cadiz to Cathay: The Story of the Long Diplomatic Struggle for the Panama Canal* (1940); and E. Taylor Parks, *Colombia and the United States, 1765–1934* (1935). Charles S. Campbell, Jr., *Anglo-American Understanding, 1898–1903* (1957) adds some details from the hitherto unused British archives.

4. *The War with Spain.* There is a crying need for a full-length analysis of this conflict and its consequences. Walter Millis, *The Martial Spirit* (1931) relies solely on printed materials and emphasizes the ludicrous. In his *Expansionists of 1898* (1936) Julius W. Pratt sketches the contours of the new manifest destiny and examines the attitudes of the business and religious community. Richard Hofstadter, "Manifest Destiny and the Philippines," in Daniel Aaron, ed., *America in Crisis* (1952), 172–200, is good on jingoism in the 1890's. Joseph E. Wisan, *The Cuban Crisis as Reflected in the New York Press* (1934) documents the familiar; more novel is George W. Auxier, "Middle Western Newspapers and the Spanish-American War, 1895–1898," *MVHR,* XXVI (1940), 523–34. For diplomatic developments, see Orestes Ferrara, *The Last Spanish War* (1937) and the third volume of Herminio Portell Vilá, *Historia de Cuba en Sus Relaciones con*

les Estados Unidos y España (4 vols., 1938–41). Leech's biography of McKinley is the fullest account of the basic decisions taken in Washington, but more remains to be said on all aspects of the war.

The peace negotiations also deserve further study. The best account of the battle in the Senate is in W. Stull Holt, *Treaties Defeated by the Senate* (1933). The personal papers of many participants have become available since Holt wrote. Leon Wolff, *Little Brown Brother* (1961) is the latest work on the Filipino insurrection, but inadequate research causes it to read like an anti-imperialist tract. William T. Sexton, *Soldiers in the Sun* (1939) is less readable but more reliable. Julius W. Pratt, *America's Colonial Experiment* (1950) is a lucid survey of some consequences of the war. Other consequences are treated in William R. Braisted, *The American Navy in the Pacific, 1897–1907* (1958); George T. Davis, *A Navy Second to None* (1940); Richard W. Leopold, *Elihu Root and the Conservative Tradition* (1954); Campbell, *Anglo-American Understanding*, cited in the preceding section; and Albert Vagts, *Deutschland und die Vereingten Staaten in der Weltpolitik, 1890–1906* (2 vols., 1935).

F. THE FIRST TEST: THE GREAT CRUSADE, 1905–21

There is no interpretive study covering the growth of American foreign policy in this period.

1. Personalities. For Roosevelt as president, in addition to the books listed in Section E1, see George E. Mowry's judicious *The Era of Theodore Roosevelt* (1958). Henry F. Pringle, *The Life and Times of William Howard Taft* (2 vols., 1938) is readable and comprehensive but fails to do justice to foreign affairs. On Wilson, all earlier works have been superseded by the writings of Arthur S. Link. His magisterial *Wilson* (3 vols., 1947–60) has reached October, 1915; his *Woodrow Wilson and the Progressive Era, 1910–1917* (1954) goes to April, 1917; his *Wilson the Diplomatist: A Look at His Major Policies* (1957) covers briefly some events to 1921. Variations of Link's interpretations appear in John M. Blum, *Woodrow Wilson and the Politics of Morality* (1956); John A. Garraty, *Woodrow Wilson: A Great Life in Brief* (1956); and Arthur Walworth, *Woodrow Wilson: American Prophet* (2 vols., 1958).

For the secretaries of state, see Philip C. Jessup, *Elihu Root* (2 vols., 1938), in addition to the brief interpretation by Leopold cited in Section E4, and Daniel M. Smith, *Robert Lansing and American Neutrality, 1914–1917* (1958). There are no full treatments of Secretaries Knox or Colby; Link's understanding portrait of Bryan in volumes II and III of his *Wilson* is the best material available on Bryan in the State Department.

Useful books on congressional and other leaders who shaped foreign policy are Garraty's life of Lodge, cited in Section E1; Belle C. and Fola La Follette, *Robert M. La Follette* (2 vols., 1953); Marian C. McKenna, *Borah* (1961); Dewey W. Grantham, *Hoke Smith and the Politics of the New South* (1958); George C. Osborn, *John Sharp Williams* (1943); Alex M. Arnett, *Claude Kitchin and the Wilson War Policies* (1937); Allan Nevins, *Henry White* (1930); and Alexander L. and Juliette L. George, *Woodrow Wilson and Colonel House: A Personality Study* (1956). There are no adequate biographies of Senators Bacon, Stone, Hitchcock, and Reed on the Democratic side or of Johnson, Norris, Brandegee, Moses, Kellogg, and McCumber on the Republican.

2. *The Caribbean and East Asia.* J. Fred Rippy, *The Caribbean Danger Zone* (1940) and three works previously cited—Pratt, *America's Colonial Experiment;* Bemis, *Latin American Policy of the United States;* and Callcott, *Caribbean Policy of the United States*—are good on the protectorate policy in general. More detailed are Howard C. Hill, *Roosevelt and the Caribbean* (1927); Russell H. Fitzgibbon, *Cuba and the United States, 1900–1935* (1935); Sumner Welles, *Naboth's Vineyard: The Dominican Republic, 1844–1924* (2 vols., 1928); Ludwell L. Montague, *Haiti and the United States, 1714–1938* (1940); and William D. McCain, *The United States and the Republic of Panama* (1937). There is no authoritative account of the Nicaraguan protectorate. Charles C. Cumberland, *Mexican Revolution: Genesis under Madero* (1952); Howard F. Cline, *The United States and Mexico* (1953); and Link, *Wilson*, II, cover the early stages of the Mexican revolution and counterrevolution.

For the peace of Portsmouth and after, consult Beale's study of Roosevelt, cited in Section E1, and Zabriskie, *American-Russian Rivalry in the Far East*, cited in Section E2. See also Hilary Conroy, *The Japanese Seizure of Korea, 1868–1910* (1960); Peter S. H. Tang, *Russian and Soviet Policy in Manchuria and Outer Mongolia, 1911–1931* (1959); and Rogers P. Churchill, *The Anglo-Russian Convention of 1907* (1939).

On tensions with Japan in 1906 and 1913, consult Thomas A. Bailey, *Theodore Roosevelt and the Japanese-American Crises* (1934); the biography of Root by Jessup; Link, *Wilson*, II; and Roy W. Curry, *Woodrow Wilson and Far Eastern Policy* (1957). The best analyses of the Chinese problem are Merebith E. Cameron, *The Reform Movement in China, 1898–1912* (1931); John G. Reid, *The Manchu Abdication and the Powers, 1908–1912* (1935); Charles Vevier, *The United States and China, 1906–1913* (1955); Tien-yi Li, *Woodrow Wilson's China Policy, 1913–1917* (1952); and Link, *Wilson*, II.

3. *Prewar Strivings for Peace.* There is no reliable study of the arbitration movement or the Hague Conference idea. Merze Tate, *The Disarmament Illusion* (1942) is a satisfactory treatment for the period to 1907, while Warren F. Kuehl, *Hamilton Holt* (1960) throws light on an advocate of world federation. Merle Curti, *Peace or War: The American Struggle, 1636–1936* (1936) is a good survey of pacifism in the United States. The milestones to Armageddon can be followed in Sidney B. Fay, *The Origins of the World War* (2 vols., 1929); Bernadotte E. Schmitt, *The Coming of the War, 1914* (2 vols., 1930); George P. Gooch, *Before the War: Studies in Diplomacy* (2 vols., 1936–8); Luigi Albertini, *The Origins of the War of 1914* (3 vols., 1952–7), first published in 1942–3; Raymond J. Sontag, *European Diplomatic History, 1871–1932* (1933); and A. J. P. Taylor, *The Struggle for Mastery in Europe, 1848–1918* (1954).

4. *The First World War.* Most of the literature on this subject written before 1941 has been superseded by the publications of the last decade. For an appraisal of the earlier writings, see Richard W. Leopold, "The Problem of American Intervention, 1917: An Historical Retrospect," *WP*, II (1950), 405–25, and Ernest R. May's nineteen-page pamphlet, *American Intervention: 1917 and 1941* (1960).

Arthur S. Link's researches on both sides of the Atlantic, revealed fully down to October, 1915, in the third volume of his biography of Wilson and briefly after that date in his other books cited above, mark the point of departure for an understanding of why the United States went to war in 1917. Broad in concept and sound in analysis is Ernest R. May's badly titled *The World War and American Isolation, 1914–1917* (1959). Specialized works which go beyond the best printed prior to 1941 include Marion C. Siney, *The Allied Blockade of Germany, 1914–1916* (1957); Karl E. Birnbaum, *Peace Moves and U-Boat Warfare* (1958), a study of German policy towards the United States with emphasis on the period from April 1916 to January 1917; Edward H. Buehrig, *Woodrow Wilson and the Balance of Power* (1955); Hans W. Gatzke, *Germany's Drive to the West* (1950), a discussion of war aims; and Armin Rappaport, *The British Press and Wilsonian Neutrality* (1951). The biographies of Roosevelt, Lodge, Root, and Lansing by Harbaugh, Garraty, Leopold, and Smith do justice to a position which received little sympathy before 1941.

Recent authors have paid more attention to the global aspects of American diplomacy during the First World War. Robert E. Quirk, *The Mexican Revolution, 1914–1915: The Convention of Aguascalientes* (1960) and Link's works are best on Wilson's involvement in Mexico. Link and the titles in Section E2 provide good accounts of the extension of the protectorate policy in the Caribbean. Charles C. Tansill, *The Purchase of the Danish West Indies* (1932) covers a final territorial addition. Link, *Wilson*, III, contains the latest analysis of the battle over the Twenty-One Demands, but the books by Curry and Li, listed in Section F2, also deal with the episode. On the Jones Act of 1916, see Garel A. Grunder and William E. Livezey, *The Philippines and the United States* (1951).

The impact of the Russian Revolution on wartime diplomacy has been dealt with masterfully by George F. Kennan in *Russia Leaves the War* (1956) and *The Decision to Intervene* (1958). Since his volumes cover only from November, 1917, to July, 1918, they must be supplemented by James W. Morley, *The Japanese Thrust into Siberia, 1918* (1957); Richard H. Ullman, *Intervention and the War* (1961), the first of two volumes on Anglo-Soviet relations in the period 1917–21; William A. Williams, *American-Russian Relations, 1781–1941* (1952); Leonid I. Strakhovsky, *Intervention at Archangel* (1944); Betty M. Unterberger, *America's Siberian Expedition, 1918–1920* (1956); and Robert D. Warth, *The Allies and the Russian Revolution: from the Fall of the Monarchy to the Peace of Brest-Litovsk* (1954).

5. *The Peacemaking.* The best introductions to the American preparations for the peace are Arthur S. Link, *Wilson the Diplomatist* (1957) and Charles Seymour, *American Diplomacy during the World War* (1934). More specialized are Ruhl J. Bartlett, *The League to Enforce Peace* (1944); Victor S. Mamatey, *The United States and East Central Europe, 1914–1918* (1957); and Louis L. Gerson, *Woodrow Wilson and the Rebirth of Poland, 1914–1918* (1953). For the European scene, see Arno J. Mayer, *Political Origins of the New Diplomacy, 1917–1918* (1959); Henry R. Winkler, *The League of Nations Movement in Great Britain, 1914–1919* (1952); Lawrence W. Martin, *Peace without Victory: Woodrow Wilson and the British Liberals* (1958); and Jere C. King, *Generals and Politicians: Conflict between France's High Command, Parliament and Government, 1914–1918* (1951). Harry R. Rudin, *Armistice 1918* (1944) is a model study. David F. Trask, *The United States in the Supreme War Council: American War Aims and Inter-Allied Strategy, 1917–1918* (1961) deals with a long-neglected subject.

The Paris Peace Conference has attracted little attention lately, in spite of the new documents available in Paul Mantoux, *Les Délibérations du Conseil des Quatre* (2 vols., 1955) and in a subseries of *Foreign Relations of the United States* (13 vols., 1942–8). France, Italy, and Japan have not printed archival materials, and the British begin their publication with July 1, 1919. Therefore Paul Birdsall, *Versailles Twenty Years After* (1941) and Thomas A. Bailey, *Woodrow Wilson and the Lost Peace* (1944) remain the best commentaries. F. S. Marston, *The Peace Conference of 1919* (1944) is excellent on organization and procedure; George F. Kennan, *Russia and the West under Lenin and Stalin* (1961) deftly handles the Russian question. Thomas Jones, *Lloyd George* (1951) and Geoffrey Bruun, *Clemenceau* (1943) are good short biographies of Wilson's chief antagonists. Seth P. Tillman, *Anglo-American Relations at the Paris Peace Conference of 1919* (1961) discusses personalities, patterns of cooperation and conflict, and political ramifications. Helpful specialized works are René Albrecht-Carrié, *Italy at the Paris Peace Conference* (1938); Philip M. Burnett, *Reparation at the Paris Peace Conference from the Standpoint of the American Delegation* (2 vols., 1940); Francis Deák, *Hungary at the Peace Conference* (1942); Russell H. Fifield, *Woodrow Wilson and the Far East: The Diplomacy of the Shantung Question* (1952); Jere C. King, *Foch versus Clemenceau: France and German Dismemberment, 1918–1919* (1960); Alma Luckau, *The German Delegation at the Paris Peace Conference* (1941); G. Bernard Noble, *Policies and Opinions at Paris, 1919* (1935); and Louis A. R. Yates, *The United States and French Security, 1917–1921* (1957). Étienne Mantoux, *The Carthaginian Peace, or the Economic Consequences of Mr. Keynes* (1946) is half tract and half history. On the peacemaking, as well as on all diplomatic problems from 1871 to 1945, the interpretations of Pierre Renouvin in the sixth, seventh, and eighth volumes of *Histoire des Relations Internationales* (8 vols., 1953–8) are most valuable.

Thomas A. Bailey, *Woodrow Wilson and the Great Betrayal* (1945) is the best general account of the battle in America. Several biographies, utilizing personal papers not available to Bailey, should be consulted—Blum and Walworth on Wilson, Garraty on Lodge, Leopold on Root, and the La Follettes on La Follette. Also helpful are the brief analyses in Link, *Wilson the Diplomatist;* Rayford W. Logan, *The Senate and the Versailles Mandate System* (1945); and Charles C. Tansill, *America and the Fight for Irish Freedom, 1866–1922* (1957).

G. INTERLUDE: THE INTERWAR COMPROMISE, 1921–39

Historians have tended to stereotype and oversimplify American foreign policy in these years. The most satisfying account is contained in the two volumes by Robert H. Ferrell, listed below, but they do not cover the entire period. Allan Nevins, *The United States in a Chaotic World* (1950) and *The New Deal in World Affairs* (1950) treat in a readable but conventional manner the years from 1918 to 1945. William A. Williams, "The Legend of Isolationism in the 1920's," *Science and Society,* XVIII (1954), 1–20, is a most useful corrective but overstates the case. For a larger view, see G. M. Gathorne-Hardy, *A Short History of International Affairs, 1920–1939* (4th ed., 1950); Hajo Holborn's brilliant condensation, *The Political Collapse of Europe* (1951); and the essays in Gordon A. Craig and Felix Gilbert, eds., *The Diplomats, 1919–1939* (1953).

1. *Personalities*. Adequate biographies of Harding, Coolidge, Hoover, and Roosevelt do not exist. The spirit of Coolidge's personality but not the shape of his foreign policy can be gleaned in William A. White, *A Puritan in Babylon* (1938) and Claude M. Fuess, *Calvin Coolidge* (1940). Robert H. Ferrell, *American Diplomacy in the Great Depression: Hoover-Stimson Foreign Policy, 1929–1933* (1957) is a model study. The chapters in James M. Burns, *Roosevelt: The Lion and the Fox* (1956) and in Dexter Perkins, *The New Age of Franklin Roosevelt, 1933–45* (1957) must suffice until Ferrell completes his third volume and until Arthur M. Schlesinger, Jr., and Frank Freidel turn their attention to Roosevelt's foreign policy. Walter Johnson, *1600 Pennsylvania Avenue: Presidents and the People, 1929–1959* (1960) is helpful on both Hoover and Roosevelt. See also Willard Range, *Franklin D. Roosevelt's World Order* (1959).

For the secretaries of state, Merlo J. Pusey, *Charles Evans Hughes* (2 vols., 1951) is detailed and uncritical, while Dexter Perkins, *Charles Evans Hughes and American Democratic Statesmanship* (1956) is short but discriminating. L. Ethan Ellis, *Frank B. Kellogg and American Foreign Relations, 1925–1929* (1961) fills a long-standing gap. Elting E. Morison, *Turmoil and Tradition* (1960) is a sensitive and discerning biography of Stimson; in briefer scope, Richard N. Current, *Secretary Stimson: A Study in Statecraft* (1954) draws different conclusions. Cordell Hull's very full *Memoirs* (2 vols., 1948) must serve until a biography appears.

Books on congressional and other leaders influencing foreign policy are deplorably few. Those on Lodge and Borah by Garraty and McKenna have been cited above. Wayne S. Cole, "Senator Key Pittman and American Neutrality Policies, 1933–1940," *MVHR*, XLVI (1960), 644–62, throws some light on an enigmatic individual.

2. *The Pacific Treaty System*. Harold and Margaret Sprout, *Toward a New Order of Sea Power* (1940) is a convenient introduction to postwar problems in the Pacific and to the Washington Conference. It should be supplemented by Griswold, *Far Eastern Policy*, cited in Section E2; John C. Vinson, *The Parchment Peace: The United States Senate and the Washington Conference, 1921–1922* (1955); the same author's "The Annulment of the Lansing-Ishii Agreement," *PHR*, XXVII (1958), 57–69; and Fifield, *Woodrow Wilson and the Far East*, cited in Section F5. For the Pacific treaty system in operation, see Dorothy Borg, *American Policy and the Chinese Revolution* (1947); Wesley R. Fishel, *The End of Extraterritoriality in China* (1952); Pauline Tompkins, *American-Russian Relations in the Far East* (1949); and Ferrell, *American Diplomacy in the Great Depression*.

Works dealing with international communism in East Asia include Benjamin I. Schwartz, *Chinese Communism and the Rise of Mao* (1951); Allen S. Whiting, *Soviet Policies in China, 1917–1924* (1954); Conrad Brandt, *Stalin's Failure in China, 1924–1927* (1958); and Robert C. North, *Moscow and the Chinese Communists* (1953). On internal developments generally, consult John K. Fairbank, *The United States and China* (2d ed., 1956); Harley F. McNair, *China in Revolution* (1931); Edwin O. Reischauer, *Japan: Past and Present* (2d ed., 1958); Hugh Borton, *Japan's Modern Century* (1954); and Robert A. Scalapino, *Democracy and the Party Movement in Prewar Japan* (1953).

3. *The Limitation of Armaments*. Merze Tate, *The United States and Armaments* (1948) is comprehensive and objective, but does not go beyond

printed materials. Fred Greene, "The Military View of American National Policy, 1904–1940," *AHR*, LXVI (1961), 354–77; Louis Morton, "War Plan ORANGE: Evolution of a Strategy," *WP*, XI (1959), 221–50; and Raymond G. O'Connor, "The 'Yardstick' and Naval Disarmament in the 1920's," *MVHR*, XLV (1958), 441–62, show what can be done by using manuscript sources. George T. Davis, *A Navy Second to None* (1940) traces the fight for complete parity. For the Washington Conference, see the works by the Sprouts and Vinson, cited in the preceding section; the Pusey biography of Hughes; and C. Leonard Hoag, *Preface to Preparedness: The Washington Conference and Public Opinion* (1941). The best treatments of the London Conference are in Ferrell, *American Diplomacy in the Great Depression* and the studies of Stimson by Morison and Current, cited in Section G1. Some insight into Japanese policy can be obtained from Tatsuji Takeuchi, *War and Diplomacy in the Japanese Empire* (1935) and Yale C. Maxon, *Control of Japanese Foreign Policy: A Study of Civil-Military Rivalry, 1930–1945* (1957).

4. *The League, the Court, and the Kellogg Pact.* A detailed and dispassionate history of the United States' relations with the League of Nations remains to be written. Denna F. Fleming, *The United States and World Organization, 1920–1933* (1938) is excessively Wilsonian in tone and out of date. Ursula P. Hubbard has compiled a useful factual survey through 1936 in *IC*, Nos. 274 (1931) and 329 (1937). F. P. Walters, *A History of the League of Nations* (2 vols., 1952) contains a splendid narrative and is as objective as can be hoped for. David D. Burks, "The United States and the Geneva Protocol of 1924: 'A New Holy Alliance'?" *AHR*, LXIV (1959), 891–905, breaks new ground in a neglected area.

The full story of the World Court in American foreign policy and politics has not been told. Denna F. Fleming, *The United States and the World Court* (1945) is interestingly written but relies on inadequate materials. The most balanced accounts of the long battle are in the biographies of Hughes and Root by Pusey and Jessup and in the books by Vinson and Ferrell cited in the next paragraph. Manley O. Hudson, *The Permanent Court of International Justice, 1920–1942* (2d ed., 1943) is the best treatise on the Court itself.

On the negotiation and ratification of the Kellogg Pact, Robert H. Ferrell, *Peace in Their Time* (1952) is excellent. Of value also are John E. Stoner, *S. O. Levinson and the Pact of Paris* (1942) and John C. Vinson, *William E. Borah and the Outlawry of War* (1957). In his second book Ferrell carries the story to 1933, while Richard N. Current, "Consequences of the Kellogg Pact," in George L. Anderson, ed., *Issues and Conflicts* (1959), 210–29, goes all the way to the Nuremberg Trials in 1945.

5. *The Good Neighbor Ideal.* Samuel F. Bemis, *The Latin American Policy of the United States* (1943) and Julius W. Pratt, *America's Colonial Experiment* (1950) contain good summaries of the retreat from the protectorate policy. Alexander DeConde, *Herbert Hoover's Latin American Policy* (1951) and Edward O. Guerrant, *Roosevelt's Good Neighbor Policy* (1950) are useful. More ambitious are Bryce Wood, *The Making of the Good Neighbor Policy* (1961), which covers the period from 1926 to 1943, and Donald M. Dozer, *Are We Good Neighbors? Three Decades of Inter-American Relations, 1930–1960* (1959). Specific issues in individual regions and countries may be studied in the following books, in addition to those listed in

Section F2: Dexter Perkins, *The United States and the Caribbean* (1947); Robert F. Smith, *The United States and Cuba: Business and Diplomacy, 1917–1960* (1960); E. David Cronon, *Josephus Daniels in Mexico* (1960); Arthur P. Whitaker, *The United States and South America: The Northern Republics* (1948); and the same author's *The United States and Argentina* (1954). Whitaker, *The Western Hemisphere Idea: Its Rise and Decline* (1954) and Laurence Duggan, *The Americas: The Search for Hemispheric Security* (1949) are good on the inter-American movement. Russell M. Cooper, *American Consultation in World Affairs* (1934) gives a factual account of the attempts to halt the Chaco War and to solve the Leticia dispute, but much remains to be done on the problem of peace in the Americas. Hubert Herring, *A History of Latin America* (2d ed., 1961) is an up-to-date treatment of its subject.

6. *The Problem of Germany and Russia.* C. E. Black and E. C. Helmreich, *Twentieth Century Europe* (2d ed., 1959) expertly distills recent scholarship on Europe between the two wars. W. M. Jordan, *Great Britain, France, and the German Problem, 1918–1939* (1943); Arnold Wolfers, *Britain and France between Two Wars: Conflicting Strategies of Peace since Versailles* (1940); and Gerhard P. Pink, *The Conference of Ambassadors* (1942), which covers the years from 1920 to 1931, are able analyses of the materials available in the 1930's. Concise, judicious, and written with greater perspective are Gordon A. Craig, *From Bismarck to Adenauer: Aspects of German Statecraft* (1958) and Philip A. Reynolds, *British Foreign Policy in the Inter-War Years* (1954). For Russo-German diplomacy, consult Edward H. Carr, *German-Soviet Relations between Two World Wars* (1951), a brief survey; Gerald Freund, *Unholy Alliance* (1957), a detailed study for the period 1917–1926; Hans Gatzke, *Stresemann and the Rearmament of Germany* (1954); Gordon A. Craig, *The Politics of the Prussian Army, 1640–1945* (1956); Paul Seabury, *The Wilhelmstrasse: A Study of German Diplomats under the Nazi Regime* (1954); George F. Kennan, *Russia and the West under Lenin and Stalin* (1961); and Max Beloff, *The Foreign Policy of Soviet Russia, 1929–1941* (2 vols., 1947–9).

The recognition of Russia is best covered by Robert P. Browder, *The Origins of Soviet-American Diplomacy* (1953), but useful background information can be found in Theodore Draper, *American Communism and Soviet Russia* (1960); William A. Williams, *American-Russian Relations, 1781–1947* (1952); and Thomas A. Bailey, *America Faces Russia* (1950).

Herbert Feis, *The Diplomacy of the Dollar: First Era, 1919–1932* (1950) and Harold G. Moulton and Leo Pasvolsky, *War Debts and World Prosperity* (1932) are good on international economic problems to 1932.

7. *The Collapse of the Compromise.* A. J. P. Taylor, *The Origins of the Second World War* (1961) is an extended, provocative essay rather than a detailed study. It covers the years from 1918 to 1939, with emphasis on the 1930's. It is frequently superficial on American policy.

For the fighting in Manchuria and Shanghai, Robert H. Ferrell, *American Diplomacy in the Great Depression* (1957) supersedes all earlier accounts, most of which were written before the pertinent volumes in the *Foreign Relations* series appeared. Variations on Ferrell's interpretation can be found in the studies of Stimson by Morison and Current, cited above, and in Richard N. Current, "The Stimson Doctrine and the Hoover Doctrine,"

AHR, LIX (1954), 513–42. F. P. Walters, *A History of the League of Nations* (2 vols., 1952) is good on developments at Geneva. For the British side, see Sir John T. Pratt, *War and Politics in China* (1943) and R. Bassett, *Democracy and Foreign Policy* (1952); for the Japanese, Maxon, *Control of Japanese Foreign Policy*, cited in Section G3; and the views of the Anglo-American ambassadors—Sir Robert Craigie, *Behind the Japanese Mask* (1945); Joseph C. Grew, *Ten Years in Japan* (1944); and the same author's *Turbulent Era* (Walter Johnson, ed., 2 vols., 1952). Publication of the British archival materials reached 1931 in 1960.

On East Asia from 1933 to 1939, see F. C. Jones, *Japan's New Order in East Asia: Its Rise and Fall, 1937–45* (1954); Robert J. C. Butow, *Tojo and the Coming of the War* (1961); Herbert Feis, *The Road to Pearl Harbor* (1950); Frank W. Iklé, *German-Japanese Relations, 1936–1940* (1956); David J. Dallin, *Soviet Russia and the Far East* (1948); and Charles B. McLane, *Soviet Policy and the Chinese Communists, 1931–1946* (1958).

There is no recent study of the collapse of the disarmament experiment. John W. Wheeler-Bennett, *The Pipe Dream of Peace* (1935) is a contemporary analysis of the conference at Geneva in 1932; Davis, *A Navy Second to None*, cited in Section G3, describes the one at London in 1935. Robert A. Divine, "Franklin D. Roosevelt and Collective Security, 1933," *MVHR*, XLVIII (1961), 42–59 shows what can be done with manuscript materials now available. Arthur M. Schlesinger, Jr., *The Coming of the New Deal* (1959) discusses the World Economic Conference of 1933.

On the resurgence of isolationism and "the new neutrality," see Selig Adler, *The Isolationist Impulse* (1957); Charles A. Beard, *American Foreign Policy in the Making, 1932–1940: A Study in Responsibilities* (1946); Charles C. Tansill, *Back Door to War: The Roosevelt Foreign Policy, 1933–1941* (1952), which begins with 1919 and devotes two thirds of the text to the period before Munich; Edwin Borchard and William P. Lage, *Neutrality for the United States* (2d ed., 1940); and Allen W. Dulles and Hamilton F. Armstrong, *Can America Stay Neutral?* (1939). Dorothy Borg, "Notes on Roosevelt's 'Quarantine' Speech," *PSQ*, LXXII (1957), 405–33, and John E. Wiltz, "The Nye Committee Revisited," *Historian*, XXIII (1961), 211–33, are two corrective articles. Julius W. Pratt, *America's Colonial Experiment* (1950) covers the retreat from empire; John M. Blum, *From the Morgenthau Diaries: Years of Crisis, 1928–1938* (1959) throws new light on the Treasury Department's influence in shaping foreign policy.

American policy during the Ethiopian conflict has not been dealt with properly. Besides the works listed in the previous paragraph, see Herbert Feis, *Seen from E. A.* (1947); Gaetano Salvemini, *Prelude to World War II* (1954); and John Norman, "Influence of Pro-Fascist Propaganda on American Neutrality, 1935–1936," in Dwight E. Lee and George E. McReynolds, eds., *Essays in History and International Relations in Honor of George Hubbard Blakeslee* (1949), 193–214. Books on the Spanish Civil War are more numerous. F. Jay Taylor, *The United States and the Spanish Civil War, 1936–1939* (1956) is narrowly conceived. Different in emphasis are Hugh Thomas, *The Spanish Civil War* (1961); P. A. M. van der Esch, *Prelude to War: The International Repercussions of the Spanish Civil War* (1951); and two works by David T. Cattell—*Communism and the Spanish Civil War* (1955) and *Soviet Diplomacy and the Spanish Civil War* (1957).

H. THE SECOND TEST: THE STRUGGLE FOR SURVIVAL, 1939–53

Of all the interpretations dealing with the revolution in American foreign policy since 1939, Walt W. Rostow, *The United States in the World Arena* (1960) is the broadest and most ambitious.

1. Personalities. Since there cannot yet be adequate biographies of the presidents, secretaries of state, congressional leaders, or others shaping foreign policy in this period, the historian must rely on memoirs and other primary sources. The best portrait of Roosevelt is in Robert E. Sherwood, *Roosevelt and Hopkins* (2d ed., 1950), while Truman emerges most clearly in his *Memoirs* (2 vols., 1955–6). Walter Johnson, *1600 Pennsylvania Avenue*, cited in Section G1, is good on both Roosevelt and Truman. Norman E. Graebner, ed., *An Uncertain Tradition* (1961) contains sketches of the secretaries of state. For Hull, see also his *Memoirs* (2 vols., 1948); for Byrnes there is his *Speaking Frankly* (1947) and *All in One Lifetime* (1958). Comparable material for Stettinius and Marshall does not exist. Acheson's ideas but not his personality are evident in McGeorge Bundy, ed., *The Pattern of Responsibility* (1952). Morison's portrait of Stimson as secretary of war may be supplemented by Henry L. Stimson and McGeorge Bundy, *On Active Service in Peace and War* (1948). Walter Millis, ed., *The Forrestal Diaries* (1951) provides some understanding of the services of the first secretary of defense.

The view from Capitol Hill is seen in Arthur H. Vandenberg, Jr., *The Private Papers of Senator Vandenberg* (1952); *My Name is Tom Connally*, as told to Alfred Steinberg (1954); and Robert A. Taft, *A Foreign Policy for Americans* (1951). H. Bradford Westerfield, *Foreign Policy and Party Politics from Pearl Harbor to Korea* (1955); Cecil V. Crabb, Jr., *Bipartisan Foreign Policy: Myth or Reality?* (1957); and John P. Armstrong, "The Enigma of Senator Taft and American Foreign Policy," *RP*, XVII (1955), 206–31, are helpful secondary works.

Winston S. Churchill, *The Second World War* (6 vols., 1948–53) and Charles de Gaulle, *War Memoirs* (3 vols., 1955–60) are indispensable.

2. The Second World War. Many of the books dealing with the involvement of the United States are already out of date. Some are based on too restricted materials; others are too concerned with blaming or exonerating Roosevelt and his advisers. For an evaluation of this literature through 1956, see Wayne S. Cole, "American Entry into World War II: A Historiographical Appraisal," *MVHR*, XLIII (1957), 595–617.

William L. Langer and S. Everett Gleason, *The Challenge to Isolation, 1937–1940* (1952) and *The Undeclared War, 1940–1941* (1953) are distinguished works of scholarship. Nonpolemical in tone, massive in detail, and global in treatment, they rest on a surprisingly wide array of sources—most of United States origin, to be sure—considering how closely they were written to the events they describe. No other books are in their class. Donald F. Drummond, *The Passing of American Neutrality, 1937–1941* (1955) is dispassionate but less comprehensive. Charles A. Beard, *President Roosevelt and the Coming of the War, 1941* (1948) is a legalistic brief on whether Roosevelt deceived the American people; Charles C. Tansill, *Back Door to War* (1952) reveals how vitriol, innuendo, and non sequiturs can debase scholarship.

The first two volumes of the Royal Institute's *Survey of International Affairs, 1939–1946* (1952, 1958) cover the last years of peace in Europe.

L. B. Namier, *Diplomatic Prelude, 1938–1939* (1948) and *Europe in Decay* (1950) are becoming outdated, while John W. Wheeler-Bennett, *Munich: Prologue to Tragedy* (1948) needs redoing. The last four chapters of A. J. P. Taylor, *The Origins of the Second World War* (1961) deal with Munich and after. For diplomatic developments in Europe from 1939 to 1941, see *Survey of International Affairs, 1939–1946*, III (1958); Gerhard L. Weinberg, *Germany and the Soviet Union, 1939–1941* (1954); and Max Jakobson, *The Diplomacy of the Winter War: An Account of the Russo-Finnish War, 1939–1940* (1961). H. L. Trefousse, *Germany and American Neutrality, 1939–1941* (1954) is a useful monograph.

Specialized studies on America's reaction to the war in Europe include Walter Johnson, *The Battle against Isolation* (1944), which deals with the Committee to Defend America by Aiding the Allies; Wayne S. Cole, *America First: The Battle against Intervention, 1940–1941* (1953); Robert Sobel, *The Origins of Interventionism: The United States and the Russo-Finnish War* (1960); and Raymond H. Dawson, *The Decision to Aid Russia: Foreign Policy and Domestic Politics* (1959). The Department of the Army's multivolume *United States Army in World War II*, more than fifty volumes of which have been published since 1947, contains a wealth of information on the interrelationship of foreign and military policy before 1941. *The Master Index: Reader's Guide*, II (1960) fully describes the volumes.

The best books on the difficulties with Japan are Robert J. C. Butow, *Tojo and the Coming of the War* (1961); Herbert Feis, *The Road to Pearl Harbor* (1950); Paul W. Schroeder, *The Axis Alliance and Japanese-American Relations, 1941* (1958), which is more critical of United States policy than the two preceding titles; F. C. Jones, *Japan's New Order in East Asia* (1954); and Ernst L. Presseisen, *Germany and Japan: A Study in Totalitarian Diplomacy, 1933–1941* (1959). Four articles of merit are Captain T. B. Kittredge, "United States Defense Policy and Strategy, 1941," *U.S. News & World Report*, December 3, 1954; Louis Morton, "The Japanese Decision for War," *USNIP*, LXXX (1954), 1325–35; Richard N. Current, "How Stimson Meant to 'Maneuver' the Japanese," *MVHR*, XL (1953), 67–74; and William L. Neumann, "How American Policy toward Japan Contributed to War in the Pacific," in Harry E. Barnes, ed., *Perpetual War for Perpetual Peace* (1953), 233–68. Most writings on the Pearl Harbor disaster are polemical. Two helpful appraisals are Louis Morton, "Pearl Harbor in Perspective: A Bibliographical Survey," *USNIP*, LXXXI (1955), 461–8 and Robert H. Ferrell, "Pearl Harbor and the Revisionists," *Historian*, XVII (1955), 215–33. Husband E. Kimmel, *Admiral Kimmel's Story* (1955) is typical of those books which accuse Roosevelt, without any evidence, of seeking war by withholding vital information from the island commanders.

Samuel E. Morison, *Strategy and Compromise* (1958); Kent R. Greenfield, *The Historian and the Army* (1954); and Hanson W. Baldwin, *Great Mistakes of the War* (1950) offer brief introductions to wartime planning. Morison opens each volume of his *History of United States Naval Operations in World War II* (14 vols., 1947–60) by analyzing the strategic situation. The *United States Army in World War II* series, mentioned above, and Wesley F. Craven and James L. Cate, eds., *The Army Air Forces in World War II* (7 vols., 1948–58) contain even more detail. Kent R. Greenfield, ed., *Command Decisions* (1958) is a collaborative treatment of key decisions. For British views, see Chester Wilmot, *The Struggle for Europe* (1952) and the three volumes published in 1956–7 in the six-volume *Grand Strategy*, edited by J. R. M. Butler.

American wartime diplomacy is treated most comprehensively by Herbert Feis in *Churchill—Roosevelt—Stalin: The War They Waged and the Peace They Sought* (1957); *The China Tangle: The American Effort in China from Pearl Harbor to the Marshall Mission* (1953); *Between War and Peace: The Postdam Conference* (1960); and *Japan Subdued: The Atomic Bomb and the End of the War in the Pacific* (1961). Churchill's volumes present his own case best. William H. McNeill, *America, Britain, & Russia: Their Co-operation and Conflict, 1941–1946* (1953) and George F. Kennan, *Russia and the West* (1961) are properly objective. The following deal with particular areas or problems: Arnold and Veronica Toynbee, eds., *The War and the Neutrals* (1956) and *The Realignment of Europe* (1955); Trumbull Higgins, *Winston Churchill and the Second Front* (1957); Arthur L. Funk, *Charles de Gaulle: The Crucial Years, 1943–1944* (1959); George Kirk, *The Middle East in the War* (1953); F. C. Jones and others, *The Far East, 1942–1946* (1955); Raymond Dennett and Joseph E. Johnson, eds., *Negotiating with the Russians* (1951); Robert J. C. Butow, *Japan's Decision to Surrender* (1954); and Paul Kecskemeti, *Strategic Surrender: The Politics of Victory and Defeat* (1958). John L. Snell, *Wartime Origins of the East-West Dilemma over Germany* (1959) and Philip E. Mosely, *The Kremlin and World Politics* (1960) describe the German problem. The literature on the Yalta agreements and the decision to drop the atomic bomb is too vast to list. The best introduction to the first issue is in John L. Snell and others, *The Meaning of Yalta* (1956); to the second, in Morison's biography of Stimson. William L. Neumann, "Allied Diplomacy in World War II," *USNIP*, LXXXI (1955), 829–34, is an early bibliographical commentary. Louis Morton's "Sources for the History of World War II," *WP*, XIII (1961), 435–53, appeared just before the *Foreign Relations* volumes on Cairo, Tehran, and Potsdam were issued.

3. *The Abortive Peace.* Since complete research is not possible for the years after 1945, the annual volumes, *The United States in World Affairs*, become indispensable. They are more usable than their British counterpart, *Survey of International Affairs*, or such short surveys as John W. Spanier, *American Foreign Policy since World War II* (1960). William Reitzel and others, *United States Foreign Policy, 1945–1955* (1956) successfully employs the problem approach.

On the United Nations, Leland M. Goodrich, *The United Nations* (1959) is a lucid and dispassionate history. Ruth B. Russell, *A History of the United Nations Charter: The Role of the United States, 1940–1945* (1958) deals fully with the Dumbarton Oaks and San Francisco Conferences. Robert E. Riggs, "Overselling the UN Charter—Fact and Myth," *IO*, XIV (1960), 277–90, reconsiders the campaign for approval in America. For the United Nations in operation, consult *Everyman's United Nations* (6th ed., 1959) and Waldo Chamberlin and others, *A Chronology of the United Nations, 1941–1958* (1959). Many books on the subject are of transitory value; those of enduring worth include Leland M. Goodrich and Anne P. Simons, *The United Nations and the Maintenance of International Peace and Security* (1955); Lincoln P. Bloomfield, *Evolution or Revolution? The United Nations and the Problem of Peaceful Territorial Change* (1957); Robert E. Asher and others, *The United Nations and the Promotion of General Welfare* (1957); Sydney D. Bailey, *The General Assembly of the United Nations* (1961); Thomas Hovet, Jr., *Bloc Politics in the United Nations* (1960); Robert E. Riggs, *Politics in the United Nations: A Study of United States Influence in the General Assembly* (1958); Francis O. Wilcox and Carl M. Marcy, *Proposals for Changes in the United Nations* (1955); and Trygve Lie, *In the Cause of Peace* (1954).

The peace treaties with Italy and the Axis satellites have not received full treatment. Resort must be had to memoirs; to the State Department's *Paris Peace Conference, 1946: Selected Documents* (1948); and the World Peace Foundation's collection of texts with commentary, *European Peace Treaties after World War II* (1954). Although it is theoretical rather than historical in method, Bernard C. Cohen, *The Political Process and Foreign Policy* (1957) is the best book on the peace treaty with Japan. For the first efforts to curb nuclear and conventional weapons, see Bernhard G. Bechhoefer, *Postwar Negotiations for Arms Control* (1961) and the State Department's massive compilation, *Documents on Disarmament, 1945–1960* (3 vols., 1960–1).

4. *The Containment of Russia*. The end of wartime unity can be traced in McNeill, *America, Britain, & Russia*, cited in Section H3. Hugh Seton-Watson, *Neither War nor Peace: The Struggle for Power in the Postwar World* (1960) and John Lukacs, *A History of the Cold War* (1961) are good analyses of the East-West conflict. The contemporary statements of two eminent Americans are in George F. Kennan, *American Diplomacy, 1900–1950* (1951), which reprints the unsigned article of July, 1947, and in Walter Lippmann, *The Cold War: A Study in U.S. Foreign Policy* (1947). For the Russian attitude, consult Kennan, *Russia and the West*; Isaac Deutscher, *Stalin: A Political Biography* (2d ed., 1960); Hugh Seton-Watson, *From Lenin to Khrushchev: The History of World Communism* (1960); and the essays by Philip E. Mosely, *The Kremlin and World Politics* (1960).

Joseph M. Jones, *The Fifteen Weeks* (1955) tells the absorbing story of how the Truman Doctrine and the Marshall offer came into being. Walter Millis and others, *Arms and the State* (1958) underscores the relationship of military and foreign policy in the postwar years; Harry B. Price, *The Marshall Plan and Its Meaning* (1955) describes fully that venture. Books on the economic and political integration of Europe include Arnold J. Zurcher, *The Struggle to Unite Europe, 1940–1958* (1958); Arthur H. Robertson, *The Council of Europe: Its Structure, Functions, and Achievements* (2d ed., 1961); and William C. Diebold, Jr., *The Schuman Plan: A Study in Economic Cooperation, 1950–1959* (1959).

Edgar McInnis and others, *The Shaping of Postwar Germany* (1960) provides the best introduction to the process of transforming a foe into a friend. More detailed are Eugene Davidson, *The Death and Life of Germany: An Account of the American Occupation* (1959); Harold Zink, *The United States in Germany, 1944–1955* (1957); and Edward H. Litchfield and others, *Governing Postwar Germany* (1950). For the crisis of 1948–9, see Lucius D. Clay, *Decision in Germany* (1950) and W. Phillips Davison, *The Berlin Blockade* (1958).

Most writings on NATO deal with technical questions of weapons and strategy or quickly become out of date. A guide to the early books and articles is Lawrence T. Kaplan, "NATO and Its Commentators: The First Five Years," *IO*, VII (1954), 447–67. For general reference, see Massimo Salvadori, *NATO: A Twentieth-Century Community of Nations* (1957) and *Facts about NATO* (1958), a NATO publication with loose-leaf supplements. The story of the negotiation and approval of the North Atlantic Treaty in the United States must be gleaned from memoir material and general works.

Richard H. Heindel and others, "The North Atlantic Treaty in the United States Senate," *AJIL*, XLIII (1949), 633–65 is of value. Robert E. Osgood, "NATO: Problems of Security and Collaboration," *APSR*, LIV (1960), 106–29, is an excellent summary. See also Ben T. Moore, *NATO and the Future of Europe* (1958); M. Margaret Ball, *NATO and the European Movement* (1959); and Klaus Knorr, ed., *NATO and American Security* (1959).

The literature on the mutual assistance and security programs is largely statistical or polemical. The American Assembly's *International Stability and Progress: United States Interest and Instruments* (1957) analyzes the basic issues. William A. Brown, Jr. and Redvers Opie, *American Foreign Assistance* (1953) is a factual account of aid rendered from 1941 to 1953; Thomas S. Loeber, *Foreign Aid: Our Tragic Experiment* (1961) is a more general treatment. Charles Wolf, Jr., *Foreign Aid: Theory and Practice in Southern Asia* (1960) probes deeply into a specific area. Eugene Staley, *The Future of Underdeveloped Countries* (2d ed., 1961) argues the case for assistance; Joseph S. Berliner, *Soviet Economic Aid* (1958) and Robert L. Allen, *Soviet Economic Warfare* (1960) describe Russia's counteroffensive. Jonathan Bingham, *Shirt-Sleeve Diplomacy: Point-4 in Action* (1954) discusses technical assistance in underdeveloped countries; George Liska, *The New Statecraft* (1960) tries to develop a theory of foreign aid as an instrument of foreign policy. Although concerned with other matters, Francis M. Bator, *The Question of Government Spending* (1960) and Peter B. Kenen, *Giant among Nations* (1960) both have relevant things to say on the subject.

5. *War and Revolution in Asia.* F. C. Jones and others, *The Far East, 1942–1946* (1955) covers the aftermath of the Second World War in East and Southeast Asia. Kenneth S. Latourette, *The American Record in the Far East, 1945–1951* (1952) is a judicious summary. The American Assembly's *The United States and the Far East* (1956) analyzes the major issues with the benefit of hindsight.

Good accounts of postwar Japan are contained in Edwin O. Reischauer, *The United States and Japan* (2d ed., 1957) and in Hugh Borton, *Japan's Modern Century* (1954). Kazuo Kawai, *Japan's American Interlude* (1960) is the best of the many books on the occupation. Internal pressures with external implications are treated in Rodger Swearingen and Paul Langer, *Red Flag in Japan: International Communism in Action, 1919–1951* (1952) and in Ivan I. Morris, *Nationalism and the Right Wing in Japan: A Study of Postwar Trends* (1960).

John K. Fairbank, *The United States and China* (2d ed., 1958) puts developments after 1945 in their proper perspective. Werner Levi, *Modern China's Foreign Policy* (1953) has some useful interpretations. Herbert Feis, *The China Tangle* (1953) describes dispassionately American diplomatic and military efforts in China from December, 1941, to November, 1945. It should be supplemented by Ambassador John L. Stuart's *Fifty Years in China* (1954); by General Albert C. Wedemeyer's *Wedemeyer Reports!* (1958); and by the three volumes of Charles F. Romanus and Riley Sunderland in the army's history—*Stilwell's Mission to China* (1953), *Stilwell's Command Problems* (1956), and *Time Runs Out in CBI* (1960). For Russia, see Max Beloff, *Soviet Policy in the Far East, 1944–1951* (1953); Charles B. McLane, *Soviet Policy and the Chinese Communists, 1931–1946* (1958); David J. Dallin, *Soviet Russia and the Far East* (1948); and Robert C. North, *Moscow and Chinese Communists* (1953). F. F. Liu, *A Military*

History of Modern China, 1924–1949 (1956) sheds light on one reason for the Nationalist debacle. Two contrasting explanations of the Chinese tragedy can be read in the State Department's "White Paper," *United States Relations with China: with Special Reference to the Period, 1944–1949* (1949), and in Chiang Kai-shek's *Russia in China: A Summing Up at Seventy* (1957). Joseph W. Ballantine, *Formosa: A Problem for United States Foreign Policy* (1952) examines one problem left by the civil war.

Carl Berger, *The Korea Knot* (1957) is a brief, unpretentious survey of the Korean issue from 1943 to 1954. Fuller detail on the emergence of two Koreas can be found in Leland M. Goodrich, *Korea: A Study of U.S. Policy in the United Nations* (1956); Leon Gordenker, *The United Nations and the Peaceful Unification of Korea* (1959); and Edward G. Meade, *American Military Government in Korea* (1951). Eric F. Goldman, *The Crucial Decade —and After: America, 1945–1960* (1961) contains an absorbing account of the popular and governmental reaction to the invasion of South Korea. Questions of diplomacy and strategy are considered in Trumbull Higgins, *Korea and the Fall of MacArthur: A Précis in Limited War* (1960); John W. Spanier, *The Truman-MacArthur Controversy and the Korean War* (1959); Walter Millis and others, *Arms and the State: Civil-Military Elements in National Policy* (1958); Arnold Wolfers, "Collective Security and the War in Korea," *YR*, XLIII (1954), 481–96; and Edwin C. Hoyt, "The United States Reaction to the Korean Attack," *AJIL*, LV (1961), 45–76. Harry S. Truman, *Memoirs* (2 vols., 1955–6) and Courtney Whitney, *MacArthur: His Rendezvous with History* (1956) offer contrasting views of a critical episode. Wilbur W. Hitchcock, "North Korea Jumps the Gun," *Current History*, XX (1951), 136–44, speculates on Communist motivation, but the explanation in *China Crosses the Yalu: The Decision to Enter the Korean War* (1960) by Allen S. Whiting, who draws upon Chinese sources, is more convincing. Admiral C. Turner Joy, *How Communists Negotiate* (1956) and William H. Vatcher, *Panmunjom* (1958) describe the armistice discussions.

6. *New Areas of Concern and Old.* See works listed in the next section.

I. THE CONTINUING TEST: NEITHER PEACE NOR WAR, 1953–61

Histories of the Eisenhower era cannot yet be written, and most of the books mentioned below will soon be out of date. But the historian is grateful for the Council on Foreign Relations' annual survey, *The United States in World Affairs* and for the State Department's systematic publication of important documents.

1. *Personalities.* On Eisenhower as president, see Robert J. Donovan, *Eisenhower: The Inside Story* (1956); Marquis Childs, *Eisenhower: Captive Hero* (1958); and Sherman Adams, *Firsthand Report: The Story of the Eisenhower Administration* (1961). John R. Beal, *John Foster Dulles: 1888–1959* (1959) is a contemporary biography; Roscoe Drummond and Gaston Coblentz, *Duel at the Brink: John Foster Dulles' Command of American Power* (1960) is an analysis by journalists. Dulles' own *War or Peace* (1950) is important for his thinking before becoming secretary of state.

2. *Trends in the Cold War.* Hugh Seton-Watson, *Neither War nor Peace* (1960); John Lukacs, *A History of the Cold War* (1961); Lionel Gelber, *America in Britain's Place: The Leadership of the West and Anglo-American Unity* (1961); David J. Dallin, *Soviet Foreign Policy after Stalin* (1961); Raymond L. Garthoff, *Soviet Strategy in the Nuclear Age* (1958); Wlady-

slaw W. Kulski, *Peaceful Co-Existence: An Analysis of Soviet Foreign Policy* (1959); Arnold Wolfers, ed., *Alliance Policy in the Cold War* (1959); and two books by Robert Strausz-Hupé and others—*Protracted Conflict* (1959) and *A Forward Strategy for America* (1961)—all have important things to say. The State Department's *Background of Heads of Government Conference, 1960* (1960) provides the documents and a narrative for appraising the attempts at summit diplomacy from 1955 to 1960. Leland M. Goodrich, *The United Nations* (1959) deals with that organization's role in the Cold War to July 1958. Lincoln P. Bloomfield, *The United Nations and U.S. Foreign Policy* (1960) and H. G. Nicholas, *The United Nations as a Political Institution* (1959) are perceptive appraisals. Two articles by Inis L. Claude, Jr. should be required reading for all citizens—"The Management of Power in the Changing United Nations," *IO*, XV (1961), 219–35, and "The United Nations and the Use of Force," *IC*, No. 532 (1961).

The futile efforts toward disarmament can be followed in Bernhard G. Bechhoefer, *Postwar Negotiations for Arms Control* (1961); in Joseph L. Nogee, *Soviet Policy toward International Control of Atomic Energy* (1961); and in the State Department's *Documents on Disarmament* (3 vols., 1960–1), covering the period 1945–60. Aspects of arms control are discussed in Donald G. Brennan, ed., *Arms Control, Disarmament, and National Security* (1961); Henry A. Kissinger, *Nuclear Weapons and Foreign Policy* (1957); Seymour Melman, ed., *Inspection for Disarmament* (1958); Thomas C. Schelling and Morton H. Halperin, *Strategy and Arms Control* (1961); and Arthur T. Hadley, *The Nation's Safety and Arms Control* (1961).

Books on the nuclear stalemate are endless. Some worth studying are Robert E. Osgood, *Limited War: The Challenge to American Strategy* (1957); Bernard Brodie, *Strategy in the Missile Age* (1959); Henry A. Kissinger, *The Necessity for Choice* (1961); William W. Kaufmann, ed., *Military Problems and National Security* (1956); Oskar Morgenstern, *The Question of National Defense* (1959); Paul Peeters, *Massive Retaliation: The Policy and Its Critics* (1958); Maxwell D. Taylor, *The Uncertain Trumpet* (1960); and Herman Kahn, *On Thermonuclear War* (1960). Paul Y. Hamond, *Organizing for Defense* (1961) is the best description and analysis of the American military establishment in the twentieth century.

3. *Europe.* Stephen Borsody, *The Triumph of Tyranny: The Nazi and Soviet Conquest of Central Europe* (1960); Hugh Seton-Watson, *The East European Revolution* (4th ed., 1961); Leften S. Stavrianos, *The Balkans since 1453* (1958); and Robert L. Wolff, *The Balkans in Our Time* (1956) offer background on the captive nations. For events in key countries, consult Edward Taborsky, *Communism in Czechoslovakia, 1948–1960* (1961); Timor Méray, *Thirteen Days that Shook the Kremlin: Imre Nagy and the Hungarian Revolution* (1959); and Frank Gibney, *The Frozen Revolution: Poland, A Study in Communist Decay* (1959). Stephen D. Kertesz, ed., *The Fate of East Central Europe: Hopes and Failures of American Foreign Policy* (1956) must suffice until a detailed study of liberation as a policy appears.

For the evolution of NATO, see books listed in Section H4 and the following titles on the Fourth and Fifth French Republics: Edgar S. Furniss, *France, Troubled Ally: De Gaulle's Heritage and Prospects* (1960); Philip Williams, *Politics in Post-War France* (1958); and Philip M. Williams and Martin Harrison, *De Gaulle's Republic* (1960). Arthur P. Whitaker, *Spain and Defense of the West: Ally and Liability* (1961) should also be read in this connection.

Edgar S. McInnis and others, *The Shaping of Postwar Germany* (1960) has two excellent chapters on divided Germany and Berlin. Gerald Freund, *Germany between Two Worlds* (1961) is an up-to-date criticism of United States policy. The Senate Foreign Relations Committee has compiled a useful set of *Documents on Germany, 1944–1959* (1959). On recent events in Berlin, see Hans Speier, *Divided Berlin: The Anatomy of Soviet Blackmail* (1961); Bruce R. L. Smith, "The Governance of Berlin," *IC*, No. 525 (1959); and O. M. von der Gablentz, *Documents on the Status of Berlin* (1959).

4. *Asia.* The books on Eisenhower and Dulles, cited in Section 11, tell of the new administration's role in securing the Korean armistice. There is little for the period 1953–61. Two State Department pamphlets set forth official policy—*The Korean Problem at the Geneva Conference, April 26—June 15, 1954* (1954) and *The Record on Korean Unification, 1943–1960* (1960). Richard C. Allen (pseud.), *Korea's Syngman Rhee* (1960) is very critical of the president and his American supporters.

On the two Chinas, A. Doak Barnett's excellent *Communist China and Asia: Challenge to American Policy* (1960) is comprehensive and has a full bibliography. H. Arthur Steiner, "Communist China in the World Community," *IC*, No. 533 (1961) contains a good brief summary. See also Peter S. H. Tang, *Communist China Today: Domestic and Foreign Policies* (2d ed., 1961) and two critical works by Richard L. Walker—*China under Communism: The First Five Years* (1955) and *The Continuing Struggle: Communist China and the Free World* (1959). O. Edmund Clubb provides background in "Formosa and the Offshore Islands in American Policy, 1950–1955," *PSQ*, LXXIV (1959), 517–31. Howard L. Boorman and others, *Moscow-Peking Axis* (1957) is a little out of date but still useful. The same is true of Allen S. Whiting's chapter on Nationalist China in the American Assembly's *The United States and the Far East* (1956).

For Japan after 1953, see Hugh Borton and others, *Japan between East and West* (1957) and Shao-chuän Leng, *Japan and Communist China* (1959). Don Kurzman, *Kishi and Japan* (1960) is a good contemporary biography.

Russell H. Fifield, *The Diplomacy of Southeast Asia, 1945–1958* (1958) describes the domestic and foreign policies of the countries in that region. Rupert Emerson, *From Empire to Nation* (1960) is a search for uniformities in the rise to self-assertion of the Asian and African peoples. Amry Vandenbosch and Richard A. Butwell, *Southeast Asia among the World Powers* (1957) also discusses the force of nationalism. Donald Lancaster, *The Emancipation of French Indo-China* (1961) supplants Ellen J. Hammer, *The Struggle for Indochina* (1954). Anglo-American disagreement in 1954 is revealed in *Full Circle: The Memoirs of Anthony Eden* (1960) and in Chalmers W. Roberts, "The Day We Didn't Go to War," *The Reporter*, September 11, 1954. Alastair M. Taylor, *Indonesian Independence and the United Nations* (1961) touches on American diplomacy. There is no reliable account of the Laotian tragedy. Sisouk Na Champassak, *Storm over Laos* (1961) is not objective on recent events, while the State Department's *The Situation in Laos* (1959) attempts to justify American policy. Little has been written about SEATO. The Chatham House Group, *Collective Defense in South East Asia: The Manila Treaty and Its Implications* (1956) is an early analysis; C. Hartley Grattan, *The United States and the Southwest Pacific* (1961) contains a recent one.

W. Norman Brown, *The United States and India and Pakistan* (1953) and Kenneth S. Latourette, *The American Record in the Far East, 1945–1951* (1952) offer brief but somewhat dated introductions to South Asia. Phillips Talbot and S. L. Poplai, *India and America* (1958) outlines major problems. Chester Bowles, *Ambassador's Report* (1954) is friendly to a country whose part in the Cold War can be followed in K. P. Karunakaran, *India in World Affairs* (2 vols., 1952–8), which goes to 1953; J. C. Kundra, *India's Foreign Policy, 1947–1954: A Study of Relations with the Western Bloc* (1955); Ross N. Berkes and Mohinder S. Bedi, *The Diplomacy of India: Indian Foreign Policy in the United Nations* (1958); and Shiv Dayal, *India's Role in the Korean Question* (1959).

5. *The Americas.* Dexter Perkins, *The United States and Latin America* (1961) is a brief but lucid discussion of contemporary problems in their historical setting. Donald M. Dozer, *Are We Good Neighbors? Three Decades of Inter-American Relations, 1930–1960* (1959) is the fullest survey. J. Fred Rippy, *Globe and Hemisphere* (1958) stresses economic factors; Arthur P. Whitaker, *The Western Hemisphere Idea* (1954) notes the subordination of the New World in United States diplomacy. Thomas W. Palmer, Jr., *Search for a Latin American Policy* (1957) and Richard N. Adams and others, *Social Change in Latin America Today: Its Implications for United States Policy* (1961) are general in nature.

The Organization of American States (1959), a study prepared by Northwestern University for the Senate Foreign Relations Committee, describes the workings of the regional organization. See also, José A. Mora, "The Organization of American States," *IO,* XIV (1960), 514–23 and Arthur P. Whitaker, "Development of American Regionalism: The Organization of American States," *IC,* No. 469 (1951).

Relations with key countries and areas are considered in Howard F. Cline, *The United States and Mexico* (1953); John D. Martz, *Central America: The Crisis and the Challenge* (1959); O. Edmund Smith, Jr., *Yankee Diplomacy: U.S. Intervention in Argentina* (1953); and two works by Arthur P. Whitaker—*The United States and Argentina* (1954) and *Argentine Upheaval* (1955). Robert F. Smith, *The United States and Cuba; Business and Diplomacy, 1917–1960* (1960) was completed before relations with the Castro regime reached their nadir. John A. Houston, *Latin America in the United Nations* (1956) is a useful study. Edwin Lieuwen, *Arms and Politics in Latin America* (1960) and Philip M. Glick, *The Administration of Technical Assistance: Growth in the Americas* (1957) discuss problems of economic and military aid.

For the Communist peril, see Robert J. Alexander, *Communism in Latin America* (1957); Robert L. Allen, *Soviet Influence in Latin America* (1959); *Soviet Bloc Latin American Activities and Their Implications for United States Foreign Policy* (1960), a study prepared for the Senate Foreign Relations Committee by the Corporation for Economic and Industrial Research; and Ronald M. Schneider, *Communism in Guatemala, 1944–1954* (1959). On the overthrow of the Arbenz government, consult Philip B. Taylor, "The Guatemalan Affair: A Critique of United States Foreign Policy," *APSR,* L (1956), 787–806; John D. Martz, *Communist Infiltration in Guatemala* (1956); Amy E. Jensen, *Guatemala: A Historical Survey* (1955); Fredrick B. Pike, "Guatemala, the United States, and Communism in the Americas," *RP*, XVII (1955), 232–61; and Daniel James, *Red Design for the Americas: Guatemalan Prelude* (1954). The State Department presented its evidence in *A Case History of Communist Penetration: Guatemala* (1957).

Canada's position in the Cold War can be studied in Hugh L. Keenleyside and Gerald S. Brown, *Canada and the United States* (2d ed., 1952) and in volumes four to eight of Frederick H. Soward and others, *Canada in World Affairs* (1950–9). See also William R. Willoughby, *The St. Lawrence Seaway: A Study in Politics and Diplomacy* (1961).

6. *Africa.* The best introductions are *Africa* (1959), a study prepared for the Senate Foreign Relations Committee by the Program of African Studies, Northwestern University, and the American Assembly's *The United States and Africa* (1958). On the revolt against colonialism, Gwendolen M. Carter, *Independence for Africa* (1960) and James Cameron, *The African Revolution* (1961) are brief; Rupert Emerson, *From Empire to Nation* (1960) and Stewart C. Easton, *The Twilight of European Colonialism* (1960) are more substantial. Raymond W. Bixler, *The Foreign Policy of the United States in Liberia* (1957) discusses America's oldest interest in Africa. Issues touching the security of the United States are considered in George H. Becker, *The Disposition of the Italian Colonies, 1941–1951* (1952); Lorna Hahn, *North Africa: Nationalism to Nationhood* (1960); Richard and Joan Brace, *Ordeal in Algeria* (1960); and Joan Gillespie, *Algeria: Rebellion and Revolution* (1960). For the Congo crisis, consult Alan P. Merriam, *Congo: Background of Conflict* (1961); Maurice N. Hennessy, *The Congo: A Brief History and Appraisal* (1961); and E. M. Miller, "Legal Aspects of the U.N. Action in the Congo," *AJIL*, LV (1961), 1–28.

7. *The Middle East.* Sydney N. Fisher, *The Middle East* (1959) is a superior history from ancient times to the present, while J. C. Hurewitz, ed., *Diplomacy in the Near and Middle East* (2 vols., 1956) is a convenient documentary record from 1535 to 1956. John A. DeNovo, "American Relations with the Middle East: Some Unfinished Business," in George L. Anderson, ed., *Issues and Conflicts* (1959), 63–98, is a valuable review with very full bibliographical notes.

The best introduction to American postwar policy is John C. Campbell, *Defense of the Middle East* (2d ed., 1960). Also helpful are J. C. Hurewitz, *Middle East Dilemmas: The Background of United States Policy* (1953); Halford L. Hoskins, *The Middle East: Problem Area in World Politics* (1954); George Kirk, *The Middle East, 1945–1950* (1954); and Ephraim A. Speiser, *The United States and the Near East* (2d ed., 1950). Walter Z. Laqueur, *Communism and Nationalism in the Middle East* (1956) combines facts and analysis. For international rivalries and the oil problem, consult George Lenczowski's two books—*The Middle East in World Affairs* (2d ed., 1956) and *Oil and State in the Middle East* (1960); Walter Z. Laqueur, ed., *The Middle East in Transition* (1958); Benjamin Shwadran, *The Middle East, Oil, and the Great Powers* (2d ed., 1959); and Raymond F. Mikesell and Hollis B. Chenery, *Arabian Oil: America's Stake in the Middle East* (1949). Russia's increased concern is reflected in Walter Z. Laqueur, *The Soviet Union and the Middle East* (1959); in Ivar Spector, *The Soviet Union and the Muslim World, 1917–1958* (1959); and in George Lenczowski, *Russia and the West in Iran, 1918–1948* (1949).

Lewis V. Thomas and Richard N. Frye, *The United States and Turkey and Iran* (1951) is one of the few studies of America's relations with individual countries. Mohammed Shafi Agwani, *The United States and the Arab World, 1945–1952* (1955) is brief and out of date; William E. Warne, *Mission for Peace: Point 4 in Iran* (1956) and Paul G. Phillips, *The Hashemite Kingdom of Jordan: Prolegomena to a Technical Assistance Program* (1954) are economic studies. For the emergence of Israel, see Paul L. Hanna, *British Policy in Palestine* (1942); Frank E. Manuel, *The Realities of American-Palestine Relations* (1949); J. C. Hurewitz, *The Struggle for Palestine* (1950); Jon and David Kimches, *A Clash of Destinies: The Arab-Jewish War and the Founding of the State of Israel* (1960); and I. Larry Leonard, "The United Nations and Palestine," *IC*, No. 454 (1949).

Benna Avram, *The Evolution of the Suez Canal Status from 1869 to 1956* (1959) and John Marlowe, *Anglo-Egyptian Relations, 1800–1953* (1954) describe the antecedents of the canal seizure. In his memoirs, *Full Circle* (1960), Eden defends himself and attacks Dulles. Guy Wint and Peter Calvocoressi offer a more objective British account in *Middle East Crisis* (1957). The books on Dulles and by Sherman Adams, cited in Section I1, are the nearest American equivalents of Eden's memoirs. Dispassionate treatments of the Suez debacle can be found in Lionel M. Gelber, *America in Britain's Place* (1961); Arnold Wolfers, ed., *Alliance Policy in the Cold War* (1959); James E. Dougherty, "The Aswan Decision in Perspective," *PSQ*, LXXIV (1959), 21–45; and M. A. Fitzsimons, "The Suez Crisis and the Containment Policy," *RP*, XIX, 419–45.

There is no adequate treatment of the Baghdad Pact and CENTO. Quincy Wright, "United States Intervention in Lebanon," *AJIL*, LIII (1959), 112–25 is a legalistic analysis.

Index

COLLECTIVE DEFENSE

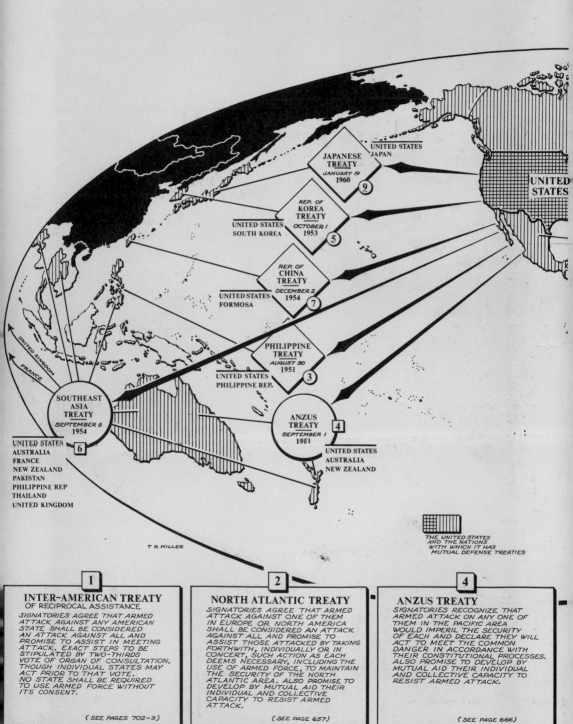

UNITED STATES
JAPAN

JAPANESE TREATY
JANUARY 19
1960
⑨

REP. OF KOREA TREATY
OCTOBER 1
1953
⑤

UNITED STATES
SOUTH KOREA

REP. OF CHINA TREATY
DECEMBER 2
1954
⑦

UNITED STATES
FORMOSA

PHILIPPINE TREATY
AUGUST 30
1951
③

UNITED STATES
PHILIPPINE REP.

UNITED
STATES

SOUTHEAST ASIA TREATY
SEPTEMBER 8
1954
⑥

UNITED STATES
AUSTRALIA
FRANCE
NEW ZEALAND
PAKISTAN
PHILIPPINE REP
THAILAND
UNITED KINGDOM

ANZUS TREATY
SEPTEMBER 1
1951
④

UNITED STATES
AUSTRALIA
NEW ZEALAND

UNITED KINGDOM

FRANCE

T R MILLER

THE UNITED STATES
AND THE NATIONS
WITH WHICH IT HAS
MUTUAL DEFENSE TREATIES

1

INTER-AMERICAN TREATY
OF RECIPROCAL ASSISTANCE

SIGNATORIES AGREE THAT ARMED ATTACK AGAINST ANY AMERICAN STATE SHALL BE CONSIDERED AN ATTACK AGAINST ALL AND PROMISE TO ASSIST IN MEETING ATTACK. EXACT STEPS TO BE STIPULATED BY TWO-THIRDS VOTE OF ORGAN OF CONSULTATION, THOUGH INDIVIDUAL STATES MAY ACT PRIOR TO THAT VOTE. NO STATE SHALL BE REQUIRED TO USE ARMED FORCE WITHOUT ITS CONSENT.

(SEE PAGES 702-3)

2

NORTH ATLANTIC TREATY

SIGNATORIES AGREE THAT ARMED ATTACK AGAINST ONE OF THEM IN EUROPE OR NORTH AMERICA SHALL BE CONSIDERED AN ATTACK AGAINST ALL AND PROMISE TO ASSIST THOSE ATTACKED BY TAKING FORTHWITH, INDIVIDUALLY OR IN CONCERT, SUCH ACTION AS EACH DEEMS NECESSARY, INCLUDING THE USE OF ARMED FORCE, TO MAINTAIN THE SECURITY OF THE NORTH ATLANTIC AREA. ALSO PROMISE TO DEVELOP BY MUTUAL AID THEIR INDIVIDUAL AND COLLECTIVE CAPACITY TO RESIST ARMED ATTACK.

(SEE PAGE 657)

4

ANZUS TREATY

SIGNATORIES RECOGNIZE THAT ARMED ATTACK ON ANY ONE OF THEM IN THE PACIFIC AREA WOULD IMPERIL THE SECURITY OF EACH AND DECLARE THEY WILL ACT TO MEET THE COMMON DANGER IN ACCORDANCE WITH THEIR CONSTITUTIONAL PROCESSES. ALSO PROMISE TO DEVELOP BY MUTUAL AID THEIR INDIVIDUAL AND COLLECTIVE CAPACITY TO RESIST ARMED ATTACK.

(SEE PAGE 666)